CORPORATIONS AND OTHER BUSINESS ORGANIZATIONS

CONTEMPORARY
LEGAL EDUCATION SERIES

Corporations and Other Business Organizations

CASES, MATERIALS, PROBLEMS

Fourth Edition

LARRY D. SODERQUIST
Professor of Law
Vanderbilt University

A.A. SOMMER, JR.
Counsel
Morgan, Lewis & Bockius
Washington, DC

PAT K. CHEW
Professor of Law
University of Pittsburgh

LINDA O. SMIDDY
Professor of Law and
Associate Dean for Academic Affairs
Vermont Law School

MICHIE
Law Publishers
CHARLOTTESVILLE, VIRGINIA

The persons and business entities in the situations in this book are fictional,
as are the events described in the situations. Neither the persons nor
business entities are intended to represent real persons or entities.

1315611

To the memory of William D. Gaillard

To Robert, Lauren, Luke,
and to my parents, Lillian and Richard Chew
—PKC

To James, Beatrice, John, and Mae
with love and gratitude
—LOS

Preface

Since the book's last edition, the law of business organizations has undergone significant and dynamic change. This edition reflects the substance and implications of these recent developments.

Most chapters of this book begin with a situation involving one or more hypothetical clients, with later situations building on earlier ones. Classroom work can involve the situations as much or as little as the teacher wishes, or it can exclude the situations entirely. For example, the situations can simply be used, as part of assigned readings, to place the cases and other materials in an understandable context. The inclusion of these situations, then, is not meant to dictate the agenda for the class.

The book is designed to be used in a three or four semester-hour corporation law or business associations course. The first two chapters deal with unincorporated business organizations. The remaining chapters focus on corporations. Some of the securities related materials have been included simply to give students a first acquaintance with a few of the more common securities law questions likely to arise in a corporate practice. Teachers who wish to deal only selectively with these questions, or to save them for another course, will find no difficulty in doing so. An introduction to the reading of financial statements is included in the appendices, as are selected provisions from the Restatement (Second) of Agency and the Model Rules of Professional Conduct. The materials on reading financial statements were designed to be understandable to students with little or no help.

Citations of authority and references of various sorts have been omitted, as have footnotes, except where inclusion or partial inclusion has served a specific purpose. These deletions generally have not been indicated. Other deletions and revisions usually have been, except for the correction of typographical errors and the deletion of paragraphs and longer portions of text appearing before or after excerpts from non-case materials, and except for a few miscellaneous deletions and revisions of a minor nature. Where footnotes have been retained, they have been renumbered. Unless otherwise indicated, the term "Model Act" refers to the Model Business Corporation Act (1984, as amended, 1994). The term "ALI" refers to the citations from *Principles of Corporate Governance: Analysis and Recommendations*, Vols. 1 & 2 (1994) which is published by the American Law Institute (ALI). We have also used the alternative titles of Chairman of the Board and Chair of the Board to designate that position. This approach reflects both the currency of the traditional term and the increasing use of the newer form.

Many people helped in the preparation of this book, and we gratefully express our thanks to all of them. Particularly, we first wish to thank the students of Professors Soderquist, Chew and Smiddy, who provided helpful research assistance. We are also grateful to Professor Soderquist's research associate on the first edition, John A. Scanlan, who did a superb job in helping with various aspects of the project over a long period of time. Our special thanks go to

Professor J. Kirkland Grant, who read drafts of the manuscript for the first edition, offered numerous helpful comments and suggestions, and provided materials that have significantly enhanced the book. We also thank Karen Cobb and Sherri Richardson for their invaluable administrative assistance, and the Rivendell Group for its support. We also want to thank the Practising Law Institute for allowing us to use material from Soderquist's and Sommer's book, *Understanding Corporation Law*, and from Chew's book, *Directors' and Officers' Liability*, both of which are published by the PLI. In addition, the authors acknowledge the numerous excerpts from the American Law Institute, *Principles of Corporate Governance: Analysis and Recommendations*, Vols. 1 & 2 (1994), copyright © 1994 by The American Law Institute and reprinted with permission, with all rights reserved; from the Model Business Corporation Act (including Official Comments) (1984, as amended, 1994), copyright © 1994 by the American Bar Foundation, also reprinted with permission, with all rights reserved; and from the Uniform Partnership Act (1914) (including Official Comments) and the Uniform Partnership Act (1994) (including Official Comments), copyright © 1918 and 1994 by the National Conference of Commissioners on Uniform State Laws, and reprinted with permission, with all rights reserved.

Larry D. Soderquist
A.A. Sommer, Jr.
Pat K. Chew
Linda O. Smiddy

Summary Table of Contents

Table of Contents

APPROACHING CORPORATE LAW

This book is about the law of business organizations, the legal rules defining the rights, responsibilities, and obligations of the individuals who own, manage and invest in businesses. The book is also about corporate lawyers. At their best, corporate lawyers are skilled practitioners with a broad understanding of business and business law and the social and ethical implications of the tasks at hand. Without this broad understanding, lawyers risk becoming little more than technicians whose limited view of their professional role diminishes the quality of their service and may even cause them to make mistakes on seemingly simple tasks. This book will help students begin to develop some of the broader perspectives that are an important component of the practice of corporate law.

SECTION I. PUTTING BUSINESS ORGANIZATIONS IN CONTEXT

A. BUSINESS ORGANIZATIONS GENERALLY

The study of corporate law is about the men and women who own, invest in, and manage businesses. It is about the corner grocer, the owner of the local plumbing supply company, the head of a multinational enterprise, the partner in a law firm, the founder of an environmental consulting firm, the movie mogul, and the art dealer. It is about individuals whose abilities to manage a company's employees and assets and make difficult financial decisions determine the fate of a business venture.

Individuals decide to become business owners for many reasons. They may need to make a living or want to earn a return on an investment. Other motivating factors are the desire to provide particular services or products, retain control over their lives, or be able to spend their working lifetimes in activities of particular interest to them. Some people want to attain money or power. Others are content with getting by. Whatever their reasons, when they do decide to go into business, their first step will be to determine whether they want to work alone or form a business organization.

A business organization typically consists of two or more people who work together for a common business purpose and who share the risks and rewards of their efforts. An individual, acting alone, is not usually considered to be a business organization, although an individual owner of a business with employees would be. People go into business with others to obtain talent, skills or money

1

that they cannot provide themselves. They may also want the companionship that comes with working with others.

Members of a business organization may be owners, employees, or investors or hold positions that combine these roles. They may actively manage the business or become passive investors who leave the management of the company to others. Their numbers may range from a very few persons to participants counted in the hundreds of thousands. Whatever the nature of their relationships or the extent of their numbers, the products of their combined efforts comprise the work of the enterprise.

In many respects, other organizations, such as labor unions, charities, and private colleges and universities, have much in common with business organizations. They often have similar governance structures. They hire employees, are operated by professional managers, own property, open bank accounts, incur debt and make money (have revenues that exceed their expenses.) The distinguishing features of business organizations are that they are formed for a business purpose, are intended to be profitable and are financed by investors who expect to make money by sharing in the company's profits. In contrast, although many non-profit organizations engage in commercial activities (such as operating a museum store, owning rental property and the like), revenues that are not needed to pay expenses are reinvested in the enterprise rather than paid out to investors.

B. THE BUSINESS LANDSCAPE

Before we comment on specific types of business organizations, we will make a few observations about the general business landscape. For the purposes of this discussion, companies will be grouped by size according to revenues earned, number of employees, or value of assets owned. We will ignore, for the time being, categories based on particular types of legal entities.

1. The Large Enterprise[1]

When one imagines a business organization, often the type that comes first to mind is a large, multinational enterprise. The economic power of companies such as these sometimes borders on incomprehensible. In 1994, General Motors was ranked as the fifth largest company in the world. Its revenues totaled $ 154.9 billion, an amount exceeding the total revenues of some small countries. In that same year, General Motors employed more people than the total population of the state of Vermont. Other U.S. companies ranked among the largest in the world

---

[1] The data in this section were drawn from information in the following sources: Statistical Abstract of the United States 530, 533, 537, 549, 562 (1995); Lisa Sanders, *The Consensual Corporation*, BUS. WK., Nov. 18, 1996, at 10; *Fortune's Global 500*, FORTUNE, August 7, 1995, at F-1.

are General Electric, International Business Machines, Mobil, Sears Roebuck, Philip Morris, Chrysler, State Farm Group, and Prudential Insurance Company of America. In five or ten years there may be additional U.S. companies on the list. The U.S. industries with the greatest growth in the 5 year period ending in 1994 were, in order of rank: health, retailing, computers/communications, consumer products and travel.

Individually and collectively, these companies have significant economic and social power. In some industry groups, a very small percentage of companies produces a disproportionate amount of revenues. Just 0.3% of manufacturing firms produced 71% of the total receipts for the industry. Similarly, 0.5% of those in the finance, insurance and real estate industry earned 80% of the total receipts.

These organizations, and others like them, wield significant influence in our lives. In the United States, large companies typically provide their employees with a range of health care and pension benefits that are governmental responsibilities in other countries. The pervasive influence of these vast enterprises was anticipated by Berle and Means in their classic work on the modern corporation:

> The rise of the modern corporation has brought a concentration of economic power which can compete on equal terms with the modern state — economic power versus political power, each strong in its own field.... The future may see the economic organism, now typified by the corporation, not only on an equal plane with the state, but possibly even superseding it as the dominant form of social organization. The law of corporations, accordingly, might well be considered as a potential constitutional law for the new economic state, while business practice is increasingly assuming the aspect of economic statesmanship.*

These companies are not static entities. The vast, world wide scope of operations of some large enterprises is reportedly causing their executives to consider replacing hierarchical organizational structures with a consensual approach to management. The recognition that one person at the top cannot be involved with and have sole responsibility for such a wide range of operations has provided a stimulus for change. Companies such as Motorola, Hewlett-Packard and Xerox have already moved in this direction. Others may follow.

Although not all of these companies are publicly held, most are. The market for shares in the largest U.S. companies continues to be dynamic. The Dow Jones Industrial index increased from a daily average of 891 in 1980 to 3,794 in 1994.

In 1997 the index exceeded the 7,000 mark. During a comparable period, the market value of all sales of stocks on all U.S. stock exchanges (excluding over the counter trading) burgeoned from 522 billion in 1980 to 2.7 trillion in 1994. Mutual funds also grew during the same time, from $ 135 billion to $ 2,162 billion. The most significant investors in mutual funds are households and nonprofit organizations, with total holdings of $ 968.5 billion or 66% of the total invested. In contrast, pension fund holdings amount to $ 150.5 billion or about 1% of the total.

2. The Small and Medium Sized Business[2]

Mega-companies are only part of the story of U.S. business. Based on numbers alone, most U.S. companies are small, whether measured by receipts, assets or employees. For example, 83% of all corporations have business receipts under a million dollars a year. Collectively, however, small and medium sized companies play an important role in the U.S. economy. In some industries, these companies, rather than large behemoths, collectively produce the greatest percentage of revenues. In the construction, and agriculture, forestry and fishing industries, the smallest companies, as measured by value of assets, produced approximately 70% of the total industry revenues. This same category of companies also produced 58% of the service industry revenues.

Small companies also employ most of the U.S. workers. Of the 92.8 million persons employed in the private sector in 1992,[3] over one-fourth worked for businesses with fewer than 20 employees, over half worked for businesses with fewer than 100 employees and over three-fourths, for companies with fewer than 500 employees. In contrast, only 6.7% worked for companies with 500 to 999 employees, and 13.2% for companies with 1,000 or more employees. These trends are likely to continue, with the smaller companies employing most of the work force. Approximately two-thirds of the 3 million new jobs in 1995 were expected to come from companies with fewer than 100 employees, half of these from firms with under 20 workers. The economic power of small and mid-sized companies is evident in other ways, as well. They reportedly produce nearly half of all U.S. exports, employ more than half of all factory workers, and account for half the total value added by U.S. manufacturing.

---

[2] The data in this section were derived from the following sources: Statistical Abstract of the United States 543-50 (1995); James Aley, *The Temp Biz Boom: Why It's Good*, FORTUNE, October 16, 1995 at 53; *Employment Levels Surging at Concerns Owned by Women*, WALL ST. J., April 12, 1995 at B2; Otis Port et al., *Small and Midsize Companies Seize the Challenge — Not a Moment Too Soon*, BUS. WK., Nov. 30, 1992, at 66.

[3] The number excludes railroad employees and self-employed persons.

3. The Changing Demographics of the Work Force[4]

During the last twenty years, the demographics of the work force have changed in two important ways. One is the shift in the structure of the employment market. The other is the change in the roles played by women and minorities.

In the last two decades, the traditional predominance of manufacturing companies has yielded to service oriented businesses. During the 1990's, the service and entertainment industries boomed, with movie production, temporary employment, computer and health care companies leading the way. At the same time, the demand for highly skilled and highly educated workers has surged. Currently, almost 40% of the U.S. work force can be characterized as "knowledge workers," with the greatest employment growth occurring in computer software and health care industries. This shift from manufacturing to service businesses requiring highly skilled employees has increased the economic gulf between skilled and unskilled workers.

The growth industry in temporary workers also signals a shift in the structure of the employment market. Since 1991, the number of temporary workers has almost doubled. Although many temporary jobs continue to be low wage, low skill positions, as many as 20% of these positions are held by highly skilled workers in technical fields and professions, including law, medicine, and engineering. In some cases, law firms and government agencies have used temporary firms as sources for recruiting new attorneys.

The business roles of women and minorities have also expanded in the last two decades. Since 1982, the number of firms owned by women and minorities has increased dramatically. Today, women-owned businesses number 7.7 million, up from 2.6 million fourteen years ago, and now comprising over one third of all U.S. businesses. Growth is likely to continue; during the past few years women have started new businesses at rates out pacing their male counterparts. Approximately 70% of female-owned businesses are in retailing and business and

---

[4] The data included in this section were compiled from the following sources: Statistical Abstract of the United States 533-35, 638-39, 543, 549-50, 553 (1995); Joann S. Lublin, *Women at Top Still Are Distant From CEO Jobs*, WALL ST. J., Feb. 28, 1996, at B1; Joann S. Lublin, *An Overseas Stint Can Be a Ticket to the Top*, WALL ST. J., Jan. 29, 1996, at B1; Udayan Gupta, *Black-Owned Businesses Rose by 46% From 1987 to '92, U.S. Survey Finds*, WALL ST. J., Dec. 12, 1995 at B2; Cynthia Fuchs Epstein et al., *Glass Ceilings and Open Doors: Women's Advancement in the Legal Profession*, 64 FORDHAM LAW REV. 291, 356-59 (1995); Stephanie N. Mehta, *Minority-Owned Businesses Are Making Headway in Marketplace, Survey Finds*, WALL ST. J., Oct. 20, 1995, at B2; James Aley, *The Temp Biz Boom: Why It's Good*, FORTUNE, Oct. 16, 1995, at 53; Pam Black, *A "New-girl" Network Starts to Take Root*, BUS. WK., Oct. 2, 1995, at 29E; Sharon Nelson, *Minority Business: The New Wave*, NATION'S BUS. Oct. 1995, at 16; Betsy Morris, *Executive Women Confront a New Kind of Midlife Crisis*, FORTUNE, Sept. 18, 1995, at 60; *Employment Levels Surging at Concerns Owned by Women*, WALL ST. J., Apr. 12, 1995, at B2; *50 Years of Progress in Corporate America*, EBONY, Apr. 1995, at 99; Keith H. Hammonds, *An Unbreakable Glass Ceiling?*, BUS. WK., Mar. 20, 1995, at 42; Michele Galan, *White "Male" and Worried*, BUS. WK., Jan. 31, 1994, at 50; *Who's News: Capital Cities/ABC, Inc.*, WALL ST. J., Jan. 6, 1994, at B2.

professional services, although more recently there has been significant growth in traditionally male fields such as manufacturing and construction.

Obtaining financing for women-owned startup companies is often difficult, and women frequently finance their businesses with credit cards. As many as 52% of women-owned businesses may take this route, compared with 18% of all small businesses. Although venture capital firms increasingly fund women-owned businesses, financing often remains elusive, particularly for service businesses lacking assets suitable to provide collateral for loans. In some industries, however, women tell a different story. Women-owned biotechnology and computer technology ventures typically receive funding at the same rate as men. Despite the difficulty of obtaining financing, women-owned businesses have become a significant force in the U.S. economy. In 1992, women-owned corporations produced revenues totaling $ 932 billion. Collectively, women-owned businesses account for approximately 11.2% of revenues generated by all U.S. businesses and employ a third more workers than the 500 largest U.S. companies combined.

In addition, women-owned businesses have played an important role in redefining accepted workplace practices. These companies have reportedly been more willing than others to offer benefits such as health-care, child-care subsidies and flexible work hours, and because of the widespread availability of these options, are often considered particularly "worker-friendly." The availability of options such as these is not confined to women-owned or small businesses, as large companies increasingly offer their employees similar opportunities.

In other segments of business the story is different. Although women comprise over 40% of professionals and managers, they hold only 5% of the senior level positions at the top 1,000 U.S. companies. Many occupy staff support positions, such as human resources and communications, rather than positions with line responsibilities offering greater opportunities for advancement to the top. Similarly, women serving as corporate officers are often the corporate secretary, treasurer or general counsel, rather than head of operations. Nevertheless, a number of business women are in the pipeline for top corporate positions and others currently hold positions such as the President of an American Airlines regional airline, and President of Chancellor Capital Management, to name just two. Women hold corporate board seats on 80% of the 500 largest U.S. companies. In addition, about 13% of the partners of the largest law firms are women, whereas less than half that number are partners in comparable accounting firms.

The profiles of minorities in the workplace are similar to those of women. Minorities, too, are making their greatest impact as entrepreneurs. At the end of the 1980's, minorities owned 1.2 million businesses in the following relative proportions: African American — 34.7%; Asian American/Pacific Islander — 29.1%; Hispanic — 34.5%; American Indian/Native Alaskan — 1.7%. Today, minority-owned businesses represent the fastest growing segment of start-up companies. From 1982 to 1992, the number of African American-owned businesses alone doubled, from over 308,260 to 620,912, with total revenues of

$ 32.2 billion. African American-owned businesses are, by themselves, a rapidly expanding force in the economy. With the increase in numbers of minority-owned businesses has come a commensurate increase in economic power. Revenues have been up as well, often outstripping by significant margins the sales of companies owned by non-minorities. Minorities own businesses in a variety of industries, with the greatest concentration in manufacturing, finance, insurance, real estate, and construction. In the mid-nineties, the health care, and technology and science industries were becoming increasingly popular.

Trends already identified in connection with women-owned companies also apply to minority-owned firms. Some difficulties with obtaining financing surface here as well, counteracted somewhat by the emergence of minority-owned venture capital firms that provide capital to and have financed public offerings for minority-owned companies. Nevertheless, like women, minority business persons at times must finance their businesses with credit cards. Minority-owned firms have also acted to help those most in need. When compared with non-minority enterprises, approximately twice as many minority-owned businesses actively recruit employees from low income neighborhoods.

Like women, minorities are generally under-represented in the executive suites of large companies. Nevertheless, some are attaining high level positions in the country's largest companies, such as Vice Chair of American Express and President of Time-Warner. Minorities hold only approximately 2% of board positions of the country's fifty largest corporations.

SECTION II. OTHER PERSPECTIVES OF BUSINESS

Members of many different disciplines study business organizations: accountants, economists, lawyers, and moral philosophers, to name a few. Each discipline focuses on particular attributes of a business, often to the exclusion of others. The view of a business through the lens of any one discipline may be very much like the proverbial description of the elephant from the perspective of one with a limited perspective. It is a partial truth that informs one's comprehension of the whole. That is why understanding the law of business organizations is aided by some familiarity with the perspectives of accountants and economists. Legal rules governing businesses may be based on principles originating in these disciplines. For example, correct application of the rules governing payment of corporate dividends requires an understanding of the underlying accounting principles.

Accountants perform several functions for businesses. They design and implement control systems that help companies avoid waste and detect wrongdoing. Accountants are also a company's financial historians. They develop systems to record business transactions as they occur and summarize the results in reports known as financial statements. Independent accountants are used to audit a company's books and records to verify that the company's financial representations are correct.

Financial statements portray a company's financial health at a particular point in time. One of these statements, the balance sheet, describes the company's assets based on their historical value and the sources of the money used to acquire the assets. A balance sheet indicates the extent to which company assets were acquired with funds provided by owner/investors, business creditors or company earnings.

One commentator has criticized the way that current systems of accounting influence our conception of company wealth. Margaret Blair has observed that:

> The accounting system that U.S. corporations use tallies returns on equipment, inventories, and other physical assets but provides no information about the return a company can earn on other kinds of investments, such as investments in the skills of its employees or in organizational capabilities. The system also fails to measure and count as wealth creation the share of the rents generated by the firm that are captured by employees [or other stakeholders]. Instead, the system "treats investment in people as a cost, biasing managers away from human capital," as David Levine has argued. Thus even directors and managers who understand their jobs to be maximizing total wealth creation and who are well motivated to pursue this goal, are generally receiving partial and misleading information about the sources of wealth in their firms.*

In contrast to accountants, business organization lawyers are mainly concerned with the legal status of a business entity and the legal rules that govern it. These rules apply to the company's formation, structure, ability to raise capital and distribute earnings, and the relationships among the company, its owners, its managerial employees and its creditors. (Issues concerning non-managerial employees are primarily covered in other areas of the law.)

Economists focus on the economic functions of the business enterprise or firm. Often taking a broader view of the business organization than either lawyers or accountants, economists consider the economic interrelationships of owners, creditors and employees within a firm, and the position of the firm within markets. Some economists view a business organization as an association of contractual relationships, whereas lawyers focus on the company's legal status as an entity created by the state. The following comments consider these differences in approach.

Henry N. Butler, The Contractual Theory of the Corporation, 11 George Mason University Law Review, 99, 100, 123 (Summer 1989)*

The contractual theory of the corporation is in stark contrast to the legal concept of the corporation as an entity created by the state. The entity theory of the corporation supports state intervention — in the form of either direct regulation or the facilitation of shareholder litigation — in the corporation on the ground that the state created the corporation by granting it a charter. The contractual theory views the corporation as founded in private contract, where the role of the state is limited to enforcing contracts. In this regard, a state charter merely recognizes the existence of a "nexus of contracts" called a corporation. Each contract in the "nexus of contracts" warrants the same legal and constitutional protections as other legally enforceable contracts. Moreover, freedom of contract requires that parties to the "nexus of contracts" must be allowed to structure their relations as they desire.

....

[T]he contractual theory of the corporation offers a new perspective on the corporation and the role of corporation law. The corporation is in no sense a ward of the state; it is, rather, the product of contracts among the owners and others. Once this point is fully recognized by the state legislators and legal commentators, the corporate form may finally be free of unnecessary and intrusive legal chains.

Other commentators are concerned with the questions of whose interests the corporation must serve.

Margaret M. Blair, Ownership and Control: Rethinking Corporate Governance for the Twenty-First Century 11-13 (1995 The Brookings Institution)**

A final development that has brought corporate governance issues to the forefront is the dramatic breakdown of the socialist economies of Eastern Europe and the former Soviet Union. In Czechoslovakia, Estonia, Latvia, Lithuania, Poland, Russia, and the Ukraine, politicians and their advisers from the West have been frantically trying to create from scratch both the governance systems that can manage and control the newly privatized industries and the legal and institutional infrastructures needed to support these governance systems and to protect and encourage further investment. The immense task is especially difficult because the existing models in the United States, Western Europe and Asia are so poorly understood.

If corporate governance questions were merely zero-sum power games (for example, does the chief executive get a larger bonus or do the shareholders get

---

a larger dividend?), the public policy questions would be interesting but not terribly compelling. But the experiences of the former socialist countries make clear that the ability of corporations to generate wealth in a sustainable way depends crucially on who has what ownership and control rights over corporate resources, how decisions get made, and what pressures, terms and conditions come into play. The U.S. system performs vastly better than the systems in most other countries of the world, but important questions remain about why it performs as well as it does and whether it performs as well as it should or could.

The debate about corporate governance is shaped by three very different clusters of views about how governance arrangements affect the performance of corporations and their ability to generate wealth and about how corporate governance rules should be reformed. Each view starts from a different set of assumptions about whether and how U.S. corporations might be performing suboptimally. Because these underlying assumptions are fundamentally at odds with each other, the debate has been confusing and not very productive. But these critical assumptions are rarely examined, and, consequently, the advocates of various reforms often talk past each other.

The first view, which I call the "finance model" holds that corporations are owned by shareholders and should therefore be managed in the interest of shareholders. But because the shares of large companies are held by tens of thousands of individuals and institutions, each holding only a tiny percentage of the total outstanding equity, shareholders are too dispersed to exercise tight control over managers. Corporate managers, therefore, often waste resources by managing companies in ways that serve their own interests, sometimes to the detriment of their "shareholder-owners." This view goes back to legal scholar A. A. Berle and economist Gardiner C. Means, who in 1932 first documented what they called the "separation of ownership from control." Reform measures that start from the finance model premise generally attempt to make managers more responsive to shareholder interests.

An opposing view is that managers are too attentive to the interests of shareholders. According to this view, financial markets are impatient and shortsighted, and shareholders do not understand what is in their own long-term interests. They prefer short-run gains to larger, but deferred, payouts and thus tend to sell out or underprice the shares of companies that emphasize sustained investments in research and development or costly market expansion strategies. Proponents of this "market myopia" point of view argue that companies under perform in some sense because management is too responsive to the short-term pressures coming from the financial markets. The reform measures they advocate focus on insulating management from this short-term pressure or, alternatively, attempting to realign the interests of shareholders by discouraging trading and encouraging long-term shareholding.

The third view is that shareholders understand fully what is in their own financial self-interest [both in the short run and in the long run], but what is optimal for shareholders often is not optimal for the rest of society. That is, the corporate policies that generate the most wealth for shareholders may not be the policies that generate the greatest total social wealth.

....

———————

Finally, some ethicists and moral philosophers view the business organization as a moral agent, accountable to groups extending beyond the enterprise constituents. Proponents of this view reject the idea that a company is only the property of its owners. They focus, instead, on the company as a social institution. According to Nesteruk and Risser:

> [C]orporate decision makers should recognize that their firms are responsible to a broader constituency than shareholders alone; a constituency including employees, customers, local communities, and the public at large. This recognition reinforces social expectations which encourage corporate decision makers to act more as public trustees, and not merely as agents for the shareholders, in the performance of their corporate roles.[5]

SECTION III. DEVELOPMENT OF AMERICAN BUSINESS CORPORATION LAW

Had we the space, and students, the time, we would recount fully the history of American business organization law. It is a compelling story. During the nineteenth century, the energy of the fledgling U.S. economy encouraged experimentation with different business forms. As the economy matured, the corporate form gained ascendancy and relegated to lesser roles other forms that had once seemed promising. The pages that follow tell the story of the rise of the modern business corporation and the influences that shaped its development. Although the discussion focuses on the corporation, the issues it raises also apply to other business forms.

A. WHAT A CORPORATION IS

One of the oldest and most interesting questions in corporation law is the question of what a corporation is. It will help in approaching that question to take as a starting point something that is incontestable: A corporation, or at least its legal form,[6] is a creation of the state. Never in the English or American

———————

[5] Jeffrey Nesteruk & David T. Risser, *Conceptions of the Corporation and Ethical Decision Making in Business*, 12 BUS. & PROF. ETHICS J., 87-88 (1993).

[6] This parenthetical is necessary because there is a body of scholarship developed by the corporate "realists" during the seventy-five-year period ending in the late 1940s that views the corporation essentially as the corporate enterprise. Adolph Berle, for example, wrote that "the entity commonly known as 'corporate entity' takes its being from the reality of the underlying enterprise." Berle, *The Theory of Enterprise Entity*, 47 COLUM. L. REV. 343 (1947).

Unlike corporations, individuals do not need state authorization to form sole proprietorships and general partnerships. Partnerships are, however, governed by state business organization law. There are no separate state business codes establishing sole proprietorships as a form of business.

experience have individuals had the power by themselves to create business corporations or, put another way, never have individuals had the power to create enterprises as corporations. In England, before the American Revolution, business corporations were formed by the sovereign or by Parliament. In the United States, business corporations have been formed by the special act of a state legislature or of Congress[7] or, more usually in modern times, by a state official acting under the authority of a general corporation statute. Under this system, someone who wishes to form a corporation, or more usually that person's lawyer, drafts the corporate charter and delivers it to the office of the proper state official, usually the secretary of state. If the charter conforms to statutory requirements, the office issues the charter in the form presented.

If a corporation, or at least its legal form, is a creation of the state, just what kind of creation is it? In American law, our earliest authoritative answer was by Chief Justice Marshall in the *Dartmouth College* case: "A corporation is an artificial being, invisible, intangible, and existing only in contemplation of law."[8] It seems clear that Marshall took part of this conception from Lord Coke, who in 1613 had said that a corporation "is only *in abstracto*; ... a corporation ... is invisible, immortal, and rests only in intendment and consideration of the law."[9] The rest of Marshall's conception, that the corporation is an artificial "being," may have originated with Pope Innocent IV, who in the thirteenth century spoke of a particular form of ecclesiastical corporation, one called a collegium or college, as a person, saying, "the college is in corporate matters figured as a person."[10] But perhaps Marshall's direct influence here was Blackstone, who in his *Commentaries* called the corporation an "artificial person."[11]

American judicial comment has tended to follow the Marshall conception, but there are some exceptions, the most notable being from *Farmers' Loan & Trust Co. v. Pierson*:

> [A] corporation is more nearly a method than a thing, and ... the law in dealing with a corporation has no need of defining it as a person or an entity, or even as an embodiment of functions, rights and duties, but may treat it as a name for a useful and usual collection of jural relations, each one of which must in every instance be ascertained, analyzed and assigned

---

[7] Probably the most famous private corporation formed by a special Act of Congress was the Second Bank of the United States, which was the subject of *McCulloch v. Maryland*, 17 U.S. 315 (1819).

[8] *Trustees of Dartmouth College v. Woodward*, 17 U.S. 518, 636 (1819).

[9] *Case of Sutton's Hospital*, 77 Eng. Rep. 937, 973 (K.B. 1613).

[10] Translation from Koessler, *The Person in Imagination or Persona Ficta of the Corporation*, 9 LA. L. REV. 435, 437 (1949).

[11] 1 William Blackstone, Commentaries on the Laws of England 467 (1765).

to its appropriate place according to the circumstances of the particular case, having due regard to the purposes to be achieved.[12]

Along this same line is *Scandia Down Corp. v. Euroquilt, Inc.*,[13] in which the Seventh Circuit said that "[t]he corporation is just a convenient name for a complex web of contracts among managers, workers, and suppliers of equity and debt capital." But even cases like *Farmers' Loan* and *Scandia Down* are not so much rejections of Marshall's conception as they are reminders that reference to that conception does not answer specific legal questions about the rights and obligations of a particular corporation and the persons involved with it.

Although the historical and judicial conceptions of the corporation are helpful, they are not complete, and their usefulness is limited. We believe that the most useful conception of the corporation begins with a view of the corporation as an entity having a legal status separate and distinct from the people who comprise it[14] and consisting of a structure within which the corporate enterprise (basically its assets and its personnel taken together as a going concern) is contained. At the heart of the structure constituting the corporation is the corporation's charter. What the state creates by the grant of a charter is an entity consisting of a legal structure. This structure is made up of (1) the rules relating to the affairs of the corporation,[15] which rules are contained in the charter, in the corporation statute, and in other laws, and (2) the right to do business within the limits specified in the charter.

We have up until now focused on the structure constituting the corporation that is created by the grant of a charter, and on the corporation's enterprise. Upon reflection it will be seen that there are some items left unaccounted for in our discussion so far. Those are items, such as the rules of corporate governance contained in the bylaws, that relate to the affairs of the corporation rather than to its business. Since these items add to and shore up the corporation's basic structure, we believe that they should be considered part of the corporate entity — not as components of that part of the entity created directly by the state, but as part of the entity as it has been added to in accordance with rules made by the state.

Taking all this into consideration, we can now go this far in saying what a corporation is: A corporation is an entity that consists of an intangible structure for the conduct of the entity's affairs and operations, the essence of which is

---

[12] 222 N.Y.S. 533, 544-45 (1927).

[13] 772 F.2d 1423 (7th Cir. 1985).

[14] In contrast, partnerships have not traditionally been treated as entities distinct from the partners, although the newer laws of some jurisdictions take this approach for some purposes.

[15] The affairs of a corporation consist of those actions relating to the corporation's internal workings as an entity as opposed to those actions relating to the conduct of the corporation's business. Examples would be the management structure laid out in the corporation statute, the rules in the statute and the bylaws about the conduct of shareholders' and directors' meetings, and the rules setting voting requirements for various corporate actions.

created by the state, and that possesses the rights and obligations given or allowed it by the state. It would help in understanding what a corporation is, of course, to know something about the rights and obligations that are given or allowed to corporations by the state. It would especially help if those rights and obligations could be categorized in such a way that a reference to the categorization itself would provide essentially the same information as would an encyclopedic listing of the rights and obligations. There already exists one basis for such a categorization. It is Blackstone's conception of the corporation as an artificial person. What we might do at this point, then, is to examine the rights and obligations of corporations in order to see the extent to which they equal or differ from those of natural persons.

The best place to start is with a corporation statute. In the sections of a corporation statute relating to purposes and powers, we find the main recitation of a corporation's rights. Using § 3.01 of the Model Business Corporation Act (1984) as a paradigm,[16] we see that a corporation may be organized under the Act for the purpose of engaging in any lawful business, unless the company is in a regulated business like banking or insurance (the idea being that there are special purpose statutes allowing the incorporation of banks and insurance companies). A corporation's purpose or purposes may be specified in its charter, but it is not necessary to do so, because according to the Official Comment to Model Act § 2.02, "a corporation formed without reference to a purpose clause will automatically have the purpose of engaging in any lawful business under section 3.01(a)."

Turning to the question of a corporation's powers, we find in Model Act § 3.02 a fifteen-item list of powers possessed by all corporations incorporated under the Act. Fourteen of these items are specific, covering the rights to own and deal in property, make contracts, sue and be sued, and so on. The last is a catchall indicating that the corporation has and may "do any other act, not inconsistent with law, that furthers the business and affairs of the corporation." So far as the corporation statute goes, then, it seems that a corporation's powers equal those of a natural person, at least in furtherance of a lawful purpose. And a further look at the statute shows that corporations in fact have the power to act in ways that do not further a lawful purpose, for in § 3.04 the statute provides that "the validity of corporate action may not be challenged on the ground that the corporation lacks or lacked power to act."

As to both rights and obligations, drafters of statutes of general applicability typically wish to include corporations along with natural persons, and they usually accomplish this by including corporations within the definition of "person." For example, § 2(a)(2) of the Securities Act of 1933 provides that "[t]he term

---

[16] The MODEL BUSINESS CORPORATION ACT (1984, as amended, 1994), hereinafter MODEL BUSINESS CORP. ACT (1984), was drafted by the Committee on Corporate Laws of the American Bar Association's Section of Business Law. It has been adopted in whole or in significant part by almost half of the states.

'person' means ... a corporation...." Seeing the wisdom of a general provision to this effect, Congress has provided at 1 U.S. Code 1 that "[i]n determining the meaning of any Act of Congress, unless the context indicates otherwise ... the [word] 'person' ... [includes] corporations." State codes often provide likewise.

The common law, has also long considered a corporation to possess the same rights and obligations as a natural person when that seems appropriate. Criminal law offers the most interesting example, with courts having a history, going back at least to the mid-seventeenth century, of treating corporations as they would natural persons in the context of some common law crimes. By the mid-nineteenth century, the context in which courts would do so had become generalized for crimes other than intentional crimes, and early in the current century this exception largely disappeared.

With respect to federal constitutional rights, the picture changes only slightly. All questions relating to the constitutional rights of corporations as persons have not been answered, but the most important have been. Corporations have the first amendment right of free speech and enjoy the due process and equal protection rights granted to persons by the fifth and fourteenth amendments. Corporations have fourth amendment protection against unreasonable searches and seizures, although the Supreme Court has indicated that this protection is not necessarily as extensive as that enjoyed by natural persons. Finally, the Supreme Court has held, in a case involving the question of whether a corporation must produce its books and papers for a grand jury, that corporations do not enjoy the fifth amendment's protection against self-incrimination. In reaching that decision, the Court developed the theory that (1) the corporation is a creature of the state, (2) the corporation received certain franchises from the state, and (3) the state therefore has a right to inquire whether these franchises "had been abused [and to] demand the production of the corporate books and papers for that purpose," whereas a natural person "owes no duty to the state ... to divulge his business, or to open his doors to investigation.... He owes no such duty to the state, since he receives nothing therefrom, beyond the protection of his life and property."[17]

From this brief survey of the rights and obligations of corporations, it may be said that corporations have largely the same rights and obligations as do natural persons, although the parallel is not exact. This conclusion allows us to complete our statement of what a corporation is: A corporation is an entity that consists of an intangible structure for the conduct of the entity's affairs and operations, the essence of which is created by the state, and that possesses the rights and obligations given or allowed it by the state, which rights and obligations more or less parallel those of natural persons.

---

[17] *Hale v. Henkel*, 201 U.S. 43, 74-75 (1906).

B. THE DEVELOPMENT OF AMERICAN BUSINESS CORPORATION LAW

The law in America relating to business corporations underwent extensive development during the nineteenth century, and that development has continued, along somewhat different lines, to the present time. It will be helpful if we examine those developments one century at a time.

1. Nineteenth Century Developments

At the beginning of the nineteenth century, American entrepreneurs could choose to form either a common law general partnership or a statutory corporation. Both were British imports. At that time, investors in both types had unlimited liability. The key differences between the two lay in their governance structures. The general partnership had a participatory form of governance; the corporation, centralized management. In the 1820's, the U.S. imported the limited partnership form from France. The form offered limited liability to partners who did not participate in management. It also avoided some of the technical requirements then characteristic of corporate formation. Over time, the corporate form shed many attributes that had originally limited its popularity. The transformation to the modern corporation resulted from three separate movements in the development of American business corporation law during the nineteenth century:

1. The movement from incorporation by special legislative acts to incorporation under the provisions of a general corporation statute.
2. The movement from restrictive toward enabling corporation statutes.
3. The movement from unlimited to limited liability of shareholders.

Each movement formed an essential step in creating the modern American business corporation and the ascendancy of the popularity of the corporate form.

a. From Special Acts to General Corporation Statutes

At the beginning of the nineteenth century, corporations were formed only by the special acts of state legislatures or, occasionally, Congress. That began to change in 1811, when New York passed what might be called the first general corporation statute, although "general" is a bit strained in this context, since the statute provided only for the incorporation of businesses engaged in the manufacture of a few specified products. Other states began following New York's lead, and in 1837 Connecticut adopted a general corporation statute that allowed the incorporation of any lawful business. This process of moving to truly general corporation statutes continued state by state throughout the rest of the nineteenth century and was complete by the century's end.

This is not to say, however, that incorporation by special legislative act ended as soon as a state passed a general corporation statute. In fact, in many states, after the passage of a general corporation statute, incorporations by special act occurred several times as frequently as did incorporations under the general statute. One reason was that those with political influence were able to induce the legislature to issue more favorable charters by special act than the legislature was willing to grant under a general statute. Also, the early general corporation statutes did not meet the needs of some businesses, and the owners or promoters of these businesses had no choice but to seek incorporation under a special act. But by the end of the nineteenth century, all states had either drastically limited or prohibited, sometimes by means of a constitutional provision, incorporation except under a general statute.

b. From Restrictive to Enabling Statutes

At the beginning of the nineteenth century, all the corporate charters granted by special legislative acts were restrictive, and that restrictiveness carried over into the general corporation statutes that states passed with increasing frequency as the century progressed. The statutory restrictions on corporations took many forms, all relating to the widely held fear of the evils that might befall society from the existence of powerful corporations. One restriction was a limit on the amount of capital a corporation could amass. As Brandeis described the reason behind that restriction, "[t]here was a sense of some insidious menace inherent in large aggregations of capital, particularly when held by corporations."[18]

The amounts of capital allowed corporations varied widely by state, and often also by the type of business a corporation was to conduct. For example, New York's original 1811 general corporation statute, which allowed the incorporation of only a few types of businesses, limited capital to $ 100,000. And when the New York legislature amended the statute in 1817 to allow the incorporation of additional types of businesses, it set lower capital limits for the newly allowed incorporations: $ 50,000 for a corporation that was to manufacture salt, for example. A nineteenth century restriction that went hand in hand with the limitation on capital was a limitation on the amount of indebtedness a corporation could maintain. Another typical provision in the restrictive statutes of the nineteenth century was a limitation on the duration of corporations, with the usual limits ranging from twenty to fifty years. In addition, until late in the century, corporation statutes usually limited the types of businesses that could be incorporated under them. Along these same lines, under the restrictive nineteenth century statutes the powers that a corporation was allowed to exercise in furtherance of its business were, by modern standards, severely limited. Among these limitations was a prohibition on a corporation's owning stock in another corporation, thus preventing a corporation from circumventing statutory restrictions by operating through subsidiaries.

---

[18] *Louis K. Liggett Co. v. Lee*, 288 U.S. 517, 549 (1933) (Brandeis, J., dissenting).

The corporate trust came into prominence in the 1870s as a way to minimize the effect of these restrictions, with the Standard Oil Trust the most famous. The nineteenth century trust was the forerunner of the modern holding company, and it operated in much the same way. Shareholders in a group of related corporations, each with a restrictive charter, deeded their shares to trustees who managed the corporate group as a single enterprise.

The nineteenth century corporate trust was short-lived, however, as a device for avoiding restrictive corporation statutes. The reason was simple: Restrictive statutes began to disappear. The movement away from restrictive corporation statutes began in 1875, when New Jersey passed the first relatively nonrestrictive (or enabling) corporation statute. Over the next two decades the New Jersey legislature amended its statute to carry the enabling philosophy further, with the process culminating in a revised and full-blown enabling statute adopted in 1896. As these statutory developments progressed, the New Jersey corporation rather than the trust became the vehicle of choice for large businesses. (The Standard Oil Trust was an early convert, incorporating in New Jersey in 1882.) During the last quarter of the nineteenth century, other states began following New Jersey's lead. As Brandeis put it, "the great industrial states yielded in order not to lose wholly the prospect of revenue and the control incident to domestic incorporation."[19] Among the states that passed enabling statutes in the nineteenth century was Delaware, but during that century neither Delaware nor any other state was able to push aside New Jersey as the haven for corporations.

c. From Unlimited to Limited Liability

Perhaps the most important nineteenth century development in corporation law was the movement from unlimited to limited liability of shareholders. When the century opened, unlimited shareholder liability was the norm for American corporations. That rule eroded as the century progressed, and by 1900 limited liability was virtually universal. In 1911, when Nicholas Murray Butler was president of Columbia University, he put the importance of these developments this way:

> I weigh my words when I say that in my judgment the limited liability corporation is the greatest single discovery of modern times.... Even steam and electricity are far less important than the limited liability corporation, and they would be reduced to comparative impotence without it.[20]

Because everyone living today takes limited shareholder liability for granted, the cost society pays for limited liability is rarely considered. Nevertheless, a cost is there, and it is substantial. And it grows every time a corporation goes

---

[19] *Id.* 559-60.

[20] *Quoted in* 1 William Meade Fletcher, Cyclopedia of the Law of Private Corporations § 21 (1917).

bankrupt leaving creditors unpaid. The point is not, however, that limited liability is bad. The point is that limited liability is not bad only to the extent of the countervailing benefits society receives from it. In the case of the business corporation, what society mainly receives are (1) an increased amount of capital invested for the provision of goods and services and (2) an increased tolerance for risk taking with the capital that is invested.

2. Twentieth Century Developments

During the twentieth century, American business corporation law has developed along three lines. First, Delaware has emerged as the leading corporate state, accompanied by a trend toward congruence with Delaware in other states' laws and approaches to corporations. The second has been a perfection of the enabling concept in corporation statutes. Third, there has been the movement from corporate regulation by the states to increasing coregulation by the federal government.

a. Emergence of Delaware and the Trend Toward Congruence in Other States

When the twentieth century began, New Jersey was the premier corporate state. That soon changed. When Woodrow Wilson became governor in 1911, he immediately mounted an effort to return to a restrictive approach to corporations. The legislature agreed and in 1913 gutted the enabling provisions from New Jersey's corporation statute. Consequences followed quickly. Corporations flocked to Delaware, which had a statute very much like the old New Jersey statute. And under the commerce clause of the federal Constitution, these corporations had the right to operate in New Jersey and in any other state so long as they were engaged in interstate commerce. From New Jersey's viewpoint the net results were these: salutary effect from corporate reforms, zero; loss of revenues from corporations, substantial. New Jersey stood that for only four years. In 1917, with Woodrow Wilson in the White House, the New Jersey legislature again amended its corporation statute, this time to undo the Wilson-era reforms.

By 1917, however, large corporations had come to like their home in Delaware, and they had no interest in moving back to New Jersey. Delaware ever since has continued to be hospitable to corporations. Its legislature has moved quickly in response to corporate desires for changes in its corporation statute. Its approach to corporate taxation has always been a gentle milking, with care being taken not to squeeze enough to hurt. Its secretary of state's office has been run like a good service business. And its courts, which like those of all states have the power to hear cases involving domestic corporations no matter where a controversy arises, have had judges who are knowledgeable in corporation law. As a result, most of America's largest corporations have been incorporated in Delaware.

During the twentieth century, however, there has developed a great congruence in corporation statutes and to a lesser degree in the ways in which the states approach corporations. All states have and have had for decades an enabling corporation statute. This has resulted from two forces. First, each state knows that having a restrictive corporation statute will cost it revenues and will have no real effect, as New Jersey learned to its great cost. Second, the Model Business Corporation Act (1969), hereinafter Model Act (1969), and its successor, the Model Act (1984), have been available for easy adoption, as a majority of the states have done. The Committee on Corporate Laws of the American Bar Association's Section of Business Law, which drafted these Model Acts, is comprised of some of the country's best corporate lawyers. The committee has worked hard to perfect these Acts to the point that they are not only generally congruent with the Delaware statute, but are in certain respects superior to the Delaware statute, at least from the point of view of corporations and their lawyers.

Perhaps because of competition from Delaware, other states also have tended at least to approach Delaware's general treatment of corporations. States have realized that it does no good to set corporate taxes that are out of line with Delaware's, and this has led to congruence. Most secretaries of state run their offices along the lines of Delaware's, or at least more like Delaware's than like a classic bureaucracy. It is in the area of judicial decisionmaking that other states are furthest from Delaware, because no other state has Delaware's high percentage of judges who are experts with respect to corporation law and because much more litigation about corporation law occurs in Delaware than in any other state.

b. Perfection of the Enabling Concept

The enabling concept has been fine-tuned throughout this century, and it also has taken on a slightly different cast than it had when the century began, for most of the examples of fine-tuning during this century have related to internal matters of corporate decisionmaking rather than to the corporation's interactions in society. Here are some examples that are found both in the Delaware statute and in both Model Acts. First, short-form mergers: If one corporation owns 90% of the stock of another corporation, the corporations can merge without the approval of either corporation's shareholders, which usually would be required in a merger. Second, preferred stock issuable in series: A corporation's charter may provide that the board of directors can set the terms of individual series of preferred stock without the approval of shareholders. Third, consents in lieu of meetings: The shareholders and the board of directors may act without a meeting, so long as each shareholder (or, under Delaware law, enough shareholders to pass on the action in question, which is usually a majority) or director agrees in writing to the action.

c. State Regulation to Coregulation with the Federal Government

At the turn of the twentieth century, the regulation of corporations was virtually the sole concern of the states, and that was especially true with respect to regulation of the internal affairs of corporations. The New Deal securities legislation, especially the Securities Exchange Act of 1934 (the Exchange Act), changed this substantially. Most of this legislation relates directly to the issuance or trading of securities and is properly considered securities regulation rather than corporate regulation. Some of this legislation, however, serves almost purely to fill gaps that Congress saw in the state scheme for the regulation of the affairs of corporations.

The best example is the regulation of the proxy solicitation process that the Exchange Act mandates for publicly held corporations. State corporation statutes provide no regulation of the solicitation of proxies, and the states are never likely to provide such regulation. Congress filled that gap with a highly formalized and detailed scheme of regulation that begins with the Exchange Act and carries over into voluminous rules of the Securities and Exchange Commission. This regulation, along with other federal securities law having regulatory attributes in common with the proxy rules, is in fact so involved in corporate regulation that it has come to be called federal corporation law. We shall return to federal corporation law later in the book.

C. TYPES OF AMERICAN CORPORATIONS

There are four types of corporations in America: business, nonprofit, government, and public. We shall take these up in reverse order, starting with the type furthest removed from the center of this book's concerns.

1. Public Corporations

Public corporations are corporations that function as governments. The most common examples are municipalities such as cities, towns, and villages. Also common are governmental authorities of various sorts that serve some special purpose, airport authorities being a common example. Public corporations are sometimes formed by a special legislative act. This would be most common in the cases of authorities and of large cities, in each case because of the need to tailor the charter to fit a unique situation. In most situations, however, incorporation is by the secretary of state or another state official acting under the authority of a general incorporation statute. Typically, under these statutes the residents of an unincorporated area that meets statutory requirements, such as level of population, vote to incorporate under a chosen name, the vote is certified by the county clerk or some other specified official, and the secretary of state then issues a charter. As in the case of all corporations, the rights and obligations of public corporations are spelled out by statute, and typically these rights and obligations are in general similar to the rights and obligations of business corporations.

Although public corporations have the basics of their existence in common with business corporations, the two types of corporations share few other characteristics, and for this reason we shall not deal with public corporations further in this book.

2. Government Corporations

Government corporations are corporations that are wholly or partly owned by a government and that were formed by that government to perform some special purpose. Examples are Amtrak and the Tennessee Valley Authority, the first of which is partly owned and the second of which is wholly owned by the federal government. These corporations and twenty-two others were formed by special Acts of Congress and are subject to a common set of laws relating, in the main, to their finances. The reason Congress formed these government corporations was to take their organization, their operations, and their finances out of the governmental sphere and place them in a more businesslike structure.

The best-known government corporation is the United States Postal Service. In the statute establishing the Postal Service, Congress avoided calling the Service a corporation, describing it instead as "an independent establishment of the executive branch of the Government of the United States." When one examines what kind of "independent establishment" the Postal Service is, however, it becomes obvious that the Postal Service is a corporation. This is seen most clearly in the sections of its establishing statute that deal with the Service's powers and organization, for these are the standard powers and organization of a corporation. The reason Congress did not call the Postal Service a corporation may well have been to distinguish it from the other government corporations, discussed in the previous paragraph, that it wished to subject to a common set of laws.

Government corporations are highly specialized entities. The legal rules relating to them are hybrids of the rules relating to business corporations and government agencies, and the affairs of government corporations are handled by only a few lawyers. For these reasons we shall not return to those corporations.

3. Nonprofit Corporations

There is a great deal of confusion in the public's mind about what it means to be a nonprofit corporation. A usual idea is that such corporations may not make profits, or that they must arrange their affairs in such a way that profits are unlikely. These ideas are far from the mark. At the heart of what distinguishes nonprofit from business corporations is the fact that nonprofit corporations do not have shareholders, or owners of any kind. They may or may not have members. If they do, the members may function very much like shareholders. In a nonprofit corporation, however, profits may not be paid to the members as dividends. This does not mean that the corporation may not or should not make profits. Many hospitals, for example, are operated by nonprofit corporations, and their managers try hard to earn profits. The difference in this respect between nonprofit and business corporations simply is in what may be done with the profits.

Nonprofit corporations are of two types: eleemosynary (or charitable) and mutual-benefit. The distinguishing characteristic is whether the purpose of the corporation is to benefit its members or to benefit some other group or groups. Hospitals, private universities, and charities of all descriptions are typically organized in the form of eleemosynary nonprofit corporations, while social clubs offer a common example of mutual-benefit nonprofit corporations.

The tax treatment of nonprofit corporations varies depending upon whether the corporation is eleemosynary or mutual-benefit. Basically, an eleemosynary corporation does not pay taxes on its profits, and contributions to the corporation are deductible by the donors. As in the case of an eleemosynary corporation, a mutual-benefit nonprofit corporation escapes taxes on its profits, but contributions to the mutual-benefit corporation are not deductible by the contributors. In each case, these tax treatments will be available only when a corporation qualifies for them under the Internal Revenue Code and when the corporation files the proper application with the Internal Revenue Service. Also, profits of nonprofit corporations that arise from essentially commercial activities are taxable in a manner comparable to profits of business corporations.

All states now have general corporation statutes for nonprofit corporations, and incorporation under these statutes usually follows the same procedure as for business corporations. But there are exceptions. Under some statutes, for example, the approval of one or more state agencies is necessary before an eleemosynary corporation may be incorporated. There is no general corporation statute for nonprofit corporations at the federal level, but Congress occasionally creates a nonprofit corporation by special Act (a relatively recent example being Vietnam Veterans of America, Inc.).

Nonprofit corporation statutes are often less detailed than are business corporation statutes, and the case law relating directly to nonprofit corporations is sparse. As a result, a lawyer dealing with a nonprofit corporation sometimes is left to wonder just what the law is on a particular point. The correct conclusion usually can be reached by making the right analysis. A good way to begin is with the idea of trying to determine what a court would decide the law to be if it got the question. Assuming there is no statutory provision or nonprofit corporation case law on the particular point in the state of incorporation, there are only two places a court reasonably could look for an answer to the question. One is the case law outside the state relating to nonprofit corporations and the other is the law of the same or other states relating to business corporations. If there is relevant case law in another state relating to nonprofit corporations, and if the nonprofit corporation statute in the other state is analogous to the one in the state in question, a court likely will accept that case law, at least if it is not contrary to the state's law relating to business corporations. In the more usual situation, however, there is available no case law on point in any jurisdiction relating to nonprofit corporations.. In that situation, a court would look to the law relating to business corporations in the state of incorporation, or in other states if necessary, to answer the question by analogy.

As may be surmised from the preceding discussion, however, much of the law relating to business corporations carries over to nonprofit corporations. To a large degree, therefore, the rest of this book can be viewed as being about business and nonprofit corporations.

4. Business Corporations

Business corporations are of two types: publicly held and closely held.[21] A number of courts have attempted at least a partial definition or characterization of the closely held corporation. Some judges have described closely held corporations as little more than chartered partnerships or incorporated partnerships. Though descriptive, these characterizations are not by themselves analytically helpful. Most courts speaking on the subject, however, have focused on specific attributes of closely held corporations. Various judges taking this approach have viewed the closely held corporation as one in which (1) the corporation's stock is held in a few hands or in a few families; and (2) the corporation's stock is never or only rarely dealt in by buying or selling; or (3) as one in which the management and ownership of the corporation are substantially identical. In the leading case of *Donahue v. Rodd Electrotype Co.,* the court, while avoiding a definition, accepted some aspects of these earlier formulations and stated that the closely held corporation is "typified by (1) a small number of stockholders, (2) no ready market for the corporate stock, and (3) substantial majority stockholder participation in the management, direction, and operations of the corporation."[22] Most scholars who have examined the nature of closely held corporations have focused on one or more of the characteristics enumerated in *Donahue,* and the largest number of these scholars seems to have regarded the last of these characteristics as the most important.

We think it is incorrect, however, in attempting to distinguish closely held from publicly held corporations, to focus on the substantial involvement of majority shareholders in the management, direction, and operations of the corporation. Certainly this involvement is typically found in closely held corpora-

---

[21] These entities are also commonly referred to as close corporations. One sometimes sees "closed" substituted for "close," perhaps because the latter strikes the unaccustomed ear as strange. "Close" is the word of choice, however, among corporate lawyers. The use of the word in this context likely was derived from its early use as a description of a piece of land that is enclosed by a fence or hedge. "Closely held" is used frequently also. It is the term of choice for the drafters of the Model Act (1984). In this text, closely held is used generally to contrast this type of corporation from a publicly held one. Corporations formed pursuant to a close corporation statute are referred to as statutory close corporations. For a fuller discussion of the matters dealt with in this section, *see* Larry A. Soderquist, *Reconciling Shareholders' Rights and Corporate Responsibility: Close and Small Public Corporations,* 33 VAND. L. REV. 1387 (1980).

[22] 328 N.E.2d 505, (Mass. 1975).

tions, but it is not always found. For example, second-generation owners of a family corporation may have no interest in the business and may turn its management over to professionals. Moreover, at some point even first-generation shareholders in a family corporation may hire professional managers because of age, health, retirement, or the desire to devote effort to other ventures. This formulation of a closely held corporation definition is, thus, too narrow. In another sense, however, it is too broad, because many corporations that have stock trading on a stock exchange and that are without question publicly held are managed by their majority owners.

Defining the closely held corporation as a corporation having few shareholders also presents problems. In most closely held corporations, there are only a few shareholders. In some, however, the concept of "few" becomes strained. In most closely held corporations, the number of shareholders will tend to increase over the years. This especially will be true if restrictions are not placed on the transfer of shares, but it will be true in any case as shares find their way into the hands of second and later generations. Moreover, while questions of how few is "few" can obviously be resolved on an ad hoc basis, one surmises that in answering the question of whether a corporation is closely held, courts or others would look to factors other than simply the number of shareholders. For example, in deciding whether a corporation with 200 shareholders meets the test of having only a few shareholders, a court might wish to know whether the corporation's stock is publicly traded or whether its shareholders are active in the management of the corporation. This definition, then, presents problems that in some cases would not be resolved by a literal interpretation of the term "few."

We believe the best way to define the closely held corporation is by reference to the other factor discussed in *Donahue:* Whether there is a ready market for the corporation's stock. For one thing, using this test as a definition avoids the problems, just discussed, that one faces when using other suggested definitions. More important, we believe that whether or not there is a ready market for a corporation's stock is the major determinant in how a shareholder views his or her relationship to the corporation. In a corporation whose stock cannot easily be traded, a shareholder is likely to take a personal, long-term interest in the corporation. This shareholder is likely to view himself or herself as an owner of the corporation in a direct sense, and one can view this kind of shareholder relationship as a secondary characteristic of a closely held corporation. In a corporation having stock with a ready market, however, a shareholder is much more likely to view himself or herself primarily as the owner of a corporation's shares rather than as an owner of the corporation itself in any real sense. The owner of a small percentage of the stock of a local foundry may say, "I own a piece of that foundry." If he or she owns a small percentage of the shares of General Motors Corporation, the statement is more likely to be, "I own some GM stock."

Finally, of course, the opposite of "closely held" is "publicly held," and when one looks at the publicly held corporation, one almost necessarily focuses on the ease with which shares of the corporation trade in the public markets, which is another way of saying that there is a ready market for the corporation's stock. To be pure in our definition, we should focus on whether the shares of a particular corporation are publicly traded with some regularity. We should, that is, consider a corporation to be a closely held corporation even if its stock is sometimes publicly traded in the over-the-counter market, so long as its stock cannot be traded there with any certainty. However, since there exists a well-known and easy-to-apply test that nearly fits the pure requirements for distinguishing between closely held and publicly held corporations, we would use that test as a rule of thumb. The test is whether the corporation is required to file the reports called for by § 13 of the Securities Exchange Act of 1934 (the Exchange Act). This filing requirement arises in one of three ways: (1) the corporation has securities registered under § 12(b) of the Exchange Act because these securities trade on a securities exchange, (2) the corporation has securities registered under § 12(g) of the Exchange Act because it has assets exceeding $ 10 million[23] and a class of equity security held of record by 500 or more persons, or (3) the corporation is required, under the provisions of Exchange Act § 15(d), to file § 13 reports because it has in the past registered securities for public sale under the Securities Act of 1933. If a corporation meets any one of these requirements, it becomes what corporation lawyers call a "reporting company." The reporting company/nonreporting company dichotomy almost exactly duplicates the publicly held/closely held corporation dichotomy insofar as corporations go, because this duplication is exactly what the Exchange Act is designed to accomplish with its reporting requirements. If a corporation's stock is traded in the public markets, Congress wanted to ensure that the corporation would make public the information that is contained in the reports required to be filed by Exchange Act § 13.

There are consequences of the determination as to whether a corporation is closely held or publicly held. First, closely held corporations sometimes are allowed greater latitude than publicly held corporations in their internal management. For example, while informal decisionmaking outside of board meetings may be unacceptable in a publicly held corporation, it may be tolerated in a closely held corporation. Moreover, some types of agreements among shareholders as to the conduct of corporate affairs may be allowed in a closely held corporation but forbidden in a publicly held corporation. (The subject of the greater latitude sometimes allowed in closely held corporations will be returned to later in the book.) The second consequence of being classified as a closely held corporation can be more important. In a series of decisions going back over three decades, courts have developed the doctrine that shareholders in closely held corporations stand in a fiduciary relationship to each other. This can have serious consequences, as will be seen in a later chapter. Finally, and what may be most

---

[23] To get to the $ 10 million test, one needs to read Exchange Act rule 12g-1 along with § 12(g). The statute contains the figure $ 1 million, but this is increased to $ 10 million by the rule.

important, corporations having securities registered under Exchange Act § 12 are subject to a whole range of special requirements and constraints under other sections of the Exchange Act. For example, these corporations must comply with the proxy rules of the Securities and Exchange Commission when soliciting proxies from their shareholders, and their officers, directors, and substantial shareholders must follow the so-called short-swing trading provisions of E Act § 16. These and other Exchange Act requirements will be introduce in the book.

These differing treatments of closely held and publicly held corporations are important, but what is more interesting is the fact that in the bulk of corporation law, closely held and publicly held corporations are treated exactly the same. For example, the typical corporation statute contains one set of provisions that applies to all corporations. What makes the statute work for the smallest, one-shareholder corporation as well as the largest publicly held multinational is the flexibility built into the statutory provisions. Model Act § 8.03, for example, allows a corporation's board of directors to "consist of one or more members." With this flexibility, the statute serves the needs of the large publicly held corporation that wishes to have a fifteen-person board and the desires of the sole shareholder who wants to be the corporation's only director. Along these same lines, Model Act §§ 7.32 and 8.01(b) provide that a corporation with a shareholder agreement authorized by § 7.32 may split management functions among the shareholders, directors, and officers as it chooses. Notwithstanding the flexibility of statutes like the Model Act, however, some states have passed statutes relating only to closely held corporations. The Model Act originally had a closely held corporation supplement, but it was repealed when § 7.32 was added.

SECTION IV. DISTINGUISHING FEATURES OF BUSINESS LAW PRACTICE

What does it take to be a business lawyer? The following article provides a brief introduction to some of the skills that are most important for an effective business lawyer to have. Some are common to all areas of law practice; others, unique to the business law attorney.

Mark A. Sargent, What Does It Take? Hallmarks of the Business Lawyer, 5 Business Law Today 11, 11-14, (July/August 1996)*

What do business lawyers *do*? Until we understand what business lawyers do (and why clients pay them for it) we can't identify the relevant skills.

We should not be too confident, however, about our ability to explain what business lawyers do, even if we limit our definition of "business lawyer" to transactional lawyers as distinct from litigators. Even so limited, the term "business lawyer" encompasses many different ways of being a lawyer and many different legal cultures with their own norms and shared expectations.

The differences arise not only from differences in practice area (a bond lawyer vs. a real estate lawyer) but from differences in scope of function (a generalist who is an all-purpose counselor to CEOs and boards vs. a specialist with technical expertise in tax or securities law), practice setting (large firm vs. small firm vs. in-house), and in local legal cultures (Silicon Valley vs. Wall Street). One way to define what business lawyers do and what skills they need, might be to engage in deep descriptions of as many of those legal cultures as possible, treating the question of what business lawyers do as a problem in ethnography.

Is there not, however, something that links the different cultures of business lawyering?...

....

[According to Professor Ronald Gilson, business lawyers] help by bridging conflicts and mitigating uncertainties, and in so doing add value to transactions net of their fees.

This compelling explanation of what business lawyers do can be made more concrete by asking *how* business lawyers do what they do.... What skills do business lawyers need?

The Ability to Penetrate the Impenetrable. When I lead my students on their first forced march through Rule 144 or Regulation S-K, their initial reaction is stupefaction, and then rebellion. How could I possibly expect them to read and be responsible for this stuff? I tell them that the ability not only to read and understand such eye-glazing minutia, but to solve problems with it, is one of the things that separates lawyers from mere mortals, and that they will become real lawyers (and not just persons with a J.D.) when they learn how to penetrate what appears impenetrable to the untutored and faint of heart.

A Sense of Where You Are.... [T]he lawyer playing on the regulatory field ... must know not only the "law," but also when the rules are clear or muddy and when the "rules" are merely implicit, informal understandings. The lawyer needs to know the limits of administrative tolerance and the direction from which private litigation is likely to come. The lawyer must understand how far the public policy implicit in a regulatory system constrains the client's choices, and where it leaves room for innovation. The ability to predict the behavior of regulators and the private enforcers of regulatory prohibitions, and to assess the purpose and strength of regulatory constraints depends ... on the ability to take in the whole picture....

... How do lawyers bridge the gaps created by informational disparities and conflicts in investment goals and perspectives, while reducing the cost of dealing with those problems? Precise answers to that question will vary from deal to deal, but some general observations are possible.

Mountains, Molehills and Knowing the Difference. Business transactions, like most human interactions, are often thick with ambiguities about desires and intentions. In this murky atmosphere, it can be difficult to discern what is really important....

The good business lawyer, exercising judgment developed through both law school training and real world experience, thus makes deals work by helping parties sort through the confusion, targeting those impediments that need attention and leaving other issues to the obscurity they deserve. This skill of discrimination may not be unique to lawyers, but in a good business lawyer, it is highly cultivated, because it is the starting point for reducing transaction costs.

When to Use the Kandy-Kolored Tangerine-Flake Streamline Baby. The Kandy-Kolored Tangerine-Flake Streamline Baby was the fabulous car described by Tom Wolfe in his essay on those obsessed with customizing cars to almost impossible perfection....

....

Knowing when to rely on [a] standard implied term and when to create explicit, nonstandard "customized" terms, such as an equal opportunity rule for shareholder redemptions, is a skill that allows business lawyers to produce the most cost-effective means of mitigating or bridging conflicts.

The Universal Translation Machine ... Business lawyers ... must be skilled translators. In a regulatory context, for example, they must translate the impenetrable language of the regulatory scheme into advice that the client can understand and follow.

Perhaps more important, they help transacting parties understand what each other wants. A lawyer counseling an entrepreneur seeking venture capital, for instance, must help translate the client's business plan into something that a venture capitalist will read and consider seriously. Without the lawyer's skill in translation, a promising business may never be recognized by the potential capital provider. The inability to speak a common language is obviously one of the major obstacles to the information exchange needed to complete a transaction. The business lawyer's skill in translation helps remove that obstacle.

The Power of Detachment.... One should not presume greater rationality on the part of lawyers than anyone else, but their ability to detach themselves from their clients' passions and fears allows business lawyers to step onto a battlefield laid waste by their clients and to ask each other quietly: "How can we work this out?" That same detachment allows them, when helping an organization achieve its goals, to probe carefully into an apparent consensus, allowing decision makers to recognize and give voice to their real preferences. Such detachment is not the exclusive product of legal education or training, but it is a skill business lawyers must develop.

A Sense of an Ending.... The term "professionalism" has many meanings, but this instinct for taking the responsibility for holding things together and moving them along is an aspect of professionalism that makes business lawyers unusually valuable to their clients.

The Capacity to Be Trusted.... The capacity to earn a client's trust is more than a matter of zealous advocacy. Every client surely appreciates an unstinting advocate, but in the transactional context, more is needed. As suggested above, a client interested only in a hired gun who can help grab a disproportionate piece of the transactional pie is ultimately engaged in a zero-sum game. Similarly, the gunslinger approach to regulatory lawyering is usually counterproductive to the clients' interests. Regulators and lawyers are repeat players who each have stakes in the smooth operation of the regulatory system.

... More important, the counseling, conflict-bridging and problem-solving functions of the lawyer as transaction cost engineer would be impossible without the client's trust.

... Informational imbalances and the resulting uncertainty can be reduced without costly information production by using lawyers as reputational intermediaries. A respected lawyer's (or law firm's) presence can be read as vouching for representations made by a client, thereby reducing the need for supporting information. In such a case the lawyer's capacity to be trusted by *both* sides is crucial.

....

... The point to remember about all such examples, however, is that trust-keeping is not only part of the business lawyer's moral imperative, it is central to the business lawyer's very function, an ethical stock-in-trade without which a business lawyer's other skills would be superfluous.

The preceding article focuses on the attributes necessary to be an accomplished business lawyer. It also touches on some of the features distinguishing the practice of business law from other practices. Some other practices share certain of these features with business practice, of course, but no other practice comes close to being quite the same. The additional features discussed below further distinguish business practice by a typical good business lawyer.

A. PROSPECTIVE VIEWPOINT

Business lawyers work as planners, viewing transactions prospectively. They take the law as a given and the basis for structuring transactions. Litigators, on the other hand, view transactions retrospectively. They take the facts as a given and attempt to portray the law, by analysis and argument, as fitting the facts in a manner favorable to the client. This prospective/retrospective dichotomy leads business lawyers and litigators to approach law quite differently. For example, whether a particular statement by a court is dictum may be important to the litigator but virtually irrelevant to the business lawyer. The litigator does not mind working in the vanguard, and sometimes that is the only place from which a case can be won. The business lawyer, on the other hand, wishes to take no avoidable chance of running afoul of the law, and so if a court has interpreted a statutory provision to say a particular act may not be done, that usually is enough to dissuade the business lawyer, whether the court's interpretation was in dicta or holding.

B. SKILL AS A DRAFTER

In much the same way as a dexterous use of the hands distinguishes the surgeon, skill as a drafter distinguishes the business lawyer. The prototypical business lawyer is a consummate drafter. Care and precision, along with elegant use of the language, are points of the business lawyer's pride. That being true, business lawyers heavily judge other business lawyers on their drafting skill. New associates rarely are careful or precise enough in drafting to satisfy the seasoned business lawyer, but that usually is forgiven if the associate seems intent on measuring up. A lack of interest in care and precision, however, will keep an associate from ever being accepted as a business lawyer.

One often hears about the predilection of surgeons to solve patients' problems by an operation. And perhaps litigators see lawsuits as the solution to clients' problems more frequently than do other lawyers. Along these same lines, business lawyers think first about drafting to solve a client's problem. If in structuring a transaction a business lawyer comes across a legal ambiguity, his or her inclination is not to do research with the hopes of resolving the ambiguity, it is rather to avoid the ambiguity by drafting around it. Here is an example. Suppose a corporation lawyer practicing in Illinois is presented with a provision in a contract that says, "This Agreement shall be governed by and construed in accordance with the laws of the State of Illinois." The lawyer probably would like the idea of using Illinois law, but might reasonably wonder what the Illinois choice-of-law rules would provide as to the contract. Would they, for example, provide that the substantive law of another place rather than Illinois would govern the contract? Rather than research the question, the business lawyer likely will rewrite this provision along these lines: "This Agreement shall be governed by and construed in accordance with the local laws of the State of Illinois and not its choice-of-law rules."

C. PREDILECTION AGAINST TELLING A CLIENT NO

The mind set of the business lawyer is to find a way to accomplish what the client basically wants. Good business lawyers not only listen to the specific questions clients ask them, but they try to discern what at base the client wants to accomplish. Business lawyers might have to say no to the specific question or the client's original proposal for accomplishing the objective, but if at all possible they will present a permissible alternative designed to accomplish the real, often unspoken, goal. A president of a client might say, for example, that the corporation wants to pay a dividend of one dollar on its common stock. Realizing that the corporation has not enough surplus available for dividends under the governing statute, the lawyer may have to say that that cannot be done. The good lawyer would not leave the matter there, however. Understanding that what the client really wants is to take one dollar per share out of the corporation and give it to its shareholders, the good lawyer would look for a permissible way to do so. If there is capital surplus available, a distribution to the extent of capital surplus will probably be allowed under the governing statute. If there is not enough capital surplus for a one dollar per share distribution, additional capital surplus can be created, if necessary, by a charter amendment changing the par value of the corporation's stock. (Each of the business concepts mentioned in this paragraph will be returned to later in the book.) The point is that a creative business lawyer will try to find permissible ways to accomplish the client's objectives.

D. INVOLVEMENT IN CLIENTS' AFFAIRS

Business lawyers do not merely give clients advice. Usually, business lawyers are intimately involved in the accomplishment of business transactions about which they give advice, and very often these transactions are accomplished almost solely by the effect of documents drafted by the lawyer. The business distribution used as an example in the preceding paragraph serves also as an example here, because the lawyer is likely to draft every document involved in the distribution, including the letter to shareholders explaining the distribution and transmitting the corporation's check. One consequence of this involvement in clients' affairs is that if anyone raises a problem about the legality or propriety of a business transaction, it is likely that the company's lawyer will be in the middle of the controversy.

E. MAIN CLIENT CONTACT

The business lawyer typically is a law firm's main contact with a business client, even if most of the firm's work for the client is done by other specialists. Here the business lawyer's role is reminiscent of that of the internist in medical practice, who tends to be the intake physician in a group practice. Another way of describing this role of the business lawyer is that it is the role of a traffic cop. One thing this means is that the business lawyer has to know enough about other specialties to decide (1) whether the client has a legal problem and (2) if the client does have a legal problem, what other lawyer to get involved.

F. CONSERVATISM

Business lawyers are conservative in their risk-taking. In everything they do for clients they ask themselves where problems might lie and what they can do to avoid them. Business lawyers often are willing to go to or have others go to whatever trouble it takes to avoid even the extremely remote possibility of a problem. For example, when a corporation opens a bank account, the bank will require that the board of directors pass a resolution defining the banking relationship. Typically, the board gives certain officers the unlimited power to borrow from the bank. However, when the corporation goes to the bank for a loan, if the bank involves its lawyer, that lawyer invariably will require that the corporation's board of directors pass a new resolution specifically authorizing the loan. But how much extra safety does the bank's lawyer add by insisting on the new resolution? Virtually none.

One can question the application of the conservative approach to a specific situation,[24] but that approach in general is exactly the correct one. The business lawyer works prospectively, but he or she continually tries to look at a transaction being planned through the eyes of a court viewing the transaction retrospectively. The good lawyer knows that what appears at the time of the transaction to be objective truth, if it exists at all, may not be nearly so important as how an opposing lawyer subsequently characterizes the facts. And finally, the good lawyer knows that it is impossible to tell when planning a transaction how a judge or jury might someday view the transaction. The lawyer's only course is to button up both the facts (by documentation) and the legalities (usually by precisely drawn contractual provisions) of a transaction so tightly that a court will have no basis for finding against the business lawyer's client.

G. COLLEGIAL APPROACH

Business lawyers working on a transaction typically find business lawyers working on the other side. The relationship between these lawyers almost invariably is collegial rather than adversarial. Negotiations on documents, for example, are characterized by good-natured civility. So much is this the case that to an outside observer it might often appear that the lawyers are working for the same client. This illusion may come partially from the fact that each client does want basically the same thing: the transaction done smoothly and quickly. It comes also from the fact that the two lawyers share approaches and values, and so they understand each other. The borrower's lawyer, for example, does not argue when the bank's lawyer requests a specific borrowing resolution from the borrower's board of directors.

H. INVOLVEMENT OF SECURITIES LAW

Business practice is intertwined with the practice of securities law to such an extent that they are virtually two parts of the same whole. Much of this intertwining arises from the fact that some federal securities law serves to fill gaps in state corporation law and is, in reality, federal corporation law. But some of the intertwining also comes from the fact that a corporation cannot avoid some

---

[24] Perhaps the conservatism of business lawyers goes back to the railroad lawyers of the nineteenth century, who knew that in many courts the railroad would lose a case brought against it if there were any basis for the plaintiff's claim.

involvement in pure securities law. All corporations need to sell stock, for example, and anytime the corporation — or one of its shareholders — sells stock, the sale involves securities law questions. This does not mean, of course, that all business lawyers need to be full-blown securities lawyers. What it does mean is that every business lawyer needs to be expert in some areas of securities law.

I. SPECIAL ETHICAL PROBLEM

Business lawyers face a special ethical problem that arises from the fact that their business clients do not exist in a form that can be dealt with directly. Everything a company does must be done through agents. The special ethical problem arises when the interest of an agent with whom the lawyer deals differs from the company's interest. The first problem of the lawyer is to see the conflict. That is not always as easy as it might seem, partly because the lawyer often does not know enough facts to discern, for example, that a proposed action is good for the company's president but bad for the enterprise. The second problem is to handle the conflict without violating the lawyer's ethical obligations and without damaging the lawyer's relationship with people in the company. That typically can be done if the lawyer exercises enough skill.

Perhaps the clearest example of this conflict arises when the president of a corporation asks the corporation's lawyer to draft the president's employment contract. Initially, the lawyer must determine whether further action is consistent with an attorney's ethical responsibilities. If it is, the lawyer would then determine whether there is an acceptable way the lawyer might handle this situation. A good and practical way would be to have the president secure the agreement of the board of directors that the lawyer will draft the contract as he or she believes the contract likely would come out if negotiated by two good business lawyers, and further that the corporation will pay for the legal work. (Essentially this would mean that the contract would include a full array of protective provisions for each party and no overreaching provisions favoring either.) This and other ethical issues that the business lawyer faces will be addressed in the following chapters.

J. PUBLIC SERVICE

One of the hallmarks of the legal profession is the opportunity to serve the public good. Business lawyers have the skills and talent to provide public service in many ways. For example, the American Bar Association Section of Business Law has joined with the National Legal Aid and Defender Association to match business lawyers with legal service organizations and public service community programs lacking the finances to hire an attorney. Some of the projects undertaken by business lawyers working pro bono with members of these organizations include assistance in securing financing for low income housing, obtaining insurance proceeds for terminal AIDS patients, and structuring loans granted by community development corporations. Other business lawyers have helped low income families form a trailer park co-operative and have provided struggling start-up companies with business formation advice. Business lawyers have also helped emerging democracies throughout the world develop constitutions, legal systems and bar associations.

Chapter 1

SOLE PROPRIETORSHIPS AND AGENCY PRINCIPLES

Situation
(This situation applies to Chapters 1 and 2)

A business client of yours recommended your law firm to William Anderson and Lila Baker, who want to start a business. An appointment was arranged, and at the appointed hour Baker and Anderson enter your office. They explain that their associate, James Phillips, will be a little late. He has been tied up at a directors' meeting but should be arriving soon. Phillips, they say, is an investment banker and also an investor in several businesses. A person of significant personal means, he made his money investing in established companies. He has a particular interest in minority-owned firms.

Baker proceeds to give you some background and explains what Anderson and she have in mind. Baker is a molecular biologist who, for the last several years, has worked in a university research laboratory. During this period she has developed a rapid, efficient process for synthesizing DNA. She is well known for this process and is often asked for advice by other laboratories around the country. Because of the considerable start-up costs required to set up a laboratory capable of performing DNA synthesis, Baker is convinced that many researchers would be interested in having this process done for them on a contract basis. Therefore, the first stage in Anderson's and Baker's plan is to set up and operate a laboratory to do this work. The second stage, which they will develop as time and money allow, is to conduct the necessary research to perfect a patentable process for using DNA manipulation to make plants disease resistant. Baker has done preliminary work in this area, but has not wanted to proceed further, as any resulting patent would be the property of her present employer.

Anderson then addresses the business details. Anderson, you learn, is the vice president for finance and administration of a small chemical supply company, where he is in charge of an office staff and has primary responsibility for managing the company's finances. He expects to handle the business end of the new enterprise. Since Baker will need to spend her time in the laboratory, Anderson plans to handle most contacts with prospective customers, except when Baker's involvement is absolutely necessary. This will be like old times, he says, since his first job with his present company involved calling on customers. He explains that he and Baker will not be able to contribute all of the required capital to the new business. Together they can raise only about $ 75,000. Anderson has been busy searching for a prospective investor, however, and has found Phillips.

Phillips is willing to contribute, or guarantee loans for, $ 200,000 to $ 300,000 if the terms are satisfactory. Baker also believes her mother-in-law may be persuaded to invest $ 75,000 to $ 100,000. She owns and operates a successful property management company, Arriz Corp. Her funding may be either a source of start-up capital or provide additional capital resources once the company is established. The parties have not developed a long term strategy for raising additional capital that may be needed.

In the ensuing general discussion, Anderson and Baker also give you the following information:

1. Neither Anderson nor Baker expects to have any substantial source of income other than what they can earn from the new business. Each requires about $ 40,000 per year to survive financially.

2. Estimated expenses, for the first year of operation, include:

Equipment and supplies		$ 200,000
Salaries:		
Anderson and Baker	$ 80,000	
Laboratory technician	25,000	
Clerical help	15,000	
		120,000
Rent		20,000
Miscellaneous office expenses		10,000
		$ 350,000

3. It is difficult to estimate first year revenues, but Anderson and Baker believe they can generate enough business to keep at least one laboratory technician busy. It will take a few months before the company can deliver and be paid for its first products. After that the two entrepreneurs should at least be able to cover expenses out of revenues.

Anderson and Baker ask you to advise them as to what kind of business entity they should form and what they should do next. Just as the meeting is about to break up, Phillips arrives. He apologizes for being late, but explains that, although he is involved in more business ventures than he has time for, he cannot resist making his presence known when his money is involved. He says that in the past he has always invested in established concerns rather than new businesses, but that he has confidence in Baker and Anderson and sees a big future for biotechnology ventures. Phillips, too, says he looks forward to having your advice on a legal structure for the new business. They would also like to know what your fees are and whether you would consider being paid with an interest in the new company. And finally, they would like to hear your opinion on the business venture itself. They know that you have many years experience in representing business clients and would like to have the benefit of that experience. In responding to their questions, you should also address applicable professional responsibility issues.

SECTION I. INTRODUCTION TO FORMS OF BUSINESS ENTITIES

Persons forming a business may choose from among eleven business organization forms. The selection process may seem daunting to someone unfamiliar with the array of possibilities. Similarly, lawyers advising clients who are starting a business must grapple with the prospect of explaining, in a cogent way, the differences between these forms, many of which overlap in some aspects, are inexplicably different in others and, taken together, may seem to lack a coherent rationale.

A company may be formed as a sole proprietorship, a general partnership, a limited liability partnership, a limited partnership, a partnership association, a general corporation, a closely held corporation, a limited liability company, a business trust, an unincorporated association such as a joint stock company or, if certain requirements are met, a professional corporation. These forms extend along a continuum, from the sole proprietorship at one end to the large, multinational corporation at the other. Not all forms, however, are widely used. Partnership associations and joint stock companies are two types that have limited appeal. Nor are all forms suitable for all types of businesses. Publicly held companies with shares traded on a securities exchange, like the New York Stock Exchange, are commonly general corporations, although some are limited partnerships. Proprietary or privately held companies, on the other hand, use a variety of established forms, including sole proprietorships, general partnerships, limited partnerships, general corporations, closely held corporations, and professional corporations. Professional corporations were developed for use by members of a licensed profession, such as doctors and lawyers. In addition, the popularity of new business forms like the limited liability company and the limited liability partnership continues to grow. Each type of business organization except the sole proprietorhip is governed by state statute. These statutes define the management and investment structure of the enterprise and control both the company's internal affairs (the rights, obligations and authority of the company's investors and managers), and some of the consequences of the company's interactions with third parties.

The drama of forming a business arises from the interactions of a stock set of characters — the company's owners/investors and its high level managers. The characters' roles vary according to the nature of their investment in the business and their expectations concerning their participation in the management of the enterprise. Some investors use real, personal or intellectual property to acquire an interest in a company, while others contribute human capital in the form of services. Some entrepreneurs plan to be active managers of the firm's day to day business operations while others have no interest in management and seek only a satisfactory return on their investments. The latter are called passive investors. Although they are not active in the business, they are nevertheless counted among the owners of the enterprise because they hold an equity interest in the company.

Their opportunities for a return on their investments are thus directly tied to the fortunes of the company, and they share the risk of the venture.

Owners' relationships with their company contrast with those who lend money to the company. Lenders have a contractual right to be repaid the principal of the loan with interest according to a specified payment schedule, whether or not the company is flourishing. The lender's rights and obligations are defined in a contract with the borrower. In contrast, state law defines the basic relationship between a company and its owners.

While all members of these groups have a common purpose, forming a successful enterprise, there are times when their individual priorities will vary and even conflict. These competing interests create challenging legal and ethical dilemmas for the lawyer forming the business.

In deciding what business form is best for a particular enterprise, lawyers and their clients should consider the questions posed below. The responses to these questions will play an important role in the ultimate choice of business organization. Business organization statutes provide answers to some questions. In some situations, the statutory rule is mandatory; in others, the statute provides a default rule that applies unless the parties choose a different approach. When you complete Chapters 1 and 2, you should be able to answer the following questions about each of the business organizations you have studied.

What is required to form and operate the business?

The formation of certain types of businesses, such as a general partnership, is relatively simple. Owners of the company are not required to file documents with state authorities or to pay franchise taxes for the privilege of forming the business. They do not even need to have a written business agreement, although one is certainly recommended. The operation and oversight of the business may be conducted with as little or as much formality as the parties wish. In contrast, other business forms, like the general corporation, require filings with the secretary of state and the payment of an annual franchise tax. In these situations, the parties must hold annual meetings and follow specified procedures for making certain types of decisions.

Who will manage the business and how will business decisions be made?

When one person owns and operates a company, a formal governance structure is unnecessary. However, as soon as a business becomes jointly owned, the question posed above must be addressed. It can be answered in several ways. Owners may manage the company themselves (participatory management) or they may hire professional managers to act on their behalf (centralized management). Participatory management is characteristic of general partnerships in which partners typically play an active role in managing the business. Centralized management is an attribute of general corporations, in which the board of directors manages the company for the benefit of the owners, the shareholders. The number of owners is one factor used to determine which type of management structure is preferred. A few owners can easily vote on all matters, but this approach becomes cumbersome if the number of owners is great. In this case, concerns with efficiency and cost may make centralized management preferable.

Joint ownership also requires the parties to determine what type of collective action will be needed to decide the many issues that inevitably arise in the operation of a business. In short, the owners will need to determine who is eligible to vote on a particular matter, how votes are allocated among those eligible to vote, and what vote is required to approve a particular action. Votes can be allocated by the amount of an owner's investment in the company or on a per capita basis. A particular decision may be made by a unanimous, super majority, majority or plurality vote. Deciding what vote is required has important implications for the allocation of power between majority and minority interests. The higher the required vote, the greater the opportunity for minority veto. The lower the required vote, the greater the power assumed by the majority.

To what extent will the investors be personally liable for the company's obligations?

In some business forms, like the sole proprietorship and the general partnership, the owners are personally liable for the company's financial obligations. If the company cannot meet its obligations, company creditors may look to the owners' personal assets to satisfy the creditors' claims. In a jointly owned business, each owner may be jointly and severally liable for company obligations, or the extent of an individual's liability for company losses may be based on a per capita allocation, the amount of the individual's ownership interest, or some other agreed upon allocation.

Other business forms, like the corporation, provide limited liability to owners. Limited liability means that owners will not be personally liable for the company's obligations beyond the amount of their original investment. They may lose the value of their investment if the business fails, but they will not be required to use their personal assets to satisfy the company's creditors. Owners can protect themselves from liability for company debts in several ways. One is to select a business form that provides limited liability. But that approach is not fool proof. A bank lending money to a business may require shareholders of a corporation to be personally responsible for the company's debts even though shareholders have limited liability under the applicable corporate statute. In some states, corporation statutes exempt wage claims from the grant of limited liability. Conversely, owners with unlimited liability can protect themselves in other ways. They can purchase insurance to cover tort liability. They may use contracts to limit their liability. Contracting parties may agree that certain creditors' claims will be satisfied only from security interests in the business personal property or mortgages on real property. The success of this approach will depend on the sophistication and relative bargaining power of the parties to the agreement.

How will the business be financed?

The question of how the business will be financed has two parts: how will the capital needed to start the company business be raised, and once the business is underway, how will it raise additional capital that it may need. The founding entrepreneurs usually provide at least some of the initial funding for a new business, and often provide additional capital once the business is a going concern.

Often, however, a company's owners are unable to provide enough capital to meet all of the start-up company's needs or to satisfy additional requirements of the business once it is underway. Consequently, the owners must look elsewhere for funding. They may want to bring in additional owners, which may be individuals or other businesses, such as venture capital firms formed for the purpose of investing in new and ongoing businesses. If it is necessary to raise capital from a significant number of investors, the company may sell ownership interests or shares to the general public. The owners may also borrow money from banks, insurance companies and other financial institutions who will be lenders, but not co-owners of the business.

How do investors receive a return on their investments?

Owners make money on their investments in a company in two ways. They may receive a portion of the company's profits or they may sell their interest in the company and thereby realize any appreciated value in their ownership interest. Shares in the profits of an ongoing venture may, like voting rights, be allocated on a per capita basis or according to the amount of each owner's investment. Some state statutes impose restrictions on the distribution of company earnings to company owners. Shareholders in a corporation may be paid a share of the profits only if the company can satisfy higher priority claims, such as those of lenders. In contrast, partners are not restricted in the distribution of company profits so long as the company is solvent.

The issue of investment liquidity becomes important when one or more owners want to leave the company and be paid the value of their ownership interests. The departure may be caused by friction among the owners, a desire to invest elsewhere, a change in the company fortunes, or the death of one of the principals. In these situations, investors in companies traded on a securities exchange have only to sell their shares to exit the company and receive the market value of their investment. Withdrawing from a privately held company that lacks a ready market for the ownership interests may be problematic, particularly when the law does not provide an exit procedure. Careful planning is a must when the investment is not liquid. Just as the voting requirements for approval of company action have important implications for the allocation of power between majority and minority interests, so do the procedures for departure from a privately held company. Permitting investors to withdraw at any time and compel payment of the value of their interests may impair the company's financial stability and jeopardize the reasonable expectations of the remaining owners. Conversely, unduly restricting individuals' opportunities to withdraw may leave minority interests at the mercy of an oppressive majority.

What are tax consequences of forming a business?

The quest for limited liability and the goal of saving taxes are two of the most important influences on the choice of business form. Even though corporations and partnerships are both aggregates of people engaged in a common business enterprise, the two forms may be treated very differently for tax purposes. Corporations are dealt with as legal taxpaying entities separate and distinct from the individuals who own and manage the business. Corporations pay income tax at the corporate tax rate on the money they earn. If corporate earnings are subsequently distributed to shareholders, the shareholders are taxed at the individual tax rate on the earnings they receive. Thus, corporate earnings are taxed twice: once when received by the corporation and a second time when distributed to shareholders. This arrangement is often referred to as a double taxation scheme. In addition, corporations are subject to state franchise taxes in all states where they are qualified to do business.

Under the Internal Revenue Code, a business taxed as a partnership is not treated as a separate, taxpaying entity. Although an informational return must be filed with the I.R.S., the business does not pay taxes. Instead, the owners are taxed at individual tax rates on their proportionate share of the business income, as though they had earned it themselves. This is referred to as pass through taxation. Tax liability is passed through the business organization directly to the owners. Unlike corporations, partnerships are not subject to state franchise taxes for the privilege of doing business. Today the federal tax treatment of most unincorporated business forms depends on whether the enterprise elects to be treated like a corporation or a partnership.[1]

Changes in corporate and individual tax rates affect the choice of business form. When corporate tax rates are significantly lower than individual rates, the corporate form is appealing. Conversely, when individual rates are more attractive, businesses eligible for pass through taxation acquire a certain cachet.

Chapters 1 and 2 focus primarily on the three predominant forms of business organizations: sole proprietorships, general partnerships, and corporations. You will also be introduced to hybrid business organization forms combining attributes of both partnerships and corporations. As tax considerations and the quest for

---

[1] Before January 1, 1997, the application of what are called the Kinter Regulations (Treas. Reg. §§ 301.7701 *et seq.*) determined whether an unincorporated business would be taxed like a corporation. An unincorporated company would be taxed like a corporation if it had three of the four following attributes: centralized management, continuity of life, free transferability of interests, and limited liability. Effective January 1, 1997, regulations §§ 301.7701-1 through 301.7701-3 were amended to permit most unincorporated business associations to elect whether to be treated as a corporation or a partnership for federal tax purposes.

limited liability increasingly affect the choice of business entity, these variant business organization forms gain in popularity.

SECTION II. SOLE PROPRIETORSHIPS

The sole proprietorship is the most popular business organization form in the United States, particularly for small start-up ventures. It is simple and easy to operate. Sometimes the form is chosen because the sole proprietorship is the best option for a particular business. Often, however, business owners choose this form without legal advice, sometimes to their regret.

A sole proprietorship is a business owned directly by one person who has sole decisionmaking authority, an exclusive claim to business profits, and direct ownership of all business assets. A sole proprietorship having employees is a business organization. Although there is only one owner, the organization is comprised of more than one person.

Since the legal identity of the sole proprietorship and its owner are one and the same, there is no business entity to form. Equally important, no formalities are required to operate the business.[2] The absence of formation and operational formalities translates to a direct cost-saving for the business owner. The absence of legal requirements also gives the owner maximum flexibility in structuring and operating the business.

The sole proprietorship suffers from serious disadvantages, however. For one thing, its single owner management structure is suitable only for small businesses with a few employees. As the company grows in scope of operations and number of employees, it will necessarily develop a number of different departments to take care of the company's internal affairs. The owner can make up a management structure, with the heads of each division or department given whatever responsibilities and titles the owner wishes, but that structure will not exist until the owner devises it, and unless the owner uses traditional business titles, the titles the owner chooses likely will not carry a widely understood meaning.

The central problem in a sole proprietorship is the unlimited liability of the owner for the company's obligations. The attribute of unlimited liability and the problem of management structure are related. In a business in which the owner is the sole decisionmaker and worker, unlimited liability is not much of a detriment if the owner's main fear is tort liability, because tortfeasors can always be sued in their individual capacity. As the operation of the business becomes complex, with a broad array of managers and workers, the sole proprietor becomes subject to an expanding risk of vicarious liability for the acts of others. In some circumstances, the risk of financial responsibility for the acts of others can be significantly reduced by the purchase of insurance or through contract. Absent those circumstances, the sole proprietorship may be an unacceptable form

---

[2]If the company is doing business under a trade name, the state may require a filing under its fictitious name statute.

for operating a business that subjects the owner to significant risks of vicarious liability.

SECTION III. AGENCY LAW AND THE LEGAL RELATIONSHIPS BETWEEN SOLE PROPRIETORS AND THEIR EMPLOYEES

A. FORMATION OF AN AGENCY RELATIONSHIP

Business organizations consist of groups of individuals — owners, managers and employees — who are participants in a common enterprise. The work of every business must be accomplished through the efforts of the people who are a part of it. The business, itself, is incapable of acting on its own behalf.

The law of agency provides the fundamental legal underpinnings of many business relationships. It creates a standard form contract that applies to the members of business associations, *inter se*, and to their interactions with third parties. When a sole proprietor employs another person to act on the owner's behalf, the common law of agency controls the relationship. The proprietor is the principal, the person on whose behalf action is to be taken. The person acting on behalf of the principal is the agent. For example, when an employer hires a purchasing agent, the agent acts on behalf of the company when dealing with company suppliers.

Employers and employees may enter into a principal/agent relationship. So may people who have independent businesses, as for example, attorneys and their clients. An agency relationship may be created expressly by an agreement between the parties or may arise as a matter of law when the parties enter into an association that has the legal attributes of an agency relationship.

The appointment of one or more agents to work on behalf of the principal enables the principal to accomplish more than would be possible if the principal were acting alone. However, the creation of an agency relationship is not cost-free. The principal will have to supervise or monitor the activities of the agent, because the agent may not always act in the principal's best interests. The principal must bear the cost when the agent's performance diverges from that which would be most beneficial to the principal.

As you read the case that follows, consider the different ways in which the agency relationships were created.

A. GAY JENSON FARMS CO. v. CARGILL, INC.

Supreme Court of Minnesota
309 N.W.2d 285 (1981)

PETERSON, JUSTICE.

Plaintiffs, 86 individual, partnership or corporate farmers, brought this action against defendant Cargill, Inc. (Cargill) and defendant Warren Grain & Seed Co.

(Warren) to recover losses sustained when Warren defaulted on the contracts made with plaintiffs for the sale of grain. After a trial by jury, judgment was entered in favor of plaintiffs, and Cargill brought this appeal. We affirm.

This case arose out of the financial collapse of defendant Warren Seed & Grain Co., and its failure to satisfy its indebtedness to plaintiffs. Warren, which was located in Warren, Minnesota, was operated by Lloyd Hill and his son, Gary Hill. Warren operated a grain elevator and as a result was involved in the purchase of cash or market grain from local farmers. The cash grain would be resold through the Minneapolis Grain Exchange or to the terminal grain companies directly. Warren also stored grain for farmers and sold chemicals, fertilizer and steel storage bins. In addition, it operated a seed business which involved buying seed grain from farmers, processing it and reselling it for seed to farmers and local elevators.

Lloyd Hill decided in 1964 to apply for financing from Cargill.[3] Cargill's officials from the Moorhead regional office investigated Warren's operations and recommended that Cargill finance Warren.

Warren and Cargill thereafter entered into a security agreement which provided that Cargill would loan money for working capital to Warren on "open account" financing up to a stated limit, which was originally set as $ 175,000.[4] Under this contract, Warren would receive funds and pay its expenses by issuing drafts drawn on Cargill through Minneapolis banks. The drafts were imprinted with both Warren's and Cargill's names. Proceeds from Warren's sales would be deposited with Cargill and credited to its account. In return for this financing, Warren appointed Cargill as its grain agent for transactions with the Commodity Credit Corporation. Cargill was also given a right of first refusal to purchase market grain sold by Warren to the terminal market.

A new contract was negotiated in 1967, extending Warren's credit line to $ 300,000 and incorporating the provisions of the original contract. It was also stated in the contract that Warren would provide Cargill with annual financial statements and that either Cargill would keep the books for Warren or an audit would be conducted by an independent firm. Cargill was given the right of access to Warren's books for inspection.

In addition, the agreement provided that Warren was not to make capital improvements or repairs in excess of $ 5,000 without Cargill's prior consent. Further, it was not to become liable as guarantor on another's indebtedness, or encumber its assets except with Cargill's permission. Consent by Cargill was required before Warren would be allowed to declare a dividend or sell and purchase stock.

---

[3] Prior to this time, Atwood Larson had provided working capital for Warren, and Warren had used Atwood Larson as its commission agent for the sale of market grain on the grain exchange.

[4] Loans were secured by a second mortgage on Warren's real estate and a first chattel mortgage on its inventories of grain and merchandise in the sum of $ 175,000 with 7% interest. Warren was to use the $ 175,000 to pay off the debt that it owed to Atwood Larson.

Officials from Cargill's regional office made a brief visit to Warren shortly after the agreement was executed. They examined the annual statement and the accounts receivable, expenses, inventory, seed, machinery and other financial matters. Warren was informed that it would be reminded periodically to make the improvements recommended by Cargill.[5] At approximately this time, a memo was given to the Cargill official in charge of the Warren account, Erhart Becker, which stated in part: "This organization (Warren) needs very strong paternal guidance."

In 1970, Cargill contracted with Warren and other elevators to act as its agent to seek growers for a new type of wheat called Bounty 208. Warren, as Cargill's agent for this project, entered into contracts for the growing of the wheat seed, with Cargill named as the contracting party. Farmers were paid directly by Cargill for the seed and all contracts were performed in full. In 1971, pursuant to an agency contract, Warren contracted on Cargill's behalf with various farmers for the growing of sunflower seeds for Cargill. The arrangements were similar to those made in the Bounty 208 contracts, and all those contracts were also completed. Both these agreements were unrelated to the open account financing contract. In addition, Warren, as Cargill's agent in the sunflower seed business, cleaned and packaged the seed in Cargill bags.

During this period, Cargill continued to review Warren's operations and expenses and recommend that certain actions should be taken.[6] Warren purchased from Cargill various business forms printed by Cargill and received sample forms from Cargill which Warren used to develop its own business forms.

Cargill wrote to its regional office in 1970 expressing its concern that the pattern of increased use of funds allowed to develop at Warren was similar to that involved in two other cases in which Cargill experienced severe losses. Cargill did not refuse to honor drafts or call the loan, however. A new security agreement which increased the credit line to $ 750,000 was executed in 1972, and a subsequent agreement which raised the limit to $ 1,250,000 was entered into in 1976.

Warren was at that time shipping Cargill 90% of its cash grain. When Cargill's facilities were full, Warren shipped its grain to other companies. Approximately

---

[5] Cargill headquarters suggested that the regional office check Warren monthly. Also, it was requested that Warren be given an explanation for the relatively large withdrawals from undistributed earnings made by the Hills, since Cargill hoped that Warren's profits would be used to decrease its debt balance. Cargill asked for written requests for withdrawals from undistributed earnings in the future.

[6] Between 1967 and 1973, Cargill suggested that Warren take a number of steps, including: (1) a reduction of seed grain and cash grain inventories; (2) improved collection of accounts receivable; (3) reduction or elimination of its wholesale seed business and its speciality grain operation; (4) marketing fertilizer and steel bins on consignment; (5) a reduction in withdrawals made by officers; (6) a suggestion that Warren's bookkeeper not issue her own salary checks; and (7) cooperation with Cargill in implementing the recommendations. These ideas were apparently never implemented, however.

25% of Warren's total sales was seed grain which was sold directly by Warren to its customers.

As Warren's indebtedness continued to be in excess of its credit line, Cargill began to contact Warren daily regarding its financial affairs. Cargill headquarters informed its regional office in 1973 that, since Cargill money was being used, Warren should realize that Cargill had the right to make some critical decisions regarding the use of the funds. Cargill headquarters also told Warren that a regional manager would be working with Warren on a day-to-day basis as well as in monthly planning meetings. In 1975, Cargill's regional office began to keep a daily debit position on Warren. A bank account was opened in Warren's name on which Warren could draw checks in 1976. The account was to be funded by drafts drawn on Cargill by the local bank.

In early 1977, it became evident that Warren had serious financial problems. Several farmers, who had heard that Warren's checks were not being paid, inquired or had their agents inquire at Cargill regarding Warren's status and were initially told that there would be no problem with payment. In April 1977, an audit of Warren revealed that Warren was $ 4 million in debt. After Cargill was informed that Warren's financial statements had been deliberately falsified, Warren's request for additional financing was refused. In the final days of Warren's operation, Cargill sent an official to supervise the elevator, including disbursement of funds and income generated by the elevator.

After Warren ceased operations, it was found to be indebted to Cargill in the amount of $ 3.6 million. Warren was also determined to be indebted to plaintiffs in the amount of $ 2 million, and plaintiffs brought this action in 1977 to seek recovery of that sum. Plaintiffs alleged that Cargill was jointly liable for Warren's indebtedness as it had acted as principal for the grain elevator....

....

The jury found that Cargill's conduct between 1973 and 1977 had made it Warren's principal.[7] Warren was found to be the agent of Cargill with regard to contracts for:

1. The purchase and sale of grain for market.
2. The purchase and sale of seed grain.
3. The storage of grain.

The court determined that Cargill was the disclosed principal of Warren. It was concluded that Cargill was jointly liable with Warren for plaintiffs' losses, and judgment was entered for plaintiffs.

---

[7] At trial, plaintiffs sought to establish actual agency by Cargill's course of dealing between 1973 and 1977 rather than "apparent" agency or agency by estoppel, so that the only issue in this case is one of actual agency.

Cargill seeks a reversal of the jury's findings or, if the jury findings are upheld, a reversal of the trial court's determination that Cargill was a disclosed principal....

... The major issue in this case is whether Cargill, by its course of dealing with Warren, became liable as a principal on contracts made by Warren with plaintiffs. Cargill contends that no agency relationship was established with Warren, notwithstanding its financing of Warren's operation and its purchase of the majority of Warren's grain. However, we conclude that Cargill, by its control and influence over Warren, became a principal with liability for the transactions entered into by its agent Warren.

Agency is the fiduciary relationship that results from the manifestation of consent by one person to another that the other shall act on his behalf and subject to his control, and consent by the other so to act. In order to create an agency there must be an agreement, but not necessarily a contract between the parties.... An agreement may result in the creation of an agency relationship although the parties did not call it an agency and did not intend the legal consequences of the relation to follow. The existence of the agency may be proved by circumstantial evidence which shows a course of dealing between the two parties. When an agency relationship is to be proven by circumstantial evidence, the principal must be shown to have consented to the agency since one cannot be the agent of another except by consent of the latter.

Cargill contends that the prerequisites of an agency relationship did not exist because Cargill never consented to the agency, Warren did not act on behalf of Cargill, and Cargill did not exercise control over Warren. We hold that all three elements of agency could be found in the particular circumstances of this case. By directing Warren to implement its recommendations, Cargill manifested its consent that Warren would be its agent. Warren acted on Cargill's behalf in procuring grain for Cargill as the part of its normal operations which were totally financed by Cargill.[8] Further, an agency relationship was established by Cargill's interference with the internal affairs of Warren, which constituted de facto control of the elevator.

A creditor who assumes control of his debtor's business may become liable as principal for the acts of the debtor in connection with the business. Restatement (Second) of Agency § 14 O (1958). It is noted in comment *a* to § 14 O that:

> A security holder who merely exercises a veto power over the business acts of his debtor by preventing purchases or sales above specified amounts does not thereby become a principal. However, if he takes over the management of the debtor's business either in person or through an agent, and directs what contracts may or may not be made, he becomes a principal,

---

[8] Although the contracts with the farmers were executed by Warren, Warren paid for the grain with drafts drawn on Cargill. While this is not in itself significant, it is one factor to be taken into account in analyzing the relationship between Warren and Cargill.

liable as a principal for the obligations incurred thereafter in the normal course of business by the debtor who has now become his general agent. The point at which the creditor becomes a principal is that at which he assumes de facto control over the conduct of his debtor, whatever the terms of the formal contract with his debtor may be.

A number of factors indicate Cargill's control over Warren, including the following:

(1) Cargill's constant recommendations to Warren by telephone;

(2) Cargill's right of first refusal on grain;

(3) Warren's inability to enter into mortgages, to purchase stock or to pay dividends without Cargill's approval;

(4) Cargill's right of entry onto Warren's premises to carry on periodic checks and audits;

(5) Cargill's correspondence and criticism regarding Warren's finances, officers['] salaries and inventory;

(6) Cargill's determination that Warren needed "strong paternal guidance";

(7) Provision of drafts and forms to Warren upon which Cargill's name was imprinted;

(8) Financing of all Warren's purchases of grain and operating expenses; and

(9) Cargill's power to discontinue the financing of Warren's operations.

We recognize that some of these elements, as Cargill contends, are found in an ordinary debtor-creditor relationship. However, these factors cannot be considered in isolation, but, rather, they must be viewed in light of all the circumstances surrounding Cargill's aggressive financing of Warren.

It is also Cargill's position that the relationship between Cargill and Warren was that of buyer-supplier rather than principal-agent. Restatement (Second) of Agency § 14 K (1958) compares an agent with a supplier as follows:

One who contracts to acquire property from a third person and convey it to another is the agent of the other only if it is agreed that he is to act primarily for the benefit of the other and not for himself.

Factors indicating that one is a supplier, rather than an agent, are:

(1) That he is to receive a fixed price for the property irrespective of price paid by him. This is the most important. (2) That he acts in his own name and receives the title to the property which he thereafter is to transfer. (3) That he has an independent business in buying and selling similar property. Restatement (Second) of Agency § 14 K, Comment *a* (1958).

Under the Restatement approach, it must be shown that the supplier has an independent business before it can be concluded that he is not an agent. The record establishes that all portions of Warren's operation were financed by Cargill and that Warren sold almost all of its market grain to Cargill. Thus, the relationship which existed between the parties was not merely that of buyer and supplier....

Further, we are not persuaded by the fact that Warren was not one of the "line" elevators that Cargill operated in its own name. The Warren operation, like the line elevator, was financially dependent on Cargill's continual infusion of capital. The arrangement with Warren presented a convenient alternative to the establishment of a line elevator. Cargill became, in essence, the owner of the operation without the accompanying legal indicia.

The amici curiae assert that, if the jury verdict is upheld, firms and banks which have provided business loans to county elevators will decline to make further loans. The decision in this case should give no cause for such concern. We deal here with a business enterprise markedly different from an ordinary bank financing, since Cargill was an active participant in Warren's operations rather than simply a financier. Cargill's course of dealing with Warren was, by its own admission, a paternalistic relationship in which Cargill made the key economic decisions and kept Warren in existence.

Although considerable interest was paid by Warren on the loan, the reason for Cargill's financing of Warren was not to make money as a lender but, rather, to establish a source of market grain for its business. As one Cargill manager noted, "We were staying in there because we wanted the grain." For this reason, Cargill was willing to extend the credit line far beyond the amount originally allocated to Warren. It is noteworthy that Cargill was receiving significant amounts of grain and that, notwithstanding the risk that was recognized by Cargill, the operation was considered profitable.

On the whole, there was a unique fabric in the relationship between Cargill and Warren which varies from that found in normal debtor-creditor situations. We conclude that, on the facts of this case, there was sufficient evidence from which the jury could find that Cargill was the principal of Warren within the definitions of agency set forth in Restatement (Second) of Agency §§ 1 and 140....

Affirmed.

A power of attorney is a document appointing an agent to act on behalf of a principal. Powers of attorney may be used in any situation involving the appointment of an agent. Persons involved in a real estate transaction who do not wish to attend the closing may use a power of attorney to authorize their lawyers to sign the documents for them. Often the power of attorney for land transactions must be created with the same formalities as those required for the conveyance of land: it must be in writing, signed and acknowledged by the grantor, and witnessed. The rule requiring the power of attorney for a transaction to be created with the same formalities as those required to complete the transaction, itself, is often referred to as the equal dignities rule. Why is it common to apply the rule to transactions involving real estate?

Ordinarily the appointment of an agent terminates if the principal becomes mentally incapacitated or incompetent. A durable power of attorney is an appointment designed to survive the principal's mental incapacity or incompetence. Durable powers of attorney may be used for a variety of reasons, as, for example, to appoint someone to manage the affairs of or to make health care decisions on behalf of an infirm person. Statutes controlling the creation of a durable power of attorney often provide that the power of attorney must be in writing, signed by the principal, and executed and witnessed in the same manner as required for wills. In addition, the writing must contain words such as "this power of attorney shall not be affected by the subsequent disability or incompetence of the principal" or words of similar import. CONN. GEN. STAT. ANN. § 45a-562. Why are these formalities required?

B. THE LEGAL CONSEQUENCES OF APPOINTING AN AGENT — THE PRINCIPAL'S LIABILITY FOR THE AGENT'S ACTS

1. Apparent Authority, Inherent Agency Power, and Estoppel

As a general rule, if an agency relationship exists and the agent's acts were authorized by the principal, third parties who have dealt with the agent may hold the principal liable for the agent's acts. The principal may establish the agent's authority by communicating with the agent directly (actual authority), by communicating with the third party dealing with the agent (apparent authority) or both.

Agency law has also developed doctrines that apply when a third party has been harmed by an agent's acts but is unable to establish that the acts were authorized. Depending on the nature of the circumstances, an aggrieved person may attempt to base recovery on the theories of estoppel or inherent agency power. These doctrines were developed to allocate fairly losses that result from an agent's unauthorized conduct.

The following case explores the doctrine of apparent authority in the context of the attorney/client relationship.

FENNELL v. TLB KENT CO.

United States Court of Appeals, Second Circuit
865 F.2d 498 (1989)

MAHONEY, CIRCUIT JUDGE:

This is an appeal from a final judgment of the United States District Court for the Southern District of New York, Louis L. Stanton, Judge, entered on June 16, 1987, which dismissed plaintiff's action and approved a $ 10,000 settlement agreement.... The attorneys for the parties negotiated a settlement and reported it to the court by telephone. Based on this conference call, the district court entered an order on January 20, 1987 which dismissed the action with prejudice, but provided that "within sixty days of the date of this order any party may apply by letter for restoration of the action to the calendar of the undersigned."

Plaintiff's counsel requested that the action be restored to the calendar on March 20, 1987. After a hearing on June 16, 1987, the district court dismissed the action and approved the settlement, finding that plaintiff's attorney had had apparent authority to settle the case and plaintiff was accordingly bound by the settlement agreement.

We reverse and remand.

Background

Plaintiff-appellant Louis Fennell commenced this action in the United States District Court for the Southern District of New York on January 7, 1985 against his employer, ... alleging wrongful discharge because of his race and age in violation of 42 U.S.C. § 1981. Fennell was represented by C. Vernon Mason and several of his associates, including Fred K. Brewington.

The case was on Judge Stanton's ready calendar on January 6, 1987. On January 16, 1987, however, Brewington and Eugene Frink, defendants' attorney, agreed to settle the case for $ 10,000 during a telephone conversation. The settlement was reported to the court by both attorneys in a telephone conference call on January 20, 1987. The district court issued an order of dismissal on the same day which provided that either party could apply to the court by letter to restore the case to the court's calendar within sixty days of the order. The settlement was conditioned upon Fennell signing a general release and a stipulation of discontinuance being filed with the court, which never occurred.

Fennell expressed his dissatisfaction with the settlement in a letter to the district court dated March 28, 1987. Fennell there contended that he had told Brewington on January 16, 1987 that he would not approve a $ 10,000 settlement, but he was willing to settle the case out of court "with the intentions of getting it out of the way and behind me." He also claimed that he had told Mason on January 20, 1987 that $ 10,000 was not a satisfactory settlement, and that he had tried several times in early February, 1987 to contact Mason's office by telephone about the case, but elicited no response. Fennell further stated that he had gone to Mason's office on February 20, 1987, at which time Mason informed him that the case has been settled for $ 10,000, whereupon Fennell reiterated his dissatisfaction with that settlement.

On February 27, 1987, Fennell wrote Mason expressing his dissatisfaction with the settlement agreement and indicating that he had "no further use of [Mason's] services." A copy of this letter was sent to the district court and received there on March 3, 1987. On March 20, 1987, Brewington wrote to the district court requesting that the "matter be restored to the calendar as the settlement which was authorized and accepted by our client is no longer acceptable to him," and that Mason and his associates be released by the court as counsel to Fennell.

Following a status conference on June 5, 1987, the district court held a hearing on June 16, 1987 to determine whether Fennell's case should be restored to the calendar. At the conclusion of the hearing, the district court dismissed the action and approved the settlement. This ruling was based upon a finding that Fennell's attorney had been clothed with "apparent authority" when he settled the case, and the court's expressed view that "[t]o allow a client to reject a settlement which has been agreed upon by his attorney with apparent authority is to open the door to a mild form of chaos."

On appeal, Fennell asserts that it was an abuse of discretion for the district court not to have vacated its order of dismissal pursuant to Fed.R.Civ.P. 60(b)(1). Appellees contend that since Fennell's attorney was clothed with apparent authority to settle the case, Fennell is bound by that settlement.

Discussion

....

We turn now to the district court's determination that Fennell's attorney was clothed with apparent authority to settle the case, resulting in denial of the motion to vacate the prior order of dismissal.

We begin with the undisputed proposition that the decision to settle is the client's to make, not the attorney's.... Model Code of Professional Responsibility EC 7-7 (1980) ("in civil cases, it is for the client to decide whether he will accept a settlement offer"). On the other hand, if an attorney has apparent authority to settle a case, and the opposing counsel has no reason to doubt that authority, the settlement will be upheld....

The district court made the following findings concerning the issue of apparent authority: 1) that Mason and his associates represented Fennell "in dealing with the other side," 2) that they were authorized to appear at conferences for him, 3) that Fennell knew that settlement was being discussed, 4) that Fennell did not tell his counsel not to continue discussing settlement, 5) that Fennell would have accepted a higher settlement figure ($ 50,000-75,000), and 6) that Fennell did not tell defendants' counsel that the authority of plaintiff's counsel was limited in any way. The district court concluded that Fennell's counsel "had every appearance of being authorized to make a binding agreement with [defendants' counsel]." The district court then applied the common law principle that an agent clothed with apparent authority binds the principal as to actions taken within the scope of that authority, together with the principle favoring settlement agreements, to conclude that Fennell was bound by the settlement agreement.

Apparent authority is "the power to affect the legal relations of another person by transactions with third persons, professedly as agent for the other, arising from and in accordance with the other's manifestations to such third persons." Restatement (Second) of Agency § 8 (1958) .... Further, in order to create apparent authority, the principal must manifest to the third party that he "consents to have the act done on his behalf by the person purporting to act for him." *Id.* § 27. Second Circuit case law supports the view that apparent authority is created only by the representations of the principal to the third party, and explicitly rejects the notion that an agent can create apparent authority by his own actions or representations.

In this case, taking the facts as the district court found them, Fennell made no manifestations to defendants' counsel that Mason and his associates were authorized to settle the case. Fennell's attorneys accordingly had no apparent authority to settle the case for $ 10,000 without Fennell's consent. The district court's findings that Mason and his associates represented Fennell, and that they were authorized to appear at conferences for him, do not prove otherwise. A client does not create apparent authority for his attorney to settle a case merely by retaining the attorney.

Further, the court's findings that Fennell knew settlement was being discussed, did not ask his attorneys not to discuss settlement, would have accepted a higher settlement figure, and did not tell defendant's counsel that the authority of plaintiff's counsel was limited in any way, do not lead to a different outcome. These findings involve only discussions between Fennell and his attorneys or things that Fennell did not say to opposing counsel. None of these findings relates to positive actions or manifestations by Fennell to defendants' counsel that would reasonably lead that counsel to believe that Fennell's attorneys were clothed with apparent authority to agree to a definitive settlement of the litigation.

....

We realize that the rule we announce here has the potential to burden, at least occasionally, district courts which must deal with constantly burgeoning calendars. A contrary rule, however, would have even more deleterious consequences. Clients should not be faced with a Hobson's choice of denying their counsel all authority to explore settlement or being bound by any settlement to which their counsel might agree, having resort only to an action against their counsel for malpractice. In any event, even if we were to consider such a rule advisable, the applicable precedents and settled principles of agency law would preclude its adoption.

Conclusion

Reversed and remanded for further proceedings not inconsistent herewith.

....

What role does Model Rules of Professional Conduct Rule 1.2(a) play in establishing a lawyer's authority with respect to representation of a client?

A corporation registering to do business in a state other than the one of incoporation is required to appoint an agent for service of process. The agent may be an individual or another company. The document creating the appointment usually must be signed by the corporation (through a representative) and by the agent and filed with the Secretary of State's office. What kind(s) of authority does the document create?

Review the facts of the *Cargill* case. Could the plaintiffs have successfully based Cargill's liability on either apparent authority or estoppel?

2. Ratification

Principals are liable for the authorized acts of their agents. Principals may be liable for unauthorized acts on the basis of inherent agency power or estoppel. The case that follows introduces the doctrine of ratification. It, too, may be used to impose liability for an agent's unauthorized acts.

CONNECTICUT JUNIOR REPUBLIC v. DOHERTY

Appeals Court of Massachusetts
478 N.E.2d 735 (1985)

KASS, JUSTICE.

Eight charities complain that a lawyer's error in drafting a codicil cost them $ 1,305,060 in bequests. A judge of the Superior Court, who heard the case without a jury, determined that, to the extent the lawyer erred, the testator consciously ratified the mistake, thus relieving the draftsman of liability. We affirm.

Here are the background facts. Richards Haskell Emerson executed a will on May 19, 1960, which provided for residuary legacies to seven charities (original charities). At that time Emerson was domiciled in Lakeville, Connecticut, to which he had retired after many years of residence in Springfield, Massachusetts. Nine years later, Emerson decided to alter the list of charitable beneficiaries. To effect that purpose, as well as some other changes in his will, he employed Mr. Paul S. Doherty, who practices law in Springfield, to draw a codicil. Mr. Doherty did so and Emerson executed the codicil on December 4, 1969. The codicil designated eleven charities (first codicil charities), of which only one, The Sharon Hospital, Inc., of Sharon, Connecticut, was included among the original charities.

Subsequent amendments to the Internal Revenue Code put in question whether some of the charitable bequests in Emerson's estate plan, which were charitable remainders of trusts, would be allowed as deductions. It had become necessary to create charitable remainder annuity trusts. The point was called to Emerson's attention in 1975 by Sager McDonald, a senior vice president of the trust department of The Third National Bank of Hampden County, the banking institution which Emerson had nominated as executor and trustee under his will. At Emerson's request, McDonald asked Mr. Doherty to make the necessary repairs by means of a second codicil.

There then occurred the fateful switch of beneficiaries which prompted this action. In drafting the second codicil, Mr. Doherty, apparently working from the original will rather than the first codicil, inadvertently substituted the original charities for the first codicil charities. He concedes he received no instruction from McDonald or from Emerson so to do. Mr. Doherty sent his draft of the second codicil to McDonald, who suggested correction of the names of two of the hospital beneficiaries, but, so far as appears, did not compare the draft with the first codicil. After making the further changes which McDonald had proposed,

Mr. Doherty sent the final version of the codicil to McDonald, who, in turn, forwarded it to Emerson. On October 24, 1975, McDonald and three other persons went to Emerson's home to preside over the execution of the second codicil. That ceremony was not a slap-dash affair.

Emerson, whom the judge found to have been "an avid reader and an intelligent and meticulous man who paid careful attention to his personal and financial affairs," met privately with McDonald before executing the second codicil. Over a period of some forty-five minutes, McDonald read aloud the second codicil, while Emerson followed a copy, and answered Emerson's questions, which focused on the effects of the new trust arrangements on the life interests he had created. Emerson made no comment about the names of the charitable remaindermen during his discussion with McDonald or immediately thereafter when he executed the codicil. Some time within the following year, however, he observed to Harvey Moses, a long-time friend and financial adviser, that he had "reverted or returned or gone back to his original list of charities." After Emerson and McDonald conferred, execution of the second codicil took place in the presence of McDonald and the three persons whom McDonald had brought with him. McDonald and two others signed the document as witnesses to the declaration by the testator that the document represented the second codicil to the will. The third person McDonald brought to the ceremony was a Connecticut notary who took the oaths of the three witnesses on a self-proving affidavit which was part of the second codicil.

Emerson died in Connecticut on October 3, 1979, at age 79. His will and the two codicils were admitted to probate in Connecticut.

These facts we have taken from the findings of the trial judge, which we accept unless clearly erroneous. Mass.R.Civ.P. 52(a), 365 Mass. 816 (1974). From her findings the judge drew the conclusion that when Emerson executed the second codicil he did so with full knowledge of all the essential facts and, therefore, ratified substitution of the original charities for the first codicil charities.

There is a presumption that a person who signs a writing that is obviously a legal document knows its contents. In the case of a will, that presumption is particularly powerful because more than ordinary care usually attends the preparation and execution of that kind of document. When, as in the instant case, the will is read to an alert testator and discussed, the proposition that the testator is acting advisedly gains still more force.

Of course it is somewhat unsatisfactory that a major shift in the donative scheme originated as a mistake rather than by instruction of the testator. One could imagine a certain suspension of critical attention by the testator and his adviser to that portion of the instrument which they could expect to be repetitive. Still, the more common experience is that the dispositive provisions of a testamentary document, i.e., the ones which say who gets it, are those which attract closer scrutiny of a testator than technical provisions. Often an estate plan may contain provisions which are idiosyncratic, disappointing, and even unthinkable to those with defeated expectations. Perhaps it is to ward off attacks from such persons that the general rule has developed that a competent testator meant what he signed and signed what he meant.

The second codicil consisted of only seven pages before the signature blocks. The remainder charities were recited twice. They were, therefore, read aloud to the testator by McDonald twice. They seem to have struck no dissonant note. Those circumstances, together with the deposition of Moses that Emerson remarked that he had reverted to the original charities, constituted sufficient basis for the judge's mixed fact and law conclusion that Emerson had ratified a return to the original charities.

Given a supportable finding of ratification, the plaintiffs' tort action against Mr. Doherty falls on the issue of proximate cause. Mr. Doherty's mistake may have set the change of beneficiaries in motion, but Emerson's ratification of the change was a superseding cause of any cognizable loss by the plaintiffs. Emerson was an intelligent testator in possession of all material information, who took full responsibility for control of the designation of beneficiaries in the second codicil to his will. Mr. Doherty had performed only a technical drafting task. Prevention of harm to the plaintiffs was fully within Emerson's control when he received and carefully read the second codicil.

We leave for another day and other facts the question whether "removed beneficiaries," as plaintiffs term themselves, can come within the scope of protection sometimes accorded to intended beneficiaries when a testator's clearly expressed intent to benefit them is frustrated because of an attorney's professional negligence. In the present case, the findings supported by the record established that, at the time of executing the second codicil, the testator did not intend to benefit the plaintiffs. We are not presented with a situation in which a third party demonstrates foreseeable and justifiable reliance upon the attorney's performance.

On the view we have taken of the case, it is not necessary to consider the other issues raised on the appeal and cross-appeal.

Judgment

Affirmed.

3. Liability for Contract — Disclosed and Undisclosed Principals

In some situations in which the agent enters into a contract on behalf of the principal, only the principal is liable on the contract. In others, both the principal and the agent are liable for the agent's acts. The agent's liability depends on whether the third party knew the identity of the principal and that the agent was acting on the principal's behalf.

AFRICAN BIO-BOTANICA, INC. v.
SALLY LEINER, T/A ECCO BELLA

Superior Court of New Jersey, Appellate Division
624 A.2d 1003 (1993)

BROCHIN, J.A.D.

Plaintiff African Bio-Botanica, Inc. sued defendant "Sally Leiner, individually and t/a Ecco Bella," in the Special Civil Part to recover $ 1530 as the unpaid purchase price of merchandise that it had sold and delivered to her. Ms. Leiner is the sole stockholder, director, and president of Ecco Bella Incorporated, a New Jersey corporation that was formed October 28, 1987, and that continued in existence during all times pertinent to the law suit. Ms. Leiner defended against plaintiff's claim solely on the ground that the merchandise had been ordered by and delivered to Ecco Bella Incorporated, and that the liability was solely that of the corporation.

The case was tried to the court. The evidence showed that plaintiff began selling merchandise to Ms. Leiner or to her corporation in December 1987. African Bio-Botanica, Inc. did not conduct any credit investigation. It did not inquire or, insofar as appears from the evidence, think about, whether its customer was an individual or a corporation. It sold the first six or seven orders for cash on delivery. Plaintiff's sales manager delivered two of the early shipments to Ms. Leiner's home, where she repackaged the merchandise for resale to retail customers. Later orders were directed to "Ecco Bella" at Ms. Leiner's address and shipped on fifteen days' credit. Initially, plaintiff's records listed Sally Leiner as the customer; subsequently, Ms. Leiner's name was whited out and the name, Ecco Bella, was substituted, without any indication that it was a corporation.

The order for the merchandise that is the subject matter of this law suit was placed either by Ms. Leiner herself or by others at her direction. Plaintiff addressed its bill for the purchase price to "Ecco Bella." That bill admittedly remains unpaid. Plaintiff received payment for prior orders by checks imprinted with the name "Ecco Bella." Ms. Leiner's company's letterhead also read "Ecco Bella." Neither the checks nor the letterhead carried the name "Ecco Bella Incorporated" or otherwise indicated that Ecco Bella was a corporation. Plaintiff's sales manager testified, without contradiction, that no one had told him Ecco Bella was a corporation and he did not know that it was.

The trial judge held that Ms. Leiner's failure to affirmatively disclose the corporate status of her company led the plaintiff to believe that it was a sole proprietorship and that, since it had not filed a trade name certificate, N.J.S.A. 14A:2-2(1)(d) required it to indicate its corporate status on its letterhead, presumably by using its full corporate name, Ecco Bella Incorporated. For those reasons, the judge ruled that Ms. Leiner was personally liable for plaintiff's unpaid bill, and he entered judgment for $ 1530, but he did not award prejudgment interest.

Ms. Leiner has appealed from the judgment. African Bio-Botanica, Inc. has cross-appealed, challenging the court's denial of pre-judgment interest. For the following reasons, we modify the judgment to award interest from the date the complaint was filed, and we otherwise affirm.

We agree with the trial judge that for Ms. Leiner to be shielded from personal liability, she was required to affirmatively disclose to plaintiff that she was acting as agent for Ecco Bella Incorporated. She failed to make her representative capacity clear. We therefore affirm, but we prefer to offer a somewhat different rationale for our decision from that adopted by the trial court.

....

A corporation acts only through its agents. In the present case, Ms. Leiner claims that when she entered into contracts with plaintiff for the purchase of its products, she did so only on behalf of her corporate principal, Ecco Bella Incorporated. Whether or not she is personally liable on those contracts must therefore be determined in accordance with the law of principal and agent.

Unless the parties agree otherwise, an agent who enters into a contract for an undisclosed or for a partly disclosed principal is personally liable on the contract; an agent who contracts on behalf of a fully disclosed principal is not personally liable on the contract. The Restatement (Second) of Agency § 4 (1958) defines "disclosed principal," "partially disclosed principal," and "undisclosed principal" as follows:

(1) If, at the time of a transaction conducted by an agent, the other party thereto has notice that the agent is acting for a principal and of the principal's identity, the principal is a disclosed principal.

(2) If the other party has notice that the agent is or may be acting for a principal but has no notice of the principal's identity, the principal for whom the agent is acting is a partially disclosed principal.

(3) If the other party has no notice that the agent is acting for a principal, the one for whom he acts is an undisclosed principal.

"Notice" is defined as follows: (1) A person has notice of a fact if he knows the fact, has reason to know it, should know it, or has been given notification of it. (2) A person is given notification of a fact by another if the latter (a) informs him of the fact by adequate or specified means or of other facts from which he has reason to know or should know the facts; ... Restatement (Second) of Agency § 9 (1958).

In the present case, the court found as a fact, with adequate support in the record, that African Bio-Botanica, Inc. was not informed and did not know that Ecco Bella was a corporation. The record gives no indication that African Bio-Botanica, Inc. was "inform[ed] of other facts from which [it] ha[d] reason to know or should [have] know[n]" that Ecco Bella was a corporation. Consequently, according to the Restatement definition, it did not have "notice" that Ecco Bella was a corporation unless the law is that it should have asked and, therefore, had "reason to know" or "should [have] know[n]" of its customer's corporate status even if it did not ask.

Fairness and expediency dictate a contrary rule. The agent who seeks protection from his status as agent has the means and the motive to communicate that status to the person with whom he is dealing. If the person with whom the agent is dealing does not know of the agency and has no reasonable way to know except by asking, the agent has the burden of disclosing his agency and the identity of his principal in order to avoid liability on contracts which he makes. In that situation the person with whom the agent is dealing has no duty to inquire. [3A William M. Fletcher, Fletcher Encyclopedia of the Law of Private Corporations (perm. Ed. Rev. vol. 1986)] § 279, states: A corporate agent is required to disclose his or her agency status in order to avoid personal liability. This is in keeping with the general agency principle that if an agent fails to reveal his or her true status as agency, he or she is bound as [a] principal. The duty of disclosure clearly lies with the agent alone, so that a third party with whom the agent deals has no duty to discover the existence of the agency or to discover the identity of the principal. Accordingly, the agent is not relieved from personal liability on the contract involving an undisclosed or partially disclosed principal merely because the party with whom he or she deals had the theoretical means of discovering that the agent was acting only in a representative capacity....

If an agent conducts business candidly as an agent for a disclosed principal, he should be readily able to prove that he disclosed his agency. The allocation of the burdens of proof between the purported agent and the third party with whom he deals reflects this reality. One bringing an action upon a contract has the burden of showing that the other is a party to it. This initial burden is satisfied if the plaintiff proves that the defendant has made a promise, the form of which does not indicate that it was given as agent. The defendant then has the burden of going forward if he wishes to show that his promise was made only as an agent and that this should have been so understood. Restatement (Second) of Agency, *supra*, § 320 Comment *b*.

In the present case, the evidence shows that Ms. Leiner entered into an oral purchase contract, either directly or through a subagent acting at her direction. She therefore has the burden of proving that she disclosed that she was buying merchandise solely as an agent on behalf of Ecco Bella Incorporated, a corporation. The trial court found that she did not sustain that burden. The fact that African Bio-Botanica, Inc. had the opportunity to inquire did not put it on notice that its customer was a corporation. If Ms. Leiner was acting as an agent for her corporation, she was an agent for an undisclosed or partially disclosed principal and she was therefore personally liable on its purchase contracts.

....

The judgment is ...

Affirmed.

Situations concerning disclosed, partially disclosed and undisclosed principals arise in a variety of contexts. One involves the purchase of property, where a buyer may want to conceal his or her identity from the seller during the negotiation process to avoid the risk of an inflated price. A convenient way to accomplish this result is to have an agent purchase the property on the buyer's behalf without disclosing the buyer's true identity. These issues may also arise because a contract did not identify the parties accurately or was not signed properly (or both).

4. Liability for Torts

When liability issues arise in tort rather than contract, the inquiry changes. In contract, the principal is liable for authorized acts. The question is whether the agent is also liable. In tort, however, the analysis focuses on the principal's liability rather than that of the agent. Agents are liable for their own tortious acts. In these cases, the principal's liability often depends on whether the agent was a servant (employee) or an independent contractor. Principals are liable for a servant's acts that are within the scope of the servant's employment. In contrast, a principal is not liable for the torts of an independent contractor unless the activity involved is inherently dangerous or the principal was negligent in selecting the contractor.

For an employer, the question whether a worker is determined to be an employee or an independent contractor has significance beyond the issue of the employer's liability for the worker's acts. An employer is subject to withholding and/or payment of payroll (FICA) and unemployment (FUTA) taxes if a worker is an employee (servant). Workers qualifying as employees (servants) under the common law agency rules will be classified as employees for federal tax purposes. The cost of these taxes may be significant sums.

Attorneys are agents of their clients. They may, however, have different types of agency relationships with their clients. Consider the following: Duane Margolis is Vice President and General Counsel of Invent Co. Susan Harris is Invent Co.'s outside counsel. Compare each attorney's relationship with Invent Co.

Comment [1] of Model Rules of Professional Conduct Rule 1.3 states, "A lawyer has professional discretion in determining the means by which a matter should be pursued." What type of agent is envisioned in this comment?

C. FIDUCIARY OBLIGATIONS OF AGENTS

Agents occupy positions of trust by dealing with their principals' property, making representations on their principals' behalf, and engaging in acts that impose legal liability on their principals. They often engage in these activities when their principals are absent. Thus, principals are not always able to monitor their agents' conduct to make sure that the agents are acting in the principals' best interests, and are not, instead, serving the interests of others, either third parties or the agents themselves. To address this situation, the law implies fiduciary obligations into every agency relationship. These obligations provide general guidelines for agents' conduct and require agents to act in their principals' best interests. As the following case demonstrates, the penalties for breaching these duties can be severe.

TARNOWSKI v. RESOP

Supreme Court of Minnesota
51 N.W.2d 801 (1952)

KNUTSON, JUSTICE.

Plaintiff desired to make a business investment. He engaged defendant as his agent to investigate and negotiate for the purchase of a route of coin-operated music machines. On June 2, 1947, relying upon the advice of defendant and the investigation he had made, plaintiff purchased such a business from Phillip Loechler and Lyle Mayer of Rochester, Minnesota, who will be referred to hereinafter as the sellers. The business was located at LaCrosse, Wisconsin, and throughout the surrounding territory. Plaintiff alleges that defendant represented to him that he had made a thorough investigation of the route; that it had 75 locations in operation; that one or more machines were at each location; that the equipment at each location was not more than six months old; and that the gross income from all locations amounted to more than $ 3,000 per month. As a matter of fact, defendant had made only a superficial investigation and had investigated only five of the locations. Other than that, he had adopted false representations of the sellers as to the other locations and had passed them on to plaintiff as his own. Plaintiff was to pay $ 30,620 for the business. He paid $ 11,000 down. About six weeks after the purchase, plaintiff discovered that the representations made to him by defendant were false, in that there were not more than 47 locations; that at some of the locations there were no machines and at others there were machines more than six months old, some of them being seven years old; and that the gross income was far less than $ 3,000 per month. Upon discovering the falsity of defendant's representations and those of the sellers, plaintiff rescinded the sale. He offered to return what he had received, and he demanded the return of his money. The sellers refused to comply, and he brought suit against them in the district court of Olmsted county. The action was tried, resulting in a verdict of $ 10,000 for plaintiff. Thereafter, the sellers paid plaintiff $ 9,500, after which the action was dismissed with prejudice pursuant to a stipulation of the parties.

In this action, brought in Hennepin county, plaintiff alleges that defendant, while acting as agent for him, collected a secret commission from the sellers for consummating the sale, which plaintiff seeks to recover under his first cause of action. In his second cause of action, he seeks to recover damages for (1) losses suffered in operating the route prior to rescission; (2) loss of time devoted to operation; (3) expenses in connection with rescission of the sale and his investigation in connection therewith; (4) nontaxable expenses in connection with prosecution of the suit against the sellers; and (5) attorneys' fees in connection with the suit. The case was tried to a jury, and plaintiff recovered a verdict of $ 5,200. This appeal is from the judgment entered pursuant thereto.

Defendant contends that after recovery of a verdict by plaintiff in his action for rescission against the sellers he cannot maintain this action against defendant. Principally, defendant argues that recovery in the action against the sellers is a bar to this action ....

1. With respect to plaintiff's first cause of action, the principle that all profits made by an agent in the course of an agency belong to the principal, whether they are the fruits of performance or the violation of an agent's duty, is firmly established and universally recognized. It matters not that the principal has suffered no damage or even that the transaction has been profitable to him. The rule and the basis therefor are well stated in *Lum v. McEwen*, 56 Minn. 278, 282, 57 N.W. 662, where, speaking through Mr. Justice Mitchell, we said: Actual injury is not the principle the law proceeds on, in holding such transactions void. Fidelity in the agent is what is aimed at, and, as a means of securing it, the law will not permit him to place himself in a position in which he may be tempted by his own private interests to disregard those of his principal.... It is not material that no actual injury to the company (principal) resulted, or that the policy recommended may have been for its best interest. Courts will not inquire into these matters. It is enough to know that the agent in fact placed himself in such relations that he might be tempted by his own interests to disregard those of his principal. The transaction was nothing more or less than the acceptance by the agent of a bribe to perform his duties in the manner desired by the person who gave the bribe. Such a contract is void. This doctrine rests on such plain principles of law, as well as common business honesty, that the citation of authorities is unnecessary.

The right to recover profits made by the agent in the course of the agency is not affected by the fact that the principal, upon discovering a fraud, has rescinded the contract and recovered that with which he parted. Restatement, Agency, § 407(2). Comment *a* on Subsection (2) reads: If an agent has violated a duty of loyalty to the principal so that the principal is entitled to profits which the agent has thereby made, the fact that the principal has brought an action against a third person and has been made whole by such action does not prevent the principal from recovering from the agent the profits which the agent has made. Thus, if the other contracting party has given a bribe to the agent to make a contract with him on behalf of the principal, the principal can rescind the transaction, recovering from the other party anything received by him, or he can maintain an action for damages against him; in either event the principal may recover from the agent the amount of the bribe.

It follows that, insofar as the secret commission of $ 2,000 received by the agent is concerned, plaintiff had an absolute right thereto, irrespective of any recovery resulting from the action against the sellers for rescission.

2. Plaintiff's second cause of action is brought to recover damages for (1) losses suffered in the operation of the business prior to rescission; (2) loss of time devoted to operation; (3) expenses in connection with rescission of the sale and investigation therewith; (4) nontaxable expenses in connection with the prosecution of the suit against the sellers; and (5) attorneys' fees in connection with the suit.

... Our inquiry is limited to a consideration of the question whether a principal may recover of an agent who has breached his trust the items of damage mentioned after a successful prosecution of an action for rescission against the third parties with whom the agent dealt for his principal.

The general rule is stated in Restatement, Agency, § 407(1), as follows: If an agent has received a benefit as a result of violating his duty of loyalty, the principal is entitled to recover from him what he has so received, its value, or its proceeds, and also the amount of damage thereby caused, except that if the violation consists of the wrongful disposal of the principal's property, the principal cannot recover its value and also what the agent received in exchange therefor.

In comment *a* on Subsection (1) we find the following: ... In either event, whether or not the principal elects to get back the thing improperly dealt with or to recover from the agent its value or the amount of benefit which the agent has improperly received, he is, in addition, entitled to be indemnified by the agent for any loss which has been caused to his interest by the improper transaction. Thus, if the purchasing agent for a restaurant purchases with the principal's money defective food, receiving a bonus therefor, and the use of the food in the restaurant damages the business, the principal can recover from the agent the amount of money improperly expended by him, the bonus which the agent received, and the amount which will compensate for the injury to the business.

The general rule with respect to damages for a tortious act is that "The wrong-doer is answerable for all the injurious consequences of his tortious act, which according to the usual course of events and the general experience were likely to ensue, and which, therefore, when the act was committed, he may reasonably be supposed to have foreseen and anticipated."

The general rule is given in Restatement, Torts, § 910, as follows: A person injured by the tort of another is entitled to recover damages from him for all harm, past, present and prospective, legally caused by the tort.

... So far as the right to recover attorneys' fees is concerned, the same may be said in this case. Plaintiff sought to return what had been received and demanded a return of his down payment. The sellers refused. He thereupon sued to accomplish this purpose, as he had a right to do, and was successful. His attorneys' fees and expenses of suit were directly traceable to the harm caused by defendant's wrongful act. As such, they are recoverable.

... The general rule applicable here is stated in 15 Am.Jur., Damages, § 144, as follows: "It is generally held that where the wrongful act of the defendant has involved the plaintiff in litigation with others or placed him in such relation with others as makes it necessary to incur expense to protect his interest, such costs and expenses, including attorneys' fees, should be treated as the legal consequences of the original wrongful act and may be recovered as damages." The same is true of the other elements of damage involved.

3. Defendant contends that plaintiff had an election of remedies and, having elected to proceed against the sellers to recover what he had paid, is now barred from proceeding against defendant. It is true that upon discovery of the fraud plaintiff had an election of remedies against the sellers. It is not true, however, that, having elected to sue for recovery of that with which he had parted, he is barred from proceeding against his agent to recover damages for his tortious conduct.... Many of the elements of damage against the agent are not available to plaintiff against the sellers. For instance, he has no right to recover attorneys' fees and expenses of the litigation against the sellers. He has that right against the agent. Plaintiff may recover profits made by the agent, irrespective of his recovery against the sellers. Losses directly flowing from the agent's tortious conduct are not recoverable against the sellers in an action for rescission, but they may be recovered against the agent, whose breach of faith has caused such losses....

Settlement of the action for rescission against the sellers is not a bar to an action against the agent to recover those elements of damages not involved in the action for rescission brought against the sellers.

Affirmed.

———

Issues of confidentiality and conflict of interest assume a particular importance in the attorney/client context. What common law rules are Model Rules 1.6, 1.7, 1.8 and 1.9 based on?

Chapter 2

TRADITIONAL BUSINESS FORMS AND THEIR PROGENY

Situation

(See Situation for Chapter 1)

SECTION I. GENERAL PARTNERSHIPS

A. INTRODUCTION

Early forms of partnership developed during the Middle Ages in the form of organizations known as *Compagnia* or *Societas*. The participants pooled their monetary and human capital resources and spread the risk of the enterprise. Although joint ownership offered efficiencies of operation unavailable to multiple, independently owned sole proprietorships, it also increased exposure to liability.

Originally, United States partnership law was a common-law creation. In the early twentieth century, however, the National Conference of Commissioners on Uniform State Laws adopted the Uniform Partnership Act (1914 Act), which was passed in all states but Louisiana. In many respects, this act was a codification of the partnership provisions that had developed in the common law. Today it forms the basis for most partnerships.

Many of the assumptions about the nature of partnerships that underlie UPA (1914) reflect the development of the law during the Middle Ages. The fundamental concept is one of a firm operated by a few members having close personal relationships. The UPA's fully participatory management structure in which all partners have equal votes (unless they agree otherwise) is suitable to a small number of members, as large numbers of owners make direct participation unwieldy. Other provisions reflect the personal nature of the members' relationships. The admission of new partners requires unanimous consent[1] and conveyance of a partner's interest confers management rights on the transferee only if the remaining partners agree.[2] The assumptions that partners know each other underlie provisions authorizing individual partners to bind the partnership and each other, thereby imposing personal liability for partnership obligations.[3] This exposure to legal liability makes sense when partners know their co-owners and

---

[1] UNIF. PARTNERSHIP ACT (1914) (hereinafter UPA (1914)) § 18(g), (U.L.A.).

[2] *Id.* § 27(1).

[3] *Id.* §§ 9(1), 13-15.

share management responsibility. It is generally less suitable to associations with large numbers of members or with passive investors. Partners' relations are essentially contractual in nature; partners can vary by agreement[4] components of the basic partnership structure.

In 1994, the National Conference adopted a revised version of the Uniform Partnership Act, which has become law in seven states as of the time of this writing. In many respects, the later Act continues the fundamental direction set by the earlier act. The two, however, do differ in key areas. Because of the continued vitality of the 1914 Act, this text will emphasize its provisions and discuss key differences in the 1994 Act.

Partnership law, like agency law, developed to meet the needs of persons jointly engaged in a business enterprise. It, too, consists of rules providing the terms of a contract for the members of a partnership. Some terms can be varied by agreement of the parties. Others are mandatory. Like agency law, partnership law defines the formation process, standards of conduct for the participants in a joint enterprise and termination of the relationship. It also addresses issues of liability among the members of the venture and between the venture and third parties. In fact, many of the provisions of partnership law are based on agency principles. Because a partnership involves multiple owners, the resolution of issues is often more complex than in situations where a single person has full decisionmaking responsibility.

The partnership is a good form for some businesses. It is relatively easy to organize and inexpensive to operate. The form, however, has some disadvantages. Two are of particular importance. The first flows from the fact that a partnership organized under UPA (1914) is generally not treated as an entity with a legal identity separate from that of the individual partners who comprise it. Instead, it is primarily treated as an aggregate of its principals. This means that the company's rights and obligations accrue to its owners and not to the business itself. It also means that the identity of a particular partnership will remain the same only so long as the same persons continue to own and operate it. A partner's retirement, bankruptcy, withdrawal or death causes what is referred to as the dissolution of the business.[5] Under the Uniform Partnership Act (1914), when one of these events occurs, the other partners must wind up the business and affairs of the partnership and distribute its assets, unless the remaining partners (and the estate of any deceased partner) agree that the business will be continued by the formation of a new partnership.[6]

---

[4]*Id.* § 18.
[5]*Id.* § 31(4).
[6]*Id.* §§ 29-43.

The detriment of aggregate status is also evident when a partner dies. Since each piece of partnership property is considered to be owned in part by the deceased partner, all of the partnership's property is subject to probate. This result can be a nuisance in any partnership. When a partnership owns property in several states, multiple probates can be an expensive nightmare.

The 1994 Act has eliminated many of these problems by treating the partnership as an entity in most respects, and by permitting the remaining partners to continue the business when one partner withdraws or dies. Although UPA (1994) expressly confers entity status on the partnership,[7] in some instances the revised act still treats the partnership as an aggregate of individuals. One example is that partners remain personally liable for partnership debts.[8]

Aggregate treatment is not always a detriment. In many respects, a partnership's legal status is immaterial. When taxes are involved, however, aggregate status can be a clear benefit, for at the federal level and usually also under state law, the partnership, itself, is not subject to income taxation unless it elects to be taxed like a corporation. The partnership merely files an information return, and then each partner pays tax on his or her proportionate share of the partnership's profits or takes a deduction for the proper share of its losses. In contrast, a corporation is treated as a separate taxable entity. Thus, the organization pays taxes on its earnings. A second tax is imposed when corporate earnings are distributed to shareholders. Since partnership earnings are taxed only to individual partners, and not also to the business entity, partnerships offer opportunities for tax savings that are not available to investors in corporations. When the marginal tax rates applied to individuals are lower than those imposed on corporations, the partnership pass through taxation scheme becomes increasingly attractive. When individual marginal tax rates are highter than corporate rates, the corporate tax rate may have some appeal. Today, partnerships, like most other unincorporated business organizations, may elect whether to be taxed like a corporation or a partnership.

The most significant detriment of the partnership form is that its owners do not enjoy limited liability. Rather, each partner is liable for all debts of the partnership.[9] Today, tax consequences and limited liability are two of the most important factors in decisions concerning what business form to use. Investment banking firms offer a good example of the increased significance of limited liability. Prior to the 1970's, almost all such firms were partnerships, and they operated with no significant problems flowing from their status as partnerships. When a changing judicial and regulatory climate fostered the widespread fear of liability, however, investment banking firms began incorporating, and during the 1970s their movement from the partnership to the corporate form became virtually complete.

---

[7] *Id.* UNIF. PARTNERSHIP ACT (1994) (hereinafter UPA (1994)) § 201, (U.L.A.).

[8] *Id.* § 306(a).

[9] UPA (1914) § 15.

Partnership remains a viable alternative for businesses whose exposure to liability may be limited by the purchase of insurance or contractual arrangements.

A joint venture is a business organization similar to a partnership. In fact, the distinctions between the two are often blurred. The term "joint venture" is usually used in connection with businesses organized to complete a specific project, such as developing a particular piece of real estate, rather than to engage in an ongoing enterprise.

B. PARTNERSHIP FORMATION

A partnership, like an agency relationship, may be created through the express agreement of the parties or may arise by operation of law when the parties have entered into an arrangement having the legal attributes of a partnership.[10] No formalities are required to form a partnership, although many states require the filing of a trade name registration, and under UPA (1994), certain filings are permitted, although not required.[11]

Persons entering into a partnership are well-advised to document their relationship in a partnership agreement addressing such issues as management and voting, sharing of profits and losses, the continuation of the business when a partner withdraws, retires or is expelled, and valuation of interests in the partnership. Preparing a partnership agreement will require the parties to discuss these matters in advance so that the partners will have common expectations when these events occur. (As you read the following materials, consider what additional issues should be addressed in a partnership agreement.) Having a partnership agreement prepared can be expensive. Very often, however, the initial investment in a carefully drafted document is more than recouped when problems arise. It is less costly, in time and impact on relationships, to decide difficult matters in advance, rather than when relations are strained and passions run high.

Because business relationships are flexible rather than static, persons dealing with a business may acquire the attributes of partners, even though they do not intend to be partners. One example is an employee having significant management responsibilities or the right to share in the profits of the enterprise. Another is a business creditor who has contracted for the right to approve certain business decisions in order to protect against the loss of funds lent to the venture. The case that follows provides examples of the problems that can arise.

---

[10] *Id.* §§ 6, 7.
[11] UPA (1994) §§ 303, 304.

MARTIN v. PEYTON

Court of Appeals of New York
158 N.E. 77 (1927)

ANDREWS, J....

Partnership results from contract, express or implied. If denied it may be proved by the production of some written instrument; by testimony as to some conversation; by circumstantial evidence. If nothing else appears the receipt by the defendant of a share of the profits of the business is enough. [UPA (1914) § 7.]

Assuming some written contract between the parties the question may arise whether it creates a partnership. If it be complete; if it expresses in good faith the full understanding and obligation of the parties, then it is for the court to say whether a partnership exists. It may, however, be a mere sham intended to hide the real relationship. Then other results follow. In passing upon it, effect is to be given to each provision. Mere words will not blind us to realities. Statements that no partnership is intended are not conclusive. If as a whole a contract contemplates an association of two or more persons to carry on as co-owners a business for profit a partnership there is. [UPA (1914) § 6] On the other hand, if it be less than this no partnership exists. Passing on the contract as a whole, an arrangement for sharing profits is to be considered. It is to be given its due weight. But it is to be weighed in connection with all the rest. It is not decisive. It may be merely the method adopted to pay a debt or wages, as interest on a loan or for other reasons.

An existing contract may be modified later by subsequent agreement, oral or written. A partnership may be so created where there was none before. And again, that the original agreement has been so modified may be proved by circumstantial evidence — by showing the conduct of the parties.

In the case before us the claim that the defendants became partners in the firm of Knauth, Nachod & Kuhne, doing business as bankers and brokers, depends upon the interpretation of certain instruments. There is nothing in their subsequent acts determinative of or indeed material upon this question. And we are relieved of questions that sometimes arise. "The plaintiff's position is not," we are told, "that the agreements of June 4, 1921, were a false expression or incomplete expression of the intention of the parties. We say that they express defendants' intention and that that intention was to create a relationship which as a matter of law constitutes a partnership." Nor may the claim of the plaintiff be rested on any question of estoppel. "The plaintiff's claim," he stipulates, "is a claim of actual partnership, not of partnership by estoppel, and liability is not sought to be predicated upon [section 16] of the [Uniform Partnership Act (1914)]."

Remitted then, as we are, to the documents themselves, we refer to circumstances surrounding their execution only so far as is necessary to make them intelligible. And we are to remember that although the intention of the parties to avoid liability as partners is clear, although in language precise and definite they deny any design to then join the firm of K. N. & K.; although they say their interests in profits should be construed merely as a measure of compensation for loans, not an interest in profits as such; although they provide that they shall not be liable for any losses or treated as partners, the question still remains whether in fact they agree to so associate themselves with the firm as to "carry on as co-owners a business for profit."

In the spring of 1921 the firm of K. N. & K. found itself in financial difficulties. John R. Hall was one of the partners. He was a friend of Mr. Peyton. From him he obtained the loan of almost $ 500,000 of Liberty bonds, which K. N. & K. might use as collateral to secure bank advances. This, however, was not sufficient. The firm and its members had engaged in unwise speculations, and it was deeply involved. Mr. Hall was also intimately acquainted with George W. Perkins, Jr., and with Edward W. Freeman. He also knew Mrs. Peyton and Mrs. Perkins and Mrs. Freeman. All were anxious to help him. He, therefore, representing K. N. & K., entered into negotiations with them. While they were pending, a proposition was made that Mr. Peyton, Mr. Perkins and Mr. Freeman or some of them should become partners. It met a decided refusal. Finally an agreement was reached. It is expressed in three documents, executed on the same day, all a part of the one transaction. They were drawn with care and are unambiguous. We shall refer to them as "the agreement," "the indenture" and "the option."

We have no doubt as to their general purpose. The respondents were to loan K. N. & K. $ 2,500,000 worth of liquid securities, which were to be returned to them on or before April 15, 1923. The firm might hypothecate them to secure loans totaling $ 2,000,000, using the proceeds as its business necessities required. To insure respondents against loss K. N. & K. were to turn over to them a large number of their own securities which may have been valuable, but which were of so speculative a nature that they could not be used as collateral for bank loans. In compensation for the loan the respondents were to receive 40 per cent of the profits of the firm until the return was made, not exceeding, however, $ 500,000 and not less than $ 100,000. Merely because the transaction involved the transfer of securities and not of cash does not prevent its being a loan within the meaning of [UPA (1914)] section [7]. The respondents also were given an option to join the firm if they or any of them expressed a desire to do so before June 4, 1923.

Many other detailed agreements are contained in the papers. Are they such as may be properly inserted to protect the lenders? Or do they go further? Whatever their purpose, did they in truth associate the respondents with the firm so that they and it together thereafter carried on as co-owners a business for profit? The answer depends upon an analysis of these various provisions.

As representing the lenders, Mr. Peyton and Mr. Freeman are called "trustees." The loaned securities when used as collateral are not to be mingled with other securities of K. N. & K., and the trustees at all times are to be kept informed of all transactions affecting them. To them shall be paid all dividends and income accruing therefrom. They may also substitute for any of the securities loaned securities of equal value. With their consent the firm may sell any of its securities held by the respondents, the proceeds to go, however, to the trustees. In other similar ways the trustees may deal with these same securities, but the securities loaned shall always be sufficient in value to permit of their hypothecation for $ 2,000,000. If they rise in price, the excess may be withdrawn by the defendants. If they fall, they shall make good the deficiency.

So far there is no hint that the transaction is not a loan of securities with a provision for compensation. Later a somewhat closer connection with the firm appears. Until the securities are returned, the directing management of the firm is to be in the hands of John R. Hall, and his life is to be insured for $ 1,000,000, and the policies are to be assigned as further collateral security to the trustees. These requirements are not unnatural. Hall was the one known and trusted by the defendants. Their acquaintance with the other members of the firm was of the slightest. These others had brought an old and established business to the verge of bankruptcy. As the respondents knew, they also had engaged in unsafe speculation. The respondents were about to loan $ 2,500,000 of good securities. As collateral they were to receive others of problematical value. What they required seems but ordinary caution. Nor does it imply an association in the business.

The trustees are to be kept advised as to the conduct of the business and consulted as to important matters. They may inspect the firm books and are entitled to any information they think important. Finally they may veto any business they think highly speculative or injurious. Again we hold this but a proper precaution to safeguard the loan. The trustees may not initiate any transaction as a partner may do. They may not bind the firm by any action of their own. Under the circumstances the safety of the loan depended upon the business success of K. N. & K. This success was likely to be compromised by the inclination of its members to engage in speculation. No longer, if the respondents were to be protected, should it be allowed. The trustees therefore, might prohibit it, and that their prohibition might be effective, information was to be furnished them. Not dissimilar agreements have been held proper to guard the interests of the lender.

As further security each member of K. N. & K. is to assign to the trustees their interest in the firm. No loan by the firm to any member is permitted and the amount each may draw is fixed. No other distribution of profits is to be made. So that realized profits may be calculated, the existing capital is stated to be $ 700,000, and profits are to be realized as promptly as good business practice will permit. In case the trustees think this is not done, the question is left to them and to Mr. Hall, and if they differ then to an arbitrator. There is no obligation that the firm shall continue the business. It may dissolve at any time. Again we conclude there is nothing here not properly adapted to secure the interest of the respondents as lenders. If their compensation is dependent on a percentage of the profits, still provision must be made to define what these profits shall be.

The "indenture" is substantially a mortgage of the collateral delivered by K. N. & K. to the trustees to secure the performance of the "agreement." It certainly does not strengthen the claim that the respondents were partners.

Finally we have the "option." It permits the respondents or any of them or their assignees or nominees to enter the firm at a later date if they desire to do so by buying 50 per cent or less of the interests therein of all or any of the members at a stated price. Or a corporation may, if the respondents and the members agree, be formed in place of the firm. Meanwhile, apparently with the design of protecting the firm business against improper or ill-judged action which might render the option valueless, each member of the firm is to place his resignation in the hands of Mr. Hall. If at any time he and the trustees agree that such resignation should be accepted, that member shall then retire, receiving the value of his interest calculated as of the date of such retirement.

This last provision is somewhat unusual, yet it is not enough in itself to show that on June 4, 1921, a present partnership was created nor taking these various papers as a whole do we reach such a result. It is quite true that even if one or two or three like provisions contained in such a contract do not require this conclusion, yet it is also true that when taken together a point may come where stipulations immaterial separately cover so wide a field that we should hold a partnership exists. As in other branches of the law a question of degree is often the determining factor. Here that point has not been reached.

The judgment appealed from should be affirmed, with costs.

CARDOZO, CH. J., POUND, CRANE, LEHMAN, KELLOGG and O'BRIEN, JJ., concur.

Judgment affirmed, etc.

Compare the result in this case with that in *Cargill*. Are the two consistent? How else could the plaintiffs in *Cargill* have characterized the relationship between Cargill and Warren? Would they have been successful?

You have been asked to prepare a partnership agreement for persons forming a partnership. Whom do you represent?

Young lawyers starting out in practice often share office space with other attorneys. Such an arrangement can be economically advantageous for everyone involved, and also provide the opportunity to discuss difficult legal issues with other professionals. What actions should they take to avoid being characterized as partners either under UPA (1914) or UPA (1994), including § 16 and § 308 respectively? For related issues on this point, consider also Model Rules of Professional Conduct Rule 1.10 Comment (1).

C. FINANCING THE BUSINESS

A partnership, like any other enterprise, needs money and other assets to conduct its business. The types and amount of assets a company should have depend on the nature of the venture. A fledgling software development company may need only a personal computer system and some office space to get started. A transportation company, on the other hand, may require substantial capital investment in equipment. The left hand side of a company's balance sheet describes the types and historical costs of its assets.

A business can raise capital through contributions of owners or by borrowing money, either from third party lenders or from company owners. The UPA (1994) anticipates the possibility that a partner may have a variety of financial arrangements with the business by recognizing that a partner may both provide capital to and lend money to the partnership.[12] Obligations to creditors, including those who are also partners, are recorded in the liabilities section of the company's balance sheet, whereas the value of partners' ownership interests appears in the equity section.

The opportunities for raising additional capital for an operating partnership are relatively few. The company may borrow money, but doing so will increase the liability of all partners. The company may take in new partners, but this action may require a change in management structure if the number of partners becomes too large. The company may also try to obtain additional capital from the current owners. Without an agreement, however, they cannot be compelled to contribute. The note that follows discusses in greater detail the issues faced by a partnership that wants to raise additional capital.

William A. Klein & John C. Coffee, Jr., Business Organization and Finance 82-85 (6th ed. 1995)*

One of the most difficult, and potentially one of the most important issues arising in the organization of small businesses has to do with the possible need for additional capital contributions after the firm has been operating for some time. Such a need can arise from a wide variety of circumstances. The firm may, for example, find itself in the happy position of having prospered and needing additional capital for expansion. On the other hand, the need may arise from the unhappy circumstance that the firm has suffered setbacks and needs new equity capital in order to be able to continue to operate. Often the partnership agreement will contain a provision dealing with the problem of additional capital contributions. This would be especially true where there is a strong possibility of need — as, for example, in an oil and gas exploration venture, where it can be anticipated that if oil is found, more money may be needed to drill additional wells, or where everyone knows that because of difficulties that may be unusual but not unforeseeable, additional funds may be needed to complete the drilling of a well. Often, however, the partnership agreement will simply ignore the issue — even where the partners are sophisticated in business affairs. It is important to bear in mind

---

[12] UPA (1994) §§ 401(e), 807(a).

in connection with this issue that, in the absence of an agreement to the contrary, a new partner cannot be added, nor can partnership shares be altered, without the unanimous consent of the partners.

....

... First, it seems plain that any knowledgeable contributor of new money will compare his or her contribution with the current value of the equity in the firm, not with the amount of the initial contribution. Second, in the case of a small business, new money may be hard to find because of the difficulty of learning what one needs to know about the business in order to be willing to invest in it. As an economist would put it, the information costs are high. This phenomenon may limit the sources of funds, which may in turn seriously affect relative bargaining positions. And finally, a supplier of new capital may be able to insist on a share of profits or control, or both, disproportionate to the relative dollar values of contributions.

Now for the moral of the story as it applies to partnership agreements. The position of an existing partner who is asked to contribute more than a *pro rata* share of any new capital is closely parallel to that of a new partner ... except that an effort by an existing partner to drive a hard bargain seems more likely to lead to bad feelings than such an effort by a stranger. To avoid the possibility of bad feelings, or of a mutually destructive impasse, the initial partners may be well advised to reach agreement in advance on a set of rules regarding additional equity capital.

Consider some of the more important issues that such an agreement must cope with and the kinds of rules that might be adopted for some of those issues. First and foremost, to what extent should some or all of the partners be obligated to supply additional capital if needed? Part of the problem in responding to this issue is that one of the partners may not have the money. If [a partner] cannot contribute, what happens to his interest? Perhaps the additional capital should come in as a loan from the wealthier partners. Beyond that, the partners may be unwilling to make a commitment to add more money to a venture in which they may have lost faith. One possible response to this kind of concern is to make additional contributions optional but to reduce the interests of the noncontributing partners to reflect not only the fact that new money is being added by less than all the partners, but also the diminution in the value of the initial contributions....

D. MANAGEMENT OF THE ENTERPRISE

Partnership acts provide a structure for the ongoing management of the business by containing default rules that determine who has a right to vote, how votes are allocated and what vote is required for approval of a proposed action. These rules may be varied by agreement of the partners. The two versions of the UPA vest in all partners the right to manage the business.[13] The right to vote is

---

[13] UPA (1914) § 18(e); UPA (1994) § 401(f).

therefore tied to one's status as a partner. This vesting of management rights in all partners is one reason partnership law requires unanimous approval for the admission of a new partner.

Both versions of the UPA allocate votes on a *per capita* basis,[14] giving every partner one vote, irrespective of the amount of the partner's capital contribution. In most situations, the vote of a majority will carry the day.[15] Extraordinary matters, such as the admission of a new partner or an act in contravention of the partnership agreement, require unanimity.[16] This requirement shifts voting power to the minority interests by creating a veto power in an individual partner who is thus able to thwart the will of the majority.

The voting structure reveals much about the assumptions on which partnership law is based. A fully participatory management structure is workable when a firm has only a few owners who are engaged in the business and are not merely passive investors. The equal allocation of votes makes sense if one assumes that all partners will work in the business as well as contribute capital. When these assumptions do not apply, either because there are many partners, or because a significant proportion are passive investors, a management structure in which owners cede decisionmaking authority to a few managers becomes desirable. This deviation from the statutory default rules can be accomplished in a partnership agreement describing who has management authority, the scope of that authority, how the authority is to be exercised, and how votes are allocated.

The allocation of voting power and the vote required for approval must be given careful consideration. In a two-person partnership, all decisions must be unanimous, because a split vote will not produce the majority required for approval of ordinary matters. Some provision should, therefore, be made for breaking deadlocks. In a three- or four-person partnership, the vote of a super majority, either ⅔ or ¾, is needed to approve an ordinary proposal or action. Similarly, the decision whether voting rights should accrue on a per capita basis, be tied to the amount of capital contribution, or allocated on a different basis requires careful thought. Persons who invest significantly more capital than their partners may want greater voting power to protect their investments, because if the partnership business takes a downturn, the largest investors will assume the greatest financial risks.

A partnership agreement may also create different classes of partners grouped by financial and/or voting rights. Law firms often use this approach, distinguishing between partners that are essentially salaried employees and those that share in the profits.

---

[14] UPA (1914) § 18(e); UPA (1994) § 401(f).
[15] UPA (1914) § 18(h); UPA (1994) § 401(j).
[16] UPA (1914) § 18(h); UPA (1994) § 401(j).

E. FIDUCIARY OBLIGATIONS

Fiduciary obligations of partners are a central component of partnership law. They are both aspirational and practical in nature. In order for a joint enterprise to function well, the members must conform their conduct according to what is in the best interests of their common venture. They must be able to trust each other to act honorably, to treat each other fairly, and to share the benefits of the enterprise. If this were not the case, then all partners would not only have to perform their own required functions, they would also have to monitor the others to make sure they were behaving appropriately, and not working solely to their own personal advantage and to the disadvantage of the enterprise and the other partners. The following case sets the standard for fiduciary obligations in a joint enterprise.

MEINHARD v. SALMON

Court of Appeals of New York
164 N.E. 545 (1928)

CARDOZO, C.J.

On April 10, 1902, Louisa M. Gerry leased to the defendant Walter J. Salmon the premises known as the Hotel Bristol at the northwest corner of Forty-Second street and Fifth avenue in the city of New York. The lease was for a term of 20 years, commencing May 1, 1902, and ending April 30, 1922. The lessee undertook to change the hotel building for use as shops and offices at a cost of $ 200,000. Alterations and additions were to be accretions to the land.

Salmon, while in course of treaty with the lessor as to the execution of the lease, was in course of treaty with Meinhard, the plaintiff, for the necessary funds. The result was a joint venture with terms embodied in a writing. Meinhard was to pay to Salmon half of the moneys requisite to reconstruct, alter, manage, and operate the property. Salmon was to pay to Meinhard 40 per cent of the net profits for the first five years of the lease and 50 per cent for the years thereafter. If there were losses, each party was to bear them equally. Salmon, however, was to have sole power to "manage, lease, underlet and operate" the building. There were to be certain preemptive rights for each in the contingency of death.

They were coadventures, subject to fiduciary duties akin to those of partners. As to this we are all agreed. The heavier weight of duty rested, however, upon Salmon. He was a coadventurer with Meinhard, but he was manager as well. During the early years of the enterprise, the building, reconstructed, was operated at a loss. If the relation had then ended, Meinhard as well as Salmon would have carried a heavy burden. Later the profits became large with the result that for each of the investors there came a rich return. For each the venture had its phases of fair weather and of foul. The two were in it jointly, for better or for worse.

When the lease was near its end, Elbridge T. Gerry had become the owner of the reversion. He owned much other property in the neighborhood, one lot adjoining the Bristol building on Fifth avenue and four lots on Forty-Second street. He had a plan to lease the entire tract for a long term to some one who would destroy the buildings then existing and put up another in their place. In the latter part of 1921, he submitted such a project to several capitalists and dealers. He was unable to carry it through with any of them. Then, in January, 1922, with less than four months of the lease to run, he approached the defendant Salmon. The result was a new lease to the Midpoint Realty Company, which is owned and controlled by Salmon, a lease covering the whole tract, and involving a huge outlay. The term is to be 20 years, but successive covenants for renewal will extend it to a maximum of 80 years at the will of either party. The existing buildings may remain unchanged for seven years. They are then to be torn down, and a new building to cost $ 3,000,000 is to be placed upon the site. The rental, which under the Bristol lease was only $ 55,000, is to be from $ 350,000 to $ 475,000 for the properties so combined. Salmon personally guaranteed the performance by the lessee of the covenants of the new lease until such time as the new building had been completed and fully paid for.

The lease between Gerry and the Midpoint Realty Company was signed and delivered on January 25, 1922. Salmon had not told Meinhard anything about it. Whatever his motive may have been, he had kept the negotiations to himself. Meinhard was not informed even of the bare existence of a project. The first that he knew of it was in February, when the lease was an accomplished fact. He then made demand on the defendants that the lease be held in trust as an asset of the venture, making offer upon the trial to share the personal obligations incidental to the guaranty. The demand was followed by refusal, and later by this suit. A referee gave judgment for the plaintiff, limiting the plaintiff's interest in the lease, however, to 25 per cent. The limitation was on the theory that the plaintiff's equity was to be restricted to one-half of so much of the value of the lease as was contributed or represented by the occupation of the Bristol site. Upon cross-appeals to the Appellate Division, the judgment was modified so as to enlarge the equitable interest to one-half of the whole lease. With this enlargement of plaintiff's interest, there went, of course, a corresponding enlargement of his attendant obligations. The case is now here on an appeal by the defendants.

Joint adventurers, like copartners, owe to one another, while the enterprise continues, the duty of the finest loyalty. Many forms of conduct permissible in a workaday world for those acting at arm's length, are forbidden to those bound by fiduciary ties. A trustee is held to something stricter than the morals of the market place. Not honesty alone, but the punctilio of an honor the most sensitive, is then the standard of behavior. As to this there has developed a tradition that is unbending and inveterate. Uncompromising rigidity has been the attitude of courts of equity when petitioned to undermine the rule of undivided loyalty by the "disintegrating erosion" of particular exceptions. Only thus has the level of conduct for fiduciaries been kept at a level higher than that trodden by the crowd. It will not consciously be lowered by any judgment of this court.

The owner of the reversion, Mr. Gerry, had vainly striven to find a tenant who would favor his ambitious scheme of demolition and construction. Baffled in the search, he turned to the defendant Salmon in possession of the Bristol, the keystone of the project. He figured to himself beyond a doubt that the man in possession would prove a likely customer. To the eye of an observer, Salmon held the lease as owner in his own right, for himself and no one else. In fact he held it as a fiduciary, for himself and another, sharers in a common venture. If this fact had been proclaimed, if the lease by its terms had run in favor of a partnership, Mr. Gerry, we may fairly assume, would have laid before the partners, and not merely before one of them, his plan of reconstruction. The preemptive privilege, or, better, the preemptive opportunity, that was thus an incident of the enterprise, Salmon appropriated to himself in secrecy and silence. He might have warned Meinhard that the plan had been submitted, and that either would be free to compete for the award. If he had done this, we do not need to say whether he would have been under a duty, if successful in the competition, to hold the lease so acquired for the benefit of a venture then about to end, and thus prolong by indirection its responsibilities and duties. The trouble about his conduct is that he excluded his coadventurer from any chance to compete, from any chance to enjoy the opportunity for benefit that had come to him alone by virtue of his agency. This chance, if nothing more, he was under a duty to concede. The price of its denial is an extension of the trust at the option and for the benefit of the one whom he excluded.

No answer is it to say that the chance would have been of little value even if seasonably offered. Such a calculus of probabilities is beyond the science of the chancery. Salmon, the real estate operator, might have been preferred to Meinhard, the woolen merchant. On the other hand, Meinhard might have offered better terms, or reinforced his offer by alliance with the wealth of others. Perhaps he might even have persuaded the lessor to renew the Bristol lease alone, postponing for a time, in return for higher rentals, the improvement of adjoining lots. We know that even under the lease as made the time for the enlargement of the building was delayed for seven years. All these opportunities were cut away from him through another's intervention. He knew that Salmon was the manager. As the time drew near for the expiration of the lease, he would naturally assume from silence, if from nothing else, that the lessor was willing to extend it for a term of years, or at least to let it stand as a lease from year to year. Not impossibly the lessor would have done so, whatever his protestations of unwillingness, if Salmon had not given assent to a project more attractive. At all events, notice of termination, even if not necessary, might seem, not unreasonably, to be something to be looked for, if the business was over and another tenant was to enter. In the absence of such notice, the matter of an extension was one that would naturally be attended to by the manager of the enterprise, and not neglected altogether. At least, there was nothing in the situation to give warning to any one that while the lease was still in being, there had come to the manager an offer of extension which he had locked within his breast to be utilized by himself alone. The very fact that Salmon was in control with exclusive powers of direction charged him the more obviously with the duty of disclosure, since only through disclosure could opportunity be equalized. If he might cut off renewal by a purchase for his own benefit when four months were to pass before the lease would have an end, he might do so with equal right while there remained as many years. He might steal a march on his comrade under cover of the darkness, and then hold the captured ground. Loyalty and comradeship are not so easily abjured.

Little profit will come from a dissection of the precedents. None precisely similar is cited in the briefs of counsel. What is similar in many, or so it seems to us, is the animating principle. Authority is, of course, abundant that one partner may not appropriate to his own use a renewal of a lease, though its term is to begin at the expiration of the partnership…. Equity refuses to confine within the bounds of classified transactions its precept of a loyalty that is undivided and unselfish. Certain at least it is that a "man obtaining his locus standi, and his opportunity for making such arrangements, by the position he occupies as a partner, is bound by his obligation to his copartners in such dealings not to separate his interest from theirs, but, if he acquires any benefit, to communicate it to them." … A constructive trust is, then, the remedial device through which preference of self is made subordinate to loyalty to others.

We have no thought to hold that Salmon was guilty of a conscious purpose to defraud. Very likely he assumed in all good faith that with the approaching end of the venture he might ignore his coadventurer and take the extension for himself. He had given to the enterprise time and labor as well as money. He had made it a success. Meinhard, who had given money, but neither time nor labor, had already been richly paid. There might seem to be something grasping in his insistence upon more. Such recriminations are not unusual when coadventurers fall out. They are not without their force if conduct is to be judged by the common standards of competitors. That is not to say that they have pertinency here. Salmon had put himself in a position in which thought of self was to be renounced, however hard the abnegation. He was much more than a coadventurer. He was a managing coadventurer. For him and for those like him the rule of undivided loyalty is relentless and supreme. A different question would be here if there were lacking any nexus of relation between the business conducted by the manager and the opportunity brought to him as an incident of management. For this problem, as for most, there are distinctions of degree. If Salmon had received from Gerry a proposition to lease a building at a location far removed, he might have held for himself the privilege thus acquired, or so we shall assume. Here the subject-matter of the new lease was an extension and enlargement of the subject-matter of the old one. A managing coadventurer appropriating the benefit of such a lease without warning to his partner might fairly expect to be reproached with conduct that was underhand, or lacking, to say the least, in reasonable candor, if the partner were to surprise him in the act of signing the new instrument. Conduct subject to that reproach does not receive from equity a healing benediction.

A question remains as to the form and extent of the equitable interest to be allotted to the plaintiff. The trust as declared has been held to attach to the lease which was in the name of the defendant corporation. We think it ought to attach at the option of the defendant Salmon to the shares of stock which were owned by him or were under his control. The difference may be important if the lessee shall wish to execute an assignment of the lease, as it ought to be free to do with the consent of the lessor. On the other hand, an equal division of the shares might lead to other hardships. It might take away from Salmon the power of control and management which under the plan of the joint venture he was to have from first to last. The number of shares to be allotted to the plaintiff should, therefore, be reduced to such an extent as may be necessary to preserve to the defendant Salmon the expected measure of dominion. To that end an extra share should be added to his half.

Subject to this adjustment, we agree with the Appellate Division that the plaintiff's equitable interest is to be measured by the value of half of the entire lease, and not merely by half of some undivided part. A single building covers the whole area. Physical division is impracticable along the lines of the Bristol site, the keystone of the whole. Division of interests and burdens is equally impracticable....

        ....

The judgment should be modified by providing that at the option of the defendant Salmon there may be substituted for a trust attaching to the lease a trust attaching to the shares of stock, with the result that one-half of such shares together with one additional share will in that event be allotted to the defendant Salmon and the other shares to the plaintiff, and as so modified the judgment should be affirmed with costs.

ANDREWS, J. (dissenting).

Where the trustee, or the partner or the tenant in common, takes no new lease but buys the reversion in good faith a somewhat different question arises. Here is no direct appropriation of the expectancy of renewal. Here is no offshoot of the original lease. The issue, then, is whether actual fraud, dishonesty, or unfairness is present in the transaction. If so, the purchaser may well be held as a trustee.

With this view of the law I am of the opinion that the issue here is simple. Was the transaction, in view of all the circumstances surrounding it, unfair and inequitable? I reach this conclusion for two reasons. There was no general partnership, merely a joint venture for a limited object, to end at a fixed time. The new lease, covering additional property, containing many new and unusual terms and conditions, with a possible duration of 80 years, was more nearly the purchase of the reversion than the ordinary renewal with which the authorities are concerned.

        ....

The one complaint made is that Mr. Salmon obtained the new lease without informing Mr. Meinhard of his intention. Nothing else. There is no claim of actual fraud. No claim of misrepresentation to any one. Here was no movable property to be acquired by a new tenant at a sacrifice to its owners. No good will, largely dependent on location, built up by the joint efforts of two men. Here was a refusal of the landlord to renew the Bristol lease on any terms; a proposal made by him, not sought by Mr. Salmon, and a choice by him and by the original lessor of the person with whom they wished to deal shown by the covenants against assignment or under-letting, and by their ignorance of the arrangement with Mr. Meinhard.

What then was the scope of the adventure into which the two men entered? It is to be remembered that before their contract was signed Mr. Salmon had obtained the lease of the Bristol property. Very likely the matter had been earlier discussed between them. The $ 5,000 advance by Mr. Meinhard indicates that fact. But it has been held that the written contract defines their rights and duties. Having the lease, Mr. Salmon assigns no interest in it to Mr. Meinhard. He is to manage the property. It is for him to decide what alterations shall be made and to fix the rents. But for 20 years from May 1, 1902, Salmon is to make all advances from his own funds and Meinhard is to pay him personally on demand one-half of all expenses incurred and all losses sustained "during the full term of said lease," and during the same period Salmon is to pay him a part of the net profits. There was no joint capital provided.

It seems to me that the venture so inaugurated had in view a limited object and was to end at a limited time. There was no intent to expand it into a far greater undertaking lasting for many years. The design was to exploit a particular lease. Doubtless in it Mr. Meinhard had an equitable interest, but in it alone. This interest terminated when the joint adventure terminated. There was no intent that for the benefit of both any advantage should be taken of the chance of renewal — that the adventure should be continued beyond that date. Mr. Salmon has done all he promised to do in return for Mr. Meinhard's undertaking when he distributed profits up to May 1, 1922. Suppose this lease, nonassignable without the consent of the lessor, had contained a renewal option. Could Mr. Meinhard have exercised it? Could he have insisted that Mr. Salmon do so? Had Mr. Salmon done so could he insist that the agreement to share losses still existed, or could Mr. Meinhard have claimed that the joint adventure was still to continue for 20 or 80 years? I do not think so. The adventure by its express terms ended on May 1, 1922. The contract by its language and by its whole import excluded the idea that the tenant's expectancy was to subsist for the benefit of the plaintiff. On that date whatever there was left of value in the lease reverted to Mr. Salmon, as it would had the lease been for thirty years instead of twenty. Any equity which Mr. Meinhard possessed was in the particular lease itself, not in any possibility of renewal. There was nothing unfair in Mr. Salmon's conduct.

POUND, CRANE, AND LEHMAN, JJ., concur with CARDOZO, C. J., for modification of the judgment appealed from and affirmance as modified.

ANDREWS, J., dissents in opinion in which KELLOGG and O'BRIEN, JJ., concur.

Judgment modified.

———

How does the standard for fiduciary obligation in *Meinhard* compare with the statutory obligations in UPA (1914) § 21, and in UPA (1994) §§ 103(b)(1)-(5), 403, 404?

What fiduciary obligations form the basis of Model Rules 1.3, 1.4, 1.6, and 1.7?

F. PARTNERS' LIABILITY TO THIRD PARTIES FOR PARTNERSHIP OBLIGATIONS

Harry G. Henn & John R. Alexander, Law of Corporations 73-75 (3d ed. 1983)*

General Partnership — Extent of Liability

....

A traditional attribute of doing business under the [UPA (1914)] partnership form is the full liability of each partner in one's personal capacity. Even in a limited partnership there must be at least one general partner with full personal liability.

The general partners are jointly and severally liable for the damages caused by any tort or breach of trust committed by a partner within the scope of partnership business. They are jointly liable for all other partnership obligations. Under joint debtor acts such joint liability may be enforced by suing them in all of their names or in the partnership name and serving one or more, in which case the resulting judgment would be enforceable against the partnership assets and the individual assets of the partners who were served.

Under the doctrine of marshaling of assets, when applicable, firm creditors must proceed against the assets of the firm before seeking satisfaction of their claims out of the individual property of the general partners.

If a partner makes any payment or incurs a personal liability in the ordinary and proper course of partnership business, the partnership is obligated to indemnify such partner for the payment so made or the liability so incurred. Thus, if a judgment on a firm obligation is satisfied out of the personal property of one partner, such partner may seek contribution against such partner's fellow

———

partners, at least where the judgment was not based upon a wrong committed by the paying partner.

Confusion as to the rights of partners with respect to contribution can and should be avoided by means of a provision in the partnership agreement. Generally, it would seem desirable to provide that tort liability will be considered as an expense of doing business and that therefore the partners will share the burdens of such liability along with other expenses. Of course, an exception should be made for willful and malicious torts and breaches of trust. Contribution among partners is not permitted until after a final accounting and settlement of partnership affairs. The partners may wish to provide in their agreement that the right to contribution will rise immediately upon the payment of the partnership debt.

A creditor of an individual partner may seek satisfaction of such claim out of the individual's property other than the debtor's interest in the partnership. Such creditor also may subject the debtor's interest in the partnership to a charging order, but cannot attach specific partnership property. A creditor who obtains a charging order may ask for dissolution of the partnership, but the remaining partners may redeem the interest so charged and thereby avoid dissolution.

An incoming partner, newly joining an established partnership, is liable personally on only those obligations incurred after joining absent voluntary assumption of the liability of a retiring partner, but the incoming partner's share in the partnership property can be used to satisfy both old and new partnership obligations.

A retiring (withdrawing) partner, absent release or novation, remains personally liable for partnership obligations incurred while a partner. As for debts incurred after withdrawal, the retiring partner is liable to those persons who had extended credit to the partnership in the past and who had no knowledge or notice of the retirement, and is also liable to new creditors, who had known of the partnership, and those who had dealt in the past with the partnership on a cash basis, but who had no knowledge or notice of such retirement, if notice of retirement had not been published in a newspaper of general circulation where the partnership business was regularly carried on. It is customary for the continuing partners to indemnify the retiring partner against further liability on firm obligations. The necessity of such complicated arrangements is a disadvantage of the partnership.

UPA (1994) makes several changes to the rules governing a partner's liability for the obligations of the partnership. One is that partners are jointly and severally liable for all partnership obligations.[17] A second change eliminates an ambiguity in the statement in UPA (1914) § 9(1) that "the act of every partner ... for apparently carrying on in the usual way the business of the partnership of

---

[17] UPA (1994) § 306(a).

which he is a member binds the partnership." That formulation was unclear as to whether the act must be of the type conducted in the business of the particular partnership in question or in the business of partnerships of the kind under consideration. UPA (1994) § 301(1) has resolved the question in favor of the latter approach.

Section 303 permits a partnership to file a statement of authority either to grant or to limit the authority of an individual partner. Although the purpose of the section is to facilitate the transfer of real property held in the partnership name by identifying which partners have the authority to make a particular transfer, it may also be used to specify the extent of a partner's authority for conducting ordinary business transactions. When properly filed and recorded in the land records, a statement of a grant or limitation of authority to transfer real estate is conclusive against third parties. UPA (1994) also avoids some procedural hurdles that third parties enforcing claims against the partnership had to contend with under the old act. The combination of eliminating joint liability for contract claims and treating a partnership as an entity that may sue and be sued in the partnership name eliminates the need to join individual partners.

KANSALLIS FINANCE LTD. v. FERN

Supreme Judicial Court of Massachusetts
659 N.E.2d 731 (1995)

FRIED, JUSTICE.

The United States Court of Appeals for the First Circuit has certified to this court, the following two questions of State law:

1. Under Massachusetts law, to find that a certain act is within the scope of a partnership for the purpose of applying the doctrine of vicarious liability, must a plaintiff show, inter alia, that the act was taken at least in part with the intent to serve or benefit the partnership?

In order that we may give the guidance that the Court of Appeals seeks, we offer the more extensive "discussion of relevant Massachusetts law" that the Court of Appeals invites in its certification order.

....

The questions arise out of an appeal by Kansallis Finance Ltd. (plaintiff) from a trial in the United States District Court for the District of Massachusetts. The Court of Appeals stated that the first question concerns an issue on which an apparent conflict exists in Massachusetts precedent, and that the second question concerns a separate issue on which there is no controlling Massachusetts precedent.

I

We summarize the facts relevant to the questions certified. Stephen Jones and the four defendants were law partners in Massachusetts when, in connection with a loan and lease financing transaction, the plaintiff sought and obtained an opinion letter from Jones. In the order of certification, the Court of Appeals states that the letter, executed in Massachusetts and issued on "Fern, Anderson, Donahue, Jones & Sabatt, P.A." letterhead, "contained several intentional misrepresentations concerning the transaction and was part of a conspiracy by Jones and others (though not any of the defendants here) to defraud Kansallis." Although Jones did not personally sign the letter, he arranged for a third party to do so, and both the District Court judge and the jury found that Jones adopted or ratified the issuance of the letter. Jones was later convicted on criminal charges for his part in the fraud, but the plaintiff was unable to collect its $ 880,000 loss from Jones or his co-conspirators.

In an effort to recover its loss, the plaintiff brought suit in the United States District Court for the District of Massachusetts seeking compensation from Jones's law partners on the theory that the partners were liable for the damage caused by the fraudulent letter.... Both the judge and jury, for different reasons, decided that defendants were not liable for Jones's conduct. The Court of Appeals affirmed both the judge's and the jury's factual findings and certified two questions to this court in order to resolve the legal issues.

On plaintiff's common law claims, the jury based their verdict on their findings that (1) Jones did not have apparent authority to issue the opinion letter[18] and (2) that his action in issuing the opinion letter was outside the scope of the partnership. On appeal to the Court of Appeals, the plaintiff contended that the jury based their second finding on an erroneous instruction directing that, to find Jones's actions within the scope of the partnership, the issuance of the letter must satisfy a three-prong test. It must have: (1) been "the kind of thing a law partner would do"; (2) "occurred substantially within the authorized time and geographic limits of the partnership; and" (3) been "motivated at least in part by a purpose to serve the partnership." Although the jury did not indicate which prong the plaintiff failed to satisfy, the plaintiff objected to the addition of the third prong, and it is on the correctness of including this third prong in the test that the Court of Appeals now seeks guidance. The Court of Appeals found our law on this issue unclear because it found that two decisions, appeared to pull in opposite directions. The Court of Appeals therefore certified this first question to us....

....

II

A

The parties have cited to us cases from this and other jurisdictions, as well as general principles set out in the Restatement (Second) of Agency and in the Uniform Partnership Act. Whatever difficulties this array of authorities presents may in part be attributed to the fact that the issue of vicarious liability has

---

[18] The judge instructed the jury that "[t]here is no contention here that Jones had actual authority from the defendants to issue this Opinion Letter."

engendered somewhat divergent formulations in the several different contexts in which it has arisen. The genus here is agency, and two of its species, for which there are special rules for determining vicarious liability, are partnership and master-servant. In the context of a partnership, the person acting and the persons who might be held liable for his actions usually stand on an equal footing and may be thought of as equally implicated in a joint enterprise. By contrast, the law of the vicarious liability of a master for the acts of his servant grew up in circumstances where the actor was often in a subordinate position and had a limited interest in the enterprise which he assists. *See* Restatement (Second) of Agency § 218 (1957). Yet both servants and partners are categorized as agents of their principals: § 9 (Uniform Partnership Act) (partners are agents of the partnership); Restatement (Second) of Agency § 218 Title B, Torts of Servants, introductory note, fourth par. (1957) (servants are agents of their master); Restatement of Agency (Second) § 14A comment *a* (1957) (partner is general agent for copartners and liable to copartners for any breach of fiduciary obligation). In the partnership context, while each partner is the agent of the partnership, he also stands in the role of a principal — a reciprocity that is lacking in the master-servant relation. Finally, there is an important practical distinction between determining vicarious liability for harms that come about through the victim's voluntary interactions with the purported agent — as in the case of contracts, of fraud and of misrepresentation — and those that are inflicted on a victim who has made no choice to deal with the agent, as in the case of an accident, an assault or a trespass. Only in the former instance is the inquiry into apparent authority particularly apt, since where the victim transacts business with the agent, the victim's ability to assess the agent's authority will bear on whether and in what ways he chooses to deal with him. By contrast, where the victim has not chosen to deal with the agent by whose act he suffers harm — as in an automobile accident — the scope of employment seems the natural determinant of vicarious liability, and that is where the concept has had its most usual application.

Standing behind these diverse concepts of vicarious liability is a principle that helps to rationalize them. This is the principle that as between two innocent parties — the principal-master and the third party — the principal-master who for his own purposes places another in a position to do harm to a third party should bear the loss. A principal who requires an agent to transact his business, and can only get that business done if third parties deal with the agent as if with the principal, cannot complain if the innocent third party suffers loss by reason of the agent's act. Similarly, the master who must put an instrument into his servant's hands in order to get his business done, must also bear the loss if the servant causes harm to a stranger in the use of that instrument as the business is transacted.

This overarching principle measures the imposition of vicarious liability in particular contexts and suggests its own limitations. Where there is actual authority to transact the very business or to do the very act that causes the harm, the agent acts as the extension of the will of his principal and the case for vicarious liability is clear. Where the authority is only apparent, vicarious liability recognizes that it is the principal who for his own purposes found it useful to create the impression that the agent acts with his authority, and therefore it is the principal who must bear the burden of the misuse to which that appearance has been put. Restatement (Second) of Agency § 8 (1957). But there is little fairness in saddling the principal with liability for acts that a reasonable third party would not have supposed were taken on the principal's behalf. Similarly, where the servant acts beyond the scope of his employment he is more like a thief who causes harm with an instrumentality he had no right to use.

Where the wrongdoer transacts business with the victim, the authority — actual or apparent — of the agent to act on the principal's behalf may be conceptualized as the dangerous instrumentality the principal has put in the agent's hands, enabling him to do harm with it. And this creates the temptation to use the concepts of apparent authority and scope of employment interchangeably. But they are not equivalent concepts. A servant or agent may sometimes act within the scope of his master's employment and yet lack apparent authority. The clearest instances are in accident cases where the victim neither knew nor cared what the wrongdoer's relation to his employer might be. Another rarer divergence may be illustrated by the present case. The scope of employment test asks the question: is this the kind of thing that in a general way employees of this kind do in employment of this kind. It does not ask the different question: whether a reasonable person in the victim's circumstances in the particular case would have taken the agent to be acting with the principal's authority. And so there arises the possibility of vicarious liability where the victim transacted business or otherwise dealt with an agent who lacked even apparent authority in the particular matter. In the case before us here, the jury instructions required the jury to consider both routes to vicarious liability. The jury found that Jones acted without actual or apparent authority, presumably because the form and circumstances of the letter were such that they concluded that no reasonable person in the plaintiff's position would have believed that the letter was issued with the partnership's authority. But then they were asked in the alternative whether Jones "acted in the scope of the partnership." This further question was taken to ask whether writing this opinion letter was the kind of thing that the partnership did — even if there was no apparent authority for this particular letter. This is the alternative theory, which the District Court labeled "vicarious liability," and under this alternative the defendants might yet be liable if the jury found all three of the conditions set out above in its charge on that issue. The rationale for this possibly more extended liability recognizes an authority in each partner to take the initiative to enlarge the partnership enterprise even without the authority — actual or apparent — of his partners, so long as what he does is within the generic description of the type of partnership involved. Whatever the harshness may be of such a rule extending vicarious liability past apparent authority, it is mitigated by the third factor, requiring that the unauthorized but law partner-like act be intended at least in part to serve the partnership. Since there is then some possibility that the partnership will benefit from the errant partner's act, then as between two innocent parties it is not unfair that the one whom the wrongful act may have and was meant to benefit must bear the burden of the harm.

B

Our cases and statutes can readily be rationalized against the background of these principles. The Uniform Partnership Act provides as general principles that: the law of agency shall apply under that chapter, [UPA (1914)] § 4(3); the act of every partner apparently carrying on in the usual way the business of the partnership binds it, [UPA (1914)] § 9(2); and an act of the partner which is not apparently for the carrying on of the business of the partnership in the usual way does not bind it unless authorized, *id.* [UPA (1914)] § 9(2). Where, however, by any wrongful act of a partner acting in the ordinary course of the business of the partnership, or with the authority of the copartners, loss or injury is caused to a third person, or a penalty is incurred, the partnership is liable therefore, [UPA (1914)] § 13.

Because the Uniform Partnership Act [(1914)] at § 4(3) specifically provides that the law of agency applies, it is appropriate to refer, as did the District Court in formulating its jury instructions, to the Restatement (Second) of Agency (1957). The District Court derived the second theory of liability, which it labeled vicarious liability and on which it instructed the jury regarding the scope of the partnership business, from § 228(1) of the Restatement (Second) of Agency. Section 228(1) provides in relevant part that conduct of a servant is within the scope of his employment, if but only if the conduct is (a) of the kind he is employed to perform, (b) within the partnership's authorized time and space limits, and (c) actuated, at least in part, by a purpose to serve the master. Subsection (2) states the complementary proposition that conduct is not within the scope of employment if it is different in kind from that authorized or too little actuated by a purpose to serve the master. Section 261 states the alternative ground of vicarious liability based on apparent authority: that a principal who puts an agent in a position which enables the agent, while apparently acting within his authority, to commit a fraud on a third party is subject to liability to the third party. And § 262 states the complementary proposition that a person who otherwise would be liable to another for the misrepresentations of one acting for him is not relieved from liability by the fact that the agent acts entirely for his own purposes, unless the other has notice of that. Thus, under § 262, if an agent has actual or apparent authority, the principal is not relieved of liability for that agent's misrepresentation even though the requirements of § 228(1)(c) have not been met.

The two cases which concerned the Court of Appeals may be understood in this light. *Wang Labs., Inc. v. Business Incentives, Inc.*, 398 Mass. 854, 501 N.E.2d 1163 (1986), a [consumer protection] case, did indeed require and find an intention to benefit the corporate principal as a condition of vicarious liability, but in that case we did not address and so did not negate the possibility of vicarious liability by the route of apparent authority. Moreover, the harm complained of in *Wang*, which was akin to the tort of intentional interference with contractual relations, did not require for its accomplishment that the victim rely on the agent's authority, and so an analysis in terms of apparent authority would have been beside the point — every bit as much as it would be in an automobile accident or an assault. By contrast, in *New England Acceptance Corp. v. American Mfrs. Mut. Ins. Corp.*, 373 N.E.2d 1385 (1977), a contract or tort case, the fraud that was worked on the plaintiff depended for its accomplishment on the plaintiff's believing that the agent was acting with his principal's authority. It is for that reason that we adopted our Appeals Court's conclusion in that case that there could be vicarious liability even though "the agents were acting entirely for their own purposes." Indeed, as we have pointed out, that will usually be the case where a dishonest agent misuses his apparent authority to work a fraud upon both his principal and a third party.

C

Accordingly, if we take the first certified question to ask whether a partner must necessarily at least in part act for the benefit of the partnership if the partnership is to be liable for his actions, the answer is "no". But the answer is "no" only because under our law — and the law of partnership and agency generally — there are two routes by which vicarious liability may be found. If the partner has apparent authority to do the act, that will be sufficient to ground vicarious liability, whether or not he acted to benefit the partnership. It is only where there is no apparent authority, which is what the jury found on the common law counts here, that there may yet be vicarious liability on the alternative ground requiring such an intent to benefit the partnership. Since there is no evidence that Jones was acting to benefit the partnership, the District Court's judgment for the defendants on the common law counts accords with our statutes and precedents. The jury instructions on the common law claims were correct.

....

IV

To summarize, we hold that under the law of the Commonwealth a partnership may be liable by one of two routes for the unauthorized acts of a partner: if there is apparent authority, or if the partner acts within the scope of the partnership at least in part to benefit the partnership. Where there is neither apparent authority nor action intended at least in part to benefit the partnership, there cannot be vicarious liability. Accordingly, we answer the first question "no," but only because even if a partner acts with no purpose to benefit the partnership, vicarious liability may yet be appropriate, if he is clothed with apparent authority. In this case, however, the jury found that there was no apparent authority....

From time to time, a lawyer may associate with an attorney who is not a member of the lawyer's firm. The association may be for a particular matter that requires special expertise the lawyer does not have. For example, a general practice attorney may retain the services of an intellectual property lawyer to assist in handling a matter. What legal and ethical issues must be addressed in order for these arrangements to work to everyone's satisfaction?

G. PARTNERSHIP PROPERTY

The 1994 UPA brought a long needed overhaul of the 1914 Act's treatment of partnership property. The earlier Act's approach reveals a statute at war with itself. To understand why that is true, we need only revisit the issue of whether a partnership should be dealt with as an aggregate of individual partners or an entity separate and distinct from its owners. The theoretical treatment of the business affects such issues as whether the business will be taxed as a separate legal entity, whether the enterprise can sue and be sued in its own name rather than in the name of the individual partners, and whether the business, itself, or the individual partners own the company property. Although UPA (1914) primarily adopts an aggregate approach, it in fact mixes the two, in wanton disregard of the muses of clarity and simplicity. The mixed approach is the product of a conflict between the views of the original drafter of the Act, Dean James Barr Ames of Harvard Law School, who adopted an entity approach, and his successor, Dean William Draper Lewis of the University of Pennsylvania Law School, who was an advocate for the aggregate approach. The provisions relating to partnership property are the battleground for the clash of those two approaches.

Section 24 of UPA (1914) groups partnership property into three categories: partners' management rights (previously described); partners' financial interests in the partnership; and the assets of the business. Partners' financial interests include partners' rights to share in the profits of the business and to be paid upon partnership dissolution, the value of their equity (their residual interest in the enterprise). A partner's financial interest is characterized as personal property. It may be transferred to a third party by the partner and levied against by a creditor of the individual partner. This type of property is discussed more fully in the following section. The most troubling component of partnership property is the last of the three, the ownership of the business assets. It is here that the uneasy mix of the entity and aggregate approaches becomes apparent.

The distinction between property belonging to the partnership and that owned by individual partners is important in determining what property can be used by the partners in the conduct of partnership business and is available to satisfy the claims of business creditors. UPA (1914) § 8 seems to be based on the entity theory. The section defines partnership property and provides that real property can be acquired in the partnership name. Section 28(1), however, applies the aggregate approach by providing that partners are co-owners of partnership property, which they hold as tenants in partnership. Subsection (2) of § 28 eliminates the usual attributes of joint ownership, such as assignment and inheritance rights. As a result, partners are co-owners of the partnership property in name only.

Fortunately, the UPA (1994) eliminates the confusion caused by this dual treatment of partnership property. The Act clearly establishes that a partnership is an entity[19] and that the partnership, not individual partners, owns partnership property. The Act eliminates the concept of tenants in partnership.[20]

H. PARTNERS' RETURN ON INVESTMENT

In a successful going concern, partners earn a return on their investments by receiving their respective shares of the profits. If the company is sold for a profit to a third party, partners receive the appreciated value of their residual shares of the business. The value of a partner's investment will also be realized if the partnership or other partners buy out a partner's interest or a partner transfers the partner's individual interest to a third party.

1. Allocation of Profits and Losses

In partnership accounting, the balance sheet capital account reflects the total value of partners' equity, the residual claim to partnership assets. The balance sheet capital account thus represents the collective value of individual partners' accounts as recorded in the company books. An individual capital account is increased by the value of the applicable partner's capital contributions and share of the profits, and decreased by the partner's share of the losses and the amounts of any draws.[21] A partner's capital contribution is the money or property the partner transfers to the partnership in exchange for a share of the business. Capital contributions may be made when the company begins and, if required, later on, when it is operating as a going concern. A partner's share of the profits is the partner's share of the earnings produced by the company's ongoing operations during a given time period. The term "draw" refers to cash distributions to partners. Whether partners receive draws and, if so, their respective amounts are determined either by a partnership agreement or by a vote of the partners. Partnership law does not restrict distributions to partners, even when the

---

[19] UPA (1994) § 201.

[20] *Id.* § 501.

[21] *Id.* § 401(a).

company is losing money. Protection of creditors depends on fraudulent conveyance statutes.

A partner's share of losses is the partner's share of company obligations that remain unmet during a particular time period. According to Comment 3 of UPA (1994) § 401(b):

> Losses are charged to each partner's account as provided in subsection (a) ... (2). It is intended to make clear that a partner is not obligated to contribute to partnership losses before his withdrawal or the liquidation of the partnership, unless the partners agree otherwise. In effect, a partner's negative account represents a debt to the partnership unless the partners agree to the contrary. Similarly each partner's share of the profits is credited to his account under subsection (a) (1). Absent an agreement to the contrary, however, a partner does not have a right to receive a current distribution of the profits credited to his account, the interim distribution of profits being a matter arising in the ordinary course of business to be decided by a majority vote of the partners.

Under both versions of the Uniform Partnership Act, partners share profits equally in the absence of an agreement.[22] Losses are shared in proportion to a partner's share of the profits,[23] which means that losses will also be shared equally if the default rules apply. These rules make sense when capital contributions to the business have parity. All partners have equal opportunities for gain and equal exposure to the financial risks of the business.

The rules are less acceptable when there is a disparity in the value of the capital contributions to the partnership. Applying a *per capita* profit-sharing rule to a situation where some partners contribute significantly more capital than the others reduces the proportional return of the investors who have made the greatest contributions, while an equal share of the profits may give a windfall to investors who have made lesser contributions. Ordinarily, in situations like this, the partnership agreement will link profit share to share of contribution. The converse is true when a *per capita* allocation applies to losses. In this case, the advantage is shifted to large contributors whose proportionate risks are reduced; smaller contributors assume a financial exposure greater than their proportionate contributions.

Assume, for purposes of illustration, that A contributes $ 80,000 to a partnership and B contributes $ 20,000. If the partnership profits for a particular year total $ 10,000, under the *per capita* rule A and B will each receive $ 5,000, a 6.25% return for A and a 25% return for B. If the profits were distributed according to capital contribution, A would receive $ 8,000 and B would receive $ 2,000, a 10% return for each. If, instead, the business lost $ 10,000 the same

---

[22] UPA (1914) § 18(a), UPA (1994) § 401(b).

[23] UPA (1914) § 18(a); UPA (1994) § 401(b).

allocations would apply to *per capita* and proportional distributions of losses. Thus, *per capita* allocation of profits is an advantage to B and a disadvantage to A, while the same allocation of losses advantages A and disadvantages B.

A related and somewhat more complicated problem arises when one partner contributes money or property to the partnership and the other contributes services, typically in the form of special skills or know-how. This problem is caused by the interplay among the UPA's rules regarding capital contributions, compensation for services, and distributions on termination of the business. Under the default rules of both versions of the UPA, contribution of capital means contribution of money or property and does not include services. Thus, when a partner contributes only services to a partnership, the capital contribution portion of that partner's account will be zero and will not reflect the value of the services rendered. If a partnership agreement does not address this issue, the services partner may be disadvantaged by the application of the rules requiring profits and losses to be shared equally. The particular outcome will depend on the proportional relationship between the actual value of the services rendered and the value of the other partners' capital contributions. If the value of the services is disproportionately higher than the other partners' capital contributions, the result will be the same as for partner A described above. If the actual value is lower, then the result will track the impact on partner B. The services partner is doubly disadvantaged because the default rules also provide that a partner may not be compensated for services performed on behalf of the business.

The problem has another dimension that emerges when the partnership is ended. When the partnership is winding up, the assets of the business are liquidated to pay partnership obligations. Creditors are paid first. Any amounts remaining are used to satisfy the residual claims of the partners based on the value in their capital accounts. Partners with negative values in their accounts must pay to the partnership the amount of the negative value. Partners with positive values in their accounts will receive distributions if surplus funds are available. This approach works against services partners in the following two ways. (For the purposes of example, assume that partner C contributed $ 50,000 worth of skill and know-how to the partnership, and partner D made a $ 50,000 capital contribution.) First, the services partner's account will be undervalued because the capital contribution component will be zero. This, in itself, diminishes this partner's opportunity to recoup the value of the original investment. Second, if after the allocation of partnership losses, partner C's account has a negative value and partner D's account has a positive value, the services partner will have to contribute to the partnership additional funds equal to the amount of the negative value. These funds may be used to repay D the value of D's capital contribution. The result is that in this situation, the services partner will not be reimbursed for the original contribution to the partnership and will have to contribute additional funds as well.

A partnership agreement that defines how profits and losses are to be allocated is essential when partners make contributions to the partnership that differ significantly in either amount or type of consideration. The options available to the parties are many. The agreement may provide that partners contributing services will be paid a salary or will have the value of their services included in their capital accounts.

Designing a compensation scheme is one of the thorniest challenges facing attorneys forming a law practice partnership. Attorneys in a large law firm may have a variety of types of relationships with the firm: partner-track associates, permanent associates, profit-sharing partners, salaried partners, contract attorneys who are paid for working on particular projects or are hired for a term, and of counsel attorneys who may be retired partners or lawyers with another type of special relationship with the firm. Some firms compensate attorneys based on their number of years at the firm. Others apply a formula based on a variety of factors including hours billed and fees collected, business generated, and capital contributed.

2. Transfer of Partnership Interest to Third Parties or to the Partnership

Shareholders in a publicly traded corporation may easily realize the current value of their investment. They have an unrestricted right to sell their shares, representing their full complement of ownership rights, at any time and to anyone they wish. In addition, established securities exchanges provide a ready market for their shares. Investors in privately held companies typically do not have these opportunities. Partners are no exception.

Under partnership law default rules, partners may freely assign to third parties only their financial interests in the partnership: the partners' share of the profits and losses and their right to receive distributions. Transferring a partner's management rights requires the permission of the remaining partners, because these interests are inextricably linked to one's status as a partner. Although the legal restrictions on transferability can be cured in a partnership agreement, unrestricted transferability may not be suitable for a business with only a few owners having a close working relationship. The absence of an available market for the interests also makes it difficult to transfer a partnership interest, as a buyer may not be found easily. The combination of the restrictions on transfer and the absence of a market make it difficult to leave an ongoing partnership.

A partnership buyout of a partner's interest provides an alternative to a sale to a third party. By statute, the partnership must compensate resigning or retiring partners for the value of their partnership interests.[24] This rule also applies to the estate of a partner who dies.[25] If, however, a partner's resignation violates the terms of the partnership agreement, the amount owed to the partner may be offset by the remaining partners' claim for damages for breach of contract.[26] The

---

[24] UPA (1914) § 38; UPA (1994) § 701(a).

[25] UPA (1914) § 38; UPA (1994) § 601(g).

[26] UPA (1914) § 602(c); UPA (1994) § 701(c).

practical difficulties that emerge in this situation are common to all privately held companies: the valuation of the interest being bought and the timing of the payments by the partnership. A partnership may not have ready cash to settle the withdrawing partner's account.

Because of the difficulties of withdrawing from a partnership, careful planning is essential. At a minimum, the agreement should identify those situations in which withdrawal is permitted, whether transfer to a third party is permitted, and, in the case of a buyout by the partnership, how the financial interest will be valued and how payments will be made. The following case addresses problems arising from the transfer of a partnership interest.

RAPOPORT v. 55 PERRY CO.

Supreme Court of New York, Appellate Division
50 A.D.2d 54 (1975)

TILZER, JUSTICE.

In 1969, Simon, Genia and Ury Rapoport entered into a partnership agreement with Morton, Jerome and Burton Parnes, forming the partnership known as 55 Perry Company. Pursuant to the agreement, each of the families owned 50% of the partnership interests. In December of 1974 Simon and Genia Rapoport assigned a 10% interest of their share in the partnership to their adult children, Daniel and Kalia. The Parnes defendants were advised of the assignment and an amended partnership certificate was filed in the County Clerk's Office indicating the addition of Daniel and Kalia as partners. However, when the plaintiffs, thereafter, requested the Parnes defendants to execute an amended partnership agreement to reflect the above changes in the partnership, the Parnes refused, taking the position that the partnership agreement did not permit the introduction of new partners without consent of all the existing partners. Thereafter, the plaintiffs Rapoport brought this action seeking a declaration that Simon and Genia Rapoport had an absolute right to assign their interests to their adult children without consent of the defendants and that such assignment was authorized pursuant to Paragraph 12 of the partnership agreement. The plaintiffs further sought to have Daniel and Kalia be declared partners in 55 Perry Company and have their names entered upon the books of the partnership as partners. The defendants Parnes interposed an answer, taking the position that the partnership agreement did not permit admission of additional partners without consent of all the existing partners and that the filing of the amended certificate of partnership was unauthorized. After joinder of issue plaintiffs moved for summary judgment and although the defendants did not cross-move for similar relief, such was, nevertheless, requested in their answering papers.

On the motion for summary judgment both parties agreed that there were no issues of fact and that there was only a question of the interpretation of the written documents which should be disposed of as a matter of law by the Court. Nevertheless, the Court below found that the agreement was ambiguous and that there was a triable issue with respect to the intent of the parties. We disagree and conclude that the agreement is without ambiguity and that pursuant to the terms of the agreement and of the Partnership Law, consent of the Parnes defendants was required in order to admit Daniel Rapoport and Kalia Shalleck to the partnership.

Plaintiffs, in support of their contention that they have an absolute right to assign their interests in the partnership to their adult children and that the children must be admitted to the partnership as partners rely on Paragraph 12 of the partnership agreement which provides as follows: "No partner or partners shall have the authority to transfer, sell ... assign or in any way dispose of the partnership realty and/or personalty and shall not have the authority to sell, transfer, assign ... his or their share in this firm, nor enter into any agreement as a result of which any person shall become interested with him in this firm, unless the same is agreed to in writing by a majority of the partners as determined by the percentage of ownership ..., except for members of his immediate family who have attained majority, in which case no such consent shall be required." As indicated, plaintiffs argue that the above provision expressly authorizes entry of their adult children into the partnership. Defendants, on the other hand, maintain that Paragraph 12 provides only for the right of a partner to assign or transfer a share of the profits in the partnership. We agree with that construction of the agreement.

A reading of the partnership agreement indicates that the parties intended to observe the differences, as set forth in the Partnership Law [UPA (1914)], between assignees of a partnership interest and the admission into the partnership itself of new partners. The Partnership Law provides that subject to any contrary agreement between the partners, "(n)o person can become a member of a partnership without the consent of all the partners." [UPA (1914) § 18(g)]. Partnership Law § 27 provides that an assignee of an interest in the partnership is not entitled "to interfere in the management or administration of the partnership business" but is merely entitled to receive "the profits to which the assigning partner would otherwise be entitled." [UPA (1914) § 27]. Additionally, [UPA (1914) § 24] indicates the differences between the rights of an assignee and a new partner. That section states that the "property rights of a partner are (a) his rights in specific partnership property, (b) his interest in the partnership, and (c) his right to participate in the management." On the other hand, as already indicated above, an assignee is excluded in the absence of agreement from interfering in the management of the partnership business and from access to the partnership books and information about partnership transactions. [UPA (1914) § 27].

The effect, therefore, of the various provisions of the Partnership Law, above discussed, is that unless the parties have agreed otherwise, a person cannot become a member of a partnership without consent of all the partners whereas an assignment of a partnership interest may be made without consent, but the assignee is entitled only to receive the profits of the assigning partner. And, as already stated, the partnership agreement herein clearly took cognizance of the differences between an assignment of an interest in the partnership as compared to the full rights of a partner as set forth in Partnership Law [UPA (1914) § 24]. Paragraph 12 of the agreement by its language has reference to Partnership Law [UPA (1914) § 27] dealing with an "assignment of partner's interest." It (Paragraph 12) refers to assignments, encumbrances and agreements "as a result of which any person shall become interested with (the assignor) in this firm." That paragraph does not contain language with respect to admitting a partner to the partnership with all rights to participate in the management of its affairs. Moreover, interpretation of Paragraph 12 in this manner is consistent with other provisions of the partnership agreement. For example, in Paragraph 15 of the agreement, the following is provided: "In the event of the death of any partner, the business of this firm shall continue with the heir, or distributee providing he has reached majority, or fiduciary of the deceased partner having the right to succeed the deceased partner with the same rights and privileges and the same obligations, pursuant to all of the terms hereof." In that paragraph, therefore, there is specific provision to succeed to all the privileges and obligations of a partner — language which is completely absent from Paragraph 12.

Accordingly, it appears that contrary to plaintiffs' contention that Paragraph 12 was intended to give the parties the right to transfer a full partnership interest to adult children, without consent of all other partners, (an agreement which would vary the rights otherwise existing pursuant to Partnership Law [UPA (1914) § 18(g)], that paragraph was instead intended to limit a partner with respect to his right to assign a partnership interest as provided for under Partnership Law [UPA (1914) § 27] (*i.e.*, the right to profits) — to the extent of prohibiting such assignments without the consent of other partners except to children of the existing partners who have reached majority. Therefore, it must be concluded that pursuant to the terms of the partnership agreement, the plaintiffs could not transfer a full partnership interest to their children and that the children only have the rights as assignees to receive a share of the partnership income and profits of their assignors.

Accordingly, the order entered July 16, 1975 should be modified on the law to grant summary judgment in favor of the defendants to the extent of declaring that the partnership agreement does not permit entry into the partnership of new partners, including adult children of the partners who have reached their majority, without consent of all the partners; that the plaintiffs, pursuant to the terms of the agreement, had the right to assign their interests to their adult children but that such children, *i.e.*, Daniel Rapoport and Kalia Shalleck, have not become partners but only have the rights of assignees to receive a share of the partnership income and profits of their assignors; that the amended partnership certificate filed with the County Clerk's Office on or about January 14, 1975 indicating the additional partners, *i.e.*, Daniel Rapoport and Kalia Shalleck, was improper and should be restated to eliminate those names as partners, and as so modified the order is affirmed without costs or disbursements.

. . . .

All concur except NUNEZ, J., who dissents in a dissenting opinion.

NUNEZ, JUSTICE (dissenting).

I agree with Special Term that the written partnership agreement providing for the assignment of partners' shares to members of their immediate families without the consent of the other partners is ambiguous and that there is a triable issue as to intent. The agreement being ambiguous, construction is a mixed question of law and fact and resolution thereof to determine the parties' intent should await a trial. Summary judgment was properly denied both parties. I would affirm.

I. DISSOLUTION OF THE PARTNERSHIP

As with so many situations in life, forming a partnership is easy, but getting out is another matter. The rules for concluding the partnership business serve two purposes. They provide for an ordered closing down of the venture, and they function as buyout provisions enabling partners to recoup their investments while the business is still ongoing.

As discussed previously, partnership default rules severely restrict partners' ability to transfer their full partnership interests to third parties. Transfer is prohibited unless the remaining partners agree. Even when transfer is permitted, finding a purchaser can be difficult because of the unavailability of a market for trading partnership interests. Withdrawing from a professional partnership may be even more difficult because other restrictions apply. The difficulty of withdrawal exacerbates struggles between minority and majority interests and the reluctance of third parties to invest in the business.

Thus, when individual partners want to recoup their investments or leave the firm for other reasons, they will turn to the procedures for concluding the business. Understanding the process of concluding a partnership requires a mastery of three terms used in UPA (1914): dissolution, winding up and termination. According to the Comment for UPA (1914) § 29, "dissolution designates the point in time when the partners cease to carry on the business together; termination is the point in time when all the partnership affairs are wound up; winding up, the process of settling partnership affairs after dissolution."

The concept of dissolution is based on the aggregate theory of partnership. Under UPA (1914), dissolution occurs when the identity and legal relations of a particular group of partners change, even if the business of the partnership is continued by some members of the original group or by a new group of partners. The Act specifies certain events that may trigger a dissolution. They include the unilateral withdrawal of a partner at any time,[27] the completion of the term of the partnership,[28] the death or bankruptcy of a partner,[29] the agreement of all partners

---

[27] UPA (1914) §§ 29, 31(1)(b), 31(d)(2).

[28] *Id.* § 31(1)(a).

[29] *Id.* § 31(3)(4).

who have not assigned their financial interests in the business to a third party,[30] the expulsion of a partner according to the terms of the partnership agreement,[31] and a court order.[32] The consequences of dissolution vary, depending on whether the triggering event violated the partnership agreement. If the triggering event was not in violation of the partnership agreement, the remaining partners may continue the partnership provided all partners, including those that are withdrawing, agree.[33] If the event was in contravention of the agreement, then the remaining partners have the right to continue the business.[34]

Winding up refers to the process of closing down the business. This is the time either to sell the company as a going concern or to liquidate its assets. The proceeds of the sale are used to settle company debts, and if there are excess funds, repay the partners' capital contributions and distribute the profits. Payments to a partner who has wrongfully dissolved the partnership will exclude the value of goodwill and may be offset by the amount of damages caused by the breach of the partnership agreement.[35] If the funds resulting from the sale are insufficient to pay off all company debts, then partners must contribute additional amounts according to their share in the profits.[36] If creditors still remain unpaid, then a dual priority rule[37] applies (also referred to as the jingle rule). With respect to claims against partnership assets, partnership creditors have priority over creditors of individual partners. With respect to the personal assets of individual partners, the claims of individual creditors take precedence over those of partnership creditors.

Under UPA (1914), partnership assets include partnership property and contributions required of individual partners to pay all partnership liabilities.[38] The Act defines partnership liabilities to include amounts owed to partnership creditors, to partners in respect of their capital, and to partners in respect of profits.[39] Under this scheme, partners with negative balances in their partnership accounts must make additional contributions to pay not only customary obligations to partnership creditors, but also to repay partners' capital contributions. This approach may disadvantage a partner contributing only services. Partnership termination occurs when the winding up process is complete and the partnership stops conducting business.

---

[30] *Id.* § 31(1)(e).
[31] *Id.* § 31(1)(c).
[32] *Id.* § 31(6).
[33] *Id.* § 31(2).
[34] *Id.* § 38(b).
[35] *Id.* § 38.
[36] *Id.* § 40(d).
[37] *Id.* § 40(h).
[38] *Id.* § 40(a).
[39] *Id.* § 40(b).

UPA (1994) continues the basic framework outlined above. Nevertheless the later act makes some changes that require attention. A partner's withdrawal from the firm is referred to as a "dissociation." Dissociation may be triggered by the same events that caused dissolution under UPA (1914).[40] Dissociation terminates one's status as a partner. Depending on the circumstances, it may lead either to a continuation of the business, with a mandatory buyout of the dissociating partner, or to dissolution and winding up of the partnership business.[41] Thus, the threat of liquidation is a constant cloud over an at-will partnership. A partnership for a term will, however, be continued at the option of the remaining partners. UPA (1994) eliminates the dual priority rule applicable to creditors' claims[42] and permits payment of the value of goodwill to a partner who wrongfully dissociates.[43]

The fundamental partnership structure common to both statutes has important implications for business law counselors and their clients. An at-will partnership, the default form provided in the statutes, is an unstable form of business. The dissolution or dissociation provisions of the respective acts can be used by an individual to compel a buyout at any time. The limitations on transferring partnership interests and the absence of a ready market for partnership shares increase the likelihood that a forced buyout will occur. Thus, when a partner wants to leave the partnership, either because the partners are not getting along or because the partner wants to invest elsewhere, compulsory buyout may be inevitable. Depending on the firm's financial position, the business may be forced to liquidate.

An individual partner's opportunities for unilateral withdrawal and compulsory buyout shift bargaining power with respect to the continuation of the business to a minority of the partners. The compelled buyout may come at a time when the company does not have ready cash to pay the departing partner or when liquidation disadvantages everyone because the company's assets are more valuable to the partnership as a going concern than to third-party purchasers. In addition, valuation of the firm may be difficult. These problems should be addressed in a partnership agreement controlling the circumstances of withdrawal, the opportunities for continuing the business, and the terms of the buyout.

The cases that follow illustrate additional issues associated with dissolution or dissociation.

---

[40] UPA (1994) § 601.
[41] Id. §§ 603(a), 701.
[42] Id. § 807.
[43] Id. §§ 602(b), 807(b).

GIRARD BANK v. HALEY

Supreme Court of Pennsylvania
332 A.2d 443 (1975)

POMEROY, JUSTICE.

This suit in equity was brought by appellants' decedent, Anna Reid, who averred in her complaint that she had dissolved a partnership between herself and the defendants, and prayed that the business of the firm be wound-up and its assets distributed. During the course of the proceedings Mrs. Reid died and the executors of her estate were substituted as parties plaintiff. The principal question for decision is whether the partnership was dissolved during Mrs. Reid's lifetime, as she averred and her personal representatives urge, or upon her death, as the trial court found.

The following facts are not in dispute. On September 28, 1958, Mrs. Reid and the three defendants, appellees here, entered into a written partnership agreement for the purpose of leasing for profit certain real property located in Montgomery County, Pennsylvania. Mrs. Reid was to manage the property, and the defendants were to perform the physical labor necessary to maintain the premises in good condition. The initial partnership assets consisted of real estate valued at $ 50,000 and $ 10,000 in cash, both contributed by Mrs. Reid, and an additional sum of $ 10,000 in cash contributed in equal shares by the three other partners. By letter addressed to her partners, the defendants, Mrs. Reid notified them that she was dissolving the partnership and requested that the partnership assets be liquidated as soon as possible.[44] Meetings between the partners following receipt of this letter failed to produce agreement for a plan for liquidation or as to the respective rights of the parties in the assets of the partnership. This suit praying for a winding up of the affairs of the partnership and a liquidation of its assets was then brought.

The chancellor found that the partnership had been dissolved, not by Mrs. Reid's letter, but rather by her death, and concluded that the defendants, as surviving partners, were entitled to exercise their option under the partnership

---

[44] The letter was undated, but the record establishes that it was sent on February 10, 1971. The text of the letter was as follows:

"Gentlemen:

I hereby notify you that I am terminating the partnership which the four of us entered into on the 28th day of September, 1958, and request that steps be taken to liquidate the assets of the Partnership as soon as possible. I hereby authorize you to deal with my attorney, J. William Wetter, Jr., in the matter of negotiating the steps necessary to bring this matter to a speedy and satisfactory conclusion.

"I trust that our friendship will continue and that you will recognize that terminating this partnership has been necessitated by my need to clarify the status of my various assets at this particular time.

Very truly yours,

Anna Reid".

agreement to purchase the interest of the deceased partner.[45] Having determined that the defendants had in fact exercised their option to purchase Mrs. Reid's interest, the chancellor entered a decree nisi ordering the defendants to pay the estate in discharge of the purchase price the sum of $ 29,165.48 plus seventy per cent of the income of the partnership for the calendar year 1971. Exceptions filed by the executors to the adjudication were dismissed and the decree nisi was adopted as the final decree. This appeal followed.

None of the parties disputes the chancellor's conclusion that the partnership has been dissolved; the dispute, as indicated at the outset, is when that event occurred. Dissolution of a partnership is statutorily defined as "the change in the relation of the partners caused by any partner ceasing to be associated in the carrying on, as distinguished from the winding up, of the business." Uniform Partnership Act (1914) § 29 ("the Act"). There is no doubt that dissolution of a partnership will be caused by the death of any partner, § 31(4) of the Act, and if Mrs. Reid's death was the cause of the dissolution here involved, the chancellor was quite correct in looking to the provisions of paragraphs 11 and 12 of the agreement ... as defining the rights and obligations of the surviving partners on the one hand and the estate of the deceased partner on the other. If, however, dissolution occurred during the lifetime of Mrs. Reid, those portions of the agreement, which are concerned solely with the effect of the death of a partner, are not germane. The agreement being otherwise silent as to winding up and liquidation, the provisions of the Act will control.

---

[45] The pertinent provisions of the partnership agreement are as follows:

"11. Upon the death of any partner, the surviving partners or any of them shall have the right to purchase the interest of the decedent in the partnership. If the surviving partners or any of them elect to purchase the interest of the decedent, they or he or she shall serve notice in writing of such election within three months after the death of the decedent, upon the executor or administrator of the decedent, or, if at the time of such election no legal representative shall have been appointed, then upon any one of the known legal heirs of the decedent at the last known address of such heir.

"12. If the surviving partners or any of them elect to purchase the interest of the decedent in the partnership, the purchase price shall be equal to the decedent's capital account on the date of his death adjusted as herein provided. The decedent's capital account on the date of his or her death shall be increased by his or her share of partnership profits, for the period from the beginning of the year in which his death occurred until the date of his death. Losses shall be treated conversely in the same manner. The real estate shall be taken at a value equivalent to the assessed value fixed by the local authorities for real estate tax purposes for the year in which such death occurs, and the decedent's capital account shall be adjusted to reflect this valuation. As thus adjusted the decedent's capital account shall be taken as shown on the books of the partnership, without any allowance for good will, trade name, or other intangible assets. In the event of the death of Anna Reid, her interest, subject to the limitations and conditions aforementioned shall be liquidated over a period of ten years following her death."

The chancellor was impressed with the fact that the decedent "was a strong willed person" who dominated the partnership enterprise, that the defendant partners had each contributed many thousands of hours of hard work and planning to the "joint venture", and that neither Mrs. Reid (who testified at the first hearing, but who then, according to the adjudication, "appeared confused and feeble") nor her personal representatives had offered "evidence to justify a termination." In supposing that justification was necessary the learned court below fell into error. Dissolution of a partnership is caused, under § 31 of the Act, "by the express will of any partner." The expression of that will need not be supported by any justification. If no "definite term or particular undertaking [is] specified in the partnership agreement," such an at-will dissolution does not violate the agreement between the partners; indeed, an expression of a will to dissolve is effective as a dissolution even if in contravention of the agreement. Ibid. We have recognized the generality of a dissolution at will. If the dissolution results in breach of contract, the aggrieved partners may recover damages for the breach and, if they meet certain conditions, may continue the firm business for the duration of the agreed term or until the particular undertaking is completed. See § 38 of the Act.

There is no doubt in our minds that Mrs. Reid's letter ... effectively dissolved the partnership between her and her three partners. It was definite and unequivocal: "I am terminating the partnership which the four of us entered into on the 28th day of September, 1958." The effective termination date is therefore February 10, 1971, and Mrs. Reid's subsequent death after this litigation was in progress is an irrelevant factor in determining the rights of the parties.

The remaining question is whether or not the unilateral dissolution made by Mrs. Reid violated the partnership agreement. The agreement contains no provision fixing a definite term, and the sole "undertaking" to which it refers is that of maintaining and leasing real property. This statement is merely one of general purpose, however, and cannot be said to set forth a "particular undertaking" within the meaning of that phrase as it is used in the Act. A "particular undertaking" under the statute must be capable of accomplishment at some time, although the exact time may be unknown and unascertainable at the date of the agreement. Leasing property, like many other trades or businesses, involves entering into a business relationship which may continue indefinitely; there is nothing "particular" about it. We thus conclude, on the record before us, that the dissolution of the partnership was not in contravention of the agreement.

In light of our conclusion that an inter-vivos dissolution took place, the provisions of the Act rather than the post-mortem provisions of the agreement, will govern the winding-up of the partnership affairs and the distribution of its assets. Because compliance with the Act requires findings and conclusions which were not made by the chancellor in view of his disposition of the case, we must remand for further proceedings.

....

Assume that you are the lawyer who completed the legal work necessary to form the business referred to in the preceding case and you have represented it ever since. Before Mrs. Reid sent her letter, the partners had been discussing whether or not to continue the business. Disagreement among the partners on this subject ultimately led Mrs. Reid to write the letter. What role(s) may you potentially play? *See* Model Rules of Professional Conduct Rules 1.7, 1.9 and 2.2. What is your role if the matter, as here, results in litigation? Rule 1.13.

What do you think were the expectations of the parties at the time the partnership was formed with respect to termination of the venture? Was the litigation the result of a drafting error on the part of the attorney who prepared the partnership agreement?

DREIFUERST v. DREIFUERST

Court of Appeals of Wisconsin
280 N.W.2d 335 (1979)

BROWN, PRESIDING JUDGE.

The plaintiffs and the defendant, all brothers, formed a partnership. The partnership operated two feed mills, one located at St. Cloud, Wisconsin and one located at Elkhart Lake, Wisconsin. There were no written Articles of Partnership governing this partnership.

On October 4, 1975, the plaintiffs served the defendant with a notice of dissolution and wind-up of the partnership. The action for dissolution and wind-up was commenced on January 27, 1976. The dissolution complaint alleged that the plaintiffs elected to dissolve the partnership. There was no allegation of fault, expulsion or contravention of an alleged agreement as grounds for dissolution. The parties were unable, however, to agree to a winding-up of the partnership.

Hearings on the dissolution were held on October 18, 1976 and March 4, 1977. Testimony was presented regarding the value of the partnership assets and each partner's equity. At the March 4, 1977 hearing, the defendant requested that the partnership be sold pursuant to [UPA (1914) § 38], and that the court allow a sale, at which time the partners would bid on the entire property. By such sale, the plaintiffs could continue to run the business under a new partnership, and the defendant's partnership equity could be satisfied in cash.

On February 20, 1978, the trial court, by written decision, denied the defendant's request for a sale and instead divided the partnership assets in-kind according to the valuation presented by the plaintiffs. The plaintiffs were given the physical assets from the Elkhart Lake mill, and the defendant was given the physical assets from the St. Cloud mill. The defendant appeals this order and judgment dividing the assets in-kind.

Under UPA (1914) § 29[46] a partnership is dissolved when any partner ceases to be associated in the carrying on of the business. The partnership is not terminated, but continues, until the winding-up of partnership is complete.[47] The action started by the plaintiffs, in this case, was an action for dissolution and wind-up. The plaintiffs were not continuing the partnership and, therefore,[48] [UPA (1914) §§ 40, 41] do not apply. The sole question in this case is whether, in the absence of a written agreement to the contrary, a partner, upon dissolution and wind-up of the partnership, can force a sale of the partnership assets.

At the outset, we note, and the parties agree, that the appellant was not in contravention of the partnership agreement since there was no partnership agreement. The partnership was a partnership at will. They also agree there was no written agreement governing distribution of partnership assets upon dissolution and wind-up. The dispute, in this case, is over the authority of the trial court to order in-kind distribution in the absence of any agreement of the partners.

[UPA (1914) § 38(1)] provides:

> When dissolution is caused in any way, except in contravention of the partnership agreement, each partner, as against his copartners and all persons claiming through them in respect to their interests in the partnership, unless otherwise agreed, may have the partnership property applied to discharge its liabilities, and the surplus applied to pay in cash the net amount owing to the respective partners.

The appellant contends this statute grants him the right to force a sale of the partnership assets in order to obtain his fair share of the partnership assets in cash upon dissolution. He claims that in the absence of an agreement of the partners to in-kind distribution, the trial court had no authority to distribute the assets in-kind. He is entitled to an in-cash settlement after judicial sale.

The respondents contend the statute does not entitle the appellant to force a sale and grants the trial court the power to distribute the assets in-kind if in-kind distribution is equitably possible and doesn't jeopardize the rights of creditors.

We do not believe that the statute can be read in any way to permit in-kind distribution unless the partners agree to in-kind distribution or unless there is a partnership agreement calling for in-kind distribution at the time of dissolution and wind-up.

A partnership at will is a partnership which has no definite term or particular undertaking and can rightfully be dissolved by the express will of any partner.

---

[46] Dissolution of partnership defined. (1) The dissolution of a partnership is the change in the relation of the partners caused by any partner ceasing to be associated in the carrying on as distinguished from the winding up of the business. [UPA (1914) § 29]

[47] On dissolution the partnership is not terminated, but continues until the winding up of partnership affairs is completed. [UPA (1914) § 30]

[48] Sections 40 and 41 deal with cases where the partnership is not wound up, but continues after one partner leaves. [UPA (1914) §§ 40, 41]

[UPA (1914) § 31(1)(b)]. In the present case, the respondents wanted to dissolve the partnership. This being a partnership at will, they could rightfully dissolve this partnership with or without the consent of the appellant. In addition, the respondents have never claimed the appellant was in violation of any partnership agreement. Therefore, neither the appellant nor the respondents have wrongfully dissolved the partnership.

Unless otherwise agreed, partners who have not wrongfully dissolved a partnership have a right to wind up the partnership. [UPA (1914) § 37]. Winding-up is the process of settling partnership affairs after dissolution. Winding-up is often called liquidation and involves reducing the assets to cash to pay creditors and distribute to partners the value of their respective interests. Thus, lawful dissolution (or dissolution which is caused in any way except in contravention of the partnership agreement) gives each partner the right to have the business liquidated and his share of the surplus paid in cash. In-kind distribution is permissible only in very limited circumstances. If the partnership agreement permits in-kind distribution upon dissolution or wind-up or if, at any time prior to wind-up, all partners agree to in-kind distribution, the court may order in-kind distribution. While at least one court has permitted in-kind distribution, absent an agreement by all partners, *Rinke v. Rinke*, 330 Mich. 615, 48 N.W.2d 201 (1951), the court's holding in that case was limited. In *Rinke*, the court stated:

> The decree of the trial court provided for dividing the assets of the partnerships rather than for the sale thereof and the distribution of cash proceeds. Appellants insist that such method of procedure is erroneous and contemplated by the uniform partnership act. Attention is directed to Section 38 of said act. Construing together pertinent provisions of the statute leads to the conclusion that it was not the intention of the legislature in the enactment of the Uniform Partnership Act to impose a mandatory requirement that, under all circumstances, the assets of a dissolved partnership shall be sold and the money received therefor divided among those entitled to it, particularly so, as in the case at bar, where there are no debts to be paid from the proceeds. The situation disclosed by the record in the present case is somewhat unusual in that no one other than the former partners is interested in the assets of the businesses. In view of this situation and of the nature of the assets, we think that the trial court was correct in apportioning them to the parties. There is no showing that appellants have been prejudiced thereby.

The Michigan court's holding was limited to situations where: (1) there were no creditors to be paid from the proceeds, (2) ordering a sale would be senseless since no one other than the partners would be interested in the assets of the business, and (3) an in-kind distribution was fair to all partners.

That is not the case here. There was no showing that there were no creditors who would be paid from the proceeds, nor was there a showing that no one other than the partners would be interested in the assets. These factors are important if an in-kind distribution is to be allowed.... [Section] 38 of the Uniform Partnership Act [is] intended to protect creditors as well as partners. In-kind distributions may affect a creditor's right to collect the debt owed since the assets of the partnership, as a whole, may be worth more than the assets once divided up. Thus, the creditor's ability to collect from the individual partners may be jeopardized. Secondly, if others are interested in the assets, a sale provides a more accurate means of establishing the market value of the assets and, thus, better assuring each partner his share in the value of the assets. Where only the partners are interested in the assets, a fair value can be determined without the necessity of a sale. The sale would be merely the partners bidding with each other without any competition. This process could be accomplished through negotiations or at trial with the court as a final arbitrator of the value of the assets. With these policy considerations in mind, we think the Michigan court's holding in *Rinke* was limited to the facts of that case. Those facts not being present in this case, we do not feel an in-kind distribution in this case was proper.

However, even assuming the respondents in this case can show that there are no creditors to be paid, no one other than the partners are interested in the assets, and in-kind distribution would be fair to all partners, we cannot read § 38 of the Uniform Partnership Act or § 178.33(1), Stats. (the Wisconsin equivalent), as permitting an in-kind distribution under any circumstances, unless all partners agree. The statute and § 38 of the Uniform Partnership Act are quite clear that if a partner may force liquidation, he is entitled to his share of the partnership assets, after creditors are paid in cash. To the extent that *Rinke v. Rinke, supra*, creates an exception to cash distribution, we decline to adopt that exception. We, therefore, must hold the trial court erred in ordering an in-kind distribution of the assets of the partnership.

The last question that arises is whether the appellant can force an actual sale of the assets or whether the trial court can determine the fair market value of the assets and order the respondents to pay the appellant in cash an amount equal to his share in the assets.

As discussed above, a sale is the best means of determining the true fair market value of the assets. Generally, liquidation envisions some form of sale. Since the statutes provide that, unless otherwise agreed, any partner who has not wrongfully dissolved the partnership has the right to wind up the partnership and force liquidation, he likewise has a right to force a sale, unless otherwise agreed. While judicial sales in some instances may cause economic hardships, these hardships can be avoided by the use of partnership agreements.

Judgment reversed and cause remanded for further proceedings not inconsistent with this opinion.

————

In the preceding case, the assets being divided were real property. The important assets of a law firm are the income streams produced by the clients. If you decide to leave your law firm, may you take your clients with you?

What if the assets of the firm include contingent fees or fees on matters for which work has been not been fully completed? How should these fees be allocated? What is the relationship between the provisions of the UPA and Model Rule 1.5?

DRASHNER v. SORENSON

Supreme Court of South Dakota
63 N.W.2d 255 (1954)

SMITH, PRESIDING JUDGE.

In January 1951 the plaintiff, C. H. Drashner, and defendants, A. D. Sorenson and Jacob P. Deis, associated themselves as co-owners in the real estate, loan and insurance business at Rapid City. For a consideration of $ 7,500 they purchased the real estate and insurance agency known as J. Schumacher Co. located in an office room on the ground floor of the Alex Johnson Hotel building. The entire purchase price was advanced for the partnership by the defendants, but at the time of trial $ 3,000 of that sum had been repaid to them by the partnership. Although, as will appear from facts presently to be outlined, their operations were not unsuccessful, differences arose and on June 15, 1951 plaintiff commenced this action in which he sought an accounting, dissolution and winding up of the partnership. The answer and counterclaim of defendants prayed for like relief.

The cause came on for trial September 4, 1951. The court among others made the following findings. "VII. 'That thereafter the plaintiff violated the terms of said partnership agreement, in that he demanded a larger share of the income of the said partnership than he was entitled to receive under the terms of said partnership agreement; that the plaintiff was arrested for reckless driving and served a term in jail for said offense; that the plaintiff demanded that the defendants permit him to draw money for his own personal use out of the moneys held in escrow by the partnership; that the plaintiff spent a large amount of time during business hours in the Brass Rail Bar in Rapid City, South Dakota, and other bars, and neglected his duties in connection with the business of the said partnership.... That the plaintiff, by his actions hereinbefore set forth, has made it impossible to carry on the partnership.'" The conclusions adopted read as follows: I "'That the defendants are entitled to continue the partnership and have the value of the plaintiff's interest in the partnership business determined, upon the filing and approval of a good and sufficient bond, conditioned upon the release of the plaintiff from any liability arising out of the said partnership, and further conditioned upon the payment by the defendants to the plaintiff of the value of plaintiff's interest in the partnership as determined by the Court.' II 'That in computing the value of the plaintiff's interest in the said partnership, the value of the good will of the business shall not be considered.' III 'That the value of the partnership shall be finally determined upon a hearing before this Court, ... ' and IV 'That the plaintiff shall be entitled to receive one-third of the value of the partnership property owned by the partnership on the 12th day of September, 1951, not including the good will of the business, after the payment of the liabilities of the partnership and the payment to the defendants of the invested capital in the sum of $ 4,500.00.'" Judgment was accordingly entered dissolving the partnership as of September 12, 1951.

After hearing at a later date the court found: I "'That the value of the said partnership property on the 12th day of September, 1951, was the sum of Four Thousand Four Hundred Ninety-eight and 90/100 Dollars ($ 4,498.90), and on said date there was due and owing by the partnership for accountant's services the sum of Four Hundred Eighty Dollars ($ 480.00), and that on said date the sum of Four Thousand Five Hundred Dollars ($ 4,500.00) of the capital invested by the defendants had not been returned to the defendants.' and II 'That there is not sufficient partnership property to reimburse the defendants for their invested capital.' Thereupon the court decreed 'That the plaintiff had no interest in the property of the said partnership', and that the defendants were the sole owners thereof.

The assignments of error are predicated upon insufficiency of the evidence to support the findings and conclusions. Of these assignments, only those which question whether the court was warranted in finding that (a) the plaintiff caused the dissolution wrongfully, and (b) the value of the partnership property, exclusive of good will, was $ 4,498.90 on the 12th day of September, 1951, merit discussion. A preliminary statement is necessary to place these issues in their framework.

The agreement of the parties contemplated an association which would continue at least until the $ 7,500 advance of defendants had been repaid from the gross earnings of the business. Hence, it was not a partnership at will. In apparent recognition of that fact, both plaintiff and defendants sought dissolution in contravention of the partnership agreement, on the ground that the adverse party had caused the dissolution wrongfully by willfully and persistently committing a breach of the partnership agreement, and by so conducting himself in matters relating to the partnership business as to render impracticable the carrying on of the business in partnership with him.

By [§ 38(2)] of the Uniform Partnership Act (1914) it is provided: "When dissolution is caused in contravention of the partnership agreement the rights of the partners shall be as follows: ... " (b) The partners who have not caused the dissolution wrongfully, if they all desire to continue the business in the same name, either by themselves or jointly with others, may do so, during the agreed term for the partnership and for that purpose may possess the partnership property, provided they secure the payment by bond approved by the Court, or pay to any partner who has caused the dissolution wrongfully, the value of his interest in the partnership at the dissolution less any damages recoverable under clause (2)(a)(2) of this section and in like manner indemnify him against all present or future partnership liabilities. "(c) A partner who has caused the dissolution wrongfully shall have: ... " (2) If the business is continued under paragraph (2)(b) of this section the right as against his copartners and all claiming through them in respect of their interests in the partnership, to have the value of his interest in the partnership, less any damages caused to his copartners by the dissolution, ascertained and paid to him in cash, or the payment secured by bond approved by the Court, and to be released from all existing liabilities of the partnership; but in ascertaining the value of the partner's interest the value of the good will of the business shall not be considered.'

....

From this background we turn to a consideration of the evidence from which the trial court inferred that plaintiff caused the dissolution wrongfully.

The breach between the parties resulted from a continuing controversy over the right of plaintiff to withdraw sufficient money from the partnership to defray his living expenses. Plaintiff was dependent upon his earnings for the support of his family. The defendants had other resources. Plaintiff claimed that he was to be permitted to draw from the earnings of the partnership a sufficient amount to support himself and family. The defendants asserted that there was a definite arrangement for the allocation of the income of the partnership and there was no agreement for withdrawal by plaintiff of more than his allotment under that plan. Defendants' version of the facts was corroborated by a written admission of plaintiff offered in evidence. From evidence thus sharply in conflict, the trial court made a finding, reading as follows: "That the oral partnership agreement between the parties provided that each of the three partners [was] to draw as compensation one-third of one-half of the commissions earned upon sales made by the partners; that the other one-half of the commissions earned on sales made by the partners and one-half of the commissions earned upon sales made by salesmen employed by the partnership, together with the earnings from the insurance business carried on by the partnership, was to be placed in a fund to be used for the payment of the operating expenses of the partnership, and after the payment of such operating expenses to be used to reimburse the defendants for the capital advanced in the purchase of the Julius Schumacher business and the capital advanced in the sum of Eight Hundred Dollars ($ 800.00) for the operating expenses of the business."

As an outgrowth of this crucial difference, there was evidence from which a court could reasonably believe that plaintiff neglected the business and spent too much time in a nearby bar during business hours. At a time when plaintiff had overdrawn his partners and was also indebted to one of defendants for personal advances, he requested $ 100 and his request was refused. In substance he then said, according to the testimony of the defendant Deis, that he would see that he "gets some money to run on", and if they "didn't give it to him he was going to dissolve the partnership and see that he got it." Thereafter plaintiff pressed his claims through counsel, and eventually brought this action to dissolve the partnership. The claim so persistently asserted was contrary to the partnership agreement found by the court.

The foregoing picture of the widening breach between the parties is drawn almost entirely from the evidence of defendants. Of course, plaintiff's version of the agreement of the parties, and of the ensuing differences, if believed, would have supported findings of a different order by the trier of the fact. It cannot be said, we think, that the trial court acted unreasonably in believing defendants, and we think it equally clear the court could reasonably conclude that the insistent and continuing demands of the plaintiff and his attendant conduct rendered it reasonably impracticable to carry on the business in partnership with him. It follows, we are of the opinion, the evidence supports the finding that plaintiff caused the dissolution wrongfully.

This brings us to a consideration of the sufficiency of the evidence to support the finding of the court that the property of the partnership was of the value of $ 4498.90 as of the date of dissolution.

Bitter complaint is made because the trial court refused to consider the good will of this business in arriving at its conclusion. The feeling of plaintiff is understandable. These partners must have placed a very high estimate upon the value of the good will of this agency because they paid Mr. Schumacher $ 7,500 to turn over that office with its very moderate fixtures and its listing of property, together with an agreement that he would not engage in the business in Rapid City for at least two years. No doubt they attached some of this good will value to the location of the business which was under only a month to month letting. Their estimate of value was borne out by the subsequent history of the business. Its real estate commissions, earned but only partly received, grossed $ 21,528.25 and its insurance commissions grossed $ 661.21 in the period January 15 to August 31, 1951. In that period the received commissions paid all expenses, including the commissions of salesmen, retired $ 3,000 of the $ 7,500 purchase price advanced by defendants, and all of $ 800 of working capital so advanced, allowed the parties to withdraw $ 1,453.02 each, and accumulated a cash balance of $ 2,221.43. In addition the partnership has commissions due which we shall presently discuss. Notwithstanding this indication of the great value of the good will of this business, the statute does not require the court to take it into consideration in valuing the property of the business in these circumstances. The statute provides such a sanction for causing the dissolution of a partnership wrongfully. The court applied the statute.

With the most valuable asset of the business eliminated, what remained? It is agreed that a group of bills receivable were of the value of $ 777.47. There was cash in the amount of $ 2,221.43. Subtracting these two amounts from $ 4,498.90, the overall value fixed by the finding, it appears that the court estimated the remaining assets to be of a value of $ 1,500. The evidence dealing with those items must be briefly examined.

The furniture and fixtures were described by Mr. Schumacher. He stated the original cost when he installed them several years before, and also stated that in his own mind he had valued them at $ 1,000 when selling the business. They were carried on the books as at a value of $ 452. They included a large desk, two smaller ones, a filing cabinet, a smaller cabinet, a typewriter, a counter, some chairs, neon signs, a partition, and some supplies.

In addition to the bills receivable above mentioned of the agreed value of $ 777.47, there were items of commission due in the amount of $ 8,100. Most of these had been placed with attorneys for collection. Plaintiff expressed the opinion that they were good, and defendants testified they were worthless. Neither one explained the deals out of which they arose, or the worth of the debtors.

Another asset was the listings of real estate for sale. Respective customers had listed real property with the agency for sale, usually at a fixed price, and had agreed that the agency should receive a 5% commission. Here again the parties took opposing extreme positions. The defendants suggested that this list of property was embraced within the good will of the business, and therefore the court was not required to consider its value. Predicated on the testimony of a witness that particular listings with which he was familiar were of the value of 5% of the sale price named therein, plaintiff asserts that the court was required to place a high estimate of value on these assets. Neither view is persuasive.

Although these listings may have resulted in part at least from the good will of customers toward the agency, we are firm in our conviction that they are not embraced within the concept of the good will described in the Uniform Partnership Act [(1914)]. According to our statutory definition "The good will of a business is the expectation of continued public patronage"' ... Elsewhere it is defined as " ... that element of value which inheres in the fixed and favorable consideration of customers, arising from an established and well-known and well-conducted business." Rather than being an element of good will value, these listings take on the aspect of going concern value.... Until such a list is established, a real estate agency is not a going concern. Money, time, energy and skill go into its establishment. Therefore, we think it would be reasonable, in fixing the over-all value of a real estate business to attach such a value to its list of property for sale as is comparable to the expense involved in its establishment. The reason it cannot be valued on an exchange basis, is that these listings are not transferable, and are revocable at will. In the instant case, we do not understand that the trial court failed to attach any value to this asset. In arriving at the conclusion that these listings should not carry a high estimate of value, the court was undoubtedly influenced by the foregoing considerations and by the further fact that plaintiff had been with the office for several years and had secured many of these listings, and therefore, the probability was not remote that some of them would follow him out of the agency. The trial court was not supplied with any very substantial basis for estimating the value of this asset.

That the $ 1,500 value placed on all of these described assets was conservative we do not question. However, after mature study and reflection we have concluded that the court's finding is not against the clear weight of the evidence appearing in this record. Hence we are not at liberty to disturb it.

....

The judgment of the trial court is

Affirmed.

All the Judges concur.

SECTION II. CORPORATIONS

Since the remaining chapters of this book will deal with corporations, we would get ahead of ourselves if we attempted to discuss the corporation completely at this point. Nevertheless, in order for you to appreciate the reasons the corporate form is usually chosen for a business, it will be helpful to examine briefly the advantages and disadvantages of operating a business as a corporation.

At the outset, however, you should distinguish between two types of corporations: those whose shares are publicly traded on a securities exchange, and those that are privately or closely held. Publicly traded corporations are organized under general corporation codes. The general corporate structure was developed to help entrepreneurs raise significant amounts of capital from many investors having little or no interest in managing the day-to-day operations of the business. Privately or closely held companies may be organized either under the general corporation codes or under close corporation statutes, which were developed expressly for privately held companies. Corporations taking the latter approach are referred to as statutory close corporations. Most corporations, large and small alike, are incorporated under general corporation statutes. Relatively few have made the statutory close corporation election.

A. ADVANTAGES OF THE CORPORATE FORM

The advantages of operating a business in the corporation are:
1. Limited liability of shareholders
2. Centralized management structure
3. Flexible capital structure
4. Separate entity status
5. Usual form for most businesses

1. Limited Liability of Shareholders

Limited liability of shareholders is the key advantage for most businesses operating in the corporate form. Limited liability means that the corporation is solely responsible for its obligations and that the personal assets of the shareholders will not be used to satisfy corporate liabilities, whether in the form of corporate debt or other third-party claims against the corporation. The few exceptions are: lending institutions may require owners of small companies personally to guarantee loans to the business; shareholders are required to satisfy any unpaid amounts of capital contributions they are obligated to pay; and, in certain circumstances, the corporate veil of limited liability may be pierced in situations where the corporation is a sham.

The importance of limited liability can best be illustrated by imagining that the liability rules of corporation and partnership law have been switched while keeping all other aspects of these laws unchanged, so that partners enjoy limited liability, but shareholders do not. Even though, as will be seen in the discussions below, the corporate form presents several advantages lacking in the partnership form, there is little doubt that many corporate businesses would switch to the partnership form if this were necessary to preserve limited liability. This conclusion is supported by the fact that all of the new business organization forms have limited liability as a central component.

This may be a good point at which to return to the enthusiastic statement of Nicholas Murray Butler, set out in the Introduction about the significance of the limited liability corporation:

> I weigh my words when I say that in my judgment the limited liability corporation is the greatest single discovery of modern times.... Even steam and electricity are far less important than the limited liability corporation, and they would be reduced to comparative impotence without it.[49]

Butler's enthusiasm is not surprising. The nineteenth century industrial revolution could not have advanced significantly without the availability of massive amounts of capital, which investors may have been unwilling to provide without the guarantee of limited liability.

2. Management Structure

As we have seen, the attribute of limited liability makes the corporation an extraordinarily effective device for amassing capital. The management structure of the general corporation makes it an equally effective device for managing capital, particularly capital raised from large numbers of people. The strengths of the corporate form in this regard flow from two factors. First, the traditional management structure created in corporation statutes works very well for most businesses. This should not be surprising, since the gradual evolution of this structure has been driven by the desire of businesses to find the most usable management structure. Second, modern corporation statutes, which provide a

---

[49] *Quoted in* 1 William Meede Fletcher, Cyclopedia of the Law of Private Corporations § 21 (1917).

default management structure, give corporations broad authority to vary the structure as their owners wish, so that any unusual needs are easily served.

The traditional management structure provided by corporate law default rules is three-tiered. It consists of shareholders, directors, and officers. In this structure, shareholders, typically passive investors of capital, elect directors and approve certain extraordinary corporate actions. As votes usually are allocated on a per-share rather than *per capita* basis, voting power is directly tied to the amount of capital contribution. Directors, acting as a board, set policy and either manage or direct the management of the corporation. The authority of the board is restricted only by the shareholders' limited powers. Directors elect officers, who manage the day-to-day operations of the corporation in whatever ways the directors authorize. This traditional structure provides substantial flexibility as directors can decide how much authority to retain and how much to delegate to officers.

Flexibility can be introduced in another way. The traditional management structure is suitable for a company with a large number of shareholders who do not want to be involved in the day-to-day operations of the company and are willing to relinquish their management authority and responsibility to a group of managers, the directors, who will serve on their behalf. In other situations, however, the traditional structure may be cumbersome because of the layers of formality. That occurs when the corporation has a few shareholders who also serve as the company managers. In this situation, the shareholders may want to take advantage of options provided in the Model Act or in close corporation statutes and either restrict the powers of the board of directors or eliminate the board altogether.

Section 8.01(b) of the Model Act offers a good example of a provision allowing variations from the traditional management structure:

> All corporate powers shall be exercised by or under authority of, and the business and affairs of the corporation managed under the direction of, its board of directors, subject to any limitation set forth in the articles of incorporation or in an agreement authorized under section 7.32.[50]

If those forming a corporation wish to eliminate the board of directors, they may either provide for this change in the corporate charter or in an agreement signed by all shareholders and included in either the charter or the corporate bylaws. The powers of the board may be given to the shareholders or to one or more officers, or the board's powers can be distributed among the shareholders

---

[50] Section 7.32(e) provides "An agreement authorized by this section that limits the discretion or powers of the board of directors shall relieve the directors of, and impose upon the person or persons in whom such discretion or powers are vested, liability for acts or omissions imposed by law on directors to the extent that the discretion or powers of the directors are limited by the agreement." MODEL BUSINESS CORP. ACT (1984) § 7.32(e).

and the officers, as the company's owners wish. The board may also be left in place but with some of its powers given to the shareholders or to the officers.

Unlike the partnership form, management rights are not tied to shareholder status. Shareholders have residual financial claims to the equity of the corporation and a limited right to vote on significant corporate matters. These attributes are associated with the shares, which are freely transferable. The fact that the shares are freely transferable means that investors generally can exit the business easily, except as limited by contract.

3. Capital Structure

The advantage of the corporate form in capital structure flows from the existence of a simple, traditional form of structure that serves the needs of most corporations, coupled with the flexibility to vary the traditional structure almost at will. In the simplest capital structure, a corporation has one class of stock, typically called common stock, which represents the sole ownership interest in the corporation. That is all the capital structure the average corporation needs when it begins its existence.

The first move away from this simple structure typically is the issuance of a promissory note to evidence a loan taken by the corporation, thus leaving the corporation with one type of equity interest, the common stock, and one type of debt interest, the note. From here the permutations in capital structure are almost endless. A corporation might have two classes of common stock, with the rights of ownership in the corporation split between the classes in any way those controlling the corporation wish. For example, the classes might be equal in every way except that one class carries the right to vote and the other does not. A corporation might have one or more classes of preferred stock in addition to common stock.[51]

Debt interests can vary as much as equity interests. A corporation might issue several different promissory notes having varying provisions with respect to interest payable and the terms of payment. The corporation might also issue a number of different bonds and debentures.[52]

One type of interest in the corporation may also be made convertible into another type of interest. For example, a bond might be convertible into common or preferred stock at the option of the bondholder, or preferred stock might be convertible into common stock. Or, for that matter, preferred stock or a class of common stock might be convertible into bonds or debentures.

---

[51] Preferred stock is simply stock that is preferred, in one or more respects, to the common stock. For example, the holders of the preferred stock might have the right to receive a certain dollar amount of dividends before any dividends are paid to the holders of the common stock.

[52] The differences between notes, bonds, and debentures are discussed in a later chapter.

In short, those controlling a corporation have virtual carte blanche to create any capital structure they wish. That being true, those wanting to exercise financial creativity have the full chance to do so. What is more important in the usual situation is that a full range of permutations in capital structure is already in existence and well known to corporate lawyers, so that the need for the creation of a unique structure is rare. What most clients want in a capital structure is available "off the shelf."

4. Separate Entity Status

The status of the corporation as a separate entity creates advantages in at least two ways. First, since the corporation is an entity separate from its owners, the death or bankruptcy of an owner, which would dissolve a partnership, has no institutional effect on the corporation. In the case of bankruptcy, a shareholder simply continues as a shareholder, and when a shareholder dies, his or her shares are distributed to the heirs as personal property.

The fact that upon the death of a shareholder his or her shares are distributed to heirs as personal property illustrates the second benefit that flows from a corporation's status as a separate entity. Remember that since under UPA (1914) a partnership is not an entity separate from its partners, a deceased partner's estate must be probated in each state where the partnership has property, because each piece of partnership property is considered to be owned in part by the deceased partner. The expense and trouble of multiple probates is avoided in a corporation, since, as personal property, corporate shares are subject to probate only in the deceased shareholder's state of domicile.

5. Usual Form

The corporation is the usual form for the operation of a jointly-owned business of any size, and the advantages of operating in the usual form should not be underestimated. In the business world, things work more smoothly if one operates in the usual way. Take, for example, something as simple as opening a bank account. When a corporation wishes to open an account, any customer service employee in the bank can provide the standard forms. This would also be true for a partnership, or, perhaps, a limited liability company, but it would not be true for a business trust or any other less common form of business. The same sort of experience will be encountered when a business wants to sign a lease or buy expensive equipment. Those on the other side of the transaction are used to dealing with corporations and are familiar with how documents are signed on behalf of corporations. With other forms of business, save the partnership, and, perhaps, the limited liability company, that usually is not the case.

B. DISADVANTAGES OF THE CORPORATE FORM

There are three clear disadvantages of operating a business in the corporate form:

1. Expense and trouble of formation and maintenance
2. Required initial and continuing formalities
3. Tax treatment

1. Expense and Trouble of Formation and Maintenance

To form a corporation, a charter needs to be drafted in accordance with the statutory requirements and then filed in one or more offices in the state of incorporation. After incorporation, bylaws need to be drafted for adoption. All this work should be done by a knowledgeable lawyer, with attendant fees of at least several hundred dollars. The state's fees will generally not be substantial for a closely held (or privately held) corporation, but they may add perhaps $ 100-$ 200 to the total costs. If the corporation is to operate in any state other than the one in which it is incorporated, it will have to qualify to do business in that state. Qualification will entail drafting and filing other forms and paying additional fees.

In addition to these one-time costs of incorporation and qualification to do business, the filing of an annual report and the payment of an annual fee will be required in the state of incorporation and in most states in which the corporation is qualified to do business. In addition to the legal fees corporations pay initially and each year in connection with the filing of annual reports, a corporation almost certainly will incur legal fees on a continuing basis for advice on corporation law, for drafting charter and bylaw amendments, for drafting minutes of meetings, and for other work relating to the corporation's internal affairs.

All such corporate expenses could be avoided in a sole proprietorship, and all could also be avoided in a partnership if the partners choose to operate without a partnership agreement. Operating without a partnership agreement is usually unwise, however, and drafting a proper partnership agreement often gives rise to higher legal fees than does the drafting of a corporation's charter and bylaws, because a partnership agreement frequently involves more custom drafting than do a corporation's charter and bylaws. Still, the total legal expenses and fees to states typically will be more in a corporation than in a partnership.

2. Required Initial and Continuing Formality

A sole proprietorship and a partnership, and to a degree a limited partnership, can be operated without formalities and without records of decisions that are made. The rules are quite different in a corporation. Both the shareholders and the directors must have meetings, or take action by formal written consent in lieu of meetings, and proper records must be kept of shareholders' and directors' actions. Further, the funds of the corporation must be kept separate from those of its owner or owners, and proper financial records must be maintained.

None of these requirements typically seems onerous to lawyers, but clients often view them as needless bothers. Unless their lawyers convince them otherwise, managers of closely held corporations tend to ignore some or all of these formalities. As will be seen in the chapters that follow, the cost of ignoring formalities might be that a court will disregard the corporate form and allow creditors to collect from a corporation's shareholders.

3. Tax Treatment

The tax disadvantage of operating in the corporate form is double taxation. A partnership as a legal entity is not subject to federal income taxation unless it elects to be taxed like a corporation, because federal tax law, tracking UPA (1914) state partnership law, treats a partnership as an aggregate of partners rather than as an entity separate from its owners. In contrast, a corporation is subject to federal income taxation precisely because, under both federal and state law, it is treated as a separate entity. Unlike a partnership, a corporation pays income taxes on its earnings. When a corporation distributes its after-tax profits to its shareholders as dividends, those dividends are subject to taxation as the ordinary income of the shareholders. Thus corporate income that is distributed to shareholders is twice subjected to taxation, once when it is earned by the corporation and again when it is distributed to shareholders.

Double taxation can be avoided in some circumstances, however, and once it is avoided, the corporate form does provide tax advantages. Congress has provided certain closely held corporations with the most straightforward way of avoiding double taxation. A corporation meeting specified requirements of the Internal Revenue Code can choose to be treated for federal tax purposes as if it were a partnership. In that case, the corporation will file merely an information return, and any corporate profits or losses will flow through to its shareholders for inclusion in their individual income tax returns. Such corporations now are called type S corporations, with that designation coming from the fact that the provisions in the Code dealing with such corporations were originally contained in subchapter S of the Internal Revenue Code of 1954. Here are the requirements for type S treatment:

1. No more than seventy-five shareholders.
2. Incorporation in the United States.
3. Only one class of stock.
4. Shareholders must be individuals, estates, or specified types of trusts.
5. No shareholder may be a nonresident alien.
6. The corporation may not be a life insurance company or certain other excluded types of businesses.
7. All shareholders must agree to the type S election.

In some corporations that have not elected type S treatment, double taxation can be avoided to an extent, or at least deferred, if the company does not pay dividends. The shareholders do not necessarily see this as a hardship, because they usually want their corporation to keep available cash invested in the corporation, rather than pay it out in dividends, so that the corporation will grow and the shareholders' shares will become more valuable. This is especially true in a closely held corporation that is owned and managed by the same group of people, since the group can take money out of the corporation as salaries and directors' fees, which are deductible expenses for the corporation, and thus not subject to double taxation.

Corporations may avoid double taxation by reinvesting available cash and paying salaries to their owner-managers; they may also minimize or at least defer even single taxation by the same means. Good managers often are able shrewdly to expand the business by using cash that otherwise would end up as a taxable profit. If the managers successfully use this approach, the corporation can become larger and more successful each year, while paying substantially minimized income taxes.

In many situations, the opportunities for using this approach may be limited and the company will look for other ways to minimize taxes. For example, some expenditures for officer and employee benefits are deductible to the corporation and not taxable to the recipients. Generally, these expenditures relate to medical payment and disability plans, group term life insurance and death benefits up to specified limits, and certain deferred compensation plans. The availability of this tax-free treatment can be especially valuable to owner-managers, because as officers or employees they themselves can receive these tax-free benefits.

Even though the impact of double taxation often can be substantially reduced, the fact that it exists as a possibility and that corporate managers must devote efforts to avoiding it makes double taxation a clear disadvantage of operating in the corporate form.

SECTION III. HYBRID FORMS OF BUSINESS ORGANIZATIONS

The current growth industry in developing or significantly revising business organization forms is the product of the very human desire to have it all. Having it all refers to business owners' desire for advantageous tax treatment, limited liability, and the flexibility to structure the company as they wish. The quest for limited liability and flexible structure continued in the late nineteenth century with the emergence of the partnership association, a form that never really took hold in the United States, although similar forms flourished in Europe. Considerations of tax consequences became important in the latter half of the twentieth century with the development of different tax treatments for corporations and partnerships. With the exception of the limited partnership, which was an early nineteenth century import from French law, the statutory forms discussed below have emerged during the past forty years, as business owners and their lawyers sought to combine the best of partnership and corporate forms.

A. STATUTORY CLOSE AND PROFESSIONAL CORPORATIONS

The development of close corporation statutes began in the late 1950's, a time when Congress began to develop a pass through taxation scheme for corporations with few owners, so that these businesses could be taxed like partnerships. At that time, corporate tax rates were lower than those imposed on individuals, and corporations could take advantage of retirement plan options then unavailable to unincorporated businesses. Small business owners also wanted a more flexible management structure than that offered by general corporation statutes. State legislatures responded by passing elective close corporation statutes that provided structural flexibility.

Statutory close corporations typically shed many attributes characteristic of general corporations and substitute those of partnerships. Their management structure can be informal. Shareholders may dispense with the Board of Directors and run the company themselves. They also may dissolve the corporation at will or on the occurrence of a particular event. In addition, share transfer restrictions are common. Although many statutory close corporations possess more noncorporate than corporate characteristics, the fact that they are organized as a corporation under state law means that, without Subchapter S, they will very likely receive corporate tax treatment. Companies making both statutory close corporation and subchapter S elections can have a pass-through taxation scheme, limited liability, flexible management structure, and corporate advantages regarding retirement plans. Today, closely held corporations not making a statutory close corporation election can achieve many of the same results by preparing shareholder agreements and taking advantage of special statutory provisions included in many general corporation statutes. Closely held corporations are discussed more fully in later chapters.

Professional Corporations developed during approximately the same period and for many of the same reasons. Licensed professionals wanted to be able to take advantage of the tax and retirement plan options available only to a corporation, a business organization form forbidden to them under state law and applicable codes of ethics, because corporate shareholders have limited liability. Ultimately, states developed the professional corporation, a form like other corporations except that it makes shareholders personally liable to their clients or patients.

B. LIMITED PARTNERSHIPS

The limited partnership developed during the Middle Ages, concurrently with the general partnership. Limited partnerships were used to finance speculative enterprises, primarily maritime trade. Small merchants and shippers needed to obtain credit and spread the risk of their venture. Investors who were owners of, rather than lenders to, an enterprise were able to increase their return on capital without violating usury laws. By the end of the Middle Ages, partnerships affording investors limited liability and freely alienable shares had begun to develop.

By the sixteenth century, the key characteristics of limited partnerships as we know them today were well established. The business organization had two classes of members. The commendators (limited partners) were passive investors whose liability was limited to the amount of their capital contribution. Tractators (general partners) had full responsibility for the conduct of the business and had unlimited liability for its obligations. Generally, the business was conducted in the tractators' names, and parties trading with the business did not know the identity of the passive investors.

In 1822, the New York Limited Partnership statute introduced this form of business organization into the United States. Other states soon followed New York's lead. Limited partnerships proved to be popular in the United States as investors sought to avoid an early court decision imposing liability on lenders to a general partnership who took a share of the profits in lieu of interest. Limited partners were protected from such a result. The limited partnership form was also attractive because corporate charters providing limited liability were difficult to obtain at that time. General corporation acts did not become common for many more years. In addition, the limited partnership form avoided technical limitations then associated with incorporation.

Today, all states except Louisiana have passed Uniform Limited Partnership Acts. The original Uniform Limited Partnership Act was adopted in 1916. That Act has now been superseded by the 1976 Uniform Limited Partnership Act in all but one state other than Louisiana. The new Act was in turn amended in 1985. It creates no revolution. In large measure, it can be viewed as a cleaning up and streamlining of limited partnership law. The new Act is, nevertheless, a helpful improvement for those involved in limited partnerships, especially those serving as limited partners, and for limited partnerships conducting business in several jurisdictions.

Both the 1916 and the 1976[53] Acts retain many of the attributes developed during the Middle Ages and considered essential to advance investment in speculative enterprises. These forms have two classes of partners: general and limited partners. General partners in a limited partnership have the same relationships to each other and to third parties as do members of a general partnership. General partners manage the business of the limited partnership, have unlimited liability for the company's debts, and cannot transfer their interests in the limited partnership without the others' consent. Their withdrawal, death or bankruptcy will cause the dissolution of the limited partnership.

Limited partners are prohibited from managing the business and the extent of their liability is limited to the amount of their investments. Their interests in the partnership may be transferred to a third party only if the other partners agree. Like the general partnership, the relationship among members of a limited partnership is essentially consensual and may be varied by agreement. An

---

[53] UNIF. LIMITED PARTNERSHIP ACT of 1976 (amended 1985) (hereinafter ULPA 1976) (U.L.A.).

important difference between general and limited partnerships is that a limited partnership cannot be created informally. In all states, forming a limited partnership requires that a certificate of limited partnership be filed in one or more state offices.

Under both the old and the new Acts, the main features that distinguish limited partners from general partners are the differences in their liability and the placement of management power solely in the hands of the general partners. It is perhaps in their treatment of the liability and management rules that the differences between the 1916 and 1976 Limited Partnership Acts are most important. The 1916 Act's provision on limited partners' liability and involvement in management is very simple: a limited partner has no liability to creditors unless he or she "takes part in the control of the business."[54] Limited partners who take part in the control of the business lose their limited liability. There can be, however, a good deal of argument about what constitutes taking part in the control of a business.

The drafters of the 1976 Uniform Limited Partnership Act started with the same concept for determining a limited partner's liability as did the drafters of the 1916 Act. Although they used essentially equivalent operative words (substituting "participates in" for "takes part in" the control of the business), they added substantial elaboration in an attempt to reduce the area of uncertainty. This elaboration takes the form of an eight-item "safe harbor" list of actions that do not constitute participation in the control of the business.[55] Examples are (1) consulting with a general partner with respect to the business of the partnership, (2) requesting or attending a meeting of partners, and (3) voting on any matter relating to the business of the partnership that under the partnership agreement is subject to the approval or disapproval of the limited partners.

The new Act also made a more fundamental change with respect to limited partners' liability. Under the new Act, a limited partner who does participate in the control of the business is liable "only to persons who transact business with the limited partnership reasonably believing, based upon the limited partner's conduct, that the limited partner is a general partner."[56] In a large percentage of cases involving conduct by a limited partner that arguably constitutes participation in the control of the business, this provision may prove to be the Act's most effective liability shield.

There is one more change from the 1916 Act to the 1976 Act that deserves attention. The old Act makes no mention of the possibility that a limited partnership may operate across state lines. This presents a substantial problem for a business operating in more than one state, because it is not clear how a particular state may treat a foreign limited partnership, with the risk being that a state will treat it as a general partnership. This uncertainty often has led careful lawyers to

---

[54] UNIF. LIMITED PARTNERSHIP ACT (1916) (hereinafter ULPA (1916)) § 7 (U.L.A.).

[55] ULPA (1976) § 303(b).

[56] Id. § 303(a).

form separate limited partnerships in each state in which a business will operate. The 1976 Act, on the other hand, devotes an entire article to the question of foreign limited partnerships and provides that limited partnerships formed in other states may register under the Act as foreign limited partnerships.

Limited partnerships tend to be used in three types of business situations. First, a business operating as a general partnership sometimes finds it convenient to recast itself as a limited partnership for the purpose of attracting new capital from investors who will share in the profits of the business, but who have no desire to participate in its management. Second, a general partnership sometimes recasts itself as a limited partnership upon the retirement of a partner who wishes to leave capital invested in the partnership, and thus share in its profits, but who does not wish to be subjected to the unlimited liability of a general partner in a business that he or she no longer manages. Family limited partnerships have also become popular planning tools in which parents give limited partnership equity interests in the business to their children without enabling the children to participate in the control of the business. These uses of the limited partnership are obviously closely related.

Limited partnerships are also used as a vehicle for tax-shelter investments, designed to take advantage of the fact that most limited partnerships are taxed like general partnerships. Until January 1, 1997, limited partnerships were generally taxed like general partnerships. Today, they may elect to be taxed either like a partnership or like a corporation. Limited partnerships are used for investments in real estate, venture capital, sports teams, and movies, to name a few. Until the 1980's, a limited partnership formed to build and operate a real estate venture, such as an apartment complex or a shopping center, offered many tax advantages. In those types of ventures, promoters looked for investors anxious to make an investment that (1) would generate losses while the project is under construction, so that the investors could write these losses off against their other income and (2) would later make profits that could be passed through to the investors without taxation at the partnership level (in each case with these tax consequences flowing from the fact that partnerships are exempt from federal and most state income taxation). The Tax Reform Act of 1986 substantially reduced the tax benefits available from the use of such tax shelters, including investors' ability to apply these losses against other income. Consequently, fewer real estate limited partnerships are now being formed.

The master limited partnership is one exception to the rule that limited partnerships were usually taxed like general partnerships. Master limited partnerships are publicly traded limited partnerships. They were originally developed to provide public markets for limited partners' interests in oil and gas tax shelters, while retaining pass through taxation and limited liability. Using the limited partnership form avoided the restrictions of Subchapter S and the impact of the corporate taxation scheme. As of 1988, however, master limited partnerships will be taxed as corporations when certain criteria are met.

Limited partnerships come into existence only when prescribed statutory formalities are followed. Under ULPA (1976) § 201, persons forming a limited partnership must file a certificate of limited partnership in the office of the Secretary of State. The certificate contains such information as the partnership's name, information about the agent for service of process, and the name and business address of each general partner, the term of the business, and any other information the general partners wish to include. The business entity is created at the time of the required filing. Although the statute does not require one, partnership agreements are an essential component of forming a limited partnership. The agreements not only define the rights and obligations of the members of the business, their provisions are used in determining tax consequences.

In limited partnerships, as in corporations, the passive investors often supply substantially all, if not all, of the capital. However, any partner's capital contribution may consist of cash, property, services rendered or a promissory note to contribute cash or property or to perform services. Partners are liable for the full amount of any promised contribution.

Partners in a limited partnership may transfer their right to receive distributions, but not other rights of the partner making the assignment. Transferring all the rights of a limited partner requires the consent of the other partners unless the partnership agreement specifies otherwise. Such a transfer does not dissolve the limited partnership. Limited partners may also withdraw with six months' prior written notice and be paid the value of their partnership interests.

A change in the identity of the limited partners does not interrupt the continuation of the partnership. In contrast, the business will generally end if the general partner withdraws for any reason. The partnership agreement may, however, provide for the continuation of the business when such an event occurs.

The limited partnership acts do not expressly address the issue of fiduciary obligations. ULPA (1976) § 403, however, imposes on the general partners the same liabilities as partners in a general partnership have to the partnership and to the other partners. Presumably this would include fiduciary obligations.

GATEWAY POTATO SALES v.
G.B. INVESTMENT CO.
Court of Appeals of Arizona
822 P.2d 490 (1991)

TAYLOR, JUDGE.

Gateway Potato Sales (Gateway), a creditor of Sunworth Packing Limited Partnership (Sunworth Packing), brought suit to recover payment for goods it had supplied to the limited partnership. Gateway sought recovery from Sunworth Packing, from Sunworth Corporation as general partner, and from G.B. Investment Company (G.B. Investment) as a limited partner, pursuant to Arizona Revised Statutes Annotated (A.R.S.) § 29-319. Under § 29-319, a limited partner may become liable for the obligations of the limited partnership under certain circumstances in which the limited partner has taken part in the control of the business.

G.B. Investment moved for summary judgment, urging that there was no evidence that the circumstances described in A.R.S. § 29-319 had occurred in this case. It argued that, as a limited partner, it was not liable to the creditors of the limited partnership except to the extent of its investment. The trial court agreed, granting G.B. Investment's motion for summary judgment.

Gateway appeals from the judgment and the denial of its motion for reconsideration, arguing the existence of conflicting evidence of material facts relating to the participation of the limited partner in the control of the partnership business. We agree and reverse the grant of summary judgment.

Facts

On review from the trial court's order granting summary judgment, the facts are viewed in the light most favorable to the party against whom judgment is entered. Sunworth Corporation and G.B. Investment formed Sunworth Packing in November 1985 for the purpose of engaging in potato farming in Arizona. The limited partnership certificate and agreement of Sunworth Packing, filed with the office of the Arizona Secretary of State, specified Sunworth Corporation as the general partner and G.B. Investment Company as the limited partner. The agreement recited that the limited partner would not participate in the control of the business. The agreement further stated that the limited partner would not become liable to the creditors of the partnership, except to the extent of its initial contribution and any liability it may incur with an Arizona bank as a signatory party or guarantor of a loan and/or line of credit.

In late 1985, Robert C. Ellsworth, the president of Sunworth Corporation, called Robert Pribula, the owner of Gateway, located in Minnesota, to see if Gateway would supply Sunworth Packing with seed potatoes. Pribula hesitated to supply the seed potatoes without receiving assurance of payment because Pribula was aware that Ellsworth had previously undergone bankruptcy. Pribula, however, decided to sell the seed potatoes to Sunworth Packing after being assured by Ellsworth that he was in partnership with a large financial institution, G.B. Investment Company, and that G.B. Investment was providing the financing, was actively involved in the operation of the business, and had approved the purchase of the seed potatoes. Thereafter, from February 1986 through April 1986, Gateway sold substantial quantities of seed potatoes to Sunworth Packing.

While supplying the seed potatoes, Pribula believed that he was doing business with a general partnership (*i.e.*, Sunworth Packing Company, formed by Sunworth Corporation and G.B. Investment Company). The sales documents used by the parties specified "Sunworth Packing Company" as the name of the partnership. Pribula was neither aware of the true name of the partnership nor that it was a limited partnership.

All of Gateway's dealings were with Ellsworth. Pribula neither contacted G.B. Investment prior to selling the seed potatoes to the limited partnership nor did he otherwise attempt to verify any of the statements Ellsworth had made about G.B. Investment's involvement. The only direct contact between G.B. Investment and Gateway occurred some time after the sale of the seed potatoes. It is, however, disputed whether G.B. Investment ever provided any assurance of payment to Gateway.

G.B. Investment's vice-president, Darl Anderson, testified in his affidavit that G.B. Investment had exerted no control over the daily management and operation of the limited partnership, Sunworth Packing. This testimony was contradicted, however, by the affidavit testimony of Ellsworth which was presented by Gateway in opposing G.B. Investment's motion for summary judgment. According to Ellsworth, G.B. Investment's employees, Darl Anderson and Thomas McHolm, controlled the day-to-day affairs of the limited partnership and made Ellsworth account to them for nearly everything he did. This day-to-day contact included but was not limited to approval of most of the significant operational decisions and expenditures and the use and management of partnership funds without Ellsworth's involvement.[57]

---

[57] Ellsworth described with some specificity the ways in which G.B. Investment's control was exerted:

a.) During the early months of the Partnership, Thomas McHolm and/or Darl Anderson were at the Partnership's offices on a daily basis directing the operation of the Partnership, and thereafter, they were at the Partnership's offices at least 2-3 times per week reviewing the operations of the business, directing changes in operations, and instructing me to make certain changes in operating the Partnership's affairs;

b.) G.B. Investment Company was solely responsible for obtaining a $ 150,000.00 line-of-credit loan for the Partnership with Valley National Bank of Arizona, and it also signed documents guaranteeing the repayment of the loan;

c.) As the President of the general partner, I was not permitted to make any significant independent business decisions concerning the operations of the Partnership, but was directed to have all business decisions approved with Darl Anderson and/or Thomas McHolm, or was directed to carry out decisions made by Darl Anderson and/or Thomas McHolm. For example, instead of using Partnership funds to pay certain creditors and suppliers, I was directed by Darl Anderson and/or Thomas McHolm to use the Partnership funds to purchase additional machinery and equipment;

d.) Prior to constructing improvements to the packaging facilities of the Partnership, Thomas McHolm and/or Darl Anderson had to approve all construction bids, individually selected some of the suppliers and subcontractors, and individually selected the equipment to be installed;

e.) Thomas McHolm and/or Darl Anderson dictated the accounting procedures to be followed by the Partnership, reviewed the Partnership's books and accounts almost continually, dictated that the Partnership use the same accounting firm as that of G.B. Investment Company to do the Partnership accounting tasks, undertook the responsibility of having prepared all Partnership tax forms and returns, and I only signed tax returns after they had been prepared by G.B. Investment Company's accountants and reviewed by Darl Anderson or some other employee/agent of G.B. Investment Company;

Ellsworth testified further that he had described G.B. Investment's control of the business operation to Pribula. Pribula confirmed that Ellsworth had informed him that G.B. Investment's employees, McHolm and Anderson, were at the partnership's office on a frequent basis, that Ellsworth reported directly to them, that daily operations of the partnership were reviewed by representatives of G.B. Investment, and that Ellsworth had to get their approval before making certain business decisions.

Discussion

Gateway argues that sufficient questions of fact exist which preclude the granting of summary judgment in favor of G.B. Investment. We will affirm the trial court's grant of summary judgment if there is no genuine issue of material fact in dispute and the moving party is entitled to judgment as a matter of law.

Subsection (a) of A.R.S. § 29-319 sets forth the general rule that a limited partner who is not also a general partner is not liable for the obligations of the

---

f.) During a great portion of the duration of the Partnership, Thomas McHolm and/or Darl Anderson oversaw the daily operations of the Partnership because I had to have all expenditures approved by Thomas McHolm and/or Darl Anderson and Darl Anderson had to approve and sign checks issued by the Partnership, including without limitation payroll checks and invoices for telephone charges, utilities, publications, interest payments, bank card charges, supplies, etc. Copies of a sampling of the invoices and the corresponding checks are attached hereto as Exhibit 2;

g.) After it was decided to add a hydrocooler to the processing and packaging facilities of the Partnership, Thomas McHolm individually selected the refrigeration equipment and chose the contractor to install the refrigeration equipment on the hydrocooler, and even saw to it that G.B. Investment Company (not the Partnership) directly paid the contractor for all of his services;

h.) Thomas McHolm insisted that the Partnership use a particular supplier, to-wit: Allied Packaging, to supply packaging materials to the Partnership, he further took an active role in reviewing and modifying the art work for use on the packaging items, and personally approved the bid submitted for the art work;

i.) At least on two separate occasions, approximately in August, 1986 and again in November, 1986, Darl Anderson caused sums of monies (approximately $ 8,000 and $ 7,000 respectively) to be withdrawn from the Partnership account (No. 2270-8018) with Valley National Bank without the prior knowledge or consent of myself, as the President of the general partner of the Partnership. These monies were paid directly to G.B. Investment, and the withdrawals caused other checks of the Partnership to be dishonored due to insufficient funds and left the Partnership without sufficient funds to meet its payroll obligations;

j. Darl Anderson and/or Thomas McHolm caused certain expenses of the Partnership to be paid directly by G.B. Investment Company, to-wit: refrigeration equipment; and

k.) After the Partnership defaulted on its loan payments to Valley National Bank, a loan which had been guaranteed by G.B. Investment Company, Darl Anderson, without my knowledge or consent, instructed the Valley National Bank to proceed with declaring the loan to be in default and to pursue its remedies under its Security Agreement with the Partnership, to-wit: to sell the equipment and machinery that it held as collateral at a foreclosure auction. At the foreclosure auction held on March 3, 1987, by Valley National Bank, Darl Anderson, on behalf of G.B. Investment Company, bought the equipment and machinery previously owned by Sunworth Corporation.

limited partnership. [A] limited partner is not liable for the obligations of a limited partnership unless he is also a general partner or, in addition to the exercise of his rights and powers as a limited partner, he takes part in the control of the business. However, if the limited partner's participation in the control of the business is not substantially the same as the exercise of the powers of a general partner, he is liable only to persons who transact business with the limited partnership with actual knowledge of his participation in control. Subsection (a) does not discuss the types of activities that might be undertaken by a limited partner which would amount to "control of the business." Subsection (b), however, does contain a listing of activities that are permissible for a limited partner to undertake without being deemed to be taking part in "control of the business."[58]

A limited partner does not participate in the control of the business within the meaning of subsection (a) solely by doing one or more of the following: (1) Being a contractor for or an agent or employee of the limited partnership or of a general partner; (2) Consulting with and advising a general partner with respect to the business of the limited partnership; (3) Acting as surety for the limited partnership; (4) Approving or disapproving an amendment to the partnership agreement; or (5) Voting on one or more of the following matters: (i) The dissolution and winding up of the limited partnership; (ii) The sale, exchange, lease, mortgage, pledge or other transfer of all or substantially all of the assets of the limited partnership other than in the ordinary course of its business; (iii) The incurrence of indebtedness by the limited partnership other than in the ordinary course of its business; (iv) A change in the nature of the business; or (v) The removal of a general partner. In addition, subsection (c) of A.R.S. § 29-319 provides that "[t]he enumeration in subsection (b) does not mean that the possession or exercise of any other powers by a limited partner constitutes participation by him in the business of the limited partnership."

In responding to the motion for summary judgment, Gateway urged the trial court to find that Gateway had presented a fact question of G.B. Investment's liability to it under A.R.S. § 29-319(a). Gateway argued that the statute imposes liability on a limited partner whose participation in the control of the business is substantially the same as the exercised power of a general partner. Gateway further argued that even if the person transacting business with the limited partnership did not know of the limited partner's participation in control, there is liability. Alternatively, Gateway argued that the statute imposes liability when the powers exercised in controlling the business might fall short of being "substantially the same as the exercise of powers of a general partner," but the person transacting business with the limited partnership had actual knowledge of the

---

[58] The drafters of the Revised Uniform Limited Partnership Act (RULPA) from which Arizona's statute is taken, refer to this listing as a "safe harbor." REVISED UNIFORM LIMITED PARTNERSHIP ACT § 303 cmt., 6 U.L.A. 239 (Supp.1991).

participation in control. Gateway asserted that the evidence it was presenting in response to the motion for summary judgment raised issues of material fact as to whether either of these situations had occurred. If either had occurred, Gateway argued, it would be entitled to recover from the limited partner, G.B. Investment.

In granting G.B. Investment's motion for summary judgment, the trial court gave two reasons for concluding that G.B. Investment could not be found liable under A.R.S. § 29-319(a) as a matter of law. First, as we interpret the trial court's comments, it read the statute as having a threshold requirement — that is, under all circumstances, a creditor of the limited partnership must have contact with the limited partner in order to impose liability on the limited partner. The evidence before the trial court showed that Gateway merely relied upon the statements made by Ellsworth, president of the general partner, and that Gateway did not contact G.B. Investment prior to transacting business with the limited partnership. Based upon these facts, the trial court concluded that liability could not be imposed upon G.B. Investment. The trial court's minute entry states, in relevant part: "[I]t is undisputed that the plaintiff contracted with and sold seed potatoes to the limited partnership, without any direct contact with the movant." In other words, at the time the sale with the limited partnership was consummated and completed — plaintiff can not by the posture of the evidence — be said to have been a person who, while transacting business with the limited partnership, did so with actual knowledge of defendant G.B. Investment Company's participation in control with the limited partnership or its general partner. Consequently, plaintiff fails to leap the first "hurdle"; and neither the court nor the trier-of-fact need review plaintiff's factual assertions regarding "safe harbor" excesses or violations, if any, under A.R.S. § 29-319(b). The only purported contact between plaintiff and defendant G.B. Investment Company occurred in the fall of 1986, well after the last of the seed potatoes were delivered by plaintiff to the limited partnership. Notwithstanding the representations made by Robert C. Ellsworth, as the president of the general partner, Sunworth Corporation, regarding the movant, plaintiff admits it never directly contacted the movant, to inquire into or verify Ellsworth's authority to bind the movant by such representations. The court finds, given the present record, that movant G.B. Investment has no liability to plaintiff arising from movant being a limited partner in Sunworth Packing Limited Partnership.

After reaching this conclusion, the trial court also found that no specific facts had been presented which would support the application of A.R.S. § 29-319 so as to impose liability on G.B. Investment. As the minute entry states: The court further finds that while the statutory protection extended to limited partners is not absolute, there are no specific facts included within the plaintiff's response, supporting statement of facts, and supporting affidavits, which would support the applicability of A.R.S. § 29-319(a) so as to impose liability in favor of plaintiff and against the movant G.B. Investment. To the extent that the trial court's ruling may have been based on a belief that a limited partner could never be liable under the statute unless the creditor had contact with the limited partner and learned directly from him of his participation and control of the business, we believe that ruling to be in error.

In A.R.S. § 29-319(a), the legislature stopped short of expressly stating that if the limited partner's participation in the control of the business is substantially the same as the exercise of the powers of a general partner, he is liable to persons who transact business with a limited partnership even though they have no knowledge of his participation and control. It has made this statement by implication, though, by stating to the opposite effect that "if the limited partner's participation in the control of the business is not substantially the same as the exercise of the powers of a general partner, he is liable only to persons who transact business with the limited partnership with actual knowledge of his participation in control." A.R.S. § 29-319(a).

We believe this interpretation is strengthened by an examination of the legislative history of Arizona's limited partnership statute. It is further strengthened by the legislature's refusal to modify this statute to correspond to the Revised Uniform Limited Partnership Act, as amended in 1985. Prior to 1982, Arizona's limited partnership statute was patterned after the Uniform Limited Partnership Act (ULPA), which was drafted in 1916. Section 7 of the ULPA provided that "[a] limited partner shall not become liable as a general partner unless, in addition to the exercise of his rights and powers as a limited partner, he takes part in the control of the business." Uniform Limited Partnership Act § 7, 6 U.L.A. 559 (1969).[59]

The Revised Uniform Limited Partnership Act (RULPA) was drafted in 1976. Revised Uniform Limited Partnership Act, 6 U.L.A. 239, 240 (Supp.1991). In 1982, the Arizona legislature adopted the RULPA after repealing its enactment of the ULPA. Presently, A.R.S. § 29-319(a), dealing with a limited partner's liability to third parties, is very similar to the 1976 version of section 303(a) of the RULPA which stated:

> Except as provided in subsection (d), a limited partner is not liable for the obligations of a limited partnership unless he is also a general partner or, and in addition to the exercise of his rights and powers as a limited partner, he takes part in the control of the business. However, if the limited partner's participation in the control of the business is not substantially the same as the exercise of the powers of a general partner, he is liable only to persons who transact business with the limited partnership with actual knowledge of his participation in control. Revised Uniform Limited Partnership Act § 303(a), 6 U.L.A. 239, 325 (Supp.1991). The drafters' comment to section 303 explained that limited partners exercising all of the powers of a general partner would not escape liability by avoiding direct dealings with third parties. The comment stated: Section 303 makes several important changes in Section 7 of the prior uniform law. The first sentence of Section 303(a)

---

[59] The language of Arizona's then § 29-307 was taken verbatim from section 7 of the ULPA....

carries over the basic test from former Section 7 whether the limited partner "takes part in the control of the business" in order to ensure that judicial decisions under the prior uniform law remain applicable to the extent not expressly changed. The second sentence of Section 303(a) reflects a wholly new concept. Because of the difficulty of determining when the "control" line has been overstepped, it was thought it unfair to impose general partner's liability on a limited partner except to the extent that a third party had knowledge of his participation in control of the business. On the other hand, in order to avoid permitting a limited partner to exercise all of the powers of a general partner while avoiding any direct dealings with third parties, the "is not substantially the same as" test was introduced.... *Id.* at 326 cmt.

In 1985, the drafters of the RULPA backtracked from the position taken in section 303(a) of the 1976 Act. The new amendments reflect a reluctance to hold a limited partner liable if the limited partner had no direct contact with the creditor. The 1985 revised RULPA section 303(a) was amended to provide as follows: Except as provided in subsection (d), a limited partner is not liable for the obligations of a limited partnership unless he is also a general partner or, in addition to the exercise of his rights and powers as a limited partner, he participates in the control of the business. However, if the limited partner participates in the control of the business, he is liable only to persons who transact business with the limited partnership reasonably believing, based upon the limited partner's conduct, that the limited partner is a general partner. *Id.* at 325. The comment to section 303 was also revised to explain the reason for the amendment. The revised comment states: Section 303 makes several important changes in Section 7 of the 1916 Act. The first sentence of section 303(a) differs from the text of Section 7 of the 1916 Act in that it speaks of participating (rather than taking part) in the control of the business; this was done for the sake of consistency with the second sentence of Section 303(a), not to change the meaning of the text. It is intended that judicial decisions interpreting the phrase "takes part in the control of the business" under the prior uniform law will remain applicable to the extent that a different result is not called for by other provisions of Section 303 and other provisions of the Act. The second sentence of Section 303(a) reflects a wholly new concept in the 1976 Act that has been further modified in the 1985 Act. It was adopted partly because of the difficulty of determining when the "control" line has been overstepped, but also (and more importantly) because of a determination that it is not sound public policy to hold a limited partner who is not also a general partner liable for the obligations of the partnership except to persons who have done business with the limited partnership reasonably believing, based on the limited partner's conduct, that he is a general partner. ... *Id.* at 326 cmt.

The Arizona legislature, however, has not revised A.R.S. § 29-319(a) to correspond to the section 303 amendments. The Arizona statute continues to impose liability on a limited partner whenever the "substantially the same as" test is met, even though the creditor has no knowledge of the limited partner's control. It follows then that no contact between the creditor and the limited partner is required to impose liability.

Moreover, whereas section 303 of the RULPA states that the creditor's reasonable belief must be "based upon the limited partner's conduct," under A.R.S. § 29-319 the only requirement is that the creditor has had "actual knowledge of [the limited partner's] participation in control." The statute does not state that this knowledge must be based upon the limited partner's conduct. The comments to the original version of section 303 of the RULPA, from which Arizona's statute is taken, make it clear that only when the "substantially the same as" test is met is direct contact not a requirement. Conversely, if the "substantially the same as" test is not met, direct contact is required. Under the facts presented in this case, Gateway had no direct contact with G.B. Investment until after the sales were concluded. We conclude, therefore, that G.B. Investment would be liable only if the "substantially the same as" test was met.

Whether a limited partner has exercised the degree of control that will make him liable to a creditor has always been a factual question. This is so regardless of whether the particular statute involved is patterned after section 7 of the ULPA or after section 303 of the RULPA. Our current Arizona statute lists activities that a limited partner may undertake without participating in controlling the business. It also states that other activities may be excluded from the definition of such control. Where activities do not fall within the "safe harbor" of A.R.S. § 29-319(b), it is necessary for a trier-of-fact to determine whether such activities amount to "control." In the absence of actual knowledge of the limited partner's participation in the control of the partnership business, there must be evidence from which a trier-of-fact might find not only control, but control that is "substantially the same as the exercise of powers of a general partner."

We conclude that the evidence Gateway presented in this case should have allowed it to withstand summary judgment. The affidavit testimony of Ellsworth raises the issue whether he was merely a puppet for the limited partner, G.B. Investment. While a few of the activities Ellsworth listed may have fallen within the protected areas listed in A.R.S. § 29-319(b), others did not. Ellsworth's detailed statement raises substantial issues of material facts.

Viewing the facts in the light most favorable to Gateway, we cannot say as a matter of law that G.B. Investment was entitled to summary judgment. We conclude that Gateway is entitled to a determination by trial of the extent of control exercised by G.B. Investment over Sunworth Packing.

For the foregoing reasons, we reverse the judgment of the trial court and remand for further proceedings.

EHRLICH, P.J., and CLABORNE, J., concur.

C. LIMITED LIABILITY COMPANIES[60]

Limited liability companies are among the latest efforts to achieve favorable tax treatment while combining the best of the partnership and corporate forms. The limited liability company offers several advantages: it usually qualifies for partnership pass through taxation while avoiding the restrictions imposed by Subchapter S and it resembles a partnership in which all members have limited liability. All states have passed limited liability company acts. Most acts have been passed since a 1988 Revenue Ruling[61] provided that limited liability companies with certain attributes qualified for partnership taxation. Today, limited liability companies, like most other unincorporated business organizations, may elect either partnership or corporate tax treatment.

One or more persons may form a limited liability company by filing articles of organization in the office of the secretary of state. Although an operating agreement is not required for formation, most acts are based on the assumption that an agreement will be prepared to address issues of company governance and operations not covered by the statute or to make elections where the statute provides options. As with other privately held firms, a well drafted operating agreement is essential for the successful operation of the company.

All LLC members have unrestricted limited liability so long as the company was properly formed, members have paid their promised capital contributions in full, and the company is not operating in a fraudulent manner. The business may be managed either by its members or by a designated group of managers, who may or may not be members of the company. The member-managed firm is very much like a partnership in the relations of the members to each other and in their ability to bind the firm through their individual acts. Each is an agent of the firm. Similarly, each manager in a manager-managed firm may also bind the firm, but individual members who are not also managers may not.

Members' capital contributions may consist of property, money, promissory notes, services performed, or agreements to contribute property, money or services. Members are liable for the full amount of their promised contributions. Distributions to members during the conduct of the company's business may be made in equal shares or according to capital contribution. A limited liability company may not make distributions to its members that would render the company insolvent. This approach is similar to that found in corporate statutes. Liability is imposed for unlawful distributions. As in partnerships, members may transfer their financial interests in the company, but the transferee does not become a member unless the other members consent or the operating agreement so provides. The transferee is entitled to receive only the distributions that the transferor had a right to receive. Members have the right to access company

---

[60] The discussion that follows is primarily based on the Uniform Limited Liability Company Act (1995), approved by the National Conference of Commissioners on Uniform State Laws in 1995.

[61] Rev. Rul. 88-76, 1988-2 C.B. 360.

records and are subject to fiduciary obligations of due care and loyalty. The scope of these obligations depends on whether the company is managed by members or by managers.

A limited liability company may be at will or be organized for a term. All members have the right to dissociate from the company at any time and to be paid the value of their interests. Dissociation does not cause dissolution of the firm unless the dissociation was wrongful.

Limited liability companies generally are taxed like partnerships. In contrast to S corporations, limited liability companies qualify for pass through taxation regardless of the number or type of members. Since tax considerations were a key factor in both the origin and continued popularity of the form and since limited liability is an essential component of the form, default provisions in the statutes usually track partnership structures so that the company will not be subject to corporate tax. Today, however, a limited liability company can elect the particular tax treatment of choice.

The following case elaborates on the implementation of this new form.

BROYHILL v. DeLUCA

United States Bankruptcy Court, E.D. Virginia
194 B.R. 65 (1996)

STEPHEN S. MITCHELL, BANKRUPTCY JUDGE.

In this action, the plaintiffs, Joel T. Broyhill and Northern Virginia Realty, Inc. Profit Sharing Trust seek a declaration that the defendants, Robert and Marilyn DeLuca, were properly removed as the managers of D & B Countryside, L.L.C., and that Joel T. Broyhill was properly appointed as the successor manager. A trial of the issues was held on September 15 and 18, 1995....

Findings of Fact

D & B Countryside, L.L.C., ("D & B Countryside") is a Virginia limited liability company that was formed on April 12, 1994 to develop a shopping center and office development in Sterling, Virginia, known as Parc City Centre. The project originally consisted of approximately 12 acres, but at the present time there remain 3.766 acres which are intended to be subdivided into four retail "pad sites."[62] The original members of the company were Joel T. Broyhill ("Broyhill") and Robert and Marilyn DeLuca ("the DeLucas"). The organization of the company was set forth in an Operating Agreement dated April 12, 1994 ("the operating agreement"), signed by Broyhill and the DeLucas. Under the terms of the operating agreement, Broyhill and the DeLucas were each 50%

---

[62] The fair market value of the property is listed on D & B Countryside's schedules at $ 3,625,000.

members,[63] and the DeLucas were named as joint managing members. The operating agreement stated that the manager of the company must be appointed by unanimous vote[64] but was silent on removal of a manager. The operating agreement further required written consent of the other members for the assignment or pledge of a member's interest. Finally, the agreement provided ... for the dissolution of the company on December 31, 2024 or the earlier occurrence of certain specified events, including:

(c) the death, resignation, expulsion, bankruptcy or dissolution of a Member ... unless the business of the Company is continued by the unanimous consent of the remaining Members.

....

With respect to termination occurring because of the death, resignation, expulsion, bankruptcy or dissolution of a member the agreement further provided:

The business of the Company shall be continued on the terms and conditions of this Agreement if, within ninety (90) days after such event, the remaining Members elect in writing that the business of the Company should be continued and, if the Affected Member was also the only Manager, elect a new Manager....

Under the terms of the operating agreement, Broyhill and the DeLucas were each to make $ 1,000,000 capital contributions; any further contributions were to be made *pro rata*. This would have resulted in $ 2,000,000 of paid-in capital, but from the testimony it appears that significantly less was actually paid in. The source of the capital funds for both Broyhill and the DeLucas was a $ 1,500,000 loan from NationsBank. Broyhill testified his understanding was that the entire loan proceeds were to be paid to D & B Countryside. In fact, as it turns out, only $ 200,000 of the loan proceeds were actually deposited in D & B Countryside's bank account.

In July 1994, the DeLucas solicited Theodore Boinis ("Boinis"), the president of Northern Virginia Realty, Inc. ("NVRI") and trustee of its profit sharing plan, to become a member and offered him a 15% interest in the company in exchange for a $ 600,000 investment. Additionally, the DeLucas offered to personally guarantee a 10% minimum rate of return on NVRI's investment. NVRI agreed to the proposal and wire-transferred the $ 600,000 to D & B Countryside's bank

---

[63] Contributions and Membership Interests. Simultaneously with the full execution of this Agreement, Broyhill shall make an initial cash contribution to the Company in an amount equal to $ 1,000,000 and R. DeLuca and M. DeLuca shall each make an initial cash contribution to the company in an amount equal to $ 1,000,000 for a total of $ 2,000,000. Thereupon, each Member shall have an interest in the Company expressed as a percentage of the whole ("Membership Interest"). The Membership Interest of R. DeLuca and M. DeLuca jointly shall be fifty percent (50%) and the Membership Interest of Broyhill shall be fifty percent (50%)."

[64] Appointment of Manager. The management of the affairs of the Company shall be vested in one or more managers (the "Manager") elected by the unanimous vote of the "Members."

account on July 22, 1994. Within a week, $ 594,300 of those funds had been transferred to other DeLuca-related entities or Robert DeLuca personally. Sometime later (apparently in September), Boinis and the DeLucas signed an Amended and Restated Operating Agreement dated "as of July 22, 1994" ("the amended operating agreement"), which assigned to the NVRI Profit Sharing Trust [NVRI] a 7.5% portion of the Deluca's interest in the company and a 7.5% portion of Broyhill's interest. Although the DeLucas told Boinis that the amended operating agreement would be sent to Broyhill for signature, it never was, and was never signed by Broyhill. Broyhill testified at trial that, although he had not seen the amended operating agreement until approximately mid-January, 1995, he had no objection to any of its provisions except for language in one paragraph acknowledging his having "received all amounts and other consideration due ... on account of this membership assignment." ... Indeed, in a memorandum to the DeLucas dated September 27, 1994, Broyhill acknowledged the existence of NVRI's 15% interest and registered no protest.

Beginning in September or October 1994, the relationship between the DeLucas and Broyhill soured, largely because the DeLucas did not respond to a number of requests by Broyhill for information concerning his investment. After Broyhill learned that almost all of the $ 600,000.00 invested by Boinis had been immediately transferred out of D & B Countryside and that the DeLucas had placed a $ 3,000,000.00 deed of trust against D & B Countryside's property without his knowledge,[65] Broyhill and NVRI Profit Sharing Trust executed a document on April 14, 1995, purporting to remove the DeLucas as D & B Countryside's managers and electing Broyhill as manager. No notice was given to the DeLucas of the meeting of Broyhill and Boinis at which the document was signed. Written notice was sent to the DeLucas that same date, however, that the action had been taken. In addition, notice was also sent that same date to the attorney who was representing the DeLucas, and who subsequently filed the chapter 11 petition on behalf of D & B Countryside, advising him that the DeLucas had been removed as managers and that he had no authority to represent D & B Countryside or to make any filings for D & B Countryside in the United States Bankruptcy Court. On May 5, 1995, the DeLucas filed a voluntary chapter 11 petition in this court, and on May 9, 1995, they caused D & B Countryside to file a voluntary chapter 11 petition. Subsequent to the DeLucas' petition, Broyhill and NVRI Profit Sharing Trust executed a document in which they elected to continue the business and confirmed the election of Broyhill as the new manager.

---

[65] The deed of trust secured a promissory note in favor of S.P. "Chip" Newell that consolidated four prior promissory notes that had been personal liabilities of the DeLucas.... At the time the deed of trust was placed on the property, the DeLucas executed a borrowing authorization on behalf of D & B Countryside in which they certified that they "are, or have the authority of, all Members" of the limited liability company. In fact, neither Broyhill nor NVRI knew of or consented to the deed of trust.

Conclusions of Law

There are two major issues raised by the complaint and the evidence. The first is whether the April 28, 1995 action by Broyhill and NVRI was effective to remove the DeLucas as the managers of D & B Countryside and to appoint Broyhill as the successor manager. If not, the second issue is whether the chapter 11 filing by the DeLucas terminated their right to act as manager and permitted Broyhill and NVRI Profit Sharing Trust to elect to continue the business with Broyhill as the manager. Each of these issues will be discussed in turn.

A. *Whether the April 28, 1995 action was effective to remove the DeLucas as managers.*

As noted above, D & B Countryside is a limited liability company. Limited liability companies, although a relatively recent innovation, have become an increasingly popular form of business organization. As explained by one commentator:

In response to favorable tax rulings, most states recently have followed the lead of Wyoming and Florida and enacted legislation for the formation and recognition of the limited liability company (LLC). The LLC is a form of legal entity that has attributes of both a corporation and a partnership but is not formally characterized as either one. Generally, an LLC offers all of its members, including any member-manager, limited liability as if they were shareholders of a corporation but treats the entity and its members as a partnership for tax purposes.

In Virginia, limited liability companies are governed by the Virginia Limited Liability Company Act, enacted in 1991. A Virginia limited liability company may engage in any lawful business that a corporation, partnership or other business entity may conduct under Virginia law. A limited liability company in Virginia is formed by filing articles of organization with the State Corporation Commission. A person that owns an interest in the company is called a "member." The members may (and in practice invariably do) also enter into an operating agreement which regulates and establishes the conduct of the company's business and the relationship of its members. Management of the company is vested in the members in proportion to their capital contributions, as adjusted for additional contributions and distributions, unless the articles of organization or the operating agreement provide that the company will be managed by one or more managers. Managers, if provided for in the articles of organization or operating agreement, are elected by the members. In a manager-managed limited liability company, only managers can contract for the company's debts or execute documents for the acquisition, mortgage or disposition of the company's property.

In order to determine whether the April 28, 1995 action by Broyhill and NVRI was effective to remove the DeLucas as managers, it is necessary first to resolve just who the members of D & B Countryside were. The DeLucas, in their pleadings and through counsel, have denied that NVRI became a member of the company because the operating agreement required unanimous consent to assign a membership interest or to admit a new member and Broyhill never signed the amended operating agreement which assigned a portion of Broyhill's and the DeLucas' membership interest to NVRI and recognized NVRI as a member. In addition, counsel for the DeLucas point out that in correspondence, counsel for NVRI referred to his client's investment in the company as a "loan."

The DeLucas themselves in testimony (as distinguished from their attorneys in argument) candidly admitted on the witness stand that they always regarded NVRI, following its $ 600,000 investment, as owning a 15% interest in the company. This is consistent with their conduct, in connection with the Regal Cinema sale, in remitting to NVRI a "15% distribution" of the net sales proceeds ($ 68,105.75 of $ 454,038.34). Additionally, D & B Countryside's schedules, signed by Robert DeLuca under penalty of perjury, reflect NVRI (although erroneously called "Virginia Realty Trust") as the holder of a 15% equity interest in the company. The DeLucas, by signing the Amended and Restated Operating Agreement, effectively (1) assigned a 7.5% portion of their own membership interest to NVRI and (2) consented to an assignment of a 7.5% portion of Broyhill's interest to NVRI. Although Broyhill never executed a writing explicitly assigning the 7.5% portion of his interest or consenting to the assignment of a similar portion of the DeLuca's interest, he testified at trial that he consented in fact to both actions, that he had never been sent the amended operating agreement to sign, and that the only reason he would not now sign the amended operating agreement was because of the language acknowledging that he had received all amounts to which he was due on account of the assignment. The requirement in the original operating agreement that any assignment and consent to assignment be in writing is clearly for the protection and benefit of the party whose interest would be adversely affected by the assignment, and that party is free to waive, as Broyhill has done in this case, the requirement of a writing. Accordingly, the court concludes that Broyhill's failure to sign the amended operating agreement did not, under the facts of this case, prevent NVRI from becoming a 15% member of D & B Countryside and that NVRI is in fact the holder of a 15% membership interest.

As discussed above, the original operating agreement required that the manager of the company be elected by unanimous vote of the members but was silent on removal of an existing manager. The plaintiffs argue, and the court concurs, that where the operating agreement is silent, resort must be had to the statute. In this connection, § 13.1-1024(F), Va.Code Ann. provides, "All managers or any lesser number may be removed in the manner provided in the articles of organization or an operating agreement. If the articles of organization or an operating agreement does not provide for the removal of managers, then all managers or any lesser number may be removed with or without cause by a majority vote of the members." ... Since Broyhill's 42.5% interest and NVRI's 15% interest clearly constituted a majority of the membership interest, their joint action removing the DeLucas as managers was, under the plain language of the statute, effective to accomplish its stated purpose. The court rejects the DeLucas' argument that, because the operating agreement required election of a manager to be unanimous, removal likewise necessarily had to be unanimous. That result simply does not follow. The obvious purpose of the operating agreement was to prevent a manager from being elected who did not enjoy the unanimous support of the members. By April 28, 1995, the DeLucas not only no longer had the unanimous support of the members, their continued retention in office was actively opposed by the majority of the members. Thus, their removal from office by the majority, pursuant to the statute, was not at all inconsistent with the requirement of the operating agreement that a manager had to be elected by unanimous vote.

At the same time, the requirement in the operating agreement for a unanimous vote in order to elect a manager presents an obvious practical difficulty. Since the manager may be removed by a majority, but less than unanimous, vote, the company could well find itself in the difficult and untenable position of having removed a manager but being unable to elect a new one, thereby leaving the company essentially paralyzed. If that were to occur, the only apparent remedy would be a judicial winding up.[66] That potentially is the situation that exists in the present case. Although the April 28, 1995 action was effective to remove the DeLucas as the managers of D & B Countryside, since the plain language of the operating agreement requires a unanimous vote to elect a manager, NVRI and Broyhill could not, by their sole act, elect Broyhill as the new manager, unless, as argued by NVRI and Broyhill, the DeLucas' subsequent chapter 11 filing in effect terminated their membership and gave NVRI and Broyhill the right under the operating agreement to elect to continue the business of the company and select a new manager. It is to that question that we must now turn.

B. *The effect of the DeLucas' chapter 11 filing on their management rights.*

As noted above, the operating agreement explicitly provided that the bankruptcy of a member would trigger the dissolution of the company,[67] but that within 90 days of the bankruptcy "event," the remaining members could elect in writing

---

[66] On application by or for a member, the circuit court of the locality in which the registered office of the limited liability company is located may decree dissolution of a limited liability company if it is not reasonably practicable to carry on the business in conformity with the articles of organization and any operating agreement.

[67] This provision of the operating agreement is consistent with § 13.1-1046, VA. CODE ANN., which at the time the DeLucas filed their chapter 7 petition, provided as follows:

A limited liability company ... is dissolved and its affairs shall be wound up upon the happening of the first to occur of the following events:

...

3. Upon the death, resignation, retirement, expulsion, bankruptcy, or dissolution of a member or occurrence of any other event that terminates the continued membership of a member in the limited liability company, unless within six months after the event the limited liability company is continued by the consent of all or such lesser percentage or number (but not less than a majority in interest) of the remaining members as may be provided in writing in the articles or organization or operating agreement of the limited liability company.

to continue the business of the company and, if the bankrupt member were also the only manager, could elect a new manager. Since Broyhill and NVRI have done precisely that, the question is whether the provisions of the operating agreement are enforceable in bankruptcy or whether, as argued by the DeLucas, they constitute an impermissible "ipso facto" clause which is unenforceable in bankruptcy.

Limited liability companies are a recent innovation. It is not surprising, therefore, that counsel have been unable to cite the court to any cases specifically dealing with this issue in the context of a limited liability company, nor has the court's own research found any such case. As discussed above, limited liability companies are a conceptual hybrid, sharing some of the characteristics of partnerships and some of corporations. "In general, the purpose of forming a limited liability company is to create an entity that offers investors the protections of limited liability and the flow-through tax status of partnerships." In order to achieve the desired goal of pass-through tax treatment, it is necessary under applicable U.S. Treasury Regulations that the company have more of the attributes of a partnership than of a corporation. Treas.Reg. § 301.7701-2(a)(1). In particular, a limited liability company will be treated as a partnership for tax purposes as long as the company does not possess the corporate characteristics of (1) continuity of life and (2) free transferability of interests. Rev.Rul. 88-76, 1988-2 C.B. 360, 361. On the other hand, simply because a limited liability company is most closely analogous to a partnership (or limited partnership) for tax purposes, does not mean that it might not be considered a corporation for other purposes. For example, the Bankruptcy Code defines a "corporation" as including, among other entities, a "partnership association organized under a law that makes only the capital subscribed responsible for the debts of such association." Under § 13.1-1019, Va.Code Ann., the members of a Virginia limited liability company are not, solely by reason of their membership interest, personally liable for the company's debts, obligations, and liabilities. Nevertheless, for the purpose of analyzing the effect of a member's bankruptcy filing upon the continued exercise of membership rights, it seems most appropriate to treat the relationship among members of a limited liability company as analogous to that of that among the partners of a partnership. In particular, the fact that membership interests in a limited liability company, unlike shares of stock in a corporation, are not freely transferable mirrors the restriction on entry of new members into a partnership, which ordinarily cannot occur without the agreement of all existing members. (Although membership interest may be assigned unless assignment is restricted by the operating agreement or articles of organization, the assignee becomes a member only if the members unanimously consent to the assignee's admission; otherwise assignment only entitles the assignees to receive the distributions to which the assignor would be entitled, and does not permit participation in the company's management or affairs.) Whether the provision in D & B Countryside's operating agreement for dissolution of the company upon the bankruptcy of a member is enforceable depends on the interplay of several sections of the bankruptcy code....

....

As an initial matter, the court is required to determine the nature of the DeLucas' interest in D & B Countryside. In the partnership context, it has been held that the interest of a debtor general partner is comprised of three components: the right to participate in profits, losses, distributions and proceeds of the partnership ("Economic Interest"); the right to participate in the management of the partnership ("Management Interest"); and the ownership share in partnership property as a tenant-in-partnership. In a limited liability company, members have no direct interest in the company's property,[68] but members have an economic interest, referred to in the statute as a "membership interest,"[69] and, in addition, both the managing member and, where the manager cannot or is not authorized to act, all members, have a management interest.

... Since the court has concluded that the DeLucas were properly removed as the managers of the company prior to the filing of their chapter 11 petition, the issue of their assuming the management functions specified in the operating agreement is not implicated, but upon their removal they would have had the right and duty to participate in the election of a successor manager, acceptable to all the members, to carry on the management function. Additionally, they would have had the right and duty to vote on any matter with respect to which a manager could not act unilaterally. Particularly in view of the highly questionable conduct of the DeLucas in having allowed a deed of trust to be recorded against the company's property to secure a personal loan and in having siphoned out of the company essentially all of NVRI's $ 600,000 investment within a week of its having been paid in, and given that the Parc City Centre project is still very much in the development phase, with important decisions to be made with respect to the sale or lease of parcels and possible further financing (which, as with the current financing, could very well require the personal guarantees of members), there is no way the identity of the DeLucas would not be material to the other members and to the success of the project. [The court concluded that the provisions of the operating agreement were not invalid under the Bankruptcy Code.] It therefore

---

[68] See § 13.1-1021, VA. CODE ANN. ("Any estate or interest in property may be acquired in the name of the limited liability company, and title to any estate or interest so acquired vests in the limited liability company."); § 13.1-1034 ("Except as provided in writing in the articles of organization or an operating agreement, a member, regardless of the nature of his or its contribution, has no right to demand and receive any distribution from a limited liability company in any form other than cash."); § 13.1-1038 ("A membership interest in a limited liability company is personal property."); § 13.1-1041 (judgment creditor has right to obtain a charging order against member's interest but "has only the rights of an assignee of the interest in the limited liability company.").

[69] "'Membership interest' or 'interest' means a member's share of the profits and the losses of the limited liability company and the right to receive distributions of the limited liability company's assets." ...

follows that the action taken by Broyhill and NVRI following the DeLucas bankruptcy "confirming" the prepetition election of Broyhill as the new manager was effective under ... the operating agreement to accomplish the election of Broyhill as the new manager, effective at least as of the date the document was signed. Such action, of course, does not deprive the DeLucas' bankruptcy estate of the economic interest — the right to share in profits, losses, and distributions — the DeLucas have as a result of their 42.5% membership interest.... Section 13.1-1041, Va.Code Ann., gives ... a creditor the right to obtain a charging order against the member's interest in the company. Such an order confers on the creditor the rights of an assignee of the member's interest, which includes, the right "to receive ... any share of profits and distributions to which the assignor would be entitled." Thus, the DeLucas' bankruptcy estate will be entitled to any distributions due on account of the DeLucas' membership interest.

....

Conclusion

For the foregoing reasons ... the court determines (1) that the DeLucas were properly removed as the managers of D & B Countryside prior to the filing of their chapter 11 petition and (2) that Broyhill was, subsequent to the DeLucas' chapter 11 filing, properly elected as the successor manager. A separate judgment will be entered consistent with this opinion.

———

Should the limited liability company make limited partnerships obsolete?

D. LIMITED LIABILITY PARTNERSHIPS

Although limited liability partnerships are children of the 1990's, their development is reminiscent of the advent of professional corporations in the 1960's. Professional corporations developed so that licensed professionals could take advantage of certain tax code provisions that gave favorable treatment to companies organized as corporations. Then, as now, in many states professionals could not organize as a limited liability business. A parallel movement has occurred in the 1990's, except that now individual tax rates are lower than corporate rates, and taxation as a partnership has become very attractive. The limited liability company was the first new form to respond to these changes. In many states, however, licensed professionals may not use this form because of the broad grant of limited liability. These professionals turned to state legislatures to provide them with some measure of protection from the wrongful acts of their partners, particularly malpractice or other similar misconduct. (In the 1980's several large law firms and their partners declared bankruptcy as a result of their inability to pay for the misconduct of a partner responsible for an exceptionally large transaction.) The result was the limited liability partnership.

The statutes vary in the scope of their grant of limited liability. Typically, partners remain liable for their own wrongdoing or negligence, and, in some cases, for that of persons under their supervision, but generally partners are shielded from liability for other partners' torts. In some statutes, partners may also be liable for partnership obligations, including contractual obligations, claims arising in the ordinary course of business and other claims of third parties not coming within the type of conduct for which protection is afforded. In other statutes, the extent of protection is much broader, approximating the broad grant of limited liability afforded shareholders. It is interesting to note that many states do not impose restrictions on limited liability partnership distributions. A few states do, however, require a minimum amount of liability insurance.

In most states, the limited liability partnership is not a separate business form but an option included in the general partnership statutes. General partnerships desiring limited liability typically must file with the secretary of state. They must also usually adopt a business name including LLP or a comparable designation indicating the company is a limited liability partnership. In some states, the general partners of a limited partnership may become a limited liability partnership, thus providing limited liability to the general as well as limited partners. The result is called a limited liability limited partnership. Limited liability partnerships, like most other unincorporated businesses, may elect either the partnership or corporate form of taxation.

Chapter 3

INCORPORATION

Situation

a. One week after your last meeting with your clients, and before you have been able to proceed further than helping them decide on incorporation, you receive an agitated phone call from Anderson. He tells you that two weeks ago, after reaching a "solid" agreement with Baker that they should go into business together, he entered into a one year lease with Southhold Properties, Inc. He signed in the name of "Biologistics Corporation" and purported to commit that corporation to pay $ 20,000 annual rent, for space in a building recently erected in an industrial park. He does not recall informing Baker of the details of the signing, but says, "She knows I did something about getting a place to set up shop, and it's O.K. by her." He is certain that Phillips knows nothing about the transaction. He said that at the time he entered into the lease, he guessed they would want to form a corporation and felt he needed to finalize the lease since someone else was interested in the space.

His call has been prompted by a recent confrontation with Southhold's rental manager, who accidentally learned of the non-existence of Biologistics Corporation. Anderson is not sure what Southhold's position ultimately is going to be, but he is concerned about the legality of the lease, which he says the enterprise needs, and also about his own possible liability.

b. After you resolve the problems relating to the Southhold lease, your clients want you to proceed as quickly as possible to form their corporation. Discussion has revealed the following:

1. If possible, your clients would like to have their organization called Biologistics, Inc.

2. They have definitely decided that Anderson, Baker, and Phillips should be on the board of directors. Baker thinks it would be a good idea to add one additional director. She proposes Professor Herbert Li, a nationally-known expert on DNA who teaches at the local university. Anderson thinks the selection would be good from the point of view of publicity, but fears dilution of his share of control over the enterprise.

3. At least in the next several years, your clients expect their corporation to have an office or laboratory only in the state where your firm has its offices. They are hoping, however, to develop a nationwide reputation and have definite plans to sell out of state.

4. Your clients want to insure that their corporation will be fully authorized to synthesize and sell DNA and to develop and exploit the DNA manipulation

147

process on which they expect to work. Baker has also pointed out that, as time goes by, they may wish to branch into related areas.

5. Anderson has heard that there might be benefits from incorporating in Delaware.

c. If your clients decide they want to incorporate in Delaware or another state where you are not licensed, may you represent them? May/should an attorney act as the incorporator? The secretary of the corporation? A member of the board of directors? (*See* Model Rule 1.7)

SECTION I. PROMOTERS' CONTRACTS

The term "promoter" is a term of art applied to persons who organize a business. They are the entrepreneurs responsible for bringing together all of the components required to transform a business opportunity into a business operation. To accomplish this result, they coordinate and complete several types of activities. They organize the business aspects of the company, such as finding investors, arranging for office space, hiring employees, purchasing capital equipment and the like, many of which involve entering into contracts. At the same time, they plan the business organization's legal structure, and have the necessary documents prepared and filed. When the company being formed is a limited liability firm, like a corporation, the interrelationships among these activities are more complicated than is the case with the formation of a sole proprietorship or general partnership. The reasons are that limited liability businesses do not legally exist until all statutory formalities have been completed, and the persons organizing the business do not expect to be personally liable for the company's obligations. Consequently, contractual obligations are often undertaken on behalf of the company to be formed, rather than by the promoters themselves.

There are many ways these contracts can be handled, some of which may have results that are not intended or desired by those who make the contracts. The rules relating to these contracts are part of the common-law doctrine of promoters' contracts, and questions relating to them can most helpfully be divided into two categories. The first category is the rights and liabilities of corporations on promoters' contracts, and the second is the rights and liabilities of promoters on promoters' contracts. These two categories will be taken up in separate sections of this chapter.

A. LIABILITIES OF CORPORATIONS ON PROMOTERS' CONTRACTS

The legal difficulties surrounding promoters' contracts stem from two circumstances. One is that although the promoter enters into the contract, all parties expect that the corporation to be formed will be responsible for contract performance. Thus, at the time of contracting, the promoter acts on behalf of a nonexistent principal. The second is that once formed, the corporation may accept or reject the contract. Consequently, no matter what a contract by its terms provides about the liabilities of a corporation that is not yet formed, the corporation is not bound by the contract unless after it is formed it takes some action to make the contract its own or takes some action that will cause a court to estop the corporation from denying that it is bound by the contract.

Ratification

The doctrine of ratification is so generally useful in the corporate context that when faced with the problem of how to make a promoter's contract a corporation's own, lawyers often think first of having the corporation ratify the acts of a promoter in making the contract. Ratification is accomplished formally when the board of directors adopts a resolution saying that the acts of the promoter in executing and delivering the contract are ratified. The problem with ratification, however, is that it relates back to the point in time when the action that is being ratified occurred. That is, the effect of ratification is retroactively to authorize whatever act is being ratified, as of the time of the act. Since, in the case of a promoter's contract, no corporation was in existence at the time the promoter executed and delivered the contract, ratification is a logical impossibility.

Adoption

In the case of promoters' contracts, the way for a corporation to bind itself to the contract is by adoption, which works in much the same way as ratification, except that adoption does not have retroactive effect. A corporation may adopt a contract in one of two ways, formally or informally. For a formal adoption, the board of directors passes a resolution stating that it adopts the contract. This is the safest course if a corporation has any question about the desire of the party on the other side of the contract to go through with the contract. Usually, however, adoption is informal, with the typical adoption scenario seeing the newly formed corporation performing obligations under the contract with knowledge of the contract's terms.

The following case discusses ratification and adoption.

McARTHUR v. TIMES PRINTING CO.

Supreme Court of Minnesota
51 N.W. 216 (1892)

MITCHELL, J.

The complaint alleges that about October 1, 1889, the defendant contracted with plaintiff for his services as advertising solicitor for one year; that in April, 1890, it discharged him, in violation of the contract. The action is to recover damages for the breach of the contract. The answer sets up two defenses: (1) That plaintiff's employment was not for any stated time, but only from week to week; (2) that he was discharged for good cause. Upon the trial there was evidence reasonably tending to prove that in September, 1889, one C. A. Nimocks and others were engaged as promoters in procuring the organization of the defendant company to publish a newspaper; that, about September 12th, Nimocks, as such promoter, made a contract with plaintiff, in behalf of the contemplated company, for his services as advertising solicitor for the period of one year from and after October 1st, — the date at which it was expected that the company would be organized; that the corporation was not, in fact, organized until October 16th, but that the publication of the paper was commenced by the promoters October 1st, at which date plaintiff, in pursuance of his arrangement with Nimocks, entered upon the discharge of his duties as advertising solicitor for the paper; that after the organization of the company he continued in its employment in the same capacity until discharged the following April; that defendant's board of directors never took any formal action with reference to the contract made in its behalf by Nimocks, but all of the stockholders, directors, and officers of the corporation knew of this contract at the time of its organization, or were informed of it soon afterwards, and none of them objected to or repudiated it, but, on the contrary, retained plaintiff in the employment of the company without any other or new contract as to his services.

There is a line of cases which hold that where a contract is made in behalf of, and for the benefit of, a projected corporation, the corporation, after its organization, cannot become a party to the contract, either by adoption or ratification of it. This, however, seems to be more a question of name than of substance; that is, whether the liability of the corporation, in such cases, is to be placed on the grounds of its adoption of the contract of its promoters, or upon some other ground, such as equitable estoppel. This court, in accordance with what we deem sound reason, as well as the weight of authority, has held that, while a corporation is not bound by engagements made on its behalf by its promoters before its organization, it may, after its organization, make such engagements its own contracts. And this it may do precisely as it might make similar original contracts; formal action of its board of directors being necessary only where it would be necessary in the case of a similar original contract. That it is not requisite that such adoption or acceptance be expressed, but it may be inferred from acts or acquiescence on part of the corporation, or its authorized agents, as any similar original contract might be shown. The right of the corporate agents to adopt an agreement originally made by promoters depends upon the purposes of the corporation and the nature of the agreement. Of course, the agreement must be one which the corporation itself could make, and one which the usual agents of the company have express or implied authority to make. That the contract in this case was of that kind is very clear; and the acts and acquiescence of the corporate officers, after the organization of the company, fully justified the jury in finding that it had adopted it as its own.

The defendant, however, claims that the contract was void under the statute of frauds, because, "by its terms, not to be performed within one year from the making thereof," which counsel assumes to be September 12th, — the date of the agreement between plaintiff and the promoter. This proceeds upon the erroneous theory that the act of the corporation, in such cases, is a ratification, which relates back to the date of the contract with the promoter, under the familiar maxim that "a subsequent ratification has a retroactive effect, and is equivalent to a prior command." But the liability of the corporation, under such circumstances, does not rest upon any principle of the law of agency, but upon the immediate and voluntary act of the company. Although the acts of a corporation with reference to the contracts made by promoters in its behalf before its organization are frequently loosely termed "ratification," yet a "ratification," properly so called, implies an existing person, on whose behalf the contract might have been made at the time. There cannot, in law, be a ratification of a contract which could not have been made binding on the ratifier at the time it was made, because the ratifier was not then in existence. What is called "adoption," in such cases, is, in legal effect, the making of a contract of the date of the adoption, and not as of some former date. The contract in this case was, therefore, not within the statute of frauds. The trial court fairly submitted to the jury all the issues of fact in this case, accompanied by instructions as to the law which were exactly in the line of the views we have expressed; and the evidence justified the verdict.

The point is made that plaintiff should have alleged that the contract was made with Nimocks, and subsequently adopted by the defendant. If we are correct in what we have said as to the legal effect of the adoption by the corporation of a contract made by a promoter in its behalf before its organization, the plaintiff properly pleaded the contract as having been made with the defendant. But we do not find that the evidence was objected to on the ground of variance between it and the complaint. The assignments of error are very numerous, but what has been already said covers all that are entitled to any special notice.

Order

Affirmed.

B. RIGHTS AND LIABILITIES OF PROMOTERS ON PROMOTERS' CONTRACTS

Promoters generally are personally liable under promoters' contracts, largely because, to be enforceable, a contract has to have at least one party on each side, and as we have just seen, a corporation cannot be bound to a contract when it is not yet in existence. In the garden-variety promoters' contract, where the promoter simply signs on behalf of the to-be-formed corporation, if the promoter were not bound by the contract, there would not be a contract. In terms of agency principles, this result is explained by the rule that if an agent purports to act for a nonexistent principal, the agent is personally bound. The general rule of promoters' liability does not always hold true, however, and whether or not a promoter is bound by a promoters' contract often turns on (1) what the parties seem to have intended and (2) how the contract is drafted.

Promoter's Liability After a Corporation's Adoption

Assume that a promoter enters into a standard promoters' contract under which he or she is bound, and assume further that the corporation that is to have the benefit of the contract is formed and adopts the contract. Is the promoter thereby released from personal liability? The promoter probably will assume so, but that is not the case. Absent a novation whereby the other contracting party releases the promoter from liability upon accepting a substituted party, the promoter will remain liable along with the now formed corporation. To guard against promoters' liability, then, either (1) language contemplating an automatic novation upon adoption of the contract by the to-be-formed corporation must be included in the contract or (2) a novation (either formal or one that can be inferred from words or actions of the other contracting party) must be effected after the to-be-formed corporation has adopted the contract.

Intent of the Parties

Care is needed in dealing with the question of intent of the parties in the context of promoters' contracts, because the question of what the parties intended needs to be approached in a special way. Suppose, as is often the case, a promoter negotiates a contract on behalf of a nonexistent corporation without telling the other party that the corporation has not yet been formed and then the promoter signs in the name of the corporation. In such a situation, the parties clearly intended that the corporation and not the promoter be bound. This situation, however, is an example of the classic, garden-variety promoters' contract that is covered by the general rule that the promoter is liable and the corporation is not. So looking for "what the parties intended" cannot be taken literally.

How a Contract Is Drafted

How a contract is drafted also significantly affects a promoter's possible liability. Any language that a court can interpret as indicating an intent that the promoter is not to be personally liable may be used by the court to relieve the promoter of liability. But unless the language is clear beyond argument, a court can be expected to be guided in its contract interpretation, subconsciously at least, by how it perceives the equities of the situation. That being the case, the only safe course for a promoter who wishes to escape personal liability on a standard promoters' contract is to include clear language in the contract saying explicitly that the other contracting party will look only to the to-be-formed corporation for performance. A pitfall to be avoided here, of course, is lack of consideration, so the promoter should ensure that the other party receives something in the bargain that will provide the necessary consideration.

Another possibility for a promoter is to secure a written option from the other contracting party by which the other party grants to the promoter, for the benefit of the to-be-formed corporation, an option to enter into a specified contract. This is often the most artful way to ensure that the promoter escapes personal liability while also assuring the right of the to-be-formed corporation to enter into a desired contract. As in the case of the standard promoters' contract, of course, the promoter needs to be sure that the option is supported by sufficient consideration.

SECTION II. WHERE AND HOW TO INCORPORATE

A. WHERE TO INCORPORATE

Key considerations. The decision where to incorporate involves consideration of three factors: the substantive provisions of state incorporation law; the cost of incorporating in a state other than the one where the company does business; and whether the company will be privately or publicly held. Substantive provisions of state corporate laws are a factor because the law of the state of incorporation governs the corporation's internal affairs. It also determines what options are available for the corporate governance and financial structures. Today, however, there is widespread congruence of corporation law among the various states. This congruence usually makes it easy to choose the state of incorporation. For the typical corporation, the clear choice is the state where the corporation is principally to operate. Virtually without exception, the corporation law of that state will be based on a modern enabling statute that offers any options needed for the efficient operation of a start-up corporation. Some desirable options admittedly may not be available in the home state's corporation statute, but for the start-up corporation, usually it is preferable to forgo such options rather than to incorporate in another state. This is not to say, of course, that home state incorporation is always desirable. Suppose, for example, that the proposed directors of a particular corporation live in different states, so that getting together for board meetings is impractical. In such a corporation, it is necessary to incorporate in a state that allows either telephone board meetings or written consents in lieu of board meetings.

The second consideration relates to the expense and trouble of incorporating in a state other than the one where the company does business. If a firm is incorporated in a state other than its home state, it will be treated as a corporation of the other state, and must therefore qualify to do business in its home state as a foreign corporation. It will also have to file reports and pay fees each year not only in its state of incorporation but in its home state as well. These additional costs may be strong negatives for the privately held corporation that does business in only one state.

For some corporations there will be tax savings to be had by incorporating other than in the home state. For the typical start-up corporation, the tax rates of the various states are irrelevant, since in almost all cases the corporation will pay the state's minimum tax, typically $ 100 or so. The rates become relevant, however, for corporations that expect to have their shares publicly held by a large number of shareholders, since taxes often are based on the number of shares that the corporation is authorized to issue.

Companies planning to operate in multiple states or to be publicly held usually give serious consideration to incorporating in Delaware. Delaware's corporation statute has a full range of options a particular corporation may find necessary or desirable. For example, it allows board meetings to be conducted by telephone and written consents in lieu of board meetings. It also contains a chapter addressing issues of closely held corporations. And when it comes to tax savings for corporations that are to have a large number of public shareholders, Delaware often wins out as the state of incorporation, since its corporate tax structure has been carefully designed to beat the competition. For the corporation that does business in many states, Delaware also is often the state of choice for incorporation because of its judiciary, which is highly competent in corporation law, and its large and well developed body of existing corporate case law, which sometimes adds a legal certainty that may be lacking in other states. For such corporations, which already have to stand the expense and trouble of qualifying to do business in many states, the possible extra expense of qualifying in the corporation's home state is too small to worry about. Also, the fast and efficient service available from the Delaware Secretary of State's office adds a benefit to Delaware incorporation. Finally, the appeal to lawyers or clients of Delaware's law on one or more particular matters, such as directors' liability, may be enough to make them settle on Delaware incorporation.

Implications of state competition for corporate charters.

Roberta Romano, The Genius of American Corporate Law 6, 8-9, 14 (1993)*

Approximately one-half of the largest industrial firms are incorporated in Delaware, and of the corporations listed on national exchanges, more are incorporated in Delaware than in any other state. Moreover, the vast majority of reincorporating firms move to Delaware. As a result, a substantial portion of the state's tax revenue — averaging more than 15 percent from 1960 to 1990 — is derived from incorporation fees. While the absolute dollars raised from franchise fees in large commercial states are greater than in Delaware, the amount is an infinitesimal proportion of their total tax revenue.... Delaware's dominance is a stable and persistent phenomenon: it has been the leading incorporation state since the 1920s.

The dynamic business environment in which firms operate places a premium on a state's responsiveness to corporations' legislative demands, that is, on a state's ability to adapt its corporation code to changing business circumstances. It also places a premium on a decentralized regime: the trial-and-error process of interjurisdictional competition enables a more accurate identification of optimal corporate arrangements when there is fluidity in business conditions. Delaware excels in both dimensions. It has consistently been the most responsive state: if Delaware is not the pioneer for a corporate law innovation, it is among the first to imitate.

....

The extraordinary success of tiny Delaware in the corporate charter market due to its responsiveness to changing corporate demands is the source, then, of a recurrent corporate law debate on the efficacy of federalism. Who benefits from the laws produced in a federal system, and, in particular, from Delaware's corporation code: managers, who select the state of incorporation, or shareholders, who ratify that selection? Does state competition produce corporation codes that mitigate the agency problem or exacerbate it? If state codes favor managers over shareholders, then from the objective of corporate law itself, the output of state competition is undesirable. Whether the current allocation of authority between the state governments and the national government should be maintained under such circumstances depends on whether the outcome would differ under a national corporation code.

....

The classic positions in the modern debate on whether state corporation codes benefit shareholders were formulated in the 1970s by William Cary, professor at Columbia Law School and former commissioner of the Securities and Exchange Commission, and Ralph Winter, professor at Yale Law School (currently a federal appeals court judge). Cary contended that Delaware's heavy reliance on incorporation fees for revenue led it to engage in a "race for the bottom" with other states to adopt laws that favor managers over shareholders. He therefore advocated national corporate law standards to end state competition. Cary's position was, for many years, the consensus view of commentators on corporate law, and his agenda still attracts support.

....

Winter identified a crucial flaw in Cary's analysis, which, when corrected, suggested that the race was more to the top than the bottom: Cary had overlooked the many markets in which firms operate — the capital, product, and corporate control markets — and that constrain managers from choosing a legal regime detrimental to the shareholders' interest. While agreeing with Cary's characterization of the power of competition in producing laws that firms demand, Winter's important point was that firms operating under a legal regime that did not maximize firm value would be outperformed by firms operating under a legal regime that did and the former would therefore have lower stock prices. A lower stock price could subject a firm's managers to either employment termination, as the firm is driven out of business because of a higher cost of capital than that of competitors operating under a value-maximizing regime, or replacement by a successful takeover bidder that could increase a firm's value by reincorporating (the term of art for a change in statutory domicile). Winter concluded that this threat of job displacement would lead managers to demand a value-maximizing regime for their shareholders and that states would provide it, as such a strategy maintains, if not enhances, a state's incorporation business. Winter's critique forced adherents of the Cary position to amend it. The contention became that markets are imperfect constraints on managers and, hence, there is sufficient slack in the system to produce non-value-maximizing state laws.

In both the Cary and the Winter positions, the goal of maximizing revenues functions as an invisible hand guiding the decentralized system of state corporation laws to codify the arrangements that firms desire. The crux of their disagreement concerns whose demand schedule for corporate charters is driving the system. Cary and the proponents of a national corporation code consider the demand function to be derived from managers' preferences. They view the state legislative process as a political market failure in which managers are better organized than the more numerous but dispersed shareholders, and they characterize managers' preferences for codes as diametrically opposed to those of shareholders'. Winter and advocates of state chartering conclude that shareholders' preferences determine firms' demand because of the constraining influence on managers of the many markets in which firms operate, which reduces or eliminates the agency problem. They further maintain that even if there is slack in the system, ... it does not follow that national legislation would do a better job than state competition at mitigating the agency problem. Of course, in the absence of conflict between shareholder and manager preferences, the debate is moot, since the substantive content of state laws would be invariant with whoever, managers or shareholders, makes the incorporation decision or lobbies state legislators. The choice of incorporation state would therefore automatically enhance the value of the firm and, accordingly, shareholder wealth.

B. HOW TO INCORPORATE

The actual process of incorporating a business is not difficult, provided it is preceded by careful planning and attention to detail. One temptation attorneys should resist is the unexamined use of pre-printed, standardized documents. If used, these documents should be carefully reviewed and modified to fit the needs of the particular corporation in question. Corporate attorneys should also develop checklists of the matters that need to be completed for a successful incorporation. The excerpt that follows raise some of the issues that incorporation involves.

Chester Rohrlich, Organizing Corporate and Other Business Enterprises 6-1 — 6-3 (5th ed. 1990)*

§ 6.01 INTRODUCTION [to Incorporation Procedure and Charter Provisions]

The mechanics of incorporating a business are largely routine. Forms, readily available from both public and private sources, provide the basic documents for

---

incorporation. There are several useful guides to procedure. For fees, lawyers can even take advantage of the several corporation service companies, which furnish incorporators and inspectors of election, file papers, act as resident agents, maintain statutory principal offices, and conduct annual stockholders' meetings.

Nonetheless, routine can lead to dangerous oversight. While a lawyer must take advantage of the aids available, he or she may soon regret their complacent use, especially when dealing in an unfamiliar jurisdiction selected for other reasons. This chapter discusses the basic procedural elements that should always be checked in a new incorporation.

§ 6.02 INCORPORATION PROCEDURE

Subject to variations required by local statutes, the usual routine followed in incorporating a company, once the state of incorporation is selected, is as follows:

(1) Arrive at general agreement among principals as to nature and scope of business and broad outline of capitalization and of distribution of securities.

(2) Select and clear the corporate name. Many delays are encountered in submitting certificates of incorporation with corporate names that are not available. This loss of time can be avoided by prior inquiry of the secretary of state. All will advise as to the availability of a given corporate name. In some states, it is possible to reserve an available name for a short period to enable the certificate to be prepared and filed. In ... states where an intended corporate name cannot be used, usually because it is deceptively similar to another, it may be possible to use a fictitious or assumed name.

(3) A few states require publication of intention to incorporate.

(4) The articles of incorporation are filed with the appropriate state official (secretary of state) and [in some states] with the appropriate local office (ordinarily the county clerk or recorder) in the county where the registered office of the corporation is located.

....

(6) A few states require publication of the articles or a notice of incorporation.

....

§ 6.03 CERTIFICATE OF INCORPORATION

Generally

The certificate of incorporation [or, in some states, the articles of incorporation] must comply with the corporation statute in the jurisdiction of incorporation. In general, this means that the certificate will be made by one or more persons that meet certain qualifications. The certificate will specify:

(1) The name of the corporation.

(2) The objects or purposes of the corporation and certain powers.

(3) The city, incorporated village, or town, and the county within the state, in which the office of the corporation will be located.

(4) The capital stock of the corporation, stated not only as to amount and class, but specifying all the rights and privileges of each class.

(5) Designation of the secretary of state as agent of the corporation upon whom process may be served and the post office address to which the secretary of state shall mail a copy of any process served upon him.

(6) The name and address of the resident agent, if the corporation is to have one.

(7) Special provisions permitted, but not required, by the statute.

Not all of the foregoing are required in every state. Some of the statutory requirements are so simple and direct as to leave no room for discretion. Other portions of the certificate, such as those dealing with capitalization, leave room for a very wide exercise of discretion .... It is generally advisable, however, to make provision in the certificate for the problems that the corporation may face in the future rather than to wait until action must be taken, perhaps, by feuding shareholders....

Model Act §§ 2.01 through 2.04 define the necessary steps for preparing and filing the articles of incorporation, and the substantive requirements for the contents of the articles. These sections are supplemented by §§ 1.20 through 1.26, which prescribe the standards for the form of the documents, such as that the documents must be typewritten or printed. According to § 2.02, the articles of incorporation at a minimum must include the corporate name, the number of authorized shares, the name and address of the registered agent, and the name and address of each incorporator. Corporations formed under the act automatically have perpetual duration, the purpose of engaging in any lawful business as provided in § 3.01(a), and a grant of limited liability to shareholders. These attributes may be modified in the articles of incorporation. The articles may also contain optional provisions concerning management structure, the use of par value for shares, limitations on director liability, and indemnification of directors. Corporate existence begins when the articles of incorporation are filed by the Secretary of State.

C. PREINCORPORATION AGREEMENTS

Attorneys often have their clients enter into preincorporation agreements spelling out the important terms and arrangements the parties have agreed to. Section 7.32 of the Model Act authorizes these agreements and gives the parties wide latitude concerning the content of these agreements. The following excerpt discusses some factors in the decision whether or not to prepare a preincorporation agreement.

1 F. Hodge O'Neal & Robert B. Thompson, O'Neal's Close Corporations Ch. 2, pp. 124-26 (3d ed. 1996)*

Need for a Preincorporation Agreement

Closely held enterprises are often organized and incorporated pursuant to informal arrangements among the prospective participants, the business bargain never being reduced to writing in the form of a preincorporation agreement. A corporation can be organized within a few days in most jurisdictions, and the participants generally can be depended on to adhere to their bargain for that period of time....

Not uncommonly, however, the possibility of disputes and litigation can be minimized by embodying the business bargain in a carefully drafted written instrument. All too often the business bargain that is not reduced to writing is little more than a vague understanding; and, where the bargain is complicated, doubt can well exist whether the participants really think the agreement through and perceive all of its ramifications until they have had it reduced to writing, examined it carefully, and caused it to be redrafted several times. But passing by the point that the drafting of a preincorporation agreement may be worthwhile just to clarify the thinking of the participants, a preincorporation agreement is usually desirable in the following circumstances:

(1) Where organization of the corporation will require a considerable period of time. In a few states, those for instance that require publication of incorporation papers or of synopses thereof, organization can be a rather slow process; and even in jurisdictions in which corporations normally can be organized expeditiously, delays can occur, perhaps delays that were entirely unanticipated, say an objection by the Secretary of State or other filing official to a key clause in the charter.

(2) Where the business bargain contemplates extensive financial commitments in advance of incorporation.

(3) Where the participants want to bind one or more of their number to commitments for possible future financing....

(4) Where one or more of the participants has been induced to engage in the enterprise by considerations other than the prospect of obtaining shares in the projected corporation. A typical inducement to a participant in a closely held enterprise is a promise by his associates that he will be employed by the corporation after it is organized.

---

(5) Where the participants plan to place restrictions on the transferability of stock in the projected corporation. The participants commonly want such restrictions in a close corporation.

(6) Where important parts of the business bargain will not (in the absence of a preincorporation agreement) be covered in writing even after the charter has been executed and the bylaws have been adopted.

A preincorporation agreement may have the limited objective of binding the participants to create and organize the enterprise according to promotion plans. It may simply set forth the state of incorporation; the money and property each participant is to contribute; the stock and other securities that are to be issued to each participant; and the principal terms to be included in the charter and bylaws. This type of preincorporation agreement is frequently referred to as a "promoters' contract." Note that it ceases to serve a purpose and becomes defunct as soon as the corporation is fully organized.

Persons contemplating the organization of a close corporation often have interests which are not protected by a simple promoters' contract. They need an agreement that will regulate the internal operations of the corporation after it has been formed and will govern the relations of the participants after they become shareholders. The agreement might cover such matters as the following: (1) variations from the traditional pattern of corporation management, such as the granting of a power to veto corporate decisions to some or all of the participants; (2) arrangements among the participants for the corporation to employ one or more of them; (3) undertakings by the participants or some of them not to acquire an interest in or participate in any way in a competing enterprise; (4) restrictions on the transferability of the corporation's stock; (5) the disposition of stock of a shareholder who dies or becomes disabled; (6) arrangements for the purchase of business insurance by the corporation or the participants; (7) undertakings by one or more of the participants to keep the others fully informed of transactions relating to the business or affecting the value of stock in the corporation; (8) provisions for arbitration or some other method of settling disputes among participants; and possibly (9) commitments for future financing. An agreement containing matters of this kind is usually referred to as a "shareholders' agreement."

Shareholders often make contracts covering matters of this kind long after the formation of the corporation. Preferably, however, the participants should come to a clear and firm agreement on these questions before incorporation. One reason is that some of the items in the agreement, if they are to be consummated properly, call for the drafting of provisions to be included in the charter and bylaws.

After the corporation is organized, the participants should cause it formally to approve and become a party to any shareholders' agreement they have made, particularly if the agreement purports to obligate the corporation in any way. The lawyer should also insert a provision in the agreement making it binding on the legal representatives of the parties to it, and he should instruct the parties to include in their wills a clause directing their executors to carry out the agreement.

D. THE PURPOSES AND POWERS CLAUSES

The purposes clause of the corporate charter designates the type(s) of business which the company may conduct. At one time, the purposes clause of corporate charters included information about the type of business conducted by the company, such as the computer software business. The designation of corporate purpose was intended to "(1) [set] the bounds of the enterprise in which the participants are making their investment; (2) ... [authorize] the directors and officers to enter into transactions and engage in activities calculated to attain the stated purposes; and (3) ... [limit] the authority of the directors and officers by impliedly excluding activities that [did] not tend to achieve those purposes."[1] Today, a stated purpose of engaging in any lawful business will satisfy the charter requirements in most states. The Model Act does not require a purposes statement in the charter. Section 3.01 provides a default purposes clause by stating that "Every corporation incorporated under this Act has the purpose of engaging in any lawful business unless a more limited purpose is set forth in the articles of incorporation."

Charter requirements concerning corporate powers have developed in a similar fashion. At one time, corporate charters were required to include a statement of powers, the types of acts a corporation could engage in to achieve its purpose. Today, statements of corporate powers are typically not required. Section 3.02 of the Model Act provides that every corporation organized under the Act "has the same powers as an individual to do all things necessary or convenient to carry out its business and affairs...." It includes a nonexclusive list of powers such as to sue and be sued in the corporate name, to acquire and convey real and personal property, to enter into contracts, to lend and borrow money, and the like.

At one time, corporate operations were limited to the confines established in the purpose clause of its charter. Anything else was *ultra vires*, or beyond the power conferred upon the corporation by the state, and could potentially be set aside as a result of successful challenges by persons conducting business with the corporation. Today, little remains of the *ultra vires* doctrine. Corporate charter purposes clauses are broad and generic; powers clauses afford corporations powers like those of natural persons. Section 3.04 of the Model Act limits challenges to corporate action based on lack of power to proceedings brought by shareholders of the corporation, by the corporation itself, or by the Attorney General.

---

[1] 1 F. Hodge O'Neal & Robert B. Thompson, O'Neal's Close Corporations Ch.3, pp. 13-14 (3d ed. 1996).

Chapter 4

CAPITALIZATION

You have been asked to work out the details of the capitalization of Biologistics, Inc. Anderson, Baker and Phillips are to share equally in the corporation's long-term profits, and are to have equal power as shareholders in corporate decisionmaking. Baker has agreed to contribute $ 30,000 and a fairly extensive list of prospective customers. Anderson has agreed to contribute $ 45,000, and it is understood that he has already performed valuable promotional services. Phillips has agreed to contribute $ 75,000 and to guarantee bank loans of up to $ 200,000, so long as Anderson and Baker also sign any guaranty. Baker's mother-in-law has decided not to invest in the business. The probable need to raise additional money to support research and development has been noted by each of your clients, and they have asked you to take this into account when advising them on how to capitalize.

Anderson and Baker are well aware that their financial resources are more limited than those of Phillips. They would like to take whatever steps are possible to insure that if the corporation wishes to sell additional stock in the future, they will have an opportunity to buy a *pro rata* share, and that if they do not have the funds to do so, neither Phillips nor anyone else will be able to do so either without their consent.

SECTION I. SOME CAPITALIZATION BASICS

Students without any business background often have initial problems with capitalization. There seem to be two reasons for this. First, many of the terms are new. Although the concepts to which they relate are quite simple, the concepts obviously cannot be understood by a student who has not been given the necessary vocabulary. Second, students sometimes expect more complexity than in fact exists. That is, they may in fact understand a concept but feel a sense of unease because they do not realize how well they understand it. Some of the matters discussed in this Chapter are introduced in Appendix B (Reading Financial Statements). Appendix B should be read or reviewed at this point. For students without a business background, Appendix B will provide all the help that is needed. Beyond this, the following discussion should help provide the necessary familiarity with terms and concepts. Perhaps it also will dispel ideas about the amount or depth of complexity involved here.

Basically, a corporation's capitalization (which we can take roughly to mean the cash or other assets put into the corporation on a long-term basis) consists of equity and, if desired, debt. With respect to the initial capitalization of a new corporation, the equity capitalization will be the cash or other assets contributed by shareholders in exchange for stock. "Equity," then, is an ownership interest in the corporation. Equity owners have a residual interest in the assets of the corporation. Their claims are paid on liquidation only after all superior claims are satisfied. "Debt," of course, is cash or other assets that are borrowed. Nothing prevents a person from contributing some capital as equity and some as debt, making the person both a shareholder and a creditor. In fact, for reasons that will be discussed below, that is often done.

A. EQUITY

1. Types of Equity Securities — Traditional Designations and the Model Act Approach

Common Stock: Equity is represented by some form of security, typically stock of one type or another. Modern corporation statutes allow great flexibility in devising forms of stock, but in most cases corporations will start out simply with common stock. In that situation, the holders of the common stock will be the only owners of the corporation, and they generally will share among themselves, in proportion to the number of shares they own, all the rights shareholders have in a corporation. Chief among those are a right to vote on certain matters, a right to the corporation's profits, and a right to the corporation's assets if the corporation is liquidated. Sometimes corporations establish more than one class of common stock, so as to distribute the traditional rights of common shareholders in some way other than equally to all common shareholders. For example, a corporation might have two classes of common stock, one of which carries the right to vote for directors and the other of which does not.

Preferred Stock: Some corporations have preferred stock in addition to common stock. Preferred stock virtually always will be preferred (have priority) over the common stock as to the shareholders' right to receive assets if the corporation is dissolved. Almost as often it will carry with it the preferred shareholders' right to receive a portion of the corporation's profits, in the form of a dividend, before the common shareholders receive a dividend. Almost always, however, the preferred shareholders' call on the corporation's profits will be limited to stated amounts. That is, preferred shareholders do not typically share in the corporation's successes beyond an agreed level. A particular preferred stock, for example, may have a per share preference as to dividends of ten dollars per year. No matter how successful the corporation becomes, an annual payment of ten dollars per share is all the dividend a holder of that stock will ever receive.

Preferred stock dividends usually are made cumulative, which means that no dividends may be paid to the common shareholders until all dividends that should have been paid to the preferred shareholders have been paid. Typically, preferred shareholders do not have a right to vote on most matters that are submitted for a shareholders' vote. If, however, preferred stock dividends are not paid for a stated period, often twelve months, many corporations give their preferred shareholders the right to elect some or all of the corporation's directors until all dividends in arrears are paid. Unlike the typical common stock, preferred stock usually is callable or redeemable at the option of the corporation. That is, the board of directors usually is able to require the preferred shareholders to sell their shares to the corporation upon the payment to them of an amount of cash that is stated in the charter. In the usual case, that amount is equal to the original purchase price of the stock plus one year's dividends. As may be apparent from this discussion, although preferred stock is technically an equity security, in practical terms it usually seems closer to debt than it does to common stock. In order to give preferred shareholders the best features of both equity and debt, however, preferred stock sometimes is made convertible into common stock upon terms specified in the charter.

Model Act: The Model Act does not use the terms "common" and "preferred" to describe types of shares, although §§ 6.01(a) and (c) expressly permit a corporation to have classes of shares that differ based on preferences, limitations and relative rights. Section 6.01(b), however, requires the articles of incorporation to authorize "(1) one or more classes of shares that together have unlimited voting rights, and (2) one or more classes of shares (which may be the same class or classes as those with voting rights) that together are entitled to receive the net assets of the corporation upon dissolution." Section 6.01(c) (2) authorizes the issuance of shares that may be redeemed at the option of either the corporation, the shareholder or a third person (such as the holder of another class of security in the same corporation) or upon the occurrence of a predetermined event.

Warrants and Rights: According to Professor Hamilton:

Warrants are transferable long-term options to acquire shares from the corporation at a specified price (that is usually fixed for the life of the warrant). Warrants have many of the qualities of an equity security since their price is a function of the market price of the underlying shares and the specified issuance price. Of course, warrants have no dividend rights while the underlying shares normally do receive some dividend. Warrants frequently are issued as a sweetener in connection with the distribution of a debt or preferred stock issue: They may be issued in connection with a public exchange offer, or as compensation for handling the public distribution of other shares. Sometimes, they are issued in a reorganization to a holder of a class of security not otherwise recognized in the reorganization.

Warrants issued by a number of corporations are traded on the New York Stock Exchange or other exchanges.

Rights are short term warrants, expiring within one year. They may also be publicly traded and listed on securities exchanges. Rights are often issued in lieu of a dividend, or in an effort to raise capital from an existing shareholder....*

2. Issuing Equity Securities

a. Par Value

Under many modern corporation statutes, any form of stock may have a "par value" stated in the corporation's charter, or the charter may state that the stock is without par value. The concept of par value often is baffling to the uninitiated. A common problem is the belief that there must be more substance to the concept than there is. In fact, there is very little to the concept of par value. The best way to view par value is as a dollar figure specified in the charter, from which certain well-defined consequences flow. Once one understands those consequences, one understands par value. We would be getting ahead of ourselves if we go too deeply into that, but here is a short introduction to the three main consequences. The consequences apply in jurisdictions whose corporate statutes are based on the concept of par.

First, stock typically cannot be issued by the corporation for less than par value. Second, when par value shares are issued by the corporation, a dollar figure equal to the par value is shown on the corporation's books as stated capital and in many states there are limitations, spelled out in the corporation statute, about what can be done with stated capital. No dividends, for example, may be paid out of it. Third, fees and taxes payable to the state of incorporation often are based on par value. A typical arrangement sets fees or taxes as a percentage of a number that is derived by multiplying par value by the number of shares authorized in the corporation's charter. Here an interesting twist is that stock without par value typically is taxed as if it had relatively high par value, such as $ 100 per share, thus making stock without par value an unpopular choice in states, such as Delaware, that follow that practice. As a result of one or more of these consequences of par value, in the case of common stock, corporations typically either choose no par value stock (in situations where there are no unfavorable tax consequences) or they choose to set par at a small fraction of the proposed selling price of the stock. One dollar par value is perhaps most usual. Largely for reasons of tradition, corporations typically set the par value of preferred stock at or near its selling price, which often is $ 100 per share.

Model Act § 6.21 significantly changed the financial provisions of corporate codes by adopting a legal capital structure that is not based on the concepts of par

---

*Reprinted with permission. Robert W. Hamilton, Fundamentals of Modern Business 360 (1989). Copyright © 1989 by Little Brown and Company. All rights reserved.

value and stated capital. The Comment to the section explains the nature of the changes and the reasons for them:

> The financial provisions of the Model Act reflect a modernization of the concepts underlying the capital structure and limitations on distributions of corporations. This process of modernization began with amendments in 1980 to the 1969 Model Act that eliminated the concepts of "par value" and "stated capital," and further modernization occurred in connection with the development of the revised Act in 1984. Practitioners and legal scholars have long recognized that the statutory structure embodying "par value" and "legal capital" concepts is not only complex and confusing, but also fails to serve the original purpose of protecting creditor and senior security holders from payments to junior security holders. Indeed, to the extent security holders are led to believe that it provides this protection, these provisions may be affirmatively misleading. The Model Act has therefore eliminated these concepts entirely and substituted a simpler and more flexible structure that provides more realistic protection to these interests....

A company may, however, continue to use the par and no par stock designations if it wishes. Section 2.02(b)(iv) of the Model Act (1984) permits the articles of incorporation to include "a par value for authorized shares or classes of shares."

The Comment to § 6.21 also distinguishes between corporate law mandates and principles of accountancy. It further provides that:

> Bookkeeping details are not the statutory responsibility of the board of directors. The statute also does not require the board of directors to determine the corresponding entry on the right-hand side of the balance sheet under owner's equity to be designated as 'stated capital' or be allocated among 'stated capital' and other surplus accounts. The corporation, however, may determine that the shareholders' equity account should be divided into these traditional categories if it wishes.

The Model Act does not make clear what consequences will follow if a corporation elects to assign par value to the shares it issues. Section 6.21 controls whether a corporation may make distributions to its shareholders. The Official Comment to § 6.21 suggests that the board may also use the traditional designations of stated capital and capital surplus if it wishes. It is unclear the extent to which these designations may be used to restrict the board's ability to make distributions to shareholders if the distributions were otherwise permissible under § 6.21.

b. Mechanics of Equity Capitalization

The best way to learn more about capitalization is to go through the mechanics involved in a corporation's equity capitalization. The starting point is a corporation statute, and here we shall use both the Delaware General Corporation Law and the Model Act as representative examples of two approaches to capitalization.

Section 102(a)(4) of the Delaware code provides that a corporation has authority to issue the number of shares that are stated in its charter, and that those shares may be divided into classes if the corporation so desires. That section also provides that the corporation must state in its charter the par value of its shares, or state that the shares are without par value.

As would be expected, § 153 of the Delaware code provides two separate rules for the consideration that a corporation must charge for its shares upon their original sale (called an "issuance") by the corporation, one rule for par value shares and the other for shares without par value. In each case, the consideration is to be that set by the board of directors. For par value shares, the board may not set the consideration at less than par value. For shares without par value, the consideration may not be less than a stated value established by the board of directors.

Section 152 needs to be read along with § 153, because it specifies what kind of consideration is allowable in payment for the issuance of shares. Basically, under § 152 the consideration must be paid in money, in property, or in labor or services actually performed for the corporation. If the stock is to be issued for an amount greater than its par or stated value, and if an amount equal to par or stated value has been paid in one of the forms of consideration just described, the corporation may accept a binding obligation of the purchaser to pay the remaining amount. No matter what form of consideration is accepted by the board, § 154 says that the board of directors must express the consideration in dollars. That allows the consideration to be entered properly in the corporation's books, which are kept in terms of dollars.

At this point it will be helpful to look at how a Delaware corporation accounts on its books for the consideration it receives upon the issuance of shares, using both par value and no par value shares as examples, and then to look at the legal consequences of that accounting. The accounting involved in our discussion will be very simple and will require no more than an understanding of how to read the most basic balance sheet.

Section 154 of the Delaware General Corporation Law provides that when a company issues shares having a par value, the amount determined to be capital must be at least equal to the aggregate par value of the outstanding shares. Thus, if a corporation issues 1,000 shares of $ 2 par value stock, capital must equal $ 2,000 ($ 2 par x 1,000 shares of stock). A corporation may issue shares for an amount greater than their par value. For example, $ 2 par stock may be issued for $ 5. In this case, the excess of the amount paid for the stock over the par value, or $ 3, will be designated as surplus. If it wishes to do so, however, the board of directors may include some or all of the excess in the capital account. For no par stock, § 154 provides that all consideration received for the issuance of shares constitutes stated capital unless the board determines that only a part of the consideration is to be stated capital. In that case, any amount the board wishes, short of all the consideration, can be designated as surplus.

It may be useful to digress briefly to review the statutory terminology and describe how the same concepts are referred to by lawyers and, as required, by accountants. The Delaware statute uses the term "capital" for par stock and "stated capital" for no par stock. Lawyers often use the term "stated capital" to refer collectively to both capital and stated capital. Under the Delaware statute, the term "surplus" includes all accounts in the equity section of the balance sheet except capital or stated capital. Lawyers and accountants distinguish among different types of surplus according to the source of the funds. The terms "earned surplus" (lawyers) and "retained earnings" (accountants) refer to company earnings that have not been distributed to shareholders as dividends. The terms "capital surplus" (lawyers) and "paid in capital in excess of par" (accountants) refer to the amount of consideration received for shares in excess of the amount of capital or stated capital. Other types of surplus will be discussed in a later chapter.

Looking at examples using lawyers' terminology will help the student understand how all of this works.

Suppose that a corporation issues 1,000 shares of one dollar par value stock for ten dollars per share. After the issuance, the corporation's balance sheet will look like this:

ASSETS		LIABILITIES	$ 0
Cash	$ 10,000	SHAREHOLDERS' EQUITY	
		Stated Capital	$ 1,000
		Capital Surplus	9,000
			$10,000
		TOTAL LIABILITIES	
TOTAL ASSETS	$ 10,000	AND EQUITY	$10,000

In the case of no par value stock the balance sheet would show $ 10,000 in stated capital unless the board of directors decided to place some portion of the consideration in capital surplus.

Suppose that the corporation then invested its $ 10,000 in some venture that returned $ 15,000 on the investment, thereby producing earnings of $ 5,000. The $ 5,000 earnings would be recorded as earned surplus. Taking into account the results of that investment, the corporation's balance sheet will look like this in the case of one dollar par value stock:

ASSETS		LIABILITIES	$ 0
Cash	$ 15,000	SHAREHOLDERS' EQUITY	
		Stated Capital	$ 1,000
		Capital Surplus	9,000
		Earned Surplus	5,000
		TOTAL EQUITY	$15,000
		TOTAL LIABILITIES	
TOTAL ASSETS	$ 15,000	AND EQUITY	$15,000

That is about all there is to the basic mechanics of equity capitalization, except that at this point we have not said anything about what difference it makes whether a particular amount appears in stated capital, capital surplus, or earned surplus. Understanding that requires a brief discussion of cash dividends. (Stock dividends are discussed in a later chapter.) In modern parlance, a cash dividend is a payment to shareholders constituting a return on their investment. According to § 170 of the Delaware code, dividends may be paid from surplus or from current profits, but not from a capital account. The account a particular amount appears in, therefore, determines whether that amount is available for the payment of dividends.

In Delaware, dividends may be paid from either the earned surplus or capital surplus accounts. These accounts indicate the source of funds used for dividends. Dividends from earned surplus constitute a payout to the shareholders of the corporation's earnings, a return *on* shareholders' investments. Distributions from capital surplus (called dividends in Delaware) generally represent a return *on* shareholders' capital rather than a payment of corporate earnings, as the usual source of capital surplus is the amount paid for shares in excess of par. Thus, distributions from capital surplus typically constitute a payback to shareholders of amounts previously invested by them in the corporation.

From the standpoint of the typical shareholder, a dividend and a distribution look very much alike. In each case, the shareholder receives a check in the amount of the per share dividend or distribution, multiplied by the number of shares owned by the shareholder. But while a dividend typically is a payout to the shareholders of a corporation's earnings, a distribution usually is a payback to shareholders of amounts previously invested by them in the corporation. (There is no provision in the Delaware code or in other corporation statutes using this approach a provision for a payback to shareholders of a corporation's stated capital.)

That is not the end of the Delaware General Corporation Law's story about the capital and surplus accounts, however, because the statute, like most others, allows certain transfers between those accounts. Under § 244, the board of directors can transfer capital surplus to stated capital, thus restricting the company's ability to make distributions. That is understandable, since the drafters of the statute had no reason to prevent a board from restricting a corporation's ability to pay dividends if the board wants to do so. However, under § 244, the directors may also transfer amounts from stated capital to capital surplus as long as the amount left in stated capital is more than equal to the total par value of the corporation's issued stock. What that comes down to is that if the board transfers an amount of capital surplus to stated capital, in the usual case the board later can transfer out of stated capital most of what the board transferred in.

Here the question may arise what happens if a corporation has a deficit in earned surplus. Suppose, in our example above, that from the corporation's investment of $ 10,000 it received only $ 5,000 in return, thus losing $ 5,000. After that loss, the corporation's balance sheet would look like this, with parentheses indicating a negative number:

ASSETS		LIABILITIES	$ 0
Cash	$ 5,000	SHAREHOLDERS' EQUITY	
		Stated Capital	$ 1,000
		Capital Surplus	9,000
		Earned Surplus	(5,000)
		TOTAL EQUITY	$ 5,000
		TOTAL LIABILITIES	
TOTAL ASSETS	$ 5,000	AND EQUITY	$ 5,000

As indicated above, if the board wishes to eliminate that earned surplus deficit, it may do so by a transfer from capital surplus. It may not, however, transfer from capital surplus any greater amount than that necessary to eliminate the deficit. If such a transfer were made, earned surplus would have a value of $ 0 and capital surplus a value of $ 4,000.

As discussed in the preceding section, the Model Act has eliminated the use of par value and the legal requirement to distinguish among capital and surplus accounts, although a company may continue with the practice if it wishes. Model Act changes to the rules governing dividends and distributions are discussed in a later chapter.

B. DEBT

1. Types of Debt

Debt capitalization involves corporate borrowing. The lender may be an independent third party or a shareholder of the corporation doing the borrowing. In all cases, the corporation promises to repay to the lender at designated times the amount borrowed (the principal) plus interest. The obligation to repay is memorialized in an agreement that contains additional terms and conditions applicable to the obligation. The most common forms of debt capitalization are short-term and long-term (one to ten years) loans from banks, private investors, or shareholders to the corporation. Such loans typically are represented by notes, which may be secured or unsecured. A note holder may be protected by contractual provisions contained in a loan agreement between the corporation and the lender.

Bonds and debentures are often encountered in larger corporations. The term "bond" is used in two different ways. It may refer generally to long-term debt instruments of ten years or more. "Bond" is also used to describe a long-term debt instrument secured by a mortgage or deed of trust on corporate property, while an unsecured long-term debt instrument usually is called a "debenture." A bond or a debenture differs from a note in that bond and debenture holders are protected by contractual provisions contained in an indenture covering a multitude of corporate financial matters. (Today, notes may also be issued subject to an indenture.) An indenture is a contract between the corporation and an indenture trustee, usually a bank, that acts for the benefit of the bond or debenture holders.

There can be many advantages to a corporation and to its shareholders in having the corporation include debt in its capital structure. From the point of view of the corporation, an important advantage of debt is that interest payments on debt are tax deductible, while payments of dividends on stock are not. If, therefore, the corporation is considering issuing either long-term notes or preferred stock, issuing notes likely will be much less expensive, largely because of the tax advantage inherent in the notes. Often shareholders wish to put into a corporation some of their total contribution as equity and some as debt, and often a prospective investor wishes to be a creditor rather than a shareholder — usually a creditor having the right to convert his or her debt into common stock if all goes well for the corporation. Of major interest to debt holders is that (1) debt may be repaid without any tax consequences, but if stock is redeemed when the corporation has had profits, the redemption may be taxed as a dividend; (2) if the corporation goes bankrupt, debt holders have prior preference, that is, the right to be repaid before any payments are made to preferred or common shareholders; and (3) if debt holders are not repaid, they can qualify for a current income tax deduction in the amount of their loss more readily than can a holder of equity who has suffered an investment loss. Largely for those reasons, owners of a corporation often wish to split their own contribution to the corporation between equity and debt, hoping to avoid some taxes if all goes well, and hoping also to salvage at least some of their investment if the corporation goes bankrupt.

During the 1980's, high-yield bonds became a popular form of security for raising new capital.

> "Junk bond" is a misleading but widely used label for high-yield bonds. The yield on such bonds is high compared with the yield on "investment grade" bonds. An investment grade bond is one that has been "rated" (by a commercial rating service) as having a low credit risk (that is, a low risk of default). Generally, investment grade bonds are issued by the largest corporations. In 1989 there were about 800 U.S. corporate issuers whose

bonds were investment grade, while there were over 23,000 other corporations with sales over $ 35 million (many of them with long histories of sound financial status) whose bonds were not (or would not be) investment grade. The bonds issued by any of the 22,000 corporations whose bonds were not rated investment grade are often called "junk" bonds.

Before 1977 there were plenty of high-yield bonds, but they were mostly "fallen angels" — that is, bonds that had been relatively low in risk, and yield, when issued but had become higher in risk and yield as a result of a decline in the fortunes of the issuer. In 1977, the investment banking firm of Drexel Burnham Lambert, Inc. began to make possible the use of the high-yield bonds for raising new capital; that is, it created a market for *original-issue* high yield bonds. The market it created (or revitalized) is both for public issues and for private placements. The use of original-issue high-yield bonds grew rapidly after 1977, though the number of new issues and their dollar volume remained far smaller than that of investment-grade bonds. (Giant corporations, especially the utilities, still issue huge amounts of traditional, investment-grade bonds.) In the early years of their use, high-yield bonds were issued primarily by modest-sized,"emerging" corporations — though these were generally well-established companies with substantial assets. Before the development of the original-issue high-yield bond market, the principal source of loans for such firms had been commercial banks or insurance companies, which sometimes imposed on the borrowers restrictions and conditions far more onerous than those commonly found in the high-yield bonds and, more important, were generally unwilling to lend long term at fixed rates. Thus, high-yield bonds have been called "securitized commercial loans."*

2. Leverage

Investors often try to achieve the competing goals of maximum safety and maximum return on their investment — in short, and very human terms, they want to have it all. Persons designing the capital structure of a corporation have similar objectives as they decide how much money to raise through equity and how much through debt. The results of their decisions determine how highly leveraged the company will be.

The word "leverage" is used to describe the financial consequences of the use of debt and equity. The use of debt ("other people's money") creates financial leverage for the equity. The greater the debt the greater the leverage. The greater the leverage the greater the potential gains and losses for the equity and the greater the risk of loss for the debt. The effects of

---

*William A. Klein & John C. Coffee, Jr., Business Organization and Finance 238-39. Reprinted with permission. Copyright © 1996 by Foundation Press. All rights reserved.

leverage result from the facts that (a) the debt holder (the lender) has a *fixed claim* (that is, a claim for a fixed amount of interest and for repayment of the amount of the loan); (b) the return on the investment or business financed by the debt is uncertain; and (c) the equity holder (the borrower) has a *residual claim* (that is, the right to whatever is left after the debt holder's claim is satisfied).*

By having their corporation borrow some of its capital from others, shareholders get the benefit of leverage. The benefits of leverage exist for the shareholders any time the corporation can make a return on borrowed money that is greater than the cost of the borrowed money. The easiest example of leverage for most people is the leverage enjoyed by homeowners during periods of rising real estate prices. Assume, for example, that a young lawyer buys a condominium for $ 100,000, paying $ 10,000 down and borrowing $ 90,000. If the lawyer later sells the condominium for $ 110,000 after expenses, the gain has been $ 10,000. If the lawyer had paid $ 100,000 cash for the house, the lawyer's gain on the invested funds would have been 10%. Since the lawyer's investment was instead highly leveraged, the gain on the $ 10,000 of invested funds was 100%. If the condominium had sold for $ 90,000 after expenses, in the leveraged transaction, the lawyer's loss would have been 100%, whereas if the lawyer had paid cash for the condominium, the loss would have been 10%. As the preceding example demonstrates, leverage can be a disadvantage as well as an advantage, because it increases the amount of risk in a particular transaction. Thus, the higher the ratio of debt to equity, the greater the impact of leverage. (Notice that the preceding example did not include interest and other costs associated with borrowing. They would have to be considered as well.)

Shareholders can use leverage in the same way as can a homeowner, by causing their corporation to borrow money at a lower rate of interest than it can earn by using the money it borrowed. If, for example, a corporation borrows from a bank $ 50,000 at 10% interest and its shareholders contribute an additional $ 50,000 in exchange for all the corporation's common stock, and then the corporation makes a 15% return on its $ 100,000 total capital, the shareholders' return on their $ 50,000 investment is $ 10,000, or 20% on the funds they had invested. That is calculated as follows: $ 15,000 profit, minus $ 5,000 interest paid on the debt, equals $ 10,000, which is 20% of the $ 50,000 that the shareholders had invested.

Since, as indicated above, preferred stock is in financial terms more like debt than it is like common stock, the common shareholders can leverage their investment by causing their corporation to issue preferred stock just as easily as they can by having the corporation issue debt. In that case, for leveraging to be

---

*William A. Klein & John C. Coffee, Jr., Business Organization and Finance 238-39. Reprinted with permission. Copyright © 1996 by Foundation Press. All rights reserved.

beneficial, the hoped-for return on the money obtained from the preferred shareholders must be greater than the dividends payable on the preferred stock.

The corporation can, of course, issue both preferred stock and debt, thus maximizing the common shareholders' leverage. Public utility corporations, for example, typically do just that, with a usual capitalization of one of those corporations being 30% common stock, 15% preferred stock, and 55% debt. One might ask why the entire leveraging amount of such a corporation is not made up of debt, since dividends on preferred stock are not tax deductible. A major reason is that public utility commissions have to approve the capital structures of public utilities, and those commissions will not allow public utilities to obligate themselves to make interest payments on more than about 55% debt. But those commissions usually will allow public utilities further to leverage their common shareholders by the issuance of perhaps 15% preferred stock. (Since preferred shareholders are not promised dividend payments, dividends are not a corporate obligation in the way that interest payments are.)

SECTION II. DULY AUTHORIZED, VALIDLY ISSUED, FULLY PAID, AND NONASSESSABLE STOCK

Corporation lawyers often are asked to give an opinion that certain shares of a corporation's stock are duly authorized, validly issued, fully paid, and nonassessable. That typically occurs when a corporation sells shares to the public or to private investors, or when a shareholder in a closely held corporation sells to a new investor. "Duly authorized" simply means that when the shares were issued, the corporation had sufficient shares authorized in its charter to cover the issuance. For example, if the opinion relates to 100 shares issued on May 1, the lawyer would check to be sure that, when the 100 shares were issued, the corporation's charter had authorized at least 100 shares in excess of the shares that were already outstanding on that date.

"Validly issued" indicates that the issuance of shares was in accordance with corporation law, including that the board and the officers of the corporation took the proper steps to issue the shares. All corporation statutes give the board the power to approve the issuance of stock.[1]

The first question for a lawyer to answer, then, is whether the board approved the issuance of stock. Another question a lawyer needs to answer is whether the consideration set by the board was in an amount and of a type allowed by the statute. In jurisdictions retaining the concept of par value, for example, the lawyer must also determine whether the consideration was at least equal to par

---

[1] That power typically is covered in the section of the statute giving the board of directors general management power. In the Model Act, that power is granted by § 8.01(b), which says: "All corporate powers shall be exercised by or under the authority of, and the business and affairs of the corporation managed under the direction of, its board of directors ...." MODEL BUSINESS CORP. ACT (1984) § 801(b).

value if the shares had par value. Yet another question is whether the officers took the proper steps to issue the stock against payment of the consideration set by the board.

"Fully paid" overlaps with "validly issued" and also with "nonassessable." It will be best if we discuss "nonassessable" first, since in almost all cases if stock is fully paid, it is nonassessable or, put another way, if stock is fully paid, the owner cannot be assessed for further payments. There are two ways that stock could be assessable. Once in a great while a corporation's charter authorizes "assessable stock," which simply means that in certain specified circumstances the corporation has the right to demand future payments from the holders of that stock. Stock also can be assessable if the consideration that was to have been paid upon its issuance was not paid.

If, on the other hand, the appropriate type and amount of consideration that was to have been paid upon issuance has been paid, the stock is "fully paid." Under a statute like the Model Act, it usually is easy to determine if the statutory requirements as to type and amount of consideration have been met, since those requirements are clearly spelled out. Model Act § 6.21(b) provides that "The board of directors may authorize shares to be issued for consideration consisting of any tangible or intangible property or benefit to the corporation, including cash, promissory notes, services performed, contracts for services to be performed, or other securities of the corporation." Other states have adopted a more restrictive approach than the Model Act by not including promissory notes and/or contracts for future services in the list of valid types of consideration.

The Comment to the Model Act explains that:

> Section 6.21(b) specifically validates contracts for future services (including promoters' services), promissory notes or "any tangible or intangible property or benefit to the corporation," as consideration for the present issue of shares. The term "benefit" should be broadly construed to include, for example, a reduction of a liability, a release of a claim, or benefits obtained by a corporation by contribution of its shares to a charitable organization or as a prize in a promotion. In the realities of commercial life, there is sometimes a need for the issuance of shares for contract rights to such intangible property or benefits. And, as a matter of business economics, contracts for future services, promissory notes, and intangible property or benefits often have value that is as real as the value of tangible property or past services, the only types of property that many older statutes permit as consideration for shares. Thus, only business judgment should determine what kind of property should be obtained for shares....

Model Act § 6.21(e) permits the corporation to hold in escrow shares issued for a contract for future services, a promissory note or other benefit until the corporation has received the full amount of the consideration. The Model Act also requires the corporation to notify shareholders when it has issued stock for promissory notes or contracts for future services.

If cash is received as consideration for the issuance of stock, it is of course easy to tell if the required amount has been received. This is not so easy to do when the consideration is property or services. The Model Act offers some assistance by vesting in the board of directors responsibility for determining that the consideration received for shares is adequate. According to § 6.21(c):

> Before the corporation issues shares, the board of directors must determine that the consideration received or to be received for shares is adequate. That determination by the board of directors is conclusive insofar as the adequacy of consideration for the issuance of shares relates to whether the shares are validly issued, fully paid and nonassessable.

Section 6.21(d) further states that "When the corporation receives the consideration for which the board of directors authorized the issuance of shares, the shares issued therefore are fully paid and nonassessable." (Note the stock is not fully paid and assessable just because the shareholder paid the amount set by the board. The consideration must also meet the statutory requirements for acceptable type.) Sections 6.21(c) and (d) leaves little doubt as to what it takes to have stock that is fully paid and nonassessable. Shareholders who have not paid the full amount of consideration for their shares remain liable for any unpaid amounts outstanding. Thus, in a Model Act jurisdiction, the only additional requirement the lawyer usually has to worry about is whether the consideration set by the board actually has been paid. In preparing a legal opinion as to whether shares are nonassessable and fully paid, the lawyer would first determine that the consideration set by the board met the statutory requirements, for example, that the transfer of a piece of real estate appraised at $ 10,000 is an acceptable type of consideration for 1,000 shares of stock. The lawyer would then check to see if title to the real estate actually passed to the corporation in exchange for the stock.

Shares issued for less than the full amount of permissible consideration set by the board are often referred to as "watered stock." So long as it is outstanding and not fully paid, watered stock dilutes the value of other issued shares because the corporation has not received full value for watered stock.

Historically, the concept of watered stock was tied to the concept of par value. It was also based on the assumption that corporate creditors relied on a corporation's balance sheet values when deciding whether or not to extend credit to the company. Stock could be "watered" in one of two ways. One is that the shareholder to whom shares were issued did not pay to the corporation an amount at least equal to the aggregate par value of the shares. Thus, if the corporation did not receive at least $ 1,000 in exhange for an issue of 100 shares of $ 10 par value stock, the stock was considered to be watered. A second way is that the value of the consideration used to pay for the stock was inflated. If 100 shares of $ 10 par value stock were issued for property actually worth only $ 500 at the time of the transfer, but recorded on the company books at the inflated amount of $ 1,000, the stock would be watered. If, therefore, either the full amount of the promised consideration, at least that equal to par, were not received by the corporation or its value is inflated at the time of transfer, the associated stock would be watered. The Model Act changed the conceptual approach to the legal capital structure by eliminating the concepts of par value and stated capital. It also expanded the types of consideration for which a corporation may issue shares. Thus, under the Model Act, the central question is whether the full amount of the promised consideration has been received by the corporation issuing shares. According to the Official Comment for Model Act § 6.21:

> Since shares need not have a par value, under section 6.21 there is no minimum price at which specific shares must be issued and therefore there can be no "watered stock" liability for issuing shares below an arbitrarily fixed price. The price at which shares are issued is primarily a matter of concern to other shareholders whose interests may be diluted if shares are issued at unreasonably low prices or for overvalued property. This problem of equality of treatment essentially involves honest and fair judgments by directors and cannot be effectively addressed by an arbitrary doctrine establishing a minimum price for shares such as "par value" provided under older statutes.

The Model Act makes a shareholder liable for the full amount of the consideration established by the board of directors. The Delaware General Corporation Law, which retains the concept of par value, takes a similar approach.

The following case demonstrates on eview of the consequences that flow from a shareholder's failure to pay the amount of consideration due.

HANEWALD v. BRYAN'S, INC.

Supreme Court of North Dakota
429 N.W.2d 414 (1988)

MESCHKE, JUSTICE.

Harold E. Hanewald appealed from that part of his judgment for $ 38,600 plus interest against Bryan's, Inc. which refused to impose personal liability upon Keith, Joan, and George Bryan for that insolvent corporation's debt. We reverse the ruling that Keith and Joan Bryan were not personally liable.

On July 19, 1984, Keith and Joan Bryan incorporated Bryan's, Inc. to "engage in and operate a general retail clothing, and related items, store...." The Certificate of Incorporation was issued by the Secretary of State on July 25, 1984. The first meeting of the board of directors elected Keith Bryan as president and Joan Bryan as secretary-treasurer of Bryan's, Inc. George Bryan was elected vice-president, appointed registered agent, and designated manager of the prospective business. The Articles of Incorporation authorized the corporation to issue "100 shares of common stock with a par value of $ 1,000 per share" with "total authorized capitalization [of] $ 100,000.00." Bryan's, Inc. issued 50 shares of stock to Keith Bryan and 50 shares of stock to Joan Bryan. The trial court found that "Bryan's, Inc. did not receive any payment, either in labor, services, money, or property, for the stock which was issued."

On August 30, 1984, Hanewald sold his dry goods store in Hazen to Bryan's, Inc. Bryan's, Inc. bought the inventory, furniture, and fixtures of the business for $ 60,000, and leased the building for $ 600 per month for a period of five years. Bryan's, Inc. paid Hanewald $ 55,000 in cash and gave him a promissory note for $ 5,000, due August 30, 1985, for the remainder of the purchase price. The $ 55,000 payment to Hanewald was made from a loan by the Union State Bank of Hazen to the corporation, personally guaranteed by Keith and Joan Bryan.

Bryan's, Inc. began operating the retail clothing store on September 1, 1984. The business, however, lasted only four months with an operating loss of $ 4,840. In late December 1984, Keith and Joan Bryan decided to close the Hazen store. Thereafter, George Bryan, with the assistance of a brother and local employees, packed and removed the remaining inventory and delivered it for resale to other stores in Montana operated by the Bryan family. Bryan's, Inc. sent a "Notice of Rescission" to Hanewald on January 3, 1985, in an attempt to avoid the lease. The corporation was involuntarily dissolved by operation of law on August 1, 1986, for failure to file its annual report with the Secretary of State.

Bryan's, Inc. did not pay the $ 5,000 promissory note to Hanewald but paid off the rest of its creditors. Debts paid included the $ 55,000 loan from Union State Bank and a $ 10,000 loan from Keith and Joan Bryan. The Bryan loan had been, according to the trial court, "intended to be used for operating costs and expenses."

Hanewald sued the corporation and the Bryans for breach of the lease agreement and the promissory note, seeking to hold the Bryans personally liable. The defendants counterclaimed, alleging that Hanewald had fraudulently misrepresented the business's profitability in negotiating its sale. After a trial without a jury, the trial court entered judgment against Bryan's, Inc. for $ 38,600 plus interest on Hanewald's claims and ruled against the defendants on their counterclaim. The defendants have not cross appealed these rulings.

The trial court, however, refused to hold the individual defendants personally liable for the judgment against Bryan's, Inc., stating: "Bryan's, Inc. was formed in a classic manner, the $ 10,000.00 loan by Keith Bryan being more than sufficient operating capital. Bryan's Inc. paid all obligations except the obligation to Hanewald in a timely fashion, and since there was no evidence of bad faith by the Bryans, the corporate shield of Bryan's Inc. should not be pierced." Hanewald appealed from the refusal to hold the individual defendants personally liable.

Insofar as the judgment fails to impose personal liability upon Keith and Joan Bryan, the corporation's sole shareholders, we agree with Hanewald that the trial court erred. We base our decision on the Bryans' statutory duty to pay for shares that were issued to them by Bryan's, Inc.

Organizing a corporation to avoid personal liability is legitimate. Indeed, it is one of the primary advantages of doing business in the corporate form. *See generally* 1 W. Fletcher, Cyclopedia of the Law of Private Corporations § 14 (1983). However, the limited personal liability of shareholders does not come free. As this court said in *Bryan v. Northwest Beverages,* 69 N.D. 274, 285 N.W. 689, 694 (1939), "[t]he mere formation of a corporation, fixing the amount of its capital stock, and receiving a certificate of incorporation, do not create anything of value upon which the company can do business." It is the shareholders' initial capital investments which protect their personal assets from further liability in the corporate enterprise. *See Cross v. Farmers' Elevator Co. of Dawson,* 31 N.D. 116, 153 N.W. 279, 282 (1915); *Jablonsky v. Klemm,* 377 N.W.2d 560, 566 (N.D.1985) (*quoting Briggs Transp. Co. v. Starr Sales Co.,* 262 N.W.2d 805, 810 (Iowa 1978)) ["shareholders should in good faith put at the risk of the business unencumbered capital reasonably adequate for its prospective liabilities."]; and J. Gillespie, *supra,* 45 N.D.L.Rev. at 388 ["Proper capitalization might be envisioned as the principal prerequisite for the insulation of limited liability."]. Thus, generally, shareholders are not liable for corporate debts beyond the capital they have contributed to the corporation. *See* 1 F. O'Neal and R. Thompson, O'Neal's Close Corporations § 1.09 (3rd ed. 1987).

This protection for corporate shareholders was codified in the statute in effect when Bryan's, Inc. was incorporated and when this action was commenced, former § 10-19-22, N.D.C.C.

"Liability of subscribers and shareholders. — A holder of or subscriber to shares of a corporation shall be under no obligation to the corporation or its creditors with respect to such shares other than the obligation to pay to the corporation the full consideration for which such shares were issued or to be issued." This statute obligated shareholders to pay for their shares as a prerequisite for their limited personal liability.

The kinds of consideration paid for corporate shares may vary. Article XII, § 9 of the state constitution says that "[n]o corporation shall issue stock or bonds except for money, labor done, or money or property actually received; and all fictitious increase of stock or indebtedness shall be void." Section 10-19-16, N.D.C.C., allowed "[t]he consideration for the issuance of shares [to] be paid, in whole or in part, in money, in other property, tangible or intangible, or in labor or services actually performed for the corporation.... [But] [n]either promissory notes nor future services shall constitute payment or part payment for shares of a corporation." And only "[w]hen payment of the consideration ... shall have been received by the corporation, [can] such shares ... be considered fully paid and nonassessable." *Id.* The purpose of these constitutional and statutory provisions is "to protect the public and those dealing with the corporation...." *Bryan v. Northwest Beverages, supra,* 285 N.W. at 694.

In this case, Bryan's, Inc. was authorized to issue 100 shares of stock each having a par value of $ 1,000. Keith Bryan and Joan Bryan, two of the original incorporators and members of the board of directors, were each issued 50 shares. The trial court determined that "Bryan's Inc. did not receive any payment, either in labor, services, money, or property, for the stock which was issued." [T]he Bryans have not challenged this finding of fact on this appeal. We hold that Bryans' failure to pay for their shares in the corporation makes them personally liable under § 10-19-22, N.D.C.C., for the corporation's debt to Hanewald.

Drafters' comments to § 25 of the Model Business Corporation Act [(1969)], upon which § 10-19-22 was based, sketched the principles: "The liability of a subscriber for the unpaid portion of his subscription and the liability of a shareholder for the unpaid balance of the full consideration for which his shares were issued are based upon contract principles. The liability of a shareholder to whom shares are issued for overvalued property or services is a breach of contract. These liabilities have not been considered to be exceptions to the absolute limited liability concept." Where statutes have been silent, courts have differed as to whether the cause of action on the liabilities of shareholders for unpaid consideration for shares issued or to be issued may be asserted by a creditor directly, by the corporation itself or its receiver, or by a creditor on behalf of the corporation. The Model Act [(1969)] is also silent on the subject for the reason that it can be better treated elsewhere. 1 Model Business Corporation Act Annotated 2d, Comment to § 25, at pp. 509-510 (1971). This court, in *Marshall-Wells Hardware Co. v. New Era Coal Co.*, 13 N.D. 396, 100 N.W. 1084 (1904), held that creditors could directly enforce shareholders' liabilities to pay for shares held by them under statutes analogous to § 10-19-22. We believe that the shareholder liability created by § 10-19-22 may likewise be enforced in a direct action by a creditor of the corporation.

Our conclusion comports with the generally recognized rule, derived from common law, that "a shareholder is liable to corporate creditors to the extent his stock has not been paid for." 18A Am.Jur.2d Corporations § 863, at p. 739 (1985). *See also, Id.* at §§ 906 and 907. One commentator has observed: "For a corporation to issue its stock as a gratuity violates the rights of existing stockholders who do not consent, and is a fraud upon subsequent subscribers, and upon subsequent creditors who deal with it on the faith of its capital stock. The former may sue to enjoin the issue of the stock, or to cancel it if it has been issued, and has not reached the hands of a bona fide purchaser; and the latter, according to the weight of authority, may compel payment by the person to whom it was issued, to such extent as may be necessary for the payment of their claims." 11 W. Fletcher, Cyclopedia of the Law of Private Corporations § 5202, at p. 450 (1986). The shareholder "is liable to the extent of the difference between the par value and the amount actually paid," and "to such an extent only as may be necessary for the satisfaction of" the creditor's claim. 11 W. Fletcher, *supra*, § 5241, at pp. 550, 551.

The defendants asserted, and the trial court ruled, that the $ 10,000 loan from Keith and Joan Bryan to the corporation was nevertheless "more than sufficient operating capital" to run the business. However, a shareholder's loan is a debt, not an asset, of the corporation. Where, as here, a loan was repaid by the corporation to the shareholders before its operations were abandoned, the loan cannot be considered a capital contribution.[2]

We conclude that the trial court, having found that Keith and Joan Bryan had not paid for their stock, erred as a matter of law in refusing to hold them personally liable for the corporation's debt to Hanewald. The debt to Hanewald does not exceed the difference between the par value of their stock and the amount they actually paid. Therefore, we reverse in part to remand for entry of judgment holding Keith and Joan Bryan jointly and severally liable for the entire corporate debt to Hanewald. The judgment is otherwise

Affirmed.

ERICKSTAD, C.J., and LEVINE, VANDE WALLE and GIERKE, JJ., concur.

How could the attorney responsible for incorporating the company have prevented the problem from arising?

Under the most traditional view of watered stock liability, a shareholder was liable for the difference between the amount paid for a share and the share's par value. That view made good sense in the nineteenth and early twentieth centuries, when most watered stock cases were decided, because the practice then was to sell stock at its par value, which traditionally was $ 100 per share. If that practice is assumed, (1) not paying par value for shares and (2) not paying the consideration set by the board in accordance with statutory requirements would come down to the same thing. Put another way, the target amount for avoiding watered stock liability would be par value under both traditional and some modern formulations, such as that in Delaware.

---

[2] There are some circumstances in which a shareholder's loan to the corporation may be treated as a capital contribution. *See* 12B W. Fletcher, Cyclopedia of the Law of Private Corporations § 5739 (1984). In bankruptcy proceedings, for example, a shareholder's loans to his corporation can be treated as capital contributions when a corporation is deemed undercapitalized. *See Pepper v. Litton*, 308 U.S. 295, 60 S.Ct. 238, 84 L.Ed. 281 (1939); *Matter of Multiponics, Inc.*, 622 F.2d 709 (5th Cir. 1980). However, the result in this class of cases is an equitable subordination of the shareholder's claim to the claims of other creditors, which is consistent in principle with the result we reach today. *See also, Jablonsky v. Klemm, supra,* 377 N.W.2d at 570 (Justice Meschke, concurring: "However, the finder of fact might also have viewed the largely uncompensated services of Klemm, the principal officer and stockholder, as additional contribution to capital, rather than as simply another liability contributing to the insolvency of the corporation.").

In the traditional view, the amount of a stock's par value was thought to have great importance to a corporation's creditors because (1) if stock is sold at its par value, the entire consideration paid for the stock goes into stated capital and, (2) as seen in the *Hanewald* case, stated capital traditionally was the basis for a corporation's credit. Even under modern statutes, stated capital arguably does provide creditors some protection in that it may be said to set a limit on what amounts can be taken out of the corporation by dividends or distributions. For example, a creditor looking at the following balance sheet could conclude rightly that at that point the corporation could take no money out of the corporation as dividends or distributions.

ASSETS		LIABILITIES	$ 0
Inventory	$ 10,000	SHAREHOLDERS' EQUITY	
		Stated Capital	$ 10,000
			$ 10,000
		TOTAL LIABILITIES	
TOTAL ASSETS	$ 10,000	AND EQUITY	$ 10,000

Notice, however, that "at that point" is an important qualifier. As discussed above in connection with Delaware's approach to these issues, if at any time stated capital exceeds the aggregate par value of a corporation's outstanding stock, the board can vote to transfer most of the excess stated capital to capital surplus, and all of a corporation's capital surplus may be taken out of the corporation by a distribution to shareholders. Also, a corporation at any time can amend its charter to change the par value of its stock so as to create an excess in stated capital that may be transferred to capital surplus. In Model Act jurisdictions, the stated capital and surplus accounts may be retained for accounting purposes, but they are not intended to impose constraints on directors wishing to issue dividends or other distributions (although a court could perhaps find otherwise). All in all, the protection that stated capital gives creditors is more illusory than real. Partly for this reason, creditors in modern times focus on corporations' income and cash flow statements (described in Appendix B), rather than on stated capital, in making credit decisions.

SECTION III. THIN INCORPORATION AND SUBORDINATION

There are dangers for shareholders if they go too far with their use of shareholder debt or if they are not careful enough in establishing and maintaining their debtor-creditor relationship with the corporation. In each case, the problem is that there may be found to exist what is called "thin incorporation." The consequences of thin incorporation fall into two categories. First, the Internal Revenue Service may consider the debt to be equity for tax purposes, causing the interest payments on the debt to be treated as nondeductible dividends. Second, a court

may subordinate the shareholders' debt to that of other creditors in the event of
bankruptcy or other financial calamity. The following materials discuss the issues
of thin incorporation and subordination.

Mortimer M. Caplin, The Caloric Count of a Thin Incorporation, Proceedings, 17th Annual N.Y.U. Institute on Federal Taxation 771 (1959)*

Introduction

....

DEFINITION

"Thin incorporation," in its original form, related to "extreme situations such
as nominal stock investments and an obviously excessive debt structure." In the
evolution of this concept, however, its meaning has broadened. Today, when we
refer to "thin incorporation," we usually are seeking to resolve one single factor:
the extent to which stockholder loans may be used to finance a corporation. A
material stock investment, or a debt structure not "obviously excessive," no
longer is deemed to obviate the issue. For as the administrators and judiciary now
view the matter, the problem lurks in any corporate financing dependent in part
on advances from stockholders.

....

Some Practical Suggestions

Practitioners must continue to wend their way through the circuitous course
plotted by conflicting thin incorporation decisions. Giving advice on this issue is
extremely difficult, often unsatisfactory both to attorney as well as to client.

Until the current confusion is ended by the courts — or until new legislation
is adopted — no quick or positive solution is possible. The following suggestions,
therefore, are intended only as a general guide....

1. Material Amount of Equity

"Material amounts" of capital should be invested in stock. This is a qualitative
test, obviously varying among different industries and among businesses within
a single industry. Ideally, the equity investment should be sufficient to acquire the
"core assets," those essential for the basic operation of the business. Explore the
economic feasibility of operating the business on a limited scale: for example,
consider the possibility of leasing arrangements. By demonstrating that the equity
was adequate to support a stripped-down version of the operation, the taxpayer
will find his position strengthened on the materiality issue.

---

2. Realistic Debt Structure

The debt structure should be planned carefully and realistically. Project the future earnings and future borrowing capacity; examine the probable cash-flow of the business. Maturities of indebtedness should be geared to these financial considerations; interest obligations should not be in excess of estimated net earnings available. If possible, repayment should be provided from the operation itself rather than through refinancing. Most important is to avoid creating a debt structure which cannot be discharged in the normal course of business and which may lead to defaults.

3. Straightforward Indebtedness

The instruments should be clear and unambiguous: an unconditional obligation to pay a sum certain at a reasonably near future date. Interest should be payable at the going rate. It should not be dependent on earnings or someone's discretion. Subordination should be avoided; and there should be no voting rights. Negotiable paper is clearly preferable.

4. Collateral

To the extent possible, the indebtedness should be secured. The presence of a mortgage or other collateral is strong evidence of the bona fides of the arrangement.

5. Corporate Formalities

Corporate records should be carefully kept, reflecting the intention to create a debtor-creditor relationship. In addition to issuing properly drawn negotiable instruments, corporations should consistently record the transactions in their minutes and financial accounts.

6. Identify Consideration

When assets are transferred for both equity and debt, care should be taken to identify the consideration given for each. Show the assets transferred for capital stock; and, as a separate transaction, show those transferred for instruments of indebtedness. Use fair valuations, backed by appraisals, in fixing the terms of the exchanges. This helps defeat a charge of indefiniteness of intent; it evidences the phase of the transaction meant to create a debtor-creditor relation.

7. Avoid *Pro Rata* Lending

Pro rata loans in proportion to stockholdings are often regarded as indicative of an intention to make capital contributions. Family lending is sometimes viewed as an entirety and compared to the group's total stockholdings. For these reasons, loans disproportionate to stockholdings should be negotiated. Borrowing from non-stockholders, for example, usually creates little problem. Similarly, when a minority stockholder finances the bulk of the later advances, debt is more likely to be found. Even when the majority stockholder makes most of the loans, the absence of proportionality is significant. In brief, try to "break the proportions" as much as possible.

8. Borrow in Stages

Funds should be borrowed only as and to the extent needed. Lump-sum lending on incorporation is more indicative of capital contribution than emergency loans made to satisfy particular needs.

9. Different Types of Indebtedness

As different loans are made, consider using various forms of debt instruments: bonds, debentures, notes. This will provide a basis for a finding that at least one earmarked portion of the transaction was intended as bona fide debt. Courts have usually followed an all-or-none approach in testing indebtedness. By distinguishing the various lending phases, a taxpayer will create a more favorable climate for partial relief.

10. Trust as Lender

Consider having stockholders create trusts for family members, transfer funds to the trustee, and induce the trustee to make loans to the corporation. As an alternative, the stockholder might make the loan directly to the corporation, with instruments of indebtedness being endorsed over or issued directly to the trustee. The presence of a trustee has been noted favorably in this type of case, as well as in other areas of the tax law. Recognition is given to the legal obligations and liabilities which result from the fiduciary relation, and courts tend to uphold trustee transactions as bona fide.

11. Guaranteed Loans

Bank loans guaranteed by stockholders have been suggested as a solution for the thin incorporation problem. A variation is to have stockholders lend collateral to the corporation, instead of endorsing its paper. While these arrangements present additional hurdles to the [Internal Revenue] Service, they are by no means insurmountable. There are indications that the courts will look through the various steps and treat the loans as made, in effect, by the stockholders themselves. However, so long as the parties recognize the risks involved, there seems little to be lost in attempting the guarantee or collateral plan. Of course, most desirable would be to have the bank make advancements on the credit of the corporation only.

12. Business Purpose

Of prime importance is the recording of the nontax reasons for issuing debt. Whether they be motivations of stockholder or corporation, they are regarded as crucial by the courts. Correspondence, minutes and other corporate documents should be at hand to reflect the contemporaneous thoughts of the parties in deciding to employ debt instruments.

13. Reasonable Expectations of Repayment

Recognition must also be given to the significance of the lender's reasonable expectations of repayment. His confidence in the success of the venture, scrutiny of the projected earnings, care in negotiating the terms of the loan and general conduct, would all be balanced against the soundness of the proposed undertaking, the risks involved and reasonableness of the capital structure. Evidence on this should be carefully preserved.

14. Acting Like Creditor

Related to his expectations of repayment is the lender's subsequent action in enforcing the debt obligations. To the extent possible, interest and principal payments should be paid on time. This again suggests the importance of planning a realistic, economically sound pay-out program. If delays are encountered, written demands should be made for payment. In extreme situations, consideration should be given to taking some form of action to collect unpaid interest or principal. This would have added weight when advances do not bear a proportionate relationship to stockholdings.

15. Ratio

Finally, mention must be made of ratio — the caloric count of a thin incorporation. This is perhaps the most difficult suggestion to make because of its varying treatment in the courts....

Perhaps all that may be added is the importance at present of exercising restraint. Under a 1:1 ratio, an investor may recapture 50% of his investment if his advances are treated as debt. At 2:1, he recaptures $66^2/_3\%$, with the corporation getting interest deductions on that percentage of the financing. Ratios, therefore, in the 1:1 to 2:1 range give sizable tax benefits and, at the same time, are regarded as not creating inferences adverse to the stockholder. While much higher ratios have been upheld — particularly where unincorporated going concerns are transferred to new corporations — the area of tax danger expands in direct proportion to the increase in ratio over 2:1....

OBRE v. ALBAN TRACTOR CO.

Court of Appeals of Maryland
179 A.2d 861 (1962)

The single question raised by this appeal is whether the Chancellor erred in his finding that a note of a corporation to its principal stockholder represented a risk capital investment in the corporation and not a bona fide debt entitling the stockholder to share as a general creditor in distribution of the corporation's assets due to insolvency.

The Annel Corporation began its existence in January, 1959, when the appellant, Henry Obre, and F. Stevens Nelson pooled certain equipment and cash for the purpose of forming the corporation to engage in the dirt moving and road building business. As his share, Obre transferred to the corporation equipment independently appraised at $ 63,874.86, plus $ 1,673.24 cash, for a total of $ 65,548.10. Nelson's contribution was equipment valued at $ 8,495.00 and $ 1,505.00 in cash, totaling $ 10,000.00.

In return, Obre received $ 20,000.00 par value non-voting preferred stock and $ 10,000.00 par value voting common stock. In addition, he received the corporation's unsecured note for $ 35,548.10, dated January 2, 1959, which was the date of the incorporation. The note, which is the subject of this appeal, was made payable five years after date and carried interest at the rate of five percent per annum, though no interest was ever actually paid. Nelson received for his contribution voting common stock of $ 10,000.00 par value.

The corporation, with Obre as president and Nelson as vice-president, experienced financial difficulty very soon after beginning its operations, requiring Obre to pay certain creditors and meet a payroll in March, 1959, by use of his own funds. For the same reason he discontinued taking his salary of $ 75.00 a week in May, 1959. In April, 1959, the corporation borrowed $ 27,079.20 from a bank, securing the loan with a chattel mortgage. During its period of operation the corporation prepared monthly financial reports in which Obre's note was listed as a debt of the corporation. In 1959 the corporation showed an operating loss of $ 14,324.67. Its continued lack of success led to the execution of a deed of trust for the benefit of creditors on October 19, 1960, and the Circuit Court for Baltimore County, sitting in equity, assumed jurisdiction of the trust.

Obre filed four separate claims in the case which were excepted to by Alban Tractor Co. and certain other trade creditors (appellees here). The Chancellor, after hearing, issued a decree sustaining the exceptions to Obre's claim on the note in question, on the ground that the note represented a contribution to the capital of the corporation and not a bona fide debt owed to Obre upon which he could share as a general creditor. The Chancellor based his decision on his finding that the corporation could not have carried on its operations without the equipment contributed by Obre. He felt that the fact that the note was given on the same day the corporation was formed, and that it was a five year note, indicated that the transaction was not a loan but was really a risk capital contribution. He held that, in view of these factors, equity required that the claim be subordinated to the claims of the general creditors. Under the circumstances of this case we are unable to agree with the conclusion of the Chancellor.

....

[A]ppellees contend that they have shown a "subordinating equity" in that the corporation, in which Obre was a dominant stockholder, was an undercapitalized venture, and that where such a situation exists, fraud or mismanagement need not be present in order to subordinate the claims of the principal stockholders. The test in such a case, it is argued, is whether the transaction can be justified within the bounds of reason and fairness. There is, principally in bankruptcy cases, some authority indicating support for this argument. See, for example, *Costello v. Fazio,* 256 F.2d 903 (C.A. 9, 1958). However, even if we assume, without deciding, that there may be situations in which the doctrine of subordination would be applied in a case short of fraud or estoppel, on general equitable principles, we do not believe that the facts present such a case here.

... Because of the expressed desire of Obre and Nelson that their control of the corporation be equal from the outset, and their ownership eventually equal, the corporate structure had to be planned carefully. Since Obre's contribution in the way of equipment was substantially greater than that of Nelson, the stock was issued so that each received an equal amount of common voting stock, but additional preferred stock was issued to Obre with the condition that it should have voting power if and when it became necessary to pass the dividend on the preferred stock. The remaining excess of assets brought in by Obre, over and above the stock issued to him, was not to be considered a capital investment since this would have made the desired end of eventual equal ownership that much more difficult. Hence the note in question was executed for the excess of $ 35,548.10. The result of this planning was that a permanent equity capital of $ 40,000 would be invested, which, as was noted in a memorandum of the firm planning the corporate structure, "all parties consider it entirely adequate for the foreseeable needs of the corporation". The note was made payable in five years, instead of in equal annual installments, for the explicit purpose of gaining tax advantage.

....

... There is no showing that $ 40,000 was inadequate capitalization for an enterprise of this size, particularly in view of the careful planning that went into determining its capital structure. What may appear hazardous by hind-sight may not have been unreasonable at the outset. It is not unusual in corporate financing to have approximately one-half of contributions put in as risk capital and the balance as loan capital. There can be no question but that, if a third party had advanced the money represented by Obre's note, he would validly be considered a creditor of the corporation.

Our view in no way compromises the position of the corporate creditor. As this Court stated in [an earlier case]:

> "So long as the corporate plan is adopted and pursued in good faith and in accordance with the ... laws of the state, those dealing with the corporation have only themselves to blame if they suffer from neglect to seek information obtainable from public records and other available sources."

It is obvious that the creditors in this case could have determined (if they actually did not do so) the financial status of the corporation by simply inspecting the stock issuance certificate filed with the State Tax Commission, or by requesting financial reports, or by obtaining credit ratings from the sources available....

In our opinion there is no basis in fact or law to justify the subordinating of appellant's claim under the note, and the decree must therefore be

Reversed.

....

FETT ROOFING AND SHEET METAL CO. v. MOORE

United States District Court, E. D. Virginia
438 F. Supp. 726 (1977)

CLARKE, DISTRICT JUDGE.

This matter comes before the Court on the appeal by plaintiff from an order of United States Bankruptcy Judge Hal J. Bonney, Jr., which dismissed plaintiffs' complaint, subordinated the note claims of the plaintiff to the claims of all other creditors and set aside deeds of trust which purported to secure the note claims. Appellant contends that the Bankruptcy Judge's findings of fact and conclusions of law were completely erroneous and that appellant's claims against the bankrupt should be reinstated....

The Facts

The record below discloses that the bankrupt, Fett Roofing and Sheet Metal Co., Inc., was owned and run prior to 1965 by plaintiff herein, Donald M. Fett, Sr., as a sole proprietorship. During 1965, Mr. Fett incorporated his business, transferring to the new corporation assets worth $ 4,914.85 for which he received 25 shares of stock. The stated capital of the corporation was never increased during the course of the corporation's existence. Mr. Fett was the sole stockholder and also the president of the corporation. The roofing business continued to be run completely by Mr. Fett much as it had been prior to its incorporation. In short, Fett Roofing was a classic "one-man" corporation. Over the years, plaintiff advanced money to his business as the need arose. Three of these transactions made in 1974, 1975 and 1976 involved the transfer to the corporation of $ 7,500, $ 40,000 and $ 30,000, respectively. In each instance plaintiff borrowed from the American National Bank, made the funds available to his business and took back demand promissory notes. On April 6, 1976, at a time his business had become insolvent, plaintiff recorded three deeds of trust intended to secure these notes with the realty, inventory, equipment and receivables of Fett Roofing and Sheet Metal Co., Inc. The deeds were backdated to indicate the dates on which the money had actually been borrowed. On November 8, 1976, an involuntary petition in bankruptcy was filed.

After a trial in which both sides presented considerable evidence and the plaintiff personally testified regarding his claim, Judge Bonney made the following findings of fact. 1. The bankrupt was undercapitalized at its inception in 1965, and remained undercapitalized throughout its existence. The capital necessary for the operation and continuation of its business was provided by the complainant in the form of so-called loans on an "as-needed" basis. Promissory notes, including the three involved herein, were given to the complainant in the course of such transactions. 2. The three deeds of trust which purport to secure the said notes were all back-dated to create the impression that they were executed contemporaneously with the advance of funds and the giving of the notes; all three were in fact executed and recorded during the first week of April 1976, when the notes were, by their terms, past due. 3. The purpose of the deeds of trust was to delay, hinder, and defraud the creditors of the bankrupt, and to give the complainant a preference over them, in the event a liquidation of assets became necessary. 4. Complainant was in sole control of the affairs of the bankrupt, and was its sole stockholder. His interests were at all times identical to and indistinguishable from that of the bankrupt; he was the alter ego of the bankrupt. 5. At the time these three deeds of trust were executed and recorded, the bankrupt was, and for several months had been, unable to meet its obligations as they came due in the ordinary course of business. Many of the debts listed in the schedules filed by the bankrupt were incurred and delinquent prior to April 1976. 6. Complainant knew that his corporation was insolvent no later than February 1976.

Based on these findings, Judge Bonney concluded that the advances made by plaintiff to his corporation were actually contributions to capital, not loans, and that claims based on them therefore should be subordinated to those of all the other creditors of the bankrupt. The Judge further found that even if the transfers had been bona fide loans, the deeds of trust intended to secure them would have been null and void as having been given with actual intent to delay, hinder and defraud creditors in violation of § 67d(2)(d) of the Bankruptcy Act, 11 U.S.C. § 107(d)(2)(d). In addition, Judge Bonney determined that such loans were given in fraud of creditors under state law and therefore were voidable under § 70(e) of the Bankruptcy Act, 11 U.S.C. § 110(e).

Because we have concluded that the Bankruptcy Judge was correct in his determination that the plaintiff's transfers of money to his corporation were capital contributions and not loans we do not consider the soundness of the last two legal findings.

The Law

At the outset the Court notes that a Bankruptcy Judge's findings of fact will be accepted unless "clearly erroneous." Bankruptcy Rule 810. In examining the entire record, the opinion and order of the Judge below and the briefs and oral argument of the parties, the Court is satisfied that substantial evidence supports the findings of fact of the Bankruptcy Judge and as they are not clearly in error, they will not be disturbed.

Although the Court is not bound by the Bankruptcy Judge's conclusions of law and is free to make its own legal deductions, an analysis of the particular facts of this case and the relevant authorities clearly shows that the determination that plaintiff made capital contributions to the bankrupt rather than loans is legally sound.

A director, officer, majority shareholder, relatives thereof or any other person in a fiduciary relation with a corporation can lawfully make a secured loan to the corporate beneficiary. However, when challenged in court a fiduciary's transaction with the corporation will be subjected to "rigorous scrutiny" and the burden will be on him "... not only to prove the good faith of the transaction but also to show its inherent fairness from the viewpoint of the corporation and those interested therein." *Pepper v. Litton*, 308 U.S. 295, 60 S.Ct. 238, 84 L.Ed. 281 (1939);

Where a director or majority shareholder asserts a claim against his own corporation, a bankruptcy court, sitting as a court of equity, will disregard the outward appearances of the transaction and determine its actual character and effect. Similar results have properly been reached in ordinary bankruptcy proceedings. Thus, salary claims of officers, directors and stockholders in the bankruptcy of "one-man" or family corporations have been disallowed or subordinated where the courts have been satisfied that allowance of the claims would not be fair or equitable to other creditors. And that result may be reached ... where on the facts the bankrupt has been used merely as a corporate pocket of the dominant stockholder, who, with disregard of the substance or form of corporate management, has treated its affairs as his own. And so-called loans or advances by the dominant or controlling stockholder will be subordinated to claims of other creditors and thus treated in effect as capital contributions by the stockholder not only in the foregoing types of situations but also where the paid-in capital is purely nominal, the capital necessary for the scope and magnitude of the operation of the company being furnished by the stockholder as a loan. *Pepper v. Litton, supra* 308 U.S. at 308-310, 60 S.Ct. at 246.

The record on this appeal reveals the bankrupt to have been a large construction contractor requiring ample amounts of capital. As indicated above, the corporation was capitalized at slightly under $ 5,000 when it was created in 1965. No increment to this initial amount was ever formally made. According to the schedule filed with the Bankruptcy Judge, the bankrupt's debt to secured creditors alone stood at $ 413,000. This is a debt-to-equity ratio of over 80 to 1. While this fact by itself will not serve to convert what is otherwise a bona fide loan into a contribution to capital, it does cast serious doubt on the advances by a person in plaintiff's special situation being considered debt rather than equity. The fact that no evidence was adduced by plaintiff to show that the "borrowings" in question were formally authorized by the corporation or that interest was ever paid on them, coupled with the undisputed day-in-and-day-out control over corporate affairs wielded by plaintiff, as president and sole stockholder leave little doubt that plaintiff, ignoring corporate formalities, was infusing new capital into his business and avoiding such necessities as charter amendment or the issuance of new stock. The record discloses that the funds transferred to the corporations were used to finance the acquisition of equipment and material necessary to the functioning of the business. Although one of the advances was used to pay a bona fide tax liability, this does not affect its character as a capital contribution under the particular circumstances of this case. The fact that plaintiff at various times characterized these advances as "re-capitalization" can only reinforce a conclusion which consideration of the entire record makes inevitable.

The Courts of this circuit have had no reluctance to pierce through surface appearances in these matters and distinguish contributions to capital from genuine loans. In *Braddy v. Randolph*, 352 F.2d 80 (4th Cir. 1965), a case with some striking similarities to the present dispute, the plaintiff, president, director and a principal stockholder of a bankrupt corporation, filed four claims based on four notes secured by deeds of trust. In affirming the rejection of these claims, the Court of Appeals stated:

> To finance this volume and to keep the business going even though operating at a loss, the Bankrupt borrowed heavily and constantly from the four officers and the North Carolina National Bank (hereinafter Bank). The money which officers, Braddy, Zeliff, Craft and Foster, "loaned" the Bankrupt was normally acquired from the Bank by use of their personal credit and personal assets. Based on the volume of business and the fact that the Bankrupt began borrowing from the officers and the Bank at the outset of operations, we think the referee and court could reasonably conclude that these "loans" were necessitated by the initial insufficiency of the Bankrupt's equity capital and that the "loans" made by the officers were, in effect, contributions to capital. Rather than invest more capital the officers and stockholders, by the use of the borrowed funds, substantially shifted and evaded the ordinary financial risks connected with this type of business enterprise and, at the same time, permitted the corporation to remain in a constant state of or in imminent danger of insolvency.

Similarly in *L & M Realty Corp. v. Leo*, 249 F.2d 668 (4th Cir. 1957), the Court of Appeals subordinated the claim of a principal shareholder, noting: While the amounts thus advanced were treated by the stockholders as loans to the corporation and it was not contemplated that stock was to be issued in payment of them, it is clear that they were not loans in the ordinary sense and were not intended to be paid in ordinary course, as were the claims of other creditors. The corporation was not adequately capitalized, the advancements were made shortly after it was organized and no steps were ever taken looking to their repayment. They were made in approximately equal amounts by the two stockholders owning the corporation, who actually paid other creditors in priority to themselves year after year, no interest was ever paid on them and the evidence is that the money was advanced as loans rather than as subscription to stock in the thought that this would be helpful for income tax purposes. In such situation, while the loans are not to be treated as investments in stock, it is clear that they were capital contributions to a corporation inadequately capitalized and that, having been made by the two stockholders, who completely owned and controlled the corporation, they should be subordinated to the claims of other creditors.

Although the advances contested here were made well after the corporation was created, there is evidence in the record that plaintiff had "loaned" the bankrupt money over the years and that the transfers here in issue were only the latest in a series of contributions made necessary by the corporation's grossly inadequate capitalization. Since these three transactions were "part of a plan of permanent personal financing," the fact that they did not occur at the outset of corporate existence is not crucial and the claims based on them are properly subordinated to those of other creditors.

Since the transfers made by plaintiff to the bankrupt were, in contemplation of law, capital contributions, the deeds of trust purporting to secure these advances were properly set aside since there was in fact "no debt to be secured."

As the cases make clear, no one fact will result in the determination that putative loans are actually contributions to capital. The Court is guided by equitable principles that look to the result of the transaction as well as to the formal indicia of its character. A person in the special position of the plaintiff "... cannot by the use of the corporate device avail himself of the privileges normally permitted outsiders in a race of creditors." *Pepper v. Litton, supra,* 308 U.S. at 311, 60 S.Ct. at 247. It is not necessary that fraud, deceit or calculated breach of trust be shown. Where, as here, a corporate insider, indeed the corporate alter ego has so arranged his dealings with his corporate principal that he achieves an unfair advantage over outside creditors dealing at arms length, the Court will subordinate his claim to theirs.

In summary, the Court has accepted the Bankruptcy Judge's findings of fact pertaining to the nature of the advances made by plaintiff and the nature of the corporation as plaintiff's alter ego, as supported by substantial evidence and not clearly erroneous. Further, it finds ample support in the facts and in the relevant authorities for treating plaintiff's advances to the bankrupt as contributions to capital and not as loans.

For the foregoing reasons, the Order appealed from is

Affirmed.

SECTION IV. PREEMPTIVE RIGHTS

Preemptive rights enable shareholders to maintain their proportionate ownership interests in a corporation when the company sells new issues of stock. Shareholders with preemptive rights are given the opportunity to buy a proportionate share of new issues of stock so that their ownership interests will not be diluted. These rights are particularly important for shareholders in a closely held corporation who often depend on the corporation for their livelihood and who may have limited opportunities to purchase additional shares other than when they are issued. Shareholders in publicly traded companies may easily increase or decrease their holdings by trading in the open market.

Although the objective of granting preemptive rights is laudable, accomplishing that goal may be difficult. One reason is that implementation is often complicated, particularly if the corporation has multiple classes of stock with different dividend and voting rights. A second reason is that broad grants of preemptive rights may make it more difficult or more costly for the corporation to accomplish legitimate business objectives, such as a merger or acquisition. Corporate attorneys should counsel their clients on maintaining the proper balance between affording shareholders the protections they desire and not unduly limiting the company's ability to act.

Corporate statutes take three approaches to grants of preemptive rights: 1) the grant of rights is mandatory; 2) preemptive rights are granted unless the corporate charter provides to the contrary (opt out provisions); or 3) the rights are granted only if the corporate charter elects them (opt-in provisions).

Model Act § 6.30 adopts the opt-in approach and requires the corporate charter expressly to state the election of preemptive rights. Under § 6.30, preemptive rights do not apply to shares or options issued as compensation for company directors and employees, shares issued within six months of incorporation, and shares sold for consideration other than money. In addition, not all shareholders may have preemptive rights. For example, the section excludes holders of shares without voting rights.

Planning for preemptive rights requires careful consideration. The following materials raise additional issues associated with the grant of preemptive rights.

1 F. Hodge O'Neal & Robert B. Thompson, O'Neal's Close Corporations Ch. 3, pp 55-57 (3d ed. 1996)*

Strengthening Shareholders' Preemptive Rights.

A good illustration of differences in the characteristics and needs of publicly held and close corporations is to be found in the area of shareholders' preemptive rights. The policy said to underlie the common law rule giving shareholders preemptive rights (*i.e.*, the privilege to purchase in proportion to their holdings new issues of stock by the corporation before the stock is offered to the public) is the protection of the existing shareholders' proportionate voting power and their proportionate interests in corporate earnings and corporate assets.

In publicly held corporations, however, the protection of proportionate interests may not be nearly as important as freeing the corporation from restrictions that might prevent its acting quickly and effectively to obtain additional financing whenever needed. Preemptive rights may be a source of almost insoluble difficulty in a corporation with a large number of shareholders. The delay and expense involved in offering a new issue of shares to thousands of shareholders, some perhaps with very small holdings, getting firm decisions from the share-

---

holders, and distributing the shares and collecting for them, may be prohibitive. Further, in a corporation with several classes of shares, the apportioning of a new share issue among the various classes of shareholders may be an exceedingly complex matter. If the various classes of shares have different par values, if they contain different numbers of shares, if some classes have voting rights while others do not or have voting rights only in certain contingencies, and if some classes have preferences in dividends in assets on liquidation, or both, it may be impossible as a practical matter to determine just what each shareholder is entitled to in the new issue. Finally, the corporation might want to sell its shares to officers or employees as an incentive, or it might want to purchase the assets of another business with shares of its own stock: obtaining the waiver of preemptive rights might be impractical in these situations. In view of these problems which preemptive rights create for publicly held corporations, most charters for corporations of that type contain a clause denying or limiting shareholders' preemptive rights, or the preemptive rights of one or more classes of shareholders, if the corporation statute in the state of organization does not deny preemptive rights.

In most closely held corporations, on the other hand, preemptive rights should not only be preserved; they should be extended and strengthened. To fully protect minority shareholders, preemptive rights must be made applicable to treasury shares, to stock issued in payment of a corporate debt, as well as to stock issued for money.

Most of the considerations that justify the elimination of preemptive rights in publicly held corporations do not apply to closely held corporations, at least not to those with a simple share structure. Preemptive rights do not create the same problems in a typical close corporation. Further, shareholders in a closely held corporation are usually vitally interested in maintaining their proportionate control and their proportionate interest in dividends and assets. A shareholder's interest in a closely held corporation is likely to be proportionately greater than the individual interest of a shareholder in a publicly held corporation. Usually the proportionate interest of a shareholder in a publicly held corporation is insignificant to begin with, and therefore an increase in the amount of the corporation's stock makes little difference to him; and if it does, he can buy additional shares on the market.

Control is more important to a shareholder in a closely held corporation than to one in a publicly held corporation because control in a closely held corporation often means employment, and the loss of control may result in a termination of employment. Issuance of new stock to some shareholders but not to others may throw out of balance an otherwise carefully formulated plan distributing control among the various participants.

A final reason for maintaining preemptive rights in a closely held corporation is that if the business prospers, its growth is likely to be due largely to the energy and skills of its shareholders. Therefore, they should be in a position to purchase new issues of the corporation's stock and thus share in its expansion and prosperity.

Charter clauses defining the preemptive rights of the shareholders apparently are valid in all jurisdictions. Some state statutes expressly grant shareholders preemptive rights subject to limitation or denial in the charter.[3] A few statutes do not explicitly refer to preemptive rights but give an implicit recognition to them by providing that the articles of incorporation may limit or deny preemptive rights. A third group of statutes deny preemptive rights except to the extent they may be provided in the charter. In the absence of a statute or charter provision denying preemptive rights, such rights are conferred on shareholders by common law. In order to "opt-in" for preemptive rights, it is of course, necessary to specify those rights in the charter. Even in those states that provide preemptive rights unless the corporation "opts-out," preemptive rights should be carefully defined in the charter. In the first place, the law of some jurisdictions recognizing preemptive rights does not clearly state the scope of the shareholders' rights. In the second place, a charter provision is desirable to require the shareholders to exercise their options to purchase within a specified time after notice is given them and to provide a time for payment. If shareholders in a corporation with several classes of shares are to have preemptive rights, special care must be used in spelling out the rights of each class. In a corporation which is to have multiple classes of shares, a sound approach to the preemptive rights problem might be to give preemptive rights only to classes of shares with voting power and to limit even their preemptive rights to a priority in the purchase of issues of voting stock. A charter clause defining preemptive rights should be protected against amendment to the prejudice of minority shareholders by a requirement of a high shareholder vote for charter amendment or for amendment of that particular clause.

Preemptive rights alone may not fully protect a shareholder against dilution of his interest in the corporation, because when new stock is issued he may not have the necessary funds to exercise his rights. Thus, a lawyer preparing incorporation papers for a closely held corporation should consider supplementary methods of protecting shareholders against that risk, *e.g.*, the use of a charter clause prohibiting without the unanimous consent of the shareholders any increase in the amount of capital stock or any allotment or reissuance of stock.

---

[3] The number of states with statutes granting preemptive rights unless limited or denied in the charter has declined in recent years....

KATZOWITZ v. SIDLER

Court of Appeals of New York
249 N.E.2d 359 (1969)

KEATING, JUDGE.

Isador Katzowitz is a director and stockholder of a close corporation. Two other persons, Jacob Sidler and Max Lasker, own the remaining securities and, with Katzowitz, comprise Sulburn Holding Corp.'s board of directors. Sulburn was organized in 1955 to supply propane gas to three other corporations controlled by these men. Sulburn's certificate of incorporation authorized it to issue 1,000 shares of no par value stock for which the incorporators established a $ 100 selling price. Katzowitz, Sidler and Lasker each invested $ 500 and received five shares of the corporation's stock.

The three men had been jointly engaged in several corporate ventures for more than 25 years. In this period they had always been equal partners and received identical compensation from the corporations they controlled. Though all the corporations controlled by these three men prospered, disenchantment with their inter-personal relationship flared into the open in 1956. At this time, Sidler and Lasker joined forces to oust Katzowitz from any role in managing the corporations. They first voted to replace Katzowitz as a director of Sullivan County Gas Company with the corporation's private counsel. Notice of directors' meetings was then caused to be sent out by Lasker and Sidler for Burnwell Gas Corporation. Sidler and Lasker advised Katzowitz that they intended to vote for a new board of directors. Katzowitz at this time held the position of manager of the Burnwell facility.

Katzowitz sought a temporary injunction to prevent the meeting until his rights could be judicially determined. A temporary injunction was granted to maintain the *status quo* until trial. The order was affirmed by the Appellate Division.

Before the issue could be tried, the three men entered into a stipulation in 1959 whereby Katzowitz withdrew from active participation in the day-to-day operations of the business. The agreement provided that he would remain on the boards of all the corporations, and each board would be limited to three members composed of the three stockholders or their designees. Katzowitz was to receive the same compensation and other fringe benefits which the controlled corporations paid Lasker and Sidler. The stipulation also provided that Katzowitz, Sidler and Lasker were "equal stockholders and each of said parties now owns the same number of shares of stock in each of the defendant corporations and that such shares of stock shall continue to be in full force and effect and unaffected by this stipulation, except as hereby otherwise expressly provided." The stipulation contained no other provision affecting equal stock interests.

The business relationship established by the stipulation was fully complied with. Sidler and Lasker, however, were still interested in disassociating themselves from Katzowitz and purchased his interest in one of the gas distribution corporations and approached him with regard to the purchase of his interest in another.

In December of 1961 Sulburn was indebted to each stockholder to the extent of $ 2,500 for fees and commissions earned up until September, 1961. Instead of paying this debt, Sidler and Lasker wanted Sulburn to loan the money to another corporation which all three men controlled. Sidler and Lasker called a meeting of the board of directors to propose that additional securities be offered at $ 100 per share to substitute for the money owed to the directors. The notice of meeting for October 30, 1961 had on its agenda "a proposition that the corporation issue common stock of its unissued common capital stock, The total par value which shall equal the total sum of the fees and commissions now owing by the corporation to its ... directors". Katzowitz made it quite clear at the meeting that he would not invest any additional funds in Sulburn in order for it to make a loan to this other corporation. The only resolution passed at the meeting was that the corporation would pay the sum of $ 2,500 to each director.

With full knowledge that Katzowitz expected to be paid his fees and commissions and that he did not want to participate in any new stock issuance, the other two directors called a special meeting of the board on December 1, 1961. The only item on the agenda for this special meeting was the issuance of 75 shares of the corporation's common stock at $ 100 per share. The offer was to be made to stockholders in "accordance with their respective preemptive rights for the purpose of acquiring additional working capital." The amount to be raised was the exact amount owed by the corporation to its shareholders. The offering price for the securities was 1/18 the book value of the stock. Only Sidler and Lasker attended the special board meeting. They approved the issuance of the 75 shares.

Notice was mailed to each stockholder that they had the right to purchase 25 shares of the corporation's stock at $ 100 a share. The offer was to expire on December 27, 1961. Failure to act by that date was stated to constitute a waiver. At about the same time Katzowitz received the notice, he received a check for $ 2,500 from the corporation for his fees and commissions. Katzowitz did not exercise his option to buy the additional shares. Sidler and Lasker purchased their full complement, 25 shares each. This purchase by Sidler and Lasker caused an immediate dilution of the book value of the outstanding securities.

On August 25, 1962 the principal asset of Sulburn, a tractor trailer truck, was destroyed. On August 31, 1962 the directors unanimously voted to dissolve the corporation. Upon dissolution, Sidler and Lasker each received $ 18,885.52 but Katzowitz only received $ 3,147.59.

The plaintiff instituted a declaratory judgment action to establish his right to the proportional interest in the assets of Sulburn in liquidation less the $ 5,000 which Sidler and Lasker used to purchase their shares in December, 1961.

Special Term (Westchester County) found the book value of the corporation's securities on the day the stock was offered at $ 100 to be worth $ 1,800. The court also found that "the individual defendants ... decided that in lieu of taking that sum in cash (the commissions and fees due the stockholders), they preferred to add to their investment by having the corporate defendant make available and offer each stockholder an additional twenty-five shares of unissued stock." The court reasoned that Katzowitz waived his right to purchase the stock or object to its sale to Lasker and Sidler by failing to exercise his preemptive right and found his protest at the time of dissolution untimely.

The Appellate Division (Second Department), two Justices, dissenting, modified the order of Special Term 29 A.D.2d 955, 289 N.Y.S.2d 324. The modification was procedural. The decretal paragraph in Special Term's order was corrected by reinstating the complaint and substituting a statement of the parties' rights. On the substantive legal issues and findings of fact, the Appellate Division was in agreement with Special Term. The majority agreed that the book value of the corporation's stock at the time of the stock offering was $ 1,800. The Appellate Division reasoned, however, that showing a disparity between book value and offering price was insufficient without also showing fraud or overreaching. Disparity in price by itself was not enough to prove fraud. The Appellate Division also found that the plaintiff had waived his right to object to his recovery in dissolution by failing to either exercise his pre-emptive rights or take steps to prevent the sale of the stock.

The concept of pre-emptive rights was fashioned by the judiciary to safeguard two distinct interests of stockholders — the right to protection against dilution of their equity in the corporation and protection against dilution of their proportionate voting control. (Ballantine, Corporations (rev. ed., 1946), § 209.) After early decisions (*Gray v. Portland Bank*, 3 Mass. 364; *Stokes v. Continental Trust Co.*, 186 N.Y. 285, 78 N.E. 1090, 12 L.R.A., N.S., 969), legislation fixed the right enunciated with respect to proportionate voting but left to the judiciary the role of protecting existing shareholders from the dilution of their equity.

It is clear that directors of a corporation have no discretion in the choice of those to whom the earnings and assets of the corporation should be distributed. Directors, being fiduciaries of the corporation, must, in issuing new stock, treat existing shareholders fairly. Though there is very little statutory control over the price which a corporation must receive for new shares, the power to determine price must be exercised for the benefit of the corporation and in the interest of all the stockholders.

Issuing stock for less than fair value can injure existing shareholders by diluting their interest in the corporation's surplus, in current and future earnings and in the assets upon liquidation. Normally, a stockholder is protected from the loss of his equity from dilution, even though the stock is being offered at less than fair value, because the shareholder receives rights which he may either exercise or sell. If he exercises, he has protected his interest and, if not, he can sell the rights, thereby compensating himself for the dilution of his remaining shares in the equity of the corporation.[4]

When new shares are issued , however at prices below fair value in a close corporation or a corporation with only a limited market for its shares, existing stockholders, who do not want to invest or do not have the capacity to invest additional funds, can have their equity interest in the corporation diluted to the vanishing point.

The protection afforded by stock rights is illusory in close corporations. Even if a buyer could be found for the rights, they would have to be sold at an inadequate price because of the nature of a close corporation. Outsiders are normally discouraged from acquiring minority interests after a close corporation has been organized. Certainly a stockholder in a close corporation is at a total loss to safeguard his equity from dilution if no rights are offered and he does not want to invest additional funds.

Though it is difficult to determine fair value for a corporation's securities and courts are therefore reluctant to get into the thicket, when the issuing price is shown to be markedly below book value in a close corporation and when the remaining shareholder-directors benefit from the issuance, a case for judicial relief has been established. In that instance, the corporation's directors must show that the issuing price falls within some range which can be justified on the basis of valid business reasons. If no such showing is made by the directors, there is no reason for the judiciary to abdicate its function to a majority of the board or stockholders who have not seen fit to come forward and justify the propriety of diverting property from the corporation and allow the issuance of securities to become an oppressive device permitting the dilution of the equity of dissident stockholders.

The defendant directors here make no claim that the price set was a fair one. No business justification is offered to sustain it. Admittedly, the stock was sold at less than book value. The defendants simply contend that, as long as all stockholders were given an equal opportunity to purchase additional shares, no stockholder can complain simply because the offering dilutes his interest in the corporation.

---

[4] There is little justification for issuing stock far below its fair value. The only reason for issuing stock below fair value exists in publicly held corporations where the problem of floating new issues through subscription is concerned. The reasons advanced in this situation is that it insures the success of the issue or that it has the same psychological effect as a dividend (Guthman and Dagell, Corporate Financial Policy (3d ed., 1955), p. 369). On rare occasions stock will be issued below book value because this indicia of value is not reflective of the actual worth of the corporation. The book value of the corporation's assets may be inflated or the company may not be glamorous to the public because it is in a declining industry or the company may be under the direction of poor management. In these circumstances there may be a business justification for a major disparity in issuing price and book value in order to inject new capital into the corporation.

The defendants' argument is fallacious.

The corollary of a stockholder's right to maintain his proportionate equity in a corporation by purchasing additional shares is the right not to purchase additional shares without being confronted with dilution of his existing equity if no valid business justification exists for the dilution.

A stockholder's right not to purchase is seriously undermined if the stock offered is worth substantially more than the offering price. Any purchase at this price dilutes his interest and impairs the value of his original holding. "A corporation is not permitted to sell its stock for a legally inadequate price at least where there is objection. Plaintiff has a right to insist upon compliance with the law whether or not he cares to exercise his option. He cannot block a sale for a fair price merely because he disagrees with the wisdom of the plan but he can insist that the sale price be fixed accordance with legal requirements." Judicial review in this area is limited to whether under all the circumstances, including the disparity between issuing price of the stock and its true value, the nature of the corporation, the business necessity for establishing an offering price at a certain amount to facilitate raising new capital, and the ability of stockholders to sell rights, the additional offering of securities should be condemned because the directors in establishing the sale price did not fix it with reference to financial considerations with respect to the ready disposition of securities.

Here the obvious disparity in selling price and book value was calculated to force the dissident stockholder into investing additional sums. No valid business justification was advanced for the disparity in price, and the only beneficiaries of the disparity were the two director-stockholders who were eager to have additional capital in the business.

It is no answer to Katzowitz' action that he was also given a chance to purchase additional shares at this bargain rate. The price was not so much a bargain as it was a tactic, conscious or unconscious on the part of the directors, to place Katzowitz in a compromising situation. The price was so fixed to make the failure to invest costly. However, Katzowitz at the time might not have been aware of the dilution because no notice of the effect of the issuance of the new shares on the already outstanding shares was disclosed. In addition, since the stipulation entitled Katzowitz to the same compensation as Sidler and Lasker, the disparity in equity interest caused by their purchase of additional securities in 1961 did not affect stockholder income from Sulburn and, therefore, Katzowitz possibly was not aware of the effect of the stock issuance on his interest in the corporation until dissolution.

No reason exists at this time to permit Sidler and Lasker to benefit from their course of conduct. Katzowitz' delay in commencing the action did not prejudice the defendants. By permitting the defendants to recover their additional investment in Sulburn before the remaining assets of Sulburn are distributed to the stockholders upon dissolution, all the stockholders will be treated equitably. Katzowitz, therefore, should receive his aliquot share of the assets of Sulburn less the amount invested by Sidler and Lasker for their purchase of stock on December 27, 1961.

Accordingly, the order of the Appellate Division should be reversed, with costs, and judgment granted in favor of the plaintiff against the individual defendants.

BURKE, SCILEPPI, BERGAN, BREITEL and JASEN, JJ., concur with KEATING, J.

FULD, C.J., dissents and votes to affirm on the opinion at the Appellate Division.

Order reversed, with costs, and case remitted to Special Term for further proceedings in accordance with the opinion herein.

What issues does the corporate attorney face when planning for preemptive rights for a corporation with multiple classes of stock with different voting, dividend and liquidation rights?

SECTION V. SHARE TRANSFER RESTRICTIONS AND BUYOUT PROVISIONS

Agreements containing share transfer restrictions and buyout provisions are commonly used in closely held corporations to accomplish two closely related purposes. One is to give remaining shareholders control over who will become shareholders when one or more shareholders want to liquidate ownership interest. The second purpose is to provide a mechanism for liquidating the interests of shareholders who die or want to terminate their relationship with the company. Provisions such as these are not used by shareholders of publicly traded companies; they generally do not care about the identity of the remaining shareholders. In addition, the public markets allow them to liquidate their holdings easily.

A. SHARE TRANSFER RESTRICTIONS

Model Act § 6.27 authorizes agreements restricting the transfer of shares. These agreements may be between the corporation and shareholders or among shareholders or both. Restrictions may be used to maintain the corporation's tax status or status as a statutory close corporation, preserve securities laws exemptions, or for any other reasonable purpose.

1 F. Hodge O'Neal & Robert B. Thompson, O'Neal's Close Corporations Ch. 7, pp 4-6, 13-15 (3d ed. 1996)*

Why Transfer Restrictions May Be Needed.

Ownership and management frequently coalesce in closely held corporations, where not uncommonly all the principal shareholders devote full time to corporate affairs. Even where one or two shareholders may be inactive, the business is normally conducted by the others without aid from nonshareholder managers. The shareholders, or most of them, are therefore in constant and intimate contact, and policy determinations are made with a minimum of formality. Typically, they take part in decisions with little or no attention to the amounts of their respective shareholdings. It is thus not surprising that shareholders in a closely held enterprise usually desire to retain the power to choose future associates.

Each shareholder wants to be in a position to prevent outsiders from entering the business if he doubts their integrity or business judgment or feels that working with them would be unpleasant or unrewarding. Participants in a closely held corporation may want to restrict the transferability of shares in order to guard against the purchase of shares by competitors or other persons unfriendly to the corporation. With a view to "boring from within," competitors sometimes buy shares in order to acquire voting rights and the privilege to inspect corporate books and records. The participants may also want to restrict the transferability of a corporation's stock to guard against one shareholder's gaining absolute control of the corporation by purchasing enough stock from other shareholders to give him a majority of the voting shares outstanding.

Whenever the shareholders' active participation in the business is necessary to its success, free transferability of shares is particularly undesirable. If a shareholder performs an essential task, the possibility that he may sell his shares to an outsider is a serious threat to the enterprise....

A purchaser interested only in investment might also be a hazard to the enterprise, for there would be a great possibility of friction with the active shareholders.... Differences would be especially likely to occur on the respective amounts to allocate to salaries and dividends. Whenever all shareholders of a closely held corporation participate full time in its affairs, they ordinarily take a substantial part of the earnings of the corporation in salaries rather than in dividends to minimize "double taxation." This practice, however, is obviously not satisfactory to a shareholder who is not on the payroll....

Parties to a shareholders' pooling agreement or shareholders' control agreement often restrict the transfer of shares subject to the agreement in order to prevent the shares from being transferred to persons not parties to the agreement or to assure that as a condition to the transfer of shares the transferees agree to become bound by the agreement. Similarly, transfer restrictions are often placed on shares subject to a voting trust.

Another reason may exist for placing restrictions on the transferability of shares. To save the expense of registering securities under the federal Securities Act of 1933, a corporation issuing securities may attempt to distribute them under the nonpublic offering exemption (the so-called "private offering" exemption) of the Act.... A resale of the securities to an unqualified purchaser could destroy the exemption for all the shares distributed by the issuer pursuant to the purported exemption and make the issuer subject to rescission of those sales or liable for damages....

Since the enactment of Subchapter S of the Internal Revenue Code, restrictions on the transferability of stock have been used to accomplish still another purpose. In the absence of transfer restrictions, any shareholder, even against the wishes of his fellow shareholder, can terminate a corporation's eligibility for Subchapter S tax status, or can terminate an election of that status already made by the corporation, simply by transferring some or all of his shares to a nonqualifying holder (*e.g.*, to a corporation) or by splitting up his holdings and transferring shares to numerous persons so as to increase the total number of shareholders in the corporation to more than the maximum of [75] shareholders permitted by Subchapter S. Carefully prepared stock transfer restrictions, by protecting against transfers of this kind, can greatly diminish the risk of arbitrary or inadvertent termination of a corporation's Subchapter S eligibility.

Statutes governing statutory close corporations or professional corporations may require the use of stock transfer restrictions or make their use advisable. Close corporation legislation in some states mandates that restrictions be placed on the transferability of a corporation's shares in order for the corporation to be defined as a statutory close corporation and thereby eligible to elect the status and privileges provided by the special statute. Close corporation statutes in other states define close corporations without reference to restrictions on share transferability but state that shares in such statutory close corporations shall be subject to designated restrictions on transfer, sometimes with specified types of transfers being set out and permitted or with power in the corporation by charter provision to depart from or modify the statutory transfer restrictions.... Statutes permitting professionals to incorporate often provide that a professional corporation's shares can be issued only to persons who are qualified to practice the profession in that state. Restrictions on the transfer of stock in a professional corporation are necessary to comply with this legal requirement as well as to insure that operation of the corporation remains consistent with professional or ethical restraints applicable in some professions.

....

Kinds of Restrictions on Transfer.

The various restrictions on the alienability of shares utilized from time to time in close corporations may be classified as follows: (1) absolute prohibitions against the transfer of shares; (2) "consent restraints," requiring approval of transfers by the shareholders, the directors or a stipulated percentage of one of these groups, (3) provisions permitting transfers only to specified classes of persons (*e.g.*, families of existing shareholders or the corporation's customers or employees) or prohibitions against transfers to other classes of persons (*e.g.*, competitors of the business); (4) "first option" provisions granting the corporation, its officers or directors, or other shareholders a preemptive right (sometimes referred to as right of "first refusal") to shares which a holder decides to sell or transfer; (5) options empowering the corporation, its officers or directors, or the other shareholders to purchase some or all of the shares of a holder on the happening of specified events (*e.g.*, a shareholder's death, his becoming disabled, his becoming bankrupt or insolvent, his moving from the city where the corporation's principal place of business is located, his acquiring an interest in a competing concern, termination of his employment with the corporation, or the exercise by the corporation of a right to call the shares at any time (6) buy-out agreements requiring the transfer of a deceased holder's shares (and perhaps those of a holder who becomes disabled) to the corporation or to the other shareholders at a stipulated price or at a valuation determined by formula; (7) provisions for the corporation's repurchase or redemption of the shares of a holder who ceases to be an employee of the corporation or provisions for the other shareholders to purchase his shares.

....

In a two-person company, provision can be made for a shareholder who wishes to sell his shares to offer them to the other shareholder at a price the offeror designates, with the offeror acquiring an option to purchase the other's shares at that price if his offer to sell is rejected. It is also possible to set up an arrangement between two shareholders which requires them to maintain equality of ownership in the company.

....

————

Regardless of the approach taken, it is important to consider who should be a party to the agreement. Generally, the more the merrier. One reason is that restrictions may not apply to shareholders who are not parties to the agreement. It is also usually advisable to make the corporation a party at the time it is organized. Having the corporation as a party can be a useful tool in enforcing terms of the agreement as the corporation may be authorized not to record on its books shares transferred in violation of the agreement.

B. BUYOUT AGREEMENTS

One of the key purposes of buyout agreements is to provide a market for shares when a shareholder dies or simply wants to exit the corporation. There are several ways to structure a buyout agreement. Each approach has special considerations.

1. Structuring the Agreement

1 F. Hodge O'Neal & Robert B. Thompson, O'Neal's Close Corporations Ch. 7, pp 52-53, 134 (3d ed. 1996)*

Validity of Mandatory Buy-Outs or Redemptions; Special Hazards If the Corporation Purchases.

....

If a buy-out agreement is among shareholders or part of them and the obligations to purchase are placed on shareholders rather than the corporation, the contract is referred to as a "buy-and-sell" agreement or as a "cross purchase agreement"; and if the obligations of the shareholders to purchase are conditioned solely on death, the contract is sometimes called a "survivor purchase" agreement. Whenever the obligations to purchase are placed on the corporation, the contract is referred to as a "corporation stock purchase," "stock purchase," "stock retirement," "stock redemption," or entity-purchase" agreement.

....

Agreements in which the corporation is to be the purchaser, as distinguished from buy-and-sell agreements among the shareholders, may be subject to a special hazard in some states. First, corporation statutes in all states restrict the funds from which a corporation can purchase its own shares. In some statutes, this permissible pool of funds is described as "surplus" or "earned surplus." More recent statutes drop surplus or similar terms and simply prevent a distribution of corporate funds (including a corporation's purchase of its own shares) if the distribution would make the corporation insolvent or would result in its assets being less than its liabilities. Under any of the statutes a corporation may lack the shares or payment for them which of course frustrates the original intentions of the parties to the agreement....

....

Combining First Options, Buy-Outs or Both with Special Dissolution Arrangements.

First option provisions or buy-out agreements can be coupled with a special provision for dissolution of the corporation on the happening of specified events in such a way as to give some protection to a shareholder who has decided to sell his shares or to the estate of a deceased shareholder. For example, if a corporation is given a first option to purchase the shares of a holder who decides to sell or who dies, it may sometimes be advisable to provide that if the corporation does not exercise the option the selling shareholder or the estate of the deceased shareholder, as the case might be, will be entitled either to sell the shares to others or have the corporation dissolved. Similarly, a buy-out agreement might bind the surviving shareholders on the death of a shareholder either to buy the shares of the deceased or vote their shares for dissolution of the corporation. Further, where an option or a buy-out provides for the purchase price for shares to be paid in installments, the selling shareholder or estate can be empowered to dissolve the corporation if payments are not made on time.

....

2. Valuation Issues

1 F. Hodge O'Neal & Robert B. Thompson, O'Neal's Close Corporations Ch. 7, pp. 136-37 (3d ed. 1996)*

One of the most difficult issues facing the corporate planner is how to provide for the valuation of shares sold under the terms of the buy-out agreement. Valuation of a closely held enterprise is difficult at any time. Preparing valuation terms in an agreement that will last over time is even more challenging.

Setting Transfer Price of Shares: General Discussion

A method or formula for fixing the transfer price of shares should always be decided on in advance and embodied in the restrictive provisions....

....

Fixing a price at which the shares are to be transferred or deciding on a formula for determining that price, even if decision is made at the time restrictions are imposed, is still a difficult task. Values involve conjecture and prediction. Transfers may and probably will occur many years after the restrictions are established, at a time when a value of the shares may have greatly changed.

No one valuation formula is equally appropriate for all businesses. The numerous methods that have been used or proposed for setting the price of shares

---

*Copyright © 1996. Reprinted with permission from 1 O'Neal's Close Corporations, published by Clark Boardman Callaghan, 155 Pfingsten Road, Deerfield, IL 60015. Toll-free 1-800-221-9428. All rights reserved.

in a closely held corporation include: (1) computing their book value, (2) setting the price at par or some other arbitrary figure mutually agreed on by the shareholders at the time the restrictions are imposed, (3) setting the price at cost to the holder plus an annual increment, (4) ascertaining the market price of the shares or the highest price that a bona fide prospective purchaser will give, (5) capitalizing earnings, (6) appraisal, (7) authorizing the board of directors or the other shareholders to set a value, (8) use of the valuation imposed by tax authorities for estate or inheritance tax purposes (this can be used of course only to determine the price at which the shares are to be transferred on the death of a holder), and (9) use of combinations of two or more of these methods.

The initial selection of a pricing formula does not end the matter. As one commentator has pointed out, "there is constant need for re-examining the valuation formula in the light of the changing financial conditions of the business and changing responsibilities of the principals."

Chapter 5

ORGANIZING THE CORPORATION

Situation

a. A few days ago you delivered Biologistics, Inc.'s Articles of Incorporation to a corporation service company for filing with the Secretary of State, and this morning the service company called and said the articles have been filed by the Secretary of State. Your clients want to begin business as soon as possible and want to know what has to be done before they can do so. They know they need to elect officers, and they have discussed bylaws with you to some extent. Anderson and Baker say that Phillips is so busy he may not be able to make all board meetings. They want you to provide in the bylaws some way that Phillips can vote on important matters without being at a meeting, perhaps by giving one of them power to vote for him. Phillips has suggested that you provide in the bylaws that neither the Articles of Incorporation nor the bylaws may be amended without the unanimous vote of the board.

b.   Some weeks ago a written consent in lieu of the organization meeting of Biologistics, Inc. was executed by which bylaws were adopted, officers were elected and other actions were taken by the board of directors. The corporation commenced business almost immediately and has entered into a number of contracts, both for the purchase of equipment and supplies and for DNA synthesis. Yesterday you noticed that the corporation service company to whom you gave Biologistics' Articles of Incorporation for filing had not sent you a copy of the document showing its filing. You called and asked them to check on it. A company representative just called back and said there has been a mistake. Biologistics' Articles, it turned out, were not filed until this morning. They were mislaid and not found until your call prompted the service company to search for them. The message you received saying they had been filed was meant for another lawyer in your office and related to the Articles of another corporation. As you determine what action to take, you should also consider the professional responsibility issues that arise in connection with an improperly formed corporation.

SECTION I. ORGANIZATION PROCEDURES

The terms "incorporation" and "organization" of a corporation often are confused. Not infrequently, lawyers use them interchangeably. Actually, incorporation and organization are two separate events in the life of a corporation. Incorporation occurs when the state issues the corporate charter. At that point only the barest corporate skeleton exists, one consisting basically of the few items covered in the charter, such as the corporation's name and the type of business in which it may engage. It is during the process of organization that the corporation is given bylaws, shareholders, officers, and often its first directors. It is only at the completion of that process that enough meat has been added to the corporate bones to establish the corporation as a legal entity ready to do business.

Organization Meeting

Corporation statutes provide for the holding of an organization meeting after the issuance of a corporation's charter, to accomplish the organization of a corporation. Model Act § 2.05(a)(1) requires a meeting to be held "... to complete the organization of the corporation by appointing officers, adopting bylaws, and carrying on any other business brought before the meeting...." Whether the meeting is to be held by the incorporator or by the directors depends on whether the directors are named in the charter, as required by some corporation statutes. If directors are named in the articles of incorporation, then they hold the organization meeting. If directors are not named in the charter, then one of the most important items on the agenda of the organization meeting is the election of the corporation's first directors.

Consent in Lieu of Meeting

Modern corporation statutes typically provide a convenient alternative to holding an organization meeting: written consent in lieu of meeting. Under statutes that allow that procedure, the incorporator or incorporators or the directors may forgo the organization meeting and act by written consent in lieu of meeting. Usually, the consent must be unanimous, but that rule is not without exception.

There is much to be said for organizing a corporation by written consent. For one thing, in cases where directors are not named in the charter and thus not available to hold an organization meeting, there typically is only one incorporator. While it is possible for a sole incorporator to hold an organization meeting, doing so is either cumbersome or strange. The cleanest way for a sole incorporator to conduct an organization meeting is to ask another person to preside as chair and then to interact with the chair. The organization meeting can also be held with only the incorporator present, with the only requirement being that the incorporator actually accomplish the necessary tasks, such as the adoption of bylaws and the election of directors and officers. The incorporator could go through the agenda out loud ("I hereby elect Mary Smith as the sole director of the corporation"), but presumably the incorporator's actions would be equally valid if done in the incorporator's head. Either way, holding a meeting with oneself is outside the norms of ordinary conduct.

Even if there is more than one person who has power to act at an organization meeting, it usually is better to organize the corporation by written consent in lieu of meeting, as provided in § 2.05(b) of the Model Act. As will be seen in the course of this chapter, there are a number of technical items to handle in connection with a corporation's organization, but at that point in a corporation's life there usually is not much that needs to be discussed at a meeting. Even critical decisions, such as who the officers are to be, typically will have been decided informally before the organization of the corporation. As a result, an organization meeting tends to be merely tedious rather than productive in terms of decisionmaking.

Finally, the kind of technical matters involved in organizing a corporation can be handled most reliably and at the least cost in a written consent drafted by the corporation's lawyer. In resolving the issue of whether to operate by written consent, an important question to consider is whether those who would conduct the meeting can be relied upon to take all the proper actions that need to be taken, and even if they can, whether they will draft proper minutes showing those actions. Considering the importance of starting the corporation's life without defects in its organization, and the expense of having a lawyer supervise the organization meeting and the preparation of accurate minutes in an attempt to ensure correctness, it turns out to be rare that holding an organization meeting makes more sense than operating by written consent.

Bylaws

The adoption of bylaws for the regulation of the corporation's affairs is the first step in organizing a corporation. Since there are many issues relating to bylaws, we will not discuss them here but rather will return to them in a subsequent section of this chapter, which is directed entirely to bylaws.

Election of Directors

If directors are not named in the charter, the incorporator typically adopts bylaws, which usually contain a provision on the number of directors, and then elects the corporation's first directors. Depending on the corporation statute involved and sometimes on the preference of the lawyer handling the organization of the corporation, the incorporator may continue with the organization or the new directors may take up the job at that point. The latter is preferable, if for no other reason than that one item that needs to be handled immediately is the sale of stock to the first shareholders. Virtually all corporation statutes require that item to be handled by the directors. Other important items, such as fixing the compensation of officers, also need to be done by the directors rather than the incorporators under most statutes, and so it usually is best simply to have the directors finish the whole task of organization. If the organization is being accomplished by consent in lieu of meeting, that simply means having two separate consents, one of the incorporator or incorporators and one of the directors.

Election of Officers

After the adoption of bylaws and, if necessary, the election of directors, the next step in organizing a corporation is the election of officers. All corporation statutes have a provision on the question of required officers, although Model Act § 8.40 provides simply that the corporation shall have "the officers described in its bylaws or appointed by the board of directors in accordance with the bylaws." Many states require certain named officers, however, and then allow the board to appoint any other officers it desires. A typical provision requires that a corporation have a president and a secretary, and some statutes go further and also require a vice president and a treasurer.

Especially in small, closely held corporations, the question arises as to whether one person may hold more than one office. The answer is that a person may hold any number of offices, with the exception in many states that a person may not hold the offices of president and secretary. The reason for that prohibition, as will better be seen in a later chapter dealing with the subject of corporate authority, is that the secretary is the principal officer who certifies the correctness of corporate actions, such as the signing of documents in the corporate name, and the president is the most likely officer to take those actions. That being so, it is not surprising that the drafters of corporate statutes usually have decided that the president and the secretary should be different persons. The Model Act, however, does not require the two offices to be held by different persons.

Bylaws typically list the officers a corporation is to have, along with a brief recitation of their basic powers and duties, and then give the board of directors (and perhaps certain officers, depending on what the corporation statute provides) the power to elect or appoint additional officers. Obviously, in planning the organization of a corporation, decisions on corporate officers need to be made before the lawyer finishes drafting the bylaws.

SECTION II. OTHER ORGANIZATIONAL MATTERS

Once a corporation has bylaws, directors, and officers, the basics of its organization have been completed. There are, however, other matters that should be handled at the time of organization. If they are not handled then, some will need to be handled almost immediately, probably to the annoyance of clients who thought the details of getting their corporation started were out of the way.

Sale of Stock

Without question, the most important of the additional organizational matters is the sale of stock to the first shareholders. Corporation statutes provide that the directors must authorize the sale of stock against consideration approved by them. If the consideration is other than cash, then the directors generally must put a dollar value on the consideration. Those details need either to be memorialized in the minutes of an organization meeting or handled in a written consent in lieu of meeting. In addition to covering such details, the directors typically authorize certain corporate officers to issue the agreed number of shares against the specified consideration.

Modern corporation statutes typically allow shares to be issued without certificates. Especially in corporations with only one or two owners, that option can be useful in achieving simplicity and minimizing costs. If the corporation is to issue stock certificates, the lawyer handling the organization of the corporation needs to obtain from a corporate stationer certificates that meet the requirements of the corporation statute. The board then should approve the form of those certificates at the time it authorizes the first stock issuance.

Promoters' Contracts and Expenses

Often, clients enter into promoters' contracts on behalf of a corporation before it is formed. Whether or not clients have entered into promoters' contracts, typically they have taken some actions on the corporation's behalf (such as having preliminary discussions with prospective suppliers and customers) and in so doing have incurred expenses. Usually, clients wish to have the board of directors adopt such actions that were taken before incorporation and ratify those taken between the corporation's incorporation and its organization. Also, clients often wish to be reimbursed by the corporation for costs they have incurred on behalf of the corporation. The clients' desires in those regards can all be taken care of at the time of organization by a simple resolution of the directors.

Compensation of Directors and Officers

At the time of organization, the directors should pass a resolution approving the compensation of directors, or at minimum approving the reimbursement of their costs, and also approving the compensation of at least the chief executive officer. It may be legally possible for the chief executive officer to approve his or her own salary, but no one believes that to be good practice. And in the typical closely held corporation, the board approves all or most officers' salaries.

Adoption of Corporate Seal

Corporation statutes do not require corporate seals, but they do authorize them. While from the standpoint of contract law seals have come to be viewed as quaint anachronisms, that is not the case for corporations. Most corporations have a seal, and the use of it often is called for in connection with the execution of corporate documents. When that is the case, it can be easier to have and use a seal than to explain that the corporation does not have one. Besides that practical benefit, the use of a corporate seal often has evidentiary effect, usually serving either as *prima facie* evidence of due authorization or due execution of the sealed document. If a corporation is to have a seal, the form of the seal should be approved in connection with the corporation's organization.

Qualification to Do Business

A domestic corporation is one that conducts business in the state where it is incorporated. A foreign corporation is one doing business in one or more states that are not the state of incorporation. Corporations doing business in other than their state of incorporation will have to qualify to do business as a foreign corporation in each state in which they intend to operate. At a minimum, the board should pass a general resolution authorizing and directing the officers to take all necessary steps to effect those qualifications. A better practice is promptly to obtain the documents that will be required for qualification and then determine if a specific board resolution is necessary in connection with any qualification.

Banking Relationship

The lawyer handling the organization of a corporation should ask the client where the corporation intends to open a bank account and then should obtain from that bank, or ask the client to obtain from the bank, the form of board of directors' resolutions the bank will require before opening an account. Those resolutions should then be passed in connection with the organization of the corporation. If that is not done, immediately after the organization is complete and the corporation has received checks from its shareholders in payment for their stock, a corporate officer will be confronted with the need for new board action to pass those resolutions as soon as the officer attempts to open a bank account.

Those resolutions authorize specified persons to open a corporate checking account, sell commercial paper, take out loans, and so on. In handling those resolutions, a lawyer can save the corporation future trouble by listing corporate offices, rather than the names of individuals, as those the board of directors authorizes to act for the corporation. That way, the banking resolutions will not have to be passed again and again as new persons are elected to corporate offices.

Agreements Among Shareholders

A later chapter deals with distributing control within the corporation, and so we would be getting ahead of ourselves if we went too deeply at this point into the kinds of agreements shareholders may wish to enter into with respect to their corporation. It is important to note two things about such agreements, however, in connection with the discussion of the organization of corporations. First, in closely held corporations owned by more than one person, there usually is a need for one or more agreements among shareholders on such matters as voting for each other as directors and officers and on such questions as to whom shareholders may sell their stock. Second, the best time for entering into such agreements is at the very beginning of a corporation's life.

Corporate Minutes

If the organization of a corporation is accomplished at an organization meeting, the question arises as to what record of the meeting must be prepared. The following excerpt deals with the question of corporate minutes.

John C. Carter, Corporate Minutes: Their Form, Contents, Inspection and Evidentiary Value, 29 The Practical Lawyer, 45, 46-52 (1983)*

....

THE LEGAL REQUIREMENTS. Either by statute or common law, all jurisdictions require that corporate minutes be kept. The statutes vary from a general require- ment to keep "records of all proceedings" to a more specific mandate that minutes of the proceedings of shareholders and boards of directors shall show the "time and place thereof, whether [the meeting was] regular or special, whether notice thereof was given, and if so in what manner, the names of those present at directors' meetings, the number of shares or members present or represented at stockholders' or membership meetings, and the proceedings...."

....

The statutes provide little indication of the scope of the minutes, typically requiring only minutes of "proceedings." In the context of a board or committee meeting, the term "proceedings" does not have a legal meaning. A proceeding in the courts, however, means an action or a suit, or a specific act in the prosecution or defense of an action or a suit. Evidently, it does not encompass the substance of the debate, argument, or discussion, but only describes the legal form. Thus, the filing of a pleading is a legal proceeding irrespective of its contents. Analogously, therefore, the statutory requirement for the keeping of minutes is purely formal, and while acts of the board of directors must be recorded in the minutes, the deliberations need not be.

....

INSPECTION OF MINUTES. Under certain circumstances, minutes must be made available to persons outside corporate management, most significantly stockhold- ers. In many cases, they can be reached by a plaintiff against the corporation through discovery. The right to inspect corporate books and records may be provided by common law, by statute, or, with respect to shareholder lists, by proxy rules established by the Securities and Exchange Commission ("SEC"). Nearly all states require a demand upon the corporation and a statement of proper purpose as a prerequisite to the exercise of inspection rights.

....

MINUTES AS EVIDENCE. Corporate minutes are private records and in most respects are subject to the rules applicable to documentary evidence generally. Thus, for the minutes to be admitted in evidence at trial, the corporate secretary or the person performing the duties of secretary at the meeting must prove their authenticity and establish that they were made in the regular course of business. Although at common law the admission of corporate minutes is limited by the rule against hearsay, minutes are generally admissible:

- To prove the so-called constitutive acts of the corporation — incorporation, organization, and performance of charter or statutory conditions;
- Against the corporation as admissions against interest; and
- Against stockholders, officers, and directors to prove participation in corporate affairs, the authority of agents, and the discharge of directors' duties of care and loyalty.

The Uniform Business Records as Evidence Act, which has been enacted in many jurisdictions, has, to a great extent, abrogated the common law on this subject by providing that any record, whether in the form of an entry in a book or otherwise, made as a memorandum or record of any act shall be admissible as evidence of that act if the record was made in the regular course of business at or near the time of the act and if, in the court's opinion, the circumstances surrounding its preparation justify its admission. This Uniform Act has been specifically applied to minutes.

OPTIONAL CONTENTS. Without regard to statutory requirements, a list of appropriate matters to be included in the minutes of the meetings of the board of directors might consist of the following:

- The date, time, and place of the meeting;
- Whether the meeting was held after due notice or notice was waived;
- Whether the meeting was regular or special;
- The names of all present;
- Whether those present constituted a quorum;
- All actions taken;
- Any dissent or abstentions from the actions taken;
- The departures and re-entries of those present;
- The substance of all reports; and
- Such matters as the board or committee may direct. Brewer & Solberg, *Corporate Minutes: What Should They Include?*, 20 BUS. LAW. 745 (1965).

If a report is in writing, it should be noted that a copy is on file with the secretary. If the report is orally presented and no written record is available, the secretary should prepare a written summary containing the substance of the report and note in the minutes that the summary is on file.

SECTION III. BYLAWS

A. POSITION OF BYLAWS IN THE HIERARCHY OF REGULATION

The adoption of bylaws is the first step in the organization of a corporation. Model Act § 2.06 provides a good starting point for discussing bylaws. The last sentence of that section provides: "The bylaws may contain any provision for managing the business and regulating the affairs of the corporation that is not inconsistent with law or the articles of incorporation." Compare that provision with the first sentence of § 8.01(b), which is the usual statement of the power of the board of directors: "All corporate powers shall be exercised by or under authority of, and the business and affairs of the corporation managed under the direction of, its board of directors, subject to any limitation set forth in the articles of incorporation or in an agreement authorized under § 7.32."

Each of those provisions relates to the hierarchy of authority in a corporation, and the first important thing to understand about bylaws is their place in that hierarchy. Notice first that § 2.06 relates to the power of the bylaws over the business and affairs of a corporation, and § 8.01(b) speaks about the power of the board over both business and affairs. Remember that the affairs of a corporation consist of those actions relating to the corporation's internal workings as an entity, as opposed to those actions relating to the conduct of the corporation's business.

This being said, one might perceive a conflict between §§ 2.06 and 8.01(b), in that § 2.06 says the bylaws may contain any provision relating to the regulation of a corporation's business and affairs "that is not inconsistent with law or the articles of incorporation" and § 8.01(b) may seem to give the board plenary power to manage the business and affairs of the corporation subject to limitations established by the articles or in an agreement authorized under § 7.32. Section 7.32 requires the agreement to be set forth in the articles of incorporation or the bylaws. In other words, under § 2.06, the hierarchy of corporate regulation with respect to a corporation's business and affairs has the bylaws directly after the charter, whereas under § 8.01(b) of directors may seem to occupy that position.

Actually, there is no conflict between §§ 2.06 and 8.01(b). In § 2.06 the drafters did intend to set out a hierarchy of corporate regulation. In § 8.01(b), on the other hand, what the drafters intended was merely to say where one would look (in the Act or the charter or the bylaws) to find exceptions to the general rules that all corporate powers are to be exercised by the directors and that all of a corporation's business and affairs are at least to be supervised by a board of directors. The Model Act contains a number of such exceptions to the plenary power of directors, as for example, the requirement that shareholders must vote to approve a charter amendment. And § 2.02(b)(2) of the Model Act provides that the charter may contain any provision for the regulation of the internal affairs of a corporation, so long as the provision is not inconsistent with law. Section 8.01(b) thus does not speak to the general position of the bylaws in the hierarchy of regulation. That being said, here is the correct corporate hierarchy, through the level of the board of directors:

1. Law
2. Charter
3. Bylaws
4. Board of Directors

B. WHAT BYLAWS COVER AND BYLAW CONFLICT

As indicated above, bylaws may contain any provision relating to the business and affairs of the corporation, so long as the provision does not conflict with law or the charter. In point of fact, however, bylaws prepared by experienced corporate lawyers are highly stylized, with the subjects covered and the way those subjects are covered being marked by little variation. A brief examination will show that these bylaws are divided into articles and sections. The major articles relate to the shareholders, the directors, and the officers, and those articles are followed by others relating to such subjects as certificates for shares and the corporate seal. Within the articles, detailed sections cover a multitude of rules relating to the subjects at hand. With respect to the shareholders, for example, each of the following is covered: annual meeting, special meetings, place of meetings, notice of meetings, fixing of record date, shareholder list, shareholder quorum and voting requirements, increasing either quorum or voting requirements, proxies, voting of shares, corporation's acceptance of votes, informal action by shareholders, voting for directors, shareholders' rights to inspect corporate records, furnishing corporate financial statements to shareholders, and dissenters' rights.

More often than the uninitiated might suppose, corporate bylaws are defective. There are many reasons. Sometimes the lawyer drafting the bylaws fails to include a provision that needs to be included, or the lawyer creates ambiguities because of inartful drafting. There are, however, other common problems: bylaws that conflict either with the corporation statute or with the corporation's own charter. This type of problem typically occurs because the lawyer uses a form of bylaws as a model without carefully checking it against the statute and charter, or because the lawyer drafts a particular bylaw provision afresh without doing this checking. Also, of course, bylaws must be kept up-to-date. Bylaws that originally are free of defects may develop them when the corporation statute or charter is amended and the bylaws are left alone. The following cases discuss the consequences of different types of bylaw conflicts.

BENINTENDI v. KENTON HOTEL, INC.

Court of Appeals of New York
60 N.E.2d 829 (1945)

DESMOND, J.

Two men who owned, in inequal amounts, all the stock of a domestic business corporation, made an agreement to vote for, and later did vote for and adopt at a stockholders' meeting, bylaws of the corporation, providing as follows: 1. That no action should be taken by the stockholders except by unanimous vote of all of them; if, however, thirty days' notice of the meeting had been given, unanimous vote of the stockholders present in person or by proxy should be sufficient; 2. That the directors of the corporation should be the three persons receiving, at the annual stockholders' meeting, the unanimous vote of all the stockholders; 3. That no action should be taken by the directors except by unanimous vote of all of them; 4. That the bylaws should not be amended except by unanimous vote of all the stockholders. The minority stockholder brought this suit to have those bylaws adjudged valid and to enjoin the other stockholder from doing anything inconsistent therewith. Special Term and the Appellate Division held that the two bylaws first above described were invalid and the other two valid. Both sides have appealed to this Court.

In striking down the bylaw (No. 2 above) which requires unanimous stock vote for election of directors, Special Term properly relied upon *Matter of Boulevard Theatre & Realty Co.* (195 App. Div. 518, *aff'd,* 231 N. Y. 615). This Court wrote no opinion in that case. The Appellate Division had ruled, however, that a provision in the Boulevard Theatre's certificate of incorporation requiring unanimous vote of all stockholders to elect directors, violated section 55 of the Stock Corporation Law, which says that directors shall be chosen "by a plurality of the votes at such election". We think it unimportant that the condemned provision was found in the certificate of incorporation in the *Boulevard Theatre* case, and in a bylaw in the present case, or that the attack on the provision is in this case made by a stockholder who agreed to vote for it and did vote for it. In 1897 a similar bylaw was invalidated in *Matter of Rapid Transit Ferry Co.* (15 App. Div. 530). The device is intrinsically unlawful because it contravenes an essential part of the State policy, as expressed in the Stock Corporation Law. An agreement by a stockholder to vote for certain persons as directors is not unlawful since the directors are still, under such an agreement, elected by a plurality of votes, as the statute mandates. But a requirement, wherever found, that there shall be no election of directors at all unless every single vote be cast for the same nominees, is in direct opposition to the statutory rule — that the receipt of a plurality of the votes entitles a nominee to election.

Although not covered by the *Boulevard Theatre* case, or any other decision we have found, the bylaw (No. 1 above) which requires unanimous action of stockholders to pass any resolution or take any action of any kind, is equally obnoxious to the statutory scheme of stock corporation management. The State, granting to individuals the privilege of limiting their individual liabilities for business debts by forming themselves into an entity separate and distinct from the persons who own it, demands in turn that the entity take a prescribed form and conduct itself, procedurally, according to fixed rules. As Special Term pointed out in this case, the Legislature, for reasons thought by it to be sufficient, has specified the various percentages of stock vote necessary to pass different kinds of resolutions. For instance, sections 36 and 37 of the Stock Corporation Law require an affirmative two-thirds vote for changing the capitalization, while section 102 of the General Corporation Law empowers the holders of a majority of the stock to force the directors to dissolve the corporation, and section 103 of that law gives the same power to holders of half the stock, if there be a deadlock on the question of dissolution. Any corporation may arrive at a condition where dissolution is the right and necessary course. The Legislature has decided that a vote of a majority of the shares, or half of them in case of a deadlock, is sufficient to force a dissolution. Yet under the bylaws of this corporation, the minority stockholder could prevent dissolution until such time as he should decide to vote for it. Those who own all the stock of a corporation may, so long as they conduct the corporate affairs in accordance with the statutory rules, deal as they will with the corporation's property (always assuming nothing is done prejudicial to creditors' rights). They may, individually, bind themselves in advance to vote in a certain way or for certain persons. But this State has decreed that every stock corporation chartered by it must have a representative government, with voting conducted conformably to the statutes, and the power of decision lodged in certain fractions, always more than half, of the stock. That whole concept is destroyed when the stockholders, by agreement, bylaw or certificate of incorporation provision as to unanimous action, give the minority interest an absolute, permanent, all-inclusive power of veto. We do not hold that an arrangement would necessarily be invalid, which, for particular decisions, would require unanimous consent of all stockholders. In *Tompkins* v. *Hale,* [284 N.Y. 675,] the stockholders of a "cooperative apartment house" had agreed in writing that such leases could be canceled and surrendered only if all the stockholder-tenants concurred. That is a far cry from a bylaw which prohibits any nonunanimous determination on any corporate question.

The bylaw numbered 3 in our list above makes it impossible for the directors to act on any matter except by unanimous vote of all of them. Such a bylaw, like the others already discussed herein, is, almost as a matter of law, unworkable and unenforceable for the reason given by the Court of King's Bench in *Dr. Hascard v. Dr. Somany,* 1 Freeman 503, in 1693: "*prima facie* in all acts done by a corporation, the major number must bind the lesser, or else differences could never be determined". The directors of a corporation are a select body, chosen by the stockholders. By section 27 of the General Corporation Law, the board as such, is given the power of management of the corporation. At common law only a majority thereof were needed for a quorum and a majority of that quorum could transact business. Section 27 modifies that common-law rule only to the extent of permitting a corporation to enact a bylaw fixing "the number of directors necessary to constitute a quorum at a number less than a majority of the board, but not less than one-third of its number." Every corporation is thus given the privilege of enacting a bylaw fixing its own quorum requirement at any fraction not less than one-third, nor more than a majority, of its directors. But the very idea of a "quorum" is that, when that required number of persons goes into session as a body, the votes of a majority thereof are sufficient for binding action. Thus, while bylaw No. 3 is not in explicit terms forbidden by section 27 (*supra*) it seems to flout the plain purpose of the Legislature in passing that statute. We have not overlooked section 28 of the General Corporation Law, the first sentence of which is as follows: "Whenever, under the provisions of any corporate law a corporation is authorized to take any action by its directors, action may be taken by the directors, regularly convened as a board, and acting by a majority of a quorum, except when otherwise expressly required by law or the bylaws and any such action shall be executed in behalf of the corporation by such officers as shall be designated by the board." Reading together sections 27 and 28 and examining their legislative history, we conclude that there never was a legislative intent so to change the common-law rule as to quorums as to authorize a bylaw like the one under scrutiny in this paragraph. A bylaw requiring for every action of the board not only a unanimous vote of a quorum of the directors, but of all the directors, sets up a scheme of management utterly inconsistent with sections 27 and 28.

....

The fourth bylaw here in dispute, requiring unanimity of action of all stockholders to amend the bylaws, is not, so far as we can find, specifically or impliedly authorized or forbidden by any statute of this State. Nor do we think it involves any public policy or interest. Every corporation is empowered to make bylaws, and bylaws of some sort or other are usually considered to be essential to the organization of a corporation. But a corporation need not provide any machinery at all for amending its bylaws — and for such an omission it could not be accused of an attempt to escape from the regulatory framework set up by law. A corporation, to function as such, must have stockholders and directors, and action and decision by both are required for the conduct of corporate business. The State has an interest in seeing to it that such "private laws" or bylaws as the corporation adopts are not inconsistent with the public law and not such as will turn the corporation into some other kind of entity. But, once proper bylaws have been adopted, the matter of amending them is, we think, no concern of the State. We, therefore, see no invalidity in bylaw numbered 4 above.

The judgment should be modified in accordance with this opinion, and, as so modified, affirmed without costs.

Review §§ 7.27 and 8.24 of the Model Act. Would the result in the preceding case change in a Model Act jurisdiction? Why?

In 1994, the New York Court of Appeals construed § 616(b) of the New York Business Corporation Law, the successor provision to the one at issue in *Benintendi*. Section 616(b) permitted supermajority provisions in a certificate of incorporation to be amended by a two-thirds vote unless the certificate specifically provided otherwise. In *Sutton v. Sutton*,[1] the court upheld a provision in a certificate of incorporation requiring unanimous shareholder approval for amendments to the certificate and invalidated an amendment lacking such approval. The provision in question had required unanimous consent of the shareholders to transact "any business ... including amendment to the certificate of incorporation." The petitioners argued unsuccessfully that such unanimity

---

[1] 637 N.E. 260 (N.Y. 1994).

provisions enabled minority shareholders to veto and thus block any corporate action.

DATAPOINT CORP. v. PLAZA SECURITIES CO.

Supreme Court of Delaware
496 A.2d 1031 (1985)

HORSEY, JUSTICE.

This appeal by Datapoint Corporation from an order of the Court of Chancery, preliminarily enjoining its enforcement of a bylaw adopted by Datapoint's board of directors, presents an issue of first impression in Delaware: whether a bylaw designed to limit the taking of corporation action by written shareholder consent in lieu of a stockholders' meeting conflicts with 8 Del.C. § 228, and thereby is invalid..[2] The Court of Chancery ruled that Datapoint's bylaw was unenforceable because its provisions were in direct conflict with the power conferred upon shareholders by 8 Del.C. § 228. We agree and affirm.

II

In December of 1984, Asher B. Edelman, general partner of both plaintiffs and beneficial owner of more than 10% of Datapoint's stock, advised the latter's chairman that he was interested in acquiring control of Datapoint. However, Datapoint's board of directors was opposed to this, and on January 11, 1985, when Edelman submitted a written proposal to acquire Datapoint, the offer was rejected the same day.

On January 24, Edelman renewed his offer and stated that if it were rejected he would consider the solicitation of consents from shareholders. Datapoint's composite certificate of incorporation then (and now) lacks any provision relating

---

[2] 8 Del.C. §228 reads, in pertinent part:

§ 228. Consent of stockholders or members in lieu of meeting.

(a) Unless otherwise provided in the certificate of incorporation, any action required by this chapter to be taken at any annual or special meeting of stockholders of a corporation, or any action which may be taken at any annual or special meeting of such stockholders, may be taken without a meeting, without prior notice and without a vote, if a consent in writing, setting forth the action so taken, shall be signed by the holders of outstanding stock having not less than the minimum number of votes that would be necessary to authorize or take such action at a meeting at which all shares entitled to vote thereon were present and voted.

. . . .

(c) Prompt notice of taking of the corporate action without a meeting by less than unanimous written consent shall be given to those stockholders or members who have not consented in writing. In the event that the action which is consented to is such as would have required the filing of a certificate under any other section of this title, if such action had been voted on by stockholders or by members at a meeting thereof, the certificate filed under such other section shall state, in lieu of any statement required by such section concerning any vote of stockholders or members, that written consent has been given as provided in this section.

to the solicitation of shareholder consents under § 228. However, the next day Texas counsel to Datapoint recommended that the Datapoint board adopt a bylaw amendment to regulate consents. Counsel stated, "While the resolution will not prevent a hostile takeover, it will provide management with additional time to explore alternatives."

On January 28, Datapoint's directors, meeting telephonically, unanimously adopted bylaw amendments (the "January bylaw") which the Chancellor later found to be "designed to establish a procedure to govern any attempt to take corporate action on Datapoint's behalf by written shareholder consent."

On January 30, 1985, Edelman withdrew his offer to buy Datapoint and announced his intention to solicit shareholder consents for removal of the board and the election of his own candidates. On February 5, plaintiffs commenced this action in the Court of Chancery for preliminary and permanent injunctive relief against enforcement of Datapoint's January bylaw amendment.

... On February 12, Datapoint's board amended its January bylaw on the recommendation, among others, of Datapoint's investment advisor, Kidder Peabody.... Datapoint's February bylaw provided, in part, that:

(1) No action by shareholder consent could take place until the 45th day after the established record date;

(2) That a record date should be fixed of not more than (or less than) 15 days after receipt of a shareholder's notice of intent to solicit consents, unless requested by the shareholder; and

(3) No shareholder consent action would become effective "until the final termination of any proceeding which may have been commenced in the Court of Chancery of the State of Delaware or any other court of competent jurisdiction for an adjudication of any legal issues incident to determining the validity of the consents, unless and until such court shall have determined that such proceedings are not being pursued expeditiously and in good faith."

On February 19, Datapoint's board, in response to Edelman's notice of intent to solicit shareholder consents, set March 4 as the record date and April 18 as the "action" date for counting shareholder consents submitted under § 228. On February 28, Datapoint filed suit in the United States District Court for the Western District of Texas to invalidate any consents obtained by plaintiffs. The suit thereby triggered the litigation "hold" mechanism of the February bylaw.

On March 5, 1985, the Court of Chancery granted plaintiffs a preliminary injunction enjoining defendant Datapoint from enforcing the February bylaw. Based on the Court's construction of § 228 and the impact of Datapoint's February bylaw, the Court concluded that plaintiffs had made "a clear and reasonable showing ... of the likelihood that the Datapoint bylaw directly conflicts with the statutory grant of power to the shareholders" under § 228; and that plaintiffs had demonstrated the likelihood of immediate irreparable harm to their efforts to solicit consents under § 228 for the purpose of removing Datapoint's present board and electing a new slate of directors.

III

On appeal, defendant asserts essentially a three-step argument in support of its contention that the Chancellor committed legal error in enjoining the enforcement of Datapoint's February bylaw. First, defendant contends that the Court erred in construing § 228 as not permitting the consent solicitation procedure — as to which § 228 is silent — to be regulated by bylaw. Second, defendant argues that the Court erred in construing § 228 as requiring a consent accomplished thereunder to be put into effect immediately and without any review of its legality being permitted. Defendant then makes a derivative argument which assumes the correctness of its first two contentions. It argues that the February bylaw constitutes a reasonable regulation of a shareholder § 228 solicitation. Defendant contends that the "delay and review" features of its bylaw are designed to prevent the possibility of "midnight raids" on an uninformed electorate. However, a further objective of the February bylaw's 45-day waiting period (actually 60 days in the aggregate), defendant concedes, is to permit management to solicit its own proxies on the subject.

As to Datapoint's first contention, defendant argues that § 228's introductory language ("Unless otherwise provided in the certificate of incorporation") means that the right of shareholders to act by written consent in lieu of meeting may only be denied shareholders by a charter provision; and that the Chancellor erroneously construed the clause to mean that the regulation of shareholder consent action may not be imposed by a board of directors through the enactment of bylaws. Since bylaws are the proper means for implementing the internal regulation of corporations, defendant reasons that corporate elections, including those accomplished under § 228, are proper subjects for regulation by bylaw.

Relating its February bylaw to general Delaware law, defendant argues that Datapoint's bylaw represents reasonable internal corporate regulation which is ... not inconsistent with § 228....

....

IV

The issue in this case is not an abstract one. Nor is the case in its present posture as multifaceted as the parties make it. The issue is not whether § 228 tolerates any delay in effectuating a shareholder consent action taken thereunder. Nor is the issue whether § 228 permits a board of directors to regulate by bylaw solicitation procedures under § 228. These threshold disputes between the parties are more theoretical than real. The injunctive relief that is here challenged was bottomed on the Court's finding of likelihood that the Datapoint bylaw "directly conflicts" with § 228's grant of power to the shareholders and the Court's conclusion that the lengthy delay provisions of the bylaw are "totally at odds" with the statutory right given shareholders to take action by written consent under § 228.

The determinative question is whether Datapoint's February bylaw conflicts with the letter and intent of § 228. The Chancellor found a clear conflict; and we agree with the Court's construction of § 228 as it applies to the bylaw before us.

Confining our ruling to this bylaw, we find it clearly in conflict with the letter and intent of § 228. Section 228 contains no language suggesting that action accomplished by stockholders through written consent "without a meeting, without prior notice and without a vote" may be lawfully deferred or thwarted on grounds not relating to the legal sufficiency of the consents obtained. The Chancellor similarly construed § 228 in stating that it "gives shareholders the right to take immediate action by written consent provided that they have at a given point in time obtained a written expression of authority on behalf of shares representing sufficient votes to take such action."

Datapoint's bylaw is not designed simply to defer consummation of shareholder action by consent in lieu of meeting until a ministerial-type review of the sufficiency of the consents has been performed by duly qualified and objective inspectors. Instead, the bylaw imposes an arbitrary delay upon shareholder action in lieu of meeting by postponing accomplishment of such action until 60 days after the corporation's receipt of a shareholder's notice of intent to solicit consents....

This delay is not only arbitrary, it is unreasonable. For the underlying intent of the bylaw is to provide the incumbent board with *time* to seek to defeat the shareholder action by management's solicitation of its own proxies, or revocations of outstanding shareholder consents.... Moreover, the bylaw's further provision staying the effective date of any shareholder consent action until termination of any lawsuits challenging such action effectively places within the incumbent board the power to stultify, if not nullify, the shareholders' statutory right. Such a result can only be found to be "repugnant to the statute" which the bylaw is intended to serve, not master.

Although we find defendant's bylaw to be invalid, we do not hold that § 228 must be construed as barring a board of directors from adopting a bylaw which would impose minimal essential provisions for ministerial review of the validity of the action taken by shareholder consent....

Model Act § 7.04 applies to shareholder action by written consent. Would the result have changed in a Model Act jurisdiction? Some states permit a majority (or a super-majority) of shareholders to act by written consents in lieu of a meeting. Is this a better approach?

PAULEK v. ISGAR

Colorado Court of Appeals
551 P.2d 213 (1976)

BERMAN, JUDGE.

Plaintiff, Victor A. Paulek, commenced this action for himself and all other similarly situated stockholders in the H.H. Ditch Co. (H.H.) to restrain the defendant officers, directors, and shareholders from proceeding to consolidate the Short Line Ditch Co. (Short Line) with H.H. From an adverse judgment in the trial court, plaintiffs appeal. We affirm.

At a special meeting of the shareholders of H.H., 56% of the shares represented at the meeting voted to consolidate the two ditch companies under the existing articles of incorporation and bylaws of H.H. At the next annual meeting of the shareholders, an amendment to the minutes of the special meeting was approved, again by majority vote. The amendment provided that as part of the consolidation Short Line was to pay a proportionate share of any indebtedness of H.H. and that all property of Short Line was to become the property of H.H.

Paulek first contends the trial court erred in its holding that series D stock of H.H. could be issued in exchange for water rights and other property of Short Line without amending its bylaws. The bylaws provide as follows:

"The capital stock of this company shall be classed in three series as follows: A series, B series, and C series, and shall be assessable for the purposes stated in the Articles of Incorporation and these Bylaws."

However, the articles of incorporation authorize the issuance of 8,000 shares of par value stock divided into four series: A, B, C, and D. Each series of stock was to be issued "in the ratio of 80 shares of stock for each cubic foot [of water] per second of time" conveyed to the company. The articles provide that series A, B, and C would be issued to the owners of rights and interests in the H.H. Ditch and subsequent enlargements, but that the D series of stock "shall be placed in the treasury of the Company to be issued at the ratio of 80 shares for each cubic foot of water per second of time … upon conveyance of such water to this Company by the owner thereof.…"

The trial court held that there was a conflict or inconsistency between the articles of incorporation and the bylaws relating to the series D stock, and concluded that the articles controlled. Paulek however contends that the series D stock could not be issued until the bylaws were amended, pursuant to the bylaw provision permitting amendment, by a two-thirds vote of the stock represented at a meeting of the shareholders held to authorize the issuance of the series D stock.

Paulek's contention ignores the fact that the articles of H.H. also provide that the board of directors, rather than shareholders, shall have the power to make the bylaws. Thus, the provision in the bylaws attempting to give this power to the shareholders is in conflict with the articles of incorporation. Where bylaws conflict with the articles of incorporation, the articles of incorporation control and the bylaws in conflict are void.

. . . .

———

The way to avoid bylaw conflicts is simple in theory (except for the kind of exotic conflict found in one of the bylaws in *Benintendi,* which admittedly would require a high degree of sophistication to avoid): Do not draft bylaws or any bylaw provision without a careful checking against the statute and corporate charter. Actually avoiding conflicts is not so simple in practice, because most corporate law firms have office forms of bylaws that lawyers are encouraged to use without much checking. Still, use of office forms without checking, even in the best firms, results in more risks than one would imagine. Meticulously check the office form bylaws in twenty good law firms, and you probably will find at least one or two problems. Not infrequently, one at least will find upon checking that the lawyer who was supposed to look after updating corporate forms has not done so frequently enough. If office form bylaws have not been updated at least as recently as the latest changes to the state's corporation statute, a lawyer should view them with more than ordinary suspicion.

C. BYLAWS AS A CONTRACT

If a particular bylaw provision is ineffective as a bylaw, a court may in some circumstances decide to interpret the bylaw as a contract between the persons who agreed to it. That only would occur in a closely held corporation, and it is much more likely to occur when the bylaw provision in question is not invalid as a bylaw because of a conflict with the statute or the corporation's charter. A provision that is ineffective as a bylaw because of a procedural defect in its passage, for example, would be the best candidate for treatment as a contract between the persons who agreed to it. The following case offers a good discussion of the treatment of invalid bylaw provisions as a contract.

JONES v. WALLACE
Supreme Court of Oregon
628 P.2d 388 (1981)

Linde, Justice.

Under the Oregon Business Corporation Act, a shareholders' meeting requires a quorum of a majority of the voting shares unless a different quorum is provided in the articles of incorporation. The issue before us here is whether a 100 percent quorum requirement that is adopted as a corporate bylaw but not in the articles, as the statute provides, nevertheless may be enforced as a binding agreement among the shareholders of a closely held corporation by setting aside corporate action taken without such a quorum.

In 1972, when defendant Wallace was the sole shareholder of Capital Credit & Collection Service, Inc. as well as one of its directors, the directors adopted bylaws which included the following:

> "At any meeting of stockholders all of the outstanding shares of the corporation entitled to vote, represented in person or by proxy, shall constitute a quorum at a meeting of stockholders."

In 1976 plaintiffs Jones and Gaarde each purchased 49½ shares of the corporation's stock. Wallace retained 100 shares, or 50.25 percent. The three shareholders also constituted the board of directors. According to plaintiffs' complaint, although not conceded by defendants, there was a directors' meeting in June, 1979, at which a majority of the directors removed Wallace as president and elected Jones president and Gaarde secretary of the corporation. Both sides agree that the following month a shareholders' meeting occurred at which Gaarde was not present in person nor represented by proxy, and at which Wallace used his majority of the voting shares to remove both the minority shareholders as directors of the corporation and to replace them with defendants Roberts and Smith.

The minority shareholders thereupon sued for a declaratory judgment that they rather than Roberts and Smith remain directors and officers of the corporation. The circuit court allowed summary judgment for defendants on the grounds that the shareholders' meeting satisfied the statutory quorum requirement, and that this requirement could not be overridden by the bylaw. The Court of Appeals reversed, accepting plaintiffs' argument that the bylaw could be enforced as a contract among assenting shareholders. As this question has not previously been decided under the Oregon Business Corporation Act, we allowed review. We reverse the Court of Appeals and affirm the judgment of the circuit court.

The choice whether an extraordinary quorum requirement can be imposed by bylaws or only in the articles of incorporation is not an unimportant technicality. The articles are on file with the Corporation Commissioner, and thus are publicly available to the original and subsequent investors as well as others doing business with the corporation; and the pertinent classes of shareholders are entitled to vote on any amendments. Bylaws, on the other hand, are adopted and changed by the board of directors without prior notice to or participation by the shareholders, unless such shareholder rights are expressly reserved. Accordingly, the statute limits bylaws to "provisions for the regulation and management of the affairs of the corporation not inconsistent with law or the articles of incorporation."

....

In view of the statute, plaintiffs do not press a claim that the bylaw on which they rely effectively requires a 100 percent quorum for a shareholders' meeting. Instead they contend, and the Court of Appeals held, that a bylaw, even if invalid, can be enforced as a contract against a shareholder who has assented to the bylaw, and that this bylaw should be so enforced.

We need not here question the general proposition that a contractual agreement may be given the form of a bylaw or, conversely, that a bylaw sometimes may incorporate a binding commitment to a corporation's shareholders or members, and that such contractual obligations may bind the parties thereto apart from the bylaw as such. The broad generalization that an invalid bylaw may be enforceable as a contract has been stated in a number of cases, although the two Oregon cases cited for this proposition involved membership associations incorporated under other statutes than the business corporation act. The decisions from other states cited on either side also are distinguishable for a variety of reasons. Some involve bylaws which were ineffective as such only because they were faultily adopted; some concern the enforcement of corporate rights against a shareholder; the older cases antedate the modern corporation statutes; or the argument made here was not presented.

Moreover, the question before us is not whether an agreement among corporate shareholders not to act at a shareholders' meeting unless all are represented, if such an agreement were actually made, could give rise to a contract cause of action by one shareholder against another or whether such an agreement would be void as contrary to ORS 57.165. The question here is whether a bylaw in existence when a shareholder buys his shares can be construed into a contract in order to enforce it by setting aside corporate action taken in accordance with the statute and the corporate articles. This contract theory, whatever its merits in other contexts, cannot be used in this fashion to circumvent the statutory procedures for corporate decisions and accomplish by indirection what the bylaw could not accomplish directly.

....

SECTION IV. DEFECTIVE INCORPORATION

A. *DE FACTO* CORPORATIONS DOCTRINE AND CORPORATIONS BY ESTOPPEL

In their early development, corporation laws set up technical multi-step procedures for establishing a corporation. For example, an incorporator might have to publish notice of intent to incorporate, file properly executed papers with the secretary of state and with one or more county officers, publish notice of those filings, and then capitalize the corporation at a certain level, all before a court would recognize the existence of what is called a *de jure* corporation, or a corporation "of right." To stumble over one of those procedures, and to operate a business that only appeared to be a corporation, was to risk being held personally liable for the business's debts. To alleviate the perceived inequities of personal liability in some of those circumstances, courts established two doctrines, the *de facto* corporation doctrine and the corporation by estoppel doctrine.

In order to establish the existence of a *de facto* corporation, there are three things that one must prove:

1. There is a law under which the purported corporation could have been incorporated;

2. There was a good faith attempt to incorporate under that law; and

3. There was a use of corporate power in the honest belief that a corporation existed.

For all of this century, the first requirement has been met in each American jurisdiction, and in situations involving real-world questions about the existence of a *de facto* corporation, the third requirement also tends to be met without much question. The real issue usually is whether there has been a good faith attempt to incorporate.

One of the more interesting modern *de facto* corporation doctrine cases is *Cantor v. Sunshine Greenery, Inc.*[3] That case nicely illustrates how the question of whether a good faith attempt has been made to incorporate can arise. In *Cantor,* the incorporators signed a corporate charter on December 3 and on that same day mailed the charter to the office of the Secretary of State. Evidently believing that the charter had been received by that office and filed, one of the incorporators signed a lease in the corporation's name on December 16. In fact, the charter was not filed by the Secretary of State until two days later. Those facts were enough to allow a New Jersey court to find a bona fide attempt to incorporate and, with the other elements of the *de facto* corporation doctrine met, also to find the existence of a *de facto* corporation. "To deny such existence because of a mere technicality caused by administrative delay in filing runs counter to the purpose of the *de facto* concept," the court said, "and would accomplish an unjust and inequitable result in favor of plaintiffs contrary to their own contractual expectations." The most important learning from *Cantor* is probably found in that quoted explanation by the court of its decision, *i.e.*, that to reach another result would be inequitable. The theme of equity in the judicial resolution of liability questions is one that runs through this chapter.

Perhaps it is the courts' appraisals of who ultimately will suffer liability that cause them to show little sympathy when it is a lawyer rather than the secretary of state who delays filing a corporate charter. For example, in *Asplund v. Marjohn Corp.*,[4] incorporation papers evidently had been signed and left with a lawyer for filing, but the lawyer had neglected to file them before a contract was entered into in the corporate name. In those circumstances, the court, which happened to be the same court that decided *Cantor,* found no bona fide attempt to incorporate and laid on personal liability. Could it be that the court was at least somewhat of the opinion that it was the lawyer, or more likely the lawyer's insurance company, who ultimately should stand the liability?

The corporation by estoppel doctrine is a misnomer. The effect of the application of that doctrine is not to create a corporation. The effect, rather, is simply

---

[3] 398 A.2d 571 (N.J. Super. Ct. App. Div. 1979).

[4] 168 A.2d 844 (N.J. Super. Ct. App. Div. 1961).

that a court in applying the doctrine will estop a plaintiff from arguing the nonexistence of a corporation that patently does not exist as a *de jure* corporation. As might be expected, the occasion for a court to invoke the doctrine relates to its appraisal of the equities of the situation before it in litigation, with the basic question for the court being, "Is it equitable to allow the plaintiff to collect from persons who thought they were officers, directors, or shareholders of a corporation?" Perhaps the best statement of the corporation by estoppel doctrine is found in one of Ballantine's classic works on corporation law:

> The so-called estoppel that arises to deny corporate capacity does not depend on the presence of the technical elements of equitable estoppel, viz., misrepresentations and change of position in reliance thereon, but on the nature of the relations contemplated, that one who has recognized the organization as a corporation in business dealings should not be allowed to quibble or raise immaterial issues on matters which do not concern him in the slightest degree or affect his substantial rights.[5]

Although some courts get confused on the subject, the corporation by estoppel doctrine and the *de facto* corporation doctrine are two distinct doctrines, and the elements of a *de facto* corporation do not have to be found before a court can find a corporation by estoppel. Some of the confusion is understandable, however, because each doctrine ultimately is underpinned by concepts of equity, and the facts that support one doctrine often also support the other. For example, a typical fact situation finds a defendant facing personal liability for a contract that both the defendant and the plaintiff believed was a corporate debt, thus leading to questions about the equity of allowing the plaintiff to collect from an individual defendant because of a technical problem in the incorporation of the defendant's corporation. A further look at the facts may indicate that they fit the required elements of the *de facto* corporation doctrine, and so the overlap between the two doctrines may be fairly extensive. Perhaps it can most helpfully be said that the usual effect of the corporation by estoppel doctrine is to backstop the *de facto* corporation doctrine by allowing courts to excuse defendants from liability, where doing so would work equity, in situations where one or more elements of the *de facto* corporation doctrine are not met.

B. STATUTORY DEVELOPMENTS

Over the last few decades, questions of defective incorporation have been answered to an increased degree by reference to corporation statutes. Those statutes, typified by the Model Act, now universally make establishing a corporation a simple one-step process, thus arguably lessening the need for the *de facto* corporation doctrine and, perhaps to a lesser extent, for the corporation by

---

[5] Henry Winthrop Ballantine, Manual of Corporation Law and Practice 92 (1930).

estoppel doctrine as well. Some of those statutes also include language speaking directly to the question of liability for those who assume to act as a corporation without authority to do so. Here are the two relevant Model Act sections:

Section 2.03 Incorporation

    (a)   Unless a delayed effective date is specified, the corporate existence begins when the articles of incorporation are filed.

    (b)   The secretary of state's filing of the articles of incorporation is conclusive proof that the incorporators satisfied all conditions precedent to incorporation except in a proceeding by the state to cancel or revoke the incorporation or involuntarily dissolve the corporation. .

Section 2.04 Liability for Preincorporation Transactions

    All persons purporting to act as or on behalf of a corporation, knowing there was no incorporation under this Act, are jointly and severally liable for all liabilities created while so acting.

The following two cases explore some of the problems raised by defective incorporation. Each was decided under a statute containing Model Act (1969) §§ 56 and 146, the predecessors to Model Act §§ 2.03 and 2.04 respectively.

ROBERTSON v. LEVY

District of Columbia Court of Appeals
197 A.2d 443 (1964)

HOOD, CHIEF JUDGE.

On December 22, 1961, Martin G. Robertson and Eugene M. Levy entered into an agreement whereby Levy was to form a corporation, Penn Ave. Record Shack, Inc., which was to purchase Robertson's business. Levy submitted articles of incorporation to the Superintendent of Corporations on December 27, 1961, but no certificate of incorporation was issued at this time. Pursuant to the contract an assignment of lease was entered into on December 31, 1961, between Robertson and Levy, the latter acting as president of Penn Ave. Record Shack, Inc. On January 2, 1962, the articles of incorporation were rejected by the Superintendent of Corporations but on the same day Levy began to operate the business under the name Penn Ave. Record Shack, Inc. Robertson executed a bill of sale to Penn Ave. Record Shack, Inc. on January 8, 1962, disposing of the assets of his business to that "corporation" and receiving in return a note providing for installment payments signed "Penn Ave. Record Shack, Inc. by Eugene M. Levy, President." The certificate of incorporation was issued on January 17, 1962. One payment was made on the note. The exact date when the payment was made cannot be clearly determined from the record, but presumably it was made after the certificate of incorporation was issued. Penn Ave. Record Shack, Inc. ceased doing business in June 1962 and is presently without assets. Robertson sued Levy for the balance due on the note as well as for additional expenses incurred in settling the lease arrangement with the original lessor. In holding for the defendant the trial court found that Code 1961, 29-950, relied upon by Robertson, did not apply and further that Robertson was estopped to deny the existence of the corporation.

The case presents the following issues on appeal: Whether the president of an "association" which filed its articles of incorporation, which were first rejected but later accepted, can be held personally liable on an obligation entered into by the "association" before the certificate of incorporation has been issued, or whether the creditor is "estopped" from denying the existence of the "corporation" because, after the certificate of incorporation was issued, he accepted the first installment payment on the note.

....

One of the reasons for enacting modern corporation statutes was to eliminate problems inherent in the *de jure*, *de facto* and estoppel concepts. Thus sections 29-921c and 950 [MBCA §§ 56 and 146] were enacted as follows:

> "§ 29-921c. Effect of issuance of incorporation.
>
> "Upon the issuance of the certificate of incorporation, the corporate existence shall begin, and such certificate of incorporation shall be conclusive evidence that all conditions precedent required to be performed by the incorporators have been complied with and that the corporation has been incorporated under this chapter, except as against the District of Columbia in a proceeding to cancel or revoke the certificate of incorporation."
>
> "§ 29-950. Unauthorized assumption of corporate powers.
>
> "All persons who assume to act as a corporation without authority so to do shall be jointly and severally liable for all debts and liabilities incurred or arising as a result thereof."

The first portion of section 29-921c sets forth a *sine qua non* regarding compliance. No longer must the courts inquire into the equities of a case to determine whether there has been "colorable compliance" with the statute. The corporation comes into existence only when the certificate has been issued. Before the certificate issues, there is no corporation *de jure*, *de facto* or by estoppel. After the certificate is issued under section 921c, the *de jure* corporate existence commences....

The authorities which have considered the problem are unanimous in their belief that section 29-921c and section 29-950 have put to rest *de facto* corporations and corporations by estoppel. Thus the Comment to section [56] of the Model Act, after noting that *de jure* incorporation is complete when the certificate is issued, states that:

> "Since it is unlikely that any steps short of securing a certificate of incorporation would be held to constitute apparent compliance, the

possibility that a *de facto* corporation could exist under such a provision is remote."

....

The portion of § 29-921c which states that the certificate of incorporation will be "conclusive evidence" that all conditions precedent have been performed eliminates the problems of estoppel and *de facto* corporations once the certificate has been issued. The existence of the corporation is conclusive evidence against all who deal with it. Under § 29-950, if an individual or group of individuals assumes to act as a corporation before the certificate of incorporation has been issued, joint and several liability attaches. We hold, therefore, that the impact of these sections, when considered together, is to eliminate the concepts of estoppel and *de facto* corporateness under the Business Corporation Act of the District of Columbia. It is immaterial whether the third person believed he was dealing with a corporation or whether he intended to deal with a corporation. The certificate of incorporation provides the cut off point; before it is issued, the individuals, and not the corporation, are liable.

Turning to the facts of this case, Penn Ave. Record Shack, Inc. was not a corporation when the original agreement was entered into, when the lease was assigned, when Levy took over Robertson's business, when operations began under the Penn Ave. Record Shack, Inc. name, or when the bill of sale was executed. Only on January 17 did Penn Ave. Record Shack, Inc. become a corporation. Levy is subject to personal liability because, before this date, he assumed to act as a corporation without any authority so to do. Nor is Robertson estopped from denying the existence of the corporation because after the certificate was issued he accepted one payment on the note. An individual who incurs statutory liability on an obligation under section 29-950 because he has acted without authority, is not relieved of that liability where, at a later time, the corporation does come into existence by complying with section 29-921c. Subsequent partial payment by the corporation does not remove this liability.

....

TIMBERLINE EQUIPMENT CO. v. DAVENPORT

Supreme Court of Oregon
514 P.2d 1109 (1973)

DENECKE, JUSTICE.

Plaintiff brought this action for equipment rentals against the defendant Dr. Bennett and two others. In addition to making a general denial, Dr. Bennett alleged as a defense that the rentals were to a *de facto* corporation, Aero-Fabb Corp., of which Dr. Bennett was an incorporator, director and shareholder. He also alleged plaintiff was estopped from denying the corporate character of the organization to whom plaintiff rented the equipment. The trial court held for plaintiff. Dr. Bennett, only, appeals.

On January 22, 1970, Dr. Bennett signed articles of incorporation for Aero-Fabb Co. The original articles were not in accord with the statutes and, therefore, no certificate of incorporation was issued for the corporation until June 12, 1970, after new articles were filed. The leases were entered into and rentals earned during the period between January 22nd and June 12th.

Prior to 1953 Oregon had adopted the common-law doctrine that prohibited a collateral attack on the legality of a defectively organized corporation which had achieved the status of a *de facto* corporation.

In 1953 the legislature adopted the Oregon Business Corporation Act. Oregon Laws 1953, ch. 549....

....

This section is virtually identical to § 56 of the Model Act. The Comment to the Model, prepared as a research project by the American Bar Foundation and edited by the American Bar Association Committee on Corporate Laws, states:

....

> "Under the unequivocal provisions of the Model Act, any steps short of securing a certificate of incorporation would not constitute apparent compliance. Therefore a *de facto* corporation cannot exist under the Model Act.
>
> "Like provisions are made throughout the Model Act in respect of the conclusiveness of the issuance by the secretary of state of the appropriate certificate in connection with filings made in his office....

....

ORS 57.793 [is virtually identical to] § 146 of the Model Act. The Comment states:

> "This section is designed to prohibit the application of any theory of de facto incorporation. The only authority to act as a corporation under the Model Act arises from completion of the procedures prescribed in sections 53 to 55 inclusive. The consequences of those procedures are specified in section 56 as being the creation of a corporation. No other means being authorized, the effect of section 146 is to negate the possibility of a de facto corporation.
>
> "Abolition of the concept of de facto incorporation, which at best was fuzzy, is a sound result. No reason exists for its continuance under general corporate laws, where the process of acquiring *de jure* incorporation is both simple and clear. The vestigial appendage should be removed." 2 Model Business Corporation Act Annotated § 146, pp. 908-909 (2d ed. 1971).

In *Robertson v. Levy*, 197 A.2d 443 (D.C. Ct. of App. 1964), the court held the president of a defectively organized corporation personally liable to a creditor of the "corporation." The applicable legislation was similar to Oregon's. The court held the legislation ended the common-law doctrine of *de facto* corporation.

....

We hold the principle of *de facto* corporation no longer exists in Oregon.

The defendant also contends that the plaintiff is estopped to deny that it contracted with a corporation.

The doctrine of "corporation by estoppel" has been recognized by this court but never fully dissected. Corporation by estoppel is a difficult concept to grasp and courts and writers have "gone all over the lot" in attempting to define and apply the doctrine....

As several writers have pointed out, in order to apply the doctrine correctly, the cases must be classified according to who is being charged with estoppel.

When a defendant seeks to escape liability to a corporation plaintiff by contending that the plaintiff is not a lawful corporate entity, courts readily apply the doctrine of corporation by estoppel. *Thompson Optical Institute v. Thompson,* [119 Or. 252, 237 P. 965 (1925)], well illustrates the equity of the doctrine in this class of cases. R. A. Thompson carried on an optical business for years. He then organized a corporation to buy his optical business and subscribed to most of the stock in this corporation. He chaired the first meeting at which the Board resolved to purchase the business from him. The corporation and Thompson entered into a contract for the sale of the business which included a covenant by Thompson not to compete. Thereafter, Thompson sold all of his stock to another individual. Some years later Thompson re-entered the optical business in violation of the covenant not to compete. The corporation brought suit to restrain Thompson from competing. Thompson defended upon the ground that the corporation had not been legally organized. We held, "The defendant cannot be heard to challenge the validity of the contract or the proper organization of the corporation." 119 Or. at 260, 237 P. at 968.

The fairness of estopping a defendant such as Thompson from denying the corporate existence of his creation is apparent.

On the other hand, when individuals such as the defendants in this case seek to escape liability by contending that the debtor is a corporation, Aero-Fabb Co., rather than the individual who purported to act as a corporation, the courts are more reluctant to estop the plaintiff from attacking the legality of the alleged debtor corporation.

The most appealing explanation of why the plaintiff may be estopped is based upon the intention of the parties. The creditor-plaintiff contracted believing it could look for payment only to the corporate entity. The associates, whatever their relationship to the supposed corporate entity, believed their only potential liability was the loss of their investment in the supposed corporate entity and that they were not personally liable.

From the plaintiff-creditor's viewpoint, such reasoning is somewhat tenuous. The creditor did nothing to create the appearance that the debtor was a legal corporate entity. The creditor formed its intention to contract with a debtor corporate entity because someone associated with the debtor represented, expressly or impliedly, that the debtor was a legal corporate entity.

We need not decide whether the doctrine of corporation by estoppel would apply in such a case as this. The trial court found that if this doctrine was still available under the Business Corporation Act defendants did not prove all the elements necessary for its application, and, moreover, it would be inequitable to apply the doctrine.

Under the explanation stated above for the application of the doctrine of estoppel in this kind of case, it is necessary that the plaintiff believe that it was contracting with a corporate entity. The evidence on this point is contradictory and the trial court apparently found against defendants.

The trial court found, and its findings are supported by the evidence, that all the defendants were partners prior to January 1970 and did business under the name "Aero-Fabb Co." Not until June 1970 were the interests in this partnership assigned to the corporation "Aero-Fabb Co." and about the same time the assumed business name "Aero-Fabb Co." was canceled.

The trial court found, and the evidence supported the finding, that two of the leases entered into by plaintiff were with "Kenneth L. Davenport, dba Aero-Fabb Co." The other was with "Kenneth L. Davenport, dba Aero-Fabb Corp." "Aero-Fabb Corp." was never the corporate name; the name of the corporation for which a certificate was finally issued was "Aero-Fabb Co." The correspondence and records of plaintiff sometimes referred to the debtor as "Aero-Fabb Co." and others as "Aero-Fabb Corp."

Plaintiff's bookkeeper testified that she thought it was a corporation because, "This was the way the information was given to me." It is uncertain whether the information was given to her by someone employed by plaintiff or by a company with whom she made a credit check. In any event, plaintiff's salesman said Mr. Davenport, speaking for the organization, stated several times that he was in a partnership with Drs. Gorman and Bennett. The salesman was dubious and checked the title to the land on which the debtors' operation was being conducted and found it was in the name of the three defendants as individuals.

A final question remains: Can the plaintiff recover against Dr. Bennett individually?

In the first third of this century the liability of persons associated with defectively organized corporations was a controversial and well-documented legal issue. The orthodox view was that if an organization had not achieved *de facto* status and the plaintiff was not estopped to attack the validity of the corporate status of the corporation, all shareholders were liable as partners. This court, however, rejected the orthodox rule. In *Rutherford v. Hill,* 22 Or. 218, 29 P. 546 (1892), we held that a person could not be held liable as a partner merely because he signed the articles of incorporation though the corporation was so defectively formed as to fall short of *de facto* status. The court stated that under this rule a mere passive stockholder would not be held liable as a partner. We went on to observe, however, that if the party actively participated in the business he might be held liable as a partner.

This controversy subsided 30 or 40 years ago probably because the procedure to achieve *de jure* corporate status was made simpler; so the problem did not arise.

The Model Act [§ 146] and the Oregon Business Corporation Act, ORS 57.793, solve the problem as follows:

"All persons who assume to act as a corporation without the authority of a certificate of incorporation issued by the Corporation Commissioner, shall be jointly and severally liable for all debts and liabilities incurred or arising as a result thereof."

We have found no decisions, comments to the Model Act, or literature attempting to explain the intent of this section.

We find the language ambiguous. Liability is imposed on "[a]ll persons who assume to act as a corporation." Such persons shall be liable "for all debts and liabilities incurred or arising as a result thereof."

We conclude that the category of "persons who assume to act as a corporation" does not include those whose only connection with the organization is as an investor. On the other hand, the restriction of liability to those who personally incurred the obligation sued upon cannot be based upon logic or the realities of business practice. When several people carry on the activities of a defectively organized corporation, chance frequently will dictate which of the several active principals directly incurs a certain obligation or whether an employee, rather than an active principal, personally incurs the obligation.

We are of the opinion that the phrase, "persons who assume to act as a corporation" should be interpreted to include those persons who have an investment in the organization and who actively participate in the policy and operational decisions of the organization. Liability should not necessarily be restricted to the person who personally incurred the obligation.

The trial court found that Dr. Bennett "acted in the business venture which was subsequently incorporated on June 12, 1970."

The proposed business of the corporation which was to be formed was to sell airplanes, recondition airplanes and give flying lessons. Land was leased for this purpose. Equipment was rented from plaintiff to level and clear for access and for other construction.

There is evidence from which the trial court could have found that while Drs. Bennett and Gorman, another defendant, entrusted the details of management to Davenport, they endeavored to and did retain some control over his management. All checks required one of their signatures. Dr. Bennett frequently visited the site and observed the activity and the presence of the equipment rented by plaintiff. He met with the organization's employees to discuss the operation of the business. Shortly after the equipment was rented and before most of the rent had accrued, Dr. Bennett was informed of the rentals and given an opinion that they were unnecessary and ill-advised. Drs. Bennett and Gorman thought they had Davenport and his management "under control."

This evidence all supports the finding that Dr. Bennett was a person who assumed to act for the organization and the conclusion of the trial court that Dr. Bennett is personally liable.

Affirmed.

Interestingly, the District of Columbia Court of Appeals, which decided *Robertson v. Levy,* did not seem inclined to follow its *Robertson* holding when the equities of a particular situation pull it in another direction. The facts in *Robertson* involved a defendant who had signed a lease in a corporate name before the certification of incorporation was issued. There was no indication in the court's decision that the defendant mistakenly thought the corporation had been formed. In those circumstances, there would seem to be no justification for the imposition of the corporation by estoppel doctrine. Two years later, the same court had before it *Namerly v. Generalcar.*[6]

In that case, the same panel that decided *Robertson* reversed field and found that a party was estopped to deny the existence of a corporation. The facts of *Namerly* easily explain the court's desire to apply an equitable doctrine. There the court was faced with a defendant who attempted to escape a contractual debt, which equitably seemed clearly to be his, on the grounds that the plaintiff — which the defendant had dealt with as a corporation — had failed to prove its corporate existence. Strangely, the *Namerly* court did not mention its decision in *Robertson.* Perhaps the court thought it best simply to ignore its earlier too-quick casting aside of its power to do equity.

The court in *American Vending Services, Inc. v. Morse*[7] interpreted Model Act (1969) §§ 56 and 146 as expressly abolishing the *de facto* corporation and corporation by estoppel doctrines. The court concluded that since a *de jure* corporation is created when the certificate of incorporation is issued, anything less than obtaining a certificate would not constitute sufficient compliance with the Act.

When the drafters of the Model Act addressed the question of personal liability for the obligations of a defectively incorporated enterprise, they found that the doctrines of *de facto* corporations, *de jure* corporations and corporations by estoppel retained a certain vitality.

The Official Comment to § 2.04 summarizes the current state of the law:

Earlier versions of the Model Act, and the statutes of many states, have long provided that corporate existence begins only with the acceptance of articles of incorporation by the secretary of state. Many states also have statutes that provide expressly that those who prematurely act as or on behalf

---

[6]217 A.2d 109 (D.C. 1966).
[7]881 P.2d 917 (Utah 1994).

of a corporation are personally liable on all transactions entered into or liabilities incurred before incorporation. A review of recent case law indicates, however, that even in states with such statutes courts have continued to rely on common law concepts of *de facto* corporations, *de jure* corporations, and corporations by estoppel that provide uncertain protection against liability for preincorporation transactions. These cases caused a review of the underlying policies represented in earlier versions of the Model Act and the adoption of a slightly more flexible or relaxed standard.

Incorporation under modern statutes is so simple and inexpensive that a strong argument may be made that nothing short of filing articles of incorporation should create the privilege of limited liability. A number of situations have arisen, however, in which the protection of limited liability arguably should be recognized even though the simple incorporation process established by modern statutes has not been completed.

(1) The strongest factual pattern for immunizing participants from personal liability occurs in cases in which the participant honestly and reasonably but erroneously believed the articles had been filed....

(2) Another class of cases, which is less compelling but in which the participants sometimes have escaped personal liability, involves the defendant who mails in articles of incorporation and then enters into a transaction in the corporate name; the letter is either delayed or the secretary of state's office refuses to file the articles after receiving them or returns them for correction....

(3) A third class of cases in which the participants sometimes have escaped personal liability involves situations where the third person has urged immediate execution of the contract in the corporate name even though he knows that the other party has not taken any steps toward incorporating....

(4) In another class of cases the defendant has represented that a corporation exists and entered into a contract in the corporate name when he knows that no corporation has been formed, either because no attempt has been made to file articles of incorporation or because he has already received rejected articles of incorporation from the filing agency. In these cases, the third person has dealt solely with the "corporation" and has not relied on the personal assets of the defendant....

(5) A final class of cases involves inactive investors who provide funds to a promoter with the instruction, "Don't start doing business until you incorporate." After the promoter does start business without incorporating, attempts have been made, sometimes unsuccessfully, to hold the investors liable as partners....

After a review of these situations, it seemed appropriate to impose liability only on persons who act as or on behalf of corporations "knowing" that no corporation exists. Analogous protection has long been accorded under the uniform limited partnership acts to limited partners who contribute capital to a partnership in the erroneous belief that a limited partnership certificate has been filed....

While no special provision is made in section 2.04, the section does not foreclose the possibility that persons who urge defendants to execute contracts in the corporate name knowing that no steps to incorporate have been taken may be estopped to impose personal liability on individual defendants. This estoppel may be based on the inequity perceived when persons, unwilling or reluctant to enter into a commitment under their own name, are persuaded to use the name of a nonexistent corporation, and then are sought to be held personally liable under section 2.04 by the party advocating that form of execution. By contrast, persons who knowingly participate in a business under a corporate name are jointly and severally liable on "corporate" obligations under section 2.04 and may not argue that plaintiffs are "estopped" from holding them personally liable because all transactions were conducted on a corporate basis.

Although the Model Act attempts to limit the doctrine of corporations by estoppel, the question remains whether courts in states adopting the Model Act will pay attention to § 2.04, or will apply the case law that precedes it. In the past, some courts deciding cases involving possible personal liability did not discuss the relevant corporation statute, but instead continued to rely on case law predating the statute. That is bad judicial decisionmaking, which may be blamed in part on lawyers who did not properly brief the courts on the corporate statutes. Nevertheless, that decisionmaking may also be taken to indicate a desire on the part of judges to retain more flexibility than the Model Act gave them in the area of defective incorporation.

Chapter 6

CORPORATE AUTHORITY

Situation

Biologistics, Inc. has been in business for a little over a year. The initial earnings projections have more than been met. After salaries and expenses, the corporation had earnings of $ 50,000 during its first year, and its prospects continue to look good. In addition to the laboratory technician and office assistant the corporation hired originally, the company has recently hired one more laboratory technician and a molecular biologist. Baker has had little opportunity to do research and development work. With the addition of more laboratory help, however, the plan is now for her to devote substantial time to this.

Over the next several months you are asked in various situations who has power to take action on behalf of the corporation. In each case, the person asking wants the action taken at the lowest corporate level that is relatively sure to be effective.   How do you respond to each of the following:

1. Purchasing laboratory and office supplies and equipment, basically to sustain the current operation, the total cost of which would be several thousand dollars annually.
2. Purchasing equipment for the research and development work, to total $ 40,000.
3. Entering into a lease on space adjoining that which the corporation currently leases under an extension of its original one-year lease. The lease is to be for five years at $ 10,000 annually.
4. Establishing a line of credit at a local bank in the amount of $ 20,000 and borrowings thereunder. Amounts are to be borrowed under the line to pay current expenses when the corporation is short of cash, and paid back as soon as cash is available.
5. Taking a five-year bank loan from the same local bank in the amount of $ 50,000, the proceeds to be used for research and development.
6. Hiring an additional laboratory assistant.

———

Corporate authority is an especially important subject for lawyers because questions about corporate authority arise frequently. Most of those questions involve one or both of the following aspects:

1. What person or corporate body has power to take action?
2. What formalities are required for the action to be taken?

245

In terms of who can take action, there are usually three choices: the shareholders, the directors, or one or more of the officers. In a general corporation, the members of the board of directors, acting collectively, have oversight responsibility for managing the corporation and making important policy decisions. The board appoints the officers, who supervise the day to day operations of the company. The shareholders elect directors and approve fundamental corporate changes, such as mergers with other companies, amendments to the articles of incorporation and the like. In closely held corporations, the shareholders may take a more active role in company management, as will be discussed below.

SECTION I. FUNCTIONS AND AUTHORITY OF SHAREHOLDERS

The role of shareholders in the management of a corporation varies according to whether the firm is a company with a large number of shareholders or one with only a few. In companies with a large number of shareholders, the functional separation between company management and company ownership is typically greater than in those companies with just a few shareholders. Management by a large number of people is unwieldy. In addition the likelihood that the owners will be widely dispersed with individual holdings amounting to only a small percentage of the total shares outstanding discourages participation in management. It is not cost effective for a shareholder with little corporate power to devote significant time to oversight of the business. Furthermore, individual shareholders may lack the necessary expertise.

Recent years have witnessed a shift in the ownership of publicly traded companies. Originally, shareholders were typically individuals. Today, stock is increasingly held by institutional investors, such as mutual funds and pension funds. Collectively, institutional ownership is a powerful market force in the ownership of publicly held companies, although the relative holdings of an individual institutional investor in any one company may be only a small percentage of the whole. Nevertheless, large institutional investors can influence company policy by communicating directly with company management.

Shareholders of closely held corporations tend to assume that they have broad powers, as shareholders, to make corporate decisions. This assumption may arise because of their close, personal identification with the corporation and because they often depend on the corporation for their livelihoods. Such was the case with the shareholders of the Rawhide Ranch Gold and Silver Mining Company when, in 1865, they met and voted to sell the corporation's mine and its other assets, thus setting the stage for one of the classic cases on shareholders' power, *Gashwiler v. Willis*.

GASHWILER v. WILLIS

Supreme Court of California
33 Cal. 11 (1867)

BY THE COURT, SAWYER, J.:

The Rawhide Ranch Gold and Silver Mining Company is a corporation duly organized under the statutes of California for the purpose of carrying on the business of mining. On the 29th of April, 1865, a special meeting of the stockholders of the corporation was held, pursuant to notice, at the office of the company, at which all the stockholders were present. At this meeting of the stockholders, all the stockholders being present and all the capital stock represented, a resolution was unanimously adopted authorizing S. S. Turner, T. N. Willis and James J. Hodges, Trustees of said corporation, for and on behalf of said corporation, to sell and convey to D. W. Barney the mine, mill, buildings, mining implements, and appurtenances belonging to said company. In pursuance of said resolution, and without any other authority shown, on the 5th of June following a conveyance was executed by said Turner, Willis, and Hodges, Trustees, the commencement and form of execution of which are as follows:

"This indenture, made the 5th day of June, A. D. 1865, between the Rawhide Ranch Gold and Silver Mining Company, a corporation under the laws of the State of California, by S. S. Turner, T. N. Willis and James J. Hodges, Trustees of said corporation, who are duly authorized and empowered by resolution and order of said corporation to sell and convey," etc.

"In witness whereof we, as the Trustees of and for and on behalf of said corporation, have hereunto set our hands and seal (the said corporation having no seal) the day and year first above written.

"T. N. WILLIS. [L. S.]
"JAMES J. HODGES. [L. S.]
"S. S. TURNER. [L. S.]

"Trustees of the Rawhide Ranch Gold and Silver Mining Company."

On the trial, after proving the adoption of the resolution before referred to at a meeting of the stockholders, as stated, the plaintiffs offered said deed in evidence, and defendants objected to its introduction on the three grounds — that it did not appear to be the act or deed of the corporation; that it had not the signature of the corporation, and that it was not sealed with the corporate seal but with the individual seals of the Trustees. The Court sustained the objection and excluded the deed, to which ruling plaintiffs excepted; and this ruling presents the question to be determined.

Under the view we take, it will only be necessary to consider the first ground of the objection, and the question is, does the instrument in question appear to be the act or deed of the corporation? If not, it was properly excluded, and the judgment must be affirmed. It is claimed by respondents that no authority is shown in the parties executing to execute the deed on behalf of the corporation.

If the deed of a natural person, purporting to have been executed by an attorney in fact, were offered in evidence, it would, clearly, be inadmissible, without first showing the authority of the attorney. The recital of the authority in the deed itself would furnish no evidence whatever of its existence. The same is true of an artificial person — a corporation — at least, where the corporate seal is not affixed.... The authority of the Trustees to execute the instrument in question must, therefore, affirmatively appear, or it does not appear to be the act or deed of the corporation.

We are not aware of anything in the law, independent of any authority expressly conferred by the corporation, which authorizes Turner, Willis and Hodges, in their official character as Trustees, to execute the instrument in question on behalf of the corporation. No law of the kind has been called to our attention, and we do not understand that any is claimed by appellants' counsel to exist. And there is nothing in the nature of those offices, as connected with the object and business of the company, from which a general power in the Trustees, when not acting as a Board, to sell and convey the mine, mill and other property of the company, could be implied. The parties executing the instrument, then, if they had any authority in the premises, must have derived it from some corporate act; and the only act proved or relied on is the resolution adopted at the stockholders' meeting before mentioned. This was a meeting of the stockholders only. It was called as such, and the proceedings all appear to have been conducted as a stockholders' meeting. The resolution authorizing the sale and conveyance of the mine, etc., in question, was adopted by the stockholders, as such, at said meeting, and not by the Board of Trustees, or at any meeting of said Board. The Board of Trustees do not appear to have ever acted at all upon the matter in the character of a Board, but the testimony shows that they acted in pursuance of the said resolution adopted at the meeting of stockholders.

Section five of the Act authorizing the formation of corporations for mining purposes provides: "That the corporate powers of the corporation shall be exercised by a Board of not less than three Trustees, who shall be stockholders," etc. And section seven provides that: "A majority of the whole number of Trustees shall form a Board for the transaction of business, and every decision of a majority of the persons duly assembled as a Board shall be valid as a corporate act." Conferring authority to sell and convey the corporate property is the exercise of a corporate power, and under these provisions the "corporate powers of the corporation" are to be exercised by the Board of Trustees when the majority are "duly assembled as a Board." When thus assembled and acting the decision of the majority "shall be valid as a corporate act." We find nothing in the Act authorizing the stockholders, either individually or collectively in a stockholders' meeting, to perform corporate acts of the character in question. The property in question was the property of the artificial being created by the statute. The whole title was in the corporation. The stockholders were not in their individual capacities owners of the property as tenants in common, joint tenants, copartners or otherwise. This proposition is so plain that no citation of authorities is needed. Had the stockholders all executed a deed to the property, they could have conveyed no title, for the reason that it was not in them and what they could not do themselves they could not by resolution or otherwise authorize another to do for them. The corporation could only act — could only speak — through the medium prescribed by law, and that is its Board of Trustees.... It is said, however, that the Trustees were also all present and participated in the proceedings at the stockholders' meeting and assented to the resolution; that the resolution therefore was approved by all of the constituents of the corporation, and the powers of the corporation were exhaustively exercised. But they were acting in their individual characters as stockholders, and not as a Board of Trustees. In this character they were not authorized to perform a corporate act of the kind in question.... The power to sell and convey could only be conferred by the Trustees when assembled and acting as a Board. This is the mode prescribed. As a Board they could perform valid corporate acts, and confer authority within the province of their powers, upon the Trustees individually or upon any other parties to perform acts as the agents of the corporation....

....

Judgment

Affirmed.

By the Court, Sawyer, J., on petition for rehearing:
The consequences assumed as the only basis of the argument in the petition for rehearing do not follow from anything determined or in any way suggested in the opinion in this case. We have nowhere held, or even intimated, that the Board of Trustees of a corporation can convey all the property of the corporation necessary to enable it to carry on the business for which it was organized, or do anything else destructive of the objects of its creation without the consent of its stockholders. We have not even held that it was competent for the Trustees, acting as a Board, to authorize the conveyance of the property now in question without the consent of the stockholders. There was no such question in the case. We simply held that the stockholders themselves could not authorize the Trustees, acting as individual Trustees, or anybody else, to convey it — that nobody could convey it unless authorized by some act of the Board of Trustees, acting as a Board. It may be conceded for the purposes of this case that the Board of Trustees itself could not authorize a conveyance of the property in question without the consent of the stockholders. But it is unnecessary to consider that question, for the case does not present or even suggest it. It will be time enough to decide that question when it arises.

Rehearing denied.

———

Although it surprises many clients, the universal rule in corporation law is that shareholders have no general power to manage a corporation. Rather, shareholders have only those powers specifically given them, mostly by the corporation statute, but in some instances by common law. The overwhelmingly important power of shareholders, of course, is to elect directors, and it is this authority to choose directors of their liking that gives shareholders their greatest power, especially when combined with the ability to remove directors at any time with or without cause,[1] which is the modern statutory norm, and when combined with the further ability to elect new directors to fill vacancies thus created.[2] Typically, all directors are elected annually, unless there are nine or more directors and their terms are staggered so that not all terms will conclude at the same time.[3]

Some corporation statutes give the shareholders the power to amend the corporation's bylaws, unless the charter provides that the directors have that power. The Model Act provides that the authority to amend bylaws resides with the shareholders and the directors, unless shareholders reserve to themselves exclusive power to amend particular provisions or the bylaws as a whole.[4]

All or almost all other instances of shareholders' powers relate to specific consents required for particular corporate actions. In each of those instances there is the statutory requirement that the board of directors first vote on the action and then send it on to the shareholders for their consent. Examples are charter amendments,[5] mergers and share exchanges,[6] sales of all or substantially all corporate assets other than in the regular course of business,[7] and voluntary dissolution.[8]

Shareholders generally exercise their powers at shareholders meetings. They elect directors at the annual meeting which is held at the time and place specified in the corporate bylaws.[9] Special meetings may be called by the board of directors, any person(s) authorized by the charter or bylaws, or the holders of at least 10 % of shares entitled to vote.[10] A written notice containing the date, time and place of the meeting must be sent to shareholders unless they waive the notice requirement.[11]

For a meeting to be properly convened, a quorum must be present. The Model Act sets quorum at a majority of shares entitled to vote on the particular matter,

---

[1] See MODEL BUSINESS CORP. ACT (1984) § 8.08(a).

[2] See id. 8.01(a)(1).

[3] See id. §§ 8.05, 8.06.

[4] See id. § 10.20.

[5] See, e.g., id. § 10.03. Id. § 10.02 authorizes the directors to amend the articles without shareholder action in certain limited situations, such as deleting names and addresses of initial directors, or deleting the name and address of the initial registered agent or registered office when a change is being made.

[6] See, e.g., id. §§ 11.01-11.03.

[7] See, e.g., id. § 12.02.

[8] See, e.g., id. § 14.02.

[9] See id. § 7.01.

[10] See id. § 7.02.

[11] See id. § 7.06.

unless a different requirement is included in the articles of incorporation.[12] In order to vote, shareholders must own their shares as of a specified record date.[13] Shareholders may vote either in person or by proxy.[14] Ordinary matters before the shareholders will be approved if the votes cast in favor of an action exceed the votes in opposition.[15] Directors are elected by a plurality of votes cast. Extraordinary matters, such as fundamental corporate changes, require approval by a majority of shareholders entitled to vote on the matter.[16] Shareholders may also take action by obtaining the written consents of all shareholders entitled to vote.[17] Although the Model Act does not restrict the use of this method, as a practical matter it is useful only for companies with a few shareholders.

Companies organized in Model Act jurisdictions must also provide shareholders with annual financial statements and statements regarding payments made to directors in connection with indemnification.[18] The Securities Exchange Act of 1934 also requires certain publicly traded corporations to provide their shareholders with financial statements. In addition, shareholders have the right to inspect and make copies of certain corporate records, such as shareholders' lists, corporate accounting records, and minutes from board of directors' meetings.[19] Shareholder lists must be available for inspection for a time beginning soon after the company sends notice of the meeting and extending through the meeting itself.[20] These lists are useful to someone trying to solicit the votes of other shareholders.

The *Pillsbury* case explores some of the issues associated with shareholders' inspection rights. As you read the case, consider whether the result would have been different if Honeywell were incorporated in a Model Act jurisdiction, and Model Act §§ 7.20, 16.01-.1603 applied.

STATE ex rel. PILLSBURY v. HONEYWELL, INC.

Supreme Court of Minnesota
191 N.W.2d 406 (1971)

KELLY, JUSTICE.

Petitioner appeals from an order and judgment of the district court denying all relief prayed for in a petition for writs of mandamus to compel respondent, Honeywell, Inc., (Honeywell) to produce its original shareholder ledger, current

---

[12] *See id.* § 7.25(a).
[13] *See id.* § 7.07.
[14] *See id.* § 7.22.
[15] *See id.* § 7.25(c).
[16] *See, e.g., id.* § 10.03(e).
[17] *See id.* § 7.04(a).
[18] *See id.* § 16.20.
[19] *See id.* § 16.02.
[20] *See id.* § 7.20.

shareholder ledger, and all corporate records dealing with weapons and munitions manufacture. We must affirm.

The issues raised by petitioner are as follows: (1) Whether Minnesota or Delaware law determines the right of a shareholder to inspect respondent's corporate books and records; (2) whether petitioner, who bought shares in respondent corporation for the purpose of changing its policy of manufacturing war munitions, had a proper purpose germane to a shareholder's interest; ...

Petitioner attended a meeting on July 3, 1969, of a group involved in what was known as the "Honeywell Project." Participants in the project believed that American involvement in Vietnam was wrong, that a substantial portion of Honeywell's production consisted of munitions used in that war, and that Honeywell should stop this production of munitions. Petitioner had long opposed the Vietnam war, but it was at the July 3rd meeting that he first learned of Honeywell's involvement. He was shocked at the knowledge that Honeywell had a large government contract to produce anti-personnel fragmentation bombs. Upset because of knowledge that such bombs were produced in his own community by a company which he had known and respected, petitioner determined to stop Honeywell's munitions production.

On July 14, 1969, petitioner ordered his fiscal agent to purchase 100 shares of Honeywell. He admits that the sole purpose of the purchase was to give himself a voice in Honeywell's affairs so he could persuade Honeywell to cease producing munitions. Apparently not aware of that purpose, petitioner's agent registered the stock in the name of a Pillsbury family nominee — Quad & Co. Upon discovering the nature of the registration, petitioner bought one share of Honeywell in his own name on August 11, 1969. In his deposition testimony petitioner made clear the reason for his purchase of Honeywell's shares:

"Q... (D)o I understand that you requested Mr. Lacey to buy these 100 shares of Honeywell in order to follow up on the desire you had to bring to Honeywell management and to stockholders these theses that you have told us about here today?

A. Yes. That was my motivation."

The "theses" referred to are petitioner's beliefs concerning the propriety of producing munitions for the Vietnam war.

During July 1969, subsequent to the July 3, 1969, meeting and after he had ordered his agent to purchase the 100 shares of Honeywell stock, petitioner inquired into a trust which had been formed for his benefit by his grandmother. The purpose of the inquiry was to discover whether shares of Honeywell were included in the trust. It was then, for the first time, that petitioner discovered that he had a contingent beneficial interest under the terms of the trust in 242 shares of Honeywell.

Prior to the instigation of this suit, petitioner submitted two formal demands to Honeywell requesting that it produce its original shareholder ledger, current shareholder ledger, and all corporate records dealing with weapons and munitions manufacture. Honeywell refused.

On November 24, 1969, a petition was filed for writs of mandamus ordering Honeywell to produce the above mentioned records. In response, Honeywell answered the petition and served a notice of deposition on petitioner, who moved that the answer be stricken as procedurally premature and that an order be issued to limit the deposition. After a hearing, the trial court denied the motion, and the deposition was taken on December 15, 1969.

In the deposition petitioner outlined his beliefs concerning the Vietnam war and his purpose for his involvement with Honeywell. He expressed his desire to communicate with other shareholders in the hope of altering Honeywell's board of directors and thereby changing its policy. To this end, he testified, business records are necessary to insure accuracy.

A hearing was held on January 8, 1970, during which Honeywell introduced the deposition, conceded all material facts stated therein, and argued that petitioner was not entitled to any relief as a matter of law. Petitioner asked that alternative writs of mandamus issue for all the relief requested in his petition. On April 8, 1970, the trial court dismissed the petition, holding that the relief requested was for an improper and indefinite purpose. Petitioner contends in this appeal that the dismissal was in error.

1. Honeywell is a Delaware corporation doing business in Minnesota. Both petitioner and Honeywell spent considerable effort in arguing whether Delaware or Minnesota law applies. The trial court, applying Delaware law, determined that the outcome of the case rested upon whether or not petitioner has a proper purpose germane to his interest as a shareholder. Del. Code Ann. tit. 8, § 220 (Supp. 1968),....

Under the Delaware statute the shareholder must prove a proper purpose to inspect corporate records other than shareholder lists. Del. Code Ann. tit. 8, § 220(c) (Supp.1968).... The case was decided solely on the pleadings and the deposition of petitioner, the court determining from them that petitioner was not entitled to relief as a matter of law. Thus, problems of burden of proof did not confront the trial court and this issue was not even raised in this court.

2. The trial court ordered judgment for Honeywell, ruling that petitioner had not demonstrated a proper purpose germane to his interest as a stockholder. Petitioner contends that a stockholder who disagrees with management has an absolute right to inspect corporate records for purposes of soliciting proxies. He would have this court rule that such solicitation is per se a "proper purpose." Honeywell argues that a "proper purpose" contemplates concern with investment return. We agree with Honeywell.

This court has had several occasions to rule on the propriety of shareholders' demands for inspection of corporate books and records. Minn. St. § 300.32, not applicable here, has been held to be declaratory of the common-law principle that a stockholder is entitled to inspection for a proper purpose germane to his business interests. While inspection will not be permitted for purposes of curiosity, speculation, or vexation, adverseness to management and a desire to gain control of the corporation for economic benefit does not indicate an improper purpose.

Several courts agree with petitioner's contention that a mere desire to communicate with other shareholders is, per se, a proper purpose. This would seem to confer an almost absolute right to inspection. We believe that a better rule would allow inspections only if the shareholder has a proper purpose for such communication....

The act of inspecting a corporation's shareholder ledger and business records must be viewed in its proper perspective. In terms of the corporate norm, inspection is merely the act of the concerned owner checking on what is in part his property. In the context of the large firm, inspection can be more akin to a weapon in corporate warfare. The effectiveness of the weapon is considerable: "Considering the huge size of many modern corporations and the necessarily complicated nature of their bookkeeping, it is plain that to permit their thousands of stockholders to roam at will through their records would render impossible not only any attempt to keep their records efficiently, but the proper carrying on of their businesses." Because the power to inspect may be the power to destroy, it is important that only those with a bona fide interest in the corporation enjoy that power.

That one must have proper standing to demand inspection has been recognized by statutes in several jurisdictions. Courts have also balked at compelling inspection by a shareholder holding an insignificant amount of stock in the corporation.

Petitioner's standing as a shareholder is quite tenuous. He only owns one share in his own name, bought for the purposes of this suit. He had previously ordered his agent to buy 100 shares, but there is no showing of investment intent. While his agent had a cash balance in the $ 400,000 portfolio, petitioner made no attempt to determine whether Honeywell was a good investment or whether more profitable shares would have to be sold to finance the Honeywell purchase. Furthermore, petitioner's agent had the power to sell the Honeywell shares without his consent. Petitioner also had a contingent beneficial interest in 242 shares. Courts are split on the question of whether an equitable interest entitles one to inspection. Indicative of petitioner's concern regarding his equitable holdings is the fact that he was unaware of them until he had decided to bring this suit.

Petitioner had utterly no interest in the affairs of Honeywell before he learned of Honeywell's production of fragmentation bombs. Immediately after obtaining this knowledge, he purchased stock in Honeywell for the sole purpose of asserting ownership privileges in an effort to force Honeywell to cease such production. We agree with the court in *Chas. A. Day & Co. v. Booth*, 123 Maine 443, 447, 123 A. 557, 558 (1924) that "where it is shown that such stockholding is only colorable, or solely for the purpose of maintaining proceedings of this kind, (we) fail to see how the petitioner can be said to be a 'person interested,' entitled as of right to inspect...." But for his opposition to Honeywell's policy, petitioner probably would not have bought Honeywell stock, would not be interested in Honeywell's profits and would not desire to communicate with Honeywell's shareholders. His avowed purpose in buying Honeywell stock was to place himself in a position to try to impress his opinions favoring a reordering of priorities upon Honeywell management and its other shareholders. Such a motivation can hardly be deemed a proper purpose germane to his economic interest as a shareholder.[21]

3. The fact that petitioner alleged a proper purpose in his petition will not necessarily compel a right to inspection. "A mere statement in a petition alleging a proper purpose is not sufficient. The facts in each case may be examined." Neither is inspection mandated by the recitation of proper purpose in petitioner's testimony. Conversely, a company cannot defeat inspection by merely alleging an improper purpose. From the deposition, the trial court concluded that petitioner had already formed strong opinions on the immorality and the social and economic wastefulness of war long before he bought stock in Honeywell. His sole motivation was to change Honeywell's course of business because that course was incompatible with his political views. If unsuccessful, petitioner indicated that he would sell the Honeywell stock.

We do not mean to imply that a shareholder with a bona fide investment interest could not bring this suit if motivated by concern with the long- or short-term economic effects on Honeywell resulting from the production of war munitions. Similarly, this suit might be appropriate when a shareholder has a bona fide concern about the adverse effects of abstention from profitable war contracts on his investment in Honeywell.

In the instant case, however, the trial court, in effect, has found from all the facts that petitioner was not interested in even the long-term well-being of Honeywell or the enhancement of the value of his shares. His sole purpose was to persuade the company to adopt his social and political concerns, irrespective of any economic benefit to himself or Honeywell. This purpose on the part of one

---

[21] We do not question petitioner's good faith incident to his political and social philosophy; nor did the trial court. In a well prepared memorandum, the lower court stated: "By enumerating the foregoing this Court does not mean to belittle or to be derisive of Petitioner's motivations and intentions because this Court cannot but draw the conclusion that the Petitioner is sincere in his political and social philosophy, but this Court does not feel that this is a proper forum for the advancement of these political-social views by way of direct contact with the stockholders of Honeywell Company or any other company. If the courts were to grant these rights on the basis of the foregoing, anyone who has a political-social philosophy which differs with that of a company in which he becomes a shareholder can secure a writ and any company can be faced with a rash and multitude of these types of actions which are not bona fide efforts to engage in a proxy fight for the purpose of taking over the company or electing directors, which the courts have recognized as being perfectly legitimate and acceptable."

buying into the corporation does not entitle the petitioner to inspect Honeywell's books and records.[22]

4. Petitioner argues that he wishes to inspect the stockholder ledger in order that he may correspond with other shareholders with the hope of electing to the board one or more directors who represent his particular viewpoint. On p. 30 of his brief he states that this purpose alone compels inspection: "... (T)his Court has said that a stockholder's motives or 'good faith' are not a test of his right of inspection, except as 'bad faith' actually manifests some recognized 'improper purpose' — such as vexation of the corporation, or purely destructive plans, or nothing specific, just pure idle curiosity, or necessarily illegal ends, or nothing germane to his interests...." While a plan to elect one or more directors is specific and the election of directors normally would be a proper purpose, here the purpose was not germane to petitioner's or Honeywell's economic interest. Instead, the plan was designed to further petitioner's political and social beliefs. Since the requisite propriety of purpose germane to his or Honeywell's economic interest is not present, the allegation that petitioner seeks to elect a new board of directors is insufficient to compel inspection.

The *Pillsbury* decision was disapproved by the Delaware Supreme Court one year later, in *Credit Bureau Reports, Inc. v. Credit Bureau of St. Paul, Inc.*, 290 A.2d 691 (Del. 1972). In *Credit Bureau*, the court required the defendant corporation to permit a shareholder, who was also a supplier to the company, to inspect the company's shareholder list. The shareholder's purpose in obtaining the list was to solicit proxies for the purpose of persuading the company to improve its treatment of its suppliers.

In order for a lawyer to be prepared for questions about the authority of shareholders, it will be helpful to understand the situations in which those

---

[22] Petitioner cites *Medical Committee for Human Rights v. S.E.C.*, 139 App.D.C. 226, 432 F.2d 659 (1970), for the proposition that economic benefit and community service may, in the motives of a shareholder, blend together. We have ruled that petitioner does not meet this test because he had no investment motivation for his inspection demands. The Medical Committee case did not reach the merits, the court ruling only that S.E.C. actions concerning the inclusion of proxy statements are reviewable. It is interesting to note, however, that the case presents an analogous factual situation. Shareholders sought to solicit proxies to stop the Dow Chemical Company's manufacture of napalm on grounds that management had "decided to pursue a course of activity which generated little profit ... and actively impaired the company's public relations and recruitment activities because Management considered this action morally and politically desirable." 139 App.D.C. 249, 432 F.2d 681. The court, in dictum, expressed its disapproval of Dow's claim that it could use its power to impose management's personal political and moral prejudices. It would be even more anomalous if an outsider with no economic concern for the corporation could attempt to adapt Honeywell's policies to his own social convictions.

questions tend to arise. One occurs when a shareholders' meeting is imminent or in progress and a lawyer is asked whether the shareholders can vote on a particular matter or whether the matter has to wait for directors' action. Another arises when it is possible to assemble a quorum of the shareholders but not of the directors or, along those same lines, where shareholders are available to sign consents in lieu of a meeting but the directors are not. When the need exists for the corporation to take action quickly, it is sometimes hard to convince shareholders that they lack the necessary power to effect the deserved action. That especially is the case where (1) the shareholders and the directors are exactly the same persons, which is a common situation in a closely held company, and (2) a quorum for a directors' meeting cannot be obtained, but a quorum for a shareholders' meeting can be (the difference being that shareholders can be represented at a meeting by proxy holders while directors cannot).

SECTION II. FUNCTIONS AND AUTHORITY OF DIRECTORS

A popular misconception about the authority of directors, which goes along with misconceptions about shareholders' power, is that the directors get their authority from the shareholders. The issue of where directors get their power is nicely explored in *Manson v. Curtis,* a case decided by the New York Court of Appeals during World War I.

MANSON v. CURTIS

Court of Appeals of New York
119 N.E. 559 (1918)

COLLIN, J.

The action is to recover the damages arising to the plaintiff by reason of the acts of the defendant. The Special Term decided ... that the complaint did not state facts sufficient to constitute a cause of action, and should be dismissed. The consequent judgment was affirmed by the Appellate Division.

[The complaint grew out of an alleged breach by the defendant of an agreement, between the plaintiff and the defendant, relating to control by the plaintiff of the Bermuda-Atlantic Steamship Company, a corporation in which each was a shareholder.]

... The fundamental and dominant purpose and intent of the parties [to the agreement] ... necessitated ... passive directors. The conditions which the parties wished to meet and their intent necessitated and contemplated the selecting of directors who should remain passive or mechanical to the will and word of the plaintiff. The management of the affairs of the corporation by its board of directors and the management of them by the plaintiff as contemplated by the agreement are irreconcilable and mutually destructive.

The prerogatives and functions of the directors of a stock corporation are sufficiently defined and established. The affairs of every corporation shall be managed by its board of directors (General Corporation Law § 34), subject, however, to the valid by-laws adopted by the stockholders (Stock Corporation Law § 30). In corporate bodies, the powers of the board of directors are, in a very important sense, original and undelegated. The stockholders do not confer, nor can they revoke, those powers. They are derivative only in the sense of being received from the state in the act of incorporation. The directors convened as a board are the primary possessors of all the powers which the charter confers, and like private principals they may delegate to agents of their own appointment the performance of any acts which they themselves can perform. The recognition of this principle is absolutely necessary in the affairs of every corporation whose powers are vested in a board of directors. All powers directly conferred by statute, or impliedly granted, of necessity, must be exercised by the directors who are constituted by the law as the agency for the doing of corporate acts. In the management of the affairs of the corporation, they are dependent solely upon their own knowledge of its business and their own judgment as to what its interests require. While the ordinary rules of law relating to an agent are applicable in considering the acts of a board of directors on behalf of a corporation when dealing with third persons, the individual directors making up the board are not mere employees, but a part of an elected body of officers constituting the executive agents of the corporation. They hold such office charged with the duty to act for the corporation according to their best judgment, and in so doing they cannot be controlled in the reasonable exercise and performance of such duty. As a general rule, the stockholders cannot act in relation to the ordinary business of the corporation, nor can they control the directors in the exercise of the judgment vested in them by virtue of their office. The relation of the directors to the stockholders is essentially that of trustee and cestui que trust. The peculiar relation that they bear to the corporation and the owners of its stock grows out of the inability of the corporation to act except through such managing officers and agents. The corporation is the owner of the property, but the directors in the performance of their duty possess it, and act in every way as if they owned it. Directors are the exclusive, executive representatives of the corporation, and are charged with the administration of its internal affairs and the management and use of its assets. Clearly the law does not permit the stockholders to create a sterilized board of directors. Corporations are the creatures of the state, and must comply with the exactions and regulations it imposes. We conclude that the agreement here is illegal and void, and its violation is not a basis for a cause of action....

....

Contemporary definitions of the roles of directors can be found in the American Law Institute Principles of Corporate Governance: Analysis and Recommendations (1994) ("ALI") and the Model Business Corporation Act (1984). The ALI has defined the role of the directors of publicly held corporations in the following way. Section 3.01 provides that:

> The management of the business of a publicly held corporation should be conducted by or under the supervision of such principal senior executives as are designated by the board of directors, and by those other officers and employees to whom the management function is delegated by the board or those executives, subject to the functions and powers of the board under § 3.02.[23]

Section 3.02 describes the powers of the board of directors as follows:

> (a) The board of directors of a publicly held corporation should perform the following functions: (1) Select, regularly evaluate, fix the compensation of, and where appropriate, replace the principal senior executives; (2) Oversee the conduct of the corporation's business to evaluate whether the business is being properly managed: (3) Review and, where appropriate, approve the corporation's financial objectives and major corporate plans and actions; (4) Review and, where appropriate, approve major changes in, and determinations of other major questions of choice respecting, the appropriate auditing and accounting principles and practices to be used in the preparation of the corporation's financial statements; (5) Perform such other functions as are prescribed by law, or assigned to the board under a standard of the corporation; (b) A board of directors also has power to: (1) Initiate and adopt corporate plans, commitments, and actions; (2) Initiate and adopt changes in accounting principles and practices; (3) Provide advice and counsel to the principal senior executives; (4) Instruct any committee, principal senior executive, or other officer and review the actions of any committee, principal senior executive, or other officer; (5) Make recommendations to shareholders; (6) Manage the business of the corporation; (7) Act as to all other corporate matters not requiring shareholder approval.[24]

Model Act § 8.01(b) is the prototypical modern statutory grant to directors of their general power over the management of a corporation. Its most essential provision is: "All corporate powers shall be exercised by or under authority of, and the business and affairs of a corporation managed under the direction of, its board of directors, subject to any limitation set forth in the articles of incorporation or in an agreement authorized under § 7.32." Section 7.32 permits shareholders of privately held corporations to enter into shareholder agreements

---

[23] American Law Institute, Principles of Corporate Governance: Analysis and Recommendations § 3.01 (1994).

[24] *Id.* at § 3.02

modifying the traditional management structure. The language of the provision makes clear that directors are not required to manage a corporation directly on a day-to-day basis, but may do so through delegation and oversight.

In Model Act § 8.01 (b), the phrase "subject to any limitation set forth in the articles of incorporation or in an agreement authorized under § 7.32" serves two purposes. First, it warns the reader that limitations on the board's power may also be imposed by provisions in the company's charter and private agreements. Second, it introduces the concept, fairly new to corporation law, that management structures other than one featuring a supremely powerful board may be established in the charter and by private agreement. That brief provision, read along with the language in Model Act § 2.02(b)(2) allowing a charter to contain any provision not inconsistent with law regarding "(ii) managing the business and regulating the affairs of the corporation; (iii) defining, limiting, and regulating the powers of the corporation, its board of directors, and shareholders..." gives corporate planners nearly carte blanche to vary the corporate management scheme. The charter could, for example, limit the board's power in specific areas or take away all the board's power and give it to the shareholders. (The Official Comment to Model Act § 7.32 affirms for privately held corporations, the validity of shareholders' agreements containing provisions "inconsistent with the statutory norms.")

Management flexibility was written into the Model Act and other statutes as a result of suggestions that traditional corporation statutes did not fit the needs of closely held corporations. It has been thought by some, for example, that it is preferable in the typical small closely held corporation to simplify corporate decisionmaking by having only shareholders and officers. This approach is allowed under some statutes. Actually, however, in many situations, the main effect of the flexible management options of modern statutes has been to show the usefulness inherent in the traditional centralized management structure. Exceptionally few corporations operate without a board, for example, and those that do may pay a high price for apparent simplicity unless their counsel has planned carefully.

Trouble may begin as soon as an officer or shareholder of a closely held corporation operating without a board of directors attempts the early corporate act of opening a bank account. Banking procedures are set up to handle accounts that have been authorized by a corporation's board of directors. The expectation is that the bank account has been authorized by the board through the adoption of an appropriate resolution at a properly convened board meeting. At minimum, the officer attempting to open an account may encounter resistance from bank employees who are unclear how to proceed in situations where a board does not exist. At maximum, the bank's officers insist on consulting their lawyers before opening an account for a directorless corporation. The result is delay and, possibly, additional cost for both parties to the transaction. That sort of problem follows such a corporation throughout its life, coming up every time the corporation wants to enter into a transaction that traditionally is accompanied by an authorizing board resolution.

The problems arising in connection with a closely held corporation that has eliminated its board of directors also apply to other forms of limited liability business forms in which the principals have opted for a participatory rather than centralized management structure. Limited liability companies and limited liability partnerships are two such forms. As the preceding banking example demonstrates, the procedures and forms for many routine business transactions are based on practices that developed when the two common business types were general partnerships and corporations. Business persons dealing with corporations knew that decisionmaking authority resulted from provisions in the articles of incorporation, the bylaws or resolutions of the board of directors. Business persons dealing with general partnerships knew that the partners have individual, unlimited liability for transactions entered into on behalf of the company. It may not be clear to third parties dealing with other limited liability firms that have eliminated centralized management just who is authorized to make binding decisions on behalf of the firm.

Referring again to *Gashwiler v. Willis,* which appears at the beginning of Section I, one may recall that the statute discussed in that case required a board of at least three directors, each of whom must be a shareholder. Those were the traditional statutory requirements. Most modern statutes have done away with such requirements, however. The Model Act, for example, requires only one director, and it does not require directors to be shareholders.[25] Experience taught that those traditional requirements serve no purpose. In the one- or two-shareholder corporation, the requirement of three directors typically ends up a meaningless formality, since any nonshareholder director can be replaced at will by the shareholder or shareholders. Similarly, the requirement that each director be a shareholder is an empty stricture in a corporation in which the number of real owners is fewer than the number of directors. Such a requirement merely leads to the issuance of what are referred to as directors' qualifying shares. Typically, a certificate representing one share is issued to each "extra" director, who immediately indorses the certificate for transfer and gives it back to the corporation with the understanding that the transfer will be effective as soon as the director's term is over.

The requirement in the statute in *Gashwiler* that the board act by majority decision at a meeting at which a majority of the whole number of directors is present also has been the traditional norm. There is a trick here for the uninitiated. Suppose that a corporation's charter or bylaws provide for a board of nine members, but that because of resignations or failures to fill all the positions the corporation has only five directors. How many directors are necessary for a quorum? The answer is "five," because the phrase "whole number of directors"

---

[25] MODEL BUSINESS CORP. ACT (1984) § 8.03.

is a term of art meaning the number of directors the corporation would have if there were no vacancies. In modern statutes, the quorum requirement is usually stated as a majority of "whole board," "full board," "entire board" or of the "fixed number of directors." Because corporation statutes generally have been drafted and refined by practical lawyers who have tried hard to make the governance portions of the statutes easily usable by corporate managers, statutory provisions usually track the expectations of those managers. The rules on quorums are one place where that is not the case. Unless they are taught otherwise, clients almost invariably assume that quorum requirements are based on the number of directors the corporation actually has, not on the number it is authorized to have.

While the *Gashwiler* statutory quorum and voting requirements stated what was the traditional norm, modern statutes generally contain some important differences. Under the Model Act, for example, both the percentage of directors that constitutes a quorum and the percentage of the quorum whose agreement is required to take action may be increased beyond a mere majority in a corporation's charter or bylaws.[26] The quorum may also be decreased to one-third of the fixed number of directors.[27] A far more important addition in modern statutes is the opportunity given directors to act by unanimous written consents in lieu of a meeting, which is a possibility that is discussed in preceding materials. Directors may also take action by conference call or other form of technology that permits all directors simultaneously to hear each other during the meeting.

Note that under neither the traditional nor the more liberal modern statutory approaches to directors' decisionmaking do directors have any power as individuals. Their power is collective only. The theory behind the traditional rule that directors may act only as a group, and only while assembled at a meeting, is that the give and take of a group discussion will help ensure the best corporate decisions. Since directors' written consents in lieu of meetings almost always must be unanimous, they fit within that theory by virtue of the idea that if all the directors are already of one mind on an issue, there would be no give and take at a meeting.

There is one final exception to the rule that directors must act together and at a meeting: under modern statutes directors may act through a committee they have established. The typical statutory provision on board committees provides that, by the vote of at least a majority of the whole board,[28] the board may

---

[26] *See id.* § 8.24.

[27] *See id.*

[28] Note the special vote required for the establishment of committees is the greater of a majority of all directors in office or the number specified in the bylaws for director action. Unless clients are reminded of that requirement, they are inclined to consider valid board action to be taken if there is an affirmative vote of a majority of a quorum, which is the usual rule in directors' decision making. What saves the situation in many cases is that votes by directors tend to be unanimous — after whatever discussion is necessary to reach consensus. Thus, if quorum requires a majority of

designate from among its members any committees it wishes, and may delegate to a committee any of the board's powers, except for certain powers that the statute prohibits to committees. The Model Act's prohibitions are representative:

> A committee may not ... (1) authorize distributions, (2) approve or propose to shareholders action that this Act requires to be approved by shareholders; (3) fill vacancies on the board of directors or on any of its committtees; (4) amend articles of incorporation ...; (5) adopt, amend, or repeal bylaws; (6) approve a plan of merger not requiring shareholder approval; (7) authorize or approve reacquisition of shares except according to a formula or method prescribed by the board of directors; or (8) authorize or approve the issuance or sale or contract for the sale of shares, or determine the designation and relative rights, preferences, and limitations of a class or a series of shares, except that the board of directors may authorize a committee (or a senior executive officer of the corporation) to do so within limits specifically prescribed by the board of directors.[29]

The first committee that a board usually appoints is an executive committee, which traditionally is a committee having all the powers of the board when the board is not in session, except those powers prohibited to a committee by statute. To call a committee an executive committee and then give it substantially different powers than that is to invite trouble, since everyone dealing with the corporation will assume that its executive committee has standard authority. Often a corporation has a board made up of both inside and outside directors.[30] Because of their everyday involvement in the corporation's affairs, inside directors usually are more available for meetings on short notice than are outside directors. Partly for that reason, it is common for an executive committee's members to be all or almost all inside directors. Other committees that are common are the nominating committee, audit committee (which selects the company's auditors) and the compensation committee.

So far, our discussion of directors has focused on what directors have the power to do — which is just about anything relating to the business and affairs of a corporation, save for those few things for which directors need the shareholders' consent. That is important, but it also is important to understand what directors actually do in corporations and what they tend to leave to others.

Here it is necessary to distinguish between corporations whose directors are substantial shareholders and those whose directors are not, because in the former

---

the full board, if a quorum is present and if a vote is unanimous, the special voting requirement of a majority of the full board (which also is the quorum requirement) is met automatically. The vote becomes problematic when the quorum requirement is less than a majority of the full board and the required majority of the full board is not present.

[29] MODEL BUSINESS CORP. ACT (1984) § 8.25.

[30] Inside directors are directors who, as officers, work full-time for the corporation. For outside directors, their directorship is their only position in the corporation.

corporations, directors can be expected to take an unusually active role in decisionmaking. Partially because the director who is a substantial shareholder is much more likely to be found in the closely held than in the publicly held corporation, closely held corporations more often have active directors than do publicly held ones. Beyond that, it is hard to generalize about what directors actually do in closely held corporations, because the distribution of real power in those corporations varies so greatly. In many closely held corporations, one majority shareholder dominates all corporate decisions, rendering board action a mere formality. In other closely held corporations, a board of equally powerful director-shareholders meets often to argue out all important decisions. On the continuum between those two extremes there exists a seemingly infinite variety of director involvement in corporate decisionmaking.

There is more consistency in the level and type of director decisionmaking in the publicly held corporation, once you set aside those publicly held corporations whose directors also are substantial shareholders. Miles Mace of the Harvard Business School conducted extensive research on what outside directors do and don't do in the typical large or medium-sized publicly held corporation. He reported his findings in a now famous book, *Directors: Myth and Reality,* and in a not so well known but more widely available article, *The President and the Board of Directors.*[31]

Mace found that in the kinds of corporations he studied, outside directors typically do three things: "[S]erve as a source of advice and counsel, offer some sort of discipline value, and act in crisis situations."[32] They do not, he found, establish objectives, strategies, or major policies, but rather leave those jobs to the corporation's officers.

From reading Mace's findings, it is easy to underestimate the value to the corporation of the things Mace says directors do. That is a mistake. In their advisory role, directors discuss troublesome corporate matters with the chief executive officer, almost exclusively on the telephone or in informal settings outside board meetings. When one considers that outside directors are familiar with the corporation in a way that management consultants typically cannot be, and that outside directors tend to be chief executive officers of other corporations or to have other significant management or professional experience, outside directors provide a chief executive officer with a source of help in decision making that is unavailable from anyone else.

Mace describes the discipline value of directors this way:

> Presidents and other members of top management in describing the discipline value of boards, indicated that the requirement of appearing formally before a board of directors consisting of respected, able people of stature, no matter how friendly, motivates the company managers to do a

---

[31] Miles Mace, *The President and the Board of Directors,* HARV. BUS. REV. 37.
[32] *See id.* at 38.

better job of thinking through their problems and of being prepared with solutions, explanations, or rationales.[33]

One also can easily see how that discipline value carries over into corporate actions generally, not just actions that are formally presented to the board. Because directors typically are given fairly broad information about their corporations, officers know that any significant decision they make may come to the directors' attention.

The role of directors in crisis situations can be a critical one. One classic crisis that Mace describes is the sudden death of the chief executive officer when succession has not been decided upon in advance. Another is when the chief executive officer's performance is so poor that a replacement must be found promptly. In situations such as those, it is only the directors who have either the statutory power or the real-world ability to act.

In the years since Mace did his research, two developments have influenced the behavior of directors. First, lawsuits against directors, alleging mismanagement, have become much more numerous. Second, there has been a widespread agreement among both scholars and corporate managers that the main function of directors should be to monitor the performance of the chief executive and other principal officers. As a result of those two developments, the first of which pushed directors toward being more active and the second of which told directors the way they should be more active, monitoring must be added to Mace's list of what directors do.

There are, however, other important aspects of board members' relationships with the corporation they serve that affect their willingness and ability to act in more than an oversight role. First, the company's chief executive officer plays an important role in selecting board members, even though the formal process of selection may be accomplished by the recommendations of a board nominating committee, with approval by the full board. Board members who wish to continue in their role must maintain a good relationship with the chief executive officer. In addition, outside directors often have other business connections with the company. They may be the company's outside counsel, a consultant, or perhaps, a supplier. These additional roles make it more difficult for an outsider to be truly independent. Second, the full board itself meets only six to twelve times a year at most and then for only a few hours at a time. The amount of information that can be presented and digested at such meetings is limited by time. And finally, much of the board's work is done in committees, which report back to the full board. Depending on the make up of the committees, outside directors may or may not play an influential role in the work of important committees.

One last point should be made about the difference between inside and outside directors' relations with the corporation they serve. Inside directors, by virtue of their positions as officers or employees, have ready access to corporate records,

---

[33] *See id.* at 39.

at least those within their sphere of operations. That is not necessarily the case with outside directors. Unlike the Model Act, which does not address the subject, § 3.03 of the Principles of Corporate Governance gives directors the right to "inspect and copy all books, records, and documents of every kind, and to inspect the physical properties, of the corporation and of its subsidiaries, domestic or foreign, at any reasonable time, in person or by an attorney or other agent." This broad grant of powers is subject to judicial enforcement.

SECTION III. FUNCTIONS AND AUTHORITY OF OFFICERS

Officers are agents of the board of directors acting collectively as the corporation, not of the shareholders. Just as the Model Act contains provisions relevant to directors' actions and obligations, corporation statutes have very similar provisions with respect to corporate officers. The structure and the substance of Model Act § 8.40 are instructive in that its provisions control what officers a corporation must have and who shall choose them. The section provides that a corporation will have "the officers described in its bylaws or appointed by the board of directors in accordance with the bylaws." The Model Act thus does not prescribe either in number or position that the company have specific officers, although it does require one officer to have "responsibility for preparing minutes of the directors' and shareholders' meetings and for authenticating records of the corporation." These functions are usually associated with the corporate secretary. In addition, under the Model Act, the "same individual may simultaneously hold more than one office in a corporation." This last provision is particularly suitable for small companies with only a few officers. It should also be noted that if authorized by the bylaws or the board of directors, "A duly appointed officer may appoint one or more officers or assistant officers...." This approach adds a measure of flexibility to the appointment of additional corporate officers. They may be chosen in any way the corporation wishes, so long as the procedure is authorized by the bylaws or the board.

The flexibility of the Model Act approach contrasts with those jurisdictions requiring specified officers, (usually at least a president and secretary, and often also a vice president and treasurer), and prohibiting the same person from acting as both president and secretary. However, even states requiring named officers typically allow corporations to have whatever other officers they wish.

So far we have discussed what officers a corporation must or may have and how they are to be chosen. The equally important question is: What are their powers? Model Act § 8.41 continues the statute's customary flexibility regarding officers' powers: "Each officer has the authority and shall perform the duties set forth in the bylaws, or, to the extent consistent with the bylaws, the duties prescribed by the board of directors or by direction of an officer authorized by the board of directors to prescribe the duties of other officers."

Although a board could establish the authority of an officer either by adopting a bylaw provision containing a general statement of the officer's powers or by adopting a resolution, in fact, the board often determines the exact powers of officers by acquiescence rather than by formal action. After that, it may "give" an officer power simply by allowing the officer to continue doing what he or she has been doing, which often is something the officer has been told to do by another officer. There is no real doubt about the effectiveness of the board's grant of power by acquiescence in such a case — there being no significant chance, for example, that a court would allow the corporation to disavow a contract signed by an officer in the exercise of such authority. Thus the Model Act provision is somewhat misleading in that it seems to require an affirmative act — adoption of bylaw or act of board or another officer — to establish the authority of an officers.

The Model Act provision we have been discussing actually is misleading in a more basic way. As indicated above, the Model Act seems to say that for an officer to have authority, the authority must either be spelled out in the bylaws or the result of an affirmative act of the board or another officer. The provision leaves unsaid anything about a number of types of authority, arising under the principles of agency law, that the board grants to officers by electing them to specified offices. Those are implied authority, incidental authority, and apparent authority.[34] Simply by being elected to a particular office with generally recognized duties, the officer is automatically granted the powers that are associated with that office, save when the board specifically indicates that the officer will not have a particular power. An example is the power of the vice president to act for the president when the president is incapacitated.

Incidental authority of an officer is the authority to perform acts that are incidental to acts for which the officer has actual authority (actual authority may include implied authority and also any authority that is specifically granted, for example in the bylaws or by the board). Suppose that the board gives the treasurer the authority to invest the corporation's funds in common stocks. In that situation, the treasurer probably would have the incidental power to contract with an investment banking firm for investment advice, so long as the terms of the contract were reasonable in the circumstances.

Apparent authority of officers can be the most troublesome form of authority for a corporation, because that form of authority cannot easily be controlled. The apparent authority of an officer is coextensive with the authority that usually resides in the office held. That sounds complicated, but in this case apparent authority is quite simple. If the board of directors elects a person to the office of vice president, but indicates that the person will not have the power to act for the president if the president becomes incapacitated, the vice president obviously will not have the actual authority to act in that situation. Nevertheless, since the power to act when the president is incapacitated usually resides in the office of vice president, the vice president will have the apparent authority to act unless third

---

[34]RESTATEMENT (SECOND) OF AGENCY § 27 cmt. a (1958).

parties dealing with the vice president know of the limitation. The result is that if, when the president is incapacitated, the vice president signs a contract that the president could have signed, the corporation ordinarily will be bound. Apparent authority is only defeated if a person dealing with an officer having apparent authority knows of the officer's lack of actual authority.

With that background in mind, it may be helpful to examine the authority associated with in the more common corporate offices: president, chair of the board, vice president, secretary, and treasurer.

A. PRESIDENT

One of the most famous cases dealing with the authority of the president is *Joseph Greenspon's Sons Iron & Steel Co. v. Pecos Valley Gas Co.* Although it is only a Delaware superior court case, its instructional value is so high that law students have studied it for decades.

JOSEPH GREENSPON'S SONS IRON & STEEL CO. v. PECOS VALLEY GAS CO.

Superior Court of Delaware
156 A. 350 (1931)

RODNEY, J., charging the Jury:

This is an action by Joseph Greenspon's Sons Iron and Steel Company, a corporation of the State of Missouri, the plaintiff, against the Pecos Valley Gas Company, a corporation of the State of Delaware, the defendant, to recover a sum of money which the plaintiff claims is due to it by reason of the alleged breach of a contract.

The plaintiff claims that the defendant, on the 7th day of January, 1929, agreed to buy from it 45 miles of 65/8" gas pipe at the sum of 61 cents a foot. The pipe was not delivered. The plaintiff has proved, and the defendant concedes that the plaintiff could have obtained the pipe at 51 cents a foot, and so the plaintiff alleges that he lost the sum of 10 cents a foot upon the amount agreed to be purchased. This by arithmetical computation amounts to $ 23,760.00 and this is the amount claimed by the plaintiff as the profits he would have made had the contract been carried out by the defendant.

The defendant denies that it is obligated to the plaintiff in any amount. It admits that Mr. Woods, the President of the defendant company, signed the contract in question, but it insists that the signature was affixed thereto in a conditional manner and was understood to be dependent upon the approval of the Board of Directors and of Mr. Burkett, the General Manager, who subsequently would not and did not approve thereof and that, therefore, no valid contract was ever entered into on behalf of the defendant company....

[The court charged the jury first to determine whether the contract was in fact conditional on the approval of the General Manager.]

If, on the other hand, you should find from the evidence that the contract was unconditional and not subject to any approval by Mr. Burkett, the General Manager, then you should further consider the matter with reference to the power of the President to bind the defendant company.

At this point I may be of some service, for as it is the duty of the jury to determine the facts of a case, so it is the duty of the Court to pronounce the law applicable thereto and the power of a corporate officer may often be a mixed question of law and fact.

A corporation is an artificial being created by law and acting under the authority of law for designated purposes. Being artificial and the mere creature of the law, it can only act by its officers and agents. Its officers are its agents or rather the agents of those who compose the corporation and many of the principles of law applicable to the relationship of principal and agent apply to the question of powers of a corporate officer. The precise question here involved is whether a corporation is bound by the contract or writing of the President alone where it involves a contract for 45 miles of pipe at 61 cents a foot involving the expenditure of $ 144,936.00, without express authority from the Board of Directors.

....

I have been asked specifically to charge you that if you should find that Albert T. Woods, President of the defendant corporation, signed the contract in question, that then the corporation would necessarily be conclusively bound by such contract, for I am requested to state that the power of a President of a corporation is as complete and effective as is the power of a Board of Directors acting pursuant to a vote of the Board.

This I decline to do as I deem it an extreme and incorrect view of the powers of a President of a corporation.

The powers of a President of a corporation, *i.e.,* the powers over its business and property, are, of course, merely the powers of an agent, for a corporation can speak in no other manner. The control over the company's business and property is vested in the Board of Directors, but subject to this control certain powers are delegated by implication to certain officers. Corporations have assumed and acquired such a position in the business world that the office of President carries with it certain implied powers of an agency. He is usually either expressly or by implied consent made the chief executive officer. Without special authority or explicitly delegated power he may perform all acts of an ordinary nature which by usage or necessity are incidents to his office and by virtue of his office he may enter into a contract and bind his corporation in matters arising from and concerning the usual course of the corporation's business. These are the implied powers of the President of the corporation and they inhere in him by virtue of the position itself. Beyond these powers — beyond the carrying out of the usual and proper functions of the corporation necessary for the proper and convenient management of the business of the corporation, the President remains as any other Director of the company, and other and further powers must be specifically conferred.

The plaintiff contends that the action of the President in ordering the pipe was an ordinary and usual duty and within the powers impliedly placed by the law in a President who is also managing executive of a corporation. Whether or not this is true in any given case depends upon all the facts of the case, including the character of the goods ordered, the amount thereof in relation to the size and condition of the company, the nature of the company, its purposes and aims, and upon many other facts and circumstances. Whether or not a specific action of a President is within his usual duties is, therefore, a question of fact for the determination of the jury.

The powers of a President of a corporation in excess of those hereinbefore suggested, that is, in excess of power over the ordinary and usual business of the corporation, must be specifically given, and the following are the usual sources of this grant of power:

1. Some provision of statutory law;
2. Corporate charter;
3. Some by-law of the company;
4. Resolution of the Board of Directors.

I am referred to no appropriate statute, charter provision or Resolution of the Board of Directors conferring additional power on the President. Section 12 of the By-laws has been admitted into evidence covering the powers of the President. It provides as follows:

"The President shall be the chief executive officer of the company; he shall preside at all meetings of the directors; he shall have general and active management of the business of the company; he shall see that all orders and resolutions of the Board are carried into effect; he shall execute all contracts and agreements authorized by the Board; he shall keep in safe custody the seal of the company and when authorized by the Board affix the seal to any instrument requiring the same and the seal when so affixed shall be attested by the signature of the Secretary or the Treasurer.

"He shall sign all certificates of stock and checks for the payment of money.

"He shall have general supervision and direction of all other officers of the company and shall see that their duties are properly performed.

"He shall submit a report of the operations of the company for the fiscal year to the Directors at their first regular meeting in each year and to the stockholders at their annual meeting and from time to time shall report to the Directors all matters within his knowledge which the interests of the company may require to be brought to their notice.

"He shall be ex officio a member of all standing committees and shall have the general powers and duties of supervision and management usually vested in the office of the President of a corporation."

This you will consider in the solution of the present question.

A fifth and perhaps the most usual source of the grant of the unusual or extraordinary powers of a President arises by implication of law from a course of conduct on the part of both the President and the corporation showing that he had been in the habit of acting in similar matters on behalf of the company and that the company had authorized him so to act and had recognized, approved and ratified his former and similar actions.

....

The plaintiff relies upon this fifth principle, and claims that the President of the defendant company had on prior occasions entered into somewhat similar contracts as here involved, which were recognized by the defendant company, and that the defendant company held out its President, Mr. Woods, to the public as having authority to enter into contracts.

The defendant denies that the President at any time signed any similar contract without express authority of the Board of Directors.

This, then, constitutes a question of fact for your determination.

If you should find from the evidence that the President, Mr. Woods, was not acting within the usual scope of his office, and that he had not in the past acted alone in the signing of contracts, and that the defendant company had never recognized any acts of the President alone or had not held him out as qualified to transact singly and alone all business dealings for the company, then your verdict must be for the defendant, for I say to you it is only upon these principles, upon the proven facts of the case, that the act of the President could bind the corporation.

If, however, you should find, as the plaintiff contends, that the President was acting within the usual scope of his employment, or that he had on prior occasions entered into contracts and bound the corporation which recognized and approved such acts and held him out as authorized so to deal with the company's officers, then your verdict may be for the plaintiff if consistent with other principles herein mentioned.

The plaintiff contends that the order or contract of January 7, 1929, was afterwards ratified and approved in a subsequent meeting in March or April. The defendant expressly denies this ratification and approval, and so the ratification becomes a disputed question of fact. I say to you that if you should find that the approval of Mr. Burkett was a condition attached to the original order, and should further find that Mr. Burkett subsequently ratified the contract, then such ratification would have the same effect as an original approval. If, however, you should find that there was no subsequent ratification by Mr. Burkett, then I say that the mere discussion of the original contract without ratification has no effect as furnishing the original approval if such be found necessary.

....

Greenspon's Sons nicely states what continues to be the general rule for a president's implied authority: The president has the power to bind the corporation in the usual course of its business. For matters outside the usual course of business, the board of directors generally must give its approval for corporate action to be valid.[35] But even though that is the general rule, courts sometimes stretch to find that a corporation is bound by the actions of the president, and less often those of another officer, that were outside the usual course of a corporation's business. The following cases are illustrative of courts' responses to these issues.

ELBLUM HOLDING CORP. v. MINTZ

Supreme Court of New Jersey
1 A.2d 204 (1938)

PERSKIE, J.

Does a president of a corporation, as such, have authority to employ and authorize an attorney to institute suit at law in behalf of his corporation?

Plaintiff is a corporation engaged in the real estate business. Its stock is owned equally by two families who are at cross-purposes with each other. An executive committee, consisting of the president, Abraham Elgart, a member of one faction, and the treasurer, Harry Mintz, a member of the other faction, manages the business during the intervals between meetings of the board of directors. The present suit was started at the behest of the president without official sanction of the directors. It is an action against the treasurer of the corporation in his individual capacity, upon two leases. The allegations are that the defendant held over after the expiration of one lease, and at the time of suit, on November 23d, 1937, owed the corporation $ 11,400 in rent. The second lease in suit was for an office, upon a month to month basis, and it is alleged that $ 270 rent is due thereon. After service of the complaint the defendant obtained a rule to show cause from Mr. Justice Parker why the complaint should not be dismissed for want of authority to file same. Affidavits were submitted. Defendant's affidavits showed, in substance, that neither the board of directors nor the executive committee authorized the bringing of the suit, and that the by-laws of the corporation do not expressly sanction such action by the president. Affidavits by the president of the corporation, on the other hand, disclose that the corporate stock is equally divided between the Elgart and Mintz families; that it is impossible to secure anything except an equally divided vote upon controversial corporate matters as between the equally contracted interests of the respective families; that defendant owed rent and that his failure to pay seriously hampered and prejudiced the corporation since it had substantial indebtedness by way of a $ 760,000 mortgage; a yearly tax bill of approximately $ 26,000; insurance premiums of

---

[35] Here it is important to remember the doctrine of ratification, under which the board could give its after-the-fact approval to an action of the president or another officer.

about $ 7,000, and an indebtedness to banks in the sum of some $ 18,000. The president of the corporation also stated the impossibility of securing corporate sanction to bring the suit; and alleges that he always managed the properties in question, and because of the seriousness of the situation concluded that it was necessary to take action....

....

... We desire at the outset to mark the fact that the question here requiring decision is one of first impression with us. Our courts have not heretofore, so far as industry of counsel and this court reveal, decided whether a president of a corporation, *qua* president, has the authority to employ and authorize an attorney to institute a suit in behalf of his corporation. Nor is there any concordance in the decisions of our sister states or in the writings of eminent and acknowledged scholars upon the subject.

Most generally stated there is, on the one hand, a respectable body of authority that, apart from the acts done by a president of a corporation in the course of its ordinary business, of acts done in pursuance of clothed, apparent authority, of acts done as incidental to his office, the powers of a president of a corporation to do a particular act depends upon the powers conferred upon him, either by statute, or by charter of his corporation, or by the by-laws, or by the directors thereof. And the mere fact he is president, without more, does not imply that he has any greater power than any other director.

On the other hand, there is also a body of respectable authority to the effect that a president of a corporation, as such, may employ and authorize counsel to institute a suit in behalf of his corporation. Which view shall be adopted? The answer to this question may be facilitated by a brief examination of the organic law of our state concerning corporations and the trend of our decisions on the point involved.

... Under our Corporation act the business of every corporation is managed by its directors, and if there be a provision in the certificate of incorporation for an executive committee, the latter, appointed by the directors, may exercise the powers of directors during the intervals between meetings of the directors. Every corporation, of course, has the power to adopt by-laws providing for the management of its property and the regulation and government of its affairs. The president of a corporation is a statutory officer.

In light of these provisions, our courts have held that the president of a corporation, as such, may, without special authority, perform all the acts, which either because of usage or necessity, are incidental to his office, and may bind the corporation by contracts arising in the usual course of its business. And beyond this he, as president, has no more control over the corporate funds than any other director. And we have held that a president of a corporation may in pursuance of a power incidental to his office, take the necessary steps in defense of litigation prosecuted against his corporation in order to preserve the corporate assets.

But, it is argued for defendant, the by-laws specifically limited the powers of the president, as was found by the learned justice, "to that of a moderator at meetings of directors, of temporary chairman at those of stockholders, and of a clerical nature in making reports and signing papers." *Ergo*, to permit plaintiff to employ counsel to institute a suit at law against a co-director is directly contrary to the contractual relationship created between the stockholders, and thus is an illegal exercise of power. It is further argued for defendant that a suit such as is here sought to be prosecuted will create strife and discord in the internal management of the corporation to the injury of the stockholders and creditors; and that if a president may institute such a suit (which is characterized as a derivative suit) by the same token he may also contract to pay counsel for his services out of corporate funds. And finally, it is argued that the only proper forum to enforce the alleged claim is the court of chancery.

We think that these arguments lack persuasion. Without, of course, trenching upon the equitable jurisdiction which might have been invoked, we are merely concerned with a simple suit brought at law to enforce a rent claim allegedly due the corporation. It is difficult to perceive what greater strife and discord in the internal affairs of the instant corporation can be created by this suit than that which already obtains by reason of the existing deadlock. How the stockholders or creditors will be injured is not made to appear. Costs incident to litigation (including counsel fees) will follow whether the litigation is in the equity or the law branch of our jurisprudence.

We are fully in accord with the views of the learned justice who observed that "what we have here is a case where the president, on the face of things, has undertaken to institute the obvious and proper step to protect the interests of his corporation; and where the defendant, by the same token, has undertaken to prejudice those very interests in favor of his own."

If, as we have seen, a president of a corporation may take the necessary steps in defense of litigation prosecuted against his corporation in order to preserve the corporate assets, so, in reason and justice, he may employ and authorize counsel to institute necessary legal proceedings for the like purpose of preserving the interests of his corporation. We so hold. For, in each instance the power exercised by the chief executive officer of the corporation is to accomplish the same results. If the president were to fail to exercise the power to protect and defend the assets of his corporation he might well be liable to his corporation for the resultant losses. And so if the president exceeds his power the corporation may likewise look to him for any damages it may have sustained.

....

LEE v. JENKINS BROTHERS

United States Court of Appeals Second Circuit
268 F.2d 357 (1959)

MEDINA, CIRCUIT JUDGE.

Bernard J. Lee appeals from a judgment dismissing his complaint in two consolidated actions against Jenkins Brothers, a corporation, and against Farnham

Yardley, to recover pension payments allegedly due under an oral agreement by Yardley on behalf of the corporation and for his own account, made in 1920. Lee's case consisted only of his own testimony and the trial judge held that there was no issue for the jury, as the claim was barred by the Connecticut Statute of Frauds and, as to the corporate defendant, was unsupported by proof that the agreement was authorized.

For the purposes of clarity and organization we shall first state our decision on the various law points involved in this interesting case....

(2) Assuming, arguendo, that there was evidence sufficient to support a finding that Yardley promised Lee a pension of not to exceed $ 1500 at the age of 60, even if not employed by Jenkins at that time, we find that, while there is no proof of actual authority, the combination of circumstances here present would, if we assume such a promise was made, make the question of apparent authority an issue for the jury.

....

The following is a summary of Lee's testimony. At the time of the alleged contract Lee was in the employ of the Crane Company, a large manufacturer of valves, fittings and plumbing supplies, at the company's Bridgeport plant. He had been with the Crane Company for thirteen years and had risen to the post of business manager, earning a salary of $ 4,000 per year. In December, 1919, the Crane Company agreed to sell its Bridgeport plant to Jenkins Brothers, a New Jersey corporation and a defendant in one of these actions. The transaction was consummated June 1, 1920 when Jenkins took over Crane's Bridgeport plant.

According to Lee's testimony this was the first venture into the manufacturing phase of the business for Jenkins, which was formerly content to be merely a customer of Crane. Jenkins was therefore extremely anxious to secure competent personnel, particularly the old Crane employees, in order to insure as smooth a transition as possible in view of the change to a relatively inexperienced management.

With this in mind Charles V. Barrington, Vice President of Jenkins in charge of manufacturing, approached Lee in February, 1920, in an attempt to induce him to join Jenkins. Lee, however, was reluctant to do so. He felt his prospects with Crane were good and he had accumulated thirteen years of pension rights under the Crane Company plan which he did not want to give up. Some time after this conversation but before June 1, 1920, Barrington arranged a meeting for Lee at his hotel suite in Bridgeport with the co-defendant Yardley, president of Jenkins, chairman of the board of directors, a substantial stockholder, son-in-law of Mr. Jenkins, and co-trustee of the Jenkins estate. Present at this meeting besides Lee and Yardley were Barrington and his wife. However, at the time of the trial in October, 1957, only Lee was alive to describe the conversation.

Yardley convinced Lee of his fine prospects with Jenkins, of the company's need for him as assistant to Barrington, and allegedly made a promise on behalf of Jenkins and a promise on his own behalf with respect to Lee's pension rights....

....

Lee testified:

"As far as the pension that I had earned with Crane Company he [Yardley] said the company (Jenkins Brothers) would pay that pension (and) if they didn't or, if anything came up, he would assume the liability himself he would guarantee payment of the pension; and in consideration of that promise I agreed to go to work for Jenkins Bros. on June 1, 1920."

.....

... Lee summarized his position:

"My claim is that the company through the chairman of the board of directors and the president, promised me credit for my 13 years of service with Crane Company, regardless of what happened I would receive a pension at the age of 60, not to exceed $ 1,500 a year. If I was discharged in 1921 or 1922 or left I would still get that pension. That is what I am asking for."

This agreement was never reduced to writing.

Lee's prospects with Jenkins turned out to be just about as bright as he had hoped. He subsequently became vice president and general manager in charge of manufacturing and a director of the company. At that time he was receiving a salary of $ 25,000 from Jenkins, $ 8,000 more from an affiliate, plus an annual 10 per cent bonus. In 1945, however, after 25 years with Jenkins, Lee was discharged at the age of 55 and his pension rights under the company's established plan were settled in full.

In 1950 the payments under the alleged pension agreement became due. Although nothing was paid under this agreement Lee waited until 1955 to institute suit against Jenkins, joining Yardley eight and one-half months later.

The Crane Company pension plan prior to June 1, 1920, to which Lee said Yardley "referred," was a gratuitous or voluntary one whereby male employees could be retired by the company at 60 or apply for retirement at 65, if they had 25 years of service. Under the plan each employee would receive 2% of his salary for each year of service at retirement, with a maximum pension of $ 1500 a year. Lee admits it was a condition of eligibility under the Crane plan that the employee had to be in the employ of the company at the time of his retirement.

Although at the start of operations on June 1, 1920, Jenkins did not have a pension plan, it soon adopted one effective as of June 1, 1920, incorporating all the features of the Crane plan. The 350 former Crane employees, including Lee, who transferred over to Jenkins were all given credit under the Jenkins plan for service with the Crane Company. Lee, however, asserts that Yardley's promise was not fulfilled by the adoption of the Jenkins plan since he had been assured of pension payments "regardless of what happened." Moreover, although Jenkins revised its plan in 1932 and Lee voluntarily took coverage thereunder, all this he claims was "over and above" the rights promised by Yardley. Lee, a member of the pension committee, admits no other employee was given such pension rights.

.....

II. *The Scope of Yardley's Authority*

In the discussion which follows we assume, arguendo, that there was evidence sufficient to support a finding that Yardley orally agreed on behalf of the corporation that Lee would be paid at the age of 60 a pension not to exceed $ 1500, and that Yardley's words "regardless of what happens" were, as Lee contends, to be interpreted as meaning that Lee would receive this pension even if he were not working for Jenkins at the time the pension became payable. Jenkins asserts that Yardley had no authority to bind it to such an "extraordinary" contract, express, implied, or apparent and the trial court so found. There is nothing in the proofs submitted by Lee to warrant any finding of actual authority in Yardley. The Certificate of Incorporation and By-Laws of Jenkins are not in evidence nor was any course of conduct shown as between the corporation and Yardley. Accordingly, on the phase of the case now under discussion, we are dealing only with apparent authority.

. . . .

Our question on this phase of the case then boils itself down to the following: can it be said as a matter of law that Yardley as president, chairman of the board, substantial stockholder and trustee and son-in-law of the estate of the major stockholder, had no power in the presence of the company's most interested vice president to secure for a "reasonable" length of time badly needed key personnel by promising an experienced local executive a life pension to commence in 30 years at the age of 60, even if Lee were not then working for the corporation, when the maximum liability to Jenkins under such a pension was $ 1500 per year.

A survey of the law on the authority of corporate officers does not reveal a completely consistent pattern. For the most part the courts perhaps have taken a rather restrictive view on the extent of powers of corporate officials, but the dissatisfaction with such an approach has been manifested in a variety of exceptions such as ratification, estoppel, and promissory estoppel. For the most part also there has been limited discussion of the problem of apparent authority, perhaps on the assumption that if authority could not be implied from a continuing course of action between the corporation and the officer, it could not have been apparent to third parties either.

Such an assumption is ill-founded. The circumstances and facts known to exist between officer and corporation, from which actual authority may be implied, may be entirely different from those circumstances known to exist as between the third party and the corporation. The two concepts are separate and distinct even though the state of the proofs in a given case may cause considerable overlap.

The rule most widely cited is that the president only has authority to bind his company by acts arising in the usual and regular course of business but not for contracts of an "extraordinary" nature. The substance of such a rule lies in the content of the term "extraordinary" which is subject to a broad range of interpretation.

The growth and development of this rule occurred during the late nineteenth and early twentieth centuries when the potentialities of the corporate form of enterprise were just being realized. As the corporation became a more common vehicle for the conduct of business it became increasingly evident that many corporations, particularly small closely held ones, did not normally function in the formal ritualistic manner hitherto envisaged. While the boards of directors still nominally controlled corporate affairs, in reality officers and managers frequently ran the business with little, if any, board supervision. The natural consequence of such a development was that third parties commonly relied on the authority of such officials in almost all the multifarious transactions in which corporations engaged. The pace of modern business life was too swift to insist on the approval by the board of directors of every transaction that was in any way "unusual."

The judicial recognition given to these developments has varied considerably. Whether termed "apparent authority" or an "estoppel" to deny authority, many courts have noted the injustice caused by the practice of permitting corporations to act commonly through their executives and then allowing them to disclaim an agreement as beyond the authority of the contracting officer, when the contract no longer suited its convenience. Other courts, however, continued to cling to the past with little attempt to discuss the unconscionable results obtained or the doctrine of apparent authority. Such restrictive views have been generally condemned by the commentators.

The summary of holdings pro and con in general on the subject of what are and what are not "extraordinary" agreements is inconclusive at best, as shown by the authorities collected in the footnote.[36] But the pattern becomes more distinct when we turn to the more limited area of employment contracts.

It is generally settled that the president as part of the regular course of business has authority to hire and discharge employees and fix their compensation. In so

---

[36] We note that the following acts have been held to be within either the implied or apparent authority of a corporate president or manager: borrowing money and executing a corporate note, even though the moneys obtained might not be used for the benefit of the corporation, pledging security for a loan, guaranteeing the note of another corporation, purchasing merchandise, authorizing an attorney to sue on a corporate claim, compromising a corporate claim, making a tax closing agreement, executing a time limitations waiver, pledging a substantial contribution to a hospital, licensing a factory spur track, sale of the corporation's only property, of all its merchandise and fixtures, or its real estate. Other courts have left the question to the jury when the matter involved was: execution of a corporate note, a promise of additional service, a promise to pay a stale debt, entering a joint venture, oral waiver of written contract provisions, and sale of the corporation's sole asset. On the other hand authority has been found lacking in the following instances: sale of all the company's assets or its major asset, a brokerage contract to effectuate a merger, modification of directors' resolutions, employing an architect in a major construction project, giving away corporate property, postponing a mortgage foreclosure, suing the corporation's chief stockholder, guaranteeing the debt of another, and contracts deemed unconscionable from the corporation's point of view.

doing he may agree to hire them for a specific number of years if the term selected is deemed reasonable. But employment contracts for life or on a "permanent" basis are generally regarded as "extraordinary" and beyond the authority of any corporate executive if the only consideration for the promise is the employee's promise to work for that period. Jenkins would have us analogize the pension agreement involved herein to these generally condemned lifetime employment contracts because it extends over a long period of time, is of indefinite duration, and involves an indefinite liability on the part of the corporation.

It is not surprising that lifetime employment contracts have met with substantial hostility in the courts, for these contracts are often oral, uncorroborated, vague in important details and highly improbable. Accordingly, the courts have erected a veritable array of obstacles to their enforcement. They have been construed as terminable at will, too indefinite to enforce, ultra vires, lacking in mutuality or consideration, abandoned or breached by subsequent acts, and the supporting evidence deemed insufficient to go to the jury, as well as made without proper authority.

However, at times such contracts have been enforced where the circumstances tended to support the plausibility of plaintiff's testimony. Thus when the plaintiff was injured in the course of employment and he agreed to settle his claim of negligence against the company for a lifetime job, authority has been generally found and the barrage of other objections adequately disposed of. And where additional consideration was given such as quitting other employment, giving up a competing business, or where the services were "peculiarly necessary" to the corporation, the courts have divided on the enforceability of the contract.

Where reasons have been given to support the conclusion that lifetime employments are "extraordinary," and hence made without authority, a scrutiny of these reasons may be helpful for their bearing on the analogous field of pension agreements. It is said that: they unduly restrict the power of the shareholders and future boards of directors on questions of managerial policy; they subject the corporation to an inordinately substantial amount of liability; they run for long and indefinite periods of time. Of these reasons the only one applicable to pension agreements is that they run for long and indefinite periods of time. There the likeness stops. Future director or shareholder control is in no way impeded; the amount of liability is not disproportionate; the agreement was not only not unreasonable but beneficial and necessary to the corporation; and pension contracts are commonly used fringe benefits in employment contracts. Moreover, unlike the case with life employment contracts, courts have often gone out of their way to find pension promises binding and definite even when labeled gratuitous by the employer. The consideration given to the employee involved is not at all dependent on profits or sales, nor does it involve some other variable suggesting director discretion.

....

The cases on executive authority to make pension agreements are few.... [T]he court then referred to two cases which reached the following conclusion: (1) [A]uthority was found lacking in the president, who acted in direct violation of a directors' resolution to promise a pension for life in return for past services. His apparent authority was not discussed. (2) [T]he vice president was found to lack authority gratuitously to promise 18 employees life pensions at half wages....

Apparent authority is essentially a question of fact. It depends not only on the nature of the contract involved, but the officer negotiating it, the corporation's usual manner of conducting business, the size of the corporation and the number of its stockholders, the circumstances that give rise to the contract, the reasonableness of the contract, the amounts involved, and who the contracting third party is, to list a few but not all of the relevant factors. In certain instances a given contract may be so important to the welfare of the corporation that outsiders would naturally suppose that only the board of directors (or even the shareholders) could properly handle it. It is in this light that the "ordinary course of business" rule should be given its content. Beyond such "extraordinary" acts, whether or not apparent authority exists is simply a matter of fact.

Accordingly, we hold that, assuming there was sufficient proof of the making of the pension agreement, Connecticut, in the particular circumstances of this case, would probably take the view that reasonable men could differ on the subject of whether or not Yardley had apparent authority to make the contract, and that the trial court erred in deciding the question as a matter of law. We do not think Connecticut would adopt any hard and fast rule against apparent authority to make pension agreements generally, on the theory that they were in the same category as lifetime employment contracts.

....

HAND, CIRCUIT JUDGE (concurring in part and dissenting in part).

My brothers have stated the facts so fully that I shall not add anything except enough to make plain my reasoning....

....

I cannot agree that Yardley, as president of the corporation, had authority to make a contract that was to last for the life of the promisee. I have not indeed found any decision, in Connecticut that decides that question; but in New York, New Jersey, Maryland, Iowa, Wyoming and West Virginia the law is settled and in Texas the same limitation was even imposed on the president's authority to make a contract for three years. There is a fairly well established exception to this doctrine when the promise is part of the settlement of a claim for personal injuries, and one case so decided when the promisee, though injured, had apparently made no claim. The distinction is a little hard to justify rationally, except for the strength of the motive that personal injury adds; however, even assuming as I do that it exists, the case at bar is not within the exception.... There being no relevant corporate by-law, I would say that the accepted doctrine is the law of Connecticut [and New Jersey].... For this reason I think that the complaint in the action against the corporation was rightly dismissed.

YUCCA MINING & PETROLEUM CO. v. HOWARD C. PHILLIPS OIL CO.

Supreme Court of New Mexico
365 P.2d 925 (1961)

CARMODY, JUSTICE.

Appellant sought damages for breach of an oil well drilling contract and alternatively for rescission and damages. From a judgment denying relief, based generally upon equitable estoppel, this appeal followed.

....

Summarizing the contract as far as material to the issues: Yucca paid $ 12,000 to Phillips to drill at least two wells on a lease owned by Phillips. If both were dry holes, no further drilling was contemplated. Appellee was to account for the money used and to assign a one-half interest in the lease to Yucca.

After the first well proved to be a dry hole, Phillips did not render an accounting nor assign the one-half interest. Thereafter, a second well was drilled on other property upon which Phillips merely had drilling rights, which, incidentally, were paid for out of the $ 12,000. This second well also proved to be unproductive and the money was exhausted.

The real basis of the controversy has to do with whether there was a valid subsequent agreement which modified the original written contract. As to this, there is a broad conflict in the evidence, the Phillips' evidence being to the effect that Yucca's president, one of the members of its board of directors, and a consulting geologist of Yucca's agreed that further drilling after the first dry hole was inadvisable on the original lease and that the second well should be attempted on a different location, somewhat deeper than originally contemplated. To the contrary, Yucca's evidence was almost diametrically opposed, at least as to the modifying of the agreement. It should be mentioned that ... Yucca's board of directors never approved the drilling of the second well....

....

The question of whether a corporation is bound by the actions of its president and other officers and agents, absent action by the board of directors, is a problem that has caused considerable difficulty. Although ordinarily a corporation can only act through its directors as to any matters that are not in the usual course of the daily operation of the business, it is recognized that, with the swift pace of modern business life, it is impossible to expect action by the directors in every transaction, even though it may be termed "unusual." Many courts have refused to permit a corporation to disclaim unauthorized agreements by officers as working an injustice as to parties dealing with the corporation, on various agency theories of "apparent authority," "implied authority," "waiver," or "estoppel," as well as ratification and acquiescence.

In the instant case, all of the actions of Richards, the president of Yucca, as well as those of Mitchell, the director who apparently acted in a liaison capacity during the drilling of the second well, and the actions of Brady, the geologist, were for the benefit of the corporation, which would have profited if the drilling had been successful. Under such circumstances, the corporation was bound by the actions taken on its behalf, and cannot be relieved by claiming lack of authority. As found by the trial court, Yucca was to have the benefits of the contract as modified, so it must also be charged with the burdens, and it is unnecessary for us to determine under which one or more of the aforementioned theories such result is reached.

....

Sometimes the president is the corporation's chief executive officer and sometimes not. Does that affect the general rule about the authority associated with the presidency? The answer is no, but that brings us to a discussion of the authority of another officer at the top of the corporate hierarchy, the chair of the board.

B. CHAIR OF THE BOARD

Most corporations do not have a chair of the board, or as often used, a "chairman." The use of that title becomes increasingly common, however, as the size of a corporation increases, and most of the largest corporations do have a chair of the board. The person with this title is usually an officer, but not always. Sometimes, especially in smaller corporations, the title is simply given to the director who is chosen to preside at meetings, without also making the director an officer.

When the chair of the board is an officer, it is not possible to identify with certainty the powers associated with the position. The widespread use of that title is relatively recent, and litigation about officers' authority is not common. Nevertheless, the opinions of courts are not too difficult to predict. Usually, if a corporation has a chair of the board, that person is also the corporation's chief executive officer. In that case, the president almost always is the chief operating officer. Whatever role the president plays, as discussed above, the president will have the power to bind the corporation in connection with the company's usual course of business. That being the case, it is virtually certain that a court faced with determining the implied authority of a chair of the board who is chief executive officer will determine that the chair of the board has the same implied powers to bind the corporation as the president. That seems especially likely when one considers how such a case is likely to arise: Typically, it would involve a corporation that attempts to avoid a contract within the corporation's usual course of business that was signed by its chair of the board. It is hard to postulate such a case in which the equities would be on the side of such a corporation, and it is highly unlikely that in such a situation a court would go against the equities.

It is not unusual, however, for the office of chair of the board to be largely ceremonial. Often, the office is occupied by a former chief executive officer who is serving out his or her time until retirement or until a suitable position outside the corporation becomes available. In such cases, there probably are no powers that are implied in the office, save arguably the power to preside at directors' meetings (and even that power is not the power of an officer, but rather of a director). Even so, corporations should not be surprised if courts do not allow them to avoid a contract entered into by a chair of the board, whatever the position's actual authority. One suspects that courts often will be inclined to make the chair of the board's corporation, rather than the other party to a contract, suffer from the ambiguity of the title "chair of the board" or "chairman of the board."

C. VICE PRESIDENT

The vice president has but one inherent power: to serve in the place of the president, most commonly in the event of the president's death, incapacity, or absence. In that connection, there are two problems. First, if there is more than one vice president, do they share those powers or is there an order of succession? Second, what constitutes "incapacity" or "absence?"

The first of those problems is the easiest to answer. In the absence of a bylaw or board action on the question, there seems to be no basis for distinguishing between vice presidents, and so each would seem to have the same power to substitute for the president. Well-drafted bylaws always speak to that question, for example, by providing that "in the event there be more than one vice president, the vice presidents in the order designated at the time of their election, or in the absence of any designation, then in the order of their appointment," shall serve in the place of the president. The usual way to set one vice president apart from others is to use a different title, such as "executive vice president" or "senior vice president." That should be enough to establish the order of succession.

Determining just when a vice president may step in for a president is more difficult. Take incapacity as an example. Is it enough that the president be home with a cold, or must the president be in a coma before he or she will be considered incapacitated? Questions such as these are particularly troubling to those on the other side of a corporate transaction, because they do not wish to run the risk that a vice president's authority later will be denied by the officer's corporation. In order to make it easier for their vice presidents to serve when needed, many corporations place in their bylaws language like the following: "The performance of any duty by a vice president shall, in respect of any other person dealing with the corporation, be conclusive evidence of the vice president's power to act."

Besides the implied power to serve in the place of the president, certain vice presidents may be given additional implied authority by virtue of their specialized titles. For example, it seems unlikely that a corporation that has elected someone to the office of vice president-purchasing could later avoid a contract for the purchase of office supplies that was signed by that vice president. Here the more interesting question relates to how far that additional authority might go. If that vice president purported to commit the corporation to purchase multimillion-dollar manufacturing equipment, for example, would the corporation be bound? Answers to those questions cannot be reached in the abstract, but will depend on how a court views the facts and, probably more important, the equities.

The following case discusses the authority of a vice president in the context of a muddled factual situation.

ANDERSON v. CAMPBELL

Supreme Court of Minnesota
223 N.W. 624 (1929)

WILSON, C. J.

....

In 1924 the Pioneer Granite Company, having three stockholders, Great Northern Granite Company, having five stockholders, and the Campbell North Star Granite Company, having three stockholders, corporations, were engaged separately in the business of monumental and construction work and operating granite quarries at St. Cloud. The stockholders in these corporations perfected a consolidation by organizing another corporation, the defendant North Star Granite Corporation, which took over the assets, except working capital, of the three corporations.

....

... The real estate of the Pioneer Granite Company was conveyed to the new corporation. A deed was prepared for the president and secretary to sign. The officers' names were apparently unknown to the scrivener, who left blank places in the acknowledgment for their insertion. When the time came for execution the president was absent and plaintiff Anderson, the vice president, executed the deed. The word "vice" was not inserted before the word president appearing below the signature nor in the acknowledgment.

The claim is now made by plaintiffs that the deed is void. It is valid on its face. It however shows Anderson to be president when he was vice president only. The president ... had the power to execute it. If the corporation had any by-laws, they did not define or limit the duties of the vice president contemplated by the articles of incorporation. His title, including the qualifying word "vice," indicates that he was to act for another, to wit, the president. This means in itself that in certain cases he may assume the duties of the president, and the most usual occasion for him so to act would be in the absence of the president. In the absence of by-laws defining or limiting his authority, he is a substitute for and when the president is absent or disqualified. Under such circumstances he is within the authority extended to the president to make the conveyance.

... When the deed was executed and delivered all the parties, including plaintiffs, intended it to be just what it purported to be. The erroneous description of Anderson as president instead of vice president was a harmless clerical inadvertence, and the plaintiffs are not in a position to take advantage thereof.

....

D. SECRETARY

Unlike the implied authority of the president and the vice president, the power associated with the office of secretary (or in the case of Model Act jurisdictions, the persons designated to perform the secretary's functions), relates only to the internal affairs of the corporation and not to its business. They are the powers to keep minutes of meetings and other nonfinancial corporate records, to have custody of the corporate seal, to attest the seal, to certify corporate records, and so on. The secretary's functions are ministerial in nature and do not vest the secretary to transact business on behalf of the corporation.

Insofar as dealings with those outside the corporation go, the certification of corporate records and particularly of minutes of meetings is by far the most important function of the secretary. Often, in connection with a corporate transaction, the person on the other side of the transaction will demand a certified copy of the board of directors' resolution approving the transaction. The person may also demand a certified list of the corporation's officers along with an attestation of the officers' signatures. The secretary has the implied power to deliver those certifications and attestations. The following case deals with the effect of such a certification or attestation.

In re DRIVE IN DEVELOPMENT CORP.

United States Court of Appeals, Seventh Circuit
371 F.2d 215 (1966)

SWYGERT, CIRCUIT JUDGE.

The principal question in this appeal relates to the circumstances which may bind a corporation to a guaranty of the obligations of a related corporation when it is contended that the corporate officer who executed the guaranty had no authority to do so. The facts giving rise to the question underlie a claim filed by the National Boulevard Bank of Chicago in an arrangement proceeding under chapter XI of the Bankruptcy Act, in which the Drive In Development Corporation was the debtor. National Boulevard's claim was disallowed by the referee, whose decision was confirmed by the district court.

[Drive In was a subsidiary of Tastee Freez, a holding company involved in franchising and supplying soft ice cream outlets. Through another of its subsidiaries, Allied Business, Tastee Freez arranged to assign conditional sales contracts to National Boulevard in return for cash. Allied Business agreed to repurchase outstanding chattel paper for the amount of any unpaid balance due in the event of a default on an installment payment. Drive In and Tastee Freez's other subsidiaries jointly and severally guaranteed Allied Business' contractual obligation. Maranz, the vice president of Drive In, signed the guaranty on behalf of Drive In as "Chairman," and Dick, the secretary, attested to its execution.

National Boulevard requested copies of the resolutions of the board of directors of each guarantor authorizing the execution of the guaranty. Drive In furnished such a resolution, which was certified, with the corporate seal affixed, by Dick.]

On September 4, 1963, Tastee Freez and each of its subsidiaries, including Drive In, filed voluntary petitions under chapter XI of the Bankruptcy Act. National Boulevard filed a claim against Drive In before the referee, asserting the guaranty executed on April 11, 1962 as the basis for it.... The referee disallowed National Boulevard's claim in its entirety.

....

Turning to the merits of the objections to National Boulevard's claim, the referee found that Drive In's minute book did not show that a resolution authorizing Maranz to sign the guaranty was adopted by the directors and that Dick could not recall a specific directors' meeting at which such a resolution was approved. From these findings, the referee concluded that Maranz, who signed the guaranty on behalf of Drive In, had no authority, "either actual or implied or apparent," to bind Drive In. This conclusion was erroneous. Drive In was estopped to deny Maranz' express authority to sign the guaranty because of the certified copy of a resolution of Drive In's board of directors purporting to grant such authority furnished to the bank by Dick, whether or not such a resolution was in fact formally adopted. Dick was the secretary of the corporation. Generally, it is the duty of the secretary to keep the corporate records and to make proper entries of the actions and resolutions of the directors. Therefore it was within the authority of Dick to certify that a resolution such as challenged here was adopted. Statements made by an officer or agent in the course of a transaction in which the corporation is engaged and which are within the scope of his authority are binding upon the corporation. Consequently Drive In was estopped to deny the representation made by Dick in the certificate forwarded to National Boulevard, in the absence of actual or constructive knowledge on the part of the bank that the representation was untrue.

[The court allowed National Boulevard's claims to the extent that they had been guaranteed.]

E. TREASURER

In terms of implied authority, the treasurer has much in common with the secretary, for the treasurer's power, too, relates to the internal affairs of the corporation. The treasurer has the power to care for the funds of the corporation. That includes depositing the funds in proper depositories and disbursing them in accordance with orders from the board of directors or a proper officer, maintaining records of the funds, and rendering reports on the corporation's funds to the board of directors. What about the implied power of a treasurer to sign a promissory note? The following case gives an illustrative answer.

JACOBUS v. JAMESTOWN MANTEL CO.

Court of Appeals of New York
105 N.E. 210 (1914)

CHASE, J.

This action is brought on a promissory note, of which the following is a copy:

"$ 2,500.00 NEW YORK, Oct. 8, 1909.

"Six months after date we promise to pay to the order of ourselves, Two thousand five hundred & 00/100 dollars at Newton Trust Co., Newton, N. J., value received.

"JAMESTOWN MANTEL CO.

GEO. M. TURNER, *Treas.*"

Said note was indorsed "Jamestown Mantel Co., Geo. M. Turner, Treas.," and it was thereafter delivered to and discounted by the Newton Trust Company, the assignor of the plaintiff. It is the last one of a series of like notes, the original of which was given in August, 1907. At the times herein mentioned the trust company had an investment committee consisting of Hough, its president, Searing, its vice-president, and George, a director.... In August, 1907, Searing was the president of the Delaware and Eastern Railroad Company. One Welch, an attorney at law, had done business as such for said railroad company and for Searing individually. Welch asserted that the railroad company and Searing owed him considerable money for services; he told Searing that he needed the money for his immediate use, and Searing said to him that the company was not in a position to pay him at that time, but that if he would borrow a note from somebody for a short time, he, Searing, would have it discounted at one of his trust companies. Welch went to Turner and told him that he wanted to borrow a note of the Jamestown Mantel Company for $ 2,500 to have it discounted, and that if he, Turner, would furnish him with such a note he would take care of it when it was due.

Turner in the name of the mantel company, and in the form shown, made and indorsed a note for $ 2,500, and gave it to Welch. Welch delivered it to Searing, who sent it to the trust company, and received in return for it a draft of $ 2,425, being the amount of the note less the discount thereon. Searing retained the proceeds of the draft and told Welch that his trust companies were not in funds to discount the note. Before the note became due, however, Searing told Welch that the note had been actually discounted and that he had used the money. It was thereafter renewed from time to time until the note now in suit became due when further renewals were refused by the mantel company and it also refused to pay the note.

....

... The treasurer of the defendant corporation had no express authority by its by-laws or otherwise to sign or indorse a promissory note. The president of the trust company had never had a transaction with the defendant corporation and did not know its treasurer. He does not remember that Searing said anything to him whatever at the time the note was sent to him for discount. It was taken by him on behalf of the trust company without inquiry ... or as to the authority of its treasurer to make a promissory note....

... One who deals with the officers or agents of a corporation is bound to know their powers and the extent of their authority.... A treasurer of a manufacturing corporation has no power to make promissory notes in its name unless such power is expressly given to such officer by the by-laws of the corporation or by resolution of its board of directors. No presumption existed that the defendant's treasurer had power to make or indorse business paper. It was necessary, therefore, for the plaintiff to show that the treasurer had authority to execute promissory notes in the name of the corporation in the ordinary course of its business, or that the defendant was estopped from denying such authority.

It is urged that there is some evidence that the treasurer of the defendant had on one or more occasions signed a promissory note in its name in the regular course of defendant's business, and that such note or notes had thereafter been paid by the corporation. It does not appear that said treasurer had ever signed such a note prior to the execution of the note which was given in August, 1907. Whether he had done so or not is of little importance for the purpose of creating an estoppel against the defendant because it affirmatively appears that the trust company did not know of any of the acts claimed to have been done by the defendant's treasurer in its name.

If the defendant had, prior to August, 1907, in the usual course of its business permitted its treasurer from time to time to make promissory notes in its name which it ratified and approved by paying them, and knowledge of such acts had come to the trust company, and it had relied upon such acts as showing authority in the defendant's treasurer to make promissory notes in its name in taking the note in controversy, a question of estoppel would have arisen as against the defendant in this action.

It is essential for one claiming that another is equitably estopped from denying liability because of his previous acts and conduct to show that he was influenced by and relied upon such acts and conduct in making the promise or performing the act upon which the liability is asserted. The defendant is not estopped from denying its liability in this case....

....

———————

One final word about the authority of officers: Most vice presidents and treasurers, and many secretaries, have substantial corporate powers in addition to those generally associated with their offices. The important thing to remember is that when considering any alleged power beyond that which is generally recognized, the power must ultimately have been given by the bylaws or the board, either directly or through another officer. The board may have granted the power formally in a bylaw or a resolution or it may have acted by acquiescence or ratification, but the bylaws or the board must have granted the power in some way — or the power does not exist.

Chapter 7

DISTRIBUTING CORPORATE CONTROL

Situation

Although the company continues to do well, Anderson and Baker believe that they will each be in a precarious position if, in future months or years, their percentage share of corporate stock is reduced as a result of raising additional capital by adding new shareholders. They understand that if one of them sides with the other shareholders, the other could be left without a voice in the business. They do not expect a falling out, but each wants protection if it happens.

Their concern is general, but they have voiced specific concerns about the following: (1) their future employment with Biologistics, Inc.; (2) the possibility that the size of the board will be increased, thus diminishing the power of any one director; (3) the possibility that one of them will be removed from the board; (4) the possibility that the charter or bylaws will be changed without the consent of both of them; and (5) the possibility of a deadlock on an important issue, as a result of which the company will be paralyzed.

They have asked your advice on each of these matters and, in general, have made it clear that each is interested in maintaining as much personal control over the company as possible. In responding to their questions, you should also consider what issues of professional responsibility are raised by their request.

The corporate lawyer has available a large number of diverse tools for fine-tuning the control relationships within a corporation. Theoretically, that fine-tuning may occur at any time during a corporation's life, but most of the tools require shareholder agreement for their use. That means that often those tools cannot be used in the midst of struggles for control or other corporate strife. For that reason, good corporate lawyers attempt to foresee possible control problems and to use those tools prophylactically. Typically, the best time for their use is at the beginning of a corporation's life.

Issues of allocation of control are particularly important in closely held corporations. One reason is that shareholders in closely held corporations usually also participate in management so that the lines demarcating the roles of shareholders and directors become blurred. Often the operation of the business more closely resembles a partnership than a general corporation. A second is that shareholders typically look to the company for their livelihood. Their financial security depends on continued receipt of salaries as employees or payment of dividends as shareholders. A third is that there generally is little or no market for the shares of a closely held corporation. Consequently, owners of such an enterprise often find themselves locked in an embrace from which there is no easy exit. For these reasons, striking a balance between majority and minority interests assumes an additional importance. Allocating too much power to the majority raises the specter of oppressive action that ignores legitimate interests of the minority. Shifting too far in the opposite direction creates the possibility that a lone voice can virtually paralyze the company's operations. The sections that follow explore structural options available to effect a balanced governance structure. The options are interrelated and function like pieces on a legal chess board; one option can be used to check the advantages of another.

SECTION I. CUMULATIVE VOTING, CLASSIFICATION OF DIRECTORS, AND CLASS VOTING

A. CUMULATIVE VOTING

You will recall from the previous chapter that directors are elected by a plurality of votes. The directors with the most votes win. Corporation statutes vary in the voting procedures required to elect directors. Most statutes mandate so-called straight voting, unless the corporate charter provides for cumulative voting. Some statutes, however, take the opposite approach and require cumulative voting unless the charter calls for straight voting. In straight voting, the shareholders have one vote per share, which they may cast to fill each vacant directorship. Under straight voting, shares are voted in blocks. If there are five directors to be elected, a shareholder having 100 shares could vote those 100 shares five times, once for each favored candidate. Notice that in this example, someone else owning as few as 101 shares could out-vote the shareholder with 100 shares and thereby fill each vacancy. In other words, under straight voting, a shareholder or shareholder group owning a majority of a corporation's voting stock can elect all of the directors.

When used effectively, cumulative voting increases the likelihood that shareholders owning minority interests in the corporation will be able to elect a director. The Model Act describes cumulative voting in the following way: shareholders "are entitled to multiply the number of votes they are entitled to cast by the number of directors for whom they are entitled to vote and cast the product for a single candidate or distribute the product among two or more candidates."[1] Under cumulative voting, the shareholder in the above example who holds 100 shares at a time when five directors are to be elected would have 500 votes (5 directors x 100 votes), and those votes could be cast for one candidate or could be spread among the candidates in any way the shareholder wishes.

---

[1] MODEL BUSINESS CORP. ACT (1984) § 7.28(c). Subsection (b) of § 7.28 makes straight voting mandatory unless the articles of incorporation provide for cumulative voting. *Id.* at § 7.28(b).

The question immediately arises, of course, as to how shareholders can use their votes most effectively. There is a formula a shareholder can use to determine how many directors can be elected with a particular number of shares. Here is the formula:

$$X = \frac{(N\text{-}1)\ (D+1)}{S}$$

X = Number of directors who can be elected with N shares
N = Number of shares controlled by a shareholder or shareholder group
D = Number of directors to be elected at the meeting
S = Number of shares to be voted by all shareholders

Here is how the formula would work, using the above example of 500 shares owned by one shareholder (N = 500) and five directors to be elected (D = 5), and assuming that all the shareholders will vote a total of 1,500 shares in the election of directors (S = 1500):

$$X = \frac{(500\text{-}1=499)\ (5+1=6)}{1500} = 2994$$

or

$$X = 1.996$$

Here the shareholder would be able to elect one director. Since 500 shares will get that shareholder so close to being able to elect two directors, perhaps an alliance can be formed to put together a few additional votes. With that in mind, the shareholder may wonder how many shares it would take to elect two directors. Here again, there is a formula the shareholder can use, this time one that will show the number of shares needed to elect a particular number of directors:[2]

$$X = \frac{S \times N}{D + 1} + 1$$

X = Number of shares needed to elect N directors
S = Number of shares to be voted by all shareholders
N = Number of directors a shareholder or shareholder group wishes to elect
D = Number of directors to be elected at the meeting

Using the numbers in the above example, here is the answer to the question of how many shares would be needed to elect two directors:

$$X = \frac{1500 \times 2 = 3000}{5+1 = 6} + 1$$

or

$$X = 501$$

---

[2] Alan M. Hoffman, Israels on Corporate Practice 148 (4th ed. 1983).

After determining the number of directors who can be elected by a given number of votes, shareholders wishing to maximize their cumulative voting power simply need to distribute their votes as evenly as possible among their candidates. In the above example, that would mean casting 251 votes for one candidate and 250 for the other.

Director removal is also an issue when cumulative voting is used. Ordinarily, a director elected cumulatively can be removed by a majority of shareholder votes unless special provisions apply. To guard against this result, Model Act § 8.08 (c) provides that a director elected cumulatively "May not be removed if the number of votes sufficient to elect him under cumulative voting is voted against his removal."

The decision whether to use cumulative voting can be a difficult one. Cumulative voting potentially gives persons with significant minority interests the opportunity to elect one or more directors and thereby make the board more truly representative of the range of shareholder interests. If, however, directors elected cumulatively regard themselves as representing a particular interest group, rather than the corporation as a whole, they may approach their obligations in a manner inconsistent with fiduciary requirements and introduce divisiveness or factionalism into board proceedings.

B. CLASSIFICATION OF DIRECTORS

As is obvious from the preceding discussion on cumulative voting, the fewer directors there are to be elected at a particular meeting, the less chance there is that a minority shareholder or shareholder group can elect even one director. In order to minimize the effective voting power of minority shareholders, corporate planners sometimes divide the directors into classes, with only one of the classes coming up for election each year. That scheme, which is called "classification of directors" or "staggering the board," is allowed by the Model Act and most other corporation statutes. Here is the heart of the provision as found in Model Act § 8.06:

> If there are nine or more directors, the articles of incorporation may provide for staggering their terms by dividing the total number of directors into two or three groups, with each group containing one half or one-third of the total, as near as may be. In that event, the terms of directors in the first group expire at the first annual shareholders' meeting after their election, the terms of the second group expire at the second annual shareholders' meeting after their election, and the terms of the third group, if any, expire at the third annual shareholders' meeting after their election. At each annual shareholders' meeting held thereafter, directors shall be chosen for a term of two years or three years, as the case may be, to succeed those whose terms expire.

Skillful classification of directors can be used to circumvent the effect of cumulative voting.

C. CLASS VOTING AND WEIGHTED VOTING

Class voting is an alternative mechanism that can be used to empower minority interests to elect directors or to make sure that all members of a small, closely held corporation have representation on the board. According to § 8.04 of the Model Act, "If the articles of incorporation authorize dividing the shares into classes, the articles may also authorize the election of all or a specified number of directors by the holders of one or more authorized classes of shares...." This approach ensures that each shareholder or group of shareholders can elect a board member.

There are many ways different classes of stock may be structured. For example, there may be two or three classes of common, Classes A, B, and C, each with the same voting, dividend and liquidation rights, the difference being that each elects one director. The classes may also differ as to voting and proprietary rights. Class A could have voting rights and no liquidation or dividend rights, while Class B could have proprietary rights but no voting rights. The possibilities are many. *Lehrman v. Cohen*[3] in Section V of this chapter provides a well known example of the uses of classified stock in a closely held corporation.

Another way to structure voting rights is to use weighted voting, which is an exception to the general rule that each share has only one vote. With weighted voting, some stock will be given super voting power, that is, more than one vote per share. Weighted voting is used in anti-takeover devices. It is also used to maintain control within a particular group without requiring proportionate investment.

In *Providence and Worcester Co. v. Baker,*[4] the Delaware Supreme Court upheld a provision in a corporation's Articles of Incorporation restricting the voting rights of investors with large share holdings. The provision limited voting rights based on the number of shares held by an individual shareholder. A shareholder was entitled to one vote for each of the first fifty shares owned, and one vote for every twenty shares in excess of fifty. No shareholder could vote in his or her own right more than one fourth of the total outstanding shares. The last restriction did not apply to the extent a shareholder was acting as proxy for other shareholders.

The plaintiff claimed the arrangement was impermissible because all shares of stock within the same class did not have uniform voting rights. The court, however, upheld the scheme, finding that it restricted the voting rights of the shareholder but did not create variations in the voting power of the stock, itself.

---

[3]222 A.2d 800 (Del. 1966).
[4]378 A.2d 121 (Del. 1977).

Not all courts have agreed with the approach taken in *Providence*. In *Asarco Inc. v. Holmes A. Court*,[5] the Asarco directors planned to issue a preferred stock dividend in response to an unwelcome takeover by a shareholder. The court enjoined the issuance of the preferred stock because it would have caused shares within the same class to have different voting rights.

The plan involved a stock dividend in which common shareholders would receive one tenth of a share of Series C Preferred stock for each common share owned. Ordinarily, the Series C shares' voting rights would be limited to matters affecting their preferential rights. The voting rights would, however, change if any person or group acquired more than 20% of either the common stock or the Series C. Preferred. In that case, each one tenth of a Series C share would have 5 votes, except Series C shares owned by the 20% holder. The latter would continue to have no voting rights. All the voting rights could be extinguished by an offer to purchase any and all of Asarco's stock for cash at a fair price.

In reviewing plaintiff's challenge to the validity of the Class C Preferred, the court stated:

> By amending its Certificate of Incorporation to provide the Series C Preferred, Asarco's Board created a situation where the same class of stock will have different voting rights. This can be viewed as occurring with respect to two classes of stock. The new preferred will have differing voting rights depending on whether it is held by a 20 percent holder. The new preferred is piggybacked onto the outstanding common stock, and therefore there has also been created a situation in which certain common stockholders — those who acquire 20 percent of the shares — will have their voting power diluted five-fold vis-à-vis the other common stockholders. This is to be distinguished from a situation where a new class of stock has superior voting rights to all common stockholders or to all stockholders holding some other class. I conclude that while the Business Corporation Act permits changes of voting rights as between classes or series of stock, it does not permit an amendment ... which would redistribute voting power within a class or series.
>
> Equality of voting power among stockholders of the same class, or at least among the same series of a class that has more than one series, is a basic concept in corporate law....
>
> The language of the New Jersey statutes clearly suggests that voting rights may be different among different classes or series, but nowhere is it suggested that voting rights may be different within a class or series....
> ....
> ...A fair reading of [New Jersey Law] compels the conclusion that it confers power on the board to alter rights and preferences between different classes of stock. There is no express authority for a board to do what Asarco's

---

[5]611 F. Supp. 468 (D.C.N.J. 1985).

Board has sought to do here — namely — change the voting powers of shareholders within a particular class vis-à-vis other members of the same class. The Series C Preferred Stock would have different voting rights within the series, depending upon whether or not a Series C share were held by a 20 percent holder. In light of the piggyback aspect of the issuance of the Preferred Stock the common stock would have different voting rights depending on presence or absence of 20 percent ownership.

In *Baker v. Providence and Worcester Co.*, ... the Delaware Supreme Court upheld an original corporate charter which limited the voting rights of large shareholders. The Chancery Court had ruled that § 151(a) of Delaware's corporation law prohibited the creation even in the original certificate of incorporation of a class of stock which has differing voting rights stating:

> [W]ithout question, a reading of Section 151(a) leaves one with the firm conviction that "classes" may be vested with differing voting rights but that particular shareholders within one class of stock may not. The statute speaks only in terms of "classes" and unequivocally and repeatedly refers to differentiating only on the grounds of class. Thus I am compelled to conclude, ... that the divergent voting rights in issue here are not permissible since they are not on a class basis.

> ....

> It requires little imagination to conjure up situations in which corporate control could be manipulated by readjustment of intra-class voting rights through the mechanism of the issuance by the Board of blank check Preferred Stock. Even granting that in the present case the Board's purposes were to implement sound business objectives, the language of the statute, the potential for abuse of this power and the radical departure from traditional corporate practice which it represents leads to the conclusion that New Jersey courts would not read this power into the statute.

> ....

> ... Neither N.J.S.A. 14A:7-2 nor any other provision of the Business Corporation Act confers upon the corporation or its directors the power to issue classes of shares which have differing voting rights within the same class or which modify previously issued classes of shares so as to confer different voting rights upon shares within that class. Asarco's Series C Preferred Stock has this effect and consequently its issuance would be ultra vires and void.[6]

Both class voting and weighted voting can be used to allocate voting power independently of the size of financial investment. As a result, shareholders in a

---

[6]*Id.* at 479-80.

closely held corporation who have made unequal capital contributions can have equal voting rights on some or all of the matters properly decided by shareholders. This, in effect, creates a partnership like structure. All of the voting options described above affect the allocation of voting power among shareholders and do not disturb the allocation of power between the directors and the shareholders. Mechanisms for accomplishing the latter result are discussed in later sections of this chapter.

SECTION II. CHARTER PROVISIONS

Modern corporation statutes allow the drafters of corporate charters and charter amendments a virtual free hand in arranging the control of a corporation in any way that suits them. The Model Act contains representative provisions, the most important of which are §§ 8.01, 2.02, and 10.01. Section 8.01(b) gives power over the management of a corporation to the board of directors, "subject to any limitation set forth in the articles of incorporation or in an agreement" authorized by the Model Act. Section 2.02, which is the Model Act's general provision on charters, allows articles of incorporation to contain "provisions, not inconsistent with law, regarding: ... (ii) managing the business and regulating the affairs of the corporation; (iii) defining, limiting, and regulating the powers of the corporation, its board of directors, and shareholders ...." And § 10.01 allows the free amendment of charters at any time.

As a result of these provisions, the power to manage a corporation can be split among its shareholders, directors, and officers in any way desirable. It is even possible to take away all of the board's powers and simply have the shareholders or one of the officers exercise those powers, although that is not generally practical. It is practical, however, to take power away from the board piecemeal. For example, a corporation's charter might provide that only a shareholders' vote is required for a merger, for the sale of all of a corporation's assets, or for dissolution, each of which usually would require the prior recommendation of the directors. Or instead of enhancing the power of shareholders, a charter could take authority away from the directors and give it to an officer. A corporation may wish to provide, for example, that all questions relating to a particular line of business will be decided by the president rather than the board.

The most common charter provision that changes the ordinary control relationships is a super-majority voting requirement. Under statutory provisions typified by Model Act §§ 7.27 and 8.24, the charter (and, in the case of directors, also the bylaws) may require a higher percentage vote of directors or shareholders than the majority vote usually specified in the statute. The super-majority requirement can be used for all actions by shareholders or directors, but usually it is limited to specified actions of particular importance. In one corporation that might be the election of directors; in another, the sale of a specified corporate asset. As a means of impeding hostile tender offers, many publicly held corporations have adopted charter provisions that require 80 to 90% majorities to approve mergers and other transactions with shareholders having a specified amount of common stock, for example, 10%. High quorum requirements are also permissible and can be used with equal effect in many situations. The danger posed by a high quorum requirement for actions by shareholders or directors is that convening a meeting will become that much more difficult and may prevent even ordinary types of business from being conducted.

When one is drafting a super-majority provision, it usually is desirable to protect the provision from being amended by a vote of the shareholders or directors that is less than the super-majority called for by the provision. That is done by specifying in the charter that a super-majority vote is required to amend the charter provision containing the super-majority requirement. The Model Act has anticipated this result by including § 7.27 (b), which provides:

> An amendment to the articles of incorporation that adds, changes, or deletes a greater quorum or voting requirement must meet the same quorum requirement and be adopted by the same vote and voting groups required to take action under the quorum and voting requirements then in effect or proposed to be adopted, whichever is greater.

SECTION III. REMOVAL OF DIRECTORS

In a closely held corporation, there often are two conflicting desires on the part of shareholders with respect to the removal of directors. First, the shareholders wish to have unlimited power to remove non-shareholder directors at will. Second, each shareholder who is also a director wants to have substantial protection against being removed personally as a director. Most modern statutes, typified by Model Act § 8.08, provide that the shareholders may remove directors with or without cause at any meeting called for the purpose. That section gives the shareholders the power they wish to have over nonshareholder directors, but it provides them little personal protection.

That circumstance raises the question of whether, under a statute like the Model Act, a corporation's charter could provide that directors who also are shareholders could be removed only for cause. The answer seems clearly to be no, since the statutory language seems unequivocally to permit shareholders to remove any or all directors without cause. One way to give shareholders substantial protection against being removed as directors is to provide for a supermajority vote for the removal without cause of any director who also is a shareholder.

The following two cases raise interesting issues relating to the removal of directors.

AUER v. DRESSEL

Court of Appeals of New York
118 N.E.2d 590 (1954)

DESMOND, J.

This ... proceeding was brought by class A stockholders of appellant R. Hoe & Co., Inc., for an order in the nature of mandamus to compel the president of Hoe to comply with a positive duty imposed on him by the corporation's by-laws. Section 2 of article I of those by-laws says that "It shall be the duty of the President to call a special meeting whenever requested in writing so to do, by stockholders owning a majority of the capital stock entitled to vote at such meeting." On October 16, 1953, petitioners submitted to the president written requests for a special meeting of class A stockholders, which writings were signed in the names of the holders of record of slightly more than 55% of the class A stock. The president failed to call the meeting and, after waiting a week, the petitioners brought the present proceeding. The answer of the corporation and its president was not forthcoming until October 28, 1953, and it contained, in response to the petition's allegation that the demand was by more than a majority of class A stockholders, only a denial that the corporation and the president had any knowledge or information sufficient to form a belief as to the stockholdings of those who had signed the requests. Since the president, when he filed that answer, had had before him for at least ten days the signed requests themselves, his denial that he had any information sufficient for a belief as to the adequacy of the number of signatures was obviously perfunctory and raised no issue whatever. There was no discretion in this corporate officer as to whether or not to call a meeting when a demand therefor was put before him by owners of the required number of shares. The important right of stockholders to have such meetings called will be of little practical value if corporate management can ignore the requests, force the stockholders to commence legal proceedings, and then, by purely formal denials, put the stockholders to lengthy and expensive litigation, to establish facts as to stockholdings which are peculiarly within the knowledge of the corporate officers. In such a situation, Special Term did the correct thing in disposing of the matter summarily....

The petition was opposed on the further alleged ground that none of the four purposes for which petitioners wished the meeting called was a proper one for such a class A stockholders' meeting. Those four stated purposes were these: (A) to vote upon a resolution indorsing the administration of petitioner Joseph L. Auer, who had been removed as president by the directors, and demanding that he be reinstated as such president; (B) voting upon a proposal to amend the charter and by-laws to provide that vacancies on the board of directors, arising from the removal of a director by stockholders or by resignation of a director against whom charges have been preferred, may be filled, for the unexpired term, by the stockholders only of the class theretofore represented by the director so removed or so resigned; (C) voting upon a proposal that the stockholders hear certain charges preferred, in the requests, against four of the directors, determine whether the conduct of such directors or any of them was inimical to the corporation and, if so, to vote upon their removal and vote for the election of their successors; and (D) voting upon a proposal to amend the by-laws so as to provide that half of the total number of directors in office and, in any event, not less than one third of the whole authorized number of directors constitute a quorum of the directors.

The Hoe certificate of incorporation provides for eleven directors, of whom the class A stockholders, more than a majority of whom join in this petition, elect nine and the common stockholders elect two. The obvious purpose of the meeting here sought to be called (aside from the indorsement and reinstatement of former president Auer) is to hear charges against four of the class A directors, to remove them if the charges be proven, to amend the by-laws so that the successor directors be elected by the class A stockholders, and further to amend the by-laws so that an effective quorum of directors will be made up of no fewer than half of the directors in office and no fewer than one third of the whole authorized number of directors. No reason appears why the class A stockholders should not be allowed to vote on any or all of those proposals.

The stockholders, by expressing their approval of Mr. Auer's conduct as president and their demand that he be put back in that office, will not be able, directly, to effect that change in officers, but there is nothing invalid in their so expressing themselves and thus putting on notice the directors who will stand for election at the annual meeting. As to purpose (B), that is, amending the charter and by-laws to authorize the stockholders to fill vacancies as to class A directors who have been removed on charges or who have resigned, it seems to be settled law that the stockholders who are empowered to elect directors have the inherent power to remove them for cause (*Matter of Koch,* 257 N.Y. 318, 321, 322). Of course, as the *Koch* case points out, there must be the service of specific charges, adequate notice and full opportunity of meeting the accusations, but there is no present showing of any lack of any of those in this instance. Since these particular stockholders have the right to elect nine directors and to remove them on proven charges, it is not inappropriate that they should use their further power to amend the by-laws to elect the successors of such directors as shall be removed after hearing, or who shall resign pending hearing. Quite pertinent at this point is *Rogers v. Hill* (289 U.S. 582, 589) which made light of an argument that stockholders, by giving power to the directors to make by-laws, had lost their own power to make them; quoting a New Jersey case, the United States Supreme Court said: "'It would be preposterous to leave the real owners of the corporate property at the mercy of their agents, and the law has not done so.'" Such a change in the by-laws, dealing with class A directors only, has no effect on the voting rights of the common stockholders, which rights have to do with the selection of the remaining two directors only. True, the certificate of incorporation authorizes the board of directors to remove any director on charges, but we do not consider that provision as an abdication by the stockholders of their own traditional, inherent power to remove their own directors. Rather, it provides an additional method. Were that not so, the stockholders might find themselves without effective remedy in a case where a majority of the directors were accused of wrongdoing and, obviously, would be unwilling to remove themselves from office.

We fail to see, in the proposal to allow class A stockholders to fill vacancies as to class A directors, any impairment or any violation of paragraph (h) of article Three of the certificate of incorporation, which says that class A stock has exclusive voting rights with respect to all matters "other than the election of directors." That negative language should not be taken to mean that class A stockholders, who have an absolute right to elect nine of these eleven directors, cannot amend their by-laws to guarantee a similar right in the class A stockholders, and to the exclusion of common stockholders, to fill vacancies in the class A group of directors.

There is urged upon us the impracticability and unfairness of constituting the numerous stockholders a tribunal to hear charges made by themselves, and the incongruity of letting the stockholders hear and pass on those charges by proxy. Such questions are really not before us at all on this appeal. The charges here are not, on their face, frivolous or inconsequential, and all that we are holding as to the charges is that a meeting may be held to deal with them. Any director illegally removed can have his remedy in the courts....

CAMPBELL v. LOEW'S, INC.

Court of Chancery of Delaware
134 A.2d 852 (1957)

SEITZ, CHANCELLOR.

This is the decision on plaintiff's request for a preliminary injunction to restrain the holding of a stockholders' meeting or alternatively to prevent the meeting from considering certain matters or to prevent the voting of certain proxies. Certain other relief is also requested.

The corporate defendant appeared and resisted the motion. The four individual defendants, who are directors, were given until September 23, to appear and as of this date (September 19, 1957) have not appeared. Consequently, reference to "defendant" will embrace only the corporation unless otherwise indicated.

Some background is in order if the many difficult and novel issues are to be understood. Two factions have been fighting for control of Loew's. One faction is headed by Joseph Tomlinson (hereafter "Tomlinson faction") while the other is headed by the President of Loew's, Joseph Vogel (hereafter "Vogel faction"). At the annual meeting of stockholders last February a compromise was reached by which each nominated six directors and they in turn nominated a thirteenth or neutral director. But the battle had only begun. Passing by much of the controversy, we come to the July 17-18 period of this year when two of the six Vogel directors and the thirteenth or neutral director resigned. A quorum is seven.

On the 19th of July the Tomlinson faction asked that a directors' meeting be called for July 30 to consider, inter alia, the problem of filling director vacancies. On the eve of this meeting one of the Tomlinson directors resigned. This left five Tomlinson directors and four Vogel directors in office. Only the five Tomlinson directors attended the July 30 meeting. They purported to fill two of the director vacancies and to take other action. This Court has now ruled that for want of a quorum the two directors were not validly elected and the subsequent action taken at that meeting was invalid. *See Tomlinson v. Loew's, Inc.,* Del. Ch., 134 A.2d 518.

On July 29, the day before the noticed directors' meeting, Vogel, as president, sent out a notice calling a stockholders' meeting for September 12 for the following purposes:

1. to fill director vacancies.
2. to amend the by-laws to increase the number of the board from 13 to 19; to increase the quorum from 7 to 10 and to elect six additional directors.
3. to remove Stanley Meyer and Joseph Tomlinson as directors and to fill such vacancies.

Still later, another notice for a September 12 stockholders' meeting as well as a proxy statement went out over the signature of Joseph R. Vogel, as president. It was accompanied by a letter from Mr. Vogel dated August 9, 1957, soliciting stockholder support for the matters noticed in the call of the meeting, and particularly seeking to fill the vacancies and newly created directorships with "his" nominees. Promptly thereafter, plaintiff began this action. An order was entered requiring that the stockholders' meeting be adjourned until October 15, to give the Court more time to decide the serious and novel issues raised.

[The court first considered the authority of Vogel, the president, to call the stockholders' meeting for the purposes announced in his September 12 notice. It concluded that he did have authority to call that meeting.]

Plaintiff next argues that the stockholders have no power between annual meetings to elect directors to fill newly created directorships.

Plaintiff argues in effect that since the Loew's by-laws provide that the stockholders may fill "vacancies," and since our Courts have construed "vacancy" not to embrace "newly created directorships" (*Automatic Steel Products v. Johnston,* 31 Del. Ch. 469, 64 A.2d 416), the attempted call by the president for the purpose of filling newly created directorships was invalid.

Conceding that "vacancy" as used in the by-laws does not embrace "newly created directorships," that does not resolve this problem. I say this because in *Moon v. Moon Motor Car Co.,* 17 Del. Ch. 176, 151 A. 298, it was held that the stockholders had the inherent right between annual meetings to fill newly created directorships. There is no basis to distinguish the *Moon* case unless it be because the statute has since been amended to provide that not only vacancies but newly created directorships "may be filled by a majority of the directors then in office ... unless it is otherwise provided in the certificate of incorporation or the bylaws ...." 8 Del. C. § 223. Obviously, the amendment to include new directors is not worded so as to make the statute exclusive. It does not prevent the stockholders from filling the new directorships.

Is there any reason to consider the absence of a reference in the by-laws to new directorships to be significant? I think not. The by-law relied upon by plaintiff was adopted long before the statutory amendment and it does not purport to be exclusive in its operation. It would take a strong by-law language to warrant the conclusion that those adopting the by-laws intended to prohibit the stockholders from filling new directorships between annual meetings. No such strong language appears here and I do not think the implication is warranted in view of the subject matter.

I therefore conclude that the stockholders of Loew's do have the right between annual meetings to elect directors to fill newly created directorships.

Plaintiff next argues that the shareholders of a Delaware corporation have no power to remove directors from office even for cause and thus the call for that purpose is invalid. The defendant naturally takes a contrary position.

While there are some cases suggesting the contrary, I believe that the stockholders have the power to remove a director for cause. See *Auer v. Dressel,* 306 N.Y. 427, 118 N.E.2d 590; compare *Bruch v. National Guarantee Credit Corp.,* 13 Del. Ch. 180, 116 A. 738. This power must be implied when we consider that otherwise a director who is guilty of the worst sort of violation of his duty could nevertheless remain on the board. It is hardly to be believed that a director who is disclosing the corporation's trade secrets to a competitor would be immune from removal by the stockholders. Other examples, such as embezzlement of corporate funds, etc., come readily to mind.

But plaintiff correctly states that there is no provision in our statutory law providing for the removal of directors by stockholder action. In contrast he calls attention to § 142 of 8 Del.C., dealing with officers, which specifically refers to the possibility of a vacancy in an office by removal. He also notes that the Loew's by-laws provide for the removal of officers and employees but not directors. From these facts he argues that it was intended that directors not be removed even for cause. I believe the statute and by-law are of course some evidence to support plaintiff's contention. But when we seek to exclude the existence of a power by implication, I think it is pertinent to consider whether the absence of the power can be said to subject the corporation to the possibility of real damage. I say this because we seek intention and such a factor would be relevant to that issue. Considering the damage a director might be able to inflict upon his corporation, I believe the doubt must be resolved by construing the statutes and by-laws as leaving untouched the question of director removal for cause. This being so, the Court is free to conclude on reason that the stockholders have such inherent power.

I therefore conclude that as a matter of Delaware corporation law the stockholders do have the power to remove directors for cause. I need not and do not decide whether the stockholders can be appropriate charter or by-law provision deprive themselves of this right.

Plaintiff next argues that the removal of Tomlinson and Meyer as directors would violate the right of minority shareholders to representation on the board and would be contrary to the policy of the Delaware law regarding cumulative voting. Plaintiff contends that where there is cumulative voting, as provided by the Loew's certificate, a director cannot be removed by the stockholders even for cause.

It is true that the Chancellor noted in the *Bruch* case that the provision for cumulative voting in the Delaware law was one reason why directors should not be considered to have the power to remove a fellow director even for cause. And it is certainly evident that if not carefully supervised the existence of a power in the stockholders to remove a director even for cause could be abused and used to defeat cumulative voting.

Does this mean that there can be no removal of a director by the stockholders for cause in any case where cumulative voting exists? The conflicting considerations involved make the answer to this question far from easy. Some states have passed statutes dealing with this problem but Delaware has not. The possibility of stockholder removal action designed to circumvent the effect of cumulative voting is evident. This is particularly true where the removal vote is, as here, by mere majority vote. On the other hand, if we assume a case where a director's presence or action is clearly damaging the corporation and its stockholders in a substantial way, it is difficult to see why that director should be free to continue such damage merely because he was elected under a cumulative voting provision.

On balance, I conclude that the stockholders have the power to remove a director for cause even where there is a provision for cumulative voting. I think adequate protection is afforded not only by the legal safeguards announced in this opinion but by the existence of a remedy to test the validity of any such action, if taken.

The foregoing points constitute all of the arguments advanced by plaintiff which go to the validity of the call of the meeting for the purposes stated. It follows from my various conclusions that the meeting was validly called by the president to consider the matters noticed.

I turn next to plaintiff's charges relating to procedural defects and to irregularities in proxy solicitation by the Vogel group.

Plaintiff's first point is that the stockholders can vote to remove a director for cause only after such director has been given adequate notice of charges of grave impropriety and afforded an opportunity to be heard.

....

[I]t is certainly true that when the shareholders attempt to remove a director for cause, "... there must be the service of specific charges, adequate notice and full opportunity of meeting the accusation ...." *See Auer v. Dressel,* above. While it involved an invalid attempt by directors to remove a fellow director for cause, nevertheless, this same general standard was recognized in *Bruch v. National*

Guarantee Credit Corp., above. The Chancellor said that the power of removal could not "be exercised in an arbitrary manner. The accused director would be entitled to be heard in his own defense."

Plaintiff asserts that no specific charges have been served upon the two directors sought to be ousted; that the notice of the special meeting fails to contain a specific statement of the charges; that the proxy statement which accompanied the notice also failed to notify the stockholders of the specific charges; and that it does not inform the stockholders that the accused must be afforded an opportunity to meet the accusations before a vote is taken.

Matters for stockholder consideration need not be conducted with the same formality as judicial proceedings. The proxy statement specifically recites that the two directors are sought to be removed for the reasons stated in the president's accompanying letter. Both directors involved received copies of the letter. Under the circumstances I think it must be said that the two directors involved were served with notice of the charges against them. It is true, as plaintiff says, that the notice and the proxy statement failed to contain a specific statement of charges. But as indicated, I believe the accompanying letter was sufficient compliance with the notice requirement.

Contrary to plaintiff's contention, I do not believe the material sent out had to advise the stockholders that the accused must be afforded an opportunity to defend the charges before the stockholders voted. Such an opportunity had to be afforded as a matter of law and the failure to so advise them did not affect the necessity for compliance with the law. Thus, no prejudice is shown.

I next consider plaintiff's contention that the charges against the two directors do not constitute "cause" as a matter of law. It would take too much space to narrate in detail the contents of the president's letter. I must therefore give my summary of its charges. First of all, it charges that the two directors (Tomlinson and Meyer) failed to cooperate with Vogel in his announced program for rebuilding the company; that their purpose has been to put themselves in control; that they made baseless accusations against him and other management personnel and attempted to divert him from his normal duties as president by bombarding him with correspondence containing unfounded charges and other similar acts; that they moved into the company's building, accompanied by lawyers and accountants, and immediately proceeded upon a planned scheme of harassment. They called for many records, some going back twenty years, and were rude to the personnel. Tomlinson sent daily letters to the directors making serious charges directly and by means of innuendos and misinterpretations.

Are the foregoing charges, if proved, legally sufficient to justify the ouster of the two directors by the stockholders? I am satisfied that a charge that the directors desired to take over control of the corporation is not a reason for their ouster. Standing alone, it is a perfectly legitimate objective which is a part of the very fabric of corporate existence. Nor is a charge of lack of cooperation a legally sufficient basis for removal for cause.

The next charge is that these directors, in effect, engaged in a calculated plan of harassment to the detriment of the corporation. Certainly a director may examine books, ask questions, etc., in the discharge of his duty, but a point can be reached when his actions exceed the call of duty and become deliberately obstructive. In such a situation, if his actions constitute a real burden on the corporation then the stockholders are entitled to relief. The charges in this area made by the Vogel letter are legally sufficient to justify the stockholders in voting to remove such directors. In so concluding I of course express no opinion as to the truth of the charges.

I therefore conclude that the charge of "a planned scheme of harassment" as detailed in the letter constitutes a justifiable legal basis for removing a director.

I next consider whether the directors sought to be removed have been given a reasonable opportunity to be heard by the stockholders on the charges made.

The corporate defendant freely admits that it has flatly refused to give the five Tomlinson directors or the plaintiff a stockholders' list. Any doubt about the matter was removed by the statement of defendant's counsel in open court at the argument that no such list would be supplied. The Vogel faction has physical control of the corporate offices and facilities. By this action the corporation through the Vogel group has deliberately refused to afford the directors in question an adequate opportunity to be heard by the stockholders on the charges made. This is contrary to the legal requirements which must be met before a director can be removed for cause.

....

There seems to be an absence of cases detailing the appropriate procedure for submitting a question of director removal for cause for stockholder consideration. I am satisfied, however, that to the extent the matter is to be voted upon by the use of proxies, such proxies may be solicited only after the accused directors are afforded an opportunity to present their case to the stockholders. This means, in my opinion, that an opportunity must be provided such directors to present their defense to the stockholders by a statement which must accompany or precede the initial solicitation of proxies seeking authority to vote for the removal of such director for cause. If not provided then such proxies may not be voted for removal. And the corporation has a duty to see that this opportunity is given the directors at its expense. Admittedly, no such opportunity was given the two directors involved. Indeed, the corporation admittedly refused to supply them with a stockholders' list.

To require anything less than the foregoing is to deprive the stockholders of the opportunity to consider the case made by both sides before voting and would make a mockery of the requirement that a director sought to be removed for cause is entitled to an opportunity to be heard before the stockholders vote....

....

SECTION IV. DEADLOCKS, OPPRESSION, AND DISSOLUTION

When shareholders in a publicly traded company are unhappy with the management or each other, they may sever their relationship with the company simply by selling their stock. In contrast, shareholders in closely held corporations, lacking such a market, find it difficult to exit from the company. This difficulty and the fact that closely held corporation shareholders often depend on the company for their livelihood exacerbate the problems caused by conflicts among participants in the enterprise. For the corporate lawyer, conflicts are particularly troublesome when they result either in deadlock or in an attempt by one group, usually the majority shareholders, to defeat the legitimate expectations of another group, usually the minority. One reason is that conflict situations raise difficult ethical issues for the counseling attorney. (*See* Model Rule 2.2.) A second reason is that the remedy is often draconian — dissolution of an economically viable corporation. The cases that follow explore these issues.

A. DEADLOCKS

Deadlocks at either the shareholder or the director level can create some of a corporation's most serious problems. There are many possible unpleasant scenarios involving deadlocks. The one that usually comes to mind is a corporation whose actions are deadlocked; it is unable to act. That can be a serious problem for a corporation and its shareholders, but it is far from the worst deadlock scenario. Since the president has the power to act for the corporation on any matter that is within the corporation's usual course of business, when the board is deadlocked, the president can operate relatively unfettered. Since the president typically also is a board member, that means that he or she can put into play many of the wishes of one board faction, perhaps to the substantial detriment of some shareholders.

Probably the worst deadlock scenarios occur when the shareholders are deadlocked and cannot replace a board that is dominated by one shareholder faction. The next case offers a good example.

HALL v. HALL

Missouri Court of Appeals
506 S.W.2d 42 (1974)

DONALD B. CLARK, SPECIAL JUDGE.

This action involves a dispute among shareholders in a closely held corporation. The facts are not in dispute.

Respondent Musselman and Hall Contractors, Inc. (hereafter the corporation) is a Missouri corporation, the corporate stock of which was wholly owned immediately prior to September 19, 1969 in equal proportions by Edward H. Hall and respondent Harry L. Hall. On the last mentioned date, Edward H. Hall died leaving his widow, appellant surviving him. Appellant thereafter succeeded to a fifty percent stock interest in the corporation in her representative capacity as the duly appointed and acting executrix of the estate of her deceased husband and is also interested as residuary devisee of the estate.

Prior to Edward Hall's death, he and respondent Harry Hall were the only directors of the corporation. Acting to fill the vacancy created by the death of Edward, respondent Harry Hall appointed his wife, respondent Florence E. Hall, as a director of the corporation and thereafter, acting as the then board of directors, they appointed themselves as president and vice-president of the corporation. To the date of the filing of this action, no further election of directors or officers has been held and the individual respondents have continued to serve as the only directors and officers of the corporation.

Upon the failure of the individual respondents to call or convene the required annual meeting of the corporation, appellant by written and published notice called an annual meeting for the second Tuesday in May, 1970, such being the date specified in the corporate by-laws. Appellant appeared at the registered office of the corporation to participate in the business of the meeting and to vote the shares held by her in her representative capacity, but respondent Harry Hall, the only other shareholder, failed and refused to attend. The equal division of stock requires the participation of both shareholders to achieve a quorum. Being unable to transact any business without the vote of the shares of the other stockholder, appellant has subsequently adjourned the 1970 annual meeting from week to week.

Subsequent to September 19, 1969, the individual respondents have been in practical control of the corporation. As no election of directors could be held, respondents have continued in office by reason of the failure to elect or qualify any successors. At a special meeting of directors held August 6, 1970, the individual respondents by resolution directed the offering and sale of 3000 shares of the capital stock of the corporation being the balance of authorized but unissued stock. The purchase or offering price was set at $ 10.00 per share. Appellant indicated her desire and ability to exercise her preemptive right to purchase one-half of the additional stock so offered but contended that the stock issue would be invalid having been approved by directors unlawfully holding office.

In her petition to the court below, appellant sought to enjoin respondent Harry Hall from refusing to attend shareholders' meetings of the corporation, to enjoin the individual respondents from establishing a terminal date for exercise of preemptive purchase rights for the new issue and from continuing to act as directors and officers of the corporation pending a meeting of shareholders. On the motion of respondents asserting failure to state a cause of action, [appellant's] petition was dismissed and this appeal has resulted.

....

The substance of appellant's complaint is that her fifty percent ownership interest in the corporation has been rendered impotent by the refusal of respondent Harry Hall to attend and participate in stockholders' meetings. Of course, such is an inevitable consequence where disputes between equal shareholders occur as [the Missouri corporation statute] constitutes a quorum as the majority of outstanding shares entitled to vote and conditions valid corporate acts on the decision of majority of the quorum. Recognizing then that the owners of fifty percent or more of the corporate stock may frustrate the conduct of business at stockholder's meetings, is such inaction unlawful and if not, do remaining stockholders have a remedy?

The very nature of the corporate form is the creation by statute of an entity separate and apart from the individuals who own, manage and operate it. One who acquires corporate stock obtains an interest in the corporate assets after payment of corporate debts and a right to participate in management which he may or may not exercise. The holder of shares is under no obligation whatever to the corporation other than to make full payment of the consideration for which the shares are issued. As participation by a shareholder in management of corporate affairs is voluntary, it necessarily follows that no shareholder may be compelled to attend or participate in shareholders' meetings. Any different rule would contradict the distinction which separates the corporate existence from the identity of its shareholders and which vests management responsibilities in the directors.

Conceding that the failure of respondent Harry Hall to attend stockholders' meetings has injured appellant in preventing her from participating in the management of the corporation, if respondent is under no legal duty to participate, how may a court of equity compel him by injunction to attend and vote at a stockholders' meeting? No maxim of equity may be invoked to destroy an existing legal right nor may equity create a right at law which does not exist....

No allegation was made by appellant of any contractual obligation on the part of respondent Harry Hall to attend and participate in stockholders' meetings and none exists by statute or rule of law. It therefore follows of necessity that a court of equity may not by injunction compel that for which no legal duty lies. The trial court was correct in refusing to grant the mandatory injunction requested.

Although appellant's petition alleged oppression by respondent Harry Hall in the matter of salary payments from corporate funds to the individual respondents and further alleged dilution, wasting and diversion of corporate assets, no suggestion is made as to why appellant may not move to dissolve the corporation under [the Missouri corporation statute], or, as the trial court suggested, try by quo warranto the right of the individual respondents to continue in the offices of directors and corporate officers when the statutory requirements for annual stockholders' meetings have been subverted. As is noted in Fletcher-Cyclopedia Corporations, Vol. 5, Chapter 13, p. 22, although quo warranto as a remedy to oust one from an office illegally held would not produce a judgment requiring an election of officers, it might produce a vacancy necessitating one. Alternative methods whereby appellant may obtain redress do not require ruling on this appeal.

....

B. OPPRESSION AND DISSENSION

Dissension among shareholders can arise in many different types of situations, as, for example, when the actions of one shareholder group work to the financial disadvantage of another. The cases and statutory provisions that follow present several approaches to dealing with dissension among shareholders, and, as appropriate, also with deadlock. Assess the merits of each approach.

DONAHUE v. RODD ELECTROTYPE CO. OF NEW ENGLAND, INC.

Supreme Judicial Court of Massachusetts
328 N.E.2d 505 (1975)

TAURO, CHIEF JUSTICE.

The plaintiff, Euphemia Donahue, a minority stockholder in the Rodd Electrotype Company of New England, Inc. (Rodd Electrotype), a Massachusetts corporation, brings this suit against the directors of Rodd Electrotype, Charles H. Rodd, Frederick I. Rodd and Mr. Harold E. Magnuson, against Harry C. Rodd, a former director, officer, and controlling stockholder of Rodd Electrotype and against Rodd Electrotype (hereinafter called defendants). The plaintiff seeks to rescind Rodd Electrotype's purchase of Harry Rodd's shares in Rodd Electrotype and to compel Harry Rodd "to repay to the corporation the purchase price of said shares, $ 36,000, together with interest from the date of purchase." The plaintiff alleges that the defendants caused the corporation to purchase the shares in violation of their fiduciary duty to her, a minority stockholder of Rodd Electrotype.

The trial judge, after hearing oral testimony, dismissed the plaintiff's bill on the merits. He found that the purchase was without prejudice to the plaintiff and implicitly found that the transaction had been carried out in good faith and with inherent fairness. The Appeals Court affirmed with costs. The case is before us on the plaintiff's application for further appellate review.

....

The evidence may be summarized as follows: In 1935, the defendant, Harry C. Rodd, began his employment with Rodd Electrotype, then styled the Royal Electrotype Company of New England, Inc. (Royal of New England). At that time, the company was a wholly-owned subsidiary of a Pennsylvania corporation, the Royal Electrotype Company (Royal Electrotype). Mr. Rodd's advancement within the company was rapid. The following year he was elected a director, and, in 1946, he succeeded to the position of general manager and treasurer.

In 1936, the plaintiff's husband, Joseph Donahue (now deceased), was hired by Royal of New England as a "finisher" of electrotype plates. His duties were confined to operational matters within the plant. Although he ultimately achieved the positions of plant superintendent (1946) and corporate vice president (1955), Donahue never participated in the "management" aspect of the business.

In the years preceding 1955, the parent company, Royal Electrotype, made available to Harry Rodd and Joseph Donahue shares of the common stock in its subsidiary, Royal of New England. Harry Rodd took advantage of the opportunities offered to him and acquired 200 shares for $ 20 a share. Joseph Donahue, at the suggestion of Harry Rodd, who hoped to interest Donahue in the business, eventually obtained fifty shares in two twenty-five share lots priced at $ 20 a share. The parent company at all times retained 725 of the 1,000 outstanding shares. One Lawrence W. Kelley owned the remaining twenty-five shares.

In June of 1955, Royal of New England purchased all 725 of its shares owned by its parent company....

The stock purchases left Harry Rodd in control of Royal of New England. Early in 1955, before the purchases, he had assumed the presidency of the company. His 200 shares gave him a dominant eighty per cent interest. Joseph Donahue, at this time, was the only minority stockholder.

Subsequent events reflected Harry Rodd's dominant influence. In June, 1960, more than a year after the last obligation to Royal Electrotype had been discharged, the company was renamed the Rodd Electrotype Company of New England, Inc. In 1962, Charles H. Rodd, Harry Rodd's son (a defendant here), who had long been a company employee working in the plant, became corporate vice president. In 1963, he joined his father on the board of directors. In 1964, another son, Frederick I. Rodd (also a defendant), replaced Joseph Donahue as plant superintendent. By 1965, Harry Rodd had evidently decided to reduce his participation in corporate management. That year Charles Rodd succeeded him as president and general manager of Rodd Electrotype.

From 1959 to 1967, Harry Rodd pursued what may fairly be termed a gift program by which he distributed the majority of his shares equally among his two sons and his daughter, Phyllis E. Mason. Each child received thirty-nine shares. Two shares were returned to the corporate treasury in 1966.

We come now to the events of 1970 which form the grounds for the plaintiff's complaint. In May of 1970, Harry Rodd was seventy-seven years old. The record indicates that for some time he had not enjoyed the best of health and that he had undergone a number of operations. His sons wished him to retire. Mr. Rodd was not averse to this suggestion. However, he insisted that some financial arrangements be made with respect to his remaining eighty-one shares of stock. A number of conferences ensued. Harry Rodd and Charles Rodd (representing the company) negotiated terms of purchase for forty-five shares which, Charles Rodd testified, would reflect the book value and liquidating value of the shares.

A special board meeting convened on July 13, 1970. As the first order of business, Harry Rodd resigned his directorship of Rodd Electrotype. The remaining incumbent directors, Charles Rodd and Mr. Harold E. Magnuson (clerk of the company and a defendant and defense attorney in the instant suit), elected Frederick Rodd to replace his father. The three directors then authorized Rodd Electrotype's president (Charles Rodd) to execute an agreement between Harry Rodd and the company in which the company would purchase forty-five shares for $ 800 a share ($ 36,000).

The stock purchase agreement was formalized between the parties on July 13, 1970. Two days later, a sale pursuant to the July 13 agreement was consummated. At approximately the same time, Harry Rodd resigned his last corporate office, that of treasurer.

Harry Rodd completed divestiture of his Rodd Electrotype stock in the following year. As was true of his previous gifts, his later divestments gave equal representation to his children. Two shares were sold to each child on July 15, 1970, for $ 800 a share. Each was given ten shares in March, 1971. Thus, in March, 1971, the shareholdings in Rodd Electrotype were apportioned as follows: Charles Rodd, Frederick Rodd and Phyllis Mason each held fifty-one shares; the Donahues held fifty shares.

A special meeting of the stockholders of the company was held on March 30, 1971. At the meeting, Charles Rodd, company president and general manager, reported the tentative results of an audit conducted by the company auditors and reported generally on the company events of the year. For the first time, the Donahues learned that the corporation had purchased Harry Rodd's shares. According to the minutes of the meeting, following Charles Rodd's report, the Donahues raised questions about the purchase. They then voted against a resolution, ultimately adopted by the remaining stockholders, to approve Charles Rodd's report. Although the minutes of the meeting show that the stockholders unanimously voted to accept a second resolution ratifying all acts of the company president (he executed the stock purchase agreement) in the preceding year, the trial judge found, and there was evidence to support his finding, that the Donahues did not ratify the purchase of Harry Rodd's shares.

A few weeks after the meeting, the Donahues, acting through their attorney, offered their shares to the corporation on the same terms given to Harry Rodd. Mr. Harold E. Magnuson replied by letter that the corporation would not purchase the shares and was not in a financial position to do so. This suit followed.

In her argument before this court, the plaintiff has characterized the corporate purchase of Harry Rodd's shares as an unlawful distribution of corporate assets to controlling stockholders. She urges that the distribution constitutes a breach of the fiduciary duty owed by the Rodds, as controlling stockholders, to her, a minority stockholder in the enterprise, because the Rodds failed to accord her an equal opportunity to sell her shares to the corporation. The defendants reply that the stock purchase was within the powers of the corporation and met the requirements of good faith and inherent fairness imposed on a fiduciary in his dealings with the corporation. They assert that there is no right to equal opportunity in corporate stock purchases for the corporate treasury. For the reasons hereinafter noted, we agree with the plaintiff and reverse the decree of the Superior Court.

However, we limit the applicability of our holding to "closely held corporations," as hereinafter defined. Whether the holding should apply to other corporations is left for decision in another case, on a proper record.

A. *Closely Held Corporations.* In previous opinions, we have alluded to the distinctive nature of the closely held corporation, but have never defined precisely what is meant by a closely held corporation. There is no single, generally accepted definition. Some commentators emphasize an "integration of ownership and management" (Note, Statutory Assistance for Closely Held Corporations, 71 Harv.L.Rev. 1498 [1958]), in which the stockholders occupy most management positions. Others focus on the number of stockholders and the nature of the market for the stock. In this view, closely held corporations have few stockholders; there is little market for corporate stock. The Supreme Court of Illinois adopted this latter view in *Galler v. Galler,* 32 Ill.2d 16, 203 N.E.2d 577 (1965): "For our purposes, a closely held corporation is one in which the stock is held in a few hands, or in a few families, and wherein it is not at all, or only rarely, dealt in by buying or selling." *Id.* at 27, 203 N.E.2d at 583. We accept aspects of both definitions. We deem a closely held corporation to be typified by: (1) a small number of stockholders; (2) no ready market for the corporate stock; and (3) substantial majority stockholder participation in the management, direction and operations of the corporation.

As thus defined, the closely held corporation bears striking resemblance to a partnership. Commentators and courts have noted that the closely held corporation is often little more than an "incorporated" or "chartered" partnership. The stockholders "clothe" their partnership "with the benefits peculiar to a corporation, limited liability, perpetuity and the like." *In the Matter of Surchin v. Approved Bus. Mach. Co., Inc.,* 55 Misc.2d 888, 889, 286 N.Y.S.2d 580, 581 (Sup.Ct.1967). In essence, though, the enterprise remains one in which ownership is limited to the original parties or transferees of their stock to whom the other stockholders have agreed, in which ownership and management are in the same hands, and in which the owners are quite dependent on one another for the success of the enterprise. Many closely held corporations are "really partnerships, between two or three people who contribute their capital, skills, experience and labor." *Kruger v. Gerth,* 16 N.Y.2d 802, 805, 263 N.Y.S.2d 1, 3, 210 N.E.2d 355, 356 (1965) (Desmond, C. J., dissenting). Just as in a partnership, the relationship among the stockholders must be one of trust, confidence and absolute loyalty if the enterprise is to succeed. Closely held corporations with substantial assets and with more numerous stockholders are no different from smaller closely held corporations in this regard. All participants rely on the fidelity and abilities of those stockholders who hold office. Disloyalty and self-seeking conduct on the part of any stockholder will engender bickering, corporate stalemates, and, perhaps, efforts to achieve dissolution.

In *Helms v. Duckworth,* 101 U.S.App.D.C. 390, 249 F.2d 482 (1957), the United States Court of Appeals for the District of Columbia Circuit had before it a stockholders' agreement providing for the purchase of the shares of a deceased stockholder by the surviving stockholder in a small "two-man" closely held corporation. The court held the surviving stockholder to a duty "to deal fairly, honestly, and openly with ... [his] fellow stockholders." *Id.* at 487. Judge Burger, now Chief Justice Burger, writing for the court, emphasized the resemblance of the two-man closely held corporation to a partnership: "In an intimate business venture such as this, stockholders of a closely held corporation occupy a position similar to that of joint adventurers and partners. While courts have sometimes declared stockholders 'do not bear toward each other that same relation of trust and confidence which prevails in partnerships,' this view ignores the practical realities of the organization and functioning of a small 'two-man' corporation organized to carry on a small business enterprise in which the stockholders, directors, and managers are the same persons." *Id.* at 486.

Although the corporate form provides the above-mentioned advantages for the stockholders (limited liability, perpetuity, and so forth), it also supplies an opportunity for the majority stockholders to oppress or disadvantage minority stockholders. The minority is vulnerable to a variety of oppressive devices, termed "freeze-outs," which the majority may employ. An authoritative study of such "freeze-outs" enumerates some of the possibilities: "The squeezers [those who employ the freeze-out techniques] may refuse to declare dividends; they may drain off the corporation's earnings in the form of exorbitant salaries and bonuses to the majority shareholder-officers and perhaps to their relatives, or in the form of high rent by the corporation for property leased from majority shareholders ... they may deprive minority shareholders of corporate offices and of employment by the company; they may cause the corporation to sell its assets at an inadequate price to the majority shareholders...." F. H. O'Neal and J. Derwin, Expulsion or Oppression of Business Associates, 42 (1961). In particular, the power of the board of directors, controlled by the majority, to declare or withhold dividends and to deny the minority employment is easily converted to a device to disadvantage minority stockholders.

The minority can, of course, initiate suit against the majority and their directors. Self-serving conduct by directors is proscribed by the director's fiduciary obligation to the corporation. However, in practice, the plaintiff will find difficulty in challenging dividend or employment policies. Such policies are considered to be within the judgment of the directors.... Although contractual provisions in an "agreement of association and articles of organization" or in by-laws have justified decrees in this jurisdiction ordering dividend declarations, generally, plaintiffs who seek judicial assistance against corporate dividend or employment policies do not prevail.

Thus, when these types of "freeze-outs" are attempted by the majority stockholders, the minority stockholders, cut off from all corporation-related revenues, must either suffer their losses or seek a buyer for their shares. Many minority stockholders will be unwilling or unable to wait for an alteration in majority policy. Typically, the minority stockholder in a closely held corporation has a substantial percentage of his personal assets invested in the corporation. The stockholder may have anticipated that his salary from his position with the corporation would be his livelihood. Thus, he cannot afford to wait passively. He must liquidate his investment in the closely held corporation in order to reinvest the funds in income-producing enterprises.

At this point, the true plight of the minority stockholder in a closely held corporation becomes manifest. He cannot easily reclaim his capital. In a large public corporation, the oppressed or dissident minority stockholder could sell his stock in order to extricate some of his invested capital. By definition, this market is not available for shares in the closely held corporation. In a partnership, a partner who feels abused by his fellow partners may cause dissolution by his "express will ... at any time" and recover his share of partnership assets and accumulated profits. If dissolution results in a breach of the partnership articles, the culpable partner will be liable in damages. By contrast, the stockholder in the closely held corporation or "incorporated partnership" may achieve dissolution and recovery of his share of the enterprise assets only by compliance with the rigorous terms of the applicable chapter of the General Laws. "The dissolution of a corporation which is a creature of the Legislature is primarily a legislative function, and the only authority courts have to deal with this subject is the power conferred upon them by the Legislature." *Leventhal v. Atlantic Fin. Corp.*, 316 Mass. 194, 205, 55 N.E.2d 20, 26 (1944). To secure dissolution of the ordinary closely held corporation subject to [the Massachusetts corporation statute], the stockholder, in the absence of corporate deadlock, must own at least fifty percent of the shares or have the advantage of a favorable provision in the articles of organization. The minority stockholder, by definition lacking fifty per cent of the corporate shares, can never "authorize" the corporation to file a petition for dissolution ... by his own vote. He will seldom have at his disposal the requisite favorable provision in the articles of organization.

Thus, in a closely held corporation, the minority stockholders may be trapped in a disadvantageous situation. No outsider would knowingly assume the position of the disadvantaged minority. The outsider would have the same difficulties. To cut losses, the minority stockholder may be compelled to deal with the majority. This is the capstone of the majority plan. Majority "freeze-out" schemes which withhold dividends are designed to compel the minority to relinquish stock at inadequate prices. When the minority stockholder agrees to sell out at less than fair value, the majority has won.

Because of the fundamental resemblance of the closely held corporation to the partnership, the trust and confidence which are essential to this scale and manner of enterprise, and the inherent danger to minority interests in the closely held corporation, we hold that stockholders in the closely held corporation owe one another substantially the same fiduciary duty in the operation of the enterprise that partners owe to one another. In our previous decisions, we have defined the standard of duty owed by partners to one another, as the "utmost good faith and loyalty." *Cardullo v. Landau*, 329 Mass. 5, 8, 105 N.E.2d 843 (1952); *DeCotis v. D'Antona*, 350 Mass. 165, 168, 214 N.E.2d 21 (1966). Stockholders in closely held corporations must discharge their management and stockholder responsibilities in conformity with this strict good faith standard. They may not act out of avarice, expediency or self-interest in derogation of their duty of loyalty to the other stockholders and to the corporation.

We contrast this strict good faith standard with the somewhat less stringent standard of fiduciary duty to which directors and stockholders of all corporations must adhere in the discharge of their corporate responsibilities. Corporate directors are held to a good faith and inherent fairness standard of conduct and are not "permitted to serve two masters whose interests are antagonistic." *Spiegel v. Beacon Participations, Inc.*, 297 Mass. 398, 411, 8 N.E.2d 895, 904 (1937). "Their paramount duty is to the corporation, and their personal pecuniary interests are subordinate to that duty." *Durfee v. Durfee & Canning, Inc.*, 323 Mass. 187, 196, 80 N.E.2d 522, 527 (1948).

The more rigorous duty of partners and participants in a joint adventure, here extended to stockholders in a closely held corporation, was described by then Chief Judge Cardozo of the New York Court of Appeals in *Meinhard v. Salmon*, 249 N.Y. 458, 164 N.E. 545 (1928): "Joint adventurers, like copartners, owe to one another, while the enterprise continues, the duty of the finest loyalty. Many forms of conduct permissible in a workaday world for those acting at arm's length, are forbidden to those bound by fiduciary ties.... Not honesty alone, but the punctilio of an honor the most sensitive, is then the standard of behavior." *Id.* at 463-464, 164 N.E. at 546.

....

... In the instant case, we extend this strict duty of loyalty to all stockholders in closely held corporations. The circumstances which justified findings of relationships of trust and confidence in these particular cases exist universally in modified form in all closely held corporations....

B. *Equal Opportunity in a Closely Held Corporation.* Under settled Massachusetts law, a domestic corporation, unless forbidden by statute, has the power to purchase its own shares. An agreement to reacquire stock "[is] enforceable, subject, at least, to the limitations that the purchase must be made in good faith and without prejudice to creditors and stockholders." *Scriggins v. Thomas Dalby Co.*, [290 Mass. 414, 418, 195 N.E. 749, 752 (1939)]; *Winchell v. Plywood Corp.*, [324 Mass. 171, 174-75, 85 N.E.2d 313, 315 (1949)]. When the corporation reacquiring its own stock is a closely held corporation, the purchase is subject to the additional requirement, in the light of our holding in this opinion, that the stockholders, who, as directors or controlling stockholders, caused the corporation to enter into the stock purchase agreement, must have acted with the utmost good faith and loyalty to the other stockholders.

To meet this test, if the stockholder whose shares were purchased was a member of the controlling group, the controlling stockholders must cause the corporation to offer each stockholder an equal opportunity to sell a ratable number of his shares to the corporation at an identical price. Purchase by the corporation confers substantial benefits on the members of the controlling group whose shares were purchased. These benefits are not available to the minority stockholders if the corporation does not also offer them an opportunity to sell their shares. The controlling group may not, consistent with its strict duty to the minority, utilize its control of the corporation to obtain special advantages and disproportionate benefit from its share ownership.

The benefits conferred by the purchase are twofold: (1) provision of a market for shares; (2) access to corporate assets for personal use. By definition, there is no ready market for shares of a closely held corporation. The purchase creates a market for shares which previously had been unmarketable. It transforms a previously illiquid investment into a liquid one. If the closely held corporation purchases shares only from a member of the controlling group, the controlling stockholder can convert his shares into cash at a time when none of the other stockholders can. Consistent with its strict fiduciary duty, the controlling group may not utilize its control of the corporation to establish an exclusive market in previously unmarketable shares from which the minority stockholders are excluded.

The purchase also distributes corporate assets to the stockholder whose shares were purchased. Unless an equal opportunity is given to all stockholders, the purchase of shares from a member of the controlling group operates as a *preferential* distribution of assets. In exchange for his shares, he receives a percentage of the contributed capital and accumulated profits of the enterprise. The funds he so receives are available for his personal use. The other stockholders benefit from no such access to corporate property and cannot withdraw their shares of the corporate profits and capital in this manner unless the controlling group acquiesces. Although the purchase price for the controlling stockholder's shares may seem fair to the corporation and other stockholders under the tests established in the prior case law, the controlling stockholder whose stock has been purchased has still received a relative advantage over his fellow stockholders, inconsistent with his strict fiduciary duty — an opportunity to turn corporate funds to personal use.

The rule of equal opportunity in stock purchases by closely held corporations provides equal access to these benefits for all stockholders. We hold that, in any case in which the controlling stockholders have exercised their power over the corporation to deny the minority such equal opportunity, the minority shall be entitled to appropriate relief. To the extent that language in *Spiegel v. Beacon Participations, Inc.,* 297 Mass. 398, 431, 8 N.E.2d 895 (1937), and other cases suggests that there is no requirement of equal opportunity for minority stockholders when a closely held corporation purchases shares from a controlling stockholder, it is not to be followed.

C. *Application of the Law to This Case.* We turn now to the application of the learning set forth above to the facts of the instant case.

The strict standard of duty is plainly applicable to the stockholders in Rodd Electrotype. Rodd Electrotype is a closely held corporation. Members of the Rodd and Donahue families are the sole owners of the corporation's stock. In actual numbers, the corporation, immediately prior to the corporate purchase of

Harry Rodd's shares, had six stockholders. The shares have not been traded, and no market for them seems to exist. Harry Rodd, Charles Rodd, Frederick Rodd, William G. Mason (Phyllis Mason's husband), and the plaintiff's husband all worked for the corporation. The Rodds have retained the paramount management positions.

Through their control of these management positions and of the majority of the Rodd Electrotype stock, the Rodds effectively controlled the corporation. In testing the stock purchase from Harry Rodd against the applicable strict fiduciary standard, we treat the Rodd family as a single controlling group. We reject the defendants' contention that the Rodd family cannot be treated as a unit for this purpose. From the evidence, it is clear that the Rodd family was a close-knit one with strong community of interest. Harry Rodd had hired his sons to work in the family business, Rodd Electrotype. As he aged, he transferred portions of his stock holdings to his children. Charles Rodd and Frederick Rodd were given positions of responsibility in the business as he withdrew from active management. In these circumstances, it is realistic to assume that appreciation, gratitude, and filial devotion would prevent the younger Rodds from opposing a plan which would provide funds for their father's retirement.

Moreover, a strong motive of interest requires that the Rodds be considered a controlling group. When Charles Rodd and Frederick Rodd were called on to represent the corporation in its dealings with their father, they must have known that further advancement within the corporation and benefits would follow their father's retirement and the purchase of his stock. The corporate purchase would take only forty-five of Harry Rodd's eighty-one shares. The remaining thirty-six shares were to be divided among Harry Rodd's children in equal amounts by gift and sale. Receipt of their portion of the thirty-six shares and purchase by the corporation of forty-five shares would effectively transfer full control of the corporation to Frederick Rodd and Charles Rodd, if they chose to act in concert with each other or if one of them chose to ally with his sister. Moreover, Frederick Rodd was the obvious successor to his father as director and corporate treasurer when those posts became vacant after his father's retirement. Failure to complete the corporate purchase (in other words, impeding their father's retirement plan) would have delayed, and perhaps have suspended indefinitely, the transfer of these benefits to the younger Rodds. They could not be expected to oppose their father's wishes in this matter. Although the defendants are correct when they assert that no express agreement involving a quid pro quo — subsequent stock gifts for votes from the directors — was proved, no express agreement is necessary to demonstrate the identity of interest which disciplines a controlling group acting in unison.

On its face, then, the purchase of Harry Rodd's shares by the corporation is a breach of the duty which the controlling stockholders, the Rodds, owed to the minority stockholders, the plaintiff and her son. The purchase distributed a portion of the corporate assets to Harry Rodd, a member of the controlling group, in exchange for his shares. The plaintiff and her son were not offered an equal opportunity to sell their shares to the corporation. In fact, their efforts to obtain an equal opportunity were rebuffed by the corporate representative. As the trial judge found, they did not, in any manner, ratify the transaction with Harry Rodd.

Because of the foregoing, we hold that the plaintiff is entitled to relief. Two forms of suitable relief are set out hereinafter. The judge below is to enter an appropriate judgment. The judgment may require Harry Rodd to remit $ 36,000 with interest at the legal rate from July 15, 1970, to Rodd Electrotype in exchange for forty-five shares of Rodd Electrotype treasury stock. This, in substance, is the specific relief requested in the plaintiff's bill of complaint. Interest is manifestly appropriate. A stockholder, who, in violation of his fiduciary duty to the other stockholders, has obtained assets from his corporation and has had those assets available for his own use, must pay for that use. In the alternative, the judgment may require Rodd Electrotype to purchase all of the plaintiff's shares for $ 36,000 without interest. In the circumstances of this case, we view this as the equal opportunity which the plaintiff should have received. Harry Rodd's retention of thirty-six shares, which were to be sold and given to his children within a year of the Rodd Electrotype purchase, cannot disguise the fact that the corporation acquired one hundred per cent of that portion of his holdings (forty-five shares) which he did not intend his children to own. The plaintiff is entitled to have one hundred per cent of her forty-five shares similarly purchased.

The final decree, in so far as it dismissed the bill as to Harry C. Rodd, Frederick I. Rodd, Charles H. Rodd, Mr. Harold E. Magnuson and Rodd Electrotype Company of New England, Inc., and awarded costs, is reversed. The case is remanded to the Superior Court for entry of judgment in conformity with this opinion.

....

In re KEMP & BEATLEY, INC.

Court of Appeals of New York
473 N.E.2d 1173 (1984)

COOKE, CHIEF JUDGE.

....

I

The business concern of Kemp & Beatley, incorporated under the laws of New York, designs and manufactures table linens and sundry tabletop items. The company's stock consists of 1,500 outstanding shares held by eight shareholders. Petitioner Dissin had been employed by the company for 42 years when, in June 1979, he resigned. Prior to resignation, Dissin served as vice-president and a director of Kemp & Beatley. Over the course of his employment, Dissin had acquired stock in the company and currently owns 200 shares.

Petitioner Gardstein, like Dissin, had been a long-time employee of the company. Hired in 1944, Gardstein was for the next 35 years involved in various aspects of the business including material procurement, product design, and plant management. His employment was terminated by the company in December 1980. He currently owns 105 shares of Kemp & Beatley stock.

Apparent unhappiness surrounded petitioners' leaving the employ of the company. Of particular concern was that they no longer received any distribution of the company's earnings. Petitioners considered themselves to be "frozen out" of the company; whereas it had been their experience when with the company to receive a distribution of the company's earnings according to their stockholdings, in the form of either dividends or extra compensation, that distribution was no longer forthcoming.

Gardstein and Dissin, together holding 20.33% of the company's outstanding stock, commenced the instant proceeding in June 1981, seeking dissolution of Kemp & Beatley pursuant to section 1104-a of the Business Corporation Law. Their petition alleged "fraudulent and oppressive" conduct by the company's board of directors such as to render petitioners' stock "a virtually worthless asset."...

....

The involuntary-dissolution statute (Business Corporation Law, § 1104-a) permits dissolution when a corporation's controlling faction is found guilty of "oppressive action" toward the complaining shareholders. The referee considered oppression to arise when "those in control" of the corporation "have acted in such a manner as to defeat those expectations of the minority stockholders which formed the basis of [their] participation in the venture." The expectations of petitioners that they would not be arbitrarily excluded from gaining a return on their investment and that their stock would be purchased by the corporation upon termination of employment, were deemed defeated by prevailing corporate policies. Dissolution was recommended in the referee's report, subject to giving respondent corporation an opportunity to purchase petitioners' stock.

Supreme Court confirmed the referee's report. It, too, concluded that due to the corporation's new dividend policy petitioners had been prevented from receiving any return on their investments. Liquidation of the corporate assets was found the only means by which petitioners would receive a fair return. The court considered judicial dissolution of a corporation to be "a serious and severe remedy." Consequently, the order of dissolution was conditioned upon the corporation's being permitted to purchase petitioners' stock. The Appellate Division affirmed, without opinion.

At issue in this appeal is the scope of section 1104-a of the Business Corporation Law. Specifically, this court must determine whether the provision for involuntary dissolution when the "directors or those in control of the corporation have been guilty of ... oppressive actions toward the complaining shareholders" was properly applied in the circumstances of this case. We hold that it was, and therefore affirm.

II

Judicially ordered dissolution of a corporation at the behest of minority interests is a remedy of relatively recent vintage in New York. Historically, this State's courts were considered divested of equity jurisdiction to order dissolution, as statutory prescriptions were deemed exclusive. Statutes permitting judicial dissolution of corporations either limited the types of corporations under their purview or restricted the parties who could petition for dissolution to the Attorney-General, or the directors, trustees, or majority shareholders of the corporation.

Minority shareholders were granted standing in the absence of statutory authority to seek dissolution of corporations when controlling shareholders engaged in certain egregious conduct. Predicated on the majority shareholders' fiduciary obligation to treat all shareholders fairly and equally, to preserve corporate assets, and to fulfill their responsibilities of corporate management with "scrupulous good faith," the courts' equitable power can be invoked when "it appears that the directors and majority shareholders 'have so palpably breached the fiduciary duty they owe to the minority shareholders that they are disqualified from exercising the exclusive discretion and the dissolution power given to them by statute.'" ....

Supplementing this principle of judicially ordered equitable dissolution of a corporation, the Legislature has shown a special solicitude toward the rights of minority shareholders of closely held corporations by enacting section 1104-a of the Business Corporation Law. That statute provides a mechanism for the holders of at least 20% of the outstanding shares of a corporation whose stock is not traded on a securities market to petition for its dissolution "under special circumstances." The circumstances that give rise to dissolution fall into two general classifications: mistreatment of complaining shareholders or misappropriation of corporate assets by controlling shareholders, directors or officers.

Section 1104-a describes three types of proscribed activity: "illegal", "fraudulent", and "oppressive" conduct. The first two terms are familiar words that are commonly understood at law. The last, however, does not enjoy the same certainty gained through long usage. As no definition is provided by the statute, it falls upon the courts to provide guidance.

The statutory concept of "oppressive actions" can, perhaps, best be understood by examining the characteristics of close corporations and the Legislature's general purpose in creating this involuntary-dissolution statute. It is widely understood that, in addition to supplying capital to a contemplated or ongoing enterprise and expecting a fair and equal return, parties comprising the ownership of a close corporation may expect to be actively involved in its management and operation. The small ownership cluster seeks to "contribute their capital, skills, experience and labor" toward the corporate enterprise.

As a leading commentator in the field has observed: "Unlike the typical shareholder in a publicly held corporation, who may be simply an investor or a speculator and cares nothing for the responsibilities of management, the share-holder in a close corporation is a co-owner of the business and wants the privileges and powers that go with ownership. His participation in that particular corporation is often his principal or sole source of income. As a matter of fact, providing employment for himself may have been the principal reason why he participated in organizing the corporation. He may or may not anticipate an ultimate profit from the sale of his interest, but he normally draws very little from the corporation as dividends. In his capacity as an officer or employee of the corporation, he looks to his salary for the principal return on his capital investment, because earnings of a close corporation, as is well known, are distributed in major part in salaries, bonuses and retirement benefits." (O'Neal, Close Corporations [2d ed.], § 1.07, at pp. 21-22 [n. omitted].)

Shareholders enjoy flexibility in memorializing these expectations through agreements setting forth each party's rights and obligations in corporate gover-nance. In the absence of such an agreement, however, ultimate decision-making power respecting corporate policy will be reposed in the holders of a majority interest in the corporation. A wielding of this power by any group controlling a corporation may serve to destroy a stockholder's vital interests and expectations.

As the stock of closely held corporations generally is not readily salable, a minority shareholder at odds with management policies may be without either a voice in protecting his or her interests or any reasonable means of withdrawing his or her investment. This predicament may fairly be considered the legislative concern underlying the provision at issue in this case; inclusion of the criteria that the corporation's stock not be traded on securities markets and that the complain-ing shareholder be subject to oppressive actions supports this conclusion.

Defining oppressive conduct as distinct from illegality in the present context has been considered in other forums. The question has been resolved by con-sidering oppressive actions to refer to conduct that substantially defeats the "reasonable expectations" held by minority shareholders in committing their capital to the particular enterprise. This concept is consistent with the apparent purpose underlying the provision under review. A shareholder who reasonably expected that ownership in the corporation would entitle him or her to a job, a share of corporate earnings, a place in corporate management, or some other form of security, would be oppressed in a very real sense when others in the corporation seek to defeat those expectations and there exists no effective means of salvaging the investment.

Given the nature of close corporations and the remedial purpose of the statute, this court holds that utilizing a complaining shareholder's "reasonable expecta-tions" as a means of identifying and measuring conduct alleged to be oppressive is appropriate. A court considering a petition alleging oppressive conduct must investigate what the majority shareholders knew, or should have known, to be the petitioner's expectations in entering the particular enterprise. Majority conduct should not be deemed oppressive simply because the petitioner's subjective hopes and desires in joining the venture are not fulfilled. Disappointment alone should not necessarily be equated with oppression.

Rather, oppression should be deemed to arise only when the majority conduct substantially defeats expectations that, objectively viewed, were both reasonable under the circumstances and were central to the petitioner's decision to join the venture. It would be inappropriate, however, for us in this case to delineate the contours of the courts' consideration in determining whether directors have been guilty of oppressive conduct. As in other areas of the law, much will depend on the circumstances in the individual case.

The appropriateness of an order of dissolution is in every case vested in the sound discretion of the court considering the application. Under the terms of this statute, courts are instructed to consider both whether "liquidation of the corporation is the only feasible means" to protect the complaining shareholder's expectation of a fair return on his or her investment and whether dissolution "is reasonably necessary" to protect "the rights or interests of any substantial number of shareholders" not limited to those complaining. Implicit in this direction is that once oppressive conduct is found, consideration must be given to the totality of circumstances surrounding the current state of corporate affairs and relations to determine whether some remedy short of or other than dissolution constitutes a feasible means of satisfying both the petitioner's expectations and the rights and interests of any other substantial group of shareholders.

By invoking the statute, a petitioner has manifested his or her belief that dissolution may be the only appropriate remedy. Assuming the petitioner has set forth a prima facie case of oppressive conduct, it should be incumbent upon the parties seeking to forestall dissolution to demonstrate to the court the existence of an adequate, alternative remedy. A court has broad latitude in fashioning alternative relief, but when fulfillment of the oppressed petitioner's expectations by these means is doubtful, such as when there has been a complete deterioration of relations between the parties, a court should not hesitate to order dissolution. Every order of dissolution, however, must be conditioned upon permitting any shareholder of the corporation to elect to purchase the complaining shareholder's stock at fair value.

One further observation is in order. The purpose of this involuntary dissolution statute is to provide protection to the minority shareholder whose reasonable expectations in undertaking the venture have been frustrated and who has no adequate means of recovering his or her investment. It would be contrary to this remedial purpose to permit its use by minority shareholders as merely a coercive tool. Therefore, the minority shareholder whose own acts, made in bad faith and undertaken with a view toward forcing an involuntary dissolution, give rise to the complained-of oppression should be given no quarter in the statutory protection.

III

There was sufficient evidence presented at the hearing to support the conclusion that Kemp & Beatley had a long-standing policy of awarding de facto dividends based on stock ownership in the form of "extra compensation bonuses." Petitioners, both of whom had extensive experience in the management of the company, testified to this effect. Moreover, both related that receipt of this compensation, whether as true dividends or disguised as "extra compensation", was a known incident to ownership of the company's stock understood by all of the company's principals. Finally, there was uncontroverted proof that this policy was changed either shortly before or shortly after petitioners' employment ended. Extra compensation was still awarded by the company. The only difference was that stock ownership was no longer a basis for the payments; it was asserted that the basis became services rendered to the corporation. It was not unreasonable for the fact finder to have determined that this change in policy amounted to nothing less than an attempt to exclude petitioners from gaining any return on their investment through the mere recharacterization of distributions of corporate income. Under the circumstances of this case, there was no error in determining that this conduct constituted oppressive action within the meaning of section 1104-a of the Business Corporation Law.

Nor may it be said that Supreme Court abused its discretion in ordering Kemp & Beatley's dissolution, subject to an opportunity for a buy-out of petitioners' shares. After the referee had found that the controlling faction of the company was, in effect, attempting to "squeeze-out" petitioners by offering them no return on their investment and increasing other executive compensation, respondents, in opposing the report's confirmation, attempted only to controvert the factual basis of the report. They suggested no feasible, alternative remedy to the forced dissolution. In light of an apparent deterioration in relations between petitioners and the governing shareholders of Kemp & Beatley, it was not unreasonable for the court to have determined that a forced buy-out of petitioners' shares or liquidation of the corporation's assets was the only means by which petitioners could be guaranteed a fair return on their investments.

Accordingly, the order of the Appellate Division should be modified, with costs to petitioners-respondents, by affirming the substantive determination of that court but extending the time for exercising the option to purchase petitioners-respondents' shares to 30 days following this court's determination.

JASEN, JONES, WACHTLER, MEYER and SIMONS, JJ., concur.

NIXON v. BLACKWELL

Supreme Court of Delaware
626 A.2d 1366 (1992)

En Banc ...

I. *Facts*

...

A. *The Parties*

Plaintiffs are 14 minority stockholders of Class B, non-voting, stock of E.C. Barton & Co. (the "Corporation"). The individual defendants are the members of the board of directors (the "Board" or the "directors"). The Corporation is also a defendant. Plaintiffs collectively own only Class B stock, and own no Class A stock. Their total holdings comprise approximately 25 percent of all the common stock outstanding as of the end of fiscal year 1989.

At all relevant times, the Board consisted of ten individuals who either are currently employed, or were once employed, by the Corporation. At the time this suit was filed, these directors collectively owned approximately 47.5 percent of all the outstanding Class A shares. The remaining Class A shares were held by certain other present and former employees of the Corporation.

B. *Mr. Barton's Testamentary Plan*

The Corporation is a non-public, closely-held Delaware corporation head-quartered in Arkansas. It is engaged in the business of selling wholesale and retail lumber in the Mississippi Delta. The Corporation was formed in 1928 by E.C. Barton ("Mr. Barton") and has two classes of common stock: Class A voting stock and Class B non-voting stock. Substantially all of the Corporation's stock was held by Mr. Barton at the time of his death in 1967.... Pursuant to Mr. Barton's testamentary plan, 49 percent of the Class A voting stock was be-queathed outright to eight of his loyal employees. The remaining 51 percent, [of the Class A stock] along with 14 percent of the Class B non-voting stock, was placed into an independently managed 15-year trust for the same eight people. Sixty-one percent of the Class B non-voting stock was bequeathed outright to Mrs. Barton. Mr. Barton's daughter and granddaughter received 21 percent of the Class B stock in trust. The non-voting Class B shares Mr. Barton bequeathed to his family represented 75 percent of the Corporation's total equity.

Ownership interests in the Corporation began to change in the early 1970s following the distribution of Mr. Barton's estate.... These transactions left Mrs. Barton's three children collectively with 30 percent of the outstanding Class B non-voting stock. The children have no voting rights despite their substantial equity interest in the Corporation. The children are also the only non-employee Class B stockholders.

There is no public market for, or trading in, either class of the Corporation's stock. This creates problems for stockholders, particularly the Class B minority stockholders, who wish to sell or otherwise realize the value of their shares. The corporation purported to address this problem in several ways over the years.

C. *The Self-Tenders*

[During the 1970's] the Corporation occasionally offered to purchase the Class B stock of the non-employee stockholders through a series of self-tender offers.... The Corporation made no further repurchase offers until May 1985, [when there was a self-tender to repurchase] at a price of $ 25 per share. The book value of the Class A stock and the Class B stock at that time was $ 38.39 and $ 26.35, respectively. The remaining children and the other plaintiffs in the present action refused to sell.

D. *The Employee Stock Ownership Plan ("ESOP")*

In November 1975 the Corporation established an ESOP designed to hold Class B non-voting stock for the benefit of eligible employees of the Corporation. The ESOP is a tax-qualified profit-sharing plan whereby employees of the Corporation are allocated a share of the assets held by the plan in proportion to their annual compensation, subject to certain vesting requirements. The ESOP is funded by annual cash contributions from the Corporation. Under the plan, terminating and retiring employees are entitled to receive their interest in the ESOP by taking Class B stock or cash in lieu of stock. It appears from the record that most terminating employees and retirees elect to receive cash in lieu of stock. The Corporation commissions an annual appraisal of the Corporation to determine the value of its stock for ESOP purposes. Thus, the ESOP provides employee Class B stockholders with a substantial measure of liquidity not available to non-employee stockholders. The Corporation had the option of repurchasing Class A stock from the employees upon their retirement or death. The estates of the employee stockholders did not have a corresponding right to put the stock to the Corporation.

E. *The Key Man Insurance Policies*

The Corporation also purchased certain key man life insurance policies with death benefits payable to the Corporation. Several early policies insuring the lives of key executives and directors were purchased during Mr. Barton's lifetime with death benefits payable to the Corporation. In 1982, the Corporation purchased additional key man policies in connection with agreements entered into between the Corporation and nine key officers and directors. Each executive executed an agreement giving the Corporation a call option to substitute Class B non-voting stock for their Class A voting stock upon the occurrence of certain events, including death and termination of employment, so that the voting shares could be reissued to new key personnel. In return, the Board adopted a resolution creating a non-binding recommendation that a portion of the key man life insurance proceeds be used to repurchase the exchanged Class B stock from the executives' estates at a price at least equal to 80 percent of their ESOP value....
[T]he ultimate decision on the use of insurance proceeds for this purpose was left to the discretion of the Corporation's management or the Board.

....

II. *Proceedings in the Court of Chancery*

....

At trial, the plaintiffs charged the defendants with (1) attempting to force the minority stockholders to sell their shares at a discount by embarking on a scheme to pay negligible dividends, (2) breaching their fiduciary duties by authorizing excessive compensation for themselves and other employees of the Corporation, and (3) breaching their fiduciary duties by pursuing a discriminatory liquidity policy that favors employee stockholders over non-employee stockholders through the ESOP and key man life insurance policies. The plaintiffs sought money damages for past dividends, a one-time liquidity dividend, and a guarantee of future dividends at a specified rate.

The Vice Chancellor held that the Corporation's low-dividend policy was within the bounds of business judgment, that the executive compensation levels were not excessive, and ruled in favor of defendants on these issues. The Vice Chancellor further held, however, that the defendant directors had breached their fiduciary duties to the minority. The basis for this ruling was that it was "inherently unfair" for the defendants to establish the ESOP and to purchase key man life insurance to provide liquidity for themselves while providing no comparable method by which the non-employee Class B stockholders may liquidate their stock at fair value. Holding that the "needs of all stockholders must be considered and addressed when providing liquidity," the court ruled that the directors breached their fiduciary duties, and granted relief to plaintiffs. The trial court ruled against the plaintiffs on all the other issues. Since plaintiffs have not appealed those rulings, they are not before this Court.

The finding for the plaintiffs and the form of the relief granted to the plaintiffs (which the defendants also contest) are set forth in paragraphs 4 and 5 of the Order and Final Judgment of March 10, 1992: 4. On the claim of the plaintiffs presented at trial that the individual defendants breached their fiduciary duty as directors and treated the plaintiffs unfairly as the non-employee, minority Class B stockholders of the Company by providing no method by which plaintiffs might liquidate their stock at fair value while providing a means through the ESOP and key-man life insurance whereby the stock of terminating employees could be purchased from them, judgment is entered in favor of the plaintiffs. 5. Pursuant to the judgment entered in paragraph 4 above, defendants shall take the following steps in order to remedy the unfair treatment of Class B stockholders: a. An amount equal to the total of all key man life insurance premiums paid to date, together with interest from the date of payment shall be used to repurchase Class B stock other than shares held by the ESOP or defendants, at a price to be set by an independent appraiser. b. Hereafter, neither the ESOP[7] nor the company shall purchase or repurchase any stock without offering to purchase the same number of shares, on the same terms and conditions, from the Class B stockholders other than defendants and the ESOP.

Plaintiffs were awarded attorneys' fees and costs in a subsequent order entered on May 20, 1992.

.....

---

[7] It is to be noted that the ESOP is not a party to the proceedings, so in all events this relief is void to the extent that it purports to bind the ESOP.

V. Applicable Principles of Substantive Law

Defendants contend that the trial court erred in not applying the business judgment rule. Since the defendants benefited from the ESOP and could have benefited from the key man life insurance beyond that which benefited other stockholders generally, the defendants are on both sides of the transaction. For that reason, we agree with the trial court that the entire fairness test applies to this aspect of the case. Accordingly, defendants have the burden of showing the entire fairness of those transactions....

The entire fairness analysis essentially requires "judicial scrutiny." Weinberger, 457 A.2d at 710. In business judgment rule cases, an essential element is the fact that there has been a business decision made by a disinterested and independent corporate decisionmaker. Aronson v. Lewis, Del.Supr., 473 A.2d 805, 812 (1984); Smith v. Van Gorkom, Del.Supr., 488 A.2d 858, 872-73 (1985). When there is no independent corporate decisionmaker, the court may become the objective arbiter.

The trial court in this case, however, appears to have adopted the novel legal principle that Class B stockholders had a right to "liquidity" equal to that which the court found to be available to the defendants. It is well established in our jurisprudence that stockholders need not always be treated equally for all purposes. See Unocal Corp. v. Mesa Petroleum Co., Del.Supr., 493 A.2d 946, 957 (1985) ("Unocal") (discriminatory exchange offer held valid); and Cheff v. Mathes, Del.Supr., 199 A.2d 548, 554-56 (1964) (selective stock repurchase held valid). To hold that fairness necessarily requires precise equality is to beg the question: Many scholars, though few courts, conclude that one aspect of fiduciary duty is the equal treatment of investors. Their argument takes the following form: fiduciary principles require fair conduct; equal treatment is fair conduct; hence, fiduciary principles require equal treatment. The conclusion does not follow. The argument depends on an equivalence between equal and fair treatment. To say that fiduciary principles require equal treatment is to beg the question whether investors would contract for equal or even equivalent treatment. Frank H. Easterbrook and Daniel R. Fischel, The Economic Structure of Corporate Law 110 (1991). This holding of the trial court overlooks the significant facts that the minority stockholders were not: (a) employees of the Corporation; (b) entitled to share in an ESOP; (c) qualified for key man insurance; or (d) protected by specific provisions in the certificate of incorporation, by-laws, or a stockholders' agreement.

There is support in this record for the fact that the ESOP is a corporate benefit and was established, at least in part, to benefit the Corporation. Generally speaking, the creation of ESOPs is a normal corporate practice and is generally thought to benefit the corporation. The same is true generally with respect to key man insurance programs. If such corporate practices were necessarily to require equal treatment for non-employee stockholders, that would be a matter for legislative determination in Delaware. There is no such legislation to that effect. If we were to adopt such a rule, our decision would border on judicial legislation.

Accordingly, we hold that the Vice Chancellor erred as a matter of law in concluding that the liquidity afforded to the employee stockholders by the ESOP and the key man insurance required substantially equal treatment for the non-employee stockholders. Moreover, the Vice Chancellor failed to evaluate and articulate, for example, whether or not and to what extent (a) corporate benefits flowed from the ESOP and the key man insurance; (b) the ESOP and key man insurance plans are novel, extraordinary, or relatively routine business practices; (c) the dividend policy was even relevant; (d) Mr. Barton's plan for employee management and benefits should be honored; and (e) the self-tenders showed defendants' willingness to provide an exit opportunity for the plaintiffs.

....

We hold on this record that defendants have met their burden of establishing the entire fairness of their dealings with the non-employee Class B stockholders, and are entitled to judgment. The record is sufficient to conclude that plaintiffs' claim that the defendant directors have maintained a discriminatory policy of favoring Class A employee stockholders over Class B non-employee stockholders is without merit. The directors have followed a consistent policy originally established by Mr. Barton, the founder of the Corporation, whose intent from the formation of the Corporation was to use the Class A stock as the vehicle for the Corporation's continuity through employee management and ownership.

Mr. Barton established the Corporation in 1928 by creating two classes of stock, not one, and by holding 100 percent of the Class A stock and 82 percent of the Class B stock. Mr. Barton himself established the practice of purchasing key man life insurance with funds of the Corporation to retain in the employ of the Corporation valuable employees by assuring them that, following their retirement or death, the Corporation will have liquid assets which could be used to repurchase the shares acquired by the employee, which shares may otherwise constitute an illiquid and unsalable asset of his or her estate. Another rational purpose is to prevent the stock from passing out of the control of the employees of the Corporation into the hands of family or descendants of the employees.

The directors' actions following Mr. Barton's death are consistent with Mr. Barton's plan. An ESOP, for example, is normally established for employees. Accordingly, there is no inequity in limiting ESOP benefits to the employee stockholders. Indeed, it makes no sense to include non-employees in ESOP benefits. The fact that the Class B stock represented 75 percent of the Corporation's total equity is irrelevant to the issue of fair dealing. The Class B stock was given no voting rights because those stockholders were not intended to have a direct voice in the management and operation of the Corporation. They were simply passive investors — entitled to be treated fairly but not necessarily to be treated equally. The fortunes of the Corporation rested with the Class A employee stockholders and the Class B stockholders benefited from the multiple increases in value of their Class B stock. Moreover, the Board made continuing efforts to buy back the Class B stock.

We hold that paragraphs 4 and 5 of the March 10, 1992 order of the trial court and the order of May 20, 1992, awarding fees and costs to plaintiffs, are reversed and remanded with instructions to conform the judgment to the findings and conclusions in this opinion.

VI. *No Special Rules For a "Closely-Held Corporation" Not Qualified as a "Close Corporation" Under Subchapter XIV of the Delaware General Corporation Law.*

We wish to address one further matter which was raised at oral argument before this Court: Whether there should be any special, judicially-created rules to "protect" minority stockholders of closely-held Delaware corporations.[8]

The case at bar points up the basic dilemma of minority stockholders in receiving fair value for their stock as to which there is no market and no market valuation. It is not difficult to be sympathetic, in the abstract, to a stockholder who finds himself or herself in that position. A stockholder who bargains for stock in a closely-held corporation and who pays for those shares (unlike the plaintiffs in this case who acquired their stock through gift) can make a business judgment whether to buy into such a minority position, and if so on what terms. One could bargain for definitive provisions of self-ordering permitted to a Delaware corporation through the certificate of incorporation or by-laws by reason of the provisions in 8 Del.C. §§ 102, 109, and 141(a). Moreover, in addition to such mechanisms, a stockholder intending to buy into a minority position in a Delaware corporation may enter into definitive stockholder agreements, and such agreements may provide for elaborate earnings tests, buy-out provisions, voting trusts, or other voting agreements. *See, e.g.*, 8 Del.C.§ 218.

The tools of good corporate practice are designed to give a purchasing minority stockholder the opportunity to bargain for protection before parting with consideration. It would do violence to normal corporate practice and our corporation law to fashion an ad hoc ruling which would result in a court-imposed stockholder buy-out for which the parties had not contracted.

In 1967, when the Delaware General Corporation Law was significantly revised, a new Subchapter XIV entitled "Close Corporations; Special Provisions," became a part of that law for the first time. While these provisions were patterned in theory after close corporation statutes in Florida and Maryland, "the Delaware provisions were unique and influenced the development of similar

---

[8] *Compare* Robert B. Thompson, *The Shareholder's Cause of Action for Oppression*, 48 BUS. LAW. 699 (1993) and F. Hodge O'Neal and Robert B. Thompson, O'Neal's Close Corporations: Law and Practice, §§ 8.07-8.09 (3d ed. 1987) (favoring court formulation of a special rule protecting the minority from oppression) with Frank H. Easterbrook and Daniel R. Fischel, The Economic Structure of Corporate Law 228-52 (1991) (noting that "courts have found the equal opportunity rule ... impossible to administer," *Id.* at 247).

legislation in a number of other states...." *See* Ernest L. Folk, III, Rodman Ward, Jr., and Edward P. Welch, 2 Folk on the Delaware General Corporation Law 404 (1988). Subchapter XIV is a narrowly constructed statute which applies only to a corporation which is designated as a "close corporation" in its certificate of incorporation, and which fulfills other requirements, including a limitation to 30 on the number of stockholders, that all classes of stock have to have at least one restriction on transfer, and that there be no "public offering." 8 Del.C.§ 342. Accordingly, subchapter XIV applies only to "close corporations," as defined in section 342. "Unless a corporation elects to become a close corporation under this subchapter in the manner prescribed in this subchapter, it shall be subject in all respects to this chapter, except this subchapter." 8 Del.C. § 341. The corporation before the Court in this matter, is not a "close corporation." Therefore it is not governed by the provisions of Subchapter XIV.[9]

One cannot read into the situation presented in the case at bar any special relief for the minority stockholders in this closely-held, but not statutory "close corporation" because the provisions of Subchapter XIV relating to close corporations and other statutory schemes[10] preempt the field in their respective areas. It would run counter to the spirit of the doctrine of independent legal significance,[11] and would be inappropriate judicial legislation for this Court to fashion a special judicially- created rule for minority investors when the entity does not fall within those statutes, or when there are no negotiated special provisions in the certificate

---

[9] We do not intend to imply that, if the Corporation had been a close corporation under Subchapter XIV, the result in this case would have been different. [S]tatutory close corporations have not found particular favor with practitioners. Practitioners have for the most part viewed the complex statutory provisions underlying the purportedly simplified operational procedures for close corporations as legal quicksand of uncertain depth and have adopted the view that the objectives sought by the subchapter are achievable for their clients with considerably less uncertainty by cloaking a conventionally created corporation with the panoply of charter provisions, transfer restrictions, by-laws, stockholders' agreements, buy-sell arrangements, irrevocable proxies, voting trusts or other contractual mechanisms which were and remain the traditional method for accomplishing the goals sought by the close corporation provisions. David A. Drexler, Lewis S. Black, Jr., and A. Gilchrist Sparks, III, Delaware Corporation Law and Practice § 43.01 (1993).

[10] It is to be noted that Delaware statutory law provides for many forms of business enterprise: partnerships pursuant to 6 Del.C. §§ 1501-43; limited partnerships pursuant to 6 Del.C. § 17-101-1109; limited liability companies pursuant to 6 Del.C. §§ 18-101-1106; business trusts pursuant to Title 12, §§ 3801-20. Compare the Close Corporation Supplement to the Model Business Corporation Act, especially Section 20 relating to "Shareholder Agreements."

[11] An important tool to practitioners in the use of the General Corporation Law is the principle of "independent legal significance." The principle holds that the validity of a transaction accomplished pursuant to a specified section or sections of the statute will be tested by the standards applicable to those sections and not by those of other provisions, even though the ultimate economic results could have been achieved through use of procedures authorized by such other provisions and even though use of such other procedures might have created different rights among those affected by the transaction.

of incorporation, by-laws, or stockholder agreements. The entire fairness test, correctly applied and articulated, is the proper judicial approach.

VII. *Conclusion*

We hold that the Court of Chancery correctly determined that the entire fairness test is applicable in reviewing the actions of the defendants in establishing and implementing the ESOP and the key man life insurance program. The Vice Chancellor erred, however, as a matter of law in concluding on this record that the defendants had not carried their burden of showing entire fairness. The trial court erroneously undertook to create a novel theory of corporation law and erroneously failed to set forth and apply articulable standards for determining fairness. Moreover, certain findings of fact by the trial court were not the product of an orderly and deductive reasoning process.

In a case such as this where the business judgment rule is not applicable and the entire fairness test is applicable, the imposition of the latter test is not, alone, outcome-determinative. The doctrine of entire fairness does not lend itself to bright line precision or rigid doctrine. Yet it does not necessarily require equality, it cannot be a matter of total subjectivity on the part of the trial court, and it cannot result in a random pattern of ad hoc determinations which could do violence to the stability of our corporation law.

Accordingly, we REVERSE the judgment of the Court of Chancery and REMAND the matter for proceedings not inconsistent with this opinion.

Remedies for deadlock, dissension and oppression may be provided either by statute or by agreements among the shareholders. The following provide representative examples.

C. STATUTORY AND CONTRACTUAL PROVISIONS

Recognizing that the issues raised above typically arise in the closely held corporation context, state corporation statutes address problems of deadlock, dissension and oppression in one of two ways. General corporation statutes may either include special provisions for closely held corporations throughout the general corporate code or they may contain a separate unit of code applicable to closely held corporations. The Model Act takes the former approach, and the Delaware code, the latter, in Subchapter XIV of the Delaware General Corporation Law. The Model Act special provisions are limited to companies whose shares are not traded on a national exchange. Delaware limits the application of the separate subchapter to companies that elect to become statutory closely held corporations. In both cases, the applicable provisions are elective and enabling. The discussion that follows focuses on the Model Act provisions, and includes Delaware code to the extent that it provides alternatives not found in the Model Act.

1. Judicial Dissolution of the Corporation

Chapter 14 of the Model Act establishes the procedures for both voluntary and involuntary dissolution of all types of corporations. Voluntary dissolution is governed by §§ 14.01 through 14.07. The Act requires that a proposal for dissolution must be recommended by the Board of Directors and approved by the shareholders. The corporation must then file articles of dissolution with the Secretary of State and proceed to liquidate its business by collecting its assets, disposing of its properties, discharging its liabilities and distributing any remaining property to its shareholders. Under § 14.30, a shareholder may initiate dissolution proceedings if the directors or shareholders are deadlocked and the deadlock cannot be broken, if the directors or those in control have acted in an illegal, oppressive or fraudulent manner, or if the corporation's assets are being wasted. The Secretary of State may initiate a dissolution proceeding if the corporation is delinquent in paying franchise taxes, filing its annual report, or notifying the Secretary of changes in its registered office or agent.[12] The Attorney General may initiate a proceeding against corporations obtaining their articles of incorporation through fraud or exceeding or abusing their authority.[13] Creditors of insolvent corporations may also initiate proceedings to recover judgment claims against insolvent corporations.[14]

Shareholders of closely held corporations may also enter into an agreement that mandates dissolution if one or more shareholders request it or if a specified event or contingency occurs.[15] This approach is that found in general partnership statutes and introduces a significant measure of instability into the corporate form.

2. Buyout of Shareholder Petitioning for Dissolution

We have already seen that shareholders may enter into an agreement restricting the transfer of shares and providing for corporate or shareholder buyout of an exiting owner. Model Act § 14.34 provides a buyout alternative to court ordered dissolution. The section permits a closely held corporation or its shareholders to elect to purchase at fair value all the shares owned by the shareholder petitioning for judicial dissolution. The Official Comment to § 14.34 states:

> The proceeding for judicial dissolution has become an increasingly important remedy for minority shareholders of closely-held corporations who believe that the value of their investment is threatened by reason of circumstances or conduct described in section 14.30(2). If the petitioning shareholder proves one or more grounds under section 14.30(2), he is entitled to some form of relief but many courts have hesitated to award

---

[12] MODEL BUSINESS CORP. ACT (1984) § 14.20.

[13] *See id.* § 14.30.

[14] *See id.*

[15] *See id.* § 7.32 (a)(7), (d).

dissolution, often the only form of relief explicitly provided, because of its adverse effects on shareholders, employees, and others who may have an interest in the continuation of the business.

Commentators have observed that it is rarely necessary to dissolve the corporation and liquidate its assets in order to provide relief: the rights of the petitioning shareholder are fully protected by liquidating only his interest and paying the fair value of his shares while permitting the remaining shareholders to continue the business. In fact, it appears that most dissolution proceedings result in a buyout of one or another of the disputants' shares either pursuant to a statutory buyout provision or a negotiated settlement.

The Model Statutory Closely Held Corporation Supplement, now withdrawn, provided a range of additional options to a court confronting deadlock, dissension or oppression in a closely held corporation. Under § 41, the court was authorized to

order one or more of the following types of relief: (1) the performance, prohibition, alteration or setting aside of any action of the corporation or of its shareholders, directors, or officers of or any other party to the proceeding; (2) the cancellation or alteration of any provision in the corporation's articles of incorporation or bylaws; (3) the removal from office of any director or officer; (4) the appointment of any individual as a director or officer; (5) an accounting with respect to any matter in dispute; (6) the appointment of a custodian to manage the business and affairs of the corporation; (7) the appointment of a provisional director (who has all the rights, powers, and duties of a duly elected director) to serve for the term and under the conditions prescribed by the court; (8) the payment of dividends; (9) the award of damages to any aggrieved party.

These options were in addition to the share purchase and dissolution options described above.

The Official Comment to § 40 noted that although the sections described above would probably "be invoked most frequently by minority shareholders, the ground for relief described in section [§§ 14.30(2), 14.34] may be used by the holders of the majority of shares to seek relief from deadlocks created by veto rights given minority shareholders which threaten the corporation's continued existence."

3. Appointment of a Custodian or Provisional Director

Delaware General Corporation Law § 352 permits a shareholder having the right to dissolve the corporation to petition for the appointment of a custodian to manage the company. Section 353 provides for the appointment of a provisional director when the board of directors is deadlocked. The Model Act § 14.32 authorizes the appointment of one or more custodians either to wind up the company's business or to manage it.

4. Contractual Provisions

Section V below will introduce you to common types of shareholder agreements used to allocate corporate control. Including an arbitration clause in these agreements may provide an effective dispute resolution mechanism for the situations described above.

> Since arbitration can play such a major role in the resolution of shareholder disputes in the closely held corporation, the arbitration remedy has been widely recommended by commentators.... If an arbitration clause is used, the extensive, expanding and rather technical body of law on arbitration and award becomes applicable. Accordingly, arbitration is the most complex of the remedies under discussion.
>
> ....
>
> *1. The Arbitration Remedy*
> Arbitration in the close corporate context actually embraces three distinct concepts. First, arbitration may be used as a litigation substitute to resolve a justiciable controversy. For example, an arbitrator might be asked to determine whether there is good cause for the discharge of a shareholder employee or whether a shareholder has diverted a corporate opportunity.... Second, arbitration may be employed as an appraisal procedure to determine the fair value of close corporate stock for purposes of a buy-out provision.... Third, arbitration may be used as a means to resolve an argument over management policy....*

SECTION V. CONTRACTUAL ARRANGEMENTS

Contractual arrangements are the most common tool shareholders use to tailor corporate control to suit their particular needs. Contractual arrangements take various forms, but most of them can be categorized as voting trusts, shareholders' agreements, or employment contracts.

A. VOTING TRUSTS AND SHAREHOLDER VOTING (OR POOLING) AGREEMENTS

Shareholders often enter into agreements designed to control how they will vote their shares with respect to the election of directors or any other matter that is subject to shareholder approval. These agreements may be limited in scope or they may apply to all matters on which shareholders are eligible to vote. They may specify in advance how the shares are to be voted or provide a mechanism

---

*Reprinted with permission. Harold D. Field, Jr., *Resolving Shareholder Disputes and Breaking Deadlocks in the Closely Held Corporation*, 58 MINN. L. REV. 985, 993-95. Copyright © 1974 by the Minnesota Law Review Foundation. All rights reserved.

for deciding at the time that the votes are to be cast. There are two forms of agreements of this type: voting trusts and pooling agreements.

The classic voting trust is a trust formed in the ordinary way under trust law with voting stock as its corpus. The shareholders who wish to participate in the trust serve as the grantors by transferring to a trustee legal title to their shares. The trustee then votes the shares according to the terms of the trust, which may be specifically enforced, and otherwise acts for the benefit of the former shareholders, who now are the beneficiaries of the trust. Trust beneficiaries will typically continue to receive any dividends declared on the stock held in the trust and, in Model Act jurisdictions, will retain their rights to inspect corporate books and records. The voting trust is an old device, going back at least as far as the mid-nineteenth century. At first it operated strictly under common law, but now the voting trust has come under supervision in corporation statutes. Commonly, modern statutes, typified by Model Act § 7.30, set an initial ten-year duration on voting trusts (with an option to extend), require that the trust agreement be in writing, and require that a copy of the agreement, and in the case of the Model Act, a list of the beneficiaries, be given to the corporation whose shares are held in trust.

Voting trusts can be used in several situations. In a family owned business, the founders may want to give a younger generation financial interests in the company without relinquishing control. They can accomplish this by putting stock issued to the younger generation in a voting trust, with a senior family member serving as trustee. A voting trust may also be used to maintain a particular control structure or to protect a creditor lending a substantial amount of money to the company. As part of the lending arrangement, shareholders can be required to transfer their stock to a voting trust, with the creditor acting as trustee. The creditor will thus be able to control the firm until the loan is repaid.

The voting trust, however, is not a popular device for controlling a corporation, partly because of its limited duration under modern statutes, but mostly because establishing a voting trust is such a drastic measure. Few shareholders wish to divest themselves of all control over their shares just for the sake of shareholder unity. For that reason, shareholder voting or pooling agreements, in which the drafters attempt to secure that unity while at the same time allowing shareholders reasonable control of their own shares, are much more popular than are voting trusts.

There is a risk, however, that if the drafter of a shareholders' agreement is not careful, the agreement may be held to be a voting trust and, what is more important, an illegal and void voting trust because the agreement does not meet the statutory requirements for a voting trust. The following case nicely presents the issues involved.

LEHRMAN v. COHEN

Supreme Court of Delaware
222 A.2d 800 (1966)

HERRMANN, JUSTICE.

The primary problem presented on this appeal involves the applicability of the Delaware Voting Trust Statute. Other questions involve the legality of stock having voting power but no dividend or liquidation rights except repayment of par value, and an alleged unlawful delegation of directorial duties and powers.

These are the material facts:

Giant Food Inc. (hereinafter the "Company") was incorporated in Delaware in 1935 by the defendant N. M. Cohen and Samuel Lehrman, deceased father of the plaintiff Jacob Lehrman. From its inception, the Company was controlled by the Cohen and Lehrman families, each of whom owned equal quantities of the voting stock, designated Class AC (held by the Cohen family) and Class AL (held by the Lehrman family) common stock. The two classes of stock have cumulative voting rights and each is entitled to elect two members of the Company's four-member board of directors.

Over the years, as may have been expected, there were differences of opinion between the Cohen and Lehrman families as to operating policies of the Company. Samuel Lehrman died in 1949; each of his children inherited part of his stock in the Company; but a dispute arose among the children regarding an *inter vivos* gift of certain shares made to the plaintiff by his father shortly before his death. To eliminate the Lehrman family dispute and its possible disruption of the affairs of the Company, an arrangement was made which settled the dispute and permitted the plaintiff to acquire all of the outstanding Class AL stock, thereby vesting in him voting power equal to that held by the Cohen family. The arrangement involved repurchase by the Company of the stock held by the plaintiff's brothers and sister, their relinquishment of any claim to the stock gift, and an equalizing surrender of certain stock by the Cohens to the Company for retirement. An essential part of the arrangement, upon the insistence of the Cohens, was the establishment of a fifth directorship to obviate the risk of deadlock which would have continued if the equal division of voting power between AL and AC stock were continued.

To implement the arrangement, on December 31, 1949, the Company's certificate of incorporation was amended, *inter alia,* to create a third class of voting stock, designated Class AD common stock, entitled to elect the fifth director. Article Fourth of the amendment to the certificate of incorporation provided for the issuance of one share of Class AD stock, having a par value of $ 10, and the following rights and powers:

> "The holder of Class AD common stock shall be entitled to all of the rights and privileges pertaining to common stock without any limitations, prohibitions, restrictions or qualifications except that the holder of said Class AD stock shall not be entitled to receive any dividends declared and paid by

the corporation, shall not be entitled to share in the distribution of assets of the corporation upon liquidation or dissolution either partial or final, except to the extent of the par value of said Class AD common stock, and in the election of Directors shall have the right to vote for and elect one of the five Directors hereinafter provided for.

"The corporation shall have the right, at any time, to redeem and call in the Class AD stock by paying to the holder thereof the par value of said stock, provided however, that such redemption or call shall be authorized and directed by the affirmative vote of four of the five Directors hereinafter provided for."

By resolution of the board of directors, the share of Class AD stock was issued forthwith to the defendant Joseph B. Danzansky, who had served as counsel to the Company since 1944. All corporate action regarding the creation and the issuance of the Class AD stock was accomplished by the unanimous vote of the AC and AL stockholders and of the board of directors. In April 1950, pursuant to the arrangement, Danzansky voted his share of AD stock to elect himself as the Company's fifth director; and he served as such until the institution of this action in 1964. During that entire period, the AC and AL stock have been voted to elect two directors each. From 1950 through 1964, Danzansky regularly attended board meetings, raised and discussed general items of business, and voted on all issues as they came before the board. He was not obliged to break any deadlock among the directors prior to October 1, 1964 because no such deadlock arose before that date.

Beginning in December 1959, 200,000 shares of non-voting common stock of the Company were sold in a public issue for over $ 3,000,000. Each prospectus published in connection with the public issue contained the following statement:

"Common Stock AD is not a participating stock, and the only purpose for the provision and issuance of such stock is to prevent a deadlock in case the Directors elected by the Common Stock AC and the Directors elected by the Common Stock AL cannot reach an agreement."

....

From the outset and until October 1, 1964, the defendant N. M. Cohen was president of the Company. On that date, a resolution was adopted at the Company's annual stockholders' meeting to give Danzansky a fifteen year executive employment contract at an annual salary of $ 67,600, and options for 25,000 shares of the non-voting common stock of the Company. The AC and AD stock were voted in favor and the AL stock was voted against the resolution. At a directors meeting held the same day, Danzansky was elected president of the Company by a 3-2 vote, the two AL directors voting in opposition. On December 11, 1964, Danzansky resigned as director and voted his share of AD stock to elect as the fifth director, Millard F. West, Jr., a former AL director and investment banker whose firm was one of the underwriters of the public issue of the Company's stock. The newly constituted board ratified the election of Danzansky as president; and, on January 27, 1965, after the commencement of this action and after a review and report by a committee consisting of the new AD director and one AL director, Danzansky's employment contract was approved and adopted with certain modifications.

The plaintiff brought this action on December 11, 1964, basing it upon two claims: The First Claim charges that the creation, issuance, and voting of the one share of Class AD stock resulted in an arrangement illegal under the law of this State for the reasons hereinafter set forth. The Second Claim, addressed to the events of October 1, 1964, charges that the election of Danzansky as president of the Company and his employment contract violated the terms of the 1959 deadlock-breaking arrangement, as made between the holders of the AC and AL stock, and constituted breaches of contract and fiduciary duty. The plaintiff and the defendants filed cross-motions for summary judgment as to the First Claim. The Court of Chancery, after considering the contentions now before us and discussed *infra,* granted summary judgment in favor of the defendants and denied the plaintiff's motion for summary judgment. The plaintiff appeals.

I

The plaintiff's primary contention is that the Class AD stock arrangement is, in substance and effect, a voting trust; that, as such, it is illegal because not limited to a ten year period as required by the Voting Trust Statute. The defendants deny that the AD stock arrangement constitutes a disguised voting trust; but they concede that if it is, the arrangement is illegal for violation of the Statute. Thus, issue is clearly joined on the point.

The criteria of a voting trust under our decisions have been summarized by this Court in *Abercrombie v. Davies,* 36 Del. Ch. 371, 130 A.2d 338 (1957). The tests there set forth, accepted by both sides of this cause as being applicable, are as follows: (1) the voting rights of the stock are separated from the other attributes of ownership; (2) the voting rights granted are intended to be irrevocable for a definite period of time; and (3) the principal purpose of the grant of voting rights is to acquire voting control of the corporation.

Adopting and applying these tests, the plaintiff says, as to the first element, that the AD arrangement provides for a divorcement of voting rights from beneficial ownership of the AC and AL stock; that the creation and issuance of the share of AD stock is tantamount to a pooling by the AC and AL stockholders of a portion of their voting stock and giving it to a trustee, in the person of the AD stockholder, to vote for the election of the fifth director; that after the creation of the AD stock, the AC and AL stockholders each hold but 40% of the voting power, and the AD stockholder holds the controlling balance of 20%; that the AD stock has no property rights except the right to a return of the $ 10 paid as the par value; and that, therefore, there has been a transfer of the voting rights devoid of any participating property rights. So runs the argument of the plaintiff in support of his contention that the first of the *Abercrombie* criteria for a voting trust is met.

The contention is unacceptable. The AD arrangement did not separate the voting rights of the AC or the AL stock from the other attributes of ownership of those classes of stock. Each AC and AL stockholder retains complete control over the voting of his stock; each can vote his stock directly; no AL or AC stockholder is divested of his right to vote his stock as he sees fit; no AL or AC stock can be voted against the shareholder's wishes; and the AL and AC stock continue to elect two directors each.

The AD stock arrangement as we view it, became a part of the capitalization of the Company. The fact that there is but a single share, or that the par value is nominal, is of no legal significance; the one share and the $ 10 par value might have been multiplied many times over, with the same consequence. It is true that the creation of the separate class of AD stock may have diluted the voting *power* which had previously existed in the AC and AL stock — the usual consequence when additional voting stock is created — but the creation of the new class did not divest and separate the voting *rights* which remain vested in each AC and AL shareholder, together with the other attributes of the ownership of that stock. The fallacy of the plaintiff's position lies in his premise that since the voting power of the AC and AL stock was reduced by the creation of the AD stock, the percentage of reduction became the *res* of a voting trust. In any recapitalization involving the creation of additional voting stock, the voting power of the previously existing stock is diminished; but a voting trust is not necessarily the result.

Since the holders of the Class AC and Class AL stock of the Company did not separate the voting rights from the other attributes of ownership of those classes when they created the Class AD stock, the first *Abercrombie* test of a voting trust is not met.

… Having held that the AC and AL stockholders have not divested themselves of their voting rights, although they may have diluted their voting powers, we do not reach the remaining *Abercrombie* tests, both of which assume the divestiture of voting rights.

In the final analysis, the essence of the question raised by the plaintiff in this connection is this: Is the substance and purpose of the AD stock arrangement sufficiently close to the substance and purpose of § 218 to warrant its being subjected to the restrictions and conditions imposed by that Statute? The answer is negative not only for the reasons above stated, but also because § 218 regulates trusts and pooling agreements amounting to trusts, not other and different types of arrangements and undertakings possible among stockholders. Compare *Ringling Bros.-Barnum & Bailey Combined Shows, Inc. v. Ringling,* 29 Del. Ch. 610, 53 A.2d 441 (1947); *Abercrombie v. Davies, supra.* The AD stock arrangement is neither a trust nor a pooling agreement.

We hold, therefore, that the Class AD stock arrangement is not controlled by the Voting Trust Statute.

II

The plaintiff's second point is that even if the Class AD stock arrangement is not a voting trust in substance and effect, the AD stock is illegal, nevertheless, because the creation of a class of stock having voting rights only, and lacking any substantial participating proprietary interest in the corporation, violates the public policy of this State as declared in § 218.

The fallacy of this argument is twofold: First, it is more accurate to say that what the law has disfavored, and what the public policy underlying the Voting Trust Statute means to control, is the separation of the vote from the stock — not from the stock ownership. 5 Fletcher Cyclopedia Corporations, § 2080, pp. 363-369; compare *Abercrombie v. Davies, supra.* Clearly, the AD stock arrangement is not violative of that public policy. Secondly, there is nothing in § 218, either expressed or implied, which requires that all stock of a Delaware corporation must have both voting rights and proprietary interests. Indeed, public policy to the contrary seems clearly expressed by 8 Del.C. § 151(a) which authorizes, in very broad terms, such voting powers and participating rights as may be stated in the certificate of incorporation. Non-voting stock is specifically authorized by § 151(a); and in the light thereof, consistency does not permit the conclusion, urged by the plaintiff, that the present public policy of this State condemns the separation of voting rights from beneficial stock ownership.

We conclude that the plaintiff's contention in this regard cannot withstand the force and effect of § 151(a). In our view, that Statute permits the creation of stock having voting rights only, as well as stock having property rights only. The voting powers and the participating rights of the Class AD stock being specified in the Company's certificate of incorporation, we are of the opinion that the Class AD stock is legal by virtue of § 151(a).

....

We are told that if the AD stock arrangement is allowed thus to stand, our Voting Trust Statute will become a "dead letter" because it will be possible to evade and circumvent its purpose simply by issuing a class of non-participating voting stock, as was done here. We have three negative reactions to this argument:

First, it presupposes a divestiture of the voting rights of the AC and AL stock — an untenable supposition as has been stated. Secondly, it fails to take into account the main purpose of a Voting Trust Statute: to avoid secret, uncontrolled combinations of stockholders formed to acquire voting control of the corporation to the possible detriment of non-participating shareholders. It may not be said that the AD stock arrangement contravenes that purpose. Finally on this point, if we misconceive the legislative intent, and if the AD stock arrangement in this case reveals a loophole in § 218 which should be plugged, it is for the General Assembly to accomplish — not for us to attempt by interstitial judicial legislation.

....

The following case raises another issue, that of the enforceability of a share-holders' voting agreement.

RINGLING BROS. — BARNUM & BAILEY COMBINED SHOWS, INC. v. RINGLING

Supreme Court of Delaware
53 A.2d 441 (1947)

PEARSON, JUDGE.

The Court of Chancery was called upon to review an attempted election of directors at the 1946 annual stockholders meeting of the corporate defendant. The pivotal questions concern an agreement between two of the three present stock-holders, and particularly the effect of this agreement with relation to the exercise of voting rights by these two stockholders. At the time of the meeting, the corporation had outstanding 1000 shares of capital stock held as follows: 315 by petitioner Edith Conway Ringling; 315 by defendant Aubrey B. Ringling Haley (individually or as executrix and legatee of a deceased husband); and 370 by defendant John Ringling North. The purpose of the meeting was to elect the entire board of seven directors. The shares could be voted cumulatively. Mrs. Ringling asserts that by virtue of the operation of an agreement between her and Mrs. Haley, the latter was bound to vote her shares for an adjournment of the meeting, or in the alternative, for a certain slate of directors. Mrs. Haley contends that she was not so bound for reason that the agreement was invalid, or at least revocable.

The two ladies entered into the agreement in 1941.... The agreement recites that each party was the owner "subject only to possible claims of creditors of the estates of Charles Ringling and Richard Ringling, respectively" (deceased husbands of the parties), of 300 shares of the capital stock of the defendant corporation; that in 1938 these shares had been deposited under a voting trust agreement which would terminate in 1947, or earlier, upon the elimination of certain liability of the corporation; that each party also owned 15 shares indi-vidually; that the parties had "entered into an agreement in April 1934 providing for joint action by them in matters affecting their ownership of stock and interest in" the corporate defendant; that the parties desired "to continue to act jointly in all matters relating to their stock ownership or interest in" the corporate defendant (and the other corporation). The agreement then provides as follows:

"Now, Therefore, in consideration of the mutual covenants and agreements hereinafter contained the parties hereto agree as follows:

'1. Neither party will sell any shares of stock or any voting trust certificates in either of said corporations to any other person whosoever, without first making a written offer to the other party hereto of all of the shares or voting trust certificates proposed to be sold, for the same price and upon the same terms and conditions as in such proposed sale, and allowing such other party a time of not less than 180 days from the date of such written offer within which to accept same.

'2. In exercising any voting rights to which either party may be entitled by virtue of ownership of stock or voting trust certificates held by them in either of said corporation, each party will consult and confer with the other and the parties will act jointly in exercising such voting rights in accordance with such agreement as they may reach with respect to any matter calling for the exercise of such voting rights.

'3. In the event the parties fail to agree with respect to any matter covered by paragraph 2 above, the question in disagreement shall be submitted for arbitration to Karl D. Loos, of Washington, D. C. as arbitrator and his decision thereon shall be binding upon the parties hereto. Such arbitration shall be exercised to the end of assuring for the respective corporations good management and such participation therein by the members of the Ringling family as the experience, capacity and ability of each may warrant. The parties may at any time by written agreement designate any other individual to act as arbitrator in lieu of said Loos."

....

The Mr. Loos mentioned in the agreement is an attorney and has represented both parties since 1937, and, before and after the voting trust was terminated in late 1942, advised them with respect to the exercise of their voting rights. At the annual meetings in 1943 and the two following years, the parties voted their shares in accordance with mutual understandings arrived at as a result of discussions. In each of these years, they elected five of the seven directors. Mrs. Ringling and Mrs. Haley each had sufficient votes, independently of the other, to elect two of the seven directors. By both voting for an additional candidate, they could be sure of his election regardless of how Mr. North, the remaining stockholder, might vote.[16]

Some weeks before the 1946 meeting, they discussed with Mr. Loos the matter of voting for directors. They were in accord that Mrs. Ringling should cast sufficient votes to elect herself and her son; and that Mrs. Haley should elect herself and her husband; but they did not agree upon a fifth director. The day before the meeting, the discussions were continued, Mrs. Haley being represented by her husband since she could not be present because of illness.... Mrs. Ringling then made a demand upon Mr. Loos to act under the third paragraph of the agreement "to arbitrate the disagreement" between her and Mrs. Haley in

---

[16] Each woman was entitled to cast 2205 votes (since each had the cumulative voting rights of 315 shares, and there were 7 vacancies in the directorate). The sum of the votes of both is 4410, which is sufficient to allow 882 votes for each of 5 persons. Mr. North, holding 370 shares, was entitled to cast 2590 votes, which obviously cannot be divided so as to give to more than two candidates as many as 882 votes each. It will be observed that in order for Mrs. Ringling and Mrs. Haley to be sure to elect five directors (regardless of how Mr. North might vote) they must act together in the sense that their combined votes must be divided among five different candidates and at least one of the five must be voted for by both Mrs. Ringling and Mrs. Haley.

connection with the manner in which the stock of the two ladies should be voted.... Mr. Loos directed Mrs. Ringling to cast her votes:

882 for Mrs. Ringling,
882 for her son, Robert, and
441 for a Mr. Dunn

[Mr. Dunn] had been a member of the board for several years. She complied. Mr. Loos directed that Mrs. Haley's votes be cast

882 for Mrs. Haley,
882 for Mr. Haley, and
441 for Mr. Dunn.

Instead of complying, Mr. Haley attempted to vote his wife's shares

1103 for Mrs. Haley, and
1102 for Mr. Haley.

Mr. North voted his shares

864 for a Mr. Woods,
863 for a Mr. Griffin, and
863 for Mr. North.

The chairman ruled that the five candidates proposed by Mr. Loos, together with Messrs. Woods and North, were elected. The Haley-North group disputed this ruling insofar as it declared the election of Mr. Dunn; and insisted that Mr. Griffin, instead, had been elected.... Soon after the meeting, Mrs. Ringling instituted this proceeding.

The Vice Chancellor determined that the agreement to vote in accordance with the direction of Mr. Loos was valid as a "stock pooling agreement" with lawful objects and purposes, and that it was not in violation of any public policy of this state. He held that where the arbitrator acts under the agreement and one party refuses to comply with his direction, "the Agreement constitutes the willing party ... an implied agent possessing the irrevocable proxy of the recalcitrant party for the purpose of casting the particular vote". It was ordered that a new election be held before a master, with the direction that the master should recognize and give effect to the agreement if its terms were properly invoked.

Before taking up defendants' objections to the agreement, let us analyze particularly what it attempts to provide with respect to voting, including what functions and powers it attempts to repose in Mr. Loos, the "arbitrator".... [The arbitrator's] role is limited to situations where the parties fail to agree upon a course of action. In such cases, the agreement directs that "the question in disagreement shall be submitted for arbitration" to Mr. Loos "as arbitrator and his decision thereon shall be binding upon the parties". These provisions are designed to operate in aid of what appears to be a primary purpose of the parties, "to act jointly"in exercising their voting rights, by providing a means for fixing a course of action whenever they themselves might reach a stalemate.

Should the agreement be interpreted as attempting to empower the arbitrator to carry his directions into effect? Certainly there is no express delegation or grant of power to do so, either by authorizing him to vote the shares or to compel either party to vote them in accordance with his directions. The agreement expresses no other function of the arbitrator than that of deciding questions in disagreement which prevent the effectuation of the purpose "to act jointly". The power to enforce a decision does not seem a necessary or usual incident of such a function.... We think the parties sought to bind each other, but to be bound only to each other, and not to empower the arbitrator to enforce decisions he might make.

From this conclusion, it follows necessarily that no decision of the arbitrator could ever be enforced if both parties to the agreement were unwilling that it be enforced, for the obvious reason that there would be no one to enforce it....

The agreement does not describe the undertaking of each party with respect to a decision of the arbitrator other than to provide that it "shall be binding upon the parties" .... The method of voting actually employed by the parties tends to show that they did not construe the agreement as creating powers to vote each other's shares; for at meetings prior to 1946 each party apparently exercised her own voting rights, and at the 1946 meeting, Mrs. Ringling, who wished to enforce the agreement, did not attempt to cast a ballot in exercise of any voting rights of Mrs. Haley. We do not find enough in the agreement or in the circumstances to justify a construction that either party was empowered to exercise voting rights of the other.

Having examined what the parties sought to provide by the agreement, we come now to defendants' contention that the voting provisions are illegal and revocable. They say that the courts of this state have definitely established the doctrine "that there can be no agreement, or any device whatsoever, by which the voting power of stock of a Delaware corporation may be irrevocably separated from the ownership of the stock, except by an agreement which complies with Section 18 of the Corporation Law, Rev.Code 1935, § 2050, and except by a proxy coupled with an interest....

....

In our view, neither the cases nor the statute sustain the rule for which the defendants contend.... [T]he statute does not purport to deal with agreements whereby shareholders attempt to bind each other as to how they shall vote their shares. Various forms of such pooling agreements, as they are sometimes called, have been held valid and have been distinguished from voting trusts. We think the particular agreement before us does not violate Section 18 or constitute an attempted evasion of its requirements, and is not illegal for any other reason. Generally speaking, a shareholder may exercise wide liberality of judgment in the matter of voting, and it is not objectionable that his motives may be for personal profit, or determined by whims or caprice, so long as he violates no duty owed his fellow shareholders. The ownership of voting stock imposes no legal duty to vote at all. A group of shareholders may, without impropriety, vote their respective shares so as to obtain advantages of concerted action. They may lawfully contract with each other to vote in the future in such way as they, or a majority of their group, from time to time determine. Reasonable provisions for cases of failure of the group to reach a determination because of an even division in their ranks seem unobjectionable.... It offends no rule of law or public policy of this state of which we are aware.

....

... With this in mind, we have concluded that the election should not be declared invalid, but that effect should be given to a rejection of the votes representing Mrs. Haley's shares. No other relief seems appropriate in this proceeding.... With respect to the election of directors, the return of the inspectors should be corrected to show a rejection of Mrs. Haley's votes, and to declare the election of the six persons for whom Mr. North and Mrs. Ringling voted.

....

An order should be entered directing a modification of the order of the Court of Chancery in accordance with this opinion.

The following case demonstrates how a combination of a pooling agreement and a buy/sell agreement can be used to address issues of control in a closely held corporation.

RAMOS v. ESTRADA

Court of Appeals of California
10 Cal. Rptr. 2d 833 (1992)

GILBERT, ASSOCIATE JUSTICE.

Defendants Tila and Angel Estrada appeal a judgment which states they breached a written corporate shareholder voting agreement. We hold that a corporate shareholders' voting agreement may be valid even though the corporation is not technically a close corporation. We affirm.

Facts

Plaintiffs Leopoldo Ramos et al. formed Broadcast Corporation for the purpose of obtaining a Federal Communications Commission (FCC) construction permit to build a Spanish language television station in Ventura County.

Ramos and his wife held 50 percent of Broadcast Corp. stock. The remaining 50 percent was issued in equal amounts to five other couples. The Estradas were one of the couples who purchased a 10 percent interest in Broadcast Corp. Tila

Estrada became president of Broadcast Corp., sometimes known as the "Broadcast Group."

In 1986, Broadcast Corp. merged with a competing applicant group, Ventura 41 Television Associates (Ventura 41), to form Costa del Oro Television, Inc. (Television Inc.). The merger agreement authorized the issuance of 10,002 shares of Television Inc. voting stock.

Initially, Television Inc. was to issue 5,000 shares to Broadcast Corp. and 5,000 to Ventura 41. Each group would have the right to elect half of an eight member board of directors. The two remaining outstanding shares were to be issued to Broadcast Corp. after the television station had operated at full power for six months. Television Inc.'s board would then increase to nine members, five of whom would be elected by Broadcast Corp.

The merger agreement contained restrictions on the transfer of stock and required each group to adopt internal shareholder agreements to carry out the merger agreement. With FCC approval, Broadcast Corp. and Ventura 41 modified their agreement to permit stock in Television Inc. to be issued directly to the respective owners of the merged entities instead of to the entities themselves. Ventura 41 sought this change so that Television Inc. would be treated as a Subchapter S corporation for tax purposes. In part, Broadcast Group agreed to this change in exchange for approval by Ventura 41 of the agreement at issue here, which is known as the June Broadcast Agreement. Among other things, the June Broadcast Agreement provides for block voting for directors by the Broadcast Group shareholders according to their ownership.

In January 1987, Broadcast Group executed a written shareholder agreement, known as the January Broadcast Agreement, to govern the voting and transfer of Broadcast Corp. shares in Television Inc. stock. At a later date, Broadcast Group drafted a written schedule showing the valuation of shares transferred pursuant to the January Broadcast Agreement. It set the price for purchase and sale of shares as their investment cost plus 8 percent per annum.

In June 1987, the shareholders of Broadcast Group executed a Master Shareholder Agreement. This agreement was designed to implement the Merger Agreement. It permits direct shareholder ownership of stock and governs various voting and transfer provisions. It requires that shareholder votes be made in the manner voted by the majority of the shareholders.

Members of Broadcast Group subscribed for shares of Television Inc. in their respective proportion of ownership pursuant to written subscription agreements attached to the Master Shareholder Agreement. The Ventura 41 group acted similarly.

Television Inc. issued stock to these subscribers in December 1987, and they elected an eight-member board. They also elected Leopoldo Ramos president, and Tila Estrada as one of the directors.

At a special directors' meeting held on October 8, 1988, Tila Estrada voted with the Ventura 41 group block to remove Ramos as president and to replace him with Walter Ulloa, a member of Ventura 41. She also joined Ventura 41 in voting to remove Romualdo Ochoa, a Broadcast Group member, as secretary and to replace him with herself.

Under the June Broadcast Agreement and the Merger Agreement, each of the groups were required to vote for the directors upon whom a majority of each respective group had agreed. The terms of that agreement expressly state that failure to adhere to the agreement constitutes an election by the shareholder to sell his or her shares pursuant to buy/sell provisions of the agreement. The agreement also calls for specific enforcement of such buy/sell provisions.

On October 15, 1988, the Broadcast Group noticed another meeting to decide how its members would vote their shares for directors at the annual meeting. All members attended except the Estradas. The group agreed to nominate another slate of directors which did not include either of the Estradas.

The Estradas unilaterally declared the June Broadcast Agreement null and void as of October 15, 1988, in a letter dictated for them by Paul Zevnik, the attorney for Ventura 41. Tila Estrada refused to recognize the October 15 vote of the majority of the Broadcast Group to replace her as a director of Television Inc. Ramos et al. sued the Estradas for breach of the June Broadcast Agreement, among other things.

The court ruled that the Estradas materially breached the valid June Broadcast Agreement, and it ordered their shares sold in accordance with the specific enforcement provisions of the June Broadcast Agreement. The court restrained the Estradas from voting their shares other than as provided in the June Broadcast Agreement.

Discussion

The Estradas contend that the June Broadcast Agreement is void because it constitutes an expired proxy which the Estradas validly revoked.

The interpretation of statutes and contracts is a matter of law subject to independent review by this court.

Corporations Code section 178 defines a proxy to be "a written authorization signed ... by a shareholder ... giving another person or persons power to vote with respect to the shares of such shareholder."

Section 7.1 of the June Broadcast Agreement details the voting arrangement among the shareholders. It states, in pertinent part: "The Stockholders agree that they shall consult with each other prior to voting their shares in the Company. They shall attempt in good faith to reach a consensus as to the outcome of any such vote. In the case of a vote for directors, they agree that no director shall be selected who is not acceptable to at least one member (*i.e.*, spousal unit) of each of Group A and Group B. (*See* P 1.2(b)(1) above [which states that: "The Stockholders shall be divided into two groups, Group 'A' being composed of Leopoldo Ramos and Cecilia Morris, and Group 'B' being composed of all the other Stockholders."].) In the case of all votes of Stockholders they agree that, following consultation and compliance with the other provisions of this paragraph, they will all vote their stock in the manner voted by a majority of the Stockholders."

No proxies are created by this agreement. The agreement has the characteristics of a shareholders' voting agreement expressly authorized by section 706, subdivision (a) for close corporations. Although the articles of incorporation do not contain the talismanic statement that "This corporation is a close corporation," the arrangements of this corporation, and in particular this voting agreement, are strikingly similar to ones authorized by the Code for close corporations.

Section 706, subdivision (a) states, in pertinent part: "an agreement between two or more shareholders of a close corporation, if in writing and signed by the parties thereto, may provide that in exercising any voting rights the shares held by them shall be voted as provided by the agreement, or as the parties may agree or as determined in accordance with a procedure agreed upon by them...."

Here, the members of this corporation executed a written agreement providing that they shall try to reach a consensus on all votes and that they shall consult with one another and vote their own stock in accordance with the majority of the stockholders. They entered into this agreement because they "mutually desire[d]" to limit the transferability of their stock to ensure "the Company does not pass into the control of persons whose interests might be incompatible with the interests of the Company and of the Stockholders, establishing their mutual rights and obligations in the event of death, and establishing a mechanism for determining how the Stockholders' voting rights in the Company shall be exercised...."

Even though this corporation does not qualify as a close corporation, this agreement is valid and binding on the Estradas. Section 706, subdivision (d) states: "This section shall not invalidate any voting or other agreement among shareholders ... which agreement ... is not otherwise illegal."

The Legislative Committee comment regarding section 706, subdivision (d) states that "[t]his subdivision is intended to preserve any agreements which would be upheld under court decisions even though they do not comply with one or more of the requirements of this section, including voting agreements of corporations other than close corporations."

The California Practice Guide indicates that such "pooling" agreements are valid not only for close corporations, but also "among any number of shareholders of other corporations as well." The Estradas cite *Dulin v. Pacific Wood and Coal Co.*, (1894) 103 Cal. 357, 35 P. 1045, and *Smith v. S.F. & N.P. Ry. Co.*, (1897) 115 Cal. 584, 47 P. 582, as support for their argument that the agreement is an expired proxy which they revoked. Their reliance on these cases is misplaced.

....

In *Smith, supra*, three individuals purchased a majority share of stock in a corporation. To keep control of the corporation, they entered into a written agreement to pool their votes so as to vote in a block for a five-year period. Although two of the three agreed on a slate for an election, the third attempted to repudiate the agreement. The two presented the vote of all the stock held by the trio in accordance with their agreement; the third attempted to vote his own stock in the manner he desired.

The court held that the express, written agreement validly called for the trio to vote their shares as a block. The court viewed the agreement as a power (to vote) coupled with an interest (in purchasing stock) which was supported by consideration. The court construed the agreement as an agency; a proxy which could not be repudiated.

There is dicta in *Smith* suggesting that the agreement in that case constituted an irrevocable proxy. Said the court: "It is not in violation of any rule or principle of law for stockholders, who own a majority of the stock in a corporation, to cause its affairs to be managed in such way as they may think best calculated to further the ends of the corporation, and, for this purpose, to appoint one or more proxies who shall vote in such a way as will carry out their plan. Nor is it against public policy for two or more stockholders to agree ... upon the officers whom they will elect, and they may do this either by themselves, or through their proxies...."

The *Smith* court also held that "[a]ny plan of procedure they [stockholders] may agree upon implies a previous comparison of views, and there is nothing illegal in an agreement to be bound by the will of the majority as to the means by which the result shall be reached. If they are in accord as to the ultimate purpose, it is but reasonable that the will of the majority should prevail as to the mode by which it may be accomplished."

In the instant case, the only difference from *Smith* is that the shareholders here chose to vote their stocks themselves, and not by proxy. What the *Smith* court held, however, is that voting agreements, like the one here, are valid. If the shareholders are unable to reach a consensus, then each shareholder must vote his or her shares according to the will of the majority.

The instant agreement is valid, enforceable and supported by consideration. It states, in pertinent part, that the stockholders entered into the agreement for the purposes of "limiting the transferability of ... stock in the Company, ensuring that the Company does not pass into the control of persons whose interests might be incompatible with the interests of the Company and of the Stockholders, establishing their mutual rights and obligations in the event of death, and establishing a mechanism for determining how the Stockholders' voting rights ... shall be exercised...."

Section 7.2 of the agreement states that "[t]he Stockholders understand and acknowledge that the purpose of the foregoing arrangement is to preserve their relative voting power in the Company.... Accordingly, in the event that a Stockholder fails to abide by this arrangement for whatever reason, that failure shall constitute on [sic] irrevocable election by the Stockholder to sell his stock in the Company, triggering the same rights of purchase provided in Article IV above."

The agreement calls for enforcement by specific performance of its terms because the stock is not readily marketable. Section 709, subdivision (c) expressly permits enforcement of shareholder voting agreements by such equitable remedies. It states, in pertinent part: "The court may determine the person entitled to the office of director or may order a new election to be held or appointment to be made, may determine the validity, effectiveness and construction of voting agreements ... and the right of persons to vote and may direct such other relief as may be just and proper."

The Estradas contend that the forced sale provision is unconscionable and oppressive. They portray themselves as naive, small-town business people who were forced to sign an adhesion agreement without reviewing its contents.

Substantial evidence supports the findings that Tila Estrada has been a licensed real estate broker. She is an astute businesswoman experienced with contracts concerning real property. The consent and signatures of the Estradas to the agreement were not procured by fraud, duress or other wrongful conduct of Ramos. The Estradas read and discussed with other members of Broadcast Group, and with their own counsel, the voting, buy/sell and other provisions of the agreement and the January Broadcast Agreement, as well as various drafts of these documents, and they freely signed these agreements.

On direct examination, under Evidence Code section 776, Tila Estrada admitted she owns and operates a real estate brokerage business; she regularly reviews a broad variety of real estate documents; she and her husband own and manage investment property; and she has considered herself "to be an astute business woman" since 1985. Tila Estrada also has been a participant and owner in another application before the FCC, for an FM radio station, before the instant suit was filed.

Ms. Estrada stated she got copies "of all the drafts and all the Shareholders Agreements." She discussed these agreements with other members of Broadcast Group and with its counsel, Mr. Howard Weiss.

The June Broadcast Agreement, including its voting and buy/sell provisions, was unanimously executed after the Estradas had a full and fair opportunity to consider it in its entirety. As the trial court found, the buy-out provisions at issue here are valid, favored by courts and enforceable by specific performance....

The Estradas breached the agreement by their written repudiation of it. Their breach constituted an election to sell their Television Inc. shares in accordance with the terms of the buy/sell provisions in the agreement. This election does not constitute a forfeiture — they violated the agreement voluntarily, aware of the consequences of their acts and they are provided full compensation, per their agreement.

The judgment is affirmed. Costs to Ramos.

STEVEN J. STONE, P.J., and YEGAN, J., concur.

———————

Model Act § 7.31 resolves two of the problems long associated with voting trusts and vote pooling agreements. The first is the issue raised in the *Lehrman* case, namely whether a pooling agreement will be recast as a voting trust and held to be invalid. Section 7.31 states that "(a) Two or more shareholders may provide for the manner in which they will vote their shares by signing an agreement for that purpose. A voting agreement created under this section is not subject to the provisions of § 7.30 [which controls voting trusts]."

The Official Comment to § 7.31(a) sheds further light on this issue. It states:

> Section 7.31(a) explicitly recognizes agreements among two or more shareholders as to the voting of shares and makes clear that these agreements are not subject to the rules relating to a voting trust. These agreements are often referred to as "pooling agreements." The only formal requirements are that they be in writing and signed by all the participating shareholders; in other respects their validity is to be judged as any other contract. They are not subject to the 10-year limitation applicable to voting trusts.

The second issue is one of enforceability. Voting trusts could be specifically enforced, whereas voting agreements could not, unless the terms of the agreement expressly provided an enforcement mechanism. Subsection (b) of § 7.31 settles that issue as well. It provides that "A voting agreement created under this section is specifically enforceable." The Official Comment to subsection (b) states:

> A voting agreement may provide its own enforcement mechanism, as by the appointment of a proxy to vote all shares subject to the agreement; the appointment may be made irrevocable under section 7.22. If no enforcement mechanism is provided, a court may order specific enforcement of the agreement and order the votes cast as the agreement contemplates. This section recognizes that damages are not likely to be an appropriate remedy for breach of a voting agreement, and also avoids the result reached in *Ringling Bros. Barnum & Bailey Combined Shows v. Ringling*, 53 A.2d 441 (Del 1947), where the court held that the appropriate remedy to enforce a pooling agreement was to refuse to permit any voting of the breaching party's shares.

B. SHAREHOLDERS' AGREEMENTS ALLOCATING CONTROL

Agreements among shareholders can contain provisions governing anything the parties wish, so long as the agreement does not constitute an illegal voting trust and so long as it does not violate public policy. We have already discussed some of the issues raised by shareholder agreements concerning voting. The agreements referred to in this section typically affect the allocation of power between shareholders and directors. Questions of public policy usually arise when a shareholders' agreement intrudes into areas governed by a state's corporation statute. Considering that all corporate issues ultimately are resolvable either by the shareholders or the directors, agreements among shareholders almost always relate to matters within the bailiwick of one or the other of those two groups.

Agreements among shareholders relating to actions within the statutory province of shareholders generally do not run into problems on public policy grounds. The general rule is that shareholders may vote their shares in any way they wish. While it is true that shareholders, especially those in closely held corporations, have fiduciary duties toward their fellow shareholders, those duties generally do not limit shareholders' ability to look out for their interests. If, therefore, shareholders believe it is in their interest to agree on such matters as whom they will vote for as directors or to whom and under what conditions they may sell their shares, the state typically will take no interest in the matter. And, in fact, agreements among shareholders on such matters are common.

The problem arises when agreements among persons who are both shareholders and directors relate to matters over which the corporation statute gives the directors control, as, for example, the oversight management of the corporation or appointment of officers. It is the job of directors to represent all of the shareholders equally, and in so doing they exercise fiduciary responsibilities to all of the shareholders. Therefore, courts traditionally have not usually favored agreements limiting the discretion or authority of the directors, including binding directors to act in the future in agreed-upon ways.

If courts wish, however, they can allow substantial leeway to shareholders and directors in closely held corporations, and sometimes courts will uphold agreements that seem, on their face, to violate public policy as reflected in the corporation statute. A leading case is *Galler v. Galler*.

GALLER v. GALLER

Supreme Court of Illinois
203 N.E.2d 577 (1964)

UNDERWOOD, JUSTICE.

Plaintiff, Emma Galler, sued in equity for an accounting and for specific performance of an agreement made in July, 1955, between plaintiff and her husband, of one part, and defendants, Isadore A. Galler and his wife, Rose, of the other. Defendants appealed from a decree of the superior court of Cook County granting the relief prayed. The First District Appellate Court reversed the decree and denied specific performance, affirming in part the order for an accounting, and modifying the order awarding master's fees. That decision is appealed here on a certificate of importance.

There is no substantial dispute as to the facts in this case. From 1919 to 1924, Benjamin and Isadore Galler, brothers, were equal partners in the Galler Drug Company, a wholesale drug concern. In 1924 the business was incorporated under the Illinois Business Corporation Act, each owning one half of the outstanding 220 shares of stock. In 1945 each contracted to sell 6 shares to an employee, Rosenberg, at a price of $ 10,500 for each block of 6 shares, payable within 10 years. They guaranteed to repurchase the shares if Rosenberg's employment were terminated, and further agreed that if they sold their shares, Rosenberg would receive the same price per share as that paid for the brothers' shares. Rosenberg was still indebted for the 12 shares in July, 1955, and continued to make payments on account even after Benjamin Galler died in 1957 and after the institution of this action by Emma Galler in 1959. Rosenberg was not involved in this litigation either as a party or as a witness, and in July of 1961, prior to the time that the master in chancery hearings were concluded, defendants Isadore and Rose Galler purchased the 12 shares from Rosenberg. A supplemental complaint was filed by the plaintiff, Emma Galler, asserting an equitable right to have 6 of the 12 shares transferred to her and offering to pay the defendants one half of the amount that the defendants paid Rosenberg. The parties have stipulated that pending disposition of the instant case, these shares will not be voted or transferred. For approximately one year prior to the entry of the decree by the chancellor in July of 1962, there were no outstanding minority shareholder interests.

In March, 1954, Benjamin and Isadore, on the advice of their accountant, decided to enter into an agreement for the financial protection of their immediate families and to assure their families, after the death of either brother, equal control of the corporation. [In July 1955 the agreement was executed.]

....

Shortly after Benjamin's death, Emma went to the office and demanded the terms of the 1955 agreement be carried out. [Isadore suggested certain modifications to the agreement.] When Emma refused to modify the agreement and sought enforcement of its terms, defendants refused and this suit followed.

During the last few years of Benjamin's life both brothers drew an annual salary of $ 42,000. [Isadore's son,] whose salary was $ 15,000 as manager of the warehouse prior to September, 1956, has since the time that Emma agreed to his acting as president drawn an annual salary of $ 20,000. In 1957, 1958, and 1959 a $ 40,000 annual dividend was paid. Plaintiff has received her proportionate share of the dividend.

The July, 1955, agreement in question here, entered into between Benjamin, Emma, Isadore and Rose, recites that Benjamin and Isadore each own 47½ % of the issued and outstanding shares of the Galler Drug Company, an Illinois corporation, and that Benjamin and Isadore desired to provide income for the support and maintenance of their immediate families.... The essential features of the contested portions of the agreement are substantially as set forth in the opinion of the Appellate Court: (2) [T]hat the bylaws of the corporation will be amended to provide for a board of four directors; that the necessary quorum shall be three directors; and that no directors' meeting shall be held without giving ten days notice to all directors. (3) The shareholders will cast their votes for the above named persons (Isadore, Rose, Benjamin and Emma) as directors at said special meeting and at any other meeting held for the purpose of electing directors. (4, 5) In the event of the death of either brother his wife shall have the right to nominate a director in place of the decedent. (6) Certain annual dividends will be declared by the corporation. The dividend shall be $ 50,000 payable out of the accumulated earned surplus in excess of $ 500,000. If 50% of the annual net profits after taxes exceeds the minimum $ 50,000, then the directors shall have discretion to declare a dividend up to 50% of the annual net profits. If the net profits are less than $ 50,000, nevertheless the minimum $ 50,000 annual dividend shall be declared, providing the $ 500,000 surplus is maintained. Earned surplus is defined. (9) The certificates evidencing the said shares of Benjamin Galler and Isadore Galler shall bear a legend that the shares are subject to the terms of this agreement. (10) A salary continuation agreement shall be entered into by the corporation which shall authorize the corporation upon the death of Benjamin Galler or Isadore Galler, or both, to pay a sum equal to twice the salary of such officer, payable monthly over a five-year period. Said sum shall be paid to the widow during her widowhood, but should be paid to such widow's children if the widow remarries within the five-year period. (11, 12) The parties to this agreement further agree and hereby grant to the corporation the authority to purchase, in the event of the death of either Benjamin or Isadore, so much of the stock of Galler Drug Company held by the estate as is necessary to provide sufficient funds to pay the federal estate tax, the Illinois inheritance tax and other administrative expenses of the estate. If as a result of such purchase from the estate of the decedent the amount of dividends to be received by the heirs is reduced, the parties shall nevertheless vote for directors so as to give the estate and heirs the same representation as before (2 directors out of 4, even though they own less stock), and also that the corporation pay an additional benefit payment equal to the diminution of the dividends. In the event either Benjamin or Isadore decides to sell his shares he is required to offer them first to the remaining shareholders and then to the corporation at book value, according each six months to accept the offer.

The Appellate Court found the 1955 agreement void because "the undue duration, stated purpose and substantial disregard of the provisions of the Corporation Act outweigh any considerations which might call for divisibility" and held that "the public policy of this state demands voiding this entire agreement."

While the conduct of defendants towards plaintiff was clearly inequitable, the basically controlling factor is the absence of an objecting minority interest, together with the absence of public detriment....

    ....

In *Schumann-Heink v. Folsom,* 328 Ill. 321, 330, 159 N.E. 250, 254, we said:

> In considering whether any contract is against public policy, it should be
> remembered that it is to the interests of the public that persons should not
> be unnecessarily restricted in their freedom to make their own contracts.
> Agreements are not held to be void, as being contrary to public policy,
> unless they be clearly contrary to what the constitution, the statutes, or the
> decisions of the courts have declared to be the public policy, or unless they
> be manifestly injurious to the public welfare. Courts must act with care in
> extending those rules which say that a given contract is void because against
> public policy, since, if there be one thing more than any other which public
> policy requires, it is that men of full age and competent understanding shall
> have the utmost liberty of contract, and that their contracts, when entered
> into fairly and voluntarily, shall be held sacred and shall be enforced by the
> courts.
>
> ....

The power to invalidate the agreements on the grounds of public policy is so
far reaching and so easily abused that it should be called into action to set aside
or annul the solemn engagement of parties dealing on equal terms only in cases
where the corrupt or dangerous tendency clearly and unequivocally appears upon
the face of the agreement itself or is the necessary inference from the matters
which are expressed, and the only apparent exception to this general rule is to be
found in those cases where the agreement, though fair and unobjectionable on its
face, is a part of a corrupt scheme and is made to disguise the real nature of the
transaction.

....

[T]here has been a definite, albeit inarticulate, trend toward eventual judicial
treatment of the closely held corporation as *sui generis*. Several shareholder-
director agreements that have technically "violated" the letter of the Business
Corporation Act have nevertheless been upheld in the light of the existing
practical circumstances, *i.e.,* no apparent public injury, the absence of a complaining minority interest, and no apparent prejudice to creditors. However, we
have thus far not attempted to limit these decisions as applicable only to closely
held corporations and have seemingly implied that general considerations
regarding judicial supervision of all corporate behavior apply.

The practical result of this series of cases, while liberally giving legal efficacy
to particular agreements in special circumstances notwithstanding literal "violations" of statutory corporate law, has been to inject much doubt and uncertainty
into the thinking of the bench and corporate bar of Illinois concerning shareholder
agreements.

It is therefore necessary, we feel, to discuss the instant case with the problems
peculiar to the closely held corporation particularly in mind.

It would admittedly facilitate judicial supervision of corporate behavior if a
strict adherence to the provisions of the Business Corporation Act were required

in all cases without regard to the practical exigencies peculiar to the closely held corporation. However, courts have long ago quite realistically, we feel, relaxed their attitudes concerning statutory compliance when dealing with close corporate behavior, permitting "slight deviations" from corporate "norms" in order to give legal efficacy to common business practice....

....

Numerous helpful textual statements and law review articles dealing with the judicial treatment of the closely held corporation have been pointed out by counsel. One article concludes with the following: "New needs compel fresh formulation of corporate 'norms.' There is no reason why mature men should not be able to adapt the statutory form to the structure they want, so long as they do not endanger other stockholders, creditors, or the public, or violate a clearly mandatory provision of the corporation laws. In a typical closely held corporation the stockholders' agreement is usually the result of careful deliberation among all initial investors. In the large public-issue corporation, on the other hand, the 'agreement' represented by the corporate charter is not consciously agreed to by the investors: they have no voice in its formulation, and very few ever read the certificate of incorporation. Preservation of the corporate norms may there be necessary for the protection of the public investors." Hornstein, "Stockholders' Agreements in the Closely Held Corporation," 59 Yale L. Journal, 1040, 1056.

....

Perhaps, as has been vociferously advanced, a separate comprehensive statutory scheme governing the closely held corporation would best serve here....

At any rate, however, the courts can no longer fail to expressly distinguish between the close and public-issue corporation when confronted with problems relating to either. What we do here is to illuminate this problem — before the bench, corporate bar, and the legislature, in the context of a particular fact situation. To do less would be to shirk our responsibility, to do more would, perhaps be to invade the province of the legislative branch.

We now, in the light of the foregoing, turn to specific provisions of the 1955 agreement.

The Appellate Court correctly found many of the contractual provisions free from serious objection, and we need not prolong this opinion with a discussion of them here. That court did, however, find difficulties in the stated purpose of the agreement as it relates to its duration the election of certain persons to specific offices for a number of years, the requirement for the mandatory declaration of stated dividends (which the Appellate Court held invalid), and the salary continuation agreement.

Since the question as to the duration of the agreement is a principal source of controversy, we shall consider it first. The parties provided no specific termination date, and while the agreement concludes with a paragraph that its terms "shall be binding upon and shall inure to the benefits of" the legal representatives, heirs and assigns of the parties, this clause is, we believe, intended to be operative only as long as one of the parties is living. It further provides that it shall be so construed as to carry out its purposes, and we believe these must be determined from a consideration of the agreement as a whole. Thus viewed, a fair construction is that its purposes were accomplished at the death of the survivor of the parties. While these life spans are not precisely ascertainable, and the Appellate Court noted Emma Galler's life expectancy at her husband's death was 26.9 years, we are aware of no statutory or public policy provision against stockholder's agreements which would invalidate this agreement on that ground.... While defendants argue that the public policy evinced by the legislative restrictions upon the duration of voting trust agreements should be applied here, this agreement is not a voting trust, but as pointed out by the dissenting justice in the Appellate Court, is a straight contractual voting control agreement which does not divorce voting rights from stock ownership....

The clause that provides for the election of certain persons to specified offices for a period of years likewise does not require invalidation. In *Kantzler v. Bensinger,* 214 Ill. 589, 73 N.E. 874, this court upheld an agreement entered into by all the stockholders providing that certain parties would be elected to the offices of the corporation for a fixed period. In *Faulds v. Yates,* 57 Ill. 416, we upheld a similar agreement among the majority stockholders of a corporation, notwithstanding the existence of a minority which was not before the court complaining thereof.

We turn next to a consideration of the effect of the stated purpose of the agreement upon its validity. The pertinent provision is: "The said Benjamin A. Galler and Isadore A. Galler desire to provide income for the support and maintenance of their immediate families." Obviously, there is no evil inherent in a contract entered into for the reason that the persons originating the terms desired to so arrange their property as to provide post-death support for those dependent upon them. Nor does the fact that the subject property is corporate stock alter the situation so long as there exists no detriment to minority stock interests, creditors or other public injury. It is, however, contended by defendants that the methods provided by the agreement for implementation of the stated purpose are, as a whole, violative of the Business Corporation Act to such an extent as to render it void *in toto.*

The terms of the dividend agreement require a minimum annual dividend of $ 50,000, but this duty is limited by the subsequent provision that it shall be operative only so long as an earned surplus of $ 500,000 is maintained. It may be noted that in 1958, the year prior to commencement of this litigation, the corporation's net earnings after taxes amounted to $ 202,759 while its earned surplus was $ 1,543,270, and this was increased in 1958 to $ 1,680,079 while earnings were $ 172,964. The minimum earned surplus requirement is designed for the protection of the corporation and its creditors, and we take no exception to the contractual dividend requirements as thus restricted.

The salary continuation agreement is a common feature, in one form or another, of corporate executive employment. It requires that the widow should receive a total benefit, payable monthly over a five-year period, aggregating twice the amount paid her deceased husband in one year. This requirement was likewise limited for the protection of the corporation by being contingent upon the payments being income tax-deductible by the corporation. The charge made in those cases which have considered the validity of payments to the widow of an officer and shareholder in a corporation is that a gift of its property by a noncharitable corporation is in violation of the rights of its shareholders and *ultra vires*. Since there are no shareholders here other than the parties to the contract, this objection is not here applicable, and its effect, as limited, upon the corporation is not so prejudicial as to require its invalidation.

....

We hold defendants must account for all monies received by them from the corporation since September 25, 1956, in excess of that theretofore authorized.

Section 7.32 of the Model Act eliminates some of the concerns associated with shareholder agreements restricting the discretion of the members of the board of directors of a closely held corporation. Section 7.32(a) provides:

> An agreement among shareholders of a corporation that complies with this section is effective among the shareholders and the corporation even though it is inconsistent with one or more other provisions of this Act in that it: (1) eliminates the board of directors or restricts the discretion or powers of the board of directors; (2) governs the authorization or making of distributions whether or not in proportion to ownership of shares, subject to the limitations in section 6.40; (3) establishes who shall be directors or officers of the corporation, or their terms of office or manner of selection or removal; (4) governs, in general or in regard to specific matters, the exercise or division of voting power by or between the shareholders and directors or by or among any of them, including use of weighted voting rights or director proxies; (6) transfers to one or more shareholders or other persons all or part of the authority to exercise the corporate powers or to manage the business and affairs of the corporation, including the resolution of any issue about which there exists a deadlock among directors or shareholders;... (8) otherwise governs the exercise of the corporate powers or the management of the business and affairs of the corporation or the relationship among the shareholders, the directors and the corporation, or among any of them, and is not contrary to public policy.

The Official Comment states:

> Shareholders of closely-held corporations, ranging from family businesses to joint ventures owned by large public corporations, frequently enter into agreements that govern the operation of the enterprise. In the past, various types of shareholder agreements were invalidated by courts for a variety of reasons, including so-called "sterilization" of the board of directors and

failure to follow the statutory norms of the applicable corporation act. *See, e.g.* Long Park, Inc. Trenton-New Brunswick Theaters Co., 297 N.Y. 174, 77 N.E.2d 633 (1948). The more modern decisions reflect a greater willingness to uphold shareholder agreements....

Rather than relying on further uncertain and sporadic development of the law in the courts, section 7.32 rejects the older line of cases. It adds an important element of predictability currently absent from the Model Act and affords participants in closely-held corporations greater contractual freedom to tailor the rules of their enterprise.

Section 7.32 is not intended to establish or legitimize an alternative form of corporation. Instead, it is intended to add, within the context of the traditional corporate structure, legal certainty to shareholder agreements that embody various aspects of the business arrangement established by the shareholders to meet their business and personal needs.... Thus, section 7.32 validates for nonpublic corporations various types of agreements among shareholders even when the agreements are inconsistent with the statutory norms contained in the Act.

C. EMPLOYMENT CONTRACTS

One contractual arrangement that can be used to distribute corporate control is the employment contract. Since in a closely held corporation shareholders often wish to work full time in their corporation, such contracts can be used along with other devices to distribute control among the shareholders. Employment agreements also can be used, of course, to place limited control in the hands of nonshareholders who will serve as officers. There are, however, significant limitations on the protections available through employment contracts, and a number of things to consider in drafting them.

Corporation statutes universally provide that a corporation's officers are to be chosen by its directors and that the officers may be removed by the directors at will. Partially for that reason, specific performance is not a remedy that will be available to an officer if a corporation breaks the officer's employment contract, except perhaps in the most extraordinary circumstances. Model Act § 8.43(b) speaks directly to the issue by providing that "A board of directors may remove any officer at any time with or without cause." Section 8.44 adds "(a) The appointment of an officer does not itself create contract rights. (b) An officer's removal does not affect the officer's contract rights, if any, with the corporation...."

To offer much protection to an officer, a salary escalator must be built into an employment contract. The simplest way to do that is to provide for minimum annual percentage increases. In financial terms, the next big choice for the drafter of an employment contract is whether to provide for liquidated damages. Although a provision for liquidated damages is not always desirable, it may make a breach of the contract too unpalatable for a board to contemplate, if breaking an employment contract is likely to cost the corporation a substantial amount of money.

In these circumstances, an officer also faces the possibility that the corporation will change the officer's job, or the duties incident to the job, in an attempt to force the officer to resign. That, in fact, often is the first thing corporate managers think of when faced with getting rid of an unwanted officer who has an employment contract. Not surprisingly, since most employment contracts are drafted by the corporation's lawyer, a usual provision in employment contracts calls for the person signing the contract to "hold such offices and perform such services as the board of directors shall provide." That obviously provides an officer with little protection.

Some protection comes from specifying the office to be held, but not so much protection as may at first seem. At the time an employment contract for the president is signed, for example, the president may be the chief executive officer. If the board of directors wants to force the president's resignation, the first thing it likely will do is elect a chair of the board and make the chair the chief executive officer. That may be followed by other actions, such as the election of a vice chair who is made chief operating officer and the removal from the president of all duties of significance. While it is true that a court may, if it wishes, interpret such corporate actions as breaches of the president's contract, there can be no assurance that that will be the case.

The best way to avoid such problems is to describe an officer's corporate role in functional terms, such as chief executive officer, chief operating officer, chief financial officer, and so on. A long-term employment contract that does that, and that has a reasonable salary escalator and perhaps a good liquidated damages clause, can give an officer substantial protection.

As a result of the increased takeover activity in recent years, many corporations have entered into so-called golden parachute contracts with their principal executives. Those contracts typically apply when there is a change of control (as defined) and an executive is either discharged without cause or is subject to a significant change of duties. Upon leaving the company, the executive is usually entitled to the continuation of any compensation, bonuses, and other benefits for a stipulated period notwithstanding any other employment the executive may secure. The Internal Revenue Code, however, by imposing confiscatory taxes, does limit the aggregate amounts that may be paid under such contracts.

Chapter 8

PIERCING THE CORPORATE VEIL

Situation

As Biologistics, Inc. continues to grow, the corporation continues to assume various obligations. For instance, the corporation is responsible for ongoing payments under its lease agreement with Southland Properties, Inc. At the same time, there are other potential liabilities. For example, what if a customer is dissatisfied with the corporation's work and successfully sues the corporation for negligent and faulty DNA analysis? The corporation's operations also use various chemicals that, if improperly disposed of, could lead to environmental law problems.

Biologistics' shareholders want assurance that they will not be held personally responsible for these corporate obligations. What advice do you offer them?

SECTION I. INTRODUCTION

As a fundamental corporate law principle, shareholders' liability for corporate obligations is limited to the amount which they contribute to the corporation in exchange for their equity interest.[1] Thus, their financial risk is limited to the amount of their deliberate investment, and creditors of the corporation cannot access shareholders' personal assets. Shareholders' limited liability also is consistent with the notion that the corporation is a separate legal entity from its shareholders.

The courts, however, have created an exception to this fundamental principle of limited liability. As we will explore in this chapter, under certain "equitable" circumstances, courts will "pierce the corporate veil." By disregarding the corporate entity, creditors of the corporation can then hold shareholders personally liable for the corporation's obligations. This shift of the loss from the corporate creditor to the shareholders effectively alters the amount of financial risk that the shareholders had anticipated and relied upon.

It is often difficult to discern the underlying legal principles in "piercing the corporate veil" cases. In part, this results from some courts' inclination to be vague about their specific reasoning, and instead defer to metaphorical but obscure rhetoric, such as describing the corporation as the "alter ego," "instrumentality," or "dummy" of the shareholders. In part, courts have not

---

[1] Model Act § 6.22(b), DEL. CODE ANN. tit. 8 § 102(b)(6).

definitively determined what extreme situations would prompt them to overcome the important presumption of limited liability.

The following cases explore various distinctions. In contract cases, where the plaintiff creditor and the corporation voluntarily entered into their relationship, should the corporation's adequate capitalization or its observance of corporate formalities be determinative? What if the shareholders misrepresented their roles in the corporation? Should tort cases be treated differently than contract cases, given that tort plaintiffs typically become corporate creditors involuntarily? Should the fact that the shareholder is a sole individual, one of many individuals, or another business enterprise make a difference?

SECTION II. TORT-BASED CLAIMS AND OTHER CONSIDERATIONS

The majority and dissenting opinions in the following two tort-based cases offer contrasting views of when it is appropriate to pierce the corporate veil. Consider how the justices' perspectives on the limits of the corporate form affect their conclusions.

BAATZ v. ARROW BAR

Supreme Court of South Dakota
452 N.W.2d 138 (1990)

SABERS, JUSTICE:

Kenny and Peggy Baatz (Baatz), appeal from summary judgment dismissing Edmond, LaVella, and Jacquette Neuroth, as individual defendants in this action.

Facts

Kenny and Peggy were seriously injured in 1982 when Roland McBride crossed the center line of a Sioux Falls street with his automobile and struck them while they were riding on a motorcycle. McBride was uninsured at the time of the accident and apparently is judgment proof.

Baatz alleges that Arrow Bar served alcoholic beverages to McBride prior to the accident while he was already intoxicated. Baatz commenced this action in 1984, claiming that Arrow Bar's negligence in serving alcoholic beverages to McBride contributed to the injuries they sustained in the accident. Baatz supports his claim against Arrow Bar with the affidavit of Jimmy Larson. Larson says he knew McBride and observed him being served alcoholic beverages in the Arrow Bar during the afternoon prior to the accident, while McBride was intoxicated....

Edmond and LaVella Neuroth formed the Arrow Bar, Inc. in May 1980. During the next two years they contributed $ 50,000 to the corporation pursuant to a stock subscription agreement. The corporation purchased the Arrow Bar business in June 1980 for $ 155,000 with a $ 5,000 down payment. Edmond and LaVella executed a promissory note personally guaranteeing payment of the $ 150,000 balance. In 1983 the corporation obtained bank financing in the amount of $ 145,000 to pay off the purchase agreement. Edmond and LaVella again personally guaranteed payment of the corporate debt. Edmond is the president of the corporation, and Jacquette Neuroth serves as the manager of the business. Based on the enactment of [S.D. Codified Laws (SDCL)] §§ 35-4-78 and 35-11-1 and advice of counsel, the corporation did not maintain dram shop liability insurance at the time of the injuries to Kenny and Peggy.

In 1987 the trial court entered summary judgment in favor of Arrow Bar and the individual defendants. Baatz appealed that judgment and we reversed and remanded to the trial court for trial. Shortly before the trial date, Edmond, LaVella, and Jacquette moved for and obtained summary judgment dismissing them as individual defendants. Baatz appeals. We affirm.

...

1. *Individual liability as employees*

SDCL § 35-4-78 protects persons from the risk of injury or death resulting from intoxication enhanced by the particular sale of alcoholic beverages. *Walz v. City of Hudson*, 327 N.W.2d 120 (S.D. 1982). Accordingly, the statute "establishes a standard of care or conduct, a breach of which is negligence as a matter of law." *Walz, supra* at 123. That standard of care may be breached either by the liquor licensee or an employee of the licensee. *Selchert v. Lien*, 371 N.W.2d 791 (S.D. 1985).

Neuroths claim there is no evidence that they individually violated the standard of care created by SDCL § 35-4-78. They claim the licensee is the corporation, Arrow Bar, Inc., leaving them liable only if one of them, as an employee, served alcoholic beverages to McBride while he was intoxicated. They claim the record is void of any evidence indicating that any one of them served McBride on the day of the accident.

Baatz argues that this court's decision in *Selchert, supra,* allowed a cause of action against both the liquor licensee and the licensee's employees. Baatz claims that each of the Neuroths admitted in deposition to being an employee of the corporation. Consequently, under his reasoning, a cause of action may be brought against the Neuroths in their individual capacities. However, Baatz reads the decision in *Selchert* too broadly.... While a cause of action may be brought against a licensee's employee, it must be established that that employee violated the standard of care established by the statute. Employee status alone is insufficient to sustain a cause of action. Baatz failed to offer evidence that any of the Neuroths personally served McBride on the day of the accident.

Baatz also argues that Jacquette Neuroth, as manager of the bar, is liable under the doctrine of *respondeat superior*. Under this doctrine, an employer may be liable for the conduct of an employee. However, in this case, Jacquette Neuroth is not the employer. The employer of the individuals who may have served McBride is the corporation, Arrow Bar, Inc. Therefore, Baatz' argument misapplies the doctrine of *respondeat superior*.

2. Individual liability by piercing the corporate veil

Baatz claims that even if Arrow Bar, Inc. is the licensee, the corporate veil should be pierced, leaving the Neuroths, as the shareholders of the corporation, individually liable. A corporation shall be considered a separate legal entity until there is *sufficient reason* to the contrary. When continued recognition of a corporation as a separate legal entity would "produce injustices and inequitable consequences," then a court has sufficient reason to pierce the corporate veil. *Farmers Feed & Seed, Inc. v. Magnum Enter., Inc.*, 344 N.W.2d 699, 701 (S.D. 1984). Factors that indicate injustices and inequitable consequences and allow a court to pierce the corporate veil are:

1) fraudulent representation by corporation directors;
2) undercapitalization;
3) failure to observe corporate formalities;
4) absence of corporate records;
5) payment by the corporation of individual obligations; or
6) use of the corporation to promote fraud, injustice, or illegalities.

Id.....

Baatz advances several arguments to support his claim that the corporate veil of Arrow Bar, Inc. should be pierced, but fails to support them with facts, or misconstrues the facts.

First, Baatz claims that since Edmond and LaVella personally guaranteed corporate obligations, they should also be personally liable to Baatz. However, the personal guarantee of a loan is a contractual agreement and cannot be enlarged to impose tort liability. Moreover, the personal guarantee creates individual liability for a corporate obligation, the opposite of factor 5, above. As such, it supports, rather than detracts from, recognition of the corporate entity.

Baatz also argues that the corporation is simply the alter ego of the Neuroths, and ... the corporate veil should be pierced. Baatz' discussion of the law is adequate, but he fails to present evidence that would support a decision in his favor in accordance with that law. When an individual treats a corporation "as an instrumentality through which he [is] conducting his personal business," a court may disregard the corporate entity. *Larson v. Western Underwriters, Inc.*, 87 N.W.2d 883, 886 (S.D. 1958). Baatz fails to demonstrate how the Neuroths were transacting personal business through the corporation. In fact, the evidence indicates the Neuroths treated the corporation separately from their individual affairs.

Baatz next argues that the corporation is undercapitalized. Shareholders must equip a corporation with a reasonable amount of capital for the nature of the business involved. Baatz claims the corporation was started with only $ 5,000 in borrowed capital, but does not explain how that amount failed to equip the corporation with a reasonable amount of capital. In addition, Baatz fails to consider the personal guarantees to pay off the purchase contract in the amount of $ 150,000, and the $ 50,000 stock subscription agreement. There simply is no evidence that the corporation's capital in whatever amount was inadequate for the operation of the business.... [S]imply asserting that the corporation is undercapitalized does not make it so. Without some evidence of the inadequacy of the capital, Baatz fails to present specific facts demonstrating a genuine issue of material fact.

Finally, Baatz argues that Arrow Bar, Inc. failed to observe corporate formalities because none of the business' signs or advertising indicated that the business was a corporation. Baatz cites SDCL § 47-2-36 as requiring the name of any corporation to contain the word corporation, company, incorporated, or limited, or an abbreviation for such a word. In spite of Baatz' contentions, the corporation is in compliance with the statute because its corporate name — Arrow Bar, Inc. — includes the abbreviation of the word incorporated. Furthermore, the "mere failure upon occasion to follow all the forms prescribed by law for the conduct of corporate activities will not justify" disregarding the corporate entity. *Larson, supra,* 87 N.W.2d at 887 (*quoting P.S. & A. Realties, Inc. v. Lodge Gate Forest, Inc.,* 127 N.Y.S.2d 315, 324 (1954)). Even if the corporation is improperly using its name, that alone is not a sufficient reason to pierce the corporate veil. This is especially so where, as here, there is no relationship between the claimed defect and the resulting harm.

....

In summary, Baatz fails to present specific facts that would allow the trial court to find the existence of a genuine issue of material fact. There is no indication that any of the Neuroths personally served an alcoholic beverage to McBride on the day of the accident. Nor is there any evidence indicating that the Neuroths treated the corporation in any way that would produce the injustices and inequitable consequences necessary to justify piercing the corporate veil. In fact, the only evidence offered is otherwise. Therefore, we affirm summary judgment dismissing the Neuroths as individual defendants.

WUEST, C.J., and MORGAN and MILLER, JJ., concur

HENDERSON, JUSTICE (dissenting):

This corporation has no separate existence. It is the instrumentality of three shareholders, officers, and employees. Here, the corporate fiction should be disregarded....

A corporate shield was here created to escape the holding of this Court relating to an individual's liability in a dram shop action....

As a result of this holding, the message is now clear: Incorporate, mortgage the assets of a liquor corporation to your friendly banker, and proceed with carefree entrepreneuring.

....

Peggy Baatz, a young mother, lost her left leg; she wears an artificial limb; Kenny Baatz, a young father, has had most of his left foot amputated; he has been unable to work since this tragic accident. Peggy uses a cane. Kenny uses crutches. Years have gone by since they were injured and their lives have been torn asunder.

Uninsured motorist was drunk, and had a reputation of being a habitual drunkard; Arrow Bar had a reputation of serving intoxicated persons. (Supported by depositions on file). An eyewitness saw uninsured motorist in an extremely intoxicated condition, shortly before the accident, being served by Arrow Bar....

Are the Neuroths subject to personal liability? It is undisputed, by the record, that the dismissed defendants (Neuroths) are immediate family members and stockholders of Arrow Bar. By pleadings, at settled record 197, it is expressed that the dismissed defendants are employees of Arrow Bar. Seller of the Arrow Bar would not accept Arrow Bar, Inc., as buyer. Seller insisted that the individual incorporators, in their individual capacity be equally responsible for the selling price. Thus, the individuals are the real party in interest and the corporate entity, Arrow Bar, Inc., is being used to justify any wrongs perpetrated by the incorporators in their individual capacity. Conclusion: Fraud is perpetrated upon the public. At a deposition of Edmond Neuroth (filed in this record), this "President" of "the corporation" was asked why the Neuroth family incorporated. His answer: "Upon advice of counsel, as a shield against individual liability." The corporation was undercapitalized (Neuroths borrowed $ 5,000 in capital)....

Clearly, it appears a question arises as to whether there is a fiction established to escape our previous holdings and the intent of our State Legislature. Truly, there are fact questions for a jury to determine: (1) negligence or no negligence of the defendants and (2) did the Neuroth family falsely establish a corporation to shield themselves from individual liability, i.e., do facts in this scenario exist to pierce the corporate veil?

....

Therefore, I respectfully dissent.

WALKOVSZKY v. CARLTON

Court of Appeals of New York
223 N.E.2d 6 (1966)

FULD, JUDGE:

This case involves what appears to be a rather common practice in the taxicab industry of vesting the ownership of a taxi fleet in many corporations, each owning only one or two cabs.

The complaint alleges that the plaintiff was severely injured four years ago in New York City when he was run down by a taxicab owned by the defendant Seon Cab Corporation and negligently operated at the time by the defendant Marchese. The individual defendant, Carlton, is claimed to be a stockholder of 10 corporations, including Seon, each of which has but two cabs registered in its name, and it is implied that only the minimum automobile liability insurance required by law (in the amount of $ 10,000) is carried on any one cab. Although seemingly independent of one another, these corporations are alleged to be "operated ... as a single entity, unit and enterprise" with regard to financing, supplies, repairs, employees and garaging, and all are named as defendants. The plaintiff asserts that he is also entitled to hold their stockholders personally liable for the damages sought because the multiple corporate structure constitutes an unlawful attempt "to defraud members of the general public" who might be injured by the cabs.

The defendant Carlton has moved, pursuant to [N.Y. Civ. Prac. L.&R. (CPLR)] § 3211(a)7, to dismiss the complaint on the ground that as to him it "fails to state a cause of action." The court at Special Term granted the motion but the Appellate Division, by a divided vote, reversed, holding that a valid cause of action was sufficiently stated. The defendant Carlton appeals to us, from the nonfinal order, by leave of the Appellate Division on a certified question.

The law permits the incorporation of a business for the very purpose of enabling its proprietors to escape personal liability but, manifestly, the privilege is not without its limits. Broadly speaking, the courts will disregard the corporate form, or, to use accepted terminology, "pierce the corporate veil," whenever necessary "to prevent fraud or to achieve equity." (*International Aircraft Trading Co. v. Manufacturers Trust Co.*, 79 N.E.2d 249, 252 [(N.Y. (1948)]). In determining whether liability should be extended to reach assets beyond those belonging to the corporation, we are guided, as Judge Cardozo noted, by "general rules of agency." (*Berkey v. Third Ave. Ry. Co.*, 155 N.E. 58, 61 [(N.Y. 1926)], 50 A.L.R. 599.) In other words, whenever anyone uses control of the corporation to further his own rather than the corporation's business, he will be liable for the corporation's acts "upon the principle of *respondeat superior* applicable even where the agent is a natural person." (*Rapid Tr. Subway Constr. Co. v. City of New York*, 259 N.Y. 472, 488, 182 N.E. 145, 150.) Such liability, moreover, extends not only to the corporation's commercial dealings but to its negligent acts as well.

In [*Mangan v. Terminal Transportation System, Inc.*, 286 N.Y.S. 666 (N.Y. App. Div. 1936)], the plaintiff was injured as a result of the negligent operation of a cab owned and operated by one of four corporations affiliated with the defendant Terminal. Although the defendant was not a stockholder of any of the operating companies, both the defendant and the operating companies were owned, for the most part, by the same parties. The defendant's name (Terminal) was conspicuously displayed on the sides of all of the taxis used in the enterprise and, in point of fact, the defendant actually serviced, inspected, repaired and dispatched them. These facts were deemed to provide sufficient cause for piercing the corporate veil of the operating company — the nominal owner of the cab which injured the plaintiff — and holding the defendant liable. The operating companies were simply instrumentalities for carrying on the business of the defendant without imposing upon it financial and other liabilities incident to the actual ownership and operation of the cabs.

In the case before us, the plaintiff has explicitly alleged that none of the corporations "had a separate existence of their own" and, as indicated above, all are named as defendants. However, it is one thing to assert that a corporation is a fragment of a larger corporate combine which actually conducts the business. (See Berle, *The Theory of Enterprise Entity*, 47 Col. L. Rev. 343, 348-350.) It is quite another to claim that the corporation is a "dummy" for its individual stockholders who are in reality carrying on the business in their personal capacities for purely personal rather than corporate ends. Either circumstance would justify treating the corporation as an agent and piercing the corporate veil to reach the principal but a different result would follow in each case. In the first, only a larger *corporate* entity would be held financially responsible while, in the other, the stockholder would be personally liable. Either the stockholder is conducting the business in his individual capacity or he is not. If he is, he will be liable; if he is not, then it does not matter — insofar as his personal liability is concerned — that the enterprise is actually being carried on by a larger "enterprise entity." (See Berle, *supra*.)

At this stage in the present litigation, we are concerned only with the pleadings[.] ... Reading the complaint in this case most favorably and liberally, we do not believe that there can be gathered from its averments the allegations required to spell out a valid cause of action against the defendant Carlton.

The individual defendant is charged with having "organized, managed, dominated and controlled" a fragmented corporate entity but there are no allegations that he was conducting business in his individual capacity. Had the taxicab fleet been owned by a single corporation, it would be readily apparent that the plaintiff would face formidable barriers in attempting to establish personal liability on the part of the corporation's stockholders. The fact that the fleet ownership has been deliberately split up among many corporations does not ease the plaintiff's burden in that respect. The corporate form may not be disregarded merely because the assets of the corporation, together with the mandatory insurance coverage of the vehicle which struck the plaintiff, are insufficient to assure him the recovery sought. If Carlton were to be held individually liable on those facts alone, the decision would apply equally to the thousands of cabs which are owned by their individual drivers who conduct their businesses through corporations organized pursuant to section 401 of the Business Corporation Law, Consol. Laws, c. 4 and carry the minimum insurance required by subdivision 1 (par. (a)) of section 370 of the Vehicle and Traffic Law, Consol. Laws, c. 71. These taxi owner-operators are entitled to form such corporations and we agree with the court at Special Term that, if the insurance coverage required by statute "is inadequate for the protection of the public, the remedy lies not with the courts but with the Legislature." It may very well be sound policy to require that certain corporations must take out liability insurance which will afford adequate compensation to their potential tort victims. However, the responsibility for imposing conditions on the privilege of incorporation has been committed by the Constitution to the Legislature (N.Y. Const., art. X, § 1) and it may not be fairly implied, from any statute, that the Legislature intended, without the slightest discussion or debate, to require of taxi corporations that they carry automobile liability insurance over and above that mandated by the Vehicle and Traffic Law.

This is not to say that it is impossible for the plaintiff to state a valid cause of action against the defendant Carlton. However, the simple fact is that the plaintiff has just not done so here. While the complaint alleges that the separate corporations were undercapitalized and that their assets have been intermingled, it is barren of any "sufficiently particular(ized) statements" (CPLR § 3013; *see* 3 Weinstein-Korn-Miller, *N.Y. Civ. Prac.*, par. 3013.01 *et seq.*, pp. 30-142 *et seq.*) that the defendant Carlton and his associates are actually doing business in their individual capacities, shuttling their personal funds in and out of the corporations "without regard to formality and to suit their immediate convenience." (*Weisser v. Mursam Shoe Corp.*, 127 F.2d 344, 345 [(2d Cir. 1942)], 145 A.L.R. 467.) Such a "perversion of the privilege to do business in a corporate form" (*Berkey*, 155 N.E. at 61, 50 A.L.R. 599, *supra*) would justify imposing personal liability on the individual stockholders. Nothing of the sort has in fact been charged, and it cannot reasonably or logically be inferred from the happenstance that the business of Seon Cab Corporation may actually be carried on by a larger corporate entity composed of many corporations which, under general principles of agency, would be liable to each other's creditors in contract and in tort.

... If it is not fraudulent for the owner-operator of a single cab corporation to take out only the minimum required liability insurance, the enterprise does not become either illicit or fraudulent merely because it consists of many such corporations. The plaintiff's injuries are the same regardless of whether the cab which strikes him is owned by a single corporation or part of a fleet with ownership fragmented among many corporations. Whatever rights he may be able to assert against parties other than the registered owner of the vehicle come into being not because he has been defrauded but because, under the principle of *respondeat superior*, he is entitled to hold the whole enterprise responsible for the acts of its agents.

In sum, then, the complaint falls short of adequately stating a cause of action against the defendant Carlton in his individual capacity.

The order of the Appellate Division should be reversed, with costs in this court and in the Appellate Division, the certified question answered in the negative and the order of the Supreme Court, Richmond County, reinstated, with leave to serve an amended complaint.

KEATING, JUDGE (dissenting):

The defendant Carlton, the shareholder here sought to be held for the negligence of the driver of a taxicab, was a principal shareholder and organizer of the defendant corporation which owned the taxicab. The corporation was one of 10 organized by the defendant, each containing two cabs and each cab having the "minimum liability" insurance coverage mandated by section 370 of the

Vehicle and Traffic Law. The sole assets of these operating corporations are the vehicles themselves and they are apparently subject to mortgages.[2]

From their inception these corporations were intentionally undercapitalized for the purpose of avoiding responsibility for acts which were bound to arise as a result of the operation of a large taxi fleet having cars out on the street 24 hours a day and engaged in public transportation. And during the course of the corporations' existence all income was continually drained out of the corporations for the same purpose.

The issue presented by this action is whether the policy of this State, which affords those desiring to engage in a business enterprise the privilege of limited liability through the use of the corporate device, is so strong that it will permit that privilege to continue no matter how much it is abused, no matter how irresponsibly the corporation is operated, no matter what the cost to the public. I do not believe that it is.

Under the circumstances of this case the shareholders should all be held individually liable to this plaintiff for the injuries he suffered. At least, the matter should not be disposed of on the pleadings by a dismissal of the complaint. "If a corporation is organized and carries on business without substantial capital in such a way that the corporation is likely to have no sufficient assets available to meet its debts, it is inequitable that shareholders should set up such a flimsy organization to escape personal liability. The attempt to do corporate business without providing any sufficient basis of financial responsibility to creditors is an abuse of the separate entity and will be ineffectual to exempt the shareholders from corporate debts. It is coming to be recognized as the policy of law that shareholders should in good faith put at the risk of the business unincumbered capital reasonably adequate for its prospective liabilities. If capital is illusory or trifling compared with the business to be done and the risks of loss, this is a ground for denying the separate entity privilege." (Ballantine, *Corporations* (Rev. ed., 1946), § 129, pp. 302-303.)

....

The policy of this State has always been to provide and facilitate recovery for those injured through the negligence of others. The automobile, by its very nature, is capable of causing severe and costly injuries when not operated in a proper manner. The great increase in the number of automobile accidents combined with the frequent financial irresponsibility of the individual driving the car led to the adoption of section 388 of the Vehicle and Traffic Law which had the effect of imposing upon the owner of the vehicle the responsibility for its negligent operation. It is upon this very statute that the cause of action against both the corporation and the individual defendant is predicated.

---

[2] It appears that the medallions, which are of considerable value, are judgment proof. (Administrative Code of City of New York, § 436-2.0.) [Eds.: Municipal governments issue a set number of "medallions," typically for a fee, that function like a license for operating a taxicab.]

In addition the Legislature, still concerned with the financial irresponsibility of those who owned and operated motor vehicles, enacted a statute requiring minimum liability coverage for all owners of automobiles. The important public policy represented by both these statutes is outlined in section 310 of the Vehicle and Traffic Law. That section provides that: "The legislature is concerned over the rising toll of motor vehicle accidents and the suffering and loss thereby inflicted. The legislature determines that it is a matter of grave concern that motorists shall be financially able to respond in damages for their negligent acts, so that innocent victims of motor vehicle accidents may be recompensed for the injury and financial loss inflicted upon them."

The defendant Carlton claims that, because the minimum amount of insurance required by the statute was obtained, the corporate veil cannot and should not be pierced despite the fact that the assets of the corporation which owned the cab were "trifling compared with the business to be done and the risks of loss" which were certain to be encountered. I do not agree.

The Legislature in requiring minimum liability insurance of $ 10,000, no doubt, intended to provide at least some small fund for recovery against those individuals and corporations who just did not have and were not able to raise or accumulate assets sufficient to satisfy the claims of those who were injured as a result of their negligence. It certainly could not have intended to shield those individuals who organized corporations, with the specific intent of avoiding responsibility to the public, where the operation of the corporate enterprise yielded profits sufficient to purchase additional insurance. Moreover, it is reasonable to assume that the Legislature believed that those individuals and corporations having substantial assets would take out insurance far in excess of the minimum in order to protect those assets from depletion. Given the costs of hospital care and treatment and the nature of injuries sustained in auto collisions, it would be unreasonable to assume that the Legislature believed that the minimum provided in the statute would in and of itself be sufficient to recompense "innocent victims of motor vehicle accidents ... for the injury and financial loss inflicted upon them."

The defendant, however, argues that the failure of the Legislature to increase the minimum insurance requirements indicates legislative acquiescence in this scheme to avoid liability and responsibility to the public. In the absence of a clear legislative statement, approval of a scheme having such serious consequences is not to be so lightly inferred.

....

The defendant contends that a decision holding him personally liable would discourage people from engaging in corporate enterprise.

What I would merely hold is that a participating shareholder of a corporation vested with a public interest, organized with capital insufficient to meet liabilities which are certain to arise in the ordinary course of the corporation's business, may be held personally responsible for such liabilities. Where corporate income is not sufficient to cover the cost of insurance premiums above the statutory minimum or where initially adequate finances dwindle under the pressure of competition, bad times or extraordinary and unexpected liability, obviously the shareholder will not be held liable.

The only types of corporate enterprises that will be discouraged as a result of a decision allowing the individual shareholder to be sued will be those such as the one in question, designed solely to abuse the corporate privilege at the expense of the public interest.

For these reasons I would vote to affirm the order of the Appellate Division.[3]

A. FACTORS

While there is no universal consensus about what is determinative in "piercing the corporate veil" cases, courts have identified a number of factors that may be relevant in a specific fact pattern. As delineated in *Laya v. Erin Homes, Inc.*,[4] they include:

(1) commingling of funds and other assets of the corporation with those of the individual shareholders;

(2) diversion of the corporation's funds or assets to noncorporate uses (to the personal uses of the corporation's shareholders);

(3) failure to maintain the corporate formalities necessary for the issuance of or subscription to the corporation's stock, such as formal approval of the stock issued by the board of directors;

(4) an individual shareholder representing to persons outside the corporation that he or she is personally liable for the debts or other obligations of the corporation;

(5) failure to maintain corporate minutes or adequate corporate records;

(6) identical equitable ownership in two entities;

(7) identity of the directors and officers of two entities who are responsible for supervision and management (a partnership or sole proprietorship and a corporation owned and managed by the same parties);

(8) failure to adequately capitalize a corporation for the reasonable risks of the corporate undertaking;

(9) absence of separately held corporate assets;

(10) use of a corporation as a mere shell or conduit to operate a single venture or some particular aspect of the business of an individual or another corporation;

---

[3] [Editor's note: On remand, the plaintiffs were able to amend their complaint to adequately allege that the defendant conducted the business in his individual capacity. *Walkovszky v. Carlton*, 287 N.Y.S.2d 546 (N.Y. App. Div. 1968), *aff'd*, 244 N.E.2d 55 (N.Y. 1968).]

[4] 352 S.E.2d 93, 98-99 (W. Va. 1986.).

(11) sole ownership of all the stock by one individual or members of a single family;

(12) use of the same office or business location by the corporation and its individual shareholder(s);

(13) employment of the same employees or attorney by the corporation and its shareholder(s);

(14) concealment or misrepresentation of the identity of the ownership, management or financial interests in the corporation, and concealment of personal business activities of the shareholders (sole shareholders do not reveal the association with a corporation, which makes loans to them without adequate security);

(15) disregard of legal formalities and failure to maintain proper arm's length relationships among related entities;

(16) use of a corporate entity as a conduit to procure labor, services or merchandise for another person or entity;

(17) diversion of corporate assets from the corporation by or to a stockholder or other person or entity to the detriment of creditors, or the manipulation of assets and liabilities between entities to concentrate the assets in one and the liabilities in another;

(18) contracting by the corporation with another person with the intent to avoid the risk of nonperformance by use of the corporate entity; or the use of a corporation as a subterfuge for illegal transactions;

(19) the formation and use of the corporation to assume the existing liabilities of another person or entity.

As illustrated in the lead cases, justices differ on how flexible the corporate form should be and, consequently, may apply the above factors differently. In both *Baatz* and *Walkovsky*, the majority and dissenting justices were presented with the same facts, but reached opposing conclusions about the appropriateness of the shareholders' conduct. Do you find the majority opinion or dissenting opinion in each case more compelling?

B. EMPIRICAL STUDY

In a review of 1,583 cases decided before 1985, Professor Thompson analyzed the factors that affected the outcomes of piercing the corporate veil cases.[5] Among a number of interesting findings, he noted that courts pierced the corporate veil in about 40% of the cases. While there were a few cases involving publicly held corporations, the corporate veil was not pierced in any of them. The doctrine's application apparently is limited to closely held corporations and corporate groups (parent and subsidiary relationships or sibling corporations). In

---

[5] Robert B. Thompson, *Piercing the Corporate Veil: An Empirical Study*, 76 CORNELL L. REV. 1036, 1047, 1054-55 (1991).

addition, the number of individual shareholders seemed to make a difference: close corporations with one shareholder were pierced in almost 50% of the cases, followed by about 46% in two or three shareholder corporations, and about 35% in corporations with more than three shareholders.

C. TORT CLAIMANT

Both *Baatz* and *Walkovsky* involved situations where the corporation's obligations resulted from a tort claim. In contrast to a contract claimant who has deliberately entered into a relationship with the corporation, the typical tort claimant has involuntarily become the corporation's creditor. Thus, one might expect courts to be more sympathetic towards the plaintiffs in tort cases in their attempts to hold the shareholders personally liable.

There is evidence to the contrary. In his survey, Professor Thompson found that courts were less inclined to pierce the veil in tort cases (30.97%), than in contract cases (41.98%).[6] This was true although more than two-thirds of the tort cases involved corporate defendants. "This combination of a corporate deep pocket and a nonvoluntary claimant suggests that the plaintiff would have a greater chance of success." The study results, however, concluded otherwise.

SECTION III. CONTRACT-BASED CLAIMS AND OTHER CONSIDERATIONS

The following case continues our exploration of the piercing the corporate veil doctrine, adopting an analytical framework found in a number of other recent cases. It organizes its analysis under two prongs: (1) Were the identities of the shareholder and the corporation so inseparable that their separate legal existences should cease? (2) Would some inequitable result occur unless the corporation's veil is pierced? The case also provides the backdrop for a discussion of these factors: undercapitalization, corporate formalities, the contract claimant, intra-enterprise liability, and equity and fraud.

SEA-LAND SERVICES, INC. v. PEPPER SOURCE

United States Court of Appeals, Seventh Circuit
941 F.2d 519 (1991)

BAUER, CHIEF JUDGE:

This spicy case finds its origin in several shipments of Jamaican sweet peppers. Appellee Sea-Land Services, Inc. ("Sea-Land"), an ocean carrier, shipped the peppers on behalf of The Pepper Source ("PS"), one of the appellants here. PS then stiffed Sea-Land on the freight bill, which was rather substantial. Sea-Land filed a federal diversity action for the money it was owed. On December 2, 1987,

---

[6] *Id.* at 1058, 1068-70.

the district court entered a default judgment in favor of Sea-Land and against PS in the amount of $ 86,767.70. But PS was nowhere to be found; it had been "dissolved" in mid-1987 for failure to pay the annual state franchise tax. Worse yet for Sea-Land, even had it not been dissolved, PS apparently had no assets. With the well empty, Sea-Land could not recover its judgment against PS. Hence the instant lawsuit.

In June 1988, Sea-Land brought this action against Gerald J. Marchese and five business entities he owns: PS, Caribe Crown, Inc., Jamar Corp., Salescaster Distributors, Inc., and Marchese Fegan Associates. Marchese also was named individually. Sea-Land sought by this suit to pierce PS's corporate veil and render Marchese personally liable for the judgment owed to Sea-Land, and then "reverse pierce" Marchese's other corporations so that they, too, would be on the hook for the $ 87,000. Thus, Sea-Land alleged in its complaint that all of these corporations "are alter egos of each other and hide behind the veils of alleged separate corporate existence for the purpose of defrauding plaintiff and other creditors." Not only are the corporations alter egos of each other, alleged Sea-Land, but also they are alter egos of Marchese, who should be held individually liable for the judgment because he created and manipulated these corporations and their assets for his own personal uses. (Hot on the heels of the filing of Sea-Land's complaint, PS took the necessary steps to be reinstated as a corporation in Illinois.)

In early 1989, Sea-Land filed an amended complaint adding Tie-Net International, Inc., as a defendant. Unlike the other corporate defendants, Tie-Net is not owned solely by Marchese: he holds half of the stock, and an individual named George Andre owns the other half. Sea-Land alleged that, despite this shared ownership, Tie-Net is but another alter ego of Marchese and the other corporate defendants, and thus it also should be held liable for the judgment against PS.

... In December 1989, Sea-Land moved for summary judgment....

In an order dated June 22, 1990, the court granted Sea-Land's motion. The court discussed and applied the test for corporate veil-piercing explicated in *Van Dorn Co. v. Future Chemical & Oil Corp.*, 753 F.2d 565 (7th Cir. 1985). Analyzing Illinois law, we held in *Van Dorn* that

> a corporate entity will be disregarded and the veil of limited liability pierced when two requirements are met:
>
> [F]irst, there must be such unity of interest and ownership that the separate personalities of the corporation and the individual [or other corporation] no longer exist; and second, circumstances must be such that adherence to the fiction of separate corporate existence would sanction a fraud or promote injustice.

... As for determining whether a corporation is so controlled by another to justify disregarding their separate identities, the Illinois cases, as we summarized them in *Van Dorn*, focus on four factors: "(1) the failure to maintain adequate corporate records or to comply with corporate formalities, (2) the commingling of funds or assets, (3) undercapitalization, and (4) one corporation treating the assets of another corporation as its own." 753 F.2d at 570.

Following the lead of the parties, the district court in the instant case laid the template of *Van Dorn* over the facts of this case. The court concluded that both halves and all features of the test had been satisfied, and, therefore, entered judgment in favor of Sea-Land and against PS, Caribe Crown, Jamar, Salescaster, Tie-Net, and Marchese individually. These defendants were held jointly liable for Sea-Land's $ 87,000 judgment, as well as for post-judgment interest under Illinois law. From that judgment Marchese and the other defendants brought a timely appeal.

. . . .

The first and most striking feature that emerges from our examination of the record is that these corporate defendants are, indeed, little but Marchese's playthings. Marchese is the sole shareholder of PS, Caribe Crown, Jamar, and Salescaster. He is one of the two shareholders of Tie-Net. Except for Tie-Net, none of the corporations ever held a single corporate meeting. (At the handful of Tie-Net meetings held by Marchese and Andre, no minutes were taken.) During his deposition, Marchese did not remember any of these corporations ever passing articles of incorporation, bylaws, or other agreements. As for physical facilities, Marchese runs all of these corporations (including Tie-Net) out of the same, single office, with the same phone line, the same expense accounts, and the like. And how he does "run" the expense accounts! When he fancies to, Marchese "borrows" substantial sums of money from these corporations — interest free, of course. The corporations also "borrow" money from each other when need be, which left at least PS completely out of capital when the Sea-Land bills came due. What's more, Marchese has used the bank accounts of these corporations to pay all kinds of personal expenses, including alimony and child support payments to his ex-wife, education expenses for his children, maintenance of his personal automobiles, health care for his pet — the list goes on and on. Marchese did not even have a personal bank account! (With "corporate" accounts like these, who needs one?)

And Tie-Net is just as much a part of this as the other corporations. On appeal, Marchese makes much of the fact that he shares ownership of Tie-Net, and that Sea-Land has not been able to find an example of funds flowing from PS to Tie-Net to the detriment of Sea-Land and PS's other creditors. So what? The record reveals that, in all material senses, Marchese treated Tie-Net like his other corporations: he "borrowed" over $ 30,000 from Tie-Net; money and "loans" flowed freely between Tie-Net and the other corporations; and Marchese charged up various personal expenses (including $ 460 for a picture of himself with

President Bush) on Tie-Net's credit card. Marchese was not deterred by the fact that he did not hold all of the stock of Tie-Net; why should his creditors be?[7]

In sum, we agree with the district court that [there] can be no doubt that the "shared control/unity of interest and ownership" part of the *Van Dorn* test is met in this case: corporate records and formalities have not been maintained; funds and assets have been commingled with abandon; PS, the offending corporation, and perhaps others have been undercapitalized; and corporate assets have been moved and tapped and "borrowed" without regard to their source. Indeed, Marchese basically punted this part of the inquiry before the district court by coming forward with little or no evidence in response to Sea-Land's extensively supported argument on these points. That fact alone was enough to do him in; opponents to summary judgment motions cannot simply rest on their laurels, but must come forward with specific facts showing that there is a genuine issue for trial. Regarding the elements that make up the first half of the *Van Dorn* test, Marchese and the other defendants have not done so. Thus, Sea-Land is entitled to judgment on these points.

The second part of the *Van Dorn* test is more problematic, however. "Unity of interest and ownership" is not enough; Sea-Land also must show that honoring the separate corporate existences of the defendants "would sanction a fraud or promote injustice." *Van Dorn*, 753 F.2d at 570. This last phrase truly is disjunctive:

> Although an intent to defraud creditors would surely play a part if established, the Illinois test does not require proof of such intent. Once the first element of the test is established, *either* the sanctioning of a fraud (intentional wrongdoing) or the promotion of injustice, will satisfy the second element.

Id. (emphasis in original). Seizing on this, Sea-Land has abandoned the language in its two complaints that make repeated references to "fraud" by Marchese, and has chosen not to attempt to *prove* that PS and Marchese intended to defraud it — which would be quite difficult on summary judgment. Instead, Sea-Land has argued that honoring the defendants' separate identities would "promote injustice."

But what, exactly, does "promote injustice" mean, and how does one establish it on summary judgment? These are the critical, troublesome questions in this case. To start with, as the above passage from *Van Dorn* makes clear, "promote

---

[7] We note that the record evidence in this case, if true, establishes that for years Marchese flagrantly has disregarded the tax code concerning the treatment of corporate funds. Yet, when we inquired at oral argument whether Marchese currently is under investigation by the IRS, his counsel informed us that to his knowledge he is not. Marchese also stated in his deposition that he never has been audited by the IRS. If these statements are true, and the IRS has so far shown absolutely no interest in Marchese's financial shenanigans with his "corporations," how and why that has occurred may be the biggest puzzles in this litigation.

injustice" means something less than an affirmative showing of fraud — but how much less? In its one-sentence treatment of this point, the district court held that it was enough that "Sea-Land would be denied a judicially-imposed recovery." Sea-Land defends this reasoning on appeal, arguing that "permitting the appellants to hide behind the shield of limited liability would clearly serve as an injustice against appellee" because it would "impermissibly deny appellee satisfaction." But that cannot be what is meant by "promote injustice." The prospect of an unsatisfied judgment looms in every veil-piercing action; why else would a plaintiff bring such an action? Thus, if an unsatisfied judgment is enough for the "promote injustice" feature of the test, then *every* plaintiff will pass on that score, and *Van Dorn* collapses into a one-step "unity of interest and ownership" test.

....

Federal district courts sitting in Illinois also have on occasion discussed what kind of "injustice" suffices under the second half of the *Van Dorn* test. *In re Conticommodity Services, Inc., Securities Litigation*, 733 F. Supp. 1555 (N.D. Ill. 1990), involved a complex, multidistrict litigation that ultimately had little to do with veil-piercing. At one point in its opinion, however, the district court considered whether a trial was necessary on the claim that a parent corporation should be pierced to satisfy a liability of one of its subsidiaries. The court concluded that the issue should go to trial, because "it may be an injustice" to allow the parent to avoid the sub's liabilities when the parent closed down the sub and left it with insufficient funds to satisfy its liabilities, and those liabilities were caused in part by a practice of the sub mandated by the parent. *Id.* at 1565. In *Boatmen's Nat'l Bank of St. Louis v. Smith*, 706 F. Supp. 30 (N.D. Ill. 1989), the court granted a judgment creditor's request to "reverse pierce" the veil of a corporation whose sole shareholder, director, and president was liable for the judgment....

Finally, *Van Dorn* itself is somewhat instructive. In that case, we affirmed the district court's decision to pierce the corporate veil of one corporation ("Future") to get at the assets held by another ("Sovereign of Illinois") for the benefit of a creditor who had shipped Future some packing cans ("Milton"). As to the second half of the test, we stated as follows:

> Eventually Future was stripped of its assets and rendered insolvent to the prejudice of Milton, its only creditor, while Sovereign of Illinois received the benefits of the Milton can shipments. The record supported the trial court's finding that such a result was unjust and warranted piercing the corporate veil between Future and Sovereign of Illinois to hold Sovereign of Illinois liable for the price of the cans.

753 F.2d at 572-73. Further, it is clear from various other passages in the opinion that the district court concluded, and the evidence showed, that Roth, the individual who controlled both Future and Sovereign of Illinois, intentionally manipulated the corporations so that Future assumed the liabilities but held no

assets, while other corporations received the assets but not the liabilities. *See, e.g., id.* at 569.

Generalizing from these cases, we see that the courts that properly have pierced corporate veils to avoid "promoting injustice" have found that, unless it did so, some "wrong" beyond a creditor's inability to collect would result: the common sense rules of adverse possession would be undermined; former partners would be permitted to skirt the legal rules concerning monetary obligations; a party would be unjustly enriched; a parent corporation that caused a sub's liabilities and its inability to pay for them would escape those liabilities; or an intentional scheme to squirrel assets into a liability-free corporation while heaping liabilities upon an asset-free corporation would be successful. Sea-Land, although it alleged in its complaint the kind of intentional asset-and liability-shifting found in *Van Dorn*, has yet to come forward with evidence akin to the "wrongs" found in these cases. Apparently, it believed, as did the district court, that its unsatisfied judgment was enough. That belief was in error, and the entry of summary judgment premature. We, therefore, reverse the judgment and remand the case to the district court.

On remand, the court should require that Sea-Land produce, if it desires summary judgment, evidence and argument that would establish the kind of additional "wrong" present in the above cases. For example, perhaps Sea-Land could establish that Marchese, like Roth in *Van Dorn*, used these corporate facades to avoid its responsibilities to creditors; or that PS, Marchese, or one of the other corporations will be "unjustly enriched" unless liability is shared by all. Of course, Sea-Land is not required fully to prove intent to defraud, which it probably could not do on summary judgment anyway. But it is required to show the kind of injustice to merit the evocation of the court's essentially equitable power to prevent "injustice." It may well be that, after more of such evidence is adduced, no genuine issue of fact exists to prevent Sea-Land from reaching Marchese's other pet corporations for PS's debt. Or it may be that only a finder of fact will be able to determine whether fraud or "injustice" is involved here. In any event, the record as it currently stands is insufficient to uphold the entry of summary judgment.

Reversed and Remanded with instructions.

A. UNDERCAPITALIZATION

Kinney Shoe Corp. v. Polan[8] and *Radaszewski v. Telecom Corp.*[9] followed an analytical framework comparable to the court in *Sea-Land*. In *Kinney*, the plaintiff Kinney Shoe Corporation argued that Lincoln Polan should have been held personally liable for the sublease obligation of his wholly-owned corporation. In *Radaszewski*, the plaintiff Konrad Radaszewski was an injured motorcyclist

---

[8] 939 F.2d 209 (4th Cir. 1991).
[9] 981 F.2d 305 (8th Cir. 1992).

who wanted to reach the assets of Telecom, which was the parent corporation of Contrux, the company whose employee injured Radaszewski.

In determining whether the two prongs of inseparable identities and equity were satisfied, both cases emphasized the role of undercapitalization. As explained in *Radaszewski*:[10]

> Undercapitalizing a subsidiary, which we take to mean creating it and putting it in business without a reasonably sufficient supply of money, has become a sort of proxy under Missouri law for the second [prong]. On the prior appeal, for example, we said that "Missouri courts will disregard the existence of a corporate entity that is operated while undercapitalized." ... The reason, we think, is not because undercapitalization, in and of itself, is unlawful (though it may be for some purposes), but rather because the creation of an undercapitalized subsidiary justifies an inference that the parent is either deliberately or recklessly creating a business that will not be able to pay its bills or satisfy judgments against it....

How would you determine what amount is necessary to meet the anticipated financial needs of the corporation, given the type, nature, and size of its business? At what point in time should the corporation be adequately capitalized? Should it be at the time of the initial incorporation, throughout the corporation's business history, or at the time when the corporation incurred the obligation at issue in the case? In *Consumer's Coop. of Walworth County v. Olsen*,[11] for example, the court concluded that the critical time was when the corporation was initially formed.

In *Radaszewski*,[12] the court distinguished between undercapitalization in the "accounting sense" and "financial responsibility."

> Here, the District Court held, and we assume, that Contrux was undercapitalized in the accounting sense. Most of the money contributed to its operation by Telecom was in the form of loans, not equity, and, when Contrux first went into business, Telecom did not pay for all of the stock that was issued to it. This is a classic instance of watered stock, of putting a corporation into business without sufficient equity investment. Telecom in effect concedes that Contrux's balance sheet was anemic, and that, from the point of view of generally accepted accounting principles, Contrux was inadequately capitalized. Telecom says, however, that this doesn't matter, because Contrux had $ 11,000,000 worth of liability insurance available to pay judgments like the one that Radaszewski hopes to obtain. No one can say, therefore, the argument runs, that Telecom was improperly motivated

---

[10] 981 F.2d 305 at 308.

[11] 419 N.W.2d 211, 218-19 (Wis. 1988).

[12] 981 F.2d 305 at 308-09.

in setting up Contrux, in the sense of either knowingly or recklessly establishing it without the ability to pay tort judgments.

... Unhappily, Contrux's insurance carrier became insolvent two years after the accident and is now in receivership.... But this insurance, Telecom points out, was sufficient to satisfy federal financial-responsibility requirements.... Contrux, at all times during its operations, was considered financially responsible by the relevant federal agency, the Interstate Commerce Commission.

Even if the corporation is clearly undercapitalized, is that a sufficient condition for piercing the corporate veil? In *Harris v. Curtis*, [87 Cal. Rptr. 614 (Cal. Ct. App. 1970)], a corporation organized for the purpose of owning and operating motels was underfinanced. The court, noting that being underfinanced was a "condition not uncommon among new small business," held that inadequate capitalization was a factor, but not determinative.

B. CORPORATE FORMALITIES

In addition to undercapitalization, *Kinney*[13] also emphasized corporate formalities. Citing from *Laya*, the court stated that ... "'[i]ndividuals who wish to enjoy limited personal liability for business activities under a corporate umbrella should be expected to adhere to the relatively simple formalities of creating and maintaining a corporate entity.'"[14] This, the court stated, is "'a relatively small price to pay for limited liability.'"

In *Kinney*, the corporation apparently had not followed corporate formalities. What kinds of formalities could the corporation have followed? "While a complete catalogue of dangerous acts is probably impossible to prepare, there appears to be a substantial risk that the separate corporate existence will be ignored when business is commenced without issuance of shares, when shareholders' meetings or directors' meetings are not held, or consents are not signed, when decisions are made by shareholders as if they were partners, when the shareholders do not sharply distinguish between corporate property and personal property, when corporate funds are used to pay personal expenses, when personal funds are used for corporate expenses without proper accounting, or when complete corporate and financial records are not maintained."[15]

Professor Thompson's study,[16] also discussed the effects of undercapitalization and corporate formalities. He found that (1) undercapitalization was present in about 19% of the contract cases and in just under 13% of the tort cases in which

---

[13] 939 F.2d 305, at 212.

[14] *Laya v. Erin Homes, Inc.*, 352 S.E.2d 93, 100 n.6 (W. Va. 1986) (*quoting Labadie Coal Co. v. Black*, 672 F.2d 92, 96-97 (D.C. Cir. 1982)).

[15] Robert W. Hamilton, *The Corporate Entity*, 49 TEX. L. REV. 979, 990 (1971).

[16] Robert B. Thompson, *Piercing the Corporate Veil: An Empirical Study*, 76 CORNELL L. REV. 1036, 1063 (1991).

the courts pierced the veil; and (2) the lack of corporate formalities was found in 20% of the contract cases and about 11% of the tort cases in which the courts pierced the veil. On the other hand, if the courts do find undercapitalization, the courts pierced the corporate veil over 73% of the time. Similarly, the absence of formalities led to piercing in about 67% of the cases.

C. CONTRACT CLAIMANT

In contrast to the tort claimant who involuntary becomes a corporate "creditor," the contract claimant has deliberately entered into a relationship with the corporation. The court in *Kinney* considered whether the Kinney Shoe Company, as a contract claimant, had assumed the risk of the corporation's insolvency.[17]

> In *Laya*, the court also noted that when determining whether to pierce a corporate veil a third prong may apply in certain cases. The court stated:

> When, under the circumstances, it would be reasonable for that particular type of a party [those contract creditors capable of protecting themselves] entering into a contract with the corporation, for example, a bank or other lending institution, to conduct an investigation of the credit of the corporation prior to entering into the contract, such party will be charged with the knowledge that a reasonable credit investigation would disclose. If such an investigation would disclose that the corporation is grossly undercapitalized, based upon the nature and the magnitude of the corporate undertaking, such party will be deemed to have assumed the risk of the gross undercapitalization and will not be permitted to pierce the corporate veil.

The court in *Kinney* declined to apply an assumption of the risk argument to the Kinney Co., questioning whether the contract distinction should be extended beyond the context of the financial institution lender. In contrast, the court in *Brunswick Corp. v. Waxman*,[18] was persuaded that the seller of bowling alley equipment was a knowledgeable bargainer who assumed the risk of selling to a "dummy" corporation.

What if the party entering an agreement with the corporation could have, but did not, investigate the corporation's financial condition? What if further inquiries or financial assurances from the corporation are inconsistent with the business customs of the industry or unrealistic given the lack of bargaining power of the contracting party?

D. INTRA-ENTERPRISE LIABILITY

In *Sea-Land*, the plaintiff was trying to pierce Pepper Source's corporate veil to reach both the corporation's sibling enterprises, sometimes called intra-

---

[17] *Kinney*, 939 F.2d 305, 212. (*citing Laya*, 352 S.E.2d at 100).
[18] 459 F. Supp. 1222 (E.D.N.Y. 1978), *aff'd*, 599 F.2d 34, 36 (2d Cir. 1979).

enterprise liability, and the individual who owns all the enterprises. Should the courts distinguish between attempts to reach enterprises, such as parent corporations or sibling corporations, and attempts to hold "living, breathing" individuals liable?

Thompson's study[19] found that a significant percentage of piercing the corporate veil cases involve corporate defendants (parents, subsidiaries, siblings). One might reasonably predict that courts would be more willing to hold corporate shareholders liable than individual shareholders. Thompson found, however, that when plaintiffs target individual shareholders, the courts pierced the veil in 43.13% of the cases; when plaintiffs target corporate defendants, courts pierced the veil in 37.21% of the cases. How would you explain this unexpected result?

When a plaintiff tries to reach the assets of a member of the corporate group who is not a shareholder of the original corporation, isn't this a more dramatic extension of the piercing the corporate veil doctrine? The sibling corporation is not the one who injured the plaintiff and also is not the owner of the corporation which has the obligation. Under what circumstances should a member of the corporate group assume this derivative liability? Should the plaintiff be required to pierce the veil to reach the common shareholder before liability can be imposed on other members of the corporate group? Should there be particular links between the original corporation and each sibling that is held liable?

E. EQUITY AND FRAUD

As in *Sea-Land*, many courts note an equity prong in their analysis. Some courts, however, do not dwell on it. They presumably reason that satisfying the first prong (requiring proof of inseparable identities) or the plaintiff's proof of an unsatisfied corporate obligation is sufficient evidence of wrongdoing, injustice, misrepresentation, or "constructive" fraud. The court in *Sea-Land* also acknowledged the difficulty of interpreting the appropriate equitable principles. Professor Thompson's study[20] found that courts which observed misrepresentation pierced the veil in approximately 94% of the cases.

Jurisdictions also differ on whether they require *fraud*. In *DeWitt Truck Brokers v. W. Ray Flemming Fruit Co.*,[21] for instance, the court concluded:

> Contrary to the basic contention of the defendant, however, proof of plain fraud is not a necessary element in a finding to disregard the corporate entity. This was made clear in *Anderson v. Abbott*, 321 U.S. 349, 362 (1944), where the Court, after stating that "fraud" has often been found to be a ground for disregarding the principle of limited liability based on the corporate fiction, declared:

---

[19] *Supra* at 1055-56.
[20] *Supra* at 1063.
[21] 540 F.2d 681, 684 (4th Cir. 1976).

" ... The cases of fraud make up part of that exception (which allow the corporate veil to be pierced, citing cases). *But they do not exhaust it....*

Texas also has chosen to emphasize fraud in its piercing the corporate veil jurisprudence. In *Castleberry v. Branscum*,[22] the Texas Supreme Court held that a jury could hold shareholders personally liable if plaintiffs could prove "a sham to perpetrate a fraud," which would involve a "flexible fact-specific approach focusing on equity." Either "actual fraud" — defined as "dishonesty of purpose or intent to deceive" — or "constructive fraud" — defined as the "breach of some legal or equitable duty which, irrespective of moral guilt, the law declares fraudulent because of its tendency to deceive others, to violate confidence, or to injure public interest."[23] In addition, the Court rejected the distinction between contract cases, where the parties negotiated the terms of their relationship, and tort cases, where the plaintiffs typically become the corporation's creditors involuntarily.

Concerned that *Castleberry*'s abstract articulation of the piercing the corporate veil doctrine excessively threatened the corporate form, Texas legislators in 1989 enacted Tex. Bus. & Com. Code Ann. § 2.21:

> A. A holder of shares, an owner of any beneficial interest in shares, or a subscriber for shares whose subscription has been accepted shall be under no obligation to the corporation or to its obligees with respect to:
>
> ....
>
> (2) any contractual obligation of the corporation on the basis that the holder, owner, or subscriber is or was the alter ego of the corporation, or on the basis of actual fraud or constructive fraud, a sham to perpetrate a fraud, or other similar theory, unless the obligee demonstrates that the holder, owner, or subscriber caused the corporation to be used for the purpose of perpetrating and did perpetrate an actual fraud on the obligee primarily for the direct personal benefit of the holder, owner, or subscriber; or
>
> (3) any contractual obligation of the corporation on the basis of the failure of the corporation to observe any corporate formality, including without limitation: (a) the failure to comply with any requirement of this Act or of the articles of incorporation or bylaws of the corporation; or (b) the failure to observe any requirement prescribed by this Act or by the articles of incorporation or bylaws for acts to be taken by the corporation, its board of directors, or its shareholders.

If *Castleberry* interpreted piercing the corporate veil doctrine too expansively, does this statute define the scope too narrowly? Which would be the applicable

---

[22]721 S.W.2d 270, 273 (Tex. 1986).
[23]*Id.* (*citing Archer v. Griffith*, 390 S.W.2d 735, 740 (Tex. 1964)).

law, *Castleberry* or the statute, if the corporation's obligation arose from a tort claim?

F. CHOICE OF LAW

As illustrated by Texas law, state laws may vary in their approach to piercing the corporate veil. In Thompson's study[24] certain states such as California were more inclined, and other states such as Pennsylvania and New York were less inclined, to pierce the corporate veil.

How is the applicable state law determined? If the "internal affairs rule" applies, then the law of the state of incorporation is used. However, it is unclear if piercing the veil cases are "internal affairs." They typically deal with claims of a third-party creditor, although the issue of shareholder liability for a corporate obligation certainly involves the shareholder and corporate relationship. If piercing cases are not considered internal affairs, then the courts would have to choose which conflict of law principle would apply. In tort cases, for instance, the traditional choice-of-law rule is to apply the law of the state in which the tort occurred.

The Texas legislature, apparently anticipating these kinds of conflict of law disputes, expressly provides that its piercing the corporate veil principles would not be applicable to corporations incorporated outside of Texas.[25]

SECTION IV. STATUTORY CLAIMS

In addition to contract and tort cases, piercing the corporate veil issues are increasingly triggered in federal and state statutory cases. In tax, workers' compensation, and environmental law cases, for example, the courts are asked whether shareholders should be liable for their corporation's statutory obligations. These statutory cases tend to emphasize the statute's purpose and policy in their determination and may even supplant traditional corporate piercing principles. The following case is illustrative.

LANSFORD-COALDALE JOINT WATER AUTHORITY v. TONOLLI CORP.

United States Court of Appeals, Third Circuit
4 F.3d 1209 (1993)

BECKER, CIRCUIT JUDGE:

The plaintiff, the Lansford-Coaldale Joint Water Authority ("Authority"), provides public water in Carbon County, Pennsylvania. The Authority's groundwater production and supply wells are adjacent to a site formerly used for lead smelting that is owned by Tonolli Pennsylvania ("Tonolli PA"). After

---

[24] *Supra* at 1050-53.
[25] TEX. BUS. & COM. CODE ANN. § 8.02.

learning that there had been releases of hazardous substances on the Tonolli site and that Tonolli PA had applied for a hazardous waste disposal permit, the Authority commissioned a study to determine whether there was or would be any contamination of its wells. Based on this study, the Authority brought suit against Tonolli PA, its sister corporation, Tonolli Canada, and its parent corporation, IFIM, alleging that they were owners or operators of the Tonolli PA facility and that hazardous discharges from their property posed a threat of future contamination to the Authority's water supply. Because Tonolli PA had become bankrupt, the Authority subsequently dropped its claims against it, and the trial proceeded against only Tonolli Canada and IFIM. The Authority's suit sought to recover response costs under the Comprehensive Environmental Response, Compensation and Liability Act (CERCLA), 42 U.S.C. § 9607(a). More specifically, the Authority sought to obtain both the costs it would incur due to the threat of future contamination, *e.g.*, the costs of obtaining an alternative water supply, and the costs it would incur in monitoring and evaluation. At the conclusion of the trial, the district court made oral findings of fact and conclusions of law denying the Authority recovery on all claims. This appeal followed.

At the heart of the Authority's appeal is an attack on the district court's fact findings. First, the Authority asserts that the findings are tainted because they were made orally only a few hours after a long and complex trial and were principally drawn verbatim from Tonolli Canada's proposed findings. Second, the Authority contends that the district court's finding that the hazardous waste releases at the Tonolli site posed no threat to the Authority's water supply, which was based upon a finding of hydrogeologic separation of the Tonolli site from the Authority site, was clearly erroneous. Third, the Authority contends that, even if that finding is upheld, we should reverse the district court's failure to authorize recovery of monitoring and evaluation costs against Tonolli Canada because it was the owner or operator of the Tonolli PA facility.

We acknowledge that the district court might have made more precise findings had it taken the time to await the trial transcript and to draft a written opinion. Moreover, the findings might have been better had they not drawn so heavily on Tonolli Canada's proposed findings. But the court's oral findings offered the distinct advantage of fresh recollection and prompt justice. We therefore reject the Authority's suggestion that the court's findings are deficient because of the nature of their construction and delivery and hold that they did not violate the requirements of *Fed. R. Civ. P.* 52(a). Pursuant to that rule, we review them only for clear error.

On the most important issue to the parties, the threat posed to the Authority's water supply, the district court was faced with a "battle of the experts." It found Tonolli Canada's expert more credible than the Authority's expert and we are satisfied that the court's findings on this claim are not clearly erroneous.

However, we will vacate the district court's judgment on the monitoring and evaluation costs claim against Tonolli Canada. In reaching its conclusion that Tonolli Canada should not be deemed an operator, the district court applied the correct inquiry for determining whether Tonolli Canada was a CERCLA operator, *i.e.*, whether it actively participated in the management of the affiliated corporation during a period of hazardous waste disposal. The federal courts are divided over this issue, but we hold that this represents the correct standard. Nevertheless, due to the district court's failure to address several critical factual issues, we will vacate the judgment on this count and remand for more detailed fact findings.

Finally, the Authority contends that the district court improperly granted judgment in favor of the parent corporation, IFIM, which never filed an answer or otherwise appeared in this case. We will affirm the judgment in favor of IFIM on the Authority's claim for the costs of obtaining a new water supply and/or treating its current supply because such a result is dictated by the rule prohibiting inconsistent judgments. However, with respect to the judgment in favor of IFIM on the monitoring and evaluation costs claim, because the district court provided no explanation for its decision and we can discern no basis for it, we will vacate this portion of the judgment and remand to the district court for further consideration.

I. *Background Facts and Procedural History*

Tonolli Canada is a Canadian Corporation engaged in the business of lead smelting and metal reclamation. In the early 1970's, Tonolli Canada decided to open a smelting facility in the northeastern United States to reduce transportation costs and improve customer service. It chose a site near Nesquehoning, Carbon County, Pennsylvania. Tonolli PA was incorporated to construct and operate the facility, and Tonolli Canada was its sole shareholder from its incorporation in 1972 until 1976. In 1976, IFIM, a Dutch corporation, purchased all of the Tonolli PA stock and also became the parent corporation of Tonolli Canada. The Nesquehoning plant commenced operations in 1975. The plant site is located approximately 3,100 feet from the Authority's production wells.

....

With respect to the Authority's more substantial monetary claim — its allegation that releases at the Tonolli site have created a threat of contamination that will cause the Authority either continuously to treat its water supply or to secure a new one — the court found squarely for the defendants. Most important-ly, the district court found that the Authority had not proved that there is any threat of future contamination to the Authority's water supply. However, with respect to the Authority's claim for monitoring and evaluation costs, the court found that a release at the Tonolli site had induced the Authority to incur monitoring and evaluation expenses (*i.e.*, the costs of the AGES study). The court nonetheless denied recovery for these costs because it concluded that the Authority had not established the other necessary elements of their claim under CERCLA....

....

IV. *Monitoring and Evaluation Costs*

....

CERCLA provides that in order to establish a *prima facie* case for the recovery of monitoring and evaluation costs, a plaintiff must establish that: 1) the defendant falls into one of four categories of "covered persons," 42 U.S.C. §§ 9607(a)(1)-(4); 2) there has been a release or a threatened release of a hazardous substance from a facility, 42 U.S.C. § 9607(a)(4); 3) this release or threatened release has caused the plaintiff to incur response costs, 42 U.S.C. § 9607(a)(4); and 4) the plaintiff's response costs are necessary and consistent with the NCP, 42 U.S.C. § 9607(a)(4)(B).

....

... Most importantly, the district court concluded that Tonolli Canada did not qualify as a "covered person" under CERCLA, 48 U.S.C. § 9607(a)(1), because it was neither an "owner" nor an "operator" of Tonolli PA....

....

C. *"Owner" and "Operator" Status Under CERCLA*

1. *Background*

Although the contours of "owner" and "operator" liability under CERCLA present an issue of first impression for this court, a number of federal courts and commentators have already considered the issue. *See, e.g.*, *United States v. Kayser-Roth Corp.*, 910 F.2d 24 (1st Cir. 1990), *cert. denied*, 498 U.S. 1084 (1991). There is general agreement that under CERCLA, "owner" liability and "operator" liability denote two separate concepts and hence require two separate standards for determining whether they apply.

Under CERCLA, a corporation may be held liable as an owner for the actions of its subsidiary corporation in situations in which it is determined that piercing the corporate veil is warranted. Operator liability, in contrast, is generally reserved for those situations in which a parent or sister corporation is deemed, due to the specifics of its relationship with its affiliated corporation, to have had substantial control over the facility in question. Courts are divided as to whether operator liability should be predicated on the actual control one corporation has over the other, or whether the corporation's capacity or authority to control is sufficient. *Compare Kayser-Roth*, 910 F.2d at 27 (applying "active involvement" test) with *Nurad, Inc. v. William E. Hooper & Sons Co.*, 966 F.2d 837 (4th Cir. 1992) (applying "authority-to-control" test), *cert. denied*, 506 U.S. 940 (1992).

In this case, the district court considered whether Tonolli Canada should be deemed either an owner or an operator under CERCLA and concluded that neither status applied. The Authority argues that the district court applied incorrect legal standards in deciding these issues and that, in the alternative, even if the district court utilized the correct standards, its conclusions that Tonolli Canada is neither an owner nor an operator are clearly erroneous. We hold that the district court, by applying the "actual control" test, applied the correct legal standard with respect to the operator liability issue. However, because the district court's factual findings fail to address a number of key facts relevant to whether or not Tonolli Canada employees exercised control over the affairs of Tonolli PA, we will remand the case to the district court for more detailed fact findings. With respect to owner liability, we conclude that the district court applied the correct standard and properly concluded that Tonolli Canada should not be held liable as an owner. We turn first to the operator liability question because it is the more difficult issue of the two.

2. Operator Liability Under CERCLA

Although congressional intent may be particularly difficult to discern with precision in CERCLA, a statute notorious for its lack of clarity and poor draftsmanship, it is at least clear that Congress has expanded the circumstances under which a corporation may be held liable for the acts of an affiliated corporation such that, when a corporation is determined to be the operator of a subsidiary or sister corporation, traditional rules of limited liability for corporations do not apply. This expansion of liability is consistent with CERCLA's broad remedial purposes, most importantly its "essential purpose" of making "those responsible for problems caused by the disposal of chemical poisons bear the costs and responsibility for remedying the harmful conditions they created." *John S. Boyd Co.*, 992 F.2d at 405 (*citing Dedham Water Co. v. Cumberland Farms Dairy, Inc.*, 805 F.2d 1074, 1081 (1st Cir. 1986)).

Courts have fashioned two competing standards for the imposition of operator liability: what we term the "actual control" test and the "authority-to-control" test. Under the actual control standard, a corporation will only be held liable for the environmental violations of another corporation when there is evidence of substantial control exercised by one corporation over the activities of the other. In contrast, under the authority-to-control test, operator liability is imposed as long as one corporation had the capability to control, even if it was never utilized.

We reject the Authority's contention that the authority-to-control standard should govern. We believe that test sweeps too broadly and we thus adopt the actual control standard, which appears to strike the appropriate middle ground, balancing the benefits of limited liability with CERCLA's remedial purposes. Under the actual control standard, while the longstanding rule of limited liability in the corporate context remains the background norm, a corporation cannot hide behind the corporate form to escape liability in those instances in which it played an active role in the management of a corporation responsible for environmental wrongdoing. In contrast, we believe that a rule which imposes liability on a corporation which never exercised its general authority over its subsidiary or sister corporation may unduly penalize the corporation for a decision by that corporation to benefit from one of the well-recognized and salutary purposes of the corporate form: specialization of management.

We follow the test adumbrated in *Kayser-Roth, supra*, and *CPC Int'l, Inc. v. Aerojet-General Corp.*, 777 F. Supp. 549 (W.D. Mich. 1991). As the *Kayser-Roth* court explained, "[t]o be an operator requires more than merely complete ownership and the concomitant general authority or ability to control that comes with ownership. At a minimum, it requires active involvement in the activities of the subsidiary." 910 F.2d at 27. Whereas a corporation's "mere oversight" of the subsidiary or sister corporation's business in a "manner appropriate and consistent with the investment relationship" does not ordinarily result in operator liability, a corporation's "actual participation and control" over the other corporations's decision-making does. *CPC Int'l*, 777 F. Supp. at 573.

The determination whether a corporation has exerted sufficient control to warrant imposition of operator liability requires an inherently fact-intensive inquiry, involving consideration of the totality of the circumstances presented. The factors courts should consider focus on the extent of the corporation's involvement in the other corporation's day-to-day operations and its policy-making decisions.[26] We understand the actual control standard to hold accountable for environmental violations those corporations which are not mere investors in other corporations, but instead have actively and substantially participated in the corporation's management.

In addition, because the essential focus of the actual control test is the control of one corporation over another, not only may a parent corporation be deemed the operator of its subsidiary, but a corporation may also be considered the operator of its sister corporation. In other words, the test is concerned with control rather than ownership and there is no reason not to hold a corporation liable when it exercises substantial management control over an affiliated corporation.

3. Should Tonolli Canada Be Deemed An Operator?

In view of the foregoing discussion, we reject the Authority's claim that the district court applied the wrong legal standard regarding operator liability, since it expressly applied the actual control test and manifested a correct understanding of it. We therefore review its application of that standard to the facts here for clear error only. Although much of the evidence supports the district court's conclusion that Tonolli Canada should not be deemed the operator of Tonolli PA, the court's findings fail to address a number of key factual issues concerning the role of several Tonolli Canada officers in the management of Tonolli PA. The dearth of findings on these issues leaves us with important unanswered questions

---

[26] We agree with the *Kayser-Roth* court that evidence of control over a sister or subsidiary corporation's environmental decisions is "indicative of the type of control necessary to hold a ... corporation liable as an operator." 910 F.2d at 27 n. 8. However, operator liability may be established even without evidence that a corporation controlled the environmental decisions of an affiliated corporation as long as there exist other factors which sufficiently demonstrate pervasive control. See *id.*

such that we cannot affirm the conclusion that Tonolli Canada was not an operator of Tonolli PA without further findings. Hence we will remand to the district court for additional proceedings.

The following basic facts were adduced at trial. From 1972 until 1976, Tonolli Canada was the parent and sole shareholder of Tonolli PA. In 1976, Tonolli Canada divested its Tonolli PA stock, selling it for value to IFIM, a company which also became the parent corporation to Tonolli Canada. Tonolli PA did not begin operations until September, 1975, which was only shortly before it was sold to IFIM. After Tonolli Canada sold its Tonolli PA stock, Tonolli PA and Tonolli Canada shared the same president, Elvio Del Sorbo, and the same chief financial officer, Vincent Bailini. From 1984 to 1985, the American Bank & Trust Company of Pennsylvania, a creditor of Tonolli PA, exercised strict, if not total, control over Tonolli PA's operations.

In support of its conclusion that the two corporations were largely self-supporting and self-sufficient entities during the period that Tonolli PA was operational, the district court made a number of subsidiary findings about the relationship between the two companies which support this conclusion and are supported by the record. For example, although Tonolli Canada had guaranteed Tonolli PA's financial liabilities when it was the latter's parent corporation, Tonolli Canada conditioned its sale of Tonolli PA stock to IFIM on the cancellation of these guarantees. The district court also found that to the extent that Tonolli Canada had advanced money to Tonolli PA during its start-up period, these advances were all repaid by Tonolli PA shortly after it began operations in 1976. It was also established that each corporation's lead smelting process was fully operational without support from the other. In addition, each corporation owned its own equipment and procured its own supplies and raw materials. Similarly, each corporation had its own customers, sales staff, legal staff, and engineering consultants.

The district court found that the two companies were kept separate in numerous other respects: they maintained separate corporate minutes; they kept their funds and assets separate; the two companies were separately audited, producing independent financial statements. Each company paid its own bills and conversely neither accepted payment for the other's products and services provided to third parties. There was no overlap among any non-officer employees, and all facets of the companies' personnel policies were separate. All of these findings are supported by the record.

The district court also found that all financial transactions between the two companies were conducted on an arm's-length basis, including, most importantly, the annual management contracts between the two companies. The Authority has argued that the management contracts are actually strong evidence of the operational and financial unity of the two companies. However, the trial testimony established that these annual contracts — in which Tonolli PA paid Tonolli Canada for services it received — were primarily to compensate Tonolli Canada for basic services it provided during the course of a year, i.e., bookkeeping work and computer consulting. There is no indication in the record that Tonolli PA's payments pursuant to these contracts amounted to anything but the market value of the services it received. In addition, there was no other evidence that the two operated on anything but an arm's-length basis; there was, for example, no evidence that Tonolli PA was undercapitalized or that Tonolli Canada siphoned off its assets or otherwise used Tonolli PA merely as a source of cash. The record, therefore, contains ample evidence supporting the district court's conclusion as to the separate nature of the two companies.

However, there are several potentially significant facts that the district court's findings do not address and which we find disquieting. The two companies shared common officers during the period in question: it is uncontroverted that Del Sorbo served as president and Bailini as chief financial officer of both Tonolli PA and Tonolli Canada. On one hand, the fact that the same people served as the president and chief financial officer for the two corporations is not, without more, enough to conclude that one corporation should be deemed the operator of the other. Because a corporate officer may be a figurehead, there must be evidence that the officer actually exerted control over both corporations. On the other hand, the existence of common high-level officers is troubling and raises serious questions about the independence of the two companies.

Despite the importance of this issue, the district court failed to make any specific findings about what role Bailini and Del Sorbo played in the management of Tonolli PA. This omission is particularly problematic in light of the fact that in 1984 Bailini signed Tonolli PA's consent order with the Pennsylvania Department of Environmental Regulation (D.E.R.), which raises questions about his involvement in Tonolli PA's environmental policies. It is further disquieting in light of a document prepared by Del Sorbo containing job descriptions and describing his responsibilities as president of Tonolli PA and Tonolli Canada as well as the responsibilities of several vice-presidents. This document, which stated an effective date of January, 1979, described the two corporations operating as one entity, with the officers of both corporations reporting to the shared president, Del Sorbo. According to this document, the president served in more than a symbolic capacity, exerting final decisionmaking authority over all facets of the two companies' operations and management.

Despite the substantial questions raised by this document, the district court made no mention of it in its findings. While it may be that the district court credited Bailini's testimony that this document was never put into effect, we simply do not know. Given the potential import of this document, the district court erred by failing to provide an explanation of its meaning and effect on the operator liability issue.

Although the district court failed to make findings about the respective roles of Bailini and Del Sorbo in the management of Tonolli PA, it did make several findings regarding Sergio Legati. Legati was the vice-president of manufacturing of Tonolli Canada and served as Tonolli PA's plant manager during 1975-1976 (the start-up period) and again in 1984-85. Legati testified that at other times he intermittently worked on behalf of the Tonolli facility. Regarding Legati's two stints as plant manager for the Tonolli facility, the district court found that, "[a]lthough Legati remained an employee of Tonolli Canada[,] ... his role was that of an individual employee temporarily on loan." Regarding Legati's part-time work for Tonolli PA, the district court found that Legati worked for the company only as a consultant.

Notwithstanding these findings about Legati, the district court's findings leave critical unanswered questions about Legati's role. More specifically, the district court failed to make any findings regarding Legati's role, if any, with respect to Tonolli PA's release of hazardous substances. Along with Bailini, Legati signed Tonolli PA's consent order with the D.E.R., raising questions about his role in environmental decisions at the Tonolli site. In addition, although the district court found that there were releases of hazardous substances into the soil at the Tonolli facility, it is unclear from both the record and the court's findings when the releases occurred. We thus cannot tell whether these releases occurred during the period *when* Legati served as a full-time plant manager for Tonolli PA. We similarly cannot tell whether they occurred when the American Bank had control over Tonolli PA.

In sum, although the district court made a number of subsidiary findings supporting its conclusion that Tonolli Canada did not exert sufficient control over Tonolli PA to be deemed an operator, its findings do not address a number of critical issues about the roles of several Tonolli Canada officers. We thus remand for the entry of more detailed findings on these issues.

4. Should Tonolli Canada Be Deemed An Owner?

It is well-established that under CERCLA a corporation may be held liable as the owner of another corporation when the attendant circumstances warrant piercing the corporate veil..... In addition, given the federal interest in uniformity in the application of CERCLA, it is federal common law, and not state law, which governs when corporate veil-piercing is justified under CERCLA.

The Authority argues that the district court failed to recognize that operator and owner liability are predicated on different inquiries. It submits that the court therefore did not apply a separate standard to determine whether Tonolli Canada should be held liable as an owner. We disagree. We cannot dispute that the district court's discussion of the owner liability issue is somewhat vague and that at one point it misspoke by referring to the owner liability issue when it apparently meant the operator liability issue. However, based on our reading of the district court's findings of fact and conclusions of law, we conclude that the district court did in fact recognize that separate standards govern the imposition of owner and operator liability, applied the appropriate standard to determine whether Tonolli Canada should be deemed an owner, and correctly concluded that it should not.

It is undisputed that Tonolli Canada sold all of its stock in Tonolli PA to IFIM for value in 1976, shortly after the Tonolli PA facility commenced operations.

Therefore, for the bulk of the relevant period — the period during which Tonolli PA was operational — Tonolli Canada was Tonolli PA's sister corporation and no longer its parent. While that fact is inconsequential with respect to the imposition of operator liability, it is generally relevant with respect to owner liability. Put simply, while Congress has provided little guidance in CERCLA as to the appropriate standard governing owner liability, having defined an "owner" circuitously to be any person owning a facility, 42 U.S.C. § 9601(20)(A)(ii), it is nonetheless clear that owner liability can ordinarily only attach if the defendant meets the common definition of that term and is at least a partial owner of the corporation responsible for the substantive CERCLA offenses. Thus, in contrast to operator liability, corporate ownership is generally a pre-requisite for this status to apply, and Tonolli Canada was not Tonolli PA's parent corporation for the bulk of the period in question here.

In addition, as we discussed above with respect to the operator liability issue, the record establishes that corporate formalities were adhered to, that the two corporations entered transactions on an arm's length basis, and that Tonolli PA was not undercapitalized. Thus, there is no indication that the circumstances warranted piercing the corporate veil. We will therefore uphold the district court's conclusion that owner liability should not be imposed.

A. CERCLA

In what ways did the court's reasoning and outcome in *Lansford-Coaldale* support the statutory intent and purpose of CERCLA? In what ways was the court's analysis similar to and different from the traditional piercing the corporate veil principles described in the prior cases in this chapter?

The federal circuits are divided about whether traditional piercing the corporate veil tests must be satisfied or whether independent CERCLA tests are a sufficient basis for imposing "operator" liability on parent corporations. Some courts agree with the court in *Lansford-Coaldale*, as illustrated in this statement from *Schiavone v. Pearce*:[27] "A recognition of direct operator liability for parent corporations is both compatible with the statutory language and consistent with CERCLA's broad remedial scheme."

In contrast, consider the view offered in *Joslyn Manufacturing Co. v. T.L. James & Co.*:[28]

> Significantly, CERCLA does not define "owners" or "operators" as including the parent company of offending wholly-owned subsidiaries. Nor does the legislative history indicate that Congress intended to alter so substantially a basic tenet of corporation law. "It is elementary that the

---

[27] 79 F.3d 248, 254 (2d Cir. 1996).
[28] 893 F.2d 80, 82-83 (5th Cir. 1990).

meaning of a statute must, in the first instance, be sought in the language in which the act is framed, and if it is plain ... the sole function of the courts is to enforce it according to its terms." *Caminetti v. United States*, 242 U.S. 470, 485 (1917). Joslyn asks this court to rewrite the language of the Act significantly and hold parents directly liable for their subsidiaries' activities. To do so would dramatically alter traditional concepts of corporation law. The "normal rule of statutory construction is that if Congress intends for legislation to change the interpretation of a judicially created concept, it makes that intent specific." *Midlantic Nat'l Bank v. New Jersey*, 474 U.S. 495, 501 (1986). Any bold rewriting of corporation law in this area is best left to Congress.

... Without an express Congressional directive to the contrary, common-law principles of corporation law, such as limited liability, govern our court's analysis....

Instead, the court in *Joslyn* applied a traditional piercing the corporate veil analysis, explaining that "[v]eil piercing should be limited to situations in which the corporate entity is used as a *sham* to perpetuate a fraud or to avoid personal liability."[29]

B. OTHER STATUTORY CLAIMS

Piercing the corporate veil issues are found in a range of statutory areas, including tax, labor, and workers' compensation law cases. Consider how the courts would consider each statute's policy in determining whether to hold shareholders liable for their corporation's obligations. For instance, in *National Labor Relations Board v. White Oak Coal Co.*,[30] the National Labor Relations Board clarified that "the corporate veil may be pierced when: (1) the shareholder and corporation have failed to maintain separate identities, and (2) adherence to the corporate structure would sanction a fraud, promote injustice, or lead to an evasion of legal obligations." Finding that the shareholders commingled the companies' funds, withdrew corporate funds for personal use, and misrepresented or interchanged the identities and obligations of their companies in legal documents, the NLRB held that the shareholders evaded their corporation's remedial and backpay obligations for unfair labor practices.

Interestingly, Thompson[31] found that courts were less inclined to pierce in some subject areas than in others. Consistent with the tax law principle that corporations and their shareholders are separate taxable entities, courts pierced the corporate veil in only 31% of the tax law cases. Courts also disfavor piercing

---

[29] *Id.* at 83.

[30] 81 F.3d 150 (1995).

[31] Robert B. Thompson, *Piercing the Corporate Veil: An Empirical Study*, 76 CORNELL L. REV. 1036, 1060-62 (1991).

arguments in workers' compensation cases, allowing piercing to occur in only 13% of the cases. In these workers' compensation cases, the defendant parent corporations often argue that the parent and subsidiary should be treated as one employing entity. If successful, this self-piercing would block plaintiffs' claims for workers' compensation against both entities.

Chapter 9

DIVIDENDS

Situation

Anderson and Baker, pleased with the company's continued growth and profitability, want to raise their salaries from $ 40,000 to $ 110,000 a year. Phillips agrees that salaries should be raised and that at current interest rates it makes sense to take some cash out of the business and borrow from the bank to help finance expansion. But rather than a $ 70,000 salary increase, Phillips suggests a $ 40,000 increase plus $ 90,000 total paid pro rata among the three shareholders as a dividend. After extensive discussion, Anderson and Baker have agreed with Phillips on a compromise salary-dividend package: Anderson and Baker's salaries are to be raised to $ 100,000, and $ 30,000 total is to be paid to the shareholders as a dividend. You have been asked to look after the legal details.

In a conversation with one of the officers, you are told that all of the surplus of the corporation has been transferred to stated capital. The officer said this was done to "make the balance sheet look better to the bank" and that the transfer was accomplished just prior to a recent bank loan.

SECTION I. MECHANICS OF DIVIDENDS AND DISTRIBUTIONS

Corporate lawyers apply the rules governing a corporation's distributions to its shareholders when they advise directors on the legality of paying a dividend or repurchasing shares of the company's stock. The legal rules that apply to corporate distributions are an attempt to accommodate the competing interests of a company's owners and creditors.

In order to attract and keep investors, a company must provide them with the opportunity to realize a return on their investment. Company owners realize such a return when they receive a part of the company's profits or when they sell their interest in the company and, if the interest has appreciated, capture the increased value. The two options are not, however, equally attractive. Owners want to be able to realize a return on an ongoing basis and not have to wait until they sell their interests in the company. Creditors, on the other hand, are loathe to have company earnings distributed to owners while company debts are outstanding. Such distributions decrease the assets of the company and increase the risk that the creditor will not be paid in full. This reduction of security is particularly problematic for creditors of corporations and limited liability companies; these creditors can look only to the company's assets for satisfaction of their claims. In contrast, creditors of general partnerships can have their claims satisfied from the personal assets of individual owners when company assets are insufficient to pay company liabilities. To provide creditors with some protection, corporation (and limited liability company) statutes restrict distributions of company profits to owners. The focus of this chapter is on the corporate law restrictions.

Lest you be deceived by the apparent simplicity of the preceding description of the desires of investors and creditors, consider the following:

Bayless Manning & James Hanks, Jr., Legal Capital 13-14 (3d ed. 1990)*

The investor who buys shares of stock in the incorporated enterprise and the investor who lends money to the incorporated enterprise are, as a matter of economics, engaged in the same kind of activity and are motivated by the same basic objectives. They are both making a capital investment; they both expect or hope to get their investment back in the long run, either by liquidating pay-out or by sale of the security; and they both expect and hope to receive income from their investment in the interim before their capital is returned to them in full.

In the stereotypic model transaction, the investor who chose to take a shareholder's position rather than a creditor's position in a particular transaction simply made a calculated economic judgment that was different from the creditor's. The shareholder estimated that he could make more money by relinquishing to creditor investors a "prior" claim for interest and a fixed principal payment on maturity, and, by opting for uncertain "dividends" and the residual claim to the assets of the enterprise that would remain after all creditors, with their fixed claims, had been paid off.

The shareholder is willing to admit the "priority" of the creditor's interest claim and claim for principal payment on maturity. That does *not* imply, however, that the shareholder is willing to stand by chronologically until such time as the creditors have been paid in full. The shareholder will usually insist, that if, as he hopes, the enterprise makes money (and perhaps even if it does not), the shareholders will receive some return on (or of) their investment from time to time, regardless of the fact that there are creditor claims outstanding. Such periodic payments to shareholders are characterized as "dividends"; and, in the usual and normal case of the healthy incorporated enterprise, it is assumed that some assets will be regularly distributed out from the corporate treasury to the shareholder investors in dividend form.

Simple as this observation may be, its implications are far-reaching. If it were the case that all creditors had to be paid off before *any* payment could be made to shareholder investors, and if shareholders received nothing until ultimate liquidation of the enterprise when they would divide the residuum left after payment of all creditors — if, in other words, the terms "prior" and "before" were chronological as well as hierarchical — the creditor would not have to worry about assets being drained away into the hands of junior claimants and he

---

*Reprinted with permission from Foundation Press. Copyright © 1990. All rights reserved.

would sleep better at night. But that arrangement would be wholly unacceptable to shareholders. Shareholders insist — and ultimately creditors must concede — that, *during the life* of the creditor's claim, assets may be passed out to an investing group that hierarchically ranks below the creditors. The question becomes unavoidable: How much of the assets in the treasury of the incorporated enterprise may be distributed to shareholders, when, and under what circumstances? (Emphasis in original.)

Company owners also have an interest in making sure the company maintains a sufficient asset base for the company to operate profitably and create earnings available for distribution to shareholders. Thus, so long as the company prospers, the competing claims of creditors and shareholders can be satisfied amicably without resort to legal rules. The situation changes, however, when the company begins to experience financial constraints, either because of a temporary downturn or because of a general decline. In these situations, the tensions between those with senior and junior claims become more pronounced.

Modern statutes take several approaches to the regulation of payment of dividends to shareholders and the repurchase by a corporation of shares of its own stock. The approaches described here are those found in the Delaware General Corporation Law and the Model Act.

Today's corporation statutes typically deal with dividends and distributions together, although analytically, dividends and distributions are different. In a pure sense, dividends represent a payment to the shareholders of a corporation's profits, whereas distributions are a return to the shareholders of a portion of their capital contributions. As will be seen in the discussions that follow, however, these distinctions between dividends and distributions have become blurred as corporation statutes treat distributions and dividends alike.

Not only do distributions technically differ from dividends, but different types of dividends differ from each other. It will be helpful if we first discuss dividends in cash or other property, then handle stock dividends (and stock splits, which are closely related), and finally turn to repurchase by a corporation of its own shares.

A. DIVIDENDS IN CASH OR OTHER PROPERTY

State corporate laws regulating dividends have common elements. One is that the board of directors declares dividends.[1] Another is that a dividend may not contravene a restriction on dividends contained in the corporation's charter.[2] However, state corporate laws regulating dividend payment use different tests to determine whether a corporation may pay dividends in cash or property to its shareholders. One is the earned surplus test: Dividends may be paid only from

---

[1] *See, e.g.*, DEL. CODE ANN. tit. 8, § 170(a); MODEL BUSINESS CORP. ACT (1984) § 6.40(a).

[2] *See, e.g., id.*

the company's earned surplus (accumulated retained earnings). A second is a balance sheet-based test: A company may pay dividends only if its assets exceed the sum of its liabilities and its stated capital. A third is the nimble dividends test: In this case, a company may pay dividends if it has current profits, even if it does not have earned surplus. A fourth approach, also based on the balance sheet, is the net worth test: It permits payment of dividends to the extent assets exceed liabilities. Net worth is equal to the total value of equity. A fifth test is called the insolvency test: A corporation may not pay a dividend if the corporation is insolvent at the time the dividend is declared or if the payment of the dividend would make the corporation insolvent. In financial usage, there are two different definitions of "insolvent." The first is insolvent in the balance sheet sense. That is, liabilities are greater than assets.[3] Here the issue is whether the company would be able to meet its obligations if it were liquidated. The second definition of insolvent is based on a different perspective, that of a company as a going concern. Referred to as insolvency in the equity sense, this definition focuses on the inability of a corporation to pay its debts as they become due in the usual course of its business.[4] As discussed below, some states use more than one test.

Model Act (1969) § 45 used the earned surplus test, which permitted dividends in cash or other property to be paid only from the company's earned surplus (accumulated retained earnings.) Model Act (1969) § 45 referred not simply to "earned surplus," but to "unreserved and unrestricted earned surplus." The board of directors may reserve a portion of earned surplus, or a specified amount of earned surplus may be restricted by a provision in the charter or some other document. Typically, reservations and restrictions are placed on earned surplus as a result of a covenant in a loan agreement, or an agreement among the shareholders, not to pay dividends unless an established amount of earned surplus will remain after the dividend. The Act also prohibited dividend payment when the company was insolvent or such payment would make it insolvent.

Delaware General Corporation Law § 170 is typical of the approach used in many modern statutory provisions governing the payment of dividends in cash or other property. Section 170 of the Delaware code provides that dividends may be declared and paid either from the company's surplus (balance sheet-based test) or, in the absence of surplus, out of its net profits for the current and preceding year (nimble dividends test). Corporations in the business of exploiting natural resources have a special rule.

You should keep in mind that when a legal rule states that dividends may be paid from surplus, the reference is to an account in the equity section of the balance sheet. Surplus is not a bank account containing cash to be used for dividends. If, however, a company does not have cash available, a dividend cannot be paid. What is surplus? Here it might help to remember that the surplus

---

[3] *See, e.g.*, DEL. CODE ANN. tit. 8, § 244 (b).
[4] *See, e.g.*, MODEL BUSINESS CORP. ACT (1984) § 6.40 (c)(1).

accounts, together with the capital account, make up the shareholders' equity section of the balance sheet. As defined in the Delaware code, § 154 surplus is "the excess of the net assets of the corporation over the amount so determined to be capital." Net assets is the amount one gets by subtracting all of the corporation's liabilities from all of its assets. Thus, the value of net assets is the same as the total value of the equity section of the balance sheet. (When one subtracts the liabilities from the assets, the remainder is the value of the equity. If Assets = Liabilities + Equity, then Assets — Liabilities = Equity). Surplus, then is the amount by which the total value of the equity section exceeds the value of the capital account(s). Some of the more advanced aspects of the definition of surplus will be discussed below in the section of this chapter entitled "Limitations on Dividends." For now, we shall confine our discussion to two types of surplus, as shown on a corporation's balance sheet: capital surplus and earned surplus.

According to the Delaware code § 154, stated capital is, at minimum, equal to the aggregate par value of outstanding shares of stock. Capital surplus (paid in capital in excess of par) is the amount shareholders pay for their shares in excess of the aggregate par value. In contrast, earned surplus (accumulated retained earnings) comes from a corporation's earnings. For example, 100 shares of one dollar par value stock issued for ten dollars a share will yield a minimum capital of one hundred dollars (one dollar par x 100 shares) and the excess of the purchase price over par value, or nine dollars, can be designated as capital surplus. If they wish, the board of directors may designate as capital a greater portion of the amount paid for stock, and thereby reduce the amount allocated to capital surplus. In the preceding example, the board could decide to allocate two dollars per share to capital, and just eight dollars per share to capital surplus. By providing that dividends may be distributed out of any type of surplus, the Delaware code has blurred the distinction between distributions (returns of capital from capital surplus) and dividends (distributions of profits from earned surplus).

Sometimes a lawyer is faced with a corporate client that wants to distribute cash or other property to its shareholders, but has neither earned nor capital surplus. The Delaware code gives the board of directors several ways to address this issue. Section 244(a)(4) provides one option. It permits the directors to transfer from stated capital to capital surplus "(ii) some or all of the capital represented by issued shares of its par value capital stock, which capital is in excess of the aggregate par value of such shares; or (iii) some of the capital represented by issued shares of its capital stock without par value." According to § 244(b), such transfers may not, however, be made unless "the assets of the corporation remaining after such reduction shall be sufficient to pay any debts of the corporation for which payment has not been otherwise provided."

A charter amendment either decreasing the par value of the corporation's shares or changing from par value to no par value stock provides another option for creating capital surplus out of which to make a distribution. If the charter amendment is approved, the directors may reduce the corporation's stated capital as described above. The amount of the reduction will become capital surplus, out of which the desired distribution may be made.

The Model Act combines the concepts of dividends and distributions by designating dividends as one kind of distribution and providing one set of rules applicable to all distributions. According to § 1.40(6) of the Model Act:

> "Distribution" means a direct or indirect transfer of money or other property (except its own shares) or incurrence of indebtedness by a corporation to or for the benefit of its shareholders in respect of any of its shares. A distribution may be in the form of a declaration or payment of a dividend; a purchase, redemption, or other acquisition of shares; a distribution of indebtedness; or otherwise.

The unitary approach to distributions is also evident in Model Act § 6.40(c), which applies to all distributions. The section, which uses a net worth approach, requires that to be validly issued, a distribution must satisfy both an equity insolvency test[5] and a balance sheet-based test.[6] According to the Official Comment, the balance sheet test:

> requires that, after giving effect to any distribution, the corporation's assets equal or exceed its liabilities plus (with some exceptions) the dissolution preferences of senior equity securities. Section 6.40(d) authorizes asset and liability determinations to be made for this purpose on the basis of either (1) financial statements prepared on the basis of accounting practices and principles that are reasonable in the circumstances or (2) a fair valuation or other method that is reasonable in the circumstances.

Thus, the Model Act does not restrict the accounts from which a distribution may be made so long as making the distribution will not render a corporation insolvent.

For brief review, it may be helpful to set out a simple balance sheet here, so that the implications of the tests just described can be seen easily. Here is a balance sheet as it would appear just after a corporation has issued 1,000 shares of one dollar par value stock for ten dollars per share:

---

[5] MODEL BUSINESS CORP. ACT (1984) § 6.40(c)(1).

[6] See id. § 6.40(c)(2).

ACADEMAIR, INC.
December 31, 199_

ASSETS		LIABILITIES	$ 0
Cash	$ 10,000		
		SHAREHOLDERS' EQUITY	
		Stated Capital	$ 1,000
		Capital Surplus	9,000
		Earned Surplus	0
TOTAL ASSETS $ 10,000		TOTAL LIABILITIES AND EQUITY $ 10,000	

Assume, for example, that Academair immediately invests its $ 10,000 cash in an option to purchase an airplane and then one month later sells that option for $ 15,000 after expenses. Here is how the new balance sheet would look after the sale of the option:

ACADEMAIR, INC.
January 31, 199_

ASSETS		LIABILITIES	$ 0
Cash	$ 15,000	SHAREHOLDERS' EQUITY	
		Stated Capital	$ 1,000
		Capital Surplus	9,000
		Earned Surplus	5,000
TOTAL ASSETS $ 15,000		TOTAL LIABILITIES AND EQUITY $ 15,000	

State corporation statutes following the basic rule of Model Act (1969) would permit dividends to be declared and paid only out of earned surplus, a total amount of $ 5,000. States using Delaware's approach permit dividends to be paid only out of surplus. Thus, a total of $ 14,000 would be available, $ 5,000 from earned surplus and $ 9,000 from capital surplus. It is important to note that only earned surplus represents the company's profitability. Dividends paid from capital surplus are actually a return of the shareholders' original capital investment. If one were in a Model Act (1984) jurisdiction, a maximum dividend of $ 15,000 would be permitted. There are no liabilities so that the company would satisfy the requirement of being able to pay its debts as they become due. There are no senior securities whose interests must be taken into account. And finally, after a $ 15,000 dividend, the corporation's assets would not be less than its liabilities. (See, however, p. 167 on par value under the Model Act.)

A number of states also follow Delaware's "nimble dividends" provision. Section 170 allows dividends to be declared and paid either out of surplus or profits of the current fiscal year and/or the prior fiscal year. The nimble dividends provision can be useful to a corporation that has had losses in previous years, which losses have prevented it from having any earned surplus even though the corporation currently is generating profits. To see how that works, it will be helpful to look at another balance sheet of Academair, Inc., this one showing the result of a $ 50,000 loss, with a $ 40,000 loan taken out to raise cash to cover the loss, in the month following the last balance sheet shown above.

ACADEMAIR, INC.
February 28, 199_

ASSETS		LIABILITIES	
Cash	$ 5,000	Note Payable	$ 40,000
		SHAREHOLDERS' EQUITY	
		Stated Capital	$ 1,000
		Capital Surplus	9,000
		Earned Surplus	(45,000)
	$ 5,000		$ 5,000

Notice that the $ 50,000 loss has wiped out the corporation's $ 5,000 earned surplus and has created a $ 45,000 deficit in earned surplus. (Deficits are shown on financial statements in parentheses.) The corporation could continue having losses, and therefore amassing deficits in earned surplus, for some time. It could then begin generating profits, but it could take some years of profits before the earned surplus deficits are eliminated. Unless the statute under which this corporation is incorporated has a nimble dividends provision, it will not be able to pay dividends until those deficits are eliminated completely. Under the Delaware code, the company potentially may begin paying dividends when it again has profits. If, for example, in the following year, the company earned a $ 3,000 profit, the earned surplus would be ($ 42,000). In a nimble dividends jurisdiction, the company would be able to pay dividends in an amount up to $ 3,000. The introduction of the nimble dividends approach reflects the continuing tension between protecting creditors and unduly restricting a going enterprise.

> The law of stated capital and pay-out restriction is the product of a continuing conflict between an urge to protect creditors by a simplistic mechanical rule, on the one hand, and on the other, the pressures of business reality. Business reality won a big round in the development of the concept of so-called 'nimble dividends'. As a practical business matter, a corporation that has accumulated large deficits and has a heavy burden of unpaid debt has no prospect of obtaining further credit unless new equity capital can be attracted to the enterprise. In turn, there is no hope of attracting additional equity capital unless there is some prospect that dividends will be paid. The old deficits must not, therefore, be allowed to block future dividends. The obvious — perhaps the only — way out is to arrange matters so that dividends can be paid if the enterprise earns a current profit

from its operations, even though the deficits piled up in previous years have not yet been eliminated.*

Although corporation statutes typically do not state explicitly how dividends are to be spread among shareholders, dividends must be paid to the various classes of shareholders (*e.g.*, preferred and common) as specified in the charter and, within classes of shareholders, pro rata on a share-for-share basis. An attempt by the directors to favor one shareholder over another in the payment of dividends, in a way not sanctioned by the charter, would be considered an illegal dividend or an unauthorized distribution of corporate assets. Under Model Act (1984) § 8.33(a), which is a representative statutory provision, directors who vote for or assent to an unauthorized distribution of corporate assets, including a dividend that is not allowed under the statute, are liable to the corporation for the amount of the distribution or dividend in excess of the amount that could have been distributed lawfully. A director held liable for an unlawful distribution is entitled to contribution from other directors who could also be held liable and from shareholders receiving the distribution, knowing it was permissible. Model Act § 8.30 affords directors some protection if they have relied on opinions, reports or financial statements prepared by public accountants or similar experts.

In all corporation statutes, the decision to declare dividends is within the board's discretion. Shareholders' legal right to receive dividends arises only when dividends are declared. Although shareholders may have every expectation that dividends will be paid annually in agreed amounts, they do not have a statutory right to have dividends paid. If a corporation has preferred stock, however, its charter typically contains provisions designed to force the declaration and payment of dividends by making the alternative unpalatable. For example, at a minimum, preferred dividends in a set amount usually are made cumulative, and the charter typically provides that no dividends may be declared on the common stock until all accumulated dividends on the preferred stock have been paid. It is not uncommon for the charter to go further and to provide that if dividends are not paid on the preferred stock for four consecutive quarters, the preferred shareholders rather than the common shareholders will have the right to elect some or all of the directors. Once dividends are declared and announced to the shareholders, they become liabilities of the corporation. At that point, shareholders can sue to collect dividends if the corporation does not pay them voluntarily.

The following passage evaluates the effectiveness of legal capital provisions.

Bayless Manning & James Hanks, Jr., Legal Capital 91-97, 176-77, 183 (3d ed. 1990)*

What has preceded has been largely descriptive of the legal capital scheme as it existed in many states until relatively recently and as it continues to exist in most states today. It is now both possible and in order to ask how well it works.

First, the legal capital machinery makes only the most marginal effort to protect groups or classes of shareholders from each other despite their often conflicting interests.

As for creditors, the system makes no attempt to ward off three of their main worries — erosion of the corporation's cash flow out of which debt will be repaid, incurrence by the corporation of additional debt liabilities and creation of secured or senior debt claims.

All the system ever purports to do is to assure that shareholders have put something into the corporate pot and that they will not redistribute corporate assets to themselves without first protecting the corporate creditors....

We have no systematic empiric studies. It is a safe generalization, however, that the statutory legal capital machinery provides little or no significant protection to creditors of corporations.... Some of the reasons are:

....

2. To the extent that the purpose of the legal capital scheme is to protect creditors from transactions that benefit shareholders but prejudice creditors, it is at least odd that the statutes should hand over all the control switches and levers to the shareholders and those whom the shareholders elect, the board of directors.... [I]n no case do the statutes provide for participation by the creditors, consultation with the creditors, or even notice to the creditors.

3. A corporation's "legal capital" is a wholly arbitrary number, unrelated in any way to any economic facts that are relevant to a creditor....

....

5. ... For purposes of the statute, cash and other quick assets are treated exactly the same as assets that would take years to liquidate for purposes of paying debts....

....

7. ....

Statutes that provide for nimble dividends admit overtly that companies with heavily-impaired legal capital may still make payments to shareholders....Where dividend payments may be made to shareholders and charged to capital surplus, the statute offers a direct invitation to the lawyer architect to design a capital structure using low par stock and creating large capital surplus accounts — an invitation that is usually accepted.

Many of the statutes permit payments to shareholders to be charged against reduction surplus, a form of surplus that is usually easy for the board to generate.

....

8. It may be, though it would be difficult to prove, that the legal capital system ... can operate as a trap. Many lawyers are not sufficiently familiar with the arcana of legal capital to recognize a related problem when it does arise and warn their clients accordingly.

....

Altogether it must be recognized that the machinery of legal capital established by our corporation acts suffers from a number of deficiencies ... is there nothing to be said for it?....

The best argument suggesting that the system has some protective consequence for creditors is the argument historical, cultural, and psychological. For nearly 150 years, it has been thought important that an enterprise have something called its "capital" and the concept has acquired its own independent aura of respectability, whatever its actual significance to real creditors in real business situations.... Deep in the consciousness of the American businessman, lawyer, accountant and banker is the general principle that distributions to shareholders are not supposed to be made "out of" capital. Everybody knows that ways are available to design around statutory restrictions; but the restrictions themselves are a reflection of that general principle....

....

A second line of speculation, unprovable, is that the statutory provisions may have a degree of actual operating impact upon corporations of the medium-size range. Those in control of the incorporated small enterprise typically manage its, and their, economic lives with little or no awareness of or regard for the niceties of procedure spelled out in legal capital provisions. Large public enterprises on the other hand, can draw on lawyers and other professionals who see to it that wide flexibility of corporate financial action and decisions is maintained while scrupulously observing the statutory mandates. But it may also be that the managers of a medium-sized incorporated enterprise may be sufficiently conscious of statutory and regulatory requirements to be affected in their behavior, and yet not served with sufficient continuity or professionality of advice to enable them to control their own destinies in the legal capital thicket. And perhaps the medium-sized corporation is the one that offers the greatest problem for the creditor; there he has not the close personal contact that grounds his extension of credit to the incorporated barbershop nor has he the institutional protections that back up a credit to General Motors.

....

Long overdue change has at last come to the field of legal capital.

In 1975 California struck out into new territory in the financial provisions of its new General Corporation Law as they substantially reconstructed the traditional edifice.... Distributions to shareholders may be made to the extent that retained earnings are available *or* certain ratios of certain assets to certain liabilities (and current assets to current liabilities) are met. (Emphasis in original)

....

... [T]he Revised Model Act presents to the world of the 1990s a shiny, new, carefully-fashioned, refined set of integrated provisions on shareholder pay-in and shareholder pay-out reflecting modern thought and practice in corporation law, finance and accounting....

....

In the Revised Model Act, the structural design for regulating distributions to shareholders is to:

(1) arrive at a dollar number as the balance sheet adjusted net worth of the corporation (assets minus liabilities, counting as a liability the liquidation claims of any outstanding senior preference shares); and,

(2) employ that single dollar number as the legal yardstick for regulating any distribution of corporate assets to any shareholder as such.

Thus, the Revised Model Act calls for no concept of stated capital or any other kind of capital account. It does not require differentiation among kinds of surplus. And it does not differentiate between capital and surplus accounts. But it does add substance to the prior liquidation claim of the holder of preference shares by according him *pro tanto* the same protection that the statute gives to a creditor of the corporation...." (emphasis in original)

As the preceding comments indicate, the effectiveness of legal capital provisions and their relevancy to modern business practices are subject to question. In fact, as Manning and Hanks point out, creditors often look to contract for protection rather than state statutory law.

B. REPURCHASE OF A CORPORATION'S OWN SHARES

Corporations have the right to repurchase previously issued shares of their own stock. When this occurs, the effect is the same as if the company had made a distribution of its assets to its shareholders. Under both the Delaware General Corporation Law and the Model Act, the provisions controlling the payment of dividends also apply to a corporation's redemption (repurchase) of its own shares. Delaware General Corporation Law § 160 (a) gives a corporation broad powers to deal in its own stock, but, with limited exceptions, prohibits the corporation from purchasing or redeeming "its own shares of capital stock for cash or other property when the capital of the corporation is impaired or when such purchase or redemption would cause any impairment of the capital of the corporation...." Thus, a corporation may repurchase its shares only out of surplus. As the Model Act considers both dividends and redemptions to be a form of distribution, § 6.40 applies equally to both.

If the repurchased stock is not retired or canceled, but is held by the corporation to be reissued later, it is often referred to as treasury stock. Model Act (1969) § 2(h) provides a standard definition:

> "Treasury shares" means shares of a corporation which have been issued, have been subsequently acquired by and belong to a corporation, and have not been canceled or restored to the status of authorized but unissued shares. Treasury shares shall be deemed to be "issued" shares, but not "outstanding" shares.

The reader may have noticed that in our earlier discussions of the rules relating to the treatment of consideration for shares, we phrased those rules as being applicable upon the "issuance" of shares, not merely on the "sale" of shares. The reason for that is that those rules typically do not apply upon the sale by a corporation of treasury stock. Treasury shares having a par value may be sold for whatever consideration the board sets, regardless of their par value. That is the case because when shares held as treasury shares initially were issued, an amount equal to their par value was placed in stated capital, and that amount remains in stated capital so long as the shares retain their status as "issued" shares. In other words, the resale of treasury shares has no relevance insofar as the rules we have discussed are concerned. (A corporation's board of directors may cancel the issuance of treasury shares and, thus, restore them to the status of authorized but unissued shares at any time it wishes. In this situation, the amount in stated capital may be reduced. If the shares are reissued, all the capitalization rules apply just as they would if the shares never had been issued.) Model Act (1984) has eliminated the concepts of par value and treasury shares (except for permitting par value shares if a corporation decides to have them). Under the Model Act, shares that would otherwise become treasury shares are designated as authorized but unissued shares.

Robert W. Hamilton, Fundamentals of Modern Business 366-68 (1989)*

An important type of distributive transaction is the purchase by the corporation of its own stock. Superficially, a purchase of stock by the corporation may not be thought of as involving a distribution at all. It appears to be the purchase of an asset rather than the making of a distribution. That analysis, however, confuses transactions in which the corporation repurchases *its own stock* and transactions in which it purchases stock *issued by another corporation*. The former is a distribution, the latter an investment. (Emphasis in original)

When a corporation buys back its own stock, it does not receive anything of value in the hands of the corporation. The remaining shareholders continue to own 100 per cent of the corporate assets (now reduced by the amount of the

---

payment used to reacquire the shares). A corporation cannot treat stock in itself that it has purchased as an asset any more than it can treat its authorized but unissued stock as an asset. One cannot own 10 percent of oneself and have one's total worth be 110 percent of the value of one's assets....

....

The difference between treasury shares and shares issued by other corporations is reflected in the accounting treatment of transactions in shares. When corporation A buys shares in corporation B, the transaction is reflected solely on the left hand side of the balance sheet: The journal entry shows a reduction of cash and an increase in an asset account "investments in other corporations." However, when a corporation buys its own shares, the reduction of cash on the left hand side of the balance sheet is offset by a reduction in one or more right hand shareholders' equity accounts. The precise account to be debited may vary depending on the status of the accounts themselves; the important point is that the transaction is reflected by adjustments to the right hand shareholders' equity accounts. A straight cash dividend is treated for accounting purposes in the same way: A reduction of the cash account on the left hand side of the balance sheet is offset by a reduction in retained earnings or similar account on the right hand side of the balance sheet.

A repurchase of shares by the corporation is a distribution even if the corporation purchases only shares owned by one shareholder rather than proportionately from each shareholder. Such a transaction is a disproportionate distribution (*i.e.*, one not shared proportionately by all shareholders). The corporation has made a distribution to a single shareholder equal to the purchase price it paid for the shares. This transaction is not all bad from the standpoint of the other shareholders, however, since it simultaneously increases their percentage interest in the corporation....

Distributions in the form of repurchases of shares are very common in real life. In closely held corporations, the elimination of one shareholder's interest in a corporation is almost routinely effected by a repurchase of shares by the corporation. Such a transaction permits the use of corporate rather than personal assets, has favorable tax consequences, and does not affect the relative interests of the remaining shareholders.

Publicly traded corporations also often go into the securities market to repurchase their own shares for a variety of possible uses, for example in compensation plans for executives or employees, for acquisitions or other corporate purposes, or simply to reduce the number of outstanding shares. A repurchase of a corporation's own shares is often preferred to the issuance of new shares because there is no dilutive effect on public shareholders and a market repurchase tends to protect or increase the market price of shares. In contrast, the use of new shares to purchase assets of uncertain value or to provide incentive compensation for senior executive officers may place downward pressure on the market price of the shares. Targets of takeover attempts may also purchase their own shares in an effort to sop up extra cash that the corporation may have and to drive up the price of their shares to make the competing offer by the aggressor unattractive.

———————

The Model Act provisions governing dividends also apply to several types of distributions by a corporation to its shareholders. The following case explores the extent to which the term "distribution" should be broadly defined.

In re C-T OF VIRGINIA, INC.
United States Court of Appeals, Fourth Circuit
958 F.2d 606 (1992)

WILKINSON, CIRCUIT JUDGE:

This case presents the question of whether the leveraged acquisition of a corporation, structured in the form of a cash-out merger and consummated at arm's length, is subject to restrictions on distributions to shareholders under Virginia law. The case involves an action brought by an official committee of unsecured creditors of a corporation now in bankruptcy against the former directors of that corporation. The creditors, suing on behalf of the corporation, claimed that the leveraged acquisition created an illegal distribution to shareholders under the Virginia Stock Corporation Act, Va.Code Ann. § 13.1-601 et seq. (Michie 1989). We agree with the district court that the merger did not create a distribution under Virginia law and therefore affirm its judgment.

I

The facts underlying this case are not in dispute. C-T of Virginia, Inc., formerly Craddock-Terry Shoe Corp., is a Virginia corporation engaged in the manufacture, wholesale, and mail-order sale of shoes. Prior to the purchase that is the subject of this action, C-T was a publicly owned corporation whose stock was traded on the over-the-counter market. In April 1985, C-T hired a financial adviser, Prudential-Bache Securities, Inc., to study the strategic alternatives available to the company. Prudential recommended that C-T's management pursue a leveraged buyout ("LBO")[7] of the company. Prudential indicated that an LBO would both realize maximum value for C-T's shareholders and maintain the viability of the post-LBO enterprise.

On May 20, 1985, C-T's board of directors accepted Prudential's recommendation and authorized management to explore the possibility of a management-sponsored LBO at $ 15 per share. (C-T common stock was trading for $ 14.25 per share when this authorization was announced.) The board retained the right to consider other proposals made to the corporation. On June 12, 1985, Southwestern General Corp. made such an unsolicited offer, which proposed a

———————

[7] In a leveraged buyout, the assets of the corporation being purchased are used as collateral for the loan(s) providing the funds to purchase the company. [Eds.]

merger at $ 17.50 per share. Southwestern withdrew this offer on August 26, 1985, however, after President Reagan refused to impose limitations on shoe imports.

C-T received a second unsolicited offer on November 11, 1985, from HH Holdings, Inc. Holdings is a Delaware holding company owned by Sidney Kimmel and Alan Salke. Neither Holdings, Kimmel, nor Salke had any prior relationship or contact with C-T or the members of its board of directors. Holdings proposed a cash merger in which C-T shareholders would receive $ 19 per share of common stock. After the directors announced this offer, several owners of substantial amounts of C-T common stock urged that the directors reject the offer and demand $ 20 per share instead. Holdings agreed to the merger at $ 20 per share, and an Agreement in Principle was signed on December 11, 1985.

The parties formalized the transaction in an Agreement and Plan of Merger executed on January 24, 1986. The merger agreement structured the purchase in the form of a reverse triangular merger. For purposes of the merger, Holdings formed HH Acquisition, Inc., a wholly owned subsidiary. The merger agreement provided that on April 30, 1986, Acquisition would merge into C-T, leaving C-T as the surviving corporation wholly owned by Holdings. The funds necessary to purchase all outstanding shares of C-T, about $ 30 million, would be deposited with the exchange agent, Sovran Bank, before or at the closing of the transaction. At the moment that the merger was effected, the outstanding shares of C-T common stock would be automatically canceled, and the former shareholders would receive the right to submit their canceled stock certificates to Sovran for payment of $ 20 per canceled share. Also at that time, the directors of C-T would resign and be replaced by Salke, John W. Baker, and Roland K. Peters.

The financing for the merger was arranged solely by Holdings. Holdings provided about $ 4 million of its own money. It obtained the balance, approximately $ 26 million, in the form of bank loans secured by C-T's assets. The pre-merger directors did not solicit proposed financing, negotiate the terms of the financing or of the security, or participate in or authorize the encumbering of C-T's assets. The merger agreement did obligate C-T to provide Holdings, Acquisition, and the financing banks access to C-T's properties, personnel, and books and records and to cooperate with Holdings' efforts to secure financing. Further, the pre-merger directors approved the repurchase of C-T's preferred stock, which was a prerequisite to effectuation of the merger.

C-T's board of directors approved the merger agreement and unanimously voted to recommend that the shareholders approve the merger, which they did on April 17, 1986. The transaction was consummated as planned on April 30. The surviving corporation struggled along for about eighteen months, and it filed for bankruptcy under Chapter 11 on October 21, 1987.

In October 1989, the Official Committee of Unsecured Creditors of C-T filed this action in federal court against the pre-merger directors and officers of the corporation. The complaint alleged that the directors and officers breached their fiduciary duties owed to the corporation and that the directors had approved a distribution in violation of Va.Code Ann. §§ 13.1-653 and 13.1- 692 (Michie 1989). The district court granted the defendants' motion to dismiss the former claim. It denied the directors' motion to dismiss the unlawful distribution claim, however, finding that under some factual circumstances the merger might have been a distribution.

Subsequently, the district court granted the directors' motion for summary judgment on the illegal distribution claim. The court found application of the restriction on distributions "inconsistent with Virginia's statutory scheme," because the merger provisions of the Virginia Stock Corporation Act — unlike the sale of corporate assets provisions--"make[ ] no mention of distributions." The court also concluded that the transaction was not "a distribution clothed in the garb of a merger" to evade the distribution restrictions. The court concluded, finally, that, even if the merger involved a distribution, the directors did not "vote[ ] for or assent[ ] to" it, a prerequisite to liability under Va.Code Ann. § 13.1-692(A) (Michie 1989). For the latter holding, the court relied on the fact that the directors did not authorize the encumbering of C-T's assets, which occurred after they had resigned their offices.

C-T appeals the summary judgment against it on the distribution claim.

II

Modern distribution statutes derive from eighteenth century restrictions on when a corporation could pay dividends to its shareholders. *See* Revised Model Business Corporation Act § 6.40 historical note 1 (1986) (hereinafter RMBCA). Restrictions on a corporation's purchase of its own shares, and on other forms of distributions, were enacted later. *See* J. Choper, J. Coffee, & C. Morris, Cases and Materials on Corporations 1007 (3d ed. 1989). All states now impose limitations on the power of a corporation to make various distributions to its shareholders, and federal courts must, of course, pay strict attention to the language of the relevant state statute.

Virginia's corporate law statute, including the distribution provisions, was substantially revised in 1985. The Virginia statute defines "distribution" as follows: "Distribution" means a direct or indirect transfer of money or other property, except its own shares, or incurrence of indebtedness by a corporation to or for the benefit of its shareholders in respect of any of its shares. A distribution may be in the form of a declaration or payment of a dividend; a purchase, redemption, or other acquisition of shares; a distribution of indebtedness of the corporation; or otherwise. Va. Code Ann. § 13.1-603 (Michie 1989). Not all distributions are unlawful. Rather, a distribution is prohibited only if, after it is made, the corporation fails either of two insolvency tests:

No distribution may be made if, after giving it effect: 1. The corporation would not be able to pay its debts as they become due in the usual course of business; or 2. The corporation's total assets would be less than the sum of its total liabilities plus (unless the articles of incorporation permit otherwise) the amount that would be needed, if the corporation were to be dissolved at the time of the distribution, to satisfy the preferential rights upon dissolution of shareholders whose preferential rights are superior to those receiving the distribution. *Id.* § 13.1-653(C).

Directors face potential personal liability when the corporation makes an unlawful distribution: Unless he complies with the applicable standards of conduct described in § 13.1-690,[8] a director who votes for or assents to a distribution made in violation of this chapter or the articles of incorporation is personally liable to the corporation and its creditors for the amount of the distribution that exceeds what could have been distributed without violating this chapter or the articles of incorporation. *Id.* § 13.1-692(A). There is, however, no provision in the Virginia Stock Corporation Act by which creditors can recover a distribution from the shareholders directly. Rather, a creditor's only remedy is against the directors, who then may seek contribution from shareholders who received the distribution. *Id.* § 13.1-692(B)(2).

III

We now address the central question in this case: whether the merger involved a distribution to shareholders within the meaning of § 13.1-603. For the reasons set forth below, we conclude that the transaction does not fall within the statutory definition of distribution and, therefore, that the directors cannot be subjected to potential liability under § 13.1-692.[9]

A

Appellant argues that the plain meaning of the statute contradicts the district court's conclusion that the merger did not create a distribution under Virginia law. It claims that the purchase of the premerger shareholders' shares in C-T entailed a distribution because the payment of the purchase price of $ 20 per share was a "transfer of money ... by a corporation to ... its shareholders." Since this purchase was funded primarily through loans secured by the assets of C-T, the argument runs, the value of the corporation — and hence the financial position of its creditors — was diminished. According to appellant, it is irrelevant whether the funds that are transferred to shareholders derive from the corporation's capital surplus, retained earnings, or new loans secured by corporate assets,

---

[8] Section 13.1-690 establishes, inter alia, the following standard of conduct for directors: "A director shall discharge his duties as a director, including his duties as a member of a committee, in accordance with his good faith business judgment of the best interests of the corporation." VA. CODE ANN. § 13.1-690(A) (Michie 1989). Because we hold that the merger in this case was not a distribution, we need not consider whether the actions of C-T's pre-merger directors satisfied § 13.1-690.

[9] Our resolution of this case makes it unnecessary to consider whether, if the merger did involve a distribution, the former directors of C-T "vote[d] for or assent[ed] to" it. VA. CODE ANN. § 13.1-692(A) (Michie 1989).

and it is likewise immaterial that the payment resulted from a cash-out merger; appellant claims that the legislature intended the statute to have "the broadest range of inclusion" and thereby "pick up all forms of transfer of the assets of a corporation to its shareholders."

We do not share appellant's view of the statute. The Virginia Stock Corporation Act provides a precise definition of the word "distribution": "[A] direct or indirect transfer of money or other property, except its own shares, or incurrence of indebtedness by a corporation to or for the benefit of its shareholders in respect of any of its shares." Va.Code Ann. § 13.1-603 (Michie 1989). Payment of the merger consideration to C-T's former shareholders simply does not fit within the plain language of this definition. The key language, for our purposes here, is the requirement that the transfer of money or property be "by a corporation to ... its shareholders." When post-merger C-T transferred $ 20 per canceled share to C-T's pre-merger shareholders, they were no longer the corporation's — "its" — shareholders, for their ownership interest had been lawfully canceled as of the effective time of the merger.

Similarly, we must reject appellant's argument that the encumbering of C-T's assets to raise sufficient funds to pay for the merger was a distribution because it represented the "incurrence of indebtedness by a corporation ... for the benefit of its shareholders." *Id.* The financing for the merger was negotiated not by C-T's pre-merger directors for the benefit of C-T's pre-merger shareholders, but by the new owners and directors of the corporation. Moreover, the financing closed simultaneously with the closing of the merger. Accordingly, at the time the encumbering was undertaken, the pre-merger shareholders' ownership interests were canceled and, therefore, C-T did not incur debt "for the benefit of its shareholders."

Appellant's attempt to shoehorn the payment of merger consideration into the statutory definition of distribution must thus prove unsuccessful, for its argument fails to appreciate the significance of the fact that the transaction at issue represented the arm's-length purchase of C-T by Holdings. The distribution statute is aimed by its terms at actions taken by a corporation to enrich unjustly its own shareholders at the expense of creditors and to the detriment of the continuing viability of the company. It does not cover third-party payments to acquire the stock of a corporation or the encumbering of assets after a change in corporate ownership, and it is not intended to obstruct an arm's-length acquisition of an enterprise by new owners who have their own plans for commercial success. The reason for this distinction is simple: A corporate acquisition, structured as a merger, is simply a different animal from a distribution. Distribution statutes, as noted above, derive from the regulation of corporate dividends and traditionally apply to situations in which shareholders, after receiving the transfer from the corporation, retain their status as owners of the corporation. Distribution statutes have not been applied to wholesale changes in corporate ownership, as is the case here, and C-T has presented no evidence that the Virginia legislature intended the statutory definition to expand the applicability of distribution restrictions beyond their traditional scope.

Appellant insists, however, that the text of the statute does not exclude from the definition of distribution transfers incident to changes in corporate control. Appellant relies on the fact that § 13.1-603 states that "[a] distribution may be in the form of ... a purchase, redemption, or other acquisition of shares." This language, however, is not nearly as broad as C-T suggests. To begin with, it is subject to the general requirement that the corporation act for the benefit of its shareholders. Further, the language functions in this context to prevent a corporation from disguising a distribution in the form of a partial acquisition of shares — e.g., by "purchasing" twenty-five percent of each shareholder's shares, which would have the effect of transferring corporate assets to the shareholders without the corporation receiving any consideration in exchange and without changing the ownership structure in the slightest. The inclusion of purchases, redemptions, and other acquisitions within the ambit of distributions, therefore, is not an indication that the statutory definition applies when all outstanding shares of the corporation are purchased at a market rate in the course of an arm's-length purchase of the corporation.

None of this discussion should suggest that the transaction in this case was not subject to extensive regulation. Article 12 of the Virginia Stock Corporation Act provides detailed procedures that govern mergers, see Va. Code Ann. §§ 13.1-716, -718 (Michie 1989), and mandates review of the articles of merger by the Virginia State Corporation Commission, see id. § 13.1-720(B). As the district court observed, Article 12 "makes no mention of distributions," and the Virginia legislature could easily have provided a cross-reference to the distribution statutes had it intended the latter to apply to mergers. 124 B.R. at 696-97. Further, Virginia law prohibits transfers of money or corporate shares that are made "with intent to delay, hinder or defraud creditors," Va. Code Ann. § 55-80 (Michie 1986), or that are "not upon consideration deemed valuable in law," id. § 55-81 (Michie Supp.1991). Finally, federal bankruptcy law provides that a trustee in bankruptcy may avoid any transfer made within one year before bankruptcy, if the debtor "received less than a reasonably equivalent value in exchange" and was insolvent at the time of, or became insolvent as a result of, the transfer. 11 U.S.C.A. § 548(a)(2)(A) and (B)(i) (West Supp. 1991). The existence of other state and federal enactments that potentially address this kind of transaction suggests the inadvisability of importing the distribution statutes into a context that the legislature did not intend.

B

Other reasons impel us to hold that the leveraged acquisition of C-T was not a distribution under Virginia law. In this case appellant asks a federal court to apply a state distribution statute in a wholly novel way. It has not directed our attention to any decision by any court, state or federal, that has applied distribution restrictions to an arm's-length merger. "Federal judges are disinclined to make bold departures in areas of law that we have no responsibility for developing." *Afram Export Corp. v. Metallurgiki Halyps*, S.A., 772 F.2d 1358, 1370 (7th Cir. 1985). Moreover, the reach of the rule of law appellant seeks is extremely broad: appellant conceded to the district court that, under its interpretation of the statutory definition, every merger would henceforth be a distribution. Accepting appellant's argument, therefore, would expose the defendants and directors of other Virginia corporations to a wholly unanticipated form of personal liability and would place a cloud over all corporate acquisitions that have closed within the past two years, *see* Va. Code Ann. § 13.1-692(C) (Michie 1989) (two-year statute of limitations for actions alleging personal liability for illegal distributions).

....

Moreover, it is difficult for us to conceive how distribution restrictions would effectively function in the corporate acquisitions context. In determining whether a proposed distribution is legal, directors must apply two sophisticated insolvency tests. *See* Va. Code Ann. § 13.1-653(C) (Michie 1989). In applying these tests, directors must assess the future business prospects and decisions of the company. *See* RMBCA § 6.40 comment 2. When, after a distribution, directors continue to operate the company and set its business policy, such a task is manageable and within their competence. In cases involving corporate acquisitions, however, the pre-acquisition directors typically depart their positions in the corporation after the transaction. Not only do they therefore lack any control over the future course of the company's business, but they also may be fully unaware of new management's plans and strategies. Indeed, the primary rationale for a change in corporate ownership and control is the new owners' belief that, by altering the company's business strategy and structure, they can make the company more profitable than it was under old management. In this situation, it seems both unrealistic and perverse to charge the old directors under the distribution statute with knowledge and responsibility for the actions of the new owners. We cannot believe that the legislature intended such a result.

We also do not share appellant's view that non-application of the distribution statute would be unfair to creditors. In this case, it is possible that the leveraged acquisition of C-T hastened or caused the company's downfall. On the other hand, C-T's creditors may have actually benefitted from the acquisition. The infusion of $ 4 million in new capital and the presence of a more effective management team may have permitted C-T to survive longer than it otherwise would have and may also have increased the chances that the company would survive over the long-term. In other words, it is impossible to conclude a priori whether a leveraged transaction such as that here on balance benefits or harms creditors of the target corporation. It is possible to say, however, that a creditor cannot avoid bearing the risk that his debtor will make a bad business decision: A creditor who lends a debtor money is taking advantage of the debtor's comparative advantage in using that money productively. A creditor necessarily defers to the debtor's skills in converting the money into other assets. The risk that both the creditor and debtor take is that the use the debtor makes of the money will benefit both parties. The creditor provides the capital, the debtor provides the know-how. The creditor is relying on the debtor's skill and judgment when it makes the loan. Only by giving the debtor discretion can the creditor hope to profit. Giving a debtor discretion, however, necessarily gives him the ability not only to make good decisions, but bad ones as well. Finally, it is important to recognize that, since LBOs are a well-known element in contemporary business life, creditors are well-positioned to protect themselves. "[T]he debtor-creditor relationship is essentially contractual." If a creditor fears the prospect of a future leveraged acquisition of its debtor, it can protect itself by bargaining for security interests or protective provisions in its loan agreements that restrict the ability of its debtor to subject itself to a leveraged acquisition without the creditor's approval. *See id.* at 834-36; *see also* Kummert, State Statutory Restrictions on Financial Distributions by Corporations to Shareholders: Part I, 55 Wash.L.Rev. 359, 374 n. 63, 395 (1980) (noting "the extensive use by large or longterm creditors of contract provisions that supersede the statutory provisions with far more rigorous restrictions on financial distributions by the corporate debtor").

In addition, we note that even if corporate acquisitions are not subject to state distribution restrictions, protection is accorded creditors by the law of creditors' rights, particularly fraudulent conveyance statutes. In contrast to state corporate law, the law of creditors' rights is designed and better equipped to protect creditors in situations such as that presented here. For example, state fraudulent conveyance statutes, enable creditors to recapture transferred funds by attacking the transaction directly. In contrast, distribution restrictions merely impose personal liability on directors, without any provision for a direct recoupment of the distributed assets from the shareholders who received them.

In attacking the transaction here, appellant fails to acknowledge all the risks inherent in it. Holdings' acquisition of C-T was an uncertain financial proposition for C-T's shareholders as well as its creditors. Although the post-merger corporation failed in this case some eighteen months after the leveraged acquisition, it was anything but clear at the time of the transaction that the corporation would enter bankruptcy. Indeed, C-T's new owners were so confident of its future success that they invested $ 4 million of their own money in it. Thus, had the domestic shoe market rebounded after the acquisition, the market price of a share in C-T may have risen substantially above the $ 20 that the pre-merger shareholders received. In that situation, the shareholders — not C-T's creditors — would be complaining today. Both this corporate acquisition and the lending of money to pre-merger C-T involved risk — the same risk that inheres in all legitimate business activity. State distribution statutes simply do not authorize courts to rearrange the losses that inevitably result from risks taken in the hope of gains.

IV

In sum, we conclude that Holdings' leveraged acquisition of C-T, accomplished in the form of an arm's-length merger between Holdings' subsidiary Acquisition and C-T, did not create a distribution under Virginia law. The judgment of the district court is therefore

Affirmed.

In *Munford, Inc. v. Valuation Research Corporation,* 958 F.2d 606 (11th Cir. 1996) the court declined to follow the approach taken in *In re C-T of Virginia, Inc.* In *Munford,* a corporation in Chapter 11 claimed that a leveraged buyout of the company which had been approved by the company's former directors violated Georgia's statutory restrictions on distributions to shareholders and the repurchase of a corporation's own stock. The bankruptcy court found the statutes had been violated and the directors appealed. The sole issue on appeal was whether Georgia's stock distribution and repurchase statutes apply to a leveraged buyout of a corporation.

Georgia's distribution and repurchase statutes prohibited distributions and repurchases made when the corporation was insolvent or when such actions would render the corporation insolvent. Both statutes imposed joint and several liability on directors voting for the distribution or repurchase to the extent the statutes were violated. The *Munford* court stated:

> In reaching its conclusion, the bankruptcy court rejected a Fourth Circuit case that refused to apply Virginia's corporate distribution statute to recapture payments made to shareholders pursuant to an LBO merger. *See C-T of Virginia, Inc. v. Barrett,* 958 F.2d 606 (4th Cir.1992). In *C-T of Virginia,* the Fourth Circuit held that the LBO merger did not constitute a distribution within the meaning of Virginia's share repurchase and distribution statutes reasoning that Virginia's distribution statute [was] not intended to obstruct an arm's-length acquisition of an enterprise by new owners who have their own plans for commercial success. The reason for this distinction is simple: a corporate acquisition, structured as a merger, is simply a different animal from a distribution. *C-T of Virginia,* 958 F.2d at 611. The court in *C-T of Virginia* further reasoned that because such distribution statutes derive from the regulation of corporate dividends, courts should limit their restrictions to situations in which shareholders, after receiving the transfer from the corporation, retain their status as owners of the corporation.
>
> The bankruptcy court, in this case, rejected this line of reasoning, reasoning that the legislature enacted the distribution and share repurchase statutes of the Georgia Code to protect creditors "by prohibiting transfers at a time when a corporation is insolvent or would be rendered insolvent." Such intent, the bankruptcy court noted, "furthers the longstanding principle that creditors are to be paid before shareholders." We agree with the district court and the reasoning of the bankruptcy court and decline to join the Fourth Circuit in holding that "[a] corporate acquisition, structured as a

merger, is simply a different animal from a distribution." *C-T of Virginia, Inc.*, 958 F.2d at 611.

We note that the LBO transaction in this case did not merge two separate operating companies into one combined entity. Instead, the LBO transaction represented a "paper merge" of Munford, Inc. and AMC, a shell corporation with very little assets of its own. To hold that Georgia's distribution and repurchase statutes did not apply to LBO mergers such as this, while nothing in these statutes precludes such a result, would frustrate the restrictions imposed upon directors who authorize a corporation to distribute its assets or to repurchase shares from stockholders when such transactions would render the corporation insolvent. We therefore affirm the district court's ruling that Georgia's restrictions on distribution and stock repurchase apply to the LBO.

In the alternative, the directors argue that their approval of the LBO merger should not subject them to liability under the distribution and repurchase statutes because they approved the merger in good faith and with the advice of legal counsel. Because we are not aware of any Georgia courts that recognize good faith or reasonable reliance on legal counsel's advice as an affirmative defense to liability under Georgia's distribution and repurchase statutes, we reject this argument.

....

For the reasons stated above, we affirm the district court's denial of the directors' motion for summary judgment on Munford, Inc.'s stock distribution and repurchase claim.

C. STOCK DIVIDENDS AND STOCK SPLITS

Stock dividends are dividends payable to a corporation's shareholders in the corporation's own stock rather than in cash or other property. Stock splits have much in common with stock dividends, in that both stock splits and stock dividends have the same effect of getting a greater number of a corporation's shares into the hands of its shareholders without their paying for the shares. In many states, however, the mechanisms involved are entirely different, as are certain of the consequences. An important consideration that should be noted at the outset is that neither a stock dividend nor a stock split changes the proportion of a shareholder's equity participation in the corporation. Each simply changes the number of shares representing that participation.

Since stock dividends and stock splits do not increase shareholders' interests in the corporation, all that either accomplishes is to cut up the corporate pie into smaller pieces. Take, for example, a corporation that has three shareholders, each owning 100 shares and having a one third interest in the corporation. If the corporation does a two-for-one stock split, each shareholder will now own 200 shares, but will still have the same one third interest in the company. Now, however, each share represents exactly half the ownership percentage that a share in the corporation used to represent. As a result, each new share will be worth exactly half of what an old share was worth. With that in mind, one might question whether there is any good reason for a corporation to pay a stock dividend or to do a stock split.

There are three primary reasons corporations issue stock dividends or do stock splits. Perhaps the most common reason is to force down the price of stock in a publicly held corporation that has risen to "too high" a level in the trading markets. Stock is traded in 100-share lots, and there is an extra commission payable for trading in odd lots. For that reason and for others relating more to tradition than logic, the markets favor shares that trade at particular levels. Assume, for example, that the preferred range is from fifteen dollars to forty dollars a share for seasoned companies. In this case, if the price of a stock approaches $ 100, a corporation may want to do a 200% stock dividend or split the stock three for one in order to drive the stock's price down to about thirty dollars per share, with the hope that its rise from there will be easier than if the price were left at $ 100.

Sometimes corporate managers issue small stock dividends, not exceeding a few percent, to communicate to shareholders that the company is prospering and would be in a position to distribute cash dividends but for the management decision to reinvest profits in the business.

Finally, a stock split or a stock dividend may occur as a necessary financial expedient when a corporation is planning to sell its shares to the public for the first time. In the typical closely held corporation, usually there are no more than a few thousand shares outstanding. An initial public offering might involve the sale of 500,000 new shares representing a 25% interest in the corporation. In that case, the corporation will need to do a stock split or stock dividend to cause the shares currently outstanding to be increased to 1,500,000, so that after the public offering that number of shares will represent a 75% interest in the corporation.

Notice that if the corporation in that example has par value stock, a stock split of the magnitude required probably would cause the stock after the split to have a par value at some fraction of a cent. That would look unusual, and the corporation would wish to avoid it. Doing so would be easy. Since the corporation will file a charter amendment to effect the stock split, it can in the same amendment change to no par value stock or change the par value of the stock to some acceptable amount, such as ten cents or one cent. The only requirement in the latter cases would be to transfer from surplus to stated capital whatever amount is necessary to have stated capital equal to at least par value times the number of shares outstanding.

Delaware General Corporation Law § 173 contains typical provisions on stock dividends and stock splits. The section distinguishes between stock dividends and stock splits. Section 173 provides:

> If the dividend is to be paid in shares of the corporation's theretofore unissued capital stock the board of directors shall, by resolution, direct that

>there be designated as capital in respect of such shares an amount which is not less than the aggregate par value of par value shares being declared as a dividend and, in the case of shares without par value being declared as a dividend, such amount as shall be determined by the board of directors....

The requirement that an amount equal to aggregate par value be allocated to stated capital is necessary if the amount of stated capital, at a minimum, is at all times to be equal to the aggregate par value of a corporation's outstanding stock, which is what is at the heart of stated capital.[10] (For stock without par value, the board must fix a stated value and then transfer to stated capital an amount equal to the stated value.)[11]

The Delaware code provision governing stock splits can be found in the last sentence of § 173. It says that "No such designation as capital shall be necessary if shares are being distributed by a corporation pursuant to a split-up or division of its stock rather than as payment of a dividend declared payable in stock of the corporation." Section 1.40 (6) of the Model Act (1984) exempts transfers by a corporation of its own shares from the definition of "distribution." Therefore, the restrictions of § 6.40 do not apply either to stock splits or to stock dividends.

In neither Delaware nor a Model Act jurisdiction is any particular statutory authority needed for a stock split. Since a stock split is accomplished by an ordinary charter amendment, the regular authorization for a charter amendment is all the authority needed.[12] The amendment to effect a stock split would first, if need be, increase the number of authorized shares. Using one dollar par value stock being split two for one as an example, the amendment would accomplish the split with language like the following: "Upon the effectiveness of this amendment, each issued share of common stock, par value $ 1, is split into two shares of common stock, par value $ .50." Stated capital will remain the same, because the aggregate par value of all the shares outstanding is exactly the same before and after the split.

In the case of stock dividends, additional stock certificates showing the newly issued shares are sent to each shareholder. The mechanics of issuing stock certificates are not so simple after a stock split involving par value stock, because all of the existing certificates will show an incorrect par value. As a result, the corporation will have to issue new certificates for all outstanding shares, which it will do by exchanging the new certificates for the old ones. All that is an expensive proposition in a publicly held corporation, and one that never can be accomplished with respect to all old certificates if the number of shareholders involved is very great, since some shareholders will not respond to requests to

---

[10] DEL. CODE ANN. tit. 8, § 154.

[11] *See Id.* § 170.

[12] *See, e.g., id.* § 242, which provides for charter amendments upon the vote of the directors and the shareholders. *Accord*, MODEL BUSINESS CORP. ACT (1984) § 10.03.

exchange their old certificates.[13] Largely for those reasons, publicly held corporations issue stock dividends much more often then stock splits. As a result, however, of financial convention and pressure from the accounting profession,[14] corporations paying stock dividends often refer to the dividend as a stock split, especially if the number of shares outstanding after the dividend is at least 20% greater than before the dividend.

SECTION II. LIMITATIONS ON DIVIDENDS

A. UNREALIZED APPRECIATION AND DEPRECIATION

The major limitation on a corporation's ability to declare and pay dividends is that, as discussed above, under a statute like Model Act (1969), dividends must be paid out of earned surplus. Delaware General Corporation Law requires only the availability of surplus for dividend payment. Over the years, one of the main questions relating to these limitations on dividends is whether a corporation can consider unrealized appreciation in its assets in calculating either type of surplus for dividend purposes. May, for example, a corporation that owns a $ 10 million piece of land, which it purchased for $ 1 million, treat for dividend purposes the $ 9 million increase in value the same way it would treat a $ 9 million profit on the sale of a piece of land?

Ask an accountant that question and he or she will think you are crazy — to accountants it is almost a sacred idea that assets are to be valued at no higher than their cost. But one might notice that judges have not necessarily listened to accountants in deciding corporation law questions (perhaps because cases are pleaded by lawyers rather than accountants) and corporation statutes do not incorporate accounting theory wholesale. Corporation statutes do not, for example, require that corporations follow generally accepted accounting principles.

One place we might begin the search for an answer to our question is with the major case on using unrealized appreciation in assets to support dividends, *Randall v. Bailey*.

RANDALL v. BAILEY

Supreme Court of New York
23 N.Y.S.2d 173 (1940)

WALTER, JUSTICE.

A trustee of Bush Terminal Company, appointed in a proceeding under Section 77B of the Bankruptcy Act, here sues former directors of that company to

---

[13] If the shares are without par value, such an exchange is not necessary.

[14] Accounting convention regards any distribution in excess of 20 or 25% of the stock outstanding as a split rather than a dividend, regardless of how the action is taken.

recover on its behalf the amount of dividends declared and paid between November 22, 1928, and May 2, 1932, aggregating $ 3,639,058.06. At the times of the declarations and payments, the company's books concededly showed a surplus which ranged from not less than $ 4,378,554.83 on December 31, 1927, down to not less than $ 2,199,486.77 on April 30, 1932. The plaintiff claims, however, that in fact there was no surplus, that the capital was actually impaired to an amount greater than the amount of the dividends, and that the directors consequently are personally liable to the corporation for the amount thereof under Section 58 of the Stock Corporation Law. Defendants claim that there was no impairment of capital and that the surplus was actually greater than the amount which plaintiff concedes as the amount shown by the books.

The claims of the plaintiff, although branching out to a multitude of items, are basically reducible to four:

1. It was improper to "write-up" the land values above cost and thereby take unrealized appreciation into account.

2. It was improper not to "write-down" to actual value the cost of investments in and advances to subsidiaries and thereby fail to take unrealized depreciation into account.

3. It was improper to include as an asset an item of so-called good will, which the company carried at $ 3,000,000.

4. It was improper to include as an asset $ 492,958.30, being the cost of properties which had been demolished.

I discuss first the item of good will.

On March 6, 1902, shortly after its organization, the Bush Terminal Company entered into a contract with Irving T. Bush, who owned or controlled Bush Company, Ltd., which was then conducting a terminal enterprise in Brooklyn, and either under that contract or some arrangement constituting in effect a modification of it or a waiver of strict performance thereof, Bush Terminal Company issued $ 2,000,000 face amount of bonds and $ 3,000,000 par value of stock and received in addition to certain services of Irving T. Bush a large tract of land nearly contiguous to that owned by Bush Company, Ltd., and equipped with piers and warehouses, and other terminal facilities, and a lease by Bush Company, Ltd., of two of the piers. The $ 3,000,000 of stock was not entered upon the books of the company until December, 1905, and then, under the same date, there was entered on the asset side of the ledger an item of good will in the same amount. It does not appear that that was done pursuant to any formal action of the board of directors fixing $ 3,000,000 as the value of any good will, but it does appear that the directors did in fact sanction the fixing of that value on such item.

Plaintiff stresses the fact that the company itself received the proceeds of the $ 2,000,000 of bonds and itself expended such proceeds in acquiring the land and erecting the piers and warehouses and other terminal facilities, and contends that it necessarily follows that the only possible asset which the company can be regarded as having received for the $ 3,000,000 of stock is the services of Mr. Bush for about two or three years. I think that is too narrow a view. Bush Company, Ltd., was an existing company which unquestionably had a good will of some value. Mr. Bush controlled that company. He also had an option to purchase the nearly contiguous land above-mentioned. In 1904 Bush Terminal Company acquired the assets of Bush Company, Ltd. The result thus was that between the time of its organization in 1902 and the end of 1905 there had been assembled under the single ownership of Bush Terminal Company the existing plant and business of Bush Company, Ltd., and nearly contiguous land which Mr. Bush had permitted it to acquire at the price at which he had it under option, and additional piers and warehouses and other terminal facilities, and the whole thereof, at least so far as appears, were being profitably operated. Such profitable operation then continued for a long period of years, and consecutively, year in and year out, for a period of over twenty years the item of $ 3,000,000 for good will was set forth upon the company's balance sheets and reported to stockholders with the approval of successive boards of directors.

Directors obviously cannot create assets by fiat, and I do not go so far as to say that, even as against the company and in favor of directors, assets can be created by laches, acquiescence, or estoppel, but whatever may now be thought of the wisdom or business judgment displayed in valuing at $ 3,000,000 in 1905 what the company received for the $ 3,000,000 of stock, I do not think that anything has been shown respecting the history of the company from its organization in 1902 to November 22, 1928, or to May 2, 1932, which warrants a finding that during the period here in question, 1928 to 1932, there did not inhere in the assembled and established plant and facilities and going business an element of value in addition to physical assets which the directors were justified in valuing at $ 3,000,000.

The term "good will" is generally used as indicating that element of value which inheres in the fixed and favorable consideration of customers arising from an established and well-known and well-conducted business, and in an enterprise of this sort, enjoying no legal monopoly, and not a public utility in a legal sense, that element of value indisputably is property for which stock may be issued, and in the absence of fraud the judgment of the directors as to its value is controlling. It also is recognized that, apart from good will in that sense, there is what in the public utility rate cases is called "going concern value", by which is meant that element of value which inheres in an assembled and established plant, doing business and earning money, over one not thus advanced, and such element of value is treated as property which must be considered in determining the base upon which the utility is entitled to earn a return, and I can perceive no reason why such "going concern value" should not be recognized here as well as in a utility rate case....

I next turn to the subject of unrealized appreciation and depreciation.

Until 1915 the company's land was carried upon its books at cost. In 1915 the land was written up to 80% of the amount at which it was then assessed for taxation, and in 1918 it was written up to the exact amount at which it was then so assessed. Those two write-ups totaled $ 7,211,791.72, and the result was that during the period here in question the land was carried on the books at $ 8,737,949.02, whereas its actual cost was $ 1,526,157.30. Plaintiff claims that the entire $ 7,211,791.72 should be eliminated because it represents merely unrealized appreciation, and dividends cannot be declared or paid on the basis of mere unrealized appreciation in fixed assets irrespective of how sound the estimate thereof may be. That obviously and concededly is another way of saying that for dividend purposes fixed assets must be computed at cost, not value, and plaintiff here plants himself upon that position, even to the point of contending that evidence of value is immaterial and not admissible. If that contention be sound, the company indisputably had a deficit at all the times here involved in an amount exceeding the dividends here in question....

It is to be emphasized at the outset that the question is not one of sound economics, or of what is sound business judgment or financial policy or of proper accounting practice, or even what the law ought to be. My views of the business acumen or financial sagacity of these directors, as well as my views as to what the legislature ought to permit or prohibit, are entirely immaterial. The question I have to decide is whether or not an existing statute has been violated. The problem is one of statutory construction.

The words of the statute, as it existed during the period here involved, are: "No stock corporation shall declare or pay any dividend which shall impair its capital or capital stock, nor while its capital or capital stock is impaired, nor shall any such corporation declare or pay any dividend or make any distribution of assets to any of its stockholders, whether upon a reduction of the number of its shares or of its capital or capital stock, unless the value of its assets remaining after the payment of such dividend, or after such distribution of assets, as the case may be, shall be at least equal to the aggregate amount of its debts and liabilities including capital or capital stock as the case may be." Stock Corporation Law, § 58.

If the part of the statute containing the words "unless the value of its assets" etc. is to be read as relating back to the beginning of the section, the lack of merit in plaintiff's contention is apparent, for the statute would then read: "No stock corporation shall declare or pay any dividend ... unless the value of its assets remaining after the payment of such dividend ... shall be at least equal to the aggregate amount of its debts and liabilities including capital or capital stock as the case may be." I think there is much to be said in support of the view that that is what was intended, but nevertheless the structure of the statute is such as to make that reading grammatically impossible, and I hence prefer to base my decision upon the assumption that the controlling words of the statute are merely these: "No stock corporation shall declare or pay any dividend which shall impair its capital or capital stock, nor while its capital or capital stock is impaired."

Before one can determine whether or not capital or capital stock has been impaired, one must determine what is capital or capital stock.... To determine its meaning in this statute it ... is essential, I think, to consider the history of the statute and what our courts have said respecting the statute's predecessors.

The earliest provisions upon the subject made it unlawful to declare dividends "excepting from the surplus profits arising from the business" or to "divide, withdraw, or in any way pay to the stockholders, or any of them, any part of the capital stock." Laws 1825, ch. 325, sec. 2; Rev. Stat. 1829, pt. 1, ch. 18, title 4, sec. 2.... In the Stock Corporation Law of 1923 ... all reference to surplus or to profits or to surplus profits was omitted.

It thus appears that after using the surplus and surplus profits terminology for practically a hundred years the legislature completely abandoned it, and I think that is quite significant as indicating a conscious intent to get away from the idea of profits earned as a result of completed transactions as the sole source of dividends. I do not say that the legislature thereby changed the existing law. On the contrary, I think that the terms capital and capital stock as used in the earlier statutes had been construed by the courts in such a way that the terms surplus and surplus profits as used therein necessarily meant any accretion or accumulation over and above debts and the liability to stockholders, and that the legislature of 1923 recognized and adopted that construction and omitted any reference to surplus or surplus profits for the very reason that by some persons those words were believed to convey the idea of and to be confined to an accumulation of net earnings resulting from completed transactions and for the express purpose of so clarifying the statute as to prevent the precise claim which plaintiff now here presses....

[The court proceeded to cite cases construing the revised statutes, all of which defined the fund available for dividends as those corporate assets over and above the corporation's stated or "chartered" capital.]

Those statements by our highest court seem to me to make it entirely plain that the terms capital and capital stock in these statutes mean an amount, *i.e.* a value, of property up to the limit of the number of dollars specified as the par value of paid-up issued shares (or as the stated value of no-par shares), and that when the amount, *i.e.* the value, of the company's property exceeds that number of dollars the excess, whether "contributed by the stockholders or otherwise obtained" is surplus or surplus profits and may be distributed as dividends until the point is reached where such dividends "deplete the assets," *i.e.* the value of the assets, "below the sum," *i.e.* below the number of dollars, specified as the par or stated value of the paid-up issued shares. In other words, the capital or capital stock referred to in these statutes is the sum of the liability to stockholders, and any value which the corporation's property has in addition to that sum is surplus. And I cannot doubt that the words "otherwise obtained" and "accumulated," as used by the court in the cases just mentioned, include an appreciation in the value of property purchased whether realized or unrealized.

....

In summary, I think that it cannot be said that there is a single case in this State which actually decides that unrealized appreciation cannot be taken into consideration, or, stated in different words, that cost and not value must be used in determining whether or not there exists a surplus out of which dividends can be paid. I think, further, that such a holding would run directly counter to the meaning of the terms capital and capital stock as fixed by decisions of the Court of Appeals construing the earlier statutes, and that such construction of those terms must be deemed to have been adopted by the legislature in enacting the statute here involved. I thus obviously cannot follow decisions to the contrary in other States or any contrary views of economists or accountants. If the policy of the law be bad it is for the legislature to change it.

Throughout the period in question the company carried upon its books as assets its investments in and advances to its subsidiaries at their face value, *i.e.* at the cost thereof, and despite his insistence that unrealized appreciation of one asset cannot be taken into consideration, the plaintiff yet insists that these investments and advances must be written down to the value thereof as shown by the books of the subsidiaries, even though the subsidiaries are still carrying on business, and, further, that those books shall be what he calls "properly adjusted," so as to cause them to show the actual value of the stock of and claims against those subsidiaries. He thus, as it seems to me, takes the inconsistent position that while unrealized appreciation cannot be considered, unrealized depreciation nevertheless must be. Defendants, also, take the equally inconsistent position that while unrealized appreciation must be considered, unrealized depreciation need not be. I am of the opinion that the same reasons which show that unrealized appreciation must be considered are equally cogent in showing that unrealized depreciation likewise must be considered. In other words, the test being whether or not the value of the assets exceeds the debts and the liability to stockholders, all assets must be taken at their actual value.

I see no cause for alarm over the fact that this view requires directors to make a determination of the value of the assets at each dividend declaration. On the contrary, I think that is exactly what the law always has contemplated that directors should do. That does not mean that the books themselves necessarily must be altered by write-ups or write-downs at each dividend period, or that formal appraisals must be obtained from professional appraisers or even made by the directors themselves. That is obviously impossible in the case of corporations of any considerable size. But it is not impossible nor unfeasible for directors to consider whether the cost of assets continues over a long period of years to reflect their fair value, and the law does require that directors should really direct in the very important matter of really determining at each dividend declaration whether or not the value of the assets is such as to justify a dividend, rather than do what one director here testified that he did, *viz.* "accept the company's figures."... When directors have in fact exercised an informed judgment with respect to the value of the company's assets, the courts obviously will be exceedingly slow to override that judgment, and clear and convincing evidence will be required to justify a finding that such judgment was not in accordance with the facts. In the last analysis, however, the issue, in any case in which it is claimed that dividends have been paid out of capital, is the value of the assets and the amount of the liabilities to creditors and stockholders at the times the dividends were declared and paid.

Upon the evidence in this case I find that the director here did in fact exercise an informed judgment with respect to the value of the good will, the value of the land of the company, and the value of the improvements thereon, and also with respect to the value of the land and improvements thereon which were owned by the subsidiaries, Bush Terminal Buildings Company and Bush Terminal Railroad Company, and that they believed and determined that the good will was worth $ 3,000,000 and that such land and improvements were worth several millions of dollars more than the amounts at which they were carried on the books....

I find that there was not the same exercise of informed judgment with respect to the value of the investments in and advances to subsidiaries. To a very large extent the value of the investments in and advances to Bush Terminal Buildings Company and Bush Terminal Railroad Company were affected by the value of the land and improvements owned by those companies, as to which I have just found that there was an exercise of an informed judgment; but on the whole I find that the directors accepted the cost of the investments in and advances to all the subsidiaries, as the same were recorded upon the books, without in fact considering the extent to which such recorded costs reflected their true values at the times of the declaration and payment of the dividends here in controversy.

... I find ample evidence to sustain and justify the judgment of the directors that the value of the land and improvements exceeded the sum at which they were carried on the books by an amount sufficient to show a surplus greater than the amount of the dividends even if all the deductions ... claimed by the plaintiff were allowed in full....

Now turning to the land, [the land and buildings were assessed for tax purposes at amounts in excess of the amounts at which they were carried on the books.] Tax assessments in this City and other cities of this State repeatedly have been recognized as competent evidence upon the question of value, and I think it not uncommon for business men to act upon them, within reasonable limits, as a rough and ready indication of value.

... I think that, at least in the absence of some extraordinary circumstance not here appearing, the figures at which the City and the taxpayer have agreed to compromise existing controversies with respect to the amount at which property should be assessed for taxation, fairly and justly may be taken as indicating the fair value of such property, and I here so find. Such figures are here also fully sustained by the testimony of a competent appraiser who here testified for defendants. It is also worthy of note that an engineering expert engaged by plaintiff to fix a value upon the properties and business as a whole accepted assessed valuations of land as at least one basis for his conclusions, and that no real estate appraiser has here attempted to fix a value of the land at lesser figures.

Each side has submitted an elaborate and detailed appraisal by an engineering appraiser of high repute. Each such appraiser has undertaken to find reproduction cost and also to arrive at a valuation by the method of capitalizing earnings, or a valuation supported by income, as it is expressed by one of them. Their views as to reproduction cost are not widely divergent despite the fact that they arrive at their conclusions upon that point by quite different methods, and under the view of either the surplus, *i.e.* the excess of asset value over liabilities to creditors and stockholders, at all times here in question, was substantially greater than the dividends paid. It is only when they come to arrive at a valuation by the method of capitalizing earnings that the views of these appraisers assume sharp contrast.... I conclude that the earnings support a value substantially as found by defendants' engineering appraiser.

It actually is unnecessary to go that far. Taking the land and improvements at the values fixed as a result of plaintiff's own compromise with the City's taxing authorities, taking the investments in and advances to subsidiaries at the values fixed by plaintiff's own witnesses ..., taking the good will at $ 3,000,000 and taking the other items of assets which have not been questioned at the values at which they appear ... (each of which things I find it proper to do) gives a total of assets far in excess of all liabilities to creditors and stockholders.

In summary, therefore, after considering all the evidence, I find that at the times these dividends were declared and paid the value of the assets exceeded the total liabilities to creditors and stockholders by an amount in excess of the total dividends, and that there accordingly was no impairment of capital or capital stock.

....

_____

The statute in *Randall v. Bailey* is now quite old-fashioned. The question therefore arises as to whether the *Randall* result would obtain under a modern statute. The Model Act (1984) provides an example. Under § 6.40(c), a dividend may be issued so long as the corporation is not insolvent or rendered insolvent by the payment of the dividend as determined by two tests: it would be able to pay its current obligations as they come due and its total assets would equal or exceed the sum of its total liabilities and the liquidation rights of priority claimants. Directors may base their determination that a dividend is permissible either on financial statements based on reasonable accounting practices or on a fair valuation.

According to the Official Comment for § 6.40(c):

> [T]he statute authorizes departures from historical cost accounting and sanctions the use of appraisal and current value methods to determine the amount available for distributions. No particular method of valuation is prescribed in the statute, since different methods may have validity depending upon the circumstances, including the type of enterprise and the

purpose for which the determination is made. For example, it is inappropriate to apply a "quick-sale liquidation" method to value an enterprise, particularly with respect to the payment of normal dividends. On the other hand, a "quick-sale liquidation valuation" method might be appropriate in certain circumstances for an enterprise in the course of reducing its asset or business base by a material degree. In most cases, a fair valuation method or a going-concern basis would be appropriate if it is believed that the enterprise will continue as a going concern.

Ordinarily a corporation should not selectively revalue assets. It should consider the value of all its material assets, whether or not reflected in the financial statements (*e.g.* a valuable executory contract). Likewise, all of a corporation's material obligations should be considered and revalued to the extent appropriate and possible. In any event, section 6.40 (d) calls for the application under section 6.40 (c)(2) of a method of determining the aggregate amount of assets and liabilities that is reasonable in the circumstances.

In jurisdictions, like Delaware, dividends are paid out of surplus. In this case, surplus can be created in three ways. As stated earlier, capital surplus is the amount of the difference between the price at which a corporation issues stock and the stock's par value. Reduction surplus is created when an amount is transferred from stated capital to surplus. Revaluation surplus is the value of the unrealized appreciation in the company's fixed assets.

The fact that directors may pay dividends based on unrealized appreciation does not mean that they will. A mistake in issuing dividends makes assenting directors liable for the impermissible amount of the distribution.

B. JUDICIAL REVIEW OF DIVIDEND POLICY

Corporation statutes provide that a corporation's board of directors may declare dividends when certain conditions are met. Those statutes never require directors to declare dividends, and for good reason. The directors may determine that retaining company earnings, or using them in another way, may present opportunities for company growth that will be lost if dividends are declared. In some situations, however, courts have been willing to require corporations to pay dividends. These cases usually involve proprietary companies. Modern cases involving suits by shareholders over nondeclaration of dividends give plaintiffs a heavy burden. That is well exemplified by *Gay v. Gay's Supermarkets, Inc.*,[15] decided by the Maine Supreme Court in 1975. There the court indicated that to

---

[15] 343 A.2d 577 (Me. 1975).

justify judicial intervention, the plaintiff must show "that the decision not to declare a dividend amounted to fraud, bad faith or an abuse of discretion on the part of the [directors]." Further, the court indicated, "If there are plausible business reasons supportive of the decision of the board of directors, and such reasons can be given credence, a Court will not interfere with a corporate board's right to make that decision."

Chapter 10

DUTY OF CARE

Situation

Biologistics, Inc., has continued to be successful. It has been in existence three years, and even with greatly increased expenses, its profits have increased incrementally. Its research and development activities have been proceeding satisfactorily, although no patentable proess has yet been perfected. The research and development work has been expensive, however, and to raise funds for these activities the corporation has taken another bank loan in the amount of $ 100,000 and has sold a total of $ 200,000 of stock to four local investors who have done business with Phillips' investment banking firm. Each new shareholder was given two and a half percent of the total outstanding common stock for $ 50,000. Anderson, Baker, and Phillips now each own 30% of the common stock.

At the time of the stock sale, the board's composition was changed. It now consists of Anderson, Baker, Phillips, Sara Martinez, who is a vice president of the corporation's local bank, and Jason Welsh, who is one of the new shareholders. In the year Welsh has been a director, there have been several board meetings, but he has been unable to attend any of them.

Notwithstanding its success, a problem recently developed that could have serious financial consequences for the corporation. Disturbing amounts of chemical pollution have been discovered recently in wells supplying some of the community's water. Newspaper reporters have focused on Biologistics, Inc. as a possible source of this pollution. The company's employees deny improperly disposing of any chemical wastes or otherwise contaminating the water, and Anderson and Baker say they are quite confident that these denials are sincere. Nevertheless, they cannot be sure.

A special directors' meeting is called for next Monday. The directors anticipate discussing and deciding what to do about the media's inquiries and the possibility that Biologistics somehow contributed to the chemical pollution. Baker has heard of a detection and filtering system for its chemical byproducts that is reportedly very effective but also very expensive. Another alternative is to close the existing facility and relocate to another community.

Meanwhile, the three new shareholders other than Welsh meet with Phillips. They are concerned about the possibility that Biologistics, Inc. is responsible for the pollution and, if so, that a suit against the corporation could bankrupt it. They obliquely raised with Phillips the possibility of suing the directors for mismanagement if this comes to pass.

The directors would like your advice prior to the Monday meeting. In particular, they are concerned about their possible liabilities and want to know ways to diminish their risk of liabilities, and they wonder whether they can make whatever decisions they like.

SECTION I. INTRODUCTION

The corporation's directors and officers are subject to two traditional fiduciary duties: the duty of care, discussed in this chapter, and the duty of loyalty, discussed in the next chapter. Other chapters on shareholder derivative litigation and changes in corporate control continue to explore how these fiduciary duties are construed in particular contexts.

These fiduciary duties impose on key corporate decisionmakers the primary corporate law parameters within which they manage corporate affairs. While courts acknowledge that directors and officers need discretion to pursue the entrepreneurial and profit-making activities of the corporation, they also recognize that directors and officers must meet certain standards of diligence, accountability, and propriety to serve the corporation and its shareholders properly.

This chapter explores how corporate law has crafted these standards of conduct — beginning with an orientation to the general standard of care, followed by a discussion of the business judgment rule and the requirements of informed decisionmaking. As the materials on the duty of care unfold, consider how the law tries to balance managerial discretion with the protection of various corporate interests including less traditional constituencies. These materials also illustrate the rich interplay between courts, legislators, and corporate management — who are collectively shaping the practices and risks of corporate decisionmaking.

SECTION II. GENERAL STANDARD OF CARE

A. THE FAILURE TO MONITOR

FRANCIS v. UNITED JERSEY BANK

Supreme Court of New Jersey
432 A.2d 814 (1981)

POLLOCK, J:

The primary issue on this appeal is whether a corporate director is personally liable in negligence for the failure to prevent the misappropriation of trust funds by other directors who were also officers and shareholders of the corporation.

Plaintiffs are trustees in bankruptcy of Pritchard & Baird Intermediaries Corp. (Pritchard & Baird), a reinsurance broker or intermediary. Defendant Lillian P. Overcash is the daughter of Lillian G. Pritchard and the executrix of her estate. At the time of her death, Mrs. Pritchard was a director and the largest single shareholder of Pritchard & Baird. Because Mrs. Pritchard died after the institution of suit but before trial, her executrix was substituted as a defendant. United Jersey Bank is joined as the administrator of the estate of Charles

Pritchard, Sr., who had been president, director and majority shareholder of Pritchard & Baird.

This litigation focuses on payments made by Pritchard & Baird to Charles Pritchard, Jr. and William Pritchard, who were sons of Mr. and Mrs. Charles Pritchard, Sr., as well as officers, directors and shareholders of the corporation. Claims against Charles, Jr. and William are being pursued in bankruptcy proceedings against them.

....

... [T]he initial question is whether Mrs. Pritchard was negligent in not noticing and trying to prevent the misappropriation of funds held by the corporation in an implied trust. A further question is whether her negligence was the proximate cause of the plaintiffs' losses. Both lower courts found that she was liable in negligence for the losses caused by the wrongdoing of Charles, Jr. and William. We affirm

I

The matrix for our decision is the customs and practices of the reinsurance industry and the role of Pritchard & Baird as a reinsurance broker. Reinsurance involves a contract under which one insurer agrees to indemnify another for loss sustained under the latter's policy of insurance. Insurance companies that insure against losses arising out of fire or other casualty seek at times to minimize their exposure by sharing risks with other insurance companies. Thus, when the face amount of a policy is comparatively large, the company may enlist one or more insurers to participate in that risk. Similarly, an insurance company's loss potential and overall exposure may be reduced by reinsuring a part of an entire class of policies (e.g., 25% of all of its fire insurance policies). The selling insurance company is known as a ceding company. The entity that assumes the obligation is designated as the reinsurer.

The reinsurance broker arranges the contract between the ceding company and the reinsurer.... In most instances, the ceding company and the reinsurer do not communicate with each other, but rely upon the reinsurance broker....

The reinsurance business was described by an expert at trial as having "a magic aura around it of dignity and quality and integrity." A telephone call which might be confirmed by a handwritten memorandum is sufficient to create a reinsurance obligation....

... When incorporated under the laws of the State of New York in 1959, Pritchard & Baird had five directors: Charles Pritchard, Sr., his wife Lillian Pritchard, their son Charles Pritchard, Jr., George Baird and his wife Marjorie. William Pritchard, another son, became director in 1960.... The corporation issued 200 shares of common stock. Charles Pritchard, Sr. acquired 120 shares, his sons Charles Pritchard, Jr., 15 and William, 15; Mr. and Mrs. Baird owned the remaining 50. In June 1964, Baird and his wife resigned as directors and sold their stock to the corporation. From that time on the corporation operated as a close family corporation with Mr. and Mrs. Pritchard and their two sons as the only directors. After the death of Charles, Sr. in 1973, only the remaining three directors continued to operate as the board. Lillian Pritchard inherited 72 of her husband's 120 shares in Pritchard & Baird, thereby becoming the largest shareholder in the corporation with 48% of the stock.

The corporate minute books reflect only perfunctory activities by the directors, related almost exclusively to the election of officers and adoption of banking resolutions and a retirement plan. None of the minutes for any of the meetings contain a discussion of the loans to Charles, Jr. and William or of the financial condition of the corporation. Moreover, upon instructions of Charles, Jr. that financial statements were not to be circulated to anyone else, the company's statements for the fiscal years beginning February 1, 1970, were delivered only to him.

Charles Pritchard, Sr. was the chief executive and controlled the business in the years following Baird's withdrawal. Beginning in 1966, he gradually relinquished control over the operations of the corporation. In 1968, Charles, Jr. became president and William became executive vice president. Charles, Sr. apparently became ill in 1971 and during the last year and a half of his life was not involved in the affairs of the business. He continued, however, to serve as a director until his death on December 10, 1973. Notwithstanding the presence of Charles, Sr. on the board until his death in 1973, Charles, Jr. dominated the management of the corporation and the board from 1968 until the bankruptcy in 1975.

Contrary to the industry custom of segregating funds, Pritchard & Baird commingled the funds of reinsurers and ceding companies with its own funds. All monies (including commissions, premiums and loss monies) were deposited in a single account. Charles, Sr. began the practice of withdrawing funds from the commingled account in transactions identified on the corporate books as "loans." As long as Charles, Sr. controlled the corporation, the "loans" correlated with corporate profits and were repaid at the end of each year. Starting in 1970, however, Charles, Jr. and William begin to siphon ever-increasing sums from the corporation under the guise of loans. As of January 31, 1970, the "loans" to Charles, Jr. were $ 230,932 and to William were $ 207,329. At least by January 31, 1973, the annual increase in the loans exceeded annual corporate revenues. By October 1975, the year of bankruptcy, the "shareholders' loans" had metastasized to a total of $ 12,333,514.47.

The trial court rejected the characterization of the payments as "loans." 162 N.J. Super. at 365, 392 A.2d 1233. No corporate resolution authorized the "loans," and no note or other instrument evidenced the debt. Charles, Jr. and William paid no interest on the amounts received. The "loans" were not repaid or reduced from one year to the next; rather, they increased annually.

    ....

The "loans" were reflected on financial statements that were prepared annually as of January 31, the end of the corporate fiscal year. Although an outside certified public accountant prepared the 1970 financial statement, the corporation prepared only internal financial statements from 1971-1975. In all instances, the statements were simple documents, consisting of three or four 8½ x 11 inch sheets.

The statements of financial condition from 1970 forward demonstrated:

	WORKING CAPITAL DEFICIT	SHAREHOLDERS' LOANS	NET BROKERAGE INCOME
1970	$ 389,022	$ 509,941	$ 807,229
1971	not available	not available	not available
1972	$ 1,684,289	$ 1,825,911	$ 1,546,263
1973	$ 3,506,460	$ 3,700,542	$ 1,736,349
1974	$ 6,939,007	$ 7,080,629	$ 876,182
1975	$ 10,176,419	$ 10,298,039	$ 551,598

Those financial statements showed working capital deficits increasing annually in tandem with the amounts that Charles, Jr. and William withdrew as "shareholders' loans." In the last complete year of business (January 31, 1974, to January 31, 1975), "shareholders' loans" and the correlative working capital deficit increased by approximately $ 3,200,000.

....

The pattern that emerges from these figures is the substantial increase in the monies appropriated by Charles Pritchard, Jr. and William Pritchard after their father's withdrawal from the business and the sharp decline in the profitability of the operation after his death. This led ultimately to the filing in December, 1975, of an involuntary petition in bankruptcy and the appointments of the plaintiffs as trustees in bankruptcy of Pritchard & Baird.

Mrs. Pritchard was not active in the business of Pritchard & Baird and knew virtually nothing of its corporate affairs. She briefly visited the corporate offices in Morristown on only one occasion, and she never read or obtained the annual financial statements. She was unfamiliar with the rudiments of reinsurance and made no effort to assure that the policies and practices of the corporation, particularly pertaining to the withdrawal of funds, complied with industry custom or relevant law. Although her husband had warned her that Charles, Jr. would "take the shirt off my back," Mrs. Pritchard did not pay any attention to her duties as a director or to the affairs of the corporation. 162 N.J. Super. at 370, 392 A.2d 1233.

After her husband died in December 1973, Mrs. Pritchard became incapacitated and was bedridden for a six-month period. She became listless at this time and started to drink rather heavily. Her physical condition deteriorated, and in 1978 she died. The trial court rejected testimony seeking to exonerate her because she "was old, was grief-stricken at the loss of her husband, sometimes consumed too much alcohol and was psychologically overborne by her sons." 162 N.J. Super. at 371, 392 A.2d 1233. That court found that she was competent to act and that the reason Mrs. Pritchard never knew what her sons "were doing was because she never made the slightest effort to discharge any of her responsibilities as a director of Pritchard & Baird." 162 N.J. Super. at 372, 392 A.2d 1233.

...

III

Individual liability of a corporate director for acts of the corporation is a prickly problem. Generally directors are accorded broad immunity and are not insurers of corporate activities. The problem is particularly nettlesome when a third party asserts that a director, because of nonfeasance, is liable for losses caused by acts of insiders, who in this case were officers, directors and shareholders. Determination of the liability of Mrs. Pritchard requires findings that she had a duty to the clients of Pritchard & Baird, that she breached that duty and that her breach was a proximate cause of their losses.

The New Jersey Business Corporation Act, which took effect on January 1, 1969, was a comprehensive revision of the statutes relating to business corporations. One section, N.J.S.A. 14A:6-14, concerning a director's general obligation makes it incumbent upon directors to

> discharge their duties in good faith and with that degree of diligence, care and skill which ordinarily prudent men would exercise under similar circumstances in like positions.

This provision was based primarily on section 43 of the Model Business Corporation Act and is derived also from section 717 of the New York Business Corporation Law (L.1961, c.855, effective September 1, 1963)....

....

... In addition to requiring that directors act honestly and in good faith, the New York courts recognized that the nature and extent of reasonable care depended upon the type of corporation, its size and financial resources. Thus, a bank director was held to stricter accountability than the director of an ordinary business....

....

As a general rule, a director should acquire at least a rudimentary understanding of the business of the corporation. Accordingly, a director should become familiar with the fundamentals of the business in which the corporation is engaged. *Campbell*, 62 N.J. Eq. at 416, 50 A. 120. Because directors are bound to exercise ordinary care, they cannot set up as a defense lack of the knowledge needed to exercise the requisite degree of care. If one "feels that he has not had sufficient business experience to qualify him to perform the duties of a director, he should either acquire the knowledge by inquiry, or refuse to act." *Ibid*.

Directors are under a continuing obligation to keep informed about the activities of the corporation. Otherwise, they may not be able to participate in the overall management of corporate affairs.... Directors may not shut their eyes to corporate misconduct and then claim that because they did not see the misconduct, they did not have a duty to look. The sentinel asleep at his post contributes nothing to the enterprise he is charged to protect.

Directorial management does not require a detailed inspection of day-to-day activities, but rather a general monitoring of corporate affairs and policies. Accordingly, a director is well advised to attend board meetings regularly. Indeed, a director who is absent from a board meeting is presumed to concur in action taken on a corporate matter, unless he files a "dissent with the secretary of the corporation within a reasonable time after learning of such action." N.J.S.A. 14A:6-13 (Supp. 1981-1982). Regular attendance does not mean that directors must attend every meeting, but that directors should attend meetings as a matter of practice. A director of a publicly held corporation might be expected to attend regular monthly meetings, but a director of a small, family corporation might be asked to attend only an annual meeting. The point is that one of the responsibilities of a director is to attend meetings of the board of which he or she is a member....

While directors are not required to audit corporate books, they should maintain familiarity with the financial status of the corporation by a regular review of financial statements. In some circumstances, directors may be charged with assuring that bookkeeping methods conform to industry custom and usage. The extent of review, as well as the nature and frequency of financial statements, depends not only on the customs of the industry, but also on the nature of the corporation and the business in which it is engaged. Financial statements of some small corporations may be prepared internally and only on an annual basis; in a large publicly held corporation, the statements may be produced monthly or at some other regular interval. Adequate financial review normally would be more informal in a private corporation than in a publicly held corporation.

....

... Sometimes the duty of a director may require more than consulting with outside counsel. A director may have a duty to take reasonable means to prevent illegal conduct by co-directors; in any appropriate case, this may include threat of suit.

A director is not an ornament, but an essential component of corporate governance. Consequently, a director cannot protect himself behind a paper shield bearing the motto, "dummy director." The New Jersey Business Corporation Act, in imposing a standard of ordinary care on all directors, confirms that dummy, figurehead and accommodation directors are anachronisms with no place in New Jersey law.... Thus, all directors are responsible for managing the business and affairs of the corporation.

The factors that impel expanded responsibility in the large, publicly held corporation may not be present in a small, close corporation. Nonetheless, a close corporation may, because of the nature of its business, be affected with a public interest. For example, the stock of a bank may be closely held, but because of the nature of banking the directors would be subject to greater liability than those of another close corporation. Even in a small corporation, a director is held to the standard of that degree of care that an ordinarily prudent director would use under the circumstances.

A director's duty of care does not exist in the abstract, but must be considered in relation to specific obligees. In general, the relationship of a corporate director to the corporation and its stockholders is that of a fiduciary. Shareholders have a right to expect that directors will exercise reasonable supervision and control over the policies and practices of a corporation. The institutional integrity of a corporation depends upon the proper discharge by directors of those duties.

While directors may owe a fiduciary duty to creditors also, that obligation generally has not been recognized in the absence of insolvency. With certain corporations, however, directors are seemed to owe a duty to creditors and other third parties even when the corporation is solvent. Although depositors of a bank are considered in some respects to be creditors, courts have recognized that directors may owe them a fiduciary duty. Directors of nonbanking corporations may owe a similar duty when the corporation holds funds of others in trust.

....

As a reinsurance broker, Pritchard & Baird received annually as a fiduciary millions of dollars of clients' money which it was under a duty to segregate. To this extent, it resembled a bank rather than a small family business. Accordingly, Mrs. Pritchard's relationship to the clientele of Pritchard & Baird was akin to that of a director of a bank to its depositors....

As a director of a substantial reinsurance brokerage corporation, she should have known that it received annually millions of dollars of loss and premium funds which it held in trust for ceding and reinsurance companies. Mrs. Pritchard should have obtained and read the annual statements of financial condition of Pritchard & Baird. Although she had a right to rely upon financial statements prepared in accordance with N.J.S.A. 14A:6-14, such reliance would not excuse her conduct. The reason is that those statements disclosed on their face the misappropriation of trust funds.

From those statements, she should have realized that, as of January 31, 1970, her sons were withdrawing substantial trust funds under the guise of "Shareholders' Loans." The financial statements for each fiscal year commencing with that of January 31, 1970, disclosed that the working capital deficits and the "loans" were escalating in tandem. Detecting a misappropriation of funds would not have required special expertise or extraordinary diligence; a cursory reading of the financial statements would have revealed the pillage. Thus, if Mrs. Pritchard had read the financial statements, she would have known that her sons were converting trust funds. When financial statements demonstrate that insiders are bleeding a corporation to death, a director should notice and try to stanch the flow of blood.

In summary, Mrs. Pritchard was charged with the obligation of basic knowledge and supervision of the business of Pritchard & Baird. Under the circumstances, this obligation included reading and understanding financial statements, and making reasonable attempts at detection and prevention of the illegal conduct of other officers and directors. She had a duty to protect the clients of Pritchard & Baird against policies and practices that would result in the misappropriation of money they had entrusted to the corporation. She breached that duty.

IV

Nonetheless, the negligence of Mrs. Pritchard does not result in liability unless it is a proximate cause of the loss. Analysis of proximate cause requires an initial determination of cause-in-fact. Causation-in-fact calls for a finding that the defendant's act or omission was a necessary antecedent of the loss, *i.e.*, that if the defendant had observed his or her duty of care, the loss would not have occurred. Further, the plaintiff has the burden of establishing the amount of the loss or damages caused by the negligence of the defendant. Thus, the plaintiff must establish not only a breach of duty, "but in addition that the performance by the director of his duty would have avoided loss, and the amount of the resulting loss." [1 G. Hornstein, Corporation Law and Practice, § 446 at 566 (1959).]

Cases involving nonfeasance present a much more difficult causation question than those in which the director has committed an affirmative act of negligence leading to the loss. Analysis in cases of negligent omissions calls for determination of the reasonable steps a director should have taken and whether that course of action would have averted the loss.

....

In this case, the scope of Mrs. Pritchard's duties was determined by the precarious financial condition of Pritchard & Baird, its fiduciary relationship to its clients and the implied trust in which it held their funds. Thus viewed, the scope of her duties encompassed all reasonable action to stop the continuing conversion. Her duties extended beyond mere objection and resignation to reasonable attempts to prevent the misappropriation of the trust funds.

A leading case discussing causation where the director's liability is predicated upon a negligent failure to act is *Barnes v. Andrews*, 298 F. 614 (S.D.N.Y. 1924). In that case the court exonerated a figurehead director who served for eight months on a board that held one meeting after his election, a meeting he was forced to miss because of the death of his mother. Writing for the court, Judge Learned Hand distinguished a director who fails to prevent general mismanagement from one such as Mrs. Pritchard who failed to stop an illegal "loan":

> When the corporate funds have been illegally lent, it is a fair inference that a protest would have stopped the loan, and that the director's neglect caused the loss. But when a business fails from general mismanagement, business incapacity, or bad judgment, how is it possible to say that a single director could have made the company successful, or how much in dollars he could have saved? [*Id.* at 616-617]

Pointing out the absence of proof of proximate cause between defendant's negligence and the company's insolvency, Judge Hand also wrote:

> The plaintiff must, however, go further than to show that [the director] should have been more active in his duties. This cause of action rests upon a tort, as much though it be a tort of omission as though it had rested upon a positive act. The plaintiff must accept the burden of showing that the performance of the defendant's duties would have avoided loss, and what loss it would have avoided. [*Id.* at 616]

....

In assessing whether Mrs. Pritchard's conduct was a legal or proximate cause of the conversion, "(l)egal responsibility must be limited to those causes which are so closely connected with the result and of such significance that the law is justified in imposing liability." [W. Prosser, Law of Torts, § 41 at 237 (4 ed. 1971).] Such a judicial determination involves not only considerations of causation-in-fact and matters of policy, but also common sense and logic. The act or the failure to act must be a substantial factor in producing the harm.

Within Pritchard & Baird, several factors contributed to the loss of the funds: commingling of corporate and client monies, conversion of funds by Charles, Jr. and William and dereliction of her duties by Mrs. Pritchard. The wrongdoing of her sons, although the immediate cause of the loss, should not excuse Mrs. Pritchard from her negligence which also was a substantial factor contributing to the loss. Her sons knew that she, the only other director, was not reviewing their conduct; they spawned their fraud in the backwater of her neglect. Her neglect of duty contributed to the climate of corruption; her failure to act contributed to the continuation of that corruption. Consequently, her conduct was a substantial factor contributing to the loss.

Analysis of proximate cause is especially difficult in a corporate context where the allegation is that nonfeasance of a director is a proximate cause of damage to a third party. Where a case involves nonfeasance, no one can say "with absolute certainty what would have occurred if the defendant had acted otherwise." Prosser, *supra*, § 41 at 242. Nonetheless, where it is reasonable to conclude that the failure to act would produce a particular result and that result has followed, causation may be inferred. *Ibid.* We conclude that even if Mrs. Pritchard's mere objection had not stopped the depredations of her sons, her consultation with an attorney and the threat of suit would have deterred them. That conclusion flows as a matter of common sense and logic from the record. Whether in other situations a director has a duty to do more than protest and resign is best left to case-by-case determinations. In this case, we are satisfied that there was a duty to do more than object and resign. Consequently, we find that Mrs. Pritchard's negligence was a proximate cause of the misappropriations.

....

The judgment of the Appellate Division is

Affirmed.

1. General Standard

In determining whether directors and officers have met their duty of care, it is helpful to distinguish between two aspects of the duty. First, in carrying out their general responsibilities, directors are subject to a general standard of conduct. As illustrated in *Francis*, this standard is often described in negligence terms: What must ordinarily prudent directors do? Have the directors excessively neglected their obligations?

Once directors actually make conscious business decisions, however, courts utilize the business judgment rule to evaluate the directors' decisionmaking process. This more frequent application of the duty of care will be explored in later cases in this chapter.

Carefully consider the language and the comments of the Model Act § 8.30(a) in its articulation of the general standard of care. Like the Model Act, ALI § 4.01(a) also embodies a reasonableness standard:

> (a) A director or officer has a duty to the corporation to perform the director's or officer's functions in good faith, in a manner that he or she reasonably believes to be in the best interests of the corporation, and with the care that an ordinarily prudent person would reasonably be expected to exercise in a like position and under similar circumstances....

The meaning of the key terms is not easily discernible and there is little case law to assist us. Do the following Comments to Model Act § 8.30(a) clarify the meanings?

(1) The reference to "ordinarily prudent person" embodies long traditions of the common law, in contrast to suggested standards that might call for some undefined degree of expertise, like "ordinarily prudent business-man." The phrase recognizes the need for innovation, essential to profit orientation, and focuses on the basic director attributes of common sense, practical wisdom, and informed judgment.

(2) The phrase "in a like position" recognizes that the "care" under consideration is that which would be used by the "ordinarily prudent person" if he were a director of the particular corporation.

(3) The combined phrase "in a like position ... under similar circumstances" is intended to recognize that (a) the nature and extent of responsibilities will vary, depending upon such factors as the size, complexity, urgency, and location of activities carried on by the particular corporation, (b) decisions must be made on the basis of the information known to the directors without the benefit of hindsight, and (c) the special background, qualifications, and management responsibilities of a particular director may be relevant in evaluating his compliance with the standard of care. Even though the quoted phrase takes into account the special background, qualifications and management responsibilities of a particular director, it does not excuse a director lacking business experience or particular

expertise from exercising the common sense, practical wisdom, and informed judgment of an "ordinarily prudent person."

These Comments suggest that directors are not required to have special expertise, but suppose they do. If Mrs. Pritchard had graduate training in business and was a financial wizard, how would that have altered her standard of conduct?

2. Oversight Responsibilities

The *Francis* case concludes that a director that does nothing does not do enough, but what specifically must directors and officers do to satisfy their basic standard of care? Corporate statutes do not define directors' and officers' functions with specificity. The provisions in corporate certificates of incorporation, bylaws, and directors' and shareholders' resolutions are typically vague.

While the *Corporate Director's Guidebook* cannot serve as legal precedent, it is a practical description of directors' basic responsibilities in most business settings. Prepared by the Section of Business Law of the American Bar Association, it is intended as corporate practice recommendations. The following excerpt describes directors' oversight tasks.

American Bar Association, Corporate Directors Guidebook, pp. 4-6 (2d ed. 1994)*

- approving fundamental operating, financial, and other corporate plans, strategies, and objectives;
- evaluating the performance of the corporation and its senior management and taking appropriate action, including removal, when warranted;
- selecting, regularly evaluating, and fixing the compensation of senior executives;
- requiring, approving, and implementing senior executive succession plans;
- adopting policies of corporate conduct, including compliance with applicable laws and regulations, and maintenance of accounting, financial, and other controls;
- reviewing the process of providing appropriate financial and operational information to decisionmakers (including board members); and
- evaluating the overall effectiveness of the board.

Stated broadly, the principal responsibility of a corporate director is to promote the best interests of the corporation and its shareholders in directing the corporation's business and affairs.

In so doing, the director should give primary consideration to long-term economic objectives. However, a director should also be concerned that the corporation conducts its affairs with due appreciation of public expectations, taking into consideration trends in the law and ethical standards. Furthermore, pursuit of the corporation's economic objectives may include consideration of the effect of corporate policies and operations upon the corporation's employees, the public, and the environment. Many states have adopted legislation expressly recognizing that corporate directors may consider the effect of corporate action on constituencies other than shareholders, such as employees, local communities, suppliers, and customers. Nevertheless, the law normally does not hold a corporate director directly responsible to constituencies other than shareholders in the formulation of corporate policy.

A director should exercise independent judgment for the overall benefit of the corporation and all of its shareholders, even if elected at the request of a controlling shareholder, a union, a creditor, or an institutional shareholder or pursuant to contractual rights.

To be effective, a director should become familiar with the corporation's business. This knowledge should enable the director to make an independent evaluation of senior management performance and allow the director to join with other directors to support, challenge, and reward management as warranted. Accordingly, all directors should have a basic understanding of the:

- principal operational and financial objectives, strategies, and plans of the corporation;
- results of operations and financial condition of the corporation and of any significant subsidiaries and business segments; and
- relative standing of the business segments within the corporation and vis-à-vis competitors.

In addition, a director should be satisfied that an effective system is in place for periodic and timely reporting to the board on the following matters:

- current business and financial performance, the degree of achievement of approved objectives, and the need to address forward-planning issues;
- financial statements, with appropriate segment or divisional breakdowns;
- compliance with law and corporate policies; and
- material litigation and regulatory matters.

Finally, directors should do their homework. They should review board and committee meeting agendas and related materials sufficiently in advance of meetings to enable them to participate in an informed manner. They should receive and review reports of all board and committee meetings.

Given these guidelines, how would you have advised Mrs. Pritchard?

The court in *Francis* held that Mrs. Pritchard breached her general standard of care, but there are surprisingly few cases that have reached the same conclusion. The ALI cites fewer than ten cases that have found "negligent liability," as indicated in ALI Reporter's Note 17 to § 4.01(a). Why? The court also appeared to place on the plaintiff the burden of showing that Mrs. Pritchard breached her general standard of care and that the breach was the proximate cause of the corporation's losses. ALI § 4.01(d) expressly agrees with this allocation of the burden. Exactly what must the plaintiff prove?

3. Type of Institution

In *Francis*, as in many financial institutions, the corporation received large sums of money in trust. Given the potential for directors' and officers' fraudulent abuse of these funds, should the directors of these institutions be held to a higher standard of conduct? While some cases have applied a higher standard, the ALI Intro. Note *d* to ALI § 4.01 has rejected this distinction as "unjustified and anachronistic." Would the court in *Francis* have reached a different decision if the corporation had been a manufacturing company?

B. DUTY TO INQUIRE

GRAHAM v. ALLIS-CHALMERS MANUFACTURING CO.

Supreme Court of Delaware
188 A.2d 125 (1963)

WOLCOTT, JUSTICE:

This is a derivative action on behalf of Allis-Chalmers against its directors and four of its non-director employees. The complaint is based upon indictments of Allis-Chalmers and the four non-director employees named as defendants herein who, with the corporation, entered pleas of guilty to the indictments. The indictments, eight in number, charged violations of the Federal anti-trust laws. The suit seeks to recover damages which Allis-Chalmers is claimed to have suffered by reason of these violations.

. . . .

The complaint alleges actual knowledge on the part of the director defendants of the anti-trust conduct upon which the indictments were based or, in the alternative, knowledge of facts which should have put them on notice of such conduct.

However, the hearing and depositions produced no evidence that any director had any actual knowledge of the anti-trust activity, or had actual knowledge of any facts which should have put them on notice that anti-trust activity was being carried on by some of their company's employees. The plaintiffs, appellants here, thereupon shifted the theory of the case to the proposition that the directors are liable as a matter of law by reason of their failure to take action designed to learn of and prevent anti-trust activity on the part of any employees of Allis-Chalmers.

By this appeal the plaintiffs seek to have us reverse the Vice Chancellor's ruling of non-liability of the defendant directors upon this theory ...

Allis-Chalmers is a manufacturer of a variety of electrical equipment. It employs in excess of 31,000 people, has a total of 24 plants, 145 sales offices, 5000 dealers and distributors, and its sales volume is in excess of $ 500,000,000 annually. The operations of the company are conducted by two groups, each of which is under the direction of a senior vice president. One of these groups is the Industries Group under the direction of Singleton, director defendant. This group is divided into five divisions. One of these, the Power Equipment Division, produced the products, the sale of which involved the anti-trust activities referred to in the indictments. The Power Equipment Division, presided over by McMullen, non-director defendant, contains ten departments, each of which is presided over by a manager or general manager.

The operating policy of Allis-Chalmers is to decentralize by the delegation of authority to the lowest possible management level capable of fulfilling the delegated responsibility. Thus, prices of products are ordinarily set by the particular department manager, except that if the product being priced is large and special, the department manager might confer with the general manager of the division. Products of a standard character involving repetitive manufacturing processes are sold out of a price list which is established by a price leader for the electrical equipment industry as a whole.

Annually, the Board of Directors reviews group and departmental profit goal budgets. On occasion, the Board considers general questions concerning price levels, but because of the complexity of the company's operations the Board does not participate in decisions fixing the prices of specific products.

The Board of Directors of fourteen members, four of whom are officers, meets once a month, October excepted, and considers a previously prepared agenda for the meeting. Supplied to the Directors at the meetings are financial and operating data relating to all phases of the company's activities. The Board meetings are customarily of several hours duration in which all the Directors participate actively. Apparently, the Board considers and decides matters concerning the general business policy of the company. By reason of the extent and complexity of the company's operations, it is not practicable for the Board to consider in detail specific problems of the various divisions.

The indictments to which Allis-Chalmers and the four non-director defendants pled guilty charge that the company and individual non-director defendants, commencing in 1956, conspired with other manufacturers and their employees to fix prices and to rig bids to private electric utilities and governmental agencies in violation of the anti-trust laws of the United States. None of the director defendants in this cause were named as defendants in the indictments. Indeed, the Federal Government acknowledged that it had uncovered no probative evidence which could lead to the conviction of the defendant directors.

The first actual knowledge the directors had of anti-trust violations by some of the company's employees was in the summer of 1959 from newspaper stories that TVA proposed an investigation of identical bids. Singleton, in charge of the Industries Group of the company, investigated but unearthed nothing. Thereafter, in November of 1959, some of the company's employees were subpoenaed before the Grand Jury. Further investigation by the company's Legal Division gave reason to suspect the illegal activity and all of the subpoenaed employees were instructed to tell the whole truth.

Thereafter, on February 8, 1960, at the direction of the Board, a policy statement relating to anti-trust problems was issued, and the Legal Division commenced a series of meetings with all employees of the company in possible areas of anti-trust activity. The purpose and effect of these steps was to eliminate any possibility of further and future violations of the antitrust laws.

As we have pointed out, there is no evidence in the record that the defendant directors had actual knowledge of the illegal anti-trust actions of the company's employees. Plaintiffs, however, point to two FTC decrees of 1937 as warning to the directors that anti-trust activity by the company's employees had taken place in the past. It is argued that they were thus put on notice of their duty to ferret out such activity and to take active steps to insure that it would not be repeated.

The decrees in question were consent decrees entered in 1937 against Allis-Chalmers and nine others enjoining agreements to fix uniform prices on condensors and turbine generators. The decrees recited that they were consented to for the sole purpose of avoiding the trouble and expense of the proceeding.

None of the director defendants were directors or officers of Allis-Chalmers in 1937. The director defendants and now officers of the company either were employed in very subordinate capacities or had no connection with the company in 1937. At the time, copies of the decrees were circulated to the heads of concerned departments and were explained to the Managers Committee.

In 1943, Singleton, officer and director defendant, first learned of the decrees upon becoming Assistant Manager of the Steam Turbine Department, and consulted the company's General Counsel as to them. He investigated his department and learned the decrees were being complied with and, in any event, he concluded that the company had not in the first place been guilty of the practice enjoined.

Stevenson, officer and director defendant, first learned of the decrees in 1951 in a conversation with Singleton about their respective areas of the company's operations. He satisfied himself that the company was not then and in fact had not been guilty of quoting uniform prices and had consented to the decrees in order to avoid the expense and vexation of the proceeding.

Scholl, officer and director defendant, learned of the decrees in 1956 in a discussion with Singleton on matters affecting the Industries Group. He was informed that no similar problem was then in existence in the company.

Plaintiffs argue that because of the 1937 consent decrees, the directors were put on notice that they should take steps to ensure that no employee of Allis-Chalmers would violate the anti-trust laws. The difficulty the argument has is that only three of the present directors knew of the decrees, and all three of them satisfied themselves that Allis-Chalmers had not engaged in the practice enjoined and had consented to the decrees merely to avoid expense and the necessity of defending the company's position. Under the circumstances, we think knowledge by three of the directors that in 1937 the company had consented to the entry of decrees enjoining it from doing something they had satisfied themselves it had never done, did not put the Board on notice of the possibility of future illegal price fixing.

Plaintiffs have wholly failed to establish either actual notice or imputed notice to the Board of Directors of facts which should have put them on guard, and have caused them to take steps to prevent the future possibility of illegal price fixing and bid rigging. Plaintiffs say that as a minimum in this respect the Board should have taken the steps it took in 1960 when knowledge of the facts first actually came to their attention as a result of the Grand Jury investigation. Whatever duty, however, there was upon the Board to take such steps, the fact of the 1937 decrees has no bearing upon the question, for under the circumstances they were [on] notice of nothing.

Plaintiffs are thus forced to rely solely upon the legal proposition advanced by them that directors of a corporation, as a matter of law, are liable for losses suffered by their corporations by reason of their gross inattention to the common law duty of actively supervising and managing the corporate affairs. Plaintiffs rely mainly upon *Briggs v. Spaulding*, 141 U.S. 132 [(1891)].

From the *Briggs* case and others cited by plaintiffs ... it appears that directors of a corporation in managing the corporate affairs are bound to use that amount of care which ordinarily careful and prudent men would use in similar circumstances. Their duties are those of control, and whether or not by neglect they have made themselves liable for failure to exercise proper control depends on the circumstances and facts of the particular case.

The precise charge made against these director defendants is that, even though they had no knowledge of any suspicion of wrongdoing on the part of the company's employees, they still should have put into effect a system of watchfulness which would have brought such misconduct to their attention in ample time to have brought it to an end. However, the *Briggs* case expressly rejects such an idea. On the contrary, it appears that directors are entitled to rely on the honesty and integrity of their subordinates until something occurs to put them on suspicion that something is wrong. If such occurs and goes unheeded, then liability of the directors might well follow, but absent cause for suspicion there is no duty upon the directors to install and operate a corporate system of espionage to ferret out wrongdoing which they have no reason to suspect exists.

The duties of the Allis-Chalmers Directors were fixed by the nature of the enterprise which employed in excess of 30,000 persons, and extended over a large geographical area. By force of necessity, the company's Directors could not know personally all the company's employees. The very magnitude of the enterprise required them to confine their control to the broad policy decisions. That they did this is clear from the record. At the meetings of the Board in which all Directors participated, these questions were considered and decided on the basis of summaries, reports and corporate records. These they were entitled to rely on, not only, we think, under general principles of the common law, but by reason of 8 Del. C. § 141(f) as well, which in [its]terms fully protects a director who relies on such in the performance of his duties.

In the last analysis, the question of whether a corporate director has become liable for losses to the corporation through neglect of duty is determined by the circumstances. If he has recklessly reposed confidence in an obviously untrustworthy employee, has refused or neglected cavalierly to perform his duty as a director, or has ignored either willfully or through inattention obvious danger signs of employee wrongdoing, the law will cast the burden of liability upon him. This is not the case at bar, however, for as soon as it became evident that there were grounds for suspicion, the Board acted promptly to end it and prevent its recurrence.

Plaintiffs say these steps should have been taken long before, even in the absence of suspicion, but we think not, for we know of no rule of law which requires a corporate director to assume, with no justification whatsoever, that all corporate employees are incipient law violators who, but for a tight check rein, will give free vent to their unlawful propensities.

We therefore affirm the Vice Chancellor's ruling that the individual director defendants are not liable as a matter of law merely because, unknown to them, some employees of Allis-Chalmers violated the anti-trust laws thus subjecting the corporation to loss.

    ....

The court in *Graham* indicated that directors can be relatively passive in their oversight responsibilities and any obligations to investigate. Would the court have reached the same conclusion if Allis-Chalmers was a small, closely held corporation as in the *Francis* case?

----

1. ALI Principles

While the Model Act § 8.30 does not refer to a duty to inquire, ALI § 4.01(a)(1), does expressly address the topic:

> The duty [of care] includes the obligation to make, or cause to be made, an inquiry when, but only when, the circumstances would alert a reasonable director or officer to the need therefor. The extent of such inquiry shall be such as the director or officer reasonably believes to be necessary.

2. Caremark International Inc.

What constitutes reasonable conduct also may change over time. In the *Caremark* case,[1] for instance, Chancellor Allen of the Delaware Court of Chancery, considered how current and future courts would interpret the *Graham* case and the duty to monitor and inquire.

> The complaint charges the director defendants with breach of their duty of attention or *care* in connection with the on-going operation of the corporation's business. The claim is that the directors allowed a situation to develop and continue which exposed the corporation to enormous legal liability and that in so doing they violated a *duty* to be active monitors of corporate performance....
>
> ... [w]hat is the board's responsibility with respect to the organization and monitoring of the enterprise to assure that the corporation functions within the law to achieve its purposes?
>
> Modernly this question has been given special importance by an increasing tendency, especially under federal law, to employ the criminal law to assure corporate compliance with external legal requirements, including environmental, financial, employee and product safety as well as assorted other health and safety regulations. In 1991, pursuant to the Sentencing Reform Act of 1984, the United States Sentencing Commission adopted Organization Sentencing Guidelines which impact importantly on the prospective effect these criminal sanctions might have on business corporations. The Guidelines set forth a uniform sentencing structure for organizations to be sentenced for violation of federal criminal statutes and provide for penalties that equal or often massively exceed those previously imposed on corporations. The Guidelines offer powerful incentives for corporations today to have in place compliance programs to detect violations of law, promptly to report violations to appropriate public officials when discovered, and to take prompt, voluntary remedial efforts.
>
> In 1963, the Delaware Supreme Court in *Graham v. Allis-Chalmers Mfg. Co.*, addressed the question of potential liability of board members for losses experienced by the corporation as a result of the corporation having violated the anti-trust laws of the United States. There was no claim in that case that the directors knew about the behavior of subordinate employees of the corporation that had resulted in the liability. Rather, as in this case, the claim asserted was that the directors ought to have known of it and if they had known they would have been under a *duty* to bring the corporation into compliance with the law and thus save the corporation from the loss. The Delaware Supreme Court concluded that, under the facts as they appeared,

---

[1] *In re Caremark International Inc. Derivative Litigation*, 1996 WL 549894 (Del. Ch. 1996).

there was no basis to find that the directors had breached a *duty* to be informed of the ongoing operations of the firm. In notably colorful terms, the court stated that "absent cause for suspicion there is no *duty* upon the directors to install and operate a corporate system of espionage to ferret out wrongdoing which they have no reason to suspect exists." The Court found that there were no grounds for suspicion in that case and, thus, concluded that the directors were blamelessly unaware of the conduct leading to the corporate liability.

How does one generalize this holding today? Can it be said today that, absent some ground giving rise to suspicion of violation of law, that corporate directors have no *duty* to assure that a corporate information gathering and reporting systems exists which represents a good faith attempt to provide senior management and the Board with information respecting material acts, events or conditions within the corporation, including compliance with applicable statutes and regulations? I certainly do not believe so. I doubt that such a broad generalization of the *Graham* holding would have been accepted by the Supreme Court in 1963. The case can be more narrowly interpreted as standing for the proposition that, absent grounds to suspect deception, neither corporate boards nor senior officers can be charged with wrongdoing simply for assuming the integrity of employees and the honesty of their dealings on the company's behalf.

A broader interpretation of *Graham v. Allis Chalmers* — that it means that a corporate board has no responsibility to assure that appropriate information and reporting systems are established by management — would not, in any event, be accepted by the Delaware Supreme Court in 1996, in my opinion. In stating the basis for this view, I start with the recognition that in recent years the Delaware Supreme Court has made it clear — especially in its jurisprudence concerning takeovers, ... the seriousness with which the corporation law views the role of the corporate board. Secondly, I note the elementary fact that relevant and timely information is an essential predicate for satisfaction of the board's supervisory and monitoring role under ... Delaware General Corporation Law. Thirdly, I note the potential impact of the federal organizational sentencing guidelines on any business organization. Any rational person attempting in good faith to meet an organizational governance responsibility would be bound to take into account this development and the enhanced penalties and the opportunities for reduced sanctions that it offers.

In light of these developments, it would, in my opinion, be a mistake to conclude that our Supreme Court's statement in *Graham* concerning "espionage" means that corporate boards may satisfy their obligation to be reasonably informed concerning the corporation, without assuring themselves that information and reporting systems exist in the organization that are reasonably designed to provide to senior management and to the board itself timely, accurate information sufficient to allow management and the board, each within its scope, to reach informed judgments concerning both the corporation's compliance with law and its business performance.

...

... Generally where a claim of directorial liability for corporate loss is predicated upon ignorance of liability creating activities within the corporation, as in *Graham* or in this case, in my opinion only a sustained or systematic failure of the board to exercise oversight — such as an utter failure to attempt to assure a reasonable information and reporting system exits — will establish the lack of good faith that is a necessary condition to liability. Such a test of liability — lack of good faith as evidenced by sustained or systematic failure of a director to exercise reasonable oversight — is quite high. But, a demanding test of liability in the oversight context is probably beneficial to corporate shareholders as a class, as it is in the board decision context, since it makes board service by qualified persons more likely, while continuing to act as a stimulus to good faith performance of *duty* by such directors.

3. Directors' Reliance on Others

Compare Model Act § 8.30(b) and (c) regarding directors' reliance on others, with ALI § 4.02 which provides:

In performing his or her duties and functions, a director or officer who acts in good faith, and reasonably believes that reliance is warranted, is entitled to rely on information, opinions, reports, statements (including financial statements and other financial data), decisions, judgments, and performance (including decisions, judgments, and performance within the scope of § 4.01(b)) prepared, presented, made, or performed by:

(a) One or more directors, officers, or employees of the corporation, or of a business organization under joint control or common control with the corporation, who the director or officer reasonably believes merit confidence; or

(b) Legal counsel, public accountants, engineers, or other persons who the director or officer reasonably believes merit confidence.

ALI § 4.03 also provides that directors may rely on a "duly authorized committee of the board upon which the director does not serve ..." In addition, ALI § 4.01(b) authorizes directors to delegate functions to "committees of the board or to directors, officers, employees, experts, or other persons ...."

Thus, both the Model Act and the ALI allow directors to rely on a wide range of types of information from a wide variety of persons when the directors reasonably believe that such reliance "merits confidence." What merits confidence in experts, in contrast to other committees of the board, varies. As stated in the Comments to Model Act § 8.30(b), "competence of an expert" ... recognizes the expectation of experience and in most instances technical skills, while the concept of confidence in committees of the board "avoid[s] any inference that technical skills are a prerequisite."

The Comments to Model Act § 8.30(b), (c) further explain how directors may rely only in "good faith."

> Also inherent in the concept of good faith is the requirement that, in order to be entitled to rely on a report, statement, opinion, or other matter, the director must have read the report or statement in question, or have been present at a meeting at which it was orally presented, or have taken other steps to become generally familiar with its contents....
>
> Section 8.30(c) expressly prevents a director from "hiding his head in the sand" and relying on information, opinions, reports, or statements when he has actual knowledge which makes reliance unwarranted.

While directors may rely on others, such reliance does not automatically substitute for their own conduct. As the Intro. Comment *c* to ALI § 4.01 states:

> The weight courts should afford to information, opinions, reports, statements, decisions, judgments, or performance on which a director or officer is "entitled to rely" ... will vary with the circumstances. Considerations affecting the weight will include the importance of the issue on which advice is sought, the nature of the advice, the complexity of the issue, the background and experience of the director or officer in the area about which advice is being given, and the precision with which the advice is followed.

4. Officers

Although a number of states have not addressed the issue of officers' reliance on others, Model Act § 8.42 and ALI § 4.02 provide that officers may rely on others. Model Act § 8.42, however, excludes committees of the board as persons on whom officers may rely. What would be the rationale for this exclusion?

SECTION III. BUSINESS JUDGMENT RULE

In carrying out their responsibilities, directors make a variety of decisions — ranging from selection of corporate officers, approval of major transactions, and approval of the general business strategy and policies of the corporation. Recognizing that directors need broad discretion in how and what decisions they make, the courts crafted an alternative analysis to the general standard of care. Thus, once directors make conscious corporate decisions, thereby exercising their business judgment, their conduct is generally subject to the "business judgment rule."

The following cases explore the business judgment rule, when it is applicable, and the consequences of its application. As this chapter and the chapters on shareholders' derivative suits and defending against tender offer attempts illustrate, the business judgment rule continues to evolve.

A. THE CLASSIC RULE

JOY v. NORTH

United States Court of Appeals, Second Circuit
692 F.2d 880 (1982)

WINTER, CIRCUIT JUDGE:

....

A. *The Liability of Corporate Directors and Officers and the Business Judgment Rule*

While it is often stated that corporate directors and officers will be liable for negligence in carrying out their corporate duties, all seem agreed that such a statement is misleading. Whereas an automobile driver who makes a mistake in judgment as to speed or distance injuring a pedestrian will likely be called upon to respond in damages, a corporate officer who makes a mistake in judgment as to economic conditions, consumer tastes or production line efficiency will rarely, if ever, be found liable for damages suffered by the corporation. Whatever the terminology, the fact is that liability is rarely imposed upon corporate directors or officers simply for bad judgment and this reluctance to impose liability for unsuccessful business decisions has been doctrinally labelled the business judgment rule. Although the rule has suffered under academic criticism, it is not without rational basis.

First, shareholders to a very real degree voluntarily undertake the risk of bad business judgment. Investors need not buy stock, for investment markets offer an array of opportunities less vulnerable to mistakes in judgment by corporate officers. Nor need investors buy stock in particular corporations. In the exercise of what is genuinely a free choice, the quality of a firm's management is often decisive and information is available from professional advisors. Since shareholders can and do select among investments partly on the basis of management, the business judgment rule merely recognizes a certain voluntariness in undertaking the risk of bad business decisions.

Second, courts recognize that after-the-fact litigation is a most imperfect device to evaluate corporate business decisions. The circumstances surrounding a corporate decision are not easily reconstructed in a courtroom years later, since business imperatives often call for quick decisions, inevitably based on less than perfect information. The entrepreneur's function is to encounter risks and to confront uncertainty, and a reasoned decision at the time made may seem a wild hunch viewed years later against a background of perfect knowledge.

Third, because potential profit often corresponds to the potential risk, it is very much in the interest of shareholders that the law not create incentives for overly cautious corporate decisions. Some opportunities offer great profits at the risk of very substantial losses, while the alternatives offer less risk of loss but also less potential profit. Shareholders can reduce the volatility[2] of risk by diversifying their holdings. In the case of the diversified shareholder, the seemingly more risky alternatives may well be the best choice since great losses in some stocks will over time be offset by even greater gains in others.[3] Given mutual funds and similar forms of diversified investment, courts need not bend over backwards to give special protection to shareholders who refuse to reduce the volatility of risk by not diversifying. A rule which penalizes the choice of seemingly riskier alternatives thus may not be in the interest of shareholders generally.

Whatever its merit, however, the business judgment rule extends only as far as the reasons which justify its existence. Thus, it does not apply in cases, *e.g.*, in which the corporate decision lacks a business purpose [or] is so egregious as to amount to a no-win decision.

---

[2]For purposes of this opinion, "volatility" is "the degree of dispersion or variation of possible outcomes." Klein, Business Organization and Finance 147 (1980).

[3]Consider the choice between two investments in an example adapted from Klein, Business Organization and Finance 147-49 (1980):

INVESTMENT A

Estimated Probability of Outcome	Outcome Profit or Loss	Value
.4	+15	6.0
.4	+ 1	.4
.2	- 13	-2.6
1.0		3.8

INVESTMENT B

Estimated Probability of Outcome	Outcome Profit or Loss	Value
.4	+6	2.4
.4	+2	.8
.2	+1	.2
1.0		3.4

Although A is clearly "worth" more than B, it is riskier because it is more volatile. Diversification lessens the volatility by allowing investors to invest in 20 or 200 A's which will tend to guarantee a total result near the value. Shareholders are thus better off with the various firms selecting A over B, although after the fact they will complain in each case of the 2.6 loss. If the courts did not abide by the business judgment rule, they might well penalize the choice of A in each such case and thereby unknowingly injure shareholders generally by creating incentives for management always to choose B.

1. The Classic Rule

The court in *Joy* describes the historic judicial tendency to defer to management discretion in corporate decisionmaking. So long as directors do not behave egregiously, the consequence of this classic business judgment rule is to substantially lower the possibility that directors will be found liable for a breach of their duty of care.

Courts have varied in their description of the standard of conduct required under this classic rule. Behavior which is not "grossly negligent" or "reckless," or decisions with "any rational business purpose," for instance, have satisfied the business judgment rule. How does this standard differ from the reasonableness and negligence standards described under the general standard of care?

The *Joy* case explores the rationale for the business judgment rule. The Introductory Note to ALI § 4.01, p. 135, further explains:

> The basic policy underpinning of the business judgment rule is that corporate law should encourage, and afford broad protection to, informed business judgments (whether subsequent events prove the judgments right or wrong) in order to stimulate risk taking, innovation, and other creative entrepreneurial activities. Shareholders accept the risk that an informed business decision — honestly undertaken and rationally believed to be in the best interests of the corporation — may not be vindicated by subsequent success. The special protection afforded business judgments is also based on a desire to limit litigation and judicial intrusiveness with respect to private-sector business decisionmaking.

2. Applicability and Exceptions

The business judgment rule applies only when directors have made "conscious" decisions. Prolonged inattention and the failure to monitor business activities, as in the *Francis* case, would clearly not be included. In contrast, decisions formally made at directors' meetings clearly would be included. What if the directors considered, but deliberately decided not to take any action?

Even if directors make a conscious decision, the business judgment rule may not be applicable. The courts have recognized at least two exceptions. Directors and officers who are "interested" in the corporate decision may be subject to a different standard of conduct, described in the chapter on the duty of loyalty. In addition, if the directors' decision itself constitutes illegal conduct, directors will not be protected by the business judgment rule. This exception was explored in *Miller v. American Telephone & Telegraph Co.*:[4]

> The suit centered upon the failure of AT&T to collect an outstanding debt of some $ 1.5 million owed to the company by the Democratic National

---

[4] 507 F.2d 759, 761-63 (3d Cir. 1974).

Committee ('DNC') for communications services provided by AT&T during the 1968 Democratic national convention....

... The failure to collect was alleged to have involved a breach of the defendant directors' duty to exercise diligence in handling the affairs of the corporation, to have resulted in affording a preference to the DNC in collection procedures in violation of § 202(a) of the Communications Act of 1934, 47 U.S.C. § 202(a) (1970), and to have amounted to AT&T's making a 'contribution' to the DNC in violation of a federal prohibition on corporate campaign spending....

....

Had plaintiffs' complaint alleged only failure to pursue a corporate claim, application of the sound business judgment rule would support the district court's ruling that a shareholder could not attack the directors' decision. Where, however, the decision not to collect a debt owed the corporation is itself alleged to have been an illegal act, different rules apply. When New York law regarding such acts by directors is considered in conjunction with the underlying purposes of the particular statute involved here, we are convinced that the business judgment rule cannot insulate the defendant directors from liability if they did in fact breach 18 U.S.C. § 610, as plaintiffs have charged.

Roth v. Robertson, 118 N.Y.S. 351 (Sup. Ct. 1909), illustrates the proposition that even though committed to benefit the corporation, illegal acts may amount to a breach of fiduciary duty in New York. In *Roth*, the managing director of an amusement park company had allegedly used corporate funds to purchase the silence of persons who threatened to complain about unlawful Sunday operation of the park. Recovery from the defendant director was sustained on the ground that the money was an illegal payment....

... In [*Abrams v. Allen*, 74 N.E.2d 305 (1947)] the court held that a cause of action was stated by an allegation in a derivative complaint that the directors of Remington Rand, Inc., had relocated corporate plants and curtailed production solely for the purpose of intimidating and punishing employees for their involvement in a labor dispute....

The alleged violation of the federal prohibition against corporate political contributions not only involves the corporation in criminal activity but similarly contravenes a policy of Congress clearly enunciated in 18 U.S.C. § 610. That statute and its predecessor reflect congressional efforts: (1) to destroy the influence of corporations over elections through financial contributions and (2) to check the practice of using corporate funds to benefit political parties without the consent of the stockholders.

3. Perspectives on the Business Judgment Rule

The business judgment rule was judicially created. The Model Act, for example, deliberately excludes it. As indicated in Official Comment to Model Act § 8.30.

> The elements of the business judgment rule and the circumstances for its application are continuing to be developed by the courts. In view of that continuing judicial development, § 8.30 does not try to codify the business judgment rule or to delineate the differences, if any, between that rule and the standards of director conduct set forth in this section. That is a task left to the courts and possibly to later revisions of this Model Act....

ALI § 4.01(c), however, does refer to the doctrine

> (c) A director or officer who makes a business judgment in good faith fulfills the duty under this Section if the director or officer:
> (1) is not interested in the subject of the business judgment;
> (2) is informed with respect to the subject of the business judgment to the extent the director or officer reasonably believes to be appropriate under the circumstances; and
> (3) rationally believes that the business judgment is in the best interests of the corporation.

As Comment *a* to § 4.01(c) explains:

> Confusion with respect to the business judgment rule has been created by the numerous varying formulations of the rule and the fact that courts have often stated the rule incompletely or with elliptical shorthand references. The relatively precise formulation of the business judgment rule set forth in § 4.01(c) avoids confusion and helps cover the myriad factual contexts in which business judgment issues arise.

It is not clear, however, if the courts agree that the business judgment rule can be so precisely articulated. The courts and commentators have described the construct of the business judgment rule in a variety of ways. Some consider it a defense against violations of, a judicial gloss on, or an alternative and less demanding standard to the general standard of care.

In *Citron v. Fairchild Camera & Instrument Corp.*,[5] the court explained:

> The business judgment rule is an extension of the fundamental principle "that the business and affairs of a corporation are managed by and under the direction of its board. *See* 8 Del. C. § 141(a)." *Pogostin v. Rice,* Del. Supr., 480 A.2d 619, 624 (1984). The rule operates as both a procedural guide for litigants and a substantive rule of law. As a rule of evidence, it

---

[5] 569 A.2d 53, 64 (Del. 1989).

creates "a presumption that in making a business decision, the directors of a corporation acted on an informed basis [*i.e.*, with due care], in good faith and in the honest belief that the action taken was in the best interest of the company." *Aronson v. Lewis*, Del. Supr., 473 A.2d 805, 812 (1984). The presumption initially attaches to a director-approved transaction within a board's conferred or apparent authority in the absence of any evidence of "fraud, bad faith, or self-dealing in the usual sense of personal profit or betterment." *Grobow v. Perot*, Del. Supr., 539 A.2d 180, 187 (1988). *See* Allaun v. Consolidated Oil Co., Del. Ch., 147 A. 257, 261 (1929). The burden falls upon the proponent of a claim to rebut the presumption by introducing evidence either of director self-interest, if not self-dealing, or that the directors either lacked good faith or failed to exercise due care. *Smith v. Van Gorkom*, Del. Supr., 488 A.2d 858, 872 (1985). If the proponent fails to meet her burden of establishing facts rebutting the presumption, the business judgment rule, as a substantive rule, will attach to protect the directors and the decisions they make...

Professor Branson in his treatise *Corporate Governance** explores the difference between the business judment rule and the duty of care:

The business judgment rule operates as a rule of judicial economy, as a presumption, or as a safe harbor. The business judgment rule, however, is not the rule of conduct, which remains the duty of care. To be sure, the business judgment rule informs conduct, especially in before-the-fact preventive law contexts in which lawyers and others may structure the decision-making process with an eye toward coming within the presumption of safe harbor. But the business judgment rule is not the legal standard itself....

Courts and commentators repeatedly gloss over or actually express their unawareness of the difference between the standard of conduct and the rule.... Other courts take the business judgment rule as the standard of conduct itself, proceeding directly to a duty of loyalty inquiry, or intrinsic fairness inquiry, if the prerequisites of the business judgment rule have not been met.

Those courts have skipped an important intermediate step. In preventive law contexts, the business judgment rule is a safe harbor. In the litigation context, among other things, the rule is a filtering device, a device for achievement of judicial economy. In the latter respect, the rule may aid a court in disposing of corporate litigation short of trial, say, by means of ruling on a dispositive motion before trial, based upon the business judgment rule. But should the defendant directors lose that motion, they are not

---

*Douglas M. Branson, Corporate Governance, 334-37 (1993). Copyright © 1993 by The Michie Company. All rights reserved. Reprinted with permission.

doomed to perdition. Those directors may then fall back and defend on substantive duty of care grounds, by means of further motions or at trial, because the ultimate legal standard is not the business judgment rule but the duty of care.

... Even after losing a first round on business judgment rule turf, directors may fall back to another duty of care argument, that whatever had occurred had not damaged the corporation, another substantive requirement of a duty of care cause of action.

B. INFORMED DECISIONMAKING

The following case prompted courts and corporate directors to rethink what the business judgment rule means. See if you agree that the case reformulated the classic rule into a more demanding standard of review.

SMITH v. VAN GORKOM

Supreme Court of Delaware
488 A.2d 858 (1985)

HORSEY, JUSTICE:

This appeal from the Court of Chancery involves a class action brought by shareholders of the defendant Trans Union Corporation ("Trans Union" or "the Company"), originally seeking rescission of a cash-out merger of Trans Union into the defendant New T Company ("New T"), a wholly-owned subsidiary of the defendant, Marmon Group, Inc. ("Marmon"). Alternate relief in the form of damages is sought against the defendant members of the Board of Directors of Trans Union, New T, and Jay A. Pritzker and Robert A. Pritzker, owners of Marmon.

....

I

The nature of this case requires a detailed factual statement. The following facts are essentially uncontradicted:

A

Trans Union was a publicly-traded, diversified holding company, the principal earnings of which were generated by its railcar leasing business. During the period here involved, the Company had a cash flow of hundreds of millions of dollars annually. However, the Company had difficulty in generating sufficient taxable income to offset increasingly large investment tax credits (ITCs). Accelerated depreciation deductions had decreased available taxable income against which to offset accumulating ITCs. The Company took these deductions, despite their effect on usable ITCs, because the rental price in the railcar leasing market had already impounded the purported tax savings.

In the late 1970's, together with other capital-intensive firms, Trans Union lobbied in Congress to have ITCs refundable in cash to firms which could not fully utilize the credit. During the summer of 1980, defendant Jerome W. Van Gorkom, Trans Union's Chairman and Chief Executive Officer, testified and lobbied in Congress for refundability of ITCs and against further accelerated depreciation. By the end of August, Van Gorkom was convinced that Congress would neither accept the refundability concept nor curtail further accelerated depreciation.

Beginning in the late 1960's, and continuing through the 1970's, Trans Union pursued a program of acquiring small companies in order to increase available taxable income. In July 1980, Trans Union Management prepared the annual revision of the Company's Five Year Forecast. This report was presented to the Board of Directors at its July, 1980 meeting. The report projected an annual income growth of about 20%. The report also concluded that Trans Union would have about $ 195 million in spare cash between 1980 and 1985, "with the surplus growing rapidly from 1982 onward." The report referred to the ITC situation as a "nagging problem" and, given that problem, the leasing company "would still appear to be constrained to a tax break even." The report then listed four alternative uses of the projected 1982-1985 equity surplus: (1) stock repurchase; (2) dividend increases; (3) a major acquisition program; and (4) combinations of the above. The sale of Trans Union was not among the alternatives. The report emphasized that, despite the overall surplus, the operation of the Company would consume all available equity for the next several years, and concluded: "As a result, we have sufficient time to fully develop our course of action."

B

On August 27, 1980, Van Gorkom met with Senior Management of Trans Union. Van Gorkom reported on his lobbying efforts in Washington and his desire to find a solution to the tax credit problem more permanent than a continued program of acquisitions. Various alternatives were suggested and discussed preliminarily, including the sale of Trans Union to a company with a large amount of taxable income.

Donald Romans, Chief Financial Officer of Trans Union, stated that his department had done a "very brief bit of work on the possibility of a leveraged buy-out." This work had been prompted by a media article which Romans had seen regarding a leveraged buy-out by management. The work consisted of a "preliminary study" of the cash which could be generated by the Company if it participated in a leveraged buy-out. As Romans stated, this analysis "was [a] very first and rough cut at seeing whether a cash flow would support what might be considered a high price for this type of transaction."

On September 5, at another Senior Management meeting which Van Gorkom attended, Romans again brought up the idea of a leveraged buy-out as a "possible strategic alternative" to the Company's acquisition program. Romans and Bruce S. Chelberg, President and Chief Operating Officer of Trans Union, had been working on the matter in preparation for the meeting. According to Romans: They did not "come up" with a price for the Company. They merely "ran the numbers" at $ 50 a share and at $ 60 a share with the "rough form" of their cash figures at the time. Their "figures indicated that $ 50 would be very easy to do but $ 60 would be very difficult to do under those figures." This work did not purport to establish a fair price for either the Company or 100% of the stock. It was intended to determine the cash flow needed to service the debt that would "probably" be incurred in a leveraged buy-out, based on "rough calculations" without "any benefit of experts to identify what the limits were to that, and so forth." These computations were not considered extensive and no conclusion was reached.

At this meeting, Van Gorkom stated that he would be willing to take $ 55 per share for his own 75,000 shares. He vetoed the suggestion of a leveraged buy-out by Management, however, as involving a potential conflict of interest for Management. Van Gorkom, a certified public accountant and lawyer, had been an officer of Trans Union for 24 years, its Chief Executive Officer for more than 17 years, and Chairman of its Board for 2 years. It is noteworthy in this connection that he was then approaching 65 years of age and mandatory retirement.

For several days following the September 5 meeting, Van Gorkom pondered the idea of a sale. He had participated in many acquisitions as a manager and director of Trans Union and as a director of other companies. He was familiar with acquisition procedures, valuation methods, and negotiations; and he privately considered the pros and cons of whether Trans Union should seek a privately or publicly-held purchaser.

Van Gorkom decided to meet with Jay A. Pritzker, a well-known corporate takeover specialist and a social acquaintance. However, rather than approaching Pritzker simply to determine his interest in acquiring Trans Union, Van Gorkom assembled a proposed per share price for sale of the Company and a financing structure by which to accomplish the sale. Van Gorkom did so without consulting either his Board or any members of Senior Management except one: Carl Peterson, Trans Union's Controller. Telling Peterson that he wanted no other person on his staff to know what he was doing, but without telling him why, Van Gorkom directed Peterson to calculate the feasibility of a leveraged buy-out at an assumed price per share of $ 55. Apart from the Company's historic stock market price,[6] and Van Gorkom's long association with Trans Union, the record is devoid of any competent evidence that $ 55 represented the per share intrinsic value of the Company.

---

[6] The common stock of Trans Union was traded on the New York Stock Exchange. Over the five year period from 1975 through 1979, Trans Union's stock had traded within a range of a high of $ 39½ and a low of $ 24¼. Its high and low range for 1980 through September 19 (the last trading day before announcement of the merger) was $ 38¼ — $ 29½.

Having thus chosen the $ 55 figure, based solely on the availability of a leveraged buy-out, Van Gorkom multiplied the price per share by the number of shares outstanding to reach a total value of the Company of $ 690 million. Van Gorkom told Peterson to use this $ 690 million figure and to assume a $ 200 million equity contribution by the buyer. Based on these assumptions, Van Gorkom directed Peterson to determine whether the debt portion of the purchase price could be paid off in five years or less if financed by Trans Union's cash flow as projected in the Five Year Forecast, and by the sale of certain weaker divisions identified in a study done for Trans Union by the Boston Consulting Group ("BCG study"). Peterson reported that, of the purchase price, approximately $ 50-80 million would remain outstanding after five years. Van Gorkom was disappointed, but decided to meet with Pritzker nevertheless.

Van Gorkom arranged a meeting with Pritzker at the latter's home on Saturday, September 13, 1980. Van Gorkom prefaced his presentation by stating to Pritzker: "Now as far as you are concerned, I can, I think, show how you can pay a substantial premium over the present stock price and pay off most of the loan in the first five years. ... If you could pay $ 55 for this Company, here is a way in which I think it can be financed."

Van Gorkom then reviewed with Pritzker his calculations based upon his proposed price of $ 55 per share. Although Pritzker mentioned $ 50 as a more attractive figure, no other price was mentioned. However, Van Gorkom stated that to be sure that $ 55 was the best price obtainable, Trans Union should be free to accept any better offer. Pritzker demurred, stating that his organization would serve as a "stalking horse" for an "auction contest" only if Trans Union would permit Pritzker to buy 1,750,000 shares of Trans Union stock at market price which Pritzker could then sell to any higher bidder. After further discussion on this point, Pritzker told Van Gorkom that he would give him a more definite reaction soon.

On Monday, September 15, Pritzker advised Van Gorkom that he was interested in the $ 55 cash-out merger proposal and requested more information on Trans Union. Van Gorkom agreed to meet privately with Pritzker, accompanied by Peterson, Chelberg, and Michael Carpenter, Trans Union's consultant from the Boston Consulting Group. The meetings took place on September 16 and 17. Van Gorkom was "astounded that events were moving with such amazing rapidity."

On Thursday, September 18, Van Gorkom met again with Pritzker. At that time, Van Gorkom knew that Pritzker intended to make a cash-out merger offer at Van Gorkom's proposed $ 55 per share. Pritzker instructed his attorney, a merger and acquisition specialist, to begin drafting merger documents. There was no further discussion of the $ 55 price. However, the number of shares of Trans Union's treasury stock to be offered to Pritzker was negotiated down to one million shares; the price was set at $ 38 — 75 cents above the per share price at the close of the market on September 19. At this point, Pritzker insisted that the Trans Union Board act on his merger proposal within the next three days, stating to Van Gorkom: "We have to have a decision by no later than Sunday [evening, September 21] before the opening of the English stock exchange on Monday morning." Pritzker's lawyer was then instructed to draft the merger documents, to be reviewed by Van Gorkom's lawyer, "sometimes with discussion and sometimes not, in the haste to get it finished."

On Friday, September 19, Van Gorkom, Chelberg, and Pritzker consulted with Trans Union's lead bank regarding the financing of Pritzker's purchase of Trans Union. The bank indicated that it could form a syndicate of banks that would finance the transaction. On the same day, Van Gorkom retained James Brennan, Esquire, to advise Trans Union on the legal aspects of the merger. Van Gorkom did not consult with William Browder, a Vice-President and director of Trans Union and former head of its legal department, or with William Moore, then the head of Trans Union's legal staff.

On Friday, September 19, Van Gorkom called a special meeting of the Trans Union Board for noon the following day. He also called a meeting of the Company's Senior Management to convene at 11:00 a.m., prior to the meeting of the Board. No one, except Chelberg and Peterson, was told the purpose of the meetings. Van Gorkom did not invite Trans Union's investment banker, Salomon Brothers or its Chicago-based partner, to attend.

Of those present at the Senior Management meeting on September 20, only Chelberg and Peterson had prior knowledge of Pritzker's offer. Van Gorkom disclosed the offer and described its terms, but he furnished no copies of the proposed Merger Agreement. Romans announced that his department had done a second study which showed that, for a leveraged buy-out, the price range for Trans Union stock was between $ 55 and $ 65 per share. Van Gorkom neither saw the study nor asked Romans to make it available for the Board meeting.

Senior Management's reaction to the Pritzker proposal was completely negative. No member of Management, except Chelberg and Peterson, supported the proposal. Romans objected to the price as being too low; he was critical of the timing and suggested that consideration should be given to the adverse tax consequences of an all-cash deal for low-basis shareholders; and he took the position that the agreement to sell Pritzker one million newly-issued shares at market price would inhibit other offers, as would the prohibitions against soliciting bids and furnishing inside information to other bidders. Romans argued that the Pritzker proposal was a "lock up" and amounted to "an agreed merger as opposed to an offer." Nevertheless, Van Gorkom proceeded to the Board meeting as scheduled without further delay.

Ten directors served on the Trans Union Board, five inside (defendants Bonser, O'Boyle, Browder, Chelberg, and Van Gorkom) and five outside (defendants Wallis, Johnson, Lanterman, Morgan and Reneker). All directors were present at the meeting, except O'Boyle who was ill. Of the outside directors, four were corporate chief executive officers and one was the former Dean of the University of Chicago Business School. None was an investment banker or trained financial analyst. All members of the Board were well informed about the Company and its operations as a going concern. They were familiar with the current financial condition of the Company, as well as operating and earnings projections reported in the recent Five Year Forecast. The Board generally received regular and detailed reports and was kept abreast of the accumulated investment tax credit and accelerated depreciation problem.

Van Gorkom began the Special Meeting of the Board with a twenty-minute oral presentation. Copies of the proposed Merger Agreement were delivered too late for study before or during the meeting.[7] He reviewed the Company's ITC and depreciation problems and the efforts theretofore made to solve them. He discussed his initial meeting with Pritzker and his motivation in arranging that meeting. Van Gorkom did not disclose to the Board, however, the methodology by which he alone had arrived at the $ 55 figure, or the fact that he first proposed the $ 55 price in his negotiations with Pritzker.

Van Gorkom outlined the terms of the Pritzker offer as follows: Pritzker would pay $ 55 in cash for all outstanding shares of Trans Union stock upon completion of which Trans Union would be merged into New T Company, a subsidiary wholly-owned by Pritzker and formed to implement the merger; for a period of 90 days, Trans Union could receive, but could not actively solicit, competing offers; the offer had to be acted on by the next evening, Sunday, September 21; Trans Union could only furnish to competing bidders published information, and not proprietary information; the offer was subject to Pritzker obtaining the necessary financing by October 10, 1980; if the financing contingency were met or waived by Pritzker, Trans Union was required to sell to Pritzker one million newly-issued shares of Trans Union at $ 38 per share.

Van Gorkom took the position that putting Trans Union "up for auction" through a 90-day market test would validate a decision by the Board that $ 55 was a fair price. He told the Board that the "free market will have an opportunity to judge whether $ 55 is a fair price." Van Gorkom framed the decision before the Board not as whether $ 55 per share was the highest price that could be obtained, but as whether the $ 55 price was a fair price that the stockholders should be given the opportunity to accept or reject.

Attorney Brennan advised the members of the Board that they might be sued if they failed to accept the offer and that a fairness opinion was not required as a matter of law.

Romans attended the meeting as chief financial officer of the Company. He told the Board that he had not been involved in the negotiations with Pritzker and knew nothing about the merger proposal until the morning of the meeting; that his studies did not indicate either a fair price for the stock or a valuation of the

---

[7] The record is not clear as to the terms of the Merger Agreement. The Agreement, as originally presented to the Board on September 20, was never produced by defendants despite demands by the plaintiffs. Nor is it clear that the directors were given an opportunity to study the Merger Agreement before voting on it. All that can be said is that Brennan had the Agreement before him during the meeting.

Company; that he did not see his role as directly addressing the fairness issue; and that he and his people "were trying to search for ways to justify a price in connection with such a [leveraged buy-out] transaction, rather than to say what the shares are worth." Romans testified:

> I told the Board that the study ran the numbers at 50 and 60, and then the subsequent study at 55 and 65, and that was not the same thing as saying that I have a valuation of the company at X dollars. But it was a way — a first step towards reaching that conclusion.

Romans told the Board that, in his opinion, $ 55 was "in the range of a fair price," but "at the beginning of the range."

Chelberg, Trans Union's President, supported Van Gorkom's presentation and representations. He testified that he "participated to make sure that the Board members collectively were clear on the details of the agreement or offer from Pritzker;" that he "participated in the discussion with Mr. Brennan, inquiring of him about the necessity for valuation opinions in spite of the way in which this particular offer was couched;" and that he was otherwise actively involved in supporting the positions being taken by Van Gorkom before the Board about "the necessity to act immediately on this offer," and about "the adequacy of the $ 55 and the question of how that would be tested."

The Board meeting of September 20 lasted about two hours. Based solely upon Van Gorkom's oral presentation, Chelberg's supporting representations, Romans' oral statement, Brennan's legal advice, and their knowledge of the market history of the Company's stock,[8] the directors approved the proposed Merger Agreement. However, the Board later claimed to have attached two conditions to its acceptance: (1) that Trans Union reserved the right to accept any better offer that was made during the market test period; and (2) that Trans Union could share its proprietary information with any other potential bidders. While the Board now claims to have reserved the right to accept any better offer received after the announcement of the Pritzker agreement (even though the minutes of the meeting do not reflect this), it is undisputed that the Board did not reserve the right to actively solicit alternate offers.

The Merger Agreement was executed by Van Gorkom during the evening of September 20 at a formal social event that he hosted for the opening of the Chicago Lyric Opera. Neither he nor any other director read the agreement prior to its signing and delivery to Pritzker.

---

[8] The Trial Court stated the premium relationship of the $ 55 price to the market history of the Company's stock as follows:

> ... the merger price offered to the stockholders of Trans Union represented a premium of 62% over the average of the high and low prices at which Trans Union stock had traded in 1980, a premium of 48% over the last closing price, and a premium of 39% over the highest price at which the stock of Trans Union had traded any time during the prior six years.

....

On Monday, September 22, the Company issued a press release announcing that Trans Union had entered into a "definitive" Merger Agreement with an affiliate of the Marmon Group, Inc., a Pritzker holding company. Within 10 days of the public announcement, dissent among Senior Management over the merger had become widespread. Faced with threatened resignations of key officers, Van Gorkom met with Pritzker who agreed to several modifications of the Agreement. Pritzker was willing to do so provided that Van Gorkom could persuade the dissidents to remain on the Company payroll for at least six months after consummation of the merger.

Van Gorkom reconvened the Board on October 8 and secured the directors' approval of the proposed amendments — sight unseen. The Board also authorized the employment of Salomon Brothers, its investment banker, to solicit other offers for Trans Union during the proposed "market test" period.

The next day, October 9, Trans Union issued a press release announcing: (1) that Pritzker had obtained "the financing commitments necessary to consummate" the merger with Trans Union; (2) that Pritzker had acquired one million shares of Trans Union common stock at $ 38 per share; (3) that Trans Union was now permitted to actively seek other offers and had retained Salomon Brothers for that purpose; and (4) that if a more favorable offer were not received before February 1, 1981, Trans Union's shareholders would thereafter meet to vote on the Pritzker proposal.

It was not until the following day, October 10, that the actual amendments to the Merger Agreement were prepared by Pritzker and delivered to Van Gorkom for execution. As will be seen, the amendments were considerably at variance with Van Gorkom's representations of the amendments to the Board on October 8; and the amendments placed serious constraints on Trans Union's ability to negotiate a better deal and withdraw from the Pritzker agreement. Nevertheless, Van Gorkom proceeded to execute what became the October 10 amendments to the Merger Agreement without conferring further with the Board members and apparently without comprehending the actual implications of the amendments.

....

Salomon Brothers' efforts over a three-month period from October 21 to January 21 produced only one serious suitor for Trans Union — General Electric Credit Corporation ("GE Credit"), a subsidiary of the General Electric Company. However, GE Credit was unwilling to make an offer for Trans Union unless Trans Union first rescinded its Merger Agreement with Pritzker. When Pritzker refused, GE Credit terminated further discussions with Trans Union in early January.

In the meantime, in early December, the investment firm of Kohlberg, Kravis, Roberts & Co. ("KKR"), the only other concern to make a firm offer for Trans Union, withdrew its offer under circumstances hereinafter detailed.

On December 19, this litigation was commenced and, within four weeks, the plaintiffs had deposed eight of the ten directors of Trans Union, including Van Gorkom, Chelberg and Romans, its Chief Financial Officer. On January 21, Management's Proxy Statement for the February 10 shareholder meeting was mailed to Trans Union's stockholders. On January 26, Trans Union's Board met and, after a lengthy meeting, voted to proceed with the Pritzker merger. The Board also approved for mailing, "on or about January 27," a Supplement to its Proxy Statement. The Supplement purportedly set forth all information relevant to the Pritzker Merger Agreement, which had not been divulged in the first Proxy Statement.

....

On February 10, the stockholders of Trans Union approved the Pritzker merger proposal. Of the outstanding shares, 69.9% were voted in favor of the merger; 7.25% were voted against the merger; and 22.85% were not voted.

II

We turn to the issue of the application of the business judgment rule to the September 20 meeting of the Board.

....

Under Delaware law, the business judgment rule is the offspring of the fundamental principle, codified in 8 Del. C. § 141(a), that the business and affairs of a Delaware corporation are managed by or under its board of directors. In carrying out their managerial roles, directors are charged with an unyielding fiduciary duty to the corporation and its shareholders. The business judgment rule exists to protect and promote the full and free exercise of the managerial power granted to Delaware directors. The rule itself "is a presumption that in making a business decision, the directors of a corporation acted on an informed basis, in good faith and in the honest belief that the action taken was in the best interests of the company." [*Aronson v. Lewis*, 473 A.2d 805, 812 (Del. 1984)]. Thus, the party attacking a board decision as uninformed must rebut the presumption that its business judgment was an informed one. *Id.*

The determination of whether a business judgment is an informed one turns on whether the directors have informed themselves "prior to making a business decision, of all material information reasonably available to them." *Id.*

Under the business judgment rule there is no protection for directors who have made "an unintelligent or unadvised judgment." *Mitchell v. Highland-Western Glass*, 167 A. 831, 833 (Del. Ch. 1933). A director's duty to inform himself in preparation for a decision derives from the fiduciary capacity in which he serves the corporation and its stockholders. Since a director is vested with the responsibility for the management of the affairs of the corporation, he must execute that duty with the recognition that he acts on behalf of others. Such obligation does not tolerate faithlessness or self-dealing. But fulfillment of the fiduciary function requires more than the mere absence of bad faith or fraud. Representation of the financial interests of others imposes on a director an affirmative duty to protect those interests and to proceed with a critical eye in assessing information of the type and under the circumstances present here.

Thus, a director's duty to exercise an informed business judgment is in the nature of a duty of care, as distinguished from a duty of loyalty. Here, there were no allegations of fraud, bad faith, or self-dealing, or proof thereof. Hence, it is presumed that the directors reached their business judgment in good faith, and considerations of motive are irrelevant to the issue before us.

The standard of care applicable to a director's duty of care has also been recently restated by this Court. In *Aronson, supra,* we stated:

> While the Delaware cases use a variety of terms to describe the applicable standard of care, our analysis satisfies us that under the business judgment rule director liability is predicated upon concepts of gross negligence.

473 A.2d at 812.

We again confirm that view. We think the concept of gross negligence is also the proper standard for determining whether a business judgment reached by a board of directors was an informed one.

In the specific context of a proposed merger of domestic corporations, a director has a duty under 8 Del. C. § 251(b), along with his fellow directors, to act in an informed and deliberate manner in determining whether to approve an agreement of merger before submitting the proposal to the stockholders. Certainly in the merger context, a director may not abdicate that duty by leaving to the shareholders alone the decision to approve or disapprove the agreement. Only an agreement of merger satisfying the requirements of 8 Del. C. § 251(b) may be submitted to the shareholders under § 251(c).

It is against those standards that the conduct of the directors of Trans Union must be tested, as a matter of law and as a matter of fact, regarding their exercise of an informed business judgment in voting to approve the Pritzker merger proposal.

III

The defendants argue that the determination of whether their decision to accept $ 55 per share for Trans Union represented an informed business judgment requires consideration, not only of that which they knew and learned on September 20, but also of that which they subsequently learned and did over the following four-month period before the shareholders met to vote on the proposal in February, 1981. The defendants thereby seek to reduce the significance of their action on September 20 and to widen the time frame for determining whether their decision to accept the Pritzker proposal was an informed one. Thus, the defendants contend that what the directors did and learned subsequent to September 20 and through January 26, 1981, was properly taken into account by the Trial Court in determining whether the Board's judgment was an informed one. We disagree with this post hoc approach.

... [T]he question of whether the directors reached an informed business judgment in agreeing to sell the Company, pursuant to the terms of the September 20 Agreement presents, in reality, two questions: (A) whether the directors reached an informed business judgment on September 20, 1980; and (B) if they did not, whether the directors' actions taken subsequent to September 20 were adequate to cure any infirmity in their action taken on September 20. We first consider the directors' September 20 action in terms of their reaching an informed business judgment.

A

On the record before us, we must conclude that the Board of Directors did not reach an informed business judgment on September 20, 1980 in voting to "sell" the Company for $ 55 per share pursuant to the Pritzker cash-out merger proposal. Our reasons, in summary, are as follows:

The directors (1) did not adequately inform themselves as to Van Gorkom's role in forcing the "sale" of the Company and in establishing the per share purchase price; (2) were uninformed as to the intrinsic value of the Company; and (3) given these circumstances, at a minimum, were grossly negligent in approving the "sale" of the Company upon two hours' consideration, without prior notice, and without the exigency of a crisis or emergency.

As has been noted, the Board based its September 20 decision to approve the cash-out merger primarily on Van Gorkom's representations. None of the directors, other than Van Gorkom and Chelberg, had any prior knowledge that the purpose of the meeting was to propose a cash-out merger of Trans Union. No members of Senior Management were present, other than Chelberg, Romans and Peterson; and the latter two had only learned of the proposed sale an hour earlier. Both general counsel Moore and former general counsel Browder attended the meeting, but were equally uninformed as to the purpose of the meeting and the documents to be acted upon.

Without any documents before them concerning the proposed transaction, the members of the Board were required to rely entirely upon Van Gorkom's 20-minute oral presentation of the proposal. No written summary of the terms of the merger was presented; the directors were given no documentation to support the adequacy of $ 55 price per share for sale of the Company; and the Board had before it nothing more than Van Gorkom's statement of his understanding of the substance of an agreement which he admittedly had never read, nor which any member of the Board had ever seen.

Under 8 Del. C. § 141(e), "directors are fully protected in relying in good faith on reports made by officers." The term "report" has been liberally construed to include reports of informal personal investigations by corporate officers, *Cheff v. Mathes*, Del. Supr., 199 A.2d 548, 556 (1964). However, there is no evidence that any "report," as defined under § 141(e), concerning the Pritzker proposal, was presented to the Board on September 20. Van Gorkom's oral presentation of his understanding of the terms of the proposed Merger Agreement, which he had not seen, and Romans' brief oral statement of his preliminary study regarding the feasibility of a leveraged buy-out of Trans Union do not qualify as § 141(e) "reports" for these reasons: The former lacked substance because Van Gorkom was basically uninformed as to the essential provisions of the very document about which he was talking. Romans' statement was irrelevant to the issues before the Board since it did not purport to be a valuation study. At a minimum for a report to enjoy the status conferred by § 141(e), it must be pertinent to the subject matter upon which a board is called to act, and otherwise be entitled to good faith, not blind, reliance. Considering all of the surrounding circumstances — hastily calling the meeting without prior notice of its subject matter, the proposed sale of the Company without any prior consideration of the issue or necessity therefor, the urgent time constraints imposed by Pritzker, and the total absence of any documentation whatsoever — the directors were duty bound to make reasonable inquiry of Van Gorkom and Romans, and if they had done so, the inadequacy of that upon which they now claim to have relied would have been apparent.

The defendants rely on the following factors to sustain the Trial Court's finding that the Board's decision was an informed one: (1) the magnitude of the premium or spread between the $ 55 Pritzker offering price and Trans Union's current market price of $ 38 per share; (2) the amendment of the Agreement as submitted on September 20 to permit the Board to accept any better offer during the "market test" period; (3) the collective experience and expertise of the Board's "inside" and "outside" directors; and (4) their reliance on Brennan's legal advice that the directors might be sued if they rejected the Pritzker proposal. We discuss each of these grounds seriatim:

(1)

A substantial premium may provide one reason to recommend a merger, but in the absence of other sound valuation information, the fact of a premium alone does not provide an adequate basis upon which to assess the fairness of an offering price. Here, the judgment reached as to the adequacy of the premium was based on a comparison between the historically depressed Trans Union market price and the amount of the Pritzker offer. Using market price as a basis for concluding that the premium adequately reflected the true value of the Company was a clearly faulty, indeed fallacious, premise, as the defendants' own evidence demonstrates.

The record is clear that before September 20, Van Gorkom and other members of Trans Union's Board knew that the market had consistently undervalued the worth of Trans Union's stock, despite steady increases in the Company's operating income in the seven years preceding the merger. The Board related this occurrence in large part to Trans Union's inability to use its ITCs as previously noted. Van Gorkom testified that he did not believe the market price accurately reflected Trans Union's true worth; and several of the directors testified that, as a general rule, most chief executives think that the market undervalues their companies' stock. Yet, on September 20, Trans Union's Board apparently believed that the market stock price accurately reflected the value of the Company for the purpose of determining the adequacy of the premium for its sale.

....

The parties do not dispute that a publicly-traded stock price is solely a measure of the value of a minority position and, thus, market price represents only the value of a single share. Nevertheless, on September 20, the Board assessed the adequacy of the premium over market, offered by Pritzker, solely by comparing it with Trans Union's current and historical stock price.

Indeed, as of September 20, the Board had no other information on which to base a determination of the intrinsic value of Trans Union as a going concern. As of September 20, the Board had made no evaluation of the Company designed to value the entire enterprise, nor had the Board ever previously considered selling the Company or consenting to a buy-out merger. Thus, the adequacy of a premium is indeterminate unless it is assessed in terms of other competent and sound valuation information that reflects the value of the particular business.

Despite the foregoing facts and circumstances, there was no call by the Board, either on September 20 or thereafter, for any valuation study or documentation of the $ 55 price per share as a measure of the fair value of the Company in a cash-out context. It is undisputed that the major asset of Trans Union was its cash flow. Yet, at no time did the Board call for a valuation study taking into account that highly significant element of the Company's assets.

We do not imply that an outside valuation study is essential to support an informed business judgment; nor do we state that fairness opinions by independent investment bankers are required as a matter of law. Often insiders familiar with the business of a going concern are in a better position than are outsiders to gather relevant information; and under appropriate circumstances, such directors may be fully protected in relying in good faith upon the valuation reports of their management....

Here, the record establishes that the Board did not request its Chief Financial Officer, Romans, to make any valuation study or review of the proposal to determine the adequacy of $ 55 per share for sale of the Company. On the record before us: The Board rested on Romans' elicited response that the $ 55 figure was within a "fair price range" within the context of a leveraged buy-out. No director sought any further information from Romans. No director asked him why he put $ 55 at the bottom of his range. No director asked Romans for any details as to his study, the reason why it had been undertaken or its depth. No director asked to see the study; and no director asked Romans whether Trans Union's finance department could do a fairness study within the remaining 36-hour period available under the Pritzker offer.

Had the Board, or any member, made an inquiry of Romans, he presumably would have responded as he testified: that his calculations were rough and preliminary; and, that the study was not designed to determine the fair value of the Company, but rather to assess the feasibility of a leveraged buy-out financed by the Company's projected cash flow, making certain assumptions as to the purchaser's borrowing needs. Romans would have presumably also informed the Board of his view, and the widespread view of Senior Management, that the timing of the offer was wrong and the offer inadequate.

The record also establishes that the Board accepted without scrutiny Van Gorkom's representation as to the fairness of the $ 55 price per share for sale of the Company — a subject that the Board had never previously considered. The Board thereby failed to discover that Van Gorkom had suggested the $ 55 price to Pritzker and, most crucially, that Van Gorkom had arrived at the $ 55 figure based on calculations designed solely to determine the feasibility of a leveraged buy-out. No questions were raised either as to the tax implications of a cash-out merger or how the price for the one million share option granted Pritzker was calculated.

We do not say that the Board of Directors was not entitled to give some credence to Van Gorkom's representation that $ 55 was an adequate or fair price. Under § 141(e), the directors were entitled to rely upon their chairman's opinion of value and adequacy, provided that such opinion was reached on a sound basis. Here, the issue is whether the directors informed themselves as to all information that was reasonably available to them. Had they done so, they would have learned of the source and derivation of the $ 55 price and could not reasonably have relied thereupon in good faith.

None of the directors, Management or outside, were investment bankers or financial analysts. Yet the Board did not consider recessing the meeting until a later hour that day (or requesting an extension of Pritzker's Sunday evening deadline) to give it time to elicit more information as to the sufficiency of the offer, either from inside Management (in particular Romans) or from Trans Union's own investment banker, Salomon Brothers, whose Chicago specialist in merger and acquisitions was known to the Board and familiar with Trans Union's affairs.

Thus, the record compels the conclusion that on September 20 the Board lacked valuation information adequate to reach an informed business judgment as to the fairness of $ 55 per share for sale of the Company.

(2)

This brings us to the post-September 20 "market test" upon which the defendants ultimately rely to confirm the reasonableness of their September 20 decision to accept the Pritzker proposal. In this connection, the directors present a two-part argument: (a) that by making a "market test" of Pritzker's $ 55 per share offer a condition of their September 20 decision to accept his offer, they cannot be found to have acted impulsively or in an uninformed manner on September 20; and (b) that the adequacy of the $ 17 premium for sale of the Company was conclusively established over the following 90 to 120 days by the most reliable evidence available — the marketplace. Thus, the defendants impliedly contend that the "market test" eliminated the need for the Board to perform any other form of fairness test either on September 20, or thereafter.

Again, the facts of record do not support the defendants' argument. There is no evidence: (a) that the Merger Agreement was effectively amended to give the Board freedom to put Trans Union up for auction sale to the highest bidder; or (b) that a public auction was in fact permitted to occur....

The Merger Agreement, specifically identified as that originally presented to the Board on September 20, has never been produced by the defendants, notwithstanding the plaintiffs' several demands for production before as well as during trial....

Van Gorkom states that the Agreement as submitted incorporated the ingredients for a market test by authorizing Trans Union to receive competing offers over the next 90-day period. However, he concedes that the Agreement barred Trans Union from actively soliciting such offers and from furnishing to interested parties any information about the Company other than that already in the public domain. Whether the original Agreement of September 20 went so far as to authorize Trans Union to receive competitive proposals is arguable. The defendants' unexplained failure to produce and identify the original Merger Agreement permits the logical inference that the instrument would not support their assertions in this regard....

....

As has been noted, nothing in the Board's Minutes supports these claims. No reference to either of the so-called "conditions" or of Trans Union's reserved right to test the market appears in any notes of the Board meeting or in the Board Resolution accepting the Pritzker offer or in the Minutes of the meeting itself. That evening, in the midst of a formal party which he hosted for the opening of the Chicago Lyric Opera, Van Gorkom executed the Merger Agreement without he or any other member of the Board having read the instruments.

The defendants attempt to downplay the significance of the prohibition against Trans Union's actively soliciting competing offers by arguing that the directors "understood that the entire financial community would know that Trans Union was for sale upon the announcement of the Pritzker offer, and anyone desiring to make a better offer was free to do so." Yet, the press release issued on September 22, with the authorization of the Board, stated that Trans Union had entered into "definitive agreements" with the Pritzkers; and the press release did not even disclose Trans Union's limited right to receive and accept higher offers. Accompanying this press release was a further public announcement that Pritzker had been granted an option to purchase at any time one million shares of Trans Union's capital stock at 75 cents above the then-current price per share.

Thus, notwithstanding what several of the outside directors later claimed to have "thought" occurred at the meeting, the record compels the conclusion that Trans Union's Board had no rational basis to conclude on September 20 or in the days immediately following, that the Board's acceptance of Pritzker's offer was conditioned on (1) a "market test" of the offer; and (2) the Board's right to withdraw from the Pritzker Agreement and accept any higher offer received before the shareholder meeting.

(3)

The directors' unfounded reliance on both the premium and the market test as the basis for accepting the Pritzker proposal undermines the defendants' remaining contention that the Board's collective experience and sophistication was a sufficient basis for finding that it reached its September 20 decision with informed, reasonable deliberation.[9] *Compare Gimbel v. Signal Companies, Inc.*, Del. Ch., 316 A.2d 599 (1974), *aff'd per curiam*, Del. Supr., 316 A.2d 619 (1974). There, the Court of Chancery preliminarily enjoined a board's sale of stock of its wholly-owned subsidiary for an alleged grossly inadequate price. It did so based on a finding that the business judgment rule had been pierced for failure of management to give its board "the opportunity to make a reasonable and reasoned decision." 316 A.2d at 615. The Court there reached this result notwithstanding the board's sophistication and experience; the company's need of immediate cash; and the board's need to act promptly due to the impact of an energy crisis on the value of the underlying assets being sold — all of its subsidiary's oil and gas interests. The Court found those factors denoting competence to be outweighed by evidence of gross negligence; that management in effect sprang the deal on the board by negotiating the asset sale without informing the board; that the buyer intended to "force a quick decision" by the board; that the board meeting was called on only one-and-a-half days' notice; that its outside directors were not notified of the meeting's purpose; that during a meeting spanning "a couple of hours" a sale of assets worth $ 480 million was approved; and that the Board failed to obtain a *current* appraisal of its oil and gas interests. The analogy of *Signal* to the case at bar is significant.

(4)

Part of the defense is based on a claim that the directors relied on legal advice rendered at the September 20 meeting by James Brennan, Esquire, who was present at Van Gorkom's request. Unfortunately, Brennan did not appear and testify at trial even though his firm participated in the defense of this action....

---

[9] Trans Union's five "inside" directors had backgrounds in law and accounting, 116 years of collective employment by the Company and 68 years of combined experience on its Board. Trans Union's five "outside" directors included four chief executives of major corporations and an economist who was a former dean of a major school of business and chancellor of a university. The "outside" directors had 78 years of combined experience as chief executive officers of major corporations and 50 years of cumulative experience as directors of Trans Union. Thus, defendants argue that the Board was eminently qualified to reach an informed judgment on the proposed "sale" of Trans Union notwithstanding their lack of any advance notice of the proposal, the shortness of their deliberation, and their determination not to consult with their investment banker or to obtain a fairness opinion.

Several defendants testified that Brennan advised them that Delaware law did not require a fairness opinion or an outside valuation of the Company before the Board could act on the Pritzker proposal. If given, the advice was correct. However, that did not end the matter. Unless the directors had before them adequate information regarding the intrinsic value of the Company, upon which a proper exercise of business judgment could be made, mere advice of this type is meaningless; and, given this record of the defendants' failures, it constitutes no defense here.

....

A second claim is that counsel advised the Board it would be subject to lawsuits if it rejected the $ 55 per share offer. It is, of course, a fact of corporate life that today when faced with difficult or sensitive issues, directors often are subject to suit, irrespective of the decisions they make. However, counsel's mere acknowledgement of this circumstance cannot be rationally translated into a justification for a board permitting itself to be stampeded into a patently unadvised act. While suit might result from the rejection of a merger or tender offer, Delaware law makes clear that a board acting within the ambit of the business judgment rule faces no ultimate liability. Thus, we cannot conclude that the mere threat of litigation, acknowledged by counsel, constitutes either legal advice or any valid basis upon which to pursue an uninformed course.

....

B

We now examine the Board's post-September 20 conduct for the purpose of determining first, whether it was informed and not grossly negligent; and second, if informed, whether it was sufficient to legally rectify and cure the Board's derelictions of September 20.

....

Trans Union's press release stated:

FOR IMMEDIATE RELEASE:
CHICAGO, IL — Trans Union Corporation announced today that it had entered into definitive agreements to merge with an affiliate of The Marmon Group, Inc. in a transaction whereby Trans Union stockholders would receive $ 55 per share in cash for each Trans Union share held. The Marmon Group, Inc. is controlled by the Pritzker family of Chicago.

The merger is subject to approval by the stockholders of Trans Union at a special meeting expected to be held sometime during December or early January. Until October 10, 1980, the purchaser has the right to terminate the merger if financing that is satisfactory to the purchaser has not been obtained, but after that date there is no such right.

In a related transaction, Trans Union has agreed to sell to a designee of the purchaser one million newly-issued shares of Trans Union common stock at a cash price of $ 38 per share. Such shares will be issued only if the merger financing has been committed for no later than October 10, 1980, or if the purchaser elects to waive the merger financing condition. In addition, the New York Stock Exchange will be asked to approve the listing of the new shares pursuant to a listing application which Trans Union intends to file shortly.

Completing of the transaction is also subject to the preparation of a definitive proxy statement and making various filings and obtaining the approvals or consents of government agencies.

....

Thus, the primary purpose of the October 8 Board meeting was to amend the Merger Agreement, in a manner agreeable to Pritzker, to permit Trans Union to conduct a "market test." Van Gorkom understood that the proposed amendments were intended to give the Company an unfettered "right to openly solicit offers down through January 31." Van Gorkom presumably so represented the amendments to Trans Union's Board members on October 8. In a brief session, the directors approved Van Gorkom's oral presentation of the substance of the proposed amendments, the terms of which were not reduced to writing until October 10. But rather than waiting to review the amendments, the Board again approved them sight unseen and adjourned, giving Van Gorkom authority to execute the papers when he received them.

....

The next day, October 9, and before the Agreement was amended, Pritzker moved swiftly to off-set the proposed market test amendment....

The next day, October 10, Pritzker delivered to Trans Union the proposed amendments to the September 20 Merger Agreement. Van Gorkom promptly proceeded to countersign all the instruments on behalf of Trans Union without reviewing the instruments to determine if they were consistent with the authority previously granted him by the Board....

....

In our view, the record compels the conclusion that the directors' conduct on October 8 exhibited the same deficiencies as did their conduct on September 20....

....

The October 9 press release, coupled with the October 10 amendments, had the clear effect of locking Trans Union's Board into the Pritzker Agreement. Pritzker had thereby foreclosed Trans Union's Board from negotiating any better "definitive" agreement over the remaining eight weeks before Trans Union was required to clear the Proxy Statement submitting the Pritzker proposal to its shareholders.

....

Next, as to the "curative" effects of the Board's post-September 20 conduct ....

....

The defendants characterize the Board's Minutes of the January 26 meeting as a "review" of the "entire sequence of events" from Van Gorkom's initiation of the negotiations on September 13 forward. The defendants also rely on the testimony of several of the Board members at trial as confirming the Minutes. On the basis of this evidence, the defendants argue that whatever information the Board lacked to make a deliberate and informed judgment on September 20, or on October 8, was fully divulged to the entire Board on January 26. Hence, the argument goes, the Board's vote on January 26 to again "approve" the Pritzker merger must be found to have been an informed and deliberate judgment.

On the basis of this evidence, the defendants assert: (1) that the Trial Court was legally correct in widening the time frame for determining whether the defendants' approval of the Pritzker merger represented an informed business judgment to include the entire four-month period during which the Board considered the matter from September 20 through January 26; and (2) that, given this extensive evidence of the Board's further review and deliberations on January 26, this Court must affirm the Trial Court's conclusion that the Board's action was not reckless or improvident.

We cannot agree. We find the Trial Court to have erred, both as a matter of fact and as a matter of law, in relying on the action on January 26 to bring the defendants' conduct within the protection of the business judgment rule.

....

IV

Whether the directors of Trans Union should be treated as one or individually in terms of invoking the protection of the business judgment rule and the applicability of 8 Del. C. § 141(c) are questions which were not originally addressed by the parties in their briefing of this case. This resulted in a supplemental briefing and a second rehearing en banc on two basic questions: (a) whether one or more of the directors were deprived of the protection of the business judgment rule by evidence of an absence of good faith; and (b) whether one or more of the outside directors were entitled to invoke the protection of 8 Del. C. § 141(e) by evidence of a reasonable, good faith reliance on "reports," including legal advice, rendered the Board by certain inside directors and the Board's special counsel, Brennan.

The parties' response, including reargument, has led the majority of the Court to conclude: (1) that since all of the defendant directors, outside as well as inside, take a unified position, we are required to treat all of the directors as one as to whether they are entitled to the protection of the business judgment rule; and (2) that considerations of good faith, including the presumption that the directors acted in good faith, are irrelevant in determining the threshold issue of whether the directors as a Board exercised an informed business judgment. For the same reason, we must reject defense counsel's ad hominem argument for affirmance: that reversal may result in a multi-million dollar class award against the defendants for having made an allegedly uninformed business judgment in a transaction not involving any personal gain, self-dealing or claim of bad faith.

....

V

The defendants ultimately rely on the stockholder vote of February 10 for exoneration. The defendants contend that the stockholders' "overwhelming" vote approving the Pritzker Merger Agreement had the legal effect of curing any failure of the Board to reach an informed business judgment in its approval of the merger.

....

The settled rule in Delaware is that "where a majority of fully informed stockholders ratify action of even interested directors, an attack on the ratified transaction normally must fail." *Gerlach v. Gillam*, Del. Ch., 139 A.2d 591, 593 (1958). The question of whether shareholders have been fully informed such that their vote can be said to ratify director action, "turns on the fairness and completeness of the proxy materials submitted by the management to the ... shareholders." *Michelson v. Duncan*, Del.Supr. 407 A.2d 211 (1979), *aff'g* in part and *rev'g* in part, Del. Ch., 386 A.2d 1144 (1978).

....

Applying this standard to the record before us, we find that Trans Union's stockholders were not fully informed of all facts material to their vote on the Pritzker Merger and that the Trial Court's ruling to the contrary is clearly erroneous.

....

The burden must fall on defendants who claim ratification based on shareholder vote to establish that the shareholder approval resulted from a fully informed electorate. On the record before us, it is clear that the Board failed to meet that burden....

....

VI

To summarize: we hold that the directors of Trans Union breached their fiduciary duty to their stockholders (1) by their failure to inform themselves of all information reasonably available to them and relevant to their decision to recommend the Pritzker merger; and (2) by their failure to disclose all material information such as a reasonable stockholder would consider important in deciding whether to approve the Pritzker offer.

We hold, therefore, that the Trial Court committed reversible error in applying the business judgment rule in favor of the director defendants in this case.

On remand, the Court of Chancery shall conduct an evidentiary hearing to determine the fair value of the shares represented by the plaintiffs' class, based on the intrinsic value of Trans Union on September 20, 1980.... Thereafter, an award of damages may be entered to the extent that the fair value of Trans Union exceeds $ 55 per share.

....

Reversed and Remanded for proceedings consistent herewith.

McNEILLY, JUSTICE, dissenting:

The majority opinion reads like an advocate's closing address to a hostile jury. And I say that not lightly. Throughout the opinion great emphasis is directed only to the negative, with nothing more than lip service granted the positive aspects of this case. In my opinion Chancellor Marvel (retired) should have been affirmed. The Chancellor's opinion was the product of well reasoned conclusions, based upon a sound deductive process, clearly supported by the evidence and entitled to deference in this appeal. Because of my diametrical opposition to all evidentiary conclusions of the majority, I respectfully dissent.

....

... The majority has spoken and has effectively said that Trans Union's Directors have been the victims of a "fast shuffle" by Van Gorkom and Pritzker. That is the beginning of the majority's comedy of errors. The first and most important error made is the majority's assessment of the directors' knowledge of the affairs of Trans Union and their combined ability to act in this situation under the protection of the business judgment rule.

... At the time the merger was proposed the inside five directors had collectively been employed by the Company for 116 years and had 68 years of combined experience as directors.... The five "outside" directors had 78 years of combined experience as chief executive officers, and 53 years cumulative service as Trans Union directors.

The inside directors wear their badge of expertise in the corporate affairs of Trans Union on their sleeves. But what about the outsiders? Dr. Wallis is or was an economist and math statistician, a professor of economics at Yale University, dean of the graduate school of business at the University of Chicago, and Chancellor of the University of Rochester. Dr. Wallis had been on the Board of Trans Union since 1962. He also was on the Board of Bausch & Lomb, Kodak, Metropolitan Life Insurance Company, Standard Oil and others.

William B. Johnson is a University of Pennsylvania law graduate, President of Railway Express until 1966, Chairman and Chief Executive of I.C. Industries Holding Company, and member of Trans Union's Board since 1968.

Joseph Lanterman, a Certified Public Accountant, is or was President and Chief Executive of American Steel, on the Board of International Harvester, Peoples Energy, Illinois Bell Telephone, Harris Bank and Trust Company, Kemper Insurance Company and a director of Trans Union for four years.

Graham Morgan is a chemist, was Chairman and Chief Executive Officer of U.S. Gypsum, and in the 17 and 18 years prior to the Trans Union transaction had been involved in 31 or 32 corporate takeovers.

Robert Reneker attended University of Chicago and Harvard Business Schools. He was President and Chief Executive of Swift and Company, director of Trans Union since 1971, and member of the Boards of seven other corporations including U.S. Gypsum and the Chicago Tribune.

Directors of this caliber are not ordinarily taken in by a "fast shuffle"....

The majority of this Court holds that the Board's decision, reached on September 20, 1980, to approve the merger was not the product of an *informed* business judgment, that the Board's subsequent efforts to amend the Merger Agreement and take other curative action were *legally and factually* ineffectual, and that the Board did *not deal with complete candor* with the stockholders by failing to disclose all material facts, which they knew or should have known, before securing the stockholders' approval of the merger. I disagree.

....

I have no quarrel with the majority's analysis of the business judgment rule. It is the application of that rule to these facts which is wrong. An overview of the entire record, rather than the limited view of bits and pieces which the majority has exploded like popcorn, convinces me that the directors made an informed business judgment which was buttressed by their test of the market.

---

1. Informed Decisionmaking

The Trans Union directors argued that their decision was "informed," given the above-market price and the market test period, their substantial expertise and experience, their reliance on expert counsel, and the shareholders' approval. How did the court dismantle each of these arguments?

How would each of these arguments fare under the classic business judgment rule analysis described in *Joy v. North*? Would the Trans Union directors have been found liable if the general standard of care, based on ordinary negligence, was the applicable standard?

By making the pivotal issue whether or not the directors' decision was "informed," the court here reminded us that the duty of care analysis focuses on the process by which corporate decisions are made, rather than on the substance and merits of the decision itself. Courts traditionally are hesitant to second-guess management's actual decisions. However, the court's detailed analysis in *Van Gorkom*, for instance, of the price reveals how difficult it is to separate the process from the substance of the decision. In addition, the selection of one decisionmaking process over another can be considered a substantive decision itself.

2. Aftermath

The parties in the *Van Gorkom* case ultimately settled, with the plaintiffs receiving $ 23.5 million. Of this amount, it was reported that the directors and their insurance carrier paid about $ 10 million, with the remainder being paid by the Pritzker group.[10]

---

[10]Bayless Manning, *Reflections and Practical Tips on Life in the Boardroom After Van Gorkom*, 41 BUS. LAW. 1 (1985).

The *Van Gorkom* case prompted a flurry of scholarly writing, many critical of the court's reasoning. The case was widely perceived to impose a higher standard of care on directors. In response, insurance companies revised their policies and increased their premiums in anticipation of increased litigation against directors — heightening directors' and officers' concerns about the availability of affordable liability insurance. Many directors, becoming increasingly concerned about the increased liability risks and the lack of insurance, considered resigning from their directors' positions. The president of the National Association of Corporate Directors indicated that *Van Gorkom* "created perilous times for corporate directors," and he called the decision "the straw that broke the camel's back" as far as directors are concerned.[11]

3. Corporate Governance Reforms

Corporate governance structures and decisionmaking processes are in transition in many publicly-held corporations. As you read the following excerpt on some of these fundamental changes, consider how directors' duty of care will be affected.

Ira M. Millstein, The Professional Board, 50 Business Lawyer 1427-31 (August 1995)*

In the past three years, a number of high-profile U.S. boards have adopted a more independent and active approach to governance responsibilities as they attempt to revitalize the corporations they serve. Numerous factors have played a role in this "activation" including, among other things: (i) undeniable and apparent performance deficiencies; (ii) prodding from institutional shareholders (primarily large public pension funds); (iii) evolving judicial interpretations of directors' duties; (iv) pressures emanating from the corporate takeovers of the 1980s; (v) the need to "re-invent" the corporate enterprise to meet newly emerging global competition efficiently; and (vi) directors' concern for their own reputations. Remarkably, the actual reordering of boardroom processes to improve directors' abilities to monitor management and corporate performance has been self-made by boards, without government intervention. This reordering is the first sign of professionalism — directors developing for themselves the standards to live by....

That fundamental change is now in process. In the spring of 1994, the General Motors (GM) board issued guidelines setting forth procedures designed to ensure active monitoring of management by an independent board. That act, by a board itself, in the right place at the right time, seemed to legitimize change in the

---

[11] Baum, *The Job Nobody Wants*, BUS. WK., Sept. 8, 1986, at 56; Mauro, *Liability in the Boardroom*, NATION'S BUS., May 1986 at 46.

boardroom. The GM guidelines have been widely praised, and the California Public Employees Retirement System has prodded other boards to consider guidelines adapted to their respective enterprises. In the past year alone, the National Association of Corporate Directors (NACD), the Conference Board, and the Business Law Section of the American Bar Association have published treatises on various aspects of corporate governance that, if followed, would significantly improve the board's ability and motivation to monitor performance. Indeed, boardroom change is going international as evidenced by the documents outlining "best practices" for boards that have been published in Canada (the Toronto Stock Exchange), the United Kingdom (the Cadbury Committee), and Australia (the Bosch Committee). It seems reasonable to assume that the European continent will not be too far behind.

While company-specific guidelines and more general codes of "best practice" properly leave with management the authority to conduct the day-to-day affairs of the corporation, they nonetheless express a change in the balance of corporate power and an extension of board powers into "grey areas" of authority that were long management's de facto province. Consider the following relatively simple changes addressed in various board guidelines that shift the balance of authority between management and the board:

(i) separation of the chairman and CEO, or at least the selection — formally or informally — by the board of a "lead director";[12]

(ii) board control over the process of nominating and retaining independent directors;[13] and,

(iii) evaluation of CEO performance by outside directors in meetings solely of outside directors.[14]

Each one of these changes increases the board's independence from the CEO as the board positions itself to gain more information about the corporation and its performance, so that it can identify and understand the early warning signals of "trouble ahead."

In defining the scope of board involvement in corporate decision-making, however, a careful line needs to be drawn between board and management responsibility. It is management which must provide both the leadership and creative force in the corporation. This implicates a major element of board professionalism, understanding and defining the limits of the board's role. Lawyers, for example, understand that in most circumstances they render advice, and that taking or leaving that advice is the client's role. The limit is when the

---

[12] The separation of the chairman and the CEO reflects the CEO's loss of domination over the board and recognition that the CEO is accountable to the board as an independent entity.

[13] When directors become the board's choice, rather than management's choice, board members address each other as peer group members not beholden to the CEO.

[14] A separate meeting of outside directors alone changes the dynamics of the CEO/board relationship.

lawyer's professional responsibilities require him or her to act when the advice is ignored.

The factors in determining the parameters of the board's role are these: Does the board have access to the same information on performance as management, and does the board have the knowledge of the business to use that information better than, or as well as, management? Will the board take the time, and is it feasible for the board to take the time, to seek out and study the information necessary for informed decision-making? Will board involvement in a particular matter improve overall corporate performance, taking into consideration any relevant costs including the cost of management becoming unnecessarily risk-averse or otherwise unable to react quickly and decisively to certain crises?

The following excerpt surveys governance reform proposals from many sources. These proposals are intended to improve the performance of boards of directors and to improve information flows and incentives. Consider whether they would achieve these objectives.

Margaret M. Blair, Ownership and Control: Rethinking Corporate Governance for the Twenty-First Century, pp. 197-201 (1995)*

Board of Directors

1.   All publicly traded companies should have a majority of outside directors.
     a.   [One model is that] outside directors should be "independent" directors; that is, they should have no business or other relationship with the firm, other than as a director and shareholder.
     b.   [Another model is that] boards of directors should include representation by significant customers, suppliers, financial advisors, employees, and community representatives.
2.   The chair of the board should be an outside director, and not the CEO.
3.   Boards should include a certain number of "professional" outside directors. These could be drawn from a pool of candidates identified by institutional investors.
4.   Each board should formally recognize a chief outside director, or, as one advocate calls it, "deputy chair of the board."
5.   Boards should be smaller. They should have no more than ten members, and outside directors should outnumber inside directors by at least two to one.
6.   CEOs should serve on no more than one other corporate board in addition to their own.
7.   Outside directors should meet alone (without the CEO or other inside directors) regularly — at least once a year; some proponents say as often as four times a year.

---

8. Directors should be required to make a specific commitment of time and should be permitted to sit on no more than three boards at once. Each day of board meetings should be matched by one to two days of preparation.

9. There should be term limits for outside directors, for example, ten to fifteen years, and a mandatory retirement age.

10. Boards should meet monthly or even bimonthly for a full day, and should have one two- to three-day strategy session each year.

11. Compensation committees should consist of no more than five people and should be staffed by independent directors. CEOs should not sit on each others' compensation committees. Compensation committees should be able to hire their own pay consultants. The board should provide the details of its compensation contract with the CEO to the shareholders.

12. Boards should have audit committees staffed only by independent directors. This committee should meet with the external auditors at least twice a year, with no executive board members present.

13. Boards should have nominating committees staffed by outside directors.

14. Outside directors should screen and recommend candidates for the board based on qualifications established by the board.

15. Directors should be allowed to contract out for professional advice.

16. To maintain control and safeguard against illegal practices, boards should formulate a specific list of matters reserved for their collective decision.

17. Directors should meet with outside shareholders, with officers and employees of the company, and, as necessary, with outside advisors, to ensure they have the information they need to do the job.

18. Companies should provide an annual informal setting in which up to ten of the larger shareholders can meet directly with the board of directors, with the goals of improving understanding between institutional shareholders and directors and thus avoiding much of the letter writing, meeting requests, board-seat requests, and proxy proposals some institutional investors have been pursuing.

19. Companies should set up a binary board structure. German AGs for example, have two-tiered boards. Another possibility is the institution of a "corporate senate," which has veto power over the actions of the board that involve conflicts of interest. The corporate bylaws would give the senators (as well as all directors) access to all corporate information and oblige each director to report any conflicts of interest to the senate. Senators would be elected on the basis of one vote per shareholder, giving small shareholders the same power as large shareholders.

20. The courts should formulate a duty of independence as a halfway point between the duty of care and the duty of loyalty. Informal, disinterested directors should be required to approve any corporate transaction in which management or any other director has a stake, other than the corporation's stake.

Enhanced Information and Internal Controls

1. Boards of directors should establish formal criteria for picking directors and formal performance standards against which they evaluate strategy, judge themselves and the CEO, and measure the long-term performance of the company.
2. Corporations should establish specific long-term quantitative performance objectives, and these objectives should be disclosed to all corporate investors. Investors and directors should periodically appraise the progress of corporate management toward reaching these goals.
3. Directors should perform an annual evaluation of CEO performance that reviews company operating performance as well as major extraordinary initiatives the CEO has set out to achieve.
4. A chosen leader of the outside directors should meet with the CEO after the performance review session to relay the main points of that discussion. The CEO should then meet with the outside directors to provide a reaction.
5. Directors should clearly communicate qualifications for board members to shareholders.
6. Before new directors are hired, they should be required to write a letter informing the CEO of their time restrictions. Corporate counsel should explicitly spell out to new directors the duties and responsibilities for which they will be accountable.
7. Independent directors should include their own statement in proxy filings (especially after a period in which the company does not meet its performance targets).
8. Outside directors should meet regularly with security analysts and selected large institutional investors.
9. Directors should be compensated in part with stock options.
10. Tax incentives for stock options and stock purchase plans should apply only to plans with restrictions on selling, such as options that cannot be activated for at least five years, or that otherwise penalize the early exercise of stock options.
11. Shareholders should have to approve compensation contracts every three years.
12. If a company under performs for three consecutive years, the board should publish a report for shareholders detailing the nature of the problems the company faces. Large shareholders would then be allowed to include statements in the proxy on management performance.
13. Companies should undergo periodic "business audits" by outside experts to provide perspective in evaluating a company's performance.
14. Management should maintain an appropriate, arms-length relationship with auditors. Firms should disclose all fees paid to the auditors for services other than the audit.

15. Auditors should have legal protection against defamation and breach of confidentiality suits when reporting suspicion of fraud. Few auditors are in a position strong enough to challenge management.

16. Companies should be required to disclose information about how compensation of the top executives is related to performance, including the performance factors that compensation is tied to and precisely how compensation would vary with variations in those factors. Companies should also be required to disclose the market value of all perquisites provided for executives.

SECTION IV. CORPORATE OBJECTIVE AND SOCIAL RESPONSIBILITY

When exercising their business judgment, directors and officers often are confronted with myriad factors. Their determination of "corporate interest" and which factors to give relevance or priority in particular factual circumstances may be complicated. Fundamental underlying issues in this determination are: (1) what is the corporation's purpose, and (2) to whom does the corporation and its directors owe their duty?

The following case considers directors' and officers' latitude regarding these fundamental issues. They are followed by materials on "other constituencies" statutes and the ALI. Finally, a corporation's statement on the topic is provided. As you study these materials, consider how they would affect the directors' corporate decisionmaking. You also may want to refer again to the discussion on the corporation's purpose in the Introduction.

A. JUDICIAL GUIDANCE

SHLENSKY v. WRIGLEY

Appellate Court of Illinois
237 N.E.2d 776 (1968)

SULLIVAN, JUSTICE:

This is an appeal from a dismissal of plaintiff's amended complaint on motion of the defendants. The action was a stockholders' derivative suit against the directors for negligence and mismanagement. The corporation was also made a defendant. Plaintiff sought damages and an order that defendants cause the installation of lights in Wrigley Field and the scheduling of night baseball games.

Plaintiff is a minority stockholder of defendant corporation, Chicago National League Ball Club (Inc.), a Delaware corporation with its principal place of business in Chicago, Illinois. Defendant corporation owns and operates the major league professional baseball team known as the Chicago Cubs. The corporation also engages in the operation of Wrigley Field, the Cubs' home park, the concessionaire sales during Cubs' home games, television and radio broadcasts of Cubs' home games, the leasing of the field for football games and other events and receives its share, as visiting team, of admission moneys from games played in other National League stadia. The individual defendants are directors of the Cubs and have served for varying periods of years. Defendant Philip K. Wrigley is also president of the corporation and owner of approximately 80% of the stock therein.

Plaintiff alleges that since night baseball was first played in 1935 nineteen of the twenty major league teams have scheduled night games. In 1966, out of a total of 1620 games in the major leagues, 932 were played at night. Plaintiff alleges that every member of the major leagues, other than the Cubs, scheduled substantially all of its home games in 1966 at night, exclusive of opening days, Saturdays, Sundays, holidays and days prohibited by league rules. Allegedly this has been done for the specific purpose of maximizing attendance and thereby maximizing revenue and income.

The Cubs, in the years 1961-65, sustained operating losses from its direct baseball operations. Plaintiff attributes those losses to inadequate attendance at Cubs' home games. He concludes that if the directors continue to refuse to install lights at Wrigley Field and schedule night baseball games, the Cubs will continue to sustain comparable losses and its financial condition will continue to deteriorate.

Plaintiff alleges that, except for the year 1963, attendance at Cubs' home games has been substantially below that at their road games, many of which were played at night.

Plaintiff compares attendance at Cubs' games with that of the Chicago White Sox, an American League club, whose weekday games were generally played at night. The weekend attendance figures for the two teams was similar; however, the White Sox week-night games drew many more patrons than did the Cubs' weekday games.

Plaintiff alleges that the funds for the installation of lights can be readily obtained through financing and the cost of installation would be far more than offset and recaptured by increased revenues and incomes resulting from the increased attendance.

Plaintiff further alleges that defendant Wrigley has refused to install lights, not because of interest in the welfare of the corporation but because of his personal opinions "that baseball is a 'daytime sport' and that the installation of lights and night baseball games will have a deteriorating effect upon the surrounding neighborhood." It is alleged that he has admitted that he is not interested in whether the Cubs would benefit financially from such action because of his concern for the neighborhood, and that he would be willing for the team to play night games if a new stadium were built in Chicago.

Plaintiff alleges that the other defendant directors, with full knowledge of the foregoing matters, have acquiesced in the policy laid down by Wrigley and have permitted him to dominate the board of directors in matters involving the installation of lights and scheduling of night games, even though they knew he was not motivated by a good faith concern as to the best interests of defendant corporation, but solely by his personal views set forth above. It is charged that the directors are acting for a reason or reasons contrary and wholly unrelated to the business interests of the corporation; that such arbitrary and capricious acts constitute mismanagement and waste of corporate assets, and that the directors have been negligent in failing to exercise reasonable care and prudence in the management of the corporate affairs.

The question on appeal is whether plaintiff's amended complaint states a cause of action....

. . . .

Plaintiff in the instant case argues that the directors are acting for reasons unrelated to the financial interest and welfare of the Cubs. However, we are not satisfied that the motives assigned to Philip K. Wrigley, and through him to the other directors, are contrary to the best interests of the corporation and the stockholders. For example, it appears to us that the effect on the surrounding neighborhood might well be considered by a director who was considering the patrons who would or would not attend the games if the park were in a poor neighborhood. Furthermore, the long run interest of the corporation in its property value at Wrigley Field might demand all efforts to keep the neighborhood from deteriorating. By these thoughts we do not mean to say that we have decided that the decision of the directors was a correct one. That is beyond our jurisdiction and ability. We are merely saying that the decision is one properly before directors and the motives alleged in the amended complaint showed no fraud, illegality or conflict of interest in their making of that decision.

While all the courts do not insist that one or more of the three elements must be present for a stockholder's derivative action to lie, nevertheless we feel that unless the conduct of the defendants at least borders on one of the elements, the courts should not interfere. The trial court in the instant case acted properly in dismissing plaintiff's amended complaint.

We feel that plaintiff's amended complaint was also defective in failing to allege damage to the corporation. The well pleaded facts must be taken as true for the purpose of judging the sufficiency of the amended complaint. However, one need not accept conclusions drawn by the pleader. Furthermore, pleadings will be construed most strongly against the pleader prior to a verdict or judgment on the merits.

There is no allegation that the night games played by the other nineteen teams enhanced their financial position or that the profits, if any, of those teams were directly related to the number of night games scheduled. There is an allegation that the installation of lights and scheduling of night games in Wrigley Field would have resulted in large amounts of additional revenues and incomes from increased attendance and related sources of income. Further, the cost of installation of lights, funds for which are allegedly readily available by financing, would be more than offset and recaptured by increased revenues. However, no allegation is made that there will be a net benefit to the corporation from such action, considering all increased costs.

Plaintiff claims that the losses of defendant corporation are due to poor attendance at home games. However, it appears from the amended complaint, taken as a whole, that factors other than attendance affect the net earnings or losses. For example, in 1962, attendance at home and road games decreased appreciably as compared with 1961, and yet the loss from direct baseball operation and of the whole corporation was considerably less.

The record shows that plaintiff did not feel he could allege that the increased revenues would be sufficient to cure the corporate deficit. The only cost plaintiff was at all concerned with was that of installation of lights. No mention was made of operation and maintenance of the lights or other possible increases in operating costs of night games and we cannot speculate as to what other factors might influence the increase or decrease of profits if the Cubs were to play night home games.

....

Finally, we do not agree with plaintiff's contention that failure to follow the example of the other major league clubs in scheduling night games constituted negligence. Plaintiff made no allegation that these teams' night schedules were profitable or that the purpose for which night baseball had been undertaken was fulfilled. Furthermore, it cannot be said that directors, even those of corporations that are losing money, must follow the lead of the other corporations in the field. Directors are elected for their business capabilities and judgment and the courts cannot require them to forego their judgment because of the decisions of directors of other companies. Courts may not decide these questions in the absence of a clear showing of dereliction of duty on the part of the specific directors and mere failure to 'follow the crowd' is not such a dereliction.

For the foregoing reasons the order of dismissal entered by the trial court is affirmed.

Affirmed.

---

1. Corporate Purpose

How did the court in *Shlensky* interpret the corporation's purpose? Did the case impose limits on directors' consideration of the needs and interests of non-shareholder groups — such as employees, communities in which the corporation is located, and customers? How, if at all, should directors and officers incorporate these other corporate constituencies into their decisionmaking?

2. *Dodge* Case

Dodge v. Ford Motor Co.,[15] is an old but classic case. Confronted with an adamant Henry Ford, the court addressed whether there were limits to directors' discretion in determining the corporation's purpose:

> "My ambition," said Mr. Ford, "is to employ still more men, to spread the benefits of this industrial system to the greatest possible number, to help them build up their lives and their homes. To do this we are putting the greatest share of our profits back in the business."
>
> ... The record, and especially the testimony of Mr. Ford, convinces that he has to some extent the attitude towards shareholders of one who has dispensed and distributed to them large gains and that they should be content to take what he chooses to give. His testimony creates the impression, also, that he thinks the Ford Motor Company has made too much money, has had too large profits, and that although large profits might be still earned, a sharing of them with the public, by reducing the price of the output of the company, ought to be undertaken....
>
> [But, a] business corporation is organized and carried on primarily for the profit of the stockholders. The powers of the directors are to be employed for that end. The discretion of directors is to be exercised in the choice of means to attain that end and does not extend to a change in the end itself, to the reduction of profits or to the nondistribution of profits among stockholders in order to devote them to other purposes.

B. OTHER CONSTITUENCIES STATUTES

Over half of the states have statues that authorize directors to consider the interests of groups other than shareholders in at least some of their corporate decisionmaking. While the statutes were originally drafted to affirm that directors defending against unsolicited tender offers could consider these nonshareholders' interests, the express statutory language typically is not limited to this context. As Pennsylvania[16] illustrates:

> (a) General rule. — In discharging the duties of their respective positions, the board of directors, committees of the board and individual directors of a business corporation may, in considering the best interests of the corporation, consider to the extent they deem appropriate:
>
> (1) The effects of any action upon any or all groups affected by such action, including shareholders, employees, suppliers, customers and creditors of the corporation, and upon communities in which offices or other establishments of the corporation are located.

---

[15] 170 N.W. 668 (1919).
[16] PA. CONS. STAT. ANN. § 1715.

(2) The short-term and long-term interests of the corporation, including benefits that may accrue to the corporation from its long-term plans and the possibility that these interests may be best served by the continued independence of the corporation.

(3) The resources, intent and conduct (past, stated and potential) of any person seeking to acquire control of the corporation.

(4) All other pertinent factors.

(b) Consideration of interests and factors. — The board of directors, committees of the board and individual directors shall not be required, in considering the best interests of the corporation or the effects of any action, to regard any corporate interest or the interests of any particular group affected by such action as a dominant or controlling interest or factor. The consideration of interests and factors in the manner described in this subsection and in subsection (a) shall not constitute a violation of section 1712 (relating to standard of care and justifiable reliance).

These other constituencies statutes are controversial.[17] Some argue that they are merely codifications of case law, which had always allowed directors to consider whatever and whomever they wanted. For example, the Delaware Supreme Court has indicated that directors may consider other constituencies in their decisionmaking so long as there is "some rationally related benefit accruing to the stockholders."[18] Others argue that these laws are an unwise departure from traditional corporate law principles. They believe that the interests of shareholders should be primary, if not exclusive, and that consideration of the interests of nonshareholders will weaken directors' loyalty to shareholders. Some also are concerned that these statutes will expose directors and officers to lawsuits by disgruntled employees, communities, and other nonshareholder constituencies.

It is not certain how these other constituencies statutes will affect the liability of directors. It appears, however, that they will probably decrease it. The statutes appear to give directors additional discretion and flexibility in determining what is in the corporation's best interest. To illustrate, if directors are considering whether to close a plant, there are numerous factors they may consider. If they decide to take into account the interests of nonshareholders, such as employees, shareholders may object because their interests were not the directors' exclusive concern. The other constituencies statutes, however, expressly allow directors to consider the interests of nonshareholders, so the objecting shareholders would have no basis for a lawsuit on these grounds. On the other hand, if the directors decide not to consider the interests of nonshareholders, they also need not worry

---

[17] *See* Committee on Corporate Laws, *Other Constituencies Statutes: Potential for Confusion*, 45 BUS. LAW. 2253 (1990).

[18] *Revlon, Inc. v. MacAndrews & Forbes Holdings, Inc.*, 506 A.2d 173, 176 (Del. 1986); *Amanda Acquisition Corp. v. Universal Foods Corp.*, 708 F. Supp. 984, 1010-15 (E.D. Wis), *aff'd on other grounds*, 877 F.2d 496 (7th Cir. 1989).

about being sued by those groups. The other constituencies statutes permit directors to consider nonshareholder interests, but they generally do not require them to do so.[19] Thus, these statutes do not appear to give the nonshareholder groups any enforceable rights.

C. ALI PRINCIPLES

ALI § 2.01 addresses the corporation's objective and how it carries out its objective. Section 6.02(b) discusses which factors directors may consider in deciding upon a reasonable response to an unsolicited tender offer. As you review these provisions, consider how they are consistent or inconsistent with the case law and the "other constituencies" statutes.

§ 2.01. The Objective and Conduct of the Corporation

(a) ... [A] corporation should have as its objective the conduct of business activities with a view to enhancing corporate profit and shareholder gain.

(b) Even if corporate profit and shareholder gain are not thereby enhanced, the corporation, in the conduct of its business:

(1) Is obliged, to the same extent as a natural person, to act within the boundaries set by law;

(2) May take into account ethical considerations that are reasonably regarded as appropriate to the responsible conduct of business; and

(3) May devote a reasonable amount of resources to public welfare, humanitarian, educational, and philanthropic purposes.

[Comment to § 2.01] *f. The economic objective.* In very general terms, Subsection (a) [to § 2.01] may be thought of as a broad injunction to enhance economic returns, while Subsection (b) [to § 2.01] makes clear that certain kinds of conduct must or may be pursued whether or not they enhance such returns (that is, even if the conduct either yields no economic return or entails a net economic loss). In most cases, however, the kinds of conduct described in Subsection (b) could be pursued even under the principle embodied in Subsection (a). Such conduct will usually be consistent with economic self-interest, because the principle embodied in Subsection (a) — that the objective of the corporation is to conduct business activities with a view to enhancing corporate profit and shareholder gain — does not mean that the objective of the corporation must be to realize corporate profit and shareholder gain in the short run. Indeed, the contrary is true: long-run profitability and shareholder gain are at the core of the economic objective. Activity that entails a short-run cost to achieve an appropriately greater long-run profit is therefore not a departure from the economic objective. An orientation toward lawful, ethical, and public-spirited activity will

---

[19] An execption in Connecticut's law, which requires that directors consider other constituencies in certain circumstances. CONN. GEN. STAT. ANN. §§ 33-756(d) (1997).

normally fall within this description. The modern corporation by its nature creates interdependencies with a variety of groups with whom the corporation has a legitimate concern, such as employees, customers, suppliers, and members of the communities in which the corporation operates. The long-term profitability of the corporation generally depends on meeting the fair expectations of such groups. Short-term profits may properly be subordinated to recognition that responsible maintenance of these interdependencies is likely to contribute to long-term corporate profit and shareholder gain. The corporation's business may be conducted accordingly.

For comparable reasons, the economic objective does not imply that the corporation must extract the last penny of profit out of every transaction in which it is involved. Similarly, under normal circumstances the economic objective is met by focusing on the business in which the corporation is actually engaged

[Comment to § 2.01] *h. Ethical considerations.* Section 2.01(b)(2) provides that a corporation may take into account ethical considerations that are reasonably regarded as appropriate to the responsible conduct of business. It is sometimes argued that because adherence to ethical principles typically involves long-run financial benefits, the concept of a long run dissolves any apparent tension between financial and ethical considerations. Certainly, a long-run profit motive may often explain conduct that appears to be based on ethical grounds.... Furthermore, when ethical considerations enter into corporate decisions, they are usually mixed with, rather than opposed to, long-run profit considerations. Nevertheless, observation suggests that corporate decisions are not infrequently made on the basis of ethical considerations even when doing so would not enhance corporate profit or shareholder gain. Such behavior is not only appropriate, but desirable. Corporate officials are not less morally obliged than any other citizens to take ethical considerations into account, and it would be unwise social policy to preclude them from doing so.

§ 6.02. Action of Directors That Has the Foreseeable Effect of Blocking Unsolicited Tender Offers

(a) The board of directors may take an action that has the foreseeable effect of blocking an unsolicited tender offer, if the action is a reasonable response to the offer.

(b) In considering whether its action is a reasonable response to the offer:

(1) The board may take into account all factors relevant to the best interests of the corporation and shareholders, including, among other things, questions of legality and whether the offer, if successful, would threaten the corporation's essential economic prospects; and

(2) The board may, in addition to the analysis under ALI § 6.02(b)(1), have regard for interests or groups (other than shareholders) with respect to which the corporation has a legitimate concern if to do so would not significantly disfavor the long-term interests of shareholders.

D. CORPORATE CODE

Most corporations do not expressly articulate their corporate objective or the factors they consider relevant in their decisionmaking. However, a few corporations include in documents such as their "Code of Conduct" an expression of their position on these issues. How would the following Code shape directors' decisionmaking?

Johnson & Johnson's Credo*

We believe our first responsibility is to the doctors, nurses and patients, to mothers and fathers and all others who use our products and services. In meeting their needs everything we do must be of high quality. We must constantly strive to reduce our costs in order to maintain reasonable prices. Customers' orders must be serviced promptly and accurately. Our suppliers and distributors must have an opportunity to make a fair profit.

We are responsible to our employees, the men and women who work with us throughout the world. Everyone must be considered as an individual. We must respect their dignity and recognize their merit. They must have a sense of security in their jobs. Compensation must be fair and adequate, and working conditions clean, orderly and safe. We must be mindful of ways to help our employees fulfill their family responsibilities. Employees must feel free to make suggestions and complaints. There must be equal opportunity for employment, development and advancement for those qualified. We must provide competent management, and their actions must be just and ethical.

We are responsible to the communities in which we live and work and to the world community as well. We must be good citizens — support good works and charities and bear our fair share of taxes. We must encourage civic improvements and better health and education. We must maintain in good order the property we are privileged to use, protecting the environment and natural resources.

Our final responsibility is to our stockholders. Business must make a sound profit. We must experiment with new ideas. Research must be carried on, innovative programs developed and mistakes paid for. New equipment must be purchased, new facilities provided and new products launched. Reserves must be created to provide for adverse times. When we operate according to these principles, the stockholders should realize a fair return.

---

*Johnson & Johnson Homepage — Our Credo (10/15/96) (http://www.jnj.com/credo/credoeng.htm). Copyright © Johnson & Johnson. Used by permission.

SECTION V. LEGISLATIVE RESPONSES TO LIABILITY

A. TYPES OF STATUTES

In response to what directors perceived as excessive liability risks created by the *Van Gorkom* case, many state legislatures quickly moved to ameliorate the crisis. They enacted laws that, in one way or another, decreased directors' liability risks. At least three types of exculpation statutes emerged

First, as illustrated by Delaware's General Corporation Law § 102(b)(7), some statutes allow individual corporations, typically through shareholder action, to include in their articles a provision limiting or eliminating their directors' liability:

> In addition to the matters required to be set forth in the certificate of incorporation by subsection (a) of this section the certificate of incorporation may also contain any or all of the following matters —
>
> A provision eliminating or limiting the personal liability of a director to the corporation or its stockholders for monetary damages for breach of fiduciary duty as a director, provided that such provision shall not eliminate or limit the liability of a director (i) for any breach of the director's duty of loyalty to the corporation or its shareholders, (ii) for acts or omissions not in good faith or which involve intentional misconduct or a knowing violation of law, (iii) under section 174 of this Title [regarding unlawful payment of dividends, etc.], or (iv) for any transaction from which the director derived an improper personal benefit...

Second, as illustrated by Virginia Code Ann. § 13.1-690(A), some laws alter the standards of fiduciary duties imposed on all corporate directors, typically lowering the standard of conduct:

> A director shall discharge his duties as a director, including his duties as a member of a committee, in accordance with his good faith business judgment of the best interests of the corporation...

Finally, another alternative is offered by the ALI § 7.19, allowing shareholders to limit the amount of directors' liability:

> Except as otherwise provided by statute, if a failure by a director or an officer to meet the standard of conduct specified in Part IV (Duty of Care and the Business Judgment Rule) did not either:
>
> (1) Involve a knowing and culpable violation of law by the director or officer;
>
> (2) Show a conscious disregard for the duty of the director or officer to the corporation under circumstances in which the director or officer was aware that the conduct or omission created an unjustified risk of serious injury to the corporation; or

(3) Constitute a sustained and unexcused pattern of inattention that amounted to an abduction of the defendant's duty to the corporation; and the director or officer, or an associate, did not receive a benefit that was improper under Part V (Duty of Fair Dealing), then a provision in a certificate of incorporation that limits damages against an officer or a director for such failure to an amount not less than such person's annual compensation from the corporation should be given effect, if the provision is adopted by a vote of disinterested shareholders after disclosure concerning the provision, may be repealed by the shareholders at any annual meeting without prior action by the board, and does not reduce liability with respect to pending actions or losses incurred prior to its adoption.

These laws also may vary in the scope of their coverage. For example, some may limit the protected group to directors, rather than extending its application to officers. Others may limit the plaintiff groups to the corporation and shareholder derivative suits, rather than including creditor or other potential plaintiff groups. Some may require the corporation to affirmatively adopt the directors' protections, while others may automatically benefit the directors without shareholders' consent.

The two cases below suggest the types of legal issues that these statutes present. As you study these cases, the first dealing with the Delaware law and the second dealing with the Virginia law described above, consider how directors' liability risks and standards of conduct are altered when these statutes are applicable. Given these changes, do these types of statutes reduce incentives for directors to effectively manage the corporation?

B. SCOPE OF STATUTES

ARNOLD v. SOCIETY FOR SAVINGS BANCORP, INC.

Supreme Court of Delaware
650 A.2d 1270 (1994)

VEASEY, CHIEF JUSTICE:

In this appeal from a judgment of the Court of Chancery in favor of defendants we consider the contention of plaintiff below-appellant Robert H. Arnold ("plaintiff") that the trial court erred in granting defendants' summary judgment motion and denying his own. This suit arose out of a merger (the "Merger") of BBC Connecticut Holding Corporation ("BBC"), a wholly-owned Connecticut subsidiary of Bank of Boston Corporation ("BoB"), a Massachusetts corporation, into Society for Savings ("Society"), a wholly-owned Connecticut subsidiary of Society for Savings Bancorp, Incorporated ("Bancorp"), a Delaware corporation. In accordance with the Merger, Bancorp ultimately merged with BoB. Plaintiff was at all relevant times a Bancorp stockholder. Plaintiff named as defendants Bancorp, BoB, BBC, and twelve of fourteen members of Bancorp's board of directors (collectively "defendants").

Plaintiff's central claim is that the trial court erred in holding that certain alleged omissions and misrepresentations in the Merger proxy statement were immaterial and need not have been disclosed. Plaintiff also claims that the Court of Chancery erroneously held that the duties enunciated in [*Revlon Inc. v. MacAndrews & Forbes Holdings, Inc.*, 506 A.2d 173 (Del. 1986)] and its progeny were not implicated. Also at issue on this appeal is whether or not the individual defendants can be held liable if a disclosure violation is found in view of the exemption from liability provision in Bancorp's certificate of incorporation, adopted pursuant to 8 Del. C. § 102(b)(7) ("Section 102(b)(7)"). For the reasons set forth below, we hold that the Court of Chancery erred in failing to find that plaintiff's claim that the partial disclosures in the Merger proxy statement made it materially misleading with respect to one particular fact. In all other respects we find that the trial court committed no reversible error.

We further hold that, in all events, the limitation provision in Bancorp's certificate of incorporation shields the individual defendants from personal liability for the disclosure violation found to exist in this case....

....

VI. *Section 102(b)(7) Protection*

Plaintiff argues that the exemption from liability in Bancorp's certificate of incorporation, adopted pursuant to Section 102(b)(7), does not extend to disclosure claims, and that, even if the provision so extended, the individual defendants' conduct here falls within two exceptions. Plaintiff further contends that his claims against Connell for disclosure violations in his capacity as an officer (rather than a director) would still survive. Finally, plaintiff argues that the individual defendants waived their Section 102(b)(7) protection in the Court of Chancery. The Court of Chancery did not reach the Section 102(b)(7) issue. In view of our finding that there was a disclosure violation, we are required to reach these questions. We hold that Section 102(b)(7), as adopted by Bancorp, shields the individual defendants from liability, and that the shield was not waived.

A. *Application of Section 102(b)(7) to Disclosure Claims*

Article XIII of Bancorp's certificate of incorporation, ... parallels the language in Section 102(b)(7).... Plaintiff claims that the legislative history of Section 102(b)(7) supports his argument that the shield is not applicable here. Plaintiff's argument, however, bypasses a logical step in statutory analysis. A court should not resort to legislative history in interpreting a statute where statutory language provides unambiguously an answer to the question at hand....

In the instant case, plaintiff's claim that Section 102(b)(7) does not extend to disclosure violations must be rejected as contrary to the express, unambiguous language of that provision. Section 102(b)(7) provides protection "for breach of fiduciary duty." Given that the fiduciary disclosure requirements were well-established when Section 102(b)(7) was enacted and were nonetheless not excepted expressly from coverage, there is no reason to go beyond the text of the statute. Thus, claims alleging disclosure violations that do not otherwise fall within any exception are protected by Section 102(b)(7) and any certificate of incorporation provision (such as Article XIII) adopted pursuant thereto. In any event, nothing in the legislative history of the adoption of Section 102(b)(7) is inconsistent with the result we reach herein.

B. *Applicability of the Exceptions to Section 102(b)(7)*

Plaintiff argues that the individual defendants' conduct implicates the duty of loyalty and the proscription against knowing, intentional violations of law. He argues that the individual defendants' conduct falls within the exceptions in Section 102(b)(7)(i) & (ii) because they: (i) "improperly interfer[ed] with the voting process by knowingly or deliberately failing to make proper disclosure"; (ii) acted in bad faith and recklessly; and (iii) improperly granted no-shop and lock-up clauses as part of the Merger. Plaintiff also contends that Connell and Stang were interested directors who violated their duty of loyalty and that Connell's actions in his role as an officer fall outside Section 102(b)(7)'s protection.

The individual defendants counter that plaintiff's claims are essentially conclusory for there is no affirmative proof that they knowingly or deliberately failed to disclose facts they knew were material. That is, they argue that they balanced in good faith which facts to disclose against those to withhold as immaterial. Next, they assert that case law does not support plaintiff's claim relating to the no-shop and lock-up clauses under the facts of this case. Finally, the individual defendants contend that the claim relating to Connell's conduct as an officer is barred pursuant to Supreme Court Rule 8 because it was not raised in the Court of Chancery. On the merits, they assert that plaintiff has failed to segregate any of Connell's actions as an officer that fall within the exceptions to Section 102(b)(7).

Plaintiff's claims are not supported by the record or Delaware law. The individual defendants did not violate the duty of loyalty under the facts of this case. Plaintiff's intentional violation argument is unsupported by the record. As to plaintiff's third claim, though the granting of no-shop and lock-up rights can under certain circumstances implicate the duty of loyalty, without any additional, supportive factual basis for his claim, sufficient at least to create a genuine issue of material fact, plaintiff's reliance on [*Mills Acquisition Co. v. MacMillan, Inc.*, 559 A.2d 1261 (Del. 1988), and *Unocal Corp. v. Mesa Petroleum Co.*, 493 A.2d 946 (Del. 1985)] is unpersuasive. Even assuming that plaintiff's final argument is not procedurally barred, it lacks merit because plaintiff has failed to highlight any specific actions Connell undertook as an officer (as distinct from actions as a director) that fall within the two pertinent exceptions to Section 102(b)(7)....

C. *Waiver of the Section 102(b)(7) Shield*

Plaintiff argues that the individual defendants can, and did, waive their Section 102(b)(7) contractual protection. The individual defendants "are prepared to assume" that the shield provided by Section 102(b)(7) can be waived, but argue that such waiver must be clear and unambiguous, which they contend is absent here. We agree.

The individual defendants did not waive their Section 102(b)(7) protection. "The standard for finding waiver in Delaware is quite exacting. 'Waiver is the voluntary and intentional relinquishment of a known right.... It implies knowledge of all material facts and intent to waive.' Moreover, 'the facts relied upon must be unequivocal in nature.'" *American Family Mortgage Corp. v. Acierno*, Del. Supr., No. 290, 1993, slip op. at 12, 1994 WL 144591 *5, Moore, J. (Mar. 28, 1994) (ORDER) (*quoting Realty Growth Inv. v. Council of Unit Owners*, Del. Supr., 453 A.2d 450, 456 (1982)) (internal citations omitted). In the instant case, the following colloquy occurred in the Court of Chancery during argument on plaintiff's motion for a preliminary injunction:

> Mr. ZIEGLER [defense counsel]: ... [T]here are remedies available to this plaintiff if in the end, after a trial, it should turn out — if there needs to be a trial — that any of these added bits of information could be determined, in fact, to have been material and not confusing, so that the balance of equities clearly favors letting this transaction proceed to a closing.
> If the Court has no questions —
> THE COURT: Finish that thought for me. I didn't really — if there were ... misleading disclosures, how would I remedy those if they weren't corrected at this stage, after a trial?
> Mr. ZIEGLER: Your Honor, it has — I believe this Court has fashioned remedies in such circumstances. In addition, in the *Ocean Drilling* case, the Court concluded in fact — denied an injunction in much more colorable circumstances than we have here on the ground that because it was a stock-for-stock exchange, a quasi-appraisal remedy could be fashioned. *I believe the Court could attempt to determine the value of non-disclosures, so to speak, or determine a quasi-appraisal remedy.*

(Emphasis added). Plaintiff's interpretation of the reference to "the value of non-disclosures" hardly constitutes the unequivocal facts necessary to find a voluntary, intentional relinquishment of the protection of Section 102(b)(7). Thus, plaintiff's waiver argument lacks merit.

....

WLR FOODS, INC. v. TYSON FOODS, INC.

United States Court of Appeals, Fourth Circuit
65 F.3d 1172 (1995)

MURNAGHAN, CIRCUIT JUDGE:

The instant case arose from an attempt by Tyson Foods, Inc. ("Tyson"), a nationwide poultry producer, to acquire WLR Foods, Inc. ("WLR"), a chicken and turkey producer. In early 1994, Tyson engaged in extensive discussions with certain members of WLR's Board of Directors ("the WLR Board") in an attempt to arrange a merger between Tyson and WLR. The WLR Board, resistant to the idea of being acquired by Tyson, adopted various defensive measures to protect WLR against the takeover. Tyson eventually presented a tender offer directly to the stockholders of WLR, but withdrew the offer several months later, claiming that, due to actions taken by the WLR Board, Tyson's offering price was no longer reflective of the value of WLR's stock. Tyson now challenges several rulings of the district court, which found that the defensive tactics adopted by the WLR Board were a valid legal means by which to respond to the threatened takeover of WLR by Tyson.

. . . .

III. *The Business Judgment Statute*

In its next assignment of error, Tyson challenges the district court's finding that the Virginia Business Judgment Statute, VA. CODE ANN. § 13.1-690 ("§ 690"), allows an inquiry only into the processes employed by corporate directors in making their decisions regarding a takeover, and not into the substance of those decisions. Pursuant to that interpretation, the district court denied Tyson access during discovery to the substantive content of the materials used by the WLR Board in responding to Tyson's takeover attempt.

. . . .

... The district court held that under the standard articulated in § 690, only the good faith business judgment of the directors was at issue in Tyson's claims, and the rationality *vel non* of the decision ultimately reached by the WLR Board was not relevant. The district court thus permitted Tyson to inquire into the procedures followed by the WLR directors during their investigation of Tyson's offer that indicated whether or not they were considering the offer in good faith, but did not allow Tyson access to the actual substantive information that was used by the directors in making their decision regarding the offer.

We find that the district court did not abuse its discretion in limiting discovery in the instant case. First, it is clear from the language of § 690 that the actions of a director are to be judged by his or her good faith in performing corporate duties, and not by the substantive merit of the director's decisions themselves. Tyson concedes that good faith is the relevant standard under § 690. However, according to Tyson, although § 690 itself does not focus on whether a director's decision is substantively correct, knowledge of the substantive content of the information that was available to the director is necessary in order to determine whether the decision was made in good faith. Tyson claims that a litigant cannot prove a director's lack of good faith without having access to all of the information on which the director relied.

In essence, Tyson hopes to prove lack of good faith in the instant case by showing that, based upon the substantive information received by the WLR Board, the Board should have reached a different result. However, that argument imports an aspect into the Virginia standard of director conduct that is not part of Virginia law. It reduces, and nearly eliminates, the ability to rely, in good faith, on experts. Whether a different person would have come to a different conclusion given the information that a director had before him is simply irrelevant to the determination of whether a director in Virginia has acted in good faith in fulfilling his corporate duties.

In fact, it is precisely such a comparison between a director and the hypothetical reasonable person that the Virginia legislature explicitly chose to reject when it enacted § 690.... The business judgment rule contained in the Model Act, like § 690, is based upon a director's good faith. By referring to an "ordinarily prudent person" and the director's "reasonabl[e] belie[f]" concerning the corporation's best interests, however, the Model Act makes clear that one of the ways in which a litigant may prove that a director did not exercise good faith is by showing that a director's decision is irrational, *i.e.*, that the decision does not comport with what a reasonable person would do under similar circumstances.

Section 690, however, contains no reference to the "reasonable person." In fact, the Virginia legislature expressly chose to reject the Model Act standard:

> [Section 690], especially subsection A, is significantly different from the Model Act's treatment of the same subject in § 8.30....
>
> ....
>
> The term "reasonable" is intentionally not used in the standard. It thereby eliminates comparison of the conduct in question with the idealized standard and removes the question of how great a deviation from this idealized standard is acceptable.

Virginia Corporation Law with Commentaries and Rules 197-98 (1992 ed.) (Joint Bar Committee Commentary); *see also* [Daniel T. Murphy, "The New Virginia Stock Corporation Act: A Primer," 20 *U. Rich. L. Rev.* 67, 108 (1985)] (Under § 690, "[t]he trier of fact need only find good faith and determine whether the conduct in question was a product of the director's own business judgment of what is in the best interest of the corporation. The director's conduct or decision is not to be analyzed in the context of whether a reasonable man would have acted similarly."); *id.* ("The statute ... may ... protect the utterly inept, but well-meaning, good faith director."). Directors' actions in Virginia are not to be judged for their reasonableness, and we, like the district court, reject Tyson's attempt to inject such a standard into Virginia law....

Chapter 11

DUTY OF LOYALTY

Situation

Concern about the possibility of a lawsuit against Biologistics, Inc. dissipated a few weeks ago after investigators for the state health department traced the local water contamination to another business in the same general area. At a board meeting shortly after these developments were announced, Baker reported that the corporation needed to contract with a machine tool company for the manufacture of approximately $ 50,000 worth of equipment for the research and development operations. She brought the matter up for board approval because the expenditure would put the project well over budget. She recommended that Olivetti Tool, Inc. be given the contract because, though their equipment is expensive, Olivetti's reputation is good. After some discussion of the budget and of Olivetti, the board unanimously approved the contract.

Anderson called you this morning and said he had just learned that Welsh is a part owner and a director of Olivetti. Anderson has no reason to doubt their contract with Olivetti is fair — though he is not sure — but he is very agitated that Welsh did not disclose his interest in Olivetti at the board meeting at which the contract was approved. He wants to know what you think should be done, and he also suggested that you call Welsh and discuss the matter with him. You did so, and Welsh said he has been bothered about his silence, but did not think he had to say anything about his interest in Olivetti because he had nothing to do with Baker's recommending the contract or the negotiations in connection with it. He said he is not an expert in such matters, but that the contract price seemed high to him. He felt, however, that he might violate a duty to Olivetti if he said anything to the Biologistics board.

SECTION I. INTRODUCTION

In addition to the duty of care, directors and officers assume a duty of loyalty to the corporation. As stated in the *Corporate Director's Guidebook*:* "The duty of loyalty requires directors to exercise their powers in the interests of the corporation and not in the directors' own interest or in the interest of another person (including a family member) or organization. Simply put, directors should not use their corporate position to make a personal profit or gain or for other personal advantage."

---

*Committee On Corporate Laws, Section of Business Law, American Bar Assoc. 4-6 (2d ed. 1994). Copyright © 1994 American Bar Association. All rights reserved. Reprinted with permission.

While the duty of loyalty can be "simply put," its meaning and requirements continue to challenge courts and legislators. As the cases in this chapter illustrate, corporate law struggles with many core questions. In order for the duty to be implicated, a conflict between the director's individual pecuniary interests and the corporation's interest must exist. Courts have identified this conflict when directors and officers enter into transactions with their corporations, *i.e.* they are on both sides of a deal, or when two corporations with common directors enter into transactions, but in what other circumstances should the duty apply? Assuming the duty is implicated, what does the basic common law test of fairness require? What is the role of the safe harbor statutes?

SECTION II. COMMON LAW TEST

LEWIS v. S. L. & E., INC.

United States Court of Appeals, Second Circuit
629 F.2d 764 (1980)

KEARSE, CIRCUIT JUDGE:

This case arises out of an intra-family dispute over the management of two closely-held affiliated corporations. Plaintiff Donald E. Lewis ("Donald"), a shareholder of S.L. & E., Inc. ("SLE"), appeals from judgments entered against him in the United States District Court for the Western District of New York, Harold P. Burke, Judge, after a bench trial of his derivative claim against directors of SLE, and of a claim asserted against him by the other corporation, Lewis General Tires, Inc. ("LGT"), which intervened in the suit. The defendants Alan E. Lewis ("Alan"), Leon E. Lewis, Jr. ("Leon, Jr."), and Richard E. Lewis ("Richard"), are the brothers of Donald; they were, at pertinent times herein, directors of SLE and officers, directors and shareholders of LGT. Donald charged that his brothers had wasted the assets of SLE by causing SLE to lease business premises to LGT from 1966 to 1972 at an unreasonably low rental. LGT was permitted to intervene in the action, and filed a complaint seeking specific performance of an agreement by Donald to sell his SLE stock to LGT in 1972. The district court held that Donald had failed to prove waste by the defendant directors, and entered judgment in their favor. The court also awarded attorneys' fees to the defendant directors and to SLE, and granted LGT specific performance of Donald's agreement to sell his SLE stock.

On appeal, Donald argues that the district court improperly allocated to him the burden of proving his claims of waste, and that since defendants failed to prove that the transactions in question were fair and reasonable, he was entitled to judgment. Donald also argues that the awards of attorneys' fees were improper. We agree with each of these contentions, and therefore reverse and remand.

I

For many years Leon Lewis, Sr., the father of Donald and the defendant directors, was the principal shareholder of SLE and LGT. LGT, formed in 1933, operated a tire dealership in Rochester, New York. SLE, formed in 1943, owned the land and complex of buildings at 260 East Avenue in Rochester. This property was SLE's only significant asset. Prior to 1956 LGT occupied SLE's premises without benefit of a lease; the rent paid was initially $ 200 per month, and had increased over the years to $ 800 per month by 1956, when additional parcels were added. On February 28, 1956, SLE granted LGT a 10-year lease on the newly expanded property ("the Property"), for a rent of $ 1,200 per month, or $ 14,400 per year. Under the terms of the lease, SLE was responsible for payment of real estate taxes on the Property, while all other current expenses were to be borne by the tenant, LGT.[1]

In 1962, Leon Lewis, Sr., transferred his SLE stock, 90 shares in all, to his six children (defendants Richard, Alan and Leon, Jr., plaintiff Donald, and two daughters, Margaret and Carol), giving 15 shares to each.[2] At that time Richard, Alan and Leon, Jr., were already shareholders, officers and directors of LGT. Contemporaneously with their receipt of SLE stock, all six of the children entered into a "shareholders' agreement" with LGT, under which each child who was not a shareholder of LGT on June 1, 1972 would be required to sell his or her SLE shares to LGT, within 30 days of that date, at a price equal to the book value of the SLE stock as of June 1, 1972.

LGT's lease on the SLE property expired on February 28, 1966. At that time the directors of SLE were Richard, Alan, Leon, Jr., Leon, Sr., and Henry Etsberger; these five were also the directors of LGT. In 1966 Alan owned 44% of LGT, Richard owned 30%, Leon, Jr., owned 19%, and Leon, Sr., owned 7%. From 1967 to 1972 Richard owned 61% of LGT and Leon, Jr., owned the remaining 39%. When the lease expired in 1966, no new lease was entered into. LGT nonetheless continued to occupy the property and to pay SLE at the old rate, $ 14,400 per year. According to the defendants' testimony at trial, there was never any thought or discussion among the SLE directors of entering into a new lease or of increasing the rent. Richard testified: "We never gave consideration to a new lease." From all that appears, the defendant directors viewed SLE as existing purely for the benefit of LGT. Richard testified, for example, that although real estate taxes rose sharply during the period 1966-1971, from approximately $ 7,800 to more than $ 11,000, to be paid by SLE out of its

---

[1] It appears that SLE was also responsible for payments due on a mortgage on the Property. In addition, LGT charged SLE for the costs of certain capital improvements, such as the major structural repairs to the principal building's facade, carried out in 1969.

[2] SLE had 150 shares outstanding, and each child thus received a ten percent interest. At the same time LGT purchased the remaining 60 outstanding shares from the elder Lewis's business partner, Henry Etsberger.

constant $ 14,400 rental income, raising the rent was never mentioned. He testified that SLE was "only a shell to protect the operating company (LGT)." When this suit was commenced there had not been a formal meeting of either the shareholders or the directors of SLE since 1962. Richard, Alan and Leon, Jr., had largely ignored SLE's separate corporate existence and disregarded the fact that SLE had shareholders who were not shareholders of LGT and who therefore could not profit from actions that used SLE solely for the benefit of LGT.

Neither Donald nor his sisters ever owned LGT stock. As the June 1972 date approached for the required sale of their SLE stock to LGT, Donald apparently came to believe that SLE's book value was lower than it should have been. He sought SLE financial information from Richard, who had been president of SLE since 1967. Richard refused to provide information. Donald therefore refused to sell his SLE shares in 1972,[3] and commenced this shareholders' derivative action in the district court in August 1973, basing jurisdiction on diversity of citizenship. The sole claim raised in the complaint was that the defendant directors had wasted the assets of SLE by "grossly undercharging" LGT for the latter's occupancy and use of the Property. Although the complaint charged such mismanagement for the period 1962 to 1973, plaintiff subsequently limited this claim to the period between February 28, 1966, the date on which the lease expired, and June 1, 1972, the date contractually set for valuation of the SLE shares which plaintiff had agreed to sell to LGT. LGT intervened and demanded specific performance of Donald's agreement to sell his SLE stock. Donald did not contest his ultimate obligation to sell, but took the position that since the book value of the shares would be increased if he prevailed on his derivative claim, specific performance should be granted only after adjudication of that claim.

There ensued an eight-day bench trial, at which plaintiff sought to prove, by the testimony of several expert witnesses, that the fair rental value of the Property was greater than the $ 14,400 per year that SLE had been paid by LGT. Defendants sought to show that the rental paid was reasonable, by offering evidence concerning the financial straits of LGT, the cost to LGT of operating the Property, the general economic decline of the East Avenue neighborhood, and rentals paid on two other properties in that neighborhood. LGT presented expert testimony that the value of plaintiff's stock as of June 1972, assuming a successful defense of the derivative claims, was $ 15,650.

... On this basis, the court held that Donald had failed to establish the rental value of the Property during the period at issue, and that defendants were therefore entitled to judgment on the derivative claims. Implicit in the district court's ruling, granting judgment for defendants upon plaintiff's failure to prove waste, was a determination that plaintiff bore the burden of proof on that issue....

---

[3] Donald's sisters Carol and Margaret sold their SLE shares to LGT in 1972 and 1973 respectively. Alan, who had sold his LGT stock in 1967, sold his SLE stock to LGT in 1972.

II

Turning first to the question of burden of proof, we conclude that the district court erred in placing upon plaintiff the burden of proving waste. Because the directors of SLE were also officers, directors and/or shareholders of LGT, the burden was on the defendant directors to demonstrate that the transactions between SLE and LGT were fair and reasonable....

Under normal circumstances the directors of a corporation may determine, in the exercise of their business judgment, what contracts the corporation will enter into and what consideration is adequate, without review of the merits of their decisions by the courts. The business judgment rule places a heavy burden on shareholders who would attack corporate transactions. But the business judgment rule presupposes that the directors have no conflict of interest. When a shareholder attacks a transaction in which the directors have an interest other than as directors of the corporation, the directors may not escape review of the merits of the transaction. At common law such a transaction was voidable unless shown by its proponent to be fair, and reasonable to the corporation. BCL § 713, in both its current and its prior versions, carries forward this common law principle, and provides special rules for scrutiny of a transaction between the corporation and an entity in which its directors are directors or officers or have a substantial financial interest.

The current version of § 713, which became effective on September 1, 1971, and governs at least so much of the dealing between SLE and LGT as occurred after that date, expressly provides that a contract between a corporation and an entity in which its directors are interested may be set aside unless the proponent of the contract "shall establish affirmatively that the contract or transaction was fair and reasonable as to the corporation at the time it was approved by the board ...." § 713(b). Thus when the transaction is challenged in a derivative action against the interested directors, they have the burden of proving that the transaction was fair and reasonable to the corporation.

The same was true under the predecessor to § 713(b), former § 713(a)(3), which was in effect prior to September 1, 1971. Section 713(a)(3) was not explicit as to the burden of proof, but simply stated that a transaction with interested directors would not be voidable "If the contract or transaction is fair and reasonable as to the corporation at the time it is approved by the board ...." The consensus among the commentators was that § 713(a)(3) carried forward the common law rule, which placed the burden of proof as to fairness on the interested directors. We agree with this construction.

During the entire period 1966-1972, Richard, Alan and Leon, Jr., were directors of both SLE and LGT; there were no SLE directors who were not also directors of LGT. Richard, Alan and Leon, Jr., were all shareholders of LGT in 1966, and from 1967 to 1972 Richard and Leon, Jr., were the sole shareholders of LGT. Under BCL § 713, therefore, Richard, Alan and Leon, Jr., had the burden of proving that $ 14,400 was a fair and reasonable annual rent for the SLE property for the period February 28, 1966 through June 1, 1972.

Our review of the record convinces us that defendants failed to carry their burden. At trial, there was no direct testimony as to what would have been a fair rental during the relevant period, *i.e.*, 1966 to 1972, and the evidence that was introduced fell far short of establishing that $ 14,400 was a fair annual rental value for those years.

Quite clearly Richard, Alan and Leon, Jr., had made no effort to determine contemporaneously what rental would be fair during the years 1966-1972. Their view was that the rent should simply cover expenses and that SLE existed for the benefit of LGT. During this period no appraisals were made; no attempts were made to sell or rent the Property; no thought whatever was given to whether $ 14,400 was a fair and reasonable rent even when real estate taxes had risen to consume nearly all of that amount.

Defendants offered instead evidence of rents paid on other properties. Among their best evidence was the expert testimony of Harvey Rosenbloom, a real estate appraiser. Rosenbloom testified that two other East Avenue buildings, which the district court found to be comparable to the 260 East Avenue premises, were leased at lower per-square-foot rentals than was paid by LGT to SLE. However, as to one of these properties, Rosenbloom testified only to rent paid in 1973 and 1974, and did not consider the 1966-1972 period. As to the other property, Rosenbloom described a fifteen year lease that was entered into in 1961. This testimony, while perhaps not wholly irrelevant to the issues in this suit, fell far short of demonstrating what rental the Property could have fetched in 1966, or in any other of the relevant years. Indeed, Rosenbloom himself testified that rental value could well be different for each year of the period. Thus, rentals that Rosenbloom testified were agreed to in 1961 or 1973 might well have been unfair in 1966 or 1967. This evidence thus could not support a finding that defendants acted fairly in maintaining an annual rental of $ 14,400 during the years from 1966 to 1972.

Defendants also produced considerable evidence that over the relevant period, the East End neighborhood had been on an economic decline; that businesses had been leaving the area; that urban renewal projects and increased crime had depressed property values there; and that the area had, in general, become a less desirable place to do business. There was also evidence of specific developments that had an adverse effect on the Property: for example, the street running along one side of the Property was made a one-way street, thus limiting customers' access to LGT's premises. The district court credited all of this testimony, and it is fair to say that defendants proved that there was a general downward trend in the value of the Property. However, as noted above, defendants did not establish what was a fair rental value for the Property in 1966. Absent such a point of reference, a general downward trend in value is of no assistance in determining whether the rental actually paid was fair and reasonable during the ensuing years.

Moreover, working in reverse, some of defendants' own evidence as to the value of the Property at the end of the relevant period suggested that $ 14,400 was less than a fair rental in 1966, and that the figure of $ 38,099, estimated by plaintiff's expert, was perhaps not far off the mark. First, there was a variety of evidence suggesting that in 1972 the Property was worth more than $ 200,000. An appraisal by defense witness Harold Grunert in 1972 set the fair market value of the Property as of June 30, 1972, at $ 220,000. In 1972 Leon, Jr., had offered personally to buy the Property for $ 200,000, an offer which Richard had rejected. And in 1971, Richard had informed Donald that evaluations by another appraiser, Harold Galloway, had set the value of the Property at $ 200,000 and $ 236,000. Second, defendants' expert witness Rosenbloom, asked what he would consider a fair rent for the property, given Grunert's 1972 valuation of $ 220,000, stated that ten percent of the value would be inadequate and that fifteen to seventeen percent would be closer to adequate. Fifteen percent of $ 220,000 would have yielded a rent of $ 33,000 on the basis of the 1972 valuation. Grunert's own expert testimony was entirely consistent with this. While he had made no estimate as to the fair rental value of the property for 1966-1972, he opined that a fair rental as of June 30, 1972, would be $ 20-21,000 with the tenant paying all expenses including real estate taxes. According to Richard, SLE's real estate taxes in 1972 were about $ 12,000. Thus Grunert's testimony, too, suggests about $ 33,000 as the fair rental value in 1972. Finally, consistent with their view of the general downward economic trend, Richard and Alan conceded that, whatever the Property was worth in 1972, it was worth more in 1966. Thus the evidence presented by defendants, far from carrying their burden of showing that $ 14,400 was a fair and reasonable annual rental in 1966-1972, suggested that the fair rental value of the Property throughout that period exceeded $ 33,000 per year.

The defendants argued, however, that LGT could not have afforded to pay SLE rent higher than $ 14,400. They produced evidence designed to show that LGT had made little profit; that this low profitability was due to the expenses of maintenance and upkeep of the 260 East Avenue property; and that LGT therefore would not have been able to pay a higher rent to SLE. The district court credited this evidence, finding that LGT had "experienced a number of years of very severe losses," that during the period from 1962-1973, LGT's overall profit was only $ 53,876, and that payment of rent at the rate of $ 39,099 per year during this period could have led to the "demise" of LGT. These findings have only a distorted relationship to this lawsuit.

The period in issue here is 1966-1972. The only "severe" losses shown, totaling nearly $ 83,000, occurred in 1963 and 1973. Their inclusion in the computation of what LGT could afford to pay in 1966-1972 was patently unfair. In fact LGT's only unprofitable year during the period in issue was 1969 when its loss was small: $ 1,168. LGT's after-tax profits in 1966-1972 in fact totaled $ 102,963, or an average of $ 14,709 per year. Thus, even on paper, LGT could have "afforded" to double its rent payments to SLE during the period in question.

Moreover, the proposition that LGT could not afford to pay as rent more than what its own books showed as profits ignores the fact that LGT was owned and managed by members of the Lewis family, some of whom were also employees of that corporation. It is entirely possible that these family members granted to themselves unusually high salaries or other perquisites, thus reducing LGT's paper profits....

Finally, even if we were to assume that LGT's financial records provided a fair basis for evaluating the SLE-LGT transactions, defendants would not have carried their burden of proof. Defendants did not demonstrate that SLE could not have found some other tenant, stronger financially than LGT, which would have been willing and able to pay a higher rental. Even given the general downward trend of the East Avenue neighborhood, it is entirely possible that at least during the early years of the 1966-1972 period, such a tenant might have been secured. No effort was made during that period to rent to anyone other than LGT.

We conclude, therefore, that defendants failed to prove that the rental paid by LGT to SLE for the years 1966-1972 was fair and reasonable. Thus, Donald is not required to sell his SLE shares to LGT without such upward adjustment in the June 1, 1972, book value of SLE as may be necessary to reflect the amount by which the fair rental value of the Property exceeded $ 14,400 in any of the years 1966-1972.

III

....

We remand to the district court (a) for the entry of judgment in favor of SLE against Richard, Alan and Leon, Jr., jointly and severally, in such amount as the district court shall determine to be equal to the amounts by which the annual fair rental value of the Property exceeded $ 14,400 in the period February 28, 1966-June 1, 1972, (b) for an accounting as to the value of Donald's SLE shares as of June 1, 1972, in light of such judgment, (c) for an order, following such accounting, of specific performance of the shareholders' agreement, and (d) for such other proceedings as are not inconsistent with this opinion.

A. FAIRNESS STANDARD

What is "fairness?" Fairness is an abstract concept and what constitutes fairness to the corporation depends on the facts of the particular case and the court's determination of what is relevant.

What factors did the court in *Lewis* use to determine if the fairness test was satisfied? Did it consider both the corporate decisionmaking process (procedural fairness) and the merits and terms of the transaction itself (substantive fairness)? How did the court's analysis differ from that used in the duty of care cases? Would the defendants' conduct in the *Lewis* case satisfy the business judgment rule test?

B. ALI PRINCIPLES

Comment to ALI § 5.02(a)(2)(A) offers this explanation of the fairness standard:

> The test of fairness is an objective test, and the director or senior executive must show that the transaction is in the "range of reasonableness" within which conflict-of-interest transactions may be sustained ... In determining fairness, the court may take into account the process by which the transaction was shaped and approved (such as whether there was undue pressure on the corporate decisionmaker who approved the transaction) and any relevant objective indicators of fairness of price (such as comparable transactions between parties dealing at arm's length).
>
> In an additional sense as well, "fairness" and the "best interests of the corporation" may need to be considered in the full business context of a transaction, particularly when it is not in the interest of the corporation to forgo a transaction with a director or senior executive. For example, a particular parcel of property or contract right held by a director or senior executive may have a special strategic value to the corporation that would warrant paying a price above general market, that is, a price higher than anyone who would not place such strategic value on the property would pay. If the corporation would be warranted in paying that price to a third party dealing at arm's length it would also be warranted in paying that price to the director or senior executive. In mandating fairness, the law does not command the board to ignore the aggregate effects on the corporation of a transaction, and to focus in an isolated fashion only on the fair value of a single component of the total transaction. Fairness will only be judged as of the time a transaction is entered into....
>
> In determining whether to enter into a transaction, the corporate decisionmaker who approves the transaction should consider not only whether the transaction will be fair to the corporation as measured by comparison with an arm's-length transaction with an unrelated third party, but whether the transaction affirmatively will be in the corporation's best interest, as in a transaction with an unrelated party. For example, the purchase of a parcel of property by the corporation from a director may be at a fair price, but the corporate decisionmaker should also determine that it is beneficial to the corporation to acquire the property for its business.
>
> ... One other issue that is of particular relevance in duty of fair dealing cases is how the transaction is initiated. If a transaction is initiated on behalf of the corporation by disinterested persons, that circumstance may under the facts of a particular case assist in supporting the fairness of the transaction to the corporation.

SECTION III. SAFE HARBOR STATUTES

A. STATUTORY INTERPRETATIONS

MARCIANO v. NAKASH

Supreme Court of Delaware
535 A.2d 400 (1987)

WALSH, JUSTICE:

This is an appeal from a decision of the Court of Chancery which validated a claim in liquidation of Gasoline, Ltd. ("Gasoline"), a Delaware corporation, placed in custodial status pursuant to 8 Del. C. § 226 by reason of a deadlock among its board of directors. Fifty percent of Gasoline is owned by Ari, Joe, and Ralph Nakash (the "Nakashes") and fifty percent by Georges, Maurice, Armand and Paul Marciano (the "Marcianos"). The Vice Chancellor ruled that $ 2.5 million in loans made by the Nakashes faction to Gasoline were valid and enforceable debts of the corporation, notwithstanding their origin in self-dealing transactions....

I

... The liquidation proceeding marked the end of a joint venture launched in 1984 by the Marcianos and the Nakashes to market designer jeans and sportswear. Through a solely owned corporation called Guess? Inc. ("Guess"), the California based Marcianos had been engaged in the design and distribution of stylized jeans for several years. In 1983 they decided to form a separate division to market copies of Guess creations in a broader retail market. In order to secure financing and broaden market exposure the Marcianos entered into negotiations with the New York based Nakash brothers, the owners of Jordache Enterprises, Inc. a leading manufacturer of jeans. Ultimately, it was agreed that the Nakashes would receive fifty percent of the stock of Guess for a consideration of $ 4.7 million. As a result, the three Nakash brothers joined three of the Marcianos on the Guess board of directors.

Similarly, when Gasoline was formed, stock ownership and board composition was shared equally by the two families. Although corporate control and direction were equally divided, from an operational standpoint Gasoline functioned in New York under the Nakashes' operational guidance while the parent, Guess, continued under the primary attention of the Marcianos. Differences between the two factions quickly surfaced with resulting deadlocks at the director level of both Guess and Gasoline....

....

... Prior to March, 1986, Gasoline had secured the necessary financing to support its inventory purchases from the Israel Discount Bank in New York. The bank advanced funds at one percent above prime rate secured by Gasoline's accounts receivable and the Nakashes' personal guarantee. Although requested to do so, the Marcianos were unwilling to participate in loan guarantees because of their dissatisfaction with the Nakashes' management. In response, the Nakashes withdrew their guarantees causing the Israel Discount Bank to terminate its outstanding loan of $ 1.6 million.

Without consulting the Marcianos, the Nakashes advanced approximately $ 2.3 million of their personal funds to Gasoline to enable the corporation to pay outstanding bills and acquire inventory. In June, 1986, the Nakashes arranged for U.F. Factors, an entity owned by them, to assume their personal loans and become Gasoline's lender. U.F. Factors charged interest at one percent over prime to which the Nakashes added one percent for their personal guarantees of the U.F. Factors loan. As of April 24, 1987, Gasoline's debt to U.F. Factors amounted to $ 2,575,000 of which $ 25,000 represented the Nakashes' guarantee fee. Another Nakash entity, Jordach Enterprises, also sought payment from Gasoline of two percent of the company's gross sales, or $ 30,000 for warehousing and invoicing services.

In November, 1986, the Nakashes had replaced the U.F. Factors loan, secured by a series of promissory notes executed by Gasoline, with a line of credit collateralized by Gasoline's assets including trademarks and copyrights. This action took place without the knowledge or consent of the custodian and was subsequently rescinded by the Nakashes. At the time of the court-ordered sale of assets, the Nakashes and their entities were general creditors of Gasoline. If allowed in full the Nakashes' claim will exhaust Gasoline's assets, leaving nothing for its shareholders.

The parties agree that the loans made by the Nakashes to Gasoline were interested transactions. The Nakashes as officers of Gasoline executed the various documents which supported the loans and at the same time guaranteed those loans extended through their wholly owned entities. It is also not disputed that, given the control deadlock, the questioned transactions did not receive majority approval of Gasoline's directors or shareholders. The Marcianos argue that the loan transaction is voidable at the option of the corporation notwithstanding its fairness or the good faith of its participants. A review of this contention, rejected by the Court of Chancery, requires analysis of the concept of director self-dealing under Delaware law.

II

It is a long-established principle of Delaware corporate law that the fiduciary relationship between directors and the corporation imposes fundamental limitations on the extent to which a director may benefit from dealings with the corporation he serves. Thus, the "voting [for] and taking" of compensation may be deemed "constructively fraudulent" in the absence of shareholder ratification, or statutory or bylaw authorization. *Cahall v. Lofland*, Del. Ch., 114 A. 224, 232 (1921). Perhaps the strongest condemnation of interested director conduct appears in *Potter v. Sanitary Co. of America*, Del. Ch., 194 A. 87 (1937), a decision which the Marcianos advance as definitive of the rule of per se voidability. In *Potter* the Court of Chancery characterized transactions between corporations having common directors and officers "constructively fraudulent," absent shareholder ratification.

Support can also be found for the per se rule of voidability in this Court's decision in *Kerbs v. California Eastern Airways Inc.*, Del. Supr., 90 A.2d 652 (1952). The *Kerbs* court, in considering the validity of a profit sharing plan, ruled that the self-interest of the directors who voted on the plan caused the transaction to be voidable. The court concluded that the profit sharing plan was voidable based on the common law rule that the vote of an interested director will not be counted in determining whether the challenged action received the affirmative vote of a majority of the board of directors.

The principle of per se voidability for interested transactions, which is sometimes characterized as the common law rule, was significantly ameliorated by the 1967 enactment of Section 144 of the Delaware General Corporation Law.[4] The Marcianos argue that section 144(a) provides the only basis for immunizing self-interested transactions and since none of the statute's component tests are satisfied the stricture of the common law per se rule applies. The Vice Chancellor agreed that the disputed loans did not withstand a section 144(a) analysis but ruled that the common law rule did not invalidate transactions determined to be intrinsically fair. We agree that section 144(a) does not provide the only validation standard for interested transactions.

It overstates the common law rule to conclude that relationship, alone, is the controlling factor in interested transactions. Although the application of the per

---

[4] Section 144 of Title 8 Del. C. now provides:

(a) No contract or transaction between a corporation and 1 or more of its directors or officers, or between a corporation and any other corporation, partnership, association, or other organization in which 1 or more of its directors or officers, are directors or officers, or have a financial interest, shall be void or voidable solely for this reason, or solely because the director or officer is present at or participates in the meeting of the board or committee which authorizes the contract or transaction, or solely because his or their votes are counted for such purpose, if:

(1) The material facts as to his relationship or interest and as to the contract or transaction are disclosed or are known to the board of directors or the committee, and the board or committee in good faith authorizes the contract or transaction by the affirmative votes of a majority of the disinterested directors, even though the disinterested directors be less than a quorum; or

(2) The material facts as to his relationship or interest and as to the contract or transaction are disclosed or are known to the shareholders entitled to vote thereon, and the contract or transaction is specifically approved in good faith by vote of the shareholders; or

(3) The contract or transaction is fair as to the corporation as of the time it is authorized, approved or ratified, by the board of directors, a committee or the shareholders.

(b) Common or interested directors may be counted in determining the presence of a quorum at a meeting of the board of directors or of a committee which authorizes the contract or transaction.

se voidability rule in early Delaware cases resulted in the invalidation of interested transactions, the result was not dictated simply by a tainted relationship. Thus in *Potter*, the Court, while adopting the rule of voidability, emphasized that interested transactions should be subject to close scrutiny. Where the undisputed evidence tended to show that the transaction would advance the personal interests of the directors at the expense of stockholders, the stockholders, upon discovery, are entitled to disavow the transaction. *Potter*, 194 A. at 91. Further, the court examined the motives of the defendant directors and the effect the transaction had on the corporation and its shareholders. *Id.*

In other Delaware cases, decided before the enactment of section 144, interested director transactions were deemed voidable only after an examination of the fairness of a particular transaction *vis-à-vis* the nonparticipating shareholders and a determination of whether the disputed conduct received the approval of a noninterested majority of directors or shareholders. The latter test is now crystallized in the ratification criteria of section 144(a), although the non-quorum restriction of *Kerbs* has been superseded by the language of subparagraph (b) of section 144.

The Marcianos view compliance with section 144 as the sole basis for avoiding the per se rule of voidability. The Court of Chancery rejected this contention and we agree that it is not consonant with Delaware corporate law. This Court in *Fliegler v. Lawrence*, Del. Supr., 361 A.2d 218 (1976), a post-section 144 decision, refused to view section 144 as either completely preemptive of the common law duty of director fidelity or as constituting a grant of broad immunity. As we stated in *Fliegler*: "It merely removes an 'interested director' cloud when its terms are met and provides against invalidation of an agreement 'solely' because such a director or officer is involved." *Id.* at 222. In *Fliegler* this Court applied a two-tiered analysis: application of section 144 coupled with an intrinsic fairness test.

If section 144 validation of interested director transactions is not deemed exclusive, as *Fliegler* clearly holds, the continued viability of the intrinsic fairness test is mandated not only by fact situations, such as here present, where shareholder deadlock prevents ratification but also where shareholder control by interested directors precludes independent review. Indeed, if an independent committee of the board, contemplated by section 144(a)(1) is unavailable, the sole forum for demonstrating intrinsic fairness may be a judicial one. In such situations the intrinsic fairness test furnishes the substantive standard against which the evidential burden of the interested directors is applied. It is this burden which was addressed by this Court in *Weinberger v. UOP, Inc.*, Del. Supr., 457 A.2d 701 (1983):

> When directors of a Delaware corporation are on both sides of a transaction, they are required to demonstrate their utmost good faith and the most scrupulous inherent fairness of the bargain.
>
> ....

The requirement of fairness is unflinching in its demand that where one stands on both sides of a transaction, he has the burden of establishing its entire fairness, sufficient to pass the test of careful scrutiny by the courts.

Id. at 710.

This case illustrates the limitation inherent in viewing section 144 as the touchstone for testing interested director transactions. Because of the shareholder deadlock, even if the Nakashes had attempted to invoke section 144, it was realistically unavailable. The ratification process contemplated by section 144 presupposes the functioning of corporate constituencies capable of providing assents. Just as the statute cannot "sanction unfairness" neither can it invalidate fairness if, upon judicial review, the transaction withstands close scrutiny of its intrinsic elements.[5]

III

On the issue of intrinsic fairness, the Court of Chancery concluded that the "U.F. Factors loans compared favorably with the terms available from unrelated lenders" and that the need for external financing had been clearly demonstrated. The Marcianos attack this ruling as factually and legally erroneous. Since the Vice Chancellor's factual findings were arrived at after an evidentiary hearing we are not free to reject them unless they are without record support or not the product of a logical deductive process. We find this standard to have been fully satisfied here.

Apart from the initial investment of $ 300,000 contributed equally by the Marcianos and the Nakashes, Gasoline's financial needs had been met through external borrowings. It is unnecessary to lay blame for the impasse which resulted in the Marcianos refusal to supply additional equity funding. It suffices to note that throughout 1985 and 1986, Gasoline was able to function only through cash advances from, and loans obtained by, the Nakashes, first through the Israel Discount Bank and later through U.F. Factors. During this period the evidence reflects the continued threat of bank overdrafts and inability to pay for purchases, particularly imported finished goods.

A finding of fairness is particularly appropriate in this case because the evidence indicates that the loans were made by the Nakashes with the *bona fide* intention of assisting Gasoline's efforts to remain in business. Directors who

---

[5] Although in this case none of the curative steps afforded under section 144(a) were available because of the director-shareholder deadlock, a non-disclosing director seeking to remove the cloud of interestedness would appear to have the same burden under section 144(a)(3), as under prior case law, of proving the intrinsic fairness of a questioned transaction which had been approved or ratified by the directors or shareholders. Folk, The Delaware General Corp. Law: A Commentary and Analysis, 86 (1972). On the other hand, approval by fully-informed disinterested directors under section 144(a)(1), or disinterested stockholders under section 144(a)(2), permits invocation of the business judgment rule and limits judicial review to issues of gift or waste with the burden of proof upon the party attacking the transaction.

advance funds to a corporation in such circumstances do not forfeit their claims as creditors merely because of relationship....

....

We hold, therefore, that the Court of Chancery properly applied the intrinsic fairness test in determining the validity of the interested director transactions and its finding of full fairness is clearly supported by the record. Accordingly, the decision is

Affirmed.

---

1. Procedures and the Fairness Test

In *Marciano*, the court found that directors' and shareholders' approvals were not possible. Consider instead if these procedures were possible and were followed. Would the fairness test still be required?

While the court in *Marciano* may not have determined unambiguously when the fairness test is required, consider the more direct holding in *Cookies Food Products v. Lakes Warehouse*:[6]

> Some commentators have supported the view that satisfaction of any one of the foregoing statutory alternatives, in and of itself, would prove that a director has fully met the duty of loyalty. We are obliged, however, to interpret statutes in conformity with the common law wherever statutory language does not directly negate it. Because the common law and [Iowa Code] section 496A.34 require directors to show "good faith, honesty, and fairness" in self-dealing, we are persuaded that satisfaction of any one of these three alternatives under the statute would merely preclude us from rendering the transaction void or voidable *outright* solely on the basis "of such [director's] relationship or interest." Iowa Code § 496A.34. To the contrary, we are convinced that the legislature did not intend by this statute to enable a court, in a shareholder's derivative suit, to rubber stamp any transaction to which a board of directors or the shareholders of a corporation have consented. Such an interpretation would invite those who stand to gain from such transactions to engage in improprieties to obtain consent. We thus require directors who engage in self-dealing to establish the additional element that they have acted in good faith, honesty, and fairness.

2. Disinterested Shareholder Approval

Forty-five states have safe-harbor statutes providing that transactions between directors and their corporations are not voidable simply because of the relationship between the parties, as indicated in ALI § 5.02 Reporter's Note 14. These statutes typically describe the three alternatives of directors' approval, sharehold-

---

[6] 430 N.W.2d 447, 452-53 (Iowa 1988).

ers' approval, and a fairness standard. They vary regarding disclosure requirements, good faith requirements, whether directors' and shareholders' approval
must be "disinterested," and whether the fairness standard is expressly required
even though directors' and shareholders' approval has occurred.

In *Fleigler v. Lawrence*,[7] referred to in the *Marciano* opinion, the defendant
directors of Agau Mines, Inc. argued that Delaware statute § 144(a)(2) did not
require "disinterested" shareholder approval. In response, the court grafted onto
the statute the applicable common-law principles:

> The purported ratification by the Agau shareholders would not affect the
> burden of proof in this case because the majority of shares voted in favor of
> exercising the option were cast by defendants in their capacity as Agau
> shareholders. Only about one-third of the "disinterested" shareholders voted,
> and we cannot assume that such non-voting shareholders either approved or
> disapproved. Under these circumstances, we cannot say that "the entire
> atmosphere has been freshened" and that departure from the objective
> fairness test is permissible....
>
> Nor do we believe the Legislature intended a contrary policy and rule to
> prevail by enacting 8 Del. C. § 144 ....
>
> ....
>
> Defendants argue that the transaction here in question is protected by
> § 144(a)(2) which, they contend, does not require that ratifying shareholders
> be "disinterested" or "independent"; nor, they argue, is there warrant for
> reading such a requirement into the statute. We do not read the statute as
> providing the broad immunity for which defendants contend....

3. Scope of the Duty

The classic duty of loyalty case deals with a director or officer that enters into
a transaction with his or her corporation. There are other circumstances,
however, when directors may not be so directly linked, but may still have a
pecuniary interest in a corporate decision. What should be the scope of the duty
of loyalty?

Model Act §§ 8.60-8.61, for instance, have attempted to answer this difficult
question. It posits that only "director's conflicting interest transactions" are
subject to its duty of loyalty provisions and offer definitions on each key term
(*e.g.*, § 8.60(1) (defining "conflicting interest"), § 8.60(2) (defining "director's
conflicting interest transaction), and § 8.60(3) (defining "related person")). A
review of § 8.60 and the Official Comments, however, results in a definitional

---

[7]361 A.2d 218, 221-22 (Del. 1976).

and situational maze that does not appear to offer a particularly simple or clear answer.

The ALI Introductory Note to Part V. Duty of Fair Dealing, begins by revisiting the term "duty of loyalty."

> Courts have traditionally analyzed the obligation of a director or officer who acts with a pecuniary interest in a matter in terms of a "duty of loyalty" to the corporation. However, courts have also used the term "duty of loyalty" in nonpecuniary contexts where a director or officer may be viewed as having conflicting interests. For clarity of analysis, ... [the ALI] avoids the use of the term "duty of loyalty," when dealing with the obligations of a person who acts with a pecuniary interest in a matter, and instead uses the term "duty of fair dealing." In doing so, ... [the ALI] does not address nonpecuniary conflict-of-interest situations which might be dealt with by the courts in appropriate cases.
>
> It is not the purpose of ... [the ALI] to set forth the duty of fair dealing as a final, complete, and unchanging concept, but rather to recognize that it is a concept that will continue to evolve as new problems and circumstances stimulate and challenge our system of corporate governance.

Rather than developing a single set of principles, the ALI offers different governing principles for varied "duty of fair dealing" fact patterns (*e.g.*, § 5.02 (directors' transactions with the corporation), § 5.03 (directors' compensation arrangements), and § 5.07 (transactions between corporations with common directors)).

B. EFFECT OF SAFE HARBOR PROCEDURES

In re WHEELABRATOR TECHNOLOGIES, INC. SHAREHOLDERS LITIGATION

Court of Chancery of Delaware
663 A.2d 1194 (1995)

JACOBS, VICE CHANCELLOR:

The question of whether or not shareholder ratification should operate to extinguish a duty of loyalty claim cannot be decided in a vacuum, divorced from the broader issue of what generally are the legal consequences of a fully-informed shareholder approval of a challenged transaction. The Delaware case law addressing that broader topic is not reducible to a single clear rule or unifying principle. Indeed, the law in that area might be thought to lack coherence because the decisions addressing the effect of shareholder "ratification" have fragmented that subject into three distinct compartments, only one of which involves "claim extinguishment."[8]

The basic structure of stockholder ratification law is, at first glance, deceptively simple. Delaware law distinguishes between acts of directors (or management) that are "void" and acts that are "voidable." As the Supreme Court stated in *Michelson v. Duncan*, 407 A.2d 211, 218-19 (1979):

> The essential distinction between voidable and void acts is that the former are those which may be found to have been performed in the interest of the corporation but beyond the authority of management, as distinguished from acts which are *ultra vires*, fraudulent, or waste of corporate assets. The practical distinction, for our purposes, is that voidable acts are susceptible to cure by shareholder approval while void acts are not.

One possible reading of *Michelson* is that all "voidable" acts are "susceptible to cure by shareholder approval." Under that reading, shareholder ratification might be thought to constitute a "full defense" (407 A.2d at 219) that would automatically extinguish all claims challenging such acts as a breach of fiduciary duty. Any such reading, however, would be overbroad, because the case law governing the consequences of ratification does not support that view and, in fact, is far more complex.

The Delaware Supreme Court has found shareholder ratification of "voidable" director conduct to result in claim-extinguishment in only two circumstances. The first is where the directors act in good faith, but exceed the board's *de jure*

---

[8]As used in our case law, even the term "shareholder ratification" has no fixed meaning, as that same term is used to describe three quite different sets of circumstances. In its "classic" or paradigmatic form, shareholder ratification describes the situation where shareholders approve board action that, legally speaking, could be accomplished without any shareholder approval.... Thus, "classic" ratification involves the voluntary addition of an independent layer of shareholder approval in circumstances where such approval is not legally required.

But, "shareholder ratification" has also been used to describe the effect of an informed shareholder vote that was statutorily required for the transaction to have legal existence. Examples are mergers, and amendments to the certificate of incorporation, both of which require shareholder approval to attain juridical existence. *See*, 8 Del. C. §§ 242, 251, *et seq.*

Even this second category is divisible into two subcategories: (a) transactions with a controlling stockholder that are expressly conditioned upon obtaining "majority of the minority" stockholder approval, and (b) transactions where shareholder approval is statutorily required yet does not involve a "majority of the minority" vote. In both sets of circumstances, the term "shareholder ratification" is used to describe the affirming shareholder vote; however, only the former category can fairly be analogized to "classic" shareholder ratification, in that it involves a condition ("majority of the minority" approval) that is not statutorily required.

That our courts have used the same term ("shareholder ratification") in such highly diverse sets of factual circumstances, without regard to their possible functional differences, suggests that "shareholder ratification" has now acquired an expanded meaning intended to describe any approval of challenged board action by a fully informed vote of shareholders, irrespective of whether that shareholder vote is legally required for the transaction to attain legal existence.

authority. In that circumstance, *Michelson* holds that "a validly accomplished shareholder ratification relates back to cure otherwise unauthorized acts of officers and directors." 407 A.2d at 219. The second circumstance is where the directors fail "to reach an informed business judgment" in approving a transaction. *Van Gorkom*, 488 A.2d at 889.

Except for these two situations, no party has identified any type of board action that the Delaware Supreme Court has deemed "voidable" for claim extinguishment purposes. More specifically, no Supreme Court case has held that shareholder ratification operates automatically to extinguish a duty of loyalty claim. To the contrary, the ratification cases involving duty of loyalty claims have uniformly held that the effect of shareholder ratification is to alter the standard of review, *or* to shift the burden of proof, *or* both. Those cases further frustrate any effort to describe the "ratification" landscape in terms of a simple rule.

The ratification decisions that involve duty of loyalty claims are of two kinds: (a) "interested" transaction cases between a corporation and its directors (or between the corporation and an entity in which the corporation's directors are also directors or have a financial interest), and (b) cases involving a transaction between the corporation and its controlling shareholder.

Regarding the first category, 8 Del. C. § 144(a)(2) pertinently provides that an "interested" transaction of this kind will not be voidable if it is approved in good faith by a majority of disinterested stockholders. Approval by fully informed, disinterested shareholders pursuant to § 144(a)(2) invokes "the business judgment rule and limits judicial review to issues of gift or waste with the burden of proof upon the party attacking the transaction." *Marciano v. Nakash*, Del. Supr., 535 A.2d 400, 405 n. 3 (1987). The result is the same in "interested" transaction cases not decided under § 144:

> Where there has been independent shareholder ratification of interested director actions, the objecting stockholder has the burden of showing that no person of ordinary sound business judgment would say that the consideration received for the options was a fair exchange for the options granted.

Michelson, 407 A.2d at 224 (*quoting Kaufman v. Shoenberg*, Del. Ch., 91 A.2d 786, 791 (1952), at 791)[.]

The second category concerns duty of loyalty cases arising out of transactions between the corporation and its controlling stockholder. Those cases involve primarily parent-subsidiary mergers that were conditioned upon receiving "majority of the minority" stockholder approval. In a parent-subsidiary merger, the standard of review is ordinarily entire fairness, with the directors having the burden of proving that the merger was entirely fair. *Weinberger v. UOP, Inc.*, 457 A.2d 701, 703. But where the merger is conditioned upon approval by a "majority of the minority" stockholder vote, and such approval is granted, the standard of review remains entire fairness, but the burden of demonstrating that the merger was unfair shifts to the plaintiff. *Kahn v. Lynch Communication Sys.*, Del. Supr., 638 A.2d 1110 (1994); *Rosenblatt v. Getty Oil Co.*, 493 A.2d 929,

937-38 (1985); *Weinberger*, at 710; Citron, at 502. That burden-shifting effect of ratification has also been held applicable in cases involving mergers with a *de facto* controlling stockholder, and in a case involving a transaction other than a merger.

....

To repeat: in only two circumstances has the Delaware Supreme Court held that a fully-informed shareholder vote operates to extinguish a claim: (1) where the board of directors takes action that, although not alleged to constitute *ultra vires*, fraud, or waste, is claimed to exceed the board's authority; and (2) where it is claimed that the directors failed to exercise due care to adequately inform themselves before committing the corporation to a transaction. In no case has the Supreme Court held that stockholder ratification automatically extinguishes a claim for breach of the directors' duty of loyalty. Rather, the operative effect of shareholder ratification in duty of loyalty cases has been either to change the standard of review to the business judgment rule, with the burden of proof resting upon the plaintiff, *or* to leave "entire fairness" as the review standard, but shift the burden of proof to the plaintiff. Thus, the Supreme Court ratification decisions do not support the defendants' position.

That being the present state of the law, the question then becomes whether there exists a policy or doctrinal basis that would justify extending the claim-extinguishing effect of shareholder ratification to cases involving duty of loyalty claims. *Van Gorkom* does not articulate a basis, and the parties have suggested none....

Do you agree with the court's holding in *Wheelbrator* on the effect of shareholders' ratification? For instance, should shareholder approval in the circumstances indicated alter the standard of review and shift the burden of proof?

Consider in the alternative Model Act § 8.61(b), the operational section of Subchapter F dealing with the duty of loyalty. As described in Model Act § 8.61 Official Comment,

> Speaking generally:
> (i) If the procedure set forth in section 8.62 [regarding directors' approval] or in section 8.63 [regarding shareholders' approval] is complied with, or if the transaction is fair to the corporation, then a director's conflicting interest transaction is immune from attack on any ground of a personal interest or conflict of interest of the director. However, the narrow scope of subchapter F must again be strongly emphasized; if the transaction is vulnerable to attack on some other ground, subchapter F does not make it less so for having been passed through the procedures of subchapter F....
> (ii) If a transaction is *not* a director's conflicting interest transaction as defined in ... [the RMBCA], then the transaction may *not* be enjoined,

rescinded, or made the basis of other sanction *on the ground of a conflict of interest of a director, whether or not it went through the procedures of subchapter F*. In that sense, subchapter F is specifically intended to be both comprehensive and exclusive.

Section 8.61's substantial directors' insulation from liability, however, is subject to the condition "that the board's action must comply with the care, best interests and good faith criteria prescribed in § 8.30(a) for all directors' actions." § 8.61(b) Official Comment.

ALI § 5.02 Reporter's Note 1 indicates:

> Most of these "safe harbor" statutes have been adopted since 1970 and there is not yet a substantial body of case law construing them. Furthermore, the decisions in which the statutes have been considered have not involved approval of transactions by disinterested directors or shareholders. However, when the issue has been raised as to the statutes' operative effect, some court have in dictum construed these statutes so as to permit judicial scrutiny of transactions even where there is disinterested approval.

SECTION IV. COMPENSATION AGREEMENTS

Directors and officers can negotiate a range of compensation packages for themselves, including cash salaries and bonuses, stock option plans, profit sharing arrangements, and retirement and termination plans. Yet as described in ALI § 5.03 Comment *c*, one can distinguish these compensation agreements from other self-interested transactions in the following ways:

> First, unlike most other self-interested transactions, which may be forgone because the corporation usually can deal on the market rather than with the director or senior executive, compensation arrangements with directors and senior executives are necessary in all cases. Second, such arrangements are sufficiently recurring and well publicized in public corporations that there is a greater opportunity for comparison of compensation arrangements and a corresponding deterrent to overreaching. Third, institutionalized procedures for disinterested decisionmaking that are now widely practiced by large public corporations may make it less likely that corporations will be disadvantaged by unfair compensation arrangements with senior executives...

With these distinctions in in mind, ALI § 5.03 provides the following review standard:

> (a) *General Rule*. A director or senior executive who receives compensation from the corporation for services in that capacity fulfills the duty of fair dealing with respect to the compensation if either:
> (1) The compensation is fair to the corporation when approved;
> (2) The compensation is authorized in advance by disinterested directors or, in the case of a senior executive who is not a director, authorized in

advance by a disinterested superior, in a manner that satisfies the standards of the business judgment rule;

(3) The compensation is ratified by disinterested directors who satisfy the requirements of the business judgment rule, provided (i) a corporate decisionmaker who was not interested in receipt of the compensation acted for the corporation in determining the compensation and satisfied the requirements of the business judgment rule; (ii) the interested director or senior executive did not act unreasonably in failing to seek advance authorization of the compensation by disinterested directors or a disinterested superior; and (iii) the failure to obtain advance authorization of the compensation by disinterested directors or a disinterested superior did not adversely affect the interests of the corporation in a significant way; or

(4) The compensation is authorized in advance or ratified by disinterested shareholders, and does not constitute a waste of corporate assets at the time of the shareholder action.

[As the accompanying Comment explains,] § 5.03 provides that compensation transactions will be subjected to the less intense judicial scrutiny provided by a business judgment review if authorized in advance by disinterested directors, or, in the case of a senior executive who is not a director, by a disinterested superior, or ratified by disinterested directors under § 5.03(a)(3). Section 5.03 does not accord the same standard of review to a situation in which a senior executive receives compensation without such advance authorization or ratification, and in such event the senior executive will have the burden of proving fairness.

Also in *Cohen v. Ayers*,[9] the court contrasts the standard of review for compensation agreements in general with self-interested compensation agreements.

Ordinarily, employee compensation and other corporate payments are not a waste or gift of assets as long as fair consideration is returned to the corporation. The question of the adequacy of consideration is committed to the sound business judgment of the corporation's directors. Thus, a plaintiff attacking a corporate payment has the heavy burden of demonstrating that no reasonable businessman could find that adequate consideration had been supplied for the payment. However, where the directors have a personal interest in the application of the corporate payments, such as where they are fixing their own compensation, the business judgment rule no longer applies and the burden shifts to the directors to demonstrate affirmatively that the transactions were engaged in with good faith and were fair, *i.e.*, that adequate

---

[9] 596 F.2d 733, 739-40 (7th Cir. 1979).

consideration had been supplied. This alteration in the burden and quantum of proof may only be avoided in two circumstances: after full disclosure the payments must have been ratified either by action of disinterested directors or by vote of the shareholders. If the payments are thus ratified, then the business judgment rule is again applicable and the plaintiff can succeed only by meeting the burden applicable to challenges of any corporate transaction. Thus, although shareholders or disinterested directors cannot ratify waste, the existence of such ratification makes proof of waste more difficult.

SECTION V. CORPORATE OPPORTUNITY DOCTRINE

The prior materials focused on transactions between the corporation and its fiduciaries and the conflicts of interest that may arise. The corporate opportunity doctrine, while a part of the duty of loyalty, focuses on a different problem. Directors and officers sometimes pursue economic opportunities on their own behalf. For instance, they buy property, start a new company, or offer consulting services in their individual capacities. In response, the corporation may argue that the opportunities really belong to it and that the directors or officers violated their duty of loyalty by taking the opportunities.

In principle, the corporate opportunity doctrine can apply to any opportunity that the corporation and the fiduciaries both claim as theirs. A survey of cases, however, reveals that most of the contested opportunities deal with opportunities that put the fiduciaries in competition with the corporation.[10] In most cases, the competition is apparent and direct. The classic example of direct competition involves fiduciaries' starting a business that offers the same services or products to the same general market as the corporation. In addition, corporate opportunity cases are much more common in small, closely held corporations than in large, publicly held corporations.

The following materials explore various judicial approaches to this problem. As you study it, consider how the courts have balanced the competing interests of the corporation and its fiduciaries.

BROZ v. CELLULAR INFORMATION SYSTEMS, INC.

Supreme Court of Delaware
673 A.2d 148 (1996)

VEASEY, CHIEF JUSTICE:

In this appeal, we consider the application of the doctrine of corporate opportunity. The Court of Chancery decided that the defendant, a corporate director, breached his fiduciary duty by not formally presenting to the corporation an opportunity which had come to the director individually and independent of

---

[10] Pat K. Chew, *Competing Interests in the Corporate Opportunity Doctrine*, 67 N.C. L. REV. 435, 436 n. 2, 444 (1989).

the director's relationship with the corporation. Here the opportunity was not one in which the corporation in its current mode had an interest or which it had the financial ability to acquire, but, under the unique circumstances here, that mode was subject to change by virtue of the impending acquisition of the corporation by another entity.

We conclude that, although a corporate director may be shielded from liability by offering to the corporation an opportunity which has come to the director independently and individually, the failure of the director to present the opportunity does not necessarily result in the improper usurpation of a corporate opportunity. We further conclude that, if the corporation is a target or potential target of an acquisition by another company which has an interest and ability to entertain the opportunity, the director of the target company does not have a fiduciary duty to present the opportunity to the target company. Accordingly, the judgment of the Court of Chancery is

Reversed.

I. *The Contentions of the Parties and the Decision Below*

Robert F. Broz ("Broz") is the President and sole stockholder of RFB Cellular, Inc. ("RFBC"), a Delaware corporation engaged in the business of providing cellular telephone service in the Midwestern United States. At the time of the conduct at issue in this appeal, Broz was also a member of the board of directors of plaintiff below-appellee, Cellular Information Systems, Inc. ("CIS"). CIS is a publicly held Delaware corporation and a competitor of RFBC.

The conduct before the Court involves the purchase by Broz of a cellular telephone service license for the benefit of RFBC.[11] The license in question, known as the Michigan-2 Rural Service Area Cellular License ("Michigan-2"), is issued by the Federal Communications Commission ("FCC") and entitles its holder to provide cellular telephone service to a portion of northern Michigan. CIS brought an action against Broz and RFBC for equitable relief, contending that the purchase of this license by Broz constituted a usurpation of a corporate opportunity properly belonging to CIS, irrespective of whether or not CIS was interested in the Michigan-2 opportunity at the time it was offered to Broz.

The principal basis for the contention of CIS is that PriCellular, Inc. ("PriCellular"), another cellular communications company which was contemporaneously engaged in an acquisition of CIS, was interested in the Michigan-2 opportunity. CIS contends that, in determining whether the Michigan-2

---

[11] The Court recognizes that the actual purchase of the Michigan-2 license was consummated by RFBC as a corporate entity, rather than by Broz acting as an individual for his own benefit. Broz is, however, the sole party in interest in RFBC and all actions taken by RFBC, including the acquisition of Michigan-2, are accomplished at the behest of Broz. Therefore, insofar as the purchase of Michigan-2 is concerned, the Court will not distinguish between the actions of Broz and those of RFBC in analyzing Broz' alleged breach of fiduciary duty.

opportunity rightfully belonged to CIS, Broz was required to consider the interests of PriCellular insofar as those interests would come into alignment with those of CIS as a result of PriCellular's acquisition plans.

....

II. *Facts*

Broz has been the President and sole stockholder of RFBC since 1992. RFBC owns and operates an FCC license area, known as the Michigan-4 Rural Service Area Cellular License ("Michigan-4"). The license entitles RFBC to provide cellular telephone service to a portion of rural Michigan. Although Broz' efforts have been devoted primarily to the business operations of RFBC, he also served as an outside director of CIS at the time of the events at issue in this case. CIS was at all times fully aware of Broz' relationship with RFBC and the obligations incumbent upon him by virtue of that relationship.

In April of 1994, Mackinac Cellular Corp. ("Mackinac") sought to divest itself of Michigan-2, the license area immediately adjacent to Michigan-4. To this end, Mackinac contacted Daniels & Associates ("Daniels") and arranged for the brokerage firm to seek potential purchasers for Michigan-2. In compiling a list of prospects, Daniels included RFBC as a likely candidate. In May of 1994, David Rhodes, a representative of Daniels, contacted Broz and broached the subject of RFBC's possible acquisition of Michigan-2. Broz later signed a confidentiality agreement at the request of Mackinac, and received the offering materials pertaining to Michigan-2.

Michigan-2 was not, however, offered to CIS. Apparently, Daniels did not consider CIS to be a viable purchaser for Michigan-2 in light of CIS' recent financial difficulties. The record shows that, at the time Michigan-2 was offered to Broz, CIS had recently emerged from lengthy and contentious Chapter 11 proceedings. Pursuant to the Chapter 11 Plan of Reorganization, CIS entered into a loan agreement that substantially impaired the company's ability to undertake new acquisitions or to incur new debt. In fact, CIS would have been unable to purchase Michigan-2 without the approval of its creditors.

The CIS reorganization resulted from the failure of CIS' rather ambitious plans for expansion. From 1989 onward, CIS had embarked on a series of cellular license acquisitions. In 1992, however, CIS' financing failed, necessitating the liquidation of the company's holdings and reduction of the company's total indebtedness. During the period from early 1992 until the time of CIS' emergence from bankruptcy in 1994, CIS divested itself of some fifteen separate cellular license systems. CIS contracted to sell four additional license areas on May 27, 1994, leaving CIS with only five remaining license areas, all of which were outside of the Midwest.

On June 13, 1994, following a meeting of the CIS board, Broz spoke with CIS' Chief Executive Officer, Richard Treibick ("Treibick"), concerning his interest in acquiring Michigan-2. Treibick communicated to Broz that CIS was not interested in Michigan-2. Treibick further stated that he had been made aware of the Michigan-2 opportunity prior to the conversation with Broz, and that any offer to acquire Michigan-2 was rejected. After the commencement of the PriCellular tender offer, in August of 1994, Broz contacted another CIS director, Peter Schiff ("Schiff"), to discuss the possible acquisition of Michigan-2 by RFBC. Schiff, like Treibick, indicated that CIS had neither the wherewithal nor the inclination to purchase Michigan-2. In late September of 1994, Broz also contacted Stanley Bloch ("Bloch"), a director and counsel for CIS, to request that Bloch represent RFBC in its dealings with Mackinac. Bloch agreed to represent RFBC, and, like Schiff and Treibick, expressed his belief that CIS was not at all interested in the transaction. Ultimately, all the CIS directors testified at trial that, had Broz inquired at that time, they each would have expressed the opinion that CIS was not interested in Michigan-2.[12]

On June 28, 1994, following various overtures from PriCellular concerning an acquisition of CIS, six CIS directors entered into agreements with PriCellular to sell their shares in CIS at a price of $ 2.00 per share. These agreements were contingent upon, *inter alia*, the consummation of a PriCellular tender offer for all CIS shares at the same price. Pursuant to their agreements with PriCellular, the CIS directors also entered into a "standstill" agreement which prevented the directors from engaging in any transaction outside the regular course of CIS' business or incurring any new liabilities until the close of the PriCellular tender offer. On August 2, 1994, PriCellular commenced a tender offer for all outstanding shares of CIS at $ 2.00 per share. The PriCellular tender offer mirrored the standstill agreements entered into by the CIS directors.

PriCellular's tender offer was originally scheduled to close on September 16, 1994. At the time the tender offer was launched, however, the source of the $ 106,000,000 in financing required to consummate the transaction was still in doubt. PriCellular originally planned to structure the transaction around bank loans. When this financing fell through, PriCellular resorted to a junk bond offering. PriCellular's financing difficulties generated a great deal of concern among the CIS insiders whether the tender offer was, in fact, viable. Financing difficulties ultimately caused PriCellular to delay the closing date of the tender offer from September 16, 1994 until October 14, 1994 and then again until November 9, 1994.

On August 6, September 6 and September 21, 1994, Broz submitted written offers to Mackinac for the purchase of Michigan-2. During this time period, PriCellular also began negotiations with Mackinac to arrange an option for the purchase of Michigan-2. PriCellular's interest in Michigan-2 was fully disclosed to CIS' chief executive, Treibick, who did not express any interest in Michigan-2,

---

[12] We assume *arguendo* that informal contacts and individual opinions of board members are not a substitute for a formal process of presenting an opportunity to a board of directors. Nevertheless, in our view such a formal process was not necessary under the circumstances of this case in order for Broz to avoid liability. These contacts with individual board members do, however, tend to show that Broz was not acting surreptitiously or in bad faith.

and was actually incredulous that PriCellular would want to acquire the license. Nevertheless, CIS was fully aware that PriCellular and Broz were bidding for Michigan-2 and did not interpose CIS in this bidding war.

In late September of 1994, PriCellular reached agreement with Mackinac on an option to purchase Michigan-2. The exercise price of the option agreement was set at $ 6.7 million, with the option remaining in force until December 15, 1994. Pursuant to the agreement, the right to exercise the option was not transferrable to any party other than a subsidiary of PriCellular. Therefore, it could not have been transferred to CIS. The agreement further provided that Mackinac was free to sell Michigan-2 to any party who was willing to exceed the exercise price of the Mackinac-PriCellular option contract by at least $ 500,000. On November 14, 1994, Broz agreed to pay Mackinac $ 7.2 million for the Michigan-2 license, thereby meeting the terms of the option agreement. An asset purchase agreement was thereafter executed by Mackinac and RFBC.

Nine days later, on November 23, 1994, PriCellular completed its financing and closed its tender offer for CIS. Prior to that point, PriCellular owned no equity interest in CIS. Subsequent to the consummation of the PriCellular tender offer for CIS, members of the CIS board of directors, including Broz, were discharged and replaced with a slate of PriCellular nominees. On March 2, 1995, this action was commenced by CIS in the Court of Chancery.

. . . .

IV. *Application of the Corporate Opportunity Doctrine*

The doctrine of corporate opportunity represents but one species of the broad fiduciary duties assumed by a corporate director or officer. A corporate fiduciary agrees to place the interests of the corporation before his or her own in appropriate circumstances. In light of the diverse and often competing obligations faced by directors and officers, however, the corporate opportunity doctrine arose as a means of defining the parameters of fiduciary duty in instances of potential conflict. The classic statement of the doctrine is derived from the venerable case of *Guth v. Loft, Inc.* In *Guth*, this Court held that:

> if there is presented to a corporate officer or director a business opportunity which the corporation is financially able to undertake, is, from its nature, in the line of the corporation's business and is of practical advantage to it, is one in which the corporation has an interest or a reasonable expectancy, and, by embracing the opportunity, the self-interest of the officer or director will be brought into conflict with that of the corporation, the law will not permit him to seize the opportunity for himself.

Guth, 5 A.2d at 510-11.

The corporate opportunity doctrine, as delineated by *Guth* and its progeny, holds that a corporate officer or director may not take a business opportunity for his own if: (1) the corporation is financially able to exploit the opportunity; (2) the opportunity is within the corporation's line of business; (3) the corporation has an interest or expectancy in the opportunity; and (4) by taking the opportunity for his own, the corporate fiduciary will thereby be placed in a position inimicable to his duties to the corporation. The Court in *Guth* also derived a corollary which states that a director or officer *may* take a corporate opportunity if: (1) the opportunity is presented to the director or officer in his individual and not his corporate capacity; (2) the opportunity is not essential to the corporation; (3) the corporation holds no interest or expectancy in the opportunity; and (4) the director or officer has not wrongfully employed the resources of the corporation in pursuing or exploiting the opportunity. *Guth*, 5 A.2d at 509.

Thus, the contours of this doctrine are well established. It is important to note, however, that the tests enunciated in *Guth* and subsequent cases provide guidelines to be considered by a reviewing court in balancing the equities of an individual case. No one factor is dispositive and all factors must be taken into account insofar as they are applicable. Cases involving a claim of usurpation of a corporate opportunity range over a multitude of factual settings. Hard and fast rules are not easily crafted to deal with such an array of complex situations. As this Court noted in *Johnston v. Greene*, Del. Supr., 121 A.2d 919 (1956), the determination of "[w]hether or not a director has appropriated for himself something that in fairness should belong to the corporation is 'a factual question to be decided by reasonable inference from objective facts.'" *Id.* at 923 (*quoting Guth*, 5 A.2d at 513). In the instant case, we find that the facts do not support the conclusion that Broz misappropriated a corporate opportunity.

We note at the outset that Broz became aware of the Michigan-2 opportunity in his individual and not his corporate capacity. As the Court of Chancery found, "Broz did not misuse proprietary information that came to him in a corporate capacity nor did he otherwise use any power he might have over the governance of the corporation to advance his own interests." 663 A.2d at 1185. This fact is not the subject of serious dispute. In fact, it is clear from the record that Mackinac did not consider CIS a viable candidate for the acquisition of Michigan-2. Accordingly, Mackinac did not offer the property to CIS. In this factual posture, many of the fundamental concerns undergirding the law of corporate opportunity are not present (*e.g.*, misappropriation of the corporation's proprietary information). The burden imposed upon Broz to show adherence to his fiduciary duties to CIS is thus lessened to some extent. *See Science Accessories Corp.*, 425 A.2d at 964 (holding that because opportunity to purchase new technology was "an "outside" opportunity not available to SAC, defendants' failure to disclose the concept to SAC and their taking it for themselves for purposes of competing with SAC cannot be found to be in breach of any agency fiduciary duty"). Nevertheless, this fact is not dispositive. The determination of whether a particular fiduciary has usurped a corporate opportunity necessitates a careful examination of the circumstances, giving due credence to the factors enunciated in *Guth* and subsequent cases.

We turn now to an analysis of the factors relied on by the trial court. First, we find that CIS was not financially capable of exploiting the Michigan-2 opportunity. Although the Court of Chancery concluded otherwise, we hold that this finding was not supported by the evidence. *Levitt*, 287 A.2d at 673. The record shows that CIS was in a precarious financial position at the time Mackinac presented the Michigan-2 opportunity to Broz. Having recently emerged from lengthy and contentious bankruptcy proceedings, CIS was not in a position to commit capital to the acquisition of new assets. Further, the loan agreement entered into by CIS and its creditors severely limited the discretion of CIS as to the acquisition of new assets and substantially restricted the ability of CIS to incur new debt.

The Court of Chancery based its contrary finding on the fact that PriCellular had purchased an option to acquire CIS' bank debt. Thus, the court reasoned, PriCellular was in a position to exercise that option and then waive any unfavorable restrictions that would stand in the way of a CIS acquisition of Michigan-2. The trial court, however, disregarded the fact that PriCellular's own financial situation was not particularly stable....

Second, while it may be said with some certainty that the Michigan-2 opportunity was within CIS' line of business, it is not equally clear that CIS had a cognizable interest or expectancy in the license.[13] Under the third factor laid down by this Court in *Guth*, for an opportunity to be deemed to belong to the fiduciary's corporation, the corporation must have an interest or expectancy in that opportunity. As this Court stated in *Johnston*, 121 A.2d at 924, "[f]or the corporation to have an actual or expectant interest in any specific property, there must be some tie between that property and the nature of the corporate business." Despite the fact that the nature of the Michigan-2 opportunity was historically close to the core operations of CIS, changes were in process. At the time the opportunity was presented, CIS was actively engaged in the process of divesting its cellular license holdings. CIS' articulated business plan did not involve any new acquisitions. Further, as indicated by the testimony of the entire CIS board, the Michigan-2 license would not have been of interest to CIS even absent CIS' financial difficulties and CIS' then current desire to liquidate its cellular license

---

[13] The language in the *Guth* opinion relating to "line of business" is less than clear:

> Where a corporation is engaged in a certain business, and an opportunity is presented to it embracing an activity as to which it has fundamental knowledge, practical experience and *ability to pursue*, which, logically and naturally, is adaptable to its business *having regard for its financial position*, and *is consonant with its reasonable needs and aspirations for expansion*, it may properly be said that the opportunity is within the corporation's line of business.

Guth, 5 A.2d at 514 (emphasis supplied). This formulation of the definition of the term "line of business" suggests that the business strategy and financial well-being of the corporation are also relevant to a determination of whether the opportunity is within the corporation's line of business. Since we find that these considerations are decisive under the other factors enunciated by the Court in *Guth*, we do not reach the question of whether they are here relevant to a determination of the corporation's line of business.

holdings. Thus, CIS had no interest or expectancy in the Michigan-2 opportunity....

Finally, the corporate opportunity doctrine is implicated only in cases where the fiduciary's seizure of an opportunity results in a conflict between the fiduciary's duties to the corporation and the self-interest of the director as actualized by the exploitation of the opportunity. In the instant case, Broz' interest in acquiring and profiting from Michigan-2 created no duties that were inimicable to his obligations to CIS. Broz, at all times relevant to the instant appeal, was the sole party in interest in RFBC, a competitor of CIS. CIS was fully aware of Broz' potentially conflicting duties. Broz, however, comported himself in a manner that was wholly in accord with his obligations to CIS. Broz took care not to usurp any opportunity which CIS was willing and able to pursue. Broz sought only to compete with an outside entity, PriCellular, for acquisition of an opportunity which both sought to possess. Broz was not obligated to refrain from competition with PriCellular. Therefore, the totality of the circumstances indicates that Broz did not usurp an opportunity that properly belonged to CIS.

A. *Presentation to the Board:*

> ....

The teaching of *Guth* and its progeny is that the director or officer must analyze the situation *ex ante* to determine whether the opportunity is one rightfully belonging to the corporation. If the director or officer believes, based on one of the factors articulated above, that the corporation is not entitled to the opportunity, then he may take it for himself. Of course, presenting the opportunity to the board creates a kind of "safe harbor" for the director, which removes the specter of a *post hoc* judicial determination that the director or officer has improperly usurped a corporate opportunity. Thus, presentation avoids the possibility that an error in the fiduciary's assessment of the situation will create future liability for breach of fiduciary duty. It is not the law of Delaware that presentation to the board is a necessary prerequisite to a finding that a corporate opportunity has not been usurped.

> ....

B. *Alignment of Interests Between CIS and PriCellular:*

> ....

... Broz was under no duty to consider the interests of PriCellular when he chose to purchase Michigan-2. As stated in *Guth*, a director's right to "appropriate [an] ... opportunity depends on the circumstances existing at the time it presented itself to him without regard to subsequent events." *Guth*, 5 A.2d at 513. At the time Broz purchased Michigan-2, PriCellular had not yet acquired CIS. Any plans to do so would still have been wholly speculative. Accordingly, Broz was not required to consider the contingent and uncertain plans of PriCellular in reaching his determination of how to proceed.

Whether or not the CIS board would, at some time, have chosen to acquire Michigan-2 in order to make CIS a more attractive acquisition target for PriCellular or to enhance the synergy of any combined enterprise, is speculative. The trial court found this to be a plausible scenario and therefore found that, pursuant to the factors laid down in *Guth*, CIS had a valid interest or expectancy in the license. This speculative finding cuts against the statements made by CIS' Chief Executive and the entire CIS board of directors and ignores the fact that CIS still lacked the wherewithal to acquire Michigan-2, even if one takes into account the possible availability of PriCellular's financing. Thus, the fact of PriCellular's plans to acquire CIS is immaterial and does not change the analysis.

In reaching our conclusion on this point, we note that certainty and predictability are values to be promoted in our corporation law. *See Williams v. Geier*, Del. Supr., 671 A.2d 1368, 1385 n. 36 (1996). Broz, as an active participant in the cellular telephone industry, was entitled to proceed in his own economic interest in the absence of any countervailing duty. The right of a director or officer to engage in business affairs outside of his or her fiduciary capacity would be illusory if these individuals were required to consider every potential, future occurrence in determining whether a particular business strategy would implicate fiduciary duty concerns. In order for a director to engage meaningfully in business unrelated to his or her corporate role, the director must be allowed to make decisions based on the situation as it exists at the time a given opportunity is presented. Absent such a rule, the corporate fiduciary would be constrained to refrain from exploiting any opportunity for fear of liability based on the occurrence of subsequent events. This state of affairs would unduly restrict officers and directors and would be antithetical to certainty in corporation law.

V. *Conclusion*

The corporate opportunity doctrine represents a judicially crafted effort to harmonize the competing demands placed on corporate fiduciaries in a modern business environment. The doctrine seeks to reduce the possibility of conflict between a director's duties to the corporation and interests unrelated to that role. In the instant case, Broz adhered to his obligations to CIS. We hold that the Court of Chancery erred as a matter of law in concluding that Broz had a duty formally to present the Michigan-2 opportunity to the CIS board. We also hold that the trial court erred in its application of the corporate opportunity doctrine under the unusual facts of this case, where CIS had no interest or financial ability to acquire the opportunity, but the impending acquisition of CIS by PriCellular would or could have caused a change in those circumstances.

Therefore, we hold that Broz did not breach his fiduciary duties to CIS. Accordingly, we *Reverse* the judgment of the Court of Chancery holding that Broz diverted a corporate opportunity properly belonging to CIS and imposing a constructive trust.

A. COMPETING INTERESTS

Corporate opportunity cases often pose conflicting interests. The corporation relies on fiduciaries to fulfill their duties in good faith and with integrity. It does not want to have to monitor the fiduciaries' honesty and fair dealing. The corporation provides them with access to information, contacts and experiences so that the fiduciaries can perform effectively. It does not want the fiduciaries' to use this information and experience to pursue interests that may conflict with and overcome the corporate interests.

On the other hand, there is society's and the individual's interest in fostering free competition. Society wants to encourage individuals to pursue opportunities that lead to the creation of new businesses and other entrepreneurial efforts. In addition, if directors' and officers' freedom of enterprise is too restricted by overly rigid corporate law rules, competent individuals will be discouraged from serving as corporate fiduciaries.

B. LINE OF BUSINESS TEST

Guth v. Loft, Inc. remains the most cited case in the corporate opportunity area. As indicated in *Broz* footnote 14, the line of business test articulated in *Guth* may be interpreted in various ways. If interpreted narrowly, it would only preclude fiduciaries from pursuing opportunities that would put fiduciaries in direct competition with the corporation. If interpreted more expansively, it could preclude fiduciaries from any opportunities to which the corporation could possibly adapt itself. Under this more expansive interpretation, corporations would be entitled to a broad range of opportunities and directors and officers would likely be found liable unless the opportunity was completely unrelated to the corporation's activities.

C. KEY INQUIRIES

Courts have used a range of approaches to resolving these disputes, several of which were noted in *Broz*. Three frequent inquiries follow:

(a) Does the corporation have a protectable *expectancy* to the opportunity? Under the circumstances, would the corporation and the fiduciary reasonably expect that the opportunity belongs to the corporation? Courts interpret "expectancy" differently. Some may require that the corporation have an express contractual right to the opportunity, such as an option to buy. Others may define expectancy more broadly, allowing the corporation to claim opportunities for which it has no contract, but for which it had some prior interest and dealings. How was "expectancy" interpreted in *Broz*

(b) Is it "*fair*" to the corporation for the fiduciary to take the opportunity? For instance, a fairness analysis may include the following:

Factors dealing with the relationship between the opportunity and the corporation:

- Whether the opportunity was of special value to the corporation;
- Whether the corporation was actively negotiating for the opportunity; and
- Whether the corporation was in a financial position to pursue the opportunity.

Factors dealing with the relationship between the opportunity and the fiduciaries:

- Whether the fiduciaries received the opportunity because of their corporate positions;
- Whether the fiduciaries were delegated to pursue the opportunity on behalf of the corporation;
- Whether the fiduciaries used the corporate resources in identifying or developing the opportunity; and
- Whether the fiduciaries intended to resell the opportunity to the corporation.

Factors dealing with the relationship between the corporation and the fiduciaries:

- Whether the fiduciaries' dealings with the corporation were fair;
- Whether the fiduciaries carried out their corporate duties in good faith;
- Whether the fiduciaries harmed the corporation by unfair bargaining; and
- Whether the fiduciaries would be put in an adverse and hostile position to the corporation.

This equity-oriented case-by-case approach allows the court to consider whatever it deems relevant, but may offer no predictable guidelines on which fiduciaries can base their future conduct

(c) Did the corporation have the actual *capacity* to develop the opportunity? If it does not, then perhaps it would serve broader efficiency and entrepreneurial objectives for fiduciaries to be allowed to pursue the opportunity. Consider, however, how an emphasis on corporate incapacity might shape fiduciaries' conduct?

In determining the corporation's capabilities, the courts may consider various corporate capacities. Does the corporation have the legal capacity to pursue the opportunity, or does the corporation's purposes, contractual obligations, or statutory limitations prohibit it from doing so? Are there organizational obstacles, such as the lack of facilities or personnel, to pursuing the opportunity? Or what if the party offering the opportunity is not inclined or refuses to deal with the corporation? The courts have particularly emphasized whether the corporation has the necessary financial resources. In *Broz*, for instance, the court concluded that CIS was not financially capable of pursuing the opportunity. Was it justified in doing so?

The following case describes the ALI's approach. As you read the case, consider the advantages and disadvantages of the approach. In what ways has the model incorporated some of the factors in the notes above and in the *Broz* case?

NORTHEAST HARBOR GOLF CLUB, INC. v. HARRIS
Supreme Judicial Court of Maine
661 A.2d 1146 (1995)

ROBERTS, JUSTICE:

Northeast Harbor Golf Club, Inc., appeals from a judgment entered in the Superior Court (Hancock County, *Atwood, J.*) following a nonjury trial. The Club maintains that the trial court erred in finding that Nancy Harris did not breach her fiduciary duty as president of the Club by purchasing and developing property abutting the golf course. Because we today adopt principles different from those applied by the trial court in determining that Harris's activities did not constitute a breach of the corporate opportunity doctrine, we vacate the judgment.

I. *The Facts*

Nancy Harris was the president of the Northeast Harbor Golf Club, a Maine corporation, from 1971 until she was asked to resign in 1990. The Club also had a board of directors that was responsible for making or approving significant policy decisions. The Club's only major asset was a golf course in Mount Desert. During Harris's tenure as president, the board occasionally discussed the possibility of developing some of the Club's real estate in order to raise money. Although Harris was generally in favor of tasteful development, the board always "shied away" from that type of activity.

In 1979, Robert Suminsby informed Harris that he was the listing broker for the Gilpin property, which comprised three noncontiguous parcels located among the fairways of the golf course. The property included an unused right-of-way on which the Club's parking lot and clubhouse were located. It was also encumbered by an easement in favor of the Club allowing foot traffic from the green of one hole to the next tee. Suminsby testified that he contacted Harris because she was the president of the Club and he believed that the Club would be interested in buying the property in order to prevent development.

Harris immediately agreed to purchase the Gilpin property in her own name for the asking price of $ 45,000. She did not disclose her plans to purchase the property to the Club's board prior to the purchase. She informed the board at its annual August meeting that she had purchased the property, that she intended to hold it in her own name, and that the Club would be "protected." The board took no action in response to the Harris purchase. She testified that at the time of the purchase she had no plans to develop the property and that no such plans took shape until 1988.

In 1984, while playing golf with the postmaster of Northeast Harbor, Harris learned that a parcel of land owned by the heirs of the Smallidge family might be available for purchase. The Smallidge parcel was surrounded on three sides by the golf course and on the fourth side by a house lot. It had no access to the road. With the ultimate goal of acquiring the property, Harris instructed her lawyer to locate the Smallidge heirs. Harris testified that she told a number of individual board members about her attempt to acquire the Smallidge parcel. At a board meeting in August 1985, Harris formally disclosed to the board that she had purchased the Smallidge property.[14] The minutes of that meeting show that she told the board she had no present plans to develop the Smallidge parcel. Harris testified that at the time of the purchase of the Smallidge property she nonetheless thought it might be nice to have some houses there. Again, the board took no formal action as a result of Harris's purchase. Harris acquired the Smallidge property from ten heirs, paying a total of $ 60,000. In 1990, Harris paid $ 275,000 for the lot and building separating the Smallidge parcel from the road in order to gain access to the otherwise landlocked parcel.

The trial court expressly found that the Club would have been unable to purchase either the Gilpin or Smallidge properties for itself, relying on testimony that the Club continually experienced financial difficulties, operated annually at a deficit, and depended on contributions from the directors to pay its bills. On the other hand, there was evidence that the Club had occasionally engaged in successful fund-raising, including a two-year period shortly after the Gilpin purchase during which the Club raised $ 115,000. The Club had $ 90,000 in a capital investment fund at the time of the Smallidge purchase.

In 1987 or 1988, Harris divided the real estate into 41 small lots, 14 on the Smallidge property and 27 on the Gilpin property. Apparently as part of her estate plan, Harris conveyed noncontiguous lots among the 41 to her children and retained others for herself. In 1991, Harris and her children exchanged deeds to reassemble the small lots into larger parcels. At the time the Club filed this suit, the property was divided into 11 lots, some owned by Harris and others by her children who are also defendants in this case. Harris estimated the value of all the real estate at the time of the trial to be $ 1,550,000.

In 1988, Harris, who was still president of the Club, and her children began the process of obtaining approval for a five-lot subdivision known as Bushwood on the lower Gilpin property. Even when the board learned of the proposed subdivision, a majority failed to take any action. A group of directors formed a separate organization in order to oppose the subdivision on the basis that it violated the local zoning ordinance. After Harris's resignation as president, the Club also sought unsuccessfully to challenge the subdivision.... Plans of Harris and her family for development of the other parcels are unclear, but the local zoning ordinance would permit construction of up to 11 houses on the land as currently divided.

---

[14] In fact, it appears that Harris did not take title to the property until October 26, 1985. She had only signed a purchase and sale agreement at the time of the August board meeting.

After Harris's plans to develop Bushwood became apparent, the board grew increasingly divided concerning the propriety of development near the golf course. At least two directors, Henri Agnese and Nick Ludington, testified that they trusted Harris to act in the best interests of the Club and that they had no problem with the development plans for Bushwood. Other directors disagreed.

In particular, John Schafer, a Washington, D.C., lawyer and long-time member of the board, took issue with Harris's conduct. He testified that he had relied on Harris's representations at the time she acquired the properties that she would not develop them. According to Schafer, matters came to a head in August 1990 when a number of directors concluded that Harris's development plans irreconcilably conflicted with the Club's interests. As a result, Schafer and two other directors asked Harris to resign as president. In April 1991, after a substantial change in the board's membership, the board authorized the instant lawsuit against Harris for the breach of her fiduciary duty to act in the best interests of the corporation. The board simultaneously resolved that the proposed housing development was contrary to the best interests of the corporation.

The Club filed a complaint against Harris, her sons John and Shepard, and her daughter-in-law Melissa Harris. As amended, the complaint alleged that during her term as president Harris breached her fiduciary duty by purchasing the lots without providing notice and an opportunity for the Club to purchase the property and by subdividing the lots for future development. The Club sought an injunction to prevent development and also sought to impose a constructive trust on the property in question for the benefit of the Club.

The trial court found that Harris had not usurped a corporate opportunity because the acquisition of real estate was not in the Club's line of business. Moreover, it found that the corporation lacked the financial ability to purchase the real estate at issue. Finally, the court placed great emphasis on Harris's good faith. It noted her long and dedicated history of service to the Club, her personal oversight of the Club's growth, and her frequent financial contributions to the Club. The court found that her development activities were "generally ... compatible with the corporation's business." This appeal followed.

II. *The Corporate Opportunity Doctrine*

Corporate officers and directors bear a duty of loyalty to the corporations they serve. As Justice Cardozo explained the fiduciary duty in *Meinhard v. Salmon*, 249 N.Y. 458, 164 N.E. 545, 546 (1928):

> A trustee is held to something stricter than the morals of the marketplace. Not honesty alone, but the punctilio of an honor the most sensitive, is then the standard of behavior. As to this there has developed a tradition that is unbending and inveterate.

Maine has embraced this "unbending and inveterate" tradition. Corporate fiduciaries in Maine must discharge their duties in good faith with a view toward furthering the interests of the corporation. They must disclose and not withhold relevant information concerning any potential conflict of interest with the corporation, and they must refrain from using their position, influence, or knowledge of the affairs of the corporation to gain personal advantage.

Despite the general acceptance of the proposition that corporate fiduciaries owe a duty of loyalty to their corporations, there has been much confusion about the specific extent of that duty when, as here, it is contended that a fiduciary takes for herself a corporate opportunity. This case requires us for the first time to define the scope of the corporate opportunity doctrine in Maine.

Various courts have embraced different versions of the corporate opportunity doctrine. The test applied by the trial court and embraced by Harris is generally known as the "line of business" test. The seminal case applying the line of business test is *Guth v. Loft, Inc.*, 5 A.2d 503 (Del. 1939). In *Guth*, the Delaware Supreme Court adopted an intensely factual test stated in general terms as follows:

> [I]f there is presented to a corporate officer or director a business opportunity which the corporation is financially able to undertake, is, from its nature, in the line of the corporation's business and is of practical advantage to it, is one in which the corporation has an interest or a reasonable expectancy, and, by embracing the opportunity, the self-interest of the officer or director will be brought into conflict with that of his corporation, the law will not permit him to seize the opportunity for himself.

Id. at 511. The "real issue" under this test is whether the opportunity "was so closely associated with the existing business activities as to bring the transaction within that class of cases where the acquisition of the property would throw the corporate officer purchasing it into competition with his company." *Id.* at 513. The Delaware court described that inquiry as "a factual question to be decided by reasonable inferences from objective facts." *Id.*

The line of business test suffers from some significant weaknesses. First, the question whether a particular activity is within a corporation's line of business is conceptually difficult to answer. The facts of the instant case demonstrate that difficulty. The Club is in the business of running a golf course. It is not in the business of developing real estate. In the traditional sense, therefore, the trial court correctly observed that the opportunity in this case was not a corporate opportunity within the meaning of the *Guth* test. Nevertheless, the record would support a finding that the Club had made the policy judgment that development of surrounding real estate was detrimental to the best interests of the Club. The acquisition of land adjacent to the golf course for the purpose of preventing future development would have enhanced the ability of the Club to implement that policy. The record also shows that the Club had occasionally considered reversing that policy and expanding its operations to include the development of surrounding real estate. Harris's activities effectively foreclosed the Club from pursuing that option with respect to prime locations adjacent to the golf course.

Second, the *Guth* test includes as an element the financial ability of the corporation to take advantage of the opportunity. The court in this case relied on the Club's supposed financial incapacity as a basis for excusing Harris's conduct. Often, the injection of financial ability into the equation will unduly favor the inside director or executive who has command of the facts relating to the finances of the corporation. Reliance on financial ability will also act as a disincentive to corporate executives to solve corporate financing and other problems. In addition, the Club could have prevented development without spending $ 275,000 to acquire the property Harris needed to obtain access to the road.

The Massachusetts Supreme Judicial Court adopted a different test in *Durfee v. Durfee & Canning, Inc.*, 323 Mass. 187, 80 N.E.2d 522 (1948). The *Durfee* test has since come to be known as the "fairness test." According to *Durfee*, the

> true basis of governing doctrine rests on the unfairness in the particular circumstances of a director, whose relation to the corporation is fiduciary, taking advantage of an opportunity [for her personal profit] when the interest of the corporation justly call[s] for protection. This calls for application of ethical standards of what is fair and equitable ... in particular sets of facts.

Id. at 529 (*quoting Ballantine on Corporations* 204-05 (rev. ed. 1946)). As with the *Guth* test, the *Durfee* test calls for a broad-ranging, intensely factual inquiry. The *Durfee* test suffers even more than the *Guth* test from a lack of principled content. It provides little or no practical guidance to the corporate officer or director seeking to measure her obligations.

The Minnesota Supreme Court elected "to combine the 'line of business' test with the 'fairness' test." *Miller v. Miller*, 301 Minn. 207, 222 N.W.2d 71, 81 (1974). It engaged in a two-step analysis, first determining whether a particular opportunity was within the corporation's line of business, then scrutinizing "the equitable considerations existing prior to, at the time of, and following the officer's acquisition." *Id.* The *Miller* court hoped by adopting this approach "to ameliorate the often-expressed criticism that the [corporate opportunity] doctrine is vague and subjects today's corporate management to the danger of unpredictable liability." *Id.* In fact, the test adopted in *Miller* merely piles the uncertainty and vagueness of the fairness test on top of the weaknesses in the line of business test.

Despite the weaknesses of each of these approaches to the corporate opportunity doctrine, they nonetheless rest on a single fundamental policy. At bottom, the corporate opportunity doctrine recognizes that a corporate fiduciary should not serve both corporate and personal interests at the same time. As we observed in *Camden Land Co. v. Lewis*, 101 Me. 78, 97, 63 A. 523, 531 (1905), corporate fiduciaries "owe their whole duty to the corporation, and they are not to be permitted to act when duty conflicts with interest. They cannot serve themselves and the corporation at the same time." The various formulations of the test are merely attempts to moderate the potentially harsh consequences of strict adherence to that policy. It is important to preserve some ability for corporate fiduciaries to pursue personal business interests that present no real threat to their duty of loyalty.

III. *The American Law Institute Approach*

In an attempt to protect the duty of loyalty while at the same time providing long-needed clarity and guidance for corporate decisionmakers, the American Law Institute has offered the most recently developed version of the corporate opportunity doctrine. *Principles of Corporate Governance* § 5.05 (May 13, 1992), provides as follows:

§ 5.05 Taking of Corporate Opportunities by Directors or Senior Executives

(a) *General Rule.* A director [§ 1.13] or senior executive [§ 1.33] may not take advantage of a corporate opportunity unless:

(1) The director or senior executive first offers the corporate opportunity to the corporation and makes disclosure concerning the conflict of interest [§ 1.14(a)] and the corporate opportunity [§ 1.14(b)];

(2) The corporate opportunity is rejected by the corporation; and

(3) Either:

(A) The rejection of the opportunity is fair to the corporation;

(B) The opportunity is rejected in advance, following such disclosure, by disinterested directors [§ 1.15], or, in the case of a senior executive who is not a director, by a disinterested superior, in a manner that satisfies the standards of the business judgment rule [§ 4.01(c)]; or

(C) The rejection is authorized in advance or ratified, following such disclosure, by disinterested shareholders [§ 1.16], and the rejection is not equivalent to a waste of corporate assets [§ 1.42].

(b) *Definition of a Corporate Opportunity.* For purposes of this Section, a corporate opportunity means:

(1) Any opportunity to engage in a business activity of which a director or senior executive becomes aware, either:

(A) In connection with the performance of functions as a director or senior executive, or under circumstances that should reasonably lead the director or senior executive to believe that the person offering the opportunity expects it to be offered to the corporation; or

(B) Through the use of corporate information or property, if the resulting opportunity is one that the director or senior executive should reasonably be expected to believe would be of interest to the corporation; or

(2) Any opportunity to engage in a business activity of which a senior executive becomes aware and knows is closely related to a business in which the corporation is engaged or expects to engage.

(c) *Burden of Proof.* A party who challenges the taking of a corporate opportunity has the burden of proof, except that if such party establishes that the requirements of Subsection (a)(3)(B) or (C) are not met, the director or the senior executive has the burden of proving that the rejection and the taking of the opportunity were fair to the corporation.

(d) *Ratification of Defective Disclosure.* A good faith but defective disclosure of the facts concerning the corporate opportunity may be cured if at any time (but no later than a reasonable time after suit is filed challenging the taking of the corporate opportunity) the original rejection of the corporate opportunity is ratified, following the required disclosure, by the board, the shareholders, or the corporate decisionmaker who initially approved the rejection of the corporate opportunity, or such decisionmaker's successor.

(e) *Special Rule Concerning Delayed Offering of Corporate Opportunities.* Relief based solely on failure to first offer an opportunity to the corporation under Subsection (a)(1) is not available if: (1) such failure resulted from a good faith belief that the business activity did not constitute a corporate opportunity, and (2) not later than a reasonable time after suit is filed challenging the taking of the corporate opportunity, the corporate opportunity is to the extent possible offered to the corporation and rejected in a manner that satisfies the standards of Subsection (a).

The central feature of the ALI test is the strict requirement of full disclosure prior to taking advantage of any corporate opportunity. *Id.*, § 5.05(a)(1). "If the opportunity is not offered to the corporation, the director or senior executive will not have satisfied § 5.05(a)." *Id.*, cmt. to § 5.05(a). The corporation must then formally reject the opportunity. *Id.*, § 505(a)(2). The ALI test is discussed at length and ultimately applied by the Oregon Supreme Court in *Klinicki v. Lundgren*, 298 Or. 662, 695 P.2d 906 (1985). As *Klinicki* describes the test, "full disclosure to the appropriate corporate body is ... an absolute condition precedent to the validity of any forthcoming rejection as well as to the availability to the director or principal senior executive of the defense of fairness." *Id.* at 920. A "good faith but defective disclosure" by the corporate officer may be ratified after the fact only by an affirmative vote of the disinterested directors or shareholders. *Principles of Corporate Governance* § 5.05(d).

The ALI test defines "corporate opportunity" broadly. It includes opportunities "closely related to a business in which the corporation is engaged." *Id.*, § 5.05(b). It also encompasses any opportunities that accrue to the fiduciary as a result of her position within the corporation. *Id.* This concept is most clearly illustrated by the testimony of Suminsby, the listing broker for the Gilpin property, which, if believed by the factfinder, would support a finding that the Gilpin property was offered to Harris specifically in her capacity as president of the Club. If the factfinder reached that conclusion, then at least the opportunity to acquire the Gilpin property would be a corporate opportunity. The state of the record concerning the Smallidge purchase precludes us from intimating any opinion whether that too would be a corporate opportunity.

Under the ALI standard, once the Club shows that the opportunity is a corporate opportunity, it must show either that Harris did not offer the opportunity to the Club or that the Club did not reject it properly. If the Club shows that the board did not reject the opportunity by a vote of the disinterested directors after full disclosure, then Harris may defend her actions on the basis that the taking of the opportunity was fair to the corporation. *Id.*, § 5.05(c). If Harris failed to offer the opportunity at all, however, then she may not defend on the basis that the failure to offer the opportunity was fair. *Id.*, cmt. to § 5.05(c).

The *Klinicki* court viewed the ALI test as an opportunity to bring some clarity to a murky area of the law. *Klinicki*, 695 P.2d at 915. We agree, and today we follow the ALI test. The disclosure-oriented approach provides a clear procedure whereby a corporate officer may insulate herself through prompt and complete disclosure from the possibility of a legal challenge. The requirement of disclosure recognizes the paramount importance of the corporate fiduciary's duty of loyalty. At the same time it protects the fiduciary's ability pursuant to the proper procedure to pursue her own business ventures free from the possibility of a lawsuit.

. . . .

IV. *Conclusion*

The question remains how our adoption of the rule affects the result in the instant case. The trial court made a number of factual findings based on an extensive record. The court made those findings, however, in the light of legal principles that are different from the principles that we today announce. Similarly, the parties did not have the opportunity to develop the record in this case with knowledge of the applicable legal standard. In these circumstances, fairness requires that we remand the case for further proceedings. Those further proceedings may include, at the trial court's discretion, the taking of further evidence.

. . . .

Remanded for further proceedings consistent with the opinion herein.

Chapter 12

DUTY OF CONTROLLING SHAREHOLDERS

Situation

a. Welsh's conflict of interest problem has been handled, but it and the possible shareholder suit for mismanagement may have left some ill feelings behind. In any case, some dissension has developed between Anderson and Baker on the one side and the other shareholders on the other. Given increasing corporate profits, Anderson and Baker want to raise their salaries again. At current revenue levels, reasonable salary increases would still leave enough profits to continue the expansion of the business, especially since bank interest rates are currently attractive and further borrowings are contemplated in any case to fuel the expansion.

Phillips and Welsh agree that it makes sense to take some cash out of the business and to borrow from the bank to help finance expansion. But rather than salary increases for Anderson and Baker, they propose instead a dividend distribution to all the shareholders paid pro rata. In that way, they say, all the shareholders can share in the corporation's success.

At a board meeting held a few days ago, Anderson and Baker wanted their salary increase approved and Phillips and Welsh pushed for their alternative suggestion. The deciding vote could have been cast by Martinez, the only disinterested director. Martinez, however, asked that the vote be put off until she could think about what she should do. She told Anderson and Baker that she realized they hold enough stock to replace her as a director if they wish, but said she hoped they would not do so until she had a chance to make her decision. She also suggested that Anderson and Baker seek your advice.

Anderson and Baker agreed to put off the vote and have spoken to you about this situation and have asked your advice. They believe the corporation's successes have come almost entirely from their efforts and that, while Phillips' investment was necessary in the beginning, he has already done very well on his investment. Also, they believe stock was sold too cheaply to Welsh and the other shareholders who purchased when he did, and they are not anxious to share current profits with them. Anderson and Baker do not want to remove Martinez from the board, but are certain she would vote their way when she realized they would remove her if need be.

b. Meanwhile, Biologistics' work has caught the attention of Daytron Corporation, a large publicly-held conglomerate. Representatives of Daytron have discretely and confidentially approached Anderson and Baker about selling their stock in Biologistics. Daytron appears willing to offer a generous premium for their controlling interest. While Daytron is vague about what it would do if it obtained controlling interest, it suggests that a merger between Daytron and Biologistics is an attractive possibility.

Anderson and Baker seek your advice about these various possibilities.

———

While shareholders ordinarily do not assume fiduciary duties, courts in certain circumstances have developed duties owed by controlling shareholders to the corporation and minority shareholders. The materials in this chapter explore these duties in three contexts: in the operation of the corporation, in the sale of control, and in merger transactions.

SECTION I. OPERATION OF CORPORATIONS

SINCLAIR OIL CORP. v. LEVIEN

Supreme Court of Delaware
280 A.2d 717 (1971)

WOLCOTT, CHIEF JUSTICE:

This is an appeal by the defendant, Sinclair Oil Corporation (hereafter Sinclair), from an order of the Court of Chancery, 261 A.2d 911 in a derivative action requiring Sinclair to account for damages sustained by its subsidiary, Sinclair Venezuelan Oil Company (hereafter Sinven), organized by Sinclair for the purpose of operating in Venezuela, as a result of dividends paid by Sinven, the denial to Sinven of industrial development, and a breach of contract between Sinclair's wholly-owned subsidiary, Sinclair International Oil Company, and Sinven.

Sinclair, operating primarily as a holding company, is in the business of exploring for oil and of producing and marketing crude oil and oil products. At all times relevant to this litigation, it owned about 97% of Sinven's stock. The plaintiff owns about 3000 of 120,000 publicly held shares of Sinven. Sinven, incorporated in 1922, has been engaged in petroleum operations primarily in Venezuela and since 1959 has operated exclusively in Venezuela.

Sinclair nominates all members of Sinven's board of directors. The Chancellor found as a fact that the directors were not independent of Sinclair. Almost without exception, they were officers, directors, or employees of corporations in the Sinclair complex. By reason of Sinclair's domination, it is clear that Sinclair owed Sinven a fiduciary duty. Sinclair concedes this.

The Chancellor held that because of Sinclair's fiduciary duty and its control over Sinven, its relationship with Sinven must meet the test of intrinsic fairness. The standard of intrinsic fairness involves both a high degree of fairness and a shift in the burden of proof. Under this standard the burden is on Sinclair to prove, subject to careful judicial scrutiny, that its transactions with Sinven were objectively fair.

Sinclair argues that the transactions between it and Sinven should be tested, not by the test of intrinsic fairness with the accompanying shift of the burden of proof, but by the business judgment rule under which a court will not interfere with the judgment of a board of directors unless there is a showing of gross and palpable overreaching....

We think, however, that Sinclair's argument in this respect is misconceived. When the situation involves a parent and a subsidiary, with the parent controlling the transaction and fixing the terms, the test of intrinsic fairness, with its resulting shifting of the burden of proof, is applied. The basic situation for the application of the rule is the one in which the parent has received a benefit to the exclusion and at the expense of the subsidiary.

Recently, this court dealt with the question of fairness in parent-subsidiary dealings in *Getty Oil Co. v. Skelly Oil Co.*, [267 A.2d 883 (Del. 1970)]. In that case, both parent and subsidiary were in the business of refining and marketing crude oil and crude oil products. The Oil Import Board ruled that the subsidiary, because it was controlled by the parent, was no longer entitled to a separate allocation of imported crude oil. The subsidiary then contended that it had a right to share the quota of crude oil allotted to the parent. We ruled that the business judgment standard should be applied to determine this contention. Although the subsidiary suffered a loss through the administration of the oil import quotas, the parent gained nothing. The parent's quota was derived solely from its own past use. The past use of the subsidiary did not cause an increase in the parent's quota. Nor did the parent usurp a quota of the subsidiary. Since the parent received nothing from the subsidiary to the exclusion of the minority stockholders of the subsidiary, there was no self-dealing. Therefore, the business judgment standard was properly applied.

A parent does indeed owe a fiduciary duty to its subsidiary when there are parent-subsidiary dealings. However, this alone will not evoke the intrinsic fairness standard. This standard will be applied only when the fiduciary duty is accompanied by self-dealing — the situation when a parent is on both sides of a transaction with its subsidiary. Self-dealing occurs when the parent, by virtue of its domination of the subsidiary, causes the subsidiary to act in such a way that the parent receives something from the subsidiary to the exclusion of, and detriment to, the minority stockholders of the subsidiary.

We turn now to the facts. The plaintiff argues that, from 1960 through 1966, Sinclair caused Sinven to pay out such excessive dividends that the industrial development of Sinven was effectively prevented, and it became in reality a corporation in dissolution.

From 1960 through 1966, Sinven paid out $ 108,000,000 in dividends ($ 38,000,000 in excess of Sinven's earnings during the same period). The Chancellor held that Sinclair caused these dividends to be paid during a period when it had a need for large amounts of cash. Although the dividends paid exceeded earnings, the plaintiff concedes that the payments were made in compliance with 8 Del. C. § 170, authorizing payment of dividends out of surplus or net profits. However, the plaintiff attacks these dividends on the ground that they resulted from an improper motive — Sinclair's need for cash. The Chancellor, applying the intrinsic fairness standard, held that Sinclair did not sustain its burden of proving that these dividends were intrinsically fair to the minority stockholders of Sinven.

Since it is admitted that the dividends were paid in strict compliance with 8 Del. C. § 170, the alleged excessiveness of the payments alone would not state a cause of action. Nevertheless, compliance with the applicable statute may not, under all circumstances, justify all dividend payments. If a plaintiff can meet his burden of proving that a dividend cannot be grounded on any reasonable business objective, then the courts can and will interfere with the board's decision to pay the dividend.

Sinclair contends that it is improper to apply the intrinsic fairness standard to dividend payments even when the board which voted for the dividends is completely dominated....

We do not accept the argument that the intrinsic fairness test can never be applied to a dividend declaration by a dominated board, although a dividend declaration by a dominated board will not inevitably demand the application of the intrinsic fairness standard. If such a dividend is in essence self-dealing by the parent, then the intrinsic fairness standard is the proper standard. For example, suppose a parent dominates a subsidiary and its board of directors. The subsidiary has outstanding two classes of stock, X and Y. Class X is owned by the parent and Class Y is owned by minority stockholders of the subsidiary. If the subsidiary, at the direction of the parent, declares a dividend on its Class X stock only, this might well be self-dealing by the parent. It would be receiving something from the subsidiary to the exclusion of and detrimental to its minority stockholders. This self-dealing, coupled with the parent's fiduciary duty, would make intrinsic fairness the proper standard by which to evaluate the dividend payments.

Consequently it must be determined whether the dividend payments by Sinven were, in essence, self-dealing by Sinclair. The dividends resulted in great sums of money being transferred from Sinven to Sinclair. However, a proportionate share of this money was received by the minority shareholders of Sinven. Sinclair received nothing from Sinven to the exclusion of its minority stockholders. As such, these dividends were not self-dealing. We hold therefore that the Chancellor erred in applying the intrinsic fairness test as to these dividend payments. The business judgment standard should have been applied.

We conclude that the facts demonstrate that the dividend payments complied with the business judgment standard and with 8 Del. C. § 170. The motives for causing the declaration of dividends are immaterial unless the plaintiff can show that the dividend payments resulted from improper motives and amounted to waste. The plaintiff contends only that the dividend payments drained Sinven of cash to such an extent that it was prevented from expanding.

The plaintiff proved no business opportunities which came to Sinven independently and which Sinclair either took to itself or denied to Sinven. As a matter of fact, with two minor exceptions which resulted in losses, all of Sinven's operations have been conducted in Venezuela, and Sinclair had a policy of exploiting its oil properties located in different countries by subsidiaries located in the particular countries.

From 1960 to 1966 Sinclair purchased or developed oil fields in Alaska, Canada, Paraguay, and other places around the world. The plaintiff contends that these were all opportunities which could have been taken by Sinven. The Chancellor concluded that Sinclair had not proved that its denial of expansion opportunities to Sinven was intrinsically fair. He based this conclusion on the following findings of fact. Sinclair made no real effort to expand Sinven. The excessive dividends paid by Sinven resulted in so great a cash drain as to effectively deny to Sinven any ability to expand. During this same period Sinclair actively pursued a company-wide policy of developing through its subsidiaries new sources of revenue, but Sinven was not permitted to participate and was confined in its activities to Venezuela.

However, the plaintiff could point to no opportunities which came to Sinven. Therefore, Sinclair usurped no business opportunity belonging to Sinven. Since Sinclair received nothing from Sinven to the exclusion of and detriment to Sinven's minority stockholders, there was no self-dealing. Therefore, business judgment is the proper standard by which to evaluate Sinclair's expansion policies.

Since there is no proof of self-dealing on the part of Sinclair, it follows that the expansion policy of Sinclair and the methods used to achieve the desired result must, as far as Sinclair's treatment of Sinven is concerned, be tested by the standards of the business judgment rule. Accordingly, Sinclair's decision, absent fraud or gross overreaching, to achieve expansion through the medium of its subsidiaries, other than Sinven, must be upheld.

Even if Sinclair was wrong in developing these opportunities as it did, the question arises, with which subsidiaries should these opportunities have been shared? No evidence indicates a unique need or ability of Sinven to develop these opportunities. The decision of which subsidiaries would be used to implement Sinclair's expansion policy was one of business judgment with which a court will not interfere absent a showing of gross and palpable overreaching. No such showing has been made here.

Next, Sinclair argues that the Chancellor committed error when he held it liable to Sinven for breach of contract.

In 1961 Sinclair created Sinclair International Oil Company (hereafter International), a wholly owned subsidiary used for the purpose of coordinating all of Sinclair's foreign operations. All crude purchases by Sinclair were made thereafter through International.

On September 28, 1961, Sinclair caused Sinven to contract with International whereby Sinven agreed to sell all of its crude oil and refined products to

International at specified prices. The contract provided for minimum and maximum quantities and prices. The plaintiff contends that Sinclair caused this contract to be breached in two respects. Although the contract called for payment on receipt, International's payments lagged as much as 30 days after receipt. Also, the contract required International to purchase at least a fixed minimum amount of crude and refined products from Sinven. International did not comply with this requirement.

Clearly, Sinclair's act of contracting with its dominated subsidiary was self-dealing. Under the contract Sinclair received the products produced by Sinven, and of course the minority shareholders of Sinven were not able to share in the receipt of these products. If the contract was breached, then Sinclair received these products to the detriment of Sinven's minority shareholders. We agree with the Chancellor's finding that the contract was breached by Sinclair, both as to the time of payments and the amounts purchased.

Although a parent need not bind itself by a contract with its dominated subsidiary, Sinclair chose to operate in this manner. As Sinclair has received the benefits of this contract, so must it comply with the contractual duties.

Under the intrinsic fairness standard, Sinclair must prove that its causing Sinven not to enforce the contract was intrinsically fair to the minority shareholders of Sinven. Sinclair has failed to meet this burden. Late payments were clearly breaches for which Sinven should have sought and received adequate damages. As to the quantities purchased, Sinclair argues that it purchased all the products produced by Sinven. This, however, does not satisfy the standard of intrinsic fairness. Sinclair has failed to prove that Sinven could not possibly have produced or someway have obtained the contract minimums. As such, Sinclair must account on this claim.

Finally, Sinclair argues that the Chancellor committed error in refusing to allow it a credit or setoff of all benefits provided by it to Sinven with respect to all the alleged damages. The Chancellor held that setoff should be allowed on specific transactions, e.g., benefits to Sinven under the contract with International, but denied an over all setoff against all damages claimed. We agree with the Chancellor, although the point may well be moot in view of our holding that Sinclair is not required to account for the alleged excessiveness of the dividend payments.

We will therefore reverse that part of the Chancellor's order that requires Sinclair to account to Sinven for damages sustained as a result of dividends paid between 1960 and 1966, and by reason of the denial to Sinven of expansion during that period. We will affirm the remaining portion of that order and remand the cause for further proceedings.

––––––––

In what ways do the duties of controlling shareholders differ from those of directors and officers? For example, *Sinclair* indicates that a "fairness" review does not automatically occur in transactions between the corporation and a controlling shareholder.

Also consider ALI § 5.11 Comment *a*:

> A number of cases have prohibited or placed limitations on a controlling shareholder's use of its position, corporate property, or material non-public corporate information for its own benefit. Although some of these cases deal with individuals who are controlling shareholders, many deal with relationships between parents and partly-owned subsidiary corporations. The cases involve such matters as misuse of position to obtain a tax benefit at the expense of a subsidiary, to influence dividend policy, to preclude a subsidiary from engaging in certain business activity, to obtain a profit from the sale of the controlled corporation's property to the exclusion of other shareholders similarly situated, and to preclude competition with the controlling shareholder. Section 5.11 synthesizes the results reached in these cases by setting forth the principle that a controlling shareholder may not, without proper disclosure and approval by disinterested minority shareholders, utilize corporate property, its controlling position, or (when trading in the corporation's securities) material non-public corporate information to secure a pecuniary benefit unless the controlling shareholder sustains the burden of proving that its conduct falls within one of the exceptions to § 5.11(a). The controlling shareholder may show that it has given value for such use, or that any resulting benefit is made proportionally available to the other similarly situated shareholders or is derived only from the use of controlling position and is not unfair to other shareholders.

SECTION II. SALE OF CONTROL

Shares constituting a controlling interest in voting power usually can be sold at a premium because of the added benefits to the buyer that flow from the ability to control the corporation. At the same time, a shareholder in general may sell his or her interest for whatever price may be obtained. Some courts have found, however, that in making such a sale a controlling shareholder has a fiduciary obligation to protect the corporation and the other shareholders.

PERLMAN v. FELDMANN

United States Court of Appeals, Second Circuit
219 F.2d 173 (1955)

CLARK, CHIEF JUDGE:

This is a derivative action brought by minority stockholders of Newport Steel Corporation to compel accounting for, and restitution of, allegedly illegal gains which accrued to defendants as a result of the sale in August, 1950, of their controlling interest in the corporation. The principal defendant, C. Russell

Feldmann, who represented and acted for the others, members of his family,[1] was at that time not only the dominant stockholder, but also the chairman of the board of directors and the president of the corporation. Newport, an Indiana corporation, operated mills for the production of steel sheets for sale to manufacturers of steel products, first at Newport, Kentucky, and later also at other places in Kentucky and Ohio. The buyers, a syndicate organized as Wilport Company, a Delaware corporation, consisted of end-users of steel who were interested in securing a source of supply in a market becoming ever tighter in the Korean War. Plaintiffs contend that the consideration paid for the stock included compensation for the sale of a corporate asset, a power held in trust for the corporation by Feldmann as its fiduciary. This power was the ability to control the allocation of the corporate product in a time of short supply, through control of the board of directors; and it was effectively transferred in this sale by having Feldmann procure the resignation of his own board and the election of Wilport's nominees immediately upon consummation of the sale.

The present action represents the consolidation of three pending stockholders' actions in which yet another stockholder has been permitted to intervene. Jurisdiction below was based upon the diverse citizenship of the parties. Plaintiffs argue here, as they did in the court below, that in the situation here disclosed the vendors must account to the non-participating minority stockholders for that share of their profit which is attributable to the sale of the corporate power. Judge Hincks denied the validity of the premise, holding that the rights involved in the sale were only those normally incident to the possession of a controlling block of shares, with which a dominant stockholder, in the absence of fraud or foreseeable looting, was entitled to deal according to his own best interests. Furthermore, he held that plaintiffs had failed to satisfy their burden of proving that the sales price was not a fair price for the stock *per se*. Plaintiffs appeal from these rulings of law which resulted in the dismissal of their complaint.

The essential facts found by the trial judge are not in dispute. Newport was a relative newcomer in the steel industry with predominantly old installations which were in the process of being supplemented by more modern facilities. Except in times of extreme shortage Newport was not in a position to compete profitably with other steel mills for customers not in its immediate geographical area. Wilport, the purchasing syndicate, consisted of geographically remote end-users of steel who were interested in buying more steel from Newport than they had been able to obtain during recent periods of tight supply. The price of $ 20 per share was found by Judge Hincks to be a fair one for a control block of stock, although the over-the-counter market price had not exceeded $ 12 and the book

---

[1] The stock was not held personally by Feldmann in his own name, but was held by the members of his family and by personal corporations. The aggregate of stock thus had amounted to 33% of the outstanding Newport stock and gave working control to the holder. The actual sale included 55,552 additional shares held by friends and associates of Feldmann, so that a total of 37% of the Newport stock was transferred.

value per share was $ 17.03. But this finding was limited by Judge Hincks' statement that "what value the block would have had if shorn of its appurtenant power to control distribution of the corporate product, the evidence does not show." It was also conditioned by his earlier ruling that the burden was on plaintiffs to prove a lesser value for the stock.

Both as director and as dominant stockholder, Feldmann stood in a fiduciary relationship to the corporation and to the minority stockholders as beneficiaries thereof. Although there is no Indiana case directly in point, the most closely analogous one emphasizes the close scrutiny to which Indiana subjects the conduct of fiduciaries when personal benefit may stand in the way of fulfillment of trust obligations. In *Schemmel v. Hill*, 169 N.E. 678, 682, 683, [(Ind. Ap. Ct. 1930)] MCMAHAN, J., said: "... In a transaction between a director and his corporation, where he acts for himself and his principal at the same time in a matter connected with the relation between them, it is presumed, where he is thus potential on both sides of the contract, that self-interest will overcome his fidelity to his principal, to his own benefit and to his principal's hurt." And the judge added: "Absolute and most scrupulous good faith is the very essence of a director's obligation to his corporation. The first principal duty arising from his official relation is to act in all things of trust wholly for the benefit of his corporation."

In Indiana, then, as elsewhere, the responsibility of the fiduciary is not limited to a proper regard for the tangible balance sheet assets of the corporation, but includes the dedication of his uncorrupted business judgment for the sole benefit of the corporation, in any dealings which may adversely affect it. Although the Indiana case is particularly relevant to Feldmann as a director, the same rule should apply to his fiduciary duties as majority stockholder, for in that capacity he chooses and controls the directors, and thus is held to have assumed their liability. This, therefore, is the standard to which Feldmann was by law required to conform in his activities here under scrutiny.

It is true, as defendants have been at pains to point out, that this is not the ordinary case of breach of fiduciary duty. We have here no fraud, no misuse of confidential information, no outright looting of a helpless corporation. But on the other hand, we do not find compliance with that high standard which we have just stated and which we and other courts have come to expect and demand of corporate fiduciaries. In the often-quoted words of Judge Cardozo: "Many forms of conduct permissible in a workaday world for those acting at arm's length, are forbidden to those bound by fiduciary ties. A trustee is held to something stricter than the morals of the market place. Not honesty alone, but the punctilio of an honor the most sensitive, is then the standard of behavior. As to this there has developed a tradition that is unbending and inveterate. Uncompromising rigidity has been the attitude of courts of equity when petitioned to undermine the rule of undivided loyalty by the 'disintegrating erosion' of particular exceptions." *Meinhard v. Salmon*, 164 N.E. 545, 546. The actions of defendants in siphoning off for personal gain corporate advantages to be derived from a favorable market situation do not betoken the necessary undivided loyalty owed by the fiduciary to his principal.

The corporate opportunities of whose misappropriation the minority stockholders complain need not have been an absolute certainty in order to support this action against Feldmann. If there was possibility of corporate gain, they are entitled to recover. In *Young v. Higbee Co.*, 324 U.S. 204, two stockholders appealing the confirmation of a plan of bankruptcy reorganization were held liable for profits received for the sale of their stock pending determination of the validity of the appeal. They were held accountable for the excess of the price of their stock over its normal price, even though there was no indication that the appeal could have succeeded on substantive grounds. And in *Irving Trust Co. v. Deutsch*, 2d Cir., 73 F.2d 121, 124, an accounting was required of corporate directors who bought stock for themselves for corporate use, even though there was an affirmative showing that the corporation did not have the finances itself to acquire the stock. Judge Swan speaking for the court pointed out that "The defendants' argument, contrary to *Wing v. Dillingham* (5th Cir., 239 F. 54), that the equitable rule that fiduciaries should not be permitted to assume a position in which their individual interests might be in conflict with those of the corporation can have no application where the corporation is unable to undertake the venture, is not convincing. If directors are permitted to justify their conduct on such a theory, there will be a temptation to refrain from exerting their strongest efforts on behalf of the corporation since, if it does not meet the obligations, an opportunity of profit will be open to them personally."

This rationale is equally appropriate to a consideration of the benefits which Newport might have derived from the steel shortage. In the past Newport had used and profited by its market leverage by operation of what the industry had come to call the "Feldmann Plan." This consisted of securing interest-free advances from prospective purchasers of steel in return for firm commitments to them from future production. The funds thus acquired were used to finance improvements in existing plants and to acquire new installations. In the summer of 1950 Newport had been negotiating for cold-rolling facilities which it needed for a more fully integrated operation and a more marketable product, and Feldmann plan funds might well have been used toward this end.

Further, as plaintiffs alternatively suggest, Newport might have used the period of short supply to build up patronage in the geographical area in which it could compete profitably even when steel was more abundant. Either of these opportunities was Newport's, to be used to its advantage only. Only if defendants had been able to negate completely any possibility of gain by Newport could they have prevailed. It is true that a trial court finding states: "Whether or not, in August, 1950, Newport's position was such that it could have entered into 'Feldmann Plan' type transactions to procure funds and financing for the further expansion and integration of its steel facilities and whether such expansion would have been desirable for Newport, the evidence does not show." This, however, cannot avail the defendants, who — contrary to the ruling below — had the burden of proof on this issue, since fiduciaries always have the burden of proof in establishing the fairness of their dealings with trust property....

Defendants seek to categorize the corporate opportunities which might have accrued to Newport as too unethical to warrant further consideration. It is true that reputable steel producers were not participating in the gray market brought about by the Korean War and were refraining from advancing their prices, although to do so would not have been illegal. But Feldmann plan transactions were not considered within this self-imposed interdiction; the trial court found that around the time of the Feldmann sale Jones & Laughlin Steel Corporation, Republic Steel Company, and Pittsburgh Steel Corporation were all participating in such arrangements. In any event, it ill becomes the defendants to disparage as unethical the market advantages from which they themselves reaped rich benefits.

We do not mean to suggest that a majority stockholder cannot dispose of his controlling block of stock to outsiders without having to account to his corporation for profits or even never do this with impunity when the buyer is an interested customer, actual or potential, for the corporation's product. But when the sale necessarily results in a sacrifice of this element of corporate good will and consequent unusual profit to the fiduciary who has caused the sacrifice, he should account for his gains. So in a time of market shortage, where a call on a corporation's product commands an unusually large premium, in one form or another, we think it sound law that a fiduciary may not appropriate to himself the value of this premium. Such personal gain at the expense of his coventurers seems particularly reprehensible when made by the trusted president and director of his company. In this case the violation of duty seems to be all the clearer because of this triple role in which Feldmann appears, though we are unwilling to say, and are not to be understood as saying, that we should accept a lesser obligation for any one of his roles alone.

Hence to the extent that the price received by Feldmann and his codefendants included such a bonus, he is accountable to the minority stockholders who sue here. And plaintiffs, as they contend, are entitled to a recovery in their own right, instead of in right of the corporation (as in the usual derivative actions), since neither Wilport nor their successors in interest should share in any judgment which may be rendered. Defendants cannot well object to this form of recovery, since the only alternative, recovery for the corporation as a whole, would subject them to a greater total liability.

The case will therefore be remanded to the district court for a determination of the question expressly left open below, namely, the value of defendants' stock without the appurtenant control over the corporation's output of steel. We reiterate that on this issue, as on all others relating to a breach of fiduciary duty, the burden of proof must rest on the defendants. Judgment should go to these plaintiffs and those whom they represent for any premium value so shown to the extent of their respective stock interests.

The judgment is therefore reversed and the action remanded for further proceedings pursuant to this opinion.

SWAN, CIRCUIT JUDGE (dissenting):

With the general principles enunciated in the majority opinion as to the duties of fiduciaries I am, of course, in thorough accord. But, as Mr. Justice Frankfurter stated in *Securities and Exchange Comm. v. Chenery Corp.*, 318 U.S. 80, 85, "to say that a man is a fiduciary only begins analysis; it gives direction to further inquiry. To whom is he a fiduciary? What obligations does he owe as a fiduciary? In what respect has he failed to discharge these obligations?" My brothers' opinion does not specify precisely what fiduciary duty Feldmann is held to have violated or whether it was a duty imposed upon him as the dominant stockholder or as a director of Newport. Without such specification I think that both the legal profession and the business world will find the decision confusing and will be unable to foretell the extent of its impact upon customary practices in the sale of stock.

The power to control the management of a corporation, that is, to elect directors to manage its affairs, is an inseparable incident to the ownership of a majority of its stock, or sometimes, as in the present instance, to the ownership of enough shares, less than a majority, to control an election. Concededly a majority or dominant shareholder is ordinarily privileged to sell his stock at the best price obtainable from the purchaser. In so doing he acts on his own behalf, not as an agent of the corporation. If he knows or has reason to believe that the purchaser intends to exercise to the detriment of the corporation the power of management acquired by the purchase, such knowledge or reasonable suspicion will terminate the dominant shareholder's privilege to sell and will create a duty not to transfer the power of management to such purchaser. The duty seems to me to resemble the obligation which everyone is under not to assist another to commit a tort rather than the obligation of a fiduciary. But whatever the nature of the duty, a violation of it will subject the violator to liability for damages sustained by the corporation. Judge Hincks found that Feldmann had no reason to think that Wilport would use the power of management it would acquire by the purchase to injure Newport, and that there was no proof that it ever was so used. Feldmann did know, it is true, that the reason Wilport wanted the stock was to put in a board of directors who would be likely to permit Wilport's members to purchase more of Newport's steel than they might otherwise be able to get. But there is nothing illegal in a dominant shareholder purchasing from his own corporation at the same prices it offers to other customers. That is what the members of Wilport did, and there is no proof that Newport suffered any detriment therefrom.

My brothers say that "the consideration paid for the stock included compensation for the sale of a corporate asset," which they describe as "the ability to control the allocation of the corporate product in a time of short supply, through control of the board of directors; and it was effectively transferred in this sale by having Feldmann procure the resignation of his own board and the election of Wilport's nominees immediately upon consummation of the sale." The implications of this are not clear to me. If it means that when market conditions are such as to induce users of a corporation's product to wish to buy a controlling block of stock in order to be able to purchase part of the corporation's output at the same mill list prices as are offered to other customers, the dominant stockholder is under a fiduciary duty not to sell his stock, I cannot agree. For reasons already stated, in my opinion Feldmann was not proved to be under any fiduciary duty as a stockholder not to sell the stock he controlled.

Feldmann was also a director of Newport. Perhaps the quoted statement means that as a director he violated his fiduciary duty in voting to elect Wilport's nominees to fill the vacancies created by the resignations of the former directors of Newport. As a director Feldmann was under a fiduciary duty to use an honest judgment in acting on the corporation's behalf. A director is privileged to resign, but so long as he remains a director he must be faithful to his fiduciary duties and must not make a personal gain from performing them. Consequently, if the price paid for Feldmann's stock included a payment for voting to elect the new directors, he must account to the corporation for such payment, even though he honestly believed that the men he voted to elect were well qualified to serve as directors. He can not take pay for performing his fiduciary duty. There is no suggestion that he did do so, unless the price paid for his stock was more than its value. So it seems to me that decision must turn on whether finding 120 and conclusion 5 of the district judge are supportable on the evidence. They are set out in the margin.[2]

Judge Hincks went into the matter of valuation of the stock with his customary care and thoroughness. He made no error of law in applying the principles relating to valuation of stock. Concededly a controlling block of stock has greater sale value than a small lot. While the spread between $ 10 per share for small lots and $ 20 per share for the controlling block seems rather extraordinarily wide, the $ 20 valuation was supported by the expert testimony of Dr. Badger, whom the district judge said he could not find to be wrong. I see no justification for upsetting the valuation as clearly erroneous. Nor can I agree with my brothers that the $ 20 valuation "was limited" by the last sentence in finding 120. The controlling block could not by any possibility be shorn of its appurtenant power to elect directors and through them to control distribution of the corporate product. It is this "appurtenant power" which gives a controlling block its value as such block. What evidence could be adduced to show the value of the block "if shorn" of such appurtenant power, I cannot conceive, for it cannot be shorn of it.

---

[2] "120. The 398,927 shares of Newport stock sold to Wilport as of August 31, 1950, had a fair value as a control block of $ 20 per share. What value the block would have had if shorn of its appurtenant power to control distribution of the corporate product, the evidence does not show."

"5. Even if Feldmann's conduct in cooperating to accomplish a transfer of control to Wilport immediately upon the sale constituted a breach of a fiduciary duty to Newport, no part of the moneys received by the defendants in connection with the sale constituted profits for which they were accountable to Newport."

....

The final conclusion of my brothers is that the plaintiffs are entitled to recover in their own right instead of in the right of the corporation. This appears to be completely inconsistent with the theory advanced at the outset of the opinion, namely, that the price of the stock "included compensation for the sale of a corporate asset." If a corporate asset was sold, surely the corporation should recover the compensation received for it by the defendants. Moreover, if the plaintiffs were suing in their own right, Newport was not a proper party....

I would affirm the judgment on appeal.

A. CURRENT TREND

The landmark *Perlman* case helps frame the issues, but the analysis in *Zetlin v. Hanson Holdings, Inc.*,[3] better represents the current legal trend.

> Plaintiff Zetlin owned approximately 2% of the outstanding shares of Gable Industries, Inc., with defendants Hanson Holdings, Inc., and Sylvestri together with members of the Sylvestri family, owning 44.4% of Gable's shares. The defendants sold their interests to Flintkote Co. for a premium price of $15 per share, at a time when Gable was selling on the open market for $7.38 per share. It is undisputed that the 44.4% acquired by Flintkote represented effective control of Gable.
>
> Recognizing that those who invest the capital necessary to acquire a dominant position in the ownership of a corporation have the right of controlling that corporation, it has long been settled law that, absent looting of corporate assets, conversion of a corporate opportunity, fraud or other acts of bad faith, a controlling stockholder is free to sell, and a purchaser is free to buy, that controlling interest at a premium price ....
>
> Certainly, minority shareholders are entitled to protection against such abuse by controlling shareholders. They are not entitled, however, to inhibit the legitimate interests of the other stockholders. It is for this reason that control shares usually command a premium price. The premium is the added amount an investor is willing to pay for the privilege of directly influencing the corporation's affairs.
>
> In this action plaintiff Zetlin contends that minority stockholders are entitled to an opportunity to share equally in any premium paid for a controlling interest in the corporation. This rule would profoundly affect the manner in which controlling stock interests are now transferred. It would require, essentially, that a controlling interest be transferred only by means of an offer to all stockholders, *i.e.*, a tender offer. This would be contrary

---

[3] 397 N.E.2d 387-89 (N.Y. 1979).

to existing law and if so radical a change is to be effected it would best be done by the Legislature.

B. ALI PRINCIPLES

§ 5.16. Disposition of Voting Equity Securities by a Controlling Shareholder to Third Parties*

A controlling shareholder has the same right to dispose of voting equity securities as any other shareholder, including the right to dispose of those securities for a price that is not made proportionally available to other shareholders, but the controlling shareholder does not satisfy the duty of fair dealing to the other shareholders if:

(a) The controlling shareholder does not make disclosure concerning the transaction to other shareholders with whom the controlling shareholder deals in connection with the transaction; or

(b) It is apparent from the circumstances that the purchaser is likely to violate the duty of fair dealing ... in such a way as to obtain a significant financial benefit for the purchaser or an associate.

As ALI § 5.16 Comment *c* explains:

Debate over whether a controlling shareholder should be allowed to sell a controlling interest in a corporation at a premium without sharing that premium with other shareholders largely has focused on the explanation for the premium. If the premium is paid for the opportunity to exploit minority shareholders, the sale should be discouraged by requiring the premium to be shared. If the premium reflects only what otherwise would have been the corporation's share of the efficiency gains that will result from the transfer of control, requiring the premium to be shared will not discourage the transfer of control, because even with a sharing requirement the sale will still make the controlling shareholder better off. If, alternatively, the premium reflects a differential in value between controlling and minority shares that is not the result of exploiting minority shareholders — for example, because control allows a controlling shareholder the opportunity to direct the fortunes of the corporation, rather than rely exclusively on independent management whose interests may diverge from those of shareholders — the argument is that there then is no reason to discourage beneficial transfers of control by a sharing requirement. There is empirical evidence that at least in publicly held corporations, premiums are generally not paid to obtain control of a corporation in order to exploit noncontrolling shareholders.

SECTION III. MERGERS

The following case describes the judicial scrutiny of a cash-out merger between a corporation and its controlling corporate shareholder.

WEINBERGER v. UOP, INC.

Supreme Court of Delaware
457 A.2d 701 (1983)

MOORE, JUSTICE:

This post-trial appeal was reheard *en banc* from a decision of the Court of Chancery. It was brought by the class action plaintiff below, a former shareholder of UOP, Inc., who challenged the elimination of UOP's minority shareholders by a cash-out merger between UOP and its majority owner, The Signal Companies, Inc. Originally, the defendants in this action were Signal, UOP, certain officers and directors of those companies, and UOP's investment banker.... The present Chancellor held that the terms of the merger were fair to the plaintiff and the other minority shareholders of UOP. Accordingly, he entered judgment in favor of the defendants.

Numerous points were raised by the parties, but we address only the following questions presented by the trial court's opinion:

1) The plaintiff's duty to plead sufficient facts demonstrating the unfairness of the challenged merger;

2) The burden of proof upon the parties where the merger has been approved by the purportedly informed vote of a majority of the minority shareholders;

3) The fairness of the merger in terms of adequacy of the defendants' disclosures to the minority shareholders;

4) The fairness of the merger in terms of adequacy of the price paid for the minority shares and the remedy appropriate to that issue...

I

The facts found by the trial court, pertinent to the issues before us, are supported by the record, and we draw from them as set out in the Chancellor's opinion.

Signal is a diversified, technically based company operating through various subsidiaries. Its stock is publicly traded on the New York, Philadelphia and Pacific Stock Exchanges. UOP, formerly known as Universal Oil Products Company, was a diversified industrial company engaged in various lines of business, including petroleum and petro-chemical services and related products, construction, fabricated metal products, transportation equipment products, chemicals and plastics, and other products and services including land development, lumber products and waste disposal. Its stock was publicly held and listed on the New York Stock Exchange.

In 1974 Signal sold one of its wholly-owned subsidiaries for $ 420,000,000 in cash. While looking to invest this cash surplus, Signal became interested in UOP as a possible acquisition. Friendly negotiations ensued, and Signal proposed to acquire a controlling interest in UOP at a price of $ 19 per share. UOP's representatives sought $ 25 per share. In the arm's length bargaining that followed, an understanding was reached whereby Signal agreed to purchase from UOP 1,500,000 shares of UOP's authorized but unissued stock at $ 21 per share.

This purchase was contingent upon Signal making a successful cash tender offer for 4,300,000 publicly held shares of UOP, also at a price of $ 21 per share. This combined method of acquisition permitted Signal to acquire 5,800,000 shares of stock, representing 50.5% of UOP's outstanding shares. The UOP board of directors advised the company's shareholders that it had no objection to Signal's tender offer at that price. Immediately before the announcement of the tender offer, UOP's common stock had been trading on the New York Stock Exchange at a fraction under $ 14 per share.

The negotiations between Signal and UOP occurred during April 1975, and the resulting tender offer was greatly oversubscribed. However, Signal limited its total purchase of the tendered shares so that, when coupled with the stock bought from UOP, it had achieved its goal of becoming a 50.5% shareholder of UOP.

Although UOP's board consisted of thirteen directors, Signal nominated and elected only six. Of these, five were either directors or employees of Signal. The sixth, a partner in the banking firm of Lazard Freres & Co., had been one of Signal's representatives in the negotiations and bargaining with UOP concerning the tender offer and purchase price of the UOP shares.

However, the president and chief executive officer of UOP retired during 1975, and Signal caused him to be replaced by James V. Crawford, a long-time employee and senior executive vice president of one of Signal's wholly-owned subsidiaries. Crawford succeeded his predecessor on UOP's board of directors and also was made a director of Signal.

By the end of 1977 Signal basically was unsuccessful in finding other suitable investment candidates for its excess cash, and by February 1978 considered that it had no other realistic acquisitions available to it on a friendly basis. Once again its attention turned to UOP.

The trial court found that at the instigation of certain Signal management personnel, including William W. Walkup, its board chairman, and Forrest N. Shumway, its president, a feasibility study was made concerning the possible acquisition of the balance of UOP's outstanding shares. This study was performed by two Signal officers, Charles S. Arledge, vice president (director of planning), and Andrew J. Chitiea, senior vice president (chief financial officer). Messrs. Walkup, Shumway, Arledge and Chitiea were all directors of UOP in addition to their membership on the Signal board.

Arledge and Chitiea concluded that it would be a good investment for Signal to acquire the remaining 49.5% of UOP shares at any price up to $ 24 each. Their report was discussed between Walkup and Shumway who, along with

Arledge, Chitiea and Brewster L. Arms, internal counsel for Signal, constituted Signal's senior management. In particular, they talked about the proper price to be paid if the acquisition was pursued, purportedly keeping in mind that as UOP's majority shareholder, Signal owed a fiduciary responsibility to both its own stockholders as well as to UOP's minority. It was ultimately agreed that a meeting of Signal's executive committee would be called to propose that Signal acquire the remaining outstanding stock of UOP through a cash-out merger in the range of $ 20 to $ 21 per share.

The executive committee meeting was set for February 28, 1978. As a courtesy, UOP's president, Crawford, was invited to attend, although he was not a member of Signal's executive committee. On his arrival, and prior to the meeting, Crawford was asked to meet privately with Walkup and Shumway. He was then told of Signal's plan to acquire full ownership of UOP and was asked for his reaction to the proposed price range of $ 20 to $ 21 per share. Crawford said he thought such a price would be "generous," and that it was certainly one which should be submitted to UOP's minority shareholders for their ultimate consideration. He stated, however, that Signal's 100% ownership could cause internal problems at UOP. He believed that employees would have to be given some assurance of their future place in a fully-owned Signal subsidiary. Otherwise, he feared the departure of essential personnel. Also, many of UOP's key employees had stock option incentive programs which would be wiped out by a merger. Crawford therefore urged that some adjustment would have to be made, such as providing a comparable incentive in Signal's shares, if after the merger he was to maintain his quality of personnel and efficiency at UOP.

Thus, Crawford voiced no objection to the $ 20 to $ 21 price range, nor did he suggest that Signal should consider paying more than $ 21 per share for the minority interests. Later, at the executive committee meeting the same factors were discussed, with Crawford repeating the position he earlier took with Walkup and Shumway. Also considered was the 1975 tender offer and the fact that it had been greatly oversubscribed at $ 21 per share. For many reasons, Signal's management concluded that the acquisition of UOP's minority shares provided the solution to a number of its business problems.

Thus, it was the consensus that a price of $ 20 to $ 21 per share would be fair to both Signal and the minority shareholders of UOP. Signal's executive committee authorized its management "to negotiate" with UOP "for a cash acquisition of the minority ownership in UOP, Inc., with the intention of presenting a proposal to [Signal's] board of directors ... on March 6, 1978." Immediately after this February 28, 1978 meeting, Signal issued a press release stating:

> The Signal Companies, Inc. and UOP, Inc. are conducting negotiations for the acquisition for cash by Signal of the 49.5 per cent of UOP which it does not presently own, announced Forrest N. Shumway, president and chief executive officer of Signal, and James V. Crawford, UOP president.

Price and other terms of the proposed transaction have not yet been finalized and would be subject to approval of the boards of directors of Signal and UOP, scheduled to meet early next week, the stockholders of UOP and certain federal agencies.

The announcement also referred to the fact that the closing price of UOP's common stock on that day was $ 14.50 per share.

Two days later, on March 2, 1978, Signal issued a second press release stating that its management would recommend a price in the range of $ 20 to $ 21 per share for UOP's 49.5% minority interest. This announcement referred to Signal's earlier statement that "negotiations" were being conducted for the acquisition of the minority shares.

Between Tuesday, February 28, 1978 and Monday, March 6, 1978, a total of four business days, Crawford spoke by telephone with all of UOP's non-Signal, *i.e.*, outside, directors. Also during that period, Crawford retained Lehman Brothers to render a fairness opinion as to the price offered the minority for its stock. He gave two reasons for this choice. First, the time schedule between the announcement and the board meetings was short (by then only three business days) and since Lehman Brothers had been acting as UOP's investment banker for many years, Crawford felt that it would be in the best position to respond on such brief notice. Second, James W. Glanville, a long-time director of UOP and a partner in Lehman Brothers, had acted as a financial advisor to UOP for many years. Crawford believed that Glanville's familiarity with UOP, as a member of its board, would also be of assistance in enabling Lehman Brothers to render a fairness opinion within the existing time constraints.

Crawford telephoned Glanville, who gave his assurance that Lehman Brothers had no conflicts that would prevent it from accepting the task. Glanville's immediate personal reaction was that a price of $ 20 to $ 21 would certainly be fair, since it represented almost a 50% premium over UOP's market price. Glanville sought a $ 250,000 fee for Lehman Brothers' services, but Crawford thought this too much. After further discussions Glanville finally agreed that Lehman Brothers would render its fairness opinion for $ 150,000.

During this period Crawford also had several telephone contacts with Signal officials. In only one of them, however, was the price of the shares discussed. In a conversation with Walkup, Crawford advised that as a result of his communications with UOP's non-Signal directors, it was his feeling that the price would have to be the top of the proposed range, or $ 21 per share, if the approval of UOP's outside directors was to be obtained. But again, he did not seek any price higher than $ 21.

Glanville assembled a three-man Lehman Brothers team to do the work on the fairness opinion. These persons examined relevant documents and information concerning UOP, including its annual reports and its Securities and Exchange Commission filings from 1973 through 1976, as well as its audited financial statements for 1977, its interim reports to shareholders, and its recent and historical market prices and trading volumes. In addition, on Friday, March 3, 1978, two members of the Lehman Brothers team flew to UOP's headquarters in Des Plaines, Illinois, to perform a "due diligence" visit, during the course of which they interviewed Crawford as well as UOP's general counsel, its chief financial officer, and other key executives and personnel.

As a result, the Lehman Brothers team concluded that "the price of either $ 20 or $ 21 would be a fair price for the remaining shares of UOP." They telephoned this impression to Glanville, who was spending the weekend in Vermont.

On Monday morning, March 6, 1978, Glanville and the senior member of the Lehman Brothers team flew to Des Plaines to attend the scheduled UOP directors meeting. Glanville looked over the assembled information during the flight. The two had with them the draft of a "fairness opinion letter" in which the price had been left blank. Either during or immediately prior to the directors' meeting, the two-page "fairness opinion letter" was typed in final form and the price of $ 21 per share was inserted.

On March 6, 1978, both the Signal and UOP boards were convened to consider the proposed merger. Telephone communications were maintained between the two meetings. Walkup, Signal's board chairman, and also a UOP director, attended UOP's meeting with Crawford in order to present Signal's position and answer any questions that UOP's non-Signal directors might have. Arledge and Chitiea, along with Signal's other designees on UOP's board, participated by conference telephone. All of UOP's outside directors attended the meeting either in person or by conference telephone.

First, Signal's board unanimously adopted a resolution authorizing Signal to propose to UOP a cash merger of $ 21 per share as outlined in a certain merger agreement and other supporting documents. This proposal required that the merger be approved by a majority of UOP's outstanding minority shares voting at the stockholders meeting at which the merger would be considered, and that the minority shares voting in favor of the merger, when coupled with Signal's 50.5% interest would have to comprise at least two-thirds of all UOP shares. Otherwise the proposed merger would be deemed disapproved.

UOP's board then considered the proposal. Copies of the agreement were delivered to the directors in attendance, and other copies had been forwarded earlier to the directors participating by telephone. They also had before them UOP financial data for 1974-1977, UOP's most recent financial statements, market price information, and budget projections for 1978. In addition they had Lehman Brothers' hurriedly prepared fairness opinion letter finding the price of $ 21 to be fair. Glanville, the Lehman Brothers partner, and UOP director, commented on the information that had gone into preparation of the letter.

Signal also suggests that the Arledge-Chitiea feasibility study, indicating that a price of up to $ 24 per share would be a "good investment" for Signal, was discussed at the UOP directors' meeting. The Chancellor made no such finding, and our independent review of the record, detailed *infra*, satisfies us by a preponderance of the evidence that there was no discussion of this document at

UOP's board meeting. Furthermore, it is clear beyond peradventure that nothing in that report was ever disclosed to UOP's minority shareholders prior to their approval of the merger.

After consideration of Signal's proposal, Walkup and Crawford left the meeting to permit a free and uninhibited exchange between UOP's non-Signal directors. Upon their return a resolution to accept Signal's offer was then proposed and adopted. While Signal's men on UOP's board participated in various aspects of the meeting, they abstained from voting. However, the minutes show that each of them "if voting would have voted yes."

On March 7, 1978, UOP sent a letter to its shareholders advising them of the action taken by UOP's board with respect to Signal's offer. This document pointed out, among other things, that on February 28, 1978 "both companies had announced negotiations were being conducted."

Despite the swift board action of the two companies, the merger was not submitted to UOP's shareholders until their annual meeting on May 26, 1978. In the notice of that meeting and proxy statement sent to shareholders in May, UOP's management and board urged that the merger be approved. The proxy statement also advised:

> The price was determined after *discussions* between James V. Crawford, a director of Signal and Chief Executive Officer of UOP, and officers of Signal which took place during meetings on February 28, 1978, and in the course of several subsequent telephone conversations. (Emphasis added.)

In the original draft of the proxy statement the word "negotiations" had been used rather than "discussions." However, when the Securities and Exchange Commission sought details of the "negotiations" as part of its review of these materials, the term was deleted and the word "discussions" was substituted. The proxy statement indicated that the vote of UOP's board in approving the merger had been unanimous. It also advised the shareholders that Lehman Brothers had given its opinion that the merger price of $ 21 per share was fair to UOP's minority. However, it did not disclose the hurried method by which this conclusion was reached.

As of the record date of UOP's annual meeting, there were 11,488,302 shares of UOP common stock outstanding, 5,688,302 of which were owned by the minority. At the meeting only 56%, or 3,208,652, of the minority shares were voted. Of these, 2,953,812, or 51.9% of the total minority, voted for the merger, and 254,840 voted against it. When Signal's stock was added to the minority shares voting in favor, a total of 76.2% of UOP's outstanding shares approved the merger while only 2.2% opposed it.

By its terms the merger became effective on May 26, 1978, and each share of UOP's stock held by the minority was automatically converted into a right to receive $ 21 cash.

II

A

A primary issue mandating reversal is the preparation by two UOP directors, Arledge and Chitiea, of their feasibility study for the exclusive use and benefit of Signal. This document was of obvious significance to both Signal and UOP. Using UOP data, it described the advantages to Signal of ousting the minority at a price range of $ 21 — $ 24 per share. Mr. Arledge, one of the authors, outlined the benefits to Signal:[4]

Purpose Of The Merger

1) Provides an outstanding investment opportunity for Signal — (Better than any recent acquisition we have seen.)

2) Increases Signal's earnings.

3) Facilitates the flow of resources between Signal and its subsidiaries — (Big factor — works both ways.)

4) Provides cost savings potential for Signal and UOP.

5) Improves the percentage of Signal's "operating earnings" as opposed to "holding company earnings."

6) Simplifies the understanding of Signal.

7) Facilitates technological exchange among Signal's subsidiaries.

8) Eliminates potential conflicts of interest.

Having written those words, solely for the use of Signal, it is clear from the record that neither Arledge nor Chitiea shared this report with their fellow directors of UOP. We are satisfied that no one else did either. This conduct hardly meets the fiduciary standards applicable to such a transaction....

. . . .

The Arledge-Chitiea report speaks for itself in supporting the Chancellor's finding that a price of up to $ 24 was a "good investment" for Signal. It shows that a return on the investment at $ 21 would be 15.7% versus 15.5% at $ 24 per share. This was a difference of only two-tenths of one percent, while it meant over $ 17,000,000 to the minority. Under such circumstances, paying UOP's minority shareholders $ 24 would have had relatively little long-term effect on Signal, and the Chancellor's findings concerning the benefit to Signal, even at a price of $ 24, were obviously correct.

Certainly, this was a matter of material significance to UOP and its shareholders. Since the study was prepared by two UOP directors, using UOP information for the exclusive benefit of Signal, and nothing whatever was done to disclose it to the outside UOP directors or the minority shareholders, a question of breach of fiduciary duty arises. This problem occurs because there were common Signal-

---

[4] The parentheses indicate certain handwritten comments of Mr. Arledge.

UOP directors participating, at least to some extent, in the UOP board's decision-making processes without full disclosure of the conflicts they faced.[5]

B

In assessing this situation, the Court of Chancery was required to:

> examine what information defendants had and to measure it against what they gave to the minority stockholders, in a context in which "complete candor" is required. In other words, the limited function of the Court was to determine whether defendants had disclosed all information in their possession germane to the transaction in issue. And by "germane" we mean, for present purposes, information such as a reasonable shareholder would consider important in deciding whether to sell or retain stock.
>
> ....

... Completeness, not adequacy, is both the norm and the mandate under present circumstances. *Lynch v. Vickers Energy Corp.*, Del. Supr., 383 A.2d 278, 281 (1977) (*Lynch I*). This is merely stating in another way the long-existing principle of Delaware law that these Signal designated directors on UOP's board still owed UOP and its shareholders an uncompromising duty of loyalty. The classic language of *Guth v. Loft, Inc.*, Del. Supr., 5 A.2d 503, 510 (1939), requires no embellishment:

> A public policy, existing through the years, and derived from a profound knowledge of human characteristics and motives, has established a rule that demands of a corporate officer or director, peremptorily and inexorably, the most scrupulous observance of his duty, not only affirmatively to protect the interests of the corporation committed to his charge, but also to refrain from doing anything that would work injury to the corporation, or to deprive it of profit or advantage which his skill and ability might properly bring to it, or to enable it to make in the reasonable and lawful exercise of its powers. The rule that requires an undivided and unselfish loyalty to the corporation demands that there shall be no conflict between duty and self-interest.

Given the absence of any attempt to structure this transaction on an arm's-length basis, Signal cannot escape the effects of the conflicts it faced, particularly when its designees on UOP's board did not totally abstain from participation in

---

[5] Although perfection is not possible, or expected, the result here could have been entirely different if UOP had appointed an independent negotiating committee of its outside directors to deal with Signal at arm's length. Since fairness in this context can be equated to conduct by a theoretical, wholly independent, board of directors acting upon the matter before them, it is unfortunate that this course apparently was neither considered nor pursued. Particularly in a parent-subsidiary context, a showing that the action taken was as though each of the contending parties had in fact exerted its bargaining power against the other at arm's length is strong evidence that the transaction meets the test of fairness.

the matter. There is no "safe harbor" for such divided loyalties in Delaware. When directors of a Delaware corporation are on both sides of a transaction, they are required to demonstrate their utmost good faith and the most scrupulous inherent fairness of the bargain. The requirement of fairness is unflinching in its demand that where one stands on both sides of a transaction, he has the burden of establishing its entire fairness, sufficient to pass the test of careful scrutiny by the courts....

There is no dilution of this obligation where one holds dual or multiple directorships, as in a parent-subsidiary context. Thus, individuals who act in a dual capacity as directors of two corporations, one of whom is parent and the other subsidiary, owe the same duty of good management to both corporations, and in the absence of an independent negotiating structure, or the directors' total abstention from any participation in the matter, this duty is to be exercised in light of what is best for both companies. The record demonstrates that Signal has not met this obligation.

C

The concept of fairness has two basic aspects: fair dealing and fair price. The former embraces questions of when the transaction was timed, how it was initiated, structured, negotiated, disclosed to the directors, and how the approvals of the directors and the stockholders were obtained. The latter aspect of fairness relates to the economic and financial considerations of the proposed merger, including all relevant factors: assets, market value, earnings, future prospects, and any other elements that affect the intrinsic or inherent value of a company's stock. However, the test for fairness is not a bifurcated one as between fair dealing and price. All aspects of the issue must be examined as a whole since the question is one of entire fairness. However, in a non-fraudulent transaction we recognize that price may be the preponderant consideration outweighing other features of the merger. Here, we address the two basic aspects of fairness separately because we find reversible error as to both.

D

Part of fair dealing is the obvious duty of candor required by *Lynch I, supra.* Moreover, one possessing superior knowledge may not mislead any stockholder by use of corporate information to which the latter is not privy. Delaware has long imposed this duty even upon persons who are not corporate officers or directors, but who nonetheless are privy to matters of interest or significance to their company. With the well-established Delaware law on the subject, and the Court of Chancery's findings of fact here, it is inevitable that the obvious conflicts posed by Arledge and Chitiea's preparation of their "feasibility study," derived from UOP information, for the sole use and benefit of Signal, cannot pass muster.

The Arledge-Chitiea report is but one aspect of the element of fair dealing. How did this merger evolve? It is clear that it was entirely initiated by Signal.

The serious time constraints under which the principals acted were all set by Signal. It had not found a suitable outlet for its excess cash and considered UOP a desirable investment, particularly since it was now in a position to acquire the whole company for itself. For whatever reasons, and they were only Signal's, the entire transaction was presented to and approved by UOP's board within four business days. Standing alone, this is not necessarily indicative of any lack of fairness by a majority shareholder. It was what occurred, or more properly, what did not occur, during this brief period that makes the time constraints imposed by Signal relevant to the issue of fairness.

The structure of the transaction, again, was Signal's doing. So far as negotiations were concerned, it is clear that they were modest at best. Crawford, Signal's man at UOP, never really talked price with Signal, except to accede to its management's statements on the subject, and to convey to Signal the UOP outside directors' view that as between the $ 20-$ 21 range under consideration, it would have to be $ 21. The latter is not a surprising outcome, but hardly arm's length negotiations. Only the protection of benefits for UOP's key employees and the issue of Lehman Brothers' fee approached any concept of bargaining.

As we have noted, the matter of disclosure to the UOP directors was wholly flawed by the conflicts of interest raised by the Arledge-Chitiea report. All of those conflicts were resolved by Signal in its own favor without divulging any aspect of them to UOP.

This cannot but undermine a conclusion that this merger meets any reasonable test of fairness. The outside UOP directors lacked one material piece of information generated by two of their colleagues, but shared only with Signal. True, the UOP board had the Lehman Brothers' fairness opinion, but that firm has been blamed by the plaintiff for the hurried task it performed, when more properly the responsibility for this lies with Signal. There was no disclosure of the circumstances surrounding the rather cursory preparation of the Lehman Brothers' fairness opinion. Instead, the impression was given UOP's minority that a careful study had been made, when in fact speed was the hallmark, and Mr. Glanville, Lehman's partner in charge of the matter, and also a UOP director, having spent the weekend in Vermont, brought a draft of the "fairness opinion letter" to the UOP directors' meeting on March 6, 1978 with the price left blank. We can only conclude from the record that the rush imposed on Lehman Brothers by Signal's timetable contributed to the difficulties under which this investment banking firm attempted to perform its responsibilities. Yet, none of this was disclosed to UOP's minority.

Finally, the minority stockholders were denied the critical information that Signal considered a price of $ 24 to be a good investment. Since this would have meant over $ 17,000,000 more to the minority, we cannot conclude that the shareholder vote was an informed one. Under the circumstances, an approval by a majority of the minority was meaningless.

Given these particulars and the Delaware law on the subject, the record does not establish that this transaction satisfies any reasonable concept of fair dealing, and the Chancellor's findings in that regard must be reversed.

E

Turning to the matter of price, plaintiff also challenges its fairness. His evidence was that on the date the merger was approved the stock was worth at least $ 26 per share. In support, he offered the testimony of a chartered investment analyst who used two basic approaches to valuation: a comparative analysis of the premium paid over market in ten other tender offer-merger combinations, and a discounted cash flow analysis.

In this breach of fiduciary duty case, the Chancellor perceived that the approach to valuation was the same as that in an appraisal proceeding. Consistent with precedent, he rejected plaintiff's method of proof and accepted defendants' evidence of value as being in accord with practice under prior case law. This means that the so-called "Delaware block" or weighted average method was employed wherein the elements of value, *i.e.*, assets, market price, earnings, etc., were assigned a particular weight and the resulting amounts added to determine the value per share. This procedure has been in use for decades. However, to the extent it excludes other generally accepted techniques used in the financial community and the courts, it is now clearly outmoded. It is time we recognize this in appraisal and other stock valuation proceedings and bring our law current on the subject.

While the Chancellor rejected plaintiff's discounted cash flow method of valuing UOP's stock, as not corresponding with "either logic or the existing law" (426 A.2d at 1360), it is significant that this was essentially the focus, *i.e.*, earnings potential of UOP, of Messrs. Arledge and Chitiea in their evaluation of the merger. Accordingly, the standard "Delaware block" or weighted average method of valuation, formerly employed in appraisal and other stock valuation cases, shall no longer exclusively control such proceedings. We believe that a more liberal approach must include proof of value by any techniques or methods which are generally considered acceptable in the financial community and otherwise admissible in court, subject only to our interpretation of 8 Del. C. § 262(h), *infra*. This will obviate the very structured and mechanistic procedure that has heretofore governed such matters.

Fair price obviously requires consideration of all relevant factors involving the value of a company....

....

Although the Chancellor received the plaintiff's evidence, his opinion indicates that the use of it was precluded because of past Delaware practice. While we do not suggest a monetary result one way or the other, we do think the plaintiff's evidence should be part of the factual mix and weighed as such. Until the $ 21 price is measured on remand by the valuation standards mandated by Delaware law, there can be no finding at the present stage of these proceedings that the price is fair. Given the lack of any candid disclosure of the material facts surrounding establishment of the $ 21 price, the majority of the minority vote, approving the merger, is meaningless.

The plaintiff has not sought an appraisal, but rescissory damages of the type contemplated by *Lynch v. Vickers Energy Corp.*, Del. Supr., 429 A.2d 497, 505-06 (1981) (*Lynch II*). In view of the approach to valuation that we announce today, we see no basis in our law for *Lynch II*'s exclusive monetary formula for relief. On remand the plaintiff will be permitted to test the fairness of the $ 21 price by the standards we herein establish, in conformity with the principle applicable to an appraisal — that fair value be determined by taking "into account all relevant factors" [*see* 8 Del. C. § 262(h), *supra*]. In our view this includes the elements of rescissory damages if the Chancellor considers them susceptible of proof and a remedy appropriate to all the issues of fairness before him. To the extent that *Lynch II*, 429 A.2d at 505-06, purports to limit the Chancellor's discretion to a single remedial formula for monetary damages in a cash-out merger, it is overruled.

While a plaintiff's monetary remedy ordinarily should be confined to the more liberalized appraisal proceeding herein established, we do not intend any limitation on the historic powers of the Chancellor to grant such other relief as the facts of a particular case may dictate. The appraisal remedy we approve may not be adequate in certain cases, particularly where fraud, misrepresentation, self-dealing, deliberate waste of corporate assets, or gross and palpable overreaching are involved. Under such circumstances, the Chancellor's powers are complete to fashion any form of equitable and monetary relief as may be appropriate, including rescissory damages. Since it is apparent that this long completed transaction is too involved to undo, and in view of the Chancellor's discretion, the award, if any, should be in the form of monetary damages based upon entire fairness standards, *i.e.*, fair dealing and fair price.

Obviously, there are other litigants, like the plaintiff, who abjured an appraisal and whose rights to challenge the element of fair value must be preserved. Accordingly, the quasi-appraisal remedy we grant the plaintiff here will apply only to: (1) this case; (2) any case now pending on appeal to this Court; (3) any case now pending in the Court of Chancery which has not yet been appealed but which may be eligible for direct appeal to this Court; (4) any case challenging a cash-out merger, the effective date of which is on or before February 1, 1983; and (5) any proposed merger to be presented at a shareholders' meeting, the notification of which is mailed to the stockholders on or before February 23, 1983. Thereafter, the provisions of 8 Del. C. § 262, as herein construed, respecting the scope of an appraisal and the means for perfecting the same, shall govern the financial remedy available to minority shareholders in a cash-out merger. Thus, we return to the well established principles of *Stauffer v. Standard Brands, Inc.*, Del. Supr., 187 A.2d 78 (1962) and *David J. Greene & Co. v. Schenley Industries, Inc.*, Del. Ch., 281 A.2d 30 (1971), mandating a stockholder's recourse to the basic remedy of an appraisal.

III

. . . .

The judgment of the Court of Chancery, finding both the circumstances of the merger and the price paid the minority shareholders to be fair, is reversed. The matter is remanded for further proceedings consistent herewith. Upon remand the plaintiff's post-trial motion to enlarge the class should be granted.

. . . .

Reversed and Remanded.

While affirming the Weinberger fairness test, the following cases extend the analysis. In these *Lynch* cases,[6] the court considers the effect of an independent negotiating committee of directors. Does it alter the standard of review or the burden of proof? How is the fairness test interpreted in this context?

KAHN v. LYNCH COMMUNICATION SYSTEMS, INC. (LYNCH I)

Supreme Court of Delaware
638 A.2d 1110 (1994)

HOLLAND, JUSTICE:

This is an appeal by the plaintiff-appellant, Alan R. Kahn ("Kahn"), from a final judgment of the Court of Chancery which was entered after a trial. The action, instituted by Kahn in 1986, originally sought to enjoin the acquisition of the defendant-appellee, Lynch Communication Systems, Inc. ("Lynch"), by the defendant-appellee, Alcatel U.S.A. Corporation ("Alcatel"), pursuant to a tender offer and cash-out merger. Kahn [a Lynch shareholder]amended his complaint to seek monetary damages after the Court of Chancery denied his request for a preliminary injunction. The Court of Chancery subsequently certified Kahn's action as a class action on behalf of all Lynch shareholders, other than the named defendants, who tendered their stock in the merger, or whose stock was acquired through the merger.

A three-day trial was held April 13-15, 1993. Kahn alleged that Alcatel was a controlling shareholder of Lynch and breached its fiduciary duties to Lynch and its shareholders. According to Kahn, Alcatel dictated the terms of the merger; made false, misleading, and inadequate disclosures; and paid an unfair price.

The Court of Chancery concluded that Alcatel was, in fact, a controlling shareholder that owed fiduciary duties to Lynch and its shareholders. It also concluded that Alcatel had not breached those fiduciary duties. Accordingly, the Court of Chancery entered judgment in favor of the defendants.

. . . .

----

[6]These are to be distinguished from *Lynch v. Vickers Energy Corp.*, Del. Supr., 383 A.2d 278 (1977) and *Lynch v. Vickers Energy Corp.*, Del. Supr., 429 A.2d 497 (1981), which the *Weinberger* court also labeled as *Lynch* cases. [Eds.]

Facts

Lynch, a Delaware corporation, designed and manufactured electronic telecommunications equipment, primarily for sale to telephone operating companies. Alcatel, a holding company, is a subsidiary of Alcatel (S.A.), a French company involved in public telecommunications, business communications, electronics, and optronics. Alcatel (S.A.), in turn, is a subsidiary of Compagnie Generale d'Electricite ("CGE"), a French corporation with operations in energy, transportation, telecommunications and business systems.

In 1981, Alcatel acquired 30.6 percent of Lynch's common stock pursuant to a stock purchase agreement. As part of that agreement, Lynch amended its certificate of incorporation to require an 80 percent affirmative vote of its shareholders for approval of any business combination. In addition, Alcatel obtained proportional representation on the Lynch board of directors and the right to purchase 40 percent of any equity securities offered by Lynch to third parties. The agreement also precluded Alcatel from holding more than 45 percent of Lynch's stock prior to October 1, 1986. By the time of the merger which is contested in this action, Alcatel owned 43.3 percent of Lynch's outstanding stock; designated five of the eleven members of Lynch's board of directors; two of three members of the executive committee; and two of four members of the compensation committee.

In the spring of 1986, Lynch determined that in order to remain competitive in the rapidly changing telecommunications field, it would need to obtain fiber optics technology to complement its existing digital electronic capabilities. Lynch's management identified a target company, Telco Systems, Inc. ("Telco"), which possessed both fiber optics and other valuable technological assets. The record reflects that Telco expressed interest in being acquired by Lynch. Because of the supermajority voting provision, which Alcatel had negotiated when it first purchased its shares, in order to proceed with the Telco combination Lynch needed Alcatel's consent. In June 1986, Ellsworth F. Dertinger ("Dertinger"), Lynch's CEO and chairman of its board of directors, contacted Pierre Suard ("Suard"), the chairman of Alcatel's parent company, CGE, regarding the acquisition of Telco by Lynch. Suard expressed Alcatel's opposition to Lynch's acquisition of Telco. Instead, Alcatel proposed a combination of Lynch and Celwave Systems, Inc. ("Celwave"), an indirect subsidiary of CGE engaged in the manufacture and sale of telephone wire, cable and other related products.

Alcatel's proposed combination with Celwave was presented to the Lynch board at a regular meeting held on August 1, 1986. Although several directors expressed interest in the original combination which had been proposed with Telco, the Alcatel representatives on Lynch's board made it clear that such a combination would not be considered before a Lynch/Celwave combination. According to the minutes of the August 1 meeting, Dertinger expressed his opinion that Celwave would not be of interest to Lynch if Celwave was not owned by Alcatel.

At the conclusion of the meeting, the Lynch board unanimously adopted a resolution establishing an Independent Committee, consisting of Hubert L. Kertz ("Kertz"), Paul B. Wineman ("Wineman"), and Stuart M. Beringer ("Beringer"), to negotiate with Celwave and to make recommendations concerning the appropriate terms and conditions of a combination with Celwave. On October 24, 1986, Alcatel's investment banking firm, Dillon, Read & Co., Inc. ("Dillon Read") made a presentation to the Independent Committee. Dillon Read expressed its views concerning the benefits of a Celwave/Lynch combination and submitted a written proposal of an exchange ratio of 0.95 shares of Celwave per Lynch share in a stock-for-stock merger.

However, the Independent Committee's investment advisors, Thomson McKinnon Securities Inc. ("Thomson McKinnon") and Kidder, Peabody & Co. Inc. ("Kidder Peabody"), reviewed the Dillon Read proposal and concluded that the 0.95 ratio was predicated on Dillon Read's overvaluation of Celwave. Based upon this advice, the Independent Committee determined that the exchange ratio proposed by Dillon Read was unattractive to Lynch. The Independent Committee expressed its unanimous opposition to the Celwave/Lynch merger on October 31, 1986.

Alcatel responded to the Independent Committee's action on November 4, 1986, by withdrawing the Celwave proposal. Alcatel made a simultaneous offer to acquire the entire equity interest in Lynch, constituting the approximately 57 percent of Lynch shares not owned by Alcatel. The offering price was $ 14 cash per share.

On November 7, 1986, the Lynch board of directors revised the mandate of the Independent Committee. It authorized Kertz, Wineman, and Beringer to negotiate the cash merger offer with Alcatel. At a meeting held that same day, the Independent Committee determined that the $ 14 per share offer was inadequate. The Independent's Committee's own legal counsel, Skadden, Arps, Slate, Meagher & Flom ("Skadden Arps"), suggested that the Independent Committee should review alternatives to a cash-out merger with Alcatel, including a "white knight" third party acquiror, a repurchase of Alcatel's shares, or the adoption of a shareholder rights plan.

On November 12, 1986, Beringer, as chairman of the Independent Committee, contacted Michiel C. McCarty ("McCarty") of Dillon Read, Alcatel's representative in the negotiations, with a counteroffer at a price of $ 17 per share. McCarty responded on behalf of Alcatel with an offer of $ 15 per share. When Beringer informed McCarty of the Independent Committee's view that $ 15 was also insufficient, Alcatel raised its offer to $ 15.25 per share. The Independent Committee also rejected this offer. Alcatel then made its final offer of $ 15.50 per share.

At the November 24, 1986 meeting of the Independent Committee, Beringer advised its other two members that Alcatel was "ready to proceed with an unfriendly tender at a lower price" if the $ 15.50 per share price was not recommended by the Independent Committee and approved by the Lynch board of directors. Beringer also told the other members of the Independent Committee that the alternatives to a cash-out merger had been investigated but were impracticable. After meeting with its financial and legal advisors, the Independent Committee voted unanimously to recommend that the Lynch board of directors approve Alcatel's $ 15.50 cash per share price for a merger with Alcatel. The Lynch board met later that day. With Alcatel's nominees abstaining, it approved the merger.

Alcatel Dominated Lynch
Controlling Shareholder Status

....

Alcatel held a 43.3 percent minority share of stock in Lynch. Therefore, the threshold question to be answered by the Court of Chancery was whether, despite its minority ownership, Alcatel exercised control over Lynch's business affairs. Based upon the testimony and the minutes of the August 1, 1986 Lynch board meeting, the Court of Chancery concluded that Alcatel did exercise control over Lynch's business decisions.

....

At the August 1 meeting, Alcatel opposed the renewal of compensation contracts for Lynch's top five managers. According to Dertinger, Christian Fayard ("Fayard"), an Alcatel director, told the board members, "[y]ou must listen to us. We are 43 percent owner. You have to do what we tell you." The minutes confirm Dertinger's testimony. They recite that Fayard declared, "you are pushing us very much to take control of the company. Our opinion is not taken into consideration."

Although Beringer and Kertz, two of the independent directors, favored renewal of the contracts, according to the minutes, the third independent director, Wineman, admonished the board as follows:

> Mr. Wineman pointed out that the vote on the contracts is a "watershed vote" and the motion, due to Alcatel's "strong feelings," might not carry if taken now. Mr. Wineman clarified that "you [management] might win the battle and lose the war." With Alcatel's opinion so clear, Mr. Wineman questioned "if management wants the contracts renewed under these circumstances." He recommended that management "think twice." Mr. Wineman declared: "I want to keep the management. I can't think of a better management." Mr. Kertz agreed, again advising consideration of the "critical" period the company is entering.

The minutes reflect that the management directors left the room after this statement. The remaining board members then voted not to renew the contracts.

At the same meeting, Alcatel vetoed Lynch's acquisition of the target company, which, according to the minutes, Beringer considered "an immediate fit" for Lynch. Dertinger agreed with Beringer, stating that the "target company is extremely important as they have the products that Lynch needs now."

Nonetheless, Alcatel prevailed. The minutes reflect that Fayard advised the board: "Alcatel, with its 44% equity position, would not approve such an acquisition as ... it does not wish to be diluted from being the main shareholder in Lynch." From the foregoing evidence, the Vice Chancellor concluded:

> ... Alcatel did control the Lynch board, at least with respect to the matters under consideration at its August 1, 1986 board meeting. The interplay between the directors was more than vigorous discussion, as suggested by defendants. The management and independent directors disagreed with Alcatel on several important issues. However, when Alcatel made its position clear, and reminded the other directors of its significant stockholdings, Alcatel prevailed. Dertinger testified that Fayard "scared [the non-Alcatel directors] to death." While this statement undoubtedly is an exaggeration, it does represent a first-hand view of how the board operated. I conclude that the non-Alcatel directors deferred to Alcatel because of its position as a significant stockholder and not because they decided in the exercise of their own business judgment that Alcatel's position was correct.

The record supports the Court of Chancery's underlying factual finding that "the non-Alcatel [independent] directors deferred to Alcatel because of its position as a significant stockholder and not because they decided in the exercise of their own business judgment that Alcatel's position was correct." The record also supports the subsequent factual finding that, notwithstanding its 43.3 percent minority shareholder interest, Alcatel did exercise actual control over Lynch by dominating its corporate affairs. The Court of Chancery's legal conclusion that Alcatel owed the fiduciary duties of a controlling shareholder to the other Lynch shareholders followed syllogistically as the logical result of its cogent analysis of the record.

Entire Fairness Requirement
Dominating Interested Shareholder

A controlling or dominating shareholder standing on both sides of a transaction, as in a parent-subsidiary context, bears the burden of proving its entire fairness. *Weinberger v. UOP, Inc.*, Del. Supr., 457 A.2d 701, 710 (1983). *See Rosenblatt v. Getty Oil Co.*, Del. Supr., 493 A.2d 929, 937 (1985).

The logical question raised by this Court's holding in *Weinberger* was what type of evidence would be reliable to demonstrate entire fairness. That question was not only anticipated but also initially addressed in the *Weinberger* opinion. *Id.* at 709-10 n.7. This Court suggested that the result "could have been entirely different if UOP had appointed an independent negotiating committee of its outside directors to deal with Signal at arm's length," because "fairness in this context can be equated to conduct by a theoretical, wholly independent, board of directors." *Id.* Accordingly, this Court stated, "a showing that the action taken was as though each of the contending parties had in fact exerted its bargaining power against the other at arm's length is strong evidence that the transaction meets the test of fairness." *Id.* (emphasis added).

....

Independent Committees
Interested Merger Transactions

It is a now well-established principle of Delaware corporate law that in an interested merger, the controlling or dominating shareholder proponent of the transaction bears the burden of proving its entire fairness. *Weinberger v. UOP, Inc.*, Del. Supr., 457 A.2d 701, 710-11 (1983). It is equally well-established in such contexts that any shifting of the burden of proof on the issue of entire fairness must be predicated upon this Court's decisions in *Rosenblatt v. Getty Oil Co.*, Del. Supr., 493 A.2d 929 (1985) and *Weinberger v. UOP, Inc.*, Del. Supr., 457 A.2d 701 (1983). In *Weinberger*, this Court noted that "[p]articularly in a parent-subsidiary context, a showing that the action taken was as though each of the contending parties had in fact exerted its bargaining power against the other at arm's length is strong evidence that the transaction meets the test of fairness." 457 A.2d at 709-10 n.7 (emphasis added). *Accord Rosenblatt v. Getty Oil Co.*, 493 A.2d at 937-38 & n.7. In *Rosenblatt*, this Court pointed out that "[an] independent bargaining structure, while not conclusive, is strong evidence of the fairness" of a merger transaction. *Rosenblatt v. Getty Oil Co.*, 493 A.2d at 938 n.7.

The same policy rationale which requires judicial review of interested cash-out mergers exclusively for entire fairness also mandates careful judicial scrutiny of a special committee's real bargaining power before shifting the burden of proof on the issue of entire fairness. A recent decision from the Court of Chancery articulated a two-part test for determining whether burden shifting is appropriate in an interested merger transaction. *Rabkin v. Olin Corp.*, Del. Ch., C.A. No. 7547 (Consolidated), Chandler, V.C., 1990 WL 47648, slip op. at 14-15 (Apr. 17, 1990), reprinted in 16 Del. J. Corp. L. 851, 861-62 (1991), *aff'd*, Del. Supr., 586 A.2d 1202 (1990). In *Olin*, the Court of Chancery stated:

> The mere existence of an independent special committee ... does not itself shift the burden. At least two factors are required. First, the majority shareholder must not dictate the terms of the merger. Second, the special committee must have real bargaining power that it can exercise with the majority shareholder on an arms length basis.

Id., ..., 16 Del. J. Corp. L. at 861-62. This Court expressed its agreement with that statement by affirming the Court of Chancery decision in *Olin* on appeal.

Lynch's Independent Committee

In the case *sub judice*, the Court of Chancery observed that although "Alcatel did exercise control over Lynch with respect to the decisions made at the August 1, 1986 board meeting, it does not necessarily follow that Alcatel also controlled the terms of the merger and its approval." This observation is theoretically accurate, as this opinion has already stated. *Weinberger v. UOP, Inc.*, 457 A.2d at 709-10 n.7. However, the performance of the Independent Committee merits careful judicial scrutiny to determine whether Alcatel's demonstrated pattern of domination was effectively neutralized so that "each of the contending parties had in fact exerted its bargaining power against the other at arm's length." *Id.* The fact that the same independent directors had submitted to Alcatel's demands on August 1, 1986 was part of the basis for the Court of Chancery's finding of Alcatel's domination of Lynch. Therefore, the Independent Committee's ability to bargain at arm's length with Alcatel was suspect from the outset.

The Independent Committee's original assignment was to examine the merger with Celwave which had been proposed by Alcatel. The record reflects that the Independent Committee effectively discharged that assignment and, in fact, recommended that the Lynch board reject the merger on Alcatel's terms. Alcatel's response to the Independent Committee's adverse recommendation was not the pursuit of further negotiations regarding its Celwave proposal, but rather its response was an offer to buy Lynch. That offer was consistent with Alcatel's August 1, 1986 expressions of an intention to dominate Lynch, since an acquisition would effectively eliminate once and for all Lynch's remaining vestiges of independence.

The Independent Committee's second assignment was to consider Alcatel's proposal to purchase Lynch. The Independent Committee proceeded on that task with full knowledge of Alcatel's demonstrated pattern of domination. The Independent Committee was also obviously aware of Alcatel's refusal to negotiate with it on the Celwave matter.

Burden of Proof Shifted
Court of Chancery's Finding

The Court of Chancery began its factual analysis by noting that Kahn had "attempted to shatter" the image of the Independent Committee's actions as having "appropriately simulated" an arm's length, third-party transaction. The Court of Chancery found that "to some extent, [Kahn's attempt] was successful." The Court of Chancery gave credence to the testimony of Kertz, one of the members of the Independent Committee, to the effect that he did not believe that $ 15.50 was a fair price but that he voted in favor of the merger because he felt there was no alternative.

The Court of Chancery also found that Kertz understood Alcatel's position to be that it was ready to proceed with an unfriendly tender offer at a lower price if Lynch did not accept the $ 15.50 offer, and that Kertz perceived this to be a threat by Alcatel. The Court of Chancery concluded that Kertz ultimately decided that, "although $ 15.50 was not fair, a tender offer and merger at that price would be better for Lynch's stockholders than an unfriendly tender offer at a significantly lower price." The Court of Chancery determined that "Kertz failed either to satisfy himself that the offered price was fair or oppose the merger."

In addition to Kertz, the other members of the Independent Committee were Beringer, its chairman, and Wineman. Wineman did not testify at trial. Beringer was called by Alcatel to testify at trial. Beringer testified that at the time of the Committee's vote to recommend the $ 15.50 offer to the Lynch board, he thought "that under the circumstances, a price of $ 15.50 was fair and should be accepted" (emphasis added).

Kahn contends that these "circumstances" included those referenced in the minutes for the November 24, 1986 Independent Committee meeting: "Mr. Beringer added that Alcatel is 'ready to proceed with an unfriendly tender at a lower price' if the $ 15.50 per share price is not recommended to, and approved by, the Company's Board of Directors." In his testimony at trial, Beringer verified, albeit reluctantly, the accuracy of the foregoing statement in the minutes: "[Alcatel] let us know that they were giving serious consideration to making an unfriendly tender" (emphasis added).

The record reflects that Alcatel was "ready to proceed" with a hostile bid. This was a conclusion reached by Beringer, the Independent Committee's chairman and spokesman, based upon communications to him from Alcatel. Beringer testified that although there was no reference to a particular price for a hostile bid during his discussions with Alcatel, or even specific mention of a "lower" price, "the implication was clear to [him] that it probably would be at a lower price."

According to the Court of Chancery, the Independent Committee rejected three lower offers for Lynch from Alcatel and then accepted the $ 15.50 offer "after being advised that [it] was fair and after considering the absence of alternatives." The Vice Chancellor expressly acknowledged the impracticability of Lynch's Independent Committee's alternatives to a merger with Alcatel:

> Lynch was not in a position to shop for other acquirors, since Alcatel could block any alternative transaction. Alcatel also made it clear that it was not interested in having its shares repurchased by Lynch. The Independent Committee decided that a stockholder rights plan was not viable because of the increased debt it would entail.

Nevertheless, based upon the record before it, the Court of Chancery found that the Independent Committee had "appropriately simulated a third-party transaction, where negotiations are conducted at arms-length and there is no compulsion to reach an agreement." The Court of Chancery concluded that the Independent Committee's actions "as a whole" were "sufficiently well informed … and aggressive to simulate an arms-length transaction," so that the burden of proof as to entire fairness shifted from Alcatel to the contending Lynch shareholder, Kahn. The Court of Chancery's reservations about that finding are apparent in its written decision.

The Power to Say No,
The Parties' Contentions,
Arm's Length Bargaining

The Court of Chancery properly noted that limitations on the alternatives to Alcatel's offer did not mean that the Independent Committee should have agreed to a price that was unfair:

> The power to say no is a significant power. It is the duty of directors serving on [an independent] committee to approve only a transaction that is in the best interests of the public shareholders, to say no to any transaction that is not fair to those shareholders and is not the best transaction available. It is not sufficient for such directors to achieve the best price that a fiduciary will pay if that price is not a fair price.

(*Quoting In re First Boston, Inc. Shareholders Litig.*, Del. Ch., C.A. 10338 (Consolidated), Allen, C., 1990 WL 78836, slip op. at 15-16 (June 7, 1990)).

The Alcatel defendants argue that the Independent Committee exercised its "power to say no" in rejecting the three initial offers from Alcatel, and that it therefore cannot be said that Alcatel dictated the terms of the merger or precluded the Independent Committee from exercising real bargaining power. The Alcatel defendants contend, alternatively, that "even assuming that such a threat [of a hostile takeover] could have had a coercive effect on the [Independent] Committee," the willingness of the Independent Committee to reject Alcatel's initial three offers suggests that "the alleged threat was either nonexistent or ineffective." *Braunschweiger v. American Home Shield Corp.*, Del. Ch., C.A. No. 10755, Allen, C., 1991 WL 3920, slip op. at 13 (Jan. 7, 1991), reprinted in 17 Del. J. Corp. L. 206, 219 (1992).

Kahn contends the record reflects that the conduct of Alcatel deprived the Independent Committee of an effective "power to say no." Kahn argues that Alcatel not only threatened the Committee with a hostile tender offer in the event its $ 15.50 offer was not recommended and approved, but also directed the affairs of Lynch for Alcatel's benefit in such a way as to make it impossible for Lynch to continue as a public company under Alcatel's control without injury to itself and its minority shareholders. In support of this argument, Kahn relies upon another proceeding wherein the Court of Chancery has been previously presented with factual circumstances comparable to those of the case *sub judice*, albeit in a different procedural posture. *See American Gen. Corp. v. Texas Air Corp.*, Del. Ch., C.A. Nos. 8390, 8406, 8650 & 8805, Hartnett, V.C., 1987 WL 6337 (Feb. 5, 1987), reprinted in 13 Del. J. Corp. L. 173 (1988).

In *American General*, in the context of an application for injunctive relief, the Court of Chancery found that the members of the Special Committee were "truly independent and ... performed their tasks in a proper manner," but it also found that "at the end of their negotiations with [the majority shareholder] the Committee members were issued an ultimatum and told that they must accept the

$ 16.50 per share price or [the majority shareholder] would proceed with the transaction without their input." *Id.*, slip op. at 11-12, 13 Del. J. Corp. L. at 181. The Court of Chancery concluded based upon this evidence that the Special Committee had thereby lost "its ability to negotiate in an arms-length manner" and that there was a reasonable probability that the burden of proving entire fairness would remain on the defendants if the litigation proceeded to trial. *Id.*, slip op. at 12, 13 Del. J. Corp. L. at 181.

Alcatel's efforts to distinguish *American General* are unpersuasive. Alcatel's reliance on *Braunschweiger* is also misplaced. In *Braunschweiger*, the Court of Chancery pointed out that "[p]laintiffs do not allege that [the management-affiliated merger partner] ever used the threat of a hostile takeover to influence the special committee." *Braunschweiger v. American Home Shield Corp.*, slip op. at 13, 17 Del. J. Corp. L. at 219. Unlike *Braunschweiger*, in this case the coercion was extant and directed to a specific price offer which was, in effect, presented in the form of a "take it or leave it" ultimatum by a controlling shareholder with the capability of following through on its threat of a hostile takeover.

Alcatel's Entire Fairness Burden Did Not Shift to Kahn

A condition precedent to finding that the burden of proving entire fairness has shifted in an interested merger transaction is a careful judicial analysis of the factual circumstances of each case. Particular consideration must be given to evidence of whether the special committee was truly independent, fully informed, and had the freedom to negotiate at arm's length.... "Although perfection is not possible," unless the controlling or dominating shareholder can demonstrate that it has not only formed an independent committee but also replicated a process "as though each of the contending parties had in fact exerted its bargaining power at arm's length," the burden of proving entire fairness will not shift. *Weinberger v. UOP, Inc.*, 457 A.2d at 709-10 n.7. *See* also *Rosenblatt v. Getty Oil Co.*, Del. Supr., 493 A.2d 929, 937-38 (1985).

Subsequent to *Rosenblatt*, this Court pointed out that "the use of an independent negotiating committee of outside directors may have significant advantages to the majority stockholder in defending suits of this type," but it does not *ipso facto* establish the procedural fairness of an interested merger transaction. *Rabkin v. Philip A. Hunt Chem. Corp.*, Del. Supr., 498 A.2d 1099, 1106 & n.7 (1985). In reversing the granting of the defendants' motion to dismiss in *Rabkin*, this Court implied that the burden on entire fairness would not be shifted by the use of an independent committee which concluded its processes with "what could be considered a quick surrender" to the dictated terms of the controlling shareholder. *Id.* at 1106. This Court concluded in *Rabkin* that the majority stockholder's "attitude toward the minority," coupled with the "apparent absence of any meaningful negotiations as to price," did not manifest the exercise of arm's length bargaining by the independent committee. *Id.*

The Court of Chancery's determination that the Independent Committee "appropriately simulated a third-party transaction, where negotiations are conducted at arm's-length and there is no compulsion to reach an agreement," is not supported by the record. Under the circumstances present in the case *sub judice*, the Court of Chancery erred in shifting the burden of proof with regard to entire fairness to the contesting Lynch shareholder-plaintiff, Kahn. The record reflects that the ability of the Committee effectively to negotiate at arm's length was compromised by Alcatel's threats to proceed with a hostile tender offer if the $ 15.50 price was not approved by the Committee and the Lynch board. The fact that the Independent Committee rejected three initial offers, which were well below the Independent Committee's estimated valuation for Lynch and were not combined with an explicit threat that Alcatel was "ready to proceed" with a hostile bid, cannot alter the conclusion that any semblance of arm's length bargaining ended when the Independent Committee surrendered to the ultimatum that accompanied Alcatel's final offer. *See Rabkin v. Philip A. Hunt Chem. Corp.*, Del. Supr., 498 A.2d 1099, 1106 (1985).

Conclusion

Accordingly, the judgment of the Court of Chancery is reversed. This matter is remanded for further proceedings consistent herewith, including a redetermination of the entire fairness of the cash-out merger to Kahn and the other Lynch minority shareholders with the burden of proof remaining on Alcatel, the dominant and interested shareholder.

KAHN v. LYNCH COMMUNICATION SYSTEMS, INC. (LYNCH II)

Supreme Court of Delaware
669 A.2d 79 (1995)

WALSH, JUSTICE:

This is the second appeal in this shareholder litigation after a Court of Chancery ruling in favor of the defendants. The underlying dispute arises from a cash-out merger of Lynch Communications System, Inc. ("Lynch") into a subsidiary of Alcatel USA, Inc. ("Alcatel"). In the previous appeal, this Court determined that Alcatel, as a controlling shareholder of Lynch, dominated the merger negotiations despite the fact that Lynch's board of directors has appointed an independent negotiating committee. *Kahn v. Lynch Communication Systems, Inc.*, Del. Supr., 638 A.2d 1110, 1112-13 (1994) ("*Lynch I*"). We concluded, however, that such a determination did not necessarily preclude a finding that the transaction was entirely fair and remanded the matter to the Court of Chancery for a determination of entire fairness, with the burden of proof upon the defendants.

Upon remand, the Court of Chancery reevaluated the record under the appropriate burden of proof and concluded that the transaction was entirely fair to the Lynch minority shareholders. The court also rejected plaintiff's claim that the defendants violated their duty of disclosure in failing to describe specifically the threat of a lower priced tender offer. We affirm in both respects.

I

The facts underlying the derivative claims are set forth extensively in *Lynch I*....

II

....

B

This Court will now review the Court of Chancery's entire fairness analysis upon remand. *Accord Cinerama, Inc. v. Technicolor, Inc.*, Del. Supr., 663 A.2d at 1172. The record reflects that the Court of Chancery followed this Court's mandate by applying a unified approach to its entire fairness examination. *Lynch I*, 638 A.2d at 1115. In doing so, the Court of Chancery properly considered "how the board of directors discharged all of its fiduciary duties with regard to each aspect of the non-bifurcated components of entire fairness: fair dealing and fair price." *Cinerama, Inc. v. Technicolor, Inc.*, Del. Supr., 663 A.2d at 1172.

In addressing the fair dealing component of the transaction, the Court of Chancery determined that the initiation and timing of the transactions were responsive to Lynch's needs. This conclusion was based on the fact that Lynch's marketing strategy was handicapped by the lack of a fiber optic technology. Alcatel proposed the merger with Celwave to remedy this competitive weakness but Lynch management and the non-Alcatel directors did not believe this combination would be beneficial to Lynch. Dertinger, Lynch's CEO, suggested to Alcatel that, under the circumstances, a cash merger with Alcatel will be preferable to a Celwave merger. Thus, the Alcatel offer to acquire the minority interests in Lynch was viewed as an alternative to the disfavored Celwave transaction.

Kahn argues that the Telco acquisition, which Lynch management strongly supported, was vetoed by Alcatel to force Lynch to accept Celwave as a merger partner or agree to a cash out merger with Alcatel. The benefits of the Telco transaction, however, are clearly debatable. Telco was not profitable and had a limited fiber optic capability. There is no assurance that Lynch's shareholders would have benefitted from the acquisition. More to the point, the timing of a merger transaction cannot be viewed solely from the perspective of the acquired entity. A majority shareholder is naturally motivated by economic self-interest in initiating a transaction. Otherwise, there is no reason to do it. Thus, mere initiation by the acquirer is not reprehensible so long as the controlling shareholder does not gain a financial advantage at the expense of the minority....

In support of its claim of coercion, Kahn contends that Alcatel timed its merger offer, with a thinly-veiled threat of using its controlling position to force the result, to take advantage of the opportunity to buy Lynch on the cheap. As will be discussed at greater length in our fair price analysis, *infra*, Lynch was experiencing a difficult and rapidly changing competitive situation. Its current financial results reflected that fact. Although its stock was trading at low levels, this may simply have been a reflection of its competitive problems. Alcatel is not to be faulted for taking advantage of the objective reality of Lynch's financial situation. Thus the mere fact that the transaction was initiated at Alcatel's discretion, does not dictate a finding of unfairness in the absence of a determination that the minority shareholders of Lynch were harmed by the timing. The Court of Chancery rejected such a claim and we agree.

C

With respect to the negotiations and structure of the transaction, the Court of Chancery, while acknowledging that the Court in *Lynch I* found the negotiations coercive, commented that the negotiations "certainly were no less fair than if there had been no negotiations at all." The court noted that a committee of non-Alcatel directors negotiated an increase in price from $ 14 per share to $ 15.50. The committee also retained two investment banking firms who were well acquainted with Lynch's prospects based on their work on the Celwave proposal. Moreover, the committee had the benefit of outside legal counsel.

It is true that the committee and the Board agreed to a price which at least one member of the committee later opined was not a fair price. But there is no requirement of unanimity in such matters either at the Independent Committee level or by the Board. A finding of unfair dealing based on lack of unanimity could discourage the use of special committees in majority dominated cash-out mergers. Here Alcatel could have presented a merger offer directly to the Lynch Board, which it controlled, and received a quick approval. Had it done so, of course, it would have born the burden of demonstrating entire fairness in the event the transaction was later questioned. Where, ultimately, it has been required to assume the same burden, it should fare no worse in a judicial review of the fairness of its negotiations with the Independent Committee.

Kahn asserts that the Court of Chancery did not properly consider our finding of coercion in *Lynch I*. Generally, as in this case, the burden rests on the party that engaged in coercive conduct to demonstrate the equity of their actions. Kahn challenges the Court of Chancery's finding of fair dealing by relying upon the holding in *Ivanhoe Partners v. Newmont Min. Corp.*, Del. Ch., 533 A.2d 585, 605-06 (1987), *aff'd*, Del. Supr., 535 A.2d 1334 (1988), for the proposition that coercion creates liability *per se*. *Ivanhoe* makes clear, however, that to be actionable, the coercive conduct directed at selling shareholders must be a "material" influence on the decision to sell.

Where other economic forces are at work and more likely produced the decision to sell, as the Court of Chancery determined here, the specter of coercion may not be deemed material with respect to the transaction as a whole, and will not prevent a finding of entire fairness. In this case, no shareholder was treated differently in the transaction from any other shareholder nor subjected to a two-tiered or squeeze-out treatment. Alcatel offered cash for all the minority shares and paid cash for all shares tendered. Clearly there was no coercion exerted which was material to this aspect of the transaction, and thus no finding of *per se* liability is required.

....

IV

In summary, after reassessing the trial record under an entire fairness standard, with the burden of proof upon Alcatel, the Court of Chancery determined that, as a result of the manner by which the board discharged its fiduciary duties, the timing and structure of negotiations and the disclosure to shareholders of such event were the product of fair dealing. Similarly, the trial court concluded that the merger price was fair. Thus the non-bifurcated standard of Weinberger was satisfied. Under our standard of review, we defer to the trial court's evidentiary findings if supported by the record and logically determined....

... We find no error in the trial court's application of legal standards and accordingly affirm.

Chapter 13

CHANGES IN CONTROL: CORPORATE COMBINATIONS AND TENDER OFFER DEFENSES

Situation

a. Daytron Corporation, a large publicly-held conglomerate, has become increasingly serious about acquiring Biologistics. Daytron's Chair of the Board and Chief Executive Officer, Lauren Lipinsky, has tracked Biologistics' success and believes that Baker's DNA research will yield very commercially valuable results sometime in the next few years. Daytron approaches Biologistic's director about a possible corporate combination. Daytron indicates a willingness to pay Baker and Anderson generous salaries but wants total ownership of Biologistics. Anderson's and Baker's initial reaction is to reject Daytron's overture; they are not ready to cash out their investment. Phillips and the other directors, however, are eager to negotiate further.

The directors ask you to identify the preliminary issues.

b. Anticipating that Biologistics' directors will reject its overture, Daytron's directors are considering their options. One possibility is for Daytron to acquire control of Biologistics by purchasing individual shareholders' stock directly.

Biologistics' directors ask you how they can defend the corporation against this unwanted "tender offer."

SECTION I. INTRODUCTION

This chapter explores two types of corporate acquisitions. In the first, corporate management decides to have the corporation merge into, consolidate with, or sell its assets to another corporation. In these corporate combinations, the acquiring corporation negotiates directly with the target corporation.

In the second type of acquisition, a tender offer, the acquiring corporation purchases directly from the shareholders of the target corporation a controlling interest in the company's stock. Chapter 18 explores what tender offers are, and the applicable federal and state regulations. This chapter discusses the fiduciary duties of directors and officers of target corporations who oppose a tender offer.

Both types of acquisitions typically involve a proposed change in who controls the target corporation. As described in the ALI Part VI Introductory Note, p. 385, these transactions pose unique issues regarding directors and officers conduct:

> First, a transaction in control or tender offer is typically the most complex business transaction in which a corporation will engage. Shareholders thus

have a need for management's expertise to be employed on their behalf in the evaluation and negotiation of transactions in control. When this face is presented, such transactions may resemble the business decisions that are protected under the business judgment rule ....

Second, a transaction in control or tender offer represents a potential conflict of interest for officers who are also directors. If they approve a proposed transaction, the approval may have been influenced by benefits formally or informally promised to be given to them after the transaction is consummated. If they reject a proposed transaction, the rejection may reflect their preference for retaining their positions. Furthermore, even non-officer directors are put in the difficult position of having to evaluate their past and future stewardship of the corporation. When this face is presented, a transaction in control or tender offer may tend to resemble an interested transaction, review of which is controlled by ... [a] more rigorous fairness standard.

Finally, transactions in control and tender offers are mechanisms through which market review of the effectiveness of management's delegated discretion can operate. Under this analysis, if management has not performed effectively, that failure will likely be reflected in the price of the corporation's securities. By purchasing those securities through such a transaction, an acquiror may displace existing management and, in effect, bet its investment on its ability to enhance shareholder value — for example, through improvement of the corporation's economic performance or creation of synergistic benefits through combining the corporation's business with the acquiror's business, or through achievement of a profit through sale of portions of the corporation's business. The existence of this market test is one of the justifications for the breadth of protection accorded the exercise of management discretion under the business judgment rule, in that there is reduced need for judicial review when effective market mechanisms are operative.

SECTION II. NEGOTIATED CHANGES IN CONTROL

A. CORPORATE COMBINATIONS

1. Acquisition Forms

The following excerpt describes the major forms of negotiated acquisitions and some of their non-tax advantages and disadvantages. In addition to the issues discussed, there are securities law implications as well.

2 Commerce Clearing House, Business Strategies, ¶ 1235 (1995)*

Purchase of Assets

From the expanding business's point of view, the purchase of a target's assets is the "cleanest" way to acquire the target. The buyer simply negotiates for those assets that it wants and can limit the liabilities that it undertakes to those specifically enumerated in the contract. Furthermore, the buyer does not inherit any of the attributes or many of the problems of the target. Theoretically, the buyer and seller could negotiate the purchase and sale of each asset separately, in which case the transaction would be nothing more than the purchase of items of plant and equipment. However, when substantially all the assets of a business are sought the purchase usually is negotiated as a package deal for a lump sum. Another reason for the lump-sum price is that the buyer is getting more than merely a number of separate assets when substantially all the assets of a going business are acquired. That the assets are assembled in an on-going business itself has value. This intangible value usually is denominated goodwill or going concern value....

Purchase of Stock

While the purchase of assets is a relatively clean transaction for the buyer, the seller's shareholders are left with the unwanted assets and the problem of what to do with the corporation and its remaining assets. A target's shareholders, therefore, may prefer a sale of their stock, rather than the sale of corporate assets. A purchase of target stock is usually, but not always, a much simpler transaction to carry out. The buyer negotiates with the target shareholders for the sale of their stock, and they are free to sell or not to sell independently of one another. A shareholder vote by the target shareholders is not required, and there is no right of appraisal. The target then becomes a subsidiary of the acquiring corporation. Of course, the more shareholders there are, the more difficult the process; and, if not all target shareholders are willing to sell, the buyer may be left with the problem of dealing with minority interests.

The purchase of stock means that the target and all of its tax, accounting, financial and legal attributes remain intact in the acquired corporate-entity. Sometimes, this is exactly what is desired by the buyer. For instance, the buyer may continue to use the target's corporate name; and agreements, contracts, etc., all remain undisturbed. If the target is unionized, the buyer is spared new labor negotiations as a result of the acquisition (but inherits the target's labor problems). On the other side of the coin, however, all the target liabilities and unwanted or unusable assets also remain in the acquired corporation, and the buyer now faces the problems of what to do with these items....

Stock for Assets

The acquiring company may want to use its own stock to acquire the assets of the target corporation. This reduces the need for cash or the creation of additional liabilities because of the acquisition. Offsetting this consideration, however, is the dilution of the equity interest of the acquiring corporation's shareholders by the issuance of additional stock, unless they have and can exercise preemptive rights to purchase additional shares. The target and its shareholders usually will accept, in fact may even want, stock when the acquiring company is a publicly traded company and, if their potential tax liability is great, the deal can be structured as a tax-free transaction. Targets and their shareholders usually do not want stock in another closely held company, especially if it would be a minority interest....

The acquiring corporation may want the acquired assets and assumed liabilities to remain outside its existing corporate structure. This can easily be accomplished through the use of a newly formed subsidiary to acquire target assets. The subsidiary may use its own voting stock or that of the parent, although the target usually will want the parent's stock if the parent corporation is a publicly traded company. Also, the acquiring corporation may not want a large block of minority stock in its subsidiary outstanding....

Stock for Stock

Just as an acquiring corporation can use its own stock to acquire assets of a target; so too, for the same reasons and with the same disadvantages, can it use its own stock to acquire the stock of a target corporation. The acquiring corporation can use a mix of stock, cash and other property to purchase the stock held by the target's shareholders, depending on what is agreeable to the parties. When mixed consideration (acquiring company stock and other property) is used, the transaction, in fact, is treated as a purchase of stock for tax and accounting purposes....

Merger

A merger is an acquisition carried out in conformity with a state's corporation law. In a merger, the target corporation is absorbed by the acquiring corporation and ceases to exist. Shareholders of the target are either bought out or become shareholders in the acquiring corporation. The major drawback to a merger as an acquisition method is the necessity to conform the transaction to state law, which usually requires approval by the shareholders of both the acquiring corporation and the target corporation. When obtaining the approval of the requisite number of shareholders in the acquiring corporation is a problem, it sometimes can be skirted with a triangular or subsidiary merger .... Another potential drawback is that the acquiring corporation becomes responsible for the target's liabilities.

The major advantage of a statutory merger is that it can qualify as a tax-free acquisition. What's more, it can so qualify even if substantial amounts of consideration other than voting stock of the acquiring corporation are used to effect the merger....

[In triangular mergers], [a]n acquiring corporation can use a controlled subsidiary (80 percent ownership) to acquire the assets of a target corporation in a tax-free merger in exchange for the parent corporation's stock.... The subsidiary can be newly created just for the purpose of carrying out the merger. A major difference between a regular merger and a triangular or subsidiary merger is that the subsidiary using its parent's stock must acquire "substantially all" the assets of the target corporation in order for the transaction to be tax free....

2. ALI Principles

§ 6.01. Role of Directors and Holders of Voting Equity Securities with Respect to Transactions in Control Proposed to the Corporation

(a) The board of directors, in the exercise of its business judgment may approve, reject, or decline to consider a proposal to the corporation to engage in a transaction in control.

(b) A transaction in control of the corporation to which the corporation is a party should require approval by the shareholders.

B. *DE FACTO* MERGERS

Under many corporate law statutes, shareholders' voting and appraisal rights are dependent on the type of transaction. For instance, shareholders of both the target and acquiring corporations typically have voting and appraisal rights in an ordinary merger, while the shareholders have more abbreviated rights in a sale of assets or short form merger. Some corporate managers respond to this regulatory scheme by shaping corporate combinations as transactions with the fewest shareholders' rights. The following cases explore the doctrine of "de facto mergers," where the court may recharacterize a corporate combination as an ordinary merger although the acquiring company labels it differently.

FARRIS v. GLEN ALDEN CORP.

Supreme Court of Pennsylvania
143 A.2d 25 (1958)

COHEN, JUSTICE:

We are required to determine on this appeal whether, as a result of a "Reorganization Agreement" executed by the officers of Glen Alden Corporation and List Industries Corporation, and approved by the shareholders of the former company, the rights and remedies of a dissenting shareholder accrue to the plaintiff.

Glen Alden is a Pennsylvania corporation engaged principally in the mining of anthracite coal and lately in the manufacture of air conditioning units and fire-fighting equipment. In recent years the company's operating revenue has declined substantially, and in fact, its coal operations have resulted in tax loss carryovers of approximately $ 14,000,000. In October 1957, List, a Delaware holding company owning interests in motion picture theaters, textile companies and real estate, and to a lesser extent, in oil and gas operations, warehouses and aluminum piston manufacturing, purchased through a wholly owned subsidiary 38.5% of Glen Alden's outstanding stock.[1] This acquisition enabled List to place three of its directors on the Glen Alden board.

On March 20, 1958, the two corporations entered into a "reorganization agreement," subject to stockholder approval, which contemplated the following actions:

1. Glen Alden is to acquire all of the assets of List, excepting a small amount of cash reserved for the payment of List's expenses in connection with the transaction. These assets include over $ 8,000,000 in cash held chiefly in the treasuries of List's wholly owned subsidiaries.

2. In consideration of the transfer, Glen Alden is to issue 3,621,703 shares of stock to List. List in turn is to distribute the stock to its shareholders at a ratio of five shares of Glen Alden stock for each six shares of List stock. In order to accomplish the necessary distribution, Glen Alden is to increase the authorized number of its shares of capital stock from $ 2,500,000 shares to 7,500,000 shares without according preemptive rights to the present shareholders upon the issuance of any such shares.

3. Further, Glen Alden is to assume all of List's liabilities including a $ 5,000,000 note incurred by List in order to purchase Glen Alden stock in 1957, outstanding stock options, incentive stock options plans, and pension obligations.

4. Glen Alden is to change its corporate name from Glen Alden Corporation to List Alden Corporation.

5. The present directors of both corporations are to become directors of List Alden.

6. List is to be dissolved and List Alden is to then carry on the operations of both former corporations.

Two days after the agreement was executed notice of the annual meeting of Glen Alden to be held on April 11, 1958, was mailed to the shareholders together with a proxy statement analyzing the reorganization agreement and recommending its approval as well as approval of certain amendments to Glen Alden's articles of incorporation and bylaws necessary to implement the agreement. At this meeting the holders of a majority of the outstanding shares, (not including those owned by List), voted in favor of a resolution approving the reorganization agreement.

---

[1] Of the purchase price of $ 8,719,109, $ 5,000,000 was borrowed.

On the day of the shareholders' meeting, plaintiff, a shareholder of Glen Alden, filed a complaint in equity against the corporation and its officers seeking to enjoin them temporarily until final hearing, and perpetually thereafter, from executing and carrying out the agreement.

The gravamen of the complaint was that the notice of the annual shareholders' meeting did not conform to the requirements of the Business Corporation Law, 15 P.S. § 2852-1 *et seq.*, in three respects: (1) It did not give notice to the shareholders that the true intent and purpose of the meeting was to effect a merger or consolidation of Glen Alden and List; (2) It failed to give notice to the shareholders of their right to dissent to the plan of merger or consolidation and claim fair value for their shares, and (3) It did not contain copies of the text of certain sections of the Business Corporation Law as required.[2]

By reason of these omissions, plaintiff contended that the approval of the reorganization agreement by the shareholders at the annual meeting was invalid and unless the carrying out of the plan were enjoined, he would suffer irreparable loss by being deprived of substantial property rights.[3]

The defendants answered admitting the material allegations of fact in the complaint but denying that they gave rise to a cause of action because the transaction complained of was a purchase of corporate assets as to which shareholders had no rights of dissent or appraisal. For these reasons the defendants then moved for judgment on the pleadings.[4]

The court below concluded that the reorganization agreement entered into between the two corporations was a plan for a *de facto* merger, and that therefore the failure of the notice of the annual meeting to conform to the pertinent requirements of the merger provisions of the Business Corporation Law rendered the notice defective and all proceedings in furtherance of the agreement void. Wherefore, the court entered a final decree denying defendants' motion for judgment on the pleadings, entering judgment upon plaintiff's complaint and granting the injunctive relief therein sought. This appeal followed.

---

[2] The proxy statement included the following declaration: "Appraisal Rights."

"In the opinion of counsel, the shareholders of neither Glen Alden nor List Industries will have any rights of appraisal or similar rights of dissenters with respect to any matter to be acted upon at their respective meetings."

[3] The complaint also set forth that the exchange of shares of Glen Alden's stock for those of List would constitute a violation of the pre-emptive rights of Glen Alden shareholders as established by the law of Pennsylvania at the time of Glen Alden's incorporation in 1917. The defendants answered that under both statute and prior common law no pre-emptive rights existed with respect to stock issued in exchange for property.

[4] Counsel for the defendants concedes that if the corporation is required to pay the dissenting shareholders the appraised fair value of their shares, the resultant drain of cash would prevent Glen Alden from carrying out the agreement. On the other hand, plaintiff contends that if the shareholders had been told of their rights as dissenters, rather than specifically advised that they had no such rights, the resolution approving the reorganization agreement would have been defeated.

When use of the corporate form of business organization first became widespread, it was relatively easy for courts to define a "merger" or a "sale of assets" and to label a particular transaction as one or the other. But prompted by the desire to avoid the impact of adverse, and to obtain the benefits of favorable, government regulations, particularly federal tax laws, new accounting and legal techniques were developed by lawyers and accountants which interwove the elements characteristic of each, thereby creating hybrid forms of corporate amalgamation. Thus, it is no longer helpful to consider an individual transaction in the abstract and solely by reference to the various elements therein determine whether it is a "merger" or a "sale". Instead, to determine properly the nature of a corporate transaction, we must refer not only to all the provisions of the agreement, but also to the consequences of the transaction and to the purposes of the provisions of the corporation law said to be applicable. We shall apply this principle to the instant case.

Section 908, subd. A of the Pennsylvania Business Corporation Law provides: "If any shareholder of a domestic corporation which becomes a party to a plan of merger or consolidation shall object to such plan of merger or consolidation ... such shareholder shall be entitled to ... [the fair value of his shares upon surrender of the share certificate or certificates representing his shares]." Act of May 5, 1933, P.L. 364, *as amended*, 15 P.S. § 2852-908, subd. A.

...[W]hen a corporation combines with another so as to lose its essential nature and alter the original fundamental relationships of the shareholders among themselves and to the corporation, a shareholder who does not wish to continue his membership therein may treat his membership in the original corporation as terminated and have the value of his shares paid to him....

Does the combination outlined in the present "reorganization" agreement so fundamentally change the corporate character of Glen Alden and the interest of the plaintiff as a shareholder therein, that to refuse him the rights and remedies of a dissenting shareholder would in reality force him to give up his stock in one corporation and against his will accept shares in another? If so, the combination is a merger within the meaning of section 908, subd. A of the corporation law....

If the reorganization agreement were consummated plaintiff would find that the "List Alden" resulting from the amalgamation would be quite a different corporation than the "Glen Alden" in which he is now a shareholder. Instead of continuing primarily as a coal mining company, Glen Alden would be transformed, after amendment of its articles of incorporation, into a diversified holding company whose interests would range from motion picture theaters to textile companies, Plaintiff would find himself a member of a company with assets of $ 169,000,000 and a long-term debt of $ 38,000,000 in lieu of a company one-half that size and with but one-seventh the long-term debt.

While the administration of the operations and properties of Glen Alden as well as List would be in the hands of management common to both companies, since all executives of List would be retained in List Alden, the control of Glen Alden would pass to the directors of List; for List would hold eleven of the seventeen directorships on the new board of directors.

As an aftermath of the transaction plaintiff's proportionate interest in Glen Alden would have been reduced to only two-fifths of what it presently is because of the issuance of an additional 3,621,703 shares to List which would not be subject to pre-emptive rights. In fact, ownership of Glen Alden would pass to the stockholders of List who would hold 76.5% of the outstanding shares as compared with but 23.5% retained by the present Glen Alden shareholders.

Perhaps the most important consequence to the plaintiff, if he were denied the right to have his shares redeemed at their fair value, would be the serious financial loss suffered upon consummation of the agreement. While the present book value of his stock is $ 38 a share after combination it would be worth only $ 21 a share. In contrast, the shareholders of List who presently hold stock with a total book value of $ 33,000,000 or $ 7.50 a share, would receive stock with a book value of $ 76,000,000 or $ 21 a share.

Under these circumstances it may well be said that if the proposed combination is allowed to take place without right of dissent, plaintiff would have his stock in Glen Alden taken away from him and the stock of a new company thrust upon him in its place. He would be projected against his will into a new enterprise under terms not of his own choosing. It was to protect dissident shareholders against just such a result that ... the legislature ... in section 908, subd. A, granted the right of dissent. And it is to accord that protection to the plaintiff that we conclude that the combination proposed in the case at hand is a merger within the intendment of section 908, subd. A.

Nevertheless, defendants contend that the 1957 amendments to sections 311 and 908 of the corporation law preclude us from reaching this result and require the entry of judgment in their favor. Subsection F of section 311 dealing with the voluntary transfer of corporate assets provides: "The shareholders of a business corporation which acquires by sale, lease or exchange all or substantially all of the property of another corporation by the issuance of stock, securities or otherwise shall not be entitled to the rights and remedies of dissenting shareholders ...."

And the amendment to section 908 reads as follows: "The right of dissenting shareholders ... shall not apply to the purchase by a corporation of assets whether or not the consideration therefor be money or property, real or personal, including shares or bonds or other evidences of indebtedness of such corporation. The shareholders of such corporation shall have no right to dissent from any such purchase." ...

...[W]e will not blind our eyes to the realities of the transaction. Despite the designation of the parties and the form employed, Glen Alden does not in fact acquire List, rather, List acquires Glen Alden, ... and under section 311, subd. D the right of dissent would remain with the shareholders of Glen Alden.

We hold that the combination contemplated by the reorganization agreement, although consummated by contract rather than in accordance with the statutory procedure, is a merger within the protective purview of sections 908, subd. A and 515 of the corporation law. The shareholders of Glen Alden should have been notified accordingly and advised of their statutory rights of dissent and appraisal. The failure of the corporate officers to take these steps renders the stockholder approval of the agreement at the 1958 shareholders' meeting invalid. The lower court did not err in enjoining the officers and directors of Glen Alden from carrying out this agreement.

Decree affirmed at appellants' cost.[5]

HARITON v. ARCO ELECTRONICS, INC.

Supreme Court of Delaware
188 A.2d 123 (1963)

SOUTHERLAND, CHIEF JUSTICE:

This case involves a sale of assets under § 271 of the corporation law, 8 Del. C. It presents for decision the question presented, but not decided, in *Heilbrunn v. Sun Chemical Corporation*, Del., 150 A.2d 755. It may be stated as follows:

A sale of assets is effected under § 271 in consideration of shares of stock of the purchasing corporation. The agreement of sale embodies also a plan to dissolve the selling corporation and distribute the shares so received to the stockholders of the seller, so as to accomplish the same result as would be accomplished by a merger of the seller into the purchaser. Is the sale legal?

The facts are these:

The defendant Arco and Loral Electronics Corporation, a New York corporation, are both engaged, in somewhat different forms, in the electronic equipment business. In the summer of 1961 they negotiated for an amalgamation of the companies. As of October 27, 1961, they entered into a "Reorganization Agreement and Plan." The provisions of this Plan pertinent here are in substance as follows:

1. Arco agrees to sell all its assets to Loral in consideration (*inter alia*) of the issuance to it of 283,000 shares of Loral.

2. Arco agrees to call a stockholders meeting for the purpose of approving the Plan and the voluntary dissolution.

3. Arco agrees to distribute to its stockholders all the Loral shares received by it as a part of the complete liquidation of Arco.

At the Arco meeting all the stockholders voting (about 80%) approved the Plan. It was thereafter consummated.

Plaintiff, a stockholder who did not vote at the meeting, sued to enjoin the consummation of the Plan on the grounds (1) that it was illegal, and (2) that it

---

[5]Following this decision, the Pennsylvania legislature acted explicitly to abolish the *de facto* merger doctrine, amending PA. CONS. STAT. ANN. § 3111(F), 1908(B). [Eds.]

was unfair. The second ground was abandoned. Affidavits and documentary evidence were filed, and defendant moved for summary judgment and dismissal of the complaint. The Vice Chancellor granted the motion and plaintiff appeals.

The question before us we have stated above. Plaintiff's argument that the sale is illegal runs as follows:

The several steps taken here accomplish the same result as a merger of Arco into Loral. In a "true" sale of assets, the stockholder of the seller retains the right to elect whether the selling company shall continue as a holding company. Moreover, the stockholder of the selling company is forced to accept an investment in a new enterprise without the right of appraisal granted under the merger statute. § 271 cannot therefore be legally combined with a dissolution proceeding under § 275 and a consequent distribution of the purchaser's stock. Such a proceeding is a misuse of the power granted under § 271, and a *de facto* merger results.

The foregoing is a brief summary of plaintiff's contention.

Plaintiff's contention that this sale has achieved the same result as a merger is plainly correct. The same contention was made to us in *Heilbrunn v. Sun Chemical Corporation*, Del., 150 A.2d 755. Accepting it as correct, we noted that this result is made possible by the overlapping scope of the merger statute and section 271, mentioned in *Sterling v. Mayflower Hotel Corporation*, 93 A.2d 107. We also adverted to the increased use, in connection with corporate reorganization plans, of § 271 instead of the merger statute....

We now hold that the reorganization here accomplished through § 271 and a mandatory plan of dissolution and distribution is legal. This is so because the sale-of-assets statute and the merger statute are independent of each other. They are, so to speak, of equal dignity, and the framers of a reorganization plan may resort to either type of corporate mechanics to achieve the desired end. This is not an anomalous result in our corporation law. As the Vice Chancellor pointed out, the elimination of accrued dividends, though forbidden under a charter amendment may be accomplished by a merger.

....

We are in accord with the Vice Chancellor's ruling, and the judgment below is

Affirmed.

As explained by the Official Comment to Model Act § 11.01, *de facto* merger problems are unlikely to occur under the Model Act since the procedural requirements for authorization and consequences of various types of transactions are largely standardized. For example, dissenters' rights are granted not only in mergers but also in share exchanges, in sales of all or substantially all the corporate assets, and in amendments to articles of incorporation that significantly affect rights of shareholders.

The following case explores a different application of the *de facto* merger doctrine. Instead of focusing on shareholders' rights in the different corporate combinations, it considers how creditors' rights are affected.

KNAPP v. NORTH AMERICAN ROCKWELL CORP.

United States Court of Appeals, Third Circuit
506 F.2d 361 (1974)

ADAMS, CIRCUIT JUDGE:

The principal question here is whether it was error to grant summary judgment on the ground that one injured by a defective machine may not recover from the corporation that purchased substantially all the assets of the manufacturer of the machine because the transaction was a sale of assets rather than a merger or consolidation.

I

Stanley Knapp, Jr., an employee of Mrs. Smith's Pie Co., was injured on October 6, 1969, when, in the course of his employment, his hand was caught in a machine known as a "Packomatic." The machine had been designed and manufactured by Textile Machine Works (TMW) and had been sold to Mrs. Smith's Pie Co. in 1966 or 1967.

On April 5, 1968, TMW entered into an agreement with North American Rockwell whereby TMW exchanged substantially all its assets for stock in Rockwell. TMW retained only its corporate seal, its articles of incorporation, its minute books and other corporate records, and $ 500,000 in cash intended to cover TMW's expenses in connection with the transfer. TMW also had the right, prior to closing the transaction with Rockwell, to dispose of land held by TMW or its subsidiary. Among the assets acquired by Rockwell was the right to use the name "Textile Machine Works." TMW was to change its name on the closing date, then to distribute the Rockwell stock to its shareholders and to dissolve TMW "as soon as practicable after the last of such distributions."

The accord reached by Rockwell and TMW also stipulated that Rockwell would assume specified obligations and liabilities of TMW, but among the liabilities not assumed were: "(a) liabilities against which TMW is insured or otherwise indemnified to the extent of such insurance or indemnification unless the insurer or indemnitor agrees in writing to insure and indemnify (Rockwell) to the same extent as it was so insuring and indemnifying TMW."

Closing took place pursuant to the agreement on August 29, 1968. Plaintiff sustained his injuries on October 6, 1969. TMW was dissolved on February 20, 1970, almost 18 months after the bulk of its assets had been exchanged for Rockwell stock.

Plaintiff filed this suit against Rockwell in the district court on March 22, 1971. He alleged that his injuries resulted from the negligence of TMW in designing and manufacturing the machine and that Rockwell, as TMW's successor, is liable for such injuries. Rockwell joined plaintiff's employer, Mrs. Smith's Pie Co., as a third-party defendant.

Rockwell moved for summary judgment in the district court on June 19, 1973. On September 6, 1973, the district court granted the motion, ruling that Rockwell had neither merged nor consolidated with TMW, that Rockwell was not a continuation of TMW, and that Rockwell had not assumed TMW's liability to Knapp. Therefore, the court concluded, Rockwell was not responsible for the obligations of TMW. On October 11, 1973, Knapp filed a motion for rehearing and reconsideration by the district court, which was denied on November 26, 1973. Knapp appealed to this Court on December 11, 1973.

II

Both parties agree that this case is controlled by the following principle of law:

> The general rule is that "a mere sale of corporate property by one company to another does not make the purchaser liable for the liabilities of the seller not assumed by it." ... There are, however, certain exceptions to this rule. Liability for obligations of a selling corporation may be imposed on the purchasing corporation when (1) the purchaser expressly or impliedly agrees to assume such obligations; (2) the transaction amounts to a consolidation or merger of the selling corporation with or into the purchasing corporation; (3) the purchasing corporation is merely a continuation of the selling corporation; or (4) the transaction is entered into fraudulently to escape liability for such obligations.

Shane v. Hobam, Inc., 332 F. Supp. 526, 527-528 (E.D. Pa.1971) (decided under New York law).

In light of this language, Knapp contends that the transaction in question "amounts to a consolidation or merger of (TMW) with or into the purchasing corporation (Rockwell)" or, alternatively, that Rockwell is a "continuation" of TMW. Although the TMW corporation technically continued to exist until its dissolution approximately 18 months after the consummation of the transaction with Rockwell, TMW was, Knapp argues, a mere shell during that period. It had none of its former assets, no active operations, and was required by the contract with Rockwell to dissolve itself "as soon as practicable." Knapp urges in effect that the transaction between TMW and Rockwell should be considered a *de facto* merger.

Rockwell asserts, in defense of the district court's grant of summary judgment, that a merger, a consolidation and a continuation all require that the corporation being merged, consolidated or continued cease to exist. TMW, Rockwell claims, did not go out of existence at the time of the exchange with Rockwell, but continued its corporate life for 18 months thereafter. Further, Rockwell argues, TMW until its dissolution possessed assets of substantial value, in the form of Rockwell stock.

III

....

No prior cases decided under Pennsylvania law have addressed the problem presently before this Court. However, when courts from other jurisdictions have considered similar questions, they have ascertained the existence *vel non* of a merger, a consolidation or a continuation on the basis of whether, immediately after the transaction, the selling corporation continued to exist as a corporate entity and whether, after the transaction, the selling corporation possessed substantial assets with which to satisfy the demands of its creditors.

....

IV

....

Denying Knapp the right to sue Rockwell because of the barren continuation of TMW after the exchange with Rockwell would allow a formality to defeat Knapp's recovery. Although TMW technically existed as an independent corporation, it had no substance. The parties clearly contemplated that TMW would terminate its existence as a part of the transaction. TMW had, in exchange for Rockwell stock, disposed of all the assets it originally held, exclusive of the cash necessary to consummate the transaction. It could not undertake any active operations. Nor was TMW permitted under the agreement to divest itself of the Rockwell stock, so that it might become an effective investment vehicle for its shareholders. Most significantly, TMW was required by the contract with Rockwell to dissolve "as soon as practicable."

On the other hand, Rockwell acquired all the assets of TMW, exclusive of certain real estate that Rockwell did not want, and assumed practically all of TMW's liabilities. Further, Rockwell required that TMW use its "best efforts," prior to the consummation of the transaction, to preserve TMW's business organization intact for Rockwell, to make available to Rockwell TMW's existing officers and employees, and to maintain TMW's relationship with its customers and suppliers. After the exchange, Rockwell continued TMW's former business operations.

If we are to follow the philosophy of the Pennsylvania courts that questions of an injured party's right to seek recovery are to be resolved by an analysis of public policy considerations rather than by a mere procrustean application of formalities, we must, in considering whether the TMW-Rockwell exchange was a merger, evaluate the public policy implications of that determination.

In resolving, where the burden of a loss should be imposed, the Pennsylvania Supreme Court has considered which of the two parties is better able to spread the loss. In *Ayala v. Philadelphia Board of Education*, [305 A.2d 877 (Pa. 1973)] a student who had been injured by a shredding machine during an upholstery class sued the Board of Education. The Court, in abolishing the doctrine of immunity in suits against local government, observed that the Board was in a better position than the student to have avoided the injury, and that "The city is a far better loss-distributing agency than the innocent and injured victim." The Court, quoting the Supreme Court of Illinois, decried the injustice of imposing upon an injured party the entire burden of his injuries, rather than distributing the responsibility throughout the community "where it could be borne without hardship upon any individual.?"

The Pennsylvania courts have also noted the importance of insurance in performing the loss-spreading function. In *Falco v. Pados*, [282 A.2d 351 (Pa. 1970)] the Court concluded that public interest mandated the abolition of parental immunity from liability for a parent's negligent injury to his child because, in the presence of wide-spread liability insurance coverage, the doctrine of parental immunity unjustly confined the burden of the loss to the injured party alone. "In a time of almost universal liability insurance, such unexpected hardship or ruin is needlessly inflicted by the immunity doctrine."

Interpreting all the allegations in the light most favorable to Knapp, as we must on a motion for summary judgment, neither Knapp nor Rockwell was ever in a position to prevent the occurrence of the injury, inasmuch as neither manufactured the defective device. As between these two parties, however, Rockwell is better able to spread the burden of the loss. Prior to the exchange with Rockwell, TMW had procured insurance that would have indemnified TMW had it been held liable to Knapp for his injuries. Rockwell could have protected itself from sustaining the brunt of the loss by securing from TMW an assignment of TMW's insurance. There is no indication in the record that such an assignment would have placed a burden on either Rockwell or TMW since TMW had already purchased the insurance protection, and the insurance was of no continuing benefit to TMW after its liability to suit was terminated by Pennsylvania statute. Rockwell has adduced no explanation, either in its brief or at oral argument, why it agreed in the contract not to take an assignment of TMW's prepaid insurance. Rockwell therefore should not be permitted to impose the weight of the loss upon a user of an allegedly defective product by delaying the formal dissolution of TMW....

....

SECTION III. DEFENDING AGAINST TENDER OFFERS

Chapter 18 describes tender offers, including applicable federal and state regulations. The following materials explore whether and if so, how directors' and officers' fiduciary duties should be modified in the tender offer context. In particular, incumbent management may oppose an unsolicited tender offer, and the directors may strategize specifically to block its successful culmination. Given shareholders' right to sell their shares without interference, when is the board justified in implementing these defensive tactics?

A. TRADITIONAL APPROACH

CHEFF v. MATHES

Supreme Court of Delaware
199 A.2d 548 (1964)

CAREY, JUSTICE:

This is an appeal from the decision of the Vice-Chancellor in a derivative suit holding certain directors of Holland Furnace Company liable for loss allegedly resulting from improper use of corporate funds to purchase shares of the company....

Holland Furnace Company, a corporation of the State of Delaware, manufactures warm air furnaces, air conditioning equipment, and other home heating equipment. At the time of the relevant transactions, the board of directors was composed of the seven individual defendants. Mr. Cheff had been Holland's Chief Executive Officer since 1933, received an annual salary of $ 77,400, and personally owned 6,000 shares of the company. He was also a director. Mrs. Cheff, the wife of Mr. Cheff, was a daughter of the founder of Holland and had served as a director since 1922. She personally owned 5,804 shares of Holland and owned 47.9 percent of Hazelbank United Interest, Inc. Hazelbank is an investment vehicle for Mrs. Cheff and members of the Cheff-Landwehr family group, which owned 164,950 shares of the 883,585 outstanding shares of Holland. As a director, Mrs. Cheff received a compensation of $ 200.00 for each monthly board meeting, whether or not she attended the meeting.

....

Prior to the events in question, Holland employed approximately 8500 persons and maintained 400 branch sales offices located in 43 states. The volume of sales had declined from over $ 41,000,000 in 1948 to less than $ 32,000,000 in 1956. Defendants contend that the decline in earnings is attributable to the artificial post-war demand generated in the 1946-1948 period. In order to stabilize the condition of the company, the sales department apparently was reorganized and certain unprofitable branch offices were closed. By 1957 this reorganization had been completed and the management was convinced that the changes were manifesting beneficial results. The practice of the company was to directly employ the retail salesman, and the management considered that practice — unique in the furnace business — to be a vital factor in the company's success.

During the first five months of 1957, the monthly trading volume of Holland's stock on the New York Stock Exchange ranged between 10,300 shares to 24,200 shares. In the last week of June 1957, however, the trading increased to 37,800 shares, with a corresponding increase in the market price. In June of 1957, Mr. Cheff met with Mr. Arnold H. Maremont, who was President of Maremont Automotive Products, Inc. and Chairman of the boards of Motor Products Corporation and Allied Paper Corporation. Mr. Cheff testified, on deposition, that Maremont generally inquired about the feasibility of merger between Motor

Products and Holland. Mr. Cheff testified that, in view of the difference in sales practices between the two companies, he informed Mr. Maremont that a merger did not seem feasible. In reply, Mr. Maremont stated that, in the light of Mr. Cheff's decision, he had no further interest in Holland nor did he wish to buy any of the stock of Holland.

None of the members of the board apparently connected the interest of Mr. Maremont with the increased activity of Holland stock. However, Mr. Trenkamp [Holland director and general counsel,] and Mr. Staal, the Treasurer of Holland, unsuccessfully made an informal investigation in order to ascertain the identity of the purchaser or purchasers. The mystery was resolved, however, when Maremont called Ames [another Holland director and a financial advisor] in July of 1957 to inform the latter that Maremont then owned 55,000 shares of Holland stock. At this juncture, no requests for change in corporate policy were made, and Maremont made no demand to be made a member of the board of Holland.

Ames reported the above information to the board at its July 30, 1957 meeting. Because of the position now occupied by Maremont, the board elected to investigate the financial and business history of Maremont and corporations controlled by him. Apart from the documentary evidence produced by this investigation, which will be considered *infra*, Staal testified, on deposition, that "leading bank officials" had indicated that Maremont "had been a participant, or had attempted to be, in the liquidation of a number of companies." Staal specifically mentioned only one individual giving such advice, the Vice President of the First National Bank of Chicago. Mr. Cheff testified, at trial, of Maremont's alleged participation in liquidation activities. Mr. Cheff testified that: "Throughout the whole of the Kalamazoo-Battle Creek area, and Detroit too, where I spent considerable time, he is well known and not highly regarded by any stretch." This information was communicated to the board.

On August 23, 1957, at the request of Maremont, a meeting was held between Mr. Maremont and Cheff. At this meeting, Cheff was informed that Motor Products then owned approximately 100,000 shares of Holland stock. Maremont then made a demand that he be named to the board of directors, but Cheff refused to consider it. Since considerable controversy has been generated by Maremont's alleged threat to liquidate the company or substantially alter the sales force of Holland, we believe it desirable to set forth the testimony of Cheff on this point: "Now we have 8500 men, direct employees, so the problem is entirely different. He indicated immediately that he had no interest in that type of distribution, that he didn't think it was modern, that he felt furnaces could be sold as he sold mufflers, through half a dozen salesmen in a wholesale way."

Testimony was introduced by the defendants tending to show that substantial unrest was present among the employees of Holland as a result of the threat of Maremont to seek control of Holland. Thus, Mr. Cheff testified that the field organization was considering leaving in large numbers because of a fear of the consequences of a Maremont acquisition; he further testified that approximately

"25 of our key men" were lost as the result of the unrest engendered by the Maremont proposal. Staal, corroborating Cheff's version, stated that a number of branch managers approached him for reassurances that Maremont was not going to be allowed to successfully gain control. Moreover, at approximately this time, the company was furnished with a Dun and Bradstreet report, which indicated the practice of Maremont to achieve quick profits by sales or liquidations of companies acquired by him. The defendants were also supplied with an income statement of Motor Products, Inc., showing a loss of $ 336,121.00 for the period in 1957.

On August 30, 1957, the board was informed by Cheff of Maremont's demand to be placed upon the board and of Maremont's belief that the retail sales organization of Holland was obsolete. The board was also informed of the results of the investigation by Cheff and Staal. Predicated upon this information, the board authorized the purchase of company stock on the market with corporate funds, ostensibly for use in a stock option plan.

Subsequent to this meeting, substantial numbers of shares were purchased and, in addition, Mrs. Cheff made alternate personal purchases of Holland stock. As a result of purchases by Maremont, Holland and Mrs. Cheff, the market price rose.... On September 4th, Maremont proposed to sell his current holdings of Holland to the corporation for $ 14.00 a share. However, because of delay in responding to this offer, Maremont withdrew the offer. At this time, Mrs. Cheff was obviously quite concerned over the prospect of a Maremont acquisition, and had stated her willingness to expend her personal resources to prevent it.

On September 30, 1957, Motor Products Corporation, by letter to Mrs. Bowles [a Hazelbank director], made a buy-sell offer to Hazelbank. At the Hazelbank meeting of October 3, 1957, Mrs. Bowles presented the letter to the board. The board took no action, but referred the proposal to its finance committee. Although Mrs. Bowles and Mrs. Putnam [another Hazelbank director] were opposed to any acquisition of Holland stock by Hazelbank, Mr. Landwehr [a Hazelbank and Holland director] conceded that a majority of the board were in favor of the purchase. Despite this fact, the finance committee elected to refer the offer to the Holland board on the grounds that it was the primary concern of Holland.

Thereafter, Mr. Trenkamp arranged for a meeting with Maremont, which occurred on October 14-15, 1957, in Chicago. Prior to this meeting, Trenkamp was aware of the intentions of Hazelbank and Mrs. Cheff to purchase all or portions of the stock then owned by Motor Products if Holland did not so act. As a result of the meeting, there was a tentative agreement on the part of Motor Products to sell its 155,000 shares at $ 14.40 per share. On October 23, 1957, at a special meeting of the Holland board, the purchase was considered. All directors, except Spatta, were present. The dangers allegedly posed by Maremont were again reviewed by the board. Trenkamp and Mrs. Cheff agree that the latter informed the board that either she or Hazelbank would purchase part or all of the block of Holland stock owned by Motor Products if the Holland board did not so act. The board was also informed that in order for the corporation to finance the purchase, substantial sums would have to be borrowed from commercial lending institutions. A resolution authorizing the purchase of 155,000 shares from Motor Products was adopted by the board. The price paid was in excess of the market price prevailing at the time, and the book value of the stock was approximately $ 20.00 as compared to approximately $ 14.00 for the net quick asset value. The transaction was subsequently consummated. The stock option plan mentioned in the minutes has never been implemented. In 1959, Holland stock reached a high of $ 15.25 a share.

On February 6, 1958, plaintiffs, owners of 60 shares of Holland stock, filed a derivative suit in the court below naming all of the individual directors of Holland, Holland itself and Motor Products Corporation as defendants. The complaint alleged that all of the purchases of stock by Holland in 1957 were for the purpose of insuring the perpetuation of control by the incumbent directors. The complaint requested that the transaction between Motor Products and Holland be rescinded and, secondly, that the individual defendants account to Holland for the alleged damages....

....

Under the provisions of 8 Del. C. § 160, a corporation is granted statutory power to purchase and sell shares of its own stock. Such a right, as embodied in the statute, has long been recognized in this State. The charge here is not one of violation of statute, but the allegation is that the true motives behind such purchases were improperly centered upon perpetuation of control. In an analogous field, courts have sustained the use of proxy funds to inform stockholders of management's views upon the policy questions inherent in an election to a board of directors, but have not sanctioned the use of corporate funds to advance the selfish desires of directors to perpetuate themselves in office. Similarly, if the actions of the board were motivated by a sincere belief that the buying out of the dissident stockholder was necessary to maintain what the board believed to be proper business practices, the board will not be held liable for such decision, even though hindsight indicates the decision was not the wisest course. *See Kors v. Carey*, Del. Ch., 158 A.2d 136. On the other hand, if the board has acted solely or primarily because of the desire to perpetuate themselves in office, the use of corporate funds for such purposes is improper. *See Bennett v. Propp*, Del., 187 A.2d 405.

Our first problem is the allocation of the burden of proof to show the presence or lack of good faith on the part of the board in authorizing the purchase of shares. Initially, the decision of the board of directors in authorizing a purchase was presumed to be in good faith and could be overturned only by a conclusive showing by plaintiffs of fraud or other misconduct. In *Kors, cited supra*, the court merely indicated that the directors are presumed to act in good faith and the burden of proof to show to the contrary falls upon the plaintiff. However, in *Bennett v. Propp, supra*, we stated:

"We must bear in mind the inherent danger in the purchase of shares with corporate funds to remove a threat to corporate policy when a threat to control is involved. The directors are of necessity confronted with a conflict of interest, and an objective decision is difficult. ... Hence, in our opinion, the burden should be on the directors to justify such a purchase as one primarily in the corporate interest." (187 A.2d 409, at page 409).

....

To say that the burden of proof is upon the defendants is not to indicate, however, that the directors have the same "self-dealing interest' as is present, for example, when a director sells property to the corporation. The only clear pecuniary interest shown on the record was held by Mr. Cheff, as an executive of the corporation, and Trenkamp, as its attorney. The mere fact that some of the other directors were substantial shareholders does not create a personal pecuniary interest in the decisions made by the board of directors, since all shareholders would presumably share the benefit flowing to the substantial shareholder. Accordingly, these directors other than Trenkamp and Cheff, while called upon to justify their actions, will not be held to the same standard of proof required of those directors having personal and pecuniary interest in the transaction.

....

Plaintiffs urge that the sale price was unfair in view of the fact that the price was in excess of that prevailing on the open market. However, as conceded by all parties, a substantial block of stock will normally sell at a higher price than that prevailing on the open market, the increment being attributable to a "control premium." Plaintiffs argue that it is inappropriate to require the defendant corporation to pay a control premium, since control is meaningless to an acquisition by a corporation of its own shares. However, it is elementary that a holder of a substantial number of shares would expect to receive the control premium as part of his selling price, and if the corporation desired to obtain the stock, it is unreasonable to expect that the corporation could avoid paying what any other purchaser would be required to pay for the stock. In any event, the financial expert produced by defendant at trial indicated that the price paid was fair and there was no rebuttal. Ames, the financial man on the board, was strongly of the opinion that the purchase was a good deal for the corporation. The Vice Chancellor made no finding as to the fairness of the price other than to indicate the obvious fact that the market price was increasing as a result of open market purchases by Maremont, Mrs. Cheff and Holland.

The question then presented is whether or not defendants satisfied the burden of proof of showing reasonable grounds to believe a danger to corporate policy and effectiveness existed by the presence of the Maremont stock ownership. It is important to remember that the directors satisfy their burden by showing good faith and reasonable investigation; the directors will not be penalized for an honest mistake of judgment, if the judgment appeared reasonable at the time the decision was made.

In holding that employee unrest could as well be attributed to a condition of Holland's business affairs as to the possibility of Maremont's intrustion, the Vice Chancellor must have had in mind one or both of two matters: (1) the pending proceedings before the Federal Trade Commission concerning certain sales practices of Holland; (2) the decrease in sales and profits during the preceding several years. Any other possible reason would be pure speculation. In the first place, the adverse decision of the F.T.C. was not announced until *after* the complained-of transaction. Secondly, the evidence clearly shows that the downward trend of sales and profits had reversed itself, presumably because of the reorganization which had then been completed. Thirdly, everyone who testified on the point said that the unrest was due to the possible threat presented by Maremont's purchases of stock. There was, in fact, no *testimony* whatever of any connection between the unrest and either the F.T.C. proceedings or the business picture.

The Vice Chancellor found that there was no substantial evidence of a liquidation posed by Maremont. This holding overlooks an important contention. The fear of the defendants, according to their testimony, was not limited to the possibility of liquidation; it included the alternate possibility of a material change in Holland's sales policies, which the board considered vital to its future success. The *unrebutted* testimony before the court indicated: (1) Maremont had deceived Cheff as to his original intentions, since his open market purchases were contemporaneous with his disclaimer of interest in Holland; (2) Maremont had given Cheff some reason to believe that he intended to eliminate the retail sales force of Holland; (3) Maremont demanded a place on the board; (4) Maremont substantially increased his purchases after having been refused a place on the board; (5) the directors had good reason to believe that unrest among key employees had been engendered by the Maremont threat; (6) the board had received advice from Dun and Bradstreet indicating the past liquidation or quick sale activities of Motor Products; (7) the board had received professional advice from the firm of Merril Lynch, Fenner & Beane, who recommended that the purchase from Motor Products be carried out; (8) the board had received competent advice that the corporation was over-capitalized; (9) Staal and Cheff had made informal personal investigations from contacts in the business and financial community and had reported to the board of the alleged poor reputation of Maremont. The board was within its rights in relying upon that investigation, since 8 Del. C. § 141(f) allows the directors to reasonably rely upon a report provided by corporate officers.

Accordingly, we are of the opinion that the evidence presented in the court below leads inevitably to the conclusion that the board of directors, based upon direct investigation, receipt of professional advice, and personal observations of the contradictory action of Maremont and his explanation of corporate purpose, believed, with justification, that there was a reasonable threat to the continued existence of Holland, or at least existence in its present form, by the plan of Maremont to continue building up his stock holdings. We find no evidence in the record sufficient to justify a contrary conclusion. The opinion of the Vice Chancellor that employee unrest may have been engendered by other factors or that the board had no grounds to suspect Maremont is not supported in any manner by the evidence.

... [T]he Vice-Chancellor found that the purpose of the acquisition was the improper desire to maintain control, but, at the same time, he exonerated those individual directors whom he believed to be unaware of the possibility of using non-corporate funds to accomplish this purpose. Such a decision is inconsistent with his finding that the motive was improper, within the rule enunciated in *Bennett*. If the actions were in fact improper because of a desire to maintain control, then the presence or absence of a non-corporate alternative is irrelevant, as corporate funds may not be used to advance an improper purpose even if there is no non-corporate alternative available. Conversely, if the actions were proper because of a decision by the board made in good faith that the corporate interest was served thereby, they are not rendered improper by the fact that some individual directors were willing to advance personal funds if the corporation did not. It is conceivable that the Vice Chancellor considered this feature of the case to be of significance because of his apparent belief that any excess corporate funds should have been used to finance a subsidiary corporation. That action would not have solved the problem of Holland's over-capitalization. In any event, this question was a matter of business judgment, which furnishes no justification for holding the directors personally responsible in this case.

Accordingly, the judgment of the court below is reversed and remanded with instruction to enter judgment for the defendants.

----

1. The Vernacular

Tender offer battles have developed colorful terms of art. The meaning of some of the more popular terms are briefly defined below and can be referred to as the terms appear in the cases in this chapter.*

Back-End Transaction is the transaction that follows the successful acquisition by an aggressor of a majority of the target's shares. In the back-end transaction, the minority shareholders in the target are eliminated through a cash-out merger. A back-end transaction is also sometimes called a Mop-Up Merger.

Bearhug is an approach by an aggressor to a target proposing a friendly acquisition. In this approach, a veiled or explicit threat may be made that if the target chooses not to negotiate, an unfriendly takeover attempt addressed directly to the target's shareholders may be undertaken.

----

*Robert W. Hamilton, Fundamentals of Modern Business, as excerpted from 535-604 (1989). Copyright © 1989, Little, Brown and Company, assigned to Aspen Law and Business, a division of Aspen Publishers, Inc.

Crown Jewels are valuable assets or lines of business owned by a potential target corporation. Such assets may be sold to third parties or placed under option at bargain prices as a device to defeat an unwanted takeover attempt.

Fair Price Amendments are amendments to Articles of Incorporation adopted by publicly held corporations that preclude subsequent mergers or related transactions with major shareholders except at prices that meet specified standards. Such amendments are designed to prevent unfair Back-End Transactions, and ultimately serve as a defense against unwanted takeovers.

Flip-in Poison Pills grant shareholders additional financial rights in the target (*e.g.*, the right to acquire additional shares or indebtedness issued by the target corporation at a bargain price) when the poison pill is triggered by a cash tender offer or a large acquisition of target shares by an aggressor.

Flip-Over Poison Pills grant shareholders additional financial rights in the aggressor when the poison pill is triggered by a cash tender offer or a large acquisition of target shares by an aggressor. The usual flip-over provision grants shareholders in the target the right to purchase shares in the aggressor at bargain prices (*e.g.*, the right to purchase $ 200 worth of the common shares of the tender offeror for $ 100 in the merger) in the event of a Back-End Merger between the target and the aggressor within a designated period after the pill is triggered.

Front-End Loaded Tender Offer is a cash tender offer in which it is announced that the Back-End Transaction will be effected at a lower price than the initial offer for the controlling interest of the target made in the tender offer itself.

Golden Parachutes are lucrative severance contracts for top management whose employment with the corporation may be terminated upon a successful takeover by an aggressor.

Greenmail is an agreement by an aggressor and a target corporation, following the acquisition by the aggressor of a substantial holding in target shares, by which the target corporation agrees to buy the target shares owned by the aggressor at a price that is usually above market and certainly above the aggressor's costs. In return the aggressor agrees to make no further purchases of target shares for an extended period.

Lock-up Options are options on Crown Jewels or on shares of the target that are granted to friendly third parties as a device to defeat an aggressor's takeover attempt.

Pac Man Defense is a defensive tactic that involves a cash tender offer by the target for a majority of the aggressor's shares.

Poison Pills in corporation law parlance are special issues of preferred shares or debt securities with rights that are designed specifically to make unwanted attempts to take over the issuing corporation difficult, impractical, or impossible. A poison pill grants additional rights to shareholders upon the occurrence of a triggering event such as an acquisition of a substantial block of shares or a tender offer by outside interests.

Shark Repellants are changes made in [the] corporation's articles of incorpora-tion or bylaws designed to make [it] difficult for a new majority shareholder to replace the incumbent board of directors or to impose additional costs on the corporation in the event of a successful takeover. These provisions are also sometimes called Porcupine Provisions.

Staggered Board of Directors is a board that has been divided into two or three groups with one group to be elected each year. A staggered board is sometimes used as defensive measure against unwanted takeover attempts.

Standstill Agreement is an agreement between a target and an aggressor under which the aggressor agrees not to increase its holding in the target beyond a specified size for a specified period of time.

Supermajority Provisions are provisions in Articles of Incorporation or Bylaws that require certain actions to be approved by more than a simple majority of the affirmative votes of shares. Supermajority provisions are widely used as takeover defenses by requiring merger transactions proposed by substantial shareholders to receive supermajority approval.

White Knight is a friendly alternative suitor for a target corporation.

2. Defense Mechanisms

The Investor Responsibility Research Center, Inc.'s *Corporate Takeover Defenses 1995* surveyed the corporate governance provisions in 1500 major corporations. The report revealed that the most popular defense mechanism — found in over four-fifths of the corporations — was a "blank check preferred stock." This stock, when authorized, gives directors broad discretion to establish dividend, voting, conversion, and other rights for the stock, if and when it is eventually issued. The stock would allow directors, for instance, to put poison pills into place.

Other popular defenses, found in over 40% of the corporations, include classified boards, golden parachutes, poison pills, and advance notice require-ments. Advance notice requirements in a corporation's articles or bylaws, for instance, may require that shareholders give advance notice of directors' nominations. These provisions, like provisions limiting shareholders' rights to call special meetings or provisions limiting shareholders' right to act by written consent (found at about 30% of the corporations) apparently are aimed at containing shareholder activism.

B. ENHANCED SCRUTINY

The *Unocal* and *Revlon* cases that follow are the key Delaware cases that reformulated the duty of care standard in the tender offer context.

UNOCAL CORP. v. MESA PETROLEUM CO.

Supreme Court of Delaware
493 A.2d 946 (1985)

MOORE, JUSTICE:

We confront an issue of first impression in Delaware — the validity of a corporation's self-tender for its own shares which excludes from participation a stockholder making a hostile tender offer for the company's stock.

The Court of Chancery granted a preliminary injunction to the plaintiffs, Mesa Petroleum Co., Mesa Asset Co., Mesa Partners II, and Mesa Eastern, Inc. (collectively "Mesa"),[6] enjoining an exchange offer of the defendant, Unocal Corporation (Unocal) for its own stock. The trial court concluded that a selective exchange offer, excluding Mesa, was legally impermissible....

I

The factual background of this matter bears a significant relationship to its ultimate outcome.

On April 8, 1985, Mesa, the owner of approximately 13% of Unocal's stock, commenced a two-tier "front loaded" cash tender offer for 64 million shares, or approximately 37%, of Unocal's outstanding stock at a price of $ 54 per share. The "back-end" was designed to eliminate the remaining publicly held shares by an exchange of securities purportedly worth $ 54 per share. However, pursuant to an order entered by the United States District Court for the Central District of California on April 26, 1985, Mesa issued a supplemental proxy statement to Unocal's stockholders disclosing that the securities offered in the second-step merger would be highly subordinated, and that Unocal's capitalization would differ significantly from its present structure. Unocal has rather aptly termed such securities "junk bonds".

Unocal's board consists of eight independent outside directors and six insiders. It met on April 13, 1985, to consider the Mesa tender offer. Thirteen directors were present, and the meeting lasted nine and one-half hours. The directors were given no agenda or written materials prior to the session. However, detailed presentations were made by legal counsel regarding the board's obligations under both Delaware corporate law and the federal securities laws. The board then received a presentation from Peter Sachs on behalf of Goldman Sachs & Co. (Goldman Sachs) and Dillon, Read & Co. (Dillon Read) discussing the bases for their opinions that the Mesa proposal was wholly inadequate. Mr. Sachs opined that the minimum cash value that could be expected from a sale or orderly liquidation for 100% of Unocal's stock was in excess of $ 60 per share. In making his presentation, Mr. Sachs showed slides outlining the valuation techniques used by the financial advisors, and others, depicting recent business

---

[6]T. Boone Pickens, Jr., is President and Chairman of the Board of Mesa Petroleum and President of Mesa Asset and controls the related Mesa entities.

combinations in the oil and gas industry. The Court of Chancery found that the Sachs presentation was designed to apprise the directors of the scope of the analyses performed rather than the facts and numbers used in reaching the conclusion that Mesa's tender offer price was inadequate.

Mr. Sachs also presented various defensive strategies available to the board if it concluded that Mesa's two-step tender offer was inadequate and should be opposed. One of the devices outlined was a self-tender by Unocal for its own stock with a reasonable price range of $ 70 to $ 75 per share. The cost of such a proposal would cause the company to incur $ 6.1 — 6.5 billion of additional debt, and a presentation was made informing the board of Unocal's ability to handle it. The directors were told that the primary effect of this obligation would be to reduce exploratory drilling, but that the company would nonetheless remain a viable entity.

The eight outside directors, comprising a clear majority of the thirteen members present, then met separately with Unocal's financial advisors and attorneys. Thereafter, they unanimously agreed to advise the board that it should reject Mesa's tender offer as inadequate, and that Unocal should pursue a self-tender to provide the stockholders with a fairly priced alternative to the Mesa proposal. The board then reconvened and unanimously adopted a resolution rejecting as grossly inadequate Mesa's tender offer. Despite the nine and one-half hour length of the meeting, no formal decision was made on the proposed defensive self-tender.

On April 15, the board met again with four of the directors present by telephone and one member still absent. This session lasted two hours. Unocal's Vice President of Finance and its Assistant General Counsel made a detailed presentation of the proposed terms of the exchange offer. A price range between $ 70 and $ 80 per share was considered, and ultimately the directors agreed upon $ 72. The board was also advised about the debt securities that would be issued, and the necessity of placing restrictive covenants upon certain corporate activities until the obligations were paid. The board's decisions were made in reliance on the advice of its investment bankers, including the terms and conditions upon which the securities were to be issued. Based upon this advice, and the board's own deliberations, the directors unanimously approved the exchange offer. Their resolution provided that if Mesa acquired 64 million shares of Unocal stock through its own offer (the Mesa Purchase Condition), Unocal would buy the remaining 49% outstanding for an exchange of debt securities having an aggregate par value of $ 72 per share. The board resolution also stated that the offer would be subject to other conditions that had been described to the board at the meeting, or which were deemed necessary by Unocal's officers, including the exclusion of Mesa from the proposal (the Mesa exclusion). Any such conditions were required to be in accordance with the "purport and intent" of the offer.

Unocal's exchange offer was commenced on April 17, 1985, and Mesa promptly challenged it by filing this suit in the Court of Chancery. On April 22, the Unocal board met again and was advised by Goldman Sachs and Dillon Read to waive the Mesa Purchase Condition as to 50 million shares. This recommendation was in response to a perceived concern of the shareholders that, if shares were tendered to Unocal, no shares would be purchased by either offeror. The directors were also advised that they should tender their own Unocal stock into the exchange offer as a mark of their confidence in it.

Another focus of the board was the Mesa exclusion. Legal counsel advised that under Delaware law Mesa could only be excluded for what the directors reasonably believed to be a valid corporate purpose. The directors' discussion centered on the objective of adequately compensating shareholders at the "back-end" of Mesa's proposal, which the latter would finance with "junk bonds". To include Mesa would defeat that goal, because under the proration aspect of the exchange offer (49%) every Mesa share accepted by Unocal would displace one held by another stockholder. Further, if Mesa were permitted to tender to Unocal, the latter would in effect be financing Mesa's own inadequate proposal.

....

On April 29, 1985, the Vice Chancellor temporarily restrained Unocal from proceeding with the exchange offer unless it included Mesa....

II

The issues we address involve these fundamental questions: Did the Unocal board have the power and duty to oppose a takeover threat it reasonably perceived to be harmful to the corporate enterprise, and if so, is its action here entitled to the protection of the business judgment rule?

Mesa contends that the discriminatory exchange offer violates the fiduciary duties Unocal owes it. Mesa argues that because of the Mesa exclusion the business judgment rule is inapplicable, because the directors by tendering their own shares will derive a financial benefit that is not available to all Unocal stockholders. Thus, it is Mesa's ultimate contention that Unocal cannot establish that the exchange offer is fair to all shareholders, and argues that the Court of Chancery was correct in concluding that Unocal was unable to meet this burden.

Unocal answers that it does not owe a duty of "fairness" to Mesa, given the facts here. Specifically, Unocal contends that its board of directors reasonably and in good faith concluded that Mesa's $ 54 two-tier tender offer was coercive and inadequate, and that Mesa sought selective treatment for itself. Furthermore, Unocal argues that the board's approval of the exchange offer was made in good faith, on an informed basis, and in the exercise of due care. Under these circumstances, Unocal contends that its directors properly employed this device to protect the company and its stockholders from Mesa's harmful tactics.

III

We begin with the basic issue of the power of a board of directors of a Delaware corporation to adopt a defensive measure of this type. Absent such authority, all other questions are moot. Neither issues of fairness nor business judgment are pertinent without the basic underpinning of a board's legal power to act.

The board has a large reservoir of authority upon which to draw. Its duties and responsibilities proceed from the inherent powers conferred by 8 Del. C. § 141(a), respecting management of the corporation's "business and affairs". Additionally, the powers here being exercised derive from 8 Del. C. § 160(a), conferring broad authority upon a corporation to deal in its own stock. From this it is now well established that in the acquisition of its shares a Delaware corporation may deal selectively with its stockholders, provided the directors have not acted out of a sole or primary purpose to entrench themselves in office.

Finally, the board's power to act derives from its fundamental duty and obligation to protect the corporate enterprise, which includes stockholders, from harm reasonably perceived, irrespective of its source. Thus, we are satisfied that in the broad context of corporate governance, including issues of fundamental corporate change, a board of directors is not a passive instrumentality.

Given the foregoing principles, we turn to the standards by which director action is to be measured. In *Pogostin v. Rice*, Del. Supr., 480 A.2d 619 (1984), we held that the business judgment rule, including the standards by which director conduct is judged, is applicable in the context of a takeover. *Id.* at 627. The business judgment rule is a "presumption that in making a business decision the directors of a corporation acted on an informed basis, in good faith and in the honest belief that the action taken was in the best interests of the company." *Aronson v. Lewis*, Del. Supr., 473 A.2d 805, 812 (1984). A hallmark of the business judgment rule is that a court will not substitute its judgment for that of the board if the latter's decision can be "attributed to any rational business purpose." *Sinclair Oil Corp. v. Levien*, Del. Supr., 280 A.2d 717, 720 (1971).

When a board addresses a pending takeover bid it has an obligation to determine whether the offer is in the best interests of the corporation and its shareholders. In that respect a board's duty is no different from any other responsibility it shoulders, and its decisions should be no less entitled to the respect they otherwise would be accorded in the realm of business judgment.... There are, however, certain caveats to a proper exercise of this function. Because of the omnipresent specter that a board may be acting primarily in its own interests, rather than those of the corporation and its shareholders, there is an enhanced duty which calls for judicial examination at the threshold before the protections of the business judgment rule may be conferred.

This Court has long recognized that:

> We must bear in mind the inherent danger in the purchase of shares with corporate funds to remove a threat to corporate policy when a threat to control is involved. The directors are of necessity confronted with a conflict of interest, and an objective decision is difficult.

Bennett v. Propp, Del. Supr., 187 A.2d 405, 409 (1962). In the face of this inherent conflict directors must show that they had reasonable grounds for believing that a danger to corporate policy and effectiveness existed because of another person's stock ownership. *Cheff v. Mathes*, 199 A.2d at 554-55. However, they satisfy that burden "by showing good faith and reasonable investigation...." *Id.* at 555. Furthermore, such proof is materially enhanced, as here, by the approval of a board comprised of a majority of outside independent directors who have acted in accordance with the foregoing standards....

IV

A

In the board's exercise of corporate power to forestall a takeover bid our analysis begins with the basic principle that corporate directors have a fiduciary duty to act in the best interests of the corporation's stockholders. As we have noted, their duty of care extends to protecting the corporation and its owners from perceived harm whether a threat originates from third parties or other shareholders. But such powers are not absolute. A corporation does not have unbridled discretion to defeat any perceived threat by any Draconian means available.

The restriction placed upon a selective stock repurchase is that the directors may not have acted solely or primarily out of a desire to perpetuate themselves in office. Of course, to this is added the further caveat that inequitable action may not be taken under the guise of law. The standard of proof established in *Cheff v. Mathes* ... is designed to ensure that a defensive measure to thwart or impede a takeover is indeed motivated by a good faith concern for the welfare of the corporation and its stockholders, which in all circumstances must be free of any fraud or other misconduct. However, this does not end the inquiry.

B

A further aspect is the element of balance. If a defensive measure is to come within the ambit of the business judgment rule, it must be reasonable in relation to the threat posed. This entails an analysis by the directors of the nature of the takeover bid and its effect on the corporate enterprise. Examples of such concerns may include: inadequacy of the price offered, nature and timing of the offer, questions of illegality, the impact on "constituencies" other than shareholders (*i.e.*, creditors, customers, employees, and perhaps even the community generally), the risk of nonconsummation, and the quality of securities being offered in the exchange. While not a controlling factor, it also seems to us that a board may reasonably consider the basic stockholder interests at stake, including those of short term speculators, whose actions may have fueled the coercive aspect of the offer at the expense of the long term investor.[7] Here, the threat posed was viewed by the Unocal board as a grossly inadequate two-tier coercive tender offer coupled with the threat of greenmail.

Specifically, the Unocal directors had concluded that the value of Unocal was substantially above the $ 54 per share offered in cash at the front end. Furthermore, they determined that the subordinated securities to be exchanged in Mesa's announced squeeze out of the remaining shareholders in the "back-end" merger were "junk bonds" worth far less than $ 54. It is now well recognized that such offers are a classic coercive measure designed to stampede shareholders into tendering at the first tier, even if the price is inadequate, out of fear of what they will receive at the back end of the transaction. Wholly beyond the coercive aspect of an inadequate two-tier tender offer, the threat was posed by a corporate raider with a national reputation as a "greenmailer".

In adopting the selective exchange offer, the board stated that its objective was either to defeat the inadequate Mesa offer or, should the offer still succeed, provide the 49% of its stockholders, who would otherwise be forced to accept "junk bonds", with $ 72 worth of senior debt. We find that both purposes are valid.

However, such efforts would have been thwarted by Mesa's participation in the exchange offer. First, if Mesa could tender its shares, Unocal would effectively be subsidizing the former's continuing effort to buy Unocal stock at $ 54 per share. Second, Mesa could not, by definition, fit within the class of shareholders being protected from its own coercive and inadequate tender offer.

Thus, we are satisfied that the selective exchange offer is reasonably related to the threats posed. It is consistent with the principle that "the minority stockholder shall receive the substantial equivalent in value of what he had before." *Sterling v. Mayflower Hotel Corp.*, Del. Supr., 93 A.2d 107, 114 (1952). This concept of fairness, while stated in the merger context, is also relevant in the area of tender offer law. Thus, the board's decision to offer what

---

[7] There has been much debate respecting such stockholder interests. One rather impressive study indicates that the stock of over 50 percent of target companies, who resisted hostile takeovers, later traded at higher market prices than the rejected offer price, or were acquired after the tender offer was defeated by another company at a price higher than the offer price. *See* [Lipton, *Takeover Bids in the Target's Boardroom*, 35 BUS. LAW. 101, 106-09, 132-33 (1979)]. Moreover, an update by Kidder Peabody & Company of this study, involving the stock prices of target companies that have defeated hostile tender offers during the period from 1973 to 1982 demonstrates that in a majority of cases the target's shareholders benefited from the defeat. The stock of 81% of the targets studied has, since the tender offer, sold at prices higher than the tender offer price. When adjusted for the time value of money, the figure is 64%. *See* [Lipton & Brownstein, *Takeover Responses and Directors' Responsibilities: An Update,* p. 10, ABA National Institute on the Dynamics of Corporate Control (Dec. 8, 1983)]. The thesis being that this strongly supports application of the business judgment rule in response to takeover threats. There is, however, a rather vehement contrary view. *See* [Easterbrook & Fischel, *Takeover Bids, Defensive Tactics, and Shareholders' Welfare*, 36 BUS. LAW. 1733, 1739-45 (1981)].

it determined to be the fair value of the corporation to the 49% of its shareholders, who would otherwise be forced to accept highly subordinated "junk bonds", is reasonable and consistent with the directors' duty to ensure that the minority stockholders receive equal value for their shares.

V

Mesa contends that it is unlawful, and the trial court agreed, for a corporation to discriminate in this fashion against one shareholder. It argues correctly that no case has ever sanctioned a device that precludes a raider from sharing in a benefit available to all other stockholders. However, as we have noted earlier, the principle of selective stock repurchases by a Delaware corporation is neither unknown nor unauthorized. The only difference is that heretofore the approved transaction was the payment of "greenmail" to a raider or dissident posing a threat to the corporate enterprise. All other stockholders were denied such favored treatment, and given Mesa's past history of greenmail, its claims here are rather ironic.

However, our corporate law is not static. It must grow and develop in response to, indeed in anticipation of, evolving concepts and needs. Merely because the General Corporation Law is silent as to a specific matter does not mean that it is prohibited. In the days when *Cheff, Bennett, Martin* and *Kors* were decided, the tender offer, while not an unknown device, was virtually unused, and little was known of such methods as two-tier "front-end" loaded offers with their coercive effects. Then, the favored attack of a raider was stock acquisition followed by a proxy contest. Various defensive tactics, which provided no benefit whatever to the raider, evolved. Thus, the use of corporate funds by management to counter a proxy battle was approved. Litigation, supported by corporate funds, aimed at the raider has long been a popular device.

More recently, as the sophistication of both raiders and targets has developed, a host of other defensive measures to counter such ever mounting threats has evolved and received judicial sanction. These include defensive charter amendments and other devices bearing some rather exotic, but apt, names: Crown Jewel, White Knight, Pac Man, and Golden Parachute. Each has highly selective features, the object of which is to deter or defeat the raider.

Thus, while the exchange offer is a form of selective treatment, given the nature of the threat posed here the response is neither unlawful nor unreasonable. If the board of directors is disinterested, has acted in good faith and with due care, its decision in the absence of an abuse of discretion will be upheld as a proper exercise of business judgment.

To this Mesa responds that the board is not disinterested, because the directors are receiving a benefit from the tender of their own shares, which because of the Mesa exclusion, does not devolve upon all stockholders equally. However, Mesa concedes that if the exclusion is valid, then the directors and all other stockholders share the same benefit. The answer of course is that the exclusion is valid, and the directors' participation in the exchange offer does not rise to the level of a disqualifying interest.

....

VI

In conclusion, there was directorial power to oppose the Mesa tender offer, and to undertake a selective stock exchange made in good faith and upon a reasonable investigation pursuant to a clear duty to protect the corporate enterprise. Further, the selective stock repurchase plan chosen by Unocal is reasonable in relation to the threat that the board rationally and reasonably believed was posed by Mesa's inadequate and coercive two-tier tender offer. Under those circumstances the board's action is entitled to be measured by the standards of the business judgment rule. Thus, unless it is shown by a preponderance of the evidence that the directors' decisions were primarily based on perpetuating themselves in office, or some other breach of fiduciary duty such as fraud, overreaching, lack of good faith, or being uninformed, a Court will not substitute its judgment for that of the board.

... If the stockholders are displeased with the action of their elected representatives, the powers of corporate democracy are at their disposal to turn the board out....

... The decision of the Court of Chancery is therefore REVERSED, and the preliminary injunction is VACATED.

---

1. Reasonable Response Standard

Unocal concludes that the target corporation's directors must do more than satisfy the ordinary business judgment rule standard of review. Do you agree that this enhanced scrutiny is justified in the tender offer context?

ALI § 6.02 provides that:

> (a) The board of directors may take an action that has the foreseeable effect of blocking an unsolicited tender offer, if the action is a reasonable response to the offer.
>
> (b) In considering whether its action is a reasonable response to the offer:
>
> (1) The board may take into account all factors relevant to the best interests of the corporation and shareholders, including, among other things, questions of legality and whether the offer, if successful, would threaten the corporation's essential economic prospects; and
>
> (2) The board may, in addition to the analysis under § 6.02(b)(1), have regard for interests or groups (other than shareholders) with respect to which the corporation has a legitimate concern if to do so would not significantly disfavor the long-term interests of shareholders.

While the ALI articulates a "reasonable response" standard consistent with *Unocal*, the ALI principles differ from *Unocal* in some other distinct ways. First, unlike *Unocal* where the directors have the burden of proving that their defensive tactics were reasonable, ALI § 6.02(c) places the burden on the plaintiffs to prove that the tactics were unreasonable. ALI § 6.02 Comment *a* and *e*. Second, ALI § 6.02(d) distinguishes between actions to enjoin or set aside corporate actions and actions to determine directors' liability. Actions to enjoin are subject to the reasonableness standards. Disinterested directors' are protected from personal liability for damages if they comply with the ordinary business judgment rule standards, even if the tactics were not reasonable. § 6.02 Comments *a* and *d*. *See* ALI § 4.01(c) (describing business judgment rule).

In addition, § 6.02(b) states more broadly than *Unocal* that directors may consider non-shareholder constituencies. Section 6.02(b)(1) links a weighing of these non-shareholder groups to the "best interests of the corporations and shareholders." Section 6.02(b)(2) goes beyond the more traditional language of § 6.02(b)(1), providing that "consideration of such other groups and interests can extend beyond the issue as to whether the best interests of shareholders may be advanced. Such groups and interests would include, for example, environmental and other community concerns, and may include groups such as employees, suppliers, and customers. However, § 6.02(b)(2) does not permit such groups or other interests to be considered in a way that would significantly disfavor long-term interests of shareholders." ALI § 6.02 Comment *c(2)*, Reporter's Note 2.

2. Duty of Loyalty

The *Unocal* and *Revlon* cases enhanced the duty of care and business judgment rule standard of review in tender offer contests. In the alternative, a few courts have concluded that incumbent management's defensive tactics are more properly analyzed under the duty of loyalty. In *Norlin Corp. v. Rooney, Pace, Inc.,*[8] Piezo Electric Products, Inc., in conjunction with Rooney, Pace, Inc., attempted to take over Norlin Corporation, a company that operated in New York. In response to this unwanted overture, the Norlin directors issued shares to Andean Enterprises, Inc., a wholly owned subsidiary, and to an Employee Stock Option Plan and Trust ("ESOP"). As a result of these stock transfers, Norlin directors controlled the votes of 49% of the corporation's outstanding stock.

In determining the appropriate standard for review, Judge Kaufman explained:[9]

[T]he business judgment rule governs only where the directors are not shown to have a self-interest in the transaction at issue. Once self-dealing or bad faith is demonstrated, the duty of loyalty supersedes the duty of care, and the burden shifts to the directors to "prove that the transaction was fair and

---

[8] 744 F.2d 255, 259 (2d Cir. 1984).
[9] *Id.* at 265-66.

reasonable to the corporation." [*Treadway Co. v. Care Corp.*, 638 F.2d 357, 382 (2d Cir. 1980).]

In this case, the evidence adduced was more than adequate to constitute a *prima facie* showing of self-interest on the board's part. All of the stock transferred to Andean and the ESOP was to be voted by the directors; indeed, members of the board were appointed trustees of the ESOP. The precipitous timing of the share issuances, and the fact that the ESOP was created the very same day that stock was issued to it, give rise to a strong inference that the purpose of the transaction was not to benefit the employees but rather to solidify management's control of the company. This is buttressed by the fact that the board offered its shareholders no rationale for the transfers other than its determination to oppose, at all costs, the threat to the company that Piezo's acquisitions ostensibly represented. Where, as here, directors amass voting control of close to a majority of a corporation's shares in their own hands by complex, convoluted and deliberate maneuvers, it strains credulity to suggest that the retention of control over corporate affairs played no part in their plans.

We reject the view, propounded by Norlin, that once it concludes that an actual or anticipated takeover attempt is not in the best interests of the company, a board of directors may take any action necessary to forestall acquisitive moves. The business judgment rule does indeed require the board to analyze carefully any perceived threat to the corporation, and to act appropriately when it decides that the interests of the company and its shareholders might be jeopardized. As we have explained, however, the duty of loyalty requires the board to demonstrate that any actions it does take are fair and reasonable. We conclude that Norlin has failed to make that showing.

3. Poison Pills

After *Unocal*, the Delaware Supreme Court considered and upheld the "poison pill" defensive tactic used in *Moran v. Household International, Inc.*[10]

> On August 14, 1984, the Board of Directors of Household International, Inc. adopted the Rights Plan by a fourteen to two vote.... Basically, the Plan provides that Household common stockholders are entitled to the issuance of one Right per common share under certain triggering conditions. There are two triggering events that can activate the Rights. The first is the announcement of a tender offer for 30 percent of Household's shares ("30% trigger") and the second is the acquisition of 20 percent of Household's shares by any single entity or group ("20% trigger").

---

[10] 500 A.2d 1346, 1348-49 (Del. 1985).

If an announcement of a tender offer for 30 percent of Household's shares is made, the Rights are issued and are immediately exercisable to purchase 1/100 share of new preferred stock for $ 100 and are redeemable by the Board for $ .50 per Right. If 20 percent of Household's shares are acquired by anyone, the Rights are issued and become non-redeemable and are exercisable to purchase 1/100 of a share of preferred. If a Right is not exercised for preferred, and thereafter, a merger or consolidation occurs, the Rights holder can exercise each Right to purchase $ 200 of the common stock of the tender offeror for $ 100. This "flip-over" provision of the Rights Plan is at the heart of this controversy.

Recall that flip-over pills, like the one described in *Moran*, would grant the target shareholders rights in the bidders' securities, while flip-in pills, such as the one described in the *Revlon* case below, would grant the target shareholders rights in the target corporation's securities.

REVLON, INC. v. MacANDREWS & FORBES HOLDINGS, INC.

Supreme Court of Delaware
506 A.2d 173 (1986)

MOORE, JUSTICE:

In this battle for corporate control of Revlon, Inc. (Revlon), the Court of Chancery enjoined certain transactions designed to thwart the efforts of Pantry Pride, Inc. (Pantry Pride) to acquire Revlon. The defendants are Revlon, its board of directors, and Forstmann Little & Co. and the latter's affiliated limited partnership (collectively, Forstmann). The injunction barred consummation of an option granted Forstmann to purchase certain Revlon assets (the lock-up option), a promise by Revlon to deal exclusively with Forstmann in the face of a takeover (the no-shop provision), and the payment of a $ 25 million cancellation fee to Forstmann if the transaction was aborted. The Court of Chancery found that the Revlon directors had breached their duty of care by entering into the foregoing transactions and effectively ending an active auction for the company. The trial court ruled that such arrangements are not illegal *per se* under Delaware law, but that their use under the circumstances here was impermissible. We agree. Thus, we granted this expedited interlocutory appeal to consider for the first time the validity of such defensive measures in the face of an active bidding contest for corporate control. Additionally, we address for the first time the extent to which a corporation may consider the impact of a takeover threat on constituencies other than shareholders.

In our view, lock-ups and related agreements are permitted under Delaware law where their adoption is untainted by director interest or other breaches of fiduciary duty. The actions taken by the Revlon directors, however, did not meet this standard. Moreover, while concern for various corporate constituencies is proper when addressing a takeover threat, that principle is limited by the requirement that there be some rationally related benefit accruing to the stockholders. We find no such benefit here.

Thus, under all the circumstances we must agree with the Court of Chancery that the enjoined Revlon defensive measures were inconsistent with the directors' duties to the stockholders. Accordingly, we affirm.

....

I

The somewhat complex maneuvers of the parties necessitate a rather detailed examination of the facts. The prelude to this controversy began in June 1985, when Ronald O. Perelman, chairman of the board and chief executive officer of Pantry Pride, met with his counterpart at Revlon, Michel C. Bergerac, to discuss a friendly acquisition of Revlon by Pantry Pride. Perelman suggested a price in the range of $ 40-50 per share, but the meeting ended with Bergerac dismissing those figures as considerably below Revlon's intrinsic value. All subsequent Pantry Pride overtures were rebuffed, perhaps in part based on Mr. Bergerac's strong personal antipathy to Mr. Perelman.

Thus, on August 14, Pantry Pride's board authorized Perelman to acquire Revlon, either through negotiation in the $ 42-$ 43 per share range, or by making a hostile tender offer at $ 45. Perelman then met with Bergerac and outlined Pantry Pride's alternate approaches. Bergerac remained adamantly opposed to such schemes and conditioned any further discussions of the matter on Pantry Pride executing a standstill agreement prohibiting it from acquiring Revlon without the latter's prior approval.

On August 19, the Revlon board met specially to consider the impending threat of a hostile bid by Pantry Pride. At the meeting, Lazard Freres, Revlon's investment banker, advised the directors that $ 45 per share was a grossly inadequate price for the company. Felix Rohatyn and William Loomis of Lazard Freres explained to the board that Pantry Pride's financial strategy for acquiring Revlon would be through "junk bond" financing followed by a break-up of Revlon and the disposition of its assets. With proper timing, according to the experts, such transactions could produce a return to Pantry Pride of $ 60 to $ 70 per share, while a sale of the company as a whole would be in the "mid 50" dollar range. Martin Lipton, special counsel for Revlon, recommended two defensive measures: first, that the company repurchase up to 5 million of its nearly 30 million outstanding shares; and second, that it adopt a Note Purchase Rights Plan. Under this plan, each Revlon shareholder would receive as a dividend one Note Purchase Right (the Rights) for each share of common stock, with the Rights entitling the holder to exchange one common share for a $ 65 principal Revlon note at 12% interest with a one-year maturity. The Rights would become effective whenever anyone acquired beneficial ownership of 20% or more of Revlon's shares, unless the purchaser acquired all the company's stock for cash at $ 65 or more per share. In addition, the Rights would not be available to the acquiror, and prior to the 20% triggering event the Revlon board could redeem the rights for 10 cents each. Both proposals were unanimously adopted.

Pantry Pride made its first hostile move on August 23 with a cash tender offer for any and all shares of Revlon at $ 47.50 per common share and $ 26.67 per preferred share, subject to (1) Pantry Pride's obtaining financing for the purchase, and (2) the Rights being redeemed, rescinded or voided.

The Revlon board met again on August 26. The directors advised the stockholders to reject the offer. Further defensive measures also were planned. On August 29, Revlon commenced its own offer for up to 10 million shares, exchanging for each share of common stock tendered one Senior Subordinated Note (the Notes) of $ 47.50 principal at 11.75% interest, due 1995, and one-tenth of a share of $ 9.00 Cumulative Convertible Exchangeable Preferred Stock valued at $ 100 per share. Lazard Freres opined that the notes would trade at their face value on a fully distributed basis. Revlon stockholders tendered 87 percent of the outstanding shares (approximately 33 million), and the company accepted the full 10 million shares on a pro rata basis. The new Notes contained covenants which limited Revlon's ability to incur additional debt, sell assets, or pay dividends unless otherwise approved by the "independent" (non-management) members of the board.

At this point, both the Rights and the Note covenants stymied Pantry Pride's attempted takeover. The next move came on September 16, when Pantry Pride announced a new tender offer at $ 42 per share, conditioned upon receiving at least 90% of the outstanding stock. Pantry Pride also indicated that it would consider buying less than 90%, and at an increased price, if Revlon removed the impeding Rights. While this offer was lower on its face than the earlier $ 47.50 proposal, Revlon's investment banker, Lazard Freres, described the two bids as essentially equal in view of the completed exchange offer.

The Revlon board held a regularly scheduled meeting on September 24. The directors rejected the latest Pantry Pride offer and authorized management to negotiate with other parties interested in acquiring Revlon. Pantry Pride remained determined in its efforts and continued to make cash bids for the company, offering $ 50 per share on September 27, and raising its bid to $ 53 on October 1, and then to $ 56.25 on October 7.

In the meantime, Revlon's negotiations with Forstmann and the investment group Adler & Shaykin had produced results. The Revlon directors met on October 3 to consider Pantry Pride's $ 53 bid and to examine possible alternatives to the offer. Both Forstmann and Adler & Shaykin made certain proposals to the board. As a result, the directors unanimously agreed to a leveraged buyout by Forstmann. The terms of this accord were as follows: each stockholder would get $ 56 cash per share; management would purchase stock in the new company by the exercise of their Revlon "golden parachutes"; Forstmann would assume Revlon's $ 475 million debt incurred by the issuance of the Notes; and Revlon would redeem the Rights and waive the Notes covenants for Forstmann or in connection with any other offer superior to Forstmann's. The board did not actually remove the covenants at the October 3 meeting, because Forstmann then lacked a firm commitment on its financing, but accepted the Forstmann capital structure, and indicated that the outside directors would waive the covenants in due course. Part of Forstmann's plan was to sell Revlon's Norcliff Thayer and Reheis divisions to American Home Products for $ 335 million. Before the merger, Revlon was to sell its cosmetics and fragrance division to Adler & Shaykin for $ 905 million. These transactions would facilitate the purchase by Forstmann or any other acquiror of Revlon.

When the merger, and thus the waiver of the Notes covenants, was announced, the market value of these securities began to fall. The Notes, which originally traded near par, around 100, dropped to 87.50 by October 8. One director later reported (at the October 12 meeting) a "deluge" of telephone calls from irate noteholders, and on October 10 the Wall Street Journal reported threats of litigation by these creditors.

Pantry Pride countered with a new proposal on October 7, raising its $ 53 offer to $ 56.25, subject to nullification of the Rights, a waiver of the Notes covenants, and the election of three Pantry Pride directors to the Revlon board. On October 9, representatives of Pantry Pride, Forstmann and Revlon conferred in an attempt to negotiate the fate of Revlon, but could not reach agreement. At this meeting Pantry Pride announced that it would engage in fractional bidding and top any Forstmann offer by a slightly higher one. It is also significant that Forstmann, to Pantry Pride's exclusion, had been made privy to certain Revlon financial data. Thus, the parties were not negotiating on equal terms.

Again privately armed with Revlon data, Forstmann met on October 11 with Revlon's special counsel and investment banker. On October 12, Forstmann made a new $ 57.25 per share offer, based on several conditions. The principal demand was a lock-up option to purchase Revlon's Vision Care and National Health Laboratories divisions for $ 525 million, some $ 100 — $ 175 million below the value ascribed to them by Lazard Freres, if another acquiror got 40% of Revlon's shares. Revlon also was required to accept a no-shop provision. The Rights and Notes covenants had to be removed as in the October 3 agreement. There would be a $ 25 million cancellation fee to be placed in escrow, and released to Forstmann if the new agreement terminated or if another acquiror got more than 19.9% of Revlon's stock. Finally, there would be no participation by Revlon management in the merger. In return, Forstmann agreed to support the par value of the Notes, which had faltered in the market, by an exchange of new notes. Forstmann also demanded immediate acceptance of its offer, or it would be withdrawn. The board unanimously approved Forstmann's proposal because: (1) it was for a higher price than the Pantry Pride bid, (2) it protected the noteholders, and (3) Forstmann's financing was firmly in place. The board further agreed to redeem the rights and waive the covenants on the preferred stock in response to any offer above $ 57 cash per share. The covenants were waived, contingent upon receipt of an investment banking opinion that the Notes would trade near par value once the offer was consummated.

Pantry Pride, which had initially sought injunctive relief from the Rights plan on August 22, filed an amended complaint on October 14 challenging the lock-up, the cancellation fee, and the exercise of the Rights and the Notes covenants. Pantry Pride also sought a temporary restraining order to prevent Revlon from placing any assets in escrow or transferring them to Forstmann. Moreover, on October 22, Pantry Pride again raised its bid, with a cash offer of $ 58 per share conditioned upon nullification of the Rights, waiver of the covenants, and an injunction of the Forstmann lock-up.

On October 15, the Court of Chancery prohibited the further transfer of assets, and eight days later enjoined the lock-up, no-shop, and cancellation fee provisions of the agreement. The trial court concluded that the Revlon directors had breached their duty of loyalty by making concessions to Forstmann, out of concern for their liability to the noteholders, rather than maximizing the sale price of the company for the stockholders' benefit.

II

To obtain a preliminary injunction, a plaintiff must demonstrate both a reasonable probability of success on the merits and some irreparable harm which will occur absent the injunction. Additionally, the Court shall balance the conveniences of and possible injuries to the parties.

A

We turn first to Pantry Pride's probability of success on the merits. The ultimate responsibility for managing the business and affairs of a corporation falls on its board of directors. 8 Del. C. § 141(a). In discharging this function the directors owe fiduciary duties of care and loyalty to the corporation and its shareholders. These principles apply with equal force when a board approves a corporate merger pursuant to 8 Del. C. § 251(b) and of course they are the bedrock of our law regarding corporate takeover issues. While the business judgment rule may be applicable to the actions of corporate directors responding to takeover threats, the principles upon which it is founded — care, loyalty and independence — must first be satisfied.

If the business judgment rule applies, there is a "presumption that in making a business decision the directors of a corporation acted on an informed basis, in good faith and in the honest belief that the action taken was in the best interests of the company." *Aronson v. Lewis*, 473 A.2d at 812. However, when a board implements anti-takeover measures there arises "the omnipresent specter that a board may be acting primarily in its own interests, rather than those of the corporation and its shareholders ..." *Unocal Corp. v. Mesa Petroleum Co.*, 493 A.2d at 954. This potential for conflict places upon the directors the burden of proving that they had reasonable grounds for believing there was a danger to corporate policy and effectiveness, a burden satisfied by a showing of good faith and reasonable investigation. *Id.* at 955. In addition, the directors must analyze the nature of the takeover and its effect on the corporation in order to ensure balance — that the responsive action taken is reasonable in relation to the threat posed. *Id.*

...

B

The first relevant defensive measure adopted by the Revlon board was the Rights Plan, which would be considered a "poison pill" in the current language of corporate takeovers — a plan by which shareholders receive the right to be bought out by the corporation at a substantial premium on the occurrence of a stated triggering event. *See generally Moran v. Household International, Inc.,* Del. Supr., 500 A.2d 1346 (1985). By 8 Del. C. §§ 141 and 122(13), the board clearly had the power to adopt the measure. Thus, the focus becomes one of reasonableness and purpose.

The Revlon board approved the Rights Plan in the face of an impending hostile takeover bid by Pantry Pride at $ 45 per share, a price which Revlon reasonably concluded was grossly inadequate. Lazard Freres had so advised the directors, and had also informed them that Pantry Pride was a small, highly leveraged company bent on a "bust-up" takeover by using "junk bond" financing to buy Revlon cheaply, sell the acquired assets to pay the debts incurred, and retain the profit for itself. In adopting the Plan, the board protected the shareholders from a hostile takeover at a price below the company's intrinsic value, while retaining sufficient flexibility to address any proposal deemed to be in the stockholders' best interests.

To that extent the board acted in good faith and upon reasonable investigation. Under the circumstances it cannot be said that the Rights Plan as employed was unreasonable, considering the threat posed. Indeed, the Plan was a factor in causing Pantry Pride to raise its bids from a low of $ 42 to an eventual high of $ 58. At the time of its adoption the Rights Plan afforded a measure of protection consistent with the directors' fiduciary duty in facing a takeover threat perceived as detrimental to corporate interests. Far from being a "show-stopper," as the plaintiffs had contended in *Moran,* the measure spurred the bidding to new heights, a proper result of its implementation.

C

The second defensive measure adopted by Revlon to thwart a Pantry Pride takeover was the company's own exchange offer for 10 million of its shares. The directors' general broad powers to manage the business and affairs of the corporation are augmented by the specific authority conferred under 8 Del. C. § 160(a), permitting the company to deal in its own stock. However, when exercising that power in an effort to forestall a hostile takeover, the board's actions are strictly held to the fiduciary standards outlined in *Unocal.* These standards require the directors to determine the best interests of the corporation and its stockholders, and impose an enhanced duty to abjure any action that is motivated by considerations other than a good faith concern for such interests.

The Revlon directors concluded that Pantry Pride's $ 47.50 offer was grossly inadequate. In that regard the board acted in good faith, and on an informed basis, with reasonable grounds to believe that there existed a harmful threat to the corporate enterprise. The adoption of a defensive measure, reasonable in relation to the threat posed, was proper and fully accorded with the powers, duties, and responsibilities conferred upon directors under our law.

....

D

However, when Pantry Pride increased its offer to $ 50 per share, and then to $ 53, it became apparent to all that the break-up of the company was inevitable. The Revlon board's authorization permitting management to negotiate a merger or buyout with a third party was a recognition that the company was for sale. The duty of the board had thus changed from the preservation of Revlon as a corporate entity to the maximization of the company's value at a sale for the stockholders' benefit. This significantly altered the board's responsibilities under the *Unocal* standards. It no longer faced threats to corporate policy and effectiveness, or to the stockholders' interests, from a grossly inadequate bid. The whole question of defensive measures became moot. The directors' role changed from defenders of the corporate bastion to auctioneers charged with getting the best price for the stockholders at a sale of the company.

III

This brings us to the lock-up with Forstmann and its emphasis on shoring up the sagging market value of the Notes in the face of threatened litigation by their holders. Such a focus was inconsistent with the changed concept of the directors' responsibilities at this stage of the developments. The impending waiver of the Notes covenants had caused the value of the Notes to fall, and the board was aware of the noteholders' ire as well as their subsequent threats of suit. The directors thus made support of the Notes an integral part of the company's dealings with Forstmann, even though their primary responsibility at this stage was to the equity owners.

The original threat posed by Pantry Pride — the break-up of the company — had become a reality which even the directors embraced. Selective dealing to fend off a hostile but determined bidder was no longer a proper objective. Instead, obtaining the highest price for the benefit of the stockholders should have been the central theme guiding director action. Thus, the Revlon board could not make the requisite showing of good faith by preferring the noteholders and ignoring its duty of loyalty to the shareholders. The rights of the former already were fixed by contract. The noteholders required no further protection, and when the Revlon board entered into an auction-ending lock-up agreement with Forstmann on the basis of impermissible considerations at the expense of the shareholders, the directors breached their primary duty of loyalty.

The Revlon board argued that it acted in good faith in protecting the noteholders because Unocal permits consideration of other corporate constituencies. Although such considerations may be permissible, there are fundamental limitations upon that prerogative. A board may have regard for various constituencies in discharging its responsibilities, provided there are rationally related benefits accruing to the stockholders. *Unocal*, 493 A.2d at 955. However, such concern for non-stockholder interests is inappropriate when an auction among active bidders is in progress, and the object no longer is to protect or maintain the corporate enterprise but to sell it to the highest bidder.

Revlon also contended that ... it had contractual and good faith obligations to consider the noteholders. However, any such duties are limited to the principle that one may not interfere with contractual relationships by improper actions. Here, the rights of the noteholders were fixed by agreement, and there is nothing of substance to suggest that any of those terms were violated. The Notes covenants specifically contemplated a waiver to permit sale of the company at a fair price. The Notes were accepted by the holders on that basis, including the risk of an adverse market effect stemming from a waiver. Thus, nothing remained for Revlon to legitimately protect, and no rationally related benefit thereby accrued to the stockholders. Under such circumstances we must conclude that the merger agreement with Forstmann was unreasonable in relation to the threat posed.

A lock-up is not *per se* illegal under Delaware law.... Such options can entice other bidders to enter a contest for control of the corporation, creating an auction for the company and maximizing shareholder profit. Current economic conditions in the takeover market are such that a "white knight" like Forstmann might only enter the bidding for the target company if it receives some form of compensation to cover the risks and costs involved. However, while those lock-ups which draw bidders into the battle benefit shareholders, similar measures which end an active auction and foreclose further bidding operate to the shareholders' detriment.

....

The Forstmann option had a similar destructive effect on the auction process. Forstmann had already been drawn into the contest on a preferred basis, so the result of the lock-up was not to foster bidding, but to destroy it. The board's stated reasons for approving the transactions were: (1) better financing, (2) noteholder protection, and (3) higher price. As the Court of Chancery found, and we agree, any distinctions between the rival bidders' methods of financing the proposal were nominal at best, and such a consideration has little or no significance in a cash offer for any and all shares. The principal object, contrary to the board's duty of care, appears to have been protection of the noteholders over the shareholders' interests.

While Forstmann's $ 57.25 offer was objectively higher than Pantry Pride's $ 56.25 bid, the margin of superiority is less when the Forstmann price is adjusted for the time value of money. In reality, the Revlon board ended the auction in return for very little actual improvement in the final bid. The principal benefit went to the directors, who avoided personal liability to a class of creditors to whom the board owed no further duty under the circumstances. Thus, when a board ends an intense bidding contest on an insubstantial basis, and where a significant by-product of that action is to protect the directors against a perceived threat of personal liability for consequences stemming from the adoption of previous defensive measures, the action cannot withstand the enhanced scrutiny which *Unocal* requires of director conduct.

In addition to the lock-up option, the Court of Chancery enjoined the no-shop provision as part of the attempt to foreclose further bidding by Pantry Pride. The no-shop provision, like the lock-up option, while not *per se* illegal, is impermissible under the *Unocal* standards when a board's primary duty becomes that of an auctioneer responsible for selling the company to the highest bidder. The agreement to negotiate only with Forstmann ended rather than intensified the board's involvement in the bidding contest.

It is ironic that the parties even considered a no-shop agreement when Revlon had dealt preferentially, and almost exclusively, with Forstmann throughout the contest. After the directors authorized management to negotiate with other parties, Forstmann was given every negotiating advantage that Pantry Pride had been denied: cooperation from management, access to financial data, and the exclusive opportunity to present merger proposals directly to the board of directors. Favoritism for a white knight to the total exclusion of a hostile bidder might be justifiable when the latter's offer adversely affects shareholder interests, but when bidders make relatively similar offers, or dissolution of the company becomes inevitable, the directors cannot fulfill their enhanced *Unocal* duties by playing favorites with the contending factions. Market forces must be allowed to operate freely to bring the target's shareholders the best price available for their equity. Thus, as the trial court ruled, the shareholders' interests necessitated that the board remain free to negotiate in the fulfillment of that duty.

. . . .

IV

Having concluded that Pantry Pride has shown a reasonable probability of success on the merits, we address the issue of irreparable harm. The Court of Chancery ruled that unless the lock-up and other aspects of the agreement were enjoined, Pantry Pride's opportunity to bid for Revlon was lost. The court also held that the need for both bidders to compete in the marketplace outweighed any injury to Forstmann. Given the complexity of the proposed transaction between Revlon and Forstmann, the obstacles to Pantry Pride obtaining a meaningful legal remedy are immense. We are satisfied that the plaintiff has shown the need for an injunction to protect it from irreparable harm, which need outweighs any harm to the defendants.

V

In conclusion, the Revlon board was confronted with a situation not uncommon in the current wave of corporate takeovers. A hostile and determined bidder sought the company at a price the board was convinced was inadequate. The initial defensive tactics worked to the benefit of the shareholders, and thus the board was able to sustain its *Unocal* burdens in justifying those measures. However, in granting an asset option lock-up to Forstmann, we must conclude that under all the circumstances the directors allowed considerations other than the maximization of shareholder profit to affect their judgment, and followed a course that ended the auction for Revlon, absent court intervention, to the ultimate detriment of its shareholders. No such defensive measure can be sustained when it represents a breach of the directors' fundamental duty of care.... In that context the board's action is not entitled to the deference accorded it by the business judgment rule. The measures were properly enjoined. The decision of the Court of Chancery, therefore, is

Affirmed.

Based on your analysis of the two cases, when are *Unocal's* reasonableness standard of conduct and *Revlon's* auctioneer standard of conduct triggered? Exactly what does each standard require?

C. REFINEMENTS OF ENHANCED SCRUTINY

Cases following *Unocal* and *Revlon* continue to clarify the meaning and applicability of the *Unocal* and *Revlon* duties. In what circumstances will the duties be triggered? How will the standards be interpreted?

PARAMOUNT COMMUNICATIONS, INC. v. TIME, INC.

Supreme Court of Delaware
571 A.2d 1140 (1989)

HORSEY, JUSTICE:

Paramount Communications, Inc. ("Paramount") and two other groups of plaintiffs ("Shareholder Plaintiffs"), shareholders of Time Incorporated ("Time"), a Delaware corporation, separately filed suits in the Delaware Court of Chancery seeking a preliminary injunction to halt Time's tender offer for 51% of Warner Communication, Inc.'s ("Warner") outstanding shares at $ 70 cash per share. The court below ... denied plaintiffs' motion. In a 50-page unreported opinion and order entered July 14, 1989, the Chancellor refused to enjoin Time's consummation of its tender offer, concluding that the plaintiffs were unlikely to prevail on the merits.

On the same day, plaintiffs filed in this Court an interlocutory appeal, which we accepted on an expedited basis. Pending the appeal, a stay of execution of Time's tender offer was entered for ten days, or until July 24, 1989, at 5:00 p.m. Following briefing and oral argument, on July 24 we concluded that the decision below should be affirmed. We so held in a brief ruling from the bench and a separate Order entered on that date. The effect of our decision was to permit

Time to proceed with its tender offer for Warner's outstanding shares. This is the written opinion articulating the reasons for our July 24 bench ruling. 565 A.2d 280, 281.

The principal ground for reversal, asserted by all plaintiffs, is that Paramount's June 7, 1989 uninvited all-cash, all-shares, "fully negotiable" (though conditional) tender offer for Time triggered duties under *Unocal Corp. v. Mesa Petroleum Co.*, Del. Supr., 493 A.2d 946 (1985), and that Time's board of directors, in responding to Paramount's offer, breached those duties. As a consequence, plaintiffs argue that in our review of the Time board's decision of June 16, 1989 to enter into a revised merger agreement with Warner, Time is not entitled to the benefit and protection of the business judgment rule.

Shareholder Plaintiffs also assert a claim based on *Revlon v. MacAndrews & Forbes Holdings, Inc.*, Del. Supr., 506 A.2d 173 (1986). They argue that the original Time-Warner merger agreement of March 4, 1989 resulted in a change of control which effectively put Time up for sale, thereby triggering *Revlon* duties. Those plaintiffs argue that Time's board breached its *Revlon* duties by failing, in the face of the change of control, to maximize shareholder value in the immediate term.

Applying our standard of review, we affirm the Chancellor's ultimate finding and conclusion under *Unocal*. We find that Paramount's tender offer was reasonably perceived by Time's board to pose a threat to Time and that the Time board's "response" to that threat was, under the circumstances, reasonable and proportionate. Applying *Unocal*, we reject the argument that the only corporate threat posed by an all-shares, all-cash tender offer is the possibility of inadequate value.

We also find that Time's board did not by entering into its initial merger agreement with Warner come under a *Revlon* duty either to auction the company or to maximize short-term shareholder value, notwithstanding the unequal share exchange. Therefore, the Time board's original plan of merger with Warner was subject only to a business judgment rule analysis. *See Smith v. Van Gorkom*, Del. Supr., 488 A.2d 858, 873-74 (1985).

I

Time is a Delaware corporation with its principal offices in New York City. Time's traditional business is publication of magazines and books; however, Time also provides pay television programming through its Home Box Office, Inc. and Cinemax subsidiaries. In addition, Time owns and operates cable television franchises through its subsidiary, American Television and Communication Corporation. During the relevant time period, Time's board consisted of sixteen directors. Twelve of the directors were "outside," nonemployee directors. Four of the directors were also officers of the company.

....

As early as 1983 and 1984, Time's executive board began considering expanding Time's operations into the entertainment industry. In 1987, Time established a special committee of executives to consider and propose corporate strategies for the 1990s. The consensus of the committee was that Time should move ahead in the area of ownership and creation of video programming.... Some of Time's outside directors had opposed this move as a threat to the editorial integrity and journalistic focus of Time.[11]

In late spring of 1987, a meeting took place between Steve Ross, CEO of Warner Brothers, and Nicholas [president and chief operating officer] of Time. Ross and Nicholas discussed the possibility of a joint venture between the two companies through the creation of a jointly-owned cable company....

On August 11, 1987, Gerald M. Levin, Time's vice chairman and chief strategist, wrote J. Richard Munro [Time's chair and CEO] a confidential memorandum in which he strongly recommended a strategic consolidation with Warner....

....

... On July 21, 1988, Time's board met, with all outside directors present. The meeting's purpose was to consider Time's expansion into the entertainment industry on a global scale. Management presented the board with a profile of various entertainment companies in addition to Warner, including Disney, 20th Century Fox, Universal, and Paramount.

Without any definitive decision on choice of a company, the board approved in principle a strategic plan for Time's expansion. The board gave management the "go-ahead" to continue discussions with Warner concerning the possibility of a merger....

The board's consensus was that a merger of Time and Warner was feasible, but only if Time controlled the board of the resulting corporation and thereby preserved a management committed to Time's journalistic integrity. To accomplish this goal, the board stressed the importance of carefully defining in advance the corporate governance provisions that would control the resulting entity. Some board members expressed concern over whether such a business combination would place Time "*in play*." The board discussed the wisdom of adopting further defensive measures to lessen such a possibility.

....

From the outset, Time's board favored an all-cash or cash and securities acquisition of Warner as the basis for consolidation. Bruce Wasserstein, Time's financial advisor, also favored an outright purchase of Warner. However, Steve Ross, Warner's CEO, was adamant that a business combination was only practicable on a stock-for-stock basis. Warner insisted on a stock swap in order

----

[11] The primary concern of Time's outside directors was the preservation of the "Time Culture." They believed that Time had become recognized in this country as an institution built upon a foundation of journalistic integrity. Time's management made a studious effort to refrain from involvement in Time's editorial policy. Several of Time's outside directors feared that a merger with an entertainment company would divert Time's focus from news journalism and threaten the Time Culture.

to preserve its shareholders' equity in the resulting corporation. Time's officers, on the other hand, made it abundantly clear that Time would be the acquiring corporation and that Time would control the resulting board. Time refused to permit itself to be cast as the "acquired" company.

Eventually Time acquiesced in Warner's insistence on a stock-for-stock deal, but talks broke down over corporate governance issues. Time wanted Ross' position as a co-CEO to be temporary and wanted Ross to retire in five years. Ross, however, refused to set a time for his retirement and viewed Time's proposal as indicating a lack of confidence in his leadership. Warner considered it vital that their executives and creative staff not perceive Warner as selling out to Time. Time's request of a guarantee that Time would dominate the CEO succession was objected to as inconsistent with the concept of a Time-Warner merger "of equals." Negotiations ended when the parties reached an impasse. Time's board refused to compromise on its position on corporate governance. Time, and particularly its outside directors, viewed the corporate governance provisions as critical for preserving the "Time Culture" through a pro-Time management at the top....

. . . .

Warner and Time resumed negotiations in January 1989. The catalyst for the resumption of talks was a private dinner between Steve Ross and Time outside director, Michael Dingman. Dingman was able to convince Ross that the transitional nature of the proposed co-CEO arrangement did not reflect a lack of confidence in Ross. Ross agreed that this course was best for the company and a meeting between Ross and Munro resulted. Ross agreed to retire in five years and let Nicholas succeed him. Negotiations resumed and many of the details of the original stock-for-stock exchange agreement remained intact. In addition, Time's senior management agreed to long-term contracts.

Time insider directors Levin and Nicholas met with Warner's financial advisors to decide upon a stock exchange ratio. Time's board had recognized the potential need to pay a premium in the stock ratio in exchange for dictating the governing arrangement of the new Time-Warner.... Warner's financial advisors informed its board that any exchange rate over .400 was a fair deal and any exchange rate over .450 was "one hell of a deal." The parties ultimately agreed upon an exchange rate favoring Warner of .465. On that basis, Warner stockholders would have owned approximately 62% of the common stock of Time-Warner.

On March 3, 1989, Time's board, with all but one director in attendance, met and unanimously approved the stock-for-stock merger with Warner. Warner's board likewise approved the merger. The agreement called for Warner to be merged into a wholly-owned Time subsidiary with Warner becoming the surviving corporation. The common stock of Warner would then be converted into common stock of Time at the agreed upon ratio. Thereafter, the name of Time would be changed to Time-Warner, Inc.

. . . .

At its March 3, 1989 meeting, Time's board adopted several defensive tactics. Time entered an automatic share exchange agreement with Warner. Time would receive 17,292,747 shares of Warner's outstanding common stock (9.4%) and Warner would receive 7,080,016 shares of Time's outstanding common stock (11.1%). Either party could trigger the exchange. Time sought out and paid for "confidence" letters from various banks with which it did business. In these letters, the banks promised not to finance any third-party attempt to acquire Time. Time argues these agreements served only to preserve the confidential relationship between itself and the banks. The Chancellor found these agreements to be inconsequential and futile attempts to "dry up" money for a hostile takeover. Time also agreed to a "no-shop" clause, preventing Time from considering any other consolidation proposal, thus relinquishing its power to consider other proposals, regardless of their merits. Time did so at Warner's insistence. Warner did not want to be left "on the auction block" for an unfriendly suitor, if Time were to withdraw from the deal.

Time's board simultaneously established a special committee of outside directors, Finkelstein, Kearns, and Opel, to oversee the merger. The committee's assignment was to resolve any impediments that might arise in the course of working out the details of the merger and its consummation.

... On May 24, 1989, Time sent out extensive proxy statements to the stockholders regarding the approval vote on the merger. In the meantime, with the merger proceeding without impediment, the special committee had concluded, shortly after its creation, that it was not necessary either to retain independent consultants, legal or financial, or even to meet. Time's board was unanimously in favor of the proposed merger with Warner; and, by the end of May, the Time-Warner merger appeared to be an accomplished fact.

On June 7, 1989, these wishful assumptions were shattered by Paramount's surprising announcement of its all-cash offer to purchase all outstanding shares of Time for $ 175 per share. The following day, June 8, the trading price of Time's stock rose from $ 126 to $ 170 per share. Paramount's offer was said to be "fully negotiable."

Time found Paramount's "fully negotiable" offer to be in fact subject to at least three conditions. First, Time had to terminate its merger agreement and stock exchange agreement with Warner, and remove certain other of its defensive devices, including the redemption of Time's shareholder rights. Second, Paramount had to obtain the required cable franchise transfers from Time in a fashion acceptable to Paramount in its sole discretion. Finally, the offer depended upon a judicial determination that section 203 of the General Corporate Law of Delaware (The Delaware Anti-Takeover Statute) was inapplicable to any Time-Paramount merger....

On June 8, 1989, Time formally responded to Paramount's offer. Time's chairman and CEO, J. Richard Munro, sent an aggressively worded letter to Paramount's CEO, Martin Davis. Munro's letter attacked Davis' personal integrity and called Paramount's offer "smoke and mirrors." Time's nonmanagement directors were not shown the letter before it was sent. However, at a board meeting that same day, all members endorsed management's response as well as the letter's content.

Over the following eight days, Time's board met three times to discuss Paramount's $ 175 offer. The board viewed Paramount's offer as inadequate and concluded that its proposed merger with Warner was the better course of action. Therefore, the board declined to open any negotiations with Paramount and held steady its course toward a merger with Warner.

In June, Time's board of directors met several times. During the course of their June meetings, Time's outside directors met frequently without management, officers or directors being present. At the request of the outside directors, corporate counsel was present during the board meetings and, from time to time, the management directors were asked to leave the board sessions. During the course of these meetings, Time's financial advisors informed the board that, on an auction basis, Time's per share value was materially higher than Warner's $ 175 per share offer. After this advice, the board concluded that Paramount's $ 175 offer was inadequate.

At these June meetings, certain Time directors expressed their concern that Time stockholders would not comprehend the long-term benefits of the Warner merger. Large quantities of Time shares were held by institutional investors. The board feared that even though there appeared to be wide support for the Warner transaction, Paramount's cash premium would be a tempting prospect to these investors. In mid-June, Time sought permission from the New York Stock Exchange to alter its rules and allow the Time-Warner merger to proceed without stockholder approval. Time did so at Warner's insistence. The New York Stock Exchange rejected Time's request on June 15; and on that day, the value of Time stock reached $ 182 per share.

The following day, June 16, Time's board met to take up Paramount's offer. The board's prevailing belief was that Paramount's bid posed a threat to Time's control of its own destiny and retention of the "Time Culture." Even after Time's financial advisors made another presentation of Paramount and its business attributes, Time's board maintained its position that a combination with Warner offered greater potential for Time. Warner provided Time a much desired production capability and an established international marketing chain. Time's advisors suggested various options, including defensive measures. The board considered and rejected the idea of purchasing Paramount in a "Pac Man" defense. The board considered other defenses, including a recapitalization, the acquisition of another company, and a material change in the present capitalization structure or dividend policy. The board determined to retain its same advisors even in light of the changed circumstances. The board rescinded its agreement to pay its advisors a bonus based on the consummation of the Time-Warner merger and agreed to pay a flat fee for any advice rendered. Finally, Time's board formally rejected Paramount's offer.

At the same meeting, Time's board decided to recast its consolidation with Warner into an outright cash and securities acquisition of Warner by Time; and Time so informed Warner. Time accordingly restructured its proposal to acquire Warner as follows: Time would make an immediate all-cash offer for 51% of Warner's outstanding stock at $ 70 per share. The remaining 49% would be purchased at some later date for a mixture of cash and securities worth $ 70 per share. To provide the funds required for its outright acquisition of Warner, Time would assume 7-10 billion dollars worth of debt, thus eliminating one of the principal transaction-related benefits of the original merger agreement. Nine billion dollars of the total purchase price would be allocated to the purchase of Warner's goodwill.

Warner agreed but insisted on certain terms. Warner sought a control premium and guarantees that the governance provisions found in the original merger agreement would remain intact. Warner further sought agreements that Time would not employ its poison pill against Warner and that, unless enjoined, Time would be legally bound to complete the transaction. Time's board agreed to these last measures only at the insistence of Warner. For its part, Time was assured of its ability to extend its efforts into production areas and international markets, all the while maintaining the Time identity and culture. The Chancellor found the initial Time-Warner transaction to have been negotiated at arms length and the restructured Time-Warner transaction to have resulted from Paramount's offer and its expected effect on a Time shareholder vote.

On June 23, 1989, Paramount raised its all-cash offer to buy Time's outstanding stock to $ 200 per share. Paramount still professed that all aspects of the offer were negotiable. Time's board met on June 26, 1989 and formally rejected Paramount's $ 200 per share second offer. The board reiterated its belief that, despite the $ 25 increase, the offer was still inadequate. The Time board maintained that the Warner transaction offered a greater long-term value for the stockholders and, unlike Paramount's offer, did not pose a threat to Time's survival and its "culture." Paramount then filed this action in the Court of Chancery.

II

The Shareholder Plaintiffs first assert a *Revlon* claim. They contend that the March 4 Time-Warner agreement effectively put Time up for sale, triggering *Revlon* duties, requiring Time's board to enhance short-term shareholder value and to treat all other interested acquirors on an equal basis. The Shareholder Plaintiffs base this argument on two facts: (i) the ultimate Time-Warner exchange ratio of .465 favoring Warner, resulting in Warner shareholders' receipt of 62% of the combined company; and (ii) the subjective intent of Time's directors as evidenced in their statements that the market might perceive the Time-Warner merger as putting Time up "for sale" and their adoption of various defensive measures.

The Shareholder Plaintiffs further contend that Time's directors, in structuring the original merger transaction to be "takeover-proof," triggered *Revlon* duties by foreclosing their shareholders from any prospect of obtaining a control premium. In short, plaintiffs argue that Time's board's decision to merge with Warner imposed a fiduciary duty to maximize immediate share value and not erect unreasonable barriers to further bids. Therefore, they argue, the Chancellor erred in finding: that Paramount's bid for Time did not place Time "for sale"; that Time's transaction with Warner did not result in any transfer of control; and that the combined Time-Warner was not so large as to preclude the possibility of the stockholders of Time-Warner receiving a future control premium.

Paramount asserts only a *Unocal* claim in which the shareholder plaintiffs join. Paramount contends that the Chancellor, in applying the first part of the *Unocal* test, erred in finding that Time's board had reasonable grounds to believe that Paramount posed both a legally cognizable threat to Time shareholders and a danger to Time's corporate policy and effectiveness. Paramount also contests the court's finding that Time's board made a reasonable and objective investigation of Paramount's offer so as to be informed before rejecting it. Paramount further claims that the court erred in applying *Unocal*'s second part in finding Time's response to be "reasonable." Paramount points primarily to the preclusive effect of the revised agreement which denied Time shareholders the opportunity both to vote on the agreement and to respond to Paramount's tender offer. Paramount argues that the underlying motivation of Time's board in adopting these defensive measures was management's desire to perpetuate itself in office.

The Court of Chancery posed the pivotal question presented by this case to be: Under what circumstances must a board of directors abandon an in-place plan of corporate development in order to provide its shareholders with the option to elect and realize an immediate control premium? As applied to this case, the question becomes: Did Time's board, having developed a strategic plan of global expansion to be launched through a business combination with Warner, come under a fiduciary duty to jettison its plan and put the corporation's future in the hands of its shareholders?

While we affirm the result reached by the Chancellor, we think it unwise to place undue emphasis upon long-term versus short-term corporate strategy. Two key predicates underpin our analysis. First, Delaware law imposes on a board of directors the duty to manage the business and affairs of the corporation. 8 Del. C. § 141(a). This broad mandate includes a conferred authority to set a corporate course of action, including time frame, designed to enhance corporate profitability. Thus, the question of "long-term" versus "short-term" values is largely irrelevant because directors, generally, are obliged to chart a course for a corporation which is in its best interests without regard to a fixed investment horizon. Second, absent a limited set of circumstances as defined under *Revlon*, a board of directors, while always required to act in an informed manner, is not under any *per se* duty to maximize shareholder value in the short term, even in the context of a takeover. In our view, the pivotal question presented by this case is: "Did Time, by entering into the proposed merger with Warner, put itself up for sale?" A resolution of that issue through application of *Revlon* has a significant bearing upon the resolution of the derivative *Unocal* issue.

A

We first take up plaintiffs' principal *Revlon* argument, summarized above. In rejecting this argument, the Chancellor found the original Time-Warner merger agreement not to constitute a "change of control" and concluded that the transaction did not trigger *Revlon* duties. The Chancellor's conclusion is premised on a finding that "[b]efore the merger agreement was signed, control of the corporation existed in a fluid aggregation of unaffiliated shareholders representing a voting majority — in other words, in the market." The Chancellor's findings of fact are supported by the record and his conclusion is correct as a matter of law. However, we premise our rejection of plaintiffs' *Revlon* claim on different grounds, namely, the absence of any substantial evidence to conclude that Time's board, in negotiating with Warner, made the dissolution or break-up of the corporate entity inevitable, as was the case in *Revlon*.

Under Delaware law there are, generally speaking and without excluding other possibilities, two circumstances which may implicate *Revlon* duties. The first, and clearer one, is when a corporation initiates an active bidding process seeking to sell itself or to effect a business reorganization involving a clear break-up of the company. However, *Revlon* duties may also be triggered where, in response to a bidder's offer, a target abandons its long-term strategy and seeks an alternative transaction involving the breakup of the company.[12] Thus, in *Revlon*, when the board responded to Pantry Pride's offer by contemplating a "bust-up" sale of assets in a leveraged acquisition, we imposed upon the board a duty to maximize immediate shareholder value and an obligation to auction the company fairly. If, however, the board's reaction to a hostile tender offer is found to constitute only a defensive response and not an abandonment of the corporation's continued existence, *Revlon* duties are not triggered, though *Unocal* duties attach.

The plaintiffs insist that even though the original Time-Warner agreement may not have worked "an objective change of control," the transaction made a "sale" of Time inevitable. Plaintiffs rely on the subjective intent of Time's board of directors and principally upon certain board members' expressions of concern that the Warner transaction *might* be viewed as effectively putting Time up for sale. Plaintiffs argue that the use of a lock-up agreement, a no-shop clause, and so-called "dry-up" agreements prevented shareholders from obtaining a control premium in the immediate future and thus violated *Revlon*.

---

[12] As we stated in *Revlon*, in both such cases, "[t]he duty of the board [has] changed from the preservation of ... [the] corporate entity to the maximization of the company's value at a sale for the stockholder's benefit.... [The board] no longer face[s] threats to corporate policy and effectiveness, or to the stockholders' interests, from a grossly inadequate bid." *Revlon v. MacAndrews & Forbes Holdings, Inc.*, Del. Supr., 506 A.2d 173, 182 (1986).

We agree with the Chancellor that such evidence is entirely insufficient to invoke *Revlon* duties; and we decline to extend *Revlon*'s application to corporate transactions simply because they might be construed as putting a corporation either "in play" or "up for sale." The adoption of structural safety devices alone does not trigger *Revlon*. Rather, as the Chancellor stated, such devices are properly subject to a *Unocal* analysis.

Finally, we do not find in Time's recasting of its merger agreement with Warner from a share exchange to a share purchase a basis to conclude that Time had either abandoned its strategic plan or made a sale of Time inevitable. The Chancellor found that although the merged Time-Warner company would be large (with a value approaching approximately $ 30 billion), recent takeover cases have proven that acquisition of the combined company might nonetheless be possible. The legal consequence is that *Unocal* alone applies to determine whether the business judgment rule attaches to the revised agreement....

B

We turn now to plaintiffs' *Unocal* claim. We begin by noting, as did the Chancellor, that our decision does not require us to pass on the wisdom of the board's decision to enter into the original Time-Warner agreement. That is not a court's task. Our task is simply to review the record to determine whether there is sufficient evidence to support the Chancellor's conclusion that the initial Time-Warner agreement was the product of a proper exercise of business judgment.

We have purposely detailed the evidence of the Time board's deliberative approach, beginning in 1983-84, to expand itself. Time's decision in 1988 to combine with Warner was made only after what could be fairly characterized as an exhaustive appraisal of Time's future as a corporation.... We find ample evidence in the record to support the Chancellor's conclusion that the Time board's decision to expand the business of the company through its March 3 merger with Warner was entitled to the protection of the business judgment rule.

The Chancellor reached a different conclusion in addressing the Time-Warner transaction as revised three months later. He found that the revised agreement was defense-motivated and designed to avoid the potentially disruptive effect that Paramount's offer would have had on consummation of the proposed merger were it put to a shareholder vote. Thus, the court declined to apply the traditional business judgment rule to the revised transaction and instead analyzed the Time board's June 16 decision under *Unocal*. The court ruled that *Unocal* applied to all director actions taken, following receipt of Paramount's hostile tender offer, that were reasonably determined to be defensive. Clearly that was a correct ruling and no party disputes that ruling.

In *Unocal*, we held that before the business judgment rule is applied to a board's adoption of a defensive measure, the burden will lie with the board to prove (a) reasonable grounds for believing that a danger to corporate policy and effectiveness existed; and (b) that the defensive measure adopted was reasonable in relation to the threat posed. *Unocal*, 493 A.2d 946. Directors satisfy the first part of the *Unocal* test by demonstrating good faith and reasonable investigation. We have repeatedly stated that the refusal to entertain an offer may comport with a valid exercise of a board's business judgment.

Unocal involved a two-tier, highly coercive tender offer. In such a case, the threat is obvious: shareholders may be compelled to tender to avoid being treated adversely in the second stage of the transaction. In subsequent cases, the Court of Chancery has suggested that an all-cash, all-shares offer, falling within a range of values that a shareholder might reasonably prefer, cannot constitute a legally recognized "threat" to shareholder interests sufficient to withstand a *Unocal* analysis. In those cases, the Court of Chancery determined that whatever threat existed related only to the shareholders and only to price and not to the corporation.

From those decisions by our Court of Chancery, Paramount and the individual plaintiffs extrapolate a rule of law that an all-cash, all-shares offer with values reasonably in the range of acceptable price cannot pose any objective threat to a corporation or its shareholders. Thus, Paramount would have us hold that only if the value of Paramount's offer were determined to be clearly inferior to the value created by management's plan to merge with Warner could the offer be viewed — objectively — as a threat.

Implicit in the plaintiffs' argument is the view that a hostile tender offer can pose only two types of threats: the threat of coercion that results from a two-tier offer promising unequal treatment for nontendering shareholders; and the threat of inadequate value from an all-shares, all-cash offer at a price below what a target board in good faith deems to be the present value of its shares. Since Paramount's offer was all-cash, the only conceivable "threat," plaintiffs argue, was inadequate value. We disapprove of such a narrow and rigid construction of *Unocal*, for the reasons which follow.

Plaintiffs' position represents a fundamental misconception of our standard of review under *Unocal* principally because it would involve the court in substituting its judgment as to what is a "better" deal for that of a corporation's board of directors. To the extent that the Court of Chancery has recently done so in certain of its opinions, we hereby reject such approach as not in keeping with a proper *Unocal* analysis.

The usefulness of *Unocal* as an analytical tool is precisely its flexibility in the face of a variety of fact scenarios. *Unocal* is not intended as an abstract standard; neither is it a structured and mechanistic procedure of appraisal. Thus, we have said that directors may consider, when evaluating the threat posed by a takeover bid, the "inadequacy of the price offered, nature and timing of the offer, questions of illegality, the impact on 'constituencies' other than shareholders ... the risk of nonconsummation, and the quality of securities being offered in the exchange." 493 A.2d at 955. The open-ended analysis mandated by *Unocal* is not intended to lead to a simple mathematical exercise: that is, of comparing the discounted value of Time-Warner's expected trading price at some future date with Paramount's offer and determining which is the higher. Indeed, in our view, precepts underlying the business judgment rule militate against a court's engaging in the process of attempting to appraise and evaluate the relative merits of a long-term versus a short-term investment goal for shareholders. To engage in such an exercise is a distortion of the *Unocal* process and, in particular, the application of the second part of *Unocal*'s test, discussed below.

In this case, the Time board reasonably determined that inadequate value was not the only legally cognizable threat that Paramount's all-cash, all-shares offer could present. Time's board concluded that Paramount's eleventh hour offer posed other threats. One concern was that Time shareholders might elect to tender into Paramount's cash offer in ignorance or a mistaken belief of the strategic benefit which a business combination with Warner might produce. Moreover, Time viewed the conditions attached to Paramount's offer as introducing a degree of uncertainty that skewed a comparative analysis. Further, the timing of Paramount's offer to follow issuance of Time's proxy notice was viewed as arguably designed to upset, if not confuse, the Time stockholders' vote. Given this record evidence, we cannot conclude that the Time board's decision of June 6 that Paramount's offer posed a threat to corporate policy and effectiveness was lacking in good faith or dominated by motives of either entrenchment or self-interest.

Paramount also contends that the Time board had not duly investigated Paramount's offer. Therefore, Paramount argues, Time was unable to make an informed decision that the offer posed a threat to Time's corporate policy. Although the Chancellor did not address this issue directly, his findings of fact do detail Time's exploration of the available entertainment companies, including Paramount, before determining that Warner provided the best strategic "fit." In addition, the court found that Time's board rejected Paramount's offer because Paramount did not serve Time's objectives or meet Time's needs. Thus, the record does, in our judgment, demonstrate that Time's board was adequately informed of the potential benefits of a transaction with Paramount. We agree with the Chancellor that the Time board's lengthy pre-June investigation of potential merger candidates, including Paramount, mooted any obligation on Time's part to halt its merger process with Warner to reconsider Paramount. Time's board was under no obligation to negotiate with Paramount. Time's failure to negotiate cannot be fairly found to have been uninformed. The evidence supporting this finding is materially enhanced by the fact that twelve of Time's sixteen board members were outside independent directors.

We turn to the second part of the *Unocal* analysis. The obvious requisite to determining the reasonableness of a defensive action is a clear identification of the nature of the threat. As the Chancellor correctly noted, this "requires an evaluation of the importance of the corporate objective threatened; alternative methods of protecting that objective; impacts of the 'defensive' action, and other relevant factors." It is not until both parts of the *Unocal* inquiry have been satisfied that the business judgment rule attaches to defensive actions of a board of directors. As applied to the facts of this case, the question is whether the record evidence supports the Court of Chancery's conclusion that the restructuring of the Time-Warner transaction, including the adoption of several preclusive defensive measures, was a *reasonable response* in relation to a perceived threat.

Paramount argues that, assuming its tender offer posed a threat, Time's response was unreasonable in precluding Time's shareholders from accepting the tender offer or receiving a control premium in the immediately foreseeable future. Once again, the contention stems, we believe, from a fundamental misunderstanding of where the power of corporate governance lies. Delaware law confers the management of the corporate enterprise to the stockholders' duly elected board representatives. 8 Del. C. § 141(a). The fiduciary duty to manage a corporate enterprise includes the selection of a time frame for achievement of corporate goals. That duty may not be delegated to the stockholders. Directors are not obliged to abandon a deliberately conceived corporate plan for a short-term shareholder profit unless there is clearly no basis to sustain the corporate strategy.

Although the Chancellor blurred somewhat the discrete analyses required under *Unocal*, he did conclude that Time's board reasonably perceived Paramount's offer to be a significant threat to the planned Time-Warner merger and that Time's response was not "overly broad." We have found that even in light of a valid threat, management actions that are coercive in nature or force upon shareholders a management-sponsored alternative to a hostile offer may be struck down as unreasonable and nonproportionate responses.

Here, on the record facts, the Chancellor found that Time's responsive action to Paramount's tender offer was not aimed at "cramming down" on its shareholders a management-sponsored alternative, but rather had as its goal the carrying forward of a pre-existing transaction in an altered form. Thus, the response was reasonably related to the threat. The Chancellor noted that the revised agreement and its accompanying safety devices did not preclude Paramount from making an offer for the combined Time-Warner company or from changing the conditions of its offer so as not to make the offer dependent upon the nullification of the Time-Warner agreement. Thus, the response was proportionate. We affirm the Chancellor's rulings as clearly supported by the record. Finally, we note that although Time was required, as a result of Paramount's hostile offer, to incur a heavy debt to finance its acquisition of Warner, that fact alone does not render the board's decision unreasonable so long as the directors could reasonably perceive the debt load not to be so injurious to the corporation as to jeopardize its well being.

C. *Conclusion*

Applying the test for grant or denial of preliminary injunctive relief, we find plaintiffs failed to establish a reasonable likelihood of ultimate success on the merits. Therefore, we affirm.

PARAMOUNT COMMUNICATIONS, INC. v. QVC NETWORK, INC.

Supreme Court of Delaware
637 A.2d 34 (1993)

VEASEY, CHIEF JUSTICE:

In this appeal we review an order of the Court of Chancery dated November 24, 1993, ... preliminarily enjoining certain defensive measures designed to facilitate a so-called strategic alliance between Viacom Inc. ("Viacom") and Paramount Communications Inc. ("Paramount") approved by the board of directors of Paramount (the "Paramount Board" or the "Paramount directors") and to thwart an unsolicited, more valuable, tender offer by QVC Network Inc. ("QVC"). In affirming, we hold that the sale of control in this case, which is at the heart of the proposed strategic alliance, implicates enhanced judicial scrutiny of the conduct of the Paramount Board under *Unocal Corp. v. Mesa Petroleum Co.*, Del. Supr., 493 A.2d 946 (1985), and *Revlon, Inc. v. MacAndrews & Forbes Holdings, Inc.*, Del. Supr., 506 A.2d 173 (1986). We further hold that the conduct of the Paramount Board was not reasonable as to process or result.

QVC and certain stockholders of Paramount commenced separate actions (later consolidated) in the Court of Chancery seeking preliminary and permanent injunctive relief against Paramount, certain members of the Paramount Board, and Viacom. This action arises out of a proposed acquisition of Paramount by Viacom through a tender offer followed by a second-step merger (the "Paramount-Viacom transaction"), and a competing unsolicited tender offer by QVC. The Court of Chancery granted a preliminary injunction.

The Court of Chancery found that the Paramount directors violated their fiduciary duties by favoring the Paramount-Viacom transaction over the more valuable unsolicited offer of QVC. The Court of Chancery preliminarily enjoined Paramount and the individual defendants (the "Paramount defendants") from amending or modifying Paramount's stockholder rights agreement (the "Rights Agreement"), including the redemption of the Rights, or taking other action to facilitate the consummation of the pending tender offer by Viacom or any proposed second-step merger, including the Merger Agreement between Paramount and Viacom dated September 12, 1993 (the "Original Merger Agreement"), as amended on October 24, 1993 (the "Amended Merger Agreement"). Viacom and the Paramount defendants were enjoined from taking any action to exercise any provision of the Stock Option Agreement between Paramount and Viacom dated September 12, 1993 (the "Stock Option Agreement"), as amended on October 24, 1993. The Court of Chancery did not grant preliminary injunctive relief as to the termination fee provided for the benefit of Viacom in Section 8.05 of the Original Merger Agreement and the Amended Merger Agreement (the "Termination Fee").

Under the circumstances of this case, the pending sale of control implicated in the Paramount-Viacom transaction required the Paramount Board to act on an informed basis to secure the best value reasonably available to the stockholders.

Since we agree with the Court of Chancery that the Paramount directors violated their fiduciary duties, we have AFFIRMED the entry of the order of the Vice Chancellor granting the preliminary injunction and have REMANDED these proceedings to the Court of Chancery for proceedings consistent herewith.

....

I. *Facts*

....

Paramount is a Delaware corporation with its principal offices in New York City. Approximately 118 million shares of Paramount's common stock are outstanding and traded on the New York Stock Exchange. The majority of Paramount's stock is publicly held by numerous unaffiliated investors. Paramount owns and operates a diverse group of entertainment businesses, including motion picture and television studios, book publishers, professional sports teams, and amusement parks.

There are 15 persons serving on the Paramount Board. Four directors are officer-employees of Paramount: Martin S. Davis ("Davis"), Paramount's Chairman and Chief Executive Officer since 1983; Donald Oresman ("Oresman"), Executive Vice-President, Chief Administrative Officer, and General Counsel; Stanley R. Jaffe, President and Chief Operating Officer; and Ronald L. Nelson, Executive Vice President and Chief Financial Officer. Paramount's 11 outside directors are distinguished and experienced business persons who are present or former senior executives of public corporations or financial institutions.

Viacom is a Delaware corporation with its headquarters in Massachusetts. Viacom is controlled by Sumner M. Redstone ("Redstone"), its Chairman and Chief Executive Officer, who owns indirectly approximately 85.2 percent of Viacom's voting Class A stock and approximately 69.2 percent of Viacom's nonvoting Class B stock through National Amusements, Inc. ("NAI"), an entity 91.7 percent owned by Redstone. Viacom has a wide range of entertainment operations, including a number of well-known cable television channels such as MTV, Nickelodeon, Showtime, and The Movie Channel. Viacom's equity co-investors in the Paramount-Viacom transaction include NYNEX Corporation and Blockbuster Entertainment Corporation.

QVC is a Delaware corporation with its headquarters in West Chester, Pennsylvania. QVC has several large stockholders, including Liberty Media Corporation, Comcast Corporation, Advance Publications, Inc., and Cox Enterprises Inc. Barry Diller ("Diller"), the Chairman and Chief Executive Officer of QVC, is also a substantial stockholder. QVC sells a variety of merchandise through a televised shopping channel. QVC has several equity co-investors in its proposed combination with Paramount including BellSouth Corporation and Comcast Corporation.

Beginning in the late 1980s, Paramount investigated the possibility of acquiring or merging with other companies in the entertainment, media, or communications industry. Paramount considered such transactions to be desirable, and perhaps necessary, in order to keep pace with competitors in the rapidly evolving field of entertainment and communications. Consistent with its goal of strategic expansion, Paramount made a tender offer for Time Inc. in 1989, but was ultimately unsuccessful. *See Paramount Communications, Inc. v. Time Inc.*, Del. Supr., 571 A.2d 1140 (1990) (*"Time-Warner"*).

Although Paramount had considered a possible combination of Paramount and Viacom as early as 1990, ... [a]fter several more meetings between Redstone and Davis, serious negotiations began taking place in early July.

It was tentatively agreed that Davis would be the chief executive officer and Redstone would be the controlling stockholder of the combined company, but the parties could not reach agreement on the merger price and the terms of a stock option to be granted to Viacom. With respect to price, Viacom offered a package of cash and stock (primarily Viacom Class B nonvoting stock) with a market value of approximately $ 61 per share, but Paramount wanted at least $ 70 per share.

....

... After a short hiatus, the parties negotiated in earnest in early September, and performed due diligence with the assistance of their financial advisors, Lazard Freres & Co. ("Lazard") for Paramount and Smith Barney for Viacom. On September 9, 1993, the Paramount Board was informed about the status of the negotiations and was provided information by Lazard, including an analysis of the proposed transaction.

On September 12, 1993, the Paramount Board met again and unanimously approved the Original Merger Agreement whereby Paramount would merge with and into Viacom. The terms of the merger provided that each share of Paramount common stock would be converted into 0.10 shares of Viacom Class A voting stock, 0.90 shares of Viacom Class B nonvoting stock, and $ 9.10 in cash. In addition, the Paramount Board agreed to amend its "poison pill" Rights Agreement to exempt the proposed merger with Viacom. The Original Merger Agreement also contained several provisions designed to make it more difficult for a potential competing bid to succeed. We focus, as did the Court of Chancery, on three of these defensive provisions: a "no-shop" provision (the "No-Shop Provision"), the Termination Fee, and the Stock Option Agreement.

First, under the No-Shop Provision, the Paramount Board agreed that Paramount would not solicit, encourage, discuss, negotiate, or endorse any competing transaction unless: (a) a third party "makes an unsolicited written, bona fide proposal, which is not subject to any material contingencies relating to financing"; and (b) the Paramount Board determines that discussions or negotiations with the third party are necessary for the Paramount Board to comply with its fiduciary duties.

Second, under the Termination Fee provision, Viacom would receive a $ 100 million termination fee if: (a) Paramount terminated the Original Merger Agreement because of a competing transaction; (b) Paramount's stockholders did not approve the merger; or (c) the Paramount Board recommended a competing transaction.

The third and most significant deterrent device was the Stock Option Agreement, which granted to Viacom an option to purchase approximately 19.9 percent (23,699,000 shares) of Paramount's outstanding common stock at $ 69.14 per share if any of the triggering events for the Termination Fee occurred. In addition to the customary terms that are normally associated with a stock option, the Stock Option Agreement contained two provisions that were both unusual and highly beneficial to Viacom: (a) Viacom was permitted to pay for the shares with a senior subordinated note of questionable marketability instead of cash, thereby avoiding the need to raise the $ 1.6 billion purchase price (the "Note Feature"); and (b) Viacom could elect to require Paramount to pay Viacom in cash a sum equal to the difference between the purchase price and the market price of Paramount's stock (the "Put Feature"). Because the Stock Option Agreement was not "capped" to limit its maximum dollar value, it had the potential to reach (and in this case did reach) unreasonable levels.

After the execution of the Original Merger Agreement and the Stock Option Agreement on September 12, 1993, Paramount and Viacom announced their proposed merger. In a number of public statements, the parties indicated that the pending transaction was a virtual certainty. Redstone described it as a "marriage" that would "never be torn asunder" and stated that only a "nuclear attack" could break the deal. Redstone also called Diller and John Malone of Tele-Communications Inc., a major stockholder of QVC, to dissuade them from making a competing bid.

Despite these attempts to discourage a competing bid, Diller sent a letter to Davis on September 20, 1993, proposing a merger in which QVC would acquire Paramount for approximately $ 80 per share, consisting of 0.893 shares of QVC common stock and $ 30 in cash. QVC also expressed its eagerness to meet with Paramount to negotiate the details of a transaction. When the Paramount Board met on September 27, it was advised by Davis that the Original Merger Agreement prohibited Paramount from having discussions with QVC (or anyone else) unless certain conditions were satisfied. In particular, QVC had to supply evidence that its proposal was not subject to financing contingencies. The Paramount Board was also provided information from Lazard describing QVC and its proposal.

On October 5, 1993, QVC provided Paramount with evidence of QVC's financing. The Paramount Board then held another meeting on October 11, and decided to authorize management to meet with QVC. Davis also informed the Paramount Board that Booz-Allen & Hamilton ("Booz-Allen"), a management consulting firm, had been retained to assess, *inter alia*, the incremental earnings potential from a Paramount-Viacom merger and a Paramount-QVC merger. Discussions proceeded slowly, however, due to a delay in Paramount signing a confidentiality agreement. In response to Paramount's request for information, QVC provided two binders of documents to Paramount on October 20.

On October 21, 1993, QVC filed this action and publicly announced an $ 80 cash tender offer for 51 percent of Paramount's outstanding shares (the "QVC tender offer"). Each remaining share of Paramount common stock would be converted into 1.42857 shares of QVC common stock in a second-step merger. The tender offer was conditioned on, among other things, the invalidation of the Stock Option Agreement, which was worth over $ 200 million by that point. QVC contends that it had to commence a tender offer because of the slow pace of the merger discussions and the need to begin seeking clearance under federal antitrust laws.

Confronted by QVC's hostile bid, which on its face offered over $ 10 per share more than the consideration provided by the Original Merger Agreement, Viacom realized that it would need to raise its bid in order to remain competitive. Within hours after QVC's tender offer was announced, Viacom entered into discussions with Paramount concerning a revised transaction. These discussions led to serious negotiations concerning a comprehensive amendment to the original Paramount-Viacom transaction. In effect, the opportunity for a "new deal" with Viacom was at hand for the Paramount Board. With the QVC hostile bid offering greater value to the Paramount stockholders, the Paramount Board had considerable leverage with Viacom.

At a special meeting on October 24, 1993, the Paramount Board approved the Amended Merger Agreement and an amendment to the Stock Option Agreement. The Amended Merger Agreement was, however, essentially the same as the Original Merger Agreement, except that it included a few new provisions. One provision related to an $ 80 per share cash tender offer by Viacom for 51 percent of Paramount's stock, and another changed the merger consideration so that each share of Paramount would be converted into 0.20408 shares of Viacom Class A voting stock, 1.08317 shares of Viacom Class B nonvoting stock, and 0.20408 shares of a new series of Viacom convertible preferred stock. The Amended Merger Agreement also added a provision giving Paramount the right not to amend its Rights Agreement to exempt Viacom if the Paramount Board determined that such an amendment would be inconsistent with its fiduciary duties because another offer constituted a "better alternative." Finally, the Paramount Board was given the power to terminate the Amended Merger Agreement if it withdrew its recommendation of the Viacom transaction or recommended a competing transaction.

Although the Amended Merger Agreement offered more consideration to the Paramount stockholders and somewhat more flexibility to the Paramount Board than did the Original Merger Agreement, the defensive measures designed to make a competing bid more difficult were not removed or modified. In particular, there is no evidence in the record that Paramount sought to use its newly-acquired leverage to eliminate or modify the No-Shop Provision, the Termination Fee, or the Stock Option Agreement when the subject of amending the Original Merger Agreement was on the table.

Viacom's tender offer commenced on October 25, 1993, and QVC's tender offer was formally launched on October 27, 1993. Diller sent a letter to the Paramount Board on October 28 requesting an opportunity to negotiate with Paramount, and Oresman responded the following day by agreeing to meet. The meeting, held on November 1, was not very fruitful, however, after QVC's proposed guidelines for a "fair bidding process" were rejected by Paramount on the ground that "auction procedures" were inappropriate and contrary to Paramount's contractual obligations to Viacom.

On November 6, 1993, Viacom unilaterally raised its tender offer price to $ 85 per share in cash and offered a comparable increase in the value of the securities being proposed in the second-step merger. At a telephonic meeting held later that day, the Paramount Board agreed to recommend Viacom's higher bid to Paramount's stockholders.

QVC responded to Viacom's higher bid on November 12 by increasing its tender offer to $ 90 per share and by increasing the securities for its second-step merger by a similar amount. In response to QVC's latest offer, the Paramount Board scheduled a meeting for November 15, 1993. Prior to the meeting, Oresman sent the members of the Paramount Board a document summarizing the "conditions and uncertainties" of QVC's offer. One director testified that this document gave him a very negative impression of the QVC bid.

At its meeting on November 15, 1993, the Paramount Board determined that the new QVC offer was not in the best interests of the stockholders. The purported basis for this conclusion was that QVC's bid was excessively conditional. The Paramount Board did not communicate with QVC regarding the status of the conditions because it believed that the No-Shop Provision prevented such communication in the absence of firm financing. Several Paramount directors also testified that they believed the Viacom transaction would be more advantageous to Paramount's future business prospects than a QVC transaction. Although a number of materials were distributed to the Paramount Board describing the Viacom and QVC transactions, the only quantitative analysis of the consideration to be received by the stockholders under each proposal was based on then-current market prices of the securities involved, not on the anticipated value of such securities at the time when the stockholders would receive them.[13]

The preliminary injunction hearing in this case took place on November 16, 1993. On November 19, Diller wrote to the Paramount Board to inform it that QVC had obtained financing commitments for its tender offer and that there was no antitrust obstacle to the offer. On November 24, 1993, the Court of Chancery issued its decision granting a preliminary injunction in favor of QVC and the plaintiff stockholders. This appeal followed.

---

[13] The market prices of Viacom's and QVC's stock were poor measures of their actual values because such prices constantly fluctuated depending upon which company was perceived to be the more likely to acquire Paramount.

II. *Applicable Principles of Established Delaware Law*

The General Corporation Law of the State of Delaware (the "General Corporation Law") and the decisions of this Court have repeatedly recognized the fundamental principle that the management of the business and affairs of a Delaware corporation is entrusted to its directors, who are the duly elected and authorized representatives of the stockholders. Under normal circumstances, neither the courts nor the stockholders should interfere with the managerial decisions of the directors. The business judgment rule embodies the deference to which such decisions are entitled.

Nevertheless, there are rare situations which mandate that a court take a more direct and active role in overseeing the decisions made and actions taken by directors. In these situations, a court subjects the directors' conduct to enhanced scrutiny to ensure that it is reasonable. The case at bar implicates two such circumstances: (1) the approval of a transaction resulting in a sale of control, and (2) the adoption of defensive measures in response to a threat to corporate control.

A. *The Significance of a Sale or Change of Control*

When a majority of a corporation's voting shares are acquired by a single person or entity, or by a cohesive group acting together, there is a significant diminution in the voting power of those who thereby become minority stockholders. Under the statutory framework of the General Corporation Law, many of the most fundamental corporate changes can be implemented only if they are approved by a majority vote of the stockholders. Such actions include elections of directors, amendments to the certificate of incorporation, mergers, consolidations, sales of all or substantially all of the assets of the corporation, and dissolution. Because of the overriding importance of voting rights, this Court and the Court of Chancery have consistently acted to protect stockholders from unwarranted interference with such rights.

In the absence of devices protecting the minority stockholders, stockholder votes are likely to become mere formalities where there is a majority stockholder. For example, minority stockholders can be deprived of a continuing equity interest in their corporation by means of a cash-out merger. Absent effective protective provisions, minority stockholders must rely for protection solely on the fiduciary duties owed to them by the directors and the majority stockholder, since the minority stockholders have lost the power to influence corporate direction through the ballot. The acquisition of majority status and the consequent privilege of exerting the powers of majority ownership come at a price. That price is usually a control premium which recognizes not only the value of a control block of shares, but also compensates the minority stockholders for their resulting loss of voting power.

In the case before us, the public stockholders (in the aggregate) currently own a majority of Paramount's voting stock. Control of the corporation is not vested in a single person, entity, or group, but vested in the fluid aggregation of unaffiliated stockholders. In the event the Paramount-Viacom transaction is consummated, the public stockholders will receive cash and a minority equity voting position in the surviving corporation. Following such consummation, there will be a controlling stockholder who will have the voting power to: (a) elect directors; (b) cause a break-up of the corporation; (c) merge it with another company; (d) cash-out the public stockholders; (e) amend the certificate of incorporation; (f) sell all or substantially all of the corporate assets; or (g) otherwise alter materially the nature of the corporation and the public stockholders' interests. Irrespective of the present Paramount Board's vision of a long-term strategic alliance with Viacom, the proposed sale of control would provide the new controlling stockholder with the power to alter that vision.

Because of the intended sale of control, the Paramount-Viacom transaction has economic consequences of considerable significance to the Paramount stockholders. Once control has shifted, the current Paramount stockholders will have no leverage in the future to demand another control premium. As a result, the Paramount stockholders are entitled to receive, and should receive, a control premium and/or protective devices of significant value. There being no such protective provisions in the Viacom-Paramount transaction, the Paramount directors had an obligation to take the maximum advantage of the current opportunity to realize for the stockholders the best value reasonably available.

B. *The Obligations of Directors in a Sale or Change of Control Transaction*

The consequences of a sale of control impose special obligations on the directors of a corporation.[14] In particular, they have the obligation of acting reasonably to seek the transaction offering the best value reasonably available to the stockholders. The courts will apply enhanced scrutiny to ensure that the directors have acted reasonably. The obligations of the directors and the enhanced scrutiny of the courts are well-established by the decisions of this Court. The directors' fiduciary duties in a sale of control context are those which generally attach....

....

In the sale of control context, the directors must focus on one primary objective — to secure the transaction offering the best value reasonably available

---

[14]We express no opinion on any scenario except the actual facts before the Court, and our precise holding herein. Unsolicited tender offers in other contexts may be governed by different precedent. For example, where a potential sale of control by a corporation is not the consequence of a board's action, this Court has recognized the prerogative of a board of directors to resist a third party's unsolicited acquisition proposal or offer. The decision of a board to resist such an acquisition, like all decisions of a properly-functioning board, must be informed, *Unocal*, 493 A.2d at 954-55, and the circumstances of each particular case will determine the steps that a board must take to inform itself, and what other action, if any, is required as a matter of fiduciary duty.

for the stockholders — and they must exercise their fiduciary duties to further that end. The decisions of this Court have consistently emphasized this goal....

In pursuing this objective, the directors must be especially diligent. In particular, this Court has stressed the importance of the board being adequately informed in negotiating a sale of control: "The need for adequate information is central to the enlightened evaluation of a transaction that a board must make." [*Barkan v. Amsted Indus., Inc.*, Del. Supr., 567 A.2d at 1279, at 1287 (1989).] This requirement is consistent with the general principle that "directors have a duty to inform themselves, prior to making a business decision, of all material information reasonably available to them."[*Aronson v. Lewis*, Del. Supr., 473 A.2d 805, at 812 (1984).] Moreover, the role of outside, independent directors becomes particularly important because of the magnitude of a sale of control transaction and the possibility, in certain cases, that management may not necessarily be impartial.

Barkan teaches some of the methods by which a board can fulfill its obligation to seek the best value reasonably available to the stockholders. 567 A.2d at 1286-87. These methods are designed to determine the existence and viability of possible alternatives. They include conducting an auction, canvassing the market, etc. Delaware law recognizes that there is "no single blueprint" that directors must follow. *Id.*

In determining which alternative provides the best value for the stockholders, a board of directors is not limited to considering only the amount of cash involved, and is not required to ignore totally its view of the future value of a strategic alliance. Instead, the directors should analyze the entire situation and evaluate in a disciplined manner the consideration being offered. Where stock or other non-cash consideration is involved, the board should try to quantify its value, if feasible, to achieve an objective comparison of the alternatives. In addition, the board may assess a variety of practical considerations relating to each alternative, including:

> [an offer's] fairness and feasibility; the proposed or actual financing for the offer, and the consequences of that financing; questions of illegality; ... the risk of non-consum[m]ation; ... the bidder's identity, prior background and other business venture experiences; and the bidder's business plans for the corporation and their effects on stockholder interests.

[*Mills Acquisition Co. v. Macmillan*, Del. Supr. 559 A.2d 1261, at 1282 n.29. (1989).] These considerations are important because the selection of one alternative may permanently foreclose other opportunities. While the assessment of these factors may be complex, the board's goal is straightforward: Having informed themselves of all material information reasonably available, the directors must decide which alternative is most likely to offer the best value reasonably available to the stockholders.

C. *Enhanced Judicial Scrutiny of a Sale or Change of Control Transaction*

Board action in the circumstances presented here is subject to enhanced scrutiny. Such scrutiny is mandated by: (a) the threatened diminution of the current stockholders' voting power; (b) the fact that an asset belonging to public stockholders (a control premium) is being sold and may never be available again; and (c) the traditional concern of Delaware courts for actions which impair or impede stockholder voting rights....

....

The key features of an enhanced scrutiny test are: (a) a judicial determination regarding the adequacy of the decisionmaking process employed by the directors, including the information on which the directors based their decision; and (b) a judicial examination of the reasonableness of the directors' action in light of the circumstances then existing. The directors have the burden of proving that they were adequately informed and acted reasonably.

Although an enhanced scrutiny test involves a review of the reasonableness of the substantive merits of a board's actions, a court should not ignore the complexity of the directors' task in a sale of control. There are many business and financial considerations implicated in investigating and selecting the best value reasonably available. The board of directors is the corporate decisionmaking body best equipped to make these judgments. Accordingly, a court applying enhanced judicial scrutiny should be deciding whether the directors made *a reasonable* decision, not *a perfect* decision. If a board selected one of several reasonable alternatives, a court should not second-guess that choice even though it might have decided otherwise or subsequent events may have cast doubt on the board's determination. Thus, courts will not substitute their business judgment for that of the directors, but will determine if the directors' decision was, on balance, within a range of reasonableness.

D. Revlon *and* Time-Warner *Distinguished*

The Paramount defendants and Viacom assert that the fiduciary obligations and the enhanced judicial scrutiny discussed above are not implicated in this case in the absence of a "break-up" of the corporation, and that the order granting the preliminary injunction should be reversed. This argument is based on their erroneous interpretation of our decisions in *Revlon* and *Time-Warner*.

In *Revlon*, we reviewed the actions of the board of directors of Revlon, Inc. ("Revlon"), which had rebuffed the overtures of Pantry Pride, Inc. and had instead entered into an agreement with Forstmann Little & Co. ("Forstmann") providing for the acquisition of 100 percent of Revlon's outstanding stock by Forstmann and the subsequent break-up of Revlon. Based on the facts and circumstances present in *Revlon*, we held that "[t]he directors' role changed from defenders of the corporate bastion to auctioneers charged with getting the best price for the stockholders at a sale of the company." 506 A.2d at 182. We further held that "when a board ends an intense bidding contest on an insubstantial basis,

... [that] action cannot withstand the enhanced scrutiny which *Unocal* requires of director conduct." *Id.* at 184.

It is true that one of the circumstances bearing on these holdings was the fact that "the break-up of the company ... had become a reality which even the directors embraced." *Id.* at 182. It does not follow, however, that a "break-up" must be present and "inevitable" before directors are subject to enhanced judicial scrutiny and are required to pursue a transaction that is calculated to produce the best value reasonably available to the stockholders. In fact, we stated in *Revlon* that "when bidders make relatively similar offers, or dissolution of the company becomes inevitable, the directors cannot fulfill their enhanced *Unocal* duties by playing favorites with the contending factions." *Id.* at 184 (emphasis added). *Revlon* thus does not hold that an inevitable dissolution or "break-up" is necessary.

The decisions of this Court following *Revlon* reinforced the applicability of enhanced scrutiny and the directors' obligation to seek the best value reasonably available for the stockholders where there is a pending sale of control, regardless of whether or not there is to be a break-up of the corporation. In *Macmillan*, this Court held:

> We stated in *Revlon*, and again here, that *in a sale of corporate control* the responsibility of the directors is to get the highest value reasonably attainable for the shareholders.

...

Although *Macmillan* and *Barkan* are clear in holding that a change of control imposes on directors the obligation to obtain the best value reasonably available to the stockholders, the Paramount defendants have interpreted our decision in *Time-Warner* as requiring a corporate break-up in order for that obligation to apply. The facts in *Time-Warner*, however, were quite different from the facts of this case, and refute Paramount's position here. In *Time-Warner*, the Chancellor held that there was no change of control in the original stock-for-stock merger between Time and Warner because Time would be owned by a fluid aggregation of unaffiliated stockholders both before and after the merger:

> If the appropriate inquiry is whether a change in control is contemplated, the answer must be sought in the specific circumstances surrounding the transaction. Surely under some circumstances a stock for stock merger could reflect a transfer of corporate control. That would, for example, plainly be the case here if Warner were a private company. But where, as here, the shares of both constituent corporations are widely held, corporate control can be expected to remain unaffected by a stock for stock merger. This in my judgment was the situation with respect to the original merger agreement. When the specifics of that situation are reviewed, it is seen that, aside from legal technicalities and aside from arrangements thought to enhance the prospect for the ultimate succession of [Nicholas J. Nicholas, Jr., president

of Time], neither corporation could be said to be acquiring the other. *Control of both remained in a large, fluid, changeable and changing market.*

The existence of a control block of stock in the hands of a single shareholder or a group with loyalty to each other does have real consequences to the financial value of "minority" stock. The law offers some protection to such shares through the imposition of a fiduciary duty upon controlling shareholders. *But here, effectuation of the merger would not have subjected Time shareholders to the risks and consequences of holders of minority shares. This is a reflection of the fact that no control passed to anyone in the transaction contemplated.* The shareholders of Time would have "suffered" dilution, of course, but they would suffer the same type of dilution upon the public distribution of new stock.

Paramount Communications Inc. v. Time Inc., Del. Ch., No. 10866, 1989 WL 79880, Allen, C. (July 17, 1989), *reprinted at* 15 Del. J. Corp. L. 700, 739 (emphasis added). Moreover, the transaction actually consummated in *Time-Warner* was not a merger, as originally planned, but a sale of Warner's stock to Time.

In our affirmance of the Court of Chancery's well-reasoned decision, this Court held that "The Chancellor's findings of fact are supported by the record and *his conclusion is correct as a matter of law*." 571 A.2d at 1150 (emphasis added). Nevertheless, the Paramount defendants here have argued that a break-up is a requirement and have focused on the following language in our *Time-Warner* decision:

> However, we premise our rejection of plaintiffs' *Revlon* claim on different grounds, namely, the absence of any substantial evidence to conclude that Time's board, in negotiating with Warner, made the dissolution or break-up of the corporate entity inevitable, as was the case in *Revlon*.
>
> Under Delaware law there are, generally speaking and *without excluding other possibilities*, two circumstances which may implicate *Revlon* duties. The first, and clearer one, is when a corporation *initiates an active bidding process seeking to sell itself* or to effect a business reorganization involving a clear break-up of the company. However, *Revlon* duties may also be triggered where, in response to a bidder's offer, a target abandons its long-term strategy and seeks an alternative transaction involving the breakup of the company.

Id. at 1150 (emphasis added) (citation and footnote omitted).

The Paramount defendants have misread the holding of *Time-Warner*. Contrary to their argument, our decision in *Time-Warner* expressly states that the two general scenarios discussed in the above-quoted paragraph are not the *only* instances where "*Revlon* duties" may be implicated. The Paramount defendants' argument totally ignores the phrase "without excluding other possibilities." Moreover, the instant case is clearly within the first general scenario set forth in

Time-Warner. The Paramount Board, albeit unintentionally, had "initiate[d] an active bidding process seeking to sell itself" by agreeing to sell control of the corporation to Viacom in circumstances where another potential acquiror (QVC) was equally interested in being a bidder.

The Paramount defendants' position that *both* a change of control *and* a break-up are *required* must be rejected. Such a holding would unduly restrict the application of *Revlon*, is inconsistent with this Court's decisions in *Barkan* and *Macmillan*, and has no basis in policy. There are few events that have a more significant impact on the stockholders than a sale of control or a corporate break-up. Each event represents a fundamental (and perhaps irrevocable) change in the nature of the corporate enterprise from a practical standpoint. It is the significance of *each* of these events that justifies: (a) focusing on the directors' obligation to seek the best value reasonably available to the stockholders; and (b) requiring a close scrutiny of board action which could be contrary to the stockholders' interests.

Accordingly, when a corporation undertakes a transaction which will cause: (a) a change in corporate control; *or* (b) a break-up of the corporate entity, the directors' obligation is to seek the best value reasonably available to the stockholders. This obligation arises because the effect of the Viacom-Paramount transaction, if consummated, is to shift control of Paramount from the public stockholders to a controlling stockholder, Viacom. Neither *Time-Warner* nor any other decision of this Court holds that a "break-up" of the company is essential to give rise to this obligation where there is a sale of control.

III. *Breach of Fiduciary Duties by Paramount Board*

We now turn to duties of the Paramount Board under the facts of this case and our conclusions as to the breaches of those duties which warrant injunctive relief.

A. *The Specific Obligations of the Paramount Board*

Under the facts of this case, the Paramount directors had the obligation: (a) to be diligent and vigilant in examining critically the Paramount-Viacom transaction and the QVC tender offers; (b) to act in good faith; (c) to obtain, and act with due care on, all material information reasonably available, including information necessary to compare the two offers to determine which of these transactions, or an alternative course of action, would provide the best value reasonably available to the stockholders; and (d) to negotiate actively and in good faith with both Viacom and QVC to that end.

Having decided to sell control of the corporation, the Paramount directors were required to evaluate critically whether or not all material aspects of the Paramount-Viacom transaction (separately and in the aggregate) were reasonable and in the best interests of the Paramount stockholders in light of current circumstances, including: the change of control premium, the Stock Option Agreement, the Termination Fee, the coercive nature of both the Viacom and

QVC tender offers, the No-Shop Provision, and the proposed disparate use of the Rights Agreement as to the Viacom and QVC tender offers, respectively.

These obligations necessarily implicated various issues, including the questions of whether or not those provisions and other aspects of the Paramount-Viacom transaction (separately and in the aggregate): (a) adversely affected the value provided to the Paramount stockholders; (b) inhibited or encouraged alternative bids; (c) were enforceable contractual obligations in light of the directors' fiduciary duties; and (d) in the end would advance or retard the Paramount directors' obligation to secure for the Paramount stockholders the best value reasonably available under the circumstances.

The Paramount defendants contend that they were precluded by certain contractual provisions, including the No-Shop Provision, from negotiating with QVC or seeking alternatives. Such provisions, whether or not they are presumptively valid in the abstract, may not validly define or limit the directors' fiduciary duties under Delaware law or prevent the Paramount directors from carrying out their fiduciary duties under Delaware law. To the extent such provisions are inconsistent with those duties, they are invalid and unenforceable.

Since the Paramount directors had already decided to sell control, they had an obligation to continue their search for the best value reasonably available to the stockholders. This continuing obligation included the responsibility, at the October 24 board meeting and thereafter, to evaluate critically both the QVC tender offers and the Paramount-Viacom transaction to determine if: (a) the QVC tender offer was, or would continue to be, conditional; (b) the QVC tender offer could be improved; (c) the Viacom tender offer or other aspects of the Paramount-Viacom transaction could be improved; (d) each of the respective offers would be reasonably likely to come to closure, and under what circumstances; (e) other material information was reasonably available for consideration by the Paramount directors; (f) there were viable and realistic alternative courses of action; and (g) the timing constraints could be managed so the directors could consider these matters carefully and deliberately.

B. *The Breaches of Fiduciary Duty by the Paramount Board*

The Paramount directors made the decision on September 12, 1993, that, in their judgment, a strategic merger with Viacom on the economic terms of the Original Merger Agreement was in the best interests of Paramount and its stockholders. Those terms provided a modest change of control premium to the stockholders. The directors also decided at that time that it was appropriate to agree to certain defensive measures (the Stock Option Agreement, the Termination Fee, and the No-Shop Provision) insisted upon by Viacom as part of that economic transaction. Those defensive measures, coupled with the sale of control and subsequent disparate treatment of competing bidders, implicated the judicial scrutiny of *Unocal, Revlon, Macmillan,* and their progeny. We conclude that the Paramount directors' process was not reasonable, and the result achieved for the stockholders was not reasonable under the circumstances.

When entering into the Original Merger Agreement, and thereafter, the Paramount Board clearly gave insufficient attention to the potential consequences of the defensive measures demanded by Viacom. The Stock Option Agreement had a number of unusual and potentially "draconian" provisions, including the Note Feature and the Put Feature. Furthermore, the Termination Fee, whether or not unreasonable by itself, clearly made Paramount less attractive to other bidders, when coupled with the Stock Option Agreement. Finally, the No-Shop Provision inhibited the Paramount Board's ability to negotiate with other potential bidders, particularly QVC which had already expressed an interest in Paramount.

Throughout the applicable time period, and especially from the first QVC merger proposal on September 20 through the Paramount Board meeting on November 15, QVC's interest in Paramount provided the *opportunity* for the Paramount Board to seek significantly higher value for the Paramount stockholders than that being offered by Viacom. QVC persistently demonstrated its intention to meet and exceed the Viacom offers, and frequently expressed its willingness to negotiate possible further increases.

The Paramount directors had the opportunity in the October 23-24 time frame, when the Original Merger Agreement was renegotiated, to take appropriate action to modify the improper defensive measures as well as to improve the economic terms of the Paramount-Viacom transaction. Under the circumstances existing at that time, it should have been clear to the Paramount Board that the Stock Option Agreement, coupled with the Termination Fee and the No-Shop Clause, were impeding the realization of the best value reasonably available to the Paramount stockholders. Nevertheless, the Paramount Board made no effort to eliminate or modify these counterproductive devices, and instead continued to cling to its vision of a strategic alliance with Viacom. Moreover, based on advice from the Paramount management, the Paramount directors considered the QVC offer to be "conditional" and asserted that they were precluded by the No-Shop Provision from seeking more information from, or negotiating with, QVC.

By November 12, 1993, the value of the revised QVC offer on its face exceeded that of the Viacom offer by over $ 1 billion at then current values. This significant disparity of value cannot be justified on the basis of the directors' vision of future strategy, primarily because the change of control would supplant the authority of the current Paramount Board to continue to hold and implement their strategic vision in any meaningful way. Moreover, their uninformed process had deprived their strategic vision of much of its credibility.

When the Paramount directors met on November 15 to consider QVC's increased tender offer, they remained prisoners of their own misconceptions and missed opportunities to eliminate the restrictions they had imposed on themselves. Yet, it was not "too late" to reconsider negotiating with QVC. The circumstances existing on November 15 made it clear that the defensive measures, taken as a whole, were problematic: (a) the No-Shop Provision could not define or limit their fiduciary duties; (b) the Stock Option Agreement had become "draconian"; and (c) the Termination Fee, in context with all the circumstances, was similarly deterring the realization of possibly higher bids. Nevertheless, the Paramount directors remained paralyzed by their uninformed belief that the QVC offer was "illusory." This final opportunity to negotiate on the stockholders' behalf and to fulfill their obligation to seek the best value reasonably available was thereby squandered.

IV. *Viacom's Claim of Vested Contract Rights*

Viacom argues that it had certain "vested" contract rights with respect to the No-Shop Provision and the Stock Option Agreement. In effect, Viacom's argument is that the Paramount directors could enter into an agreement in violation of their fiduciary duties and then render Paramount, and ultimately its stockholders, liable for failing to carry out an agreement in violation of those duties. Viacom's protestations about vested rights are without merit. This Court has found that those defensive measures were improperly designed to deter potential bidders, and that such measures do not meet the reasonableness test to which they must be subjected. They are consequently invalid and unenforceable under the facts of this case.

The No-Shop Provision could not validly define or limit the fiduciary duties of the Paramount directors. To the extent that a contract, or a provision thereof, purports to require a board to act or not act in such a fashion as to limit the exercise of fiduciary duties, it is invalid and unenforceable.... Despite the arguments of Paramount and Viacom to the contrary, the Paramount directors could not contract away their fiduciary obligations. Since the No-Shop Provision was invalid, Viacom never had any vested contract rights in the provision.

As discussed previously, the Stock Option Agreement contained several "draconian" aspects, including the Note Feature and the Put Feature. While we have held that lock-up options are not *per se* illegal, no options with similar features have ever been upheld by this Court. Under the circumstances of this case, the Stock Option Agreement clearly is invalid. Accordingly, Viacom never had any vested contract rights in that Agreement.

Viacom, a sophisticated party with experienced legal and financial advisors, knew of (and in fact demanded) the unreasonable features of the Stock Option Agreement. It cannot be now heard to argue that it obtained vested contract rights by negotiating and obtaining contractual provisions from a board acting in violation of its fiduciary duties. As the Nebraska Supreme Court said in rejecting a similar argument in *ConAgra, Inc. v. Cargill, Inc.*, 222 Neb. 136, 382 N.W.2d 576, 587-88 (1986), "To so hold, it would seem, would be to get the shareholders coming and going." Likewise, we reject Viacom's arguments and hold that its fate must rise or fall, and in this instance fall, with the determination that the actions of the Paramount Board were invalid.

V. *Conclusion*

The realization of the best value reasonably available to the stockholders became the Paramount directors' primary obligation under these facts in light of the change of control. That obligation was not satisfied, and the Paramount Board's process was deficient. The directors' initial hope and expectation for a strategic alliance with Viacom was allowed to dominate their decisionmaking process to the point where the arsenal of defensive measures established at the outset was perpetuated (not modified or eliminated) when the situation was dramatically altered. QVC's unsolicited bid presented the opportunity for significantly greater value for the stockholders and enhanced negotiating leverage for the directors. Rather than seizing those opportunities, the Paramount directors chose to wall themselves off from material information which was reasonably available and to hide behind the defensive measures as a rationalization for refusing to negotiate with QVC or seeking other alternatives. Their view of the strategic alliance likewise became an empty rationalization as the opportunities for higher value for the stockholders continued to develop.

It is the nature of the judicial process that we decide only the case before us — a case which, on its facts, is clearly controlled by established Delaware law. Here, the proposed change of control and the implications thereof were crystal clear. In other cases they may be less clear. The holding of this case on its facts, coupled with the holdings of the principal cases discussed herein where the issue of sale of control is implicated, should provide a workable precedent against which to measure future cases.

After your analysis of the preceding cases, how would you determine when *Revlon* duties are triggered? In what ways did the cases clarify or confuse the required standard of conduct?

---

1. Applicability of the *Unocal* Analysis

In *Williams v. Greier*,[15] the directors of Cincinnati Miacron, Inc., in consultation with outside financial and legal counsel, devised a recapitalization plan to be effected through an amendment to the certificate of incorporation. Under the plan, which shareholders approved, all stockholders owning common stock on the effective date of the plan, would be entitled to ten votes per share. Upon the issuance of new shares, or the sale or other transfer of ownership of existing shares, the voting rights of each share would revert to a single vote per share until the new shareholder held the share for three years. This "tenure voting plan" was in response to a number of corporate objectives, including maximization of the long-term value for shareholders and reduction of the corporation's exposure to corporate raiders.

Josephine Williams, a minority shareholder, challenged the recapitalization as an impermissible attempt at management entrenchment which disproportionately

---

[15] 671 A.2d 1368, 1377-78 (Del. 1996).

disfavored minority shareholders. In considering the applicable standard of review, Chief Justice Veasey stated:

> A *Unocal* analysis should be used only when a board unilaterally (*i.e.*, without stockholder approval) adopts defensive measures in reaction to a perceived threat. *Unocal*, 493 A.2d at 954-55. *Unocal* is a landmark innovation of the dynamic takeover era of the 1980s. It has stood the test of time, and was recently explicated by this Court in *Unitrin, Inc. v. American General Corp.*, Del. Supr., 651 A.2d 1361 (1995). Yet, it is inapplicable here because there was no unilateral board action.
>
> ....
>
> The instant case does not involve either unilateral director action in the face of a claimed threat or an act of disenfranchisement. Rather, the instant case implicates the traditional review of disinterested and independent director action in recommending, and the vote of the stockholders in approving, the Amendment and the resulting Recapitalization....
>
> ....
>
> The Board's action in recommending the Recapitalization to the stockholders pursuant to Section 242(b)(1) is protected by the presumption of the business judgment rule unless that presumption is rebutted....

2. Judicial Deference Under the *Unocal* Standard

Unitrin, Inc. was the target of an unsolicited tender offer by American General Corporation.[16] Unitrin's board responded to American General's unwanted bid with a poison pill and a stock repurchase plan. After determining that *Unocal* provided the proper standard of review of these defensive actions, the court recognized that the ultimate question was the amount of judicial deference to be given to directors under *Unocal*. In response, Justice Holland stated:

> An examination of the cases applying *Unocal* reveals a direct correlation between findings of proportionality or disproportionality and the judicial determination of whether a defensive response was draconian because it was either coercive or preclusive in character. In *Time*, for example, this Court concluded that the Time board's defensive response was reasonable and proportionate since it was not aimed at "cramming down" on its shareholders a management-sponsored alternative, *i.e.*, was not coercive, and because it did not preclude Paramount from making an offer for the combined Time-Warner company, *i.e.*, was not preclusive....
>
> ....
>
> More than a century before *Unocal* was decided, Justice Holmes observed that the common law must be developed through its application and "cannot

---

[16] *Unitrin, Inc. v. American Gen. Corp.*, 651 A.2d 1361, 1387-88 (Del. 1995).

be dealt with as if it contained only the axioms and corollaries of a book of mathematics." Oliver Wendell Holmes, Jr., The Common Law 1 (1881). As common law applications of *Unocal*'s proportionality standard have evolved, at least two characteristics of draconian defensive measures taken by a board of directors in responding to a threat have been brought into focus through enhanced judicial scrutiny. In the modern takeover lexicon, it is now clear that since *Unocal*, this Court has consistently recognized that defensive measures which are either preclusive or coercive are included within the common law definition of draconian.

If a defensive measure is not draconian, however, because it is not either coercive or preclusive, the *Unocal* proportionality test requires the focus of enhanced judicial scrutiny to shift to "the range of reasonableness." *Paramount Communications, Inc. v. QVC Network, Inc.*, Del. Supr., 637 A.2d 34, 45-46 (1994). Proper and proportionate defensive responses are intended and permitted to thwart perceived threats. When a corporation is not for sale, the board of directors is the defender of the metaphorical medieval corporate bastion and the protector of the corporation's shareholders. The fact that a defensive action must not be coercive or preclusive does not prevent a board from responding defensively before a bidder is at the corporate bastion's gate.[17]

Do tests like "draconian" responses that are "coercive or preclusive in character" and "range of reasonableness" inform us about the amount of judicial deference to be given to directors?

---

[17] This Court's choice of the term "draconian" in *Unocal* was a recognition that the law affords boards of directors substantial latitude in defending the perimeter of the corporate bastion against perceived threats. Thus, continuing with the medieval metaphor, if a board reasonably perceives that a threat is on the horizon, it has broad authority to respond with a panoply of individual or combined defensive precautions, *e.g.*, staffing the barbican, raising the drawbridge, and lowering the portcullis. Stated more directly, depending upon the circumstances, the board may respond to a reasonably perceived threat by adopting individually or sometimes in combination: advance notice by-laws, supermajority voting provisions, shareholder rights plans, repurchase programs, etc.

Chapter 14

SHAREHOLDER DERIVATIVE LITIGATION AND OTHER RESOLUTION PROCESSES

Situation

One of the minority shareholders, Herbert Li, called Phillips this morning to inform him that he intends to initiate a shareholder derivative suit. He claims that Biologistics' directors have repeatedly mismanaged the corporation's operations, thereby breaching their fiduciary duties. He argues, in particular, that they improperly handled the chemical pollution accusations which resulted in the loss of goodwill among employees and the community; that they improperly approved the equipment purchase from Olivetti because the terms were unnecessarily costly; and that they have compensated Anderson and Baker excessively while denying dividends to the shareholders. In addition, Li is especially angered by Anderson's and Baker's opposition to Daytron's interest in acquiring the company.

The directors are aghast. They seek your advice and want to know the following:

1. Can Li proceed with the litigation without the corporation's support?
2. Can the directors terminate the litigation if they think that is the appropriate thing to do?
3. Are there alternative ways to resolve the dispute?

SECTION I. INTRODUCTION

Shareholders who are dissatisfied with management decisions have a number of options. One is the shareholder derivative suit. For example, shareholders, technically on behalf of the corporation, may initiate a lawsuit against the directors for an alleged breach of their fiduciary duties to the corporation. As the materials in this chapter reveal, however, the derivative action raises a number of complex policy and legal issues.

A. THE DERIVATIVE ACTION

ALI, The Derivative Action, Introductory Note

... Since at least the middle of the 19th century, it has been accepted in this country that the law should permit shareholders to sue derivatively on their corporation's behalf under appropriate conditions. The problem has been to determine what these conditions should be. Here, competing considerations need to be balanced. On the one hand, the availability of legal recourse is essential if management's obligations to its shareholders are to constitute more than a precatory body of law. Some judicial mechanism for the enforcement of fiduciary duties must therefore exist that is independent of management's control. On the other hand, few intracorporate transactions are not susceptible to differences of opinion; nor are courts infallible. Thus, corporate directors might have reason to view their position as exposed and vulnerable if every transaction or alleged omission subjected them to the prospect of significant liability at the behest of a single shareholder.

In striking a proper balance, this Chapter recognizes that the derivative action is neither the initial nor the primary protection for shareholders against managerial misconduct. A variety of social and market forces also operate to hold corporate officials accountable: the professional standards of managers, oversight by outside directors, the disciplinary power of the market, and shareholder voting — all these mechanisms plus the regulatory authority of governmental agencies would constitute significant protections in the absence of private litigation. Even if dissatisfied shareholders had no other recourse than to sell their shares, such action, taken collectively, might also inhibit managerial overreaching, to the extent it depressed the value of the corporation's stock, which management typically also holds. Yet, no single technique of accountability (including market and legal remedies) is likely to be optimal under all circumstances. Each has its characteristic and well-known limitations, and, as a result, shareholders are best served by an overlapping system of protections. When properly structured, the derivative action should enhance the capabilities of these other mechanisms of accountability by (1) ensuring a measure of judicial oversight, (2) providing for a remedy that does not depend upon the ability of widely dispersed shareholders to take coordinated action, and (3) protecting transactions in corporate control from unreasonable interferences. In addition, the derivative action may offer the only effective remedy in those circumstances in which a control group has the ability to engage in self-dealing transactions with the corporation.

The social utility of the derivative action must also be judged in terms of the alternative of greater public regulation, to which society would likely turn if private mechanisms of enforcement proved inadequate. Over the long run, the availability of private enforcement should reduce the need for public enforcement and bureaucratic oversight of corporate conduct. Moreover, private enforcement multiplies society's enforcement resources, and also probably minimizes enforcement costs, because the private enforcer will be restrained by the fact that it is typically compensated only when successful....

Nonetheless, private enforcement, as represented by the derivative action, should not be idealized. Experience suggests that the social costs associated with intracorporate litigation can sometimes outweigh the benefits. In overview, two problems stand out: First, the threat of liability for violations of the duty of care may reduce managerial incentives to take business risks, with resulting loss to shareholders and to the economy generally. Given that the fees received by directors are relatively modest in proportion to their overall income, the threat of litigation could also deter many qualified persons from serving as directors, especially in the case of financially troubled companies. Second, in both class and derivative litigation, incentives exist for a private enforcer to bring a nonmeritorious action for its nuisance or settlement value. Frequently, a litigation-cost differential favoring the plaintiff exists, which the plaintiff can exploit to obtain a favorable settlement even of a nonmeritorious case. Even in meritorious cases, a private enforcer can reach an inadequate or even collusive settlement that exchanges a low corporate recovery for a high award of attorneys' fees that is paid by the corporation. Unlike most other forms of litigation, in which the plaintiff's gain essentially comes at the defendant's expense, the derivative action is a three-sided litigation with three necessary parties: plaintiff, defendant, and the corporation. As a practical matter, the first two parties can pass the costs of the litigation onto the third by reaching a settlement that maximizes their own interests, but does not benefit the corporation. *See Saylor v. Lindsley*, 456 F.2d 896 (2d Cir. 1972). Although judicial oversight of the settlement process can reduce the severity of this problem, the court's capacity to prevent improper settlements is limited, and other safeguards are therefore also desirable.

B. RULE 23.1 OF THE FEDERAL RULES OF CIVIL PROCEDURE: DERIVATIVE ACTIONS BY SHAREHOLDERS

In a derivative action brought by one or more shareholders or members to enforce a right of a corporation or of an unincorporated association, the corporation or association having failed to enforce a right which may properly be asserted by it, the complaint shall be verified and shall allege (1) that the plaintiff was a shareholder or member at the time of the transaction of which the plaintiff complains or that the plaintiff's share or membership thereafter devolved on the plaintiff by operation of law, and (2) that the action is not a collusive one to confer jurisdiction on a court of the United States which it would not otherwise have. The complaint shall also allege with particularity the efforts, if any, made by the plaintiff to obtain the action the plaintiff desires from the directors or comparable authority and, if necessary, from the shareholders or members, and the reasons for the plaintiff's failure to obtain the action or for not making the effort. The derivative action may not be maintained if it appears that the plaintiff does not fairly and adequately represent the interests of the shareholders or members similarly situated in enforcing the right of the corporation or association. The action shall not be dismissed or compromised without the approval of the court, and notice of the proposed dismissal or compromise shall be given to shareholders or members in such manner as the court directs.

SECTION II. DISTINGUISHING DERIVATIVE SUITS

A threshold issue in shareholder litigation is whether a particular action is personal or derivative. Personal direct actions are those brought by shareholders to enforce their own rights or to remedy their own injuries. Derivative actions are brought by shareholders, in the name of their corporation, to enforce a right of the corporation or to remedy a corporate injury. Each type of lawsuit has distinctive procedural requirements, as illustrated in Fed. R. Civ. P. 23.1 above. As the following materials explain, it is sometimes difficult in particular fact patterns to distinguish between the two types of suits.

EISENBERG v. FLYING TIGER LINE, INC.

United States Court of Appeals, Second Circuit
451 F.2d 267 (1971)

KAUFMAN, CIRCUIT JUDGE:

Max Eisenberg, a resident of New York, "as stockholder of The Flying Tiger Line, Inc. [Flying Tiger], on behalf of himself and all other stockholders of said corporation similarly situated" commenced this action in the Supreme Court of the State of New York to enjoin the effectuation of a plan of reorganization and merger....

Flying Tiger pleaded several affirmative defenses and moved for an order to require Eisenberg to comply with New York Business Corporation Law § 627, ... which requires a plaintiff suing derivatively on behalf of a corporation to post security for the corporation's costs. Judge Travia granted the motion without opinion and afforded Eisenberg thirty days to post security in the sum of $ 35,000. Eisenberg did not comply, his action was dismissed and he appeals. We find Eisenberg's cause of action to be personal and not derivative within the meaning of § 627. We therefore reverse the dismissal.

In this action, Eisenberg is seeking to overturn a reorganization and merger which Flying Tiger effected in 1969. He charges that a series of corporate maneuvers were intended to dilute his voting rights. In order to achieve this end, he alleges, Flying Tiger in July 1969 organized a wholly owned Delaware subsidiary, the Flying Tiger Corporation ("FTC"). In August, FTC in turn organized a wholly owned subsidiary, FTL Air Freight Corporation ("FTL"). The three Delaware corporations then entered into a plan of reorganization, subject to stockholder approval, by which Flying Tiger merged into FTL and only FTL survived. A proxy statement dated August 11 was sent to stockholders, who approved the plan by the necessary two-thirds vote at the stockholders' meeting held on September 15.

Upon consummation of this merger Flying Tiger ceased as the operating company, FTL took over operations and Flying Tiger shares were converted into an identical number of FTC shares. Thereafter, FTL changed its name to "Flying Tiger Line, Inc.," for the obvious purpose of continuing without disruption the business previously conducted by Flying Tiger. The approximately 4,500,000 shares of the company traded on the New York and Pacific Coast stock exchanges are now those of the holding company, FTC, rather than those of the operating company, Flying Tiger. The effect of the merger is that business operations are now confined to a wholly owned subsidiary of a holding company whose stockholders are the former stockholders of Flying Tiger.

...

Eisenberg argues, however, that New York courts would refuse to invoke § 627 in the instant case because the section applies exclusively to derivative actions specified in Business Corporation Law § 626. He urges that his class action is representative and not derivative.

We are told that if the gravamen of the complaint is injury to the corporation the suit is derivative, but "if the injury is one to the plaintiff as a stockholder and to him individually and not to the corporation," the suit is individual in nature and may take the form of a representative class action. 13 Fletcher, *Private Corporation* § 5911 (1970 Rev. Vol.). This generalization is of little use in our case which is one of those "borderline cases which are more or less troublesome to classify." *Id.* The essence of Eisenberg's claimed injury is that the reorganization has deprived him and fellow stockholders of their right to vote on the operating company affairs and that this right in no sense ever belonged to Flying Tiger itself. This right, he says, belonged to the stockholders per se. Flying Tiger notes, however, that the stockholders were harmed, if at all, only because their company was dissolved, and their vote can be restored only if that company is revived. It insists, therefore, that stockholders are affected only secondarily or derivatively because we must first breathe life back into their dissolved corporation before the stockholders can be helped.

... New York cases which have distinguished between derivative and representative actions are of some interest. In *Horwitz v. Balaban*, 112 F. Supp. 99 (S.D.N.Y. 1949), a stockholder sought to restrain the exercise of conversion rights that the corporation had granted to its president. The court found the action representative and refused to require security, setting forth the test as "[w]here the corporation has no right of action by reason of the transaction complained of, the suit is representative, not derivative." *Id.* at 101. Similarly, actions to compel the dissolution of a corporation have been held representative, since the corporation could not possibly benefit therefrom.... *Lennan v. Blakely*, 80 N.Y.S.2d 288 (N.Y. Sup. Ct. 1948), teaches that an action by preferred stockholders against directors is not derivative. And *Lehrman v. Godchaux Sugars, Inc.*, [138 N.Y.S. 163 (N.Y. Sup. Ct. 1955)], discloses that an action by a stockholder complaining that a proposed recapitalization would unfairly benefit holders of another class of stock was representative. These cases are totally consistent with the postulates of the leading treatises. *See, e.g.,* ... 3B J. Moore, *Federal Practice* ¶ 23.1.16[1] (2d ed. 1969). Professor Moore instructs that "where a shareholder sues on behalf of himself and all others similarly situated to ... enjoin a proposed merger or consolidation ... he is not enforcing a derivative right; he is, by an appropriate type of class suit enforcing a right common to all the shareholders which runs against the corporation."

Eisenberg's position is even stronger than it would be in the ordinary merger case. In routine merger circumstances the stockholders retain a voice in the operation of the company, albeit a corporation other than their original choice. Here, however, the reorganization deprived him and other minority stockholders of any voice in the affairs of their previously existing operating company.

...

Furthermore, we view as an objective of a requirement for security for costs the prevention of strike suits and collusive settlements. Where directors are sued for mismanagement, the risk of personal monetary liability is a strong motive for bringing the suit and inducing settlement. Here, no monetary damages are sought, and no individuals will be liable.

Perhaps the strongest string in Eisenberg's bow is one he helped to fashion when he made an investment some forty years ago in Central Zone Property Corp. In 1952 that New York corporation obtained stockholder approval to transfer its assets to a new Delaware corporation in return for the new company's stock. The stock was to be held by trustees in a voting trust, and the former stockholders received voting trust certificates. Eisenberg complained that this effectively deprived him of a voice in the operation of his company which would be run in the future by the trustees of the voting trust. The Court of Appeals agreed that New York law did not permit such a reorganization. *Eisenberg v. Central Zone Property Corp.*, 116 N.Y.S.2d 154, *aff'd*, 115 N.E.2d 652 (1953). Although we have emphasized that we do not reach the merits of Eisenberg's present complaint, it is of some interest that security for costs was neither sought nor was it discussed in the *Central Zone* opinions, even though Eisenberg did not own five percent of the shares of the corporation. It was clear to all that the allegations of the complaint, quite similar in character to the instant one, stated a representative cause of action. We cannot conceive that the question of security for costs was not considered by the able counsel for the corporation or by the court, particularly since [*Gordon v. Elliman*, 119 N.E.2d 331 (N.Y. 1954)] had been decided in the Appellate Division less than one year before the *Central Zone* decision in the Court of Appeals and extensive commentaries had already appeared. We believe Eisenberg's action should not have been dismissed for failure to post security pursuant to § 627.

Reversed.

———

A. DIRECT CLAIMS

A number of cases have considered the following claims to be direct actions: (a) a claim to dividends, (b) the right to inspect corporate books and records, (c) the right to vote, (d) a claim that a transaction will improperly dilute the shareholder's proportionate interest in the corporation or violate preemptive rights, (e) claims that corporate officials sought to "entrench" themselves or manipulate the corporate machinery so as to frustrate plaintiff's attempt to secure representation or obtain control, (f) a claim that proposed corporate action should be enjoined as *ultra vires*, fraudulent, or designed to harm a specific shareholder illegitimately, (g) a claim that minority shareholders have been oppressed or that corporate dissolution or similar equitable relief is justified, and (h) claims that a proposed corporate control transaction, recapitalization, redemption, or similar defensive transaction unfairly affects the plaintiff shareholder. ALI § 7.01 Reporter's Note, note 1.

B. POLICY AND OTHER CONSIDERATIONS

As further explained in ALI § 7.01 Comment *d*:

... In borderline cases [between direct versus derivative suits], the following policy considerations deserve to be given close attention by the court:

First, a derivative action distributes the recovery more broadly and evenly than a direct action. Because the recovery in a derivative action goes to the corporation, creditors and others having a stake in the corporation benefit financially from a derivative action and not from a direct one. Similarly, although all shareholders share equally, if indirectly, in the corporate recovery that follows a successful derivative action, the injured shareholders other than the plaintiff will share in the recovery from a direct action only if the action is a class action brought on behalf of all these shareholders.

Second, once finally concluded, a derivative action will have a preclusive effect that spares the corporation and the defendants from being exposed to a multiplicity of suits.

Third, a successful plaintiff, is entitled to an award of attorneys' fees in a derivative action directly from the corporation, but in a direct action the plaintiff must generally look to the fund, if any, created by the action.

Finally, characterizing the suit as derivative may entitle the board to take over the action or to seek dismissal of the action.... Thus, in some circumstances the characterization of the action will determine the available defenses.

In practice, the most important result of characterizing an action as direct or derivative is the tendency for derivative actions to be more complex procedurally and to impose additional restrictions on the eligibility of the plaintiffs who may maintain them. For these reasons, the plaintiff usually wishes to characterize the action as direct, while the defendant prefers to characterize it as derivative. In general, courts have been more prepared to permit the plaintiff to characterize the action as direct when the plaintiff is seeking only injunctive or prospective relief. In such situations, the policy considerations favoring a derivative action are less persuasive, because typically the requested relief will not involve significant financial damages against corporate officials, the period in which the corporation is exposed to multiple suits will be relatively brief, and the relief will benefit all shareholders proportionately.

SECTION III. THE DEMAND REQUIREMENT

Under both federal and most state laws, as illustrated by Fed. R. Civ. P. 23.1, shareholders in a derivative action are required to ask the directors to pursue the lawsuit on the corporation's behalf, unless the plaintiff shareholders can demonstrate a sufficient reason for their failure to make such a "demand." As explored in the following cases, courts will often excuse demand if it would be "futile."

The materials in this section and the section on special litigation committees also revisit the business judgment rule in the context of shareholder derivative litigation. Consider, for example, that corporate directors may make a number of decisions in this context, including whether the corporation (1) should pursue the litigation initiated by the shareholders, (2) should seek a dismissal of the derivative suit, or (3) should address and, if appropriate, internally remedy the allegations raised by the shareholders.

ARONSON v. LEWIS

Supreme Court of Delaware
473 A.2d 805 (1984)

MOORE, JUSTICE:

... [W]hen is a stockholder's demand upon a board of directors, to redress an alleged wrong to the corporation, excused as futile prior to the filing of a derivative suit? We granted this interlocutory appeal to the defendants, Meyers Parking System, Inc. (Meyers), a Delaware corporation, and its directors, to review the Court of Chancery's denial of their motion to dismiss this action, pursuant to Chancery Rule 23.1, for the plaintiff's failure to make such a demand or otherwise demonstrate its futility. The Vice Chancellor ruled that plaintiff's allegations raised a "reasonable inference" that the directors' action was unprotected by the business judgment rule. Thus, the board could not have impartially considered and acted upon the demand.

We cannot agree with this formulation of the concept of demand futility. In our view demand can only be excused where facts are alleged with particularity which create a reasonable doubt that the directors' action was entitled to the protections of the business judgment rule. Because the plaintiff failed to make a demand, and to allege facts with particularity indicating that such demand would be futile, we reverse the Court of Chancery and remand with instructions that plaintiff be granted leave to amend the complaint.

I

The issues of demand futility rest upon the allegations of the complaint. The plaintiff, Harry Lewis, is a stockholder of Meyers. The defendants are Meyers and its ten directors, some of whom are also company officers.

In 1979, Prudential Building Maintenance Corp. (Prudential) spun off its shares of Meyers to Prudential's stockholders. Prior thereto Meyers was a wholly owned subsidiary of Prudential. Meyers provides parking lot facilities and related services throughout the country. Its stock is actively traded over-the-counter.

This suit challenges certain transactions between Meyers and one of its directors, Leo Fink, who owns 47% of its outstanding stock. Plaintiff claims that these transactions were approved only because Fink personally selected each director and officer of Meyers.

Prior to January 1, 1981, Fink had an employment agreement with Prudential which provided that upon retirement he was to become a consultant to that company for ten years. This provision became operable when Fink retired in April 1980. Thereafter, Meyers agreed with Prudential to share Fink's consulting services and reimburse Prudential for 25% of the fees paid Fink. Under this arrangement Meyers paid Prudential $ 48,332 in 1980 and $ 45,832 in 1981.

On January 1, 1981, the defendants approved an employment agreement between Meyers and Fink for a five year term with provision for automatic renewal each year thereafter, indefinitely. Meyers agreed to pay Fink $ 150,000 per year, plus a bonus of 5% of its pre-tax profits over $ 2,400,000. Fink could terminate the contract at any time, but Meyers could do so only upon six months' notice. At termination, Fink was to become a consultant to Meyers and be paid $ 150,000 per year for the first three years, $ 125,000 for the next three years, and $ 100,000 thereafter for life. Death benefits were also included. Fink agreed to devote his best efforts and substantially his entire business time to advancing Meyers' interests. The agreement also provided that Fink's compensation was not to be affected by any inability to perform services on Meyers' behalf. Fink was 75 years old when his employment agreement with Meyers was approved by the directors. There is no claim that he was, or is, in poor health.

Additionally, the Meyers board approved and made interest-free loans to Fink totalling $ 225,000. These loans were unpaid and outstanding as of August 1982 when the complaint was filed. At oral argument defendants' counsel represented that these loans had been repaid in full.

The complaint charges that these transactions had "no valid business purpose," and were a "waste of corporate assets" because the amounts to be paid are "grossly excessive," that Fink performs "no or little services," and because of his "advanced age" cannot be "expected to perform any such services." The plaintiff also charges that the existence of the Prudential consulting agreement with Fink prevents him from providing his "best efforts" on Meyers' behalf. Finally, it is alleged that the loans to Fink were in reality "additional compensation" without any "consideration" or "benefit" to Meyers.

The complaint alleged that no demand had been made on the Meyers board because:

> [Paragraph] 13.... such attempt would be futile for the following reasons:
>
> (a) All of the directors in office are named as defendants herein and they have participated in, expressly approved and/or acquiesced in, and are personally liable for, the wrongs complained of herein.
>
> (b) Defendant Fink, having selected each director, controls and dominates every member of the Board and every officer of Meyers.
>
> (c) Institution of this action by present directors would require the defendant-directors to sue themselves, thereby placing the conduct of this action in hostile hands and preventing its effective prosecution.

The relief sought included the cancellation of the Meyers-Fink employment contract and an accounting by the directors, including Fink, for all damage sustained by Meyers and for all profits derived by the directors and Fink.

...

III

The defendants make two arguments, one policy-oriented and the other, factual. First, they assert that the demand requirement embraces the policy that directors, rather than stockholders, manage the affairs of the corporation. They contend that this fundamental principle requires the strict construction and enforcement of Chancery Rule 23.1. Second, the defendants point to four of plaintiff's basic allegations and argue that they lack the factual particularity necessary to excuse demand. Concerning the allegation that Fink dominated and controlled the Meyers board, the defendants point to the absence of any facts explaining how he "selected each director." With respect to Fink's 47% stock interest, the defendants say that absent other facts this is insufficient to indicate domination and control. Regarding the claim of hostility to the plaintiff's suit, because defendants would have to sue themselves, the latter assert that this bootstrap argument ignores the possibility that the directors have other alternatives, such as cancelling the challenged agreement. As for the allegation that directorial approval of the agreement excused demand, the defendants reply that such a claim is insufficient, because it would obviate the demand requirement in almost every case. The effect would be to subvert the managerial power of a board of directors. Finally, as to the provision guaranteeing Fink's compensation, even if he is unable to perform any services, the defendants contend that the trial court read this out of context. Based upon the foregoing, the defendants conclude that the plaintiff's allegations fall far short of the factual particularity required by Rule 23.1.

IV

A

A cardinal precept of the General Corporation Law of the State of Delaware is that directors, rather than shareholders, manage the business and affairs of the corporation. 8 Del. C. § 141(a).... The existence and exercise of this power carries with it certain fundamental fiduciary obligations to the corporation and its shareholders. Moreover, a stockholder is not powerless to challenge director action which results in harm to the corporation. The machinery of corporate democracy and the derivative suit are potent tools to redress the conduct of a torpid or unfaithful management. The derivative action developed in equity to enable shareholders to sue in the corporation's name where those in control of the company refused to assert a claim belonging to it. The nature of the action is two-fold. First, it is the equivalent of a suit by the shareholders to compel the corporation to sue. Second, it is a suit by the corporation, asserted by the shareholders on its behalf, against those liable to it.

By its very nature the derivative action impinges on the managerial freedom of directors. Hence, the demand requirement of Chancery Rule 23.1 exists at the threshold, first to insure that a stockholder exhausts his intracorporate remedies, and then to provide a safeguard against strike suits. Thus, by promoting this form of alternate dispute resolution, rather than immediate recourse to litigation, the demand requirement is a recognition of the fundamental precept that directors manage the business and affairs of corporations.

In our view the entire question of demand futility is inextricably bound to issues of business judgment and the standards of that doctrine's applicability. The business judgment rule is an acknowledgment of the managerial prerogatives of Delaware directors under Section 141(a). It is a presumption that in making a business decision the directors of a corporation acted on an informed basis, in good faith and in the honest belief that the action taken was in the best interests of the company. Absent an abuse of discretion, that judgment will be respected by the courts. The burden is on the party challenging the decision to establish facts rebutting the presumption.

The function of the business judgment rule is of paramount significance in the context of a derivative action. It comes into play in several ways — in addressing a demand, in the determination of demand futility, in efforts by independent disinterested directors to dismiss the action as inimical to the corporation's best interests, and generally, as a defense to the merits of the suit. However, in each of these circumstances there are certain common principles governing the application and operation of the rule.

First, its protections can only be claimed by disinterested directors whose conduct otherwise meets the tests of business judgment. From the standpoint of interest, this means that directors can neither appear on both sides of a transaction nor expect to derive any personal financial benefit from it in the sense of self-dealing, as opposed to a benefit which devolves upon the corporation or all stockholders generally. Thus, if such director interest is present, and the transaction is not approved by a majority consisting of the disinterested directors, then the business judgment rule has no application whatever in determining demand futility.

Second, to invoke the rule's protection directors have a duty to inform themselves, prior to making a business decision, of all material information reasonably available to them. Having become so informed, they must then act with requisite care in the discharge of their duties. While the Delaware cases use a variety of terms to describe the applicable standard of care, our analysis satisfies us that under the business judgment rule director liability is predicated upon concepts of gross negligence.

However, it should be noted that the business judgment rule operates only in the context of director action. Technically speaking, it has no role where directors have either abdicated their functions, or absent a conscious decision, failed to act. But it also follows that under applicable principles, a conscious decision to refrain from acting may nonetheless be a valid exercise of business judgment and enjoy the protections of the rule.

...

Delaware courts have addressed the issue of demand futility on several earlier occasions. The rule emerging from these decisions is that where officers and directors are under an influence which sterilizes their discretion, they cannot be considered proper persons to conduct litigation on behalf of the corporation. Thus, demand would be futile.

However, those cases cannot be taken to mean that any board approval of a challenged transaction automatically connotes "hostile interest" and "guilty participation" by directors, or some other form of sterilizing influence upon them. Were that so, the demand requirements of our law would be meaningless, leaving the clear mandate of Chancery Rule 23.1 devoid of its purpose and substance.

The trial court correctly recognized that demand futility is inextricably bound to issues of business judgment, but stated the test to be based on allegations of fact, which, if true, "show that there is a reasonable inference" the business judgment rule is not applicable for purposes of a pre-suit demand.

The problem with this formulation is the concept of reasonable inferences to be drawn against a board of directors based on allegations in a complaint. As is clear from this case, and the conclusory allegations upon which the Vice Chancellor relied, demand futility becomes virtually automatic under such a test. Bearing in mind the presumptions with which director action is cloaked, we believe that the matter must be approached in a more balanced way.

Our view is that in determining demand futility the Court of Chancery in the proper exercise of its discretion must decide whether, under the particularized facts alleged, a reasonable doubt is created that: (1) the directors are disinterested and independent and (2) the challenged transaction was otherwise the product of a valid exercise of business judgment. Hence, the Court of Chancery must make two inquiries, one into the independence and disinterestedness of the directors and the other into the substantive nature of the challenged transaction and the board's approval thereof. As to the latter inquiry the court does not assume that the transaction is a wrong to the corporation requiring corrective steps by the board. Rather, the alleged wrong is substantively reviewed against the factual background alleged in the complaint. As to the former inquiry, directorial independence and disinterestedness, the court reviews the factual allegations to decide whether they raise a reasonable doubt, as a threshold matter, that the protections of the business judgment rule are available to the board. Certainly, if this is an "interested" director transaction, such that the business judgment rule is inapplicable to the board majority approving the transaction, then the inquiry ceases. In that event futility of demand has been established by any objective or subjective standard.[1] This includes situations involving self-dealing directors.

However, the mere threat of personal liability for approving a questioned transaction, standing alone, is insufficient to challenge either the independence or disinterestedness of directors, although in rare cases a transaction may be so egregious on its face that board approval cannot meet the test of business judgment, and a substantial likelihood of director liability therefore exists. In sum the entire review is factual in nature. The Court of Chancery in the exercise of its sound discretion must be satisfied that a plaintiff has alleged facts with particularity which, taken as true, support a reasonable doubt that the challenged transaction was the product of a valid exercise of business judgment. Only in that context is demand excused.

B

Having outlined the legal framework within which these issues are to be determined, we consider plaintiff's claims of futility here: Fink's domination and control of the directors, board approval of the Fink-Meyers employment agreement, and board hostility to the plaintiff's derivative action due to the directors' status as defendants.

Plaintiff's claim that Fink dominates and controls the Meyers' board is based on: (1) Fink's 47% ownership of Meyers' outstanding stock, and (2) that he "personally selected" each Meyers director. Plaintiff also alleges that mere approval of the employment agreement illustrates Fink's domination and control of the board. In addition, plaintiff argued on appeal that 47% stock ownership,

---

[1] We recognize that drawing the line at a majority of the board may be an arguably arbitrary dividing point. Critics will charge that we are ignoring the structural bias common to corporate boards throughout America, as well as the other unseen socialization processes cutting against independent discussion and decisionmaking in the boardroom. The difficulty with structural bias in a demand futile case is simply one of establishing it in the complaint for purposes of Rule 23.1. We are satisfied that discretionary review by the Court of Chancery of complaints alleging specific facts pointing to bias on a particular board will be sufficient for determining demand futility.

though less than a majority, constituted control given the large number of shares outstanding, 1,245,745.

Such contentions do not support any claim under Delaware law that these directors lack independence. In *Kaplan v. Centex Corp.*, Del. Ch., 284 A.2d 119 (1971), the Court of Chancery stated that "[s]tock ownership alone, at least when it amounts to less than a majority, is not sufficient proof of domination or control". *Id.* at 123. Moreover, in the demand context even proof of majority ownership of a company does not strip the directors of the presumptions of independence, and that their acts have been taken in good faith and in the best interests of the corporation. There must be coupled with the allegation of control such facts as would demonstrate that through personal or other relationships the directors are beholden to the controlling person. To date the principal decisions dealing with the issue of control or domination arose only after a full trial on the merits. Thus, they are distinguishable in the demand context unless similar particularized facts are alleged to meet the test of Chancery Rule 23.1.

The requirement of director independence inhers in the conception and rationale of the business judgment rule. The presumption of propriety that flows from an exercise of business judgment is based in part on this unyielding precept. Independence means that a director's decision is based on the corporate merits of the subject before the board rather than extraneous considerations or influences. While directors may confer, debate, and resolve their differences through compromise, or by reasonable reliance upon the expertise of their colleagues and other qualified persons, the end result, nonetheless, must be that each director has brought his or her own informed business judgment to bear with specificity upon the corporate merits of the issues without regard for or succumbing to influences which convert an otherwise valid business decision into a faithless act.

Thus, it is not enough to charge that a director was nominated by or elected at the behest of those controlling the outcome of a corporate election. That is the usual way a person becomes a corporate director. It is the care, attention and sense of individual responsibility to the performance of one's duties, not the method of election, that generally touches on independence.

We conclude that in the demand-futile context a plaintiff charging domination and control of one or more directors must allege particularized facts manifesting "a direction of corporate conduct in such a way as to comport with the wishes or interests of the corporation (or persons) doing the controlling". *Kaplan*, 284 A.2d at 123. The shorthand shibboleth of "dominated and controlled directors" is insufficient. In recognizing that Kaplan was decided after trial and full discovery, we stress that the plaintiff need only allege specific facts; he need not plead evidence. Otherwise, he would be forced to make allegations which may not comport with his duties under Chancery Rule 11.

Here, plaintiff has not alleged any facts sufficient to support a claim of control. The personal-selection-of-directors allegation stands alone, unsupported. At best it is a conclusion devoid of factual support. The causal link between Fink's control and approval of the employment agreement is alluded to, but nowhere specified. The director's approval, alone, does not establish control, even in the face of Fink's 47% stock ownership. The claim that Fink is unlikely to perform any services under the agreement, because of his age, and his conflicting consultant work with Prudential, adds nothing to the control claim. Therefore, we cannot conclude that the complaint factually particularizes any circumstances of control and domination to overcome the presumption of board independence, and thus render the demand futile.

C

Turning to the board's approval of the Meyers-Fink employment agreement, plaintiff's argument is simple: all of the Meyers directors are named defendants, because they approved the wasteful agreement; if plaintiff prevails on the merits all the directors will be jointly and severally liable; therefore, the directors' interest in avoiding personal liability automatically and absolutely disqualifies them from passing on a shareholder's demand.

Such allegations are conclusory at best. In Delaware mere directorial approval of a transaction, absent particularized facts supporting a breach of fiduciary duty claim, or otherwise establishing the lack of independence or disinterestedness of a majority of the directors, is insufficient to excuse demand. Here, plaintiff's suit is premised on the notion that the Meyers-Fink employment agreement was a waste of corporate assets. So, the argument goes, by approving such waste the directors now face potential personal liability, thereby rendering futile any demand on them to bring suit. Unfortunately, plaintiff's claim falls in its initial premise. The complaint does not allege particularized facts indicating that the agreement is a waste of corporate assets. Indeed, the complaint as now drafted may not even state a cause of action, given the directors' broad corporate power to fix the compensation of officers.

In essence, the plaintiff alleged a lack of consideration flowing from Fink to Meyers, since the employment agreement provided that compensation was not contingent on Fink's ability to perform any services. The bare assertion that Fink performed "little or no services" was plaintiff's conclusion based solely on Fink's age and the *existence* of the Fink-Prudential employment agreement. As for Meyers' loans to Fink, beyond the bare allegation that they were made, the complaint does not allege facts indicating the wastefulness of such arrangements. Again, the mere existence of such loans, given the broad corporate powers conferred by Delaware law, does not even state a claim.

In sustaining plaintiff's claim of demand futility the trial court relied on *Fidanque v. American Maracaibo Co.*, Del. Ch., 92 A.2d 311, 321 (1952), which held that a contract providing for payment of consulting fees to a retired president/director was a waste of corporate assets. In *Fidanque*, the court found after trial that the contract and payments were in reality compensation for past services. This was based upon facts not present here: the former president/director was a 70 year old stroke victim, neither the agreement nor the record spelled out his consulting duties at all, the consulting salary equalled the individual's salary when he was president and general manager of the corporation, and the contract was silent as to continued employment in the event that the retired president/director again became incapacitated and unable to perform his duties. Contrasting the facts of *Fidanque* with the complaint here, it is apparent that plaintiff has not alleged facts sufficient to render demand futile on a charge of corporate waste, and thus create a reasonable doubt that the board's action is protected by the business judgment rule.

D

Plaintiff's final argument is the incantation that demand is excused because the directors otherwise would have to sue themselves, thereby placing the conduct of the litigation in hostile hands and preventing its effective prosecution. This bootstrap argument has been made to and dismissed by other courts. Its acceptance would effectively abrogate Rule 23.1 and weaken the managerial power of directors. Unless facts are alleged with particularity to overcome the presumptions of independence and a proper exercise of business judgment, in which case the directors could not be expected to sue themselves, a bare claim of this sort raises no legally cognizable issue under Delaware corporate law.

V

In sum, we conclude that the plaintiff has failed to allege facts with particularity indicating that the Meyers directors were tainted by interest, lacked independence, or took action contrary to Meyers' best interests in order to create a reasonable doubt as to the applicability of the business judgment rule. Only in the presence of such a reasonable doubt may a demand be deemed futile. Hence, we reverse the Court of Chancery's denial of the motion to dismiss, and remand with instructions that plaintiff be granted leave to amend his complaint to bring it into compliance with Rule 23.1 based on the principles we have announced today.[2]

RALES v. BLASBAND

Supreme Court of Delaware
634 A.2d 927 (1993)

VEASEY, CHIEF JUSTICE:

This certified question of law comes before the Court pursuant to Article IV, Section 11(9) of the Delaware Constitution and Supreme Court Rule 41. The question of law was certified by the United States District Court for the District of Delaware (the "District Court"), and was accepted by this Court on June 16, 1993....

---

[2] On remand, the court held that demand was excused because the plaintiff's amended complaint alleged sufficient facts to create a reasonable doubt regarding the board's independence. *Lewis v. Aronson*, Del. Ch. C.A. No. 6919, Hartnett, V.C. (May 1, 1985).[Eds.]

The underlying action pending in the District Court is a stockholder derivative action filed on March 25, 1991, by Alfred Blasband ("Blasband") on behalf of Danaher Corporation, a Delaware corporation ("Danaher").... Following Blasband's filing of an amended complaint (the "amended complaint"), the defendants filed a motion to dismiss and moved to certify the following question of law to this Court:

> In the context of this novel action, which is neither a simple derivative suit nor a double derivative suit, but which the United States Court of Appeals for the Third Circuit describes as a "first cousin to a double derivative suit," has plaintiff Alfred Blasband, in accordance with the substantive law of the State of Delaware, alleged facts to show that demand is excused on the board of directors of Danaher Corporation, a Delaware corporation?

After consideration of the allegations of the amended complaint, the briefs, and the oral argument of the parties in this Court, it is our conclusion that the certified question must be answered in the affirmative. Because the amended complaint does not challenge a decision of the board of directors of Danaher (the "Board"), the test enunciated in *Aronson v. Lewis*, Del. Supr., 473 A.2d 805 (1984) is not implicated. In the unusual context of this case, demand on the Board is excused because the amended complaint alleges particularized facts creating a reasonable doubt that a majority of the Board would be disinterested or independent in making a decision on a demand.

I. *Facts*

Blasband is currently a stockholder of Danaher. Prior to 1990 Blasband owned 1100 shares of Easco Hand Tools, Inc., a Delaware corporation ("Easco"). Easco entered into a merger agreement with Danaher in February 1990 whereby Easco became a wholly-owned subsidiary of Danaher (the "Merger").

Steven M. Rales and Mitchell P. Rales (the "Rales brothers") have been directors, officers, or stockholders of Easco and Danaher at relevant times. Prior to the Merger, the Rales brothers were directors of Easco, and together owned approximately 52 percent of Easco's common stock. They continued to serve as directors of Easco after the Merger.

The Rales brothers also own approximately 44 percent of Danaher's common stock. Prior to the Merger, Mitchell Rales was President and Steven Rales was Chief Executive Officer of Danaher. The Rales brothers resigned their positions as officers of Danaher in early 1990, but continued to serve as members of the Board. The Board consists of eight members. The other six members are Danaher's President and Chief Executive Officer, George Sherman ("Sherman"), Donald E. Ehrlich ("Ehrlich"), Mortimer Caplin ("Caplin"), George D. Kellner ("Kellner"), A. Emmett Stephenson, Jr. ("Stephenson"), and Walter Lohr ("Lohr"). A number of these directors have business relationships with the Rales brothers or with entities controlled by them.

The central focus of the amended complaint is the alleged misuse by the Easco board of the proceeds of a sale of that company's 12.875% Senior Subordinated Notes due 1998 (the "Notes"). On or about September 1, 1988, Easco sold $ 100 million of the Notes in a public offering (the "Offering").... The prospectus further stated that "[p]ending such uses, the Company will invest the balance of the net proceeds from this offering in government and other marketable securities which are expected to yield a lower rate of return than the rate of interest borne by the Notes."

Blasband alleges that the defendants did not invest in "government and other marketable securities," but instead used over $ 61.9 million of the proceeds to buy highly speculative "junk bonds" offered through Drexel Burnham Lambert Inc. ("Drexel"). Blasband alleges that these junk bonds were bought by Easco because of the Rales brothers' desire to help Drexel at a time when it was under investigation and having trouble selling such bonds....

The amended complaint alleges that these investments have declined substantially in value, resulting in a loss to Easco of at least $ 14 million. Finally, Blasband complains that the Easco and Danaher boards of directors refused to comply with his request for information regarding the investments.

II. *Scope and Standard of Review*

...

The parties have raised a threshold issue regarding this Court's ability to consider the legal standards which are applicable to the certified question. Blasband contends that the role of this Court in responding to the certified question is limited to a mechanical application of the two-part test set forth in *Aronson v. Lewis*. The defendants disagree, and argue that the Court should apply a test more stringent than the *Aronson* test to protect corporations against strike suits.

... The certified question does not limit the issue presented to the mere application of the *Aronson* test, but instead calls upon this Court to decide whether Blasband's amended complaint establishes that demand is excused under the "substantive law of the State of Delaware." It is therefore necessary for this Court to determine what the applicable "substantive law" is before we can decide whether demand on the Board should be excused. Accordingly, the language of the question certified to this Court requires a consideration of the appropriate legal principles, including the applicability of the *Aronson* test in this unusual context, so that we may properly decide the issue presented to us.

III. *The Standards for Determining Whether Demand is Excused in This Derivative Suit*

...

Because such derivative suits challenge the propriety of decisions made by directors pursuant to their managerial authority, we have repeatedly held that the stockholder plaintiffs must overcome the powerful presumptions of the business judgment rule before they will be permitted to pursue the derivative claim....

Although these standards are well-established, they cannot be applied in a vacuum. Not all derivative suits fall into the paradigm addressed by *Aronson* and its progeny. The essential predicate for the *Aronson* test is the fact that a *decision* of the board of directors is being challenged in the derivative suit....

Under the unique circumstances of this case, an analysis of the Board's ability to consider a demand requires a departure here from the standards set forth in *Aronson*. The Board did not approve the transaction which is being challenged by Blasband in this action. In fact, the Danaher directors have made no decision relating to the subject of this derivative suit. Where there is no conscious decision by directors to act or refrain from acting, the business judgment rule has no application. The absence of board action, therefore, makes it impossible to perform the essential inquiry contemplated by *Aronson* — whether the directors have acted in conformity with the business judgment rule in approving the challenged transaction.

Consistent with the context and rationale of the *Aronson* decision, a court should not apply the *Aronson* test for demand futility where the board that would be considering the demand did not make a business decision which is being challenged in the derivative suit. This situation would arise in three principal scenarios: (1) where a business decision was made by the board of a company, but a majority of the directors making the decision have been replaced;[3] (2) where the subject of the derivative suit is not a business decision of the board; and (3) where, as here, the decision being challenged was made by the board of a different corporation.

Instead, it is appropriate in these situations to examine whether the board that would be addressing the demand can impartially consider its merits without being influenced by improper considerations. Thus, a court must determine whether or

---

[3] This first scenario was addressed by the Court of Chancery in *Harris v. Carter*, Del.Ch., 582 A.2d 222 (1990):

> In the special case, however, where there is a change in board control between the date of the challenged transaction and the date of suit, it might open the way to error to focus on the board existing at the time of the challenged transaction. What, in the end, is relevant is not whether the board that approved the challenged transaction was or was not interested in that transaction but whether the present board is or is not disabled from exercising its right and duty to control corporate litigation.
>
> *I do not consider that Aronson intended to determine that demand under Rule 23.1 upon an independent board that has come into existence after the time of the "challenged transaction" would be excused if the board that approved the challenged transaction did not qualify for business judgment protection.*

Id. at 230 (emphasis added). Because the new board in *Harris* was not yet in place at the time of the original complaint in that case, the Court of Chancery did not need to determine how, or if, *Aronson* would apply where there was a change in the board prior to the derivative suit being filed.

not the particularized factual allegations of a derivative stockholder complaint create a reasonable doubt that, as of the time the complaint is filed, the board of directors could have properly exercised its independent and disinterested business judgment in responding to a demand. If the derivative plaintiff satisfies this burden, then demand will be excused as futile.

In so holding, we reject the defendants' proposal that, for purposes of this derivative suit and future similar suits, we adopt either a universal demand requirement or a requirement that a plaintiff must demonstrate a reasonable probability of success on the merits. The defendants seek to justify these stringent tests on the need to discourage "strike suits" in situations like the present one. This concern is unfounded.

A plaintiff in a double derivative suit is still required to satisfy the *Aronson* test in order to establish that demand on the subsidiary's board is futile. The *Aronson* test was designed, in part, with the objective of preventing strike suits by requiring derivative plaintiffs to make a threshold showing, through the allegation of particularized facts, that their claims have some merit. *Aronson*, 473 A.2d at 811-12. Moreover, defendants' proposal of requiring demand on the parent board in all double derivative cases, even where a board of directors is interested, is not the appropriate protection against strike suits. While defendants' alternative suggestion of requiring a plaintiff to demonstrate a reasonable probability of success is more closely related to the prevention of strike suits, it is an extremely onerous burden to meet at the pleading stage without the benefit of discovery.[4] Because a plaintiff must satisfy the *Aronson* test in order to show that demand is excused on the subsidiary board, there is no need to create an unduly onerous test for determining demand futility on the parent board simply to protect against strike suits.

---

[4] Although derivative plaintiffs may believe it is difficult to meet the particularization requirement of *Aronson* because they are not entitled to discovery to assist their compliance with Rule 23.1, ..., they have many avenues available to obtain information bearing on the subject of their claims. For example, there is a variety of public sources from which the details of a corporate act may be discovered, including the media and governmental agencies such as the Securities and Exchange Commission. In addition, a stockholder who has met the procedural requirements and has shown a specific proper purpose may use the summary procedure embodied in 8 DEL.C. § 220 to investigate the possibility of corporate wrongdoing.... Surprisingly, little use has been made of section 220 as an information-gathering tool in the derivative context. Perhaps the problem arises in some cases out of an unseemly race to the court house, chiefly generated by the "first to file" custom seemingly permitting the winner of the race to be named lead counsel. The result has been a plethora of superficial complaints that could not be sustained. Nothing requires the Court of Chancery, or any other court having appropriate jurisdiction, to countenance this process by penalizing diligent counsel who has employed these methods, including section 220, in a deliberate and thorough manner in preparing a complaint that meets the demand excused test of *Aronson*.

IV. *Whether the Board is Interested or Lacks Independence*

In order to determine whether the Board could have impartially considered a demand at the time Blasband's original complaint was filed, it is appropriate to examine the nature of the decision confronting it. A stockholder demand letter would, at a minimum, notify the directors of the nature of the alleged wrongdoing and the identities of the alleged wrongdoers. The subject of the demand in this case would be the alleged breaches of fiduciary duty by the Easco board of directors in connection with Easco's investment in Drexel "junk bonds." The allegations of the amended complaint, which must be accepted as true in this procedural context, claim that the investment was made solely for the benefit of the Rales brothers, who were acting in furtherance of their business relationship with Drexel and not with regard to Easco's best interests. Such conduct, if proven, would constitute a breach of the Easco directors' duty of loyalty.

The task of a board of directors in responding to a stockholder demand letter is a two-step process. First, the directors must determine the best method to inform themselves of the facts relating to the alleged wrongdoing and the considerations, both legal and financial, bearing on a response to the demand. If a factual investigation is required, it must be conducted reasonably and in good faith. Second, the board must weigh the alternatives available to it, including the advisability of implementing internal corrective action and commencing legal proceedings. In carrying out these tasks, the board must be able to act free of personal financial interest and improper extraneous influences. We now consider whether the members of the Board could have met these standards.

A. *Interest*

The members of the Board at the time Blasband filed his original complaint were Steven Rales, Mitchell Rales, Sherman, Ehrlich, Caplin, Kellner, Stephenson, and Lohr. The Rales brothers and Caplin were also members of the Easco board of directors at the time of the alleged wrongdoing. Blasband's amended complaint specifically accuses the Rales brothers of being the motivating force behind the investment in Drexel "junk bonds." The Board would be obligated to determine whether these charges of wrongdoing should be investigated and, if substantiated, become the subject of legal action.

A director is considered interested where he or she will receive a personal financial benefit from a transaction that is not equally shared by the stockholders. Directorial interest also exists where a corporate decision will have a materially detrimental impact on a director, but not on the corporation and the stockholders. In such circumstances, a director cannot be expected to exercise his or her independent business judgment without being influenced by the adverse personal consequences resulting from the decision.

We conclude that the Rales brothers and Caplin must be considered interested in a decision of the Board in response to a demand addressing the alleged wrongdoing described in Blasband's amended complaint. Normally, "the mere threat of personal liability for approving a questioned transaction, standing alone, is insufficient to challenge either the independence or disinterestedness of directors...." *Aronson*, 473 A.2d at 815. Nevertheless, the Third Circuit has already concluded that "Blasband has pleaded facts raising at least a reasonable doubt that the [Easco board's] use of proceeds from the Note Offering was a valid exercise of business judgment." This determination is part of the law of the case, and is therefore binding on this Court. Such determination indicates that the potential for liability is not "a mere threat" but instead may rise to "a substantial likelihood." *See Aronson*, 473 A.2d at 815.

Therefore, a decision by the Board to bring suit against the Easco directors, including the Rales brothers and Caplin, could have potentially significant financial consequences for those directors. Common sense dictates that, in light of these consequences, the Rales brothers and Caplin have a disqualifying financial interest that disables them from impartially considering a response to a demand by Blasband.

B. *Independence*

Having determined that the Rales brothers and Caplin would be interested in a decision on Blasband's demand, we must now examine whether the remaining Danaher directors are sufficiently independent to make an impartial decision despite the fact that they are presumptively disinterested. As explained in *Aronson*, "[i]ndependence means that a director's decision is based on the corporate merits of the subject before the board rather than extraneous considerations or influences." 473 A.2d at 816. To establish lack of independence, Blasband must show that the directors are "beholden" to the Rales brothers or so under their influence that their discretion would be sterilized. *Id.* at 815. We conclude that the amended complaint alleges particularized facts sufficient to create a reasonable doubt that Sherman and Ehrlich, as members of the Board, are capable of acting independently of the Rales brothers.

Sherman is the President and Chief Executive Officer of Danaher. His salary is approximately $ 1 million per year. Although Sherman's continued employment and substantial remuneration may not hinge solely on his relationship with the Rales brothers, there is little doubt that Steven Rales' position as Chairman of the Board of Danaher and Mitchell Rales' position as Chairman of its Executive Committee place them in a position to exert considerable influence over Sherman. In light of these circumstances, there is a reasonable doubt that Sherman can be expected to act independently considering his substantial financial stake in maintaining his current offices.

Ehrlich is the President of Wabash National Corp. ("Wabash"). His annual compensation is approximately $ 300,000 per year. Ehrlich also has two brothers who are vice presidents of Wabash. The Rales brothers are directors of Wabash and own a majority of its stock through an investment partnership they control. As a result, there is a reasonable doubt regarding Ehrlich's ability to act independently since it can be inferred that he is beholden to the Rales brothers in light of his employment.

Therefore, the amended complaint pleads particularized facts raising a reasonable doubt as to the independence of Sherman and Ehrlich. Because of their alleged substantial financial interest in maintaining their employment positions, there is a reasonable doubt that these two directors are able to consider impartially an action that is contrary to the interests of the Rales brothers.

V. *Conclusion*

We conclude that, under the "substantive law" of the State of Delaware, the *Aronson* test does not apply in the context of this double derivative suit because the Board was not involved in the challenged transaction. Nevertheless, we do not agree with the defendants' argument that a more stringent test should be applied to deter strike suits. Instead, the appropriate inquiry is whether Blasband's amended complaint raises a reasonable doubt regarding the ability of a majority of the Board to exercise properly its business judgment in a decision on a demand had one been made at the time this action was filed. Based on the existence of a reasonable doubt that the Rales brothers and Caplin would be free of a financial interest in such a decision, and that Sherman and Ehrlich could act independently in light of their employment with entities affiliated with the Rales brothers, we conclude that the allegations of Blasband's amended complaint establish that DEMAND IS EXCUSED on the Board. The certified question is therefore answered in the

Affirmative.

A. UNIVERSAL DEMAND

Model Act § 7.42 and ALI § 7.03 offer an alternative approach to Delaware law. Rather than assessing whether demand would be futile in certain circumstances, they provide that shareholders should always make a written demand upon the board of directors ("universal demand"). Under ALI § 7.03(b), demand should be excused "only if the plaintiff makes a specific showing that irreparable injury to the corporation would otherwise result."

As explained in Model Act § 7.42 Official Comment:

> Section 7.42 requires a written demand on the corporation in all cases. The demand must be made at least 90 days before commencement of suit unless irreparable injury to the corporation would result. This approach has been adopted for two reasons. First, even though no director may be independent, the demand will give the board of directors the opportunity to reexamine the act complained of in the light of a potential lawsuit and take corrective action. Secondly, the provision eliminates the time and expense of the litigants and the court involved in litigating the question whether

demand is required. It is believed that requiring a demand in all cases does not impose an onerous burden since a relatively short waiting period of 90 days is provided and this period may be shortened if irreparable injury to the corporation would result by waiting for the expiration of the 90 day period. Moreover, the cases in which demand is excused are relatively rare. Many plaintiffs' counsel as a matter of practice make a demand in all cases rather than litigate the issue whether demand is excused.

B. NEW YORK APPROACH

You may also want to consider New York's articulation of demand futility in *Marx v. Akers*:[5]

> Although instructive, neither the universal demand requirement nor the Delaware approach to demand futility is adopted here. Since New York's demand requirement is codified in Business Corporation Law § 626(c), a universal demand may only be adopted by the Legislature. Delaware's approach, which resembles New York law in some respects, incorporates a "reasonable doubt" standard which has provoked criticism as confusing and overly subjective....
>
> ...
>
> [Under New York law,] conclusory allegations of wrongdoing against each member of the board are not sufficient to excuse demand ... [Various courts] have misinterpreted [*Barr v. Wackman*, 329 N.E.2d 180 (1975),] as excusing demand whenever a majority of the board members who approved the transaction are named as defendants .... The problem with such an approach is that it permits plaintiffs to frame their complaint in such a way as to automatically excuse demand, thereby allowing the exception to swallow the rule.
>
> We thus deem it necessary to offer the following elaboration of *Barr*'s demand/futility standard. (1) Demand is excused because of futility when a complaint alleges with particularity that a majority of the board of directors is interested in the challenged transaction. Director interest may either be self-interest in the transaction at issue or a loss of independence because a director with no direct interest in a transaction is "controlled" by a self-interested director. (2) Demand is excused because of futility when a complaint alleges with particularity that the board of directors did not fully inform themselves about the challenged transaction to the extent reasonably appropriate under the circumstances. (3) Demand is excused because of futility when a complaint alleges with particularity that the challenged transaction was so egregious on its face that it could not have been the product of sound business judgment of the directors.

---

[5] 666 N.E.2d 1034, 1039-40 (N.Y. 1996).

SECTION IV. DIRECTORS' AUTHORITY TO TERMINATE A SUIT AND SPECIAL LITIGATION COMMITTEES

The special litigation committee has become a formidable obstacle to shareholders who wish to pursue derivative suits. When some impropriety is alleged against the officers or directors, the board of directors often appoints a special litigation committee. This committee typically consists of directors whose conduct is not in question, and they are asked to determine whether the corporation should bring suit. Boards also frequently appoint such committees after a shareholders' derivative action has been filed. In those situations, the committee's task is to decide whether the corporation should seek a dismissal of the suit.

The following cases describe the judicial review of directors' authority to terminate derivative suits. The first case describes New York's approach and the second case describes Delaware law. Consider whether, and if so how, these courts have modified the general standards of conduct.

AUERBACH v. BENNETT

Court of Appeals of New York
393 N.E.2d 994 (1979)

JONES, JUDGE:

In the summer of 1975 the management of General Telephone & Electronics Corporation, in response to reports that numerous other multinational companies had made questionable payments to public officials or political parties in foreign countries, directed that an internal preliminary investigation be made to ascertain whether that corporation had engaged in similar transactions. On the basis of the report of this survey, received in October, 1975, management brought the issue to the attention of the corporation's board of directors. At a meeting held on November 6 of that year the board referred the matter to the board's audit committee. The audit committee retained as its special counsel the Washington, D. C., law firm of Wilmer, Cutler & Pickering which had not previously acted as counsel to the corporation. With the assistance of such special counsel and Arthur Andersen & Co., the corporation's outside auditors, the audit committee engaged in an investigation into the corporation's worldwide operations, focusing on whether, in the period January 1, 1971 to December 31, 1975, corporate funds had been (1) paid directly or indirectly to any political party or person or to any officer, employee, shareholder or director of any governmental or private customer, or (2) used to reimburse any officer of the corporation or other person for such payments.

On March 4, 1976 the audit committee released its report which was filed with the Securities and Exchange Commission and disclosed to the corporation's shareholders in a proxy statement prior to the annual meeting of shareholders held in April, 1976. The audit committee reported that it had found evidence that in the period from 1971 to 1975 the corporation or its subsidiaries had made payments abroad and in the United States constituting bribes and kickbacks in amounts perhaps totaling more than 11 million dollars and that some of the individual defendant directors had been personally involved in certain of the transactions.

Almost immediately Auerbach, a shareholder in the corporation, instituted the present shareholders' derivative action on behalf of the corporation against the corporation's directors, Arthur Andersen & Co. and the corporation. The complaint alleged that in connection with the transactions reported by the audit committee defendants, present and former members of the corporation's board of directors and Arthur Andersen & Co., are liable to the corporation for breach of their duties to the corporation and should be made to account for payments made in those transactions.

On April 21, 1976 the board of directors of the corporation adopted a resolution creating a special litigation committee "for the purpose of establishing a point of contract between the Board of Directors and the Corporation's General Counsel concerning the position to be taken by the Corporation in certain litigation involving shareholder derivative claims on behalf of the Corporation against certain of its directors and officers" and authorizing that committee "to take such steps from time to time as it deems necessary to pursue its objectives including the retention of special outside counsel." The special committee comprised three disinterested directors who had joined the board after the challenged transactions had occurred. The board subsequently additionally vested in the committee "all of the authority of the Board of Directors to determine, on behalf of the Board, the position that the Corporation shall take with respect to the derivative claims alleged on its behalf" in the present and similar shareholder derivative actions.

The special litigation committee reported under date of November 22, 1976. It found that defendant Arthur Andersen & Co. had conducted its examination of the corporation's affairs in accordance with generally accepted auditing standards and in good faith and concluded that no proper interest of the corporation or its shareholders would be served by the continued assertion of a claim against it. The committee also concluded that none of the individual defendants had violated the New York State statutory standard of care, that none had profited personally or gained in any way, that the claims asserted in the present action are without merit, that if the action were allowed to proceed the time and talents of the corporation's senior management would be wasted on lengthy pretrial and trial proceedings, that litigation costs would be inordinately high in view of the unlikelihood of success, and that the continuing publicity could be damaging to the corporation's business. The committee determined that it would not be in the best interests of the corporation for the present derivative action to proceed, and, exercising the authority delegated to it, directed the corporation's general counsel to take that position in the present litigation as well as in pending comparable shareholders' derivative actions.

On December 17, 1976 the corporation and the four individual defendants who had been served moved for an order ... dismissing the complaint or in the alternative for an order ... for summary judgment. On January 7, 1977 Arthur Andersen & Co. made a similar motion. On May 13, 1977 Supreme Court, Special Term, granted the motions of all defendants and dismissed the complaint on the merits.

...

As all parties and both courts below recognize, the disposition of this case on the merits turns on the proper application of the business judgment doctrine, in particular to the decision of a specially appointed committee of disinterested directors acting on behalf of the board to terminate a shareholders' derivative action. That doctrine bars judicial inquiry into actions of corporate directors taken in good faith and in the exercise of honest judgment in the lawful and legitimate furtherance of corporate purposes. "Questions of policy of management, expediency of contracts or action, adequacy of consideration, lawful appropriation of corporate funds to advance corporate interests, are left solely to their honest and unselfish decision, for their powers therein are without limitation and free from restraint, and the exercise of them for the common and general interests of the corporation may not be questioned, although the results show that what they did was unwise or inexpedient." (*Pollitz v. Wabash R.R. Co.*, 100 N.E. 721, 724 [(N.Y. 1912)].)

In this instance our inquiry, to the limited extent to which it may be pursued, has a two-tiered aspect. The complaint initially asserted liability on the part of defendants based on the payments made to foreign governmental customers and privately owned customers, some unspecified portions of which were allegedly passed on to officials of the customers, *i.e.*, the focus was on first-tier bribes and kickbacks. Then subsequent to the service of the complaint there came the report of a special litigation committee, particularly appointed by the corporation's board of directors to consider the merits of the present and similar shareholders' derivative actions, and its determination that it would not be in the best interests of the corporation to press claims against defendants based on their possible first-tier liability. The motions for summary judgment were predicated principally on the report and determination of the special litigation committee and on the contention that this second-tier corporate action insulated the first-tier transactions from judicial inquiry and was itself subject to the shelter of the business judgment doctrine. The disposition at Special Term was predicated on this analysis; its decision focused on the actions of the special litigation committee, and the motions for summary judgment were granted on the ground that the business judgment doctrine precluded the courts from going back of the decision of the special litigation committee on behalf of the corporation not to pursue the claims alleged in the complaint. Similarly the reversal at the Appellate Division was based on that court's perception of the proper application of the business judgment rule to the actions and determination of the special litigation committee. We proceed on the same analysis, concluding, however, on the record before us, at variance with the Appellate Division, that the determination of the special litigation committee forecloses further judicial inquiry in this case.

It appears to us that the business judgment doctrine, at least in part, is grounded in the prudent recognition that courts are ill equipped and infrequently called on to evaluate what are and must be essentially business judgments. The authority and responsibilities vested in corporate directors both by statute and decisional law proceed on the assumption that inescapably there can be no available objective standard by which the correctness of every corporate decision may be measured, by the courts or otherwise. Even if that were not the case, by definition the responsibility for business judgments must rest with the corporate directors; their individual capabilities and experience peculiarly qualify them for the discharge of that responsibility. Thus, absent evidence of bad faith or fraud (of which there is none here) the courts must and properly should respect their determinations.

Derivative claims against corporate directors belong to the corporation itself. As with other questions of corporate policy and management, the decision whether and to what extent to explore and prosecute such claims lies within the judgment and control of the corporation's board of directors. Necessarily such decision must be predicated on the weighing and balancing of a variety of disparate considerations to reach a considered conclusion as to what course of action or inaction is best calculated to protect and advance the interests of the corporation. This is the essence of the responsibility and role of the board of directors, and courts may not intrude to interfere.

In the present case we confront a special instance of the application of the business judgment rule and inquire whether it applies in its full vigor to shield from judicial scrutiny the decision of a three-person minority committee of the board acting on behalf of the full board not to prosecute a shareholder's derivative action. The record in this case reveals that the board is a 15-member board, and that the derivative suit was brought against four of the directors. Nothing suggests that any of the other directors participated in any of the challenged first-tier transactions. Indeed the report of the audit committee on which the complaint is based specifically found that no other directors had any prior knowledge of or were in any way involved in any of these transactions. Other directors had, however, been members of the board in the period during which the transactions occurred. Each of the three director members of the special litigation committee joined the board thereafter.

The business judgment rule does not foreclose inquiry by the courts into the disinterested independence of those members of the board chosen by it to make the corporate decision on its behalf here the members of the special litigation committee. Indeed the rule shields the deliberations and conclusions of the chosen representatives of the board only if they possess a disinterested independence and do not stand in a dual relation which prevents an unprejudicial exercise of judgment.

We examine then the proof submitted by defendants. It is not disputed that the members of the special litigation committee were not members of the corporation's board of directors at the time of the first-tier transactions in question. Howard Blauvelt, chairman of the board of Continental Oil Company, had been elected to the corporation's board of directors on October 9, 1975. Dr. John T. Dunlop, Lamont University professor at the Graduate School of Business Administration of Harvard University had been elected to the board on April 21, 1976. James R. Barker, chairman of the board and chief executive officer of Moore McCormack Resources, Inc., was added as the third member of the committee when he was elected to the board on July 19, 1976. None of the three had had any prior affiliation with the corporation. Notwithstanding the vigorous and imaginative hypothesizing and innuendo of counsel there is nothing in this record to raise a triable issue of fact as to the independence and disinterested status of these three directors.

The contention of Wallenstein that any committee authorized by the board of which defendant directors were members must be held to be legally infirm and may not be delegated power to terminate a derivative action must be rejected. In the very nature of the corporate organization it was only the existing board of directors which had authority on behalf of the corporation to direct the investigation and to assure the cooperation of corporate employees, and it is only that same board by its own action or as here pursuant to authority duly delegated by it which had authority to decide whether to prosecute the claims against defendant directors. The board in this instance, with slight adaptation, followed prudent practice in observing the general policy that when individual members of a board of directors prove to have personal interests which may conflict with the interests of the corporation, such interested directors must be excluded while the remaining members of the board proceed to consideration and action. Courts have consistently held that the business judgment rule applies where some directors are charged with wrongdoing, so long as the remaining directors making the decision are disinterested and independent.

To accept the assertions of the intervenor and to disqualify the entire board would be to render the corporation powerless to make an effective business judgment with respect to prosecution of the derivative action. The possible risk of hesitancy on the part of the members of any committee, even if composed of outside, independent, disinterested directors, to investigate the activities of fellow members of the board where personal liability is at stake is an inherent, inescapable, given aspect of the corporation's predicament. To assign responsibility of the dimension here involved to individuals wholly separate and apart from the board of directors would, except in the most extraordinary circumstances, itself be an act of default and breach of the nondelegable fiduciary duty owed by the members of the board to the corporation and to its shareholders, employees and creditors. For the courts to preside over such determinations would similarly work an ouster of the board's fundamental responsibility and authority for corporate management.

We turn then to the action of the special litigation committee itself which comprised two components. First, there was the selection of procedures appropriate to the pursuit of its charge, and second, there was the ultimate substantive decision, predicated on the procedures chosen and the data produced thereby, not to pursue the claims advanced in the shareholders' derivative actions. The latter, substantive decision falls squarely within the embrace of the business judgment doctrine, involving as it did the weighing and balancing of legal, ethical, commercial, promotional, public relations, fiscal and other factors familiar to the resolution of many if not most corporate problems. To this extent the conclusion reached by the special litigation committee is outside the scope of our review. Thus, the courts cannot inquire as to which factors were considered by that committee or the relative weight accorded them in reaching that substantive decision "the reasons for the payments, the advantages or disadvantages accruing to the corporation by reason of the transactions, the extent of the participation or profit by the respondent directors and the loss, if any, of public confidence in the corporation which might be incurred" [*Auerbach v. Bennett*, 408 N.Y.S.2d 83, 107 (N.Y. App. Div. 1978)]. Inquiry into such matters would go to the very core of the business judgment made by the committee. To permit judicial probing of such issues would be to emasculate the business judgment doctrine as applied to the actions and determinations of the special litigation committee. Its substantive evaluation of the problems posed and its judgment in their resolution are beyond our reach.

As to the other component of the committee's activities, however, the situation is different, and here we agree with the Appellate Division. As to the methodologies and procedures best suited to the conduct of an investigation of facts and the determination of legal liability, the courts are well equipped by long and continuing experience and practice to make determinations. In fact they are better qualified in this regard than are corporate directors in general. Nor do the determinations to be made in the adoption of procedures partake of the nuances or special perceptions or comprehensions of business judgment or corporate activities or interests. The question is solely how appropriately to set about to gather the pertinent data.

While the court may properly inquire as to the adequacy and appropriateness of the committee's investigative procedures and methodologies, it may not under the guise of consideration of such factors trespass in the domain of business judgment. At the same time those responsible for the procedures by which the business judgment is reached may reasonably be required to show that they have pursued their chosen investigative methods in good faith. What evidentiary proof may be required to this end will, of course, depend on the nature of the particular investigation, and the proper reach of disclosure at the instance of the shareholders will in turn relate inversely to the showing made by the corporate representatives themselves. The latter may be expected to show that the areas and subjects to be examined are reasonably complete and that there has been a good-faith pursuit of inquiry into such areas and subjects. What has been uncovered and the relative weight accorded in evaluating and balancing the several factors and considerations are beyond the scope of judicial concern. Proof, however, that the investigation has been so restricted in scope, so shallow in execution, or otherwise so Pro forma or halfhearted as to constitute a pretext or sham, consistent with the principles underlying the application of the business judgment doctrine, would raise questions of good faith or conceivably fraud which would never be shielded by that doctrine.

In addition to the issue of the disinterested independence of the special litigation committee, addressed above, the disposition of the present appeal turns, then, on whether on defendants' motions for summary judgment predicated on the investigation and determination of the special litigation committee, Wallenstein by tender of evidentiary proof in admissible form has shown facts sufficient to require a trial of any material issue of fact as to the adequacy or appropriateness of the Modus operandi of that committee or has demonstrated acceptable excuse for failure to make such tender. We conclude that the requisite showing has not been made on this record.

. . .

On the submissions made by defendants in support of their motions, we do not find either insufficiency or infirmity as to the procedures and methodologies chosen and pursued by the special litigation committee. That committee promptly engaged eminent special counsel to guide its deliberations and to advise it. The committee reviewed the prior work of the audit committee, testing its completeness, accuracy and thoroughness by interviewing representatives of Wilmer, Cutler & Pickering, reviewing transcripts of the testimony of 10 corporate officers and employees before the Securities and Exchange Commission, and studying documents collected by and work papers of the Washington law firm. Individual interviews were conducted with the directors found to have participated in any way in the questioned payments, and with representatives of Arthur Andersen & Co. Questionnaires were sent to and answered by each of the corporation's nonmanagement directors. At the conclusion of its investigation the special litigation committee sought and obtained pertinent legal advice from its special counsel. The selection of appropriate investigative methods must always turn on the nature and characteristics of the particular subject being investigated, but we find nothing in this record that requires a trial of any material issue of fact concerning the sufficiency or appropriateness of the procedures chosen by this special litigation committee. Nor is there anything in this record to raise a triable issue of fact as to the good-faith pursuit of its examination by that committee.

. . .

For the reasons stated the order of the Appellate Division should be modified, with costs to defendants, by reversing so much thereof as reversed the order of Supreme Court, and, as so modified,

Affirmed.

ZAPATA CORP. v. MALDONADO

Supreme Court of Delaware
430 A.2d 779 (1981)

QUILLEN, JUSTICE:

This is an interlocutory appeal from an order entered on April 9, 1980, by the Court of Chancery denying appellant-defendant Zapata Corporation's (Zapata) alternative motions to dismiss the complaint or for summary judgment. The issue to be addressed has reached this Court by way of a rather convoluted path.

In June, 1975, William Maldonado, a stockholder of Zapata, instituted a derivative action in the Court of Chancery on behalf of Zapata against ten officers and/or directors of Zapata, alleging, essentially, breaches of fiduciary duty. Maldonado did not first demand that the board bring this action, stating instead such demand's futility because all directors were named as defendants and allegedly participated in the acts specified. In June, 1977, Maldonado commenced an action in the United States District Court for the Southern District of New York against the same defendants, save one, alleging federal security law violations as well as the same common law claims made previously in the Court of Chancery.

By June, 1979, four of the defendant-directors were no longer on the board, and the remaining directors appointed two new outside directors to the board. The board then created an "Independent Investigation Committee" (Committee), composed solely of the two new directors, to investigate Maldonado's actions, as well as a similar derivative action then pending in Texas, and to determine whether the corporation should continue any or all of the litigation. The Committee's determination was stated to be "final, ... not ... subject to review by the Board of Directors and ... in all respects ... binding upon the Corporation."

Following an investigation, the Committee concluded, in September, 1979, that each action should "be dismissed forthwith as their continued maintenance is inimical to the Company's best interests ...." Consequently, Zapata moved for dismissal or summary judgment in the three derivative actions. On January 24, 1980, the District Court for the Southern District of New York granted Zapata's motion for summary judgment, holding, under its interpretation of Delaware law, that the Committee had the authority, under the "business judgment" rule, to require the termination of the derivative action. Maldonado appealed that decision to the Second Circuit Court of Appeals.

On March 18, 1980, the Court of Chancery, in a reported opinion, the basis for the order of April 9, 1980, denied Zapata's motions, holding that Delaware law does not sanction this means of dismissal. More specifically, it held that the "business judgment" rule is not a grant of authority to dismiss derivative actions and that a stockholder has an individual right to maintain derivative actions in certain instances. *Maldonado v. Flynn*, Del.Ch., 413 A.2d 1251 (1980) (herein *Maldonado*). Pursuant to the provisions of Supreme Court Rule 42, Zapata filed an interlocutory appeal with this Court shortly thereafter. The appeal was accepted by this Court on June 5, 1980. On May 29, 1980, however, the Court of Chancery dismissed Maldonado's cause of action, its decision based on principles of *res judicata*, expressly conditioned upon the Second Circuit affirming the earlier New York District Court's decision. The Second Circuit appeal was ordered stayed, however, pending this Court's resolution of the appeal from the April 9th Court of Chancery order denying dismissal and summary judgment.

Thus, Zapata's observation that it sits "in a procedural gridlock" appears quite accurate, and we agree that this Court can and should attempt to resolve the particular question of Delaware law. As the Vice Chancellor noted, "it is the law of the State of incorporation which determines whether the directors have this power of dismissal ..." We limit our review in this interlocutory appeal to whether the Committee has the power to cause the present action to be dismissed.

We begin with an examination of the carefully considered opinion of the Vice Chancellor which states, in part, that the "business judgment" rule does not confer power "to a corporate board of directors to terminate a derivative suit." His conclusion is particularly pertinent because several federal courts, applying Delaware law, have held that the business judgment rule enables boards (or their committees) to terminate derivative suits, decisions now in conflict with the holding below.

As the term is most commonly used, and given the disposition below, we can understand the Vice Chancellor's comment that "the business judgment rule is irrelevant to the question of whether the Committee has the authority to compel the dismissal of this suit." Corporations, existing because of legislative grace, possess authority as granted by the legislature. Directors of Delaware corporations derive their managerial decision making power, which encompasses decisions whether to initiate, or refrain from entering, litigation, from 8 Del. C. § 141 (a). This statute is the fount of directorial powers. The "business judgment" rule is a judicial creation that presumes propriety, under certain circumstances, in a board's decision. Viewed defensively, it does not create authority. In this sense the "business judgment" rule is not relevant in corporate decision making until after a decision is made. It is generally used as a defense to an attack on the decision's soundness. The board's managerial decision making power, however, comes from § 141(a). The judicial creation and legislative grant are related because the "business judgment" rule evolved to give recognition and deference to directors' business expertise when exercising their managerial power under § 141(a).

In the case before us, although the corporation's decision to move to dismiss or for summary judgment was, literally, a decision resulting from an exercise of the directors' (as delegated to the Committee) business judgment, the question of "business judgment," in a defensive sense, would not become relevant until and unless the decision to seek termination of the derivative lawsuit was attacked as improper. This question was not reached by the Vice Chancellor because he determined that the stockholder had an individual right to maintain this derivative action.

Thus, the focus in this case is on the power to speak for the corporation as to whether the lawsuit should be continued or terminated. As we see it, this issue in the current appellate posture of this case has three aspects: the conclusions of the Court below concerning the continuing right of a stockholder to maintain a derivative action; the corporate power under Delaware law of an authorized board committee to cause dismissal of litigation instituted for the benefit of the corporation; and the role of the Court of Chancery in resolving conflicts between the stockholder and the committee.

Accordingly, we turn first to the Court of Chancery's conclusions concerning the right of a plaintiff stockholder in a derivative action. We find that its determination that a stockholder, once demand is made and refused, possesses an independent, individual right to continue a derivative suit for breaches of fiduciary duty over objection by the corporation as an absolute rule, is erroneous.

. . .

Consistent with the purpose of requiring a demand, a board decision to cause a derivative suit to be dismissed as detrimental to the company, after demand has been made and refused, will be respected unless it was wrongful.[6]

. . .

The question to be decided becomes: When, if at all, should an authorized board committee be permitted to cause litigation, properly initiated by a derivative stockholder in his own right, to be dismissed? As noted above, a board has the power to choose not to pursue litigation when demand is made upon it, so long as the decision is not wrongful. If the board determines that a suit would be detrimental to the company, the board's determination prevails. Even when demand is excusable, circumstances may arise when continuation of the litigation would not be in the corporation's best interests. Our inquiry is whether, under such circumstances, there is a permissible procedure under § 141(a) by which a corporation can rid itself of detrimental litigation. If there is not, a single stockholder in an extreme case might control the destiny of the entire corporation.... But, when examining the means, including the committee mechanism examined in this case, potentials for abuse must be recognized. This takes us to the second and third aspects of the issue on appeal.

. . .

At the risk of stating the obvious, the problem is relatively simple. If, on the one hand, corporations can consistently wrest bona fide derivative actions away

---

[6] In other words, when stockholders, after making demand and having their suit rejected, attack the board's decision as improper, the board's decision falls under the "business judgment" rule and will be respected if the requirements of the rule are met. That situation should be distinguished from the instant case, where demand was not made, and the power of the board to seek a dismissal, due to disqualification, presents a threshold issue.... We recognize that the two contexts can overlap in practice.

from well-meaning derivative plaintiffs through the use of the committee mechanism, the derivative suit will lose much, if not all, of its generally-recognized effectiveness as an intra-corporate means of policing boards of directors. If, on the other hand, corporations are unable to rid themselves of meritless or harmful litigation and strike suits, the derivative action, created to benefit the corporation, will produce the opposite, unintended result. It thus appears desirable to us to find a balancing point where bona fide stockholder power to bring corporate causes of action cannot be unfairly trampled on by the board of directors, but the corporation can rid itself of detrimental litigation.

As we noted, the question has been treated by other courts as one of the "business judgment" of the board committee. If a "committee, composed of independent and disinterested directors, conducted a proper review of the matters before it, considered a variety of factors and reached, in good faith, a business judgment that (the) action was not in the best interest of (the corporation)," the action must be dismissed. *See, e.g., Maldonado v. Flynn, supra,* 485 F. Supp. at 282, 286. The issues become solely independence, good faith, and reasonable investigation. The ultimate conclusion of the committee, under that view, is not subject to judicial review.

We are not satisfied, however, that acceptance of the "business judgment" rationale at this stage of derivative litigation is a proper balancing point. While we admit an analogy with a normal case respecting board judgment, it seems to us that there is sufficient risk in the realities of a situation like the one presented in this case to justify caution beyond adherence to the theory of business judgment.

The context here is a suit against directors where demand on the board is excused. We think some tribute must be paid to the fact that the lawsuit was properly initiated. It is not a board refusal case. Moreover, this complaint was filed in June of 1975 and, while the parties undoubtedly would take differing views on the degree of litigation activity, we have to be concerned about the creation of an "Independent Investigation Committee" four years later, after the election of two new outside directors. Situations could develop where such motions could be filed after years of vigorous litigation for reasons unconnected with the merits of the lawsuit.

Moreover, notwithstanding our conviction that Delaware law entrusts the corporate power to a properly authorized committee, we must be mindful that directors are passing judgment on fellow directors in the same corporation and fellow directors, in this instance, who designated them to serve both as directors and committee members. The question naturally arises whether a "there but for the grace of God go I" empathy might not play a role. And the further question arises whether inquiry as to independence, good faith and reasonable investigation is sufficient safeguard against abuse, perhaps subconscious abuse.

...

Whether the Court of Chancery will be persuaded by the exercise of a committee power resulting in a summary motion for dismissal of a derivative action, where a demand has not been initially made, should rest, in our judgment, in the independent discretion of the Court of Chancery. We thus steer a middle course between those cases which yield to the independent business judgment of a board committee and this case as determined below which would yield to unbridled plaintiff stockholder control. In pursuit of the course, we recognize that "(t)he final substantive judgment whether a particular lawsuit should be maintained requires a balance of many factors ethical, commercial, promotional, public relations, employee relations, fiscal as well as legal." *Maldonado v. Flynn, supra,* 485 F. Supp. at 285. But we are content that such factors are not "beyond the judicial reach" of the Court of Chancery which regularly and competently deals with fiduciary relationships, disposition of trust property, approval of settlements and scores of similar problems. We recognize the danger of judicial overreaching but the alternatives seem to us to be outweighed by the fresh view of a judicial outsider. Moreover, if we failed to balance all the interests involved, we would in the name of practicality and judicial economy foreclose a judicial decision on the merits. At this point, we are not convinced that is necessary or desirable.

After an objective and thorough investigation of a derivative suit, an independent committee may cause its corporation to file a pretrial motion to dismiss in the Court of Chancery. The basis of the motion is the best interests of the corporation, as determined by the committee. The motion should include a thorough written record of the investigation and its findings and recommendations. Under appropriate Court supervision, akin to proceedings on summary judgment, each side should have an opportunity to make a record on the motion. As to the limited issues presented by the motion noted below, the moving party should be prepared to meet the normal burden under Rule 56 that there is no genuine issue as to any material fact and that the moving party is entitled to dismiss as a matter of law. The Court should apply a two-step test to the motion.

First, the Court should inquire into the independence and good faith of the committee and the bases supporting its conclusions. Limited discovery may be ordered to facilitate such inquiries. The corporation should have the burden of proving independence, good faith and a reasonable investigation, rather than presuming independence, good faith and reasonableness. If the Court determines either that the committee is not independent or has not shown reasonable bases for its conclusions, or, if the Court is not satisfied for other reasons relating to the process, including but not limited to the good faith of the committee, the Court shall deny the corporation's motion. If, however, the Court is satisfied under Rule 56 standards that the committee was independent and showed reasonable bases for good faith findings and recommendations, the Court may proceed, in its discretion, to the next step.

The second step provides, we believe, the essential key in striking the balance between legitimate corporate claims as expressed in a derivative stockholder suit and a corporation's best interests as expressed by an independent investigating committee. The Court should determine, applying its own independent business judgment, whether the motion should be granted. This means, of course, that instances could arise where a committee can establish its independence and sound bases for its good faith decisions and still have the corporation's motion denied. The second step is intended to thwart instances where corporate actions meet the criteria of step one, but the result does not appear to satisfy its spirit, or where corporate actions would simply prematurely terminate a stockholder grievance deserving of further consideration in the corporation's interest. The Court of Chancery of course must carefully consider and weigh how compelling the corporate interest in dismissal is when faced with a non-frivolous lawsuit. The Court of Chancery should, when appropriate, give special consideration to matters of law and public policy in addition to the corporation's best interests.

If the Court's independent business judgment is satisfied, the Court may proceed to grant the motion, subject, of course, to any equitable terms or conditions the Court finds necessary or desirable.

A. *ALFORD v. SHAW*

The range of views regarding the appropriate standard of review for special litigation committees is illustrated not only by the *Auerbach* and *Zapata* cases, but also by *Alford v. Shaw*, the Model Act, and the ALI Principles. Consider the rationale of each.

In *Alford v. Shaw*,[7] the court compared the *Auerbach* and *Zapata* approaches, and ultimately offered an alternative model:

> The sole issue raised by this appeal is whether a special litigation committee's decision to terminate plaintiff minority shareholders' derivative action against defendant corporate directors is binding upon the courts....
>
> ...
>
> The recent trend among courts which have been faced with the choice of applying an *Auerbach*-type rule of judicial deference or a *Zapata*-type rule of judicial scrutiny has been to require judicial inquiry on the merits of the special litigation committee's report....
>
> ... We interpret the trend away from *Auerbach* among other jurisdictions as an indication of growing concern about the deficiencies inherent in a rule giving great deference to the decisions of a corporate committee whose institutional symbiosis with the corporation necessarily affects its ability to render a decision that fairly considers the interest of plaintiffs forced to bring suit on behalf of the corporation. Such concerns are legitimate ones and, upon further reflection, we find that they must be resolved not by slavish adherence to the business judgment rule, but by careful interpretation of the provisions of our own Business Corporation Act. We conclude from

---

[7] 358 S.E.2d 323 (N.C. 1987).

our analysis of the pertinent statutes that a modified *Zapata* rule, requiring judicial scrutiny of the merits of the litigation committee's recommendation, is most consistent with the intent of our legislature and is therefore the appropriate rule to be applied in our courts....

. . .

Although the recommendation of the special litigation committee is not binding on the court, in making this determination the court may choose to rely on such recommendation. To rely blindly on the report of a corporation-appointed committee which assembled such materials on behalf of the corporation is to abdicate the judicial duty to consider the interests of shareholders imposed by the statute. This abdication is particularly inappropriate in a case such as this one, where shareholders allege serious breaches of fiduciary duties owed to them by the directors controlling the corporation.

. . .

The *Zapata* Court limited its two-step judicial inquiry to cases in which demand upon the corporation was futile and therefore excused. However, we find no justification for such limitation in our statutes.... Thus, court approval is required for disposition of all derivative suits, even where the directors are not charged with fraud or self-dealing, or where the plaintiff and the board agree to discontinue, dismiss, compromise, or settle the lawsuit.

. . .

When N.C.G.S. §§ 55-55 and 55-30(b)(3) are read in pari materia, they indicate that when a stockholder in a derivative action seeks to establish self-dealing on the part of a majority of the board, the burden should be upon those directors to establish that the transactions complained of were just and reasonable to the corporation when entered into or approved. The fact that a special litigation committee appointed by those directors charged with self-dealing recommends that the action should not proceed, while carrying weight, is not binding upon the trial court. Rather, the court must make a fair assessment of the report of the special committee, along with all the other facts and circumstances in the case, in order to determine whether the defendants will be able to show that the transaction complained of was just and reasonable to the corporation. If this appears evident from the materials before the court, then in a proper case summary judgment may be allowed in favor of the defendants.

B. ALI AND MODEL ACT APPROACHES

The ALI and Model Act are similar to *Zapata* to the extent that they have bifurcated steps in their standards of review. The basis for and consequences of the bifurcation however differ.

ALI § 7.10 adopts a dual standard of review regarding the corporation's motion requesting dismissal of a derivative suit which is dependent on the nature of the allegations. If the "gravamen of the actions allege only a violation of the duty of care," it is subject to a business judgment rule standard of review. On the other hand, if more serious violations are alleged, such as cases based on the duty of loyalty or "cases in which the gravamen of the claim is that the defendant committed a knowing and culpable violation of law," the court will consider whether the special litigation committee "was adequately informed under the circumstances and reasonably determined that dismissal was in the best interests of the corporation, based on grounds that the court deems to warrant reliance." See § 7.10 and Comment *c*, pp. 134-35.

Model Act § 7.44(a) provides that the court will grant a motion for dismissal if it is based on a determination "in good faith after conducting a reasonable inquiry upon which its conclusions are based that the maintenance of the derivative proceeding is not in the best interests of the corporation." The pleading rules and allocation of the burden of proof, however, is dependent on who makes the determination. If the determination is made by a majority vote of independent directors or a court appointed panel of "independent persons," the plaintiff assumes the pleading and burden of proof. "If there is not independent majority, the burden is on the corporation on the issues delineated in § 7.44(a). In this case, the corporation must prove both the independence of the decisionmakers and the propriety of the inquiry and determination." § 7.44 Official Comment 2.

SECTION V. ALTERNATIVE DISPUTE RESOLUTION PROCESSES

A. EMERGING TREND

The complexity and high costs of litigation, such as shareholder derivative suits, have prompted disputants to consider alternative ways to resolve their problems. As the following materials explore, these alternative dispute resolution ("ADR") processes have certain attractions but may not be appropriate for every corporate dispute. Consider in what circumstances you would advise their use.

Linda R. Singer, Settling Disputes: Conflict Resolution in Business, Families, and the Legal System, at 55-57, 70, 74-75, 78-80 (2d ed. 1994)*

What began in the 1970s as a movement to settle interpersonal conflicts, racial tensions, and what the legal establishment considered "minor" disputes was quickly seized on by important parts of corporate America as a way of keeping business conflicts out of court. To a large extent, according to law professor Eric Green, corporate interest in ADR constitutes a consumer movement at the upper

---

end of the legal market. "ADR" is the term adopted by corporate managers and their counsel to describe any way of resolving a dispute short of a full courtroom trial.

In the past twenty-five years, managers have felt besieged by the escalating costs of disputing. Their perception is that businesses, both large and small, are facing an avalanche of litigation. In fact, there has been a significant increase in commercial litigation since the early 1970s. The number of contract cases filed each year in federal courts increased from 14,000 during the 1960s to over 47,000 by 1986. A study of these cases in the Southern District of New York (Manhattan), the federal court with the largest commercial caseload, revealed that the average number of pending contract cases increased from 365 during the 1960s to 1,273 (and sometimes exceeding 1,400) from 1973 to 1990. Economist Ronald Gilson suggests that this surge in commercial litigation may have been caused by the end of the previous taboo against large companies suing one another.

The types and complexity of cases going to court also have increased. Claims for injuries to consumers by products manufactured or sold by business, for workers' exposure to occupational hazards, and for damage to the environment, all of which have grown in number, involve complicated causal relationships and scientific uncertainty.

Although reform efforts are proliferating, judicial discovery rules, designed to develop facts and narrow legal issues before trial, permit questioning virtually every officer of a corporation and examining literally thousands of documents in the course of litigating a single dispute–all of which adds to both the cost and the difficulty of steering a business case through the courts. Law firms that represent corporations have expanded dramatically in response to the complexity of corporate litigation. This expansion, some charge, may have prompted still greater proliferation of lawsuits. Juries also seem more ready to compensate (some would say overcompensate) the injured than they once were. For whatever reason, the business costs devoted to disputing have skyrocketed. With the growth of legal expenses having greatly outstripped that of the gross national product, managers increasingly find that full adjudication of disputes is a luxury their companies cannot afford and a burden they need not tolerate.

In an effort to seize control of their companies' runaway legal expenses, many managers have become actively involved in overseeing the resolution of business disputes. Lawyers employed full-time by corporations, whose jobs once were limited to dealing with the outside law firms that handled the companies' legal business, now are taxed with managing litigation in such a way as to keep costs under control. Many of these corporate counsel have become actively involved in seeking alternative, less costly ways of resolving disputes; a 1992 Harris Executive Poll of 400 senior corporate executives showed that an overwhelming 97 percent favor such alternative methods over litigation. In 1979, general counsel of several Fortune 500 companies banded together to form the Legal Program to Reduce the Costs of Business Disputes, under the auspices of the

Center for Public Resources (CPR) in New York. Since then, 600 U.S. corporations, representing nearly one-half of the gross national product, have signed a pledge with CPR to explore alternatives to litigation whenever they have disputes with other signatories.

Beyond cutting costs, a significant and growing minority of the more sophisticated managers and their lawyers is coming to recognize that, for many disputes, various alternatives offer the possibility of producing better results than do trials. Judges are constrained by the need to respond to the issues as they are presented by the litigants' attorneys and to follow legal precedents. They often lack the technical or managerial expertise that may be required to understand technical disputes. These straightjackets need not confine private mediators, neutral experts, or arbitrators. As they become more personally involved in the business of resolving disputes, some managers are recognizing that they can apply their own business knowledge and creativity to developing solutions better suited to their needs than courts and lawyers alone could devise.

...

Mediation: The "Sleeping Giant"

A 1985 guide for business executives with legal disputes termed mediation the "sleeping giant" of business dispute resolution, potentially the most powerful means of bringing the parties to terms. Since that time the giant has awakened, and the use of mediation to resolve conflicts among businesses has increased exponentially.

Because of its flexibility, mediation is adaptable to business disputes of all sizes and complexity. Except for the opportunity to observe lawyers' presentation of a case, which may be unnecessary or excessively expensive for most business conflicts, mediation has the advantages of minitrials without some of the complications. Mediation puts business managers in control of resolving their own disputes. Lawyers generally (although not always) participate as advisors and, often, as spokespersons. The process emphasizes solving problems rather than establishing who did what to whom in the past. In the hands of skilled mediators, representatives of sparring businesses can be helped to focus on their future relationships. In the case of suppliers of necessary materials, ongoing construction, or other time sensitive relationships, this focus can be critical. It also may be critical in disputes that involve ongoing business or mixed business and personal relationships. For example, in my experience in dissolving corporations or partnerships or dealing with the withdrawal of key principals, I have found that the mixture of financial and emotional elements is the same as in a divorce, with mediation the most responsive way to deal with the hidden issues behind division of assets and liabilities. Finally, in an effort to prevent a recurrence of the impasse, mediators can help parties to determine in advance how they will resolve any future disputes.

Several courts have begun to discover the potential of mediation for settling complex business disputes. In Chicago, U.S. District Judge Marvin E. Aspen has appointed law professor and mediator Stephen Goldberg to serve as a special master for the purpose of mediating cases involving allegations of fraud, breach of contract, antitrust, and employment discrimination. Claims for damages have ranged from $ 250,000 to $ 30 million. According to Goldberg, the judge chose those cases for mediation because each was complex and likely to require a lengthy trial, yet appeared susceptible to settlement. Becoming personally involved in settlement efforts might take more time than the judge himself could afford and involve him more deeply in the substance of the dispute than he considered appropriate.

... Goldberg's only ground rules involve confidentiality: No communications from one party to the mediator outside the presence of the other party will be communicated to the other party without permission, and nothing the parties tell the mediator will be disclosed to the judge. Like most other mediators, Goldberg approaches mediation of cases referred by courts in the same way he deals with private mediation: "My goal is to assist the parties to reach a mutually acceptable settlement that accommodates the vital interests of each, and is viewed by each as preferable to the costs and risks of litigation. I do this by encouraging the parties to focus on their vital interests and to generate options for settlement that accommodate those interests." ...

When Does a Settlement Process Make Sense?

Disputing businesses and their lawyers now have an array of settlement processes from which to choose. Over 90 percent of all civil cases filed in U.S. courts do settle before the court decides. In most cases, however, settlements continue to take place "on the courthouse steps," whether figuratively or literally, or even mid-trial, when treasuries are depleted and emotions spent. Thus, when to focus on settlement, as well as which process to use, is a critical question. Although there is no litmus test, several considerations may be helpful:

1. What is the relationship of the disputing firms or their principals? The greater the potential of ongoing business relations, the more critical it is to find a settlement option that will preserve them. Disputes between businesses with ongoing relationships are particularly appropriate for mediation. They also cry out for speedy resolution — before any remaining desire for continued dealings is frayed beyond repair.

2. What kind of outcome is desirable? The need for establishing a principle to govern future cases (or, occasionally, for sending a message to future litigants that they cannot sue a particular company without fear of annihilation) may argue against any settlement. The difficulty is that principles often get lost in the fray of litigation and end up being settled anyway — much less effectively than if the business managers were in a position to discuss them from the start. Alternatively, principles sometimes can be established by business experts instead of by courts. Particularly when creative options are

imaginable — be they tradeoffs of different property, reciprocal actions, or joint ventures — settlement processes should be considered.

3. How useful would it be to have the business principals themselves involved in developing the outcome? The benefits of active participation argue strongly for negotiation, mediation, or minitrials — all with principals present.

4. How high are emotions running? Although anger and thirst for revenge may propel litigants into the courtroom, face-to-face mediation, with ample opportunity for everyone to vent emotions, often clears the air and permits disputants to focus on future results.

5. Are the costs of battle likely to be high in proportion to the expected returns? Even managers who order their lawyers to pursue a "scorched earth" strategy sometimes become interested in alternatives once they receive their first litigation-spawned legal bill.

6. Is speed important? Virtually all the settlement options are faster than litigation. Yet many lawyers become stymied by their need for more information about the details of a dispute before they believe they responsibly can advise their clients to pursue settlement. The need for speed (and its effect on litigation-related costs) argues for finding creative ways of obtaining needed information without waiting for the discovery process run its course.

7. What kinds of information do the parties need before they can focus on settlement? Information on the facts surrounding a particular incident can be obtained in a number of ways. One of the most obvious is to use pretrial discovery tools — but in a limited, carefully crafted way. If the parties are in mediation, they can agree on what information they need and how to go about getting it. Technical information may require the services of one or more experts; early agreement on a neutral expert can speed resolution. The need for information on the probable outcome of a particular factual dispute — or of an entire case if it were to go to trial — argues for using a minitrial or a summary jury trial. If the outcome in a case may turn on the credibility of particular witnesses with differing versions of an event or transaction, the parties might consider having those witnesses questioned in front of the business principals, who then may be ready to negotiate (or mediate) a settlement based on what they have learned. Finally, information on the interests and priorities of the disputants can be obtained best by involving them directly in negotiations — with a mediator if they are unwilling to confide in one another.

8. How important is it to keep private the details of a particular dispute, such as one involving trade secrets? All of the settlement options discussed offer greater privacy than a public trial. Mediation, which permits confidential discussions between the parties and the mediator, offers the greatest amount of privacy.

———

Professor Seligman has described an alternative process to derivative litigation and the special litigation committee, where the court appoints a "distinterested person" who investigates and determines whether a derivative proceeding is not in the best interests of the corporation.[8] In comparison to a special litigation committee, the disinterested person procedure is more "neutral and should provide a good faith, intellectually honest effort to evaluate the merits of a derivative claim." In smaller companies, Professor Seligman suggests, the disinterested person who also is a lawyer may be viewed as a "bargain" compared to the special litigation committee. Fewer special counsels are necessary and the disinterested person can perform a "role trying to inspire settlements...." In cases involving complex claims and facts, the disinterested person can perform a useful "triage" role, by helping the court and the parties better understand the facts and distinguish between meritorious and nonmeritorious claims.

Do you agree that the disinterested person procedure is preferable to a special litigation committee?

B. CHARACTERISTICS OF ADR PROCESSES

The following tables from Professors Goldber, Sander, and Rogers efficiently summarize various dispute resolution processes. It introduces and compares the different methods (including litigation, arbitration, mediation, negotiation, and other hybrid dispute resolution processes) by key characteristics. Keep in mind, however, that the particular characteristics of most private ADR methods are negotiated by the parties themselves. If you were to shape an ADR process to suit the needs of the disputants in the problems we have encountered in the duty of care and duty of loyalty chapters or the materials focusing on closely held corporations, for instance, which of the following characteristics would it have?

---

[8] Joel Seligman, *The Disinterested Person: An Alternative to Shareholder Derivative Litigation*, LAW & CONTEMP. PROB., 357, 362-65, 376-77 (1992).

Stephen B. Goldberg, Frank E.A. Sander, and Nancy H. Rogers, Dispute Resolution: Negotiation, Mediation, and Other Processes, pp. 4-5 (2d ed. 1992)*

"Primary" Dispute Resolution Processes

Characteristics	Adjudication	Arbitration[*]	Mediation	Negotiation
Voluntary/Involuntary	Involuntary	Voluntary	Voluntary	Voluntary
Binding/Nonbinding	Binding; subject to appeal	Binding, subject to review on limited grounds	If agreement, enforceable as contract	If agreement, enforceable as contract
Third Party	Imposed, third-party neutral decisionmaker, generally with no specialized expertise in dispute subject	Party-selected third-party decisionmaker, often with specialized subject expertise	Party-selected outside facilitator	No third-party facilitator
Degree of formality	Formalized and highly structured by predetermined, rigid rules	Procedurally less formal; procedural rules and substantive law may be set by parties	Usually informal, un-structured	Usually informal, un-structured
Nature of proceeding	Opportunity for each party to present proofs and arguments	Opportunity for each party to present proofs and arguments	Unbounded presentation of evidence, arguments and interests	Unbounded presentation of evidence, arguments and interests
Outcome	Principled decision, supported by reasoned opinion	Sometimes principled decision supported by reasoned opinion; sometimes compromise without opinion	Mutually acceptable agreement sought	Mutually acceptable agreement sought
Private/Public	Public	Private, unless judicial review sought	Private	Private

*Copyright © 1992. Little, Brown and Company, assigned to Aspen Law & Business, a division of Aspen Publishers, Inc. Reprinted with permission.

[*]Court-annexed arbitration is involuntary, nonbinding, and public.

"Hybrid" Dispute Resolution Processes

Characteristics	Private Judging	Neutral Expert Fact-Finding	MiniTrial	Ombuds[person]	Summary Jury Trial
Voluntary/ Involuntary	Voluntary	Voluntary or involuntary under FRE 706	Voluntary	Voluntary	Voluntary or involuntary …
Binding/Nonbinding	Binding, subject to appeal	Nonbinding but results may be admissible	If agreement, enforceable as contract	Nonbinding	Nonbinding
Third party	Party-selected third-party decisionmaker, may have to be former judge or lawyer	Third-party neutral with specialized subject matter expertise; may be selected by the parties or the court	Party-selected neutral advisor, sometimes with specialized subject expertise	Third-party selected by institution	Mock jury impaneled by court
Degree of formality	Statutory procedure but highly flexible as to timing, place, and procedures	Informal	Less formal than adjudication; procedural rules may be set by parties	Informal	Procedural rules fixed; less formal than adjudication
Nature of proceeding	Opportunity for each party to present proofs and arguments	Investigatory	Opportunity and responsibility to present summary proofs and arguments	Investigatory	Opportunity for each side to present summary proofs and arguments
Outcome	Principled decision, sometimes supported by findings of fact and conclusions of law	Report or testimony	Mutually acceptable agreement sought	Report	Advisory verdict
Private/Public	Private, unless judicial enforcement sought	Private, unless disclosed in court	Private	Private	Usually public …

Chapter 15

INDEMNIFICATION AND INSURANCE

Situation

Biologistics' directors now realize that their corporate decisionmaking may lead to personal liabilities. They want to know how the corporation can help protect them, including the possibility of reimbursing them for any expenses and liabilities they may incur for breaches of their duties to the corporation. What strategies would you recommend?

SECTION I. INTRODUCTION

Surveys reveal the most common types of lawsuits against directors and officers. The most likely plaintiff group is shareholders, who allege that directors and officers act improperly in mergers, acquisitions, tender offers, and other major corporate transactions. Much of the material in this casebook explores these types of claims. The second most likely plaintiff group is employees, who make claims involving wrongful termination, employment discrimination, or breach of the employment contract. Finally, the third largest plaintiff class is customers and clients.[1]

Given these risks, the corporation can significantly alter the actual personal liability of directors and officers in at least three ways. First, the corporation can utilize exculpation statutes. Recall, as discussed in Chapter 10, Duty of Care, these state corporate laws take various forms. Some allow the corporation, typically through its articles of incorporation, to diminish or eliminate directors' liability for certain breaches of duty. Others may alter the standards of conduct or impose a cap on the amount of liability that directors may incur personally.

Second, the corporation may advance to or reimburse directors for the expenses and liabilities they incur as a result of their corporate decisionmaking. For instance, directors who are found personally liable for a breach of their duty of care may seek corporate assistance under mandatory, permissive, and court-ordered indemnification statutes. If they are successful, the financial burden will effectively be shifted from the directors to the corporation.

Finally, the corporation can purchase insurance to cover the cost of directors' and officers' liabilities. Insurance policies may provide for repayment to the

---

[1] BNA, *Cost of Litigation Against Directors Reaches Record Levels, Survey Finds*, CORP. COUNS. WKLY., Mar. 15, 1995, at 2 (describing results of 1994 Wyatt Company survey of over 1200 companies covering the past nine years); ALI § 7.20 Reporter's Note 8 (describing 1992 Wyatt Company survey).

corporation for its indemnification of directors' liabilities. In addition, the policies may cover directors' liabilities for which they were not indemnified.

Keep in mind, however, there is a difference between what exculpation, permissive indemnification, and insurance statutes allow and what money directors in a specific case actually receive. For instance, these statutes typically authorize, but do not require, a corporation to provide the maximum benefits allowed under the law. Directors can rely only on their particular agreement with the corporation, as documented in a contract or in the corporate articles or bylaws. In negotiating this agreement, the corporation may have lesser standards than the individual directors and officers for what constitutes adequate protection. Because of the expense, a corporation may want to obtain only the minimum amount of insurance coverage for the risks of directors' and officers' liability.

In addition, while corporate agreements may provide for indemnification, receiving payments according to those agreements may be a problem. New management may be resistant to reimbursing disfavored directors and officers. Or the corporation may be experiencing financial problems that make indemnification payments from the corporation's general cash funds scarce or simply unavailable. Thus, directors may need to safeguard against these risks with reserve funds or escrow arrangements.

This chapter explores some of the legal and policy issues raised by indemnification and insurance. Consider whether the legal rules encourage fiduciaries to serve in corporate positions, yet do not prompt improper conduct.

SECTION II. INDEMNIFICATION

As Model Act Subchapter E, Indemnification, Introductory Comment 1 explains:

> Indemnification (including advance for expenses) provides financial protection by the corporation for its directors against exposure to expenses and liabilities that may be incurred by them in connection with legal proceedings based on an alleged breach of duty in their service to or on behalf of the corporation. Today, when both the volume and the cost of litigation have increased dramatically, it would be difficult to persuade responsible persons to serve as directors if they were compelled to bear personally the cost of vindicating the propriety of their conduct in every instance in which it might be challenged.
>
> If permitted too broadly, however, indemnification may violate equally basic tenets of public policy. It is inappropriate to permit management to use corporate funds to avoid the consequences of certain conduct. For example, a director who intentionally inflicts harm on the corporation should not expect to receive assistance from the corporation for legal or other expenses and should be required to satisfy from his personal assets not only any adverse judgment but also expenses incurred in connection with the

proceeding. Any other rule would tend to encourage socially undesirable conduct.

A further policy issue is raised in connection with indemnification against liabilities or sanctions imposed under state or federal civil or criminal statutes. A shift of the economic cost of these liabilities from the individual director to the corporation by way of indemnification may in some instances frustrate the public policy of those statutes.

The fundamental issue that must be addressed by an indemnification statute is the establishment of policies consistent with these broad principles: to ensure that indemnification is permitted only where it will further sound corporate policies and to prohibit indemnification where it might protect or encourage wrongful or improper conduct. As phrased by one commentator, the goal of indemnification is to "seek the middle ground between encouraging fiduciaries to violate their trust, and discouraging them from serving at all." Johnston, *Corporate Indemnification and Liability Insurance for Directors and Officers*, 33 BUS. LAW. 1993, 1994 (1978). The increasing number of suits against directors, the increasing cost of defense, and the increasing emphasis on diversifying the membership of boards of directors all militate in favor of workable arrangements to protect directors against liability to the extent consistent with established principles.

A. MANDATORY INDEMNIFICATION

The corporation is required to indemnify directors and officers in certain circumstances. In most states, directors are entitled by statute to be indemnified for expenses if they are "successful on the merits" in their lawsuits.

MERRITT-CHAPMAN & SCOTT CORP. v. WOLFSON

Superior Court of Delaware
321 A.2d 138 (1974)

BALICK, JUDGE.

These actions arise over claims of Louis Wolfson, Elkin Gerbert, Joseph Kosow and Marshal Staub (claimants) for indemnification by Merritt-Chapman & Scott Corporation (MCS) against expenses incurred in a criminal action. All parties seek summary judgment.

Claimants were charged by indictment with participation in a plan to cause MCS to secretly purchase hundreds of thousands of shares of its own common stock. Count one charged all claimants with conspiracy to violate federal securities laws. Count two charged Wolfson and count three charged Gerbert with perjury before the Securities and Exchange Commission (SEC). Counts four and five charged Wolfson, Gerbert, and Staub with filing false annual reports for 1962 and 1963 respectively with the SEC and New York Stock Exchange.

At the first trial the court dismissed part of the conspiracy count but the jury returned guilty verdicts on all charges against all claimants. At that stage this court held that Wolfson, Gerbert, and Kosow were not entitled to partial indemnification. *Merritt-Chapman & Scott v. Wolfson*, 264 A.2d 358 (Del. Super. 1970). Thereafter the convictions were reversed. *United States v. Wolfson*, 437 F.2d 862 (2d Cir. 1970).

There were two retrials of the perjury and filing false annual report charges against Wolfson and Gerbert. At the first retrial the court entered a judgment of acquittal on count four at the end of the State's case, and the jury could not agree on the other counts. At the second retrial the jury returned a guilty verdict on count three, but could not agree further.

The charges were then settled as follows: Wolfson entered a plea of *nolo contendere* to count five and the other charges against him were dropped. He was fined $ 10,000 and given a suspended sentence of eighteen months. Gerbert agreed not to appeal his conviction of count three, on which he was fined $ 2,000 and given a suspended sentence of eighteen months, and the other charges against him were dropped. The prosecution also dropped the charges against Kosow and Staub.

Indemnification of corporate agents involved in litigation is the subject of legislation in Delaware. Title 8 Delaware Code § 145. Subsection (a), which permits indemnification, and subsection (c), which requires indemnification, provide as follows:

> (a) A corporation may indemnify any person who was or is a party or is threatened to be made a party to any threatened, pending or completed action, suit or proceeding, whether civil, criminal, administrative or investigative (other than an action by or in the right of the corporation) by reason of the fact that he is or was a director, officer, employee or agent of the corporation, or is or was serving at the request of the corporation as a director, officer, employee or agent of another corporation, partnership, joint venture, trust or other enterprise, against expenses (including attorneys' fees), judgments, fines and amounts paid in settlement actually and reasonably incurred by him in connection with such action, suit or proceeding if he acted in good faith and in a manner he reasonably believed to be in or not opposed to the best interests of the corporation, and, with respect to any criminal action or proceeding, had no reasonable cause to believe his conduct was unlawful. The termination of any action, suit or proceeding by judgment, order, settlement, conviction, or upon a plea of *nolo contendere* or its equivalent, shall not, of itself, create a presumption that the person did not act in good faith and in a manner which he reasonably believed to be in or not opposed to the best interests of the corporation, and, with respect to any criminal action or proceeding, had reasonable cause to believe that his conduct was unlawful.
>
> ...
>
> (c) To the extent that a director, officer, employee or agent of a corporation has been successful on the merits or otherwise in defense of any

action, suit or proceeding referred to in [subsection (a)], or in defense of any claim, issue or matter therein, he shall be indemnified against expenses (including attorneys' fees) actually and reasonably incurred by him in connection therewith.

The policy of the statute and its predecessor has been described as follows, Folk, *The Delaware General Corporation Law* 98 (1972):

> The invariant policy of Delaware legislation on indemnification is to "promote the desirable end that corporate officials will resist what they consider" unjustified suits and claims, "secure in the knowledge that their reasonable expenses will be borne by the corporation they have served if they are vindicated." [*Essential Enterprises Corp. v. Automatic Steel Prods., Inc.*, 39 Del. Ch. 371, 164 A.2d 437, 441-442 (Del. Chanc. 1960).] Beyond that, its larger purpose is "to encourage capable men to serve as corporate directors, secure in the knowledge that expenses incurred by them in upholding their honesty and integrity as directors will be borne by the corporation they serve." [*Mooney v. Willys-Overland Motors, Inc.*, 204 F.2d 888, 898 (3d Cir. 1953)].

MCS argues that the statute and sound public policy require indemnification only where there has been vindication by a finding or concession of innocence. It contends that the charges against claimants were dropped for practical reasons, not because of their innocence, and that in light of the conspiracy charged in the indictment, the judgment of acquittal on count four alone is not vindication.

The statute requires indemnification to the extent that the claimant "has been successful on the merits or otherwise." Success is vindication. In a criminal action, any result other than conviction must be considered success. Going behind the result, as MCS attempts, is neither authorized by subsection (c) nor consistent with the presumption of innocence.

The statute does not require complete success. It provides for indemnification to the extent of success "in defense of any claim, issue or matter" in an action. Claimants are therefore entitled to partial indemnification if successful on a count of an indictment, which is an independent criminal charge, even if unsuccessful on another, related count.

. . . .

---

1. Settlements

As described in Joseph P. Montelone & Nicholas J. Conca, *Directors and Officers Indemnification and Liability Insurance: An Overview of Legal and Practical Issues*," 51 BUS. LAW. 573, 575 (1996):

> The purpose of [Delaware's] mandatory indemnification provision is to give vindicated directors and officers a judicially enforceable right to

indemnification. The person to be indemnified need not demonstrate his or her own good faith or that he or she was free from wrongdoing, but only that the claim asserted against him or her was without merit.

Given that most D&O claims are settled, a question in many directors' and officers' minds is whether the mandatory indemnification provision applies to settlements. The answer appears to be that a settlement that is with prejudice and results in the dismissal of the case without any payment or assumption of liability may be considered a "success" within the meaning of that provision. Settlements that are without prejudice to a claimant's right to assert further claims against an officer are not "successes" under section 145(c) of the Delaware statute.

2. "Wholly" and "Otherwise"

While Delaware law allows for mandatory indemnification "to the extent" possible, consider the alternative approach illustrated by Model Act § 8.52 requiring that the director be "wholly" successful. As indicated in § 8.52 Official Comment:

> ...The word "wholly" is added to avoid the argument accepted in *Merritt-Chapman & Scott Corp. v. Wolfson*, 321 A.2d 138 (Del. 1974), that a defendant may be entitled to partial mandatory indemnification if, by plea bargaining or otherwise, he was able to obtain the dismissal of some but not all counts of an indictment. A defendant is "wholly successful" only if the entire proceeding is disposed of on a basis which does not involve a finding of liability.

Consistent with Delaware law, Model Act § 8.52 allows for mandatory indemnification if successful "on the merits or otherwise." Section 8.52 Official Comment explains the significance of the word "otherwise:"

> ... While this standard may result in an occasional defendant becoming entitled to indemnification because of procedural defenses not related to the merits, *e.g.*, the statute of limitations or disqualification of the plaintiff, it is unreasonable to require a defendant with a valid procedural defense to undergo a possibly prolonged and expensive trial on the merits in order to establish eligibility for mandatory indemnification.

B. PERMISSIVE INDEMNIFICATION

In contrast to the mandatory indemnification situation where the corporation is required by statute to indemnify, permissive indemnification empowers but does not require the corporation to indemnify directors and officers in a wide range of other circumstances. The following cases consider who is entitled to permissive indemnification and whether permissive indemnification statutes set the exclusive parameters for discretionary corporate indemnification.

HEFFERNAN v. PACIFIC DUNLOP GNB CORP.

United States Court of Appeals, Seventh Circuit
965 F.2d 369 (1992)

ESCHBACH, SENIOR CIRCUIT JUDGE.

Litigation is an occupational hazard for corporate directors, albeit one that may often be shifted to the corporation through indemnification. In this diversity case, we consider whether Delaware law precludes a former director from obtaining indemnification from the corporations he served. For the reasons that follow, we hold that the district court prematurely dismissed this case under Rule 12(b)(6) by concluding that it was one in which the director could prove no set of facts entitling him to indemnification. Accordingly, we reverse and remand for further proceedings.

I

Daniel E. Heffernan is a former director and 6.7% shareholder of GNB Holdings, Inc. (Holdings) and its wholly-owned subsidiary, GNB Inc. (GNB). In October 1987, a third firm, Pacific Dunlop Holdings, Inc. (Pacific) acquired control of Holdings (and in turn, GNB) pursuant to a stock purchase transaction whereby Pacific acquired approximately 60% of Holdings' stock, boosting its total ownership to 92%. Prior to Pacific's stock purchase, Holdings had filed a registration statement with the Securities and Exchange Commission (SEC) in contemplation of an initial public offering of its stock. Holdings later abandoned the public offering, opting instead to structure a private transaction with Pacific. The transaction was pursuant to an agreement (the Stock Purchase Agreement) by and among Pacific, Holdings, certain management shareholders, Heffernan and Allen & Co. (an investment company that owned approximately 20% of Holdings' stock and for which Heffernan was a vice president). Pursuant to the Stock Purchase Agreement, which apparently incorporated the material that Holdings previously had prepared for the SEC, Heffernan sold Pacific his 6.7% interest in Holdings and ceased to be a director.

Litigation subsequently arose out of the Stock Purchase Agreement. In September 1990, Pacific sued Heffernan and Allen & Co. under section 12(2) of the Securities Act of 1933, 15 U.S.C. § 77l(2), and under Illinois securities law. Pacific sought to rescind its purchase of Heffernan's and Allen & Co.'s shares in Holdings on the ground that the Stock Purchase Agreement was materially misleading in regard to its disclosure of certain liabilities facing Holdings and GNB. At oral argument, the parties indicated that Pacific has sued some of the other parties to the Stock Purchase Agreement as well, although the record leaves unclear specifically whom it sued. Heffernan requested indemnification and an advance on his litigation expenses from Holdings and GNB pursuant to section 145 of the Delaware General Corporation Law and the companies' corporate bylaws. When Holdings refused (and GNB failed to respond to) Heffernan's request, he initiated this action against the two companies seeking to establish his rights to indemnification and advances.

Under Delaware law, "a corporation may indemnify any person who was or is a party to any [suit] by reason of the fact that he is or was a director...." § 145(a). Holdings' and GNB's bylaws make mandatory the provision for permissive indemnification in section 145(a). Holdings' bylaws state that "the Corporation shall, to the fullest extent permitted by the Delaware General Corporation law ... indemnify and hold harmless any person who is or was a party [to] any [suit] by reason of his status as, or the fact that he is or was or has agreed to become, a director [of] the Corporation or of an affiliate, and as to acts performed in the course of the [director's] duty to the Corporation...." GNB's bylaws simply state that "[t]he corporation shall indemnify its officers, directors, employees and agents to the extent permitted by the law of Delaware."

Heffernan does not argue that there is a material difference between the statutory requirement that a director be sued "by reason of the fact that" he was a director and Holdings' bylaw requirement that a director be sued "by reason of his status as, or the fact that" he was a director. And Holdings' brief footnote argument that its bylaw standard is narrower in scope than the statutory one fails in light of its bylaws' stated objective to indemnify directors "to the fullest extent permitted" by Delaware law. Thus, we focus our inquiry on whether Pacific may have sued Heffernan "by reason of the fact that" he was a director of Holdings and GNB.

II

The district court dismissed Heffernan's complaint, holding that he was not entitled to indemnification under the terms of the statute and bylaws because he had been sued for "wrongs he committed as an individual, not as a director." Furthermore, the district court reasoned that because "Heffernan's status as a director is not a necessary element of the section 12(2) claim" he was not sued by reason of the fact that he was a director. On appeal, Heffernan argues that although he was sued over a transaction in which he sold his own stock in Holdings, it does not necessarily follow as a matter of law that he was not sued "by reason of the fact that" he was a director of Holdings and GNB. He asserts that Delaware's "by reason of the fact that" phrase reaches Pacific's suit against him because the suit involves his status as a director. Conversely, appellees Holdings and GNB contend that Pacific's complaint against Heffernan has nothing whatsoever to do with Heffernan's former status as a director for Holdings and GNB. They argue that Delaware's "by reason of the fact that" requirement means that a director must be sued for a breach of duty to the corporation or for a wrong committed on behalf of the corporation to be entitled to indemnification. Accordingly, Holdings and GNB assert that Heffernan is not entitled to indemnification because the "sale of his stock was a personal transaction which did not involve his duties or status as a director."

Despite a surprising dearth of case law addressing the reach of Delaware's "by reason of the fact that" language, our review of the substance of Pacific's complaint against Heffernan in light of the language and purpose of Delaware'[s] indemnification law convinces us that the district court's view of Pacific's complaint and Delaware's indemnification law is too restrictive. Standing alone, neither the fact that Heffernan sold his own shares in Holdings during the transaction nor the particular statutory provision on which Pacific's suit is based thwarts Heffernan's right to indemnification as a matter of law. Rather, the substance of Pacific's allegations and the nature and context of the transaction giving rise to the complaint indicate that Heffernan may have been sued, at least in part, because he was a director of Holdings and GNB. Furthermore, we find no support in the language and purpose of Delaware's indemnification statute for the defendants' argument that it limits indemnification to suits asserted against a director for breaching a duty of his directorship or for acting wrongfully on behalf of the corporation he serves. Thus, we conclude that Heffernan's complaint was improperly dismissed; it does not appear beyond doubt that Heffernan can prove no set of facts in support of his claim that would entitle him to the advances or indemnification he requests.

III

To determine whether Heffernan was sued "by reason of the fact" that he was a director of Holdings and GNB, we begin by reviewing the allegations in the underlying action's complaint. Here, the underlying complaint is based on Heffernan's sale of his shares in Holdings to Pacific pursuant to the Stock Purchase Agreement. More specifically, Pacific contends that Heffernan violated section 12(2) of the Securities Act by selling those securities pursuant to a misleading prospectus — that is, the Stock Purchase Agreement. Under section 12(2), a person who offers or sells a security through a prospectus or oral communication containing a material misrepresentation or omission may be liable to the purchaser. To avoid liability, the seller must prove that he did not know, and in the exercise of reasonable care could not have known, of the misrepresentation or omission.

In complaining of Heffernan's alleged failure to disclose environmental and other liabilities of Holdings and GNB in the Stock Purchase Agreement, Pacific's complaint repeatedly states that Heffernan's status as a director put him in a position where, in the performance of his duties as a director, he either learned or should have learned of those liabilities. Because Pacific realleges these provisions under both counts of its complaint, its argument that Heffernan's status as a director was not specifically alleged in the complaint is without merit. Moreover, assuming for the moment that Pacific's section 12(2) claim against Heffernan is viable, his status as a director is directly relevant to his defense. As noted earlier, to avoid liability under section 12(2), a defendant must prove that he did not know, and in the exercise of reasonable care could not have known, of the misrepresentation or omission. The defendant's position gives content to the term "reasonable care." For instance, reasonable care for a director requires more than does reasonable care for an individual owning a few shares of stock with no other connection to the corporation. It is accordingly no answer to our inquiry as to whether Heffernan was sued "by reason of the fact that" he was a director to label his participation in Pacific's acquisition of Holdings a "personal" transaction. Despite the fact that Heffernan sold his own shares to Pacific, a nexus exists between Heffernan's status as a director and Pacific's suit.

Moreover, the transaction at the heart of Pacific's complaint is not a purely personal transaction of Heffernan's. Despite Holdings' and GNB's arguments to the contrary, Heffernan was not "trading securities for his own account" in the usual meaning of that phrase. That is, this is not a situation in which Heffernan maintained a personal trading portfolio and encountered litigation over his individual sale of a security in an unrelated company. In such a scenario, "there is no reason why the corporation should be obligated or permitted to bear the executives' [litigation] expenses." Joseph W. Bishop, Jr., *The Law of Corporate Officers and Directors: Indemnification and Insurance* § 2.03 at 4 (1988). Rather, this was a structured sale of control transaction pursuant to one agreement — all of the stock that Pacific acquired in this transaction was pursuant to the Stock Purchase Agreement. We decline to distort the context in which Pacific's complaint arose by accepting Holdings' and GNB's unsupported invitation to carve Pacific's acquisition of Holdings' into various component parts.

Furthermore, neither the specific statutory provision under which a director is sued nor the mere form of the underlying complaint is dispositive of his right to indemnification. The logical extension of the district court's reliance on the "necessary elements" of section 12(2) in denying Heffernan indemnification as a matter of law is that Delaware did not intend for any suit under section 12(2) to fall within its indemnification provisions. Delaware's case-by-case approach to indemnification counsels against such a formalistic gloss. Otherwise, a director could be forced to bear the costs of unfounded, harassing litigation just because the particular cause of action does not specify a breach of a duty to the corporation, regardless of the connection between the suit and the individual's service as a director. As a practical matter, it is unsurprising that Pacific's complaint is not more explicit in its reliance on Heffernan's role as a director of Holdings and GNB. Because Pacific now controls Holdings and GNB, those three corporations' interests are aligned; thus Pacific has the incentive and opportunity to structure its complaint so as to avoid triggering its subsidiaries' duty of indemnification. Nevertheless, artful drafting cannot disguise the fact that the gravamen of Pacific's complaint is that Heffernan, at least in part because he was a director of Holdings and GNB, either knew or should have known that Holdings and GNB may be subject to environmental and other liabilities inadequately reflected in the Stock Purchase Agreement. We recognize that because Heffernan wore three hats — director, shareholder and investment banker — his director status may not be the *only* reason that he was sued by Pacific. But at this stage of this litigation, we cannot, as a matter of law, rule out the fact that it may have been one reason.

IV

Having established that Pacific's complaint is connected to Heffernan's status as a director, we now turn to whether Delaware's "by reason of" requirement necessarily requires more than the nexus present here. Without delineating the precise contours of the "by reason of" phrase, we conclude that it may be broad enough to encompass the litigation that Heffernan has incurred, at least in part, because of his status as a director of Holdings and GNB. Both the language and the purpose of Delaware's indemnification statute support interpreting its scope expansively.

First, Delaware is no neophyte in corporate law matters. Had it desired to limit permissible indemnification solely to those suits in which a director is sued for breaching a duty of his directorship or for certain enumerated causes of action, it would have jettisoned the supple "by reason of the fact that" phrase in favor of more specific language. Had Delaware desired to so limit its indemnification statute, we are confident that it could have found the words. Holdings and GNB have given us no reason to doubt that Delaware's choice of language was anything but purposeful and strategic. We believe that Delaware's "by reason of the fact that" phrase is broad enough to encompass suits against a director in his official capacity as well as suits against a director that arise more tangentially from his role, position or status as a director. Flexibility of language is vexing as well as liberating. In employing its "by reason of" phrase, Delaware is able to cover a myriad of potential factual scenarios that cannot be anticipated *ex ante* by the legislature or by corporate officials in drafting their articles and bylaws. The task of giving content to that flexible phrase, however, falls on the courts when the parties encounter interpretive differences.

Finally, we think that the policy of Delaware's indemnification statute supports permitting Heffernan to proceed to establish his right to advances and indemnification from Holdings and GNB. One of the primary purposes of Delaware's indemnification statute is to encourage capable individuals "to serve as corporate directors, secure in the knowledge that expenses incurred by them in upholding their honesty and integrity as directors will be borne by the corporation they serve." *MCI Telecommunications Corp. v. Wanzer*, 1990 Del. Super. Lexis 222. Additionally, the statute ought to promote the "desirable end that corporate officials will resist what they consider unjustified suits and claims, secure in the knowledge that their reasonable expenses will be borne by the corporation they have served if they are vindicated." *Id.* Delaware has effectuated these policies by gradually expanding its indemnification provisions to cover the everchanging contexts in which a director may encounter litigation. The district court's restrictive interpretation of Heffernan's claim diminishes the broad and expansive flavor of Delaware's indemnification provisions.

V

In sum, while a fine line often separates those suits emanating purely from a director's personal transactions and those suits emanating from a director's duties, role or status, we think the district court erred in prematurely concluding that Pacific's suit against Heffernan fell squarely on the personal side. We emphasize that our inquiry in this case has been a narrow one, confined to whether Heffernan's indemnification and advances claim against Holdings and GNB should be allowed to proceed. We express no opinion on the merits of Heffernan's right to advances, or on his ultimate right to indemnification. We hold only that his suit was prematurely dismissed under an unduly restrictive reading of Delaware's indemnification law. Holdings' bylaws have numerous prerequisites that a director must meet before being entitled to indemnification. Those remain to be explored in the district court. In addition, on remand the district court should first consider Heffernan's right to advances, which the Delaware Supreme Court has recently indicated may present a prior and distinct inquiry from a director's ultimate right to indemnification.

Reversed and Remanded.

1. Model Act Approach

Model Act § 8.51 offers a complicated set of rules governing permissive indemnification, beginning with a general basis for permissive indemnification, followed by rules on the broadening or narrowing of indemnification. Section 8.51(a)(1) begins with the general basis, emphasizing the director's "good faith" and the "corporation's best interests" standards. So long as these two standards are met, the director is allowed indemnification even though he or she may not satisfy the general duty of care standard in Model Act § 8.30. Official Comment 1 to § 8.51.

In addition to this general basis for permissive indemnification, § 8.51(a)(2) allows the corporation to broaden indemnification through a provision in its articles of incorporation. The charter provision may provide indemnification to a director for liability "to any person for any action taken, or any failure to take any action, as a director," subject to exceptional circumstances such as the director's intentionally harming the corporation or improper financial benefit. *See* Model Act §§ 2.02(b)(5), 8.58(a). As the Official Comment 1 to § 8.51 further explains:

> [S]ection 8.51(a)(2) permits indemnification in connection with claims by third parties and, through section 8.56, applies to officers as well as directors. (This goes beyond the scope of a charter provision adopted pursuant to section 2.02(b)(4), which can only limit liability of directors against claims by the corporation or its shareholders.) Section 8.51(a)(2) is subject to the prohibition ... against indemnification of settlements and

judgments in derivative suits [and the prohibition] ... against indemnification for receipt of an improper financial benefit....

At the same time Model Act § 8.58(c) indicates that the corporation in its articles of incorporation may limit any rights to indemnification.

In addition, as described in Official Comment 4 to § 8.51:

> This subsection makes clear that indemnification is not permissible under section 8.51 in two situations: (i) a proceeding brought by or in the right of a corporation that results in a settlement or a judgment against the director and (ii) a proceeding that results in a judgment that the director received an improper financial benefit as a result of his conduct.
>
> Permitting indemnification of settlements and judgments in derivative proceedings would give rise to a circularity in which the corporation receiving payment of damages by the director in the settlement or judgment (less attorneys' fees) would then immediately return the same amount to the director (including attorneys' fees) as indemnification. Thus, the corporation would be in a poorer economic position than if there had been no proceeding. This situation is most egregious in the case of a judgment against the director. Even in the case of a settlement, however, prohibiting indemnification is not unfair. Under the revised procedures of section 7.44, upon motion by the corporation, the court must dismiss any derivative proceeding which independent directors (or a court-appointed panel) determine in good faith, after a reasonable inquiry, is not in the best interests of the corporation. Furthermore, under section 2.02(b)(4), the directors have the opportunity to propose to shareholders adoption of a provision limiting the liability of directors in derivative proceedings. In view of these considerations, it is unlikely that directors will be unnecessarily exposed to meritless actions....
>
> Indemnification under section 8.51 is also prohibited if there has been an adjudication that a director received an improper financial benefit (*i.e.*, a benefit to which he is not entitled), even if, for example, he acted in a manner not opposed to the best interests of the corporation. For example, improper use of inside information for financial benefit should not be an action for which the corporation may elect to provide indemnification, even if the corporation was not thereby harmed.

2. Good Faith

Permissive indemnification statutes typically include a "good faith" requirement, but there is little case law guidance on its meaning. In *In re Landmark Land Co. of Carolina*,[2] Judge Donald Russell addressed both the meaning of the requirement and who may determine if the directors have acted in "good faith:"

---

[2] 76 F.3d 553, 562-65 (4th Cir. 1996), *cert. denied*, 117 S. Ct. 59 (1996).

Thus, there are two requirements for permissive indemnification under [Cal. Corp. Code] § 317(b): (1) the corporation must authorize the indemnification, and (2) the agent must have acted in good faith and in the best interests of the corporation. It is not clear, however, whether the good faith determination should be made by a court or by the corporation itself.... At first glance, § 317(e) suggests that the corporation's finding of good faith settles the matter, and that the court's role is limited to ensuring that the corporation made its finding of good faith by proper procedures.

We do not agree that the court's role is so narrow. Although a corporation has to find that the agent acted in good faith before authorizing indemnification, nothing in § 317(e) restricts a court's authority under § 317(b) to make an independent assessment of the agent's good faith. Section 317(b) allows permissive indemnification where the agent has acted in good faith, not where the corporation finds that the agent has acted in good faith. Reading § 317(b) together with § 317(e), we conclude that the issue of an agent's good faith is a question for the courts to decide.

....

In the instant case, it is not clear whether the district court — the indemnification court in this case — recognized the proper scope of its "good faith" determination. In finding that the Directors acted in good faith and in the best interest of the Debtors when they filed the petitions for bankruptcy, the district court offered little explanation on how it reached its finding.... [I]mportantly, the district court did not explain how the Directors could have acted in good faith if the OTS [Office of Thrift Supervision] charges filed against them were true.

....

According to the OTS charges, the OTS investigated the Bank on June 4, 1990 and found that the Bank was inadequately capitalized and had demonstrated a pattern of repeated losses. The OTS directed the Bank to infuse sufficient capital to meet the minimum capitalization requirement, but the Bank did not submit an acceptable plan. Because of the Bank's inability to meet the requirement, the OTS forced the Bank directors to sign a Consent Agreement on January 15, 1991, signalling to the Directors that an OTS takeover was imminent. Instead of working with the OTS to correct the Bank's capitalization problem, the Directors filed the bankruptcy petitions to prevent the OTS from exercising control of the Bank's subsidiaries.

We cannot conclude that the Directors' action was taken in good faith. If the OTS charges are accurate, the Director's action to place the Debtors in bankruptcy was a deliberate attempt to prevent the OTS from exercising control over the Bank's assets, thus hindering the OTS's ability to deal effectively with a failing savings and loan.... [T]he OTS therefore had a statutory duty to force the Bank's management to comply with the capitalization requirement. The Directors acknowledged the OTS's regulatory authority when they signed the Consent Agreement and agreed that the

Bank's subsidiaries would not enter into any material transaction without prior approval from the OTS. When the OTS threatened to take control of the Bank, however, the Directors' used the bankruptcy code to stymie the OTS, even though their action breached the Consent Agreement with the OTS and violated their fiduciary duties to the Bank. We cannot condone the Directors' blatant attempt to circumvent the OTS's regulatory authority by holding that they acted in good faith.

Even if the bankruptcy filings benefitted the Debtors, we still could not conclude that the Directors acted in good faith. An agent who has intentionally participated in illegal activity or wrongful conduct against third persons cannot be said to have acted in good faith, even if the conduct benefits the corporation. "For example, corporate executives who participate in a deliberate price-fixing conspiracy with competing firms could not be found to have acted in good faith, even though they may have reasonably believed that a deliberate flouting of the antitrust laws would increase the profits of the corporation." 1 Harold Marsh, Jr. and R. Roy Finkle, *Marsh's California Corporation Law* (3d ed.) § 10.43, at 751. We recognize that the Directors did not break any law by filing the bankruptcy petitions, and that the OTS has not filed criminal charges against the Directors. Nonetheless, we find that a deliberate attempt to undermine the regulatory authority of a government agency cannot constitute good faith conduct, even if such actions benefit the corporation.

The Directors intentionally breached their fiduciary duties to the Bank and their Consent Agreement with the OTS in order to prevent the OTS from exercising the powers granted to it under FIRREA. The Directors knew the impropriety of their actions, and one of the Directors ... resigned his position when he learned of the scheme. We therefore conclude that the Directors did not act in good faith when they placed the Debtors in bankruptcy.

3. Court-Ordered Indemnification

Under corporate law statutes, directors and officers can seek judicial assistance in obtaining advances for expenses or indemnification. To illustrate, Model Act § 8.54 provides for court-ordered indemnification in three situations: (1) if a director is entitled to mandatory indemnification; (2) if a director is entitled to permissive indemnification to which the corporation has agreed to in a provision in the articles or bylaws, by board or shareholder resolution, or by contract; or (3) if the "court determines, in view of all the relevant circumstances, that it is fair and reasonable" to provide indemnification or advances. Under this third situation, the court in its discretion may order indemnification even if the director has not met the "good faith" and "corporation's best interests" standards provided in the permissive indemnification statute (Model Act § 8.51(a)) or is otherwise ineligible for indemnification. This judicial discretion, however, is limited under the Model Act in the following way. If there is an adverse judgment in a derivative proceeding or a proceeding charging receipt of an improper financial benefit, the court may order only the payment of expenses.[3]

C. NON-EXCLUSIVITY STATUTES

The mandatory, permissive, and court-ordered indemnification discussed above may or may not exhaust the forms of indemnification available in a particular state. Whether the corporation can indemnify officers and directors further depends on whether the statutes described above are considered exclusive or nonexclusive.

WALTUCH v. CONTICOMMODITY SERVICES, INC.

United States District Court, S.D. New York
833 F. Supp. 302 (1993)

LASKER, DISTRICT JUDGE:

Norton Waltuch brings this action for indemnification of $ 2,346,586.67 in legal expenses and related cost against his former employer, ContiCommodity Services, Inc. ("Conti") and its parent corporation, Continental Grain Company ("Conti Grain"). All these costs arose out of litigation in connection with Waltuch's activities in the silver market as an employee of Conti in 1979-80. Waltuch's indemnity claims are based on provisions of Conti's Certificate of Incorporation and by-laws as well as Delaware General Corporation Law.

After the last of the underlying actions had been settled, Waltuch presented his indemnification claim to Conti and Conti Grain.... Conti Grain appointed a three-member *ad hoc* Special Committee and the Special Committee retained independent legal counsel to advise it. On November 19, 1991 the Special Committee, having reviewed voluminous written submissions by the parties, issued a detailed report in which it concluded that Waltuch was not entitled to indemnification. Conti Grain's Board of Directors adopted the report and its conclusion.

Approximately two months later, Waltuch commenced this action. Waltuch now moves for summary judgment on his claim against Conti.... In addition, Conti Grain moves for an order dismissing the complaint for failure to state a cause of action against it.

....

II

Count I of the complaint sets forth Waltuch's indemnification claim against Conti under Article Ninth of Conti's Certificate of Incorporation. Article Ninth provides:

---

[3] Official Comment to § 8.54. *See also* DEL. CODE ANN. tit. 8, § 145(b) and ALI § 7.20(c).

> The Corporation shall indemnify and hold harmless each of its incumbent or former directors, officers, employees and agents ... against expenses actually and necessarily incurred by him in connection with the defense of any action, suit or proceeding threatened, pending or completed, in which he is made a party, by reason of his serving in or having held such position or capacity, except in relation to matters as to which he shall be adjudged in such action, suit or proceeding to be liable for negligence or misconduct in the performance of duty.

The Special Committee denied the claim on the grounds that indemnification would violate the public policy limitations expressed in Section 145 of the Delaware General Corporation Law. Both Conti and Waltuch move for summary judgment.

There is no dispute that Article Ninth is facially satisfied since Waltuch has not been "adjudged ... liable for negligence or misconduct in the performance of duty." Nevertheless, Conti argues that Article Ninth cannot be enforced as literally written because to do so would violate Section 145 of the Delaware General Corporation Law which requires a person seeking indemnification to show that he acted in good faith and in a manner he reasonably believed to be in or not opposed to the corporation's best interests. Conti contends that Waltuch cannot meet that burden and accordingly is not entitled to indemnification.

Waltuch disputes both Conti's legal theory and its version of the facts. He points out that he has satisfied the literal terms of Article Ninth and argues that this should "end the matter." Waltuch also maintains that, even if this does not end the matter, subsection (f) of Section 145 of the Delaware General Corporation Law, the so-called "non-exclusive" clause, permits indemnification pursuant to Article Ninth of Conti's Charter and that he therefore need not make any additional showing to be indemnified under Article Ninth. Finally, Waltuch argues that, in any event, he did act in good faith and so should recover his legal expenses.

Article Ninth, by itself, does not "end the matter." Conti's Certificate of Incorporation is subject to the law of Delaware. Section 102(b)(1) of the Delaware General Corporation law specifically provides that a certificate of incorporation may include "[a]ny provision for the management of the business and conduct of the affairs of the corporation ... if such provisions are not contrary to the laws of this State." Del. Gen. Corp. L. § 102(b)(1). Accordingly, Waltuch cannot recover under Article Ninth unless he can also satisfy the requirements of Section 145 of the Delaware General Corporation Law.

Section 145 is the statutory authority for indemnification. It applies to any person involved in actual or threatened litigation or an investigation by reason of the status of such a person as an officer, director, employee or agent of the corporation. Subsections (a) and (b) of the statute permit indemnification by the corporation "against expenses (including attorneys' fees), judgments, fines and amounts paid in settlement actually and reasonably incurred" provided that the indemnitee "acted in good faith and in a manner he reasonably believed to be in or not opposed to the best interests of the corporation." Subsection (c) mandates indemnification against "expenses (including attorneys' fees) actually and reasonably incurred" if the indemnitee "has been successful on the merits or otherwise in defense of any action suit or proceeding referred to in subsections (a) and (b), or in defense of any claim, issue or matter therein."

These provisions are all critically affected by the language of subsection (f) which provides:

The indemnification provided by this section shall not be deemed exclusive of any other rights to which those seeking indemnification may be entitled under any by-law, agreement, vote of stockholders or disinterested directors or otherwise.

The dispute between the parties concerns the meaning of subsection (f) — the so-called "non-exclusive" clause....

....

There is no question that subsection 145(f) allows a corporation to "grant indemnification rights beyond those provided by the [rest of] the statute." *Hibbert v. Hollywood Park, Inc.*, 457 A.2d 339 (Del. 1983). However, subsection (f) is not a blanket authorization to indemnify directors or officers against all expenses of whatever nature regardless of conduct. Although one court has described the other subsections of Section 145 as "simply 'fall back' provisions which a Delaware corporation may or may not adopt," *PepsiCo, Inc. v. Continental Casualty Co.*, 640 F. Supp. 656, 661 (S.D.N.Y. 1986), other courts and commentators agree that "[i]t is questionable whether a Delaware court would be quite this sweeping in its language in a case properly presented to it involving the outer limits of the authority provided in Section 145(f)." R. Franklin Balotti & Jesse A. Finkelstein, *The Delaware Law of Corporations and Business Organizations* § 4.16, at 4-318 (2d ed. Supp. 1992).

Be that as it may, it has been generally agreed that there are public policy limits on indemnification under Section 145(f).

The more difficult question is to define precisely what limitations on indemnification public policy imposes. Waltuch maintains that Article Ninth of Conti's Charter — which requires that the indemnitee has not been adjudged liable for negligence or misconduct in the performance of duty — by itself satisfies Delaware public policy....

What guidance there is on the precise limits to indemnification imposed by public policy comes from commentators. To the extent that they have addressed the subject, they side with Conti's position. Thus, one commentator has expressly stated that "[a]ny agreement or by-law adopted pursuant to the authority of Section 145(f) would be subject to the public policy limitations reflected by the ... specific statutory provisions" of the rest of section 145. [R. Franklin] Balotti & [Jesse A.] Finkelstein, [*The Delaware Law of Corporations and Business Organizations*] § 4. 16, at 4-320 [(2d ed. Supp. 1992)]. Another has agreed, albeit more tentatively, that "an argument can be made that indemnification which is uncategorically prohibited under subsections (a) and (b) ... [is] contrary to public policy and hence cannot be the subject of subsection (f) indemnification." A. Gilchrist Sparks, III et al., *Indemnification, Directors and Officers Liability Insurance and Limitations of Director Liability Pursuant to Statutory Authorization: The Legal Framework under Delaware Law*, 696 PLI/Corp. 941, 976 (May 7, 1990). Finally, one commentator has noted that "[a]lthough there is no case law on point, it is probable that a Delaware court would not allow indemnification ... when [i]t is prohibited by law or public policy. To the extent that the statute can be read to embody the public policy limitations of indemnification, a by-law or agreement purporting to expand these limits would likely be void as violative of public policy." E. Norman Veasey et al., *Delaware Law Supports Directors with a Three-Legged Stool of Limited Liability, Indemnification, and Insurance*, 42 BUS. LAW. 399, 414 (1987).

In addition to the weight of this authority, there is a compelling argument on Conti's side. It is simply that there would be no point to the carefully crafted provisions of Section 145 spelling out the permissible scope of indemnification under Delaware law if subsection (f) allowed indemnification in additional circumstances without regard to these limits. The exception would swallow the rule.

It is not true, as Waltuch maintains, that on this approach, the rule swallows the exception. Even when circumscribed by the limitations set forth in the other subsections, subsection (f) still "may authorize the adoption of various procedures and presumptions to make the process of indemnification more favorable to the indemnitee without violating the statute." Balotti & Finkelstein, *supra*, § 4.16, at 4-320.

In sum, subsection (f) does not permit indemnification without regard to the limitations set forth in the other subsections of Section 145. Thus, Waltuch must show either that he "acted in good faith and in a manner he reasonably believed to be in or not opposed to the best interests of the corporation" or that he "has been successful on the merits or otherwise" in defense of the actions against him.[4]

PepsiCo, Inc. v. Continental Casualty Co.,[5] offers a contrasting view of the meaning of nonexclusivity statutes. Corporate officers and directors there were accused of violating federal securities laws. In the course of the proceedings, including settlement agreements, the corporation indemnified its officers and directors.

The insurance company argued that the corporation had not complied with Delaware's permissive indemnification statutes. It argued that the corporation had

---

[4] The Second Circuit subsequently affirmed the District Court on these issues. *Waltuch v. Conticommodity Services, Inc.*, 88 F.3d 87, 89-95 (2d Cir. 1996).

[5] 640 F. Supp. 656, 660 (S.D.N.Y. 1986).

not determined that the defendants acted in "good faith" and in the "best interests of the corporation." In addition, the corporation had not followed the proper process for determining if these standards were met. Furthermore, the insurance company contended, the corporation's indemnification of liabilities resulting from securities laws violations was against public policy. The corporation responded that its bylaws broadened its ability to indemnify. The bylaws made indemnification of directors and officers "the rule rather than the exception."

The court agreed with the corporation. It indicated that the standards and processes of the Delaware permissive indemnification statutes were "simply 'fall back' provisions which a Delaware corporation may or may not adopt." *Id.* at 661. The corporation's decision to supplant the terms of the statute with its own standards and processes for indemnification was permitted under the statute's nonexclusivity provisions. Public policy did not preclude the enforcement of the bylaw terms.

SECTION III. INSURANCE

Corporate law statutes allow corporations to buy directors' and officers' liability insurance. The corporation may purchase this insurance "whether or not the corporation would have the power to indemnify" against such liabilities under the indemnification provisions. Model Act § 8.57. In other words, the corporation may purchase insurance coverage under circumstances where the permissive indemnification statutes would often prohibit indemnification — for instance, to cover the amounts paid in settlement or adverse judgments in derivative actions. Consequently, insurance theoretically can fill the gap between the directors' and officers' total amount of liability and the amount that the corporation indemnified.

Most state statutes, however, do impose some limits. As ALI § 7.20(b)(2) illustrates:

> A corporation should not be entitled to purchase insurance ... to the extent that the insurance would furnish protection against liability for conduct directly involving a knowing and culpable violation of law or involving a significant pecuniary benefit obtained by an insured person to which the person is not legally entitled.

The typical directors' and officers' liability insurance policy, commonly called "D & O" liability insurance, contains two types of coverage: the first covers the corporation for its responsibility to indemnify directors and officers ("Company Reimbursement") and the second covers losses incurred by the directors and officers which the corporation is not permitted or required to indemnify ("Directors and Officers Liability"). The policy contains provisions defining the rights of those insured and the obligations of the insurance company. A description of the coverage, for instance, indicates the limits of the coverage, deductibles for which the corporation and individual directors and officers are responsible, and the policy period.

Policies also provide that certain types of liabilities are excluded from coverage. One survey of D & O policies, for instance, found that over half of the policies excluded coverage for liabilities arising from pending or prior litigation, pollution and environmental damage, or illegal payments or commissions. Other exclusions included liabilities arising from mergers and acquisitions, tender offers and tender offer rejections, and a number of securities law violations. ALI § 7.20 Reporter's Note 8, p. 287 (describing 1987 Wyatt D & O Survey).

Not surprisingly, there is substantial litigation between insurance companies who claim that the policy does not cover the particular claim and the corporations, directors, and officers who believe that they are entitled to coverage under the policy terms. Two of the recurrent issues are described in the following excerpt.

Joseh P. Montelone & Nicholas J. Conca, Directors and Officers Indemnification and Liability Insurance: An Overview of Legal and Practical Issues, 51 Business Lawyer 573, 598-603, 607-08 (1996)*

Policy Exclusions

Because the grant of coverage under the typical D&O policy form is so broad, the exclusions in the policy in a sense define the coverage more than any other policy provisions.... Typically, between the specimen and added endorsements, the policy will contain somewhere between ten and twenty separate exclusions. Subject to negotiation among the insured corporation, the insurer, and the broker, various combinations of these exclusions may be used for given risks.... In examining a policy form, one needs to examine the *entire* policy very carefully, as not all of the exclusions are always contained in the policy section discreetly labeled as "Exclusions."

... The D&O policy exclusions can be characterized broadly as falling into either of two categories: corporate governance exclusions and those excluding matters that should be covered under other insurance. These exclusions have their origin in principles of good corporate governance and, in particular, state statutory law regarding indemnification of directors and officers by the corporation and recently, laws exculpating directors and officers from liability in certain circumstances....

Generally, much of the conduct excluded by "dishonesty" and "personal profit" exclusions is the very conduct for which the statutes of many states and/or federal law, rules, and regulations prohibit indemnification, if such conduct is established. Many of the recent statutory enactments which exculpate directors (and sometimes officers as well) from liability to the corporation and/or its

---

shareholders make exceptions for fraudulent conduct, willful violations of law, and unentitled personal profit....

Courts have not had a great deal of difficulty in identifying or defining "dishonesty." One question that directors and officers *may* ask, however, is whether certain breaches of fiduciary duty may implicate the dishonesty exclusion in their D&O policies. One case suggests the answer is "yes." In *Leucadia, Inc. v. Reliance Insurance Co.*, 864 F.2d 964 (2d Cir. 1988), *cert. denied*, 109 S. Ct. 3160 (1989), the Second Circuit, in the context of interpreting the coverage afforded under a fidelity bond, held that there need not be a finding of fraud in order to have dishonesty: "New York law does not ... consider the words fraud and dishonesty to be synonymous. Dishonesty is broader and may cover acts which fall short of constituting fraud."

... A second group of exclusions bars from coverage matters which should be covered under some other liability insurance policy held by the corporation for its own and its directors' and officers' benefit.

....

Allocation

The concept of allocation is inherent in the makeup of a D&O policy. To state the concept simply, D&O policies afford coverage only to specific classes of insureds, *i.e.*, the directors and officers of the insured organization, and not the insured organization itself. Additionally, D&O policies cover only specified types of wrongful acts, and do not insure conduct which is excluded or beyond the scope of coverage. The end result is that D&O coverage will attach only if covered claims are asserted against covered parties (the directors and officers). On occasion, a claim may only be partially covered: hence the need for allocation.

Allocation comes into play when (i) covered and noncovered claims are asserted against covered parties; (ii) a claim is asserted against both covered and noncovered parties; or (iii) covered parties are alleged to have committed wrongful acts in both insured and noninsured capacities. Once it is determined whether one or more of these scenarios is present in a given claim, the parties should agree upon an appropriate allocation, *i.e.*, what portion of the defense costs, settlement, or judgment amounts should be borne by the D&O insurer.

Unfortunately, although the courts have offered some broad criteria for determining allocations, no court has formulated a specific mechanism by which an appropriate allocation can be derived. As a result, most practitioners agree that the derivation of allocations is an inexact science and typically is the subject of negotiation between the interested parties.

Chapter 16

IMPACT OF SECURITIES LAWS ON CORPORATIONS

Situation

Biologistics, Inc. has been in existence just over five years, and it has had continuing success. Earnings have increased steadily, with those for the last year reaching almost $ 600,000. What may be more important, the corporation has just patented a process for manipulating the DNA of plants so as to create increased resistance to certain diseases. Developing efficient production techniques will be expensive, however. Further bank borrowings or sales of securities will be necessary if the process is to be exploited fully.

Phillips has discussed with Anderson and Baker the possibility of selling perhaps 25% of the corporation to a small group of wealthy investors. He believes that his investment banking firm could sell common stock representing that much ownership for $ 3 million. Alternatively, he has suggested that the corporation do, through his firm, a $ 3 million public offering of the corporation's common stock. That, of course, would make Biologistics a publicly held rather than a closely held corporation. Anderson and Baker would like your advice about those alternatives.

Many and various corporate transactions have securities law implications. So pervasive, in fact, is the involvement of securities law in corporate transactions that it is impossible to practice corporate law without also practicing securities law, at least to a limited extent. Any lawyer handling corporate matters needs to have a good basic understanding of the Securities Act of 1933 (the Securities Act), along with at least rudimentary knowledge of some of the provisions in the Securities Exchange Act of 1934 (the Exchange Act). In addition, the corporate lawyer needs to know something of the securities laws of the state or states involved in the lawyer's corporate transactions. The materials that follow in this chapter are designed to provide introductions to some provisions of the Securities Act and the Exchange Act, and to some extent to state securities laws also.

Robert A. Kessler, The Effect of the Securities Laws Upon the Small Business, The Practical Lawyer, September 1, 1982 at 11*

No business, however small, is immune from federal law. Every business must raise capital, and its owners may want to transfer their interests. Those transactions can pose problems under federal and state securities laws.

---

*Copyright 1982 by the author. Reprinted with permission. This article is a condensed and modified version of Chapter 18 of New Jersey Close Corporations (Callaghan & Co.) and New York Close Corporations (William S. Hein & Co., Inc.), also by the author.

....

[T]he federal securities acts [having the greatest effect on the small business] are the Securities Act of 1933 ("1933 Act"), and the Securities Exchange Act of 1934 ("1934 Act")....

The 1933 Act

Unless some exemption is available, the 1933 Act:

- Applies to all offers to sell and sales of securities by their issuers, controlling shareholders, and those acting as distributors for either, whenever the mail or some interstate commerce instrumentality is used;
- Provides that a "registration statement" be filed with the Securities Exchange Commission ("SEC") prior to the public offering; and
- Requires that a prospectus, which is typically incorporated in the registration statement, be furnished to prospective investors.

Both the registration statement and prospectus must follow a prescribed form.

Since the purpose of the 1933 Act is full and fair disclosure, criminal penalties are imposed and a civil right of action is given for failure to comply with the registration and prospectus requirements and for any false or misleading statements in either document.

The 1933 Act is difficult to avoid on jurisdictional grounds. In *United States v. Wolfson,* 405 F.2d 779 (2d Cir. 1968), the defendants were held criminally liable when third parties — brokers — confirmed by mail the sales by the defendants. Since the use of the mails by the brokers was reasonably foreseeable, the defendants were considered to have "caused" the mails to be used and hence met the jurisdictional requirement for liability.

The 1934 Act

The primary function of the 1934 Act is to protect through adequate disclosure investors in securities listed on national securities exchanges. The Securities Act Amendments of 1964 extend this protection to investors in securities issued by companies with assets of over $ 1 million[1] and 500 or more shareholders, even though the securities are traded only over the counter — *i.e.,* are not "listed." Although the 1934 Act is generally applicable to corporations whose securities were issued to the public, at least one provision, section 10(b), applies to close corporations.

Since the 1934 Act also requires only the use of the mails or some instrumentality of interstate commerce — which has been held to include even an intrastate phone call — it, too, is difficult to avoid on jurisdictional grounds.

---

[1] Under Exchange Act Rule 12g-1, the threshold is now $ 10 million [Eds.]

Focus

The focus of the 1933 Act is on the sale of securities. Although the 1934 Act contains numerous provisions on such diverse subjects as the regulation of broker-dealers, stock exchanges, corporate takeover bids, and proxy solicitations in public corporations, the one section of the 1934 Act of primary concern to closely-held businesses [section 10(b)] also deals with transactions involving securities. Accordingly, the first matter requiring discussion is what constitutes a security within the meaning of both acts.

Definition of Security — The term "security" under both Acts is broadly defined. Section 2[(a)](1) of the 1933 Act provides:

> The term "security" means any note, stock, treasury stock, bond, debenture, evidence of indebtedness, certificate of interest or participation in any profit-sharing agreement, collateral trust certificate, preorganization certificate or subscription, transferable share, investment contract, voting trust certificate, certificate of deposit for a security, fractional undivided interest in oil, gas, or other mineral rights, any put, call, straddle, option, or privilege on any security, certificate of deposit, or group or index of securities (including any interest therein or based on the value thereof), or any put, call, straddle, option, or privilege entered into on a national securities exchange relating to foreign currency, or, in general, any interest or instrument commonly known as a "security," or any certificate of interest or participation in, temporary or interim certificate for, receipt for, guarantee of, or warrant or right to subscribe to or purchase, any of the foregoing.

Except as to "notes," [t]he definition in the 1934 Act is substantially the same.

Although the Supreme Court, looking at the economic realities, has held in *United Housing Foundation, Inc. v. Forman,* 421 U.S. 837 (1975), that stock in a publicly supported housing project was not a security, it is clear that stock in an ordinary business corporation, even a stock subscription, is ... a security....

Any long-term debt, such as a note maturing over nine months after issuance, is normally a covered security. Even a shorter term note is not automatically exempt under either Act as interpreted by the courts.

Thus, the attorney for a small business must be aware of the possibility that any form of financing will subject his clients to the federal securities laws whenever the jurisdictional requirements of the Acts are met....

Exemptions Under the 1933 Act — Because compliance with the registration and prospectus requirements of the 1933 Act is extremely costly, the most important question for the average practitioner is whether his client may ignore those requirements. The answer depends on the exemption provisions of sections 3 and 4 of the 1933 Act. Section 3 deals with exempted securities, and section 4 with exempted transactions. The principal exemptions applicable to the close corporation are contained in sections 3(a)(11), 3(b), 4(2), and ... section 4(6).

Prior to the 1970's, the only guidance on the availability of the various exemptions came from the statute itself, the relatively few judicial decisions on the subject, and vague administrative interpretations by the SEC — collectively known as the "statutory law." Recognizing both the vagueness and the frequent inconsistency of this statutory law, during the past few years the SEC has attempted to introduce greater certainty by promulgating "safe harbor" rules, compliance with which will insure exemption from the registration provisions of the 1933 Act.

Many small businesses should be able to comply with the new rules. Those that cannot completely meet their requirements should attempt to do so to the extent possible. Since the vague statutory law is at least flexible, it may grant immunity for partial compliance.

The Intrastate Exemption — Section 3(a)(11) exempts:

> Any security which is part of an issue offered and sold only to persons resident within a single State or Territory, where the issuer of such security is a person resident and doing business within, or, if a corporation, incorporated by and doing business within, such State or Territory.

Thus, if three or four New Jersey residents wish to form a New Jersey corporation to do only a local business and to own only local property and they intend to keep all of the stock for themselves, the incorporators will not have to comply with the 1933 Act.

To take advantage of this exemption, not only must the entire issue of securities be sold to persons domiciled in the same state as the issuing corporation, but also no offer to sell may be made to any nonresident.

Furthermore, the entire issue must end up only in the hands of residents. Although later sales to nonresidents by the resident who, in good faith, purchased the securities for investment and not for resale will not destroy the exemption, such resales, especially if they take place shortly after the sale to the residents, may create an inference that the original sale was an attempt to circumvent the 1933 Act. Therefore, it is advisable to secure a statement from each purchaser that he is a resident of the state of incorporation and that the securities are being purchased solely for investment and not for resale. Obviously, this self-serving declaration will not be conclusive when the facts show that the original purchase was, in reality, made for resale and not investment.

Since the burden of proof to establish an exemption is on the person claiming it, the attorney relying solely on the statutory law should advise his clients that they need not comply with the 1933 Act only if the facts clearly show the truly intrastate character of the offering.

Moreover, unless the business conducted is strictly local, the exemption may not be available. Thus, even when the persons to whom the securities are offered are all residents of the same state, the offering is not exempt when the proceeds are to be used to refurbish an out-of-state hotel, purchase out-of-state oil and gas interests, or make loans to out-of-state land developers.

Rule 147

As a "safe harbor" for the intrastate exemption, the SEC adopted Rule 147, SEC Securities Act Release No. 33-5450 (Jan. 7, 1974). Prudence dictates compliance with all of the Rule's requirements....

A newly formed corporation in Illinois, for example, will qualify under Rule 147 if:

- At least 80 per cent of its assets are located in Illinois;
- At least 80 per cent of the net proceeds from the sale of the securities are intended to be, and are, used in Illinois;
- The corporation's principal office is in Illinois;
- Offers and sales of the securities are made only to Illinois residents;
- No resales are made to nonresidents for nine months after the last sale of securities under the Rule;
- A legend is placed on the securities stating that they are not registered under the 1933 Act and cannot be resold to nonresidents for nine months after the last sale under the Rule;
- A notation is made in the corporate records — like the stock book — barring the recognition of transfers in violation of the Rule;
- A written representation is obtained from each purchaser that he is an Illinois resident; and
- The corporation discloses in writing to each person to whom the securities are offered the restrictions on transfer, including the fact that the securities will be legended, that prohibited transfers to nonresidents will not be recognized, and that any new certificates for securities that are part of the same issue will be subject to the same limitations.

....

The Small Issues Exemption — Section 3(b) of the 1933 Act empowers the SEC to "add any class of securities to the securities exempted" if the offering price to the public does not exceed $ 5 million and the SEC finds that, "by reason of the small amount involved or the limited character of the public offering," enforcement of the Act is not necessary.

....

Recently, the SEC promulgated, under the authority of section 3(b), Rules 504 and 505.... Moreover, in new section 4(6) of the 1933 Act, added by the Small Business Investment Incentive Act of 1980, Congress provided its own statutory small issues exemption supplementing section 3(b). These changes have been included in new Regulation D, SEC Securities Act Release No. 33-6389 (Mar. 8, 1982), which will be discussed later....

The Nonpublic Offering Exemption — To the average practitioner, the most important statutory exemption provision may be contained in section 4(2), exempting "transactions by an issuer not involving any public offering."

Although it might seem obvious that the formation of a small business is a transaction not involving any public offering, this is by no means certain. The term "public offering" is not defined in the statute, nor is its converse, a nonpublic offering or a private placement. Accordingly, the boundaries of the exemption have been left to administrative and judicial determination. Under these interpretations, even the formation of the small corporation and later financing attempts may not be exempt under section 4(2).

SEC Criteria

The SEC very early formulated certain criteria for determining what is a public, as opposed to a private, offering or placement. [F]actors to be considered are:

- The number of offerees and their relationships to each other and the issuer.
- The number of units offered. Since a large number of shares of stock of small denominations are more apt to get into the hands of the general public, the offering is more likely to be a public one.
- The size of the offering. Even though the number of securities offered is initially small, the offering is more likely to be public if the offering is part of a larger one made to the public.
- The manner of offering the securities. If the offer is made in face-to-face negotiations, it is less likely to be a public offering than if effected through a brokerage firm or underwriter.

The Ralston Purina Test

The Supreme Court has refused to lay down any hard and fast rule as to the effect of the number of offerees and their relationship to one another upon whether an offering is public or private. Instead, it provided a flexible test for the availability of the exemption:

> Since exempt transactions are those as to which "there is no practical need for [the bill's] application," the applicability of § 4(1) [now § 4(2)] should turn on whether the particular class of persons affected need the protection of the Act. An offering to those who are shown to be able to fend for themselves is a transaction "not involving any public offering." *SEC v. Ralston Purina Co.,* 346 U.S. 119, 125 (1953).

Thus, when some of the persons to whom the securities are offered are apt to be unsophisticated — a strong possibility whenever numbers of persons are involved — the issue must be considered a public one. Furthermore, as the case intimates, even an offer to one unsophisticated person unable to "fend for himself" may constitute such a public offering. The number of offerees is significant in imposing liability, not in excluding it. Finally, by stating that "[t]he employees [offerees] here were not shown to have access to the kind of information which registration would disclose," the Court suggests that there must not only be sophistication, but access to detailed information.

Some of the lower federal courts have not hesitated to apply the *Ralston Purina* test expansively to convert what many would regard as private placements into nonexempt public offerings. Both sophistication and access to the same information that registration would disclose have generally been required. Furthermore, in *Lively v. Hirschfeld,* 440 F.2d 631, 633 (10th Cir. 1971), sophistication was held to require "exceptional business experience," while in *Lawler v. Gilliam,* 569 F.2d 1283 (4th Cir. 1978), the court held that even a sale of only two unique notes to an allegedly sophisticated single investor was not exempt when he did not have access to the information that a registration statement would show.

This statutory law remains intact. Nonetheless, since the requirements of Regulation D for offerings of $ [1 million] or less are so easy to meet and the more onerous requirements applicable when greater amounts of capital are needed over a relatively short period of time have the advantage of greater certainty, the statutory law should be utilized by the small businessman only as a last resort — as for a litigation defense — and not for planning purposes.

However, when certain institutional investors may be unwilling to accept securities with legends restricting their negotiability or the lawyer may have neglected to file the necessary SEC form, most likely the exemptions under Regulation D — including Rule 506, the private placement rule — will not be available. Then ultimate reliance will have to be placed on the statutory law, although compliance with as many of the provisions of Regulation D as possible will be desirable.

ABA Position Paper

Although conceding that "it is difficult, if not impossible, to state accurately what the Statutory Law is," a position paper of the Federal Regulation of Securities Committee of the American Bar Association, 31 Bus. Law. 485, 486 (1975), offers guidelines, compliance with which, it argues, should, in the hortatory sense, be sufficient for the private placement exemption despite failure to comply with specific SEC exemptive rules. The guidelines consist of four essential factors — offeree qualification, availability of information, manner of offering, and absence of distribution.

In regard to offeree qualification, "[t]he relevant inquiry should be whether the investor can understand and evaluate the nature of the risk based upon the information supplied to him." This suggests that sophistication and the amount of disclosure are to a certain extent reciprocal. If the disclosure is painstaking, the degree of sophistication may not have to be as high.

Great sophistication, however, may not be essential. "[O]fferees in a private placement should be deemed qualified on any one of several bases." Thus, although wealth alone may not be enough if the investor has no understanding of financial matters and no competent advisor, wealth or "a personal relationship to the issuer or a promoter" should be sufficient to qualify an offeree, even though he lacks a high degree of sophistication.

The information to be supplied need not be as extensive as that in Schedule A to the 1933 Act — the information required in a registration statement. Basic information concerning the issuer's financial condition, the results of its operations, and its business, property, and management may suffice. Although a written list of risk factors may be desirable, the other information can be presented more informally, whether orally, through a tour of the physical facilities or inspection of the products, or by allowing the offeree to communicate directly with the issuer's customers, suppliers, and bankers.

The manner of offering should be direct communication with the person to whom the security is offered. All forms of general advertising and mass media circulation should be avoided.

The last factor, absence of distribution, calls for the legending of securities, investment letters, and stop-transfer orders, though the necessity of these actions in a "purely private company where there is no reasonable expectation that a trading market for its securities will develop" is questionable. Even though the investors did not have "investment intent," if no public resales are, in fact, made, the exemption should be available.

Despite the *Ralston Purina* holding that the burden of proof is on the person claiming an exemption, the paper concludes that

> once the party relying on the exemption has shown that the transaction was generally conducted in a proper manner, the burden of going forward should and probably will shift to the adverse party to demonstrate some material defect in the transaction.

While the conclusions of the paper are qualified as a result of the acknowledged uncertainties of the statutory law, they should, because of their source, be persuasive to courts in determining whether a private placement exemption is available. However, if these minimal requirements for a private placement under the statutory law are correct, they impose what may well be as great a burden on the issuer as that of Regulation D for raising very significant amounts of money, and certainly a greater burden than that imposed by Rule 504 when amounts up to $ [1 million] are involved. Accordingly, failure to meet the Regulation D requirements should never occur inadvertently, but only when full compliance is for some reason impossible.

Regulation D. —

　....

General Provisions

Perhaps the most important requirement of Regulation D is that five copies of a notice — Form D — must be filed with the SEC in Washington regardless of the amount of money being raised. Rule 503. [Although one can now get the benefits of the Regulation if the form is not filed.]

Furthermore, [unless] the offering is made under Rule 504, ... any form of "general solicitation" is banned and limitations on the resale of securities are imposed. Rules 502(c) and (d).

Other requirements depend on the amount of money being raised and on the persons to whom the offer to sell is made. Rule 504 deals with offers and sales of [up to $ 1 million], Rule 505, with those up to $ 5,000,000, and Rule 506 has no monetary limit.

Central to Regulation D is the concept of the "accredited investor." When all the prospective purchasers fall into this category, specific information need not be furnished them, nor must they meet any sophistication test. There is also no limit on the number of purchasers.

When, however, any nonaccredited investor is approached, unless the offer or sale falls within ... Rule 504, specified information must be furnished to all purchasers prior to sale and the number of nonaccredited purchasers cannot exceed 35, although certain purchasers, such as the spouse of a purchaser who has the same principal residence, will not be counted. Rules 502(b) and 501(e).

Furthermore, when any nonaccredited investor is involved and Rule 506 must be used because the monetary limits of Rule 505 will be exceeded, the issuer must "reasonably believe immediately prior to making any sale that each purchaser who is not an accredited investor either alone or with his purchaser representative(s) has such knowledge and experience in financial and business matters that he is capable of evaluating the merits and risks of the prospective investment." Rule 506(b)(2)(ii).... Such sophistication is only required, however, for offerings under Rule 506, not for those under Rules 504 or 505.

Rule 506

Rule 506 ... allows an issuer to raise an unlimited amount of money if the investors are furnished with specified information — unless all are accredited. Still, it imposes a sophistication requirement when nonaccredited purchasers are involved and, except for accredited investors, generally permits no more than 35 purchasers. *See* Rule 501(e) for calculating the number.

Because new Rules 504 and 505 provide more satisfactory means of raising smaller amounts of money, Rule 506 will probably only be utilized by issuers seeking to raise over $ 5 million in any 12-month period, and it is, therefore, of limited interest to closely-held businesses.

Rule 505

Although Rules 504 and 505, like their predecessors, were adopted under section 3(b) of the 1933 Act, securities issued under them will, with an exception to be discussed below, have the same status as though they had been acquired in a private placement under section 4(2). Rule 502(d). An important effect of this characterization is a restriction on the investor's right to resell his securities.

Businessmen needing $ 5 million or less can rely on either section 4(6) of the 1933 Act or Rule 505. The most significant difference between the two is that, under the statute, offers and sales may only be made to accredited investors, while under the Rule, sales may also be made to as many as 35 other investors, provided specified information is made available to all purchasers, including the accredited ones, prior to the sale. Since the Rule goes beyond the statutory provision, it has, in effect, made section 4(6) superfluous.

Accredited Investors

For purposes of both the statute and the Rule, accredited investors include [, along with others]:

- Banks and insurance companies;
- Certain business development companies;
- [Certain other organizations and trusts]
- Persons whose net worth [with one's spouse] exceeds $ 1 million;
- Persons whose income exceeded $ 200,000 in each of the two preceding years [or $ 300,000 with one's spouse, in either case where there is a reasonable expectation of reaching such income level] for the current year; and
- Directors, executive officers, or general partners of the issuer. Rule 501(a).

"Executive officer" includes the president, "any vice president in charge of a principal business unit, division or function (such as sales, administration or finance)," and[, basically,] any other person who performs a policy making function. Rule 501(f).

Thus, in the small business, all of the active participants will ordinarily qualify as accredited, at least after the business is formed. When, however, any of the securities are to be sold to a passive investor — a limited partner or a shareholder who will not act as officer or director — the exemption will not be available unless all of the nondirectors and nonofficers are accredited or all the purchasers, including the accredited ones, are furnished with [extensive specified information]. *See* Rule 502(b).

In addition to the written disclosure of transfer restrictions, the issuer taking advantage of Rules 505 or 506 is required to give to each nonaccredited purchaser a brief written description of any additional written information supplied to any accredited investor and, prior to his purchase, any portion or all of this information that the unaccredited purchaser requests. Rule 502(b)(2)(iv). The issuer must also provide each prospective purchaser with an opportunity to ask questions and receive answers concerning the terms and conditions of the offering and to obtain any information it has or can reasonably acquire in order to verify the accuracy of the information supplied in the registration statement. Rule 502(b)(2)(v). Preliminary Note 1 to Regulation D also cautions that "such further material information, if any, as may be necessary to make the information required under this regulation, in light of the circumstances under which it is furnished, not misleading" may have to be furnished.

There are more information requirements for business combinations and reporting companies, but the latter are, by definition, not closely-held businesses.

Rule 504

Most closely-held businesses will not need to raise more than $ [1 million] on formation or in any 12-month period thereafter. Rule 504 ... will, therefore, be most important for small businessmen. While containing a ... monetary limit, it imposes no limit on the number of purchasers, no necessity that the investors be accredited or sophisticated, ... no requirement that they be furnished with any specific information[, and essentially no other limitations or requirement for obtaining the exemption.]

....

Resales — The SEC has always sought to prevent an exempt offering from being used as a means of circumventing the 1933 Act requirements. The law would become meaningless if a sale of all of a corporation's stock to a single sophisticated investor ... were to be immune as a private placement, even though that shareholder immediately sold all of his shares to a number of uninformed and unsophisticated third parties.

A person who participates in such a public distribution will be considered a "statutory underwriter" under the 1933 Act and subject to severe penalties. Such a public resale by a shareholder may also subject the issuer to liability, especially when it has notice that resales are contemplated, by destroying the private placement or [Rule 505 or 506] exemptions that otherwise would have been available to it.

Safe Harbor [Rule]

Since the term "statutory underwriter" is elusive, the SEC has promulgated [a] "safe harbor" [rule] that [allows] shareholders to dispose of limited quantities of "restricted" securities — [which includes] those received in a private placement or a limited offering under [Rule 505 or 506] — without being considered statutory underwriters.

....

Rule 144

Rule 144 allows a shareholder who received his shares in a bona fide private placement or exempt transaction to dispose of them publicly when certain requirements are met — most notably, the shareholder's holding of the securities for [one year] before the sale and the availability to the public of adequate information about the issuer. After filing an appropriate notice with the SEC, the shareholder can sell the restricted securities in limited quantities without registration.

[T]he shareholders of a close corporation will have difficulty meeting the requirement for adequate public information [, but this requirement, along with those relating to] the quantity limits and the manner of sale and notice requirements, is relaxed by Rule 144(k) in the case of [most] noncontrolling security holders who have held their securities for [two] or more years ....

....

Control Persons

Because of the limitations of [Rule 144, the Rule does not assure] an exemption for such common close-corporation transactions as a sale of all of a participant's shares to a third party or even to fellow shareholders....

According to one expert, only three avenues are open to control persons who wish to sell their company's securities:

- Under a registration statement and in full compliance with the 1933 Act;
- By way of a Regulation A offering, which is almost as burdensome; and
- Through "an exempt transaction such as a nondistributive sale." S. Goldberg, *Private Placements and Restricted Securities* § 8.2[b] (Clark Boardman, New York City, 1975).

The last — and the only practical alternative for most close-corporation participants unless the corporation decides to go public — is called the "section 4(1½) exemption" by securities lawyers. The reason for the name is that this exemption, recognized in practice but not given express statutory sanction, is midway between section 4(1), which exempts transactions "by any person other than an issuer, underwriter or dealer," and section 4(2), which exempts transactions by an issuer "not involving any public offering." The section $4(1^1/_2)$ exemption is, therefore, a kind of private placement by a security holder, and most close-corporation shareholders, like many institutional investors, will have to rely on it to sell their shares.

....

Recommendations — The 1933 Act is broad enough to apply to the formation of a close corporation and to any efforts to obtain later financing. Furthermore, even if the initial issuance of securities escapes the sweep of the 1933 Act, later resales may subject either the sellers to liability as control persons or both the sellers and the corporation to the prohibition against resales by statutory underwriters.

Neither the statute itself nor any of the exemptive rules promulgated by the SEC offers a completely safe exemption from the 1933 Act. The best exemption for a small business is Rule 504, since the issuer may easily comply with its requirements....

....

A written statement — frequently called an investment letter — by the initial investors that they are not taking the shares with a view to distribution is [usually] wise, since, if they are honest, it may protect a private placement exemption under the statutory law and help to insure an exemption under many state blue sky laws. Preferably, the statement should assert that the securities will be held for investment. If applicable, the statement should also indicate that the shareholders are all residents of the same state as the corporation.

The shareholders should also agree not to transfer the shares in violation of the 1933 Act. When more than one person is involved in the formation of the close corporation, usually restrictions on the transfer of shares will prevent a public distribution, and, when applicable, protect an intrastate exemption.

In addition, the share certificates [issued in other than a Rule 504 transaction] should carry a legend that the shares are not registered under the 1933 Act and that resales are prohibited unless they comply with that Act. When the intrastate exemption is available, the legend should also state that resales to nonresidents will not be permitted except as provided in the rules and regulations promulgated under the 1933 Act.

... A notation should also be made in the stock book that transfers will not be recognized if they violate the 1933 Act or any of the rules or regulations promulgated thereunder. Finally, Form D should be filed [if the transaction is under Regulation D or Section 4(6)].

....

Although some of the precautions may seem overly fastidious to the lawyer setting up a small business, it is worth remembering that the SEC has not hesitated to bring actions against lawyers who carelessly advised clients to proceed with transactions later held to violate the securities laws. Complicity in securities laws violations may also result in loss of the right to practice under state law.

The principal danger of failure to comply with the federal or state securities laws will, however, probably come not from the SEC, but from investors in the business who are disappointed and seek to recoup all, or at least a portion, of their money. Moreover, the purchaser seeking rescission [under section 12(a)(1) of the 1933 Act] need not have been the victim of the violation. Thus, if, in an attempted statutory private placement, an offer is made to an unsophisticated potential investor who does not purchase, a sophisticated investor who does buy the securities may have the right to rescind, because the exemption has been destroyed by the improper offer.

Obviously, the danger of potential liability increases as "outsiders" — those not original participants in the business — are approached, unless an exemption is clearly available. Even greater precautions may be necessary when the business seeks financing later.

Antifraud Provisions — Even if an exemption from registration is established, the antifraud provisions of both the 1933 and the 1934 Acts will apply....

....

Section 10(b) of the 1934 Act and its implementing Rule 10b-5 [provide the main] remedy for fraud in a securities transaction....

Section 10(b) makes it unlawful for any person, in connection with the purchase or sale of any security, to use by any means or instrumentality of interstate commerce or of the mails ... any manipulative or deceptive device or contrivance in contravention of such rules and regulations as the Commission may prescribe....

Under the authority thus given it, the SEC has promulgated Rule 10b-5, which provides as follows:

> It shall be unlawful for any person, directly or indirectly, by the use of any means or instrumentality of interstate commerce, or of the mails, or of any facility of any national securities exchange,
>
> (a) to employ any device, scheme, or artifice to defraud,
>
> (b) to make any untrue statement of a material fact or to omit to state a material fact necessary in order to make the statements made, in the light of the circumstances under which they were made, not misleading, or
>
> (c) to engage in any act, practice, or course of business which operates or would operate as a fraud or deceit upon any person, in connection with the purchase or sale of any security.

Paragraph (b) not only forbids positive misrepresentations, but also half-truths. It has also been held to create civil liability against insider purchasers for mere nondisclosure of factors affecting the market value of the shares. Those who fail to disclose material information have even been held liable to the purchasers of the stock for the profits made by those sellers to whom they passed the information — their tippees. [Scienter is, however, required to be proven (though most courts have found that recklessness is enough to constitute scienter.)]

Rule 10b-5 applies to the sale or issuance of its own stock by a corporation.
....

Even when the registration and prospectus requirements of the 1933 Act are avoided by means of the intrastate, limited, or private offering exemptions, the civil [and criminal] liabilities of section 10(b) of the 1934 Act and those of the 1933 Act may still apply if the jurisdictional prerequisites — use of the mails or the instrumentalities of interstate commerce — are present.

... Full disclosure of all the facts concerning the security is the best protection against liability under these provisions.

State Regulation — Under section 18 of the 1933 Act and section 28(a) of the 1934 Act, federal securities laws are in addition to, and generally do not supersede, regulations that the individual states impose upon the issue and sale of securities. Thus, a business desiring to market its securities must comply not only with federal law, but also with the rules of any state in which they are offered.

Every state now has a "blue sky" law. Unfortunately, the statutes differ widely from one state to another. Although the laws in such important states as California and New York are uninfluenced by the Uniform Securities Act, a significant number of states follow it. The Uniform Securities Act exempts "any isolated nonissuer transaction, whether effected through a broker-dealer or not" and "any transaction pursuant to an offer directed by the offeror to not more than ten persons ... in this state during any period of twelve consecutive months ... if (A) the seller reasonably believes that all the buyers ... are purchasing for investment, and (B) no commission or other remuneration is paid or given directly or indirectly for soliciting any prospective buyer...." §§ 402(b)(1) and (9). As to the 10-offeree exemption, the Uniform Securities Act empowers the State Blue Sky Administrator to "withdraw or further condition this exemption, or increase or decrease the number of offerees permitted, or waive the conditions in Clauses (A) and (B)...." § 402(b)(9).

These two provisions would generally exempt at least the formation of a small business and most later resales of interests in it. Nevertheless, even in states that have adopted these sections verbatim, the exact scope of the small business exemptions is uncertain without consulting judicial interpretations of the meaning of "isolated non-issuer transaction" and the administrative regulations promulgated under the authority of section 402(b)(9).

The Uniform Securities Act ... expressly provides for the civil liability of the seller for misleading statements in the sale of securities. § 410(a)(2).

Because of the relaxation of federal requirements in the area of small offerings, as evidenced by the adoption of Regulation D, the imposition of additional state requirements can be anticipated.

Obviously, the lawyer must check his state law through the Blue Sky Law Reporter, published by Commerce Clearing House, and the office of the local Blue Sky Administrator to determine what, if any, state law requirements must be met in addition to the federal ones, especially since the state statutes may apply even when federal registration can be avoided.

HILL YORK CORP. v. AMERICAN INTERNATIONAL FRANCHISES, INC.

United States Court of Appeals, Fifth Circuit
448 F.2d 680 (1971)

CLARK, CIRCUIT JUDGE:

This appeal raises substantial and complex questions involving the Securities Act of 1933. Defendants-Appellants, the Freemans and Browne, have appealed from a jury verdict awarding rescission of certain stock sales and punitive damages to plaintiffs-stock purchasers. Basically the issues revolve around whether the defendants have violated Sections 5 and [12(a)(1)], but in order to resolve these issues a detailed consideration of the facts is necessary in addition to a microscopic view of various provisions of the Act. Since the jury, in answer to interrogatories on the material elements of Section 5 and Section [12(a)(1)] violations, found against the defendants on all questions of liability, this Court is "duty bound to accept all evidence in favor of the verdict as true and to give such evidence the benefit of all permissible inferences that would help sustain the jury's decision." *Little v. Green,* 428 F.2d 1061, 1066 (5th Cir. 1970).

The evidence viewed in this light indicates that the Freemans and Browne had developed a franchise promotion scheme designed to funnel funds from the sale of stock in certain franchise sales centers to themselves as stockholders of American International Franchises, Inc. (American). The Freemans formed American in Springfield, Missouri, in July 1967 with Browne joining one month later as Executive Vice President. These three individuals comprised all of the officers and stockholders of American.

The franchising concept conceived by the Freemans involved the marketing of two restaurant franchises called Hickory Corral and Italian Den. The Chairman of the Board of Directors of Hickory Corral was Gurn Freeman, and the Chairman of the Board of Italian Den was Jack Freeman. The only restaurant of either type to be operated was one Hickory Corral which opened in Springfield, Missouri, and closed shortly thereafter. Under the plan commonly used, American would seek out local investors to incorporate a state-wide or regional franchise sales center. The payment of a franchise fee to American conferred upon this sales center the exclusive right to sell Hickory Corral and Italian Den franchises within the state or region. The local investors who formed the franchise sales center corporation would sell stock in the corporation to a small number of persons who would be most likely to furnish supplies and services to the restaurants; for instance, a real estate firm, an air conditioning company or a builder. American was also in the franchise consulting business and was to assist the local investors in organizing and developing the business of the sales center.

....

During the first year of operation, the defendants formed the following franchise sales centers: Texas Franchise Systems, Inc.; Midwest Franchise Systems, Inc.; Georgia Franchise Systems, Inc.; Southeastern Franchise Systems, Inc.; Colorado Franchise Systems, Inc.; and Florida Franchise Systems, Inc. (Florida Franchise), the sales center involved in this case. During the period of the stock sales in Florida Franchise, the defendants' other sales centers were the object of investigations by various state securities commissions. Shortly after all of the stock of Florida Franchise had been sold, two of the sales centers, Texas Franchise and Southeastern Franchise, were ordered to cease and desist operations, although this order was later lifted for Southeastern Franchise.

Florida Franchise was formed by dispatching Browne and William Osborne to Miami for the purpose of soliciting preincorporation subscriptions from Florida investors. An advertisement was placed in a local newspaper seeking a "Vice President of Marketing" for the proposed franchise sales center. When responses to the advertisement were received, the applicant was interviewed and asked to complete a financial statement indicating his net worth. If the applicant's net worth statement reflected an ability to invest in the proposed sales center, he was then told that to be hired by American, he would have to invest 5,000 dollars. The three applicants thus chosen to incorporate Florida Franchise were Shepherd, Quinn and McDaniel. The initial capitalization of 15,000 dollars invested by these three men was utilized to pay salaries and the expenses of Browne and Osborne in organizing the new sales center. Shepherd, Quinn and McDaniel were instructed by the defendants as to the solicitation of additional capitalization for Florida Franchise. This instruction included advice on what kind of investors to approach and the nature of the introductory language or "sales pitch" to be used. Between July 1968 and December 1968, Shepherd, Quinn and McDaniel, utilizing the instructions of Browne and Osborne, sold the remaining stock to plaintiffs. To induce them to purchase stock, the plaintiffs were shown promotional literature prepared by American, were told that Browne was an experienced capitalization consultant, and were given glowing reports on the operations of the other sales centers. Browne admitted at trial that the statement ascribed to him was false. The plaintiffs were never informed of the S.E.C. investigation of Nationwide nor of the State investigations of the other sales centers. Indeed, when Shepherd contacted the other sales centers, he received nothing but glowing reports from them.

American purchased 10,000 dollars worth of stock out of the 70,000 dollars worth of stock available in Florida Franchise. During the formative stages of Florida Franchise, American required that two of the five directors be representatives of American. American also required that Mickey Viles, an employee of American, become the secretary-treasurer of Florida Franchise, and in addition, Browne became the Chairman of the Board and chief executive officer. Browne later resigned, and Shepherd assumed these positions. American provided all stationery, promotional material, and sales and franchise literature. Florida Franchise was required to keep all of its corporate minute books and accounting books and records at American's office in Springfield, Missouri. All bank statements of Florida Franchise were sent directly from the bank to American in Missouri. American provided a set of recommended by-laws which were adopted by Florida Franchise. Finally, American prohibited Florida Franchise from marketing any franchises unless they were supplied by American.

On October 4, 1968, American and Florida Franchise entered into a franchise agreement, utilizing a form agreement drafted by American. The price to Florida Franchise for this exclusive right to sell was 25,000 dollars. Subsequent to the payment of the 25,000 dollars, on October 22, American insisted that Florida Franchise enter into a new agreement which provided for an additional franchise fee of 1,000 dollars per month.

Plaintiffs, alleging that these activities amounted to a pyramiding scheme to funnel money to American, brought this suit for rescission of the stock sales and the return of their investments. The jury awarded rescission and a return of the stock purchase monies paid by all but two of the plaintiffs and in addition, assessed punitive damages of 60,000 dollars against American, 15,000 dollars each against the Freemans, and 10,000 dollars against Browne. Plaintiffs Quinn and McDaniel were held to be estopped to recover their investments because they had served on the Board of Directors of Florida Franchise. They have not appealed that jury determination. The third local member of the Florida Franchise board, Shepherd, did not join in this suit. American did not appeal.

Plaintiffs based their right of recovery on Section [12(a)(1)] of the 1933 Securities Act....

Section [12(a)(1)] Recovery for Section 5 Violation

Section [12(a)(1)] of the 1933 Securities Act states:

Any person who —

(1) offers or sells a security in violation of Section [5] ... shall be liable to the person purchasing such security from him, who may sue either at law or in equity in any court of competent jurisdiction, to recover the consideration paid for such security with interest thereon, less the amount of any income received thereon, upon the tender of such security, or for damages if he no longer owns the security.

Section 5(a) and (c) of the Securities Act of 1933 provides:

(a) Unless a registration statement is in effect as to a security, it shall be unlawful for any person, directly or indirectly —

(1) To make use of any means or instruments of transportation or communication in interstate commerce or of the mails to sell such security through the use or medium of any prospectus or otherwise; or (2) to carry or cause to be carried through the mails or in interstate commerce by any means or instruments of transportation, any such security for the purpose of sale or for delivery after sale ....

(c) It shall be unlawful for any person, directly or indirectly, to make use of any means or instruments of transportation or communication in interstate commerce or of the mails to offer to sell or offer to buy through the use or medium of any prospectus or otherwise any security, unless a registration statement has been filed as to such security ....

Thus it is evident that Section 5 establishes and defines proscribed conduct and that Section [12(a)(1)] provides a remedy for a Section 5 violation. The basic question then is whether or not Section 5 was violated by the defendants.

In order to establish a prima facie case for a Section 5 violation, a plaintiff must prove three elements. First, it must be shown that no registration statement was in effect as to the securities. Second, it must be established that the defendant sold or offered to sell these securities, and finally, the use of interstate transportation or communication or of the mails in connection with the sale or offer of sale must be proved.

It is conceded that no registration statement had been filed with the S.E.C. in connection with this offering of securities. The defendants contend, however, that the transactions come within the exemptions to registration found in [Section 4(2)]. Specifically, they contend that the offering of securities was not a public offering.

In the past the S.E.C. has utilized the arbitrary figure of twenty-five offerees as a litmus test of whether an offering was public. A leading commentator in the field has noted, however, that in recent years the S.E.C. has increasingly disavowed any safe numerical test. Initially, the figure of twenty-five was probably no more than a rule of administrative convenience. In any case, such an arbitrary figure is inappropriate as an absolute in a private civil lawsuit. The Supreme Court has put it thus: "No particular numbers are prescribed. Anything from two to infinity may serve: perhaps even one ...." *S.E.C. v. Ralston Purina Co.*, 346 U.S. 119, 73 S. Ct. 981 (1953). Obviously, however, the more offerees, the more likelihood that the offering is public. The relationship between the offerees and the issuer is most significant. If the offerees know the issuer and have special knowledge as to its business affairs, such as high executive officers of the issuer would possess, then the offering is apt to be private. The Supreme Court laid special stress on this consideration in *Ralston Purina* by stating that "[t]he focus of the inquiry should be on the need of the offerees for the protections afforded by registration. The employees here were not shown to have access to the kind of information which registration would disclose." 73 S. Ct. at 985. Also to be considered is the relationship between the offerees and their knowledge of each other. For example, if the offering is being made to a diverse and unrelated group, *i.e.* lawyers, grocers, plumbers, etc., then the offering would have the appearance of being public; but an offering to a select group of high executive officers of the issuer who know each other and of course have similar interests and knowledge of the offering would more likely be characterized as a private offering.

At the threshold of this contention we deem it appropriate to consider the instructions under which the public offering phase of the exemption issue was decided ....

The S.E.C. has stated that the question of public offering is one of fact and must depend upon the circumstances of each case. We agree with this approach. It is of course apparent that presenting an issue of fact to S.E.C. analysts is totally different from presenting a question of fact to a jury unsophisticated and untrained in the niceties of securities law. Although courts accord a marked deference to the expertise of such an agency which is charged with broad regulation of a specific field when reviewing their regulatory action, we do not intimate that their procedures are binding precedent. However, to be consistent — which is the constant aim if not the invariable result of the law — and, most vitally, because we find S.E.C. criteria both legally accurate and meaningfully sufficient for testing the issue, we hold that a jury should consider the factors enumerated below which the S.E.C. considers, together with the policies embodied in the Act.

The following specific factors are relevant:

1. The number of offerees and their relationship to each other and to the issuer.

2. The number of units offered.

Here again there is no fixed magic number. Of course, the smaller the number of units offered, the greater the likelihood the offering will be considered private.

3. The size of the offering.

The smaller the size of the offering, the more probability it is private.

4. The manner of offering.

A private offering is more likely to arise when the offer is made directly to the offerees rather than through the facilities of public distribution such as investment bankers or the securities exchanges. In addition, public advertising is incompatible with the claim of private offering.

Even an objective testing of these factors without determining whether a more comprehensive and generalized prerequisite has been met, is insufficient. "The natural way to interpret the private offering exemption is in light of the statutory purpose." *S.E.C. v. Ralston Purina Co., supra* at 984. "The design of the statute is to protect investors by promoting full disclosure of information thought necessary to informed investment decisions." *Id.* Thus the ultimate test is whether "'the particular class of persons affected need the protection of the Act.'" *Id.* The Act is remedial legislation entitled to a broad construction. Conversely, its exemptions must be narrowly viewed. Thus, only where the practical need for the enforcement of the safeguards afforded by the Act or the public benefit derived from such enforcement can confidently be said to be remote with respect to the transaction is the private offering exemption met.

....

It is well-settled law that the defendants have the burden of proving their affirmative defense of private offering. The defendants, however, adduced no evidence on this issue, relying instead on the evidence introduced by the plaintiffs to prove these sales were exempt from registration. The evidence indicates that this offering was limited to sophisticated businessmen and attorneys who planned to do business with the new firm. The thirteen actual purchasers paid 5,000 dollars each for their stock. In order to be exempt from the Florida Blue Sky Law, the total number of purchasers in the first year of stock sales was deliberately kept below fifteen and the number of original subscribers below five, pursuant to advice these plaintiff-purchasers obtained from independent legal counsel who they retained to render advice on the Blue Sky and S.E.C. laws. Finally, the defendants assert that the plaintiffs had access to all the information they desired. We take this to mean that the plaintiffs had access to all information concerning Florida Franchise. We also interpret it to mean that the plaintiffs could have obtained any information they desired concerning American and the background of the individual defendants if they had just asked.

The defendants rely most strongly on the fact that the offering was made only to sophisticated businessmen and lawyers and not the average man in the street. Although this evidence is certainly favorable to the defendants, the level of sophistication will not carry the point. In this context, the relationship between the promoters and the purchasers and the "access to the kind of information which registration would disclose" become highly relevant factors. Relying specifically upon the words just quoted from *Ralston Purina,* the S.E.C. has rejected the position which the defendants posit here, stating: "'The Supreme Court's language does not support the view that the availability of an exemption depends on the sophistication of the offerees or buyers, rather than their possession of, or access to, information regarding the issuer....'" I Loss, Securities Regulation 657 n. 53 (2d ed. 1961). Obviously if the plaintiffs did not possess the information requisite for a registration statement, they could not bring their sophisticated knowledge of business affairs to bear in deciding whether or not to invest in this franchise sales center. There is abundant evidence to support the conclusion that the plaintiffs did not in fact possess the requisite information....

While defendants allude to other evidence in this case, the paucity of evidence pertaining to the relevant considerations remains stark. The record contains no evidence as to the number of offerees. The fact that there were only thirteen actual purchasers is of course irrelevant. We do know that the purchasers were a diverse and unrelated group, or at least this was so at the time the offering occurred. Furthermore, the defendants admit that the plaintiffs had never met or in any way communicated with them prior to purchasing their stock. As previously stated, there were only thirteen units sold the first year, but there is no evidence to show whether or not more units were to be offered in subsequent years. The same is true for the size of the offering. Although only 65,000 dollars worth of stock was offered, the evidence does not negate the existence of plans for offering additional securities. It must be remembered that the number of purchasers was deliberately kept below fifteen the first year in order to comply with the Florida Blue Sky law. This intentional limitation is fully consistent with a program that would bring additional offerings in subsequent years. Finally, there is no evidence as to the manner in which the offering was carried out. The most likely inference from the evidence is that the plaintiffs were contacted personally by Shepherd, Quinn or McDaniel, but again there is no hard and fast evidence.

....

The judgment ordering rescission of the stock sales and return of the purchase price was correct....

....

Lawyers' Responsibilities Under the Securities Laws

Lawyers working on securities matters often find themselves in a somewhat special position. In many securities transactions, a lawyer's opinion as to the legality of the transaction is required before one party or the other will proceed. Not infrequently, the protections the securities laws offer participants in these transactions — and those they offer members of the public who may be affected by the transactions — depend in large measure on the lawyers who give or withhold their opinions. In addition, lawyers tend to be involved in securities transactions not only as advisors and opinion givers, but as those who do the physical acts required to accomplish the transactions. For example, the main documents by which securities are offered for sale by issuers (a registration statement in a registered public offering and an offering memorandum in an exempt offering) typically are drafted by the issuer's law firm.

Because of the lawyer's special role in securities matters, some have argued that here lawyers have responsibilities not only to their clients, but to the public at large. In support of this position, proponents sometimes analogize the position of lawyers to that of certified public accountants, who have long been held to owe obligations to the public in addition to those they owe their clients. The push toward special responsibilities for lawyers has taken various forms. One is a heightened interest, on the part of the Securities and Exchange Commission and private plaintiffs, in including lawyers as defendants in securities lawsuits, either as aiders and abettors (in actions brought by the Commission) or as principals. The following case will serve as a brief introduction to this phenomenon.

SECURITIES AND EXCHANGE COMMISSION v. SPECTRUM, LTD.

United States Court of Appeals, Second Circuit
489 F.2d 535 (1973)

IRVING R. KAUFMAN, CHIEF JUDGE:

The securities laws provide a myriad of safeguards designed to protect the interests of the investing public. Effective implementation of these safeguards, however, depends in large measure on the members of the bar who serve in an advisory capacity to those engaged in securities transactions. The standard of diligence demanded of the legal profession to meet this responsibility is a matter on which we are required to comment in the resolution of this appeal.

On April 2, 1971, the Securities and Exchange Commission [SEC] filed a complaint charging twelve defendants, including the appellee, Stuart Schiffman, with participation in a partially successful scheme to distribute over one million unregistered shares of the common stock of Spectrum, Ltd. in violation of the registration provisions of the Securities Act of 1933 [the 1933 Act] [Section 5] and the antifraud provisions of that Act [Section 17(a)] and of the Securities Exchange Act of 1934 [the 1934 Act] [Section 10(b)]. Although the Commission has obtained permanent injunctions against at least ten of the defendants, it was unsuccessful in its effort to gain preliminary injunctive relief against Schiffman, an attorney who allegedly prepared an opinion letter on the basis of which some of the unregistered securities were sold. Judge Tenney, after reviewing the affidavits, cross-affidavits, exhibits, and depositions filed by the SEC and by Schiffman, denied the SEC's request for an evidentiary hearing, on the grounds that there were no material facts in dispute, and concluded that Schiffman's conduct, although perhaps negligent, did not rise to a violation of the securities laws. Upon a careful examination of the record, we find the existence of a highly material factual conflict. Accordingly, we reverse and remand to Judge Tenney for an evidentiary hearing in which the disputed issues can be resolved.

I

....

In September, 1969, Louis Marder, representing the Westward Investment Corporation, and Bernard Goldenberg and Joseph Dye, representing Spectrum, Ltd., agreed to a merger of Westward into Spectrum. The purpose of this merger was to provide a vehicle for the distribution of unregistered Spectrum securities which could later be sold to an unwitting public.

Section 5(c) of the 1933 Act states that "it shall be unlawful for any person, directly or indirectly ... to sell ... any security unless a registration statement has been filed as to such security." To avoid this registration requirement, a plan was devised, principally by Marder and Goldenberg, which relied on a two-step procedure for securing exemption from Section 5. First, a large block of unregistered Spectrum common stock would be issued to the shareholders of Westward in the merger of Westward into Spectrum. This stock would be exempt from the registration mandate of Section 5 pursuant to [now rescinded] Commission Rule 133, which provided that the exchange of shares between a surviving corporation and the shareholders of a disappearing corporation in the course of a merger would not be considered a "sale" within the purview of Section 5. Second, under Section 4(1) of the 1933 Act, the recipients of this unregistered Spectrum Stock would be able to dispose of these securities, again without the filing of a registration statement as a predicate to the transaction, as long as the seller was not deemed to be "an issuer, underwriter or dealer" under the Act.

For Marder, who controlled Westward, successful implementation of this plan presented one obvious stumbling block — Rule 133 classified a controlling shareholder of the "constituent corporation" (Westward) as an "underwriter" and, therefore, a person not qualified for exemption under Section 4(1). Accordingly, prior to the merger Marder commenced distributing some of his Westward shares to various friends, many of whom, as the court below found, were in fact unaware of their status as Westward shareholders. Following the merger, Marder intended to effect the sale of the Spectrum stock received by his acquaintances in transactions which, because of the stock's nominal ownership by non-controlling former Westward shareholders, would appear to satisfy the criteria for a Section 4(1) exemption.

The stage was set for the successful charade upon consummation of the Spectrum-Westward merger on November 10, 1969. Of the 4,596,465 shares of Spectrum stock issued in the exchange, approximately one million shares went to Marder's corps of nominees. By obtaining the necessary stock powers from these individuals, Marder was in a position to begin the illicit sale of unregistered Spectrum securities.

On the day of the merger, November 10, Spectrum's general counsel, Morton Berger, wrote an opinion letter to Spectrum's transfer agent in which he instructed the agent on the proper classification of the Spectrum shares then being issued. Berger's letter, based upon representations by Goldenberg and Marder, included his opinion that the merger complied with the requirements of Rule 133 and that certain recipients of the newly-issued Spectrum stock should receive shares labelled "restricted" *i.e.,* not for public sale because these former Westward shareholders, whom Berger listed, were considered to be "underwriters" pursuant to Rule 133(c). Berger included his letter by opining that the remaining former Westward shareholders, whose names Berger did not recite, could be issued Spectrum securities without a restrictive legend.

On November 25, 1969, Berger wrote a second letter, this time to the president of Spectrum, in which he listed those persons who had received unrestricted shares of Spectrum stock pursuant to the merger. This letter, however, was not in the form of an opinion letter.

Retracing our steps, on November 13 and November 28, 1969, Marder delivered for sale a total of 125,000 shares of unrestricted Spectrum stock, nominally owned by William and John Doyen, to Michael Gardner, a principal at the registered broker-dealer firm of Gardner Securities. Gardner balked at the sale of these unregistered securities, despite their unrestricted nature, insisting upon an opinion letter which stated that these shares were considered exempt from the registration requirements of Section 5. Although Marder possessed the Berger letters of November 10 and November 25, Gardner viewed them as insufficient, apparently because the November 10 letter failed to specify the individuals entitled to exemption, while the November 25 letter did not purport to be an opinion letter.

Although Gardner called Berger about preparing the requisite opinion letter, Berger refused to issue such a letter on behalf of any shareholder. Because of this refusal, Gardner communicated with Schiffman stating that he wished to discuss a securities matter the details of which Gardner failed to provide on the telephone. Schiffman responded by meeting Gardner at his office.

It is at this juncture — Schiffman debut so to speak — that the crucial factual controversy arises. According to Schiffman's affidavit submitted in opposition to the motion for a preliminary injunction, he visited Gardner's office twice in late November. On the first occasion, he and Gardner spoke in general terms about Gardner's securities business and Gardner introduced him to James Morse, one of Gardner's clients. At the second meeting, several days later, Morse was again present at Gardner's office. On this occasion, Morse mentioned that a friend of his, a Mr. Doyen, was in need of some help and asked Schiffman if he would speak to Doyen. After Schiffman agreed, Morse telephoned Doyen. Morse handed the instrument to Schiffman and Doyen proceeded to explain to Schiffman that he owned some unregistered stock in Spectrum, Ltd. for which he wanted an opinion letter that would indicate that the securities could be sold without registration. Schiffman allegedly responded that since he had no knowledge of the underlying transactions, he would be hesitant to write such a letter. But, Schiffman claims that his reluctance was overcome when Morse showed him the two Berger letters. Schiffman then proceeded to advise Doyen that he would prepare an opinion letter which would "verify" Berger's opinion.

Schiffman's version of these meetings at Gardner's office is sharply in conflict with Gardner's recollection of the events, as described in his affidavit submitted by the SEC. Gardner recalls only one meeting with Schiffman at which not only Morse was present but Louis Marder as well. Gardner's affidavit then notes, quite specifically, that

> I [Gardner] introduced Schiffman to Marder and Morse for the purpose of Schiffman representing Marder and Morse. Marder and Morse asked Schiffman, in my presence, to prepare an opinion letter for securities of Spectrum that were going to be sold *by Marder and Morse.* [Emphasis added.]

The affidavit concludes with the statement:

> I do not recall at any time ... Morse telephoning one William Doyen, giving the telephone to Schiffman, and Schiffman speaking to Doyen about an opinion letter to be prepared by Schiffman concerning either Doyen's stock, or any other stock.

In any event, Gardner was evidently satisfied that Schiffman would write the opinion letter because, sometime before its preparation, he proceeded to sell 50,000 shares of Spectrum stock jointly owned by the Doyens. As for Schiffman, he claims to have arranged a conference with Berger so that he could learn more about the Spectrum stock for which he had agreed to write an opinion letter. What transpired at this meeting between Schiffman and Berger is also the subject of conflicting documentary versions. Both men agree that Berger gave Schiffman the two letters dated November 10 and November 25. Berger, however, in his affidavit submitted in the preliminary injunction proceeding, added that he warned Schiffman that he "suspected that this stock [the unregistered Spectrum securities] was going to be traded by a control person and therefore the stock should not be freely traded." This account did not appear in Berger's two prior depositions, also part of the record below. Schiffman, on the other hand, in his reply affidavit, denied that Berger uttered any warning whatsoever.

It is uncontroverted that following this meeting Schiffman prepared an opinion letter which closely paralleled the Berger opinion letter of November 10 with one key addition — it contained the names of those shareholders, mentioned only as a group by Berger, who could sell their Spectrum stock in a transaction exempt from the registration requirement of Section 5. Although Schiffman's letter, dated December 4, was addressed to Doyen, Schiffman delivered it to Gardner's office because Schiffman had never received Doyen's address. Subsequently, on December 8, Schiffman sent a second letter to Doyen, again through Gardner's office, in which Schiffman stated that his opinion letter of December 4 was not to be used for the sale of unregistered Spectrum stock. No such caveat, however, was incorporated in the December 4 letter.

The use to which Schiffman's opinion letter of December 4 was put is a matter of some uncertainty. The SEC has alleged that in January, 1970, Marder showed the Schiffman letter to "Canadian citizen #1" in order to assure this anonymous Canadian that the Spectrum shares that he had agreed to purchase from Marder could be traded without registration. The SEC charges that "Canadian citizen #1" subsequently sold 15,000 shares of this unregistered Spectrum stock in the Canadian market. Although these allegations were never contested by Schiffman, they also remain unsupported by any independent evidence.

Eighteen months after this documentary joust commenced, Judge Tenney, on October 10, 1972, denied the SEC's request for a preliminary injunction to enjoin Schiffman from further violations of §§ 5(a), 5(c) and 17(a) of the 1933 Act and § 10(b) of the 1934 Act. He concluded that there was no evidence, apart from the bare allegations by the SEC, that any unregistered Spectrum stock had been sold on the basis of Schiffman's opinion letter. Recognizing that Schiffman might still have violated the securities laws as an aider and abettor, the district court, after pronouncing a standard of liability which required actual knowledge of the illegal scheme, found a dearth of credible evidence in the papers before him to sustain a finding of such knowledge on Schiffman's part. Judge Tenney finally noted that even if Schiffman were considered negligent in preparing his opinion letter, there had been no showing that, unless enjoined, he would be likely to run afoul of the law in the future.

II

We should note, at the outset, that had the denial of temporary injunctive relief been based solely on the failure to demonstrate a propensity for future violations, we would hesitate before disturbing such conclusion. Judge Tenney, however, went well beyond this rationale, finding no evidence whatsoever of any violation, nor even sufficient factual uncertainty to justify an evidentiary hearing. It is especially as to this latter holding, the declination to hold an evidentiary hearing, that we find error for we believe that the district judge failed to properly heed our admonition that "a judge should not resolve a factual dispute on affidavits or depositions for then he is merely showing a preference for 'one piece of paper to another.' *Sims v. Greene,* 161 F.2d 87, 88 (3d Cir. 1947)." *Dopp v. Franklin National Bank,* 461 F.2d 873, 879 (2d Cir. 1972).

... Examination of this record, moreover, discloses a sharp factual conflict bearing heavily on the critical question of Schiffman's actual knowledge of the scheme to illicitly distribute unregistered Spectrum stock at the time he agreed to draft the December 4 opinion letter.

On Schiffman's part, he has steadfastly maintained that he was ignorant of the Marder plan. Yet, these protestations of innocence are met squarely on two fronts by the affidavits of Gardner and Berger. Although we do not disagree with the district court that the Berger affidavit would seem to be incredible on its face in light of Berger's failure to make any mention of his alleged warning to Schiffman in the course of two prior depositions, we cannot overlook the dispute between Gardner and Schiffman over the events and participants at the crucial meeting at Gardner's office in late November, 1969. If Gardner's statement that Marder personally asked Schiffman for an opinion letter so that Marder could sell unregistered Spectrum stock is true — and only a hearing could determine this — then Schiffman's claim of unawareness of the scheme would appear thin. To be sure, Gardner's veracity may be questioned, but no more nor less than Schiffman's, in view of Schiffman's stake in the outcome of this lawsuit. Accordingly, since oral testimony is a medium far superior for evaluating credibility than the cold written word, we consider an evidentiary hearing essential to the proper disposition of this case.

....

For the reasons stated, the order of the district court is reversed and the case remanded for further proceedings.

....

Carl W. Schneider, Joseph M. Manko & Robert S. Kant, Going Public: Practice, Procedure and Consequences, Bowne & Co., Inc. (1996)*

Introduction

When a company wishes to "go public" it faces a complex and challenging process. It is the purpose of this article to focus on the sections of the Securities Act of 1933 (the '33 Act) dealing with registration as it applies to companies selling securities to the public for the first time "going public" or engaging in an initial public offering (IPO). The authors' aim is to cover the practice and procedure, as well as certain important consequences, of going public. In a nutshell, the '33 Act is designed to prohibit the public distribution of securities without disclosure of relevant information to the investor. In this context, distribution refers to a public offering by the company itself a "primary offering." The '33 Act also covers certain offerings by existing security holders, who

---

may or may not be those persons who control the company "secondary offerings" or, more opprobriously, "bailouts."

....

Advantages and Disadvantages of Going Public

Among the more common advantages of going public are the following:

1. Funds are obtained from the offering. When the securities are sold for the account of the company, the money derived may be used for such common purposes as increasing working capital, performing research and development, expanding plant and equipment, retiring existing indebtedness, or diversifying company operations. In a secondary offering, the proceeds, of course, go to the selling security holders.

2. A public offering of stock will improve net worth, enabling the company to obtain capital or borrowings on more favorable terms. Once a public market is created, and if the stock performs well in the continuing aftermarket, substantial additional equity capital can be raised from the public and also privately from institutional investors on favorable terms. The company can offer investors a security with liquidity and an ascertainable market value. Thus, management's future financing alternatives are increased following an initial public offering.

3. Many companies contemplate expansion through acquisitions of other businesses. A company with publicly-traded stock is in a position to make acquisitions for its own securities without depleting its cash.

4. The business may be better able to attract and retain personnel if it can offer them stock having a public market or options to purchase such stock. The use of stock and stock options may make it possible for employees to realize capital gains for tax purposes, in lieu of ordinary income. Currently, capital gains generally are taxed at a lower rate than ordinary income. In addition to the lower tax rate for the capital gains, employees may derive other benefits from realizing capital gains rather than ordinary income.

5. Through public ownership of its securities, the company may gain prestige, become better known, and thereby improve its business operations. In addition, the company's customers and suppliers often become shareholders and thus acquire an interest in purchasing its products or services. This reason for going public is especially applicable to companies distributing consumer goods or otherwise dealing with the public at large.

6. Liquidity is achieved for the owners, including venture capital and other professional investors, that require an exit strategy in order to achieve returns on their investment. Before going public, ownership of a fractional part or even the whole of a closely held business is normally an asset with no ready market. Once the company becomes publicly owned, there will be a ready market for as little as 100 shares, or even less, which may present a fraction of one percent of the outstanding equity. As noted below, however, controlling shareholders may not sell the securities of the company they control as freely as securities of other

corporations that they do not control. There are some very important limitations to the sale of control stock, and considerable advance planning is often required when a disposition is to be made.

7. Public ownership may enable company principals to eliminate existing personal guarantees to lenders, landlords, and suppliers and generally to avoid any future personal guarantees.

8. By establishing a public market for the stock of a company, the owners usually achieve a psychological sense of financial success and self-fulfillment as well as a high degree of liquidity for their own investment.

Among the disadvantages of going public, aside from the relatively high expense, are the following:

1. Once the public is admitted to ownership, information must be disclosed. Owners may be reluctant to make public such information as salaries and transactions with management. Owners of a privately held business often fear that disclosure of certain information, such as sales, profits, competitive position, mode of operation, and material contracts, would place them at a severe competitive disadvantage, although the significant adverse consequences which were envisioned rarely occur in the authors' experience.

2. By incurring a responsibility to the public, the owners of a business lose some flexibility in management. There are practical, if not legal, limitations on salaries and fringe benefits, relatives on the payroll, and many other operating procedures. Certain business or investment opportunities, which might have been available personally to the former owners, may have to be turned over to the company they control. Ability to act quickly may be lost, especially when approval is required of shareholders or outside directors.

3. Once a company is publicly owned, management inevitably will consider the impact on the market price of its stock when making various decisions. For example, a decision whether to undertake a research and development program, which can adversely affect income in the short run, or a decision whether to risk a strike in a labor negotiation, might then be considered in light of its impact on the stock. While it is felt that management's preoccupation with day-to-day stock market price fluctuations is unwholesome and should be avoided, there are no doubt some situations in which a legitimate concern for stock market impact properly limits the practical alternatives of a public company.

4. There are many additional expenses, typically ranging from $ 50,000 to $ 200,000 annually, and administrative problems for a publicly owned company. Routine legal and accounting fees can increase materially. Recurring expenses include the preparation and distribution of proxy material and annual reports to shareholders, the preparation and filing with the Securities and Exchange Commission (the SEC or Commission) of reports under the Securities Exchange Act of 1934 (the '34 Act), including the costs of complying with the electronic filing requirements described below, and the expenditure of fees for a transfer agent, a registrar and, sometimes, a public relations consultant. There is also a

cost that may be considerable in terms of executive time devoted to shareholder relations and public disclosures.

5. Insiders may be threatened with the loss of control of the company if a sufficiently large proportion of the shares are sold to the public. The number of shares to be sold is a matter of negotiation between the owners of the company, who are fearful of a dilution of management control, and the underwriters, who are hopeful of assuring a sufficiently large floating supply of the stock after the offering. In addition, once the public is admitted to ownership, progressive dilution of the insiders' holdings by subsequent public offerings, secondary financings, and acquisitions must be contemplated. Control is often bolstered through various means, including staggered terms for directors, supermajority voting provisions, voting trust agreements, and special classes of stock.

6. In the current legal environment, a public company and its officers and directors may become subject to a class action or derivative lawsuit alleging violations of corporate and securities laws. Even if the claim has no merit, establishing a defense can be time-consuming, distracting, and expensive.

7. The owners of a privately held business are often in high tax brackets and prefer that the company pay either no or low dividends, although the underwriters may require otherwise. Such problems are often resolved in the underwriters' favor, occasionally with the owners arranging to waive some or all dividends, or to hold a special stock which bears no dividends, for certain periods.

8. One frequently mentioned advantage of going public is to have an equity interest in the business that can be converted readily into cash to pay estate taxes. It is often noted that a public market tends to simplify the question of valuation. It should not be overlooked, however, that a public offering also can be very disadvantageous from an estate tax point of view. When the public evaluates the security, as it often does, at a great many times its book value and at a very high multiple of earnings, the estate tax valuation, which is determined at least in part by reference to the public market price, may be considerably higher than the valuation that would have been established if the business were privately owned.

Eligibility for Public Financing

In evaluating the advisability of going public, as well as pricing the company's stock, the underwriters will consider the amount and trend of the company's sales and earnings (compared with the trend in its industry), the adequacy of its present and projected working capital and cash flow positions, the experience, integrity, and quality of its management, the likelihood of management's being able to accept the burden of responsibility to a public shareholder group, and the growth potential of its business. Other factors evaluated include the nature and number of its customers, its sources of supply, its inclination and ability to diversify, and its relative competitive position. In terms of what underwriters will require, there is often a direct relationship between the company's sales and earnings record and the existence of growth potential in the company's industry the less growth potential for the company the underwriters perceive, the more historic earnings they will require.

....

Selection of an Underwriter

Once the decision has been made to go public, the parties immediately face perhaps the most important decision to be made selecting the managing underwriter. Investment banking firms vary widely in prestige, financial strength, and ability to provide the various services that the company can expect. Some underwriters are not ordinarily interested in first offerings, while others specialize in them. Some underwriters have particular stature and experience in specific industries. Underwriters may have pre-existing relationships with customers, suppliers, or competitors of a prospective company going public, which can be both an advantage and a disadvantage from varying points of view. In short, a managing underwriter appropriate for one company may be wholly inappropriate for another.

....

Several services can be expected from the underwriters. Initially, the managing underwriter will take the lead in forming the underwriting syndicate that is, a group of underwriters that will jointly share the responsibilities, rewards, and risks of selling the stock to the public. The managing underwriter and certain members of the underwriting syndicate also are expected to provide aftermarket support for the security being sold. They may serve as over-the-counter market makers that stand ready to purchase or sell the stock in the interdealer market; they may purchase the stock for their own account; and they may take the initiative in bringing the stock to the attention of analysts and investors, including their own customers....

In addition, managing underwriters traditionally supply other investment banking services to the company following the offering. They will assist in obtaining additional financing from public or private sources as the need arises, advise the company concerning possible acquisitions, and generally make available their expertise as financial institutions. In some cases, they will recommend (and in isolated cases supply) experienced persons to become members of the company's board of directors or to serve as officers or key employees.

....

Alternative methods of raising capital may be increasing. The SEC recently allowed a company to use the Internet to offer and sell its own stock directly to the public. In addition, some companies are seeking to achieve public ownership through the "back door" approach of merging into a publicly traded company typically one with minimal assets and operations or a business much smaller than the company going public through this technique. As a result, the former stockholders of the previously private company own the bulk of the outstanding stock of the post-merger public company.

Structure of the Offering

Once a company has decided to make a public offering, it must determine, in consultation with its managing underwriter, what class of securities should be offered. Most first offerings include common stock. Some first offerings consist of a package including other securities such as debentures, which may or may not be convertible into common stock, or warrants to purchase common stock....

There are two other interrelated variables to consider: the number of shares offered and the offering price per share. It is generally felt that a minimum of 500,000 to 750,000 shares, and preferably 1,000,000 shares or even more, is desirable in the public "float" to constitute a broad national distribution and to support an active trading market thereafter. As to price level, many of the larger investment banking firms and many investors are not particularly interested in dealing with securities offered at less than $ 10 per share, with the $ 12 to $ 20 range being preferred. The $ 5 level is often another psychological break-point below which many investment bankers and investors lose interest. In addition, many larger brokerage firms prohibit their brokers from soliciting orders for stocks trading under $ 5 per share. Any offering with an initial price of $ 20 or more is likely to import a prestige image. During some periods of interest in new issues, however, many high risk issues have been marketed at or below $ 1 per share.

For an offering of $ 10,000,000, 1,000,000 shares at $ 10 per share would be considered in the optimum range. If the offering is below $ 10,000,000, a decrease in the offering price per share is recommended, rather than a reduction in the number of shares offered below 1,000,000. These are matters of judgment, however, which should be reviewed carefully with the underwriters in each situation....

In today's increasingly institutional market, total offering size has increased and offerings of less than $ 20 million generally are underwritten by local or regional investment banking firms....

Small Business Issuers

As part of the Commission's so-called Small Business Initiative, the Commission in August 1992 made comprehensive changes to its rules and forms designed to decrease the burdens of raising capital for small business issuers. Among other matters, these changes affected the process by which securities are registered for public sale, the exemptions that permit unregistered sales of securities both publicly and privately, and the ongoing periodic reporting requirements that are applicable to publicly owned companies, all of which are described below. The reduced burdens apply to "small business issuers" that generally include companies meeting the following criteria: the company has annual revenue less than $ 25 million; its "public float" (*i.e.* the aggregate market value of its outstanding securities held by non-affiliates) does not exceed $ 25 million which, in the case of an initial public offering, is computed on the basis of the number of shares outstanding prior to the offering and the estimated public offering price of the securities; it is a U.S. or Canadian issuer; it is not an investment company; and it is not a majority owned subsidiary of a non-small business issuer. For this purpose, the term "affiliate" generally encompasses persons who control the company, which typically includes for small businesses most if not all directors, senior officers, and principal shareholders. Transitional rules detail the time periods for applying these tests to determine when an issuer phases into and out of small business issuer status. Various forms and regulations available for the use of small business issuers have an "SB" denomination and generally follow in a somewhat simplified version the overall form and content of the corresponding traditional forms.

The Registration Statement

The registration statement is the disclosure document required to be filed with the SEC in connection with a registered offering. It consists physically of two principal parts. Part I of the registration statement is the prospectus, which is the only part that normally goes to the public offerees of the securities. It is the legal offering document. Part II of the registration statement contains supplemental information, which is available for public inspection at the office of the SEC.

The registration forms, Regulation S-K or Regulation S-B (as discussed below), Regulation S-X, and the Industry Guides (when applicable) specify the information to be contained in the registration statement. Regulation S-K or S-B sets forth detailed disclosure requirements, which are applicable in various contexts under the securities laws; Regulation S-X similarly sets forth financial statement requirements for certain offerings; and the Industry Guides require specific disclosure applicable to certain prescribed businesses such as oil and gas and banking. In addition, Regulation C sets forth certain general requirements as to the registration of securities including filing fees, the number of copies of the registration statements and amendments to be filed, signature requirements, paper and type size, and other mechanical aspects of registration.

The registration forms contain a series of "items" and instructions (generally referring to the disclosure requirements contained in Regulation S-K or Regulation S-B) in response to which disclosures must be made. But they are not forms in the sense that they have blanks to be completed like a tax return. Traditionally, the prospectus describes the company's business and responds to all the disclosures required in narrative rather than item-and-answer form. It is prepared as a brochure describing the company and the securities to be offered. The usual prospectus is a fairly stylized document, and there is a customary sequence for organizing the material. The material typically is presented under descriptive captions, such as "Business," "Management," "Dividend Policy," "Use of Proceeds," and "Underwriting," with the disclosures responding to all of the information required by the items in the form, but with the information presented in a different sequence and under different captions than those called for by the form.

Form S-1 traditionally has been the most common registration form. Form S-1 filings are made at the Commission's principal office in Washington, D.C.

As part of the Small Business Initiative, the Commission adopted a simpler Form SB-2 to be used for cash offerings by small business issuers. Form SB-2 may be used to register an unlimited amount of securities by any small business issuer whether or not a reporting company....

Form SB-2 may be used for offerings by the issuer of newly issued securities as well as secondary offerings of outstanding securities as long as the consideration received is cash. Form SB-2 filings for initial public offerings [are] made at the SEC's principal office in Washington, D.C....

The principal advantages of Form SB-2 over Form S-1 are its somewhat less demanding requirements regarding financial statements....

Form SB-1 may be used to register securities in offerings of up to $ 10 million in any continuous 12-month period.... Form SB-1 permits a small business issuer to [write the registration statement in question and answer format.] ....

....

In preparing a prospectus, the applicable form is merely the beginning. The forms are quite general and apply to all types of businesses, securities, and offerings, except for a few industries or limited situations for which special forms have been prepared. In the course of administration over the years, the Commission has given specific content to the general disclosure requirements. It often requires disclosures on a number of points within the scope of the form, but not explicitly covered by the form itself. Furthermore, in addition to the information that the form expressly requires, the company must add any information necessary to make the statements made not misleading.[2] Thus, the prospectus may not contain a half-truth — a statement that may be literally true but is misleading in context.

....

The Commission also has evolved certain principles of emphasis in highlighting disclosures of adverse facts. It cannot prohibit an offering from being made if disclosure is adequate, but its policies on disclosure can make the offering look highly unattractive....

....

The SEC, which reviews the registration statement, has no authority to pass on the merits of a particular offering. The SEC has no general power to prohibit an offering because it considers the investment opportunity to be a poor risk. The sole thrust of the federal statute is disclosure of relevant information. No matter how speculative the investment, no matter how poor the risk, the offering will comply with federal law if all the required facts are disclosed. By contrast, some state securities, or "blue sky" laws, which are applicable in the jurisdictions in which the distribution takes place, do regulate the merits of the securities.

---

[2] SEC Securities Act Rule 408.

Typically, their standards are very indefinite, often expressed in terms of offerings which are "fair, just and equitable." In practice, state administrators exercise broad discretion in determining which offerings may be sold in their states.

....

The prospectus is a somewhat schizophrenic document, having two purposes which often present conflicting pulls. On the one hand, it is a selling document. It is used by the managing underwriter to form the underwriting syndicate and a dealer group and by the underwriters and dealers to sell the securities to the public. From this point of view, it is desirable to present the best possible image. On the other hand, the prospectus is a disclosure document, an insurance policy against liability. With the view toward protection against liability, there is a tendency to resolve all doubts against the company and to make things look as bleak as possible....

Many years ago, it was traditional to confine prospectuses principally to objectively verifiable statements of historic fact. It is now considered proper, and in some instances essential, to include some information in a prospectus, either favorable or adverse to the company, which is predictive or based upon opinions or subjective evaluations. However, no such "soft information" should be included in the prospectus unless it has a reasonable basis in fact and represents management's good faith judgment.

Preparing the Registration Statement

The "quarterback" in preparing the registration statement is normally the attorney for the company. Company counsel is principally responsible for preparing the non-financial parts of the registration statement. The managing underwriter or its counsel may play an active role in drafting various sections of the prospectus, particularly those that will assist in marketing the shares. Drafts are circulated to all concerned. There are normally at least a few "all hands" drafting sessions prior to filing the registration statement, attended by management personnel of the company, counsel for the company, the company's auditors, representatives of the managing underwriter, and underwriters' counsel. Although the degree of input from each of the participants may differ depending on various factors, such as the quality of the initial draft, the experience level of the participants, the uniqueness of the company, and the particular issues in question, major revisions generally result from these drafting sessions. Close cooperation is required among counsel for the company, the underwriters' counsel, the accountants, and the printer. Unless each knows exactly what the others expect, additional delay, expense, and irritation are predictable.

....

Review by the SEC

After the registration statement is filed initially, the Commission's Division of Corporation Finance reviews it to see that it responds appropriately to the applicable form. The Division's staff almost always finds some actual or perceived deficiencies, which are communicated through a "letter of comments" or possibly (especially after the initial comments have been given) by telephone call, typically directed to company counsel. Amendments to the registration statement then are filed in response to the comments. Quite often, there are additional comments, conveyed either by letter or telephone, on amended filings. When the comments are reflected to the satisfaction of the SEC staff, the SEC issues an order allowing the registration statement to become effective. Only after the registration statement is effective may sales to the public take place.

....

Pre-Effective and Post-Effective Offers

Prior to the initial filing of the registration statement, no public offering, either orally or in writing, is permitted. For this purpose, the concept of offering has been given an expansive interpretation. Publicity about the company or its products may be considered an illegal offering, in the sense that it is designed to stimulate an interest in the securities, even if the securities themselves are not mentioned. A violation of this prohibition is often referred to as "gun jumping." Under a specific rule, limited announcements concerning the proposal to make a public offering through a registration statement are permitted.

In the interval between the first filing with the Commission (or sometimes after a second filing responding to comments) and the effective date, the so-called "waiting period," the company and the underwriters distribute preliminary or "red herring" prospectuses, officially referred to as a "prospectus subject to completion." The term "red herring" derives from the legend historically required to be printed in red ink on the cover of any prospectus that is distributed before the effective date of the registration statement. The legend is to the effect that a registration statement has been filed but has not become effective, that the information contained in the registration statement is subject to completion or amendment, and that the securities may not be sold nor may offers to buy be accepted prior to the effective date of the registration statement.

....

During the waiting period, oral selling efforts are permitted but no written sales literature that is, "free writing" is permitted other than the preliminary prospectus. Tombstone advertisements, so-called because the very limited notice of the offering which is permitted is often presented in a form resembling a tombstone, are not considered selling literature and may be published during the waiting period,[3] although it is much more common for them to be published after the effective date. In addition, publicly held companies must continue to make timely disclosure of factual information concerning themselves and their products during this waiting period so as not to interrupt the normal flow of information;

---

[3] Securities Act of 1933 § 2[(a)](10)(b). *See also* SEC Securities Act Rule 134.

of course, they may not do so to instigate publicity to facilitate the sale of stock. Through the use of a red herring prospectus and by making oral offers by telephone or otherwise, the underwriters may offer the security and may accept "indications of interest" from purchasers prior to the effective date. However, as indicated, no sales can be made during the waiting period.

. . . .

In a bow to cyberspace, the SEC has authorized the delivery of electronic prospectuses....

. . . .

The Underwriting Agreement

. . . .

In a "firm commitment" underwriting agreement, the underwriters agree that they will purchase the shares being offered for the purpose of resale to the public. The underwriters must pay for and hold the shares for their own account if they are not successful in finding public purchasers. This form of underwriting almost always is used by the larger underwriters and provides the greater assurance of raising the desired funds. In the other common type of underwriting arrangement, the underwriters agree to use their "best efforts" to sell the issue as the company's agent. To the extent that purchasers cannot be found, the issue is not sold. Some best efforts agreements provide that no shares will be sold unless buyers can be found for all shares, while others set a lower minimum such as 50 percent. For certain special types of securities, such as limited partnership offerings, even the major underwriters normally use the best efforts or agency underwriting relationship.

. . . .

The binding firm underwriting agreement normally is not signed until the effective date of the registration statement or shortly thereafter. Thus, throughout the process of preparing the registration statement and during the waiting period, the company has incurred very substantial expenses with no assurance that the offering will take place. It is not uncommon for an offering to abort, especially for small and highly speculative offerings, if there are adverse market developments during the waiting period.

. . . .

Timetable

Although businesspersons find it difficult to believe, the average first public offering normally requires two to three months of intensive work before the registration statement can be filed....

. . . .

The SEC's current policy calls for the issuance of an initial letter of comments within 30 days of the filing of a registration statement....

The overall time lapse between the beginning of preparation of a company's first registration statement and the final effective date may well exceed six months. Rarely will it be less than three months.

....

Expenses

A major expense in going public is usually the underwriters' compensation. The underwriting cash discount or cash commission on a new issue generally ranges from seven percent to ten percent of the public offering price. The maximum amount of direct and indirect underwriting compensation is regulated by the [National Association of Securities Dealers, Inc. (NASD)]. Normally, the three largest additional expenses are legal fees, accounting fees, and printing costs. The following are general estimates of the expenses for a typical medium size offering on Form S-1.

Legal fees for a first offering can vary over a wide range, depending on the size and complexity of the offering, the ease with which information can be assembled and verified, the extent of risk factors or other difficult disclosures, and other factors. Fees in the range of $ 150,000 to $ 450,000 would be typical....

Accounting fees can vary significantly, depending on the complexity of the business .... If there have been no prior audits, new accountants are engaged at the time of the offering, or the business or businesses of the company going public are being restructured, fees ranging from $ 100,000 to $ 250,000 would not be unusual....

....

Printing expenses for registration statements and various underwriting documents typically are in a range of $ 75,000 to $ 175,000, but larger charges are not unusual. Color printing, maps, charts, and other graphics, if used, can add significantly to the printing expense....

For each registration statement, there is a filing fee at the rate of 1/33rd of one percent of the maximum aggregate offering price of the securities[, decreasing each year through fiscal year 2006], which fee is non-refundable.

Among the other expenses to be borne are transfer taxes (in the event of a secondary offering), if applicable, transfer agent and registrar fees, printing of stock certificates, and "blue sky" expenses. The company generally is required to reimburse the underwriter for the NASD filing fee, which is computed at the rate of $ 500 plus 0.01 percent of the maximum aggregate offering price of the securities, with a maximum fee of $ 30,500. Especially for smaller offerings with smaller underwriters, the company may agree to pay an expense allowance (sometimes on an accountable basis and sometimes on a non-accountable basis) to the underwriters. This is a negotiated figure, which can range from several thousand dollars to $ 100,000 or more in some cases, with three percent of the total offering price being the upper limit....

....

For a normal first public stock offering in the $ 10 million to $ 50 million range, total expenses in the $ 400,000 to $ 1,000,000 range would be typical, exclusive of the underwriting discount or commission, but inclusive of any expense allowance (whether or not accountable) payable to the underwriters....

....

In addition to cash disbursements, there are other costs to consider when going public. As part of the arrangement, underwriters sometimes insist upon receiving options or warrants exercisable over a number of years to purchase the securities being offered at a price usually equal to or above the offering price....

....

Another cost of going public arises out of the heavy burden and time demand it may impose on the company's administrative and executive personnel. Throughout the period of selecting the underwriters and preparing the registration statement, these activities can, and often do, absorb a significant amount of executive time.

Liabilities

Under the '33 Act and related statutes, civil and criminal liability may arise from material misstatements or omissions in a registration statement when it becomes effective, including the final prospectus; from failure to comply with applicable registration requirements; from failure to supply a final prospectus in connection with specified activities; and from engaging in fraudulent transactions. Under various provisions, directors, certain officers who must sign the registration statement, underwriters, controlling persons, and experts (such as accountants but normally not attorneys) participating in the registration also may be subject to the same liabilities as are imposed upon the company. The parties named are jointly and severally liable and their potential civil liability is the full sales price of the security.

Under the '33 Act, the company is absolutely liable for material deficiencies in the registration statement irrespective of good faith or the exercise of due diligence. However, certain "due diligence" defenses against liability are available to directors, officers who sign the registration statement, underwriters, experts, and controlling persons if they neither knew of the deficiencies in the registration statement nor had reason to know of them upon the exercise of due diligence....

....

'34 Act Consequences of Going Public

....

There are certain continuing consequences arising under the '34 Act once a company goes public. If any company has total assets of more than $ 10 million and a class of equity securities held by [at least] 500 persons at any fiscal year end, such class of equity securities must be registered under Section 12(g) within

120 days after the first fiscal year end on which the company meets these tests. Likewise, any company that has a class of securities listed on a stock exchange must register those securities under Section 12(b). These registrations under Section 12 of the '34 Act are one time registrations, which apply to that entire class of securities, and should be distinguished from registrations under the '33 Act, which relate only to specific securities involved in a particular offering.

Registration under the '34 Act involves five separate sets of legal obligations relating to periodic reporting, proxy solicitation, insider trading, tender offers and related matters, and the Foreign Corrupt Practices Act.

Periodic Reporting

The company must file certain periodic reports with the Commission. Companies with exchange listed securities also file copies with the exchange. The required reports include a Form 10-K or Form 10-KSB report, which is filed with the SEC on an annual basis. The Form 10-K or Form 10-KSB report requires a description of the company's business, property, and financial condition. The wording of the disclosure items is substantially similar to the corresponding disclosure items in the '33 Act registration form applicable to the company for applicable periods. The general philosophy of the current Form 10-K or Form 10-KSB is to keep the full range of '33 Act registration statement disclosures current on an annual basis. However, many companies have a more condensed disclosure in their Form 10-Ks or Form 10-KSBs than in their '33 Act prospectuses.

In addition, the company must file interim quarterly reports on Form 10-Q or Form 10-QSB. The principal content of Form 10-Q or Form 10-QSB is unaudited quarterly financial information, but there are also other items which call for disclosures only if specific reportable events have occurred during the period covered by the report. Furthermore, for certain significant events, a report must be filed on Form 8-K, which is normally due within 15 calendar days or, in two circumstances, five business days after the reportable event.

Companies that have filed a registration statement under the '33 Act are required under Section 15(d) of the '34 Act to file periodic reports for the balance of the year in which the registration statement becomes effective and for each subsequent year if they have 300 or more holders of the registered security at the start of the fiscal year....

Proxy Solicitation

If any person, including the company itself or its management, solicits proxies from the holders of a class of securities registered under Section 12(b) or (g) of the '34 Act, such person must comply with the Commission's proxy rules promulgated under Section 14(a) of the '34 Act. These rules require a proxy statement describing the matters being submitted to a vote of the security holders together with a form of proxy on which they can vote for or against each matter being submitted. The extent of the disclosure required on any matter being submitted to a vote is substantially equivalent to the disclosure required on the same such matter in the applicable '33 Act registration statement and may vary depending on whether the company is a small business issuer. The proxy material is reviewed by the Commission in a manner generally similar to the procedure used for '33 Act registration statements but in a shorter period of time.

The proxy rules also require that an annual report to shareholders must be distributed with or before the solicitation of proxies for the annual election of directors. The proxy rules prescribe certain disclosure requirements for the company's annual report to shareholders. If a matter is being submitted to a vote of security holders of a registered class and the company does not solicit proxies, it is required to supply an information statement that contains substantially the same information as would appear in a proxy statement.

Insider Trading Under Section 16

Section 16(a) of the '34 Act requires certain reports to be filed by directors and officers of any company with a class of equity securities registered under the '34 Act, and also by beneficial holders of more than 10 percent of any class of such securities. Such "reporting persons" must report their beneficial holdings of all equity securities of the company .... There are detailed rules as to what constitutes beneficial holdings, which can include indirect holdings through entities such as partnerships, trusts, and estates, and may also include securities owned by certain close relatives of the reporting person.

....

The reporting persons are also subject to the "short-swing profit recapture" provisions of Section 16(b) of the '34 Act. If any reporting person realizes any profit, with certain exceptions, on a purchase and subsequent sale, or sale and subsequent purchase, of any class of equity security within a six-month period, that person may be required to pay such profit over to the company....

....

Under Section 16(c), reporting persons are prohibited from selling securities "short" or selling securities that they own but do not plan to deliver currently, so-called "short sales against the box."

Tender Rules and Related Matters

The '34 Act includes several provisions relating generally to tender offers for securities registered under the '34 Act. Related provisions apply to persons owning beneficially more than five percent of such securities, even if no tender offer has been involved. If, after '34 Act registration of a class of equity securities, any person or group acting in concert becomes the owner of more than five percent of the securities of any such class or makes a tender offer that would result in that person becoming an owner of more than five percent of such class, that person must make certain disclosures to the SEC, the company and, in some instances, the company's shareholders. There also are substantive requirements relating to the mechanics of tender offers, including limitations on activities by the company in resisting the tender offer and purchasing its own shares while the tender offer is pending.

Foreign Corrupt Practices Act

The Foreign Corrupt Practices Act, which amended the '34 Act, requires a company to make and keep books, records, and accounts which, in reasonable detail, accurately and fairly reflect a company's transactions and dispositions of assets and to devise and maintain a system of internal accounting controls. These are very significant substantive provisions that are not related in any way to either foreign activities or corrupt practices, as suggested by the title of the Act. There are other provisions of this Act that relate, in fact, to irregular payments abroad and matters that would be considered to be corrupt foreign practices.

Other Consequences of Going Public

Apart from the specific requirements under the '34 Act that become applicable once a publicly owned company registers under that act, there are other requirements generally applicable to all publicly owned companies and their insiders.

Timely Disclosure of Material Developments

Good corporate practice and, to a significant degree, the antifraud provisions under the '33 and '34 Acts, require publicly held companies to make timely disclosure to the public at large of any developments in their affairs that would be material to public investors, whether favorable or unfavorable. Such disclosures normally take place through press releases, which may be supplemented by communications directly to shareholders. The SEC requires prompt and accurate public disclosure of material corporate developments. Companies with securities listed on a stock exchange are subject to the exchange's requirements to make timely disclosures. Companies whose securities are traded in the Nasdaq system must conform to NASD policies on timely disclosures. While the scope of these various disclosure requirements is difficult to define with precision, the general trend has been toward requiting higher standards of disclosure. The possible consequences of failing to comply with these disclosure standards include civil liability, criminal penalties, suspension of trading, various injunctive remedies, and disgorgement of any profits realized from improper trading on inside information.

Restrictions on Trading on Undisclosed Inside Information

Until such time as information concerning material developments has been disclosed adequately to the public, it is unlawful for any person deriving such information from the company to trade on the basis of such information. While it is customary to speak of these restrictions as dealing with "insiders" and "inside information," they clearly apply to anyone deriving the information from the company. Thus, the restricted group may include not only directors and top executives, but also lower level employees and even persons not affiliated with the company, so-called "tippees," who may receive the information from an informed source within the company.

....

Sale of Restricted and Control Stock

Even after a company becomes publicly owned, persons holding restricted stock (generally shares acquired in private placements) and controlling shareholders holding any stock (including shares acquired on the open market) are not completely free to sell their own shares in the public securities markets without registration. There are, however, certain specific "leakage" provisions under Rule 144 that permit limited sales under defined circumstances for securities of companies that meet specified tests regarding the public availability of current information....

....

Mandated Electronic Filing Under the Edgar System

Under the Commission's Electronic Data Gathering, Analysis and Retrieval System (EDGAR), a company that files a registration statement for its initial public offering is required to submit its filings electronically. Once a company has securities registered under either the '33 Act or '34 Act, virtually all documents flied with the Commission must be filed electronically....

....

Conclusion

The process of going public is a major development in the business life of any company. It is a step to be taken only after a thorough analysis of the advantages, disadvantages, consequences, and alternative means of financing. Going public is a relatively time consuming and expensive means of raising capital, although the commensurate benefits may more than outweigh these disadvantages in the appropriate situation.

....

Chapter 17

PROXY REGULATION

Situation

Before Biologistics, Inc., got very far in its thinking about raising cash through a sale of securities, it found itself presented with another opportunity. Daytron Corporation, a large conglomerate that is incorporated in the same state as Biologistics and whose common stock is traded on a national stock exchange, became interested in acquiring Biologistics. Daytron's officers said they would wish to retain current management and would give them a free hand so long as Biologistics remains successful. Daytron would provide the needed cash for exploitation of the just patented process along with production and marketing assistance.

Daytron and the shareholders of Biologistics, Inc. have now come to an agreement on an exchange of stock. Certain Daytron shareholders are against Daytron's doing further acquisitions, however, and have indicated that they may fight this acquisition by one means or another. Daytron does not have any authorized but unissued shares, so it will have to amend its Articles of Incorporation to increase its number of authorized shares. It will hold a special meeting of its shareholders to approve the amendment and will solicit shareholders' proxies for the meeting. In its proxy materials it will describe Biologistics, Inc. and its business, and because of this has asked that your firm assist in the drafting of the proxy materials.

Anderson and Baker have agreed that you should help Daytron's lawyers with the proxy work. In light of the opposition of some Daytron shareholders to the acquisition, Anderson and Baker want you to discuss with them the chance that Daytron will not be able to proceed with the exchange of stock.

———

Shareholders may vote either in person or by proxy. To do the latter, a shareholder simply appoints someone else as his or her agent for the purpose of voting. State corporation statutes typically say very little about proxy voting, leaving to agency law most of its regulation at the state level. This is probably all the law that is needed in the typical close corporation, where a shareholder is likely to be personally involved in the corporation, or at least is likely to know whoever solicits his or her proxy. What is missing in state law, however, is regulation to protect shareholders of publicly held corporations from being asked to give their proxies, to persons they do not know, for purposes that are not fully explained.

The Securities Exchange Act of 1934 has filled this gap in state proxy law. The federal proxy regulation scheme is found in § 14 of the Exchange Act and the rules of the Securities and Exchange Commission. The thrust of the regulation is disclosure. That is, with minor exceptions neither Congress nor the SEC has attempted to regulate who may solicit proxies or under what circumstances proxies may be solicited. In the main, the regulation simply requires full and detailed disclosure of prescribed information anytime proxies are solicited in respect of securities (other than exempted securities) that are registered under the Exchange Act. This is covered in § 14(a) and its rules. Much of the litigation under § 14 has involved Rule 14a-9, which prohibits false or misleading statements, or material omissions, in connection with proxy solicitations.

The cases that follow deal with some of the more interesting questions relating to proxy solicitations.

SECTION I. GENERAL

MILLS v. ELECTRIC AUTO-LITE CO.

United States Supreme Court
396 U.S. 375 (1970)

MR. JUSTICE HARLAN delivered the opinion of the Court.

This case requires us to consider a basic aspect of the implied private right of action for violation of § 14(a) of the Securities Exchange Act of 1934, recognized by this Court in *J. I. Case Co. v. Borak,* 377 U.S. 426 (1964). As in *Borak* the asserted wrong is that a corporate merger was accomplished through the use of a proxy statement that was materially false or misleading. The question with which we deal is what causal relationship must be shown between such a statement and the merger to establish a cause of action based on the violation of the Act.

I

Petitioners were shareholders of the Electric Auto-Lite Company until 1963, when it was merged into Mergenthaler Linotype Company. They brought suit on the day before the shareholders' meeting at which the vote was to take place on the merger, against Auto-Lite, Mergenthaler, and a third company, American Manufacturing Company, Inc. The complaint sought an injunction against the voting by Auto-Lite's management of all proxies obtained by means of an allegedly misleading proxy solicitation; however, it did not seek a temporary restraining order, and the voting went ahead as scheduled the following day. Several months later petitioners filed an amended complaint, seeking to have the merger set aside and to obtain such other relief as might be proper.

In Count II of the amended complaint, which is the only count before us, petitioners predicated jurisdiction on § 27 of the 1934 Act. They alleged that the proxy statement sent out by the Auto-Lite management to solicit shareholders' votes in favor of the merger was misleading, in violation of § 14(a) of the Act and SEC Rule 14a-9 thereunder. Petitioners recited that before the merger Mergenthaler owned over 50% of the outstanding shares of Auto-Lite common stock, and had been in control of Auto-Lite for two years. American Manufacturing in turn owned about one-third of the outstanding shares of Mergenthaler, and for two years had been in voting control of Mergenthaler and, through it, of Auto-Lite. Petitioners charged that in light of these circumstances the proxy statement was misleading in that it told Auto-Lite shareholders that their board of directors recommended approval of the merger without also informing them that all 11 of Auto-Lite's directors were nominees of Mergenthaler and were under the "control and domination of Mergenthaler." Petitioners asserted the right to complain of this alleged violation both derivatively on behalf of Auto-Lite and as representatives of the class of all its minority shareholders.

On petitioners' motion for summary judgment with respect to Count II, the District Court for the Northern District of Illinois ruled as a matter of law that the claimed defect in the proxy statement was, in light of the circumstances in which the statement was made, a material omission. The District Court concluded, from its reading of the *Borak* opinion, that it had to hold a hearing on the issue whether there was "a causal connection between the finding that there has been a violation of the disclosure requirements of § 14(a) and the alleged injury to the plaintiffs" before it could consider what remedies would be appropriate.

After holding such a hearing, the court found that under the terms of the merger agreement, an affirmative vote of two-thirds of the Auto-Lite shares was required for approval of the merger, and that the respondent companies owned and controlled about 54% of the outstanding shares. Therefore, to obtain authorization of the merger, respondents had to secure the approval of a substantial number of the minority shareholders. At the stockholders' meeting, approximately 950,000 shares, out of 1,160,000 shares outstanding, were voted in favor of the merger. This included 317,000 votes obtained by proxy from the minority shareholders, votes that were "necessary and indispensable to the approval of the merger." The District Court concluded that a causal relationship had thus been shown, and it granted an interlocutory judgment in favor of petitioners on the issue of liability, referring the case to a master for consideration of appropriate relief.

The District Court made the certification required by 28 U.S.C. § 1292(b), and respondents took an interlocutory appeal to the Court of Appeals for the Seventh Circuit. That court affirmed the District Court's conclusion that the proxy statement was materially deficient, but reversed on the question of causation. The court acknowledged that, if an injunction had been sought a sufficient time before the stockholders' meeting, "corrective measures would have been appropriate." 403 F.2d 429, 435 (1968). However, since this suit was brought too late for preventive action, the courts had to determine "whether the misleading statement and omission caused the submission of sufficient proxies," as a prerequisite to a determination of liability under the Act. If the respondents could show, "by a preponderance of probabilities, that the merger would have received a sufficient vote even if the proxy statement had not been misleading in the respect found," petitioners would be entitled to no relief of any kind. *Id.*, at 436.

The Court of Appeals acknowledged that this test corresponds to the common-law fraud test of whether the injured party relied on the misrepresentation. However, rightly concluding that "[r]eliance by thousands of individuals, as here, can scarcely be inquired into" (*id.*, at 436, n. 10), the court ruled that the issue was to be determined by proof of the fairness of the terms of the merger. If respondents could show that the merger had merit and was fair to the minority shareholders, the trial court would be justified in concluding that a sufficient number of shareholders would have approved the merger had there been no deficiency in the proxy statement. In that case respondents would be entitled to a judgment in their favor.

Claiming that the Court of Appeals has construed this Court's decision in *Borak* in a manner that frustrates the statute's policy of enforcement through private litigation, the petitioners then sought review in this Court. We granted certiorari, believing that resolution of this basic issue should be made at this stage of the litigation and not postponed until after a trial under the Court of Appeals' decision.

II

As we stressed in *Borak,* § 14(a) stemmed from a congressional belief that "[f]air corporate suffrage is an important right that should attach to every equity security bought on a public exchange." H.R. Rep. No. 1383, 73d Cong., 2d Sess., 13. The provision was intended to promote "the free exercise of the voting rights of stockholders" by ensuring that proxies would be solicited with "explanation to the stockholder of the real nature of the questions for which authority to cast his vote is sought." *Id.*, at 14; S. Rep. No. 792, 73d Cong., 2d Sess., 12. The decision below, by permitting all liability to be foreclosed on the basis of a finding that the merger was fair, would allow the stockholders to be bypassed, at least where the only legal challenge to the merger is a suit for retrospective relief after the meeting has been held. A judicial appraisal of the merger's merits could be substituted for the actual and informed vote of the stockholders.

The result would be to insulate from private redress an entire category of proxy violations — those relating to matters other than the terms of the merger. Even outrageous misrepresentations in a proxy solicitation, if they did not relate to the terms of the transaction, would give rise to no cause of action under § 14(a). Particularly if carried over to enforcement actions by the Securities and Exchange Commission itself, such a result would subvert the congressional purpose of ensuring full and fair disclosure to shareholders.

Further, recognition of the fairness of the merger as a complete defense would confront small shareholders with an additional obstacle to making a successful challenge to a proposal recommended through a defective proxy statement. The risk that they would be unable to rebut the corporation's evidence of the fairness of the proposal, and thus to establish their cause of action, would be bound to discourage such shareholders from the private enforcement of the proxy rules that "provides a necessary supplement to Commission action." *J. I. Case Co. v. Borak,* 377 U.S., at 432.[1]

Such a frustration of the congressional policy is not required by anything in the wording of the statute or in our opinion in the *Borak* case. Section 14(a) declares it "unlawful" to solicit proxies in contravention of Commission rules, and SEC Rule 14a-9 prohibits solicitations "containing any statement which ... is false or misleading with respect to any material fact, or which omits to state any material fact necessary in order to make the statements therein not false or misleading ...." Use of a solicitation that is materially misleading is itself a violation of law, as the Court of Appeals recognized in stating that injunctive relief would be available to remedy such a defect if sought prior to the stockholders' meeting. In *Borak,* which came to this Court on a dismissal of the complaint, the Court limited its inquiry to whether a violation of § 14(a) gives rise to "a federal cause of action for rescission or damages," 377 U.S., at 428. Referring to the argument made by petitioners there "that the merger can be dissolved only if it was fraudulent or non-beneficial, issues upon which the proxy material would not bear," the Court stated: "But the causal relationship of the proxy material and the merger are questions of fact to be resolved at trial, not here. We therefore do not discuss this point further." *Id.,* at 431. In the present case there has been a hearing specifically directed to the causation problem. The question before the Court is whether the facts found on the basis of that hearing are sufficient in law to establish petitioners' cause of action, and we conclude that they are.

Where the misstatement or omission in a proxy statement has been shown to be "material," as it was found to be here, that determination itself indubitably embodies a conclusion that the defect was of such a character that it might have been considered important by a reasonable shareholder who was in the process of deciding how to vote. This requirement that the defect have a significant *propensity* to affect the voting process is found in the express terms of Rule 14a-9, and it adequately serves the purpose of ensuring that a cause of action cannot

---

[1] The Court of Appeals' ruling that "causation" may be negated by proof of the fairness of the merger also rests on a dubious behavioral assumption. There is no justification for presuming that the shareholders of every corporation are willing to accept any and every fair merger offer put before them; yet such a presumption is implicit in the opinion of the Court of Appeals. That court gave no indication of what evidence petitioners might adduce, once respondents had established that the merger proposal was equitable, in order to show that the shareholders would nevertheless have rejected it if the solicitation had not been misleading. Proof of actual reliance by thousands of individuals would, as the court acknowledged, not be feasible; and reliance on the *nondisclosure* of a fact is a particularly difficult matter to define or prove. In practice, therefore, the objective fairness of the proposal would seemingly be determinative of liability. But, in view of the many other factors that might lead shareholders to prefer their current position to that of owners of a larger, combined enterprise, it is pure conjecture to assume that the fairness of the proposal will always be determinative of their vote.

be established by proof of a defect so trivial, or so unrelated to the transaction for which approval is sought, that correction of the defect or imposition of liability would not further the interests protected by § 14(a).

There is no need to supplement this requirement, as did the Court of Appeals, with a requirement of proof of whether the defect actually had a decisive effect on the voting. Where there has been a finding of materiality, a shareholder has made a sufficient showing of causal relationship between the violation and the injury for which he seeks redress if, as here, he proves that the proxy solicitation itself, rather than the particular defect in the solicitation materials, was an essential link in the accomplishment of the transaction. This objective test will avoid the impracticalities of determining how many votes were affected, and, by resolving doubts in favor of those the statute is designed to protect, will effectuate the congressional policy of ensuring that the shareholders are able to make an informal choice when they are consulted on corporate transactions.[2]

III

Our conclusion that petitioners have established their case by showing that proxies necessary to approval of the merger were obtained by means of a materially misleading solicitation implies nothing about the form of relief to which they may be entitled. We held in *Borak* that upon finding a violation the courts were "to be alert to provide such remedies as are necessary to make effective the congressional purpose," noting specifically that such remedies are not to be limited to prospective relief. 377 U.S., at 433, 434. In devising retrospective relief for violation of the proxy rules, the federal courts should consider the same factors that would govern the relief granted for any similar illegality or fraud. One important factor may be the fairness of the terms of the merger. Possible forms of relief will include setting aside the merger or granting other equitable relief, but, as the Court of Appeals below noted, nothing in the statutory policy "requires the court to unscramble a corporate transaction merely because a violation occurred." 403 F.2d, at 436. In selecting a remedy the lower courts should exercise "'the sound discretion which guides the determinations of courts of equity,'" keeping in mind the role of equity as "the instrument for nice adjustment and reconciliation between the public interest and private needs as well as between competing private claims." *Hecht Co. v. Bowles,* 321 U.S. 321, 329-330 (1944), *quoting from Meredith v. Winter Haven,* 320 U.S. 228, 235 (1943).

We do not read § 29(b) of the Act, which declares contracts made in violation of the Act or a rule thereunder "void ... as regards the rights of" the violator and

---

[2] We need not decide in this case whether causation could be shown where the management controls a sufficient number of shares to approve the transaction without any votes from the minority. Even in that situation, if the management finds it necessary for legal or practical reasons to solicit proxies from minority shareholders, at least one court has held that the proxy solicitation might be sufficiently related to the merger to satisfy the causation requirement....

knowing successors in interest, as requiring that the merger be set aside simply because the merger agreement is a "void" contract. This language establishes that the guilty party is precluded from enforcing the contract against an unwilling innocent party, but it does not compel the conclusion that the contract is a nullity, creating no enforceable rights even in a party innocent of the violation. The lower federal courts have read § 29(b), which has counterparts in the Holding Company Act, the Investment Company Act, and the Investment Advisers Act, as rendering the contract merely voidable at the option of the innocent party. This interpretation is eminently sensible. The interests of the victim are sufficiently protected by giving him the right to rescind; to regard the contract as void where he has not invoked that right would only create the possibility of hardships to him or others without necessarily advancing the statutory policy of disclosure.

The United States, as *amicus curiae,* points out that as representatives of the minority shareholders, petitioners are not parties to the merger agreement and thus do not enjoy a statutory right under § 29(b) to set it aside. Furthermore, while they do have a derivative right to invoke Auto-Lite's status as a party to the agreement, a determination of what relief should be granted in Auto-Lite's name must hinge on whether setting aside the merger would be in the best interests of the shareholders as a whole. In short, in the context of a suit such as this one, § 29(b) leaves the matter of relief where it would be under *Borak* without specific statutory language — the merger should be set aside only if a court of equity concludes, from all the circumstances, that it would be equitable to do so.

Monetary relief will, of course, also be a possibility. Where the defect in the proxy solicitation relates to the specific terms of the merger, the district court might appropriately order an accounting to ensure that the shareholders receive the value that was represented as coming to them. On the other hand, where, as here, the misleading aspect of the solicitation did not relate to terms of the merger, monetary relief might be afforded to the shareholders only if the merger resulted in a reduction of the earnings or earnings potential of their holdings. In short, damages should be recoverable only to the extent that they can be shown. If commingling of the assets and operations of the merged companies makes it impossible to establish direct injury from the merger, relief might be predicated on a determination of the fairness of the terms of the merger at the time it was approved. These questions, of course, are for decision in the first instance by the District Court on remand, and our singling out of some of the possibilities is not intended to exclude others.

....

For the foregoing reasons we conclude that the judgment of Court of Appeals should be vacated and case remanded to that court for further proceedings consistent with this opinion.

TSC INDUSTRIES, INC. v. NORTHWAY, INC.

United States Supreme Court
426 U.S. 438 (1976)

MR. JUSTICE MARSHALL delivered the opinion of the Court.

The proxy rules promulgated by the Securities and Exchange Commission under the Securities Exchange Act of 1934 bar the use of proxy statements that are false or misleading with respect to the presentation or omission of material facts. We are called upon to consider the definition of a material fact under those rules, and the appropriateness of resolving the question of materiality by summary judgment in this case.

....

The question of materiality, it is universally agreed, is an objective one, involving the significance of an omitted or misrepresented fact to a reasonable investor. Variations in the formulation of a general test of materiality occur in the articulation of just how significant a fact must be or, put another way, how certain it must be that the fact would affect a reasonable investor's judgment.

The Court of Appeals in this case concluded that material facts include "all facts which a reasonable shareholder *might* consider important." 512 F.2d, at 330 (emphasis added). This formulation of the test of materiality has been explicitly rejected by at least two courts as setting too low a threshold for the imposition of liability under Rule 14a-9. *Gerstle v. Gamble-Skogmo, Inc.,* 478 F.2d 1281, 1301-1302 (CA2 1973); *Smallwood v. Pearl Brewing Co.,* 489 F.2d 579, 603-604 (CA5 1974). In these cases, panels of the Second and Fifth Circuits opted for the conventional tort test of materiality — whether a reasonable man *would* attach importance to the fact misrepresented or omitted in determining his course of action. *Gerstle v. Gamble-Skogmo, supra,* at 1302, also approved the following standard, which had been formulated with reference to statements issued in a contested election: "whether, taking a properly realistic view, there is a substantial likelihood that the misstatement or omission may have led a stockholder to grant a proxy to the solicitor or to withhold one from the other side, whereas in the absence of this he would have taken a contrary course." *General Time Corp. v. Talley Industries, Inc.,* 403 F.2d 159, 162 (CA2 1968), cert. denied, 393 U.S. 1026 (1969).

In arriving at its broad definition of a material fact as one that a reasonable shareholder *might* consider important, the Court of Appeals in this case relied heavily upon language of this Court in *Mills v. Electric Auto-Lite Co.,* [386 U.S. 375 (1970)]. That reliance was misplaced. The *Mills* Court did characterize a determination of materiality as at least "embod[ying] a conclusion that the defect was of such a character that it might have been considered important by a reasonable shareholder who was in the process of deciding how to vote." 396 U.S., at 384. But if any language in *Mills* is to be read as suggesting a general notion of materiality, it can only be the opinion's subsequent reference to materiality as a "requirement that the defect have a significant *propensity* to affect the voting process." *Ibid.* (emphasis in original). For it was that requirement that the Court said "adequately serves the purpose of ensuring that a cause of action cannot be established by proof of a defect so trivial, or so unrelated to the transaction for which approval is sought, that correction of the defect or imposition of liability would not further the interests protected by § 14(a)." *Ibid.* Even this language must be read, however, with appreciation that the Court specifically declined to consider the materiality of the omissions in *Mills.* The references to materiality were simply preliminary to our consideration of the sole question in the case — whether proof of the materiality of an omission from a proxy statement must be supplemented by a showing that the defect actually caused the outcome of the vote. It is clear, then, that *Mills* did not intend to foreclose further inquiry into the meaning of materiality under Rule 14a-9.

....

In formulating a standard of materiality under Rule 14a-9, we are guided, of course, by the recognition in *Borak* and *Mills* of the Rule's broad remedial purpose. That purpose is not merely to ensure by judicial means that the transaction, when judged by its real terms, is fair and otherwise adequate, but to ensure disclosures by corporate management in order to enable the shareholders to make an informed choice. As an abstract proposition, the most desirable role for a court in a suit of this sort, coming after the consummation of the proposed transaction, would perhaps be to determine whether in fact the proposal would have been favored by the shareholders and consummated in the absence of any misstatement or omission. But as we recognized in *Mills, supra,* at 382 n. 5, such matters are not subject to determination with certainty. Doubts as to the critical nature of information misstated or omitted will be commonplace. And particularly in view of the prophylactic purpose of the Rule and the fact that the content of the proxy statement is within management's control, it is appropriate that these doubts be resolved in favor of those the statute is designed to protect.

We are aware, however, that the disclosure policy embodied in the proxy regulations is not without limit. Some information is of such dubious significance that insistence on its disclosure may accomplish more harm than good. The potential liability for a Rule 14a-9 violation can be great indeed, and if the standard of materiality is unnecessarily low, not only may the corporation and its management be subjected to liability for insignificant omissions or misstatements, but also management's fear of exposing itself to substantial liability may cause it simply to bury the shareholders in an avalanche of trivial information — a result that is hardly conducive to informed decisionmaking. Precisely these dangers are presented, we think, by the definition of a material fact adopted by the Court of Appeals in this case — a fact which a reasonable shareholder *might* consider important. We agree with Judge Friendly, speaking for the Court of Appeals in *Gerstle,* that the "might" formulation is "too suggestive of mere possibility, however unlikely." 478 F.2d, at 1302.

The general standard of materiality that we think best comports with the policies of Rule 14a-9 is as follows: An omitted fact is material if there is a substantial likelihood that a reasonable shareholder would consider it important in deciding how to vote. This standard is fully consistent with *Mills'* general description of materiality as a requirement that "the defect have a significant *propensity* to affect the voting process." It does not require proof of a substantial likelihood that disclosure of the omitted fact would have caused the reasonable investor to change his vote. What the standard does contemplate is a showing of a substantial likelihood that, under all the circumstances, the omitted fact would have assumed actual significance in the deliberations of the reasonable shareholder. Put another way, there must be a substantial likelihood that the disclosure of the omitted fact would have been viewed by the reasonable investor as having significantly altered the "total mix" of information made available.

....

The issue of materiality may be characterized as a mixed question of law and fact, involving as it does the application of a legal standard to a particular set of facts. In considering whether summary judgment on the issue is appropriate, we must bear in mind that the underlying objective facts, which will often be free from dispute, are merely the starting point for the ultimate determination of materiality. The determination requires delicate assessments of the inferences a "reasonable shareholder" would draw from a given set of facts and the significance of those inferences to him, and these assessments are peculiarly ones for the trier of fact. Only if the established omissions are "so obviously important to an investor, that reasonable minds cannot differ on the question of materiality" is the ultimate issue of materiality appropriately resolved "as a matter of law" by summary judgment.

....

COLE v. SCHENLEY INDUSTRIES, INC.

United States Court of Appeals, Second Circuit
563 F.2d 35 (1977)

J. JOSEPH SMITH, CIRCUIT JUDGE:

This is an appeal from a final judgment entered in the United States District Court for the Southern District of New York, Richard Owen, Judge, dismissing a consolidated complaint challenging the merger of Schenley Industries, Inc. ("Schenley"), a subsidiary of Glen Alden Corporation ("Glen Alden"), with a wholly-owned subsidiary of Glen Alden....

The pertinent facts leading to the instant action are as follows. In March 1968, during a contest for control of Schenley, Glen Alden purchased 18 percent of Schenley's common stock at $ 53.33 ⅓ per share from Lewis S. Rosenstiel, founder and chairman of the board of Schenley. The agreement of purchase and sale with Rosenstiel recited that it was the intention of the parties that the remaining minority holders of Schenley common stock were to be afforded an opportunity to sell their shares to Glen Alden at a price comparable to or more favorable than the price paid to Rosenstiel. In August 1968 Glen Alden made a formal offer to purchase the common stock of the remaining shareholders of Schenley for $ 58.66 2/3 per share. Through open market purchases followed by this tender offer Glen Alden acquired more than 86 percent of Schenley's common stock.

In February 1971 Glen Alden announced a proposed merger with Schenley. Under the terms of the merger, Glen Alden offered Schenley's minority common shareholders a cash payment of $ 5 and a 7½ percent Glen Alden debenture in the principal amount of $ 30 due in 1985 in exchange for each share. Schenley's preferred shareholders were offered a cash payment of $ 4.50 and a 7½ percent Glen Alden debenture in the principal amount of $ 27 due in 1985 in exchange for each share. It is undisputed that the fair market value of this offer was $ 29 per share of common stock and $ 26.10 per share of preferred stock. On June 17, 1971 Schenley and Glen Alden Subsidiary Corporation, a wholly-owned subsidiary of Glen Alden, merged, with Schenley surviving as the resulting corporation.

....

A lengthy proxy statement, dated May 21, 1971, was sent to the shareholders in connection with a shareholders' meeting scheduled for June 17, 1971. Appellants claim that this proxy statement violated § 14(a) of the 1934 Act and SEC Rule 14a-9, in three principal ways: (1) the proxy statement did not accurately show how much cash Schenley had, (2) the proxy statement did not adequately reveal how much cash would be transferred from Schenley to Glen Alden, and (3) the proxy statement did not adequately reveal the value of a share of Schenley stock.

In May 1971 Glen Alden owned about 84 percent of the voting power of the outstanding capital stock of Schenley, and the proxy statement said that Glen Alden intended to vote its shares in favor of the merger. The threshold question is whether "the proxy solicitation itself ... was an essential link in the accomplishment of the transaction." *Mills v. Electric Auto-Lite Co.,* 396 U.S. 375, 385 (1970).

A Schenley minority shareholder had four options in May 1971: (1) accept Glen Alden's offer, (2) seek appraisal rights under Delaware law, (3) threaten to seek appraisal rights in an attempt to force Glen Alden to improve its offer, and (4) seek to enjoin the merger. The minority shareholders owned about 1.1 million shares of common stock and about 2.5 million shares of preferred stock of Schenley; if all, or a substantial portion, had exercised, or threatened to exercise, their appraisal rights, Schenley would have had to set aside a considerable sum of cash and the merger might not have been consummated. It was also possible that if additional information could be extracted the minority shareholders would have been able to enjoin the merger under Delaware law. We need not decide whether such a suit would have been successful under Delaware law. In view of these three alternatives to accepting the Glen Alden offer, we hold that the proxy solicitation was an essential part of the merger.

....

VIRGINIA BANKSHARES, INC. v. SANDBERG

United States Supreme Court
501 U.S. 1083 (1991)

JUSTICE SOUTER delivered the opinion of the court.

....

The questions before us are whether a statement couched in conclusory or qualitative terms purporting to explain directors' reasons for recommending certain corporate action can be materially misleading within the meaning of Rule 14a-9, and whether causation of damages compensable under § 14(a) can be shown by a member of a class of minority shareholders whose votes are not required by law or corporate bylaw to authorize the corporate action subject to the proxy solicitation. We hold that knowingly false statements of reasons may be actionable even though conclusory in form, but that respondents have failed to demonstrate the equitable basis required to extend the § 14(a) private action to such shareholders when any indication of congressional intent to do so is lacking.

I

In December 1986, First American Bankshares, Inc. (FABI), a bank holding company, began a "freeze-out" merger, in which the First American Bank of Virginia (Bank) eventually merged into Virginia Bankshares, Inc., (VBI), a wholly owned subsidiary of FABI. VBI owned 85% of the Bank's shares, the remaining 15% being in the hands of some 2,000 minority shareholders. FABI hired the investment banking firm of Keefe, Bruyette & Woods (KBW) to give an opinion on the appropriate price for shares of the minority holders, who would lose their interests in the Bank as a result of the merger. Based on market quotations and unverified information from FABI, KBW gave the Bank's executive committee an opinion that $ 42 a share would be a fair price for the minority stock. The executive committee approved the merger proposal at that price, and the full board followed suit.

Although Virginia law required only that such a merger proposal be submitted to a vote at a shareholders' meeting, and that the meeting be preceded by circulation of a statement of information to the shareholders, the directors nevertheless solicited proxies for voting on the proposal at the annual meeting set for April 21, 1987. In their solicitation, the directors urged the proposal's adoption and stated they had approved the plan because of its opportunity for the minority shareholders to achieve a "high" value, which they elsewhere described as a "fair" price, for their stock.

Although most minority shareholders gave the proxies requested, respondent Sandberg did not, and after approval of the merger she sought damages in the United States District Court for the Eastern District of Virginia from VBI, FABI, and the directors of the Bank. She pleaded two counts, one for soliciting proxies in violation of § 14(a) and Rule 14a-9, and the other for breaching fiduciary duties owed to the minority shareholders under state law. Under the first count,

Sandberg alleged, among other things, that the directors had not believed that the price offered was high or that the terms of the merger were fair, but had recommended the merger only because they believed they had no alternative if they wished to remain on the board. At trial, Sandberg invoked language from this Court's opinion in *Mills v. Electric Auto-Lite Co.*, 396 U.S. 375, 385 (1970), to obtain an instruction that the jury could find for her without a showing of her own reliance on the alleged misstatements, so long as they were material and the proxy solicitation was an "essential link" in the merger process.

The jury's verdicts were for Sandberg on both counts, after finding violations of Rule 14a-9 by all defendants and a breach of fiduciary duties by the Bank's directors. The jury awarded Sandberg $ 18 a share, having found that she would have received $ 60 if her stock had been valued adequately.

While Sandberg's case was pending, a separate action on similar allegations was brought against petitioners in the United States District Court for the District of Columbia by several other minority shareholders including respondent Weinstein, who, like Sandberg, had withheld his proxy. This case was transferred to the Eastern District of Virginia. After Sandberg's action had been tried, the Weinstein respondents successfully pleaded collateral estoppel to get summary judgment on liability.

On appeal, the United States Court of Appeals for the Fourth Circuit affirmed the judgments, holding that certain statements in the proxy solicitation were materially misleading for purposes of the Rule, and that respondents could maintain their action even though their votes had not been needed to effectuate the merger....

II

The Court of Appeals affirmed petitioners' liability for two statements found to have been materially misleading in violation of § 14(a) of the Act, one of which was that "The Plan of Merger has been approved by the Board of Directors because it provides an opportunity for the Bank's public shareholders to achieve a high value for their shares." Petitioners argue that statements of opinion or belief incorporating indefinite and unverifiable expressions cannot be actionable as misstatements of material fact within the meaning of Rule 14a-9, and that such a declaration of opinion or belief should never be actionable when placed in a proxy solicitation incorporating statements of fact sufficient to enable readers to draw their own, independent conclusions.

A

We consider first the actionability *per se* of statements of reasons, opinion or belief. Because such a statement by definition purports to express what is consciously on the speaker's mind, we interpret the jury verdict as finding that the directors' statements of belief and opinion were made with knowledge that the directors did not hold the beliefs or opinions expressed, and we confine our discussion to statements so made. That such statements may be materially significant raises no serious question.... Shareholders know that directors usually have knowledge and expertness far exceeding the normal investor's resources, and the directors' perceived superiority is magnified even further by the common knowledge that state law customarily obliges them to exercise their judgment in the shareholders' interest. Naturally, then, the share owner faced with a proxy request will think it important to know the directors' beliefs about the course they recommend, and their specific reasons for urging the stockholders to embrace it.

B

1

But, assuming materiality, the question remains whether statements of reasons, opinions, or beliefs are statements "with respect to ... material fact[s]" so as to fall within the strictures of the Rule....

....

... Such statements are factual in two senses: as statements that the directors do act for the reasons given or hold the belief stated and as statements about the subject matter of the reason or belief expressed.... Reasons for directors' recommendations or statements of belief are ... characteristically matters of corporate record subject to documentation, to be supported or attacked by evidence of historical fact outside a plaintiff's control. Such evidence would include not only corporate minutes and other statements of the directors themselves, but circumstantial evidence bearing on the facts that would reasonably underlie the reasons claimed and the honesty of any statement that those reasons are the basis for a recommendation or other action, a point that becomes especially clear when the reasons or beliefs go to valuations in dollars and cents.

It is no answer to argue, as petitioners do, that the quoted statement on which liability was predicated did not express a reason in dollars and cents, but focused instead on the "indefinite and unverifiable" term, "high" value, much like the similar claim that the merger's terms were "fair" to shareholders. The objection ignores the fact that such conclusory terms in a commercial context are reasonably understood to rest on a factual basis that justifies them as accurate, the absence of which renders them misleading....

....

2

Under § 14(a), then, a plaintiff is permitted to prove a specific statement of reason knowingly false or misleadingly incomplete, even when stated in conclusory terms. In reaching this conclusion we have considered statements of reasons of the sort exemplified here, which misstate the speaker's reasons and also mislead about the stated subject matter (*e.g.*, the value of the shares). A statement of belief may be open to objection only in the former respect, however, solely as a misstatement of the psychological fact of the speaker's belief in what he says. In this case, for example, the Court of Appeals alluded to just such limited falsity in observing that "the jury was certainly justified in believing that the directors did not believe a merger at $ 42 per share was in the minority stockholders' interest but, rather, that they voted as they did for other reasons, *e.g.*, retaining their seats on the board."

The question arises, then, whether disbelief, or undisclosed belief or motivation, standing alone, should be a sufficient basis to sustain an action under § 14(a), absent proof by the sort of objective evidence described above that the statement also expressly or impliedly asserted something false or misleading about its subject matter. We think that proof of mere disbelief or belief undisclosed should not suffice for liability under § 14(a), and if nothing more had been required or proven in this case we would reverse for that reason.

....

[T]o recognize liability on mere disbelief or undisclosed motive without any demonstration that the proxy statement was false or misleading about its subject would authorize § 14(a) litigation confined solely to what one skeptical court spoke of as the "impurities" of a director's "unclean heart." *Stedman v. Storer*, 308 F. Supp. 881, 887 (SDNY 1969) (dealing with § 10(b)).... While it is true that the liability, if recognized, would rest on an actual, not hypothetical, psychological fact, the temptation to rest an otherwise nonexistent § 14(a) action on psychological enquiry alone would threaten ... strike suits and attrition by discovery.... We therefore hold disbelief or undisclosed motivation, standing alone, insufficient to satisfy the element of fact that must be established under § 14(a).

C

Petitioners' fall-back position assumes the same relationship between a conclusory judgment and its underlying facts that we described in Part II-B-1, *supra*. [P]etitioners argue that even if conclusory statements of reason or belief can be actionable under § 14(a), we should confine liability to instances where the proxy material fails to disclose the offending statement's factual basis. There would be no justification for holding the shareholders entitled to judicial relief, that is, when they were given evidence that a stated reason for a proxy recommendation was misleading, and an opportunity to draw that conclusion themselves.

The answer to this argument rests on the difference between a merely misleading statement and one that is materially so. While a misleading statement will not always lose its deceptive edge simply by joinder with others that are true, the true statements may discredit the other one so obviously that the risk of real deception drops to nil. Since liability under § 14(a) must rest not only on deceptiveness but materiality as well (*i.e.*, it has to be significant enough to be important to a reasonable investor deciding how to vote), petitioners are on perfectly firm ground insofar as they argue that publishing accurate facts in a proxy statement can render a misleading proposition too unimportant to ground liability.

But not every mixture with the true will neutralize the deceptive. If it would take a financial analyst to spot the tension between the one and the other, whatever is misleading will remain materially so, and liability should follow. The point of a proxy statement, after all, should be to inform, not to challenge the reader's critical wits Only when the inconsistency would exhaust the misleading conclusion's capacity to influence the reasonable shareholder would a § 14(a) action fail on the element of materiality.

Suffice it to say that the evidence invoked by petitioners in the instant case fell short of compelling the jury to find the facial materiality of the misleading statement neutralized....

III

The second issue before us, left open in *Mills v. Electric Auto-Lite Co.*, is whether causation of damages compensable through the implied private right of action under § 14(a) can be demonstrated by a member of a class of minority shareholders whose votes are not required by law or corporate bylaw to authorize the transaction giving rise to the claim....

Although a majority stockholder in *Mills* controlled just over half the corporation's shares, a two-thirds vote was needed to approve the merger proposal.... In [*Mills*], the Court found the solicitation essential, as contrasted with one addressed to a class of minority shareholders without votes required by law or by-law to authorize the action proposed, and left it for another day to decide whether such a minority shareholder could demonstrate causation.

In this case, respondents address *Mills'* open question by proffering two theories that the proxy solicitation addressed to them was an "essential link" under the *Mills* causation test. They argue, first, that a link existed and was essential simply because VBI and FABI would have been unwilling to proceed with the merger without the approval manifested by the minority shareholders' proxies, which would not have been obtained without the solicitation's express misstatements and misleading omissions. On this reasoning, the causal connection would depend on a desire to avoid bad shareholder or public relations, and the essential character of the causal link would stem not from the enforceable terms of the parties' corporate relationship, but from one party's apprehension of the ill will of the other.

In the alternative, respondents argue that the proxy statement was an essential link between the directors' proposal and the merger because it was the means to satisfy a state statutory requirement of minority shareholder approval, as a condition for saving the merger from voidability resulting from a conflict of interest on the part of one of the Bank's directors, Jack Beddow, who voted in favor of the merger while also serving as a director of FABI. Under the terms of Va. Code § 13.1-691(A) (1989), minority approval after disclosure of the material facts about the transaction and the director's interest was one of three avenues to insulate the merger from later attack for conflict, the two others being ratification by the Bank's directors after like disclosure, and proof that the merger was fair to the corporation. On this theory, causation would depend on the use of the proxy statement for the purpose of obtaining votes sufficient to bar a minority shareholder from commencing proceedings to declare the merger void.

Although respondents have proffered each of these theories as establishing a chain of causal connection in which the proxy statement is claimed to have been an "essential link," neither theory presents the proxy solicitation as essential in the sense of *Mills'* causal sequence, in which the solicitation links a directors' proposal with the votes legally required to authorize the action proposed. As a consequence, each theory would, if adopted, extend the scope of [*J.I. Case Co. v. Borak*, 377 U.S. 426 (1964),] actions beyond the ambit of *Mills*, and expand the class of plaintiffs entitled to bring *Borak* actions to include shareholders whose initial authorization of the transaction prompting the proxy solicitation is unnecessary.

Assessing the legitimacy of any such extension or expansion calls for the application of some fundamental principles governing recognition of a right of action implied by a federal statute, the first of which was not, in fact, the considered focus of the *Borak* opinion. The rule that has emerged in the years since *Borak* and *Mills* came down is that recognition of any private right of action for violating a federal statute must ultimately rest on congressional intent to provide a private remedy, *Touche Ross & Co. v. Redington*, 442 U.S. 560, 575 (1979). From this the corollary follows that the breadth of the right once recognized should not, as a general matter, grow beyond the scope congressionally intended.

This rule and corollary present respondents with a serious obstacle, for we can find no manifestation of intent to recognize a cause of action (or class of plaintiffs) as broad as respondents' theory of causation would entail....

Looking to the Act's text and legislative history ... reveals little that would help toward understanding the intended scope of any private right....

The congressional silence that is thus a serious obstacle to the expansion of cognizable *Borak* causation is not, however, a necessarily insurmountable barrier. This is not the first effort in recent years to expand the scope of an action originally inferred from the Act without "conclusive guidance" from Congress, *see Blue Chip Stamps v. Manor Drug Stores*, 421 U.S. [729, 737 (1975)], and we may look to that earlier case for the proper response to such a plea for expansion. There, we accepted the proposition that where a legal structure of private statutory rights has developed without clear indications of congressional intent, the contours of that structure need not be frozen absolutely when the result would be demonstrably inequitable to a class of would-be plaintiffs with claims comparable to those previously recognized. Faced in that case with such a claim for equality in rounding out the scope of an implied private statutory right of action, we looked to policy reasons for deciding where the outer limits of the right should lie. We may do no less here, in the face of respondents' pleas for a private remedy to place them on the same footing as shareholders with votes necessary for initial corporate action.

A

Blue Chip Stamps set an example worth recalling as a preface to specific policy analysis of the consequences of recognizing respondents' first theory, that a desire to avoid minority shareholders' ill will should suffice to justify recognizing the requisite causality of a proxy statement needed to garner that minority support. It will be recalled that in *Blue Chip Stamps* we raised concerns about the practical consequences of allowing recovery, under § 10(b) of the Act and Rule 10b-5, on evidence of what a merely hypothetical buyer or seller might have done on a set of facts that never occurred, and foresaw that any such expanded liability would turn on "hazy" issues inviting self-serving testimony, strike suits, and protracted discovery, with little chance of reasonable resolution by pretrial process. These were good reasons to deny recognition to such claims in the absence of any apparent contrary congressional intent.

The same threats of speculative claims and procedural intractability are inherent in respondents' theory of causation linked through the directors' desire for a cosmetic vote. Causation would turn on inferences about what the corporate directors would have thought and done without the minority shareholder approval unneeded to authorize action. A subsequently dissatisfied minority shareholder would have virtual license to allege that managerial timidity would have doomed corporate action but for the ostensible approval induced by a misleading statement, and opposing claims of hypothetical diffidence and hypothetical boldness on the part of directors would probably provide enough depositions in the usual case to preclude any judicial resolution short of the credibility judgments that can only come after trial. Reliable evidence would seldom exist. Directors would understand the prudence of making a few statements about plans to proceed even without minority endorsement, and discovery would be a quest for recollections of oral conversations at odds with the official pronouncements, in hopes of finding support for *ex post facto* guesses about how much heat the directors would have stood in the absence of minority approval. The issues would be hazy, their litigation protracted, and their resolution unreliable. Given a choice, we would reject any theory of causation that raised such prospects, and we reject this one.

B

The theory of causal necessity derived from the requirements of Virginia law dealing with postmerger ratification seeks to identify the essential character of the proxy solicitation from its function in obtaining the minority approval that would preclude a minority suit attacking the merger. Since the link is said to be a step in the process of barring a class of shareholders from resort to a state remedy otherwise available, this theory of causation rests upon the proposition of policy that § 14(a) should provide a federal remedy whenever a false or misleading proxy statement results in the loss under state law of a shareholder plaintiff's state remedy for the enforcement of a state right. Respondents agree with the suggestions of counsel for the SEC and FDIC that causation be recognized, for example, when a minority shareholder has been induced by a misleading proxy statement to forfeit a state-law right to an appraisal remedy by voting to approve a transaction, or when such a shareholder has been deterred from obtaining an order enjoining a damaging transaction by a proxy solicitation that misrepresents the facts on which an injunction could properly have been issued. Respondents claim that in this case a predicate for recognizing just such a causal link exists in Va. Code § 13.1-691(A)(2)(1989), which sets the conditions under which the merger may be insulated from suit by a minority shareholder seeking to void it on account of Beddow's conflict.

This case does not, however, require us to decide whether § 14(a) provides a cause of action for lost state remedies, since there is no indication in the law or facts before us that the proxy solicitation resulted in any such loss. The contrary appears to be the case. Assuming the soundness of respondents' characterization of the proxy statement as materially misleading, the very terms of the Virginia statute indicate that a favorable minority vote induced by the solicitation would not suffice to render the merger invulnerable to later attack on the ground of the conflict. The statute bars a shareholder from seeking to avoid a transaction tainted by a director's conflict if, *inter alia*, the minority shareholders ratified the transaction following disclosure of the material facts of the transaction and the conflict. Assuming that the material facts about the merger and Beddow's interests were not accurately disclosed, the minority votes were inadequate to ratify the merger under state law, and there was no loss of state remedy to connect the proxy solicitation with harm to minority shareholders irredressable under state law. Nor is there a claim here that the statement misled respondents into entertaining a false belief that they had no chance to upset the merger, until the time for bringing suit had run out.

. . . .

FRADKIN v. ERNST

United States District Court, Northern District of Ohio
571 F. Supp. 829 (1983)

Dowd, District Judge.

This case involves a challenge to the implementation of the 1983 stock option plan (Plan) for the senior executives of Mohawk Rubber Company (Mohawk). The Plan was approved by Mohawk's Directors on January 4, 1983, and presented to and allegedly approved by the shareholders at Mohawk's Annual Meeting. Plaintiff contends that a proxy statement issued to shareholders describing the Plan prior to the Annual Meeting violated [Section 14(a) of the Securities Exchange Act of 1934 and Rule 14a-9 thereunder].

. . . .

Defendants argue that plaintiff must show that they acted with scienter in order to prove their claim under Rule 14a-9. While the Supreme Court has imposed a scienter requirement in the context of the private right of action under Rule 10b-5, *Ernst & Ernst v. Hochfelder,* 425 U.S. 185 (1976), the issue remains unresolved in the context of the Rule 14a-9 cause of action.

The leading case on the scienter requirement in a 14a-9 action brought against a corporate defendant is *Gerstle v. Gamble-Skogmo, Inc.,* 478 F.2d 1281 (2d Cir.1973). The Court relied on the differences between the statutory authorization for Rules 10b-5 and 14a-9 to suggest that the scienter requirement under Rule 10b-5 need not be extended to Rule 14a-9. Further, the Court found that general principles of tort law indicated that where "the transaction redounded directly to the benefit of the defendant, ... the common law would provide the remedies of rescission and restitution without proof of scienter." Further, the Court concluded that "a broad standard of culpability ... will serve to reinforce the high duty of care owed by a controlling corporation to minority shareholders in the preparation of a proxy statement ...." The Court, therefore, held that when the plaintiffs "are seeking compensation from the beneficiary who is responsible for the preparation of the [proxy] statement, they are not required to establish any evil motive or even reckless disregard of the facts. Liability would be imposed upon individuals who "merely negligently drafted" a proxy statement.

The Sixth Circuit addressed the issue of a Rule 14a-9 scienter requirement in a slightly different context in *Adams v. Standard Knitting Mills, Inc.,* 623 F.2d 422 (6th Cir. 1980). In that case, the Sixth Circuit reversed a judgment assessing damages against a firm of certified public accountants for the negligent preparation of a proxy statement used to obtain shareholder approval of a merger. In that case, the Court concluded that "scienter should be an element of liability in private suits under the proxy provisions as they apply to outside accountants." The Court distinguished the scienter requirements for outside accountants and corporate issuers. Reviewing the legislative history of the Exchange Act, the Court found that the principal concern of the drafters of the proxy rules was that of "corporate officers using the proxy mechanism to ratify their own frauds upon the shareholders." The critical distinction, therefore, is that

> the accountant here, unlike the corporate issuer, does not directly benefit from the proxy vote and is not in privity with the stockholder.... Federal courts ... have a special responsibility to consider the consequences of their rulings and to mold liability fairly to reflect the circumstances of the parties.... The preparation of financial statements to be appended to proxies and to other reports is the daily fare of accountants, and the accountant's potential liability for relatively minor mistakes would be enormous under a negligence standard.

The Court, therefore, distinguishing between outside accountants and the coprporate issuer, imposed a scienter requirement in a private action brought under Rule 14a-9 against outside accountants.

In light of these authorities, the Court must now consider the applicability of a scienter requirement to the corporate issuer under Rule 14a-9. While the leading cases apply a negligence standard to corporate insiders, the Sixth Ciruit has imposed a scienter requirement for finding outside accountants liable under Rule 14a-9. The issue, therefore, is whether the Court should distinguish between the scienter requirement imposed in the context of corporate issuers and outside accountants under Rule 14a-9 or whether the Court should extend the scienter requirement for outside accountants developed in *Adams* to a case involving a corporate issuer.

Upon review, the Court concludes that a distinction between the liability of a corporate issuer and outside accountants is appropriate, and a negligence standard should apply to the corporation issuing the proxy statement. Where the *Gerstle* court concluded that a negligence standard would be appropriate where the "transaction redounded directly to the benefit of the defendant," the *Adams* court imposed a scienter requirement where the outside accountant "does not directly benefit from the proxy vote." In the Court's view, these two precedents are harmonious. Where the defendant is the corporate issuer, and the corporate officals are responsible for drafting the proxy statement, the *Gerstle* neligence standard applies, but not the *Adams* scienter requirement. As a matter of law, the preparation of a proxy statement by corporate insiders containing materially false or misleading statements or omitting a material fact is sufficient to satisfy the *Gerstle* negligence standard.

. . . .

SECTION II. SHAREHOLDERS' PROPOSALS

Rule 14a-8, relating to proposals of shareholders, is an anomaly in the federal party regulation scheme in that it essentially has nothing to do with disclosure by proxy solicitors. Rather, it sets up an elaborate mechanism by which a shareholder may, if certain conditions are met, have a proposal of shareholders' action included in the proxy statement management sends to the shareholders. If a shareholder's proposal is included in the proxy statement, management will also have to provide a means by which all the shareholders can instruct the proxyholder how to vote on the proposal. If management opposes a shareholder's proposal, and it usually does, the shareholder must be given the opportunity to include a supporting statement in management's proxy materials.

The cases that follow represent the two forms of shareholder activism typically seen. The first involves a struggle by a shareholder to secure from the corporation rights intended to benefit the shareholders in a traditional sense. The second presents a situation where a shareholder uses the shareholder proposal mechanism to work toward greater corporate social responsibility.

SECURITIES AND EXCHANGE COMMISSION v.
TRANSAMERICA CORP.

United States Court of Appeals, Third Circuit
163 F.2d 511 (1947)

BIGGS, CIRCUIT JUDGE.

There are two appeals at bar. One is that of Transamerica Corporation, the other is the appeal of the Securities and Exchange Commission. Both are from an order of the United States District Court for the District of Delaware....

Transamerica, a Delaware corporation subject to the provisions of Section 14(a) of the Securities Exchange Act of 1934, has outstanding approximately 9,935,000 shares of $ 2 par value capital stock registered with the Commission and listed on national security exchanges .... Transamerica's shares are held by approximately 151,000 persons.

On January 2, 1946, Gilbert, the owner of record of seventeen shares of Transamerica's stock, wrote the management, submitting four proposals which he desired to present for action by shareholders at the next annual stockholders' meeting to be held on April 25, 1946. The first, second, and fourth of these proposals were as follows:

(1) To have independent public auditors of the books of Transamerica elected by the stockholders, beginning with the annual meeting of 1947, a representative of the auditing firm last chosen to attend the annual meeting each year.

(2) To amend By-Law 47 in order to eliminate therefrom the requirement that notice of any proposed alteration or amendment of the by-laws be contained in the notice of meeting.

(4) To require an account or a report of the proceedings at the annual meeting to be sent to all stockholders.

It appears that proposal (1) was in the form of a by-law amendment; Gilbert, the Commission and the corporation all so regarding it. Gilbert identified the second proposal also as a by-law amendment. The fourth proposal was designated by Gilbert as "a straight resolution." The Commission demanded of Transamerica that it accede to Gilbert's proposals. The corporation refused the Commission's demands.

The Commission therefore filed a complaint in the court below to enjoin Transamerica and its officers, *inter alia*, from making use of any proxy solicited by it for use at the annual meeting, from making use of the mails or any instrumentality of interstate commerce to solicit proxies or from making use of any soliciting material without complying with the Commission's demands, and for other relief which need not be detailed here.

The court below, finding its jurisdiction based on Sections 14(a), 23(a) and Section 21(e) and Section 27 of the Securities Exchange Act of 1934, to enforce compliance with the proxy rules of the Commission, concluded that the primary question in respect to Gilbert's proposals was whether they constituted proper subjects for action by stockholders at the annual meeting and stated that the question must be answered "not by federal but by Delaware law." *See* D.C., 67 F. Supp. 326, 329. No substantial question of fact being in dispute, the learned trial judge disposed of the case on the Commission's motion for summary judgment. He concluded as to proposal (1) that nothing in the General Corporation Law of Delaware or in the charter or by-laws of Transamerica required the corporation to give stockholders notice in the notice of meeting of any by-law amendment which a shareholder desired to submit to an annual meeting of stockholders, but that there was "no special reason why the vote on independent auditors should be required to assume the form of a new by-law." He held that such a vote is simply a mandate from the stockholders to the directors which may be carried into execution by following its terms. He ordered management to notice and set forth Gilbert's proposal for independent auditors for a vote of stockholders at the adjourned meeting of the company. As to proposal (2), the court concluded that Transamerica's management was not compelled to give notice in the notice of meeting of a stockholder's proposal to change By-Law 47 and hence the management was entitled to rule, notice not being given, the proposal out of order. As to proposal (4) the court concluded that the Commission was not entitled to make good the demand that an account or a report of the proceedings at annual meetings be sent to all stockholders. He enjoined the corporation from proceeding to hold the annual meeting unless complying with Proxy Rules X-14A-7 and X-14A-2 of the Commission by giving notice in the proxy of Gilbert's proposal. Following the hearing and its opinions the court ordered the adjourned meeting to be convened for consideration of the auditor proposal, Gilbert's proposal (1). Both the Commission and Transamerica have appealed; the Commission, from the failure of the court below to enforce its demands respecting Gilbert's proposals (2) and (4); Transamerica, from the court's decision to enforce the Commission's demand as to Gilbert's proposal (1).

We think it will be of assistance in understanding what is involved if we deal first with the respective major contentions of each of the parties; then treat with the specific proposals involved, some of the contentions of the parties in respect to them and the applicable rulings of the court below. Respecting the major contentions of the parties, it will be observed that the decision in the case at bar must turn in some part on the interpretation to be placed on that portion of Proxy Rule X-14A-7 which provides that if a qualified security holder has given the management reasonable notice that he intends to present for action at a meeting of security holders "a proposal which is a proper subject for action by security holders" the management shall set forth the proposal and provide means by which the security holders can vote on the proposal as provided in Proxy Rule X-14A-2. Much of the briefs of the parties and most of the argument have been devoted to a discussion of what is "a proper subject" for action by the stockholders of Transamerica. Speaking broadly, it is the position of the Commission that "a proper subject" for stockholder action is one in which the stockholders may properly be interested under the law of Delaware. Transamerica takes the position that a stockholder may interest himself with propriety only in a subject in respect to which he is entitled to vote at a stockholders' meeting when every requirement of Delaware law and of the provisions of the charter and by-laws, including notice, has been fulfilled. Putting Transamerica's position in its full technical abundance, as we understand it, it says that since Section 5(8) of the Delaware Corporation Law provides that a certificate of incorporation may set forth provisions which limit, regulate and define the powers and functions of the directors and stockholders, and since Article XIII of Transamerica's charter states that all the powers of the corporation shall be vested in the board of directors, the power to control corporate acts rests in the board of directors and not in the stockholders; in other words that the incorporators by the notice requirement of By-Law 47 curbed the power of the stockholders to vote on any by-law amendment of which notice was not included in the notice of meeting and in effect vested in Transamerica's board of directors the power to decide whether any proposed by-law amendment should be voted on at an annual meeting of stockholders. In short, management insists that it is entitled to use the notice requirement of By-Law 47 as a block or strainer to prevent any proposal to amend the by-laws, which it may deem unsuitable, from reaching a vote at an annual meeting of stockholders.

We will now treat specifically with Gilbert's three proposals, with some of the contentions of the parties in regard to them and with the rulings of the court below. Transamerica contends, as we have indicated, that since Article XIII of Transamerica's charter vests in the Board of Directors all powers of corporate management, not prohibited to them by the law of Delaware, this comprehensive grant renders the question of auditors not a proper subject for action by Transamerica's stockholders. The court below took the view, in our opinion, fully supportable, that the stockholders as the beneficial owners of the enterprise may prefer to consider the selection of independent auditors to review "what is no more than the trust relationship which exists between the directors and stockholders." *See* D.C., 67 F. Supp. at page 334. Assuredly, it is no less than this. It is necessary to go no further in order to sustain the Commission's contention that the auditing of the books of a corporation is a proper subject for stockholder consideration and action. Surely the audit of a corporation's books may not be considered to be peculiarly within the discretion of the directors. A corporation is run for the benefit of its stockholders and not for that of its managers.

Stockholders are entitled to employ watchmen to eye the guardians of their enterprise, the directors. Section 9 of the Delaware Corporation Law does not militate against this view nor is it important whether Gilbert's proposal be considered as a proposal to amend the by-laws or, as the court below considered it, "a mandate from the stockholders to the directors" to be carried into execution by following its terms. Setting to one side the notice provision of By-Law 47, to be dealt with hereinafter, the employment of independent auditors to be selected by the stockholders beyond any question is a proper subject for action by the stockholders.

As to (2), the proposal to amend By-Law 47 in order to eliminate the requirement that notice be given in the notice of any meeting of any proposed alteration or amendment of the by-laws, the court below decided in favor of Transamerica and against the Commission. As the learned District Judge pointed out, as Transamerica has contended and as has been stated herein, By-Law 47 provides that the by-laws may be altered or amended by an affirmative vote of a majority of the stock issued and outstanding and entitled to vote at any regular or special meeting of stockholders if notice of the proposed alteration or amendment is contained in the notice of the meeting. The court below took the view that because notice was not given by management, management was entitled to rule out of order any proposal to amend this by-law. But Gilbert had made his intention plain. He did not intend to deny notice to the stockholders for notice would have been given if Transamerica obeyed the Commission's direction and its proxy rules. Gilbert stated to Transamerica that the proposed by-law amendment was "to be introduced only if the management again resorts to what I consider the extremely undemocratic method of trying to avoid a vote, for approval or rejection, of the other resolutions, by ruling them out of order."

That the law of Delaware will permit stockholders of a Delaware corporation to act validly on a stockholder's proposal to amend by-laws is clear beyond any doubt. Section 12 of the General Corporation Law of Delaware provides that "The original by-laws of a corporation may be adopted by the incorporators. Thereafter, the power to make, alter or repeal by-laws shall be in the stockholders, but any corporation may, in the certificate of incorporation, confer that power upon the directors." Transamerica's charter imposes no impediment for Article X of the charter provides: "In furtherance and not in limitation of the powers conferred by statute, the board of directors is expressly authorized: (a) To make and alter the by-laws of this corporation, without any action on the part of the stockholders; but the by-laws made by the directors and the power so conferred may be altered or repealed by the stockholders." In short if it were not for the block interposed by the notice provisions of By-Law 47, it would be clear that Gilbert's second proposal would be a proper subject for stockholder action.

As to (4), the proposal to require a report of the proceeding of the annual meeting to be sent to all stockholders, we can perceive no logical basis for concluding that it is not a proper subject for action by the security holders. The security holders numbered approximately 151,000 persons holding approximately 9,935,000 shares of stock. Certainly it is proper for the stockholders to desire and to receive a report as to what transpired at the annual meeting of their company. True it may cost Transamerica $ 20,000 annually, but accurate information as to what transpires respecting the corporation is an absolute necessity if stockholders are to act for their joint interest. If stockholders cannot act together, they cannot act effectively.

The propriety of proposal (4) seems to us to be scarcely arguable and we conclude that no further discussion is necessary, any question of notice under By-Law 47 aside.

The conclusions reached by the court below in respect to Gilbert's proposals (2) and (4) may be supported only by applying the notice provision of By-Law 47 in all its strictness. Admittedly, so long as the notice provision of By-Law 47 remains in effect unless management sees fit to include notice of a by-law amendment proposed by a stockholder in the notice of meeting the proposed amendment can never come before the stockholders' meeting with complete correctness. The same would be true even if one per centum of the stockholders backed the proposed amendment. But Transamerica's position is overnice and is untenable. In our opinion Gilbert's proposals are proper subjects for stockholder action within the purview of Proxy Rule X-14A-7 since all are subjects in respect to which stockholders have the right to act under the General Corporation Law of Delaware.

But assuming arguendo that this was not so, we think that we have demonstrated that Gilbert's proposals are within the reach of security-holder action were it not for the insulation afforded management by the notice provision of By-Law 47. If this minor provision may be employed as Transamerica seeks to employ it, it will serve to circumvent the intent of Congress in enacting the Securities Exchange Act of 1934. It was the intent of Congress to require fair opportunity for the operation of corporate suffrage. The control of great corporations by a very few persons was the abuse at which Congress struck in enacting Section 14(a). We entertain no doubt that Proxy Rule X-14A-7 represents a proper exercise of the authority conferred by Congress on the Commission under Section 14(a). This seems to us to end the matter. The power conferred upon the Commission by Congress cannot be frustrated by a corporate by-law.

. . . .

ROOSEVELT v. E.I. DU PONT DE NEMOURS & CO.

United States Court of Appeals, District of Columbia Circuit
958 F.2d 416 (1992)

RUTH BADER GINSBURG, CIRCUIT JUDGE.

Amelia Roosevelt appeals the district court's judgment that E.I. Du Pont de Nemours & Co. ("Du Pont") could omit her shareholder proposal from its proxy materials for the 1992 annual meeting. The district court concluded that Roosevelt's proposal "deals with a matter relating to the conduct of [Du Pont's] ordinary business operations," and is therefore excludable under Securities and Exchange Commission ("SEC") Rule 14a-8(c)(7)....

I. Background

Prior to Du Pont's 1991 annual shareholder meeting, Friends of the Earth Oceanic Society ("Friends of the Earth") submitted a proposal, on behalf of Roosevelt, regarding: (1) the timing of Du Pont's phase out of the production of chlorofluorocarbons ("CFCs") and halons; and (2) the presentation to shareholders of a report detailing (a) research and development efforts to find environmentally sound substitutes, and (b) marketing plans to sell those substitutes. Du Pont opposed inclusion of the proposal in its proxy materials; as required by SEC rule, the company notified the SEC staff of its intention to omit the proposal and its reasons for believing the omission proper. Friends of the Earth filed with the staff a countersubmission on Roosevelt's behalf urging that the proposal was not excludable.

The SEC staff issued a "no-action letter"; citing the Rule 14a-8(c)(7) exception for matters "relating to the conduct of the [company's] ordinary business operations," the staff stated that it would not recommend Commission enforcement action against Du Font if the company excluded the proposal. Roosevelt did not seek Commission review of the staff's disposition [, but rather brought suit.]

....

III. *Roosevelt's Proposals and the Rule 14a-8(c)(7) Exception for "Ordinary Business Operations"*

... In reviewing [the district court's] ruling, we emphasize that Roosevelt's disagreement with Du Pont's current policy is not about whether to eliminate CFC production or even whether to do so at once. The former is an end to which Du Pont is committed, and immediate cessation, before environmentally safe alternatives are available, is not what Roosevelt proposes.

Roosevelt differs with Du Pont on a less fundamental matter — the rapidity with which the near-term phase out should occur. Roosevelt seeks a target no later than 1995 ("surpassing [Du Pont's] global competitors which have set a 1995 target date"). In contrast, when this litigation began, Du Pont had set a target of "as soon as possible, but at least by the year 2000."

In recent months and days, the "at least by" year has moved ever closer to Roosevelt's target. Prior to oral argument, Roosevelt informed the court that Du Pont had issued a press release reiterating its "as soon as possible" policy, but "advancing the end point to year-end 1994 for Halons and 1996 for CFCs." Following oral argument, Du Pont informed the court that, "in response to an announcement issued by the White House today regarding an accelerated phaseout of CFCs and Halons," the company "will accelerate its CFC end date to no later than December 31, 1995 in developed countries." Du Pont Statement on Accelerated CFC Phaseout, Feb. 12, 1992.

Although the regulation necessary to give effect to the President's announcement has not yet been adopted, Du Pont immediately reported that it "supports the Administration's position," and that it will phase out CFC production by December 31, 1995. We accept that public statement as the company's current timetable. While the SEC staff and the district court considered Roosevelt's proposal with the company's year-2000 end point in view, we think it proper to take account of the current reality: Roosevelt's proposal would have Du Pont surpass its global competitors' target of 1995; Du Pont projects completion of the phase out "as soon as possible," but no later than year-end 1995.

Roosevelt has confirmed that the first, or phase-out portion of her proposal is the "core issue" and that, if necessary, she would withdraw the second, or report-to-shareholders portion, so that the first portion could be included in Du Pont's 1992 proxy materials. We therefore consider separately the two portions of Roosevelt's proposal.

Because both parts of Roosevelt's proposal must be measured against the Rule 14a-8(c)(7) "ordinary business operations" exception, we set out here the Commission's general understanding of that phrase. When the Commission adopted the current version of the "ordinary business operations" exception, it announced its intention to interpret the phrase both "more restrictively" and "more flexibly than in the past." Adoption of Amendments Relating to Proposals by Security Holders, Exchange Act Release No. 12,999, 41 FR 52,994, 52,998 (1976) ("*1976 Rule 14a-8 Amendments*"). Specifically, the Commission explained:

> [T]he term "ordinary business operations" has been deemed on occasion to include certain matters which have significant policy, economic or other implications inherent in them. For instance, a proposal that a utility company not construct a proposed nuclear power plant has in the past been considered excludable under [the predecessor of (c)(7)]. In retrospect, however, it seems apparent that the economic and safety considerations attendant to nuclear power plants are of such magnitude that a determination whether to construct one is not an "ordinary" business matter. Accordingly, proposals of that nature, as well as others that have major implications, will in the future be considered beyond the realm of an issuer's ordinary business operations....

Id. The Commission contrasted with matters of such moment as a decision not to build a nuclear power plant, "matters ... mundane in nature [that] do not involve any substantial policy ... considerations." *1976 Rule 14a-8 Amendments*, 41 Fed. Reg. at 52,998. Proposals of that genre, the Commission said, may be safely omitted from proxy materials.

In its brief as amicus curiae, the SEC stated that it regarded the first portion of Roosevelt's proposal, on the timing of the CFC phase out, as not excludable under Rule 14a-8(c)(7), but the second part, on research and development programs and marketing plans, as fitting within the "ordinary business operations" exception. The Commission noted that "[its] staff, in contrast, viewed the timing of the phase-out as an ordinary business matter." We agree with the Commission on the second part of Roosevelt's proposal but not on the first.

A. *The Phase Out Target Date*

It is not debated in this case that CFCs contribute intolerably to depletion of the ozone layer and that their manufacture has caused a grave environmental hazard. However, Roosevelt's proposal, we emphasize again, relates not to *whether* CFC production should be phased out, but *when* the phase out should be completed.

Timing questions no doubt reflect "significant policy" when large differences are at stake. That would be the case, for example, if Du Pont projected a phase-out period extending into the new century. On the other hand, were Roosevelt seeking to move up Du Pont's target date by barely a season, the matter would appear much more of an "ordinary" than an extraordinary business judgment. In evaluating the Commission's classification of the timing question here as extraordinary, *i.e.*, one involving "fundamental business strategy" or "long-term goals," we are mindful that the SEC conceived of a five-year interval, not an interval now cut to one year.

We are furthermore mindful that we sit in this case as a court of review and owe respect to the findings made by the district court. The trial judge concluded from the record that "Du Pont's 'as soon as possible' policy," contrary to Roosevelt's argument, "does not lack definition." The judge found the policy genuine based on evidence that Du Pont had already spent more than $ 240 million developing alternatives to CFCs and had just announced the shutdown of the facility that had been the largest CFC plant in the world. Du Pont, the district court also observed, continues to work "toward a global policy of phasing out CFCs" and "with CFC consumers to phase out their use of CFCs."

Stressing the undisputed need for the responsible development of safe substitutes, and the acknowledged irresponsibility of suddenly cutting off all CFC production, the trial judge highlighted the essential difference between this case and the nuclear power plant in the Commission's *1976 Rule 14a-8 Amendments* example. Phasing out CFC production is not a go/no go matter. The phase out takes work "day-to-day ... with equipment manufacturers to help develop the technology needed for alternative compounds." It takes careful planning "in sensitive areas, such as the storage of perishable food and medical products (like vaccines and transfusable blood)," and expertise "in technical fields, such as the sterilization of temperature-sensitive surgical instruments."

We recognize that "ordinary business operations" ordinarily do not attract the interest of both the executive and legislative branches of the federal government. But government regulation of the CFC phase out, even the President's headline-attracting decision to accelerate the schedule initially set by Congress, does not automatically elevate shareholder proposals on timing to the status of "significant policy." What the President and Congress have said about CFCs is not the subject of our closest look. Instead, Rule 14a-8(c)(7) requires us to home in on Roosevelt's proposal, to determine whether her request dominantly implicates ordinary business matters. The gap between her proposal and the company's schedule is now one year, not five. The steps to be taken to accomplish the phase out are complex; as the district court found, the company, having agreed on the essential policy, must carry it out safely, using "business and technical skills" day-to-day that are not meant for "shareholder debate and participation."

In sum, the parties agree that CFC production must be phased out, that substitutes must be developed, and that both should be achieved sooner rather than later. Du Pont has undertaken to eliminate the products in question by year-end 1995, and has pledged to do so sooner if "possible." The trial judge has found Du Pont's "as soon as possible" pledge credible. In these circumstances, we conclude that what is at stake is the "implementation of a policy," "the timing for an agreed-upon action," *see* Brief of the Securities and Exchange Commission, Amicus Curiae, at 31, and we therefore hold the target date for the phase out a matter excludable under Rule 14a-8(c)(7).

B. *The Report to Shareholders*

The second part of Roosevelt's proposal solicits a report from management within six months detailing research and development efforts on environmentally safe substitutes and a marketing plan to sell those substitutes. This portion of the proposal, the SEC concluded in agreement with its staff, "requires detailed information about the company's day-to-day business operations [and] is subject to exclusion pursuant to [Rule 14a-8(c)(7)]." Roosevelt concedes that the report is not central to her proposal, and we find no cause to place the matter outside the "ordinary business operations" exception.

For a time, the Commission staff "ha[d] taken the position that proposals requesting issuers to prepare reports on specific aspects of their business or to form [study committees] would not be excludable under Rule 14a-8(c)(7)." *Amendments to Rule 14a-8 Under the Securities Exchange Act of 1934 Relating to Proposals by Security Holders*, Exchange Act Rel. No. 20,091, 48 FR 38,218, 38,221 (Aug. 23, 1983). The Commission has changed that position. Pointing out that the staff's interpretation "raise[d] form over substance," the Commission instructed the staff to "consider whether the subject matter of the [requested] report or [study] committee involves a matter of ordinary business: where it does, the proposal [is] excludable under Rule 14a-8(c)(7)." *Id.*

We need not linger over the report issue. The staff's no-action letters in this respect are unremarkable and entirely in keeping with current practice. *See, e.g.,* Carolina Power & Light Co., SEC No-Action Letter (available Mar. 8, 1990) (shareholder proposal requesting preparation of a report on specific aspects of company's nuclear operations, covering, *inter alia*, safety, regulatory compliance, emissions problems, hazardous waste disposal and related cost information, may be omitted as relating to ordinary business operations).

Just as the Commission has clarified that requests for special reports or committee studies are not automatically includable in proxy materials, we caution that such requests are not inevitably excludable. But Roosevelt has not shown that the detailed research and development or marketing information she seeks implicates significant policy issues, and not merely implementation arrangements. She does not, for example, suggest that Du Pont is developing or planning to market hazardous substitutes. *Cf. Lovenheim v. Iroquois Brands, Ltd.*, 618 F. Supp. 554, 556, 561 (D.D.C. 1985) (in light of "ethical and social significance" of proposal, court granted preliminary injunction barring corporation from excluding from its proxy materials shareholder proposal that requested formation of committee to study, and submission of report to shareholders about, whether company's supplier produced pate de foie gras in a manner involving undue pain or suffering to animals and whether distribution should be discontinued until a more humane method is developed).

In agreement with the district judge, the Commission, and the staff, we hold that the second part of Roosevelt's proposal falls within the "ordinary business operations" exception.

Conclusion

... Roosevelt's proposal ... may be excluded by Du Pont because, in both of its parts, the proposal falls within the exception furnished by Rule 14a-8(c)(7) for matters relating to "ordinary business operations." ...

SECTION III. PROXY CONTESTS

The shareholder proposal mechanism of Rule 14a-8, while providing shareholders a means of being heard by management, does not serve as a tool for wresting control from management. If this is desired, a shareholder or shareholder group must solicit proxies for use at a shareholders' meeting. Since management will do so also, what will develop is a proxy contest.

Proxy contests in publicly held corporations go in and out of fashion. They were popular in the 1950's, then were eclipsed by tender offers as the preferred way to take over a corporation, and now have reemerged to a limited extent as an alternative to the tender offer. Economics is one of the most important reasons for a reemergence. Proxy contests are expensive. For a publicly held corporation of any size, millions of dollars will need to be spent to have any real chance of success. But, if the alternative is a cash tender offer for at least majority ownership, a proxy contest will be several times cheaper. Also, shareholders who win proxy contests can typically have the corporation reimburse them for their expenses.

What one obtains through a tender offer is, of course, quite different from what can be gained as the result of a proxy contest. In the tender offer it is stock ownership and in the proxy contest voting control, sometimes control over only one question (for example, as illustrated in the immediately following case, whether the corporation should merge with another), but more often over the choosing of directors at a particular meeting (as was the situation in the second case below). Since, however, boards essentially are self-perpetuating — except when a proxy contest is won by insurgents — winning one election typically will lead to long-term management control (except in the case of a staggered board, where obtaining control is more difficult).

UNION PACIFIC RAILWAY CO. v. CHICAGO
AND NORTH WESTERN RAILWAY CO.

United States District Court, Northern District of Illinois
226 F. Supp. 400 (1964)

JULIUS J. HOFFMAN, DISTRICT JUDGE.

This action is the judicial culmination of a struggle between two of the nation's major railroads, the Union Pacific and the North Western, competing in their efforts to take over a third, the Rock Island. The contest in this phase concerns the efforts of these competitors to win the support of the Rock Island stockholders. Each has claimed a foul by the other in the solicitation of proxies for these stockholders' votes in a meeting scheduled for November 15, 1963, called for the purpose of approving a proposal for merger of the Rock Island with the Union Pacific.

....

I

The background of the controversy has been developed at length in the evidence and briefs. A summary will suffice for the disposition of this action. [Both parties submitted merger proposals to the directors of Rock Island. The directors of Rock Island supported Union Pacific's offer and scheduled a special shareholders' meeting to approve the sale. Publicity was generated by both sides, and several lawsuits were brought charging irregularities in the proxy campaign. One suit was brought by eight Rock Island shareholders, opponents of the merger with Union Pacific, seeking to obtain corporate shareholder lists. In this effort they were successful. The dissident Rock Island shareholders also formed a "Committee" opposing the merger.]

II

On October 1, 1963, formal proxy solicitation began with the mailing of proxy statements, forms, and supporting materials to Rock Island shareholders by both the Rock Island management and the so-called Committee.... In the following six weeks a number of mailings were made by the Rock Island management to the Rock Island shareholders, seeking support for and approval of the plan of merger with the Union Pacific to be voted on at the meeting scheduled for November 15. In opposition, the so-called Committee and the North Western, acting in its own behalf, separately sent out a number of mailings to the Rock Island stockholders. All three railroads made use of their employees as proxy solicitors, telephoning or calling personally upon the shareholders and seeking their proxies.

Since the Rock Island stock is registered on the New York Stock Exchange, all solicitation activities were subject to the Securities Exchange Act of 1934 and to the regulations promulgated by the Securities and Exchange Commission under that authority. The staff of the SEC, in considering materials filed with it by the Committee and the North Western prior to distribution, made a number of comments, requests, and objections to the proposed materials. The North Western and the Committee acquiesced to some of these positions so taken by the SEC and made changes, deletions, or withdrawals. In other instances these defendants proceeded in spite of the staff positions. Objections and protests on behalf of the Union Pacific were repeatedly made to the SEC concerning the materials sent out by the so-called Committee and the North Western. Finally the Union Pacific requested that the Commission take judicial action to adjourn the scheduled meeting for a period of 60 days to permit resolicitation. The Commission replied on November 13 that it declined to take action as requested. On November 14, the following day and the very eve of the November 15 meeting, this action was filed.

....

III

The controversy is governed by the Securities Exchange Act of 1934, enacted for the protection of the investing public in securities transactions....

....

... Basic to the regulatory plan is Rule 14a-6, which requires that preliminary copies of proxy soliciting material be filed with the Commission before such material is sent or given to security holders. This requirement affords the Commission staff an opportunity to examine materials in advance, in the interests of protecting the investing public. The standard against which soliciting materials are to be measured is set down by the SEC in its Rule 14a-9, which proscribes [materially false or misleading statements and material omissions].

....

IV

The plaintiffs have charged a number of alleged violations of these rules by the Committee and the North Western during the period of proxy solicitation between October 1, 1963, and November 14, 1963. Prominent among the communications complained of is the so-called Hayden, Stone Report.

Hayden, Stone & Co., Incorporated, is a New York firm engaged as broker and dealer in the securities business, with branch offices and correspondents in other large cities. On October 4, 1963, the record date fixing eligibility to vote at the scheduled stockholders' meeting, the firm was record owner of 13,000 shares of Rock Island stock. On October 16, 1963, during the solicitation period, the firm released and distributed a four-page letter or pamphlet entitled "Progress Report: Union Pacific-Chicago North Western-Chicago, Rock Island & Pacific Railroad Merger Controversy." The Report was written by Pierre R. Bretey, an investment analyst in the firm who was described in the evidence as a dean of railroad analysts. The North Western management supplied information to Mr. Bretey during the preparation of the Report, and two North Western officers consulted with him. A draft of the Report was submitted to the North Western for review before release, and a North Western officer made certain changes or suggestions of a minor nature.

Some 7,500 copies of the Report were printed. Approximately 5,000 of these were distributed to the regular customers of Hayden, Stone and its branch offices and correspondents. Most of the remainder were distributed to the North Western. Copies of the Report were furnished by some North Western proxy solicitors to Rock Island shareholders in the course of proxy solicitation. Other shareholders received copies of the Report in the mail from undisclosed sources. A number of copies came into the hands of broker-dealer firms who might be in a position to advise Rock Island stockholders concerning their votes, and of institutional investors such as banks, insurance companies, pension funds, and investment companies.

This Hayden, Stone Report was cast in the form of advice to Rock Island stockholders and concluded, in various phrasings, that the North Western offer was "far more attractive" than that of the Union Pacific. It thus constituted a communication to the stockholders "reasonably calculated to result in the procurement, withholding or revocation of a proxy" within the meaning of Rule 14a-1 of the SEC's regulations, and was thereby subject to the requirement of prior filing under Rule 14a-6, as the Commission staff determined when the Report came to its attention. At no time, however, was the Report filed with the SEC as required.

The North Western has candidly and repeatedly admitted in open court that the use of the Report constituted a violation of the SEC regulations and was therefore unlawful under the Securities Exchange Act of 1934. By way of exculpation, however, it is said that the offense of failure to file is merely a technical violation. The offense cannot be so easily dismissed. It deprives the Commission of an opportunity to consider the solicitation material and thereby evades the first line of enforcement. A solicitor by failing to file circumvents the agency primarily responsible for protection of the investor and speculates upon the decision of the court. In any event, the violation committed here cannot be passed as mere technicality, since when the Report did in fact receive SEC consideration, the staff found it to be sufficiently objectionable to request that distribution cease. In response to this request, Hayden, Stone destroyed undistributed copies and called for the return of copies in the hands of its branches and correspondents. The North Western, also at the SEC's request, directed its proxy solicitors to make no further use of the Report and returned remaining copies.

Objections to the content of the Report concern principally the predictions, estimates, and opinions which it contains. There is no need to determine whether such statements would support a common law action for fraud or deceit. The Congressional purpose was to elevate standards in the securities field above those generally prevailing. In applying the Commission's command that proxy solicitations be neither false nor misleading, the court is admonished to keep that goal in view. Since the Commission in its supervisory role is in constant touch with the problems of investor protection and aware of the needed safeguards, its findings and recommendations deserve weight and respect. The words to be interpreted here are the language of the SEC, exercising its power to prescribe standards, and the meaning of those words is illuminated by the intent revealed in their application by the SEC itself.

... Bald statements contrary to concrete and historic fact run the risk of ready refutation and exposure, and to that degree are self-policing. Predictions, estimates, and opinions are more elusive and may present graver dangers of misleading the investing public. They lend themselves to this evil by allowing facts to be suggested or implied without direct statement. Even if they do not tend to induce belief in any particular fact, they nonetheless import the existence of unspecified facts which support the conclusion. The shareholder may be led readily to assume, contrary to fact, that the predictor has special knowledge or unique information to bear out fully his prediction, and be induced to rely upon a supposed expert judgment of the mysteries of finance.... Whether the prediction is the product of an intent to mislead or of innocent overenthusiasm, the misleading effect upon the investing public is the same.

The Hayden, Stone Report, used for proxy solicitation, plainly offended against these principles. It advises that there should be added to the past earnings record of the North Western "merger savings of twenty-five million dollars which are anticipated when Rock Island and North Western actually merge." The dollar figure so stated was not arrived at by disinterested study but adopted from the prediction of North Western's management. The SEC staff had objected to the use of the figure as proposed for inclusion in materials prepared by the North Western, where it was more guardedly described as an estimate, which could not be guaranteed, indicated by North Western management studies. In considering the North Western filing, the staff had also objected to any assumptions of a North Western-Rock Island merger, since its realization was remote, contingent, and conjectural. The Hayden, Stone Report went further, however, and predicted "potential savings" of seventy-five million dollars from an assumed three-way merger in which the Milwaukee Road would be added to the North Western and Rock Island.

In the same vein, the Report presented specific earnings for a merged North Western-Rock Island on the basis of an appended pro forma tabulation of a kind which had been deleted from North Western's proxy solicitation materials as the result of discussions with the SEC. An additional prediction of specific earnings was offered for the assumed three-way merger including the Milwaukee. Combining a prediction of the trend in the market price of the bond to be offered in exchange by the North Western and a prediction of the future value of North Western stock, the Report predicted that "work out values" of the package offered by the North Western "should reach well above forty dollars per share" as compared with a value "between twenty-eight dollars and twenty-nine dollars per share on the Union Pacific exchange offer." As an additional reason for preferring the North Western offer, the Report predicted: "In our judgment, the [Interstate Commerce] Commission is not likely to approve the Union Pacific's acquisition of the Rock Island since such acquisition would doubtless seriously injure the North Western and Milwaukee Systems." The SEC staff had recommended the deletion of a similar prediction from the solicitation materials filed by the North Western because of "its extremely speculative nature and possibly misleading effects."

The court is constrained to agree with the judgment of the SEC staff that such predictions mislead by conveying a certitude which inherently they cannot possess. Viewed as a whole, the Hayden, Stone Report was misleading in the circumstances of its use. Whatever its value for other purposes, it was inappropriate for use in proxy solicitation under the demanding standards of conduct established in the public interest for all sides in such a contest. In the light of this finding, it is unnecessary to decide whether the somewhat similar predictions contained in the materials of the North Western and of the so-called Committee also crossed the line of propriety.

....

VI

Contributing to the misleading effect of the proxy campaign was the role of the self-styled Chicago, Rock Island & Pacific Railroad Company's Stockholders' Committee for North Western's Exchange Offer and Against Rock Island-U. P. Merger, the so-called Committee. Its title conveys the impression of a group of shareholders, representing the interests of all, acting independently upon their own considered conclusions. In fact the so-called Committee consisted of some seven shareholders representing an aggregate of 950 of the nearly three million shares of Rock Island stock held by more than 11,000 owners. Some 500 of these shares had been purchased after the Union Pacific-North Western controversy arose. In fact these persons simply lent their names to the campaign at the suggestion of a broker who contacted the attorney for them. In fact they did not meet or deliberate or contribute their views or opinions, to each other or their attorney. In fact they furnished no financial support for any of the activities of the Committee and assumed no obligations. In any ordinary or meaningful sense of the term, there was in fact no committee.

Still the major portion of the proxy campaign was carried on in the Committee's name. The proxy forms distributed bore its title. The illusion of substantial, separate, and impartial support for the North Western offer was heightened by the repetition, in proxy solicitation materials, of such phrases as "The Committee has made a study ...," "The Committee is of the opinion ...," "the Committee believes ...," and "the Committee has considered.. .." The impression thus created was not dispelled by the disclosures, in the Committee proxy statement, that "The North Western has agreed to pay a substantial amount, if not all, of the expenses of the Committee except expenses of members of the Committee incurred prior to September 16, 1963, which expenses aggregated approximately $ 5,000.00." In fact the so-called members consented to the use of their names as a "Committee" only upon condition that the North Western assume all expenses. The technique of employing an ostensibly independent organization to gain public support has been judicially recognized as deceptive.. ..

... Nor is it a defense that this third-party technique may have become a common manipulative device in modern mass persuasion. The beneficial requirement of meticulous disclosure demanded by the federal securities laws cannot be evaded by measurement against the lowest common moral denominator in communications. As Mr. Justice Goldberg recently explained, "A fundamental purpose, common to these statutes, was to substitute a philosophy of full disclosure for the philosophy of *caveat emptor* and thus to achieve a high standard of business ethics in the securities industry. As we recently said in a related context, 'It requires but little appreciation ... of what happened in this country during the 1920's and 1930's to realize how essential it is that the highest ethical standards prevail' in every facet of the securities industry." *Securities and Exchange Commission v. Capital Gains Research Bureau, Inc.,* 375 U.S. 180, 186-187 (1963).

....

Accordingly, an order will be entered enjoining the holding of a meeting of the Rock Island shareholders to vote on the proposed merger into the Union Pacific until such date, not earlier than 60 days from the date of the order, as may be fixed and announced by the Rock Island directors. The record date for determining eligibility of shareholders to vote at the meeting shall be fixed by the Rock Island directors as well. The parties will be enjoined from voting at this meeting any proxy received on or before the date of the order. Solicitation of proxies for the new meeting shall be conducted in accordance with the applicable regulations of the SEC. In view of these restrictions the plaintiffs' demand for a mandatory injunction directing that the so-called Committee be disbanded is denied. The order having been entered, the temporary restraining order will be dissolved.

....

KENNECOTT COPPER CORP. v. CURTISS-WRIGHT CORP.

United States Court of Appeals, Second Circuit
584 F.2d 1195 (1978)

VAN GRAAFEILAND, CIRCUIT JUDGE:

Curtiss-Wright Corporation has appealed from a judgment of the United States District Court for the Southern District of New York entered in the midst of a proxy fight between Curtiss-Wright and Kennecott Copper Corporation. At issue was the election of directors to the board of Kennecott, in which Curtiss-Wright had become a minority shareholder. The judgment, dated May 1, 1978, permanently enjoined Curtiss-Wright from further solicitation of Kennecott proxies and from voting the shares and proxies it then held at the May 2, 1978, annual meeting of Kennecott. On May 2, 1978, prior to the meeting, this Court granted a stay of the district court's judgment and an expedited appeal. For reasons that follow, we have concluded that the judgment must, in substantial part, be reversed.

In 1968, Kennecott, the largest producer of copper in the United States, sought to diversify by acquiring Peabody Coal Company. This acquisition was attacked by the Federal Trade Commission on antitrust grounds, and in 1977, following the Commission's order to divest, Peabody was sold. As consideration, Kennecott received $ 809 million in cash and some five per cent subordinated income notes due in 2007, which were in the face amount of $ 400 million but were carried on Kennecott's balance sheet at a value of $ 171 million. A number of shareholders urged the company to distribute the proceeds of the sale, either by making a cash tender offer for outstanding shares or by declaring an extraordinary cash dividend. Indeed, one shareholder commenced a shareholders' suit, the underlying purpose of which was to force such a distribution. Instead of acceding to these requests, Kennecott, in January 1978, purchased the Carborundum Company for $ 567 million in cash.

In November 1977, Curtiss-Wright, a diversified manufacturing company, decided to acquire an interest in Kennecott. By March 13, 1978, ... it had acquired 9.9 per cent of the outstanding Kennecott shares at a cost of approximately $ 77 million. On March 15, officials of Curtiss-Wright met with Kennecott officials to determine whether they could work together, and Curtiss-Wright suggested the nomination of a joint slate of candidates for Kennecott's board which would give Curtiss-Wright's nominees a minority position on the board. When these overtures were rejected, Curtiss-Wright, on March 23, 1978, announced its own slate and a campaign platform which, in effect, took up the cause of the shareholders who had sought distribution of the Peabody proceeds. In essence, Curtiss-Wright proposed that Kennecott try to sell Carborundum at or above the $ 567 million which Kennecott had paid for it and use the proceeds and other Kennecott funds to make either a tender offer for half the outstanding Kennecott shares at $ 40 per share, or a $ 20 per share cash distribution.

Kennecott did not wait for the battle lines thus to be drawn; it struck first. On [March 21, 1978,] Kennecott commenced the instant action in the District Court for the Southern District of New York.

Kennecott's original complaint alleged both securities and antitrust law violations arising out of Curtiss-Wright's acquisition of Kennecott stock. On April 5, 1978, Curtiss-Wright counterclaimed, alleging improper proxy solicitation by Kennecott. On April 17, 1978, the district court permitted Kennecott to amend its complaint to allege improper proxy solicitation by Curtiss-Wright. Each party sought injunctive relief. The trial commenced on April 24 and was completed on April 27.

The district court held that ... Curtiss-Wright's proxy solicitations had violated section 14(a) of the Securities Exchange Act of 1934 and Rule 14a-9(a) of the Commission, but Kennecott's solicitations had not .... The court enjoined Curtiss-Wright from voting its shares and proxies, while permitting Kennecott's annual meeting to go forward....

....

Rule 14a-9(a) Disclosures

Rule 14a-9(a) prohibits solicitation by a proxy statement that is false or misleading with respect to a material fact or which omits to state a material fact needed to make other statements therein not false or misleading. This rule, a typical securities regulation, was enacted to implement a "philosophy of full disclosure." *Santa Fe Industries, Inc. v. Green,* 430 U.S. 462 (1977). If full and fair disclosure is made, the wisdom and fairness of the program for which support is solicited are of tangential concern.

Curtiss-Wright's program, which followed upon its investment of $ 77 million in Kennecott, was not created in a vacuum. Although its officers were not privy to the inner workings of Kennecott, they studied the annual reports of Kennecott and its competitors and publications of the financial and copper industries. Curtiss-Wright's executive vice-president analyzed Kennecott's balance sheet, made a number of suggestions as to how it could be improved, and prepared a pro forma balance sheet showing the effect of Curtiss-Wright's proposals. However, Curtiss-Wright's consideration of the effect of its proposed plan was limited in nature, and it said so. Its April 4 proxy statement contained the following caveat:

> Curtiss-Wright has not made a detailed study of the consequences to Kennecott of the program described above. It and the nominees believe, however, that the program would not result in Kennecott's inability to continue its metals operations or to finance them. This belief is based upon the following: In the approximately nine years during which Kennecott owned Peabody it contributed approximately $ 532 million to Peabody's capital. Peabody thus represented a very substantial cash drain on Kennecott during the period it operated Peabody. Despite this Kennecott was able to continue its metals operations and to finance them.

The sale of Peabody produced $ 809 million in cash plus $ 400 million in subordinated income notes which are now valued by Kennecott at $ 171 million. The Peabody sale thus yielded approximately $ 980 million in present value of assets, of which $ 567 million was invested in Carborundum. The program of the nominees, described above, envisages the sale of Carborundum for about the same price and a distribution equivalent to approximately $ 20 per share, or $ 663 million in the aggregate. This would leave the Kennecott metal operations with approximately $ 317 million more in assets than were available to them at the time Kennecott owned Peabody, and without the need for continued cash contributions to Peabody.

Despite this clear and unequivocal statement by Curtiss-Wright that it had not made a "detailed study of the consequences to Kennecott of the program," the district judge held that its "proxy materials misled shareholders to believe that the feasibility of the plan had been thoroughly studied." He based this holding on a belief that Curtiss-Wright's disclaimer of a "detailed study" did not fully disclose that it had not conducted a thorough investigation. In making a Rule 14a-9(a) violation out of this semantic differentiation between "detailed study" and "thorough investigation," the district court erred.

Rare indeed is the proxy statement whose language could not be improved upon by a judicial craftsman sitting in the serenity of his chambers. This is particularly so where the statement is prepared in the "hurly-burly" of a contested election. "[N]ot every corporate counsel is a Benjamin Cardozo ...", *Ash v. LFE Corp.*, 525 F.2d 215, 221 (3d Cir. 1975), and nit-picking should not become the name of the game.

Assuming for the argument that the words "thorough investigation" would have been more descriptive than "detailed study," the latter term conveyed a sufficiently accurate picture so as not to mislead. Fair accuracy, not perfection, is the appropriate standard.

....

Because of the stay granted by this Court, Kennecott's annual meeting went on as scheduled; and this Court has been informed that management's slate was elected by a narrow margin. There is a strong likelihood, however, that the election results were influenced by the criticism of Curtiss-Wright contained in the district court's election-eve decision. Equity demands, therefore, that the proceedings of the 1978 annual meeting be voided in whole or in part so as to permit a new election of directors.

Because there must be another election in any event, we need not dwell upon Curtiss-Wright's allegations of improper solicitation by Kennecott. However, several of Curtiss-Wright's charges of wrongdoing merit comment. The first of these charges concerns alleged misstatements regarding Kennecott's inability to survive if Curtiss-Wright's plan was adopted. In a letter to its shareholders dated March 31, 1978, Kennecott stated:

> At the time of the Peabody divestiture your Board of Directors considered in depth what to do with the proceeds of the divestiture. To assist the Board it retained a major national investment banking firm to evaluate Kennecott's financial situation and opportunities.
>
> Among the alternatives considered was the possibility of a substantial direct distribution or the reacquisition of Kennecott shares. The Board concluded that this alternative would not be consistent with the maintenance of Kennecott as a viable company.

"Viable" in this context must mean capable of existing as an economic unit or able to generate enough income to pay expenses. That this was the meaning that Kennecott intended is shown by its statement in its April 17 mailing that "the Board and Management believe no other cause of action [save diversification] was possible if the Company were to survive."

The district court held that, inasmuch as the Kennecott board and its financial consultant, Morgan Stanley & Co., had investigated and rejected a plan of cash distribution of the Peabody proceeds, the March 31 material did not misstate facts in this regard. We disagree. There is nothing in the board minutes or the report of Kennecott's investment banking firm indicating that a conclusion concerning non-viability was reached. Moreover, Kennecott's board chairman conceded at the trial that the board did not examine the question whether the use of the Peabody proceeds for any other purpose except diversification was possible if the company was to survive. A conclusion reached by a company's board of directors that the company will not survive a proposed change is obviously a material matter. It should not be misstated.

Curtiss-Wright also contends that Kennecott misstated facts concerning the calling of certain loans. On March 31, 1978, just after the proxy contest had begun, Kennecott negotiated a new $ 450 million line of credit with a consortium of banks, against which it borrowed $ 234 million. This agreement contains several negative covenants, some of which would be breached if Curtiss-Wright's program were adopted. The agreement also provides that, if such a breach occurs, any bank holding forty per cent or more of the notes outstanding "may" terminate the bank's commitments and declare the entire principal to be due and payable.

On April 12, 1978, Kennecott advised its shareholders that adoption of the Curtiss-Wright program would result in a default under the loan agreement and would "trigger" the repayment of the $ 234 million. In its April 17 mailing Kennecott said that the sale of Carborundum and the distribution of the proceeds would result in a default and that "current borrowings would have to be repaid." The record discloses that Kennecott had attempted unsuccessfully to induce the major lending banks to sign a letter stating that, if requested to waive the covenants in question, they would refuse and, if Curtiss-Wright's program were carried out, they would require immediate repayment of their loaned funds. The shareholders were never notified that this conference took place.

The district court ignored Curtiss-Wright's argument that the above quoted words in Kennecott's proxy solicitations were misleading, holding only that the record supported Kennecott's statements that the Curtiss-Wright plan would breach certain negative covenants in the credit agreement. The question, however, was not whether the covenants would be breached, but whether the banks "would" require repayment of the loans. It seems to us that Kennecott was less than forthright in its disclosures on this point.

Curtiss-Wright's final complaint regarding Kennecott's proxy materials involves an alleged misstatement of figures. Curtiss-Wright's program envisioned the distribution to Kennecott shareholders of $ 663 million of the $ 980 million derived from the sale of Peabody, which, Curtiss-Wright stated, would leave an unused balance of $ 317 million. In Kennecott's mailing of April 12, 1978, it stated that Curtiss-Wright was ignoring the fact that $ 235 million of the Peabody proceeds had been used to reduce indebtedness. The mailing then continued:

This simply means that even if all of the opposition group's other premises are assumed to be correct and constant, then without this $ 235,000,000, in order for Kennecott to repurchase one-half of its outstanding stock with the resources assumed by the opposition group's soliciting material, the purchase price would have to be reduced by more than $ 14.17 per share — from the promised $ 40.00 to less than $ 25.83 per share.

What Kennecott was saying, in a somewhat convoluted fashion, was that, inasmuch as $ 235 million had been used to reduce indebtedness, the company would not end up with a balance of $ 317 million unless it paid no more than $ 25.83 per share for redeemed stock. We would not endorse this poor, or perhaps clever, choice of language as a Rule 14a-9(a) model. However, we think that Curtiss-Wright's characterization of it as "false and misleading" puts the matter too strongly.

Curtiss-Wright does not contend that Kennecott should have been unconditionally enjoined from voting its proxies at the 1978 annual meeting because of its alleged wrongful statements. Indeed, such a contention would be inconsistent with Curtiss-Wright's argument that the district judge erred in granting such drastic relief against it. The appropriate remedy, says Curtiss-Wright, would have been to adjourn the annual meeting and permit resolicitation, because then the shareholders who opted for the wrongdoing party would not have been disenfranchised. This, in effect, is the remedy we now provide by ordering a new election.

The district court will make the necessary orders to see that a new election is promptly scheduled, that further solicitation of proxies by both parties is permitted, and that proxy materials used in the solicitation comply with SEC rules and the decision of this Court.

....

Chapter 18

TENDER OFFERS

Situation

Daytron completed the purchase of Biologistics, Inc. with minimal shareholder opposition. Shortly thereafter, Daytron decides to attempt an acquisition of Harvest Electronics Corporation, a publicly held corporation headquartered in your state. Daytron's management believes that Harvest can only be acquired by means of a tender offer directed at its shareholders. It also believes that Harvest's management will fight the acquisition, among other things by filing a lawsuit in the local federal district court. Because of the expected litigation, Daytron has retained your firm as local counsel and wants you to be prepared to help defend its tender offer.

A tender offer is a form of acquisition in which the acquiring corporation goes directly to the shareholders of the target corporation and asks them to "tender" their shares in exchange for whatever the acquiring corporation is willing to offer. Typically it offers cash or some security, usually its own common stock. Sometimes tender offers are "friendly," in that they have the blessing of the target corporation's management. More often they are not. In a "hostile" tender offer, management of the target typically engages in various defenses in an attempt to fight off the acquisition. Martin Lipton and Erica H. Steinberger have well described the situation allegorically in the prologue to their book *Takeovers & Freezeouts*:*

> Modern corporate takeover battles resemble closely the feudal wars of the Middle Ages. A corporation that fears a raid by a Black Knight builds a Castle of charter amendments and changes in its corporate structure designed to make a takeover difficult. Then it attempts to establish a reputation for fierce resistance to takeovers by strongly rejecting all proposals to discuss alliance by merger. At the same time the serfs are pacified with increased dividends and a shareholder relations campaign. The Count warns his noblemen against fraternization with raiders. Frequently mercenaries, lawyers specializing in takeover battles, are specially retained to advise as to the design of the Castle, to periodically check the ramparts and smooth the glacis and to be available on short notice in the event of a surprise —

*Copyright 1984 by the authors. Reprinted with permission.

Saturday Night Special — attack. The King is petitioned repeatedly to promulgate a takeover law banning from the Kingdom all raids and raiders or at least making raids well nigh impossible. If a raid does come, the Council is convened, the Clergy is consulted and the mercenaries, if not already on retainer, are hired.

The Board of Directors is the Council. Like the feudal Council, it is often subservient to the Count. However, corporate presidents are not divine right rulers and the Board has a critical role in a takeover war. Without the full support of the Council, takeover defense is almost impossible and the Castle will quickly be lost. It is only the Council that can make the ultimate decision to reject the takeover bid and defend against a takeover raid. Here the power of the Council is supreme. The King demands that the Council act in good faith and on a reasonable basis to further the best interests of the serfs, not the Count and his noblemen. The Council almost always obeys the King's command for they know that they live in the Kingdom of the shareholder derivative lawsuit and the SEC enforcement proceeding.

The investment bankers are the Clergy. They consult the scriptures by Moody and Standard and Poor and damn the takeover bid as unfair or inadequate. They review the household accounts and bless the continued independence of the Castle. They comfort the serfs. They strengthen the resolve of the Count and the Council. They know the Bishops of Wall Street and can read their signs as they appear on the tape. They know the mercenaries and can reach them at any hour of the day or night. If the need arises, they act as emissaries to the neighboring Castles in the sometimes desperate last-minute quest for a White Knight.

The shields of the mercenaries are their legal opinions; the pikestaffs are their lawsuits. Their religion is loyalty, persistence and ingenuity. Their Holy Grail is the showstopper defense. They advise that with the blessing of the Clergy, the Council has a reasonable basis for rejecting the takeover bid and defending against the raid. This protects the Council against being held to account by the King's commissioners or the judge of the serfs' derivative lawsuit. They march against the Black Knight in court and regulatory agencies, probing his lines for weak spots and fighting at every turn. Their mission is to lift the siege. Or, at the very least to hold the Castle until the Clergy have found a White Knight.

If, despite the incantations of the Clergy and the sorties of the mercenaries, the Castle is about to be invested and the serfs are about to rebel, in rides the White Knight. He is a neighboring Count or foreign potentate of greater resources than the Black Knight. He too has mercenaries in his train. He vanquishes the Black Knight, repacifies the serfs and rebuilds the Castle. But alas, it is the White Knight's men who now sit at the Council table. The Count either swears fealty to his new overlord or joins his fellow exiles in Palm Beach or La Jolla.

So goeth the takeover wars.

Tender offers in which the acquiring corporation offers some security in exchange for the target's stock always have been regulated to some extent by the Securities Act of 1933. Under the Securities Act, the security to be offered has to be registered, unless an exemption is available. Since an exemption in this circumstance is a rarity, the target corporation's shareholders are almost always provided with the full disclosures that accompany registration.

Cash tender offers have been a different story. Until 1968 they were unregulated by the securities laws. In that year Congress, concerned about various abuses, passed legislation known as the Williams Act. That Act added §§ 13(d) and (e), and 14(d), (e) and (f), to the Securities Exchange Act of 1934. The bulk of this regulation, which covers both cash and non-cash tender offers, takes three forms: (1) disclosure requirements, (2) mandated tender offer provisions, and (3) an anti-fraud provision. But before examining Williams Act issues, it is important to look at the question of just what a tender offer is.

SECTION I. WHAT IS A TENDER OFFER?

The Williams Act does not define "tender offer," and the Securities and Exchange Commission has never defined it by rule. The next case provides a good introduction to judicial interpretations of the term.

HANSON TRUST PLC v. SCM CORP.

United States Court of Appeals, Second Circuit
774 F.2d 47 (1985)

MANSFIELD, CIRCUIT JUDGE:

Hanson Trust PLC, HSCM Industries, Inc., and Hanson Holdings Netherlands B.V. (hereinafter sometimes referred to collectively as "Hanson") appeal from an order of the Southern District of New York ... granting SCM Corporation's motion for a preliminary injunction restraining them, their officers, agents, employees and any persons acting in concert with them, from acquiring any shares of SCM and from exercising any voting rights with respect to 3.1 million SCM shares acquired by them on September 11, 1985. The injunction was granted on the ground that Hanson's September 11 acquisition of the SCM stock through five private and one open market purchases amounted to a "tender offer" for more than 5% of SCM's outstanding shares, which violated §§ 14(d)(1) and (6) of the Williams Act, and rules promulgated by the Securities and Exchange Commission (SEC) thereunder. We reverse.

The setting is the familiar one of a fast-moving bidding contest for control of a large public corporation: first, a cash tender offer of $ 60 per share by Hanson, an outsider, addressed to SCM stockholders; next, a counterproposal by an "insider" group consisting of certain SCM managers and their "White Knight," Merrill Lynch Capital Markets (Merrill), for a "leveraged buyout" at a higher price ($ 70 per share); then an increase by Hanson of its cash offer to $ 72 per share, followed by a revised SCM-Merrill leveraged buyout offer of $ 74 per share with a "crown jewel" irrevocable lock-up option to Merrill designed to discourage Hanson from seeking control by providing that if any other party (in this case Hanson) should acquire more than one-third of SCM's outstanding shares ($66^2/_3\%$ being needed under N.Y.Bus.L. § 903(a)(2) to effectuate a merger) Merrill would have the right to buy SCM's two most profitable businesses (consumer foods and pigments) at prices characterized by some as "bargain basement." The final act in this scenario was the decision of Hanson, having been deterred by the SCM-Merrill option (colloquially described in the market as a "poison pill"), to terminate its cash tender offer and then to make private purchases, amounting to 25% of SCM's outstanding shares, leading SCM to seek and obtain the preliminary injunction from which this appeal is taken....

....

Since ... the material relevant facts in the present case are not in dispute, this appeal turns on whether the district court erred as a matter of law in holding that when Hanson terminated its offer and immediately thereafter made private purchases of a substantial share of the target company's outstanding stock, the purchases became a "tender offer" within the meaning of § 14(d) of the Williams Act. Absent any express definition of "tender offer" in the Act, the answer requires a brief review of the background and purposes of § 14(d).

....

The typical tender offer, as described in the Congressional debates, hearings and reports on the Williams Act, consisted of a general, publicized bid by an individual or group to buy shares of a publicly-owned company, the shares of which were traded on a national securities exchange, at a price substantially above the current market price. The offer was usually accompanied by newspaper and other publicity, a time limit for tender of shares in response to it, and a provision fixing a quantity limit on the total number of shares of the target company that would be purchased.

... The average shareholder, pressured by the fact that the tender offer would be available for only a short time and restricted to a limit number of shares, was forced "with severely limited information, [to] decide what course of action he should take." H.R. Rep. No. 1711, 90th Cong., 2d Sess. 2 (1968)....

The purpose of the Williams Act was, accordingly, to protect the shareholders from that dilemma by insuring "that public shareholders who are confronted by a cash tender offer for their stock will not be required to respond without adequate information." *Piper v. Chris-Craft Industries,* 430 U.S. 1, 35 (1977).

....

Although § 14(d)(1) clearly applies to "classic" tender offers of the type described above, courts soon recognized that in the case of privately negotiated transactions or solicitations for private purchases of stock many of the conditions leading to the enactment of § 14(d) for the most part do not exist. The number and percentage of stockholders are usually far less than those involved in public offers. The solicitation involves less publicity than a public tender offer or none. The solicitees, who are frequently directors, officers or substantial stockholders of the target, are more apt to be sophisticated, inquiring or knowledgeable concerning the target's business, the solicitor's objectives, and the impact of the solicitation on the target's business prospects. In short, the solicitee in the private transaction is less likely to be pressured, confused, or ill-informed regarding the businesses and decisions at stake than solicitees who are the subjects of a public tender offer.

These differences between public and private securities transactions have led most courts to rule that private transactions or open market purchases do not qualify as a "tender offer" requiring the purchaser to meet the pre-filing strictures of § 14(d). The borderline between public solicitations and privately negotiated stock purchases is not bright and it is frequently difficult to determine whether transactions falling close to the line or in a type of "no man's land" are "tender offers" or private deals. This has led some to advocate a broader interpretation of the term "tender offer" than that followed by us in *Kennecott Copper Corp. v. Curtiss-Wright Corp.,* and to adopt the eight-factor "test" of what is a tender offer, which was recommended by the SEC and applied by the district court in *Wellman v. Dickinson,* 475 F. Supp. 783, 823-24 (S.D.N.Y. 1979), and by the Ninth Circuit in *SEC v. Carter Hawley Hale Stores, Inc.,* [760 F.2d 945 (9th Cir. 1985)]. The eight factors are:

(1) active and widespread solicitation of public shareholders for the shares of an issuer;
(2) solicitation made for a substantial percentage of the issuer's stock;
(3) offer to purchase made at a premium over the prevailing market price;
(4) terms of the offer are firm rather than negotiable;
(5) offer contingent on the tender of a fixed number of shares, often subject to a fixed maximum number to be purchased;
(6) offer open only for a limited period of time;
(7) offeree subjected to pressure to sell his stock;
....
[(8)] public announcements of a purchasing program concerning the target company precede or accompany rapid accumulation of large amounts of the target company's securities.

Although many of the above-listed factors are relevant for purposes of determining whether a given solicitation amounts to a tender offer, the elevation of such a list to a mandatory "litmus test" appears to be both unwise and unnecessary. As even the advocates of the proposed test recognize, in any given case a solicitation may constitute a tender offer even though some of the eight factors are absent or, when many factors are present, the solicitation may nevertheless not amount to a tender offer because the missing factors outweigh those present.

We prefer to be guided by the principle followed by the Supreme Court in deciding what transactions fall within the private offering exemption provided by § 4(1) of the Securities Act of 1933, and by ourselves in *Kennecott Copper* in determining whether the Williams Act applies to private transactions. That principle is simply to look to the statutory purpose. In *SEC v. Ralston Purina Co.*, 346 U.S. 119 (1953), the Court stated, "the applicability of § 4(1) should turn on whether the particular class of persons affected need the protection of the Act. An offering to those who are shown to be able to fend for themselves is a transaction 'not involving any public offering.'" Similarly, since the purpose of § 14(d) is to protect the ill-informed solicitee, the question of whether a solicitation constitutes a "tender offer" within the meaning of § 14(d) turns on whether, viewing the transaction in the light of the totality of circumstances, there appears to be a likelihood that unless the pre-acquisition filing strictures of that statute are followed there will be a substantial risk that solicitees will lack information needed to make a carefully considered appraisal of the proposal put before them.

Applying this standard, we are persuaded on the undisputed facts that Hanson's September 11 negotiation of five private purchases and one open market purchase of SCM shares, totalling 25% of SCM's outstanding stock, did not under the circumstances constitute a "tender offer" within the meaning of the Williams Act. Putting aside for the moment the events preceding the purchases, there can be little doubt that the privately negotiated purchases would not, standing alone, qualify as a tender offer, for the following reasons:

(1) In a market of 22,800 SCM shareholders the number of SCM sellers here involved, six in all, was minuscule compared with the numbers involved in public solicitations of the type against which the Act was directed.

(2) At least five of the sellers were highly sophisticated professionals, knowledgeable in the market place and well aware of the essential facts needed to exercise their professional skills and to appraise Hanson's offer, including its financial condition as well as that of SCM, the likelihood that the purchases might block the SCM-Merrill bid, and the risk that if Hanson acquired more than $33^1/_3\%$ of SCM's stock the SCM-Merrill lockup of the "crown jewel" might be triggered....

(3) The sellers were not "pressured" to sell their shares by any conduct that the Williams Act was designed to alleviate, but by the forces of the market place....

(4) There was no active or widespread advance publicity or public solicitation, which is one of the earmarks of a conventional tender offer....

(5) The price received by the six sellers, $ 73.50 per share, unlike that appearing in most tender offers, can scarcely be dignified with the label "premium." The stock market price on September 11 ranged from $ 72.50 to $ 73.50 per share....

(6) Unlike most tender offers, the purchases were not made contingent upon Hanson's acquiring a fixed minimum number or percentage of SCM's outstanding shares....

(7) Unlike most tender offers, there was no general time limit within which Hanson would make purchases of SCM stock....

There remains the question whether Hanson's private purchases take on a different hue, requiring them to be treated as a "*de facto*" continuation of its earlier tender offer, when considered in the context of Hanson's earlier acknowledged tender offer, the competing offer of SCM-Merrill and Hanson's termination of its tender offer. After reviewing all of the undisputed facts we conclude that the district court erred in so holding.

In the first place, we find no record support for the contention by SCM that Hanson's September 11 termination of its outstanding tender offer was false, fraudulent or ineffective. Hanson's termination notice was clear, unequivocal and straightforward. Directions were given, and presumably are being followed, to return all of the tendered shares to the SCM shareholders who tendered them. Hanson also filed with the SEC a statement pursuant to § 14(d)(1) of the Williams Act terminating its tender offer. As a result, at the time when Hanson made its September 11 private purchases of SCM stock it owned no SCM stock other than those shares revealed in its § 14(d) pre-acquisition report filed with the SEC on August 26, 1985.

....

Nor does the record support SCM's contention that Hanson had decided, before terminating its tender offer, to engage in each purchases.... Absent evidence or a finding that Hanson had decided to seek control of SCM through purchases of its stock, no duty of disclosure existed under the federal securities laws.

Second, Hanson had expressly reserved the right in its August 26, 1985, pre-acquisition tender offer filing papers, whether or not tendered shares were purchased, "*thereafter* ... to purchase additional Shares in the open market, in privately negotiated transactions, through another tender offer or otherwise." (Emphasis added). Thus, Hanson's privately negotiated purchases could hardly have taken the market by surprise. Indeed, professional arbitrageurs and market experts rapidly concluded that it was Hanson which was making the post-termination purchase.

Last, Hanson's prior disclosures of essential facts about itself and SCM in the pre-acquisition papers it filed on August 26, 1985, with the SEC pursuant to § 14(d)(1), are wholly inconsistent with the district court's characterization of Hanson's later private purchases as "a deliberate attempt to do an 'end run' around the requirements of the Williams Act." On the contrary, the record shows that Hanson had already filed with the SEC and made public substantially the same information as SCM contends that Hanson should have filed before making the cash purchases....

It may well be that Hanson's private acquisition of 25% of SCM's shares after termination of Hanson's tender offer was designed to block the SCM-Merrill leveraged buyout group from acquiring the $66^2/_3$% of SCM's stock needed to effectuate a merger. It may be speculated that such a blocking move might induce SCM to buy Hanson's 25% at a premium or lead to negotiations between the parties designed to resolve their differences. But we know of no provision in the federal securities laws or elsewhere that prohibits such tactics in "hardball" market battles of the type encountered here....

....

The order of the district court is reversed, the preliminary injunction against Hanson is vacated, and the case is remanded for further proceedings in accordance with this opinion....

SECTION II. WILLIAMS ACT ISSUES

As indicated above, the Williams Act added to the Exchange Act §§ 13(d) and (e) and 14(d), (e), and (f). Section 13(d) is aimed at tender offers only indirectly. It requires a person who owns more that 5% of a class of equity security registered under the Exchange Act to provide certain information to the issuer and to the Commission within ten days after the acquisition of securities that triggers the reporting requirement. The other Williams Act provision in § 13 is § 13(e). It gives the Commission the power to regulate repurchases by issuers of their own equity securities.

The centerpiece of the Williams Act is § 14(d). Under that provision, it is unlawful, unless certain filings are made, to make a tender offer for an Exchange Act-registered equity security and certain other securities[1] if success in the offer would result in ownership of more than 5% of the class. Section 14(d) also contains a limited amount of substantive regulation of tender offers. For example, it provides that if a tender offeror increases the price offered, it must pay the higher price to security holders who already name tendered at a lower price.

The Williams Act also contains an antifraud provision, § 14(e), that makes it unlawful to make a tender offer on the basis of materially false or misleading information. Unlike other provisions in the Williams Act, that section relates not only to tender offers for specified types of securities (basically those registered under the Exchange Act), but to tender offers for any kind of security.

Section 14(f) is a specialized provision that calls for certain disclosures to the Commission and to security holders when a majority of a corporation's directorships are to be filled, otherwise than at a meeting of security holders, following an acquisition of securities that is subject to the requirements of § 13(d) or 14(d). The usual trigger of that provision is the filling of vacant directorships by sitting directors, which generally is allowed under state corporation law. That provision is intended to deal with the situation in which control of the corporation is sold and, as a part of the transaction, it is agreed that the existing directors will resign seriatim and that the remaining directors will elect new directors who are chosen by the entity acquiring control.

---

[1] These are an insurance company's equity securities that would be required to be registered under the Exchange Act save for a registration exemption and equity securities issued by a closed-end investment company registered under the Investment Company Act of 1940.

The following cases touch on many of the important Williams Act issues that have arisen in litigation.

PIPER v. CHRIS-CRAFT INDUSTRIES, INC.

United States Supreme Court
430 U.S. 1 (1977)

MR. CHIEF JUSTICE BURGER delivered the opinion of the Court.

We granted certiorari in these cases to consider, among other issues, whether an unsuccessful tender offeror in a contest for control of a corporation has an implied cause of action for damages under § 14(e) of the Securities Exchange Act of 1934, as amended by the Williams Act of 1968 ..., based on alleged antifraud violations by the successful competitor, its investment adviser, and individuals comprising the management of the target corporation.

I

Background

The factual background of this complex contest for control, including the protracted litigation culminating in the case now before us, is essential to a full understanding of the contending parties' claims.

The three petitions present questions of first impression, arising out of a "sophisticated and hard fought contest" for control of Piper Aircraft Corporation, a Pennsylvania-based manufacturer of light aircraft. Piper's management consisted principally of members of the Piper family, who owned 31% of Piper's outstanding stock. Chris-Craft Industries, Inc., a diversified manufacturer of recreational products, attempted to secure voting control of Piper through cash and exchange tender offers for Piper common stock. Chris-Craft's takeover attempt failed, and Bangor Punta Corporation, with the support of the Piper family, obtained control of Piper in September 1969. Chris-Craft brought suit under § 14(e) of the Securities Exchange Act of 1934 ..., alleging that Bangor Punta achieved control of the target corporation as a result of violations of the federal securities laws by the Piper family, Bangor Punta, and Bangor Punta's underwriter, First Boston Corporation, who together had successfully repelled Chris-Craft's takeover attempt.

The struggle for control of Piper began in December 1968. At that time, Chris-Craft began making cash purchases of Piper common stock. By January 22, 1969, Chris-Craft had acquired 203,700 shares, or approximately 13% of Piper's 1,644,790 outstanding shares. On the next day, following unsuccessful preliminary overtures to Piper by Chris-Craft's president, Herbert Siegel, Chris-Craft publicly announced a cash tender offer for up to 300,000 Piper shares at $ 65 per share, which was approximately $ 12 above the then current market price. Responding promptly to Chris-Craft's bid, Piper's management met on the same day with the company's investment banker, First Boston, and other advisers. On January 24, the Piper family decided to oppose Chris-Craft's tender offer. As part of its resistance to Chris-Craft's takeover campaign, Piper management sent several letters to the company's stockholders between January 25-27, arguing against acceptance of Chris-Craft's offer. On January 27, a letter to shareholders from W. T. Piper, Jr., president of the company, stated that the Piper Board "has carefully studied this offer and is convinced that it is inadequate and not in the best interests of Piper's shareholders."

In addition to communicating with shareholders, Piper entered into an agreement with Grumman Aircraft Corporation on January 29, whereby Grumman agreed to purchase 300,000 authorized but unissued Piper shares at $ 65 per share. The agreement increased the amount of stock necessary for Chris-Craft to secure control and thus rendered Piper less vulnerable to Chris-Craft's attack. A Piper press release and letter to shareholders announced the Grumman transaction but failed to state either that Grumman had a "put" or option to sell the shares back to Piper at cost, plus interest, or that Piper was required to maintain the proceeds of the transaction in a separate fund free from liens.

Despite Piper's opposition, Chris-Craft succeeded in acquiring 304,606 shares by the time its cash tender offer expired on February 3. To obtain the additional 17% of Piper stock needed for control, Chris-Craft decided to make an exchange offer of Chris-Craft securities for Piper stock. Although Chris-Craft filed a registration statement and preliminary prospectus with the SEC in late February 1969, the exchange offer did not go into effect until May 15, 1969.

In the meantime, Chris-Craft made cash purchases of Piper stock on the open market until Mr. Siegel, the company's president, was expressly warned by SEC officials that such purchases, when made during the pendency of an exchange offer, violated SEC Rule 10b-6. At Mr. Siegel's direction, Chris-Craft immediately complied with the SEC's directive and canceled all outstanding orders for purchases of Piper stock.

While Chris-Craft's exchange offer was in registration, Piper in March 1969 terminated the agreement with Grumman and entered into negotiations with Bangor Punta. Bangor had initially been contacted by First Boston about the possibility of a Piper takeover in the wake of Chris-Craft's initial cash tender offer in January. With Grumman out of the picture, the Piper family agreed on May 8, 1969, to exchange their 31% stockholdings in Piper for Bangor Punta securities. Bangor also agreed to use its best efforts to achieve control of Piper by means of an exchange offer of Bangor securities for Piper common stock. A press release issued the same day announced the terms of the agreement, including a provision that the forthcoming exchange offer would involve Bangor securities to be valued, in the judgment of First Boston, "at not less than $ 80 per Piper share."

While awaiting the effective date of its exchange offer, Bangor in mid-May 1969 purchased 120,200 shares of Piper stock in privately negotiated, off-exchange transactions from three large institutional investors. All three purchases were made after the SEC's issuance of a release on May 5 announcing proposed Rule 10b-13, a provision which, upon becoming effective in November 1969, would expressly prohibit a tender offeror from making purchases of the target company's stock during the pendency of an exchange offer. The SEC release stated that the proposed rule was "in effect, a codification of existing interpretations under Rule 10b-6," the provision invoked by SEC officials against Mr. Siegel of Chris-Craft a month earlier. Bangor officials, although aware of the release at the time of the three off-exchange purchases, made no attempt to secure an exemption for the transactions from the SEC, as provided by Rule 10b-6(f). The Commission, however, took no action concerning these purchases as it had with respect to Chris-Craft's open market transactions.

With these three block purchases, amounting to 7% of Piper stock, Bangor Punta in mid-May took the lead in the takeover contest. The contest then centered upon the competing exchange offers. Chris-Craft's first exchange offer, which began in mid-May 1969, failed to produce tenders of the specified minimum number of Piper shares (80,000). Meanwhile, Bangor Punta's exchange offer, which had been announced on May 8, became effective on July 18. The registration materials which Bangor filed with the SEC in connection with the exchange offer included financial statements, reviewed by First Boston, representing that one of Bangor's subsidiaries, the Bangor and Aroostock Railroad (BAR), had a value of $ 18.4 million. This valuation was based upon a 1965 appraisal by investment bankers after a proposed sale of the BAR failed to materialize. The financial statements did not indicate that Bangor was considering the sale of BAR or that an offer to purchase the railroad for $ 5 million had been received.

In the final phase of the see-saw of competing offers, Chris-Craft modified the terms of its previously unsuccessful exchange offer to make it more attractive. The revised offer succeeded in attracting 112,089 additional Piper shares, while Bangor's exchange offer, which terminated on July 29, resulted in the tendering of 110,802 shares. By August 4, 1969, at the conclusion of both offers, Bangor Punta owned a total of 44.5%, while Chris-Craft owned 40.6% of Piper stock. The remainder of Piper stock, 14.9%, remained in the hands of the public.

After completion of their respective exchange offers, both companies renewed market purchases of Piper stock, but Chris-Craft, after purchasing 29,200 shares for cash in mid-August, withdrew from competition. Bangor Punta continued making cash purchases until September 5, by which time it had acquired a majority interest in Piper. The final tally in the nine-month takeover battle showed that Bangor Punta held over 50% and Chris-Craft held 42% of Piper stock.

II

Before either side had achieved control, the contest moved from the marketplace to the courts. Then began more than seven years of complex litigation growing out of the contest for control of Piper Aircraft.

[Chris-Craft first filed suit, seeking damages and injunctive relief, in May 1969. Over the next six years the District Court and the Court of Appeals issued several opinions with respect to various aspects of the litigation. Ultimately the

Court of Appeals held that Chris-Craft had standing to sue under § 14(e), that Piper had violated § 14(e) and that Chris-Craft was entitled to damages, the amount of which to be set by the District Court. The District Court then set damages at $ 1,673,988, measured by comparing the value of Chris-Craft's Piper stock prior and subsequent to Bangor's achieving control. The District Court also granted an award of prejudgment interest.]

Court of Appeals Opinion on Relief
April 11, 1975

In the final phase of the litigation, the Court of Appeals reversed on the damages issue and calculated Chris-Craft's damages without further remand to the District Court. The Court of Appeals fixed damages as the difference between what Chris-Craft had actually paid for Piper shares and the price at which the large minority block could have been sold at the earliest point after Bangor Punta gained control. Application of this formula produced damages in the amount of $ 36.98 per Piper share held by Chris-Craft, or a total of $ 25,793,365. The court instructed the District Court to recompute prejudgment interest based on the revised damage award. This new computation increased Chris-Craft's prejudgment interest from $ 600,000 to approximately $ 10 million.

It is this judgment which is now under review.

III

The Williams Act

....

Besides requiring disclosure and providing specific benefits for tendering shareholders, the Williams Act ... contains a broad antifraud prohibition, which is the basis of Chris-Craft's claim. Section 14(e) of the Act provides:

> It shall be unlawful for any person to make any untrue statement of a material fact or omit to state any material fact necessary in order to make the statements made, in the light of the circumstances under which they are made, not misleading, or to engage in any fraudulent, deceptive, or manipulative acts or practices, in connection with any tender offer or request or invitation for tenders, or any solicitation of security holders in opposition to or in favor of any such offer, request, or invitation.

This provision was expressly directed at the conduct of a broad range of persons, including those engaged in making or opposing tender offers or otherwise seeking to influence the decision of investors or the outcome of the tender offer.

The threshold issue in these cases is whether tender offerors such as Chris-Craft, whose activities are regulated by the Williams Act, have a cause of action for damages against other regulated parties under the statute on a claim that antifraud violations by other parties have frustrated the bidder's efforts to obtain control of the target corporation. Without reading such a cause of action into the Act, none of the other issues need be reached.

IV

Our analysis begins, of course, with the statute itself. Section 14(e), like § 10(b), makes no provision whatever for a private cause of action, such as those explicitly provided in other sections of the 1933 and 1934 Acts. This Court has nonetheless held that in some circumstances a private cause of action can be implied with respect to the 1934 Act's antifraud provisions, even though the relevant provisions are silent as to remedies. *J. I. Case Co. v. Borak,* 377 U.S. 426 (1964) (§ 14(a)); *Superintendent of Insurance v. Bankers Life & Cas. Co.,* 404 U.S. 6, 13 n. 9 (1971) (§ 10(b)).

The reasoning of these holdings is that, where congressional purposes are likely to be undermined absent private enforcement, private remedies may be implied in favor of the particular class intended to be protected by the statute. For example, in *J. I. Case Co. v. Borak, supra,* recognizing an implied right of action in favor of a shareholder complaining of a misleading proxy solicitation, the Court concluded as to such a shareholder's right:

> While [§ 14(a)] makes no specific reference to a private right of action, among its chief purposes is *"the protection of investors,"* which certainly implies the availability of judicial relief *where necessary to achieve that result.* 377 U.S., at 432. (Emphasis supplied.)

Indeed, the Court in *Borak* carefully noted that because of practical limitations upon the SEC's enforcement capabilities, "[p]rivate enforcement of the proxy rules provides *a necessary supplement to Commission action." Ibid.* (Emphasis added.)...

Against this background we must consider whether § 14(e), which is entirely silent as to private remedies, permits this Court to read into the statute a damages remedy for unsuccessful tender offerors. To resolve that question we turn to the legislative history to discern the congressional purpose underlying the specific statutory prohibition in § 14(e). Once we identify the legislative purpose, we must then determine whether the creation by judicial interpretation of the implied cause of action asserted by Chris-Craft is necessary to effectuate Congress' goals.

.....

The legislative history thus shows that Congress was intent upon regulating takeover bidders, theretofore operating covertly, in order to protect the shareholders of target companies. That tender offerors were not the intended beneficiaries of the bill was graphically illustrated by the statements of Senator Kuchel, cosponsor of the legislation, in support of requiring takeover bidders, whom he described as "corporate raiders" and "takeover pirates," to disclose their activities.

Today there are those individuals in our financial community who seek to reduce our proudest businesses into nothing but corporate shells. They seize control of the corporation with unknown assets, sell or trade away the best assets, and later split up the remains among themselves. The tragedy of such collusion is that the corporation can be financially raped without management *or shareholders* having any knowledge of the acquisitions.... The corporate raider may thus act under a cloak of secrecy while obtaining the shares needed to put him on the road to a successful capture of the company. 113 Cong. Rec. 857-858 (Jan. 18, 1967) (remarks of Sen. Kuchel). (Emphasis supplied.)

....

Moreover, the Senate Subcommittee heard the testimony of Professor Hayes, speaking on behalf of himself and his co-author of a comprehensive study on takeover attempts, who stated:

The two major protagonists — the bidder and the defending management — *do not need any additional protection,* in our opinion. They have the resources and the arsenal of moves and countermoves which can adequately protect their interests. Rather, *the investor* — who is the subject of these entreaties of both major protagonists — *is the one who needs a more effective champion....* Senate Hearings, at 57. (Emphasis supplied.)

... In this Court, however, Chris-Craft and the SEC contend that Congress clearly intended to protect tender offerors as part of a "pervasive scheme of federal regulation of tender offers." In support of their reading of the legislative history, they emphasize, first, that in enacting the legislation Congress was intent upon establishing a policy of even-handedness in takeover regulation. Congress was particularly anxious, Chris-Craft argues "to avoid tipping the balance of regulation...."

Congress was indeed committed to a policy of neutrality in contests for control, but its policy of even-handedness does not go either to the purpose of the legislation or to whether a private cause of action is implicit in the statute. Neutrality is, rather, but one characteristic of legislation directed toward a different purpose — the protection of investors. Indeed, the statements concerning the need for Congress to maintain a neutral posture in takeover attempts are contained in the section of the Senate Report entitled, "Protection of Investors." Taken in their totality, these statements confirm that what Congress had in mind was the protection of shareholders, the "pawn[s] in a form of industrial warfare."...

....

Accordingly, the congressional policy of "even-handedness" is nonprobative of the quite disparate proposition that the Williams Act was intended to confer rights for money damages upon an injured takeover bidder.

Besides the policy of even-handedness, Chris-Craft emphasizes that the matter of implied private causes of action was raised in written submissions to the Senate Subcommittee. Specifically, Chris-Craft points to the written statements of Professors Israels and Painter, who made reference to *J. I. Case v. Borak, supra.* Chris-Craft contends, therefore, that Congress was aware that private actions were implicit in § 14(e).

But this conclusion places more freight on the passing reference to *Borak* than can reasonably be carried. Even accepting the value of written statements received without comment by the committee and without cross-examination, the statements do not refer to implied private actions by *offeror-bidders*. For example, Professor Israels' statement on this subject reads:

> [A] private litigant could seek similar relief before or after the significant fact *such as the acceptance of his tender of securities.* Senate Report, at 67. (Emphasis supplied.)

Similarly, Professor Painter in his written submission referred to "injured investors." *Id.,* at 140. Neither Israels nor Painter discussed or even alluded to remedies potentially available to takeover bidders.

More important, these statements referred to a case in which the remedy was afforded to shareholders — the *direct* and *intended* beneficiaries of the legislation. In *Borak,* the Court emphasized that § 14(a), the proxy provision, was adopted expressly for "the protection of investors," 377 U.S., at 432, the very class of persons there seeking relief. The Court found no difficulty in identifying the legislative objective and concluding that remedies should be available if necessary "to make effective the congressional purpose." *Id.,* at 433. *Borak* did not involve, and the statements in the legislative history relied upon by Chris-Craft do not implicate, the interests of parties such as offeror-bidders who are outside the scope of the concerns articulated in the evolution of this legislation.

. . . .

Finally, Chris-Craft emphasizes what it perceives as the Commission's express concern with the plight of takeover bidders faced with "unfair tactics by entrenched management." The SEC Chairman did indeed speak in the Subcommittee Hearings of the need to "regulate improper practices by management and others opposing a tender offer ...." Senate Hearings, at 184. But in so doing, he was not pleading the cause of takeover bidders; on the contrary, he testified that imposing disclosure duties upon management would "make it much easier for *stockholders* to evaluate the offer on its merits." *Ibid.* (Emphasis supplied.)

In short, by extending the statute's coverage to solicitations in opposition to tender offers, Congress was seeking to broaden the scope of protection afforded to shareholders confronted with competing claims ....

The legislative history thus shows that the sole purpose of the Williams Act was the protection of investors who are confronted with a tender offer. As we stated in *Rondeau v. Mosinee Paper Corp.,* 422 U.S., at 58: "The purpose of the Williams Act is to insure that public shareholders who are confronted by a cash tender offer for their stock will not be required to respond without adequate information ...." We find no hint in the legislative history, on which respondent so heavily relies, that Congress contemplated a private cause of action for damages by one of several contending offerors against a successful bidder or by a losing contender against the target corporation.

.....

Our conclusion as to the legislative history is confirmed by the analysis in *Cort v. Ash,* 422 U.S. 66 (1975). There, the Court identified four factors as "relevant" in determining whether a private remedy is implicit in a statute not expressly providing one. The first is whether the plaintiff is "'one of the class for whose *especial* benefit the statute was enacted ....'" As previously indicated, examination of the statute and its genesis shows that Chris-Craft is not an intended beneficiary of the Williams Act, and surely is not one "for whose *especial* benefit the statute was enacted."...

Second, in *Cort v. Ash* we inquired whether there was "any indication of legislative intent, explicit or implicit, either to create such a remedy or to deny one." Although the historical materials are barren of any express intent to deny a damages remedy to tender offerors as a class, there is, as we have noted, no indication that Congress intended to create a damages remedy in favor of the loser in a contest for control....

.....

Third, *Cort v. Ash* tells us that we must ascertain whether it is "consistent with the underlying purposes of the legislative scheme to imply such a remedy for the plaintiff." We conclude that it is not. As a disclosure mechanism aimed especially at protecting shareholders of target corporations, the Williams Act cannot consistently be interpreted as conferring a monetary remedy upon regulated parties, particularly where the award would not redound to the direct benefit of the protected class....

.....

Fourth, under the *Cort v. Ash* analysis, we must decide whether "the cause of action [is] one traditionally relegated to state law ...." Despite the pervasiveness of federal securities regulation, the Court of Appeals concluded in these cases that Chris-Craft's complaint would give rise to a cause of action under common-law principles of interference with a prospective commercial advantage. Although Congress is, of course, free to create a remedial scheme in favor of contestants in tender offers, we conclude, as we did in *Cort v. Ash,* that "it is entirely appropriate in this instance to relegate [the offeror-bidder] and others in [that] situation to whatever remedy is created by state law," at least to the extent that the offeror seeks damages for having been wrongfully denied a "fair opportunity" to compete for control of another corporation.

.....

We therefore conclude that Chris-Craft, as a defeated tender offeror, has no implied cause of action for damages under § 14(e).

.....

INDIANA NATIONAL CORP. v. RICH

United States Court of Appeals, Seventh Circuit
712 F.2d 1180 (1983)

CUDAHY, CIRCUIT JUDGE.

This case requires us to decide whether there is an implied private right of action for an issuer corporation to seek injunctive relief under Section 13(d) of the Securities Exchange Act (the "Act"). Section 13(d) requires any person acquiring more than 5% of a class of registered securities of a corporation to send to the issuer and to file with the S.E.C. a statement disclosing certain information about the person's identity and purposes. The other federal courts of appeal which have considered this question have concluded that an issuer corporation has an implied right of action to obtain injunctive relief against violations of Section 13(d). We agree, and in so doing reverse the judgment of the district court in this case.

I

Plaintiff, Indiana National Corporation ("Indiana National"), is a bank holding company which engages principally in the banking business through its wholly owned subsidiary, Indiana National Bank. Indiana National's stock is registered pursuant to Section 12 of the Securities Exchange Act and is traded in the over-the-counter market. The defendants are a group of investors who acquired more than 5% of Indiana National's stock during 1981 and 1982. As required by Section 13(d) of the Act, they filed a Schedule 13D on September 4, 1981, and subsequently amended it six times between then and August 10, 1982.

On July 21, 1982, Indiana National filed a complaint in which it was alleged that the defendants' Schedule 13D contained materially false and misleading information, in that it failed to disclose the defendants' intention to acquire control of Indiana National, the Federal Reserve Bank's prior denial of an application by certain of the defendants for control of another bank, certain information concerning the members of the group and the true source of the funds used to acquire the shares. The plaintiffs sought a court order compelling defendants to file an amended Schedule 13D with full disclosure in the respects noted, as well as enjoining defendants from acquiring more shares of Indiana National, and compelling them to divest themselves of the shares they already held, which were alleged to have been unlawfully acquired.

In response, the defendants filed a motion to dismiss the complaint on the grounds, in relevant part, that Indiana National, as the issuer of the stock, had no standing to assert a claim under Section 13(d) of the Act. On December 30, 1982, the district court granted the defendants' motion to dismiss on the ground that an issuer corporation does not have an implied right of action under Section 13(d) of the Act....

II

In the course of the last decade, the Supreme Court has given us substantial guidance about when to imply a private right of action in the face of statutory silence. In 1975, the Court outlined a four-part test to determine the appropriateness of such a remedy: (1) whether the plaintiff is a member of a class for whose especial benefit the statute was enacted; (2) whether there is any explicit or implicit indication of congressional intent to create or deny a private remedy; (3) whether a private remedy would be consistent with the underlying purposes of the legislative scheme; and (4) whether the cause of action is one traditionally relegated to state law. *Cort v. Ash,* 422 U.S. 66, 78 (1975). Several years later, however, the Court indicated that these factors were not of equal weight but that the central inquiry, at which the first three factors were all directed, was one of congressional intent. *Touche Ross & Co. v. Redington,* 442 U.S. 560, 575 (1979); *Transamerica Mortgage Advisors, Inc. (TAMA) v. Lewis,* 444 U.S. 11, 15-16 (1979).

The reduction of these questions to one of congressional intent imposes on us the challenging task of divining, as of a moment in the past, the collective state of mind of a body of legislators. But on this question as well, recent Supreme Court cases have shed additional light. In perusing the legislative history for signs of congressional intent, we are directed to pay particular attention to the contemporary legal context in which the statute was enacted. *See Cannon v. University of Chicago,* 441 U.S. 677, 694-703 (1979); *Merrill Lynch, Pierce, Fenner & Smith, Inc. v. Curran,* 456 U.S. 353, 378-82 (1982). Thus in *Cannon* the Supreme Court, in finding that there was a private right of action implied in Title IX of the Education Amendments of 1972, emphasized that Title IX was patterned after Title VI of the Civil Rights Act of 1964 and was enacted at a time when Title VI had been construed as creating a private remedy. Thus, the Court reasoned, Congress must be presumed to have been aware of the previous five years of judicial interpretation of Title VI and to have expected its enactment (Title IX) to be interpreted in conformity with those precedents. In *Merrill Lynch,* the Court described this approach in more detail:

> In determining whether a private cause of action is implicit in a federal statutory scheme when the statute by its terms is silent on that issue, the initial focus must be on the state of the law at the time the legislation was enacted.... When Congress acts in a statutory context in which an implied private remedy has already been recognized by the courts, the inquiry logically is different. Congress need not have intended to create a new remedy, since one already existed; the question is whether Congress intended to preserve the pre-existing remedy.

Thus the Court was led to conclude that, when Congress undertook reexamination and significant amendment of a statute while leaving intact the provisions under which the federal courts had implied a cause of action, the evidence was that

Congress had affirmatively intended to preserve that remedy. This approach, construing a statute in light of the contemporary legal context in order to determine whether Congress intended that a private right of action be implied, has recently been reaffirmed by the Supreme Court in *Herman & MacLean v. Huddleston,* 103 S. Ct. 683, 689 (1983); and we shall make use of it in analyzing the case at hand.

III

The Williams Act amendments to the Securities Exchange Act were passed in 1968 in response to the growing use of cash tender offers as a means for achieving corporate takeovers. *Piper v. Chris-Craft Industries, Inc.,* 430 U.S. 1, 22 (1977). The purpose of the Williams Act was to insure that public shareholders facing a tender offer or the acquisition by a third party of a large block of shares possibly involving a contest for control be armed with adequate information about the qualifications and intentions of the party making the offer or acquiring the shares. Whereas corporate acquisitions by proxy solicitations or by exchange offers of securities were subject to registration and disclosure requirements, tender offers or acquisitions of substantial amounts of stock having a potential for control were not subject to similar requirements.

....

At the time it was enacted ... the Williams Act was consciously patterned upon the protections already available in the proxy rules, Section 14(a) of the Act. As former S.E.C. Chairman Manuel F. Cohen explained at the Senate hearings:

> The procedures provided by the bill in the case of contested tender offers are analogous to those now followed when contending factions solicit proxies under the Commission's proxy rules.

Hearings on S. 510 Before the Subcomm. on Securities of the Senate Comm. on Banking and Currency, 90th Cong., 1st Sess. 16 (1967). And in 1968 it was already established that an issuer corporation had an implied private right of action under Section 14(a). Thus, although the Williams Act did not itself contain an explicit private right of action, the statute upon which it was modeled had already been held to contain such a right by implication. We are justified in assuming, as did the Supreme Court in an analogous situation in *Cannon,* that Congress was aware of this precedent when the Williams Act was enacted upon the model of a prior statute.

More important, the Williams Act has itself been twice amended; and on neither occasion did Congress avail itself of the opportunity to overturn the accumulating precedents for a private right of action for issuer corporations under Section 13(d). When the Act was amended in 1970, this Court had already assumed the existence of such a right of action; and by the time of the 1977 amendments, the Court of Appeals for the Second Circuit had explicitly addressed the issue and concluded in a landmark decision that a private right of action for issuer corporations must be implied under Section 13(d). Moreover, the Supreme

Court had assumed, without directly confronting the issue, that such a private right was available to issuer corporations, at least with respect to injunctive relief. *See Rondeau v. Mosinee Paper Corp.,* 422 U.S. 49, 59 n. 9 (1975). We are justified in presuming that Congress was aware of these judicial interpretations when the Williams Act was amended. *See Cannon v. University of Chicago,* 441 U.S. at 696-99. Since Congress amended the Act while leaving this remedy intact, we conclude that the legislature affirmatively intended to preserve the remedy of a private right of action for issuer corporations under Section 13(d). *See Merrill Lynch, Pierce, Fenner & Smith v. Curran,* 456 U.S. at 381-82.

In reaching a conclusion opposite to the one we reach here, the district court, following *Gateway Industries, Inc. v. Agency Rent A Car, Inc.,* 495 F. Supp. 92 (N.D. Ill. 1980), emphasized that the Securities Exchange Act expressly includes several methods for enforcing the disclosure requirements of Section 13(d), most notably, remedies available through action by the S.E.C. itself. The district court also noted that other sections of the Securities Exchange Act expressly provide for private rights of action, and concluded that the provision of these explicit remedies was evidence that Congress intended *not* to provide a private right under Section 13(d).

We do not believe that this argument, based on the doctrine that *expressio unius est exclusio alterius,* compels such a conclusion in this case. The Supreme Court's most recent case on implied private rights of action explicitly rejects the notion that the availability of an express remedy in a statute precludes the implication of a private right of action as well. *Herman & MacLean v. Huddleston,* 103 S. Ct. at 687-90. The Court in *Huddleston* also reaffirmed the analysis, based on *Cannon* and *Merrill Lynch,* that revision of the securities laws in light of a line of cases allowing private suit, without overturning those precedents, should be taken as evidence (like that in the case before us) that Congress assumed the existence of the private remedy and intended to ratify it.

Our conclusion is further bolstered by the fact that such an interpretation of the statutory provision at issue is the only construction which can make the Section 13(d) disclosure requirements effective at all. The filing required by Section 13(d) is sent to the S.E.C. and to the issuer corporation; it is not disseminated to the shareholders, for whose protection the information is required. The S.E.C., as friend of the court, has told us that it is unreasonable to expect the Commission to police possible Section 13(d) filing violations. The only party with both the capability and incentive to pursue these violations is the issuer corporation. Our conclusion that Congress intended that a private right of action for an issuer corporation be implied under Section 13(d) is thus inescapable if the objectives of the statute are to be realized.

IV

The appellees contend, however, that an issuer corporation has no right of action under Section 13(d) under the analysis outlined by the Supreme Court in *Cort v. Ash,* 422 U.S. 66, 95 S. Ct. 2080, 45 L. Ed. 2d 26 (1975). First of all, we doubt whether the *Cort* four-factor analysis is still the proper test to apply in circumstances such as this. The Supreme Court seems to have put an entirely new gloss upon the *Cort* test in its most recent opinions. Instead of *Cort,* as such, it has moved to a direct consideration of the underlying issue of legislative intent. *See Merrill Lynch,* 456 U.S. at 393; *Transamerica Mortgage Advisors,* 444 U.S. at 23; *Touche Ross,* 442 U.S. at 575....

....

Our conclusion that an issuer corporation has a right of action under Section 13(d) brings the law in this circuit into accord with the conclusions of all the other circuits which have considered this question.[2] In *GAF Corp. v. Milstein,* 453 F.2d 709, the Second Circuit concluded that "the obligation to file *truthful* statements is implicit in the obligation to file with the issuer, and, *a fortiori,* the issuer has standing under Section 13(d) to seek relief in the event of a false filing." The First Circuit in *General Aircraft Corp. v. Lampert,* 556 F.2d 90 (1977), held that when there is a finding that a Schedule 13D is incomplete, inaccurate or false, the corporation has a right to injunctive relief "until the Schedule 13D is amended to reflect accurately their [the investing person's] intentions." Similarly, the Eighth Circuit has upheld a target corporation's standing to maintain an equitable action involving the completeness and truthfulness of a section 13(d) filing and to secure equitable relief requiring the purchaser to file an accurate, truthful and complete Schedule 13D in order to make a "full and fair disclosure." *Chromalloy American Corp. v. Sun Chemical Corp.,* 611 F.2d 240, 248 n. 16 (1979). Moreover, the Fourth Circuit, following the reasoning in all these cases, concluded that a target corporation has the right to seek injunctive relief to enforce the filing of a complete and accurate Schedule 13D. *Dan River, Inc. v. Unitex Ltd.,* 624 F.2d 1216, 1224 (1980). Insofar as our conclusion that the issuer corporation in the case at hand has a similar right to seek injunctive relief under Section 13(d) conflicts with *Gateway Industries, Inc. v. Agency Rent A Car, Inc.,* 495 F. Supp. 92 (N.D. Ill. 1980), and *Sta-Rite Industries, Inc. v. Nortek, Inc.,* 494 F. Supp. 358 (E.D. Wis. 1980), we disapprove the conclusions in those cases.

....

---

[2] In 1984 the Eleventh Circuit broke with the other circuits, in *Liberty Nat'l Ins. Holding Co. v. Charter Co.,* 734 F.2d 545 (11th Cir. 1984), by finding that neither Exchange Act Section 13(d) nor Section 14(d) or (e) impliedly authorizes a suit by a target brought to require the tender offeror to divest itself of all target shares. However, in 1985 a different panel of the Eleventh Circuit, distinguishing *Liberty National,* held that a target does have standing to sue under these Exchange Act sections when seeking corrective disclosures rather than divestiture. *Florida Commercial Banks v. Culverhouse,* 772 F.2d 1513 (11th Cir. 1985). [Eds.]

SCHREIBER v. BURLINGTON NORTHERN, INC.

United States Supreme Court
472 U.S. 1 (1985)

CHIEF JUSTICE BURGER delivered the opinion of the Court.

We granted certiorari to resolve a conflict in the Circuits over whether misrepresentation or nondisclosure is a necessary element of a violation of § 14(e) of the Securities Exchange Act of 1934.

I

On December 21, 1982, Burlington Northern, Inc., made a hostile tender offer for El Paso Gas Co. Through a wholly owned subsidiary, Burlington proposed to purchase 25.1 million El Paso shares at $ 24 per share. Burlington reserved the right to terminate the offer if any of several specified events occurred. El Paso management initially opposed the takeover, but its shareholders responded favorably, fully subscribing the offer by the December 30, 1982 deadline.

Burlington did not accept those tendered shares; instead, after negotiations with El Paso management, Burlington announced on January 10, 1983, the terms of a new and friendly takeover agreement. Pursuant to the new agreement, Burlington undertook, *inter alia,* to (1) rescind the December tender offer, (2) purchase 4,166,667 shares from El Paso at $ 24 per share, (3) substitute a new tender offer for only 21 million shares at $ 24 per share, (4) provide procedural protections against a squeeze-out merger[3] of the remaining El Paso shareholders, and (5) recognize "golden parachute"[4] contracts between El Paso and four of its

---

[3] A "squeeze-out" merger occurs when Corporation A, which holds a controlling interest in Corporation B, uses its control to merge B into itself or into a wholly owned subsidiary. The minority shareholders in Corporation B are, in effect, forced to sell their stock. The procedural protection provided in the agreement between El Paso and Burlington required the approval of non-Burlington members of El Paso's board of directors before a squeeze-out merger could proceed. Burlington eventually purchased all the remaining shares of El Paso for $ 12 cash and one quarter share of Burlington preferred stock per share. The parties dispute whether this consideration was equal to that paid to those tendering during the January tender offer.

[4] Petitioner alleged in her complaint that respondent Burlington failed to disclose that four officers of El Paso had entered into "golden parachute" agreements with El Paso for "extended employment benefits in the event El Paso should be taken over, which benefits would give them millions of dollars of extra compensation." The term "golden parachute" refers generally to agreements between a corporation and its top officers which guarantee those officers continued employment, payment of a lump sum, or other benefits in the event of a change of corporate ownership. As described in the Schedule 14D-9 filed by El Paso with the Commission on January 12, 1983, El Paso entered into "employment agreements" with two of its officers for a period of not less than five years, and with two other officers for a period of three years. The Schedule 14D-9 also disclosed that El Paso's Deferred Compensation Plan had been amended "to provide that for the purposes of such Plan a participant shall be deemed to have retired at the instance of the Company if his duties as a director, officer or employee of the Company have been diminished or curtailed by the Company in any material respect."

senior officers. By February 8, more than 40 million shares were tendered in response to Burlington's January offer, and the takeover was completed.

The rescission of the first tender offer caused a diminished payment to those shareholders who had tendered during the first offer. The January offer was greatly oversubscribed and consequently those shareholders who retendered were subject to substantial proration. Petitioner Barbara Schreiber filed suit on behalf of herself and similarly situated shareholders, alleging that Burlington, El Paso, and members of El Paso's board violated § 14(e)'s prohibition of "fraudulent, deceptive or manipulative acts or practices ... in connection with any tender offer." She claimed that Burlington's withdrawal of the December tender offer coupled with the substitution of the January tender offer was a "manipulative" distortion of the market for El Paso stock. Schreiber also alleged that Burlington violated § 14(e) by failing ... to disclose the "golden parachutes" offered to four of El Paso's managers. She claims that this January nondisclosure was a deceptive act forbidden by § 14(e).

The District Court dismissed the suit for failure to state a claim....

The Court of Appeals for the Third Circuit affirmed....

....

II

A

We are asked in this case to interpret § 14(e) of the Securities Exchange Act. The starting point is the language of the statute. Section 14(e) provides:

> It shall be unlawful for any person to make any untrue statement of a material fact or omit to state any material fact necessary in order to make the statements made, in the light of the circumstances under which they are made, not misleading, or to engage in any fraudulent, deceptive or manipulative acts or practices, in connection with any tender offer or request or invitation for tenders, or any solicitation of security holders in opposition to or in favor of any such offer, request, or invitation....

Petitioner relies on a construction of the phrase, "fraudulent, deceptive or manipulative acts or practices." Petitioner reads the phrase "fraudulent, deceptive or manipulative acts or practices" to include acts which, although fully disclosed, "artificially" affect the price of the takeover target's stock. Petitioner's interpretation relies on the belief that § 14(e) is directed at purposes broader than providing full and true information to investors.

Petitioner's reading of the term "manipulative" conflicts with the normal meaning of the term. We have held in the context of an alleged violation of § 10(b) of the Securities Exchange Act:

> Use of the word "manipulative" is especially significant. It is and was virtually a term of art when used in connection with the securities markets. It connotes intentional or willful conduct *designed to deceive or defraud*

investors by controlling or artificially affecting the price of securities. *Ernst & Ernst v. Hochfelder,* 425 U.S. 185, 199 (1976) (emphasis added).

Other cases interpreting the term reflect its use as a general term comprising a range of misleading practices.... The meaning the Court has given the term "manipulative" is consistent with the use of the term at common law, and with its traditional dictionary definition.

....

B

Our conclusion that "manipulative" acts under § 14(e) require misrepresentation or nondisclosure is buttressed by the purpose and legislative history of the provision....

It is clear that Congress relied primarily on disclosure to implement the purpose of the Williams Act. Senator Williams, the Bill's Senate sponsor, stated in the debate:

> Today, the public shareholder in deciding whether to accept or reject a tender offer possesses limited information. No matter what he does, he acts without adequate knowledge to enable him to decide rationally what is the best course of action. This is precisely the dilemma which our securities laws are designed to prevent. 113 Cong. Rec. 24664 (1967) (remarks of Sen. Williams).

The expressed legislative intent was to preserve a neutral setting in which the contenders could fully present their arguments....

....

While legislative history specifically concerning § 14(e) is sparse, the House and Senate Reports discuss the role of § 14(e). Describing § 14(e) as regulating "fraudulent transactions," and stating the thrust of the section:

> This provision would affirm the fact that persons engaged in making or opposing tender offers or otherwise seeking to influence the decision of investors or the outcome of the tender offer are under an obligation to make *full disclosure* of material information to those with whom they deal. H.R. Rep. No. 1711, 90th Cong., 2d Sess., 11 (1968) (emphasis added); S.R. Rep. No. 550, 90th Cong., 1st Sess., 11 (1967) (emphasis added).

Nowhere in the legislative history is there the slightest suggestion that § 14(e) serves any purpose other than disclosure, or that the term "manipulative" should be read as an invitation to the courts to oversee the substantive fairness of tender offers; the quality of any offer is a matter for the marketplace.

To adopt the reading of the term "manipulative" urged by petitioner would not only be unwarranted in light of the legislative purpose but would be at odds with it. Inviting judges to read the term "manipulative" with their own sense of what constitutes "unfair" or "artificial" conduct would inject uncertainty into the tender offer process. An essential piece of information — whether the court would deem the fully disclosed actions of one side or the other to be "manipulative" — would not be available until after the tender offer had closed. This uncertainty would directly contradict the expressed Congressional desire to give investors full information.

Congress' consistent emphasis on disclosure persuades us that it intended takeover contests to be addressed to shareholders. In pursuit of this goal, Congress, consistent with the core mechanism of the Securities Exchange Act, created sweeping disclosure requirements and narrow substantive safeguards. The same Congress that placed such emphasis on shareholder choice would not at the same time have required judges to oversee tender offers for substantive fairness. It is even less likely that a Congress implementing that intention would express it only through the use of a single word placed in the middle of a provision otherwise devoted to disclosure.

C

We hold that the term "manipulative" as used in § 14(e) requires misrepresentation or nondisclosure. It connotes "conduct designed to deceive or defraud investors by controlling or artificially affecting the price of securities." *Ernst & Ernst v. Hochfelder,* 425 U.S., at 199. Without misrepresentation or nondisclosure, § 14(e) has not been violated.

Applying that definition to this case, we hold that the actions of respondents were not manipulative. The amended complaint fails to allege that the cancellation of the first tender offer was accompanied by any misrepresentation, nondisclosure or deception. The District Court correctly found, "All activity of the defendants that could have conceivably affected the price of El Paso shares was done openly."

Petitioner also alleges that El Paso management and Burlington entered into certain undisclosed and deceptive agreements during the making of the second tender offer. The substance of the allegations is that, in return for certain undisclosed benefits, El Paso managers agreed to support the second tender offer. But both courts noted that petitioner's complaint seeks redress only for injuries related to the cancellation of the first tender offer. Since the deceptive and misleading acts alleged by the petitioner all occurred with reference to the making of the second tender offer — when the injuries suffered by petitioner had already been sustained — these acts bear no possible causal relationship to petitioner's alleged injuries....

....

SECTION III. STATE REGULATION

Shortly after passage of the Williams Act, state legislatures began adopting their own takeover statutes. Finally, over two-thirds of the states passed such a statute in one form or the other. While the Williams Act is generally viewed as neutral on takeovers, the state statutes tended to be protective of "local" target corporation management. The reasons for that seem clear enough. First, managements of in-state corporations have substantial political power in state legislatures, while those of outside corporations have very little. Second, legislatures properly fear that industry is less likely to be responsive to local needs, and also is more likely to be moved out of state, if decisionmaking power is in the hands of distant management.

During the years when most of those state statutes were being passed, there was much controversy about their constitutionality. It was argued that they impermissibly burdened interstate commerce and that they were preempted by the Williams Act. In 1982 the Supreme Court, in the following case, decided the issue with respect to the Illinois law, which was representative of a substantial number of those statutes.

EDGAR v. MITE CORP.

United States Supreme Court
457 U.S. 624 (1982)

JUSTICE WHITE delivered an opinion, Parts I, II, and V-B of which are the opinion of the Court.[5]

The issue in this case is whether the Illinois Business Takeover Act is unconstitutional under the Supremacy and Commerce Clauses of the Federal Constitution.

I

Appellee MITE Corp. and its wholly owned subsidiary, MITE Holdings, Inc., are corporations organized under the laws of Delaware with their principal executive offices in Connecticut. Appellant James Edgar is the Secretary of State of Illinois and is charged with the administration and enforcement of the Illinois Act. Under the Illinois Act any takeover offer for the shares of a target company must be registered with the Secretary of State. A target company is defined as a corporation or other issuer of securities of which shareholders located in Illinois own 10% of the class of equity securities subject to the offer, or for which any two of the following three conditions are met: the corporation has its principal executive office in Illinois, is organized under the laws of Illinois, or has at least 10% of its stated capital and paid-in surplus represented within the State. An offer becomes registered 20 days after a registration statement is filed with the Secretary unless the Secretary calls a hearing. The Secretary may call a hearing at any time during the 20-day waiting period to adjudicate the substantive fairness of the offer if he believes it is necessary to protect the shareholders of the target

---

[5] THE CHIEF JUSTICE joins the opinion in its entirety; JUSTICE BLACKMUN joins Parts I, II, III, and IV; JUSTICE POWELL joins Parts I and V-B; and JUSTICE STEVENS and JUSTICE O'CONNOR join Parts I, II, and V.

company, and a hearing must be held if requested by a majority of a target company's outside directors or by Illinois shareholders who own 10% of the class of securities subject to the offer. If the Secretary does hold a hearing, he is directed by the statute to deny registration to a tender offer if he finds that it "fails to provide full and fair disclosure to the offerees of all material information concerning the take-over offer, or that the take-over offer is inequitable or would work or tend to work a fraud or deceit upon the offerees ...."

On January 19, 1979, MITE initiated a cash tender offer for all outstanding shares of Chicago Rivet & Machine Co., a publicly held Illinois corporation, by filing a Schedule 14D-1 with the Securities and Exchange Commission in order to comply with the Williams Act. The Schedule 14D-1 indicated that MITE was willing to pay $ 28 per share for any and all outstanding shares of Chicago Rivet, a premium of approximately $ 4 over the then-prevailing market price. MITE did not comply with the Illinois Act, however, and commenced this litigation on the same day by filing an action in the United States District Court for the Northern District of Illinois. The complaint asked for a declaratory judgment that the Illinois Act was pre-empted by the Williams Act and violated the Commerce Clause. In addition, MITE sought a temporary restraining order and preliminary and permanent injunctions prohibiting the Illinois Secretary of State from enforcing the Illinois Act.

Chicago Rivet responded three days later by bringing suit in Pennsylvania, where it conducted most of its business, seeking to enjoin MITE from proceeding with its proposed tender offer on the ground that the offer violated the Pennsylvania Takeover Disclosure Law. After Chicago Rivet's efforts to obtain relief in Pennsylvania proved unsuccessful, both Chicago Rivet and the Illinois Secretary of State took steps to invoke the Illinois Act. On February 1, 1979, the Secretary of State notified MITE that he intended to issue an order requiring it to cease and desist further efforts to make a tender offer for Chicago Rivet. On February 2, 1979, Chicago Rivet notified MITE by letter that it would file suit in Illinois state court to enjoin the proposed tender offer. MITE renewed its request for injunctive relief in the District Court and on February 2 the District Court issued a preliminary injunction prohibiting the Secretary of State from enforcing the Illinois Act against MITE's tender offer for Chicago Rivet.

MITE then published its tender offer in the February 5 edition of the Wall Street Journal. The offer was made to all shareholders of Chicago Rivet residing throughout the United States. The outstanding stock was worth over $ 23 million at the offering price. On the same day Chicago Rivet made an offer for approximately 40% of its own shares at $ 30 per share. The District Court entered final judgment on February 9, declaring that the Illinois Act was pre-empted by the Williams Act and that it violated the Commerce Clause. Accordingly, the District Court permanently enjoined enforcement of the Illinois statute against MITE. Shortly after final judgment was entered, MITE and Chicago Rivet entered into an agreement whereby both tender offers were withdrawn and MITE was given 30 days to examine the books and records of Chicago Rivet. Under the agreement

MITE was either to make a tender offer of $ 31 per share before March 12, 1979, which Chicago Rivet agreed not to oppose, or decide not to acquire Chicago Rivet's shares or assets. On March 2, 1979, MITE announced its decision not to make a tender offer.

The United States Court of Appeals for the Seventh Circuit affirmed *sub nom. MITE Corp. v. Dixon,* 633 F.2d 486 (1980). It agreed with the District Court that several provisions of the Illinois Act are pre-empted by the Williams Act and that the Illinois Act unduly burdens interstate commerce in violation of the Commerce Clause. We noted probable jurisdiction and now affirm.

II

The Court of Appeals specifically found that this case was not moot, reasoning that because the Secretary has indicated he intends to enforce the Act against MITE, a reversal of the judgment of the District Court would expose MITE to civil and criminal liability for making the February 5, 1979, offer in violation of the Illinois Act. We agree. It is urged that the preliminary injunction issued by the District Court is a complete defense to civil or criminal penalties. While, as JUSTICE STEVENS' concurrence indicates, that is not a frivolous question by any means, it is an issue to be decided when and if the Secretary of State initiates an action. That action would be foreclosed if we agree with the Court of Appeals that the Illinois Act is unconstitutional. Accordingly, the case is not moot.

III

We first address the holding that the Illinois Take-Over Act is unconstitutional under the Supremacy Clause. We note at the outset that in passing the Williams Act, which is an amendment to the Securities Exchange Act of 1934, Congress did not also amend § 28(a) of the 1934 Act. In pertinent part, § 28(a) provides as follows:

> Nothing in this title shall affect the jurisdiction of the securities commission (or any agency or officer performing like functions) of any State over any security or any person insofar as it does not conflict with the provisions of this title or the rules and regulations thereunder.

Thus Congress did not explicitly prohibit States from regulating takeovers; it left the determination whether the Illinois statute conflicts with the Williams Act to the courts. Of course, a state statute is void to the extent that it actually conflicts with a valid federal statute; and

> [a] conflict will be found "where compliance with both federal and state regulations is a physical impossibility ... ," *Florida Lime & Avocado Growers, Inc. v. Paul,* 373 U.S. 132, 142-143 (1963), or where the state "law stands as an obstacle to the accomplishment and execution of the full purposes and objectives of Congress." *Hines v. Davidowitz,* 312 U.S. 52, 67 (1941).

Our inquiry is further narrowed in this case since there is no contention that it would be impossible to comply with both the provisions of the Williams Act and the more burdensome requirements of the Illinois law. The issue thus is, as it was in the Court of Appeals, whether the Illinois Act frustrates the objectives of the Williams Act in some substantial way.

The Williams Act, passed in 1968, was the congressional response to the increased use of cash tender offers in corporate acquisitions, a device that had "removed a substantial number of corporate control contests from the reach of existing disclosure requirements of the federal securities laws." *Piper v. Chris-Craft Industries, Inc.*, 430 U.S. 1, 22 (1977). The Williams Act filled this regulatory gap. The Act imposes several requirements....

There is no question that in imposing these requirements, Congress intended to protect investors. *Piper v. Chris-Craft Industries, Inc.*, *supra*, at 35; *Rondeau v. Mosinee Paper Corp.*, 422 U.S. 49, 58 (1975); S. Rep. No. 550, 90th Cong., 1st Sess., 3-4 (1967) (Senate Report). But it is also crystal clear that a major aspect of the effort to protect the investor was to avoid favoring either management or the takeover bidder. As we noted in *Piper*, the disclosure provisions originally embodied in S. 2731 "were avowedly pro-management in the target company's efforts to defeat takeover bids." But Congress became convinced "that takeover bids should not be discouraged because they serve a useful purpose in providing a check on entrenched but inefficient management." Senate Report, at 3. It also became apparent that entrenched management was often successful in defeating takeover attempts. As the legislation evolved, therefore, Congress disclaimed any "intention to provide a weapon for management to discourage takeover bids," *Rondeau v. Mosinee Paper Corp.*, *supra*, at 58, and expressly embraced a policy of neutrality. As Senator Williams explained: "We have taken extreme care to avoid tipping the scales either in favor of management or in favor of the person making the takeover bids." 113 Cong. Rec. 24664 (1967). This policy of "evenhandedness," *Piper v. Chris-Craft Industries, Inc.*, *supra*, at 31, represented a conviction that neither side in the contest should be extended additional advantages vis-à-vis the investor, who if furnished with adequate information would be in a position to make his own informed choice. We, therefore, agree with the Court of Appeals that Congress sought to protect the investor not only by furnishing him with the necessary information but also by withholding from management or the bidder any undue advantage that could frustrate the exercise of an informed choice.

To implement this policy of investor protection while maintaining the balance between management and the bidder, Congress required the latter to file with the Commission and furnish the company and the investor with all information adequate to the occasion. With that filing, the offer could go forward, stock could be tendered and purchased, but a stockholder was free within a specified time to withdraw his tendered shares. He was also protected if the offer was increased. Looking at this history as a whole, it appears to us, as it did to the Court of Appeals, that Congress intended to strike a balance between the investor, management, and the takeover bidder. The bidder was to furnish the investor and the target company with adequate information but there was no "inten[tion] to do ... more than give incumbent management an opportunity to express and explain its position." *Rondeau v. Mosinee Paper Corp., supra,* at 58. Once that opportunity was extended, Congress anticipated that the investor, if he so chose, and the takeover bidder should be free to move forward within the time frame provided by Congress.

IV

The Court of Appeals identified three provisions of the Illinois Act that upset the careful balance struck by Congress and which therefore stand as obstacles to the accomplishment and execution of the full purposes and objectives of Congress. We agree with the Court of Appeals in all essential respects.

A

The Illinois Act requires a tender offeror to notify the Secretary of State and the target company of its intent to make a tender offer and the material terms of the offer 20 business days before the offer becomes effective. During that time, the offeror may not communicate its offer to the shareholders. Meanwhile, the target company is free to disseminate information to its shareholders concerning the impending offer. The contrast with the Williams Act is apparent. Under that Act, there is no precommencement notification requirement; the critical date is the date a tender offer is "first published or sent or given to security holders."

We agree with the Court of Appeals that by providing the target company with additional time within which to take steps to combat the offer, the precommencement notification provisions furnish incumbent management with a powerful tool to combat tender offers, perhaps to the detriment of the stockholders who will not have an offer before them during this period. These consequences are precisely what Congress determined should be avoided, and for this reason, the precommencement notification provision frustrates the objectives of the Williams Act.

It is important to note in this respect that in the course of events leading to the adoption of the Williams Act, Congress several times refused to impose a precommencement disclosure requirement. In October 1965, Senator Williams introduced S. 2731, a bill which would have required a bidder to notify the target company and file a public statement with the Securities and Exchange Commission at least 20 days before commencement of a cash tender offer for more than 5% of a class of the target company's securities. The Commission commented on the bill and stated that "the requirement of a 20-day advance notice to the issuer and the Commission is unnecessary for the protection of security holders ...." 112 Cong. Rec. 19005 (1966). Senator Williams introduced a new bill in 1967, S. 510, which provided for a confidential filing by the tender offeror with the Commission five days prior to the commencement of the offer. S. 510 was enacted as the Williams Act after elimination of the advance disclosure requirement. As the Senate Report explained:

> At the hearings it was urged that this prior review was not necessary and in some cases might delay the offer when time was of the essence. In view of the authority and responsibility of the Securities and Exchange Commission to take appropriate action in the event that inadequate or misleading information is disseminated to the public to solicit acceptance of a tender offer, the bill as approved by the committee requires only that the statement be on file with the Securities and Exchange Commission at the time the tender offer is first made to the public. Senate Report, at 4.

Congress rejected another precommencement notification proposal during deliberations on the 1970 amendments to the Williams Act.

B

For similar reasons, we agree with the Court of Appeals that the hearing provisions of the Illinois Act frustrate the congressional purpose by introducing extended delay into the tender offer process. The Illinois Act allows the Secretary of State to call a hearing with respect to any tender offer subject to the Act, and the offer may not proceed until the hearing is completed. The Secretary may call a hearing at any time prior to the commencement of the offer, and there is no deadline for the completion of the hearing. Although the Secretary is to render a decision within 15 days after the conclusion of the hearing, that period may be extended without limitation. Not only does the Secretary of State have the power to delay a tender offer indefinitely, but incumbent management may also use the hearing provisions of the Illinois Act to delay a tender offer. The Secretary is required to call a hearing if requested to do so by, among other persons, those who are located in Illinois "as determined by post office address as shown on the records of the target company and who hold of record or beneficially, or both, at least 10% of the outstanding shares of any class of equity securities which is the subject of the take-over offer." Since incumbent management in many cases will control, either directly or indirectly, 10% of the target company's shares, this provision allows management to delay the commencement of an offer by insisting on a hearing. As the Court of Appeals observed, these provisions potentially afford management a "powerful weapon to stymie indefinitely a takeover." In enacting the Williams Act, Congress itself "recognized that delay can seriously impede a tender offer" and sought to avoid it. *Great Western United Corp. v. Kidwell,* 577 F.2d 1256, 1277 (CA5 1978); Senate Report, at 4.

....

As we have said, Congress anticipated investors and the takeover offeror be free to go forward without unreasonable delay. The potential for delay provided by the hearing provisions upset the balance struck by Congress by favoring management at the expense of stockholders. We therefore agree with the Court of Appeals that these hearing provisions conflict with the Williams Act.

C

The Court of Appeals also concluded that the Illinois Act is pre-empted by the Williams Act insofar as it allows the Secretary of State of Illinois to pass on the substantive fairness of a tender offer. Under the Illinois law, the Secretary is required to deny registration of a takeover offer if he finds that the offer "fails to provide full and fair disclosure to the offerees ... *or that the take-over offer is inequitable ...*" (emphasis added). The Court of Appeals understood the Williams Act and its legislative history to indicate that Congress intended for investors to be free to make their own decisions. We agree. Both the House and Senate Reports observed that the Act was "designed to make the relevant facts known so that shareholders have a fair opportunity to make their decision." H. R. Rep. No. 1711, 90th Cong., 2d Sess., 4 (1968); Senate Report, at 3. Thus, as the Court of Appeals said, "[t]he state thus offers investor protection at the expense of investor autonomy — an approach quite in conflict with that adopted by Congress."

V

The Commerce Clause provides that "Congress shall have Power ... [t]o regulate Commerce ... among the several states." U. S. Const., Art. I, § 8, cl. 3. "[A]t least since *Cooley v. Board of Wardens,* 12 How. 299 (1852), it has been clear that 'the Commerce Clause ... even without implementing legislation by Congress is a limitation upon the power of the States.'" *Great Atlantic & Pacific Tea Co. v. Cottrell,* 424 U.S. 366, 370-371 (1976), *quoting Freeman v. Hewitt,* 329 U.S. 249, 252 (1946). Not every exercise of state power with some impact on interstate commerce is invalid. A state statute must be upheld if it "regulates even-handedly to effectuate a legitimate local public interest, and its effects on interstate commerce are only incidental ... unless the burden imposed on such commerce is clearly excessive in relation to the putative local benefits." *Pike v. Bruce Church, Inc.,* 397 U.S. 137, 142 (1970), *citing Huron Cement Co. v. Detroit,* 362 U.S. 440, 443 (1960). The Commerce Clause, however, permits only *incidental* regulation of interstate commerce by the States; direct regulation is prohibited. *Shafer v. Farmers Grain Co.,* 268 U.S. 189, 199 (1925). The Illinois Act violates these principles for two reasons. First, it directly regulates and prevents, unless its terms are satisfied, interstate tender offers which in turn would generate interstate transactions. Second, the burden the Act imposes on interstate commerce is excessive in light of the local interests the Act purports to further.

A

States have traditionally regulated intrastate securities transactions, and this Court has upheld the authority of States to enact "blue-sky" laws against Commerce Clause challenges on several occasions. *Hall v. Geiger-Jones Co.,* 242 U.S. 539 (1917). The Court's rationale for upholding blue-sky laws was that they only regulated transactions occurring within the regulating States. "The provisions of the law ... apply to dispositions of securities *within* the State and while information of those issued in other States and foreign countries is required to be filed .. ., they are only affected by the requirement of a license of one who deals with them *within* the State.... Such regulations affect interstate commerce in [securities] only incidentally." *Hall v. Geiger-Jones Co., supra,* at 557-558. Congress has also recognized the validity of such laws governing intrastate securities transactions in § 28(a) of the Securities Exchange Act, a provision "designed to save state blue-sky laws from pre-emption." *Leroy v. Great Western United Corp.,* 443 U.S. 173, 182, n. 13 (1979).

The Illinois Act differs substantially from state blue-sky laws in that it directly regulates transactions which take place across state lines, even if wholly outside the State of Illinois. A tender offer for securities of a publicly held corporation is ordinarily communicated by the use of the mails or other means of interstate commerce to shareholders across the country and abroad. Securities are tendered and transactions closed by similar means. Thus, in this case, MITE Corp., the tender offeror, is a Delaware corporation with principal offices in Connecticut. Chicago Rivet is a publicly held Illinois corporation with shareholders scattered around the country, 27% of whom live in Illinois. MITE's offer to Chicago Rivet's shareholders, including those in Illinois, necessarily employed interstate facilities in communicating its offer, which, if accepted, would result in transactions occurring across state lines. These transactions would themselves be interstate commerce. Yet the Illinois law, unless complied with, sought to prevent MITE from making its offer and concluding interstate transactions not only with Chicago Rivet's stockholders living in Illinois, but also with those living in other States and having no connection with Illinois. Indeed, the Illinois law on its face would apply even if not a single one of Chicago Rivet's shareholders were a resident of Illinois, since the Act applies to every tender offer for a corporation meeting two of the following conditions: the corporation has its principal executive office in Illinois, is organized under Illinois laws, or has at least 10% of its stated capital and paid-in surplus represented in Illinois. Thus the Act could be applied to regulate a tender offer which would not affect a single Illinois shareholder.

It is therefore apparent that the Illinois statute is a direct restraint on interstate commerce and that it has a sweeping extraterritorial effect. Furthermore, if Illinois may impose such regulations, so may other States; and interstate commerce in securities transactions generated by tender offers would be thoroughly stifled. In *Shafer v. Farmers Grain Co., supra,* at 199, the Court held that "a state statute which by its necessary operation directly interferes with or burdens [interstate] commerce is a prohibited regulation and invalid, regardless of the purpose with which it was enacted." The Commerce Clause also precludes the application of a state statute to commerce that takes place wholly outside of the State's borders, whether or not the commerce has effects within the State. In *Southern Pacific Co. v. Arizona,* 325 U.S. 761, 775 (1945), the Court struck down on Commerce Clause grounds a state law where the "practical effect of such regulation is to control [conduct] beyond the boundaries of the state ...." The limits on a State's power to enact substantive legislation are similar to the limits on the jurisdiction of state courts. In either case, "any attempt 'directly' to assert extraterritorial jurisdiction over persons or property would offend sister States and exceed the inherent limits of the State's power." *Shaffer v. Heitner*, 433 U.S. 186, 197 (1977).

Because the Illinois Act purports to regulate directly and to interdict interstate commerce, including commerce wholly outside the State, it must be held invalid as were the laws at issue in *Shafer v. Farmers Grain Co.* and *Southern Pacific*.

B

The Illinois Act is also unconstitutional under the test of *Pike v. Bruce Church, Inc.*, 397 U.S., at 142, for even when a state statute regulates interstate commerce indirectly, the burden imposed on that commerce must not be excessive in relation to the local interests served by the statute. The most obvious burden the Illinois Act imposes on interstate commerce arises from the statute's previously described nationwide reach which purports to give Illinois the power to determine whether a tender offer may proceed anywhere.

The effects of allowing the Illinois Secretary of State to block a nationwide tender offer are substantial. Shareholders are deprived of the opportunity to sell their shares at a premium. The reallocation of economic resources to their highest valued use, a process which can improve efficiency and competition, is hindered. The incentive the tender offer mechanism provides incumbent management to perform well so that stock prices remain high is reduced.

Appellant claims the Illinois Act furthers two legitimate local interests. He argues that Illinois seeks to protect resident security holders and that the Act merely regulates the internal affairs of companies incorporated under Illinois law. We agree with the Court of Appeals that these asserted interests are insufficient to outweigh the burdens Illinois imposes on interstate commerce.

While protecting local investors is plainly a legitimate state objective, the State has no legitimate interest in protecting nonresident shareholders. Insofar as the Illinois law burdens out-of-state transactions, there is nothing to be weighed in the balance to sustain the law. We note, furthermore, that the Act completely exempts from coverage a corporation's acquisition of its own shares. Thus Chicago Rivet was able to make a competing tender offer for its own stock without complying with the Illinois Act, leaving Chicago Rivet's shareholders to depend only on the protections afforded them by federal securities law, protections which Illinois views as inadequate to protect investors in other contexts. This distinction is at variance with Illinois' asserted legislative purpose, and tends to undermine appellant's justification for the burdens the statute imposes on interstate commerce.

We are also unconvinced that the Illinois Act substantially enhances the shareholders' position. The Illinois Act seeks to protect shareholders of a company subject to a tender offer by requiring disclosures regarding the offer, assuring that shareholders have adequate time to decide whether to tender their shares, and according shareholders withdrawal, proration, and equal consideration rights. However, the Williams Act provides these same substantive protections. As the Court of Appeals noted, the disclosures required by the Illinois Act which go beyond those mandated by the Williams Act and the regulations pursuant to it may not substantially enhance the shareholders' ability to make informed decisions. It also was of the view that the possible benefits of the potential delays required by the Act may be outweighed by the increased risk that the tender offer will fail due to defensive tactics employed by incumbent management. We are unprepared to disagree with the Court of Appeals in these respects, and conclude that the protections the Illinois Act affords resident security holders are, for the most part, speculative.

Appellant also contends that Illinois has an interest in regulating the internal affairs of a corporation incorporated under its laws. The internal affairs doctrine is a conflict of laws principle which recognizes that only one State should have the authority to regulate a corporation's internal affairs — matters peculiar to the relationships among or between the corporation and its current officers, directors, and shareholders — because otherwise a corporation could be faced with conflicting demands. That doctrine is of little use to the State in this context. Tender offers contemplate transfers of stock by stockholders to a third party and do not themselves implicate the internal affairs of the target company. Furthermore, the proposed justification is somewhat incredible since the Illinois Act applies to tender offers for any corporation for which 10% of the outstanding shares are held by Illinois residents. The Act thus applies to corporations that are not incorporated in Illinois and have their principal place of business in other States. Illinois has no interest in regulating the internal affairs of foreign corporations.

We conclude with the Court of Appeals that the Illinois Act imposes a substantial burden on interstate commerce which outweighs its putative local benefits. It is accordingly invalid under the Commerce Clause.

The judgment of the Court of Appeals is

Affirmed.

In the years following *MITE*, a number of states passed new statutes designed to avoid the constitutional problems disclosed in that case. The only such statute that has been subjected to constitutional review in the Supreme Court is one passed in Indiana in 1986. The case in which that review took place is *CTS Corp. v. Dynamics Corp. of America*. (After the *CTS* case, a number of other states passed statutes like the one in Indiana.)

CTS CORP. v. DYNAMICS CORP. OF AMERICA

United States Supreme Court
481 U.S. 69 (1987)

JUSTICE POWELL delivered the opinion of the Court.

This case presents the questions whether the Control Share Acquisitions Chapter of the Indiana Business Corporation Law is pre-empted by the Williams Act or violates the Commerce Clause of the Federal Constitution.

I

A

On March 4, 1986, the Governor of Indiana signed a revised Indiana Business Corporation Law. That law included the Control Share Acquisitions Chapter (Indiana Act or Act). Beginning on August 1, 1987, the Act will apply to any corporation incorporated in Indiana unless the corporation amends its articles of incorporation or bylaws to opt out of the Act. The Act applies only to "issuing public corporations." The term "corporation" includes only businesses incorporated in Indiana. An "issuing public corporation" is defined as:

a corporation that has:
(1)   one hundred (100) or more shareholders;
(2)   its principal place of business, its principal office, or substantial assets within Indiana; and
(3)   either:
  (A)   more than ten percent (10%) of its shareholders resident in Indiana;
  (B)   more than ten percent (10%) of its shares owned by Indiana residents; or
  (C)   ten thousand (10,000) shareholders resident in Indiana.

The Act focuses on the acquisition of "control shares" in an issuing public corporation. Under the Act, an entity acquires "control shares" whenever it acquires shares that, but for the operation of the Act, would bring its voting power in the corporation to or above any of three thresholds: 20%, 33$\frac{1}{3}$%, or 50%. An entity that acquires control shares does not necessarily acquire voting rights. Rather, it gains those rights only "to the extent granted by resolution approved by the shareholders of the issuing public corporation." Section 9 requires a majority vote of all disinterested shareholders holding each class of stock for passage of such a resolution. The practical effect of this requirement is to condition acquisition of control of a corporation on approval of a majority of the pre-existing disinterested shareholders.

The shareholders decide whether to confer rights on the control shares at the next regularly scheduled meeting of the shareholders, or at a specially scheduled meeting. The acquiror can require management of the corporation to hold such a special meeting within 50 days if it files an "acquiring person statement," requests the meeting, and agrees to pay the expenses of the meeting. If the shareholders do not vote to restore voting rights to the shares, the corporation may redeem the control shares from the acquiror at fair market value, but it is not required to do so. Similarly, if the acquiror does not file an acquiring person statement with the corporation, the corporation may, if its bylaws or articles of incorporation so provide, redeem the shares at any time after 60 days after the acquiror's last acquisition.

B

On March 10, 1986, appellee Dynamics Corporation of America (Dynamics) owned 9.6% of the common stock of appellant CTS Corporation, an Indiana corporation. On that day, six days after the Act went into effect, Dynamics announced a tender offer for another million shares in CTS; purchase of those shares would have brought Dynamics' ownership interest in CTS to 27.5%. Also on March 10, Dynamics filed suit in the United States District Court for the Northern District of Illinois, alleging that CTS had violated the federal securities laws in a number of respects no longer relevant to these proceedings....

[Dynamics then amended its complaint to challenge the constitutionality of the Indiana Act. The district court ultimately found the Act to be unconstitutional under both the Supremacy and Commerce Clauses of the federal constitution, and the Seventh Circuit affirmed.]

II

The first question in this cause is whether the Williams Act pre-empts the Indiana Act....

....

B

The Indiana Act differs in major respects from the Illinois statute that the Court considered in *Edgar v. MITE Corp.*, 457 U.S. 624 (1982)....

....

C

As the plurality opinion in *MITE* did not represent the views of a majority of the Court, we are not bound by its reasoning. We need not question that reasoning, however, because we believe the Indiana Act passes muster even under the broad interpretation of the Williams Act articulated by JUSTICE WHITE in *MITE*. [T]he overriding concern of the *MITE* plurality was that the Illinois statute considered in that case operated to favor management against offerors, to the detriment of shareholders. By contrast, the statute now before the Court protects the independent shareholder against both of the contending parties....

The Indiana Act operates on the assumption, implicit in the Williams Act, that independent shareholders faced with tender offers often are at a disadvantage. By allowing such shareholders to vote as a group, the Act protects them from the coercive aspects of some tender offers. If, for example, shareholders believe that a successful tender offer will be followed by a purchase of nontendering shares at a depressed price, individual shareholders may tender their shares — even if they doubt the tender offer is in the corporation's best interest — to protect themselves from being forced to sell their shares at a depressed price.... In such a situation under the Indiana Act, the shareholders as a group, acting in the corporation's best interest, could reject the offer, although individual shareholders might be inclined to accept it. The desire of the Indiana Legislature to protect shareholders of Indiana corporations from this type of coercive offer does not conflict with the Williams Act. Rather, it furthers the federal policy of investor protection.

In implementing its goal, the Indiana Act avoids the problems the plurality discussed in *MITE*. Unlike the *MITE* statute, the Indiana Act does not give either management or the offeror an advantage in communicating with the shareholders about the impending offer. The Act also does not impose an indefinite delay on tender offers. Nothing in the Act prohibits an offeror from consummating an offer on the 20th business day, the earliest day permitted under applicable federal regulations. Nor does the Act allow the state government to interpose its views of fairness between willing buyers and sellers of shares of the target company. Rather, the Act allows *shareholders* to evaluate the fairness of the offer collectively.

D

The Court of Appeals based its finding of pre-emption on its view that the practical effect of the Indiana Act is to delay consummation of tender offers until 50 days after the commencement of the offer....

The Act does not impose an absolute 50-day delay on tender offers, nor does it preclude an offeror from purchasing shares as soon as federal law permits. If the offeror fears an adverse shareholder vote under the Act, it can make a conditional tender offer, offering to accept shares on the condition that the shares receive voting rights within a certain period of time....

Even assuming that the Indiana Act imposes some additional delay, nothing in *MITE* suggested that *any* delay imposed by state regulation, however short, would create a conflict with the Williams Act. The plurality argued only that the offeror should "be free to go forward without *unreasonable* delay." (emphasis added.) In that case, the Court was confronted with the potential for indefinite delay and presented with no persuasive reason why some deadline could not be established. By contrast, the Indiana Act provides that full voting rights will be vested — if this eventually is to occur — within 50 days after commencement of the offer. This period is within the 60-day maximum period Congress established for tender offers in [the Williams Act]. We cannot say that a delay within that congressionally determined period is unreasonable.

....

... Accordingly, we hold that the Williams Act does not pre-empt the Indiana Act.

III

As an alternative basis for its decision, the Court of Appeals held that the Act violates the Commerce Clause of the Federal Constitution....

A

The principal objects of dormant Commerce Clause scrutiny are statutes that discriminate against interstate commerce. The Indiana Act is not such a statute. It has the same effects on tender offers whether or not the offeror is a domiciliary or resident of Indiana....

... Because nothing in the Indiana Act imposes a greater burden on out-of-state offerors than it does on similarly situated Indiana offerors, we reject the contention that the Act discriminates against interstate commerce.

B

This Court's recent Commerce Clause cases also have invalidated statutes that adversely may affect interstate commerce by subjecting activities to inconsistent regulations. The Indiana Act poses no such problem. So long as each State regulates voting rights only in the corporations it has created, each corporation will be subject to the law of only one State. No principle of corporation law and practice is more firmly established than a State's authority to regulate domestic corporations, including the authority to define the voting rights of shareholders. Accordingly, we conclude that the Indiana Act does not create an impermissible risk of inconsistent regulation by different States.

C

The Court of Appeals did not find the Act unconstitutional for either of these threshold reasons. Rather, its decision rested on its view of the Act's potential to hinder tender offers. We think the Court of Appeals failed to appreciate the significance for Commerce Clause analysis of the fact that state regulation of corporate governance is regulation of entities whose very existence and attributes are a product of state law. As Chief Justice Marshall explained:

> A corporation is an artificial being, invisible, intangible, and existing only in contemplation of law. Being the mere creature of law, it possesses only those properties which the charter of its creation confers upon it, either expressly, or as incidental to its very existence. These are such as are supposed best calculated to effect the object for which it was created. *Trustees of Dartmouth College v. Woodward,* 4 Wheat. 518, 636 (1819).

Every State in this country has enacted laws regulating corporate governance. By prohibiting certain transactions, and regulating others, such laws necessarily affect certain aspects of interstate commerce. This necessarily is true with respect to corporations with shareholders in States other than the State of incorporation. Large corporations that are listed on national exchanges, or even regional exchanges, will have shareholders in many States and shares that are traded frequently. The markets that facilitate this national and international participation in ownership of corporations are essential for providing capital not only for new enterprises but also for established companies that need to expand their businesses. This beneficial free market system depends at its core upon the fact that a corporation — except in the rarest situations — is organized under, and governed by, the law of a single jurisdiction, traditionally the corporate law of the State of its incorporation.

These regulatory laws may affect directly a variety of corporate transactions. Mergers are a typical example. In view of the substantial effect that a merger may have on the shareholders' interests in a corporation, many States require supermajority votes to approve mergers. By requiring a greater vote for mergers than is required for other transactions, these laws make it more difficult for corporations to merge. State laws also may provide for "dissenters' rights" under which minority shareholders who disagree with corporate decisions to take particular actions are entitled to sell their shares to the corporation at fair market value. By requiring the corporation to purchase the shares of dissenting shareholders, these laws may inhibit a corporation from engaging in the specified transactions.

It thus is an accepted part of the business landscape in this country for States to create corporations, to prescribe their powers, and to define the rights that are acquired by purchasing their shares. A State has an interest in promoting stable relationships among parties involved in the corporations it charters, as well as in ensuring that investors in such corporations have an effective voice in corporate affairs.

There can be no doubt that the Act reflects these concerns. The primary purpose of the Act is to protect the shareholders of Indiana corporations. It does this by affording shareholders, when a takeover offer is made, an opportunity to decide collectively whether the resulting change in voting control of the corporation, as they perceive it, would be desirable. A change of management may have important effects on the shareholders' interests; it is well within the State's role as overseer of corporate governance to offer this opportunity. The autonomy provided by allowing shareholders collectively to determine whether the takeover is advantageous to their interests may be especially beneficial where a hostile tender offer may coerce shareholders into tendering their shares.

Dynamics argues ... that the State has "'no legitimate interest in protecting the nonresident shareholders.'" Dynamics relies heavily on the statement by the *MITE* Court that "[i]nsofar as the ... law burdens out-of-state transactions, there is nothing to be weighed in the balance to sustain the law." But that comment was made in reference to an Illinois law that applied as well to out-of-state corporations as to in-state corporations. We agree that Indiana has no interest in protecting nonresident shareholders *of nonresident corporations*. But this Act applies only to corporations incorporated in Indiana. We reject the contention that Indiana has no interest in providing for the shareholders of its corporations the voting autonomy granted by the Act. Indiana has a substantial interest in preventing the corporate form from becoming a shield for unfair business dealing. Moreover, unlike the Illinois statute invalidated in *MITE,* the Indiana Act applies only to corporations that have a substantial number of shareholders in Indiana. Thus, every application of the Indiana Act will affect a substantial number of Indiana residents, whom Indiana indisputably has an interest in protecting.

....

IV

On its face, the Indiana Control Share Acquisitions Chapter evenhandedly determines the voting rights of shares of Indiana corporations. The Act does not conflict with the provisions or purposes of the Williams Act. To the limited extent that the Act affects interstate commerce, this is justified by the State's interests in defining the attributes of shares in its corporations and in protecting shareholders. Congress has never questioned the need for state regulation of these matters. Nor do we think such regulation offends the Constitution. Accordingly, we reverse the judgment of the Court of Appeals.

....

SECTION IV. PERSPECTIVES

Passage of the Williams Act only fueled the debate about the proper regulatory response to tender offers and, more basically, about how tender offers ought to be viewed: as beneficial to society or detrimental. There are strongly held and well articulated views on each end of the spectrum, and at most points in between. Some, for example, argue that tender offers serve a useful purpose in monitoring the performance of management and in encouraging better performance. Roughly stated, the argument is that the fittest survive as managers and the ineffectual see their corporations taken over by new management. Others believe that tender offers largely serve to divert the attention of management, both in acquiring corporations and targets, from their real tasks of efficiently providing products and services. Those who view tender offers with favor, as one would expect, view defensive tactics by targets with disfavor, and vice versa. The following articles state two sides of the tender offer issue.

Daniel R. Easterbrook and Frank H. Fischel, Is Takeover Defense in Shareholders' Best Interest?, Legal Times of Washington, August 10, 1981 at 42*

A cash tender offer typically presents shareholders of a target corporation an opportunity to sell all or part of their shares quickly and at a substantial premium

---

above the market price. Even though shareholders are generally all too willing to sell their shares and realize considerable profits, it has become commonplace for managers of target corporations to resist offers, calling them contrary to the shareholders' best interests or those of the corporation itself. To ensure that the shareholder will not make the mistake of selling at a profit, a target's management may initiate litigation against the bidder, sell new shares to make the acquisition of control more difficult, create an antitrust problem by acquiring one of the bidder's competitors, or engage in a wide variety of other defensive tactics.

This managerial resistance may defeat the offer altogether, or it may result in a higher price paid for the target's shares. Regardless of the outcome, however, a strong argument can be made that defensive strategies by a target's management reduce shareholders' welfare. To see why requires an understanding of the function of tender offers, and how defensive tactics affect the number of tender offers, the price if an offer is made, and the price of the stock in the event that no offer is made.

Functions of Tender Offers

A cash tender offer at a premium above the market price gives each shareholder the opportunity to obtain a return exceeding the current market value of his stock. Despite this, managers of target companies frequently claim that the offer should be rejected because it is inadequate and is an attempt to buy the company at bargain basement prices.

Such declarations ask the shareholders to ignore the facts. The market price of a stock is the best guess of what the firm is worth under current management. If this were not the case and there were significant divergences between market price and value, investors could reap substantial gains by identifying and buying underpriced shares and selling overpriced shares. As investors bought and sold on the basis of their information, the divergence between price and value would disappear. This process of arbitrage would continue until the cost of discovering mispriced securities exceeded any trading gains that could be realized.

The result of this process is that stock prices reflect all of the available information about the value of shares. It necessarily follows that a tender offer at a price higher than the prevailing one also exceeds the market's best guess about the value of the stock. Therefore, statements by a target's managers that the stock is really worth more than the tender offer price are simply not believable.

Any attempt to steal a corporation on the basis of information known to the bidder but not to the market would lead to disclosure by the target's managers, a reevaluation of the shares in the market, and a failure of the offer. Tender offers at a premium thus benefit the target's shareholders.

Why Pay Premium?

That the target's shareholders benefit from tender offers does not explain why the bidder is willing to make an offer above the market price. How can a bidder identify underpriced securities if market professionals cannot?

The answer is that the bidder's willingness to pay a premium is not explained by its ability to identify a company whose shares are priced less than their true worth. A far more plausible explanation for the bidder's willingness to pay a premium in an unfriendly takeover is its belief that the transaction will produce a real economic benefit. Indeed, the bidder would be acting irrationally in paying a premium if this were not the case.

Suppose, for example, that a bidder purchases 1,000 shares of the target's stock at $ 15 when the current price is $ 10. The bidder must anticipate a gain of more than $ 5,000 as a result of the tender offer. Otherwise it would be committing the irrational act of paying a premium of $ 5,000 and receiving less than that in return.

There are several possible sources of gains from tender offers. Perhaps there are economies of scale if the two firms combine; perhaps the acquired firm has idle cash that could be profitably invested by the bidder. The most probable explanation for unfriendly takeover, however, emphasizes the role of the bidder in disciplining corporate managers who do not perform well in their role as agents for the firm. Anyone who hires an agent (such as the managers of a corporation) must find some way to control the agent's conduct. Otherwise, the agent will have an incentive to siphon off profits, fritter away time, or make bad managerial decisions.

We do not mean to suggest that managers of corporations are lazy or not interested in doing a good job. Our point is simply that managers, like other employees, respond to incentives. This is why corporations, like all organizations, have systems for monitoring employees' work in order to reward good performance while penalizing poor performance.

It is inconceivable that shareholders in a publicly held firm could monitor the performance of the corporation's managers. No one shareholder has the right incentives, because each can obtain only a trivial share of the gain from better performance. And shareholders have no device for controlling management. Proxy contests are notoriously difficult to wage, and incumbents win most contested elections.

Passive Shareholders

The reason for this phenomenon is obvious. Most shareholders are passive investors who ignore contested elections, as well as other questions of corporate governance, because no one shareholder's vote will affect the outcome. Thus the initiator of the proxy fight must invest substantial resources in learning about the firm's affairs and formulating proposals for change, only to have other shareholders disregard the contest.

Even if the contest is successful, the leaders receive benefits only in proportion to their holdings. Most of the benefits are captured by shareholders who watched the contest from the sidelines and took no risk. Under these circumstances, it is easy to see why few are willing to devote the time and resources to waging a proxy fight — it pays to be a passive shareholder.

Tender offers are another, and far more effective, method of monitoring the work of management teams. Prospective bidders monitor the performance of managerial teams by comparing a corporation's potential value with its value (as reflected by share prices) under current management. When the difference between the market price of a firm's shares and the price those shares might have traded at becomes too great, a bidder can profit by buying the firm and improving its management. The source of the premium, therefore, is the expected gains from improved management, which makes the firm's assets worth more in the hands of the successful bidder than they were worth under current management.

The extensive empirical evidence on the economic effects of tender offers supports this interpretation. This evidence shows, roughly, that the share prices of target firms decline relative to the market for some 40 months before the offer, that they rise at or shortly before the time of the offer, and that untendered shares continue to trade at the higher price after the tendered shares have been accepted. Thus the stock market data show that target firms perform worse than anticipated, and that tender offers restore prices that had prevailed before the erosion. The acquiring firms typically make an ordinary profit in the transaction.

All Benefit

It is important to emphasize that all parties benefit in this process. The bidder makes an ordinary profit on the transaction. The target's shareholders receive a premium above market price. Perhaps most important, shareholders benefit even if their corporation never is the subject of a tender offer. The process of monitoring by prospective bidders poses a continuous threat of takeover if performance lags. Because of this threat, managers have strong incentives to reduce agency costs, raise share prices, and thus make tender offers less likely.

Some claim that tender offers have adverse consequences for the economy. It has been argued, for example, that the threat of tender offers forces firms to focus on short-run profits at the expense of long-term planning. This argument is specious. If long-term plans are needed, they will be made by incumbent managers and new ones alike, a successful long-term plan will lead to higher share prices that discourage takeovers. Moreover, no rational firm would make a tender offer that disrupted an established and profitable plan. There is no profit in paying a premium for assets that will be worth less after the takeover than before.

The argument that tender offers divert resources from capital investments also is misguided. The funds paid to the target's shareholders do not disappear but rather are shifted from the bidder to shareholder, much as dividend payments. There is no presumption that these shareholders will waste this money, any more than the money received from the 40 to 50 million shares sold in the market every day is wasted. Similarly, there is no presumption that funds will be invested if tender offers are prohibited. Such funds could be distributed to shareholders or put to other non-investment uses.

Shareholders' Welfare

Since takeovers are beneficial to both shareholders and society, it follows that defensive strategies designed to prevent takeovers do not improve shareholders' welfare. The costs of defensive tactics, and the costs incurred by bidders to overcome defensive tactics are sheer waste. If the company is successful in maintaining a policy of independence, the shareholders lose whatever premium the bidder offered, or would have offered, but for the resistance or the prospect of resistance. This loss can be substantial as the abortive attempt by Carter Hawley Hale to take over Marshall Field shows. As a result of the policy of intransigent resistance followed by Field's management, its shareholders lost the ability to sell their shares at a premium of more than 100 percent. Any policy of remaining independent is bound to deprive shareholders of premium offers and cause share prices to fall as monitoring by bidders becomes less and less effective.

The detriment to shareholders is less clear, however, if the purpose of defensive tactics is to trigger a bidding contest for the target. Indeed the ability of some recent targets such as St. Joe Minerals and Conoco to orchestrate an auction appears to have benefitted the shareholders of those firms. But the situation is far more complicated than it first appears.

Even where resistance leads to a higher price for the firm's shares, shareholders as a whole do not necessarily benefit. The value of any stock can be understood as the sum of two components: (1) the price in the event that there is no offer multiplied by the likelihood that there will be none; and (2) the price that will be paid in a future tender offer multiplied by the likelihood that some offer will succeed. The rational shareholder would prefer a legal rule that maximized the sum of these two components.

Given the existence of an offer, the target's shareholders are pleased by defensive tactics that produce a higher price. When shareholders are considering what the optimal legal rule should be, however, they must give substantial weight to the effect of those instructions on the likelihood that a tender offer will be made and on the market price in the event there is no takeover. If managers are allowed to engage in defensive tactics, the number of tender offers is reduced because they become more expensive. Empirical evidence demonstrates that the number of tender offers has indeed decreased in recent years as takeover statutes make defensive tactics easier.

When the number of tender offers falls, the effectiveness of monitoring also decreases, and with it the pre-offer price of shares. Indeed, the higher the costs faced by bidders in overcoming defensive tactics, the lower the price can fall before attracting the interest of bidders. Thus it is quite possible that the higher premiums observed in recent years result from depressed pre-offer prices rather than from higher offer prices being paid by bidders.

There is another related consequence of defensive tactics. No firm has an incentive to monitor and bid for prospective targets unless it can recover its costs. The first bidder must not only pay the premium but also must make substantial expenditures to identify prospective targets. Once it makes a bid, however, the identity of the target and many of the pertinent facts are revealed.

Subsequent bidders, especially those receiving the cooperation of the target's managers, can conduct their investigations at lower costs, confining their attention to the identified firm. These lower costs enable subsequent bidders to make higher bids and prevail in an auction. If the first bidder is at a disadvantage because of the defensive tactics, who would want to be the first bidder? And if there is no first bidder, there will be no higher subsequent bidder. Defensive tactics for the purpose of triggering an auction, therefore, also make shareholders as a whole worse off.

Other Explanations

There is one other possible explanation for defensive tactics that must be considered. A target's managers may not even attempt to justify resistance as increasing shareholders' welfare. Rather, they may argue that concerns such as protecting the interests of employees, suppliers or creditors require resistance; alternatively, they may argue that defense is necessary to prevent an antitrust violation.

Neither rationale for resistance is convincing. Advocates of the view that managers must consider the interests of non-investor groups make no attempt to explain why a successful tender offer would be harmful to the corporation's employees, suppliers or creditors. The new owner cannot improve the firm's performance by discarding valuable employees or suppliers or by disrupting relationships with established creditors. The new owner would be harming itself in the process of harming the firm. If, on the other hand, suppliers or employees are performing inefficiently, a change is in order whether or not the firm is taken over. Indeed, the failure of the current management to take this step may be indicative of the inferior performance that leads to the takeover in the first place.

Resistance for the purpose of preventing an antitrust violation is equally unpersuasive. Why should the management of a target have a duty to prevent an antitrust violation? Only the acquirer can violate the antitrust laws; the target's shareholders are not exposed to any risk of penalty. Moreover, the target's shareholders do not suffer any injury. The acquired company generally becomes stronger not weaker, as a result of an anticompetitive acquisition. Consumers might be injured, but the target is not.

We are left with the conclusion that defensive tactics disserve the interests of shareholders and cannot be justified for any other reason. Managers' ability to frustrate a tender bid by engaging in defensive tactics should be sharply curtailed.

Managers of target companies should remain passive when confronted with a tender offer. Passivity does not require managers to ignore the corporation's ordinary business if they suspect or are confronted with a tender offer. But it does mean that managers should not take any action, other than issuing a press release, designed to frustrate a tender offer.

Thus management should not propose anti-takeover charter or bylaw amendments, file suits against the bidder, acquire a competitor of the bidder in order to create an antitrust obstacle to the tender offer, buy or sell shares in order to make the offer more costly, give away to some potential White Knight valuable corporate information that might call forth a competing bid, or initiate any other defensive tactic to defeat a tender offer. Any departure by management from passivity should, in our view, be a per se breach of fiduciary duty.

The business judgment rule properly understood supports this position. The fundamental premise of the rule is that managers, rather than courts or shareholders, are best able to make business decisions that maximize shareholders' welfare. The rule serves the salutary purpose of preventing courts from second-guessing business decisions made by managers. But this presumption in favor of management's decision-making has never been applied in situations where managers have acute conflicts of interest. In these situations, courts have not applied the business judgment rule because of the risk that managers will not act in the shareholders' best interests.

The target's managers have an acute conflict of interest when faced with a tender offer. Successful bidders often replace incumbent managers. In light of the serious and unavoidable conflict of interest accompanying any decision to resist one's own ouster, managers have little claim to the business judgment rule's shield against judicial review.

More importantly for our purposes, the rationale underlying the rule — the inability of courts to make better decisions than managers — is inapplicable in the tender offer context. For the reasons we have stated, shareholders' welfare is maximized if managers are passive when confronted with a tender offer. There is, therefore, no business decision for managers (or a committee of disinterested directors) to make; all they need do is remain passive. Similarly, the implementation of a rule of managerial passivity does not require courts to become involved in making business decisions, let alone better business decisions than managers. All they need do is determine whatever managers were passive.

We disagree, therefore, with several recent judicial decisions that hold or suggest that defensive tactics by a target's management are protected by the business judgment rule. These decisions are based on a misunderstanding of the business judgment rule and are inimical to the goal of maximizing shareholders' welfare.

Peter F. Drucker, Taming the Corporate Takeover, The Wall Street Journal, October 30, 1984 at 30*

What explains the takeover wave that is engulfing American industry? Should it be stopped? And can it be stopped before it does irreparable harm? I am asked these questions every time I sit down with senior executives, middle managers or union leaders. The questions are also increasingly being asked by bankers or Wall Street people despite the immediate gains they derive from unfriendly takeovers.

It is increasingly hard to defend the unfriendly takeover as benefiting anyone other than the raider (and a few investment bankers and merger lawyers). Anyone working with management people knows that fear of the raider paralyzes our executives. Worse, it forces them into making decisions they know to be stupid and to damage the enterprise in their charge. A good many experienced business leaders I know now hold takeover fear to be a main cause of the decline in America's competitive strength in the world economy — and a far more potent cause than the high dollar. It contributes to the obsession with the short term and the slighting of tomorrow in research, product development, market development and marketing, and in quality and service — all to squeeze out a few more dollars in next quarter's "bottom line."

Employees Demoralized

But also, employees, from senior middle managers down to the rank and file in the office or factory floor, are increasingly being demoralized — a thoughtful union leader of my acquaintance calls it "traumatized" — by the fear of a takeover raid.

The very shareholders who accept the raider's bid clearly do not believe it to be in the best interest of either the acquiring company or the one about to be acquired. Announcement of an unfriendly bid is followed almost as a matter of routine by a drop in the share price of the bidding company. After they have voted to accept the raider's bid, most of the former holders of the acquired company at once sell the securities they received in exchange, thus giving the acquirer a rousing vote of nonconfidence. Indeed, the great majority of companies acquired through an unfriendly takeover have done worse under the new ownership than they did when they were independent. One reason for this is that the successful raider immediately strips his new acquisition of its best assets and drains it of cash — both to repay what he borrowed to buy the business and to make a quick killing.

It is thus highly debatable whether the unfriendly takeover is even in the best interest of the shareholders. It may be more nearly correct to say — as a banker friend of mine said recently — that in its opposition to any restriction on takeovers, the SEC, founded to protect the investor against the financial wolves, has now become the protector of the wolves.

And yet neither the shareholders who accept a takeover bid they know to be deleterious, nor the SEC, have much choice. The holders whose votes decide the outcome have a legal duty to accept the bid. They cannot exercise the owner's right — indeed, the owner's responsibility — to make a decision, *e.g.* to weigh long term vs. short term. They are fiduciaries. At least one-third of the equity of our publicly owned companies — 50% for the big ones — is held by "trustees" — pension funds foremost, mutual funds second. And fiduciaries have a legal duty to accept whatever gives their beneficiaries the highest immediate return. If, for example, the fiduciaries turn down a raider's bid that was a little higher than the stock-exchange quotation, they are liable for severe damages if the company's stock then does not go up, and soon. The pension-fund and mutual-fund managers whose votes decide the outcome may doubt the wisdom of a proposed merger or its benefits to either the acquiring or the acquired company — and they do have doubts most of the time. But they are legally bound to accept the bid. The wave of unfriendly takeovers is thus the price we pay for that great achievement, the pension fund.

But is it a necessary price? More and more people doubt it. We can expect — maybe no later than the next big, bitter, controversial takeover battles — several proposals to ban, or at least to curtail, unfriendly takeovers.

One proposal being quietly discussed by Washington's congressional staffers and by senior officials in the Treasury, Commerce and Labor departments is to have the Comptroller of the Currency forbid banks to make loans to finance takeover bids. I expect this proposal to surface the next time Congress debates regulation or deregulation of financial institutions. Some lawyers argue that the Comptroller already has the power to stop such loans. And with the Comptroller being pushed by the troubles of a few big banks into becoming more "activist," he may well, in a new administration, do something that, however unpopular with the banks and with Wall Street, would be applauded on "Main Street." Such a ban would put a stop to most, perhaps all, unfriendly takeovers.

A second proposal is being considered seriously in a few states with strong and politically powerful "high-tech" enterprises: Massachusetts, Minnesota, California, Colorado. It is to build legal delays into takeover proposals: a waiting period of nine months; a holding period of a year before the successful acquirer can sell any assets or touch the cash of the acquired business; or delaying the vote on the acquisition until the bidder has submitted a detailed and legally binding plan in which he outlines what he will do with the company he intends to buy. An approach favored by one powerful state official is to demand that the bidding company commit itself in advance to specific performance goals for the target company in respect to investment, sales, profit and employment, with penalties payable to shareholders and former employees should the goals not be reached.

Finally, there is increasing interest in the way the British are tackling the problem. They have a "Take-Over Panel" to which the government routinely refers unfriendly takeover bids for a final "yes" or "no." The advantage of this approach is that it allows takeovers, no matter how highly contested, if deemed justified and beneficial. But do we really need or want another government agency?

In one of these ways — or in a way no one has thought of yet — we will, I am reasonably sure, do something to curb the unfriendly takeover, and fairly soon. It is likely to go the way of the equally prominent financial ploy of the 1920s, the pyramided public-utility holding company. But there is a danger that the policies we adopt will be punitive rather than remedial, and will encroach on the freedom of business enterprise rather than strengthen it. This only means, however, that business had better think through what the policies should be instead of waiting for the "scandal" that pushes the politicians into demagoguery.

The Shift of Voting Power

And none of the policies we are likely to adopt will solve the basic problem, the one created by the shift of voting power from "owners" to "fiduciaries." The classical defense of ownership has always been that the "owner" has an abiding, long-term interest in the welfare of his property and that, therefore, his decisions are more likely than those of anyone else to balance and optimize the interests of all who have a stake in the enterprise: those of the owner, to be sure, but also those of employees, creditors, suppliers, customers, the economy and society in general.

The owner's self-interest, argued the Roman lawyers 2,000 years ago when they developed the legal concept we now call "property," was most nearly compatible with the true interest of the enterprise. But the new legal "owners" of our publicly owned businesses are forbidden as fiduciaries even to consider the interest of the enterprise. Can and will any society tolerate this? Can it even be defended as legitimate power? And how do we reconcile the justified interest of beneficiaries who need to be "investors" rather than "owners," and whose priorities therefore are quite properly liquidity and the fast buck, with the welfare of society's wealth- and job-producing asset: the going concern, the enterprise?

Chapter 19

INSIDER TRADING AND OTHER SECURITIES FRAUD

Situation

Biologistics, Inc. has been a wholly-owned subsidiary of Daytron Corporation for a year, and your firm remains its counsel. Anderson and Baker continue as officers and, three months ago, Baker joined Daytron's Board of Directors.

Anderson and Baker each acquired a substantial number of Daytron shares in exchange for their Biologistics shares. During the last year each has purchased, on the stock exchange, a total of several thousand more Daytron shares. These purchases began shortly after the acquisition and have continued at intervals of a month or two. At the time of the share exchange, Daytron stock was selling at $ 55 per share. Since the Biologistics acquisition, Daytron stock has been rising in price, and is currently selling at $ 75 per share.

Daytron has recently sent Anderson and Baker a questionnaire inquiring about purchases of Daytron stock. The questionnaire is worded in such a way as to make them suspect there may be problems with their purchases, and they have asked your advice.

SECTION I. INSIDER TRADING AND OTHER SECURITIES FRAUD UNDER STATE LAW

The regulation of improper "insider trading" (basically the buying or selling of securities, by those having some duty not to do so, on the basis of information not publicly available) has become in recent decades largely the province of federal law. But not the entire province. State regulation in this area has continued importance, with a number of questions remaining unanswered. As indicated in the following cases, one of the more interesting of these questions relates to the circumstances under which shareholders having evidence of insider trading may bring a derivative action alleging a state law claim.

Beyond state case law, there are statutes in many states governing insider trading and other acts that can loosely be called securities fraud. Some of these statutes are patterned after Rule 10b-5 under the Securities Exchange Act of 1934, which serves as the basis for much of the federal regulation. In this sense, at least, federal law also has become state law.

DIAMOND v. OREAMUNO

Court of Appeals of New York
24 N.Y.2d 494, 248 N.E.2d 910 (1969)

FULD, CHIEF JUDGE.

Upon this appeal from an order denying a motion to dismiss the complaint as insufficient on its face, the question presented — one of first impression in this court — is whether officers and directors may be held accountable to their corporation for gains realized by them from transactions in the company's stock as a result of their use of material inside information.

The complaint was filed by a shareholder of Management Assistance, Inc. (MAI) asserting a derivative action against a number of its officers and directors to compel an accounting for profits allegedly acquired as a result of a breach of fiduciary duty. It charges that two of the defendants — Oreamuno, chairman of the board of directors, and Gonzalez, its president — had used inside information, acquired by them solely by virtue of their positions, in order to reap large personal profits from the sale of MAI shares and that these profits rightfully belong to the corporation. Other officers and directors were joined as defendants on the ground that they acquiesced in or ratified the assertedly wrongful transactions.

MAI is in the business of financing computer installations through sale and lease back arrangements with various commercial and industrial users. Under its lease provisions, MAI was required to maintain and repair the computers but, at the time of this suit, it lacked the capacity to perform this function itself and was forced to engage the manufacturer of the computers, International Business Machines (IBM), to service the machines. As a result of a sharp increase by IBM of its charges for such service, MAI's expenses for August of 1966 rose considerably and its net earnings declined from $ 262,253 in July to $ 66,233 in August, a decrease of about 75%. This information, although earlier known to the defendants, was not made public until October of 1966. Prior to the release of the information, however, Oreamuno and Gonzalez sold off a total of 56,500 shares of their MAI stock at the then current market price of $ 28 a share.

After the information concerning the drop in earnings was made available to the public, the value of a share of MAI stock immediately fell from the $ 28 realized by the defendants to $ 11. Thus, the plaintiff alleges, by taking advantage of their privileged position and their access to confidential information, Oreamuno and Gonzalez were able to realize $ 800,000 more for their securities than they would have had this inside information not been available to them. Stating that the defendants were "forbidden to use [such] information ... for their own personal profit or gain," the plaintiff brought this derivative action seeking to have the defendants account to the corporation for this difference. A motion by the defendants to dismiss the complaint ... for failure to state a cause of action was granted by the court at Special Term. The Appellate Division, with one dissent, modified Special Term's order by reinstating the complaint as to the defendants Oreamuno and Gonzalez. The appeal is before us on a certified question.

In reaching a decision in this case, we are, of course, passing only upon the sufficiency of the complaint and we necessarily accept the charges contained in that pleading as true.

It is well established, as a general proposition, that a person who acquires special knowledge or information by virtue of a confidential or fiduciary relationship with another is not free to exploit that knowledge or information for his own personal benefit but must account to his principal for any profits derived therefrom. This, in turn is merely a corollary of the broader principle, inherent in the nature of the fiduciary relationship, that prohibits a trustee or agent from extracting secret profits from his position of trust.

In support of their claim that the complaint fails to state a cause of action, the defendants take the position that, although it is admittedly wrong for an officer or director to use his position to obtain trading profits for himself in the stock of his corporation, the action ascribed to them did not injure or damage MAI in any way. Accordingly, the defendants continue, the corporation should not be permitted to recover the proceeds. They acknowledge that, by virtue of the exclusive access which officers and directors have to inside information, they possess an unfair advantage over other shareholders and, particularly, the persons who had purchased the stock from them but, they contend, the corporation itself was unaffected and, for that reason, a derivative action is an inappropriate remedy.

It is true that the complaint before us does not contain any allegation of damages to the corporation but this has never been considered to be an essential requirement for a cause of action founded on a breach of fiduciary duty. This is because the function of such an action, unlike an ordinary tort or contract case, is not merely to compensate the plaintiff for wrongs committed by the defendant but, as this court declared many years ago (*Dutton v. Willner,* 52 N.Y. 312, 319), "to *prevent* them, by removing from agents and trustees all inducement to attempt dealing for their own benefit in matters which they have undertaken for others, or to which their agency or trust relates." (Emphasis supplied.)

Just as a trustee has no right to retain for himself the profits yielded by property placed in his possession but must account to his beneficiaries, a corporate fiduciary, who is entrusted with potentially valuable information, may not appropriate that asset for his own use even though, in so doing, he causes no injury to the corporation. The primary concern, in a case such as this, is not to determine whether the corporation has been damaged but to decide, as between the corporation and the defendants, who has a higher claim to the proceeds derived from the exploitation of the information. In our opinion, there can be no justification for permitting officers and directors, such as the defendants, to retain for themselves profits which, it is alleged, they derived solely from exploiting information gained by virtue of their inside position as corporate officials.

In addition, it is pertinent to observe that, despite the lack of any specific allegation of damage, it may well be inferred that the defendants' actions might have caused some harm to the enterprise. Although the corporation may have little concern with the day-to-day transactions in its shares, it has a great interest in maintaining a reputation of integrity, an image of probity, for its management and in insuring the continued public acceptance and marketability of its stock. When officers and directors abuse their position in order to gain personal profits, the effect may be to cast a cloud on the corporation's name, injure stockholder relations and undermine public regard for the corporation's securities....

....

... In *Brophy v. Cities Serv. Co.* (31 Del. Ch. 241, 70 A.2d 5), [o]ne of the defendants ... was an employee who had acquired inside information that the corporate plaintiff was about to enter the market and purchase its own shares. On the basis of this confidential information, the employee ... bought a large block of shares and, after the corporation's purchases had caused the price to rise, resold them at a profit. The court sustained the complaint in a derivative action brought for an accounting, stating that "[p]ublic policy will not permit an employee occupying a position of trust and confidence toward his employer to abuse that relation to his own profit, regardless of whether his employer suffers a loss." And a similar view has been expressed in the Restatement, 2d, Agency (§ 388, comment *c*):

> c. Use of confidential information. An agent who acquires confidential information in the course of his employment or in violation of his duties has a duty ... to account for any profits made by the use of such information, although this does not harm the principal.... So, if [a corporate officer] has "inside" information that the corporation is about to purchase or sell securities, or to declare or to pass a dividend, profits made by him in stock transactions undertaken because of his knowledge are held in constructive trust for the principal.

....

Accepting the truth of the complaint's allegations, there is no question but that the defendants were guilty of withholding material information from the purchasers of the shares and, indeed, the defendants acknowledge that the facts asserted constitute a violation of [federal] rule 10b-5. The remedies which the Federal law provides for such violation, however, are rather limited. An action could be brought, in an exceptional case, by the SEC for injunctive relief. This, in fact, is what happened in the *Texas Gulf Sulphur* case (401 F.2d 833). The purpose of such an action, however, would appear to be more to establish a principle than to provide a regular method of enforcement. A class action under the Federal rule might be a more effective remedy but the mechanics of such an action have, as far as we have been able to ascertain, not yet been worked out by the Federal courts and several questions relating thereto have never been resolved. These include the definition of the class entitled to bring such an action, the measure of damages, the administration of the fund which would be recovered and its distribution to the members of the class. Of course, any individual purchaser, who could prove an injury as a result of a rule 10b-5 violation can bring his own action for rescission but we have not been referred to a single case in which such an action has been successfully prosecuted where the public sale of securities is involved. The reason for this is that sales of securities, whether through a stock exchange or over-the-counter, are characteristically anonymous transactions, usually handled through brokers, and the matching of the ultimate buyer with the ultimate seller presents virtually insurmountable obstacles....

In view of the practical difficulties inherent in an action under the Federal law, the desirability of creating an effective common-law remedy is manifest. "Dishonest directors should not find absolution from retributive justice," Ballantine observed in his work on Corporations ([rev. ed., 1946], p. 216), "by concealing their identity from their victims under the mask of the stock exchange." There is ample room in a situation such as is here presented for a "private Attorney General" to come forward and enforce proper behavior on the part of corporate officials through the medium of the derivative action brought in the name of the corporation. Only by sanctioning such a cause of action will there be any effective method to prevent the type of abuse of corporate office complained of in this case.

There is nothing in the Federal law which indicates that it was intended to limit the power of the States to fashion additional remedies to effectuate similar purposes. Although the impact of Federal securities regulation has on occasion been said to have created a "Federal corporation law," in fact, its effect on the duties and obligations of directors and officers and their relation to the corporation and its shareholders is only occasional and peripheral. The primary source of the law in this area ever remains that of the State which created the corporation. Indeed, Congress expressly provided against any implication that it intended to pre-empt the field by declaring, in section 28(a) of the Securities Exchange Act of 1934, that "[t]he rights and remedies provided by this title shall be in addition to any and all other rights and remedies that may exist at law or in equity."

Nor should we be deterred, in formulating a State remedy, by the defendants' claim of possible double liability. Certainly, as already indicated if the sales in question were publicly made, the likelihood that a suit will be brought by purchasers of the shares is quite remote. But, even if it were not, the mere possibility of such a suit is not a defense nor does it render the complaint insufficient. It is not unusual for an action to be brought to recover a fund which may be subject to a superior claim by a third party. If that be the situation, a defendant should not be permitted to retain the fund for his own use on the chance that such a party may eventually appear. A defendant's course, if he wishes to protect himself against double liability, is to interplead any and all possible claimants and bind them to the judgment.

In any event, though, no suggestion has been made either in brief or on oral argument that any purchaser has come forward with a claim against the defendants or even that anyone is in a position to advance such a claim. As we have stated, the defendants' assertion that such a party may come forward at some future date is not a basis for permitting them to retain for their own benefit the fruits of their allegedly wrongful acts. For all that appears, the present derivative action is the only effective remedy now available against the abuse by these defendants of their privileged position.

....

FREEMAN v. DECIO

United States Court of Appeals, Seventh Circuit
584 F.2d 186 (1978)

HARLINGTON WOOD, JR., CIRCUIT JUDGE.

The principal question presented by this case is whether under Indiana law the plaintiff may sustain a derivative action against certain officers and directors of the Skyline Corporation for allegedly trading in the stock of the corporation on the basis of material inside information. The district court granted summary judgment for the defendants on the ground that in light of the defendants' affidavits and documentary evidence, the plaintiff had failed to create a genuine dispute as to whether the defendants' sales of stock were based on material inside information. Alternatively, the court held that the plaintiff had failed to state a cause of action in that Indiana law has never recognized a right in a corporation to recover profits from insider trading and is not likely to follow the lead of the New York Court of Appeals in *Diamond v. Oreamuno,* 24 N.Y.2d 494, 301 N.Y.S.2d 78, 248 N.E.2d 910 (1969), in creating such a cause of action. We affirm....

Plaintiff-appellant Marcia Freeman is a stockholder of the Skyline Corporation, a major producer of mobile homes and recreational vehicles. Skyline is a publicly owned corporation whose stock is traded on the New York Stock Exchange (NYSE). Defendant Arthur J. Decio is the largest shareholder of Skyline, the chairman of its board of directors, and until September 25, 1972, was also the president of the company. Defendant Dale Swikert is a director of Skyline and prior to assuming the presidency from Decio in 1972 was Skyline's executive vice president and chief operating officer. Defendants Samuel P. Mandell and Ira J. Kaufman are outside directors of Skyline.

Throughout the 1960's and into 1972 Skyline experienced continual growth in sales and earnings. At the end of fiscal 1971 the company was able to report to its shareholders that over the previous five years sales had increased at a 40% average compound rate and that net income had grown at a 64% rate. This enormous success was reflected in increases in the price of Skyline stock. By April of 1972 Skyline common had reached a high of $ 72.00 per share, representing a price/earnings ratio of greater than 50 times earnings. Then, on December 22, 1972, Skyline reported that earnings for the quarter ending November 30, 1972, declined from $ 4,569,007 to $ 3,713,545 compared to the comparable period of the preceding year, rather than increasing substantially as they had done in the past. The NYSE immediately suspended trading in the stock. Trading was resumed on December 26 at $ 34.00 per share, down $ 13.50 from the preannouncement price. This represented a drop in value of almost 30%.

Plaintiff alleges that the defendants sold Skyline stock on the basis of material inside information during two distinct periods. Firstly, it is alleged that the financial results reported by Skyline for the quarters ending May 31 and August 31, 1972, significantly understated material costs and overstated earnings. It is further alleged that Decio, Kaufman and Mandell made various sales of Skyline stock totalling nearly $ 10 million during the quarters in question, knowing that earnings were overstated. Secondly, plaintiff asserts that during the quarter ending November 30 and up to December 22, 1972, Decio and Mandell made gifts and sales of Skyline stock totaling nearly $ 4 million while knowing that reported earnings for the November 30 quarter would decline....

After three years of extensive discovery both sides moved for summary judgment. The district court granted the defendants' Fed. R. Civ. P. 56 motions on the insider trading counts on the ground that Indiana law does not provide for a derivative cause of action on behalf of a corporation to recover profits from insider trading. Alternatively, the court found that, in view of the defendants' affidavits and depositions, the plaintiff had not succeeded in creating a genuine dispute as to whether the defendants' stock sales were made on the basis of material inside information.

....

I. *Diamond v. Oreamuno and Indiana Law*

Both parties agree that there is no Indiana precedent directly dealing with the question of whether a corporation may recover the profits of corporate officials who trade in the corporation's securities on the basis of inside information. However, the plaintiff suggests that were the question to be presented to the Indiana courts, they would adopt the holding of the New York Court of Appeals in *Diamond v. Oreamuno,* 24 N.Y.2d 494, 301 N.Y.S.2d 78, 248 N.E.2d 910 (1969). There, building on the Delaware case of *Brophy v. Cities Service Co.,* 31 Del. Ch. 241, 70 A.2d 5 (1949), the court held that the officers and directors of a corporation breached their fiduciary duties owed to the corporation by trading in its stock on the basis of material non-public information acquired by virtue of their official positions and that they should account to the corporation for their profits from those transactions. Since *Diamond* was decided, few courts have had an opportunity to consider the problem there presented. In fact, only one case has been brought to our attention which raised the question of whether *Diamond* would be followed in another jurisdiction. In *Schein v. Chasen,* 478 F.2d 817 (2d Cir. 1973), *vacated and remanded sub nom., Lehman Bros. v. Schein,* 416 U.S. 386 (1974), *on certification to the Fla. Sup. Ct.,* 313 So. 2d 739 (Fla. 1975), the Second Circuit, sitting in diversity, considered whether the Florida courts would permit a *Diamond*-type action to be brought on behalf of a corporation. The majority not only tacitly concluded that Florida would adopt *Diamond,* but that the *Diamond* cause of action should be extended so as to permit recovery of the profits of non-insiders who traded in the corporation's stock on the basis of inside information received as tips from insiders. Judge Kaufman, dissenting, agreed with the policies underlying a *Diamond*-type cause of action, but disagreed with the extension of liability to outsiders. He also failed to understand why the panel was not willing to utilize Florida's certified question statute so as to bring the question of law before the Florida Supreme Court. Granting *certiorari,* the United States Supreme Court agreed with the dissent on this last point and on remand the case was certified to the Florida Supreme Court. That court not only stated that it would not "give the unprecedented expansive reading to *Diamond* sought by appellants" but that, furthermore, it did not "choose to adopt the innovative ruling of the New York Court of Appeals in *Diamond* [itself]." Thus, the question here is whether the Indiana courts are more likely to follow the New York Court of Appeals or to join the Florida Supreme Court in refusing to undertake such a change from existing law.

It appears that from a policy point of view it is widely accepted that insider trading should be deterred because it is unfair to other investors who do not enjoy the benefits of access to inside information. The goal is not one of equality of possession of information — since some traders will always be better "informed" than others by dint of greater expenditures of time and resources, greater experience, or greater analytical abilities — but rather equality of access to information....

....

[T]he New York Court of Appeals in *Diamond* found the existing remedies for controlling insider trading to be inadequate. Although the court felt that the device of a class action under the federal securities laws held out hope of a more effective remedy in the future, it concluded that "the desirability of creating an effective common-law remedy is manifest." It went on to do so by engineering an innovative extension of the law governing the relation between a corporation and its officers and directors. The court held that corporate officials who deal in their corporation's securities on the basis of non-public information gained by virtue of their inside position commit a breach of their fiduciary duties to the corporation. This holding represents a departure from the traditional common law approach, which was that a corporate insider did not ordinarily violate his fiduciary duty to the corporation by dealing in the corporation's stock, unless the corporation was thereby harmed.

....

There are a number of difficulties with the *Diamond* court's ruling. Perhaps the thorniest problem was posed by the defendants' objection that whatever the ethical status of insider trading, there is no injury to the corporation which can serve as a basis for recognizing a right of recovery in favor of the latter. The Court of Appeals' response to this argument was two-fold, suggesting first that no harm to the corporation need be shown and second that it might well be inferred that the insiders' activities did in fact cause some harm to the corporation.... Some might see the *Diamond* court's decision as resting on a broad, strict-trust notion of the fiduciary duty owed to the corporation: no director is to receive any profit, beyond what he receives from the corporation, solely because of his position. Although, once accepted, this basis for the *Diamond* rule would obviate the need for finding a potential for injury to the corporation, it is not at all clear that current corporation law contemplates such an extensive notion of fiduciary duty. It is customary to view the *Diamond* result as resting on a characterization of inside information as a corporate asset. The lack of necessity for looking for an injury to the corporation is then justified by the traditional "no inquiry" rule with respect to profits made by trustees from assets belonging to the trust *res*. However, to start from the premise that all inside information should be considered a corporate asset may presuppose an answer to the inquiry at hand. It might be better to ask whether there is any potential loss to the corporation from the use of such information in insider trading before deciding to characterize the inside information as an asset with respect to which the insider owes the corporation a duty of loyalty (as opposed to a duty of care). This approach would be in keeping with the modern view of another area of application of the duty of loyalty — the corporate opportunity doctrine. Thus, while courts will require a director or officer to automatically account to the corporation for diversion of a corporate opportunity to personal use, they will first inquire to see whether there was a possibility of a loss to the corporation — *i.e.*, whether the corporation was in a position to potentially avail itself of the opportunity — before deciding that a corporate opportunity in fact existed. Similarly, when scrutinizing transactions between a director or officer and the corporation under the light of the duty of loyalty, most courts now inquire as to whether there was any injury to the corporation, *i.e.*, whether the transaction was fair and in good faith, before permitting the latter to avoid the transaction. An analogous question might be posed with respect to the *Diamond* court's unjust enrichment analysis: is it proper to conclude that an insider has been unjustly enriched *vis-à-vis* the corporation (as compared to other traders in the market) when there is no way that the corporation could have used the information to its own profit, just because the insider's trading was made possible by virtue of his corporate position?

Not all information generated in the course of carrying on a business fits snugly into the corporate asset mold. Information in the form of trade secrets, customer lists, etc., can easily be categorized as a valuable or potentially valuable corporate "possession," in that it can be directly used by the corporation to its own economic advantage. However, most information involved in insider trading is not of this ilk, *e.g.*, knowledge of an impending merger, a decline in earnings, etc. If the corporation were to attempt to exploit such non-public information by dealing in its own securities, it would open itself up to potential liability under federal and state securities laws, just as do the insiders when they engage in insider trading. This is not to say that the corporation does not have any interests with regard to such information. It may have an interest in either preventing the information from becoming public or in regulating the timing of disclosure. However, insider trading does not entail the disclosure of inside information, but rather its use in a manner in which the corporation itself is prohibited from exploiting it.

... It must be conceded that the unfairness that is the basis of the widespread disapproval of insider trading is borne primarily by participants in the securities markets, rather than by the corporation itself. By comparison, the harm to corporate goodwill posited by the *Diamond* court pales in significance. At this point, the existence of such an indirect injury must be considered speculative, as there is no actual evidence of such a reaction. Furthermore, it is less than clear to us that the nature of this harm would form an adequate basis for an action for an accounting based on a breach of the insiders' duty of loyalty, as opposed to an action for damages based on a breach of the duty of care. The injury hypothesized by the *Diamond* court seems little different from the harm to the corporation that might be inferred whenever a responsible corporate official commits an illegal or unethical act using a corporate asset. Absent is the element of loss of opportunity or potential susceptibility to outside influence that generally is present when a corporate fiduciary is required to account to the corporation.

....

A second problem presented by the recognition of a cause of action in favor of the corporation is that of potential double liability. The *Diamond* court thought that this problem would seldom arise, since it thought it unlikely that a damage suit would be brought by investors where the insiders traded on impersonal exchanges. The court further reasoned that:

> ... A defendant's course, if he wishes to protect himself against double liability, is to interplead any and all possible claimants and bind them to the judgment (CPLR 1006, subd. [b])....

Since the *Diamond* court's action was motivated in large part by its perception of the inadequacy of existing remedies for insider trading, it is noteworthy that over the decade since *Diamond* was decided, the 10b-5 class action has made substantial advances toward becoming the kind of effective remedy for insider trading that the court of appeals hoped that it might become. Most importantly, recovery of damages from insiders has been allowed by, or on the behalf of, market investors even when the insiders dealt only through impersonal stock exchanges, although this is not yet a well-settled area of the law. In spite of other recent developments indicating that such class actions will not become as easy to maintain as some plaintiffs had perhaps hoped, it is clear that the remedies for insider trading under the federal securities laws now constitute a more effective deterrent than they did when *Diamond* was decided.

[H]aving carefully examined the decision of the New York Court of Appeals in *Diamond,* we are of the opinion that although the court sought to ground its ruling in accepted principles of corporate common law, that decision can best be understood as an example of judicial securities regulation. Although the question is a close one, we believe that were the issue to be presented to the Indiana courts at the present time, they would most likely join the Florida Supreme Court in refusing to adopt the New York court's innovative ruling.

....

SECTION II. INSIDER TRADING AND OTHER SECURITIES FRAUD UNDER FEDERAL LAW

Rule 10b-5 was passed in the early 1940's in response to an enforcement need of the Securities and Exchange Commission. Section 17(a) of the Securities Act of 1933 prohibited a variety of fraudulent conduct in connection with the sale of securities, but neither this nor any other provision prohibited fraudulent acts in connection with the purchase of securities. The SEC plugged this hole by rewriting § 17(a) and adopting it as a rule under § 10(b) of the Securities Exchange Act of 1934. Here is the text of the rule:

> It shall be unlawful for any person, directly or indirectly, by the use of any means or instrumentality of interstate commerce, or of the mails, or of any facility of any national securities exchange,
> (a) to employ any device, scheme, or artifice to defraud,
> (b) to make any untrue statement of a material fact or to omit to state a material fact necessary in order to make the statements made, in the light of the circumstances under which they were made, not misleading, or
> (c) to engage in any act, practice, or course of business which operates or would operate as a fraud or deceit upon any person, in connection with the purchase or sale of any security.

The enforcement need that triggered the passage of Rule 10b-5 was one involving insider trading, and the regulation of insider trading has been the main thrust of the rule all along. But not its only thrust. The rule has been pressed into service to cover various kinds of "fraud" somehow connected to the buying or selling of securities. Most, but not all, of the uses of the rule will show up in the cases that follow. Left for a course in securities regulation are examples of its use against market manipulation (basically effecting trades for the purpose of influencing the market price of a security) and various misdeeds by securities professionals, such as "churning" (buying and selling securities for a customer's account, over which a securities firm has discretionary authority, for the purpose of generating commissions).

All the cases in this section save one are presented in subsections dealing with a particular issue under the rule. Before beginning a reading of those cases, two items of background may be helpful. First, as to who can bring actions under the rule and, second, as to the stages of the rule's evolution.

As is apparent from its language ("It shall be unlawful...."), Rule 10b-5 is a criminal provision. Section 32 of the Exchange Act provides that a willful violation of such a rule is a felony. Criminal actions may be brought only by the

Justice Department, not by the SEC. Under authority of §§ 21 and 21A of the Exchange Act, however, the SEC does have power to bring actions in court seeking injunctions against violations of the Act and its rules and requesting the court to impose civil penalties. Exchange Act §§ 21B and 21C give the SEC power to impose civil penalties in administrative actions heard in its quasi-judicial capacity and to issue its own cease-and-desist orders. In addition, Exchange Act §§ 20, 20A, and 20D cover the liability of controlling persons, of aiders and abettors, and of certain inside traders, and also provide for limitations on damages and proportionate liability. Also, courts have long held that an implied private right of action exists under Rule 10b-5, making its use available to private individuals who meet the standing requirement.

From the adoption of Rule 10b-5 in 1942 until the 1960's, the rule evolved slowly, with courts and lawyers feeling their way. One turning point in the rule's evolution was an SEC opinion, which it rendered while sitting in its quasi-judicial capacity, in an insider trading case involving a securities firm. The case was *In re Cady, Roberts & Co.*[1] One might view *Cady, Roberts* as a sort of spark that ignited Rule 10b-5. If so, the first case included below, *SEC v. Texas Gulf Sulphur Co.*, was a gasoline hose turned loose on the flame. From this point until the mid-1970's, the reach of the rule was continuously expanding as courts used it more and more aggressively in new and newer contexts. This era is typified by cases such as *Superintendent of Insurance of New York v. Bankers Life & Casualty Co.* and *Shapiro v. Merrill Lynch, Pierce, Fenner & Smith, Inc.*, each of which is included below.

In 1975 and 1976 the Supreme Court handed down *Blue Chip Stamps v. Manor Drug Stores* and *Ernst & Ernst v. Hochfelder*. The first involves the issue of standing and the second the degree of fault required in a private right of action case. As a technical matter, these opinions are important for their holdings. They are, however, much more important for the signals they sent about the court's inclination away from a continued expansion of Rule 10b-5. This is easily seen by comparing the tenor of *Bankers Life* with that of *Blue Chip,* decided only four years later. Both *Blue Chip* and *Hochfelder* appear in this chapter.

Since the mid-1970's the rule has had relatively little growth, and some retrenchment. This, again, will easily be seen in comparing cases from era to era. The most striking comparison may be between *Shapiro* and two later cases, included in this chapter, that discuss it: *Fridrich v. Bradford* and *Elkind v. Liggett & Myers, Inc.*

---

[1] 40 S.E.C. 907 (1961).

Remarks of Milton Freeman, 22 Business Lawyer 922 (1967)*

[S]ince people keep talking about 10b-5 as my rule, and since I have told a lot of people about it, I think it would be appropriate for me now to make a brief statement of what actually happened when 10b-5 was adopted, where it would be written down and be available to everybody, not just the people who are willing to listen to me.

It was one day in the year 1943, I believe. I was sitting in my office in the S.E.C. building in Philadelphia and I received a call from Jim Treanor who was then the Director of the Trading and Exchange Division. He said, "I have just been on the telephone with Paul Rowen," who was then the S.E.C. Regional Administrator in Boston, "and he has told me about the president of some company in Boston who is going around buying up the stock of his company from his own shareholders at $ 4.00 a share, and he has been telling them that the company is doing very badly, whereas, in fact, the earnings are going to be quadrupled and will be $ 2.00 a share for this coming year. Is there anything we can do about it?" So he came upstairs and I called in my secretary and I looked at Section 10(b) and I looked at Section 17, and I put them together, and the only discussion we had there was where "in connection with the purchase or sale" should be, and we decided it should be at the end.

We called the Commission and we got on the calendar, and I don't remember whether we got there that morning or after lunch. We passed a piece of paper around to all the commissioners. All the commissioners read the rule and they tossed it on the table, indicating approval. Nobody said anything except Sumner Pike who said, "Well," he said, "we are against fraud, aren't we?" That is how it happened.

... I never thought that twenty-odd years later it would be the biggest thing that had ever happened. It was intended to give the Commission power to deal with this problem. It had no relation in the Commission's contemplation to private proceedings. How it got into private proceedings was by the ingenuity of members of the private Bar starting with the *Kardon* case. It has been developed by the private lawyers, the members of the Bar, with the assistance or, if you don't like it, connivance of the federal judiciary, who thought this was a very fine fundamental idea and that it should be extended....

Myself, I tend to think that judges do not extend principles that do not appeal to their basic sense of fairness and equity. I would be inclined to say that whether the development comes from a rule or from a congressional adoption, the result would be in broad outline approximately the same....

SECURITIES AND EXCHANGE COMMISSION
v. TEXAS GULF SULPHUR CO.

United States Court of Appeals, Second Circuit
401 F.2d 833 (1968)

WATERMAN, CIRCUIT JUDGE:

This action was commenced in the United States District Court for the Southern District of New York by the Securities and Exchange Commission (the SEC) pursuant to Sec. 21(e) of the Securities Exchange Act of 1934 (the Act) against Texas Gulf Sulphur Company (TGS) and several of its officers, directors and employees, to enjoin certain conduct by TGS and the individual defendants said to violate Section 10(b) of the Act and Rule 10b-5 (the Rule), promulgated thereunder, and to compel the rescission by the individual defendants of securities transactions assertedly conducted contrary to law. The complaint alleged (1) that defendants Fogarty, Mollison, Darke, Murray, Huntington, O'Neill, Clayton, Crawford, and Coates had either personally or through agents purchased TGS stock or calls thereon from November 12, 1963 through April 16, 1964 on the basis of material inside information concerning the results of TGS drilling in Timmins, Ontario, while such information remained undisclosed to the investing public generally or to the particular sellers; (2) that defendants Darke and Coates had divulged such information to others for use in purchasing TGS stock or calls or recommended its purchase while the information was undisclosed to the public or to the sellers; that defendants Stephens, Fogarty, Mollison, Holyk, and Kline had accepted options to purchase TGS stock on Feb. 20, 1964 without disclosing the material information as to the drilling progress to either the Stock Option Committee or the TGS Board of Directors; and (4) that TGS issued a deceptive press release on April 12, 1964....

....

The Factual Setting

This action derives from the exploratory activities of TGS begun in 1957 on the Canadian Shield in eastern Canada. In March of 1959, aerial geophysical surveys were conducted over more than 15,000 square miles of this area by a group led by defendant Mollison, a mining engineer and a Vice President of TGS. The group included defendant Holyk, TGS's chief geologist, defendant Clayton, an electrical engineer and geophysicist, and defendant Darke, a geologist. These operations resulted in the detection of numerous anomalies, *i.e.*, extraordinary variations in the conductivity of rocks, one of which was on the Kidd 55 segment of land located near Timmins, Ontario.

On October 29 and 30, 1963, Clayton conducted a ground geophysical survey on the northeast portion of the Kidd 55 segment which confirmed the presence of an anomaly and indicated the necessity of diamond core drilling for further evaluation. Drilling of the initial hole, K-55-1, at the strongest part of the anomaly was commenced on November 8 and terminated on November 12 at a depth of 655 feet. Visual estimates by Holyk of the core of K-55-1 indicated an average copper content of 1.15% and an average zinc content of 8.64% over a length of 599 feet. This visual estimate convinced TGS that it was desirable to acquire the remainder of the Kidd 55 segment, and in order to facilitate this acquisition TGS President Stephens instructed the exploration group to keep the results of K-55-1 confidential and undisclosed even as to other officers, directors, and employees of TGS. The hole was concealed and a barren core was intentionally drilled off the anomaly. Meanwhile, the core of K-55-1 had been shipped to Utah for chemical assay which, when received in early December, revealed an average mineral content of 1.18% copper, 8.26% zinc, and 3.94% ounces of silver per ton over a length of 602 feet. These results were so remarkable that neither Clayton, an experienced geophysicist, nor four other TGS expert witnesses, had ever seen or heard of a comparable initial exploratory drill hole in a base metal deposit. So, the trial court concluded, "There is no doubt that the drill core of K-55-1 was unusually good and that it excited the interest and speculation of those who knew about it." By March 27, 1964, TGS decided that the land acquisition program had advanced to such a point that the company might well resume drilling, and drilling was resumed on March 31.

During this period, from November 12, 1963 when K-55-1 was completed, to March 31, 1964 when drilling was resumed, certain of the individual defendants ... and persons ... said to have received "tips" from them, purchased TGS stock or calls thereon. Prior to these transactions these persons had owned 1135 shares of TGS stock and possessed no calls; thereafter they owned a total of 8235 shares and possessed 12,300 calls.

On February 20, 1964, also during this period, TGS issued stock options to 26 of its officers and employees whose salaries exceeded a specified amount, five of whom were the individual defendants Stephens, Fogarty, Mollison, Holyk, and Kline. Of these, only Kline was unaware of the detailed results of K-55-1, but he, too, knew that a hole containing favorable bodies of copper and zinc ore had been drilled in Timmins. At this time, neither the TGS Stock Option Committee nor its Board of Directors had been informed of the results of K-55-1, presumably because of the pending land acquisition program which required confidentiality. All of the foregoing defendants accepted the options granted them.

When drilling was resumed on March 31, hole K-55-3 was commenced 510 feet west of K-55-1 and was drilled easterly at a 45' angle so as to cross K-55-1 in a vertical plane. Daily progress reports of the drilling of this hole K-55-3 and of all subsequently drilled holes were sent to defendants Stephens and Fogarty (President and Executive Vice President of TGS) by Holyk and Mollison. Visual estimates of K-55-3 revealed an average mineral content of 1.12% copper and 7.93% zinc over 641 of the hole's 876-foot length. On April 7, drilling of a third hole, K-55-4, 200 feet south of and parallel to K-55-1 and westerly at a 45' angle, was commenced and mineralization was encountered over 366 of its 579-foot length. Visual estimates indicated an average content of 1.14% copper and 8.24% zinc. Like K-55-1, both K-55-3 and K-55-4 established substantial copper mineralization on the eastern edge of the anomaly. On the basis of these findings relative to the foregoing drilling results, the trial court concluded that the vertical plane created by the intersection of K-55-1 and K-55-3, which measured at least 350 feet wide by 500 feet deep extended southward 200 feet to its intersection with K-55-4, and that "There was real evidence that a body of commercially mineable ore might exist."

On April 8 TGS began with a second drill rig to drill another hole, K-55-6, 300 feet easterly of K-55-1. This hole was drilled westerly at an angle of 60' and was intended to explore mineralization beneath K-55-1. While no visual estimates of its core were immediately available, it was readily apparent by the evening of April 10 that substantial copper mineralization had been encountered over the last 127 feet of the hole's 569-foot length. On April 10, a third drill rig commenced drilling yet another hole, K-55-5, 200 feet north of K-55-1 parallel to the prior holes, and slanted westerly at a 45' angle. By the evening of April 10 in this hole, too, substantial copper mineralization had been encountered over the last 42 feet of its 97-foot length.

Meanwhile, rumors that a major ore strike was in the making had been circulating throughout Canada. On the morning of Saturday, April 11, Stephens at his home in Greenwich, Conn. read in the New York Herald Tribune and in the New York Times unauthorized reports of the TGS drilling which seemed to infer a rich strike from the fact that the drill cores had been flown to the United States for chemical assay. Stephens immediately contacted Fogarty at his home in Rye, N. Y., who in turn telephoned and later that day visited Mollison at Mollison's home in Greenwich to obtain a current report and evaluation of the drilling progress. The following morning, Sunday, Fogarty again telephoned Mollison, inquiring whether Mollison had any further information and told him to return to Timmins with Holyk, the TGS Chief Geologist, as soon as possible "to move things along." With the aid of one Carroll, a public relations consultant, Fogarty drafted a press release designed to quell the rumors, which release, after having been channeled through Stephens and Huntington, a TGS attorney, was issued at 3:00 P. M. on Sunday, April 12, and which appeared in the morning newspapers of general circulation on Monday, April 13. It read in pertinent part as follows:

> NEW YORK, April 12 — The following statement was made today by Dr. Charles F. Fogarty, executive vice president of Texas Gulf Sulphur Company, in regard to the company's drilling operations near Timmins, Ontario, Canada. Dr. Fogarty said:
>
> "During the past few days, the exploration activities of Texas Gulf Sulphur in the area of Timmins, Ontario, have been widely reported in the press, coupled with rumors of a substantial copper discovery there. These reports exaggerate the scale of operations, and mention plans and statistics of size and grade of ore that are without factual basis and have evidently originated by speculation of people not connected with TGS.

"The facts are as follows. TGS has been exploring in the Timmins area for six years as part of its overall search in Canada and elsewhere for various minerals — lead, copper, zinc, etc. During the course of this work, in Timmins as well as in Eastern Canada, TGS has conducted exploration entirely on its own, without the participation by others. Numerous prospects have been investigated by geophysical means and a large number of selected ones have been core-drilled. These cores are sent to the United States for assay and detailed examination as a matter of routine and on advice of expert Canadian legal counsel. No inferences as to grade can be drawn from this procedure.

"Most of the areas drilled in Eastern Canada have revealed either barren pyrite or graphite without value; a few have resulted in discoveries of small or marginal sulphide ore bodies.

"Recent drilling on one property near Timmins has led to preliminary indications that more drilling would be required for proper evaluation of this prospect. The drilling done to date has not been conclusive, but the statements made by many outside quarters are unreliable and include information and figures that are not available to TGS.

"The work done to date has not been sufficient to reach definite conclusions and any statement as to size and grade of ore would be premature and possibly misleading. When we have progressed to the point where reasonable and logical conclusions can be made, TGS will issue a definite statement to its stockholders and to the public in order to clarify the Timmins project."

The release purported to give the Timmins drilling results as of the release date, April 12. From Mollison Fogarty had been told of the developments through 7:00 P. M. on April 10, and of the remarkable discoveries made up to that time, detailed supra, which discoveries, according to the calculations of the experts who testified for the SEC at the hearing, demonstrated that TGS had already discovered 6.2 to 8.3 million tons of proven ore having gross assay values from $ 26 to $ 29 per ton. TGS experts, on the other hand, denied at the hearing that proven or probable ore could have been calculated on April 11 or 12 because there was then no assurance of continuity in the mineralized zone.

The evidence as to the effect of this release on the investing public was equivocal and less than abundant. On April 13 the New York Herald Tribune in an article head-noted "Copper Rumor Deflated" quoted from the TGS release of April 12 and backtracked from its original April 11 report of a major strike but nevertheless inferred from the TGS release that "recent mineral exploratory activity near Timmins, Ontario, has provided preliminary favorable results, sufficient at least to require a step-up in drilling operations." Some witnesses who testified at the hearing stated that they found the release encouraging. On the other hand, a Canadian mining security specialist, Roche, stated that "earlier in the week [before April 16] we had a Dow Jones saying that they [TGS] didn't have anything basically" and a TGS stock specialist for the Midwest Stock Exchange became concerned about his long position in the stock after reading the release. The trial court stated only that "While, in retrospect, the press release may appear gloomy or incomplete, this does not make it misleading or deceptive on the basis of the facts then known."

Meanwhile, drilling operations continued. By morning of April 13, in K-55-5, the fifth drill hole, substantial copper mineralization had been encountered to the 580 foot mark, and the hole was subsequently drilled to a length of 757 feet without further results. Visual estimates revealed an average content of 0.82% copper and 4.2% zinc over a 525-foot section. Also by 7:00 A. M. on April 13, K-55-6 had found mineralization to the 946-foot mark. On April 12 a fourth drill rig began to drill K-55-7, which was drilled westerly at a 45' angle, at the eastern edge of the anomaly. The next morning the 137 foot mark had been reached, fifty feet of which showed mineralization. By 7:00 P. M. on April 15, the hole had been completed to a length of 707 feet but had only encountered additional mineralization during a 26-foot length between the 425 and 451-foot marks. A mill test hole, K-55-8, had been drilled and was complete by the evening of April 13 but its mineralization had not been reported upon prior to April 16. K-55-10 was drilled westerly at a 45' angle commencing April 14 and had encountered mineralization over 231 of its 249-foot length by the evening of April 15. It, too, was drilled at the anomaly's eastern edge.

While drilling activity ensued to completion, TGS officials were taking steps toward ultimate disclosure of the discovery. On April 13, a previously-invited reporter for The Northern Miner, a Canadian mining industry journal, visited the drillsite, interviewed Mollison, Holyk and Darke, and prepared an article which confirmed a 10 million ton ore strike. This report, after having been submitted to Mollison and returned to the reporter unamended on April 15, was published in the April 16 issue. A statement relative to the extent of the discovery, in substantial part drafted by Mollison, was given to the Ontario Minister of Mines for release to the Canadian media. Mollison and Holyk expected it to be released over the airways at 11 P. M. on April 15th, but, for undisclosed reasons, it was not released until 9:40 A. M. on the 16th. An official detailed statement, announcing a strike of at least 25 million tons of ore, based on the drilling data set forth above, was read to representatives of American financial media from 10:00 A. M. to 10:10 or 10:15 A. M. on April 16, and appeared over Merrill Lynch's private wire at 10:29 A. M. and, somewhat later than expected, over the Dow Jones ticker tape at 10:54 A. M.

Between the time the first press release was issued on April 12 and the dissemination of the TGS official announcement on the morning of April 16, the only defendants before us on appeal who engaged in market activity were Clayton and Crawford and TGS director Coates. Clayton ordered 200 shares of TGS stock through his Canadian broker on April 15 and the order was executed that day over the Midwest Stock Exchange. Crawford ordered 300 shares at midnight on the 15th and another 300 shares at 8:30 A. M. the next day, and these orders were executed over the Midwest Exchange in Chicago at its opening on April 16. Coates left the TGS press conference and called his broker son-in-law Haemisegger shortly before 10:20 A. M. on the 16th and ordered 2,000 shares of TGS for family trust accounts of which Coates was a trustee but not a beneficiary; Haemisegger executed this order over the New York and Midwest Exchanges, and he and his customers purchased 1500 additional shares.

During the period of drilling in Timmins, the market price of TGS stock fluctuated but steadily gained overall. On Friday, November 8, when the drilling began, the stock closed at 173/8; on Friday, November 15, after K-55-1 had been completed, it closed at 18. After a slight decline to 163/8 by Friday, November 22, the price rose to 207/8 by December 13, when the chemical assay results of K-55-1 were received, and closed at a high of 241/8 on February 21, the day after the stock options had been issued. It had reached a price of 26 by March 31, after the land acquisition program had been completed and drilling had been resumed, and continued to ascend to 301/8 by the close of trading on April 10, at which time the drilling progress up to then was evaluated for the April 12th press release. On April 13, the day on which the April 12 release was disseminated, TGS opened at 301/8, rose immediately to a high of 32 and gradually tapered off to close at 307/8. It closed at 30¼ the next day, and at 293/8 on April 15. On April 16, the day of the official announcement of the Timmins discovery, the price climbed to a high of 37 and closed at 363/8. By May 15, TGS stock was selling at 58¼.

I. *The Individual Defendants*

A. *Introductory*

....

... The essence of [Rule 10b-5] is that anyone who, trading for his own account in the securities of a corporation has "access, directly or indirectly, to information intended to be available only for a corporate purpose and not for the personal benefit of anyone" may not take "advantage of such information knowing it is unavailable to those with whom he is dealing," *i.e.*, the investing public. *Matter of Cady, Roberts & Co.*, 40 SEC 907, 912 (1961). Insiders, as directors or management officers are, of course, by this Rule, precluded from so unfairly dealing, but the Rule is also applicable to one possessing the information who may not be strictly termed an "insider" within the meaning of Sec. 16(b) of the Act. *Cady, Roberts, supra.* Thus, anyone in possession of material inside information must either disclose it to the investing public, or, if he is disabled from disclosing it in order to protect a corporate confidence, or he chooses not to do so, must abstain from trading in or recommending the securities concerned while such inside information remains undisclosed. So, it is here no justification for insider activity that disclosure was forbidden by the legitimate corporate objective of acquiring options to purchase the land surrounding the exploration site; if the information was, as the SEC contends, material, its possessors should have kept out of the market until disclosure was accomplished. *Cady, Roberts, supra* at 911.

B. *Material Inside Information*

An insider is not, of course, always foreclosed from investing in his own company merely because he may be more familiar with company operations than are outside investors. An insider's duty to disclose information or his duty to abstain from dealing in his company's securities arises only in "those situations which are essentially extraordinary in nature and which are reasonably certain to have a substantial effect on the market price of the security if [the extraordinary situation is] disclosed." Fleischer, Securities Trading and Corporate Information Practices: The Implications of the Texas Gulf Sulphur Proceeding, 51 Va. L. Rev. 1271, 1289.

Nor is an insider obligated to confer upon outside investors the benefit of his superior financial or other expert analysis by disclosing his educated guesses or predictions. The only regulatory objective is that access to material information be enjoyed equally, but this objective requires nothing more than the disclosure of basic facts so that outsiders may draw upon their own evaluative expertise in reaching their own investment decisions with knowledge equal to that of the insiders.

This is not to suggest, however, as did the trial court, that "the test of materiality must necessarily be a conservative one, particularly since many actions under Section 10(b) are brought on the basis of hindsight," in the sense that the materiality of facts is to be assessed solely by measuring the effect the knowledge of the facts would have upon prudent or conservative investors. As we stated in *List v. Fashion Park, Inc.,* 340 F.2d 457, 462, "The basic test of materiality ... is whether a *reasonable* man would attach importance ... in determining his choice of action in the transaction in question." ... Thus, material facts include not only information disclosing the earnings and distributions of a company but also those facts which affect the probable future of the company and those which may affect the desire of investors to buy, sell, or hold the company's securities.

In each case, then, whether facts are material within Rule 10b-5 when the facts relate to a particular event and are undisclosed by those persons who are knowledgeable thereof will depend at any given time upon a balancing of both the indicated probability that the event will occur and the anticipated magnitude of the event in light of the totality of the company activity. Here, notwithstanding the trial court's conclusion that the results of the first drill core, K-55-1, were "too 'remote' ... to have had any significant impact on the market, *i.e.,* to be deemed material," knowledge of the possibility, which surely was more than marginal, of the existence of a mine of the vast magnitude indicated by the remarkably rich drill core located rather close to the surface (suggesting mineability by the less expensive open-pit method) within the confines of a large anomaly (suggesting an extensive region of mineralization) might well have affected the price of TGS stock and would certainly have been an important fact to a reasonable, if speculative, investor in deciding whether he should buy, sell, or hold. After all, this first drill core was "unusually good and ... excited the interest and speculation of those who knew about it."

... Our survey of the facts found below conclusively establishes that knowledge of the results of the discovery hole, K-55-1, would have been important to a reasonable investor and might have affected the price of the stock.[2] On April 16, The Northern Miner, a trade publication in wide circulation among mining stock specialists, called K-55-1, the discovery hole, "one of the most impressive drill holes completed in modern times." Roche, a Canadian broker whose firm specialized in mining securities, characterized the importance to investors of the results of K-55-1. He stated that the completion of "the first drill hole" with "a 600 foot drill core is very very significant ... anything over 200 feet is considered very significant and 600 feet is just beyond your wildest imagination.".…

Finally, a major factor in determining whether the K-55-1 discovery was a material fact is the importance attached to the drilling results by those who knew about it. In view of other unrelated recent developments favorably affecting TGS, participation by an informed person in a regular stock-purchase program, or even sporadic trading by an informed person, might lend only nominal support to the inference of the materiality of the K-55-1 discovery; nevertheless, the timing by those who knew of it of their stock purchases and their purchases of *short-term* calls — purchases in some cases by individuals who had never before purchased calls or even TGS stock — virtually compels the inference that the insiders were influenced by the drilling results. This insider trading activity, which surely constitutes highly pertinent evidence and the only truly objective evidence of the materiality of the K-55-1 discovery, was apparently disregarded by the court below in favor of the testimony of defendants' expert witnesses, all of whom "agreed that one drill core does not establish an ore body, much less a mine." Significantly, however, the court below, while relying upon what these defense experts said the defendant insiders *ought* to have thought about the worth to TGS of the K-55-1 discovery, and finding that from November 12, 1963 to April 6, 1964 Fogarty, Murray, Holyk and Darke spent more than $ 100,000 in purchasing TGS stock and calls on that stock, made no finding that the insiders were motivated by any factor other than the extraordinary K-55-1 discovery when they bought their stock and their calls. No reason appears why outside investors,

---

[2] We do not suggest that material facts must be disclosed immediately; the timing of disclosure is a matter for the business judgment of the corporate officers entrusted with the management of the corporation within the affirmative disclosure requirements promulgated by the exchanges and by the SEC. Here, a valuable corporate purpose was served by delaying the publication of the K-55-1 discovery. We do intend to convey, however, that where a corporate purpose is thus served by withholding the news of a material fact, those persons who are thus quite properly true to their corporate trust must not during the period of non-disclosure deal personally in the corporation's securities or give to outsiders confidential information not generally available to all the corporations' stockholders and to the public at large.

perhaps better acquainted with speculative modes of investment and with, in many cases, perhaps more capital at their disposal for intelligent speculation, would have been less influenced, and would not have been similarly motivated to invest if they had known what the insider investors knew about the K-55-1 discovery.

....

The core of Rule 10b-5 is the implementation of the Congressional purpose that all investors should have equal access to the rewards of participation in securities transactions. It was the intent of Congress that all members of the investing public should be subject to identical market risks, — which market risks include, of course the risk that one's evaluative capacity or one's capital available to put at risk may exceed another's capacity or capital. The insiders here were not trading on an equal footing with the outside investors. They alone were in a position to evaluate the probability and magnitude of what seemed from the outset to be a major ore strike; they alone could invest safely, secure in the expectation that the price of TGS stock would rise substantially in the event such a major strike should materialize, but would decline little, if at all, in the event of failure, for the public, ignorant at the outset of the favorable probabilities would likewise be unaware of the unproductive exploration, and the additional exploration costs would not significantly affect TGS market prices. Such inequities based upon unequal access to knowledge should not be shrugged off as inevitable in our way of life, or, in view of the congressional concern in the area, remain uncorrected.

We hold, therefore, that all transactions in TGS stock or calls by individuals apprised of the drilling results of K-55-1 were made in violation of Rule 10b-5. Inasmuch as the visual evaluation of that drill core (a generally reliable estimate though less accurate than a chemical assay) constituted material information, those advised of the results of the visual evaluation as well as those informed of the chemical assay traded in violation of law. The geologist Darke possessed undisclosed material information and traded in TGS securities. Therefore we reverse the dismissal of the action as to him and his personal transactions....

....

C. *When May Insiders Act?*

Appellant Crawford, who ordered the purchase of TGS stock shortly before the TGS April 16 official announcement, and defendant Coates, who placed orders with and communicated the news to his broker immediately after the official announcement was read at the TGS-called press conference, concede that they were in possession of material information. They contend, however, that their purchases were not proscribed purchases for the news had already been effectively disclosed. We disagree.

Crawford telephoned his orders to his Chicago broker about midnight on April 15 and again at 8:30 in the morning of the 16th, with instructions to buy at the opening of the Midwest Stock Exchange that morning. The trial court's finding that "he sought to, and did, 'beat the news,'" is well documented by the record....

... The reading of a news release, which prompted Coates into action, is merely the first step in the process of dissemination required for compliance with the regulatory objective of providing all investors with an equal opportunity to make informed investment judgments. Assuming that the contents of the official release could instantaneously be acted upon, at the minimum Coates should have waited until the news could reasonably have been expected to appear over the media of widest circulation, the Dow Jones broad tape, rather than hastening to insure an advantage to himself and his broker son-in-law.

....

E. *May Insiders Accept Stock Options Without Disclosing Material Information to the Issuer?*

On February 20, 1964, defendants Stephens, Fogarty, Mollison, Holyk and Kline accepted stock options issued to them and a number of other top officers of TGS, although not one of them had informed the Stock Option Committee of the Board of Directors or the Board of the results of K-55-1, which information we have held was then material. The SEC sought rescission of these options. The trial court, in addition to finding the knowledge of the results of the K-55 discovery to be immaterial, held that Kline had no detailed knowledge of the drilling progress and that Holyk and Mollison could reasonably assume that their superiors, Stephens and Fogarty, who were directors of the corporation, would report the results if that was advisable; indeed all employees had been instructed not to divulge this information pending completion of the land acquisition program. Therefore, the court below concluded that only directors Stephens and Fogarty, of the top management, would have violated the Rule by accepting stock options without disclosure, but it also found that they had not acted improperly as the information in their possession was not material. In view of our conclusion as to materiality we hold that Stephens and Fogarty violated the Rule by accepting them. However, as they have surrendered the options and the corporation has canceled them, we find it unnecessary to order that the injunctions prayed for be actually issued. We point out, nevertheless, that the surrender of these options after the SEC commenced the case is not a satisfaction of the SEC claim, and a determination as to whether the issuance of injunctions against Stephens and Fogarty is advisable in order to prevent or deter future violations of regulatory provisions is remanded for the exercise of discretion by the trial court.

Contrary to the belief of the trial court that Kline had no duty to disclose his knowledge of the Kidd project before accepting the stock option offered him, we believe that he, a vice president, who had become the general counsel of TGS in January 1964, but who had been secretary of the corporation since January 1961, and was present in that capacity when the options were granted, and who was in charge of the mechanics of issuance and acceptance of the options, was a member of top management and under a duty before accepting his option to disclose any material information he may have possessed, and, as he did not disclose such information to the Option Committee we direct rescission of the option he received. As to Holyk and Mollison, the SEC has not appealed the holding below that they, not being then members of top management (although Mollison was a vice president) had no duty to disclose their knowledge of the drilling before accepting their options. Therefore, the issue of whether, by accepting, they violated the Act, is not before us, and the holding below is undisturbed.

II. *The Corporate Defendant*

[A.] *Introductory*

At 3:00 P.M. on April 12, 1964, evidently believing it desirable to comment upon the rumors concerning the Timmins project, TGS issued the press release quoted in pertinent part [above]. The SEC argued below and maintains on this appeal that this release painted a misleading and deceptive picture of the drilling progress at the time of its issuance, and hence violated Rule 10b-5(2). TGS relies on the holding of the court below that "The issuance of the release produced no unusual market action" and "In the absence of a showing that the purpose of the April 12 press release was to affect the market price of TGS stock to the advantage of TGS or its insiders, the issuance of the press release did not constitute a violation of Section 10(b) or Rule 10b-5 since it was not issued 'in connection with the purchase or sale of any security'" and, alternatively, "even if it had been established that the April 12 release was issued in connection with the purchase or sale of any security, the Commission has failed to demonstrate that it was false, misleading or deceptive."

Before further discussing this matter it seems desirable to state exactly what the SEC claimed in its complaint and what it seeks. The specific SEC allegation in its complaint is that this April 12 press release "... was materially false and misleading and was known by certain of defendant Texas Gulf's officers and employees, including defendants Fogarty, Mollison, Holyk, Darke and Clayton, to be materially false and misleading."

The specific relief the SEC seeks is, pursuant to Section 21(e) of Securities Exchange Act of 1934, a permanent injunction restraining the issuance of any further materially false and misleading publicly distributed informative items.

B. *The "In Connection With ..." Requirement*

In adjudicating upon the relationship of this phrase to the case before us it would appear that the court below used a standard that does not reflect the congressional purpose that prompted the passage of the Securities Exchange Act of 1934.

....

[I]t seems clear from the legislative purpose Congress expressed in the Act, and the legislative history of Section 10(b) that Congress when it used the phrase "in connection with the purchase or sale of any security" intended only that the device employed, whatever it might be, be of a sort that would cause reasonable investors to rely thereon, and, in connection therewith, so relying, cause them to purchase or sell a corporation's securities. There is no indication that Congress intended that the corporations or persons responsible for the issuance of a misleading statement would not violate the section unless they engaged in related securities transactions ....

....

C. Did the Issuance of the April 12 Release Violate Rule 10b-5?

Turning first to the question of whether the release was misleading, *i.e.,* whether it conveyed to the public a false impression of the drilling situation at the time of its issuance, we note initially that the trial court did not actually decide this question. Its conclusion that "the Commission has failed to demonstrate that it was false, misleading or deceptive," seems to have derived from its views that "The defendants are to be judged *on the facts known to them* when the April 12 release was issued" (emphasis supplied), that the draftsmen "exercised reasonable business judgment under the circumstances," and that the release was not "misleading or deceptive *on the basis of the facts then known,*" (emphasis supplied) rather than from an appropriate primary inquiry into the meaning of the statement to the reasonable investor and its relationship to truth....

....

We hold only that, in an action for injunctive relief, the district court has the discretionary power under Rule 10b-5 and Section 10(b) to issue an injunction, if the misleading statement resulted from a lack of due diligence on the part of TGS. The trial court did not find it necessary to decide whether TGS exercised such diligence and has not yet attempted to resolve this issue. While the trial court concluded that TGS had exercised "reasonable *business* judgment under the circumstances," (emphasis supplied) it applied an incorrect *legal* standard in appraising whether TGS should have issued its April 12 release on the basis of the facts known to its draftsmen at the time of its preparation, and in assuming that disclosure of the full underlying facts of the Timmins situation was not a viable alternative to the vague generalities which were asserted.

....

The choice of an ambiguous general statement rather than a summary of the specific facts cannot reasonably be justified by any claimed urgency. The avoidance of liability for misrepresentation in the event that the Timmins project failed, a highly unlikely event as of April 12 or April 13, did not forbid the accurate and truthful divulgence of detailed results which need not, of course, have been accompanied by conclusory assertions of success. Nor is it any justification that such an explicit disclosure of the truth might have "encouraged the rumor mill which they were seeking to allay."

We conclude, then, that, having established that the release was issued in a manner reasonably calculated to affect the market price of TGS stock and to influence the investing public, we must remand to the district court to decide whether the release was misleading to the reasonable investor and if found to be misleading, whether the court in its discretion should issue the injunction the SEC seeks.

....

A. CAUSATION AND RELIANCE; MATERIALITY

SHAPIRO v. MERRILL LYNCH, PIERCE, FENNER & SMITH, INC.

United States Court of Appeals, Second Circuit
495 F.2d 228 (1974)

TIMBERS, CIRCUIT JUDGE:

This appeal presents important questions, some of first impression, involving the scope of the antifraud provisions of the federal securities laws in their application to transactions on a national securities exchange when material inside information has not been disclosed.

Specifically, the questions presented are (1) whether Section 10(b) of the Securities Exchange Act of 1934 and Rule 10b-5 were violated by a prospective managing underwriter of a debenture issue and the underwriter's officers, directors and employees when they divulged material inside information to the underwriter's customers for the purpose of protecting the latters' investments in the stock of the issuer; (2) whether the same antifraud provisions of the securities laws were violated by the underwriter's customers when they traded in the stock of the issuer without disclosing the material inside information which had been divulged to them by the underwriter; and (3) whether those referred to above, if they did violate the antifraud provisions of the securities laws, are liable in damages to those persons who during the same period purchased stock in the same company in the open market without knowledge of the material inside information. In short, this case involves the liability of non-trading "tippers" and trading "tippees" under Section 10(b) and Rule 10b-5.

Defendants appeal ... from an order entered in the Southern District of New York, Charles H. Tenney, District Judge, denying their motion for judgment on the pleadings on the ground that the complaint failed to state a claim upon which relief can be granted.

The action was brought to recover damages claimed to have been sustained as the result of defendants' trading or recommending trading of common stock of Douglas Aircraft Company, Inc. (Douglas) on the New York Stock Exchange (NYSE) in 1966. Such acts or transactions are alleged to have violated [Section] 10(b) ... of the Securities Exchange Act of 1934 [and Rule 10b-5 thereunder].

Applying to the admitted facts before us what we believe to be controlling principles of law as enunciated by the Supreme Court and by our Court, we affirm.

I

In summarizing here the facts necessary to a determination of the legal issues raised on this appeal, we must take as admitted the well-pleaded material facts alleged in the complaint, as the district court did, since the order under review denied defendants' motion for judgment on the pleadings ....

The course of events which culminated in the instant action occurred during the period April 1966 through July 1966. During this period, Merrill Lynch, Pierce, Fenner & Smith Inc. (Merrill Lynch) was engaged as the prospective managing underwriter of a proposed Douglas offering of $ 75,000,000 principal amount of a new issue of 4¾ % convertible subordinated debentures. A registration statement for this offering was filed with the SEC on June 7; it became effective on July 12, with Merrill Lynch the managing underwriter. On June 7, Douglas had released an earnings statement which reported the results of operations for the first five months of its 1966 fiscal year, *i.e.*, through April 30, 1966. This statement indicated that Douglas had earned 85 cents per share on its common stock during that period.

During the period June 17 through June 22, Merrill Lynch and certain of its officers, directors and employees (the individual defendants) were advised by Douglas' management of certain material adverse inside information regarding Douglas' earnings. This information was essentially that (a) Douglas would report substantially lower earnings for the entire first six months than it had reported for the first five months of its 1966 fiscal year; (b) Douglas had sharply lowered its estimate of earnings for its full 1966 fiscal year in that it now expected to have little or no profit for that year; and (c) Douglas had substantially reduced its projection of earnings for its 1967 fiscal year. This information was given to Merrill Lynch solely because of its position as the prospective underwriter for the Douglas debenture issue. The individual defendants and Merrill Lynch knew or should have known that the information had not yet been publicly announced.

During the period June 20 through June 24, Merrill Lynch and the individual defendants disclosed this confidential information to [a number of] Merrill Lynch customers (the selling defendants), most of whom were institutional investors ....

During the period June 20 through June 23, the selling defendants either sold from existing positions or made short sales of more than 165,000 shares of Douglas common on the NYSE. This was approximately one-half of the total number of Douglas shares sold on the NYSE during this period. These sales were made prior to Douglas' public disclosure of the revised earnings information on June 24 and without the sellers having disclosed this information to the investing public, including plaintiffs. As a result of these sales, the individual defendants and Merrill Lynch received commissions from the execution of the selling defendants' orders and also received compensation in the form of customer directed "give-ups" — *i.e.* division of commissions earned by other brokers who executed orders for the selling defendants.

On June 23, plaintiff Gibson purchased an unspecified number of shares of Douglas common on the NYSE; his purchase was prior to the public release on June 24 of Douglas' revised earnings report. The other four plaintiffs — Maurice Shapiro, Isadore Shapiro, Naigles and Saxe — purchased an unspecified number of shares of Douglas common on the NYSE on June 24; their purchases were made without knowledge of the material adverse earnings information released by Douglas that day.

Beginning about June 22 or 23, the market price of Douglas common on the NYSE took a sudden and substantial drop. This coincided with and, according to the complaint, was caused by the substantial sales by the selling defendants on the basis of material inside information, the disclosure of which after plaintiffs' purchases precipitated a further severe drop in the market price of Douglas common.

On August 21, 1970, plaintiffs commenced the instant action in the Southern District of New York. They sued on behalf of themselves and all others similarly situated who purchased Douglas common during the period June 21 through June 24, 1966. Essentially the complaint alleges that defendants were under a duty to disclose to the general investing public, including plaintiffs, the material inside information regarding Douglas' earnings; that defendants defrauded plaintiffs by not disclosing such information, in violation of the antifraud provisions of the securities laws; that plaintiffs would not have purchased Douglas stock if they had known of the information withheld by defendants; and that plaintiffs sustained substantial damages as a result of the acts of defendants. Plaintiffs do not claim to have purchased specific shares of Douglas stock sold by any of the selling defendants. The complaint demands damages sustained by plaintiffs and an accounting of profits realized by defendants.

....

II

Upon the basis of the foregoing summary of the facts and prior proceedings, we turn directly to the legal questions presented. They are essentially whether defendants violated Section 10(b) and Rule 10b-5 and, if so, whether they are liable in damages to plaintiffs for such violations. The district court held as a matter of pleading that both questions must be answered in the affirmative. We agree.

....

As we have stated time and again, the purpose behind Section 10(b) and Rule 10b-5 is to protect the investing public and to secure fair dealing in the securities markets by promoting full disclosure of inside information so that an informed judgment can be made by all investors who trade in such markets. We recently held in *Radiation Dynamics, Inc. v. Goldmuntz*, 464 F.2d 876, 890 (2d Cir. 1972), that "[t]he essential purpose of Rule 10b-5 ... is to prevent corporate insiders and their tippees from taking unfair advantage of the uninformed outsiders."

Moreover, in applying the antifraud provisions of the securities laws to the facts of this case, it is important to bear in mind that "Congress intended securities legislation enacted for the purpose of avoiding frauds to be construed 'not technically and restrictively, but flexibly to effectuate its remedial purposes.'" *Affiliated Ute Citizens v. United States,* 406 U.S. 128, 151 (1972), *quoting from SEC v. Capital Gains Research Bureau, Inc.,* 375 U.S. 180, 195 (1963)....

Here, upon the question of whether Section 10(b) and Rule 10b-5 were violated, the critical facts — admitted for purposes of this appeal — are that Merrill Lynch, a prospective managing underwriter of a Douglas debenture issue, and some of the officers, directors and employees of Merrill Lynch, divulged to certain of its customers, the selling defendants, material adverse inside information regarding Douglas' earnings; the selling defendants, without disclosing to the investing public this inside information, sold Douglas common stock on a national securities exchange; and as a result of such trading Merrill Lynch and the individual defendants received commissions and other compensation, the selling defendants minimized their losses, but the investing public comprised of uninformed outsiders, including plaintiffs, who purchased Douglas stock during the same period sustained substantial losses.

Our holding that such conduct on the part of all defendants violated Section 10(b) and Rule 10b-5 is based chiefly on our decision in *SEC v. Texas Gulf Sulphur Co.,* [401 F.2d 833], where we stated that

> anyone in possession of material inside information must either disclose it to the investing public, or, if he is disabled from disclosing it ..., must abstain from trading in or recommending the securities concerned while such inside information remains undisclosed. 401 F.2d at 848.

....

... We hold that defendants owed a duty — for the breach of which they may be held liable in this private action for damages not only to the purchasers of the actual shares sold by defendants (in the unlikely event they can be identified) but to all persons who during the same period purchased Douglas stock in the open market without knowledge of the material inside information which was in the possession of defendants.

We find untenable the contentions of the respective defendants that, upon the issue of whether they violated the antifraud provisions of the securities laws, a distinction should be drawn between their roles as non-trading "tippers" and trading "tippees."

With respect to Merrill Lynch and the individual defendants (the non-trading "tippers"), their divulging of confidential material inside information to their customers who sold Douglas stock on the basis of such information clearly violated Section 10(b) and Rule 10b-5....

With respect to the selling defendants (the trading "tippees"), *Texas Gulf* strongly suggests that the same duty to "abstain or disclose" should be imposed upon them. Although the issue of "tippee" liability was not squarely before us in *Texas Gulf*, we did say:

> As Darke's 'tippees' are not defendants in this action, we need not decide whether, if they acted with actual or constructive knowledge that the material information was undisclosed, their conduct is as equally violative of the Rule as the conduct of their insider source, though we note that it certainly could be equally reprehensible. 401 F.2d at 852-53.

In *Ross v. Licht*, 263 F. Supp. 395, 410 (S.D.N.Y. 1967), the court observed, "If [defendants] were not insiders, they would seem to have been 'tippees' ... and subject to the same duty as insiders." We are not persuaded by the selling defendants' argument that as tippees they were not able to make effective public disclosure of information about a company with which they were not associated; for the duty imposed is not a naked one to disclose, but a duty to abstain from trading unless they do disclose. Since upon the admitted facts before us the selling defendants knew or should have known of the confidential corporate source of the revised earnings information and they knew of its non-public nature, they were under a duty not to trade in Douglas stock without publicly disclosing such information.

In short, for the reasons set forth above, we hold that all defendants violated Section 10(b) and Rule 10b-5.

III

We turn next to the remaining major legal question presented: assuming that defendants did violate the antifraud provisions of the securities laws by trading in or recommending trading in Douglas common stock (as we have held above), whether they are liable in a private action for damages to plaintiffs who during the same period purchased Douglas stock in the open market without knowledge of the material inside information which was in the possession of defendants.

The essential argument of defendants on this question is that, even if they did violate Section 10(b) and Rule 10b-5, their conduct did not "cause" damage to plaintiffs; that it was Douglas' precarious financial condition, not defendants' securities law violations, which precipitated the sudden, substantial drop in the market price of Douglas stock and hence the losses sustained by plaintiffs; that, since plaintiffs had no prior or contemporaneous knowledge of defendants' actions, they would have purchased Douglas stock regardless of defendants' securities law violations; and that, since defendants' sales were unrelated to plaintiffs' purchases and all transactions took place on anonymous public stock exchanges, there is lacking the requisite connection between defendants' alleged violations and the alleged losses sustained by plaintiffs.

The short, and we believe conclusive, answer to defendants' assertion that their conduct did not "cause" damage to plaintiffs is the "causation in fact" holding by the Supreme Court in *Affiliated Ute Citizens v. United States*, 406 U.S. 128, 153-54 (1972), upon the authority of which we conclude that the requisite element of causation in fact has been established here by the uncontroverted facts that defendants traded in or recommended trading in Douglas stock without disclosing material inside information which plaintiffs as reasonable investors might have considered important in making their decision to purchase Douglas stock.

....

We consistently have held that causation is a necessary element of a private action for damages under Rule 10b-5. Indeed, we have refused "to facilitate outsiders' proof of insiders' fraud" by "reading out of [Rule 10b-5] so basic an element of tort law as the principle of causation in fact." *List v. Fashion Park, Inc.*, 340 F.2d 457, 463 (2d Cir.), *cert. denied*, 382 U.S. 811 (1965). This is consistent with "the basic concept that causation must be proved else defendants could be held liable to all the world." *Globus v. Law Research Service, Inc.*, 418 F.2d 1276, 1292 (2d Cir. 1969), *cert. denied*, 397 U.S. 913 (1970). And we have recognized that the aim of Rule 10b-5 "is to qualify, as between insiders and outsiders, the doctrine of *caveat emptor* — not to establish a scheme of investors' insurance." *List v. Fashion Park, Inc., supra*, 340 F.2d at 463.

As one branch of their absence of causation argument, defendants contend that there was no privity between themselves and plaintiffs. We hold here, as we have held before, that privity between plaintiffs and defendants is not a requisite element of a Rule 10b-5 cause of action for damages. For example, we have upheld Rule 10b-5 claims for relief where there have been no direct transactions between plaintiffs and defendants. As the Tenth Circuit stated in *Mitchell v. Texas Gulf Sulphur Co.*, 446 F.2d 90, 101 (10th Cir.), *cert. denied*, 404 U.S. 1004 (1971), "[p]erhaps the first step is to realize that the common law requirement of privity has all but vanished from 10b-5 proceedings while the distinguishable 'connection' element is retained." And we recognized in *Globus v. Law Research Service, Inc., supra*, 418 F.2d at 1291, that "[b]efore there may be a violation of the securities acts there need not be present all of the same elements essential to a common law fraud...." In short, causation as an element of a rule 10b-5 cause of action can be established notwithstanding lack of privity.

As a further refinement of their absence of causation argument, defendants contend that, even if privity between plaintiffs and defendants is not required, it is still necessary to show a "connection" between defendants' nondisclosure conduct and plaintiffs' purchase of Douglas stock — in the sense that the former induced the latter — before a Rule 10b-5 claim can be established. It is true that prior to the Supreme Court decision in *Affiliated Ute* the so-called connection requirement was stated in terms of causation and reliance.... While the concepts of reliance and causation have been used interchangeably in the context of a Rule 10b-5 claim, the proper test to determine whether causation in fact has been established in a non-disclosure case is "whether the plaintiff would have been influenced to act differently than he did act if the defendant had disclosed to him the undisclosed fact." *List v. Fashion Park, Inc., supra*, 340 F.2d at 463.

....

[W]e believe that the Supreme Court's decision in *Affiliated Ute* — which we regard as controlling on the issue of causation in the instant case — is a logical sequel to our prior decisions.... Moreover, *Affiliated Ute* specifically applied to a Rule 10b-5 damage action the causation in fact standard enunciated by Mr. Justice Harlan in *Mills v. Electric Auto-Lite Co.*, 396 U.S. 375, 385 (1970), where, in a case involving a cognate provision of the 1934 Act (Section 14(a)), the Court approved dispensing with any requirement of proof of reliance as a prerequisite to recovery in a private damage action....

In *Affiliated Ute*, members of a large class of holders of stock deposited in a bank alleged that two employees of the bank in arranging for sales of this stock had failed to disclose to plaintiffs facts regarding the bank's and the employees' positions as market makers and facts regarding the true value of the stock, in violation of Rule 10b-5. The Supreme Court, in reversing the Court of Appeals which had held that there could be no recovery under Section 10(b) and Rule 10b-5 without a showing of reliance, stated:

> Under the circumstances of this case, involving primarily a failure to disclose, positive proof of reliance is not a prerequisite to recovery. *All that is necessary is that the facts withheld be material in the sense that a reasonable investor might have considered them important in the making of this decision....* This obligation to disclose and this withholding of a material fact establish the requisite element of causation in fact. 406 U.S. at 153-54. (citations omitted) (emphasis added).

As applied to the instant case, this holding in *Affiliated Ute* surely warrants our conclusion that the requisite element of causation in fact has been established by the admitted withholding by defendants of material inside information which they were under an obligation to disclose, such information being clearly material in the sense that plaintiffs as reasonable investors might have considered it important in making their decision to purchase Douglas stock.

Defendants argue that the *Affiliated Ute* rule of causation in fact should be confined to the facts of that case which involved face-to-face transactions. We disagree. That rule is dependent not upon the character of the transaction — face-to-face versus national securities exchange — but rather upon whether the defendant is obligated to disclose the inside information. Here, as we have held above, defendants were under a duty to the investing public, including plaintiffs, not to trade in or to recommend trading in Douglas stock without publicly disclosing the revised earnings information which was in their possession. They breached that duty. Causation in fact therefore has been established.

[T]he underlying purpose of Section 10(b) and Rule 10b-5 [is] "to prevent inequitable and unfair practices and to insure fairness in securities transactions generally, whether conducted face-to-face, over the counter, or on the exchanges.... The Act and the Rule apply to the transactions here, all of which were consummated on exchanges." *SEC v. Texas Gulf Sulphur Co.*, 401 F.2d 833,

847-48 (2d Cir. 1968), *cert. denied sub nom. Kline v. SEC,* 394 U.S. 976 (1969) (citations omitted).

For the reasons set forth above, we hold that defendants are liable in this private action for damages to plaintiffs who, during the same period that defendants traded in or recommended trading in Douglas common stock, purchased Douglas stock in the open market without knowledge of the material inside information which was in the possession of defendants.

IV

Finally, having held that all defendants violated Section 10(b) and Rule 10b-5 and that they are liable to plaintiffs in this private action for damages, we leave to the district court the appropriate form of relief to be granted, including the proper measure of damages....

... Among the questions to be determined which will have an important bearing on the form of relief is whether the action is to be maintained as a class action and, if so, the parameters of the class.... Another closely related question bearing upon the relief to be granted as to which the district court had insufficient data upon which to make a determination is just when Douglas' news release regarding its revised earnings forecast on the morning of June 24, 1966 became effectively disseminated, especially in the light of *SEC v. Texas Gulf Sulphur Co.,* 401 F.2d 833, 854 n.18 (2d Cir. 1968). Other questions bearing upon the appropriate form of relief which must await trial include the extent of the selling defendants' trading in Douglas stock, whether such trading effectively impaired the integrity of the market, what compensation if any was paid by the selling defendants to Merrill Lynch for the inside information, what profits or other benefits were realized by defendants, what expenses were incurred and what losses were sustained by plaintiffs, and what should be the difference, if any, in the extent of liability imposed on the individual defendants and the selling defendants, respectively. Moreover, we do not foreclose the possibility that an analysis by the district court of the nature and character of the Rule 10b-5 violations committed may require limiting the extent of liability imposed on either class of defendants.

....

In short, we decide today only those legal questions properly before us on this appeal from the interlocutory order denying defendants' motion for judgment on the pleadings. We leave all other issues to the district court, including the fashioning of appropriate relief.

Affirmed.

FRIDRICH v. BRADFORD

United States Court of Appeals, Sixth Circuit
542 F.2d 307 (1976)

ENGEL, CIRCUIT JUDGE.

On April 27, 1972 J. C. Bradford, Jr. purchased 1,225 shares of common stock of Old Line Life Insurance Company (Old Line). The shares were purchased on inside information Bradford, Jr. had received on a tip from his father. The shares were purchased on the over-the-counter market from J. C. Bradford and Co., a Nashville brokerage firm of which Bradford, Jr. and his father are managing partners. Subsequent to the purchase, Old Line stock increased in value and on July 27, 1972, Bradford, Jr. sold the 1,225 shares, reaping a profit of $ 13,000 on the transaction.

The Securities and Exchange Commission investigated Bradford, Jr.'s stock transaction. As a result of a consent decree entered into between the Commission and Bradford, Jr., he was required to disgorge the entire $ 13,000 profit, was permanently enjoined from any further violation of § 10(b) of the Securities Exchange Act of 1934 and Rule 10b-5, and was suspended from performing any business activities as a broker-dealer for twenty working days.

Thereafter plaintiffs filed this civil action, alleging that Bradford, Jr.'s trading activities violated Rule 10b-5. By the judgment of the district court appealed from here, Bradford, Jr. has been rendered jointly and severally liable to plaintiffs for the sum of $ 361,186.75. He has been held liable, although plaintiffs never sold their stock to him or his associates, nor did they sell on the same day or even in the same month in which he bought. There was no proof that Bradford, Jr.'s trading activities had any impact upon the market price of Old Line stock or upon plaintiff's decision to trade in it. As we read the district court judgment, Bradford, Jr.'s liability would have been the same even though he had purchased only five shares of Old Line and made a profit of less than $ 53.00.

While Bradford, Jr. is only one of five defendants in this appeal, we have focused on his liability at the outset in order to illustrate the "Draconian liability" to which persons who trade on inside information may be subjected under the district court's interpretation of Rule 10b-5. Because we conclude that under the circumstances of this case imposition of civil liability constitutes an unwarranted extension of the judicially created private cause of action under Rule 10b-5, we reverse the judgment of the district court.

....

IV

Few early cases brought under § 10(b) and Rule 10b-5 dealt with non-disclosure by insiders trading in the open market. Development of the law in this area is largely traceable to the "abstain or disclose rule" developed in *SEC v. Texas Gulf Sulphur Co.,* 401 F.2d 833 (2d Cir. 1968).... [This case] involved an SEC enforcement action against the company and several corporate investors. That particular case did not involve an attempt to impose civil liability for damages upon insiders who trade in the open market without disclosure of inside information.

An early effort to impose civil liability in the context of non-disclosure of inside information is found in *Joseph v. Farnsworth Radio and Television Corp.,* 99 F. Supp. 701 (S.D.N.Y. 1951) *aff'd* 198 F.2d 883 (2d Cir. 1952), where District Judge Sugarman framed the issue thus:

> The issue is narrowed to merely this: May A, who purchased stock of the F Corporation on November 12th and B, who likewise purchased stock of the same corporation on December 13th, each on a national stock exchange and each at a price higher than he would have paid therefore had he known the true financial condition of F, recover from C, D and E, the director and officers of the corporation, the difference between that paid and that which would have been paid had C, D and E disclosed, between the previous March 19 and October 30th when they were unloading their own stock in F, that F was in a straitened financial condition?

In granting a defense motion to dismiss for failure to state a claim upon which relief could be granted, Judge Sugarman observed:

> Nothing in the history of the Act or the Rule permits the far-reaching effect sought herein by the plaintiffs. A semblance of privity between the vendor and purchaser of the security in connection with which the improper act, practice or course of business was invoked seems to be requisite and it is entirely lacking here.

A similar result was reached, but for different reasons, in *Reynolds v. Texas Gulf Sulphur Co.,* 309 F. Supp. 548 (D. Utah 1970), *aff'd as modified,* 446 F.2d 90 (10th Cir. 1971), a private 10b-5 action arising out of the same transactions challenged by the SEC in *SEC v. Texas Gulf Sulphur Co., supra.* There one of the plaintiffs, Lawrence A. Karlson, sought damages for profits he claimed to have lost when he sold his TGS stock on December 11, 1963. It was established, in particular, that the defendant Fogarty, a vice-president of TGS, had purchased TGS stock prior to and after Karlson had sold his shares without publicly disclosing the inside information he possessed. Both Karlson and Fogarty had traded through a national stock exchange. The district judge noted that there was no face-to-face transaction and that Fogarty did not purchase the particular shares sold by Karlson. In denying recovery to Karlson, the district judge noted that while it was not necessary that he establish privity of contract in order to recover, it was nevertheless necessary for Karlson to prove "some causative effect":

> In the case brought against Texas Gulf Sulphur Company, Fogarty and other TGS officials and employees, by the Securities and Exchange Commission, the Circuit Court found that Fogarty had violated Section 10(b) and Rule 10b-5 by purchasing TGS stock without publicly disclosing the

insider information he possessed. It does not follow that such purchases by Fogarty, some of which were made prior to the time Karlson sold his stock, caused any damage to Karlson, and the record before us does not support any such contention.

A different result has been indicated in *Shapiro v. Merrill Lynch, Pierce, Fenner and Smith, Inc.*, 353 F. Supp. 264 (S.D.N.Y. 1973) *aff'd*, 495 F.2d 228 (2d Cir. 1974)....

....

In *Shapiro*, plaintiffs did not allege that they had actually traded with the defendants. Neither does it appear from the opinion that defendants' act of trading had any influence upon their own decision to purchase. In their motion to dismiss, defendants contended that their violation of Rule 10b-5, even if proved, did not cause any damage to plaintiffs and that since plaintiffs would have bought the stock in any event, no injury to plaintiffs was occasioned. Judge Tenney rejected this analysis:

> But therein lies the fallacy of defendants' reasoning: it is not the act of trading which causes plaintiffs' injury, *it is the act of trading without disclosing material insider information which causes plaintiff's injury*. Had Merrill Lynch and the individual defendants refrained from divulging the earnings information to the selling defendants, or had the selling defendants decided not to trade, there would have been no liability for plaintiffs' injury due to the eventual public disclosure of Douglas' poor financial position. But defendants did not choose to follow that course of action, and by trading in Douglas stock on a national securities exchange they assumed the duty to disclose the information to all potential buyers. It is the breach of this duty which gives rise to defendants' liability.

The Second Circuit, in affirming the district court judgment, agreed with Judge Tenney's analysis and further concluded that any argument defendants might make that their conduct did not cause plaintiffs' damage was precluded by the Supreme Court holding in *Affiliated Ute Citizens v. United States*, 406 U.S. 128 (1972):

> The short, and we believe conclusive, answer to defendants' assertion that their conduct did not "cause" damage to plaintiffs is the "causation in fact" holding by the Supreme Court in *Affiliated Ute Citizens v. United States*, 406 U.S. 128, 153-54 (1972), upon the authority of which we conclude that the requisite element of causation in fact has been established here by the uncontroverted facts that defendants traded in or recommended trading in Douglas stock without disclosing material inside information which plaintiffs as reasonable investors might have considered important in making their decision to purchase Douglas stock.

While neither court endeavored to rule upon the measure of any damages which might ultimately be allowed, the Second Circuit observed:

> Moreover, we do not foreclose the possibility that an analysis by the district court of the nature and character of the Rule 10b-5 violations committed may require limiting the extent of liability imposed on either class of defendants.

Thus it appears that both the district court and the Second Circuit in their respective opinions in *Shapiro, supra,* were ready and willing to extend the 10b-5 private right of action to accord relief to those who traded upon an impersonal market where the defendants were charged with violation of the "abstain or disclose" rule in *SEC v. Texas Gulf Sulphur, supra.*

As the foregoing cases illustrate, extension of the private civil remedy under Rule 10b-5 where shares have been traded upon an impersonal market has eluded uniform analysis by judicial writers. The courts and legal writers seem to agree that the plaintiff must establish a causal connection between the defendant's misconduct and his loss, but what exactly plaintiff must show to establish this causal element is unclear.

V

We conclude that upon the facts of this case defendants' conduct caused no injury to plaintiffs and the judgment of the district court must be reversed. It is undisputed that defendants did not purchase any shares of stock from plaintiffs, and that defendants' acts of trading in no way affected plaintiffs' decision to sell.

We are unable to agree with the observation of the district judge in *Shapiro* that "... it is the act of trading without disclosing material inside information which causes plaintiffs' injury.... Having breached that obligation [to abstain or disclose], the defendants are liable for plaintiffs' injuries." The flaw in this logic, we conclude, is that it assumes the very injury which it then declares compensable. It does so by presupposing that the duty to disclose is absolute, and that the plaintiff is injured when the information is denied him. The duty to disclose, however, is not an absolute one, but an alternative one, that of either disclosing or abstaining from trading. We conceive it to be the act of trading which essentially constitutes the violation of Rule 10b-5, for it is this which brings the illicit benefit to the insider, and it is this conduct which impairs the integrity of the market and which is the target of the rule. If the insider does not trade, he has an absolute right to keep material information secret. Investors must be prepared to accept the risk of trading in an open market without complete or always accurate information. Defendants' trading did not alter plaintiffs' expectations when they sold their stock, and in no way influenced plaintiffs' trading decision.

We hold, therefore, the defendants' act of trading with third persons was not causally connected with any claimed loss by plaintiffs who traded on the impersonal market and who were otherwise unaffected by the wrongful acts of the insider.

Likewise, we are not persuaded, as was the Second Circuit in its decision in *Shapiro, supra,* that *Affiliated Ute Citizens v. United States, supra,* mandates a "short, and ... conclusive answer" to the contrary.

In *Affiliated Ute,* certain members of the Ute Indian tribe brought suit against a bank and two of its employees under Rule 10b-5. The basis of the complaint was that the bank, which held certain shares of stock owned by plaintiffs, had arranged sales of the stock without disclosing to the plaintiffs certain material information, including the fact that defendants were making a market in the stock, purchasing some of it for their own account, and that the stock was sold for a substantially higher price to nonmembers of the tribe. The district judge entered judgment for plaintiffs. The Court of Appeals reversed, holding there could be no recovery under § 10(b) and Rule 10b-5 without proof that the plaintiffs had relied upon some misrepresentation by defendants. In reversing the Court of Appeals, the Supreme Court held:

> Under the circumstances of this case, involving primarily a failure to disclose, positive proof of reliance is not a prerequisite to recovery. All that is necessary is that the facts withheld be material in the sense that a reasonable investor might have considered them important in the making of this decision. This obligation to disclose and this withholding of a material fact establish the requisite element of causation in fact. *Chasins v. Smith, Barney & Co.,* 438 F.2d [1167] at 1172 (CA2).

It is this language which the Second Circuit, in *Shapiro,* felt to be controlling upon it. We are unable to construe the language quoted so broadly. It was shown in *Affiliated Ute* that the defendant bank employees had engaged in prior business dealings with the plaintiff Indians. They entered into a deliberate scheme to induce the plaintiffs to sell their stock without disclosure of material facts which would have influenced the decision to sell. The resulting sales were a direct result of the scheme. Thus it comes as no surprise that the Supreme Court concluded that "[U]nder the circumstances of this case," all that was necessary was that the information withheld be material in order to establish the requisite causation.

That the quoted language was not intended to produce such a far-reaching result we think is indicated by Justice Blackmun's reference therein to *Chasins v. Smith, Barney & Co.,* 438 F.2d 1167 (2d Cir. 1970). *Chasins,* like *Affilated Ute,* involved direct dealings between Chasins, an investor, and Smith, Barney & Co. as his broker-dealer. It was charged that Smith, Barney & Co., in handling Chasins' accounts, had violated Rule 10b-5 by failing to disclose when it strongly recommended certain stocks to Chasins that it was also a market maker in those same stocks. The question immediately before the court was whether, as part of his proofs, Chasins must show that in making his purchases he in fact relied upon the recommendation made. Under the facts of the case, the court concluded that positive proof of reliance was not required:

To the extent that reliance is necessary for a finding of a 10b-5 violation in a non-disclosure case such as this, the test is properly one of tort "causation in fact." *Crane Co. v. Westinghouse Air Brake Co.*, 419 F.2d 787 (2d Cir. 1969). Chasins relied upon Smith, Barney's recommendations of purchase made without the disclosure of a material fact, purchased the securities recommended, and suffered a loss in their resale. Causation in fact or adequate reliance was sufficiently shown by Chasins.

Here, unlike *Affiliated Ute,* defendants did not perpetrate any scheme to induce defendants to sell their stock. Plaintiffs and defendants here had no relationship whatever during the period in question. The plaintiffs in *Affiliated Ute* had a right to expect that the defendant bank officials would fully disclose all material information concerning the stock while inducing them to sell. When defendants did not make full disclosure, they breached Rule 10b-5 and became liable for plaintiffs' foreseeable damages. The type of relationship existing between plaintiffs and defendants in *Affiliated Ute* is totally absent here.

VI

Neither do we believe that sound policy considerations support the result reached by the district court. Logic, at first blush, tends to support extension of the civil remedy to persons trading in an impersonal market in the context presented here. Congress certainly never intended § 10(b) to be limited in its scope solely to face-to-face transactions. Indeed since the Securities Exchange Act of 1934 is aimed at nationwide practices, H.R. No. 1383, 73rd Cong., 2nd Sess. 11 (1934), it would be idle to exclude from its operation those over-the-counter and national stock exchange transactions which are most characteristic of the national market.

The key issue, as we see it, is not whether the proscriptions of § 10(b) and Rule 10b-5 should encompass open market transactions, which they should, but whether the civil remedy must invariably be coextensive in its reach with the reach of the SEC, which under the Act, was designated by the Congress as the primary vehicle of its enforcement. We reject such a view where its application leads us inexorably to an unjust and unworkable result.[3] By so extending the liability of defendants here beyond that which has already been imposed through the SEC enforcement action, we believe we would be doing violence to the intent of the statute and rule, creating a windfall for those fortuitous enough to be aware

---

[3] We specifically do not reach the question of availability of the remedy to open market situations where the insider trading with resultant price changes has in fact induced the plaintiffs to buy or sell to their injury. Here there was no proof that defendants' insider trading had any impact whatever upon the value of Old Line stock.

of their nebulous legal rights, and imposing what essentially must be considered punitive damages almost unlimited in their potential scope.[4]

Where private civil actions under Rule 10b-5 have been employed in essentially face-to-face situations, the potential breadth of the action was usually contained. However, extension of the private remedy to impersonal market cases where plaintiffs have neither dealt with defendants nor been influenced in their trading decisions by any act of the defendants would present a situation wholly lacking in the natural limitations on damages present in cases dealing with face-to-face transactions. We think the potential liability of Bradford, Jr. in this case, noted earlier, is sufficiently illustrative of the dangers posed.[5]

....

While we hold to the view that the private action should be compensatory, it is to be observed that in any event the 1934 Act provides a number of non-compensatory sanctions to deter insider misconduct, including SEC investigations and criminal sanctions. Further, the SEC may ask the federal district court, in the exercise of its equity jurisdiction under § 27 of the 1984 Act, to require an insider to disgorge any profits he may have made from his illegal trading, *SEC v. Texas Gulf Sulphur Co.*, 446 F.2d 1301 (2d Cir. 1971), or even an amount in excess of the amount of illicit profits which the insider has made. *SEC v. Shapiro*, 494 F.2d 1301, 1309 (2d Cir. 1974). Finally, state law may provide various sanctions against insider trading.

Whether the sanctions imposed upon the defendants here together with others which were also available amount to a sufficient vindication of the public rights and to an adequate deterrent to future misconduct we need not say. We may at least observe that the impact is bound to be significant.

Finally, it has been suggested that the problem of unlimited damages can be avoided by allowing recovery to all plaintiffs who traded during the period of non-disclosure, but limiting recovery to the amount of defendants' profits from insider trading....

---

[4] We express concern similar to that noted by Judge Friendly in his concurring opinion in *SEC v. Texas Gulf Sulphur, supra,* that broad extension of the civil remedy under rule 10b-5 in open market cases "will lead to large judgments, payable in the last analysis by innocent investors, for the benefit of speculators and their lawyers...." 401 F.2d 833, 867.

[5] Plaintiffs sold Old Line stock in the over-the-counter market in various lots on June 13, 14 and 15, 1972. Based upon the market data received in evidence at the trial, if all of the persons who had sold their shares of Old Line stock on those days alone had joined in the instant lawsuit, Bradford Jr.'s potential liability in damages would have totalled approximately $ 800,000. If a class action had been brought which included all investors who sold Old Line stock between April 21 and June 29, 1972, the damages could have totalled approximately $ 3,700,000. If the class had been further expanded to those selling up to November 20, 1972 (and the holding appealed from admits of no limitation short thereof), the damages would have run in excess of $ 7,000,000.00. As noted earlier, Bradford, Jr.'s profit from his illegal purchases, already disgorged in an SEC proceeding, amounted to about $ 13,000.

As compared to Congress or administrative agencies such as the SEC, we think the courts are ill-fitted to the task of rulemaking which would be required. As we see no connection between defendants' violation of Rule 10b-5 and plaintiffs' alleged losses, we decline to base our decision upon a rule of limitation of damages here.

....

BASIC, INC. v. LEVINSON

United States Supreme Court
485 U.S. 224 (1988)

JUSTICE BLACKMUN delivered the opinion of the Court.

This case requires us to apply the materiality requirement of § 10(b) of the Securities Exchange Act of 1934 and the Securities and Exchange Commission's Rule 10b-5, promulgated thereunder, in the context of preliminary corporate merger discussions. We must also determine whether a person who traded a corporation's shares on a securities exchange after the issuance of a materially misleading statement by the corporation may invoke a rebuttable presumption that, in trading, he relied on the integrity of the price set by the market.

I

Prior to December 20, 1978, Basic Incorporated was a publicly traded company primarily engaged in the business of manufacturing chemical refractories for the steel industry....

Beginning in September 1976, Combustion [Engineering, Inc.] representatives had meetings and telephone conversations with Basic officers and directors, including petitioners here, concerning the possibility of a merger. During 1977 and 1978, Basic made three public statements denying that it was engaged in merger negotiations.[6] On December 18, 1978, Basic asked the New York Stock

---

[6] On October 21, 1977, after heavy trading and a new high in Basic stock, the following news item appeared in the Cleveland Plain Dealer:

[Basic] President Max Muller said the company knew no reason for the stock's activity and that no negotiations were under way with any company for a merger. He said Flintkote recently denied Wall Street rumors that it would make a tender offer of $ 25 a share for control of the Cleveland-based maker of refractories for the steel industry.

On September 25, 1978, in reply to an inquiry from the New York Stock Exchange, Basic issued a release concerning increased activity in its stock and stated that

management is unaware of any present or pending company development that would result in the abnormally heavy trading activity and price fluctuation in company shares that have been experienced in the past few days.

On November 6, 1978, Basic issued to its shareholders a "Nine Months Report 1978." This Report stated:

With regard to the stock market activity in the Company's shares we remain unaware of any present or pending developments which would account for the high volume of trading and price fluctuations in recent months.

Exchange to suspend trading in its shares and issued a release stating that it had been "approached" by another company concerning a merger. On December 19, Basic's board endorsed Combustion's offer of $ 46 per share for its common stock and on the following day publicly announced its approval of Combustion's tender offer for all outstanding shares.

Respondents are former Basic shareholders who sold their stock after Basic's first public statement of October 21, 1977, and before the suspension of trading in December 1978. Respondents brought a class action against Basic and its directors, asserting that the defendants issued three false or misleading public statements and thereby were in violation of § 10(b) of the 1934 Act and of Rule 10b-5. Respondents alleged that they were injured by selling Basic shares at artificially depressed prices in a market affected by petitioners' misleading statements and in reliance thereon.

... On the merits, ... the District Court granted summary judgment for the defendants....

The United States Court of Appeals for the Sixth Circuit ... reversed the District Court's summary judgment, and remanded the case....

....

II

....

... The Court ... explicitly has defined a standard of materiality under the securities laws, *see TSC Industries, Inc. v. Northway, Inc.*, 426 U.S. 438 (1976), concluding in the proxy-solicitation context that "[a]n omitted fact is material if there is a substantial likelihood that a reasonable shareholder would consider it important in deciding how to vote." Acknowledging that certain information concerning corporate developments could well be of "dubious significance," the Court was careful not to set too low a standard of materiality; it was concerned that a minimal standard might bring an overabundance of information within its reach, and lead management "simply to bury the shareholders in an avalanche of trivial information — a result that is hardly conducive to informed decisionmaking." It further explained that to fulfill the materiality requirement "there must be a substantial likelihood that the disclosure of the omitted fact would have been viewed by the reasonable investor as having significantly altered the 'total mix' of information made available." We now expressly adopt the *TSC Industries* standard of materiality for the § 10(b) and Rule 10b-5 context.

III

The application of this materiality standard to preliminary merger discussions is not self-evident. Where the impact of the corporate development on the target's fortune is certain and clear, the *TSC Industries* materiality definition admits straightforward application. Where, on the other hand, the event is contingent or speculative in nature, it is difficult to ascertain whether the "reasonable investor" would have considered the omitted information significant at the time. Merger negotiations, because of the ever-present possibility that the contemplated transaction will not be effectuated, fall into the latter category.

A

Petitioners urge upon us a Third Circuit test for resolving this difficulty. Under this approach, preliminary merger discussions do not become material until "agreement-in-principle" as to the price and structure of the transaction has been reached between the would-be merger partners. By definition, then, information concerning any negotiations not yet at the agreement-in-principle stage could be withheld or even misrepresented without a violation of Rule 10b-5.

Three rationales have been offered in support of the "agreement-in-principle" test. The first derives from the concern expressed in *TSC Industries* that an investor not be overwhelmed by excessively detailed and trivial information, and focuses on the substantial risk that preliminary merger discussions may collapse: because such discussions are inherently tentative, disclosure of their existence itself could mislead investors and foster false optimism. The other two justifications for the agreement-in-principle standard are based on management concerns: because the requirement of "agreement-in-principle" limits the scope of disclosure obligations, it helps preserve the confidentiality of merger discussions where earlier disclosure might prejudice the negotiations; and the test also provides a usable, bright-line rule for determining when disclosure must be made.

None of these policy-based rationales, however, purports to explain why drawing the line at agreement-in-principle reflects the significance of the information upon the investor's decision. The first rationale, and the only one connected to the concerns expressed in *TSC Industries,* stands soundly rejected, even by a Court of Appeals that otherwise has accepted the wisdom of the agreement-in-principle test. "It assumes that investors are nitwits, unable to appreciate — even when told — that mergers are risky propositions up until the closing." *Flamm v. Eberstadt,* 814 F.2d [1169, 1175 (CA7 1987)]. Disclosure, and not paternalistic withholding of accurate information, is the policy chosen and expressed by Congress. We have recognized time and again, a "fundamental purpose" of the various securities acts, "was to substitute a philosophy of full disclosure for the philosophy of *caveat emptor* and thus to achieve a high standard of business ethics in the securities industry." *SEC v. Capital Gains Research Bureau, Inc.,* 375 U.S. 180, 186 (1963). The role of the materiality requirement is not to "attribute to investors a child-like simplicity, an inability to grasp the probabilistic significance of negotiations," *Flamm v. Eberstadt,* 814 F.2d, at 1175, but to filter out essentially useless information that a reasonable investor would not consider significant, even as part of a larger "mix" of factors to consider in making his investment decision. *TSC Industries, Inc. v. Northway, Inc.,* 426 U.S., at 448-449.

The second rationale, the importance of secrecy during the early stages of merger discussions, also seems irrelevant to an assessment whether their existence is significant to the trading decision of a reasonable investor. To avoid a "bidding war" over its target, an acquiring firm often will insist that negotiations remain confidential, and at least one Court of Appeals has stated that "silence pending settlement of the price and structure of a deal is beneficial to most investors, most of the time." *Flamm v. Eberstadt,* 814 F.2d, at 1177.

We need not ascertain, however, whether secrecy necessarily maximizes shareholder wealth — although we note that the proposition is at least disputed as a matter of theory and empirical research — for this case does not concern the *timing* of a disclosure; it concerns only its accuracy and completeness. We face here the narrow question whether information concerning the existence and status of preliminary merger discussions is significant to the reasonable investor's trading decision. Arguments based on the premise that some disclosure would be "premature" in a sense are more properly considered under the rubric of an issuer's duty to disclose. The "secrecy" rationale is simply inapposite to the definition of materiality.

The final justification offered in support of the agreement-in-principle test seems to be directed solely at the comfort of corporate managers. A bright-line rule indeed is easier to follow than a standard that requires the exercise of judgment in the light of all the circumstances. But ease of application alone is not an excuse for ignoring the purposes of the securities acts and Congress' policy decisions. Any approach that designates a single fact or occurrence as always determinative of an inherently fact-specific finding such as materiality, must necessarily be over- or underinclusive. In *TSC Industries* this Court explained: "The determination [of materiality] requires delicate assessments of the inferences a 'reasonable shareholder' would draw from a given set of facts and the significance of those inferences to him...." After much study, the Advisory Committee on Corporate Disclosure cautioned the SEC against administratively confining materiality to a rigid formula. Courts also would do well to heed this advice.

We therefore find no valid justification for artificially excluding from the definition of materiality information concerning merger discussions, which would otherwise be considered significant to the trading decision of a reasonable investor, merely because agreement-in-principle as to price and structure has not yet been reached by the parties or their representatives.

B

The Sixth Circuit explicitly rejected the agreement-in-principle test, as we do today, but in its place adopted a rule that, if taken literally, would be equally insensitive, in our view, to the distinction between materiality and the other elements of an action under Rule 10b-5:

> When a company whose stock is publicly traded makes a statement, as Basic did, that 'no negotiations' are underway, and that the corporation knows of 'no reason for the stock's activity,' and that 'management is unaware of any present or pending corporate development that would result in the abnormally heavy trading activity,' information concerning ongoing acquisition

discussions becomes material *by virtue of the statement denying their existence*....

....

... In analyzing whether information regarding merger discussions is material such that it must be affirmatively disclosed to avoid a violation of Rule 10b-5, the discussions and their progress are the primary consider- ations. However, once a statement is made denying the existence of any discussions, even discussions that might not have been material in absence of the denial are material because they make the statement made untrue. (emphasis in original.)

This approach, however, fails to recognize that, in order to prevail on a Rule 10b-5 claim, a plaintiff must show that the statements were *misleading* as to a *material* fact. It is not enough that a statement is false or incomplete, if the misrepresented fact is otherwise insignificant.

C

Even before this Court's decision in *TSC Industries,* the Second Circuit had explained the role of the materiality requirement of Rule 10b-5, with respect to contingent or speculative information or events, in a manner that gave that term meaning that is independent of the other provisions of the Rule. Under such circumstances, materiality "will depend at any given time upon a balancing of both the indicated probability that the event will occur and the anticipated magnitude of the event in light of the totality of the company activity." *SEC v. Texas Gulf Sulphur Co.,* 401 F.2d [833, 849 (CA2 1968)]. Interestingly, neither the Third Circuit decision adopting the agreement-in-principle test nor petitioners here take issue with this general standard. Rather, they suggest that with respect to preliminary merger discussions, there are good reasons to draw a line at agreement on price and structure.

In a subsequent decision, the late Judge Friendly, writing for a Second Circuit panel, applied the *Texas Gulf Sulphur* probability/magnitude approach in the specific context of preliminary merger negotiations. After acknowledging that materiality is something to be determined on the basis of the particular facts of each case, he stated:

Since a merger in which it is bought out is the most important event that can occur in a small corporation's life, to wit, its death, we think that inside information, as regards a merger of this sort, can become material at an earlier stage than would be the case as regards lesser transactions — and this even though the mortality rate of mergers in such formative stages is doubtless high.

SEC v. Geon Industries, Inc., 531 F.2d 39, 47-48 (CA2 1976). We agree with that analysis.

Whether merger discussions in any particular case are material therefore depends on the facts. Generally, in order to assess the probability that the event will occur, a factfinder will need to look to indicia of interest in the transaction at the highest corporate levels. Without attempting to catalog all such possible factors, we note by way of example that board resolutions, instructions to investment bankers, and actual negotiations between principals or their intermediaries may serve as indicia of interest. To assess the magnitude of the transaction to the issuer of the securities allegedly manipulated, a factfinder will need to consider such facts as the size of the two corporate entities and of the potential premiums over market value. No particular event or factor short of closing the transaction need be either necessary or sufficient by itself to render merger discussions material.[7]

As we clarify today, materiality depends on the significance the reasonable investor would place on the withheld or misrepresented information. The fact-specific inquiry we endorse here is consistent with the approach a number of courts have taken in assessing the materiality of merger negotiations. Because the standard of materiality we have adopted differs from that used by both courts below, we remand the case for reconsideration of the question whether a grant of summary judgment is appropriate on this record.

IV

A

We turn to the question of reliance and the fraud-on-the-market theory. Succinctly put:

> The fraud on the market theory is based on the hypothesis that, in an open and developed securities market, the price of a company's stock is

---

[7]To be actionable, of course, a statement must also be misleading. Silence, absent a duty to disclose, is not misleading under Rule 10b-5. "No comment" statements are generally the functional equivalent of silence. *See In re Carnation Co.* [Exchange Act Release No. 22214, 33 SEC Docket 1025 (1985)]. *See also* New York Stock Exchange Listed Company Manual § 202.01, reprinted in 3 CCH Fed. Sec. L. Rep. ¶23,515 (premature public announcement may properly be delayed for valid business purpose and where adequate security can be maintained); American Stock Exchange Company Guide §§ 401-405, reprinted in 3 CCH Fed. Sec. L. Rep. ¶¶23,124A-23,124E (similar provisions).

It has been suggested that given current market practices, a "no comment" statement is tantamount to an admission that merger discussions are underway. *See Flamm v. Eberstadt*, 814 F.2d, at 1178. That may well hold true to the extent that issuers adopt a policy of truthfully denying merger rumors when no discussions are underway, and of issuing "no comment" statements when they are in the midst of negotiations. There are, of course, other statement policies firms could adopt; we need not now advise issuers as to what kind of practice to follow, within the range permitted by law. Perhaps more importantly, we think that creating an exception to a regulatory scheme founded on a prodisclosure legislative philosophy, because complying with the regulation might be "bad for business," is a role for Congress, not this Court. *See also id.*, at 1182 (opinion concurring in the judgment and concurring in part).

determined by the available material information regarding the company and its business.... Misleading statements will therefore defraud purchasers of stock even if the purchasers do not directly rely on the misstatements.... The causal connection between the defendants' fraud and the plaintiffs' purchase of stock in such a case is no less significant than in a case of direct reliance on misrepresentations. *Peil v. Speiser,* 806 F.2d 1154, 1160-1161 (CA3 1986).

Our task, of course, is not to assess the general validity of the theory, but to consider whether it was proper for the courts below to apply a rebuttable presumption of reliance, supported in part by the fraud-on-the-market theory.

... In their amended complaint, the named plaintiffs alleged that in reliance on Basic's statements they sold their shares of Basic stock in the depressed market created by petitioners. Requiring proof of individualized reliance from each member of the proposed plaintiff class effectively would have prevented respondents from proceeding with a class action, since individual issues then would have overwhelmed the common ones. The District Court found that the presumption of reliance created by the fraud-on-the-market theory provided "a practical resolution to the problem of balancing the substantive requirement of proof of reliance in securities cases against the procedural requisites of [Fed. Rule Civ. Proc.] 23." The District Court thus concluded that with reference to each public statement and its impact upon the open market for Basic shares, common questions predominated over individual questions, as required by Fed. Rule Civ. Proc. 23(a)(2) and (b)(3).

Petitioners and their *amici* complain that the fraud-on-the-market theory effectively eliminates the requirement that a plaintiff asserting a claim under Rule 10b-5 prove reliance. They note that reliance is and long has been an element of common-law fraud and argue that because the analogous express right of action includes a reliance requirement, so too must an action implied under § 10(b).

We agree that reliance is an element of a Rule 10b-5 cause of action. Reliance provides the requisite causal connection between a defendant's misrepresentation and a plaintiff's injury. There is, however, more than one way to demonstrate the causal connection. Indeed, we previously have dispensed with a requirement of positive proof of reliance, where a duty to disclose material information had been breached, concluding that the necessary nexus between the plaintiffs' injury and the defendant's wrongful conduct had been established. *See Affiliated Ute Citizens v. United States,* 406 U.S. [128, 153-154 (1972)]. Similarly, we did not require proof that material omissions or misstatements in a proxy statement decisively affected voting, because the proxy solicitation itself, rather than the defect in the solicitation materials, served as an essential link in the transaction. *See Mills v. Electric Auto-Lite Co.,* 396 U.S. 375, 384-385 (1970).

The modern securities markets, literally involving millions of shares changing hands daily, differ from the face-to-face transactions contemplated by early fraud cases, and our understanding of Rule 10b-5's reliance requirement must encompass these differences.

> In face-to-face transactions, the inquiry into an investor's reliance upon information is into the subjective pricing of that information by that investor. With the presence of a market, the market is interposed between seller and buyer and, ideally, transmits information to the investor in the processed form of a market price. Thus the market is performing a substantial part of the valuation process performed by the investor in a face-to-face transaction. The market is acting as the unpaid agent of the investor, informing him that given all the information available to it, the value of the stock is worth the market price. *In re LTV Securities Litigation,* 88 F.R.D. 134, 143 (N.D. Tex. 1980).

B

Presumptions typically serve to assist courts in managing circumstances in which direct proof, for one reason or another, is rendered difficult. The courts below accepted a presumption, created by the fraud-on-the-market theory and subject to rebuttal by petitioners, that persons who had traded Basic shares had done so in reliance on the integrity of the price set by the market, but because of petitioners' material misrepresentations that price had been fraudulently depressed. Requiring a plaintiff to show a speculative state of facts, *i.e.,* how he would have acted if omitted material information had been disclosed, or if the misrepresentation had not been made, would place an unnecessarily unrealistic evidentiary burden on the Rule 10b-5 plaintiff who has traded on an impersonal market.

Arising out of considerations of fairness, public policy, and probability, as well as judicial economy, presumptions are also useful devices for allocating the burdens of proof between parties. The presumption of reliance employed in this case is consistent with, and, by facilitating Rule 10b-5 litigation, supports, the congressional policy embodied in the 1934 Act. In drafting that Act, Congress expressly relied on the premise that securities markets are affected by information, and enacted legislation to facilitate an investor's reliance on the integrity of those markets:

> No investor, no speculator, can safely buy and sell securities upon the exchanges without having an intelligent basis for forming his judgment as to the value of the securities he buys or sells. The idea of a free and open public market is built upon the theory that competing judgments of buyers and sellers as to the fair price of a security brings [*sic*] about a situation where the market price reflects as nearly as possible a just price. Just as artificial manipulation tends to upset the true function of an open market, so the hiding and secreting of important information obstructs the operation of the markets as indices of real value. H.R. Rep. No. 1383, [73d Cong., 2d Sess., 11 (1934)].

The presumption is also supported by common sense and probability. Recent empirical studies have tended to confirm Congress' premise that the market price of shares traded on well-developed markets reflects all publicly available information, and, hence, any material misrepresentations.[8] It has been noted that "it is hard to imagine that there ever is a buyer or seller who does not rely on market integrity. Who would knowingly roll the dice in a crooked crap game?" *Schlanger v. Four-Phase Systems Inc.,* 555 F. Supp. 535, 538 (S.D.N.Y. 1982). Indeed, nearly every court that has considered the proposition has concluded that where materially misleading statements have been disseminated into an impersonal, well-developed market for securities, the reliance of individual plaintiffs on the integrity of the market price may be presumed. Commentators generally have applauded the adoption of one variation or another of the fraud-on-the-market theory. An investor who buys or sells stock at the price set by the market does so in reliance on the integrity of that price. Because most publicly available information is reflected in market price, an investor's reliance on any public material misrepresentations, therefore, may be presumed for purposes of a Rule 10b-5 action.

C

The Court of Appeals found that petitioners "made public, material misrepresentations and [respondents] sold Basic stock in an impersonal, efficient market. Thus the class, as defined by the district court, has established the threshold facts for proving their loss." The court acknowledged that petitioners may rebut proof of the elements giving rise to the presumption, or show that the misrepresentation in fact did not lead to a distortion of price or that an individual plaintiff traded or would have traded despite his knowing the statement was false.

Any showing that severs the link between the alleged misrepresentation and either the price received (or paid) by the plaintiff, or his decision to trade at a fair market price, will be sufficient to rebut the presumption of reliance. For example, if petitioners could show that the "market makers" were privy to the truth about the merger discussions here with Combustion, and thus that the market price would not have been affected by their misrepresentations, the causal connection could be broken: the basis for finding that the fraud had been transmitted through market price would be gone. Similarly, if, despite petitioners'

---

[8] *See In re LTV Securities Litigation,* 88 F.R.D. 134, 144 (ND Tex. 1980) (*citing* studies); Fischel, *Use of Modern Finance Theory in Securities Fraud Cases Involving Actively Traded Securities,* 38 BUS. LAW. 1, 4, n.9 (1982) (*citing* literature on efficient-capital-market theory); Dennis, *Materiality and the Efficient Capital Market Model: A Recipe for the Total Mix,* 25 WM. & MARY L. REV. 373, 374-381, and n.1 (1984). We need not determine by adjudication what economists and social scientists have debated through the use of sophisticated statistical analysis and the application of economic theory. For purposes of accepting the presumption of reliance in this case, we need only believe that market professionals generally consider most publicly announced material statements about companies, thereby affecting stock market prices.

allegedly fraudulent attempt to manipulate market price, news of the merger discussions credibly entered the market and dissipated the effects of the misstatements, those who traded Basic shares after the corrective statements would have no direct or indirect connection with the fraud. Petitioners also could rebut the presumption of reliance as to plaintiffs who would have divested themselves of their Basic shares without relying on the integrity of the market. For example, a plaintiff who believed that Basic's statements were false and that Basic was indeed engaged in merger discussions, and who consequently believed that Basic stock was artificially underpriced, but sold his shares nevertheless because of other unrelated concerns, *e.g.,* potential antitrust problems, or political pressures to divest from shares of certain businesses, could not be said to have relied on the integrity of a price he knew had been manipulated.

....

B. "IN CONNECTION WITH" REQUIREMENT

SUPERINTENDENT OF INSURANCE OF NEW YORK v. BANKERS LIFE & CASUALTY CO.

United States Supreme Court
404 U.S. 6 (1971)

MR. JUSTICE DOUGLAS delivered the opinion of the Court.

Manhattan Casualty Co., now represented by petitioner, New York's Superintendent of Insurance, was, it is alleged, defrauded in the sale of certain securities in violation of § 17(a) of the Securities Act of 1933 and of § 10(b) of the Securities Exchange Act of 1934. The District Court dismissed the complaint, and the Court of Appeals affirmed, by a divided bench. The case is here on a petition for a writ of certiorari which we granted.

It seems that Bankers Life & Casualty Co., one of the respondents, agreed to sell all of Manhattan's stock to one Begole for $ 5,000,000. It is alleged that Begole conspired with one Bourne and others to pay for this stock, not out of their own funds, but with Manhattan's assets. They were alleged to have arranged, through Garvin, Bantel & Co. — a note brokerage firm — to obtain a $ 5,000,000 check from respondent Irving Trust Co., although they had no funds on deposit there at the time. On the same day they purchased all the stock of Manhattan from Bankers Life for $ 5,000,000 and as stockholders and directors, installed one Sweeny as president of Manhattan.

Manhattan then sold its United States Treasury bonds for $ 4,854,552.67.[9] That amount, plus enough cash to bring the total to $ 5,000,000, was credited to an account of Manhattan at Irving Trust and the $ 5,000,000 Irving Trust check was

---

[9] Manhattan's Board of Directors was allegedly deceived into authorizing this sale by the misrepresentation that the proceeds would be exchanged for a certificate of deposit of equal value.

charged against it. As a result, Begole owned all the stock of Manhattan, having used $ 5,000,000 of Manhattan's assets to purchase it.

To complete the fraudulent scheme, Irving Trust issued a second $ 5,000,000 check to Manhattan which Sweeny, Manhattan's new president, tendered to Belgian-American Bank & Trust Co. which issued a $ 5,000,000 certificate of deposit in the name of Manhattan. Sweeny endorsed the certificate of deposit over to New England Note Corp., a company alleged to be controlled by Bourne. Bourne endorsed the certificate over to Belgian-American Banking Corp.[10] as collateral for a $ 5,000,000 loan from Belgian-American Banking to New England. Its proceeds were paid to Irving Trust to cover the latter's second $ 5,000,000 check.

Though Manhattan's assets had been depleted, its books reflected only the sale of its Government bonds and the purchase of the certificate of deposit and did not show that its assets had been used by Begole to pay for his purchase of Manhattan's shares or that the certificate of deposit had been assigned to New England and then pledged to Belgian-American Banking.

Manhattan was the seller of Treasury bonds and, it seems to us, clearly protected by § 10(b) of the Securities Exchange Act, which makes it unlawful to use "in connection with the purchase or sale" of any security "any manipulative or deceptive device or contrivance" in contravention of the rules and regulations of the Securities and Exchange Commission.

There certainly was an "act" or "practice" within the meaning of Rule 10b-5 which operated as "a fraud or deceit" on Manhattan, the seller of the Government bonds. To be sure, the full market price was paid for those bonds; but the seller was duped into believing that it, the seller, would receive the proceeds. We cannot agree with the Court of Appeals that "no investor [was] injured" and that the "purity of the security transaction and the purity of the trading process were unsullied."

Section 10(b) outlaws the use "in connection with the purchase or sale" of any security of "any manipulative or deceptive device or contrivance." The Act protects corporations as well as individuals who are sellers of a security. Manhattan was injured as an investor through a deceptive device which deprived it of any compensation for the sale of its valuable block of securities.

The fact that the fraud was perpetrated by an officer of Manhattan and his outside collaborators is irrelevant to our problem. For § 10(b) bans the use of any deceptive device in the "sale" of any security by "any person." And the fact that the transaction is not conducted through a securities exchange or an organized over-the-counter market is irrelevant to the coverage of § 10(b). *Hooper v. Mountain States Securities Corp.*, 282 F.2d 195, 201. Likewise irrelevant is the

---

[10] Belgian-American Banking at the same time made a loan to New England Note in the amount of $ 250,000 which was distributed in part as follows: Belgian-American Banking $ 100,000, Bourne $ 50,000, Begole $ 50,000, and Garvin, Bantel $ 25,000.

fact that the proceeds of the sale that were due the seller were misappropriated. As the Court of Appeals for the Fifth Circuit said in the *Hooper* case, "Considering the purpose of this legislation, it would be unrealistic to say that a corporation having the capacity to acquire $ 700,000 worth of assets for its 700,000 shares of stock has suffered no loss if what it gave up was $ 700,000 but what it got was zero."

The Congress made clear that "disregard of trust relationships by those whom the law should regard as fiduciaries, are all a single seamless web" along with manipulation, investor's ignorance, and the like. H. R. Rep. No. 1383, 73d Cong., 2d Sess., 6. Since practices "constantly vary and where practices legitimate for some purposes may be turned to illegitimate and fraudulent means, broad discretionary powers" in the regulatory agency "have been found practically essential." *Id.,* at 7. Hence we do not read § 10(b) as narrowly as the Court of Appeals; it is not "limited to preserving the integrity of the securities markets," though that purpose is included. Section 10(b) must be read flexibly, not technically and restrictively. Since there was a "sale" of a security and since fraud was used "in connection with" it, there is redress under § 10(b), whatever might be available as a remedy under state law.

We agree that Congress by § 10(b) did not seek to regulate transactions which constitute no more than internal corporate mismanagement. But we read § 10(b) to mean that Congress meant to bar deceptive devices and contrivances in the purchase or sale of securities whether conducted in the organized markets or face to face. And the fact that creditors of the defrauded corporate buyer or seller of securities may be the ultimate victims does not warrant disregard of the corporate entity. The controlling stockholder owes the corporation a fiduciary obligation — one "designed for the protection of the entire community of interests in the corporation — creditors as well as stockholders." *Pepper v. Litton,* 308 U.S. 295, 307.

The crux of the present case is that Manhattan suffered an injury as a result of deceptive practices touching its sale of securities as an investor. As stated in *Shell v. Hensley,* 430 F.2d 819, 827:

> When a person who is dealing with a corporation in a securities transaction denies the corporation's directors access to material information known to him, the corporation is disabled from availing itself of an informed judgment on the part of its board regarding the merits of the transaction. In this situation the private right of action recognized under Rule 10b-5 is available as a remedy for the corporate disability.

The case was before the lower courts on a motion to dismiss.

Bankers Life urges that the complaint did not allege, and discovery failed to disclose, any connection between it and the fraud and that therefore, the dismissal of the complaint as to it was correct and should be affirmed. We make no ruling on this point.

The case must be remanded for trial. We intimate no opinion on the merits, as we have dealt only with allegations and with the question of law whether a cause of action as respects the sale by Manhattan of its Treasury bonds has been charged under § 10(b). We think it has been so charged and accordingly we reverse and remand for proceedings consistent with this opinion.

All defenses except our ruling on § 10(b) will be open on remand.

Reversed.

BROWN v. IVIE

United States Court of Appeals, Fifth Circuit
661 F.2d 62 (1981)

FRANK M. JOHNSON, JR., CIRCUIT JUDGE:

Plaintiff L. M. Brown filed suit alleging that the defendants Ivie and Lightsey violated the federal Securities Act antifraud provisions by inducing him to enter into an agreement to sell his stock. The district court dismissed the case, holding that plaintiff had failed to state a cause of action under the federal securities laws, and plaintiff appeals. We reverse.

Brown and two defendants were each an officer, a director and a one-third shareholder in a closely held corporation, United Power Distributors, Inc. Brown and Lightsey were also employed as salesmen for the corporation. In 1976 the three stockholders entered into a "buy-sell agreement" that required shareholders no longer employed with the corporation to sell their stock back to the corporation at book value. By setting the purchase price at book value, the 1976 agreement insured that a shareholder would receive less than fair market value for the stock. The 1976 agreement also contained a provision requiring that a restrictive endorsement be placed on all stock certificates stating that any transfer to stock was subject to the terms of the 1976 agreement. Brown avers that the stock certificates were never properly indorsed, thereby rendering the 1976 agreement unenforceable.

In 1979 the defendants decided to oust Brown from the corporation and force him to sell his stock back to the corporation at less than fair value. Ivie and Lightsey recognized, however, that the 1976 agreement was unenforceable and could not be used to force Brown to sell his stock. As a result, the defendants drafted a new agreement that embodied terms substantially identical to those in the 1976 agreement. The 1979 agreement required shareholders leaving the corporation to sell their shares back to the corporation at book value and to surrender possession of the stock certificates to a trustee. Brown was presented with the 1979 agreement and informed that the new agreement was necessary to effectuate a change in insurance companies and to increase the amount of insurance held by the corporation on each shareholder. The defendants omitted to tell Brown that they intended to oust him from the corporation and would be using the 1979 agreement to obtain his stock at less than fair value. Brown signed the agreement and seven days later defendants terminated his employment.

Shortly thereafter Brown was also removed as officer and director. The defendants insisted that Brown sell his stock back to the corporation in accordance with the terms of the 1979 agreement. Brown refused and brought suit alleging that the defendants violated Section 10(b) of the Securities Exchange Act of 1934 and Rule 10b-5 by fraudulently inducing him to enter into the 1979 agreement. Ivie and Lightsey counterclaimed for specific performance of the agreement. The district court dismissed Brown's suit, concluding that the alleged fraud had not been made "in connection with" the sale of a security as required by Rule 10b-5 and, alternatively, that the facts alleged by Brown involved an internal corporate dispute of the type not properly cognizable as a federal securities violation. The court also dismissed the defendants' counterclaims for lack of pendent jurisdiction of the subject matter.

A necessary element of a Rule 10b-5 offense is that the fraud or deceit be "in connection with" the sale of a security. *Superintendent of Insurance v. Banker's Life & Cas. Co.*, 404 U.S. 6 (1971). In *Alley v. Miramon*, 614 F.2d 1372 (5th Cir. 1980), the Court determined that "in connection with" is to be flexibly applied but requires that there be a nexus between the defendant's fraud and the securities "sale". However, the "plaintiff in a Rule 10b-5 case need not establish a direct or close relationship between the fraudulent transaction and the purchase or sale, but only that the transaction [involving the sale] 'touch' the transaction involving the defendant's fraud." *Id.* at 1378 n.11. Whether fraudulent omissions or misrepresentation are too remote to be "in connection with" the sale of a security depends upon the individual facts of each case. Applying the "touch" test enunciated in *Alley*, we conclude that the alleged fraud by the defendants was made "in connection with" the sale of a security.

The district court determined that "[a]ny alleged misrepresentation by the [defendants] as to why they wanted [Brown] to sign the [1979] agreement, is too remote to be 'in connection with' a securities transaction," and relied primarily upon *Ketchum v. Green*, 557 F.2d 1022 (3d Cir. 1977), to support the conclusion. *Ketchum* is, however, readily distinguishable from the present case. In *Ketchum* the plaintiffs alleged that they were ousted from the corporation as a result of defendants' misrepresentations and required by the terms of a "stock-retirement agreement" to sell their stock back to the corporation at less than fair value. The *Ketchum* court concluded that the fraud was too remote to be "in connection with" the sale of a security. The court stressed that the objective of defendants' alleged fraud was to expel plaintiffs from the corporation in order to gain control and that the resulting sale of securities was simply an "indirect" consequence of plaintiffs' expulsion. Significantly, the defendants in *Ketchum* did not as an integral part of their scheme induce the plaintiffs to enter into the stock-retirement agreement; the agreement had been executed over seven years prior to the alleged fraud. Thus, a nexus between the fraud and the securities transaction was clearly absent.

The facts, as alleged, in the instant case demonstrate a more direct causal connection between the fraud and the sale of securities than was present in

Ketchum. Unlike the situation in *Ketchum,* Ivie and Lightsey collectively controlled two-thirds of the corporate stock and had the power to terminate Brown's employment at any time. It is alleged, however, that Ivie and Lightsey did not have an enforceable agreement that required Brown to sell his stock back to the corporation upon termination of employment. As a result, the plaintiff contends that the defendants fraudulently induced him to sign the 1979 agreement, thereby guaranteeing that they would obtain his stock at book value. Thus, accepting the fraud as alleged, there is a direct connection between it and the execution of the 1979 agreement obligating Brown to sell his stock for less than fair value. Since a contract for the sale or disposition of stock constitutes a sale of a security for purposes of the federal securities laws, the defendants' fraud, as alleged, is "in connection with" the sale of a security.

. . . .

The district court also found that the corporate struggle between Brown, a minority shareholder, and the two defendants, the majority shareholders, was beyond the purview of Rule 10b-5 under the rationale articulated by the Supreme Court in *Santa Fe Industries, Inc. v. Green,* 430 U.S. 462 (1977). In *Santa Fe,* the Supreme Court concluded that Rule 10b-5 did not encompass claims by a minority shareholder concerning a breach of fiduciary duty by the majority shareholders where there were no allegations of misrepresentation or nondisclosure. The Fifth Circuit has interpreted *Santa Fe* as precluding application of Rule 10b-5 only if the breach of fiduciary duty does not involve misrepresentations or nondisclosures. This interpretation of *Santa Fe* has been adopted by other circuits. Brown has averred the requisite nondisclosures and misrepresentations necessary to overcome the hurdles presented by *Sante Fe.* The complaint contains affirmative allegations that the defendants fraudulently misrepresented that the purpose of the 1979 agreement was to alter the insurance provisions and provide increased compensation in the event of a shareholder's death or disability, and that the defendants fraudulently omitted to inform Brown that they sought the agreement in order to obtain his stock at less than fair value. Because of the presence of these allegations of fraud, Brown's claim is not beyond the scope of Rule 10b-5.

. . . .

C. STANDING

BLUE CHIP STAMPS v. MANOR DRUG STORES

United States Supreme Court
421 U.S. 723 (1975)

MR. JUSTICE REHNQUIST delivered the opinion of the Court.

This case requires us to consider whether the offerees of a stock offering, made pursuant to an antitrust consent decree and registered under the Securities Act of 1933 (1933 Act), may maintain a private cause of action for money damages where they allege that the offeror has violated the provisions of Rule 10b-5 of the Securities and Exchange Commission, but where they have neither purchased nor sold any of the offered shares. *See Birnbaum v. Newport Steel Corp.,* 193 F.2d 461 (CA2), *cert. denied,* 343 U.S. 956 (1952).

I

In 1963 the United States filed a civil antitrust action against Blue Chip Stamp Co. (Old Blue Chip), a company in the business of providing trading stamps to retailers, and nine retailers who owned 90% of its shares. In 1967 the action was terminated by the entry of a consent decree. The decree contemplated a plan of reorganization whereby Old Blue Chip was to be merged into a newly formed corporation, Blue Chip Stamps (New Blue Chip). The holdings of the majority shareholders of Old Blue Chip were to be reduced, and New Blue Chip, one of the petitioners here, was required under the plan to offer a substantial number of its shares of common stock to retailers who had used the stamp service in the past but who were not shareholders in the old company. Under the terms of the plan, the offering to nonshareholder users was to be proportional to past stamp usage and the shares were to be offered in units consisting of common stock and debentures.

The reorganization plan was carried out, the offering was registered with the SEC as required by the 1933 Act, and a prospectus was distributed to all offerees as required by § 5 of that Act. Somewhat more than 50% of the offered units were actually purchased. In 1970, two years after the offering, respondent, a former user of the stamp service and therefore an offeree of the 1968 offering, filed this suit in the United States District Court for the Central District of California. Defendants below and petitioners here are Old and New Blue Chip, eight of the nine majority shareholders of Old Blue Chip, and the directors of New Blue Chip (collectively called Blue Chip).

Respondent's complaint alleged, *inter alia,* that the prospectus prepared and distributed by Blue Chip in connection with the offering was materially misleading in its overly pessimistic appraisal of Blue Chip's status and future prospects. It alleged that Blue Chip intentionally made the prospectus overly pessimistic in order to discourage respondent and other members of the allegedly large class whom it represents from accepting what was intended to be a bargain offer, so that the rejected shares might later be offered to the public at a higher price. The complaint alleged that class members because of and in reliance on the false and misleading prospectus failed to purchase the offered units. Respondent therefore sought on behalf of the alleged class some $ 21,400,000 in damages representing the lost opportunity to purchase the units; the right to purchase the previously rejected units at the 1968 price; and in addition, it sought some $ 25,000,000 in exemplary damages.

The only portion of the litigation thus initiated which is before us is whether respondent may base its action on Rule 10b-5 of the Securities and Exchange Commission without having either bought or sold the securities described in the allegedly misleading prospectus. The District Court dismissed respondent's complaint for failure to state a claim upon which relief might be granted. On appeal to the United States Court of Appeals for the Ninth Circuit, respondent pressed only its asserted claim under Rule 10b-5, and a divided panel of the Court of Appeals sustained its position and reversed the District Court. After the Ninth Circuit denied rehearing en banc, we granted Blue Chip's petition for certiorari. Our consideration of the correctness of the determination of the Court of Appeals requires us to consider what limitations there are on the class of plaintiffs who may maintain a private cause of action for money damages for violation of Rule 10b-5, and whether respondent was within that class.

II

....

[In 1952] the Court of Appeals for the Second Circuit concluded that the plaintiff class for purposes of a private damages action under § 10(b) and Rule 10b-5 was limited to actual purchasers and sellers of securities. *Birnbaum v. Newport Steel Corp., supra.*

The Court of Appeals in this case did not repudiate *Birnbaum*.... But in this case a majority of the Court of Appeals found that the facts warranted an exception to the *Birnbaum* rule. For the reasons hereinafter stated, we are of the opinion that *Birnbaum* was rightly decided, and that it bars respondent from maintaining this suit under Rule 10b-5.

III

The panel which decided *Birnbaum* consisted of Chief Judge Swan and Judges Learned Hand and Augustus Hand: the opinion was written by the last named. Since both § 10(b) and Rule 10b-5 proscribed only fraud "in connection with the purchase or sale" of securities, and since the history of § 10(b) revealed no congressional intention to extend a private civil remedy for money damages to other than defrauded purchasers or sellers of securities, ... the court concluded that the plaintiff class in a Rule 10b-5 action was limited to actual purchasers and sellers.

[V]irtually all lower federal courts facing the issue in the hundreds of reported cases presenting this question over the past quarter century have reaffirmed *Birnbaum*'s conclusion that the plaintiff class for purposes of § 10(b) and Rule 10b-5 private damage actions is limited to purchasers and sellers of securities.

In 1957 and again in 1959, the Securities and Exchange Commission sought from Congress amendment of § 10(b) to change its wording from "in connection with the purchase or sale of any security" to "in connection with the purchase or sale of, *or any attempt to purchase or sell,* any security." In the words of a memorandum submitted by the Commission to a congressional committee, the purpose of the proposed change was "to make section 10(b) also applicable to manipulative activities in connection with any attempt to purchase or sell any security." Opposition to the amendment was based on fears of the extension of civil liability under § 10(b) that it would cause. Neither change was adopted by Congress.

The longstanding acceptance by the courts, coupled with Congress' failure to reject *Birnbaum's* reasonable interpretation of the wording of § 10(b), wording which is directed toward injury suffered "in connection with the purchase or sale" of securities, argues significantly in favor of acceptance of the *Birnbaum* rule by this Court.

Available evidence from the texts of the 1933 and 1934 Acts as to the congressional scheme in this regard, though not conclusive, supports the result reached by the *Birnbaum* court....

....

Having said all this, we would by no means be understood as suggesting that we are able to divine from the language of § 10(b) the express "intent of Congress" as to the contours of a private cause of action under Rule 10b-5. When we deal with private actions under Rule 10b-5, we deal with a judicial oak which has grown from little more than a legislative acorn.... It is therefore proper that we consider, in addition to the factors already discussed, what may be described as policy considerations when we come to flesh out the portions of the law with respect to which neither the congressional enactment nor the administrative regulations offer conclusive guidance.

Three principal classes of potential plaintiffs are presently barred by the *Birnbaum* rule. First are potential purchasers of shares, either in a new offering or on the Nation's post-distribution trading markets, who allege that they decided not to purchase because of an unduly gloomy representation or the omission of favorable material which made the issuer appear to be a less favorable investment vehicle than it actually was. Second are actual shareholders in the issuer who allege that they decided not to sell their shares because of an unduly rosy representation or a failure to disclose unfavorable material. Third are shareholders, creditors, and perhaps others related to an issuer who suffered loss in the value of their investment due to corporate or insider activities in connection with the purchase or sale of securities which violate Rule 10b-5. It has been held that shareholder members of the second and third of these classes may frequently be able to circumvent the *Birnbaum* limitation through bringing a derivative action on behalf of the corporate issuer if the latter is itself a purchaser or seller of securities. But the first of these classes, of which respondent is a member, cannot claim the benefit of such a rule.

A great majority of the many commentators on the issue before us have taken the view that the *Birnbaum* limitation on the plaintiff class in a Rule 10b-5 action for damages is an arbitrary restriction which unreasonably prevents some deserving plaintiffs from recovering damages which have in fact been caused by violations of Rule 10b-5. The Securities and Exchange Commission has filed an *amicus* brief in this case espousing that same view. We have no doubt that this is indeed a disadvantage of the *Birnbaum* rule, and if it had no countervailing advantages it would be undesirable as a matter of policy, however much it might be supported by precedent and legislative history. But we are of the opinion that there are countervailing advantages to the *Birnbaum* rule, purely as a matter of policy, although those advantages are more difficult to articulate than is the disadvantage.

There has been widespread recognition that litigation under Rule 10b-5 presents a danger of vexatiousness different in degree and in kind from that which accompanies litigation in general. This fact was recognized by Judge Browning in his opinion for the majority of the Court of Appeals in this case and by Judge Hufstedler in her dissenting opinion when she said:

> The purchaser-seller rule has maintained the balances built into the congressional scheme by permitting damage actions to be brought only by those persons whose active participation in the marketing transaction promises enforcement of the statute without undue risk of abuse of the litigation process and without distorting the securities market.

Judge Friendly in commenting on another aspect of Rule 10b-5 litigation has referred to the possibility that unduly expansive imposition of civil liability "will lead to large judgments, payable in the last analysis by innocent investors, for the benefit of speculators and their lawyers...." *SEC v. Texas Gulf Sulphur Co.*, 401 F.2d 833, 867 (CA2 1968) (concurring opinion).

We believe that the concern expressed for the danger of vexatious litigation which could result from a widely expanded class of plaintiffs under Rule 10b-5 is founded in something more substantial than the common complaint of the many defendants who would prefer avoiding lawsuits entirely to either settling them or trying them. These concerns have two largely separate grounds.

The first of these concerns is that in the field of federal securities laws governing disclosure of information even a complaint which by objective standards may have very little chance of success at trial has a settlement value to the plaintiff out of any proportion to its prospect of success at trial so long as he may prevent the suit from being resolved against him by dismissal or summary judgment. The very pendency of the lawsuit may frustrate or delay normal business activity of the defendant which is totally unrelated to the lawsuit.

Congress itself recognized the potential for nuisance or "strike" suits in this type of litigation, and in Title II of the 1934 Act amended § 11 of the 1933 Act to provide that:

> In any suit under this or any other section of this title the court may, in its discretion, require an undertaking for the payment of the costs of such suit, including reasonable attorney's fees....

....

The potential for possible abuse of the liberal discovery provisions of the Federal Rules of Civil Procedure may likewise exist in this type of case to a greater extent than they do in other litigation. The prospect of extensive deposition of the defendant's officers and associates and the concomitant opportunity for extensive discovery of business documents, is a common occurrence in this and similar types of litigation.... [T]o broadly expand the class of plaintiffs who may sue under Rule 10b-5 would appear to encourage the least appealing aspect of the use of the discovery rules.

Without the *Birnbaum* rule, an action under Rule 10b-5 will turn largely on which oral version of a series of occurrences the jury may decide to credit, and therefore no matter how improbable the allegations of the plaintiff, the case will be virtually impossible to dispose of prior to trial other than by settlement....

The *Birnbaum* rule, on the other hand, permits exclusion prior to trial of those plaintiffs who were not themselves purchasers or sellers of the stock in question. The fact of purchase of stock and the fact of sale of stock are generally matters which are verifiable by documentation, and do not depend upon oral recollection, so that failure to qualify under the *Birnbaum* rule is a matter that can normally be established by the defendant either on a motion to dismiss or on a motion for summary judgment.

... The *Birnbaum* rule undoubtedly excludes plaintiffs who have in fact been damaged by violations of Rule 10b-5, and to that extent it is undesirable. But it also separates in a readily demonstrable manner the group of plaintiffs who actually purchased or actually sold, and whose version of the facts is therefore more likely to be believed by the trier of fact, from the vastly larger world of potential plaintiffs who might successfully allege a claim but could seldom succeed in proving it. And this fact is one of its advantages.

The second ground for fear of vexatious litigation is based on the concern that, given the generalized contours of liability, the abolition of the *Birnbaum* rule would throw open to the trier of fact many rather hazy issues of historical fact the proof of which depended almost entirely on oral testimony.... The Commission suggests that in particular cases additional requirements of corroboration of testimony and more limited measure of damages would correct the dangers of an expanded class of plaintiffs.

But the very necessity, or at least the desirability, of fashioning unique rules of corroboration and damages as a correlative to the abolition of the *Birnbaum* rule suggests that the rule itself may have something to be said for it.

　　....

In today's universe of transactions governed by the 1934 Act, privity of dealing or even personal contact between potential defendant and potential plaintiff is the exception and not the rule. The stock of issuers is listed on financial exchanges utilized by tens of millions of investors, and corporate representations reach a potential audience, encompassing not only the diligent few who peruse filed corporate reports or the sizable number of subscribers to financial journals, but the readership of the Nation's daily newspapers....

[I]n the absence of the *Birnbaum* rule, it would be sufficient for a plaintiff to prove that he had failed to purchase or sell stock by reason of a defendant's violation of Rule 10b-5. The manner in which the defendant's violation caused the plaintiff to fail to act could be as a result of the reading of a prospectus, as respondent claims here, but it could just as easily come as a result of a claimed reading of information contained in the financial pages of a local newspaper. Plaintiff's proof would not be that he purchased or sold stock, a fact which would be capable of documentary verification in most situations, but instead that he decided *not* to purchase or sell stock. Plaintiff's entire testimony could be dependent upon uncorroborated oral evidence of many of the crucial elements of his claim, and still be sufficient to go to the jury. The jury would not even have the benefit of weighing the plaintiff's version against the defendant's version, since the elements to which the plaintiff would testify would be in many cases totally unknown and unknowable to the defendant. The very real risk in permitting those in respondent's position to sue under Rule 10b-5 is that the door will be open to recovery of substantial damages on the part of one who offers only his own testimony to prove that he ever consulted a prospectus of the issuer, that he paid any attention to it, or that the representations contained in it damaged him. The virtue of the *Birnbaum* rule, simply stated, in this situation, is that it limits the class of plaintiffs to those who have at least dealt in the security to which the prospectus, representation, or omission relates. And their dealing in the security, whether by way of purchase or sale, will generally be an objectively demonstrable fact in an area of the law otherwise very much dependent upon oral testimony....

....

Thus we conclude that what may be called considerations of policy, which we are free to weigh in deciding this case, are by no means entirely on one side of the scale. Taken together with the precedential support for the *Birnbaum* rule over a period of more than 20 years, and the consistency of that rule with what we can glean from the intent of Congress, they lead us to conclude that it is a sound rule and should be followed.

IV

The majority of the Court of Appeals in this case expressed no disagreement with the general proposition that one asserting a claim for damages based on the violation of Rule 10b-5 must be either a purchaser or seller of securities. However, it noted that prior cases have held that persons owning contractual rights to buy or sell securities are not excluded by the *Birnbaum* rule. Relying on these cases, it concluded that respondent's status as an offeree pursuant to the terms of the consent decree served the same function, for purposes of delimiting the class of plaintiffs, as is normally performed by the requirement of a contractual relationship.

....

... While the *Birnbaum* rule has been flexibly interpreted by lower federal courts, we have been unable to locate a single decided case from any court in the 20-odd years of litigation since the *Birnbaum* decision which would support the right of persons who were in the position of respondent here to bring a private suit under Rule 10b-5. Respondent was not only not a buyer or seller of any security but it was not even a shareholder of the corporate petitioners.

....

Beyond the difficulties evident in an extension of standing to this respondent, we do not believe that the *Birnbaum* rule is merely a shorthand judgment on the nature of a particular plaintiff's proof. As a purely practical matter, it is doubtless true that respondent and the members of its class, as offerees and recipients of the prospectus of New Blue Chip, are a smaller class of potential plaintiffs than would be all those who might conceivably assert that they obtained information violative of Rule 10b-5 and attributable to the issuer in the financial pages of their local newspaper. And since respondent likewise had a prior connection with some of petitioners as a result of using the trading stamps marketed by Old Blue Chip, and was intended to benefit from the provisions of the consent decree, there is doubtless more likelihood that its managers read and were damaged by the allegedly misleading statements in the prospectus than there would be in a case filed by a complete stranger to the corporation.

But respondent and the members of its class are neither "purchasers" nor "sellers," as those terms are defined in the 1934 Act, and therefore to the extent that their claim of standing to sue were recognized, it would mean that the lesser practical difficulties of corroborating at least some elements of their proof would be regarded as sufficient to avoid the *Birnbaum* rule. While we have noted that these practical difficulties, particularly in the case of a complete stranger to the corporation, support the retention of that rule, they are by no means the only factor which does so. The general adoption of the rule by other federal courts in the 20-odd years since it was announced, and the consistency of the rule with the statutes involved and their legislative history, are likewise bases for retaining the rule. Were we to agree with the Court of Appeals in this case, we would leave the *Birnbaum* rule open to endless case-by-case erosion depending on whether a particular group of plaintiffs was thought by the court in which the issue was being litigated to be sufficiently more discrete than the world of potential purchasers at large to justify an exception. We do not believe that such a shifting and highly fact-oriented disposition of the issue of who may bring a damages claim for violation of Rule 10b-5 is a satisfactory basis for a rule of liability imposed on the conduct of business transactions. Nor is it as consistent as a straightforward application of the *Birnbaum* rule with the other factors which support the retention of that rule. We therefore hold that respondent was not entitled to sue for violation of Rule 10b-5, and the judgment of the Court of Appeals is

Reversed.

D. FAULT REQUIRED

ERNST & ERNST v. HOCHFELDER

United States Supreme Court
425 U.S. 185 (1976)

MR. JUSTICE POWELL delivered the opinion of the Court.

The issue in this case is whether an action for civil damages may lie under § 10(b) of the Securities Exchange Act of 1934 (1934 Act), and Securities and Exchange Commission Rule 10b-5, in the absence of an allegation of intent to deceive, manipulate, or defraud on the part of the defendant.

I

Petitioner, Ernst & Ernst, is an accounting firm. From 1946 through 1967 it was retained by First Securities Company of Chicago (First Securities), a small brokerage firm and member of the Midwest Stock Exchange and of the National Association of Securities Dealers, to perform periodic audits of the firm's books and records. In connection with these audits Ernst & Ernst prepared for filing with the Securities and Exchange Commission (the Commission) the annual reports required of First Securities under § 17(a) of the 1934 Act. It also prepared for First Securities responses to the financial questionnaires of the Midwest Stock Exchange (the Exchange).

Respondents were customers of First Securities who invested in a fraudulent securities scheme perpetrated by Leston B. Nay, president of the firm and owner of 92% of its stock. Nay induced the respondents to invest funds in "escrow" accounts that he represented would yield a high rate of return. Respondents did so from 1942 through 1966, with the majority of the transactions occurring in the 1950's. In fact, there were no escrow accounts as Nay converted respondents' funds to his own use immediately upon receipt. These transactions were not in the customary form of dealings between First Securities and its customers. The respondents drew their personal checks payable to Nay or a designated bank for his account. No such escrow accounts were reflected on the books and records of First Securities, and none was shown on its periodic accounting to respondents in connection with their other investments. Nor were they included in First Securities' filings with the Commission or the Exchange.

This fraud came to light in 1968 when Nay committed suicide, leaving a note that described First Securities as bankrupt and the escrow accounts as "spurious." Respondents subsequently filed this action for damages against Ernst & Ernst in the United States District Court for the Northern District of Illinois under § 10(b) of the 1934 Act. The complaint charged that Nay's escrow scheme violated § 10(b) and Commission Rule 10b-5, and that Ernst & Ernst had "aided and abetted" Nay's violations by its "failure" to conduct proper audits of First Securities. As revealed through discovery, respondents' cause of action rested on a theory of negligent nonfeasance. The premise was that Ernst & Ernst had failed to utilize "appropriate auditing procedures" in its audits of First Securities, thereby failing to discover internal practices of the firm said to prevent an effective audit. The practice principally relied on was Nay's rule that only he could open mail addressed to him at First Securities or addressed to First Securities to his attention, even if it arrived in his absence. Respondents contended that if Ernst & Ernst had conducted a proper audit, it would have discovered this "mail rule." The existence of the rule then would have been disclosed in reports to the Exchange and to the Commission by Ernst & Ernst as an irregular procedure that prevented an effective audit. This would have led to an investigation of Nay that would have revealed the fraudulent scheme. Respondents specifically disclaimed the existence of fraud or intentional misconduct on the part of Ernst & Ernst.

After extensive discovery the District Court granted Ernst & Ernst's motion for summary judgment and dismissed the action [and the Court of Appeals reversed].

....

We granted certiorari to resolve the question whether a private cause of action for damages will lie under § 10(b) and Rule 10b-5 in the absence of any allegation of "scienter" intent to deceive, manipulate, or defraud.[11] We conclude that it will not and therefore we reverse.

II

....

... During the 30-year period since a private cause of action was first implied under § 10(b) and Rule 10b-5, a substantial body of case law and commentary has developed as to its elements. Courts and commentators long have differed with regard to whether scienter is a necessary element of such a cause of action, or whether negligent conduct alone is sufficient. In addressing this question, we turn first to the language of § 10(b), for "[t]he starting point in every case involving construction of a statute is the language itself." *Blue Chip Stamps, supra,* at 756 (Powell, J., concurring).

A

Section 10(b) makes unlawful the use or employment of "any manipulative or deceptive device or contrivance" in contravention of Commission rules. The words "manipulative or deceptive" used in conjunction with "device or contriv-

---

[11] ....

In this opinion the term "scienter" refers to a mental state embracing intent to deceive, manipulate, or defraud. In certain areas of the law recklessness is considered to be a form of intentional conduct for purposes of imposing liability for some act. We need not address here the question whether, in some circumstances, reckless behavior is sufficient for civil liability under § 10(b) and Rule 10b-5.

Since this case concerns an action for damages we also need not consider the question whether scienter is a necessary element in an action for injunctive relief under § 10(b) and Rule 10b-5.

ance" strongly suggest that § 10(b) was intended to proscribe knowing or intentional misconduct.

In its *amicus curiae* brief, however, the Commission contends that nothing in the language "manipulative or deceptive device or contrivance" limits its operation to knowing or intentional practices. In support of its view, the Commission cites the overall congressional purpose in the 1933 and 1934 Acts to protect investors against false and deceptive practices that might injure them. The Commission then reasons that since the "effect" upon investors of given conduct is the same regardless of whether the conduct is negligent or intentional, Congress must have intended to bar all such practices and not just those done knowingly or intentionally. The logic of this effect-oriented approach would impose liability for wholly faultless conduct where such conduct results in harm to investors, a result the Commission would be unlikely to support. But apart from where its logic might lead, the Commission would add a gloss to the operative language of the statute quite different from its commonly accepted meaning. The argument simply ignores the use of the words "manipulative," "device," and "contrivance," terms that make unmistakable a congressional intent to proscribe a type of conduct quite different from negligence. Use of the word "manipulative" is especially significant. It is and was virtually a term of art when used in connection with securities markets. It connotes intentional or willful conduct designed to deceive or defraud investors by controlling or artificially affecting the price of securities.

In addition to relying upon the Commission's argument with respect to the operative language of the statute, respondents contend that since we are dealing with "remedial legislation," *Tcherepnin v. Knight,* 389 U.S. 332, 336 (1967), it must be construed "'not technically and restrictively, but flexibly to effectuate its remedial purposes.'" *Affiliated Ute Citizens v. United States, supra,* 406 U.S. at 151, quoting *SEC v. Capital Gains Research Bureau, supra,* 375 U.S., at 186. They argue that the "remedial purposes" of the Acts demand a construction of § 10(b) that embraces negligence as a standard of liability. But in seeking to accomplish its broad remedial goals, Congress did not adopt uniformly a negligence standard even as to express civil remedies. In some circumstances and with respect to certain classes of defendants, Congress did create express liability predicated upon a failure to exercise reasonable care. *E.g.,* 1933 Act § 11(b)(3)(B) (liability of "experts," such as accountants for misleading statements in portions of registration statements for which they are responsible). But in other situations good faith is an absolute defense. 1934 Act § 18 (misleading statements in any document filed pursuant to the 1934 Act). And in still other circumstances Congress created express liability regardless of the defendant's fault, 1933 Act § 11(a) (issuer liability for misleading statements in the registration statement).

It is thus evident that Congress fashioned standards of fault in the express civil remedies in the 1933 and 1934 Acts on a particularized basis.... In view of the language of § 10(b) which so clearly connotes intentional misconduct, and mindful that the language of a statute controls when sufficiently clear in its context, further inquiry may be unnecessary. We turn now, nevertheless, to the legislative history of the 1934 Act to ascertain whether there is support for the meaning attributed to § 10(b) by the Commission and respondents.

B

Although the extensive legislative history of the 1934 Act is bereft of any explicit explanation of Congress' intent, we think the relevant portions of that history support our conclusion that § 10(b) was addressed to practices that involve some element of scienter and cannot be read to impose liability for negligent conduct alone.

....

[T]he intended scope of § 10(b) [is not] revealed explicitly in the legislative history of the 1934 Act, which deals primarily with other aspects of the legislation. There is no indication, however, that § 10(b) was intended to proscribe conduct not involving scienter. The extensive hearings that preceded passage of the 1934 Act touched only briefly on § 10, and most of the discussion was devoted to the enumerated devices that the Commission is empowered to proscribe under § 10(a). The most relevant exposition of the provision that was to become § 10(b) was by Thomas G. Corcoran, a spokesman for the drafters. Corcoran indicated:

> Subsection (c) [§ 9(c) of H.R. 7852 — later § 10(b)] says, "Thou shalt not devise any other cunning devices."
>
> ....
>
> ... Of course subsection (c) is a catch-all clause to prevent manipulative devices. I do not think there is any objection to that kind of clause. The Commission should have the authority to deal with new manipulative devices.

Hearings on H.R. 7852 and H.R. 8720 before the House Comm. on Interstate and Foreign Commerce, 73d Cong., 2d Sess., 115 (1934). This brief explanation of § 10(b) by a spokesman for its drafters is significant. The section was described rightly as a "catch-all" clause to enable the Commission "to deal with new manipulative [or cunning] devices." It is difficult to believe that any lawyer, legislative draftsman, or legislator would use these words if the intent was to create liability for merely negligent acts or omissions....

The legislative reports do not address the scope of § 10(b) or its catch-all function directly. In considering specific manipulative practices left to Commission regulation, however, the reports indicate that liability would not attach absent scienter, supporting the conclusion that Congress intended no lesser standard under § 10(b)....

In the portion of the general analysis section of the Report entitled "Manipulative Practices," however, there is a discussion of specific practices that were considered so inimical to the public interest as to require express prohibition such as "wash" sales and "matched" orders,[12] and of other practices that might in some cases serve legitimate purposes, such as stabilization of security prices and grants of options. These latter practices were left to regulation by the Commission. 1934 Act §§ 9(a)(6), (c). Significantly, we think, in the discussion of the need to regulate even the latter category of practices when they are manipulative, there is no indication that any type of criminal or civil liability is to attach in the absence of scienter. Furthermore, in commenting on the express civil liabilities provided in the 1934 Act, the Report explains:

> ... [I]f an investor has suffered loss by reason of illicit practices, it is equitable that he should be allowed to recover damages from the guilty party.... The bill provides that any person who unlawfully manipulates the price of a security, or who induces transactions in a security by means of false or misleading statements, or who makes a false or misleading statement in the report of a corporation, shall be liable in damages to those who have bought or sold the security at prices affected by such violation or statement. In such case the burden is on the plaintiff to show the violation or the fact that the statement was false or misleading, and that he relied thereon to his damage. The defendant may escape liability by showing that the statement was made in *good faith*. *Id.*, at 12-13 (emphasis supplied).

....

C

The 1933 and 1934 Acts constitute interrelated components of the federal regulatory scheme governing transactions in securities.... Recognizing this, respondents and the Commission contrast § 10(b) to other sections of the Acts to support their contention that civil liability may be imposed upon proof of negligent conduct. We think they misconceive the significance of the other provisions of the Acts.

The Commission argues that Congress has been explicit in requiring willful conduct when that was the standard of fault intended, citing § 9 of the 1934 Act, which generally proscribes manipulation of securities prices.... From this the Commission concludes that since § 10(b) is not by its terms explicitly restricted to willful, knowing, or purposeful conduct, it should not be construed in all cases to require more than negligent action or inaction as a precondition for civil liability.

The structure of the Acts does not support the Commission's argument. In each instance that Congress created express civil liability in favor of purchasers or

---

[12] "Wash" sales are transactions involving no change in beneficial ownership. "Matched" orders are orders for the purchase sale of a security that are entered with the knowledge that orders of substantially the same size, at substantially the same time and price, have been or will be entered by the same or different persons for the
sale/purchase of such security....

sellers of securities it clearly specified whether recovery was to be premised on knowing or intentional conduct, negligence, or entirely innocent mistake....

We also consider it significant that each of the express civil remedies in the 1933 Act allowing recovery for negligent conduct, see §§ 11, 12(2), 15, is subject to significant procedural restrictions not applicable under § 10(b).... We think these procedural limitations indicate that the judicially created private damage remedy under § 10(b) — which has no comparable restrictions — cannot be extended, consistently with the intent of Congress, to actions premised on negligent wrongdoing. Such extension would allow causes of action covered by § 11, § 12(2), and § 15 to be brought instead under § 10(b) and thereby nullify the effectiveness of the carefully drawn procedural restrictions on these express actions....

D

We have addressed, to this point, primarily the language and history of § 10(b). The Commission contends, however, that subsections (2) and (3) of Rule 10b-5 are cast in language which if standing alone — could encompass both intentional and negligent behavior. These subsections respectively provide that it is unlawful "[t]o make any untrue statement of a material fact or to omit to state a material fact necessary in order to make the statements made, in light of the circumstances under which they were made, not misleading ..." and "to engage in any act, practice, or course of business which operates or would operate as a fraud or deceit upon any person...." Viewed in isolation the language of subsection (2), and arguably that of subsection (3), could be read as proscribing, respectively, any type of material misstatement or omission, and any course of conduct, that has the effect of defrauding investors, whether the wrongdoing was intentional or not.

We note first that such a reading cannot be harmonized with the administrative history of the rule, a history making clear that when the Commission adopted the rule it was intended to apply only to activities that involved scienter. More importantly, Rule 10b-5 was adopted pursuant to authority granted the Commission under § 10(b). The rulemaking power granted to an administrative agency charged with the administration of a federal statute is not the power to make law. Rather, it is "'the power to adopt regulations to carry into effect the will of Congress as expressed by the statute.'" *Dixon v. United States,* 381 U.S. 68, 74 (1965), quoting *Manhattan General Equipment Co. v. Commissioner,* 297 U.S. 129, 134 (1936). Thus, despite the broad view of the Rule advanced by the Commission in this case, its scope cannot exceed the power granted the Commission by Congress under § 10(b). For the reasons stated above, we think the Commission's original interpretation of Rule 10b-5 was compelled by the language and history of § 10(b) and related sections of the Acts....

....

The judgment of the Court of Appeals is

Reversed.

....

MR. JUSTICE BLACKMUN, with whom MR. JUSTICE BRENNAN joins, dissenting.

Once again — *see Blue Chip Stamps v. Manor Drug Stores,* 421 U.S. 723, 730 (1975) — the Court interprets § 10(b) of the Securities Exchange Act of 1934 and the Securities and Exchange Commission's Rule 10b-5, restrictively and narrowly and thereby stultifies recovery for the victim. This time the Court does so by confining the statute and the Rule to situations where the defendant has "scienter," that is, the "intent to deceive, manipulate, or defraud." Sheer negligence, the Court says, is not within the reach of the statute and the Rule, and was not contemplated when the great reforms of 1933, 1934, and 1942 were effectuated by Congress and the Commission.

Perhaps the Court is right, but I doubt it. The Government and the Commission doubt it too, as is evidenced by the thrust of the brief filed by the Solicitor General on behalf of the Commission, as *amicus curiae.* The Court's opinion, *ante,* to be sure, has a certain technical consistency about it. It seems to me, however, that an investor can be victimized just as much by negligent conduct as by positive deception, and that it is not logical to drive a wedge between the two, saying that Congress clearly intended the one but certainly not the other.

No one questions the fact that the respondents here were the victims of an intentional securities fraud practiced by Leston B. Nay. What is at issue, of course, is the petitioner-accountant firm's involvement and that firm's responsibility under Rule 10b-5. The language of the Rule, making it unlawful for any person "in connection with the purchase or sale of any security"

> (b) To make any untrue statement of a material fact or to omit to state a material fact necessary in order to make the statements made, in the light of the circumstances under which they were made, not misleading, or
>
> (c) To engage in any act, practice, or course of business which operates or would operate as a fraud or deceit upon any person,

seems to me, clearly and succinctly, to prohibit negligent as well as intentional conduct of the kind proscribed, to extend beyond common law fraud, and to apply to negligent omission and commission. This is consistent with Congress' intent, repeatedly recognized by the Court, that securities legislation enacted for the purpose of avoiding frauds be construed "not technically and restrictively, but flexibly to effectuate its remedial purposes."

On motion for summary judgment, therefore, the respondents' allegations, in my view, were sufficient, and the District Court's dismissal of the action was improper to the extent that the dismissal rested on the proposition that suit could not be maintained under § 10(b) and Rule 10b-5 for mere negligence. The opposite appears to be true, at least in the Second Circuit, with respect to suits by the SEC to enjoin a violation of the Rule....

The critical importance of the auditing accountant's role in insuring full disclosure cannot be overestimated. The SEC has emphasized that in certifying statements the accountant's duty "is to safeguard the public interest, not that of his client." *In re Touche, Niven, Bailey & Smart,* 37 S.E.C. 629, 670-671 (1957). "In our complex society the accountant's certificate and the lawyer's opinion can be instruments for inflicting pecuniary loss more potent than the chisel or the crowbar." *United States v. Benjamin,* 328 F.2d 854, 863 (CA2), *cert. denied sub nom. Howard v. United States,* 377 U.S. 953 (1964). In this light, the initial inquiry into whether Ernst & Ernst's preparation and certification of the financial statements of First Securities Company of Chicago were negligent, because of the failure to perceive Nay's extraordinary mail rule and in other alleged respects, and thus whether Rule 10b-5 was violated, should not be thwarted.

But the Court today decides that it is to be thwarted; and so once again it rests with Congress to rephrase and to re-enact, if investor victims, such as these, are ever to have relief under the federal securities laws that I thought had been enacted for their broad, needed, and deserving benefit.

From a technical standpoint, one of the more interesting things about *Ernst & Ernst v. Hochfedler* is what it left undecided. First, it left for another time the question of whether scienter is required in a Rule 10b-5 injunction action brought by the Securities and Exchange Commission. Second, it left open whether in a Rule 10b-5 case recklessness is enough by itself to constitute scienter. The Supreme Court answered the first of these questions in *Aaron v. SEC.*[13] Using essentially the same reasoning presented in *Hochfelder,* the Court said scienter is required in an SEC injunction action brought under Rule 10b-5. The second question is still open at the Supreme Court level, but virtually all the circuit and district courts that have addressed the issue have agreed that recklessness meets the Rule 10b-5 scienter requirement.

E. PERSONS SUBJECT TO TRADING CONSTRAINTS

CHIARELLA v. UNITED STATES

United States Supreme Court
445 U.S. 222 (1980)

MR. JUSTICE POWELL delivered the opinion of the Court.

The question in this case is whether a person who learns from the confidential documents of one corporation that it is planning an attempt to secure control of a second corporation violates § 10(b) of the Securities Exchange Act of 1934 if he fails to disclose the impending takeover before trading in the target company's securities.

I

Petitioner is a printer by trade. In 1975 and 1976, he worked as a "markup man" in the New York composing room of Pandick Press, a financial printer.

---

[13] 446 U.S. 680 (1980).

Among documents that petitioner handled were five announcements of corporate takeover bids. When these documents were delivered to the printer, the indentities of the acquiring and target corporations were concealed by blank spaces or false names. The true names were sent to the printer on the night of the final printing.

The petitioner, however, was able to deduce the names of the target companies before the final printing from other information contained in the documents. Without disclosing his knowledge, petitioner purchased stock in the target companies and sold the shares immediately after the takeover attempts were made public. By this method, petitioner realized a gain of slightly more than $ 30,000 in the course of 14 months. Subsequently, the Securities and Exchange Commission (Commission or SEC) began an investigation of his trading activities. In May 1977, petitioner entered into a consent decree with the Commission in which he agreed to return his profits to the sellers of the shares. On the same day, he was discharged by Pandick Press.

In January 1978, petitioner was indicted on 17 counts of violating § 10(b) of the Securities Exchange Act of 1934 (1934 Act) and SEC Rule 10b-5. After petitioner unsuccessfully moved to dismiss the indictment, he was brought to trial and convicted on all counts.

The Court of Appeals for the Second Circuit affirmed petitioner's conviction. We granted certiorari, and we now reverse.

II

....

This case concerns the legal effect of the petitioner's silence. The District Court's charge permitted the jury to convict the petitioner if it found that he willfully failed to inform sellers of target company securities that he knew of a forthcoming takeover bid that would make their shares more valuable. In order to decide whether silence in such circumstances violates § 10(b), it is necessary to review the language and legislative history of that statute as well as its interpretation by the Commission and the federal courts.

Although the starting point of our inquiry is the language of the statute, § 10(b) does not state whether silence may constitute a manipulative or deceptive device. Section 10(b) was designed as a catchall clause to prevent fraudulent practices. But neither the legislative history nor the statute itself afford specific guidance for the resolution of this case. When Rule 10b-5 was promulgated in 1942, the SEC did not discuss the possibility that failure to provide information might run afoul of § 10(b).

The SEC took an important step in the development of § 10(b) when it held that a broker-dealer and his firm violated that section by selling securities on the basis of undisclosed information obtained from a director of the issuer corporation who was also a registered representative of the brokerage firm. In *Cady, Roberts & Co.*, 40 S.E.C. 907 (1961), the Commission decided that a corporate insider must abstain from trading in the shares of his corporation unless he has first disclosed all material inside information known to him.... The Commission emphasized that the duty arose from (i) the existence of a relationship affording access to inside information intended to be available only for a corporate purpose, and (ii) the unfairness of allowing a corporate insider to take advantage of that information by trading without disclosure.

That the relationship between a corporate insider and the stockholders of his corporation gives rise to a disclosure obligation is not a novel twist of the law. At common law, misrepresentation made for the purpose of inducing reliance upon the false statement is fraudulent. But one who fails to disclose material information prior to the consummation of a transaction commits fraud only when he is under a duty to do so. And the duty to disclose arises when one party has information "that the other [party] is entitled to know because of a fiduciary or other similar relation of trust and confidence between them."[14] In its *Cady, Roberts* decision, the Commission recognized a relationship of trust and confidence between the shareholders of a corporation and those insiders who have obtained confidential information by reason of their position with that corporation.[15] This relationship gives rise to a duty to disclose because of the "necessity of preventing a corporate insider from ... tak[ing] unfair advantage of the uninformed minority stockholders." *Speed v. Transamerica Corp.*, 99 F. Supp. 808, 829 (Del. 1951).

The federal courts have found violations of § 10(b) where corporate insiders used undisclosed information for their own benefit. *E.g., SEC v. Texas Gulf Sulphur Co.*, 401 F.2d 883 (CA2 1968). The cases also have emphasized, in accordance with the common-law rule, that "[t]he party charged with failing to disclosed market information must be under a duty to disclose it." *Frigitemp Corp. v. Financial Dynamics Fund, Inc.*, 524 F.2d 275, 282 (CA2 1975). Accordingly, a purchaser of stock who has no duty to a prospective seller because he is neither an insider nor a fiduciary has been held to have no obligation to reveal material facts. *See General Time Corp. v. Talley Industries, Inc.*, 403 F.2d 159, 164 (CA2 1968).

This Court followed the same approach in *Affiliated Ute Citizens v. United States*, 406 U.S. 128 (1972). A group of American Indians formed a corporation to manage joint assets derived from tribal holdings. The corporation issued stock

---

[14]Restatement (Second) of Torts § 551 (2)(a) (1976)....

[15] ....

The dissent of MR. JUSTICE BLACKMUN suggests that the "special facts" doctrine may be applied to find that silence constitutes fraud where one party has superior information to another. This Court has never so held. In *Strong v. Repide*, 213 U. S. 419, 431-434 (1909), this Court applied the special-facts doctrine to conclude that a corporate insider had a duty to disclose to a shareholder. In that case, the majority shareholder of a corporation secretly purchased the stock of another shareholder without revealing that the corporation, under the insider's direction, was about to sell corporate assets at a price that would greatly enhance the value of the stock. The decision in *Strong v. Repide* was premised upon the fiduciary duty between the corporate insider and the shareholder.

to its Indian shareholders and designated a local bank as its transfer agent. Because of the speculative nature of the corporate assets and the difficulty of ascertaining the true value of a share, the corporation requested the bank to stress to its stockholders the importance of retaining the stock. Two of the bank's assistant managers aided the shareholders in disposing of stock which the managers knew was traded in two separate markets — a primary market of Indians selling to non-Indians through the bank and a resale market consisting entirely of non-Indians. Indian sellers charged that the assistant managers had violated § 10(b) and Rule 10b-5 by failing to inform them of the higher prices prevailing in the resale market. The Court recognized that no duty of disclosure would exist if the bank merely had acted as a transfer agent. But the bank also had assumed a duty to act on behalf of the shareholders, and the Indian sellers had relied upon its personnel when they sold their stock. Because these officers of the bank were charged with a responsibility to the shareholders, they could not act as market makers inducing the Indians to sell their stock without disclosing the existence of the more favorable non-Indian market.

Thus, administrative and judicial interpretations have established that silence in connection with the purchase or sale of securities may operate as a fraud actionable under § 10(b) despite the absence of statutory language or legislative history specifically addressing the legality of nondisclosure. But such liability is premised upon a duty to disclose arising from a relationship of trust and confidence between parties to a transaction. Application of a duty to disclose prior to trading guarantees that corporate insiders, who have an obligation to place the shareholder's welfare before their own, will not benefit personally through fraudulent use of material, nonpublic information.

III

In this case, the petitioner was convicted of violating § 10(b) although he was not a corporate insider and he received no confidential information from the target company. Moreover, the "market information" upon which he relied did not concern the earning power or operations of the target company, but only the plans of the acquiring company. Petitioner's use of that information was not a fraud under § 10(b) unless he was subject to an affirmative duty to disclose it before trading. In this case, the jury instructions failed to specify any such duty. In effect, the trial court instructed the jury that petitioner owed a duty to everyone; to all sellers, indeed, to the market as a whole. The jury simply was told to decide whether petitioner used material, nonpublic information at a time when "he knew other people trading in the securities market did not have access to the same information."

The Court of Appeals affirmed the conviction by holding that "[a]nyone — corporate insider or not — who regularly receives material nonpublic information may not use that information to trade in securities without incurring an affirmative duty to disclose." Although the court said that its test would include only persons who regularly receive material, nonpublic information, its rationale for that limitation is unrelated to the existence of a duty to disclose. The Court of Appeals, like the trial court, failed to identify a relationship between petitioner and the sellers that could give rise to a duty. Its decision thus rested solely upon its belief that the federal securities laws have "created a system providing equal access to information necessary for reasoned and intelligent investment decisions." The use by anyone of material information not generally available is fraudulent, this theory suggests, because such information gives certain buyers or sellers an unfair advantage over less informed buyers and sellers.

This reasoning suffers from two defects. First, not every instance of financial unfairness constitutes fraudulent activity under § 10(b). *See Santa Fe Industries, Inc. v. Green,* 430 U.S. 462, 474-477 (1977). Second, the element required to make silence fraudulent — a duty to disclose — is absent in this case. No duty could arise from petitioner's relationship with the sellers of the target company's securities, for petitioner had no prior dealings with them. He was not their agent, he was not a fiduciary, he was not a person in whom the sellers had placed their trust and confidence. He was, in fact, a complete stranger who dealt with the sellers only through impersonal market transactions.

We cannot affirm petitioner's conviction without recognizing a general duty between all participants in market transactions to forgo actions based on material, nonpublic information. Formulation of such a broad duty, which departs radically from the established doctrine that duty arises from a specific relationship between two parties, should not be undertaken absent some explicit evidence of congressional intent.

As we have seen, no such evidence emerges from the language or legislative history of § 10(b). Moreover, neither the Congress nor the Commission ever has adopted a parity-of-information rule. Instead the problems caused by misuse of market information have been addressed by detailed and sophisticated regulation that recognizes when use of market information may not harm operation of the securities markets. For example, the Williams Act limits but does not completely prohibit a tender offeror's purchases of target corporation stock before public announcement of the offer. Congress' careful action in this and other areas contrasts, and is in some tension, with the broad rule of liability we are asked to adopt in this case.

Indeed, the theory upon which the petitioner was convicted is at odds with the Commission's view of § 10(b) as applied to activity that has the same effect on sellers as the petitioner's purchases. "Warehousing" takes place when a corporation gives advance notice of its intention to launch a tender offer to institutional investors who then are able to purchase stock in the target company before the tender offer is made public and the price of shares rises. In this case, as in warehousing, a buyer of securities purchases stock in a target corporation on the basis of market information which is unknown to the seller. In both of these situations, the seller's behavior presumably would be altered if he had the nonpublic information. Significantly, however, the Commission has acted to bar warehousing under its authority to regulate tender offers after recognizing that action under § 10(b) would rest on a "somewhat different theory" than that previously used to regulate insider trading as fraudulent activity.

We see no basis for applying such a new and different theory of liability in this case. As we have emphasized before, the 1934 Act cannot be read "'more broadly than its language and the statutory scheme reasonably permit.'" *Toucher Ross & Co. v. Redington,* 442 U.S. 560, 578 (1979), quoting *SEC v. Sloan,* 436 U.S. 103, 116 (1978). Section 10(b) is aptly described as a catchall provision, but what it catches must be fraud. When an allegation of fraud is based upon nondisclosure, there can be no fraud absent a duty to speak. We hold that a duty to disclose under § 10(b) does not arise from the mere possession of nonpublic market information. The contrary result is without support in the legislative history of § 10(b) and would be inconsistent with the careful plan that Congress has enacted for regulation of the securities markets.

IV

In its brief to this Court, the United States offers an alternative theory to support petitioner's conviction. It argues that petitioner breached a duty to the acquiring corporation when he acted upon information that he obtained by virtue of his position as an employee of a printer employed by the corporation. The breach of this duty is said to support a conviction under § 10(b) for fraud perpetrated upon both the acquiring corporation and the sellers.

We need not decide whether this theory has merit for it was not submitted to the jury. The jury was told, in the language of Rule 10b-5, that it could convict the petitioner if it concluded that he either (i) employed a device, scheme, or artifice to defraud or (ii) engaged in an act, practice, or course of business which operated or would operate as a fraud or deceit upon any person. The trial judge stated that a "scheme to defraud" is a plan to obtain money by trick or deceit and that "a failure by Chiarella to disclose material, non-public information in connection with his purchase of stock would constitute deceit." Accordingly, the jury was instructed that the petitioner employed a scheme to defraud if he "did not disclose ... material non-public information in connection with the purchases of the stock."

Alternatively, the jury was instructed that it could convict if "Chiarella's alleged conduct of having purchased securities without disclosing material, non-public information would have or did have the effect of operating as a fraud upon a seller." The judge earlier had stated that fraud "embraces all the means which human ingenuity can devise and which are resorted to by one individual to gain an advantage over another by false misrepresentation, suggestions or by suppression of the truth."

The jury instructions demonstrate that petitioner was convicted merely because of his failure to disclose material, non-public information to sellers from whom he bought the stock of target corporations. The jury was not instructed on the nature or elements of a duty owed by petitioner to anyone other than the sellers. Because we cannot affirm a criminal conviction on the basis of a theory not presented to the jury, we will not speculate upon whether such a duty exists, whether it has been breached, or whether such a breach constitutes a violation of § 10(b).[16]

The judgment of the Court of Appeals is

Reversed.

SECURITIES AND EXCHANGE COMMISSION v. MATERIA
United States Court of Appeals, Second Circuit
745 F.2d 197 (1984)

IRVING R. KAUFMAN, CIRCUIT JUDGE.

Our era aptly has been styled, and well may be remembered as, the "age of information." Francis Bacon recognized nearly 400 years ago that "knowledge is power," but only in the last generation has it risen to the equivalent of the coin of the realm. Nowhere is this commodity more valuable or volatile than in the world of high finance, where facts worth fortunes while secret may be rendered worthless once revealed.

At a certain point, amorphous data must be translated into the written word. In the financial field, this transmogrification requires masses of information — much of it highly sensitive — to be channeled through the financial printing firms that service our great commercial centers. It was in one such firm that Anthony Materia worked. Materia stole information to which he was privy in his work, and traded on that information to his pecuniary advantage. The Securities and Exchange Commission ("SEC" or "Commission") sought — and the district court granted — an injunction against Materia, restraining him from such activities in the future and requiring him to disgorge his ill-gotten gains. In light of the broad prophylactic coverage of the antifraud provisions of the securities laws, particularly where they are sought to be enforced by the SEC, we affirm the decision below, and hold that Materia's misappropriation of material nonpublic information, and his subsequent trading on that information, violate Section 10(b) and

---

[16] The dissent of THE CHIEF JUSTICE relies upon a single phrase from the jury instructions, which states that the petitioner held a "confidential position" at Pandick Press, to argue that the jury was properly instructed on the theory "that a person who has misappropriated nonpublic information has an absolute duty to disclose that information or to refrain from trading." The few words upon which this thesis is based do not explain to the jury the nature and scope of the petitioner's duty to his employer, the nature and scope of petitioner's duty, if any, to the acquiring corporation, or the elements of the tort of misappropriation. Nor do the jury instructions suggest that a "confidential position" is a necessary element of the offense for which petitioner was charged. Thus, we do not believe that a "misappropriation" theory was included in the jury instructions.

The conviction would have to be reversed even if the jury had been instructed that it could convict the petitioner either (1) because of his failure to disclose material, nonpublic information to sellers or (2) because of a breach of a duty to the acquiring corporation. We may not uphold a criminal conviction if it is impossible to ascertain whether the defendant has been punished for noncriminal conduct.

Rule 10b-5 of the Securities Exchange Act of 1934. Recognizing the complexity attendant to an examination of Section 10(b) and Rule 10b-5, we find it necessary to set forth the facts in this dispute.

I

Anthony Materia was employed by Bowne of New York City, Inc. (Bowne), a firm specializing in the printing of financial documents, including many used by its corporate clients in connection with proposed tender offers. Because even a hint of an upcoming tender offer may send the price of the target company's stock soaring, information regarding the identity of a target is extremely sensitive and zealously guarded. It is customary, therefore, for offerors (or their law firms, which ordinarily draft such documents) to omit information that might tend to identify a target company until the last possible moment. Code names are used, blanks are left to be filled in on the eve of publication, and occasionally misinformation is even included in early drafts. In sum, a quick reading of preliminary versions of these sensitive papers would not reveal the information sought to be guarded.

Anthony Materia did not read such material quickly. In his job as a "copyholder," Materia read clients' drafts aloud to a proofreader, who in turn checked to make certain that page proofs conformed to the copy received from the client. If copyholding was Materia's vocation, the stock market appears to have been equally consuming. Notwithstanding scrupulous efforts by Bowne and its clients to keep confidential information confidential,[17] Materia was able to divine the identities of at least four tender offer targets in the period between December 1980 and September 1982. Within hours of each discovery, he purchased stock, and within days — after the offer had been made public — he sold his holdings at substantial gains.

Soon after Materia completed his purchase and sale of securities in the fourth target company, the Securities and Exchange Commission filed an enforcement action, charging that he had violated and was about to violate [Section 10(b)] of the Securities Exchange Act of 1934 and [Rule 10b-5]. The basis of its complaint was Materia's trading in securities on the basis of material nonpublic information he had misappropriated from his employer and its clients.

Following a fourteen-day nonjury trial, Judge Brieant delivered an opinion and order from the bench. He found that Materia had, in fact, traded on the basis of confidential data stolen from Bowne and the offerors. Moreover, he explicitly found that Materia had breached a fiduciary duty to his employer and its clients to maintain their confidences. Finally, he concluded that Materia had actual knowledge of this duty, and thus had acted with scienter.... The court issued a

---

[17] Not wishing to rely solely on the difficulties inherent in deciphering codes and filling in blanks, Bowne had a policy explicitly forbidding its employees from trading on information they might come across in the course of their work. Written statements of this prohibition were posted conspicuously in Bowne's plant, and copies were distributed to all employees.

permanent injunction, restraining him from continuing violations. In addition, Materia was ordered to disgorge his illegally obtained profits of $ 99,862.50. Final judgment was entered on Judge Brieant's order, and Materia timely filed this appeal.

....

III

Materia does not contest the district court's finding that he misappropriated confidential information and traded on it to his advantage. His sole argument is that such activity does not contravene Section 10(b) and Rule 10b-5. In light of this court's holding in *United States v. Newman,* 664 F.2d 12 (2d Cir. 1981), we hold that such actions do, indeed, lie within the proscriptive purview of the antifraud provisions of the securities laws.

Newman addressed the criminal liability under Section 10(b) and Rule 10b-5 of an individual defendant charged with participating in a scheme to misappropriate confidential information regarding upcoming tender offers. Along with his co-conspirators, employees of two investment banking firms, Newman surreptitiously gathered and traded on this nonpublic data. The court held that Newman's "conduct ... could be found to constitute a criminal violation of Section 10(b) and Rule 10b-5...." The facts in the instant appeal are sufficiently similar to those in *Newman* for us to affirm on the authority of that precedent alone. To delineate the contours of what may still be perceived as a novel theory of liability under the antifraud provisions, we choose, however, to elucidate the bases for our holding.

a

... As in *Newman,* "we need spend little time on the issue of fraud and deceit." Materia "misappropriated — stole to put it bluntly — valuable nonpublic information entrusted to him in the utmost confidence." *United States v. Chiarella,* 445 U.S. 222, 245 (Burger, C.J., dissenting). We hold that such activity falls squarely within the "fraud or deceit" language of the Rule. Legislative history to the Securities Exchange Act of 1934 makes clear that the antifraud provision was intended to be broad in scope, encompassing all "manipulative and deceptive practices which have been demonstrated to fulfill no useful function." S. Rep. No. 792, 73d Cong., 2d Sess., 6 (1934). This language negates the suggestion that the provision was aimed solely at the eradication of fraudulent trading by corporate insiders. Against this expansive construction of "fraud or deceit," Materia's theft of information was indeed as fraudulent as if he had converted corporate funds for his personal benefit.

In an effort to circumvent this conclusion, Materia attempts to argue that he could not have defrauded his employer, since he was unaware of the confidential nature of the information he handled in the course of his work. Judge Brieant explicitly found that Bowne's diligent efforts to communicate the need for secrecy vitiated this claim, and the record contains ample support for such a finding. We find similarly unavailing Materia's argument that Bowne was not injured as a result of his misappropriation of client information. Among a financial printer's most valuable assets is its reputation as a safe repository for client secrets. By purloining and trading on confidences entrusted to Bowne, it cannot be gainsaid that Materia undermined his employer's integrity. Accordingly, we are driven to the conclusion that, by his misappropriation of material nonpublic information, Materia perpetrated a fraud upon Bowne.[18]

Such a determination, however, merely begins a tripartite inquiry. We turn next to Materia's contention that the only fraud properly giving rise to an action under 10(b) and 10b-5 is one premised upon a duty to disclose.

b

With the barrage of private civil actions, it is "easy to forget that Section 10(b) was written as both a regulatory and criminal piece of legislation." *Newman, supra,* at 16.... Only by fashioning the private right with which we are by now so familiar, were courts forced to deal with ancillary issues such as standing, and whether a defendant has breached a duty to a particular plaintiff. Indeed, these issues are germane only in the context of private civil litigation. In reviewing an enforcement action such as this, our concern "must be with the scope of the Rule," *Newman, supra,* at 17, rather than the precise direction in which a duty may have been owed. For this reason, Materia's attempted reliance on *Chiarella v. United States,* 445 U.S. 222 (1980), is misplaced.

Chiarella, like Materia, was an employee of a financial printing firm. He, too, divined the identities of tender offer targets from confidential documents and traded on that information for his personal gain. Affirming his criminal conviction under Section 10(b), this court held that Chiarella had breached an affirmative duty to disclose material nonpublic information to those from whom he purchased securities. Additionally, we ruled that liability could be premised upon his having misappropriated the information from his employer and its clients. Although the Supreme Court explicitly reversed on the first theory, holding that the mere possession of confidential information is insufficient to create a duty to disclose that information to those on the other side of the market, it did not similarly disavow the misappropriation theory. Rather, a majority held that the theory could not support Chiarella's conviction because it had not been submitted to the jury. Accordingly, "resolution of this issue [was left] for another day." *Id.* at 238 (Stevens, J., concurring).

---

[18] It is axiomatic that

> an agent is subject to a duty to the principal not to use or communicate information confidentially given to him by the principal or acquired by him during the course of or on account of his agency....

Restatement (Second) of Agency § 359 (1958).

As Judge Pierce made clear at oral argument, in this circuit that day arrived in October 1981, with the filing of the *Newman* decision. We announced then, and reiterate now, that one who misappropriates nonpublic information in breach of a fiduciary duty and trades on that information to his own advantage violates Section 10(b) and Rule 10b-5.

Moss v. Morgan Stanley Co., [719 F.2d 295 (2d Cir. 1983)], relied on by Materia, does not suggest otherwise. That case, arising out of the same facts as *Newman,* was a private action brought by shareholders who unwittingly sold stock to Newman and his cohorts. This court affirmed the dismissal of the action on the same limited grounds announced by the Supreme Court in *Chiarella*. The defendants owed no duty to the plaintiffs. At the risk of repetition, we stress that such analysis bears only on the type of question raised in a private suit for damages; it is not relevant to an inquiry into whether the Rule was or was not contravened.

....

Accordingly, the decision of the district court is

Affirmed.

DIRKS v. SECURITIES AND EXCHANGE COMMISSION

United States Supreme Court
463 U.S. 646 (1983)

JUSTICE POWELL delivered the opinion of the Court.

....

[Raymond] Dirks was an officer of a New York broker-dealer firm who specialized in providing investment analysis of insurance company securities to institutional investors.... Dirks received information from Ronald Secrist, a former officer of Equity Funding of America. Secrist alleged that the assets of Equity Funding, a diversified corporation primarily engaged in selling life insurance and mutual funds, were vastly overstated as the result of fraudulent corporate practices.... He urged Dirks to verify the fraud and disclose it publicly.

[Dirks investigated, and as he did so "he openly discussed the information he had obtained with a number of clients and investors," some of whom sold Equity Funding securities. After the Equity Funding fraud came to light publicly, the Securities and Exchange Commission censured Dirks after determining that he had aided and abetted violations of Rule 10b-5 "by repeating the allegations of fraud to members of the investment community." The court of appeals affirmed the decision of the SEC, and the Supreme Court granted certiorari.]

We were explicit in *Chiarella* in saying that there can be no duty to disclose where the person who has traded on inside information "was not [the corporation's] agent, ... was not a fiduciary, [or] was not a person in whom the sellers [of the securities] had placed their trust and confidence." Not to require such a fiduciary relationship, we recognized, would "depar[t] radically from the established doctrine that duty arises from a specific relationship between two parties" and would amount to "recognizing a general duty between all participants in market transactions to forgo actions based on material, nonpublic information." This requirement of a specific relationship between the shareholders and the individual trading on inside information has created analytical difficulties for the SEC and courts in policing tippees who trade on inside information. Unlike insiders who have independent fiduciary duties to both the corporation and its shareholders, the typical tippee has no such relationships.[19] In view of this absence, it has been unclear how a tippee acquires the ... duty to refrain from trading on inside information.

....

In determining whether a tippee is under an obligation to disclose or abstain, it ... is necessary to determine whether the insider's "tip" constituted a breach of the insider's fiduciary duty [, and the test for this] is whether the insider personally will benefit ... from his disclosure....

... This requires courts to focus on objective criteria, *i.e.,* whether the insider receives a direct or indirect personal benefit from the disclosure, such as a pecuniary gain or a reputational benefit that will translate into future earnings.... The elements of fiduciary duty and exploitation of nonpublic information also exist when an insider makes a gift of confidential information to a trading relative or friend....

....

Under the insider-trading and tipping rules set forth above, we find that there was no actionable violation by Dirks.... Unless the insiders breached their ... duty to shareholders in disclosing the nonpublic information to Dirks, he breached no duty when he passed it on to investors....

It is clear that neither Secrist nor the other Equity Funding employees violated their ... duty to the corporation's shareholders by providing information to Dirks.... As the facts of this case clearly indicate, the tippers were motivated by a desire to expose the fraud. In the absence of a breach of duty to shareholders by the insiders, there was no derivative breach by Dirks....

....

---

[19] Under certain circumstances, such as where corporate information is revealed legitimately to an underwriter, accountant, lawyer, or consultant working for the corporation, these outsiders may become fiduciaries of the shareholders. The basis for recognizing this fiduciary duty is not simply that such persons acquired nonpublic corporate information, but rather that they have entered into a special confidential relationship in the conduct of the business of the enterprise and are given access to information solely for corporate purposes. When such a person breaches his fiduciary relationship, he may be treated more properly as a tipper than a tippee. For such a duty to be imposed, however, the corporation must expect the outsider to keep the disclosed nonpublic information confidential, and the relationship at least must imply such a duty.

UNITED STATES v. BRYAN

United States Court of Appeals, Fourth Circuit
58 F.3d 933 (1995)

LUTTIG, CIRCUIT JUDGE:

Appellant, Elton "Butch" Bryan, is a former director of the West Virginia Lottery. In September 1993, a federal jury in Charleston, West Virginia found Bryan guilty of ... one count of securities fraud in violation of [Exchange Act section 10(b) and Rule 10b-5. This conviction] stemmed from ... Bryan's use of confidential, non-public information in the purchase of securities of companies doing business with the West Virginia Lottery....

....

I

....

Bryan's [conviction] for securities fraud [was] based upon his trading in the shares of companies doing business with the West Virginia Lottery. In 1991 and 1992, Bryan purchased shares of [International Game Technology] and GTech, both of which were bidding for valuable contracts before the Lottery, and in September 1992, soon after the decision had been made to select [Video Lottery Consultants] as the exclusive supplier of terminals in the statewide expansion of video lottery, Bryan purchased 300 shares of [Video Lottery Consultants] stock. Bryan made all of these trades on the basis of nonpublic, confidential information entrusted to him in his capacity as Lottery Director.

....

IV

Bryan ... challenges his conviction for securities fraud under section 10(b) of the Securities Exchange Act of 1934 and Rule 10b-5. The government proceeded against Bryan under the so-called "misappropriation theory" of securities fraud liability, a theory that, although novel to this circuit, has been embraced by the Second, Seventh, and Ninth Circuits. *See United States v. Newman*, 664 F.2d 12 (2d Cir. 1981); *United States v. Chestman*, 947 F.2d 551 (2d Cir. 1991) (*en banc*); *SEC v. Cherif*, 933 F.2d 403 (7th Cir. 1991); *SEC v. Clark*, 915 F.2d 439 (9th Cir. 1990).[20] The Supreme Court has yet to address whether the misappropriation theory is reconcilable with the language and purposes of section 10(b) and Rule 10b-5, having evenly divided on the validity of a conviction based on this theory in *Carpenter v. United States*, 484 U.S. 19, 24. *See also Chiarella v.*

---

[20] As do many of the courts that have addressed the misappropriation theory, the government also identifies the Third Circuit as having adopted the theory, *citing Rothberg v. Rosenbloom*, 771 F.2d 818 (3d Cir. 1985), *rev'd after remand*, 808 F.2d 252 (1986). The court in *Rothberg*, however, merely adverted to the theory in a single sentence, and even then, not by name.

United States, 445 U.S. 222, 235-36 (1980) (declining to address merit of misappropriation theory because theory not submitted to jury).

We conclude that neither the language of section 10(b), Rule 10b-5, the Supreme Court authority interpreting these provisions, nor the purposes of these securities fraud prohibitions, will support convictions resting on the particular theory of misappropriation adopted by our sister circuits. Section 10(b), insofar as concerns us, prohibits only the use of deception, in the form of material misrepresentations or omissions, to induce action or inaction by purchasers or sellers of securities, or that affects others with a vested interest in a securities transaction. In contravention of this established principle, the misappropriation theory authorizes criminal conviction for simple breaches of fiduciary duty and similar relationships of trust and confidence, whether or not the breaches entail deception within the meaning of section 10(b) and whether or not the parties wronged by the breaches were purchasers or sellers of securities, or otherwise connected with or interested in the purchase or sale of securities. Finding no authority for such an expansion of securities fraud liability indeed, finding the theory irreconcilable with applicable Supreme Court precedent we reject application of the theory in this circuit. We hold therefore that the district court plainly erred in instructing the jury that it could convict Bryan of securities fraud on the basis of the misappropriation theory of Rule 10b-5 liability.

A

Those courts that have adopted the misappropriation theory with which we are concerned in this case have read section 10(b) and Rule 10b-5 to authorize the criminal conviction of a person who

> (1) misappropriates material nonpublic information (2) by breaching a duty arising out of a relationship of trust and confidence and (3) uses that information in a securities transaction, (4) regardless of whether he owed any duties to the shareholders of the traded stock.

Clark, 915 F.2d at 443. Under this misappropriation theory, the "fraud" requirement of Rule 10b-5 is deemed to be satisfied when a person "misappropriates material nonpublic information in breach of a fiduciary duty or similar relationship of trust and confidence." *Chestman*, 947 F.2d at 566. The source of the nonpublic information need not be a purchaser or seller of securities, be affiliated with a purchaser or seller, or be in any way connected to or even interested in the purchase or sale of securities. Even though the defendant owes no duty of disclosure to the purchaser or seller of the securities, the completed fraud (*i.e.*, the misappropriation) is deemed to be "in connection with the purchase or sale of [a] security," because the misappropriated information is thereafter used in a securities transaction.

. . . .

Manipulation and deception are the touchstones of section 10(b) liability: "The language of § 10(b) gives no indication that Congress meant to prohibit any conduct not involving manipulation or deception." *Santa Fe Indus., Inc. v. Green*, 430 U.S. 462, 473 (1977). Section 10(b) thus makes it "unlawful for any person ... to use or employ, in connection with the purchase or sale of any security ... any *manipulative* or *deceptive* device or contrivance," in contravention of SEC rules. (emphasis added) For purposes of assessing the validity of the misappropriation theory, we need focus solely on the scope of the statutory phrase "deception" "in connection with" a securities transaction and the Rule 10b-5 phrase "fraud" "in connection with" a securities transaction, because "manipulation" is "virtually a term of art" in the securities context, *see Santa Fe Indus.*, 430 U.S. at 476 (*quoting Ernst & Ernst v. Hochfelder*, 425 U.S. 185, 199 (1976)), referencing "practices, such as wash sales, matched orders, or rigged prices," that are "intended to mislead investors by artificially affecting market activity," *id*. Our specific concern is whether the Rule's prohibition of "fraud" "in connection with the purchase or sale of any security," which can be read no more broadly than the statutory prohibition of "deception" "in connection with the purchase or sale of any security," *see infra* note 17, may extend to breaches of fiduciary duty involving the misappropriation of confidential information from one who is neither a purchaser nor seller of securities, or otherwise connected with a securities transaction.

....

In light of the [Supreme] Court's consistent interpretation of section 10(b) as proscribing only the deception, by material misrepresentation or omission, of a purchaser or seller of securities, or of a person in some way connected with or having a stake in an actual or proposed purchase or sale of securities, we believe that the misappropriation theory cannot be defended. Although the misappropriation of information in breach of a fiduciary duty may, in a generalized sense, involve deception, in most cases such misappropriation will not constitute a "misrepresentation" or "nondisclosure." In any event, by its own terms, the misappropriation theory does not even require deception, but rather allows the imposition of liability upon the mere breach of a fiduciary relationship or similar relationship of trust and confidence. Such a theory obviously cannot be squared with the holding of *Santa Fe Industries* that a breach of fiduciary duty, even in connection with a purchase or sale of securities, does not give rise to liability under section 10(b), absent deception.

Even if the misappropriation theory required deception, or deception were otherwise present, the theory still does not require deception violative of a duty of fair representation or disclosure owed to a market participant, *i.e.*, deception in connection with a purchase or sale of securities. Section 10(b), it bears repeating, reaches only deception of persons with some connection to, or some interest or stake in, an actual or proposed purchase or sale of securities. The misappropriation of information from an individual who is in no way connected to, or even interested in, securities is simply not the kind of conduct with which the securities laws, as presently written, are concerned.[21] In essence, the misappropriation theory disregards the specific statutory requirement of deception, in favor of a requirement of a mere fiduciary breach, and then artificially divides into two discrete requirements — *a* fiduciary breach and *a* purchase or sale of securities — the single indivisible requirement of deception upon the purchaser or seller of securities, or upon some other person intimately linked with or affected by a securities transaction. In so doing, the theory effectively eliminates the requirement that a person in some way connected to a securities transaction be deceived, allowing conviction not only where the "defrauded" person has no connection with a securities transaction, but where no investor or market participant has been deceived. In allowing the statute's unitary requirement to be satisfied by any fiduciary breach (whether or not it entails deceit) that is followed by a securities transaction (whether or not the breach is of a duty owed to a purchaser or seller of securities, or to another market participant), the misappropriation theory transforms section 10(b) from a rule intended to govern and protect relations among market participants who are owed duties under the securities laws into a federal common law governing and protecting any and all trust relationships. If, as the Supreme Court has held, the fraud-on-the-market theory is insupportable because section 10(b) does not ensure equal information to all investors, *Chiarella*, 445 U.S. at 233-34, *a fortiori* such a general fraud-on-the-source theory in pursuit of the same parity of information cannot be defended.

Though the text of section 10(b) as interpreted by the Supreme Court is itself a sufficient basis upon which to reject the misappropriation theory, the principles that inform interpretation of the securities fraud provisions also counsel rejection of the theory. The Supreme Court has repeatedly emphasized that the securities

---

[21] Those courts that have adopted the misappropriation theory have reconciled the theory with the statute's requirement that deception occur "in connection with the purchase or sale of any security" by concluding that the deception need only "touch" a securities transaction, *citing* dicta from *Superintendent of Ins. v. Bankers Life & Casualty Co.*, 404 U.S. 6, 12-13 (1971) ("The crux of the present case is that Manhattan suffered an injury as a result of deceptive practices *touching* its sale of securities as an investor." (emphasis added)).

Not only can the isolated passage from *Bankers Life* not fairly be read to eliminate the requirement of fraud upon a purchaser or seller, or some other person linked to a securities transaction, it would not occur to us to so read it, given that the fraud victim in *Bankers Life* was the seller of securities, who suffered injuries "as an investor." *Bankers Life*, 404 U.S. at 10. In fact, in *Bankers Life* the Court stated its understanding that section 10(b) only "bar[red] deceptive devices and contrivances *in the purchase or sale of* securities." *Id.* at 12 (emphasis added). We therefore remain as skeptical today as we were a decade ago about reading too much into the "touch" language of *Bankers Life*:

> The *Bankers Life* "*de minimis* touch test" might be read literally and expansively to make any securities transaction actionable under Rule 10b-5 so long as there was some deceptive practice remotely "touching" the transaction. But we think the test could not have been intended to be applied in so unlimited a way.

Head v. Head, 759 F.2d 1172, 1175 (4th Cir. 1985).

market "demands certainty and predictability," *Central Bank of Denver* [, *N.A. v. First Interstate Bank of Denver, N.A.*, 114 S.Ct. 1439, 1454 (1994)].... Absent clearly defined rules, investors find themselves the targets of *ad hoc* decisionmaking or pawns in an overall litigation strategy known only to the SEC.

It would be difficult to overstate the uncertainty that has been introduced into the already uncertain law governing fraudulent securities transactions through adoption of the misappropriation theory, with its linchpin the breach of a fiduciary duty.... Indeed, although fifteen years have passed since the theory's inception, no court adopting the misappropriation theory has offered a principled basis for distinguishing which types of fiduciary or similar relationships of trust and confidence can give rise to Rule 10b-5 liability and which cannot. After repeatedly grappling with its own misappropriation theory, the only guidance that the Second Circuit has been able to provide, apart from its observation that the misappropriation theory rests on general notions of "dependency and influence," [*Chestman*, 947 F.2d] at 569, is that it "will not apply outer permutations of chancery relief in addressing" whether a fiduciary duty or similar relationship of trust and confidence has been breached, *id.* at 570.

Thus far, the misappropriation theory has been invoked by federal prosecutors and securities regulators to regulate such diverse relationships as that between an employer and employee, between an employer and an employee's tippees, between a newspaper and its reporters, between an employer and a former employee, between a psychiatrist and his patient, between a husband and wife, between a father and son, and, as in this case, between a government official and his constituency. If a categorical rule applicable to each class of relationship were possible, the scope of the theory would yet be broad. But whether a fiduciary or similar relationship of trust and confidence will be held to exist can be expected to vary from state to state, from family to family, from employer to employer, and from division to division and even from employee to employee within a single employer. Moreover, while the courts adopting the misappropriation theory incant that the breach of a fiduciary relationship is a necessary element of the offense, in principle, if not in reality, these courts would be obliged to find liability in the case of simple theft by an employee, even where no fiduciary duty has been breached, for the *raison d'etre* of the misappropriation theory in fact is concern over "the unfairness inherent in trading on [stolen] information." *Chiarella*, 445 U.S. at 241 (Burger, C.J., dissenting).

The only alternative to the inevitable patchwork of criminal standards that will develop under the theory would be the effective federalization of relationships historically regulated by the states. The superimposition of a "federal fiduciary principle," *Santa Fe Indus.*, 430 U.S. at 479, however, would usurp the states' common law and statutory authority over fiduciary relationships, violating the Court's injunction in *Santa Fe Industries* against use of the federal securities laws to regulate areas of conduct "traditionally relegated to state law." Though there may well be a need for uniform federal standards governing the handling of confidential, market-sensitive information within the many common-law relationships customarily regulated by state law, the Court has instructed that such standards "should not be supplied by judicial extension of § 10(b) and Rule 10b-5 to 'cover the corporate universe.'" *Id.* at 480.

....

Accordingly, we hold that criminal liability under section 10(b) cannot be predicated upon the mere misappropriation of information in breach of a fiduciary duty owed to one who is neither a purchaser nor seller of securities, or in any other way connected with, or financially interested in, an actual or proposed purchase or sale of securities, even when such a breach is followed by the purchase or sale of securities. Such conduct simply does not constitute fraud in connection with the purchase or sale of securities, within the meaning of section 10(b). Section 10(b) is not concerned with the general fairness of securities transactions themselves, so long as there is no evidence of deception in connection with a securities transaction, in the form of material misrepresentations or omissions made to persons connected with a securities transaction. It should come as no surprise that the provision is unconcerned with the fairness of conduct toward persons such as family members, employers, medical patients, or other parties to the infinite number of similar trust relationships who are not in any way connected with or even interested in a purchase or sale of securities.

B

We do not believe that rejection of the particular misappropriation theory that we address today will ultimately have a notable impact on federal efforts to combat fraud in the securities markets. Much of the conduct rendered criminal under the misappropriation theory is already criminalized under section 10(b) as interpreted in *Chiarella* and *Dirks* [*v. SEC*, 463 U.S. 646 (1983)], or under the mail and wire fraud statutes, 18 U.S.C. §§ 1341, 1343, as interpreted by the Court in *Carpenter* and as expanded by Congress in 18 U.S.C. § 1346.

Many of the people who would fall within the ambit of the misappropriation theory urged in this case already owe a duty to purchasers and sellers of securities to disclose or abstain from trading, duties recognized by the Supreme Court in *Chiarella* and *Dirks* as legitimate predicates for criminal liability under section 10(b)....

Those who trade on purloined information but who do not come within the *Chiarella/Dirks* definition of "insider" are still almost certain to be subject to criminal liability for federal mail or wire fraud. Under *Carpenter's* expansive notion of "fraud," the embezzlement of confidential information, coupled with the use of mail or wire to execute a securities transaction, will likely be sufficient to establish criminal liability under sections 1341 and 1343. *Carpenter* itself, in which the Court unanimously affirmed the defendant's wire fraud convictions but divided evenly over the securities fraud conviction, is illustrative.

Congress' recent adoption of 18 U.S.C. § 1346, which prohibits "a scheme or artifice to deprive another of the intangible right of honest services," further ensures that many of the fiduciary breaches giving rise to criminal liability under the misappropriation theory may also serve as the predicate fraud under the mail and wire fraud statutes, leaving only the use of wire or the mails to complete the crime. Finally, we are also confident that the fiduciary breaches proscribed by the misappropriation theory will in many instances give rise to criminal and civil liability under the array of state laws addressing fraud and unethical conduct.

....

CENTRAL BANK OF DENVER, N. A. v. FIRST INTERSTATE BANK OF DENVER, N. A.

United States Supreme Court
511 U.S. 164 (1994)

JUSTICE KENNEDY delivered the opinion of the Court.

As we have interpreted it, § 10(b) of the Securities Exchange Act of 1934 imposes private civil liability on those who commit a manipulative or deceptive act in connection with the purchase or sale of securities. In this case, we must answer a question reserved in two earlier decisions: whether private civil liability under § 10(b) extends as well to those who do not engage in the manipulative or deceptive practice but who aid and abet the violation.

....

II

....

With respect ... to ... the scope of conduct prohibited by § 10(b), the text of the statute controls our decision. In § 10(b), Congress prohibited manipulative or deceptive acts in connection with the purchase or sale of securities. It envisioned that the SEC would enforce the statutory prohibition through administrative and injunctive actions. Of course, a private plaintiff now may bring suit against violators of § 10(b). But the private plaintiff may not bring a 10b-5 suit against a defendant for acts not prohibited by the text of § 10(b)....

....

Our consideration of statutory duties, especially in cases interpreting § 10(b), establishes that the statutory text controls the definition of conduct covered by § 10(b). That bodes ill for respondents, for "the language of Section 10(b) does not in terms mention aiding and abetting." Brief for SEC as *Amicus Curiae* 8....

Congress knew how to impose aiding and abetting liability when it chose to do so. If, as respondents seem to say, Congress intended to impose aiding and abetting liability, we presume it would have used the words "aid" and "abet" in the statutory text. But it did not.

We reach the uncontroversial conclusion, accepted even by those courts recognizing a § 10(b) aiding and abetting cause of action, that the text of the 1934 Act does not itself reach those who aid and abet a § 10(b) violation. Unlike those courts, however, we think that conclusion resolves the case. It is inconsistent with settled methodology in § 10(b) cases to extend liability beyond the scope of conduct prohibited by the statutory text. To be sure, aiding and abetting a wrongdoer ought to be actionable in certain instances. The issue, however, is not whether imposing private civil liability on aiders and abettors is good policy but whether aiding and abetting is covered by the statute.

As in earlier cases considering conduct prohibited by § 10(b), we again conclude that the statute prohibits only the making of a material misstatement (or omission) or the commission of a manipulative act. The proscription does not include giving aid to a person who commits a manipulative or deceptive act. We cannot amend the statute to create liability for acts that are not themselves manipulative or deceptive within the meaning of the statute.

....

As a result of the *Central Bank* case, it was uncertain whether the SEC had authority to bring aiding and abetting actions for Rule 10b-5 violations (and, indeed, for other violations). This uncertainty was cleared up when Congress amended Exchange Act Section 20 to give the SEC such power in the case of any violation of an Exchange Act section or rule. (There never has been a question about the Justice Department's ability to bring criminal aiding and abetting actions for Exchange Act violations, because 18 U.S.C. § 2 creates aiding and abetting liability in the case of all federal crimes.)

F. ISSUER'S DUTY TO DISCLOSE

The *Texas Gulf Sulphur* case, which begins this chapter, involved, among other things, the duty of an issuer of publicly held securities to disclose, in certain circumstances, material inside information relating to the issuer. The following case serves as a further beneficial introduction to the tricky questions involved in this area of Rule 10b-5 law.

STRANSKY v. CUMMINS ENGINE CO.

United States Court of Appeals, Seventh Circuit
51 F.3d 1329 (1995)

KANNE, CIRCUIT JUDGE.

The predicate for this case is a familiar one: a company makes optimistic predictions about future performance, the predictions turn out to be less than prophetic, and shareholders cry foul, or more specifically, fraud. Alan Stransky and Raphael Warkel filed a class action suit against Cummins Engine Company, Inc. (Cummins), alleging securities fraud. The district court dismissed with prejudice....

Cummins is a leading designer and manufacturer of inline and v-type diesel engines. Because of new emissions standards promulgated by the U.S. Environmental Protection Agency, in 1988 Cummins began producing redesigned engines. Stransky claims that "in internal technical memoranda, Cummins admitted that it had 'rushed' its design and production to comply with the new standards, that there was insufficient time for evaluation of the engines, and that the technical division had relied too much on the testing of prototype hardware rather than on the testing of the final production product." Cummins typically warranted its engines for two years or 100,000 miles, whichever came first.

Stransky alleges that beginning in the fall of 1988 and extending through the spring of 1989, Cummins' board of directors was informed that the newly designed engines were experiencing problems due to faulty design and that costs associated with fixing the engines (warranty costs) were rising....

Of course, to state a securities fraud claim, Stransky must allege fraud. To this end, Stransky alleges that during the fall of 1988, the directors of Cummins became concerned that the Hanson Group (USA) Ltd. (Hanson), a known corporate takeover company, was preparing a hostile takeover. To thwart this effort, the directors conceived a plan known among the directors as "Project Diesel." By March 1989, the directors' research into Hanson indicated that it typically took over companies whose stock was undervalued. As is true in many hostile takeovers, Hanson would fire the company's management and replace them with its own group. Thus, Stransky alleges that in order to entrench themselves against the takeover, the directors plotted to increase the value of Cummins' stock by suppressing the news of the redesigned engines' problems.

Mere silence about even material information is not fraudulent absent a duty to speak. Stransky alleges that Cummins' silence about the rising warranty costs violated SEC Rule 10b-5 because a duty to disclose the warranty problems arose when Cummins made public statements that related to warranty costs and were misleading because of the withheld information about the problems. If one speaks, he must speak the whole truth. In general, to prevail on a Rule 10b-5 claim, a plaintiff must prove that the defendant: 1) made a misstatement or omission, 2) of material fact, 3) with scienter, 4) in connection with the purchase or sale of securities; 5) upon which the plaintiff relied; and 6) that reliance proximately caused the plaintiff's injury. The avenues of proving a false or misleading statement or omission are still uncertain. The most common and obvious method is by demonstrating that the defendant fraudulently made a statement of material fact or omitted a fact necessary to prevent a statement from being misleading. Two other avenues have been kicked around by courts, litigants and academics alike: a "duty to correct" and a "duty to update." Litigants often fail to distinguish between these theories (as did Stransky in this case) and to delineate their exact parameters. The former applies when a company makes a historical statement that, at the time made, the company believed to be true, but as revealed by subsequently discovered information actually was not. The company then must correct the prior statement within a reasonable time. *See, e.g., Backman v. Polaroid Corp.*, 910 F.2d 10, 16-17 (1st Cir. 1990).

Some have argued that a duty to update arises when a company makes a forward-looking[22] statement a projection[23] that because of subsequent events becomes untrue. *See, e.g., Backman*, 910 F.2d at 17. This court has never embraced such a theory, and we decline to do so now.

... The rule implicitly precludes basing liability on circumstances that arise after the speaker makes the statement. In addition, the securities laws typically do not act as a Monday Morning Quarterback. "The securities laws approach matters from an *ex ante* perspective: just as a statement true when made does not become fraudulent because things unexpectedly go wrong, so a statement materially false when made does not become acceptable because it happens to come true." *Pommer v. Medtest Corp.*, 961 F.2d 620, 623 (7th Cir. 1992). These considerations give us serious pause in imposing a duty to update.[24]

Courts differ on how they examine forward-looking statements. One method, adopted by the Fourth Circuit, has focused on the requirement that the misleading statement be material. In *Howard v. Haddad*, 962 F.3d 328 (4th Cir. 1992), Howard claimed that Haddad induced him, through misrepresentations, to buy stock in a bank that subsequently went under. The alleged misrepresentations were statements by Haddad "that it was a growing bank, and that it was [a] good investment." The Fourth Circuit held that such "puffery" could not lead to liability because it "lacks the materiality essential to a securities fraud allegation." In *Raab v. General Physics Corp.*, 4 F.3d 286 (4th Cir. 1993), the Fourth Circuit expanded on this rationale by stating, "'Soft,' 'puffing' statements ... generally lack materiality because the market price of a share is not inflated by vague statements predicting growth.... No reasonable investor would rely on those statements, and they are certainly not specific enough to perpetrate a fraud on the market."[25]

While it often may be the case that predictions of growth are not material, we hesitate to impose a *per se* rule to this effect. The Supreme Court has cautioned

---

[22] No duty to update an historical statement can logically exist. By definition an historical statement is addressing only matters at the time of the statement. Thus, that circumstances subsequently change cannot render an historical statement false or misleading. Absent a duty to speak, a company cannot commit fraud by failing to disclose changed circumstances, with respect to a historical statement.

[23] As Stransky contests only statements that were predictions or projections about the performance of Cummins' products, we limit our analysis to whether a duty to update such predictions exists. We express no opinion on whether the outcome would be the same if a plaintiff contested statements of intent to take a certain action.

[24] SEC Rule 175 provides a safe harbor for forward-looking statements contained in certain documents that are filed with the SEC. The SEC is currently considering expanding the safe harbor to include forward-looking statements in non-filed statements. [Congress provided this expansion in Exchange Act Section 21E. Eds.]

[25] Other circuits have similarly held that predictions about future performance are not material under Rule 10b-5. *See, e.g., Krim v. BancTexas Group, Inc.*, 989 F.2d 1435, 1446 (5th Cir. 1993); *Friedman v. Mohasco Corp.*, 929 F.2d 77, 79 (2nd Cir. 1991).

that materiality is typically an issue to be resolved by the finder of fact. A blanket rule that forward-looking statements are not material does not allow for the contextual, fact-specific nature of the inquiry and would potentially allow companies to engage in conjecture with impunity.

Moreover, current SEC policy contradicts the rationale that investors do not rely *at all* on projections. Until the late 1970s, SEC policy forbade companies from making forward-looking statements in mandatory disclosure documents. After years of study and public comment, in 1978 the SEC reversed itself and adopted a policy that encouraged disclosure of management projections....

Another avenue of analysis is available. In *Virginia Bankshares, Inc. v. Sandberg*, 501 U.S. 1083 (1991), the Supreme Court held that statements by a board of directors of reasons for taking action and statements of present opinion or belief are statements "with respect to ... material facts" within the meaning of SEC Rule 14(a)-9. The Court reasoned that, "such statements are factual in two senses: as statements that the directors do act for the reasons given or hold the belief stated and as statements about the subject matter of the reason or belief expressed."

Applying this framework to forward-looking statements, in *Kowal v. MCI Communications Corp.*, 16 F.3d 1271 (D.C. Cir. 1994), the D.C. Circuit stated that the "only truly factual elements involved in a projection are the implicit representations that the statements are made in good faith and with a reasonable basis." (Internal quotations and citations omitted.) We believe this is correct. This analysis remains true to the wording of the rule, as well as limiting liability to the small number of statements that are most harmful in the marketplace. Thus, a projection can lead to liability under Rule 10b-5 only if it was not made in good faith or was made without a reasonable basis. With this discussion in mind, we turn to the facts of the case before us.

....

We first look to the complaint to determine whether Stransky has alleged facts that, if true, could lead to Rule 10b-5 liability under any theory. The complaint, as it relates to Stransky, alleges that four press releases lead to liability.... Nothing in [two of the] press releases related directly to warranty costs, and therefore Stransky cannot rely on them for alleging that Cummins violated Rule 10b-5.

Stransky also alleges that two April press releases can support liability. The complaint alleges the following about an April 4, 1989 press release.

43. [The press release] indicated that Cummins expected its First Quarter earnings to exceed $ 1.50 per share and that Second Quarter results were expected to be stronger than the First Quarter. The press release further stated that the shift by the Company to sales of their new engines had a dramatic influence on profitability since each of these products were coming down on their cost curves and were making progress toward their targets. As set forth above, however, the new engines were, in fact, beginning to

show design defects and increased product and warranty costs from January to April of 1989.

Stransky admits in the next paragraph of the complaint that Cummins' expectations about First Quarter earnings were correct, and therefore the statement concerning earnings per share cannot lead to liability. However, the press release also made two historical statements that may relate to warranty costs: that the engines "were coming down on their cost curves," and that the engines "were making progress toward their targets." These statements, at least as represented in the complaint, are ambiguous. We can think of at least four ways in which "cost curves" can be interpreted. It could refer to only production costs, as the district court seems to have concluded, in which case warranty costs would indeed be unrelated. On the other hand, it could refer to overall costs of a product, which conceivably, although not necessarily, include warranty costs. If warranty costs were rising so precipitously as to outweigh the decrease in other costs, thereby causing overall costs to rise, the statement could be false. Additionally, "cost curves" was stated in the plural; this could lead to two additional interpretations. One can imagine a company breaking up its overall cost curve into its derivative costs (*i.e.*, raw materials, labor, marketing, warranty, among others) and charting and following these more particularized costs. Thus, "cost curves" could have referred to each of these derivative costs. However, the plural could have stemmed from the press releases' discussion of multiple products. The statement is unclear. What is clear is that on a motion to dismiss we should make all reasonable inferences in favor of Stransky and should not resolve the interpretation of the press release against Stransky. Similarly, if Cummins had "targets" for its warranty costs, as suggested in the complaint, then the fact that warranty costs were rising could make incorrect the statement that the engines were making progress toward their targets.

The complaint also recounts an April 20, 1989 press release that "indicated that B & C engines were now profitable and that profit margins on these engines should improve as the costs of these engines continued to decline." This statement appears to contain one historical statement, that the costs of the engines are now declining, and two predictions, 1) that profit margins should improve, and 2) that the costs of the engines should decline from current levels. The analysis of the historical statement alleged here follows that set out above and will not be repeated. The forward-looking statements can lead to liability only if they were unreasonable in light of the facts known at the time (and such unreasonableness was due to rising warranty costs as Stransky has alleged no other reason) or they were not made in good faith. We must remand to the district court for further resolution of these issues.

....

G. DAMAGES AND PENALTIES

ELKIND v. LIGGETT & MYERS, INC.

United States Court of Appeals, Second Circuit
635 F.2d 156 (1980)

MANSFIELD, CIRCUIT JUDGE.

This case presents a number of issues arising out of what has become a form of corporate brinkmanship — non-public disclosure of business-related information to financial analysts. The action is a class suit by Arnold B. Elkind on behalf of certain purchasers ... of the stock of Liggett & Myers, Inc. (Liggett) against it. They seek damages for alleged failure of its officers to disclose certain material information with respect to its earnings and operations and for their alleged wrongful tipping of inside information to certain persons who then sold Liggett shares on the open market.

... The [district] court found ... that on July 10, 1972, and July 17, 1972, officers of Liggett disclosed material inside information to individual financial analysts, leading to sale of Liggett stock by investors to whom this information was conveyed. Damages were computed on the basis of the difference between the price which members of the plaintiff class (uninformed buyers of Liggett stock between the time of the first tip and subsequent public disclosure) paid and what the stock sold for after the later disclosure....

....

Liggett is a diversified company, with traditional business in the tobacco industry supplemented by acquisitions in such industries as liquor (Paddington Corp., importer of J&B Scotch), pet food (Allen Products Co. and Perk Foods Co., manufacturer of Alpo dog food), cereal, watchbands, cleansers and rugs. Its common stock is listed on the New York Stock Exchange.

In 1969 Liggett officers concluded that the company's stock was underpriced, due in part to lack of appreciation in the financial community for the breadth of its market activity. To cure this perceived deficiency, Liggett initiated an "analyst program," hiring a public relations firm and encouraging closer contact between analysts and company management. This included meetings with analysts at which Liggett officials discussed operations. Liggett also reviewed and commented on reports which the analysts were preparing, to correct errors and other misunderstandings.

Liggett had a record year in 1971, with earnings of $ 4.22 per share (up from $ 3.56 in 1970). The first quarter of 1972 was equally auspicious. On March 22, Liggett issued a press release reporting that sales of the non-tobacco lines had continued to increase in the first two months, but noting that current stockpiling of J&B Scotch by customers (in anticipation of a price increase) could affect sales. On May 3, 1972, the company released its first quarter figures, showing earnings of $ 1.00 per share (compared to $ .81 in the first quarter of 1971).

This quarterly operations report led to considerable optimism in the financial community over Liggett's prospects. Management did nothing to deflate the enthusiasm. A number of reports containing predictions that 1972 earnings would increase about 10% over 1971 earnings were reviewed by officials of Liggett during the first five months of 1972. While company personnel corrected factual errors in these reports, they did not comment (or make noncommittal or evasive comments) on the earnings projections, according to the findings below, which are supported by the record. At group meetings with analysts in February and March, management indicated that it was making "good progress" with certain products and that it was "well-positioned" to take advantage of industry trends. At the end of March, Liggett successfully made a public offering of $ 50 million of debentures. At an April 25 stockholders' meeting, Liggett's Executive Vice President expressed general optimism that the company was continuing to make good progress. On May 3, the first quarter earnings were released. At a May 16 meeting with analysts in New York, officials reiterated their vague but quieting pronouncements. Similar comments, to the effect that 1972 was expected to be a "good year," were voiced at a June 5 presentation in London.

Despite the company's outward appearance of strength, Liggett's management was less sanguine intramurally. Internal budget projections called for only a two percent increase in earnings in 1972. In April and May, a full compilation of updated figures was ordered, and new projections were presented to the Board of Directors on May 15[.] April was marked by a sharp decline, with earnings of only $ .03 per share (compared to $ .30 the previous April). The 1972 earnings projection was revised downward from $ 4.30 to $ 3.95 per share. May earnings, which the Board received on June 19, rebounded somewhat to $ .23 per share (compared to $ .27 in May 1971 and original budget projections of $ .34). At meetings with analysts during this period, Liggett officials took a more negative tone, emphasizing, for example, various cost pressures. There was no public disclosure of the adverse financial developments at this time. Beginning in late June, 1972, the price of Liggett's common stock steadily declined.

On July 17, preliminary earnings data for June and six-month totals became available to the Board of Directors. June earnings were $ .20 per share (compared to $ .44 in June 1971). The first half earnings for 1972 were approximately $ 1.46 per share, down from $ 1.82 the previous year. The Board decided to issue a press release the following day. That release, issued at about 2:15 P.M. on July 18, disclosed the preliminary earnings figures and attributed the decline to shortcomings in all of Liggett's product lines.

The district court found two "tips" of material inside information in the days before the July 18 press release. On July 10, analyst Peter Barry of Kuhn Loeb & Co. spoke by telephone with Daniel Provost, Liggett's Director of Corporate Communications. According to Barry's deposition testimony, apparently adopted by the court below, Provost confirmed Barry's suggestions that J&B sales were slowing due to earlier stockpiling and that a new competing dog food was affecting Alpo sales adversely. Barry asked if a projection of a 10% earnings decline would be realistic, and received what he characterized as a noncommittal response. Barry testified that Provost told him that a preliminary earnings statement would be coming out in a week or so. Since Barry knew of no prior instances in which Liggett had issued such a preliminary statement, he deduced that the figures would be lower than expected. Barry sent a wire ... to Kuhn Loeb's offices. The information was conveyed to three clients. Two of them, holders of a total of over 600,000 shares did not sell. A third client sold the 100 shares he owned. No other Kuhn Loeb customers sold between the time of the July 10 "tip" and the release of preliminary earnings figures on July 18; Kuhn Loeb customers bought some 5,000 shares during this period.

The second "tip" occurred on July 17, one day before the preliminary earnings figures for the first half were released. Analyst Robert Cummins of Loeb Rhoades & Co. questioned Ralph Moore, Liggett's chief financial officer, about the recent decline in price of Liggett's common stock, as well as performance of the various subsidiaries. According to Cummins' deposition, he asked Moore whether there was a good possibility that earnings would be down, and received an affirmative ("grudging") response. Moore added that this information was confidential. Cummins sent a wire to his firm, and spoke with a stockholder who promptly sold 1,800 shares of Liggett stock on behalf of his customers.

The district court held that each of these disclosures was a tip of material information in violation of Rule 10b-5, rendering Liggett liable to all persons who bought the company's stock during the period from July 11 to July 18, 1972, inclusive, without knowledge of the tipped information. However, the court rejected plaintiff's claims that Liggett was under a legal obligation to correct the analysts' earlier erroneous predictions, relying on this court's decision in *Electronic Specialty Co. v. International Controls Corp.*, 409 F.2d 937 (2d Cir. 1969). It also rejected plaintiff's claims that Liggett's earlier statements to analysts and stockholders were misrepresentations and that Liggett was under a duty to issue a preliminary earnings statement in June when it received its May figures.

In computing damages for the July 10 and 17 tips, the court attempted to award the difference between the amount plaintiff class members paid for their stock and the value they received. The latter was interpreted to be the price at which the stock would have sold had there been public disclosure of the tipped information. The court ruled that plaintiff's expert testimony on this point was speculative and unsupported by the record. Instead, following *Mitchell v. Texas Gulf Sulphur Co.*, 446 F.2d 90 (10th Cir.), it looked to the actual market price at the end of "a reasonable period" (eight trading days) following the July 18 release of earnings figures as an approximation of what the price would have been had the tipped information been disclosed publicly. Thus damages amounted to the difference between the plaintiff class members' purchase prices (generally in the vicinity of $ 60 per share) and $ 43, the price of the stock eight trading days after disclosure. Based on the total volume of trading transactions from July 11 to July 18, the court awarded damages amounting to $ 740,000 on condition that any unclaimed portion would revert to Liggett. To this the court added prejudgment interest of approximately $ 300,000.

....

Discussion

....

Damages

This case presents a question of measurement of damages which we have previously deferred, believing that damages are best addressed in a concrete setting. *See Shapiro v. Merrill Lynch, Pierce, Fenner & Smith, Inc.,* [495 F.2d 228, 241-42 (2d Cir. 1974)]. We ruled in *Shapiro* that defendants selling on inside information would be liable to those who bought on the open market and sustained "substantial losses" during the period of insider trading.[26]

The district court looked to the measure of damages used in cases where a buyer was induced to purchase a company's stock by materially misleading statements or omissions. In such cases of fraud by a fiduciary intended to induce others to buy or sell stock the accepted measure of damages is the "out-of-pocket" measure. This consists of the difference between the price paid and the "value" of the stock when [bought] (or when the buyer committed himself to buy, if earlier).[27] Except in rare face-to-face transactions, however, uninformed traders on an open, impersonal market are not induced by representations on the part of the tipper or tippee to buy or sell. Usually they are wholly unacquainted with and uninfluenced by the tippee's misconduct. They trade independently and voluntarily but without the benefit of information known to the trading tippee.

In determining what is the appropriate measure of damages to be awarded to the outside uninformed investor as the result of tippee-trading through use of information that is not equally available to all investors [it] must be remembered that investors who trade in a stock on the open market have no absolute right to know inside information. They are, however, entitled to an honest market in which those with whom they trade have no confidential corporate information.... It is the combination of the tip and the tippee's trading that poses the evil against

---

[26] The Sixth Circuit has since reached the opposite conclusion. *Fridrich v. Bradford*, 542 F.2d 307, 318 (6th Cir. 1976).

[27] Some cases have suggested the availability as an alternative measure of damages of a modified rescissionary measure, consisting of the difference between the price the defrauded party paid and the price at the time he learned or should have learned the true state of affairs. The theory of this measure is to restore the plaintiff to the position where he would have been had he not been fraudulently induced to trade. *See, e.g., Mitchell v. Texas Gulf Sulphur Co.*, 446 F.2d 90, 104-06 (10th Cir. [1971]). The soundness of this measure has been vigorously disputed in the case of open market trading. *Green v. Occidental Petroleum Corp.*, 541 F.2d 1335, 1341-44 (9th Cir. 1976) (Sneed, J., concurring). While the district court cited to *Mitchell,* its opinion makes clear that it was applying the out-of-pocket measure of damages. Since the district court did not apply this modified rescissionary measure, we need not pass on it here.

which the open market investor must be protected. The reason for the "disclose or abstain" rule is the unfairness in permitting an insider to trade for his own account on the basis of material inside information not available to others. The tipping of material information is a violation of the fiduciary's duty but no injury occurs until the information is used by the tippee. The entry into the market of a tippee with superior knowledge poses the threat that if he trades on the basis of the inside information he may profit at the expense of investors who are disadvantaged by lack of the inside information. For this both the tipper and the tippee are liable. If the insider chooses not to trade, on the other hand, no injury may be claimed by the outside investor, since the public has no right to the undisclosed information.

Recognizing the foregoing, we in *Shapiro* suggested that the district court must be accorded flexibility in assessing damages, after considering

> the extent of the selling defendants' trading in Douglas stock, whether such trading effectively impaired the integrity of the market, ... what profits or other benefits were realized by defendants [and] what expenses were incurred and what losses were sustained by plaintiffs.... Moreover, we do not foreclose the possibility that an analysis by the district court of the nature and character of the Rule 10b-5 violations committed may require limiting the extent of liability imposed on either class of defendants....

Within the flexible framework thus authorized for determining what amounts should be recoverable by the uninformed trader from the tipper and tippee trader, several measurers are possible. First, there is the traditional out-of-pocket measure used by the district court in this case. For several reasons this measure appears to be inappropriate. In the first place, as we have noted, it is directed toward compensating a person for losses directly traceable to the defendant's fraud upon him. No such fraud or inducement may be attributed to a tipper or tippee trading on an impersonal market. Aside from this the measure poses serious proof problems that may often be insurmountable in a tippee-trading case. The "value" of the stock traded during the period of nondisclosure of the tipped information (*i.e.*, the price at which the market would have valued the stock if there had been a disclosure) is hypothetical. Expert testimony regarding that "value" may, as the district court found in the present case, be entirely speculative. This has led some courts to conclude that the drop in price of the stock after actual disclosure and after allowing a period of time to elapse for the market to absorb the news may sometimes approximate the drop which would have occurred earlier had the tip been disclosed. The court below adopted this approach of using post-public disclosure market price as *nunc pro tunc* evidence of the "value" of the stock during the period of non-disclosure.

Whatever may be the reasonableness of the *nunc pro tunc* "value" method of calculating damages in other contexts, it has serious vulnerabilities here. It rests on the fundamental assumptions (1) that the tipped information is substantially the same as that later disclosed publicly, and (2) that one can determine how the market would have reacted to the public release of the tipped information at an earlier time by its reaction to that information at a later, proximate time. This theory depends on the parity of the "tip" and the "disclosure." When they differ, the basis of the damage calculation evaporates. One could not reasonably estimate how the public would have reacted to the news that the Titanic was near an iceberg from how it reacted to news that the ship had struck an iceberg and sunk. In the present case, the July 10 tip that preliminary earnings would be released in a week is not comparable to the later release of the estimated earnings figures on July 18. Nor was the July 17 tipped information that there was a good possibility that earnings would be down comparable to the next day's release of the estimated earnings figures.

An equally compelling reason for rejecting the theory is its potential for imposition of Draconian, exorbitant damages, out of all proportion to the wrong committed, lining the pockets of all interim investors and their counsel at the expense of innocent corporate stockholders. Logic would compel application of the theory to a case where a tippee sells only 10 shares of a heavily traded stock (e.g., IBM), which then drops substantially when the tipped information is publicly disclosed. To hold the tipper and tippee liable for the losses suffered by every open market buyer of the stock as a result of the later decline in value of the stock after the news became public would be grossly unfair. While the securities laws do occasionally allow for potentially ruinous recovery, we will not readily adopt a measure mandating "large judgments, payable in the last instance by innocent investors [here, Liggett shareholders], for the benefit of speculators and their lawyers," *SEC v. Texas Gulf Sulphur Co., supra,* 401 F.2d at 867 (Friendly, J., concurring); *cf. Blue Chip Stamps v. Manor Drug Stores,* 421 U.S. 723, 739-40 (1975), unless the statute so requires.

An alternative measure would be to permit recovery of damages caused by erosion of the market price of the security that is traceable to the tippee's wrongful trading, i. e., to compensate the uninformed investor for the loss in market value that he suffered as a direct result of the tippee's conduct. Under this measure an innocent trader who bought Liggett shares at or after a tippee sold on the basis of inside information would recover any decline in value of his shares caused by the tippee's trading. Assuming the impact of the tippee's trading on the market is measurable, this approach has the advantage of limiting the plaintiffs to the amount of damage actually caused in fact by the defendant's wrongdoing and avoiding windfall recoveries by investors at the expense of stockholders other than the tippee trader, which could happen in the present action against Liggett. The rationale is that if the market price is not affected by the tippee's trading, the uninformed investor is in the same position as he would have been had the insider abstained from trading. In such event the equilibrium of the market has not been disturbed and the outside investor has not been harmed by the informational imbalance. Only where the market has been contaminated by the wrongful conduct would damages be recoverable.

This causation-in-fact approach has some disadvantages. It allows no recovery for the tippee's violation of his duty to disclose the inside information before trading. Had he fulfilled this duty, others, including holders of the stock, could then have traded on an equal informational basis. Another disadvantage of such a measure lies in the difficult [if] not impossible burden it would impose on the uninformed trader of proving the time when and extent to which the integrity of the market was affected by the tippee's conduct.[28] In some cases, such as *Mitchell, supra* and *Shapiro, supra,* the existence of very substantial trading by the tippee, coupled with a sharp change in market price over a short period, would provide the basis for measuring a market price movement attributable to the wrongful trading. On the other hand, in a case where there was only a modest amount of tippee trading in a heavy-volume market in the stock, accompanied by other unrelated factors affecting the market price, it would be impossible as a practical matter to isolate such rise or decline in market price, if any, as was caused by the tippee's wrongful conduct. Moreover, even assuming market erosion caused by this trading to be provable and that the uninformed investor could show that it continued after his purchase, there remains the question of whether the plaintiff would not be precluded from recovery on the ground that any post-purchase decline in market price attributable to the tippee's trading would not be injury to him as a purchaser, *i.e.*, "in connection with the purchase and sale of securities," but injury to him as a stockholder due to a breach of fiduciary duty by the company's officers, which is not actionable under § 10(b) of the 1934 Act or Rule 10b-5 promulgated thereunder. *Blue Chip Stamps v. Manor Drug Stores,* 421 U.S. 723 (1975). For these reasons, we reject this strict direct market-repercussion theory of damages.

A third alternative is (1) to allow any uninformed investor, where a reasonable investor would either have delayed his purchase or not purchased at all if he had had the benefit of the tipped information, to recover any post-purchase decline in market value of his shares up to a reasonable time after he learns of the tipped information or after there is a public disclosure of it but (2) limit his recovery to the amount gained by the tippee as a result of his selling at the earlier date rather than delaying his sale until the parties could trade on an equal informational basis. Under this measure if the tippee sold 5,000 shares at $ 50 per share on the basis of inside information and the stock thereafter declined to $ 40 per share within a reasonable time after public disclosure, an uninformed purchaser, buying shares during the interim (*e.g.,* at $ 45 per share) would recover the difference between his purchase price and the amount at which he could have sold the shares on an equal informational basis (*i.e.,* the market price within a reasonable time after public disclosure of the tip), subject to a limit of $ 50,000, which is the

---

[28] Although the approach that damages cannot be recovered unless causally connected with the trading on inside information has been recognized, it has also been observed that such connection is difficult to establish. *Fridrich v. Bradford,* 542 F.2d 307, 320 n. 27 (1976).

amount gained by the tippee as a result of his trading on the inside information rather than on an equal basis. Should the intervening buyers, because of the volume and price of their purchases, claim more than the tippee's gain, their recovery (limited to that gain) would be shared *pro rata*.

This third alternative, which may be described as the disgorgement measure, has in substance been recommended by the American Law Institute in its 1978 Proposed Draft of a Federal Securities Code, §§ 1603, 1703(b), 1708(b), 1711(j). It offers several advantages. To the extent that it makes the tipper and tippees liable up to the amount gained by their misconduct, it should deter tipping of inside information and tippee-trading. On the other hand, by limiting the total recovery to the tippee's gain, the measure bars windfall recoveries of exorbitant amounts bearing no relation to the seriousness of the misconduct. It also avoids the extraordinary difficulties faced in trying to prove traditional out-of-pocket damages based on the true "value" of the shares purchased or damages claimed by reason of market erosion attributable to tippee trading. A plaintiff would simply be required to prove (1) the time, amount, and price per share of his purchase, (2) that a reasonable investor would not have paid as high a price or made the purchase at all if he had had the information in the tippee's possession, and (3) the price to which the security had declined by the time he learned the tipped information or at a reasonable time after it became public, whichever event first occurred. He would then have a claim and, up to the limits of the tippee's gain, could recover the decline in market value of his shares before the information became public or known to him. In most cases the damages recoverable under the disgorgement measure would be roughly commensurate to the actual harm caused by the tippee's wrongful conduct. In a case where the tippee sold only a few shares, for instance, the likelihood of his conduct causing any substantial injury to intervening investors buying without benefit of his confidential information would be small. If, on the other hand, the tippee sold large amounts of stock, realizing substantial profits, the likelihood of injury to intervening uninformed purchasers would be greater and the amount of potential recovery thereby proportionately enlarged.

We recognize that there cannot be any perfect measure of damages caused by tippee trading. The disgorgement measure, like others we have described, does have some disadvantages. It modifies the principle that ordinarily gain to the wrongdoer should not be a prerequisite to liability for violation of Rule 10b-5. It partially duplicates disgorgement remedies available in proceedings by the SEC or others. Under some market conditions such as where the market price is depressed by wholly unrelated causes, the tippee might be vulnerable to heavy damages, permitting some plaintiffs to recover undeserved windfalls. In some instances the total claims could exceed the wrongdoer's gain, limiting each claimant to a pro rata share of the gain. In other situations, after deducting the cost of recovery, including attorneys' fees, the remainder might be inadequate to make a class action worthwhile. However, as between the various alternatives we are persuaded, after weighing the pros and cons, that the disgorgement measure, despite some disadvantages, offers the most equitable resolution of the difficult problems created by conflicting interests.

In the present case the sole Rule 10b-5 violation was the tippee-trading of 1,800 Liggett shares on the afternoon of July 17, 1972. Since the actual preliminary Liggett earnings were released publicly at 2:15 P.M. on July 18 and were effectively disseminated in a Wall Street Journal article published on the morning of July 19, the only outside purchasers who might conceivably have been damaged by the insider-trading were those who bought Liggett shares between the afternoon of July 17 and the opening of the market on July 19. Thereafter all purchasers bought on an equal informational footing, and any outside purchaser who bought on July 17 and 18 was able to decide within a reasonable time after the July 18-19 publicity whether to hold or sell his shares in the light of the publicly-released news regarding Liggett's less favorable earnings.

The market price of Liggett stock opened on July 17, 1972, at $ 55⅝, and remained at substantially the same price on that date, closing at $ 55¼. By the close of the market on July 18 the price declined to $ 52½ per share. Applying the disgorgement measure, any member of the plaintiff class who bought Liggett shares during the period from the afternoon of July 17 to the close of the market on July 18 and met the reasonable investor requirement would be entitled to claim a *pro rata* portion of the tippee's gain, based on the difference between their purchase price and the price to which the market price declined within a reasonable time after the morning of July 19. By the close of the market on July 19 the market price had declined to $ 46⅜ per share. The total recovery thus would be limited to the gain realized by the tippee from the inside information, *i.e.*,1,800 shares multiplied by approximately $ 9.35 per share.

The finding of liability based on the July 10, 1972, tip is reversed. The award of damages is also reversed and the case is remanded for a determination of damages recoverable for tippee-trading based on the July 17, 1972, tip, to be measured in accordance with the foregoing. Each party will bear [its] own costs.

As might be imagined, the *Elkind* case engendered mixed reactions. Among those who wanted Rule 10b-5 used aggressively against insider trading, it was viewed as a step backward. Congress took a countervailing step by amending the Securities Exchange Act of 1934. Under § 21A, the Securities and Exchange Commission may request, and a federal court may levy, a civil penalty on inside traders and on persons who control inside traders of up to three times the profit gained or the loss prevented by insider trading (except in the case of controlling persons, whose penalties can be as high as $ 1 million regardless of profit gained or loss avoided).

In 1988, Congress added § 20A to the Exchange Act, and this section had the effect of softening somewhat the toughness added to the Act by § 21A. In § 20A, Congress mandated the disgorgement measure of damages in civil liability cases brought by persons whose claims are based on the fact that they traded contemporaneously with the defendant, but who cannot show that the defendant violated a pre-existing duty owed to them individually.

In 1990, Congress again amended the Exchange Act to stiffen its penalty provisions. Under § 21B, the SEC is given the power to impose civil penalties in certain administrative actions heard in its quasi-judicial capacity. Section 21C gives the SEC the power to issue its own cease-and-desist orders and to order accountings and disgorgements of unlawful gains. Also, under § 21(d)(2) courts are given the authority to prohibit a violator of § 10(b) from serving as an officer or director of an Exchange Act reporting company, and under § 21(d)(3) the SEC's power to seek civil penalties is extended to cover anyone who violates and provision of the Exchange Act, any of its rules, or any Exchange Act cease-and-desist order.

As part of the Litigation Reform Act of 1995, Congress added § 21D to the Exchange Act. This section relates to a limitation on damages and to proportionate liability. The limitation on damages comes into play when a plaintiff seeks to establish damages by reference to the market price of a security. Basically under this section, damages cannot exceed the difference between the plaintiff's purchase or sale price and the mean trading price (as defined) "during the 90-day period beginning on the date on which the information correcting the misstatement or omission that is the basis for the action is disseminated to the market."

Some of the basic aspects of the proportionate liability provision in § 21D are that in private actions under the Exchange Act, (i) a defendant is usually liable solely for the portion of a judgment that corresponds to the percentage of responsibility of that defendant, (ii) a defendant is liable for damages jointly and severally only when the trier of fact specifically determines that the defendant knowingly committed a violation of the securities laws; and (iii) a defendant has a right of contribution, based on proportionate liability.

Also relevant to the issue of liability is Exchange Act § 20. This section provides for the liability of persons who control violators of the Exchange Act or its rules and of aiders and abettors of such violations.

Chapter 20

SHORT-SWING TRADING: SECTION 16 OF THE SECURITIES EXCHANGE ACT OF 1934

Situation

In the course of working on questions relating to purchases of Daytron stock by Anderson and Baker, you learn that in the past year both Anderson and Baker have sold Daytron stock on the stock exchange. Baker sold shares both before and after she became a Daytron director, and Anderson sold at three points spread fairly evenly over the year. The shares they sold were ones purchased on the stock exchange since the Daytron-Biologistics acquisition.

Anderson and Baker assure you that they had no negative inside information at the times of their sales, and that they sold shares simply to take care of immediate cash needs. Because there has not been any announcement of negative information by Daytron, because the price of its stock has risen rather than declined, and because Anderson and Baker each purchased more Daytron shares within a few weeks of the sales, the facts seem to support them.

Rule 10b-5 is now a fairly refined weapon for getting at insider trading. During all of the life of this rule, § 16 of the Securities Exchange Act of 1934 has existed alongside of it. Section 16 was also designed to regulate insider trading, but, compared to Rule 10b-5, it is a spring gun that can hit the innocent as easily as the guilty. The method by which this section gets at the abuse of inside information is the regulation of so-called "short-swing trading." Its most basic provisions are these:

1. Section 16(a) requires that each beneficial owner of more than 10% of any equity security registered under the Exchange Act (except an exempt security), and each director and officer of an issuer of such a security, file reports with the Securities and Exchange Commission and relevant stock exchanges concerning their holdings of all equity securities of such issuer and changes in such holdings.

2. Section 16(b) provides that any profit realized by any of the above persons on any purchase and sale, or sale and purchase, of any non-exempt equity security of such an issuer, within any period of less than six months, "shall inure to and be recoverable by the issuer" (unless the security was acquired in good faith in connection with a debt previously contracted).

3. Section 16(c) makes it unlawful for any of the above persons to sell any non-exempt equity security of such an issuer if (a) the person does not own the

security (*i.e.,* a "short sale") or (b) if owning the security, does not deliver the security against the sale within prescribed periods.

The most interesting and troublesome of these provisions is § 16(b), as will be seen in the cases that follow. Its interpretations contain many quirks that probably are not expected. Interpretations aside, § 16(b) is on its face unusual in that it does not prohibit short-swing trading. In a statute filled with provisions making this or that conduct unlawful, Congress chose not to do so here. Instead, it simply provided that any profits on short-swing trading are to go to the issuer. It should be noted that many of the trickiest questions involving § 16 are answered in the rules the SEC has passed under the section.

SECTION I. PROFIT REALIZED

SMOLOWE v. DELENDO CORP.

United States Court of Appeals, Second Circuit
136 F.2d 231 (1943)

CLARK, CIRCUIT JUDGE.

The issue on appeal is ... the construction ... of § 16(b) of the Securities Exchange Act of 1934, rendering directors, officers, and principal stockholders liable to their corporation for profits realized from security tradings within any six months' period. Plaintiffs, Smolowe and Levy, stockholders of the Delendo Corporation, brought separate actions under this statute on behalf of themselves and other stockholders for recovery by the Corporation — joined as defendant — against defendants Seskis and Kaplan, both directors and president and vice-president respectively of the Corporation.... After trial at which the facts were stipulated, the district court in a careful opinion held the named defendants liable for the maximum profit shown by matching their purchases and sales of corporate stock, some transacted privately and some upon a national securities exchange, between December 1, 1939, and May 30, 1940, in conceded good faith and without any "unfair" use of inside information.

The named defendants had been connected with the Corporation (whose name was Oldetyme Distillers Corporation until after the transactions here involved) since 1933, and each owned around 12 per cent (approximately 100,000 shares) of the 800,000 shares of $ 1 par value stock issued by the Corporation and listed on the New York Curb Exchange. The Corporation had negotiated for a sale of all its assets to Schenley Distillers Corporation in 1935-1936; but the negotiations were then terminated because of Delendo's contingent liability for a tax claim of the United States against a corporation acquired by it, then in litigation. This claim, originally in the amount of $ 3,600,000, had been reduced by agreement to $ 487,265, with the condition that trial was to be postponed (to await the trial of other cases) until, but not later than, December 31, 1939. The Corporation was, therefore, pressing for trial when on February 29, 1940, the present attorney for the defendants submitted to the Attorney General a formal offer of settlement of $ 65,000, which was accepted April 2 and publicly announced April 5, 1940. Negotiations with Schenley's were reopened on April 11 and were consummated by sale on April 30, 1940, for $ 4,000,000, plus the assumption of certain of the Corporation's liabilities. Proceedings for dissolution of the Corporation were thereupon initiated and on July 16, 1940, an initial liquidating dividend of $ 4.35 was paid.

During the six months here in question from December 1, 1939, to May 30, 1940, Seskis purchased 15,504 shares for $ 25,150.20 and sold 15,800 shares for $ 35,550, while Kaplan purchased 22,900 shares for $ 48,172 and sold 21,700 shares for $ 53,405.16. Seskis purchased 584 shares on the Curb Exchange and the rest from a corporation; he made the sale at one time thereafter to Kaplan at $ 2.25 per share — 15,583 shares in purported satisfaction of a loan made him by Kaplan in 1936 and 217 shares for cash. Kaplan's purchases, in addition to the stock received from Seskis, were made on the Curb Exchange at various times prior to April 11, 1940; he sold 200 shares on February 15, and the remaining shares between April 16 and May 14, 1940 (both to private individuals and through brokers on the Curb). Except as to 1,700 shares, the certificates delivered by each of them upon selling were not the same certificates received by them on purchases during the period. The district court held the transactions within the statute and by matching purchases and sales to show the highest profits held Seskis for $ 9,733.80 and Kaplan for $ 9,161.05 to be paid to the Corporation. Both the named defendants and the Corporation have appealed.

....

The controversy as to the construction of the statute involves both the matter of substantive liability and the method of computing "such profit." The first turns primarily upon the preamble, viz., "For the purpose of preventing the unfair use of information which may have been obtained by such beneficial owner, director, or officer by reason of his relationship to the issuer." Defendants would make it the controlling grant and limitation of authority of the entire section, and liability would result only for profits from a proved unfair use of inside information. We cannot agree with this interpretation.

....

The primary purpose of the Securities Exchange Act — as the declaration of policy in § 2 makes plain — was to insure a fair and honest market, that is, one which would reflect an evaluation of securities in the light of all available and pertinent data. Furthermore, the Congressional hearings indicate that § 16(b), specifically, was designed to protect the "outside" stockholders against at least short-swing speculation by insiders with advance information. It is apparent too, from the language of § 16(b) itself, as well as from the Congressional hearings, that the only remedy which its framers deemed effective for this reform was the imposition of a liability based upon an objective measure of proof....

A subjective standard of proof, requiring a showing of an actual unfair use of inside information, would render senseless the provisions of the legislation limiting the liability period to six months, making an intention to profit during that period immaterial, and exempting transactions wherein there is a bona fide acquisition of stock in connection with a previously contracted debt. It would also torture the conditional "may" in the preamble into a conclusive "shall have" or "has." And its total effect would be to render the statute little more of an incentive to insiders to refrain from profiteering at the expense of the outside stockholder than are the common-law rules of liability; it would impose a more stringent statute of limitation upon the party aggrieved at the same time that it allowed the wrongdoer to share in the spoils of recovery.

Had Congress intended that only profits from an actual misuse of inside information should be recoverable, it would have been simple enough to say so. Significantly, however, it makes recoverable the profit from any purchase and sale, or sale and purchase, within the period. The failure to limit the recovery to profits gained from misuse of information justifies the conclusion that the preamble was inserted for other purposes than as a restriction on the scope of the Act. The legislative custom to insert declarations of purpose as an aid to constitutionality is well known. Moreover, the preamble here serves the desirable purpose of guide to the Commission in the latter's exercise of its rule-making authority.

....

The present case would seem to be of the type which the statute was designed to include. Here it is conceded that the defendants did not make unfair use of information they possessed as officers at the time of the transactions. When these began they had no offer from Schenley's. But they knew they were pressing the tax suit; and they, of course, knew of the corporate offer to settle it which reestablished the offer to purchase and led to the favorable sale. It is naive to suppose that their knowledge of their own plans as officers did not give them most valuable inside knowledge as to what would probably happen to the stock in which they were dealing. It is difficult to find this use "unfair" in the sense of illegal; it is certainly an advantage and a temptation within the general scope of the legislature's intended prohibition.

The legislative history of the statute is perhaps more significant upon a determination of the method of computing profits — defendants' second line of attack upon the district court's construction of the statute. They urge that even if the statute be not construed to impose liability only for unfair use of inside information, in any event profits should be computed according to the established income tax rule which first looks to the identification of the stock certificate, and if that is not established, then applies the presumption which is hardly more than a rule of administrative convenience of "first in, first out." Defendants rely on the deletion from early drafts of the statute, H.R. 7852, H.R. 8720, and S. 2693, of a provision that profit should be calculated irrespective of certificates received or delivered. H.R. 9323, which was finally passed by the House, failed even to penalize short-swing speculations, other than to prohibit short sales. But

H.R. 8720 was never discussed by a House Committee of the Whole, and the omission of the penalty provision in H.R. 9323 suggests at most only an opinion of the Committee on Interstate and Foreign Commerce which drafted it, and one which concerns merely the advisability of any penalty, not the method for its computation.

Actually the Act as passed is a combination of H.R. 9323 and S. 3420. In the process § 16(b) was taken bodily from S. 3420 and written into H.R. 9323. S. 3420 was introduced into the Senate after elaborate hearings on S. 2693 were closed. And its failure to specify a method of computation may well be thought more of a sanction of the formula devised in S. 2693 than an expression of hostility towards it.

Such a conclusion can be reached upon the face of the Act. "Purchase" is defined in § 3(a)(13) to include "any contract to buy," and "sale," in § 3(a)(14), to include "any contract to sell." "Equity security" is defined in § 3(a)(11) as "any stock or similar security." Section 16(b) then appears simply as a statement that any profit from any contract to purchase and any contract to sell — or vice versa — any stock or similar security shall be recoverable by the corporate issuer. There is no express limitation in this language; its generality permits and points to the matching of purchases and sales followed below. The fact that purchases and sales may be thus coupled, regardless of the intent of the insider with respect to a particular purchase or a particular sale and without limitation to a specific stock certificate, points to an arbitrary matching to achieve the showing of a maximum profit. Thus, where an insider purchases one certificate and sells another, the purchase and sale may be connected, even though the insider contends that he is holding the purchased security for sale after six months.

. . . .

The statute is broadly remedial. Recovery runs not to the stockholder, but to the corporation. We must suppose that the statute was intended to be thoroughgoing, to squeeze all possible profits out of stock transactions, and thus to establish a standard so high as to prevent any conflict between the selfish interest of a fiduciary officer, director, or stockholder and the faithful performance of his duty. The only rule whereby all possible profits can be surely recovered is that of lowest price in, highest price out — within six months — as applied by the district court. We affirm it here, defendants having failed to suggest another more reasonable rule.

. . . .

While it is well settled that in a stockholder's or creditor's representative action to recover money belonging to the class the moving party is entitled to lawyer's fees from the sum recovered, this was not strictly an action for money belonging to either class, but for a penalty payable to the corporation. Ordinarily the corporate issuer must bring the action; and only upon its refusal or delay to do so, as here, may a security holder act for it in its name and on its behalf. But this in effect creates a derivative right of action in every stockholder, regardless of the fact that he has no holdings from the class of security subjected to a short-swing operation or that he can receive no tangible benefits, directly or indirectly, from an action because of his position in the security hierarchy. And a stockholder who is successful in maintaining such an action is entitled to reimbursement for reasonable attorney's fees on the theory that the corporation which has received the benefit of the attorney's services should pay the reasonable value thereof....

While the allowance made here was quite substantial, we are not disposed to interfere with the district court's well-considered determination. Since in many cases such as this the possibility of recovering attorney's fees will provide the sole stimulus for the enforcement of § 16(b), the allowance must not be too niggardly.

Affirmed.

The "lowest price in, highest price out" method of calculating profits sometimes results in confusion on three points. First, to find a match for any particular purchase or sale, one looks at transactions within six months before *and* after the purchase or sale. That is, the total period involved in possible matching is just short of one year, not six months. Second, a multi-share transaction may be split as needed for purposes of matching. That is, a 100 share purchase on July 1 could be matched with a 50 share sale on February 1 and another 50 share sale on December 1. Third, any losses during the period are ignored. It is entirely possible to have profits for purposes of § 16(b) when, in fact, one has suffered a loss when all transactions during a period are taken into account.

Perhaps a comprehensive example will be helpful. Assume the following transactions:

> February 1: sold 50 shares at $ 75
> March 1: purchased 100 shares at $ 75
> July 1: purchased 100 shares at $ 50
> August 1: sold 200 shares at $ 50
> November 1: purchased 100 shares at $ 75
> December 1: sold 50 shares at $ 75

Profits for purposes of § 16(b) were $ 2,500. This is calculated by matching the 50 shares sold at $ 75 on each of February 1 and December 1 ($ 7,500) against the 100 shares purchased on July 1 at $ 50 ($ 5,000). The fact that matching the other transactions results in a loss of $ 5,000 (a total of 200 shares purchased at $ 75 matched against 200 shares sold at $ 50) is irrelevant under § 16(b).

SECTION II. WHO IS A DIRECTOR?

BLAU v. LEHMAN

United States Supreme Court
368 U.S. 403 (1962)

MR. JUSTICE BLACK delivered the opinion of the Court.

The petitioner Blau, a stockholder in Tide Water Associated Oil Company, brought this action in a United States District Court on behalf of the company under § 16(b) of the Securities Exchange Act of 1934 to recover with interest "short swing" profits, that is, profits earned within a six months' period by the purchase and sale of securities, alleged to have been "realized" by respondents in Tide Water securities dealings. Respondents are Lehman Brothers, a partnership engaged in investment banking, securities brokerage and in securities trading for its own account, and Joseph A. Thomas, a member of Lehman Brothers and a director of Tide Water. The complaint alleged that Lehman Brothers "deputed … Thomas, to represent its interests as a director on the Tide Water Board of Directors," and that within a period of six months in 1954 and 1955 Thomas, while representing the interests of Lehman Brothers as a director of Tide Water and "by reason of his special and inside knowledge of the affairs of Tide Water advised and caused the defendants, Lehman Brothers, to purchase and sell 50,000 shares of … stock of Tide Water, realizing profits thereon which did not inure to and [were] not recovered by Tide Water."

The case was tried before a district judge without a jury. The evidence showed that Lehman Brothers had in fact earned profits out of short-swing transactions in Tide Water securities while Thomas was a director of that company. But as to the charges of deputization and wrongful use of "inside" information by Lehman Brothers, the evidence was in conflict.

First, there was testimony that respondent Thomas had succeeded Hertz, another Lehman partner, on the board of Tide Water; that Hertz had "joined Tidewater Company thinking it was going to be in the interests of Lehman Brothers"; and that he had suggested Thomas as his successor partly because it was in the interest of Lehman. There was also testimony, however, that Thomas, aside from having mentioned from time to time to some of his partners and other people that he thought Tide Water was "an attractive investment" and under "good" management, had never discussed the operating details of Tide Water affairs with any member of Lehman Brothers; that Lehman had bought the Tide Water securities without consulting Thomas and wholly on the basis of public announcements by Tide Water that common shareholders could thereafter convert their shares to a new cumulative preferred issue; that Thomas did not know of Lehman's intent to buy Tide Water stock until after the initial purchases had been made; that upon learning about the purchases he immediately notified Lehman that he must be excluded from "any risk of the purchase or any profit or loss from the subsequent sale"; and that this disclaimer was accepted by the firm.

From the foregoing and other testimony the District Court found that "there was no evidence that the firm of Lehman Brothers deputed Thomas to represent its interests as director on the board of Tide Water" and that there had been no actual use of inside information, Lehman Brothers having bought its Tide Water stock "solely on the basis of Tide Water's public announcements and without consulting Thomas."

On the basis of these findings the District Court refused to render a judgment, either against the partnership or against Thomas individually, for the $ 98,686.77 profits which it determined that Lehman Brothers had realized holding:

> The law is now well settled that the mere fact that a partner in Lehman Brothers was a director of Tide Water, at the time that Lehman Brothers had this short swing transaction in the stock of Tide Water, is not sufficient to make the partnership liable for the profits thereon, and that Thomas could not be held liable for the profits realized by the other partners from the firm's short swing transactions. *Rattner v. Lehman,* 2d Cir., 1952, 193 F.2d 564, 565, 567. This precise question was passed upon in the *Rattner* decision.

Despite its recognition that Thomas had specifically waived his share of the Tide Water transaction profits, the trial court nevertheless held that within the meaning of § 16(b) Thomas had "realized" $ 3,893.41, his proportionate share of the profits of Lehman Brothers. The court consequently entered judgment against Thomas for that amount but refused to allow interest against him. On appeal, taken by both sides, the Court of Appeals for the Second Circuit adhered to the view it had taken in *Rattner v. Lehman,* 193 F.2d 564, and affirmed the District Court's judgment in all respects, Judge Clark dissenting. The Securities and Exchange Commission then sought leave from the Court of Appeals *en banc* to file an *amicus curiae* petition for rehearing urging the overruling of the *Rattner* case. The Commission's motion was denied, Judges Clark and Smith dissenting. We granted certiorari on the petition of Blau, filed on behalf of himself, other stockholders and Tide Water, and supported by the Commission. The questions presented by the petition are whether the courts below erred: (1) in refusing to render a judgment against the Lehman partnership for the $ 98,686.77 profits they were found to have "realized" from their "short-swing" transactions in Tide Water stock, (2) in refusing to render judgment against Thomas for the full $ 98,686.77 profits, and (3) in refusing to allow interest on the $ 3,893.41 recovery allowed against Thomas.

Petitioner apparently seeks to have us decide the questions presented as though he had proven the allegations of his complaint that Lehman Brothers actually deputized Thomas to represent its interests as a director of Tide Water, and that it was his advice and counsel based on his special and inside knowledge of Tide Water's affairs that caused Lehman Brothers to buy and sell Tide Water's stock. But the trial court found otherwise and the Court of Appeals affirmed these findings. Inferences could perhaps have been drawn from the evidence to support petitioner's charges, but examination of the record makes it clear to us that the findings of the two courts below were not clearly erroneous. Moreover, we cannot agree with the Commission that the courts' determinations of the disputed factual issues were conclusions of law rather than findings of fact. We must therefore decide whether Lehman Brothers, Thomas or both have an absolute liability under § 16(b) to pay over all profits made on Lehman's Tide Water stock dealings even though Thomas was not sitting on Tide Water's board to represent Lehman and even though the profits made by the partnership were on its own initiative, independently of any advice or "inside" knowledge given it by director Thomas.

First. The language of § 16 does not purport to impose its extraordinary liability on any "person," "fiduciary" or not, unless he or it is a "director," "officer" or "beneficial owner of more than 10 per centum of any class of any equity security ... which is registered on a national securities exchange." Lehman Brothers was neither an officer nor a 10% stockholder of Tide Water, but petitioner and the Commission contend that the Lehman partnership is or should be treated as a director under § 16(b).

(a) Although admittedly not "literally designated" as one, it is contended that Lehman is a director. No doubt Lehman Brothers, though a partnership, could for purposes of § 16 be a "director" of Tide Water and function through a deputy, since § 3(a)(9) of the Act provides that "'person' means ... partnership" and § 3(a)(7) that "'director' means any director of a corporation or any person performing similar functions with respect to any organization, whether incorporated or unincorporated." Consequently, Lehman Brothers would be a "director" of Tide Water, if as petitioner's complaint charged Lehman actually functioned as a director through Thomas, who had been deputized by Lehman to perform a director's duties not for himself but for Lehman. But the findings of the two courts below, which we have accepted, preclude such a holding. It was Thomas, not Lehman Brothers as an entity, that was the director of Tide Water.

(b) It is next argued that the intent of § 3(a)(9) in defining "person" as including a partnership is to treat a partnership as an inseparable entity. Because Thomas, one member of this inseparable entity, is an "insider," it is contended that the whole partnership should be considered the "insider." But the obvious intent of § 3(a)(9), as the Commission apparently realizes, is merely to make it clear that a partnership can be treated as an entity under the statute, not that it must be. This affords no reason at all for construing the word "director" in § 16(b) as though it read "partnership of which the director is a member." And the fact that Congress provided in § 3(a)(9) for a partnership to be treated as an entity in its own right likewise offers no support for the argument that Congress wanted a partnership to be subject to all the responsibilities and financial burdens of its members in carrying on their other individual business activities.

(c) Both the petitioner and the Commission contend on policy grounds that the Lehman partnership should be held liable even though it is neither a director, officer, nor a 10% stockholder. Conceding that such an interpretation is not justified by the literal language of § 16(b) which plainly limits liability to directors, officers, and 10% stockholders, it is argued that we should expand § 16(b) to cover partnerships of which a director is a member in order to carry out the congressionally declared purpose "of preventing the unfair use of information which may have been obtained by such beneficial owner, director, or officer by reason of his relationship to the issuer...." Failure to do so, it is argued, will leave a large and unintended loophole in the statute — one "substantially eliminating the great Wall Street trading firms from the statute's operation." 286 F.2d, at 799. These firms it is claimed will be able to evade the Act and take advantage of the "inside" information available to their members as insiders of countless corporations merely by trading "inside" information among the various partners.

The argument of petitioner and the Commission seems to go so far as to suggest that § 16(b)'s forfeiture of profits should be extended to include all persons realizing "short swing" profits who either act on the basis of "inside" information or have the possibility of "inside" information. One may agree that petitioner and the Commission present persuasive policy arguments that the Act should be broadened in this way to prevent "the unfair use of information" more effectively than can be accomplished by leaving the Act so as to require forfeiture of profits only by those specifically designated by Congress to suffer those losses. But this very broadening of the categories of persons on whom these liabilities are imposed by the language of § 16(b) was considered and rejected by Congress when it passed the Act. Drafts of provisions that eventually became § 16(b) not only would have made it unlawful for any director, officer or 10% stockholder to disclose any confidential information regarding registered securities, but also would have made all profits received by *anyone,* "insider" or not, "to whom such unlawful disclosure" had been made recoverable by the company.

Not only did Congress refuse to give § 16(b) the content we are now urged to put into it by interpretation, but with knowledge that in 1952 the Second Circuit Court of Appeals refused, in the *Rattner* case, to apply § 16(b) to Lehman Brothers in circumstances substantially like those here, Congress has left the Act as it was. And so far as the record shows this interpretation of § 16(b) was the view of the Commission until it intervened last year in this case.... Congress can and might amend § 16(b) if the Commission would present to it the policy arguments it has presented to us, but we think that Congress is the proper agency to change an interpretation of the Act unbroken since its passage, if the change is to be made.

Second. The petitioner and the Commission contend that Thomas should be required individually to pay to Tide Water the entire $ 98,686.77 profit Lehman Brothers realized on the ground that under partnership law he is co-owner of the entire undivided amount and has therefore "realized" it all. "[O]nly by holding the partner-director liable for the *entire* short-swing profits realized by his firm," it is urged, can "an effective prophylactic to the stated statutory policy ... be fully enforced." But liability under § 16(b) is to be determined neither by general partnership law nor by adding to the "prophylactic" effect Congress itself clearly prescribed in § 16(b). That section leaves no room for judicial doubt that a director is to pay to his company only "any profit realized *by him*" from short-swing transactions. (Emphasis added.) It would be nothing but a fiction to say that Thomas "realized" all the profits earned by the partnership of which he was a member. It was not error to refuse to hold Thomas liable for profits he did not make.

Third. It is contended that both courts below erred in failing to allow interest on the recovery of Thomas' share of the partnership profits. Section 16(b) says nothing about interest one way or the other. This Court has said in a kindred situation that "interest is not recovered according to a rigid theory of compensation for money withheld, but is given in response to considerations of fairness. It is denied when its exaction would be inequitable." *Board of Commissioners v. United States,* 308 U.S. 343, 352. Both courts below denied interest here and we cannot say that the denial was either so unfair or so inequitable as to require us to upset it.

Affirmed.

MR. JUSTICE DOUGLAS, with whom THE CHIEF JUSTICE concurs, dissenting.

What the Court does today is substantially to eliminate "the great Wall Street trading firms" from the operation of § 16(b), as Judge Clark stated in his dissent in the Court of Appeals. This result follows because of the wide dispersion of partners of investment banking firms among our major corporations. Lehman Bros. has partners on 100 boards. Under today's ruling that firm can make a rich harvest on the "inside information" which § 16 of the Act covers because each partner need account only for his distributive share of the firm's profits on "inside information," the other partners keeping the balance. This is a mutilation of the Act.

....

We forget much history when we give § 16 a strict and narrow construction. Brandeis in *Other People's Money* spoke of the office of "director" as "a happy hunting ground" for investment bankers. He said that "The goose that lays golden eggs has been considered a most valuable possession. But even more profitable is the privilege of taking the golden eggs laid by somebody else's goose. The investment bankers and their associates now enjoy that privilege."

The hearings that led to the Securities Exchange Act of 1934 are replete with episodes showing how insiders exploited for their personal gain "inside information" which came to them as fiduciaries and was therefore an asset of the entire body of security holders. The Senate Report labeled those practices as "predatory operations." S. Rep. No. 1455, 73d Cong., 2d Sess., p. 68. It said:

> Among the most vicious practices unearthed at the hearings before the subcommittee was the flagrant betrayal of their fiduciary duties by directors and officers of corporations who used their positions of trust and the confidential information which came to them in such positions, to aid them

in their market activities. Closely allied to this type of abuse was the unscrupulous employment of inside information by large stockholders who, while not directors and officers, exercised sufficient control over the destinies of their companies to enable them to acquire and profit by information not available to others. *Id.,* at 55. *See also* S. Rep. No. 792, 73d Cong., 2d Sess., p. 9.

The theory embodied in § 16 was the one Brandeis espoused. It was stated by Sam Rayburn as follows: "Men charged with the administration of other people's money must not use inside information for their own advantage." H.R. Rep. No. 1383, 73d Cong., 2d Sess. 13.

What we do today allows all but one partner to share in the feast which the one places on the partnership table. They in turn can offer feasts to him in the 99 other companies of which they are directors. This result is a dilution of the fiduciary principle that Congress wrote into § 16 of the Act. It is, with all respect, a dilution that is possible only by a strained reading of the law. Until now, the courts have given this fiduciary principle a cordial reception. We should not leave to Congress the task of restoring the edifice that it erected and that we tear down.

SECTION III. WHAT IS A SALE?

KERN COUNTY LAND CO. v. OCCIDENTAL PETROLEUM CORP.

United States Supreme Court
411 U.S. 582 (1973)

MR. JUSTICE WHITE delivered the opinion of the Court.

Section 16(b) of the Securities Exchange Act of 1934 provides that officers, directors, and holders of more than 10% of the listed stock of any company shall be liable to the company for any profits realized from any purchase and sale or sale and purchase of such stock occurring within a period of six months. Unquestionably, one or more statutory purchases occur when one company, seeking to gain control of another, acquires more than 10% of the stock of the latter through a tender offer made to its shareholders. But is it a § 16(b) "sale" when the target of the tender offer defends itself by merging into a third company and the tender offeror then exchanges his stock for the stock of the surviving company and also grants an option to purchase the latter stock that is not exercisable within the statutory six-month period? This is the question before us in this case.

I

On May 8, 1967, after unsuccessfully seeking to merge with Kern County Land Co. (Old Kern), Occidental Petroleum Corp. (Occidental) announced an offer, to expire on June 8, 1967, to purchase on a first-come, first-served basis 500,000 shares of Old Kern common stock at a price of $ 83.50 per share plus a brokerage commission of $ 1.50 per share. By May 10, 1967, 500,000 shares, more than 10% of the outstanding shares of Old Kern, had been tendered. On May 11, Occidental extended its offer to encompass an additional 500,000 shares. At the close of the tender offer, on June 8, 1967, Occidental owned 887,549 shares of Old Kern.

Immediately upon the announcement of Occidental's tender offer, the Old Kern management undertook to frustrate Occidental's takeover attempt. A management letter to all stockholders cautioned against tender and indicated that Occidental's offer might not be the best available, since the management was engaged in merger discussions with several companies. When Occidental extended its tender offer, the president of Old Kern sent a telegram to all stockholders again advising against tender. In addition, Old Kern undertook merger discussions with Tenneco, Inc. (Tenneco), and, on May 19, 1967, the Board of Directors of Old Kern announced that it had approved a merger proposal advanced by Tenneco. Under the terms of the merger, Tenneco would acquire the assets, property, and goodwill of Old Kern, subject to its liabilities, through "Kern County Land Co." (New Kern), a new corporation to be formed by Tenneco to receive the assets and carry on the business of Old Kern. The shareholders of Old Kern would receive a share of Tenneco cumulative convertible preference stock in exchange for each share of Old Kern common stock which they owned. On the same day, May 19, Occidental, in a quarterly report to stockholders, appraised the value of the new Tenneco stock at $ 105 per share.

... Realizing that, if the Old Kern-Tenneco merger were approved and successfully closed, Occidental would have to exchange its Old Kern shares for Tenneco stock and would be locked into a minority position in Tenneco. Occidental took other steps to protect itself. Between May 30 and June 2, it negotiated an arrangement with Tenneco whereby Occidental granted Tenneco Corp., a subsidiary of Tenneco, an option to purchase at $ 105 per share all of the Tenneco preference stock to which Occidental would be entitled in exchange for its Old Kern stock when and if the Old Kern-Tenneco merger was closed. The premium to secure the option, at $ 10 per share, totaled $ 8,866,230 and was to be paid immediately upon the signing of the option agreement. If the option were exercised, the premium was to be applied to the purchase price. By the terms of the option agreement, the option could not be exercised prior to December 9, 1967, a date six months and one day after expiration of Occidental's tender offer. On June 2, 1967, within six months of the acquisition by Occidental of more than 10% ownership of Old Kern, Occidental and Tenneco Corp. executed the option. Soon thereafter, Occidental announced that it would not oppose the Old Kern-Tenneco merger and dismissed its state court suits against Old Kern.

The Old Kern-Tenneco merger plan was presented to and approved by Old Kern shareholders at their meeting on July 17, 1967. Occidental refrained from voting its Old Kern shares, but in a letter read at the meeting Occidental stated that it had determined prior to June 2 not to oppose the merger and that it did not consider the plan unfair or inequitable. Indeed, Occidental indicated that, had it been voting, it would have voted in favor of the merger.

Meanwhile, the Securities and Exchange Commission had refused Occidental's request to exempt from possible § 16(b) liability Occidental's exchange of its Old Kern stock for the Tenneco preference shares that would take place when and if the merger transaction were closed....

The Old Kern-Tenneco merger transaction was closed on August 30. Old Kern shareholders thereupon became irrevocably entitled to receive Tenneco preference stock, share for share in exchange for their Old Kern stock. Old Kern was dissolved and all of its assets, including "all claims, demands, rights and choses in action accrued or to accrue under and by virtue of the Securities Exchange Act of 1934 ...," were transferred to New Kern.

The option granted by Occidental on June 2, 1967, was exercised on December 11, 1967....

On October 17, 1967, New Kern instituted a suit under § 16(b) against Occidental to recover the profits which Occidental had realized as a result of its dealings in Old Kern stock. The complaint alleged that the execution of the Occidental-Tenneco option on June 2, 1967, and the exchange of Old Kern shares for shares of Tenneco to which Occidental became entitled pursuant to the merger closed on August 30, 1967, were both "sales" within the coverage of § 16(b). Since both acts took place within six months of the date on which Occidental became the owner of more than 10% of the stock of Old Kern, New Kern asserted that § 16(b) required surrender of the profits realized by Occidental. New Kern eventually moved for summary judgment, and, on December 27, 1970, the District Court granted summary judgment in favor of New Kern. The District Court held that the execution of the option on June 2, 1967, and the exchange of Old Kern shares for shares of Tenneco on August 30, 1967, were "sales" under § 16(b). The Court ordered Occidental to disgorge its profits plus interest. In a supplemental opinion, Occidental was also ordered to refund the dividends which it had received plus interest.

On appeal, the Court of Appeals reversed and ordered summary judgment entered in favor of Occidental. The Court held that neither the option nor the exchange constituted a "sale" within the purview of § 16(b). We granted certiorari. We affirm.

II

... As specified in its introductory clause, § 16(b) was enacted "[f]or the purpose of preventing the unfair use of information which may have been obtained by [a statutory insider] ... by reason of his relationship to the issuer." Congress recognized that short-swing speculation by stockholders with advance, inside information would threaten the goal of the Securities Exchange Act to "insure the maintenance of fair and honest markets." Insiders could exploit information not generally available to others to secure quick profits. As we have noted, "the only method Congress deemed effective to curb the evils of insider trading was a flat rule taking the profits out of a class of transactions in which the possibility of abuse was believed to be intolerably great." *Reliance Electric Co. v. Emerson Electric Co.,* 404 U.S. 418, 422 (1972). As stated in the report of the Senate Committee, the bill aimed at protecting the public "by preventing directors, officers, and principal stockholders of a corporation ... from speculating in the stock on the basis of information not available to others." S. Rep. No. 792, 73d Cong., 2d Sess., 9 (1934).

Although traditional cash-for-stock transactions that result in a purchase and sale or a sale and purchase within the six-month statutory period are clearly within the purview of § 16(b), the courts have wrestled with the question of inclusion or exclusion of certain "unorthodox" transactions. The statutory definitions of "purchase" and "sale" are broad and, at least arguably, reach many transactions not ordinarily deemed a sale or purchase. In deciding whether borderline transactions are within the reach of the statute, the courts have come to inquire whether the transaction may serve as a vehicle for the evil which Congress sought to prevent — the realization of short-swing profits based upon access to inside information — thereby endeavoring to implement congressional objectives without extending the reach of the statute beyond its intended limits. The statute requires the inside, short-swing trader to disgorge all profits realized on all "purchases" and "sales" within the specified time period, without proof of actual abuse of insider information, and without proof of intent to profit on the basis of such information. Under these strict terms, the prevailing view is to apply the statute only when its application would serve its goals. "[W]here alternative constructions of the terms of § 16(b) are possible, those terms are to be given the construction that best serves the congressional purpose of curbing short-swing speculation by corporate insiders." *Reliance Electric Co. v. Emerson Electric Co.,* 404 U.S., at 424. Thus, "[i]n interpreting the terms 'purchase' and 'sale,' courts have properly asked whether the particular type of transaction involved is one that gives rise to speculative abuse." *Reliance Electric Co. v. Emerson Electric Co., supra,* at 424, n. 4.

In the present case, it is undisputed that Occidental became a "beneficial owner" within the terms of § 16(b) when, pursuant to its tender offer, it "purchased" more than 10% of the outstanding shares of Old Kern. We must decide, however, whether a "sale" within the ambit of the statute took place either when Occidental became irrevocably bound to exchange its shares of Old Kern for shares of Tenneco pursuant to the terms of the merger agreement between Old Kern and Tenneco or when Occidental gave an option to Tenneco to purchase from Occidental the Tenneco shares so acquired.

III

On August 30, 1967, the Old Kern-Tenneco merger agreement was signed, and Occidental became irrevocably entitled to exchange its shares of Old Kern stock for shares of Tenneco preference stock. Concededly, the transaction must be viewed as though Occidental had made the exchange on that day. But, even so, did the exchange involve a "sale" of Old Kern shares within the meaning of § 16(b)? We agree with the Court of Appeals that it did not, for we think it totally unrealistic to assume or infer from the facts before us that Occidental either had or was likely to have access to inside information, by reason of its ownership of more than 10% of the outstanding shares of Old Kern, so as to afford it an opportunity to reap speculative, short-swing profits from its disposition within six months of its tender-offer purchases.

It cannot be contended that Occidental was an insider when, on May 8, 1967, it made an irrevocable offer to purchase 500,000 shares of Old Kern stock at a price substantially above market. At that time, it owned only 1,900 shares of Old Kern stock, far fewer than the 432,000 shares needed to constitute the 10% ownership required by the statute....

It is also wide of the mark to assert that Occidental, as a sophisticated corporation knowledgeable in matters of corporate affairs and finance, knew that its tender offer would either succeed or would be met with a "defensive merger." If its takeover efforts failed, it is argued, Occidental knew it could sell its stock to the target company's merger partner at a substantial profit. Calculations of this sort, however, whether speculative or not and whether fair or unfair to other stockholders or to Old Kern, do not represent the kind of speculative abuse at which the statute is aimed, for they could not have been based on inside information obtained from substantial stockholdings that did not yet exist....

By May 10, 1967, Occidental had acquired more than 10% of the outstanding shares of Old Kern. It was thus a statutory insider when, on May 11, it extended its tender offer to include another 500,000 shares. We are quite unconvinced, however, that the situation had changed materially with respect to the possibilities of speculative abuse of inside information by Occidental. Perhaps Occidental anticipated that extending its offer would increase the likelihood of the ultimate success of its takeover attempt or the occurrence of a defensive merger. But, again, the expectation of such benefits was unrelated to the use of information unavailable to other stockholders or members of the public with sufficient funds and the intention to make the purchases Occidental had offered to make before June 8, 1967.

The possibility that Occidental had, or had the opportunity to have, any confidential information about Old Kern before or after May 11, 1967, seems extremely remote....

There is, therefore, nothing in connection with Occidental's acquisition of Old Kern stock pursuant to its tender offer to indicate either the possibility of inside information being available to Occidental by virtue of its stock ownership or the potential for speculative abuse of such inside information by Occidental. Much the same can be said of the events leading to the exchange of Occidental's Old Kern stock for Tenneco preferred, which is one of the transactions that is sought to be classified a "sale" under § 16(b). The critical fact is that the exchange took place and was required pursuant to a merger between Old Kern and Tenneco. That merger was not engineered by Occidental but was sought by Old Kern to frustrate the attempts of Occidental to gain control of Old Kern. Occidental obviously did not participate in or control the negotiations or the agreement between Old Kern and Tenneco....

Once the merger and exchange were approved, Occidental was left with no real choice with respect to the future of its shares of Old Kern. Occidental was in no position to prevent the issuance of a ruling by the Internal Revenue Service that the exchange of Old Kern stock for Tenneco preferred would be tax free; and, although various lawsuits were begun in state and federal courts seeking to postpone the merger closing beyond the statutory six-month period, those efforts were futile. The California Corporation Commissioner issued the necessary permits for the closing that took place on August 30, 1967. The merger left no right in dissenters to secure appraisal of their stock. Occidental could, of course, have disposed of its shares of Old Kern for cash before the merger was closed. Such an act would have been a § 16(b) sale and would have left Occidental with a prima facie § 16(b) liability. It was not, therefore, a realistic alternative for Occidental as long as it felt that it could successfully defend a suit like the present one. We do not suggest that an exchange of stock pursuant to a merger may never result in § 16(b) liability. But the involuntary nature of Occidental's exchange, when coupled with the absence of the possibility of speculative abuse of inside information, convinces us that § 16(b) should not apply to transactions such as this one.

IV

Petitioner also claims that the Occidental-Tenneco option agreement should itself be considered a sale, either because it was the kind of transaction the statute was designed to prevent or because the agreement was an option in form but a sale in fact. But the mere execution of an option to sell is not generally regarded as a "sale."... And we do not find in the execution of the Occidental-Tenneco option agreement a sufficient possibility for the speculative abuse of inside information with respect to Old Kern's affairs to warrant holding that the option agreement was itself a "sale" within the meaning of § 16(b)....

Neither does it appear that the option agreement, as drafted and executed by the parties, offered measurable possibilities for speculative abuse. What Occidental granted was a "call" option. Tenneco had the right to buy after six months, but Occidental could not force Tenneco to buy. The price was fixed at $ 105 for each share of Tenneco preferred. Occidental could not share in a rising market for the Tenneco stock. If the stock fell more than $ 10 per share, the option might not be exercised, and Occidental might suffer a loss if the market further deteriorated to a point where Occidental was forced to sell....

The option, therefore, does not appear to have been an instrument with potential for speculative abuse, whether or not Occidental possessed inside information about the affairs of Old Kern. In addition the option covered Tenneco preference stock, a stock as yet unissued, unregistered, and untraded.... If Occidental had inside information when it negotiated and signed the option agreement, it was inside information with respect to Old Kern. Whatever it may have known or expected as to the future value of Old Kern stock, Occidental had no ownership position in Tenneco giving it any actual or presumed insights into the future value of Tenneco stock. That was the critical item of intelligence if Occidental was to use the option for purposes of speculation....

Nor can we agree that we must reverse the Court of Appeals on the ground that the option agreement was in fact a sale because the premium paid was so large as to make the exercise of the option almost inevitable, particularly when coupled with Tenneco's desire to rid itself of a potentially troublesome stockholder.... We see no satisfactory basis or reason for disagreeing with the judgment of the Court of Appeals in this respect.

The judgment of the Court of Appeals is affirmed.

SECTION IV. TIMING ISSUES

RELIANCE ELECTRIC CO. v. EMERSON ELECTRIC CO.

United States Supreme Court
404 U.S. 418 (1972)

MR. JUSTICE STEWART delivered the opinion of the Court.

Section 16(b) of the Securities Exchange Act of 1934 provides, among other things, that a corporation may recover for itself the profits realized by an owner of more than 10% of its shares from a purchase and sale of its stock within any six-month period, provided that the owner held more than 10% "both at the time of the purchase and sale." In this case, the respondent, the owner of 13.2% of a corporation's shares, disposed of its entire holdings in two sales, both of them within six months of purchase. The first sale reduced the respondent's holdings to 9.96%, and the second disposed of the remainder. The question presented is whether the profits derived from the second sale are recoverable by the corporation under § 16(b). We hold that they are not.

I

On June 16, 1967, the respondent, Emerson Electric Co., acquired 13.2% of the outstanding common stock of Dodge Manufacturing Co., pursuant to a tender offer made in an unsuccessful attempt to take over Dodge. The purchase price for this stock was $ 63 per share. Shortly thereafter, the shareholders of Dodge approved a merger with the petitioner, Reliance Electric Co. Faced with the certain failure of any further attempt to take over Dodge, and with the prospect of being forced to exchange its Dodge shares for stock in the merged corporation in the near future, Emerson, following a plan outlined by its general counsel, decided to dispose of enough shares to bring its holdings below 10%, in order to immunize the disposal of the remainder of its shares from liability under § 16(b). Pursuant to counsel's recommendation, Emerson on August 28 sold 37,000 shares of Dodge common stock to a brokerage house at $ 68 per share. This sale reduced Emerson's holdings in Dodge to 9.96% of the outstanding common stock. The remaining shares were then sold to Dodge at $ 69 per share on September 11.

After a demand on it by Reliance for the profits realized on both sales, Emerson filed this action seeking a declaratory judgment as to its liability under § 16(b). Emerson first claimed that it was not liable at all, because it was not a 10% owner at the time of the *purchase* of the Dodge shares. The District Court disagreed, holding that a purchase of stock falls within § 16(b) where the purchaser becomes a 10% owner by virtue of the purchase. The Court of Appeals affirmed this holding, and Emerson did not cross-petition for certiorari. Thus that question is not before us.

....

Among the "objective standards" contained in § 16(b) is the requirement that a 10% owner be such "both at the time of the purchase and sale ... of the security involved." Read literally, this language clearly contemplates that a statutory insider might sell enough shares to bring his holdings below 10%, and later — but still within six months — sell additional shares free from liability under the statute. Indeed, commentators on the securities laws have recommended this exact procedure for a 10% owner who, like Emerson, wishes to dispose of his holdings within six months of their purchase.

Under the approach urged by Reliance, and adopted by the District Court, the apparent immunity of profits derived from Emerson's second sale is lost where the two sales, though independent in every other respect, are "interrelated parts of a single plan." But a "plan" to sell that is conceived within six months of purchase clearly would not fall within § 16(b) if the sale were made after the six months had expired, and we see no basis in the statute for a different result where the 10% requirement is involved rather than the six-month limitation.

....

To be sure, where alternative constructions of the terms of § 16(b) are possible, those terms are to be given the construction that best serves the congressional purpose of curbing short-swing speculation by corporate insiders. But a construction of the term "at the time of ... sale" that treats two sales as one upon proof of a pre-existing intent by the seller is scarcely in harmony with the congressional design of predicating liability upon an "objective measure of proof." *Smolowe v. Delendo Corp.,* [136 F.2d 231, 235 (2d Cir. 1943)]. Were we to adopt the approach urged by Reliance, we could be sure that investors would not in the future provide such convenient proof of their intent as Emerson did in this case. If a "two-step" sale of a 10% owner's holdings within six months of purchase is thought to give rise to the kind of evil that Congress sought to correct through § 16(b), those transactions can be more effectively deterred by an amendment to the statute that preserves its mechanical quality than by a judicial search for the will-o'-the-wisp of an investor's "intent" in each litigated case.

....

FOREMOST-McKESSON, INC. v. PROVIDENT SECURITIES CO.

United States Supreme Court
423 U.S. 232 (1976)

MR. JUSTICE POWELL delivered the opinion of the Court.

This case presents an unresolved issue under § 16(b) of the Securities Exchange Act of 1934 (Act).... Section 16(b)'s last sentence ... provides that it "shall not be construed to cover any transaction where such beneficial owner was not such both at the time of the purchase and sale, or the sale and purchase, of the security involved ...." The question presented here is whether a person purchasing securities that put his holdings above the 10% level is a beneficial owner "at the time of the purchase" so that he must account for profits realized on a sale of those securities within six months. The United States Court of Appeals for the Ninth Circuit answered this question in the negative. We affirm.

....

The meaning of the exemptive provision has been disputed since § 16(b) was first enacted. The discussion has focused on the application of the provision to a purchase-sale sequence, the principal disagreement being whether "at the time of the purchase" means "before the purchase" or "immediately after the purchase." The difference in construction is determinative of a beneficial owner's liability in cases such as Provident's where such owner sells within six months of purchase the securities the acquisition of which made him a beneficial owner. The commentators divided immediately over which construction Congress intended, and they remain divided. The Courts of Appeals also are in disagreement over the issue.

....

The Court of Appeals considered this case against the background ... of ambiguity in the pertinent statutory language, continued disagreement among the commentators, and a perceived absence in the relatively few decided cases of a full consideration of the purpose and legislative history of § 16(b). The court found unpersuasive the rationales offered in [*Stella v. Graham-Paige Motors Corp.*, 232 F.2d 299 (1956),] and its progeny for the "immediately after the purchase" construction. It noted that construing the provision to require that beneficial-ownership status exist before the purchase in a purchase-sale sequence would not foreclose an "immediately after the purchase" construction in a sale-repurchase sequence. More significantly, the Court of Appeals challenged directly the premise of the earlier cases that a "before the purchase" construction in a purchase-sale sequence would allow abuses Congress intended to abate. The court reasoned that in § 16(b) Congress intended to reach only those beneficial owners who both bought and sold on the basis of inside information, which was presumptively available to them only after they became statutory "insiders."

....

The general purpose of Congress in enacting § 16(b) is well known. Congress recognized that insiders may have access to information about their corporations not available to the rest of the investing public. By trading on this information, these persons could reap profits at the expense of less well informed investors. In § 16(b) Congress sought to "curb the evils of insider trading [by] ... taking the profits out of a class of transactions in which the possibility of abuse was believed to be intolerably great." *Reliance Electric Co.* [*v. Emerson Electric Co.*, 404 U.S. 418, 422 (1972)]. It accomplished this by defining directors, officers, and beneficial owners as those presumed to have access to inside information and enacting a flat rule that a corporation could recover the profits these insiders made on a pair of security transactions within six months.

Foremost points to this purpose, and invokes the observation in *Reliance Electric Co.* that "where alternative constructions of the terms of § 16(b) are possible, those terms are to be given the construction that best serves the congressional purpose of curbing short-swing speculation by corporate insiders." From these premises Foremost argues that the Court of Appeals' construction of the exemptive provision must be rejected because it makes § 16(b) inapplicable to some possible abuses of inside information that the statute would reach under the *Stella* construction. We find this approach unsatisfactory in its focus on situations that § 16(b) may not reach rather than on the language and purpose of the exemptive provision itself. Foremost's approach also invites an imposition of § 16(b)'s liability without fault that is not consistent with the premises upon which Congress enacted the section.

....

The exemptive provision, which applies only to beneficial owners and not to other statutory insiders, must have been included in § 16(b) for a purpose. Although the extensive legislative history of the Act is bereft of any explicit explanation of Congress' intent, the evolution of § 16(b) from its initial proposal through passage does shed significant light on the purpose of the exemptive provision.

The original version of what would develop into the Act was S. 2693, 73d Cong., 2d Sess. (1934). It provided in § 15(b):

> It shall be unlawful for any director, officer, or owner of securities, owning as of record and/or beneficially more than 5 per centum of any class of stock of any issuer, any security of which is registered on a national securities exchange —
>
> (1) To purchase any such registered security with the intention or expectation of selling the same security within six months; and any profit made by such person on any transaction in such a registered security extending over a period of less than six months shall inure to and be recoverable by the issuer, irrespective of any intention or expectation on his part in entering into such transaction of holding the security purchased for a period exceeding six months.

In the next version of the legislation, H.R. 8720, 73d Cong., 2d Sess. (1934), § 15(b) read almost identically to § 16(b) as it was eventually enacted:

> Any profit realized by such beneficial owner, director, or officer from any purchase and sale or sale and purchase of any such registered equity security within a period of less than six months, unless such security was acquired in good faith in connection with a debt previously contracted, shall inure to and be recoverable by the issuer, irrespective of any intention on the part of such beneficial owner, director, or officer in entering into such transaction of holding the security purchased or of not repurchasing the security sold for a period exceeding six months.... This subsection shall not be construed to cover any transaction where such beneficial owner was not such both at the time of the purchase and sale or sale and purchase of the security involved, nor any transaction or transactions which the Commission by rules and regulations may exempt as not comprehended within the purpose of this subsection of preventing the unfair use of information which may have been obtained by such beneficial owner, director, or officer by reason of his relationship to the issuer.

Thomas G. Corcoran, a spokesman for S. 2693's drafters, introduced § 15(b) as forbidding an insider "to carry on any short-term specu[la]tions in the stock. He cannot, with his inside information get in and out of stock within six months." Hearings on H.R. 7852 and H.R. 8720 before the House Committee on Interstate and Foreign Commerce, 73d Cong., 2d Sess., 133 (1934). The Court of Appeals concluded that § 15(b) of S. 2693 would have applied only to a beneficial owner who had that status before a purchase-sale sequence was initiated, 506 F.2d, at 609, and we agree. Foremost appears not to contest this point. The question thus becomes whether H.R. 8720's change in the language imposing liability and its addition of the exemptive provision were intended to change S. 2693's result in a purchase-sale sequence by a beneficial owner. We think the legislative history shows no such intent.

....

The legislative record ... reveals that the drafters focused directly on the fact that S. 2693 covered a short-term purchase-sale sequence by a beneficial owner only if his status existed before the purchase, and no concern was expressed about the wisdom of this requirement. But the explicit requirement was omitted from the operative language of the section when it was restructured to cover sale-repurchase sequences. In the same draft, however, the exemptive provision was added to the section. On this record we are persuaded that the exemptive provision was intended to preserve the requirement of beneficial ownership before the purchase. Later discussions of the present § 16(b) in the hearings are consistent with this interpretation. We hold that, in a purchase-sale sequence, a beneficial owner must account for profits only if he was a beneficial owner "before the purchase."

....

SECTION V. STANDING TO SUE

GOLLUST v. MENDELL

United States Supreme Court
501 U.S. 115 (1991)

JUSTICE SOUTER delivered the opinion of the Court.

....

... This case ... requires us to address a plaintiff's standing under [1934 Act] § 16(b) and, in particular, the requirements for continued standing after the institution of an action. We hold that a plaintiff, who properly "instituted [a § 16(b) action as] the owner of [a] security of the issuer," may continue to prosecute the action after his interest in the issuer is exchanged in a merger for stock in the issuer's new corporate parent.

I

In January 1987, respondent Ira L. Mendell filed a complaint under § 16(b) against petitioners in the United States District Court for the Southern District of New York, stating that he owned common stock in Viacom International, Inc. (International) and was suing on behalf of the corporation. He alleged that petitioners, a collection of limited partnerships, general partnerships, individual partners and corporations, "operated as a single unit" and were, for purposes of this litigation, a "single ... beneficial owner of more than ten per centum of the common stock" of International. Respondent claimed that petitioners were liable to International under § 16(b) for approximately $ 11 million in profits earned by them from trading in International's common stock between July and October 1986. The complaint recited that respondent had made a demand upon International and its Board of Directors to bring a § 16(b) action against petitioners and that more than 60 days had passed without the institution of an action.

In June 1987, less than six months after respondent had filed his § 16(b) complaint, International was acquired by Arsenal Acquiring Corp., a shell corporation formed by Arsenal Holdings, Inc. (now named Viacom, Inc.) (Viacom) for the purpose of acquiring International. By the terms of the acquisition, Viacom's shell subsidiary was merged with International, which then became Viacom's wholly owned subsidiary and only asset. The stockholders of International received a combination of cash and stock in Viacom in exchange for their International stock.

As a result of the acquisition, respondent, who was a stockholder in International when he instituted this action, acquired stock in International's new parent corporation and sole stockholder, Viacom. Respondent amended his complaint to reflect the restructuring by claiming to prosecute the § 16(b) action on behalf of Viacom as well as International.

Following the merger, petitioners moved for summary judgment, arguing that respondent had lost standing to maintain the action when the exchange of stock and cash occurred, after which respondent no longer owned any security of International, the "issuer." The District Court held that § 16(b) actions "may be prosecuted only by the issuer itself or the holders of its securities," and granted the motion because respondent no longer owned any International stock. The court concluded that only Viacom, as International's sole security holder, could continue to prosecute this action against petitioners.

A divided Court of Appeals reversed....

We granted certiorari ... to determine whether a stockholder who has properly instituted a § 16(b) action to recover profits from a corporation's insiders may continue to prosecute that action after a merger involving the issuer results in exchanging the stockholder's interest in the issuer for stock in the issuer's new corporate parent.

II

A

....

... The only textual restrictions on the standing of a party to bring suit under § 16(b) are that the plaintiff must be the "owner of [a] security" of the "issuer" at the time the suit is "instituted."

Although plaintiffs seeking to sue under the statute must own a "security," § 16(b) places no significant restriction on the type of security adequate to confer standing.... Nor is there any restriction in terms of either the number or percentage of shares, or the value of any other security, that must be held. In fact, the terms of the statute do not even require that the security owner have had an interest in the issuer at the time of the defendant's short-swing trading, and the courts to have addressed this issue have held that a subsequent purchaser of the issuer's securities has standing to sue for prior short-swing trading.

The second requirement for § 16(b) standing is that the plaintiff own a security of the "issuer" whose stock was traded by the insider defendant. An "issuer" of a security is defined under § 3(a)(8) of the 1934 Act as the corporation that actually issued the security and does not include parent or subsidiary corporations. While this requirement is strict on its face, it is ostensibly subject to mitigation in the final requirement for § 16(b) standing, which is merely that the plaintiff own a security of the issuer at the time the § 16(b) action is "instituted." Today, as in 1934, the word "institute" is commonly understood to mean "inaugurate or commence; as to institute an action." Black's Law Dictionary 985-986 (3d ed. 1933) (citing cases); *see* Black's Law Dictionary 800 (6th ed. 1990) (same definition). Congressional intent to adopt this common understanding is confirmed by Congress' use of the same word elsewhere to mean the commencement of an action. *See, e.g.*, 8 U.S.C. § 1503(a) ("action ... may be instituted only within five years after ... final administrative denial"); 42 U.S.C. § 405(g) ("Any action instituted in accordance with this subsection shall survive notwithstanding any change in the person occupying the office of Secretary or any vacancy in such office").

The terms of § 16(b), read in context, thus provide standing of signal breadth, expressly limited only by conditions existing at the time an action is begun. Petitioners contend, however, that the statute should at least be read narrowly enough to require the plaintiff owning a "security" of the "issuer" at the time the action is "instituted" to maintain ownership of the issuer's security throughout the period of his participation in the litigation. But no such "continuous ownership requirement" is found in the text of the statute, nor does § 16(b)'s legislative history reveal any congressional intent to impose one.

This is not to say, of course, that a § 16(b) action could be maintained by someone who is subsequently divested of any interest in the outcome of the litigation. Congress clearly intended to put "a private-profit motive behind the uncovering of this kind of leakage of information, [by making] the stockholders [its] policemen." Hearings on H. R. 7852 and H. R. 8720 before the House Committee on Interstate and Foreign Commerce, 73d Cong., 2d. Sess., 136 (1934) (testimony of Thomas G. Corcoran). The sparse legislative history on this question, which consists primarily of hearing testimony by one of the 1934 Act's drafters, merely confirms this conclusion.

Congress must, indeed, have assumed any plaintiff would maintain some continuing financial stake in the litigation for a further reason as well. For if a security holder were allowed to maintain a § 16(b) action after he had lost any financial interest in its outcome, there would be serious constitutional doubt whether that plaintiff could demonstrate the standing required by Article III's case or controversy limitation on federal court jurisdiction....

Hence, we have no difficulty concluding that, in the enactment of § 16(b), Congress understood and intended that, throughout the period of his participation, a plaintiff authorized to sue insiders on behalf of an issuer would have some continuing financial interest in the outcome of the litigation, both for the sake of furthering the statute's remedial purposes by ensuring that enforcing parties maintain the incentive to litigate vigorously, and to avoid the serious constitutional question that would arise from a plaintiff's loss of all financial interest in the outcome of the litigation he had begun.

B

The conclusion that § 16(b) requires a plaintiff security holder to maintain some financial interest in the outcome of the litigation does not, however, tell us whether an adequate financial stake can be maintained when the plaintiff's interest in the issuer has been replaced by one in the issuer's new parent. We think it can be.

The modest financial stake in an issuer sufficient to bring suit is not necessarily greater than an interest in the original issuer represented by equity ownership in the issuer's parent corporation. A security holder eligible to institute suit will have no direct financial interest in the outcome of the litigation, since any recovery will inure only to the issuer's benefit. Yet the indirect interest derived through one share of stock is enough to confer standing, however slight the potential marginal increase in the value of the share. A bondholder's sufficient financial interest may be even more attenuated, since any recovery by the issuer will increase the value of the bond only because the issuer may become a slightly better credit risk.

Thus, it is difficult to see how such a bondholder plaintiff, for example, is likely to have a more significant stake in the outcome of a § 16(b) action than a stockholder in a company whose only asset is the issuer. Because such a bondholder's attenuated financial stake is nonetheless sufficient to satisfy the statute's initial standing requirements, the stake of a parent company stockholder like respondent should be enough to meet the requirements for continued standing, so long as that is consistent with the text of the statute. It is consistent, of course, and in light of the congressional policy of lenient standing, we will not read any further condition into the statute, beyond the requirement that a § 16(b) plaintiff maintain a financial interest in the outcome of the litigation sufficient to motivate its prosecution and avoid constitutional standing difficulties.

III

In this case, respondent has satisfied the statute's requirements. He owned a "security" of the "issuer" at the time he "instituted" this § 16(b) action. In the aftermath of International's restructuring, he retains a continuing financial interest in the outcome of the litigation derived from his stock in International's sole stockholder, Viacom, whose only asset is International. Through these relationships, respondent still stands to profit, albeit indirectly, if this action is successful, just as he would have done if his original shares had not been exchanged for stock in Viacom. Although a calculation of the values of the respective interests in International that respondent held as its stockholder and holds now as a Viacom stockholder is not before us, his financial interest is actually no less real than before the merger and apparently no more attenuated than the interest of a bondholder might be in a § 16(b) suit on an issuer's behalf.

The judgment of the Court of Appeals is, accordingly,

Affirmed.

Appendix A

SOME AGENCY CONCEPTS

Since business organizations exist only as legal conceptions, every act of a business must be done through an agent. It should not be surprising, then, that agency concepts permeate the law of business organizations. Included below are some of the basic sections of the Restatement (Second) of Agency. The object here is to provide a basis for an introductory knowledge of some of the agency concepts likely to be encountered during a study of business organization law.

RESTATEMENT (SECOND) OF AGENCY*

INTRODUCTORY MATTERS

Definitions

§ 1. Agency; Principal; Agent

(1) Agency is the fiduciary relation which results from the manifestation of consent by one person to another that the other shall act on his behalf and subject to his control, and consent by the other so to act.

(2) The one for whom action is to be taken is the principal.

(3) The one who is to act is the agent.

Comment on Subsection (1):

a. The relation of agency is created as the result of conduct by two parties manifesting that one of them is willing for the other to act for him subject to his control, and that the other consents so to act.... Either of the parties to the relation may be a natural person, groups of natural persons acting for this purpose as a unit such as a partnership, joint undertakers, or a legal person, such as a corporation.

b.... Agency is a legal concept which depends upon the existence of required factual elements: the manifestation by the principal that the agent shall act for him, the agent's acceptance of the undertaking and the understanding of the parties that the principal is to be in control of the undertaking. The relation which the law calls agency does not depend upon the intent of the parties to create it, nor their belief that they have done so.

---

§ 2. Master; Servant; Independent Contractor

(1) A master is a principal who employs an agent to perform service in his affairs and who controls or has the right to control the physical conduct of the other in the performance of the service.

(2) A servant is an agent employed by a master to perform service in his affairs whose physical conduct in the performance of the service is controlled or is subject to the right to control by the master.

(3) An independent contractor is a person who contracts with another to do something for him but who is not controlled by the other nor subject to the other's right to control with respect to his physical conduct in the performance of the undertaking. He may or may not be an agent.

Comment:

a.... A master is a species of principal, and a servant is a species of agent. The words "master" and "servant" are herein used to indicate the relation from which arises both the liability of an employer for the physical harm caused to third persons by the tort of an employee ... and the special duties and immunities of an employer to the employee.

§ 4. Disclosed Principal; Partially Disclosed Principal; Undisclosed Principal

(1) If, at the time of a transaction conducted by an agent, the other party thereto has notice that the agent is acting for a principal and of the principal's identity, the principal is a disclosed principal.

(2) If the other party has notice that the agent is or may be acting for a principal but has no notice of the principal's identity, the principal for whom the agent is acting is a partially disclosed principal.

(3) If the other party has no notice that the agent is acting for a principal, the one for whom he acts is an undisclosed principal.

Comment:

...

c.... Whether a principal is a disclosed principal, a partially disclosed principal or an undisclosed principal depends upon the manifestations of the principal or agent and the knowledge of the other party at the time of the transaction.

§ 7. Authority

Authority is the power of the agent to affect the legal relations of the principal by acts done in accordance with the principal's manifestations of consent to him.

Comment:

a.... Thus there is no authority unless the principal has capacity to enter into the legal relation sought to be created by the agent....

§ 8. Apparent Authority

Apparent authority is the power to affect the legal relations of another person by transactions with third persons, professedly as agent for the other, arising from and in accordance with the other's manifestations to such third persons.

Comment:

...

b. The manifestation of the principal may be made directly to a third person, or may be made to the community, by signs, by advertising, by authorizing the agent to state that he is authorized, or by continuously employing the agent....

c.... Apparent authority exists only to the extent that it is reasonable for the third person dealing with the agent to believe that the agent is authorized. Further, the third person must believe the agent to be authorized.

d.... Apparent authority is based upon the principle which has led to the objective theory of contracts, namely that in contractual relations one should ordinarily be bound by what he says rather than by what he intends....

Estoppel ... is essentially a principle in the law of torts developed in order to prevent loss to an innocent person.... Like apparent authority, it is based on the idea that one should be bound by what he manifests irrespective of fault; but it operates only to compensate for loss to those relying upon the words and not to create rights in the speaker.... [O]ne basing his claim upon the rules of estoppel must show not merely reliance, which is required when the claim is based upon apparent authority, but also such a change of position that it would be unjust for the speaker to deny the truth of his words.

§ 8 A. Inherent Agency Power

Inherent agency power is a term used in the restatement of this subject to indicate the power of an agent which is derived not from authority, apparent authority or estoppel, but solely from the agency relation and exists for the protection of persons harmed by or dealing with a servant or other agent.

Comment:

a. Rationale. The power of an agent to bind his principal is the distinctive feature of the Anglo-American agency relation. In many situations, however, its existence and extent can be based upon other legal principles. Thus, the liability of a principal for the authorized acts and contracts of an agent is responsive to the tort rule that one is liable for what he intentionally causes, and to the rule in contracts that one who manifests assent to another is bound by the resulting transaction. Contractual liability based upon apparent authority, or its close relation, estoppel, can equally be referred to tort or to contract principles. Likewise restitutional principles may require a principal to surrender property by which he has been unjustly enriched.

However, there are situations in which the principal is made liable because of an act done or a transaction entered into by an agent even though there is no tort, contract, or restitutional theory upon which the liability can be rested. A principle which will explain such cases can be found if it is assumed that a power can exist purely as a product of the agency relation. Because such a power is derived solely from the agency relation and is not based upon principles of contracts or torts, the term inherent agency power is used to distinguish it from other powers of an agent which are sustained upon contract or tort theories.

The principles of agency have made it possible for persons to utilize the services of others in accomplishing far more than could be done by their unaided efforts. Although the agency relation may exist without reference to mercantile affairs, as in the case of domestic servants, its primary function in modern life is to make possible the commercial enterprises which could not exist otherwise. The common law has properly been responsive to the needs of commerce, permitting what older systems of law denied, namely a direct relation between the principal and a third person with whom the agent deals, even when the principal is undisclosed. Partnerships and corporations, through which most of the work of the world is done today, depend for their existence upon agency principles. The rules designed to promote the interests of these enterprises are necessarily accompanied by rules to police them. It is inevitable that in doing their work, either through negligence or excess of zeal, agents will harm third persons or will deal with them in unauthorized ways. It would be unfair for an enterprise to have the benefit of the work of its agents without making it responsible to some extent for their excesses and failures to act carefully. The answer of the common law has been the creation of special agency powers or, to phrase it otherwise, the imposition of liability upon the principal because of unauthorized or negligent acts of his servants and other agents. These powers or liabilities are created by the courts primarily for the protection of third persons, either those who are harmed by the agent or those who deal with the agent. In the long run, however, they enure to the benefit of the business world and hence to the advantage of employers as a class, the members of which are plaintiffs as well as defendants in actions brought upon authorized transactions conducted by agents.

b.... Inherent agency powers fall into two groups. The first and most familiar is the power of a servant to subject his employer to liability for faulty conduct in performing his master's business. The liability of the master in such cases cannot be based upon any ordinary tort theory, since in many cases the employment is not a causative factor in any accepted sense. The liability results purely from the relation. Its existence depends in most cases upon the fact that the servant is acting in his employer's business and intends so to act; it does not depend upon a connection between the principal's conduct and the harm done.

The other type of inherent power subjects the principal to contractual liability or to the loss of his property when an agent has acted improperly in entering into contracts or making conveyances....

§ 8 B. Estoppel — Change of Position

(1) A person who is not otherwise liable as a party to a transaction purported to be done on his account, is nevertheless subject to liability to persons who have changed their positions because of their belief that the transaction was entered into by or for him, if

(a) he intentionally or carelessly caused such belief, or

(b) knowing of such belief and that others might change their positions because of it, he did not take reasonable steps to notify them of the facts.

....

(3) Change of position, as the phrase is used in the restatement of this subject, indicates payment of money, expenditure of labor, suffering a loss or subjection to legal liability.

Comment:

a.... Estoppel is fundamentally a doctrine in the law of torts, sometimes operating by creating liability, sometimes by denying a cause of action which might otherwise accrue.

Essential Characteristics of Relation

§ 13. Agent as a Fiduciary

An agent is a fiduciary with respect to matters within the scope of his agency.

Comment:

a.... The agreement to act on behalf of the principal causes the agent to be a fiduciary, that is a person having a duty, created by his undertaking, to act primarily for the benefit of another in matters connected with his undertaking. Among the agent's fiduciary duties to the principal is the duty to account for profits arising out of the employment, the duty not to act as, or on account of, an adverse party without the principal's consent, the duty not to compete with the principal on his own account or for another in matters relating to the subject matter of the agency, and the duty to deal fairly with the principal in all transactions between them.

§ 14 C. Agent or Director

Neither the board of directors nor an individual director of a business is, as such, an agent of the corporation or of its members.

§ 14 K. Agent or Supplier

One who contracts to acquire property from a third person and convey it to another is the agent of the other only if it is agreed that he is to act primarily for the benefit of the other and not for himself.

§ 14 N. Agent and Independent Contractor

One who contracts to act on behalf of another and subject to the other's control except with respect to his physical conduct is an agent and also an independent contractor.

§ 14 O. Security Holder Becoming a Principal

A creditor who assumes control of his debtor's business for the mutual benefit of himself and his debtor may become a principal, with liability for the acts and transactions of the debtor in connection with the business.

CREATION OF RELATION

§ 15. Manifestations of Consent

An agency relation exists only if there has been a manifestation by the principal to the agent that the agent may act on his account, and consent by the agent so to act.

CREATION AND INTERPRETATION OF AUTHORITY AND APPARENT AUTHORITY

Methods of Manifesting Consent

§ 26. Creation of Authority; General Rule

Except for the execution of instruments under seal or for the performance of transactions required by statute to be authorized in a particular way, authority to do an act can be created by written or spoken words or other conduct of the principal which, reasonably interpreted, causes the agent to believe that the principal desires him so to act on the principal's account.

§ 27. Creation of Apparent Authority; General Rule

Except for the execution of instruments under seal or for the conduct of transactions required by statute to be authorized in a particular way, apparent authority to do an act is created as to a third person by written or spoken words or any other conduct of the principal which, reasonably interpreted, causes the third person to believe that the principal consents to have the act done on his behalf by the person purporting to act for him.

Interpretation of Authority and Apparent Authority

§ 35. When Incidental Authority is Inferred

Unless otherwise agreed, authority to conduct a transaction includes authority to do acts which are incidental to it, usually accompany it, or are reasonably necessary to accomplish it.

§ 43. Acquiescence by Principal in Agent's Conduct

(1) Acquiescence by the principal in conduct of an agent whose previously conferred authorization reasonably might include it, indicates that the conduct was authorized; if clearly not included in the authorization, acquiescence in it indicates affirmance.

(2) Acquiescence by the principal in a series of acts by the agent indicates authorization to perform similar acts in the future.

§ 49. Interpretation of Apparent Authority Compared with Interpretation of Authority

The rules applicable to the interpretation of authority are applicable to the interpretation of apparent authority except that:

(a) manifestations of the principal to the other party to the transaction are interpreted in light of what the other party knows or should know instead of what the agent knows or should know, and

(b) if there is a latent ambiguity in the manifestations of the principal for which he is not at fault, the interpretation of apparent authority is based on the facts known to the principal.

RATIFICATION

Definitions

§ 82. Ratification

Ratification is the affirmance by a person of a prior act which did not bind him but which was done or professedly done on his account, whereby the act, as to some or all persons, is given effect as if originally authorized by him.

Comment:

a.... [R]atification connotes that the act was done or purported to be done for a person who acquired no rights or liabilities because of it, except the right to elect to become a party to it....

§ 83. Affirmance

Affirmance is either

(a) a manifestation of an election by one on whose account an unauthorized act has been done to treat the act as authorized, or

(b) conduct by him justifiable only if there were such an election.

When Affirmance Results in Ratification

§ 84. What Acts Can Be Ratified

(1) An act which, when done, could have been authorized by a purported principal, or if an act of service by an intended principal, can be ratified if, at the time of affirmance, he could authorize such an act.

(2) An act which, when done, the purported or intended principal could not have authorized, he cannot ratify, except an act affirmed by a legal representative whose appointment relates back to or before the time of such act.

§ 91. Knowledge of Principal at Time of Affirmance

(1) If, at the time of affirmance, the purported principal is ignorant of material facts involved in the original transaction, and is unaware of his ignorance, he can thereafter avoid the effect of the affirmance.

(2) Material facts are those which substantially affect the existence or extent of the obligations involved in the transaction, as distinguished from those which affect the values or inducements involved in the transaction.

TERMINATION OF AGENCY POWERS

§ 118. Revocation or Renunciation

Authority terminates if the principal or the agent manifests to the other dissent to its continuance.

Termination of Powers Given As Security

§ 138. Definition

A power given as security is a power to affect the legal relations of another, created in the form of an agency authority, but held for the benefit of the power holder or a third person and given to secure the performance of a duty or to protect a title, either legal or equitable, such power being given when the duty or title is created or given for consideration.

§ 139. Termination of Powers Given as Security

(1) Unless otherwise agreed, a power given as security is not terminated by:

(a) revocation by the creator of the power;

(b) surrender by the holder of the power, if he holds for the benefit of another;

(c) the loss of capacity during the lifetime of either the creator of the power or the holder of the power; or

(d) the death of the holder of the power, or, if the power is given as security for a duty which does not terminate at the death of the creator of the power, by his death.

(2) A power given as security is terminated by its surrender by the beneficiary, if of full capacity; or by the happening of events which, by its terms, discharges the obligations secured by it, or which makes its execution illegal or impossible.

LIABILITY OF PRINCIPAL TO THIRD PERSONS: CONTRACTS AND CONVEYANCES

General Principles

§ 140. Liability Based upon Agency Principles

The liability of the principal to a third person upon a transaction conducted by an agent, or the transfer of his interests by an agent, may be based upon the fact that:

(a) the agent was authorized;

(b) the agent was apparently authorized; or

(c) the agent had a power arising from the agency relation and not dependent upon authority or apparent authority.

Comment:

a.... In transactions in which there is neither authority or apparent authority, the principal may be subjected to liability because, in view of the relations of the parties or the subject matter involved, policy requires that the agent should have power to bind the principal, described ... as inherent agency powers....

Disclosed or Partially Disclosed Principal

§ 144. General Rule

A disclosed or partially disclosed principal is subject to liability upon contracts made by an agent acting within his authority if made in proper form and with the understanding that the principal is a party.

Interpretation of Written Instruments as to Parties

§ 156. Instrument in Which Fact of Agency or Name of Principal Appears

In the absence of a manifestation to the contrary therein, an unsealed written instrument is interpreted as the instrument of the principal and not of the agent if, in the signature or description of the parties, the name of the principal and agent both appear, the agent indicating his agency. The addition of the word 'agent' to the signature or description of the signer does not of itself prevent the inference that such person is a party to the contract.

UNDISCLOSED PRINCIPAL

§ 186. General Rule

An undisclosed principal is bound by contracts and conveyances made on his account by an agent acting within his authority....

Comment:

....

b.... [A]n agent who makes a contract for an undisclosed principal is personally liable upon the contract as a party to it. The rule stated in this section gives to the other party the election ... of holding the principal liable when discovered.

LIABILITY OF PRINCIPAL TO THIRD PERSON; TORTS

§ 213 Principal Negligent or Reckless

A person conducting an activity through servants or other agents is subject to liability for harm resulting from his conduct if he is negligent or reckless:

....

(b) in the employment of improper persons or instrumentalities in work involving risk of harm to others;

Torts of Servants

§ 219. When Master is Liable for Torts of His Servants

(1) A master is subject to liability for the torts of his servants committed while acting in the scope of their employment....

§ 220. Definition of a Servant

(1) A servant is a person employed to perform services in the affairs of another and who with respect to the physical conduct in the performance of the services is subject to the other's control or right to control.

(2) In determining whether one acting for another is a servant or an independent contractor, the following matters of fact, among others are considered:

(a) the extent of control which, by the agreement, the master may exercise over the details of the work;

(b) whether or not the one employed is engaged in a distinct occupation or business;

(c) the kind of occupation, with reference to whether, in the locality, the work is usually done under the direction of the employer or by a specialist without supervision;

(d) the skill required in the particular occupation;

(e) whether the employer or the workman supplies the instrumentalities, tools and the place of work for the person doing the work;

(f) the length of time for which the person is employed;

(g) the method of payment, whether by the time or by the job;

(h) whether or not the work is a part of the regular business of the employer;

(i) whether or not the parties believe they are creating the relation of master and servant; and

(j) whether the principal is or is not in business.

Scope of Employment

§ 228 General Statement

(1) conduct of a servant is within the scope of employment if, but only if:

(a) it is of the kind he is employed to perform;

(b) it occurs substantially within the authorized time and space limits;

(c) it is actuated, at least in part, by a purpose to serve the master; and

(d) if force is intentionally used by the servant against another, the use of force is not unexpectable by the master.

(2) conduct of a servant is not within the scope of employment if it is different in kind from that authorized, far beyond the authorized time or space limits, or too little actuated by a purpose to serve the master.

LIABILITY OF THIRD PERSON TO PRINCIPAL

Contracts; Disclosed Agency

§ 292. General Rule

The other party to a contract made by an agent for a disclosed or partially disclosed principal, acting within his authority, apparent authority or other agency power, is liable to the principal as if he had contracted directly with the principal, unless the principal is excluded as a party by the form or terms of the contract.

Contracts; Undisclosed Agency

§ 301. General Rule

A person who makes a contract with an agent of an undisclosed principal, intended by the agent to be on account of his principal and within the power of such agent to bind his principal, is liable to the principal as if the principal himself had made the contract with him, unless he is excluded by the form or terms of the contract, unless his existence is fraudulently concealed or unless there is set-off or a similar defense against the agent.

LIABILITY OF AGENT TO THIRD PERSONS

Contracts and Conveyances

§ 320. Principal Disclosed

Unless otherwise agreed, a person making or purporting to make a contract with another as agent for a disclosed principal does not become a party to the contract.

§ 321. Principal Partially Disclosed

Unless otherwise agreed, a person purporting to make a contract with another for a partially disclosed principal is a party to the contract.

§ 322. Principal Undisclosed

An agent purporting to act upon his own account, but in fact making a contract on account of an undisclosed principal, is a party to the contract.

§ 326. Principal Known to be Non existent or Incompetent

Unless otherwise agreed, a person who, in dealing with another, purports to act as agent for a principal whom both know to be nonexistent or wholly incompetent, becomes a party to such a contract.

Comment:

a. A person may knowingly go through the form of entering into a contract with a nonexistent or incompetent person, known by him to be such, as where one deals with the promoter of a corporation to be formed, or with the representative of one who both know to be insane. If the understanding of the parties is that, at all events, the one purporting to act as agent is not to be a party, he is not subject to liability either upon the contract or otherwise, unless he has been guilty of some misstatement in the transaction. On the other hand, there is an inference that a person intends to make a present contract with an existing person. If, therefore, the other party knows that there is no principal capable of entering into such a contract, there is a rebuttable inference that, although the contract is nominally in the name of the nonexistent person, the parties intend that the person signing as agent should be a party, unless there is some indication to the contrary....

b. Promoters. The classic illustration of the rule stated in this Section is the promoter. When a promoter makes an agreement with another on behalf of a corporation to be formed, the following alternatives may represent the intent of the parties:

(1) They may understand that the other party is making a revocable offer to the nonexistent corporation which will result in a contract if the corporation is formed and accepts the offer prior to withdrawal. This is the normal understanding.

(2) They may understand that the other party is making an irrevocable offer for a limited time. Consideration to support the promise to keep the offer open can be found in an express or limited promise by the promoter to reorganize the corporation and use his best efforts to cause it to accept the offer.

(3) They may agree to a present contract by which the promoter is bound, but with an agreement that his liability terminates if the corporation is formed and manifests its willingness to become a party. There can be no ratification by the newly formed corporation, since it was not in existence when the agreement was made....

(4) They may agree to a present contract on which, even though the corporation becomes a party, the promoter remains liable either primarily or as surety for the performance of the corporation's obligation.

Which one of these possible alternatives, or variants thereof, is intended is a matter of interpretation on the facts of the individual case.

§ 328. Liability of Authorized Agent for Performance of Contract

An agent, by making a contract only on behalf of a competent disclosed or partially disclosed principal whom he has power so to bind, does not thereby become liable for its nonperformance.

Comment:

a. One who makes a contract only on account of another ordinarily does not himself contemplate responsibility for its performance. His function is performed if he causes a contract to be made between his principal and the third person.

DUTIES AND LIABILITIES OF AGENT TO PRINCIPAL

Duties of Service and Obedience

§ 379. Duty of Care and Skill

(1)   Unless otherwise agreed, a paid agent is subject to a duty to the principal to act with standard care and with the skill which is standard in the locality for the kind of work which he is employed to perform and, in addition, to exercise any special skill that he has.

§ 381. Duty to Give Information

Unless otherwise agreed, an agent is subject to a duty to use reasonable efforts to give his principal information which is relevant to affairs entrusted to him and which, as the agent has notice, the principal would desire to have and which can be communicated without violating a superior duty to a third person.

§ 382. Duty to Keep and Render Accounts

Unless otherwise agreed, an agent is subject to a duty to keep, and render to his principal, an account of money or other things which he has received or paid out on behalf of the principal.

Duties of Loyalty

§ 387. General Principle

Unless otherwise agreed, an agent is subject to a duty to his principal to act solely for the benefit of the principal in all matters connected with his agency.

§ 388. Duty to Account for Profits Arising out of Employment

Unless otherwise agreed, an agent who makes a profit in connection with transactions conducted by him on behalf of the principal is under a duty to give such profit to the principal.

§ 393. Competition as to Subject Matter of Agency

Unless otherwise agreed, an agent is subject to a duty not to compete with the principal concerning the subject matter of his agency.

§ 394. Acting for One with Conflicting Interests

Unless otherwise agreed, an agent is subject to a duty not to act or to agree to act during the period of his agency for persons whose interests conflict with those of the principal in matters in which the agent is employed.

§ 395. Using or Disclosing Confidential Information

Unless otherwise agreed, an agent is subject to a duty to the principal not to use or to communicate information confidentially given him by the principal or acquired by him during the course of or on account of his agency or in violation of his duties as agent, in competition with or to the injury of the principal, on his own account or on behalf of another, although such information does not relate to the transaction in which he is then employed, unless the information is a matter of general knowledge.

Comment:

...

b. Scope of rule. The rule stated in this Section applies not only to those communications which are stated to be confidential, but also to information which the agent should know his principal would not care to have revealed to others or used in competition with him....

§ 396. Using Confidential Information after Termination of Agency

Unless otherwise agreed, after the termination of the agency, the agent:

(a) has no duty not to compete with the principal;

(b) has a duty to the principal not to use or to disclose to third persons, on his own account or on account of others, in competition with the principal or to his injury, trade secrets, written lists of names, or other similar confidential matters given to him only for the principal's use or acquired by the agent in violation of duty The agent is entitled to use general information concerning the method of business of the principal and the names of the customers retained in his memory, if not acquired in violation of his duty as agent;

(c) has a duty to account for profits made by the sale or use of trade secrets and other confidential information, whether or not in competition with the principal;

(d) has a duty to the principal not to take advantage of a still subsisting confidential relation created during the prior agency relation.

Appendix B

READING FINANCIAL STATEMENTS

Lawyers advising business clients need to know accounting fundamentals in order to be effective counselors. Accounting issues arise in connection with organizing and financing businesses, distributing company earnings to its owners, structuring business transactions, and buying, selling and investing in companies. Although accountants are available to provide expert advice on these issues, lawyers must know when an expert is needed and be able to discuss accounting issues intelligently with both the expert and the client.

The business organization law student can approach accounting as one might approach parachute jumping. To be really good at either parachute jumping or accounting requires a lot of knowledge and skill; to be good enough to survive at either requires little knowledge or skill, but what each requires, it requires absolutely. The basics of jumping can be found in four lines of verse:

Stand up, buckle up, shuffle to the door.
Jump right out and count to four.
If your chute don't open wide,
Pull that rip cord by your side.

We cannot quite get the essentials of accounting pared down this far, but we think the next few pages will work as well for the business organization law student as these lines do for a parachute jumper. They will provide enough accounting basics to read most financial statements.

SECTION I. INTRODUCTION TO ACCOUNTING

The first known accounting system was developed sometime in the fifteenth century to keep track of daily business transactions and, in the process, to determine if mistakes were being made or, worse, if someone was up to no good. Accounting systems provide a set of controls designed to reduce waste, prevent dishonesty and provide information about the company's financial position. More recently, accounting data has also been used as a factor in determining a company's value. Whether it should be so used is a matter of debate. Courts and lawyers often do use accounting data for valuation purposes. Economists typically focus on the control and monitoring functions of accounting.

The use of an accounting system involves two types of activities: keeping records of business transactions as they occur and producing reports that summarize the results of the transactions. The reports, called financial statements, are typically prepared according to generally accepted accounting principles

(GAAP). The most basic and most frequently encountered financial statements are the balance sheet and the income statement. These are discussed below somewhat fully. Two subsidiary statements, the retained earnings statement and the statement of cash flows, are mentioned briefly. These statements are designed to provide financial information useful to persons making economic decisions about a company, including the company's owners, managers, investors, and creditors.

Financial statements are prepared based on several common principles. Each statement deals with a particular time period, such as a quarter or a year. Businesses are regarded as going concerns. They are also treated as entities separate and distinct from their owners, even when state law considers them to be one and the same. Usually, financial statement values reflect historical cost rather than current market value, and all transactions are recorded in the same currency, in our case, the U.S. dollar. Companies are expected to be consistent in the way they record transactions from year to year.

A. BALANCE SHEET

The balance sheet shows a company's assets (what it owns) and liabilities (what it owes), plus the owners' equity in the business (the amount left over for the owners) at a particular point in time, such as at the close of business on December 31. The simplest corporate balance sheet possible, showing only totals and leaving out all detail, might look like this:

ACME CORPORATION
Balance Sheet
December 31, 199_

Assets	$385,000	Liabilities	$ 285,000
		Shareholders' Equity	$ 100,000
		Total Liabilities and Shareholders'	
Total Assests	$385,000	Equity	$ 385,000

In this example, the assets are equal to the liabilities plus the shareholders' equity (which might be called "proprietor's equity" in a proprietorship or "partners' capital" in a partnership). This is always true for a balance sheet, because what a balance sheet shows is simply how much the company owns (its assets), how much it owes (its liabilities) and how much is left over for the company's owners (equity). Another way to look at the balance sheet is to say that it states the types of assets held by the company and the persons (creditors and owners) with claims to the assets. The following two equations may be helpful in understanding balance sheets:

assets = liabilities + equity
assets − liabilities = equity

The first of these equations reflects the way information is organized on the balance sheet, with assets listed on the left and liabilities and equity on the right. The equation also shows why this financial statement is called a balance sheet. Just like the equation, the two sides of the balance sheet must equal each other. The equation also reflects the way information is recorded in the company records and on the balance sheet. Since one must keep the equation in balance, company transactions are recorded using what is called the double entry bookkeeping system. Every transaction will cause two changes on the accounting statements. A transaction affecting one side of the equation will also affect the other side, unless there are two offsetting entries on one side. For example, a $2,000 increase in assets will also require one of the following: an offsetting $2,000 decrease in assets (if, for example, a new asset worth $2,000 was purchased with $2,000 cash); a $2,000 increase in liabilities (if the company borrowed the $2,000 needed to buy the asset); or a $2,000 increase in equity (if a $2,000 increase in the equity, the amount contributed by the company's owners, provided the funds to buy the asset).

With this background, we now can turn to a balance sheet showing details. This balance sheet will show the types of assets a company has, the types of obligations it has incurred, and the types of equity (owners' investments in the company and company earnings). A more detailed version of the balance sheet shown above might look like this:

ACME CORPORATION
Balance Sheet
December 31, 199_

ASSETS			LIABILITIES		
Current Assets			Current Liabilities		
Cash	$ 50,000		Accounts payable		$ 60,000
Accounts receivable	75,000		Notes payable		40,000
(net of allowance			(including current		
for bad debts			portion of long-		
of $5,000)			term debt)		
Inventory (FIFO)	125,000		Income taxes payable		25,000
Total current			Total current		
assets	$ 250,000		liabilities		$ 125,000
Fixed Assets					
Land	$ 50,000				
Building	75,000		Long Term Liabilities		
Equipment	50,000		5-year notes payable		$ 160,000
	$ 175,000				
Less: Accumulated					
depreciation	50,000		Total Liabilities		$ 285,000
Net fixed					
assets	$ 125,000		SHAREHOLDERS' EQUITY		
			Common stock ($1.00 par		
Intangibles			value; 1,000 shares		
Patents	$ 10,000		authorized, issued		
			and outstanding)		$ 1,000
			Paid-in capital in excess		
			of par value		49,000
			Retained earnings		50,000
			Total Shareholders'		
			Equity		$ 100,000
			Total Liabilities		
			and Shareholders'		
Total Assets	$ 385,000		Equity		$ 385,000

Even without further discussion, it is now possible to "read" a good deal of this balance sheet, since much of the detail that has been added is self-explanatory. To understand this detail, however, some explanation is in order. Each item on the balance sheet is called an account. Increases and decreases in each account are recorded in the company's books and ultimately reflected on the balance sheet. The most common accounts are described below.

1. Assets

The assets accounts on the balance sheet show how the company has used the money it has obtained from lenders, investors, and company earnings. Assets can be grouped according to whether they are monetary (cash and accounts receivables), liquid (whether they can easily be converted to cash) or whether they are tangible or intangible. The assets of this corporation are shown under three headings: current assets, fixed assets and intangibles. Current assets consist of cash and those items, such as accounts receivable, that are normally expected to be converted into cash within one year. Fixed assets are the company's more or less permanent physical assets, such as its land, buildings, machinery and equipment. Intangible assets include, among other things, such items as patents and trademarks. An asset can be valued in several ways: 1) how much it cost to acquire it (historical cost); 2) its current market value; 3) its value in use; 4) its liquidation value based on its sale after use. Assets are typically recorded on financial statements at their historical cost expressed in dollars. Current assets and fixed assets are discussed below.

i. Current Assets

Cash. — Cash includes not only currency, which a company might keep in "petty cash," but also bank deposits and other "cash equivalents."

Accounts Receivable. — If a company sells goods or services on credit, the amounts owed to the company by the purchasers are "accounts receivable." The company must, however, anticipate that some of the accounts receivable will not be received. An account, which might be called "allowance for bad debts," therefore is established in the company's books and set-off against, or subtracted from, the accounts receivable shown in the balance sheet. This is necessary in order to present a fair picture of how much the company will likely receive from its credit sales.

Inventory. — In a manufacturing company, inventory includes raw materials, work in process and finished goods. Other types of companies have other types of inventory. For example, a retail store has in inventory only the purchased goods it sells. Service companies, of course, have no inventory. In preparing a balance sheet, a company must first determine what its inventory is (preferably by physically counting it) and then place a value on that inventory. The generally accepted method of valuation is to record the inventory at its cost or market value, whichever is lower (here "market value" is not retail value, but what it would cost the company to replace the inventory). For simplicity, we will ignore the methods a manufacturing company would use in measuring the cost of goods that are in various stages of the manufacturing process and deal only with the valuation of purchased goods a company has in inventory. The following are two common ways to measure the "cost" of inventory that has been purchased at different times and at varying prices.

(a) *First-in, first-out ("FIFO")*. Under the FIFO method of valuation, the items of inventory that are purchased first are deemed to be sold first. Under this method, the most recent purchase prices are deemed to represent the cost of the items remaining. For example, suppose that the purchases and sales of a particular item are as follows:

	Quantity	Cost per item	Total Cost
Jan. Purchase	100	$ .60	$ 60
March Purchase	500	.70	$ 350
June Purchase	300	.80	$ 240
Sept. Purchase	100	.90	$ 90
Total purchases	1,000		$ 740
Less sales	700		
Ending inventory	300		

Under the FIFO method of valuation, the cost of the ending inventory of 300 items would be deemed to be $250 ($.90 each for 100 and $.80 each for 200). Obviously, in times of rising prices, use of the FIFO method will result in inventory being shown on the balance sheet at the highest possible amount.

(b) *Last-in, first-out ("LIFO")*. Under the LIFO method of valuation, the items of inventory that are purchased last are deemed to be sold first, and so the cost of the ending inventory is deemed to be the cost of the items that were purchased first. In the situation described above, the cost of the ending inventory of 300 items would be deemed to be $200 ($.60 for each 100 items and $.70 each for 200 items).

ii. Fixed Assets

As indicated above, fixed assets include such items as land, buildings, machinery and equipment. Fixed assets are typically shown on the balance sheet at their cost, less accumulated depreciation. "Depreciation" is the term used to describe the allocation of the cost of certain fixed assets, such as buildings, machinery and equipment, over their estimated useful lives. The term "depletion" rather than "depreciation" is used in the case of "wasting assets," such as oil and gas fields. "Amortization" is the term used when intangible assets, such as patents or trademarks, are involved. Land is not depreciated, since it does not have (at least for accounting purposes) a limited useful life.

When a fixed asset is depreciated, the cost of the asset is allocated over its expected useful life, and each annual installment of depreciation is added to an account in the company's books called "accumulated depreciation." On the balance sheet, accumulated depreciation is set-off against the total fixed assets (shown at their total cost at time of purchase). Notice that appreciation in the value of assets, which is likely for certain assets in times of rising prices, is not reflected on the balance sheet.

Several methods are used to calculate depreciation. Here are two of the most frequently encountered.

Straight-line method. — The straight line depreciation method is the most common. Under this method, depreciation is calculated by dividing the cost of the asset, less its salvage value, by the estimated useful life of the asset. For example, a computer costing $50,000, with a salvage value of $10,000 and an estimated useful life of 5 years, would have annual depreciation of $8,000 ($50,000 − $10,000 = $40,000; $40,000 ÷ 5 = $8,000), or 20% per year.

Double declining balance method. — Under the double declining balance method, depreciation is calculated by taking twice the straight-line depreciation percentage rate and multiplying this percentage rate by either the initial cost of the asset, which is what is done the first year depreciation is calculated, or, in succeeding years, by each declining balance figure that results from subtracting previously calculated depreciation from the initial cost. Salvage value does not enter into the computation, but under this method an asset is not depreciated below a reasonable salvage value. Using the example above, the depreciation percentage rate would be 40% (20% doubled). This rate multiplied by $50,000 (the initial cost of the computer) gives a result of $20,000, which would be the amount of depreciation for the first year. For the following year, depreciation would be calculated by multiplying the "declining balance" of $30,000 ($50,000 − $20,000) by 40%, to give a result of $12,000. This method of calculating annual depreciation would continue until a reasonable salvage figure is reached. The double declining balance method, and certain other methods not discussed here, are called accelerated depreciation methods because they produce a greater amount of depreciation in the initial years of an asset's life than does the straight-line method.

2. Liabilities

The second portion of the balance sheet consists of the liabilities of the company. Liabilities are usually separated into two categories: current liabilities and long-term liabilities. Current liabilities consist of those debts that are to be paid within a year. Accounts payable, short-term notes payable and income taxes payable are typical current liabilities. Long-term liabilities are often in the form of long-term notes or bonds, but include any debt that is not due within one year. In the case of a debt that is partially due within one year and partially due in future years, the portion of the debt payable within one year is shown as a current liability and the rest as a long-term liability.

3. Equity

The third and final portion of a balance sheet represents the owners' equity. In a company owned by only one person (sole proprietorship), this section would have only one entry: proprietor's equity. In a partnership, the equity section has only one account: partners' capital. In the case of a corporation, the equity portion usually is subdivided into three categories. These categories are given various names in state corporation statutes. In many they are called stated capital, capital surplus and earned surplus. Irrespective of the names used in corporation statutes, however, accountants use their own terms on balance sheets. Thus, what a corporation statute calls stated capital is shown on the ACME balance sheet as "common stock;" capital surplus is shown as "paid-in capital in excess of par value" and earned surplus as "retained earnings." In the discussion below, we will use the "lawyers' terms" commonly found in statutes. The accountants' terms will be noted in parentheses. To explain these terms fully would take more space and time than is warranted here, particularly since these terms are discussed in Chapters 4 and 9. Briefly, stated capital (here shown as common stock) is calculated by multiplying the number of shares of stock outstanding by the par value of each share. (In this discussion of stated capital and both categories of surplus, we will ignore stock without par value and will also ignore the possibility of transfers between these categories of shareholders' equity, which is allowed by corporation statutes in some circumstances.) In the case of the balance sheet shown above, the par value of the corporation's common stock is $1.00 per share and 1,000 shares have been issued, yielding a stated capital of $1,000. For current purposes, par value is perhaps best explained as being simply an arbitrary dollar figure assigned to the stock, the major purpose of which is to determine the amount of stated capital. The importance of this is that some corporation statutes place restrictions on what a corporation can do with its stated capital.

Capital surplus (paid in capital in excess of par) is basically the difference between what shareholders paid the corporation for their stock and the par value of the stock. In the case of the balance sheet shown above, it appears that the 1,000 shares of common stock were sold by the corporation for $50 each, or $50,000 in total ($49,000 shown in paid-in capital in excess of par value plus $1,000 shown in common stock). Some corporation statutes also restrict what a corporation can do with its capital surplus, although the restrictions are different from those for stated capital.

Again ignoring transfers between categories of shareholders' equity, earned surplus (retained earnings) shows the total amount of profits and losses of the corporation since its formation, decreased by any dividends paid the shareholders. One might ask what happens if the corporation has had losses rather than profits. In this case, earned surplus is shown as a negative number (indicated by placing the number in parenthesis).

B. BALANCE SHEET ANALYSIS

Robert W. Hamilton, Fundamentals of Modern Business 204-08 (1989)*

Most financial statements contain, either as part of the statements themselves or in the notes, historical information or summaries relating to prior accounting

---

periods that are comparable to the information provided for the current period. Significant insights may be gained by considering trends over several accounting periods. Such analysis may show, for example, whether the position of the company is improving or declining over time. Analysis of the single period covered by the most recent statements is usually enriched by historical perspective. When practicable, the ratios discussed below should be computed for several years, and changes in the ratios should be evaluated.

....

Several widely used ratios concentrate exclusively on the balance sheet. These tend to be the most traditional analytic techniques.

Net Working Capital

A basic question is whether a business has sufficient economic strength to continue in operation for a reasonable period. It may be recalled that current assets are those that involve cash, cash equivalents, and assets that should be reduced to cash within a year, while current liabilities are those that come due within a year. A simple measure of short-term stability of the business is to ascertain that current assets exceed current liabilities. The difference is called *net working capital:*

Net working capital = current assets - current liabilities

....

The Current Ratio

A widely used measure of the adequacy of working capital is the *current ratio*, which is the ratio between current assets and current liabilities:

$$\text{Current ratio} = \frac{\text{current assets}}{\text{current liabilities}}$$

... As a broad rule of thumb, a solid current ratio for an industrial company is 2 to 1. However, lower current ratios may be entirely adequate for many businesses. In general terms, the smaller the inventory levels required and the more easily collectible the amounts receivable, the lower the current ratio that is acceptable....

The Acid Test

Bankers and others considering short-term loans to a business often rely on quick asset analysis. *Quick assets* are assets that can be used to cover an immediate emergency. They differ from current assets in that they exclude inventories. Quick assets are obviously never greater than current assets.

$$\text{Quick assets} = \text{Cash} + \text{marketable securities} + \text{current receivables}$$

$$\text{Net quick assets} = \text{Quick assets} - \text{current liabilities}$$

$$\text{Quick assets ratio} = \frac{\text{quick assets}}{\text{current liabilities}}$$

The quick assets ratio is usually referred to as the *acid test*....

A quick asset ratio of 1.0 or better shows that a company is able to meet its current liabilities without liquidating inventory. Ratios of less than 1.0 do not necessarily signify danger, however. An analysis of anticipated cash flow over the period of the loan may show that the company is able to repay the loan without difficulty despite a ratio of less than 1.0. It all depends on how promptly liquidation or turnover of inventories occurs.

Book Value of Shares

Book value of shares is an important concept that simply means the value of those shares calculated from the books of the company using the values shown on the books. Book value does *not* mean market value. For example, shares of closely held corporations have book value even though the shares have never been bought or sold and no one has any idea of their value. Book value also does not mean liquidation value or "real" value, since the financial statements are constructed on historical cost rather than current market value of assets....

Book value ... of common shares is computed simply by subtracting liabilities from the book value of assets and dividing by the number of outstanding shares:

$$\text{Book value} = \frac{\text{assets - liabilities}}{\text{number of shares}}$$

Asset Coverage of Debt

... A measure of how secure the holder of [long term] debt is can be obtained simply by subtracting current liabilities from total assets and dividing by the amount of the debt, all computed at book value:

$$\text{Asset coverage} = \frac{\text{total assets - current liabilities}}{\text{long-term debt}}$$

... In this calculation, no account is taken of the interests of the holders of the common shares since the rights of the holders of the long-term debt are senior to those of shareholders, that is the bondholders must be paid in full before the shareholders get anything.

Debt/Equity Ratio

The debt/equity ratio recognizes that long-term debt is part of the permanent capitalization of the business; the ratio is computed by dividing long term debt by the total shareholders' equity in the corporation:

$$\text{Debt/equity ratio} = \frac{\text{long-term debt}}{\text{total equity}}$$

... The debt/equity ratio gives a picture of what proportion of the company's permanent capital is borrowed and what proportion is contributed (or internally generated as retained earnings). Because borrowed capital carries with it an obligation to pay interest, while dividends are usually discretionary with management, large amounts of debt in the capital structure are more risky than smaller amounts. A company with a high debt/equity ratio is said to be *heavily leveraged.* A heavily leveraged corporation with most of the debt held by the corporation's shareholders is called a *thin corporation* or a *thinly capitalized corporation.*

From the standpoint of a lender, the debt/equity ratio measures the relative size of the equity "cushion" available for repayment of the debt in the case of default. A high debt/equity ratio means that each lender has a relatively small cushion and therefore an increased risk that the debt will not be fully collectible in the event of a default.

Is it appropriate to consider long-term debt as a kind of capital? Debt ultimately has to be repaid. Nevertheless, the treatment of debt as part of the permanent capitalization is certainly reasonable if the repayment date is far distant in the future, or sometimes even if shorter-term debt is involved. Financial statements treat debt as current only if it falls due within 12 months. Debt maturing beyond that time is permanent within the context of the financial statement. Also, debt falling due within two or three years may reasonably be viewed as long-term capital if it is anticipated that new loans will be obtained to repay the debt when it matures, a very common phenomenon in business. This is often referred to as *rolling over* the debt.

Shorter-term debt may be excluded from the debt/equity ratio calculation if its repayment is adequately provided for and no roll-over is contemplated.

C. INCOME STATEMENT

Unlike the balance sheet, which shows a company's financial status at a particular point in time (such as on December 31), the income statement shows the results of a company's operations over a period of time (such as for the year ending December 31). Stated simply, it shows the company's revenues and expenses, and how much the company made in profits. An income statement for Acme Corporation might look like this:

ACME CORPORATION
Income Statement
Year ended December 31, 199__

Net sales	$ 500,000
Cost of goods sold and operating expenses	
Cost of goods sold	$ 304,000
Depreciation	15,000
Selling and administrative expenses	100,000
	$ 419,000
Operating Income	$ 81,000
Interest on long-term notes	13,000
Income before income taxes	$ 68,000
Income taxes	18,000
Net income	$ 50,000
Net income per share (1,000 shares outstanding)	$ 50

Some explanation of specific income statement items may be helpful.

Net Sales. — Net sales is calculated by totaling all sales during the period, and then subtracting the sales price of all returned goods and all allowances made because of damaged or defective goods.

Cost of Goods Sold. — Calculating the cost of goods sold begins where calculating the cost of ending inventory for balance sheet purposes ends. In the case of goods that are sold in the form in which they are purchased, the cost of goods sold during a period (assuming there is no "operating inventory" at the beginning of the period) is calculated by subtracting the cost of ending inventory from the total cost of the purchased goods. In our example above, relating to inventory valuation, the total cost of the purchases of the item in question were $740. Under the FIFO method of valuation the cost of ending inventory was $250 and under the LIFO method $200. Under these methods, the cost of goods sold for this item would be $490 ($740 minus $250) and $540 ($740 minus $200).

Obviously, the cost of goods sold has a direct effect on the amount of income shown on a company's income statement. As can easily be seen, the amount of income shown may vary, sometimes to a great extent, depending on the method of inventory valuation used.

Depreciation. — We have already discussed depreciation as it is shown on the balance sheet. There, the total amount of depreciation over the past life of fixed assets is shown as a set-off from the total cost of these assets. On the income statement, only depreciation for the period covered by the statement is shown. In the case of the above income statement, this is one year's depreciation.

By using an accelerated depreciation method, such as the double declining balance method, the depreciation over the first few years of an asset's life will be much greater than it would be if the straight line method were used. This, of course, will result in lower income — and lower taxes — during these years. A company's decisions with respect to the estimated useful life of assets also affects the amount of depreciation, and therefore income, shown on its income statement. For example, within the limits of what are called "generally accepted accounting principles" (GAAP), a company might estimate the useful life of a particular piece of machinery as five years, or ten years, or any number of years in between, thus causing a possible variation in depreciation of as much as 100 percent.

Selling and Administrative Expenses. — Selling and administrative expenses are exactly what one would expect. This item generally encompasses all the expenses of a company not included under another heading (called "line items" on financial statements) on the income statement.

Interest on Long-term Notes. — The interest accrued on long-term debt during the period covered by an income statement is generally shown as a line item separate from other expenses. In the case of Acme Corporation, the long-term debt is in the form of notes. In the case of other corporations, it could be represented by other debt instruments, such as bonds.

Income Taxes. — Income taxes are also shown as a separate line item, allowing the reader of the income statement to see at a glance what the company's income was both before and after taxes.

Net Income Per Share. — This item is simply net income divided by the number of shares outstanding.

D. INCOME STATEMENT ANALYSIS

Robert W. Hamilton, Fundamentals of Modern Business 208-10, 212 (1989)*

For most analytic purposes, information about past earnings and prospects of future earnings is more useful than information about property and assets. An old axiom is that assets are worth only what they can earn. Assets that have no earning capacity are salable only for scrap. Hence, more reliance is usually placed on the income statement ratios described below than the balance sheet ratios.... Actually, income statement ratios is not an entirely accurate term, since income statement analysis often involves ratios between items appearing on the balance sheet as well as on the income statement.

....

Earnings per Share

Another fundamental measure of profitability, which is of particular interest to shareholders, is *earnings per share,* computed as the net income divided by the number of shares outstanding.

$$\text{Earnings per share} = \frac{\text{Net income}}{\text{Outstanding shares}}$$

....

Return on Equity

Return on equity is simply the ratio of net income to net worth.

$$\text{Return on equity} = \frac{\text{Net income}}{\text{Net worth}}$$

... This is one of the more widely used ratios since it describes how much the company is earning on each dollar of shareholders' investment. When applied to GAAP statements, it is also broadly comparable from company to company and from industry to industry even though it is affected to some extent by the accounting conventions that have been adopted....

Return on equity is a relatively universal measure of profitability. Information is widely available on the return on equity for thousands of publicly held corporations. In 1986, the composite return on equity for the nation's 1,000 largest companies was 10.9 percent.

E. ACCUMULATED RETAINED EARNINGS STATEMENT

The term "earnings" refers to the amount of money a company makes as a result of conducting its business. Retained earnings is an accountant's term used to refer to earnings that have been retained by the business and have not been distributed to shareholders as dividends. (Lawyers refer to this as earned surplus.) Earnings kept in the business are accumulated from accounting period to accounting period. Accumulated retained earnings thus refers to the total amount of retained earnings a company has at the beginning of an accounting period increased by the earnings retained during the current accounting period. The amount of retained earnings at the end of an accounting period is recorded in the retained earnings (earned surplus) account on the balance sheet.

The accumulated retained earnings statement shows increases and decreases in the corporation's retained earnings (earned surplus) during the period covered by the income statement it accompanies. An accumulated retained earnings statement showing changes during a calendar year would show (i) the amount of accumulated retained earnings (earned surplus) on January 1, (ii) any additions to accumulated retained earnings arising from profits during the year, (iii) any decreases arising from dividends paid to shareholders, or from transfers to capital surplus or stated capital, and (iv) the amount of accumulated retained earnings on December 31. The amount of accumulated retained earnings on December 31 would also appear in the accumulated retained earnings (earned surplus) account on the balance sheet.

F. STATEMENT OF CASH FLOWS

The statement of cash flows involves some concepts that are beyond the needs of students in a basic corporation law course and will not be discussed here in detail. Basically, this statement covers the same period as the income statement it accompanies and shows from what sources the company received its cash flow (which is net income plus an add-back of depreciation and other non-cash charges that were subtracted from the company's revenues when calculating its net income.)

The financial statements shown above do not include all of the items that one will find on other financial statements. And, the discussion of these statements, and the accounting concepts they embody, was simplified. One will find, however, that even the most complicated balance sheets and income statements for the largest corporations are, in the main, simply more detailed versions of the statements included here. If one understands these simple statements, more complex ones will be understandable to a fair degree.

SECTION II. VALUATION OF BUSINESSES

The business organization lawyer encounters issues related to business valuation in several contexts: when a company is being sold; when an owner in a company wants to be bought out; when interests in a company are being valued for estate tax purposes or as part of divorce proceedings. Although lawyers are not expected to determine the valuation, they must understand some of the basics when addressing related legal questions. There are many ways to value a business. Three of the more common are briefly described below.

Book value is based on a company's balance sheet and is equated with the net worth (or equity) of the business, the value remaining after liabilities are subtracted from assets. Book value is relatively easy to calculate. The problem with this approach is that financial statements typically reflect historical cost and do not accurately represent either the current value of the company's assets or the value of the company as a going concern. Book value will also not reflect the value of goodwill[1] or of the company's earnings potential.

Liquidation value is the net amount remaining after a business is brought to an end, its assets are sold individually, and its creditors are paid. This value may be difficult to calculate if the business is large and has a sizeable number of assets. Assets also are often worth more when valued based on their productive use in the context of a going concern, rather than when they are sold piecemeal.

Company cash flow or earnings is the most popular method for valuing a company. It assumes that the business is a going concern. Here, the value of the company is based on projections of what its earnings or cash flow is likely to be in the future. The approach requires the use of several variables to arrive at a value. For example, although one may reasonably predict future cash flows or earnings for certain types of businesses, for others that determination may be somewhat speculative. However, including such factors as the company's historical performance, its current earnings and cash flow, and comparison with comparable companies may reduce some of the uncertainty associated with this approach.

———

1. What is the ultimate effect on the Acme Balance Sheet[2] of each of the following transactions? Consider each transaction separately.

    a. Acme purchases a parcel of land for $20,000 cash.
    b. Acme borrows $20,000, payable in 3 years at 8% interest, to purchase a parcel of land.
    c. Acme collects $5,000 of accounts receivable.
    d. Acme buys $10,000 of inventory on credit, with the total amount payable in 6 months.
    e. Acme pays off $5,000 of a note due in 180 days.

---

[1]Goodwill is the value a business derives from having a strong brand name, excellent reputation, exceptional management, loyal customers, good location or other similar attributes. The value of goodwill equals the amount by which the price paid for a company as a going concern exceeds the fair market value of its assets minus liabilities. Classified as an intangible asset, goodwill is recorded on a company's books only when it is acquired in connection with the purchase of the company.

[2]The balance sheet is a financial statement that periodically summarizes a company's financial condition. Individual transactions are recorded in a company's books as the transactions occur. At the end of the reporting period, the results of those transactions are summarized on the balance sheet. Nevertheless, considering the way a particular transaction will ultimately affect the balance sheet helps one understand the interrelationships of the balance sheet entries.

2. What is the value of each of the following and what does each tell you about Acme?

- a. Net working capital.
- b. Current ratio.
- c. Net quick assets.
- d. Quick assets ratio.
- e. Book value of common shares.
- f. Asset coverage of debt.
- g. Debt/equity ratio.
- h. Earnings per share
- i. Return on equity

3. Consider each of the following ways to value a business. What are the advantages and disadvantages of each approach?

- a. Book value
- b. Liquidation value
- c. Cash flow or earnings

AMERICAN BAR ASSOCIATION
MODEL RULES OF PROFESSIONAL CONDUCT*
CLIENT-LAWYER RELATIONSHIP

Rule 1.1. Competence

A lawyer shall provide competent representation to a client. Competent representation requires the legal knowledge, skill, thoroughness and preparation reasonably necessary for the representation.

Comment

Legal Knowledge and Skill

[1] In determining whether a lawyer employs the requisite knowledge and skill in a particular matter, relevant factors include the relative complexity and specialized nature of the matter, the lawyer's general experience, the lawyer's training and experience in the field in question, the preparation and study the lawyer is able to give the matter and whether it is feasible to refer the matter to, or associate or consult with, a lawyer of established competence in the field in question. In many instances, the required proficiency is that of a general practitioner. Expertise in a particular field of law may be required in some circumstances.

[2] A lawyer need not necessarily have special training or prior experience to handle legal problems of a type with which the lawyer is unfamiliar. A newly admitted lawyer can be as competent as a practitioner with long experience. Some important legal skills, such as the analysis of precedent, the evaluation of evidence and legal drafting, are required in all legal problems. Perhaps the most fundamental legal skill consists of determining what kind of legal problems a situation may involve, a skill that necessarily transcends any particular specialized knowledge. A lawyer can provide adequate representation in a wholly novel field through necessary study. Competent representation can also be provided through the association of a lawyer of established competence in the field in question.

[3] In an emergency a lawyer may give advice or assistance in a matter in which the lawyer does not have the skill ordinarily required where referral to or consultation or association with another lawyer would be impractical. Even in an emergency, however, assistance should be limited to that reasonably necessary

---

in the circumstances, for ill-considered action under emergency conditions can jeopardize the client's interest.

[4] A lawyer may accept representation where the requisite level of competence can be achieved by reasonable preparation. This applies as well to a lawyer who is appointed as counsel for an unrepresented person. See also Rule 6.2.

Thoroughness and Preparation

[5] Competent handling [of] a particular matter includes inquiry into and analysis of the factual and legal elements of the problem, and use of methods and procedures meeting the standards of competent practitioners. It also includes adequate preparation. The required attention and preparation are determined in part by what is at stake; major litigation and complex transactions ordinarily require more elaborate treatment than matters of lesser consequence.

Maintaining Competence

[6] To maintain the requisite knowledge and skill, a lawyer should engage in continuing study and education. If a system of peer review has been established, the lawyer should consider making use of it in appropriate circumstances.

Model Code Comparison

DR 6-101(A)(1) provided that a lawyer shall not handle a matter "which he knows or should know that he is not competent to handle, without associating himself with a lawyer who is competent to handle it." DR 6-101(A)(2) required "preparation adequate in the circumstances." Rule 1.1 more fully particularizes the elements of competence. Whereas DR 6-101(A)(3) prohibited the "[n]eglect of a legal matter," Rule 1.1 does not contain such a prohibition. Instead, Rule 1.1 affirmatively requires the lawyer to be competent.

Rule 1.2. Scope of Representation

(a) A lawyer shall abide by a client's decisions concerning the objectives of representation, subject to paragraphs (c), (d) and (e), and shall consult with the client as to the means by which they are to be pursued. A lawyer shall abide by a client's decision whether to accept an offer of settlement of a matter. In a criminal case, the lawyer shall abide by the client's decision, after consultation with the lawyer, as to a plea to be entered, whether to waive jury trial and whether the client will testify.

(b) A lawyer's representation of a client, including representation by appointment, does not constitute an endorsement of the client's political, economic, social or moral views or activities.

(c) A lawyer may limit the objectives of the representation if the client consents after consultation.

(d) A lawyer shall not counsel a client to engage, or assist a client, in conduct that the lawyer knows is criminal or fraudulent, but a lawyer may discuss the legal consequences of any proposed course of conduct with a client and may counsel or assist a client to make a good faith effort to determine the validity, scope, meaning or application of the law.

(e) When a lawyer knows that a client expects assistance not permitted by the rules of professional conduct or other law, the lawyer shall consult with the client regarding the relevant limitations on the lawyer's conduct.

Comment

Scope of Representation

[1] Both lawyer and client have authority and responsibility in the objectives and means of representation. The client has ultimate authority to determine the purposes to be served by legal representation, within the limits imposed by law and the lawyer's professional obligations. Within those limits, a client also has a right to consult with the lawyer about the means to be used in pursuing those objectives. At the same time, a lawyer is not required to pursue objectives or employ means simply because a client may wish that the lawyer do so. A clear distinction between objectives and means sometimes cannot be drawn, and in many cases the client-lawyer relationship partakes of a joint undertaking. In questions of means, the lawyer should assume responsibility for technical and legal tactical issues, but should defer to the client regarding such questions as the expense to be incurred and concern for third persons who might be adversely affected. Law defining the lawyer's scope of authority in litigation varies among jurisdictions.

[2] In a case in which the client appears to be suffering mental disability, the lawyer's duty to abide by the client's decisions to be guided by reference to Rule 1.14.

Independence from Client's Views or Activities

[3] Legal representation should not be denied to people who are unable to afford legal services, or whose cause is controversial or the subject of popular disapproval. By the same token, representing a client does not constitute approval of the client's views or activities.

Services Limited in Objectives or Means

[4] The objectives or scope of services provided by a lawyer may be limited by agreement with the client or by the terms under which the lawyer's services are made available to the client. For example, a retainer may be for a specifically defined purpose. Representation provided through a legal aid agency may be subject to limitations on the types of cases the agency handles. When a lawyer has been retained by an insurer to represent an insured, the representation may be limited to matters related to the insurance coverage. The terms upon which representation is undertaken may exclude specific objectives or means. Such

limitations may exclude objectives or means that the lawyer regards as repugnant or imprudent.

[5] An agreement concerning the scope of presentation must accord with the Rules of Professional Conduct and other law. Thus, the client may not be asked to agree to representation so limited in scope as to violate Rule 1.1, or to surrender the right to terminate the lawyer's services or the right to settle litigation that the lawyer might wish to continue.

Criminal, Fraudulent and Prohibited Transactions

[6] A lawyer is required to give an honest opinion about the actual consequences that appear likely to result from a client's conduct. The fact that a client uses advice in a course of action that is criminal or fraudulent does not, of itself, make a lawyer a party to the course of action. However, a lawyer may not knowingly assist a client in criminal or fraudulent conduct. There is a critical distinction between presenting an analysis of legal aspects of questionable conduct and recommending the means by which a crime or fraud might be committed with impunity.

[7] When the client's course of action has already begun and is continuing, the lawyer's responsibility is especially delicate. The lawyer is not permitted to reveal the client's wrongdoing, except where permitted by Rule 1.6. However, the lawyer is required to avoid furthering the purpose, for example, by suggesting how it might be concealed. A lawyer may not continue assisting a client in conduct that the lawyer originally supposes is legally proper but then discovers is criminal or fraudulent. Withdrawal from the representation, therefore, may be required.

[8] Where the client is fiduciary, the lawyer may be charged with special obligations in dealings with a beneficiary.

[9] Paragraph (d) applies whether or not the defrauded party is a party to the transaction. Hence, a lawyer should not participate in a sham transaction; for example, a transaction to effectuate criminal or fraudulent escape of tax liability. Paragraph (d) does not preclude undertaking a criminal defense incident to a general retainer for legal services to a lawful enterprise. The last clause of paragraph (d) recognizes that determining the validity or interpretation of a statute or regulation may require a course of action involving disobedience of the statute or regulation or of the interpretation placed upon it by governmental authorities.

Model Code Comparison

Paragraph (a) has no counterpart in the Disciplinary Rules of the Model Code. EC 7-7 stated: "In certain areas of legal representation not affecting the merits of the cause or substantially prejudicing the rights of a client, a lawyer is entitled to make decisions on his own. But otherwise the authority to make decisions is exclusively that of the client...." EC 7-8 stated that "[I]n the final analysis, however, the ... decision whether to forego legally available objectives or methods because of nonlegal factors is ultimately for the client.... In the event that the client in a nonadjudicatory matter insists upon a course of conduct that is contrary to the judgment and advice of the lawyer but not prohibited by Disciplinary Rules, the lawyer may withdraw from the employment." DR 7-101(A)(1) provided that a lawyer "shall not intentionally ... fail to seek the lawful objectives of his client through reasonably available means permitted by law.... A lawyer does not violate this Disciplinary Rule, however, by ... avoiding offensive tactics...."

Paragraph (b) has no counterpart in the Model Code.

With regard to Paragraph (c), DR 7-101(B)(1) provided that a lawyer may, "where permissible, exercise his professional judgment to waive or fail to assert a right or position of his client."

With regard to Paragraph (d), DR 7-102(A)(7) provided that a lawyer shall not "counsel or assist his client in conduct that the lawyer knows to be illegal or fraudulent." DR 7-102(A)(6) provided that a lawyer shall not "participate in the creation or preservation of evidence when he knows or it is obvious that the evidence is false." DR 7-106 provided that a lawyer shall not "advise his client to disregard a standing rule of a tribunal or a ruling of a tribunal ... but he may take appropriate steps in good faith to test the validity of such rule or ruling." EC 7-5 stated that a lawyer "should never encourage or aid his client to commit criminal acts or counsel his client on how to violate the law and avoid punishment therefor."

With regard to Paragraph (e), DR 2-110(C)(1)(c) provided that a lawyer may withdraw from representation if a client "insists" that the lawyer engage in "conduct that is illegal or that is prohibited under the Disciplinary Rules." DR 9-101(C) provided that "a lawyer shall not state or imply that he is able to influence improperly ... any tribunal, legislative body or public official."

Rule 1.3. Diligence

A lawyer shall act with reasonable diligence and promptness in representing a client.

Comment

[1] A lawyer should pursue a matter on behalf of a client despite opposition, obstruction or personal inconvenience to the lawyer, and may take whatever lawful and ethical measures are required to vindicate a client's cause or endeavor. A lawyer should act with commitment and dedication to the interests of the client and with zeal in advocacy upon the client's behalf. However, a lawyer is not bound to press for every advantage that might be realized for a client. A lawyer has professional discretion in determining the means by which a matter should be pursued. See Rule 1.2. A lawyer's work load should be controlled so that each matter can be handled adequately.

[2] Perhaps no professional shortcoming is more widely resented than procrastination. A client's interests often can be adversely affected by the passage

of time or the change of conditions; in extreme instances, as when a lawyer overlooks a statute of limitations, the client's legal position may be destroyed. Even when the client's interests are not affected in substance, however, unreasonable delay can cause a client needless anxiety and undermine confidence in the lawyer's trustworthiness.

[3] Unless the relationship in terminated as provided in Rule 1.16, a lawyer should carry through [to] conclusion all matters undertaken for a client. If a lawyer's employment is limited to a specific matter, the relationship terminates when the matter has been resolved. If a lawyer has served a client over a substantial period in a variety of matters, the client sometimes may assume that the lawyer will continue to serve on a continuing basis unless the lawyer gives notice of withdrawal. Doubt about whether a client-lawyer relationship still exists should be clarified by the lawyer, preferably in writing, so that the client will not mistakenly suppose the lawyer is looking after the client's affairs when the lawyer has ceased to do so. For example, if a lawyer has handled a judicial or administrative proceeding that produced a result adverse to the client but has not been specifically instructed concerning pursuit of an appeal, the lawyer should advise the client of the possibility of appeal before relinquishing responsibility for the matter.

Model Code Comparison

DR 6-101(A)(3) required that a lawyer not "[n]eglect a legal matter entrusted to him." EC 6-4 stated that a lawyer should "give appropriate attention to his legal work." Canon 7 stated that "a lawyer should represent a client zealously within the bounds of the law." DR 7-101(A)(1) provided that a lawyer "shall not intentionally ... fail to seek the lawful objectives of his client through reasonably available means permitted by law and the Disciplinary Rules...." DR 7-101(A)(3) provided that a lawyer "shall not intentionally ... [p]rejudice or damage his client during the course of the relationship...."

Rule 1.4. Communication

(a) A lawyer shall keep a client reasonably informed about the status of a matter and promptly comply with reasonable requests for information.

(b) A lawyer shall explain a matter to the extent reasonably necessary to permit the client to make informed decisions regarding the representation.

Comment

[1] The client should have sufficient information to participate intelligently in decisions concerning the objectives of the representation and the means by which they are to be pursued, to the extent the client is willing and able to do so. For example, a lawyer negotiating on behalf of a client should provide the client with facts relevant to the matter, inform the client of communications from another party and take other reasonable steps that permit the client to make a decision

regarding a serious offer from another party. A lawyer who receives from opposing counsel an offer of settlement in a civil controversy or a proffered plea bargain in a criminal case should promptly inform the client of its substance unless prior discussions with the client have left it clear that the proposal will be unacceptable. See Rule 1.2(a). Even when a client delegates authority to the lawyer, the client should be kept advised of the status of the matter.

[2] Adequacy of communication depends in part on the kind of advice or assistance involved. For example, in negotiations where there is time to explain a proposal, the lawyer should review all important provisions with the client before proceeding to an agreement. In litigation a lawyer should explain the general strategy and prospects of success and ordinarily should consult the client on tactics that might injure or coerce others. On the other hand, a lawyer ordinarily cannot be expected to describe trial or negotiation strategy in detail. The guiding principle is that the lawyer should fulfill reasonable client expectations for information consistent with the duty to act in the client's best interests, and the client's overall requirements as to the character of representation.

[3] Ordinarily, the information to be provided is that appropriate for a client who is a comprehending and responsible adult. However, fully informing the client according to this standard may be impracticable, for example, where the client is a child or suffers from mental disability. See Rule 1.14. When the client is an organization or group, it is often impossible or inappropriate to inform every one of its members about its legal affairs; ordinarily, the lawyer should address communications to the appropriate officials of the organization. See Rule 1.13. Where many routine matters are involved, a system of limited or occasional reporting may be arranged with the client. Practical exigency may also require a lawyer to act for a client without prior consultation.

Withholding Information

[4] In some circumstances, a lawyer may be justified in delaying transmission of information when the client would be likely to react imprudently to an immediate communication. Thus, a lawyer might withhold a psychiatric diagnosis of a client when the examining psychiatrist indicates that disclosure would harm the client. A lawyer may not withhold information to serve the lawyer's own interest or convenience. Rules or court orders governing litigation may provide that information supplied to a lawyer may not be disclosed to the client. Rule 3.4(c) directs compliance with such rules or orders.

Model Code Comparison

Rule 1.4 has no direct counterpart in the Disciplinary Rules of the Model Code. DR 6-101(A)(3) provided that a lawyer shall not "[n]eglect a legal matter entrusted to him." DR 9-102(B)(1) provided that a lawyer shall "[p]romptly notify a client of the receipt of his funds, securities, or other properties." EC 7-8 stated that a lawyer "should exert his best efforts to insure that decisions of his client are made only after the client has been informed of relevant considerations." EC 9-2 stated that "a lawyer should fully and promptly inform his client of material developments in the matters being handled for the client."

Rule 1.5. Fees

(a) A lawyer's fee shall be reasonable. The factors to be considered in determining the reasonableness of a fee include the following:

(1) the time and labor required, the novelty and difficulty of the questions involved, and the skill requisite to perform the legal service properly;

(2) the likelihood, if apparent to the client, that the acceptance of the particular employment will preclude other employment by the lawyer;

(3) the fee customarily charged in the locality for similar legal services;

(4) the amount involved and the results obtained;

(5) the time limitations imposed by the client or by the circumstances;

(6) the nature and length of the professional relationship with the client;

(7) the experience, reputation, and ability of the lawyer or lawyers performing the services; and

(8) whether the fee is fixed or contingent.

(b) When the lawyer has not regularly represented the client, the basis or rate of the fee shall be communicated to the client, preferably in writing, before or within a reasonable time after commencing the representation.

(c) A fee may be contingent on the outcome of the matter for which the service is rendered, except in a matter in which a contingent fee is prohibited by paragraph (d) or other law. A contingent fee agreement shall be in writing and shall state the method by which the fee is to be determined, including the percentage or percentages that shall accrue to the lawyer in the event of settlement, trial or appeal, litigation and other expenses to be deducted from the recovery, and whether such expenses are to be deducted before or after the contingent fee is calculated. Upon conclusion of a contingent fee matter, the lawyer shall provide the client with a written statement stating the outcome of the matter and, if there is a recovery, showing the remittance to the client and the method of its determination.

(d) A lawyer shall not enter into an arrangement for, charge, or collect:

(1) any fee in a domestic relations matter, the payment or amount of which is contingent upon the securing of a divorce or upon the amount of alimony or support, or property settlement in lieu thereof; or

(2) a contingent fee for representing a defendant in a criminal case.

(e) A division of a fee between lawyers who are not in the same firm may be made only if:

(1) the division is in proportion to the services performed by each lawyer or, by written agreement with the client, each lawyer assumes joint responsibility for the representation;

(2) the client is advised of and does not object to the participation of all the lawyers involved; and

(3) the total fee is reasonable.

Comment

Basis or Rate of Fee

[1] When the lawyer has regularly represented a client, they ordinarily will have evolved an understanding concerning the basis or rate of the fee. In a new client-lawyer relationship, however, an understanding as to the fee should be promptly established. It is not necessary to recite all the factors that underlie the basis of the fee, but only those that are directly involved in its computation. It is sufficient, for example, to state that the basic rate is an hourly charge or a fixed amount or an estimated amount, or to identify the factors that may be taken into account in finally fixing the fee. When developments occur during the representation that render an earlier estimate substantially inaccurate, a revised estimate should be provided to the client. A written statement concerning the fee reduces the possibility of misunderstanding. Furnishing the client with a simple memorandum or a copy of the lawyer's customary fee schedule is sufficient if the basis or rate of the fee is set forth.

Terms of Payment

[2] A lawyer may require advance payment of a fee, but is obliged to return any unearned portion. See Rule 1.16(d). A lawyer may accept property in payment for services, such as an ownership interest in an enterprise, providing this does not involve acquisition of a proprietary interest in the cause of action or subject matter of the litigation contrary to Rule 1.8(j). However, a fee paid in property instead of money may be subject to special scrutiny because it involves questions concerning both the value of the services and the lawyer's special knowledge of the value of the property.

[3] An agreement may not be made whose terms might induce the lawyer improperly to curtail services for the client or perform them in a way contrary to the client's interest. For example, a lawyer should not enter into an agreement whereby services are to be provided only up to a stated amount when it is foreseeable that more extensive services probably will be required, unless the situation is adequately explained to the client. Otherwise, the client might have to bargain for further assistance in the midst of a proceeding or transaction. However, it is proper to define the extent of services in light of the client's ability to pay. A lawyer should not exploit a fee arrangement based primarily on hourly charges by using wasteful procedures. When there is doubt whether a contingent fee is consistent with the client's best interest, the lawyer should offer the client alternative bases for the fee and explain their implications. Applicable law may impose limitations on contingent fees, such as a ceiling on the percentage.

Division of Fee

[4] A division of fee is a single billing to a client covering the fee of two or more lawyers who are not in the same firm. A division of fee facilitates

association of more than one lawyer in a matter in which neither alone could serve the client as well, and most often is used when the fee is contingent and the division is between a referring lawyer and a trial specialist. Paragraph (e) permits the lawyers to divide a fee on either the basis of the proportion of services they render or by agreement between the participating lawyers if all assume responsibility for the representation as a whole and the client is advised and does not object. It does not require disclosure to the client of the share that each lawyer is to receive. Joint responsibility for the representation entails the obligations stated in Rule 5.1 for purposes of the matter involved.

Disputes over Fees

[5] If a procedure has been established for resolution of fee disputes, such as an arbitration or mediation procedure established by the bar, the lawyer should conscientiously consider submitting to it. Law may prescribe a procedure for determining a lawyer's fee, for example, in representation of an executor or administrator, a class or a person entitled to a reasonable fee as part of the measure of damages. The lawyer entitled to such a fee and a lawyer representing another party concerned with the fee should comply with the prescribed procedure.

Model Code Comparison

DR 2-106(A) provided that a lawyer "shall not enter into an agreement for charge, or collect an illegal or clearly excessive fee." DR 2-106(B) provided that a fee is "clearly excessive when, after a review of the facts, a lawyer of ordinary prudence would be left with a definite and firm conviction that the fee is in excess of a reasonable fee." The factors of a reasonable fee in Rule 1.5(a) are substantially identical to those listed in DR 2-106(B). EC 2-17 states that a lawyer "should not charge more than a reasonable fee...."

There was no counterpart to paragraph (b) in the Disciplinary Rules of the Model Code. EC 2-19 stated that it is "usually beneficial to reduce to writing the understanding of the parties regarding the fee, particularly when it is contingent."

There was also no counterpart to paragraph (c) in the Disciplinary Rules of the Model Code. EC 2-20 provided that "[c]ontingent fee arrangements in civil cases have long been commonly accepted in the United States," but that "a lawyer generally should decline to accept employment on a contingent fee basis by one who is able to pay a reasonable fixed fee...."

With regard to paragraph (d), DR 2-106(C) prohibited "a contingent fee in a criminal case." EC 2-20 provided that "contingent fee arrangements in domestic relation cases are rarely justified."

With regard to paragraph (e), DR 2-107(A) permitted division of fees only if:

"(1) The client consents to employment of the other lawyer after a full disclosure that a division of fees will be made.

(2) The division is in proportion to the services performed and responsibility assumed by each.

(3) The total fee does not exceed clearly reasonable compensation...." Paragraph (e) permits division without regard to the services rendered by each lawyer if they assume joint responsibility for the representation.

Rule 1.6. Confidentiality of Information

(a) A lawyer shall not reveal information relating to representation of a client unless the client consents after consultation, except for disclosures that are impliedly authorized in order to carry out the representation, and except as stated in paragraph (b):

(b) A lawyer may reveal such information to the extent the lawyer reasonably believes necessary:

(1) to prevent the client from committing a criminal act that the lawyer believes is likely to result in imminent death or substantial bodily harm; or

(2) to establish a claim or defense on behalf of the lawyer in a controversy between the lawyer and the client, to establish a defense to a criminal charge or civil claim against the lawyer based upon conduct in which the client was involved, or to respond to allegations in any proceeding concerning the lawyer's representation of the client.

Comment

[1] The lawyer is part of a judicial system charged with upholding the law. One of the lawyer's functions is to advise clients so that they avoid any violation of the law in the proper exercise of their rights.

[2] The observance of the ethical obligation of a lawyer to hold inviolate confidential information of the client not only facilitates the full development of facts essential to proper representation of the client but also encourages people to seek early legal assistance.

[3] Almost without exception, clients come to lawyers in order to determine what their rights are and what is, in the maze of laws and regulations, deemed to be legal and correct. The common law recognizes that the client's confidences must be protected from disclosure. Based upon experience, lawyers know that almost all clients follow the advice given, and the law is upheld.

[4] A fundamental principle in the client-lawyer relationship is that the lawyer maintain confidentiality of information relating to the representation. The client is thereby encouraged to communicate fully and frankly with the lawyer even as to embarrassing or legally damaging subject matter.

[5] The principle of confidentiality is given effect in two related bodies of law, the attorney-client privilege (which includes the work product doctrine) in the law of evidence and the rule of confidentiality established in professional ethics. The attorney-client privilege applies in judicial and other proceedings in which a lawyer may be called as a witness or otherwise required to produce evidence

concerning a client. The rule of client-lawyer confidentiality applies in situations other than those where evidence is sought from the lawyer through compulsion of law. The confidentiality rule applies not merely to matters communicated in confidence by the client but also to all information relating to the representation, whatever its source. A lawyer may not disclose such information except as authorized or required by the Rules of Professional Conduct or other law. See also Scope.

[6] The requirement of maintaining confidentiality of information relating to representation applies to government lawyers who may disagree with the policy goals that their representation is designed to advance.

Authorized Disclosure

[7] A lawyer is impliedly authorized to make disclosures about a client when appropriate in carrying out the representation, except to the extent that the client's instructions or special circumstances limit that authority. In litigation, for example, a lawyer may disclose information by admitting a fact that cannot properly be disputed, or in negotiation by making a disclosure that facilitates a satisfactory conclusion.

[8] Lawyers in a firm may, in the course of the firm's practice, disclose to each other information relating to a client of the firm, unless the client has instructed that particular information be confined to specified lawyers.

Disclosure Adverse to Client

[9] The confidentiality rule is subject to limited exceptions. In becoming privy to information about a client, a lawyer may foresee that the client intends serious harm to another person. However, to the extent a lawyer is required or permitted to disclose a client's purposes, the client will be inhibited from revealing facts which would enable the lawyer to counsel against a wrongful course of action. The public is better protected if full and open communication by the client is encouraged than if it is inhibited.

[10] Several situations must be distinguished.

[11] First, the lawyer may not counsel or assist a client in conduct that is criminal or fraudulent. See Rule 1.2(d). Similarly, a lawyer has a duty under Rule 3.3(a)(4) not to use false evidence. This duty is essentially a special instance of the duty prescribed in Rule 1.2(d) to avoid assisting a client in criminal or fraudulent conduct.

[12] Second, the lawyer may have been innocently involved in past conduct by the client that was criminal or fraudulent. In such a situation the lawyer has not violated Rule 1.2(d), because to "counsel or assist" criminal or fraudulent conduct requires knowing that the conduct is of that character.

[13] Third, the lawyer may learn that a client intends prospective conduct that is criminal and likely to result in imminent death or substantial bodily harm. As stated in paragraph (b)(1), the lawyer has professional discretion to reveal information in order to prevent such consequences. The lawyer may make a

disclosure in order to prevent homicide or serious bodily injury which the lawyer reasonably believes is intended by a client. It is very difficult for a lawyer to "know" when such a heinous purpose will actually be carried out, for the client may have a change of mind.

[14] The lawyer's exercise of discretion requires consideration of such factors as the nature of the lawyer's relationship with the client and with those who might be injured by the client, the lawyer's own involvement in the transaction and factors that may extenuate the conduct in question. Where practical, the lawyer should seek to persuade the client to take suitable action. In any case, a disclosure adverse to the client's interest should be no greater than the lawyer reasonably believes necessary to the purpose. A lawyer's decision not to take preventive action permitted by paragraph (b)(1) does not violate this Rule.

Withdrawal

[15] If the lawyer's services will be used by the client in materially furthering a course of criminal or fraudulent conduct, the lawyer must withdraw, as stated in Rule 1.16(a)(1).

[16] After withdrawal the lawyer is required to refrain from making disclosure of the client's confidences, except as otherwise provided in Rule 1.6. Neither this rule nor Rule 1.8(b) nor Rule 1.16(d) prevents the lawyer from giving notice of the fact of withdrawal, and the lawyer may also withdraw or disaffirm any opinion, document, affirmation, or the like.

[17] Where the client is an organization, the lawyer may be in doubt whether contemplated conduct will actually be carried out by the organization. Where necessary to guide conduct in connection with this Rule, the lawyer may make inquiry within the organization as indicated in Rule 1.13(b).

Dispute Concerning a Lawyer's Conduct

[18] Where a legal claim or disciplinary charge alleges complicity of the lawyer in a client's conduct or other misconduct of the lawyer involving representation of the client, the lawyer may respond to the extent the lawyer reasonably believes necessary to establish a defense. The same is true with respect to a claim involving the conduct or representation of a former client. The lawyer's right to respond arises when an assertion of such complicity has been made. Paragraph (b)(2) does not require the lawyer to await the commencement of an action or proceeding that charges such complicity, so that the defense may be established by responding directly to a third party who has made such an assertion. The right to defend, of course, applies where a proceeding has been commenced. Where practicable and not prejudicial to the lawyer's ability to establish the defense, the lawyer should advise the client of the third party's assertion and request that the client respond appropriately. In any event, disclosure should be no greater than the lawyer reasonably believes is necessary to vindicate innocence, the disclosure should be made in a manner which limits access to the information to the tribunal or others persons having a need to know

it, and appropriate protective orders or others arrangements should be sought by the lawyer to the fullest extent practicable.

[19] If the lawyer is charged with wrongdoing in which the client's conduct is implicated, the rule of confidentiality should not prevent the lawyer from defending against the charge. Such a charge can arise in a civil, criminal or professional disciplinary proceeding, and can be based on a wrong allegedly committed by the lawyer against the client, or on a wrong alleged by a third person; for example, a person claiming to have been defrauded by the lawyer and client acting together. A lawyer entitled to a fee is permitted by paragraph (b)(2) to prove the services rendered in an action to collect it. This aspect of the rule expresses the principle that the beneficiary of a fiduciary relationship may not exploit it to the detriment of the fiduciary. As stated above, the lawyer must make every effort practicable to avoid unnecessary disclosure of information relating to a representation, to limit disclosure to those having the need to know it, and to obtain protective orders or make other arrangements minimizing the risk of disclosure.

Disclosures Otherwise Required or Authorized

[20] The attorney-client privilege is differently defined in various jurisdictions. If a lawyer is called as a witness to give testimony concerning a client, absent waiver by the client, paragraph (a) requires the lawyer to invoke the privilege when it is applicable. The lawyer must comply with the final orders of a court or other tribunal of competent jurisdiction requiring the lawyer to give information about the client.

[21] The Rules of Professional Conduct in various circumstances permit or require a lawyer to disclose information relating to the representation. See Rules 2.2, 2.3, 3.3 and 4.1. In addition to these provisions, a lawyer may be obligated or permitted by other provisions of law to give information about a client. Whether another provision of law supersedes Rule 1.6 is a matter of interpretation beyond the scope of these Rules, but a presumption should exist against such a supersession.

Former Client

[22] The duty of confidentiality continues after the client-lawyer relationship has terminated.

Model Code Comparison

Rule 1.6 eliminates the two-pronged duty under the Model Code in favor of a single standard protecting all information about a client "relating to representation." Under DR 4-101, the requirement applied to information protected by the attorney-client privilege and to information "gained in" the professional relationship that "the client has requested be held inviolate or the disclosure of which would be embarrassing or would be likely to be detrimental to the client." EC 4-4 added that the duty differed from the evidentiary privilege in that it existed "without regard to the nature or source of information or the fact that others share the knowledge." Rule 1.6 imposes confidentiality on information relating to the representation even if it is acquired before or after the relationship existed. It does not require the client to indicate information that is to be confidential, or permit the lawyer to speculate whether particular information might be embarrassing or detrimental.

Paragraph (a) permits a lawyer to disclose information where impliedly, authorized to do so in order to carry out the representation. Under DR 4-101(B) and (C), a lawyer was not permitted to reveal "confidences" unless the client first consented after disclosure.

Rule 1.7. Conflict of Interest: General Rule

(a) A lawyer shall not represent a client if the representation of that client will be directly adverse to another client, unless:

    (1) the lawyer reasonably believes the representation will not adversely affect the relationship with the other client; and

    (2) each client consents after consultation.

(b) A lawyer shall not represent a client if the representation of that client may be materially limited by the lawyer's responsibilities to another client or to a third person, or by the lawyer's own interests, unless:

    (1) the lawyer reasonably believes the representation will not be adversely affected; and

    (2) the client consents after consultation.

When representation of multiple clients in a single matter is undertaken, the consultation shall include explanation of the implications of the common representation and the advantages and risks involved.

Comment

Loyalty to a Client

[1] Loyalty is an essential element in the lawyer's relationship to a client. An impermissible conflict of interest may exist before representation is undertaken, in which event the representation should be declined. The lawyer should adopt reasonable procedures, appropriate for the size and type of firm and practice, to determine in both litigation and non-litigation matters the parties and issues involved and to determine whether there are actual or potential conflicts of interest.

[2] If such a conflict arises after representation has been undertaken, the lawyer should withdraw from the representation. See Rule 1.16. Where more than one client is involved and the lawyer withdraws because a conflict arises after representation, whether the lawyer may continue to represent any of the clients is determined by Rule 1.9. See also Rule 2.2(c). As to whether a client-lawyer

relationship exists or, having once been established, is continuing, see Comment to Rule 1.3 and Scope.

[3] As a general proposition, loyalty to a client prohibits undertaking representation directly adverse to that client without that client's consent. Paragraph (a) expresses that general rule. Thus, a lawyer ordinarily may not act as advocate against a person the lawyer represents in some other matter, even if it is wholly unrelated. On the other hand, simultaneous representation in unrelated matters of clients whose interests are only generally adverse, such as competing economic enterprises, does not require consent of the respective clients. Paragraph (a) applies only when the representation of one client would be directly adverse to the other.

[4] Loyalty to a client is also impaired when a lawyer cannot consider, recommend or carry out an appropriate course of action for the client because of the lawyer's other responsibilities or interests. The conflict in effect forecloses alternatives that would otherwise be available to the client. Paragraph (b) addresses such situations. A possible conflict does not itself preclude the representation. The critical questions are the likelihood that a conflict will eventuate and, if it does, whether it will materially interfere with the lawyer's independent professional judgment in considering alternatives or foreclose courses of action that reasonably should be pursued on behalf of the client. Consideration should be given to whether the client wishes to accommodate the other interest involved.

Consultation and Consent

[5] A client may consent to representation notwithstanding a conflict. However, as indicated in paragraph (a)(1) with respect to representation directly adverse to a client, and paragraph (b)(1) with respect to material limitations on representation of a client, when a disinterested lawyer would conclude that the client should not agree to the representation under the circumstances, the lawyer involved cannot properly ask for such agreement or provide representation on the basis of the client's consent. When more than one client is involved, the question of conflict must be resolved as to each client. Moreover, there may be circumstances where it is impossible to make the disclosure necessary to obtain consent. For example, when the lawyer represents different clients in related matters and one of the clients refuses to consent to the disclosure necessary to permit the other client to make an informed decision, the lawyer cannot properly ask the latter to consent.

Lawyer's Interests

[6] The lawyer's own interests should not be permitted to have an adverse effect on representation of a client. For example, a lawyer's need for income should not lead the lawyer to undertake matters that cannot be handled competently and at a reasonable fee. See Rules 1.1 and 1.5. If the probity of a lawyer's own conduct in a transaction is in serious question, it may be difficult or

impossible for the lawyer to give a client detached advice. A lawyer may not allow related business interests to affect representation, for example, by referring clients to an enterprise in which the lawyer has an undisclosed interest.

Conflicts in Litigation

[7] Paragraph (a) prohibits representation of opposing parties in litigation. Simultaneous representation of parties whose interests in litigation may conflict, such as coplaintiffs or codefendants, is governed by paragraph (b). An impermissible conflict may exist by reason of substantial discrepancy in the parties' testimony, incompatibility in positions in relation to an opposing party or the fact that there are substantially different possibilities of settlement of the claims or liabilities in question. Such conflicts can arise in criminal cases as well as civil. The potential for conflict of interest in representing multiple defendants in a criminal case is so grave that ordinarily a lawyer should decline to represent more than one codefendant. On the other hand, common representation of persons having similar interests is proper if the risk of adverse effect is minimal and the requirements of paragraph (b) are met. Compare Rule 2.2 involving intermediation between clients.

[8] Ordinarily, a lawyer may not act as advocate against a client the lawyer represents in some other matter, even if the other matter is wholly unrelated. However, there are circumstances in which a lawyer may act as advocate against a client. For example, a lawyer representing an enterprise with diverse operations may accept employment as an advocate against the enterprise in an unrelated matter if doing so will not adversely affect the lawyer's relationship with the enterprise or conduct of the suit and if both clients consent upon consultation. By the same token, government lawyers in some circumstances may represent government employees in proceedings in which a government agency is the opposing party. The propriety of concurrent representation can depend on the nature of the litigation. For example, a suit charging fraud entails conflict to a degree not involved in a suit for a declaratory judgment concerning statutory interpretation.

[9] A lawyer may represent parties having antagonistic positions on a legal question that has arisen in different cases, unless representation of either client would be adversely affected. Thus, it is ordinarily not improper to assert such positions in cases pending in different trial courts, but it may be improper to do so in cases pending at the same time in an appellate court.

Interest of Person Paying for a Lawyer's Service

[10] A lawyer may be paid from a source other than the client, if the client is informed of that fact and consents and the arrangement does not compromise the lawyer's duty of loyalty to the client. See Rule 1.8(f). For example, when an insurer and its insured have conflicting interests in a matter arising from a liability insurance agreement, and the insurer is required to provide special counsel for the insured, the arrangement should assure the special counsel's

professional independence. So also, when a corporation and its directors or employees are involved in a controversy in which they have conflicting interests, the corporation may provide funds for separate legal representation of the directors or employees, if the clients consent after consultation and the arrangement ensures the lawyer's professional independence.

Other Conflict Situations

[11] Conflicts of interest in contexts other than litigation sometimes may be difficult to assess. Relevant factors in determining whether there is potential for adverse effect include the duration and intimacy of the lawyer's relationship with the client or clients involved, the functions being performed by the lawyer, the likelihood that actual conflict will arise and the likely prejudice to the client from the conflict if it does arise. The question is often one of proximity and degree.

[12] For example, a lawyer may not represent multiple parties to a negotiation whose interests are fundamentally antagonistic to each other, but common representation is permissible where the clients are generally aligned in interest even though there is some difference of interest among them.

[13] Conflict questions may also arise in estate planning and estate administration. A lawyer may be called upon to prepare wills for several family members, such as husband and wife, and, depending upon the circumstances, a conflict of interest may arise. In estate administration the identity of the client may be unclear under the law of a particular jurisdiction. Under one view, the client is the fiduciary; under another view the client is the estate or trust, including its beneficiaries. The lawyer should make clear the relationship to the parties involved.

[14] A lawyer for a corporation or other organization who is also a member of its board of directors should determine whether the responsibilities of the two roles may conflict. The lawyer may be called on to advise the corporation in matters involving actions of the directors. Consideration should be given to the frequency with which such situations may arise, the potential intensity of the conflict, the effect of the lawyer's resignation from the board and the possibility of the corporation's obtaining legal advice from another lawyer in such situations. If there is material risk that the dual role will compromise the lawyer's independence of professional judgment, the lawyer should not serve as a director.

Conflict Charged by an Opposing Party

[15] Resolving questions of conflict of interest is primarily the responsibility of the lawyer undertaking the representation. In litigation, a court may raise the question when there is reason to infer that the lawyer has neglected the responsibility. In a criminal case, inquiry by the court is generally required when a lawyer represents multiple defendants. Where the conflict is such as clearly to call in question the fair or efficient administration of justice, opposing counsel may properly raise the question. Such an objection should be viewed with caution, however, for it can be misused as a technique of harassment. See Scope.

Model Code Comparison

DR 5-101(A) provided that "[e]xcept with the consent of his client after full disclosure, a lawyer shall not accept employment if the exercise of his professional judgment on behalf of the client will be or reasonably may be affected by his own financial, business, property, or personal interests." DR 5-105(A) provided that a lawyer "shall decline proffered employment if the exercise of his independent professional judgment in behalf of a client will be or is likely to be adversely affected by the acceptance of the proffered employment, or if it would be likely to involve him in representing differing interests, except to the extent permitted under DR 5-105(C)." DR 5-105(C) provided that "a lawyer may represent multiple clients if it is obvious that he can adequately represent the interest of each and if each consents to the representation after full disclosure of the possible effect of such representation on the exercise of his independent professional judgment on behalf of each." DR 5-107(B) provided that a lawyer "shall not permit a person who recommends, employs, or pays him to render legal services for another to direct or regulate his professional judgment in rendering such services."

Rule 1.7 clarifies DR 5-105(A) by requiring that when the lawyer's other interests are involved, not only must the client consent after consultation but also that, independent of such consent, the representation reasonably appears not to be adversely affected by the lawyer's other interests. This requirement appears to be the intended meaning of the provision in DR 5-105(C) that "it is obvious that he can adequately represent" the client, and was implicit in EC 5-2, which stated that a lawyer "should not accept proffered employment if his personal interests or desires will, or there is a reasonable probability that they will, affect adversely the advice to be given or services to be rendered the prospective client."

Rule 1.8. Conflict of Interest: Prohibited Transactions

(a) A lawyer shall not enter into a business transaction with a client or knowingly acquire an ownership, possessory, security or other pecuniary interest adverse to a client unless:

(1) the transaction and terms on which the lawyer acquires the interest are fair and reasonable to the client and are fully disclosed and transmitted in writing to the client in a manner which can be reasonably understood by the client;

(2) the client is given a reasonable opportunity to seek the advice of independent counsel in the transaction; and

(3) the client consents in writing thereto.

(b) A lawyer shall not use information relating to representation of a client to the disadvantage of the client unless the client consents after consultation, except as permitted or required by Rule 1.6 or Rule 3.3.

(c) A lawyer shall not prepare an instrument giving the lawyer or a person related to the lawyer as parent, child, sibling, or spouse any substantial gift from a client, including a testamentary gift, except where the client is related to the donee.

(d) Prior to the conclusion of representation of a client, a lawyer shall not make or negotiate an agreement giving the lawyer literary or media rights to a portrayal or account based in substantial part on information relating to the representation.

(e) A lawyer shall not provide financial assistance to a client in connection with pending or contemplated litigation, except that:

> (1) a lawyer may advance court costs and expenses of litigation, the repayment of which may be contingent on the outcome of the matter; and
> (2) a lawyer representing an indigent client may pay court costs and expenses of litigation on behalf of the client.

(f) A lawyer shall not accept compensation for representing a client from one other than the client unless:

> (1) the client consents after consultation;
> (2) there is no interference with the lawyer's independence of professional judgment or with the client-lawyer relationship; and
> (3) information relating to representation of a client is protected as required by Rule 1.6.

(g) A lawyer who represents two or more clients shall not participate in making an aggregate settlement of the claims of or against the clients, or in a criminal case an aggregated agreement as to guilty or nolo contendere pleas, unless each client consents after consultation, including disclosure of the existence and nature of all the claims or pleas involved and of the participation of each person in the settlement.

(h) A lawyer shall not make an agreement prospectively limiting the lawyer's liability to a client for malpractice unless permitted by law and the client is independently represented in making the agreement, or settle a claim for such liability with an unrepresented client or former client without first advising that person in writing that independent representation is appropriate in connection therewith.

(i) A lawyer related to another lawyer as parent, child, sibling or spouse shall not represent a client in a representation directly adverse to a person whom the lawyer knows is represented by the other lawyer except upon consent by the client after consultation regarding the relationship.

(j) A lawyer shall not acquire a proprietary interest in the cause of action or subject matter of litigation the lawyer is conducting for a client, except that the lawyer may:

> (1) acquire a lien granted by law to secure the lawyer's fee or expenses; and
> (2) contract with a client for a reasonable contingent fee in a civil case.

Comment

Transactions Between Client and Lawyer

[1] As a general principle, all transactions between client and lawyer should be fair and reasonable to the client. In such transactions a review by independent counsel on behalf of the client is often advisable. Furthermore, a lawyer may not exploit information relating to the representation to the client's disadvantage. For example, a lawyer who has learned that the client is investing in specific real estate may not, without the client's consent, seek to acquire nearby property where doing so would adversely affect the client's plan for investment. Paragraph (a) does not, however, apply to standard commercial transactions between the lawyer and the client for products or services that the client generally markets to others, for example, banking or brokerage services, medical services, products manufactured or distributed by the client, and utilities' services. In such transactions, the lawyer has no advantage in dealing with the client, and the restrictions in paragraph (a) are unnecessary and impracticable.

[2] A lawyer may accept a gift from a client, if the transaction meets general standards of fairness. For example, a simple gift such as a present given at a holiday or as a token of appreciation is permitted. If effectuation of a substantial gift requires preparing a legal instrument such as a will or conveyance, however, the client should have the detached advice that another lawyer can provide. Paragraph (c) recognizes an exception where the client is a relative of the donee or the gift is not substantial.

Literary Rights

[3] An agreement by which a lawyer acquires literary or media rights concerning the conduct of the representation creates a conflict between the interests of the client and the personal interests of the lawyer. Measures suitable in the representation of the client may detract from the publication value of an account of the representation. Paragraph (d) does not prohibit a lawyer representing a client in a transaction concerning literary property from agreeing that the lawyer's fee shall consist of a share in ownership in the property, if the arrangement conforms to Rule 1.5 and paragraph (j).

Person Paying for a Lawyer's Services

[4] Paragraph (f) requires disclosure of the fact that the lawyer's services are being paid for by a third party. Such an arrangement must also conform to the requirements of Rule 1.6 concerning confidentially and Rule 1.7 concerning conflict of interest. Where the client is a class, consent may be obtained on behalf of the class by court-supervised procedure.

Limiting Liability

[5] Paragraph (h) is not intended to apply to customary qualifications and limitations in legal opinions and memoranda.

Family Relationships Between Lawyers

[6] Paragraph (i) applies to related lawyers who are in different firms. Related lawyers in the same firm are governed by Rules 1.7, 1.9, and 1.10. The disqualification stated in paragraph (i) is personal and is not imputed to members of firms with whom the lawyers are associated.

Acquisition of Interest in Litigation

[7] Paragraph (j) states the traditional general rule that lawyers are prohibited from acquiring a proprietary interest in litigation. This general rule, which has its basis in common law champerty and maintenance, is subject to specific exceptions developed in decisional law and continued in these Rules, such as the exception for reasonable contingent fees set forth in Rule 1.5 and the exception for certain advances of the costs of litigation set forth in paragraph (e).

Model Code Comparison

With regard to paragraph (a), DR 5-104(A) provided that a lawyer "shall not enter into a business transaction with a client if they have differing interests therein and if the client expects the lawyer to exercise his professional judgment therein for the protection of the client, unless the client has consented after full disclosure." EC 5-3 stated that a lawyer "should not seek to persuade his client to permit him to invest in an undertaking of his client nor make improper use of his professional relationship to influence his client to invest in an enterprise in which the lawyer is interested."

With regard to paragraph (b), DR 4-101(B)(3) provided that a lawyer should not use "a confidence or secret of his client for the advantage of himself, or of a third person, unless the client consents after full disclosure."

There was no counterpart to paragraph (c) in the Disciplinary Rules of the Model Code. EC 5-5 stated that a lawyer "should not suggest to his client that a gift be made to himself or for his benefit. If a lawyer accepts a gift from his client, he is peculiarly susceptible to the charge that he unduly influenced or overreached the client. If a client voluntarily offers to make a gift to his lawyer, the lawyer may accept the gift, but before doing so, he should urge that the client secure disinterested advice from an independent, competent person who is cognizant of all the circumstances. Other than in exceptional circumstances, a lawyer should insist that an instrument in which his client desires to name him beneficially be prepared by another lawyer selected by the client."

Paragraph (d) is substantially similar to DR 5-104(B), but refers to "literary or media" rights, a more generally inclusive term than "publication" rights.

Paragraph (e)(1) is similar to DR 5-103(B), but eliminates the requirement that "the client remains ultimately liable for such expenses."

Paragraph (e)(2) has no counterpart in the Model Code.

Paragraph (f) is substantially identical to DR 5-107(A)(1).

Paragraph (g) is substantially identical to DR 5-106.

The first clause of paragraph (h) is similar to DR 6-102(A). There was no counterpart in the Model Code to the second clause of paragraph (h).

Paragraph (i) has no counterpart in the Model Code.

Paragraph (j) is substantially identical to DR 5-103(A).

Rule 1.9. Conflict of Interest: Former Client

(a) A lawyer who has formerly represented a client in a matter shall not thereafter represent another person in the same or a substantially related matter in which that person's interests are materially adverse to the interests of the former client unless the former client consents after consultation.

(b) A lawyer shall not knowingly represent a person in the same or a substantially related matter in which a firm with which the lawyer formerly was associated had previously represented a client

    (1) whose interests are materially adverse to that person; and

    (2) about whom the lawyer had acquired information protected by Rules 1.6 and 1.9(c) that is material to the matter; unless the former client consents after consultation.

(c) A lawyer who has formerly represented a client in a matter or whose present or former firm has formerly represented a client in a matter shall not thereafter:

    (1) use information relating to the representation to the disadvantage of the former client except as Rule 1.6 or Rule 3.3 would permit or require with respect to a client, or when the information has become generally known; or

    (2) reveal information relating to the representation except as Rule 1.6 or Rule 3.3 would permit or require with respect to a client.

Comment

[1] After termination of a client-lawyer relationship, a lawyer may not represent another client except in conformity with this Rule. The principles in Rule 1.7 determine whether the interests of the present and former client are adverse. Thus, a lawyer could not properly seek to rescind on behalf of a new client a contract drafted on behalf of the former client. So also a lawyer who has prosecuted an accused person could not properly represent the accused in a subsequent civil action against the government concerning the same transaction.

[2] The scope of a "matter" for purposes of this Rule may depend on the facts of a particular situation or transaction. The lawyer's involvement in a matter can also be a question of degree. When a lawyer has been directly involved in a specific transaction, subsequent representation of other clients with materially adverse interests clearly is prohibited. On the other hand, a lawyer who recurrently handled a type of problem for a former client is not precluded from later representing another client in a wholly distinct problem of that type even though the subsequent representation involves a position adverse to the prior

client. Similar considerations can apply to the reassignment of military lawyers between defense and prosecution functions within the same military jurisdiction. The underlying question is whether the lawyer was so involved in the matter that the subsequent representation can be justly regarded as a changing of sides in the matter in question.

Lawyers Moving Between Firms

[3] When lawyers have been associated within a firm but then end their association, the question of whether a lawyer should undertake representation is more complicated. There are several competing considerations. First, the client previously represented by the former firm must be reasonably assured that the principle of loyalty to the client is not compromised. Second, the rule should not be so broadly cast as to preclude other persons from having reasonable choice of legal counsel. Third, the rule should not unreasonably hamper lawyers from forming new associations and taking new clients after having left a previous association. In this connection, it should be recognized that today many lawyers practice in firms, that many lawyers to some degree limit their practice to one field or another, and that many move from one association to another several times in their careers. If the concept of imputation were applied with unqualified rigor, the result would be radical curtailment of the opportunity of clients to change counsel.

[4] Reconciliation of these competing principles in the past has been attempted under two rubrics. One approach has been to seek per se rules of disqualification. For example, it has been held that a partner in a law firm is conclusively presumed to have access to all confidences concerning all clients of the firm. This presumption might properly be applied in some circumstances, especially where the client has been extensively represented, but may be unrealistic where the client was represented only for limited purposes. Furthermore, such a rigid rule exaggerates the difference between a partner and an associate in modern law firms.

[5] The other rubric formerly used for dealing with disqualification is the appearance of impropriety proscribed in Canon 9 of the ABA Model Code of Professional Responsibility. This rubric has a two-fold problem. First, the appearance of impropriety can be taken to include any new client-lawyer relationship that might make a former client feel anxious. If that meaning were adopted, disqualification would become little more than a question of subjective judgment by the former client. Second, since "impropriety" is undefined, the term "appearance of impropriety" is question-begging. It therefore has to be recognized that the problem of disqualification cannot be properly resolved either by simple analogy to a lawyer practicing alone or by the very general concept of appearance of impropriety.

Confidentiality

[6] Preserving confidentiality is a question of access to information. Access to information, in turn, is essentially a question of fact in particular circumstances, aided by inferences, deductions or working presumptions that reasonably may be made about the way in which lawyers work together. A lawyer may have general access to files of all clients of a law firm and may regularly participate in discussions of their affairs; it should be inferred that such a lawyer in fact is privy to all information about all the firm's clients. In contrast, another lawyer may have access to the files of only a limited number of clients and participate in discussions of the affairs of no other clients; in the absence of information to the contrary, it should be inferred that such a lawyer in fact is privy to information about the clients actually served but not those of other clients.

[7] Application of paragraph (b) depends on a situation's particular facts. In such an inquiry, the burden of proof should rest upon the firm whose disqualification is sought.

[8] Paragraph (b) operates to disqualify the lawyer only when the lawyer involved has actual knowledge of information protected by Rules 1.6 and 1.9(b). Thus, if a lawyer while with one firm acquired no knowledge or information relating to a particular client of the firm, and that lawyer later joined another firm, neither the lawyer individually nor the second firm is disqualified from representing another client in the same or a related matter even though the interests of the two clients conflict. See Rule 1.10(b) for the restrictions on a firm once a lawyer has terminated association with the firm.

[9] Independent of the question of disqualification of a firm, a lawyer changing professional association has a continuing duty to preserve confidentiality of information about a client formerly represented. See Rules 1.6 and 1.9.

Adverse Positions

[10] The second aspect of loyalty to a client is the lawyer's obligation to decline subsequent representations involving positions adverse to a former client arising in substantially related matters. This obligation requires abstention from adverse representation by the individual lawyer involved, but does not properly entail abstention of other lawyers through imputed disqualification. Hence, this aspect of the problem is governed by Rule 1.9(a). Thus, if a lawyer left one firm for another, the new affiliation would not preclude the firms involved from continuing to represent clients with adverse interests in the same or related matters, so long as the conditions of paragraphs (b) and (c) concerning confidentiality have been met.

[11] Information acquired by the lawyer in the course of representing a client may not subsequently be used or revealed by the lawyer to the disadvantage of the client. However, the fact that a lawyer has once served a client does not preclude the lawyer from using generally known information about that client when later representing another client.

[12] Disqualification from subsequent representation is for the protection of former clients and can be waived by them. A waiver is effective only if there is disclosure of the circumstances, including the lawyer's intended role in behalf of the new client.

[13] With regard to an opposing party's raising a question of conflict of interest, see Comment to Rule 1.7. With regard to disqualification of a firm with which a lawyer is or was formerly associated, see Rule 1.10.

Model Code Comparison

There was no counterpart to this Rule in the Disciplinary Rules of the Model Code. Representation adverse to a former client was sometimes dealt with under the rubric of Canon 9 of the Model Code, which provided: "A lawyer should avoid even the appearance of impropriety." Also applicable were EC 4-6 which stated that the "obligation of a lawyer to preserve the confidences and secrets of his client continues after the termination of his employment" and Canon 5 which stated that "[a] lawyer should exercise independent professional judgment on behalf of a client."

The provision for waiver by the former client in paragraphs (a) and (b) is similar to DR 5-105(C).

The exception in the last clause of paragraph (c)(1) permits a lawyer to use information relating to a former client that is in the "public domain," a use that was also not prohibited by the Model Code, which protected only "confidences and secrets." Since the scope of paragraphs (a) and (b) is much broader than "confidences and secrets," it is necessary to define when a lawyer may make use of information about a client after the client-lawyer relationship has terminated.

Rule 1.10. Imputed Disqualification: General Rule

(a) While lawyers are associated in a firm, none of them shall knowingly represent a client when any one of them practicing alone would be prohibited from doing so by Rules 1.7, 1.8(c), 1.9 or 2.2.

(b) When a lawyer has terminated an association with a firm, the firm is not prohibited from thereafter representing a person with interests materially adverse to those of a client represented by the formerly associated lawyer and not currently represented by the firm, unless:

(1) the matter is the same or substantially related to that in which the formerly associated lawyer represented the client; and

(2) any lawyer remaining in the firm has information protected by Rules 1.6 and 1.9 (c) that is material to the matter.

(c) A disqualification prescribed by this rule may be waived by the affected client under the conditions stated in Rule 1.7.

Comment

Definition of Firm

[1] For purposes of the Rules of Professional conduct, the term "firm" includes lawyers in a private firm, and lawyers in the legal department of a corporation or other organization, or in a legal services organization. Whether two or more lawyers constitute a firm within this definition can depend on the specific facts. For example, two practitioners who share office space and occasionally consult or assist each other ordinarily would not be regarded as constituting a firm. However, if they present themselves to the public in a way suggesting that they are a firm or conduct themselves as a firm, they should be regarded as a firm for the purposes of the rules. The terms of any formal agreement between associated lawyers are relevant in determining whether they are a firm, as is the fact that they have mutual access to information concerning the clients they serve. Furthermore, it is relevant in doubtful cases to consider the underlying purpose of the rule that is involved. A group of lawyers could be regarded as a firm for purposes of the rule that the same lawyer should not represent opposing parties in litigation while it might not be so regarded for purposes of the rule that information acquired by one lawyer is attributed to the other.

[2] With respect to the law department of an organization, there is ordinarily no question that the members of the department constitute a firm within the meaning of the Rules of Professional Conduct. However, there can be uncertainty as to the identity of the client. For example, it may not be clear whether the law department of a corporation represents a subsidiary or an affiliated corporation, as well as the corporation by which the members of the department are directly employed. A similar question can arise concerning an unincorporated association and its local affiliates.

[3] Similar questions can also arise with respect to lawyers in legal aid. Lawyers employed in the same unit of a legal service organization constitute a firm, but not necessarily those employed in separate units. As in the case of independent practitioners, whether the lawyers should be treated as associated with each other can depend on the particular rule that is involved, and on the specific facts of the situation.

[4] Where a lawyer has joined a private firm after having represented the government, the situation is governed by Rule 1.11(a) and (b); where a lawyer represents the government after having served private clients, the situation is governed by Rule 1.11(c)(1). The individual lawyer involved is bound by the Rules generally, including Rules 1.6, 1.7 and 1.9.

[5] Different provisions are thus made for movement of a lawyer from one private firm to another and for movement of a lawyer between a private firm and the government. The government is entitled to protection of its client confidences and, therefore, to the protections provided in Rules 1.6, 1.9 and 1.11. However, if the more extensive disqualification in Rule 1.10 were applied to former government lawyers, the potential effect on the government would be unduly

burdensome. The government deals with all private citizens and organizations and, thus has a much wider circle of adverse legal interests than does any private law firm. In these circumstances, the government's recruitment of lawyers would be seriously impaired if Rule 1.10 were applied to the government. On balance, therefore, the government is better served in the long run by the protections stated in Rule 1.11.

Principals of Imputed Disqualification

[6] The rule of imputed disqualification stated in paragraph (a) gives effect to the principle of loyalty to the client as it applies to lawyers who practice in a law firm. Such situations can be considered from the premise that a firm of lawyers is essentially one lawyer for purposes of the rules governing loyalty to the client, or from the premise that each lawyer is vicariously bound by the obligation of loyalty owed by each lawyer with whom the lawyer is associated. Paragraph (a) operates only among the lawyers currently associated in a firm. When a lawyer moves from one firm to another, the situation is governed by Rules 1.9(b) and 1.10(b).

[7] Rule 1.10(b) operates to permit a law firm, under certain circumstances, to represent a person with interests directly adverse to those of a client represented by a lawyer who formerly was associated with the firm. The Rule applies regardless of when the formerly associated lawyer represented the client. However, the law firm may not represent a person with interests adverse to those of a present client of the firm, which would violate Rule 1.7. Moreover, the firm may not represent the person where the matter is the same or substantially related to that in which the formerly associated lawyer represented the client and any other lawyer currently in the firm has material information protected by Rules 1.6 and 1.9(c).

Model Code Comparison

DR 5-105(D) provided that "[i]f a lawyer is required to decline or to withdraw from employment under a Disciplinary Rule, no partner, or associate, or any other lawyer affiliated with him or his firm, may accept or continue such employment."

Rule 1.13. Organization as Client

(a) A lawyer employed or retained by an organization represents the organization acting through its duly authorized constituents.

(b) If a lawyer for an organization knows that an officer, employee or other person associated with the organization is engaged in action, intends to act or refuses to act in a matter related to the representation that is a violation of law which reasonably might be imputed to the organization, and is likely to result in substantial injury to the organization, the lawyer shall proceed as is reasonably necessary in the best interest of the organization. In determining how to proceed, the lawyer shall give due consideration to the seriousness of the violation and its consequences, the scope and nature of the lawyer's representation, the responsibility in the organization and the apparent motivation of the person involved, the policies of the organization concerning such matters and any other relevant considerations. Any measures taken shall be designed to minimize disruption of the organization and the risk of revealing information relating to the representation to persons outside the organization. Such measures may include among others:

(1) asking reconsideration of the matter;

(2) advising that a separate legal opinion on the matter be sought for presentation to appropriate authority in the organization; and

(3) referring the matter to higher authority in the organization, including, if warranted by the seriousness of the matter, referral to the highest authority that can act in behalf of the organization as determined by applicable law.

(c) If, despite the lawyer's efforts in accordance with paragraph (b), the highest authority that can act on behalf of the organization insists upon action, or a refusal to act, that is clearly a violation of law and is likely to result in substantial injury to the organization, the lawyer may resign in accordance with Rule 1.16.

(d) In dealing with an organization's directors, officers, employees, members, shareholders or other constituents, a lawyer shall explain the identity of the client when it is apparent that the organization's interests are adverse to those of the constituents with whom the lawyer is dealing.

(e) A lawyer representing an organization may also represent any of its directors, officers, employees, members, shareholders or other constituents, subject to the provisions of Rule 1.7. If the organization's consent to the dual representation is required by Rule 1.7, the consent shall be given by an appropriate official of the organization other than the individual who is to be represented, or by the shareholders.

Comment

The Entity as the Client

[1] An organizational client is a legal entity, but it cannot act except through its officers, directors, employees, shareholders and other constituents. Officers, directors, employees and shareholders are the constituents of the corporate organizational client. The duties defined in this Comment apply equally to unincorporated associations. "Other constituents" as used in this Comment means the positions equivalent to officers, directors, employees and shareholders held by persons acting for organizational clients that are not corporations.

[2] When one of the constituents of an organizational client communicates with the organization's lawyer in that person's organizational capacity, the communication is protected by Rule 1.6. Thus, by way of example, if an organizational client requests its lawyer to investigate allegations of wrongdoing, interviews

made in the course of that investigation between the lawyer and the client's employees or other constituents are covered by Rule 1.6. This does not mean, however, that constituents of an organizational client are the clients of the lawyer. The lawyer may not disclose to such constituents information relating to the representation except for disclosures explicitly or impliedly authorized by the organizational client in order to carry out the representation or as otherwise permitted by Rule 1.6.

[3] When constituents of the organization make decisions for it, the decisions ordinarily must be accepted by the lawyer even if their utility or prudence is doubtful. Decisions concerning policy and operations, including ones entailing serious risk, are not as such in the lawyer's province. However, different considerations arise when the lawyer knows that the organization may be substantially injured by action of a constituent that is in violation of law. In such a circumstance, it may be reasonably necessary for the lawyer to ask the constituent to reconsider the matter. If that fails, or if the matter is of sufficient seriousness and important to the organization, it may be reasonably necessary for the lawyer to take steps to have the matter reviewed by a higher authority in the organization. Clear justification should exist for seeking review over the head of the constituent normally responsible for it. The stated policy of the organization may define circumstances and prescribe channels for such review, and a lawyer should encourage the formulation of such a policy. Even in the absence of organization policy, however, the lawyer may have an obligation to refer a matter to higher authority, depending on the seriousness of the matter and whether the constituent in question has apparent motives to act at variance with the organization's interest. Review by the chief executive officer or by the board of directors may be required when the matter is of importance commensurate with their authority. At some point it may be useful or essential to obtain an independent legal opinion.

[4] In an extreme case, it may be reasonably necessary for the lawyer to refer the matter to the organization's higher authority. Ordinarily, that is the board of directors or similar governing body. However, applicable law may prescribe that under certain conditions highest authority reposes elsewhere, for example, in the independent directors of a corporation.

Relation to Other Rules

[5] The authority and responsibility provided in paragraph (b) are concurrent with the authority and responsibility provided in other Rules. In particular, this Rule does not limit or expand the lawyer's responsibility under Rule 1.6, 1.8, 1.16, 3.3 or 4.1. If the lawyer's services are being used by an organization to further a crime or fraud by the organization, Rule 1.2(d) can be applicable.

Government Agency

[6] The duty defined in this Rule applies to governmental organizations. However, when the client is a governmental organization, a different balance may

be appropriate between maintaining confidentiality and assuring that the wrongful official act is prevented or rectified, for public business is involved. In addition, duties of lawyers employed by the government or lawyers in military service may be defined by statutes and regulation. Therefore, defining precisely the identity of the client and prescribing the resulting obligations of such lawyers may be more difficult in the government context. Although in some circumstances the client may be a specific agency, it is generally the government as a whole. For example, if the action or failure to act involves the head of a bureau, either the department of which the bureau is a part or the government as a whole may be the client for purpose of this Rule. Moreover, in a matter involving the conduct of government officials, a government lawyer may have authority to question such conduct more extensively than that of a lawyer for a private organization in similar circumstances. This Rule does not limit that authority. See note on Scope.

Clarifying the Lawyer's Role

[7] There are times when the organization's interests may be or become adverse to those of one or more of its constituents. In such circumstances the lawyer should advise any constituent, whose interest the lawyer finds adverse to that of the organization of the conflict or potential conflict of interest, that the lawyer cannot represent such constituent, and that such person may wish to obtain independent representation. Care must be taken to assure that the individual understands that, when there is such adversity of interest, the lawyer for the organization cannot provide legal representation for that constituent individual, and that discussions between the lawyer for the organization and the individual may not be privileged.

[8] Whether such a warning should be given by the lawyer for the organization to any constituent individual may turn on the facts of each case.

Dual Representation

[9] Paragraph (e) recognizes that a lawyer for an organization may also represent a principal officer or major shareholder.

Derivative Actions

[10] Under generally prevailing law, the shareholders or members of a corporation may bring suit to compel the directors to perform their legal obligations in the supervision of the organization. Members of unincorporated associations have essentially the same right. Such an action may be brought nominally by the organization, but usually is, in fact, a legal controversy over management of the organization.

[11] The question can arise whether counsel for the organization may defend such an action. The proposition that the organization is the lawyer's client does not alone resolve the issue. Most derivative actions are a normal incident of an organization's affairs, to be defended by the organization's lawyer like any other suit. However, if the claim involves serious charges of wrongdoing by those in

control of the organization, a conflict may arise between the lawyer's duty to the organization and the lawyer's relationship with the board. In those circumstances, Rule 1.7 governs who should represent the directors and the organization.

Model Code Comparison

There was no counterpart to this Rule in the Disciplinary Rules of the Model Code. EC 5-18 stated that a "lawyer employed or retained by a corporation or similar entity owes his allegiance to the entity and not to a stockholder, director, officer, employee, representative, or other person connected with the entity. In advising the entity, a lawyer should keep paramount its interests and his professional judgment should not be influenced by the personal desires of any person or organization. Occasionally, a lawyer for an entity is requested by a stockholder, director, officer, employee, representative, or other person connected with the entity to represent him in an individual capacity; in such case the lawyer may serve the individual only if the lawyer is convinced that differing interests are not present." EC 5-24 stated that although a lawyer "may be employed by a business corporation with non-lawyers serving as directors or officers, and they necessarily have the right to make decisions of business policy, a lawyer must decline to accept direction of his professional judgment from any layman." DR 5-107(B) provided that a lawyer "shall not permit a person who ... employs ... him to render legal services for another to direct or regulate his professional judgment in rendering such legal services."

COUNSELOR

Rule 2.1. Advisor

In representing a client, a lawyer shall exercise independent professional judgment and render candid advice. In rendering advice, a lawyer may refer not only to law but to other considerations such as moral, economic, social and political factors, that may be relevant to the client's situation.

Comment

Scope of Advice

[1] A client is entitled to straightforward advice expressing the lawyer's honest assessment. Legal advice often involves unpleasant facts and alternatives that a client may be disinclined to confront. In presenting advice, a lawyer endeavors to sustain the client's morale and may put advice in as acceptable a form as honesty permits. However, a lawyer should not be deterred from giving candid advice by the prospect that the advice will be unpalatable to the client.

[2] Advice couched in narrowly legal terms may be of little value to a client, especially where practical considerations, such as cost or effects on other people, are predominant. Purely technical legal advice, therefore, can sometimes be

inadequate. It is proper for a lawyer to refer to relevant moral and ethical considerations in giving advice. Although a lawyer is not a moral advisor as such, moral and ethical considerations impinge upon most legal questions and may decisively influence how the law will be applied.

[3] A client may expressly or impliedly ask the lawyer for purely technical advice. When such a request is made by a client experienced in legal matters, the lawyer may accept it at face value. When such a request is made by a client inexperienced in legal matters, however, the lawyer's responsibility as advisor may include indicating that more may be involved than strictly legal considerations.

[4] Matters that go beyond strictly legal questions may also be in the domain of another profession. Family matters can involve problems within the professional competence of psychiatry, clinical psychology or social work; business matters can involve problems within the competence of the accounting profession or of financial specialists. Where consultation with a professional in another field is itself something a competent lawyer would recommend, the lawyer should make such a recommendation. At the same time, a lawyer's advice at its best often consists of recommending a course of action in the face of conflicting recommendations of experts.

Offering Advice

[5] In general, a lawyer is not expected to give advice until asked by the client. However, when a lawyer knows that a client proposes a course of action that is likely to result in substantial adverse legal consequences to the client, duty to the client under Rule 1.4 may require that the lawyer act if the client's course of action is related to the representation. A lawyer ordinarily has no duty to initiate investigation of a client's affairs or to give advice that the client has indicated is unwanted, but a lawyer may initiate advice to a client when doing so appears to be in the client's interest.

Model Code Comparison

There was no direct counterpart to this Rule in the Disciplinary Rules of the Model Code. DR 5-107(B) provided that a lawyer "shall not permit a person who recommends, employs, or pays him to render legal services for another to direct or regulate his professional judgment in rendering such legal services." EC 7-8 stated that "[a]dvice of a lawyer to his client need not be confined to purely legal considerations.... In assisting his client to reach a proper decision, it is often desirable for a lawyer to point out those factors which may lead to a decision that is morally just as well as legally permissible.... In the final analysis, however, ... the decision whether to forego legally available objectives or methods because of nonlegal factors is ultimately for the client...."

Rule 2.2. Intermediary

(a) A lawyer may act as intermediary between clients if:

    (1) the lawyer consults with each client concerning the implications of the common representation, including the advantages and risks involved, and the effect on the attorney-client privilege, and obtains each client's consent to the common representation;

    (2) the lawyer reasonably believes that the matter can be resolved on terms compatible with the clients' best interests, that each client will be able to make adequately informed decisions in the matter and that there is little risk of material prejudice to the interests of any of the clients if the contemplated resolution is unsuccessful; and

    (3) the lawyer reasonably believes that the common representation can be undertaken impartially and without improper effect on other responsibilities the lawyer has to any of the clients.

(b) While acting as intermediary, the lawyer shall consult with each client concerning the decisions to be made and the considerations relevant in making them, so that each client can make adequately informed decisions.

(c) A lawyer shall withdraw as intermediary if any of the clients so requests, or if any of the conditions stated in paragraph (a) is no longer satisfied. Upon withdrawal, the lawyer shall not continue to represent any of the clients in the matter that was the subject of the intermediation.

Comment

[1] A lawyer acts as intermediary under this Rule when the lawyer represents two or more parties with potentially conflicting interests. A key factor in defining the relationship is whether the parties share responsibility for the lawyer's fee, but the common representation may be inferred from other circumstances. Because confusion can arise as to the lawyer's role where each party is not separately represented, it is important that the lawyer make clear the relationship.

[2] The Rule does not apply to a lawyer acting as arbitrator or mediator between or among parties who are not clients of the lawyer, even where the lawyer has been appointed with the concurrence of the parties. In performing such a role the lawyer may be subject to applicable codes of ethics, such as the Code of Ethics for Arbitration in Commercial Disputes prepared by a joint Committee of the American Bar Association and the American Arbitration Association.

[3] A lawyer acts as intermediary in seeking to establish or adjust a relationship between clients on an amicable and mutually advantageous basis; for example, in helping to organize a business in which two or more clients are entrepreneurs, working out the financial reorganization of an enterprise in which two or more clients have an interest, arranging a property distribution in settlement of an estate or mediating a dispute between clients. The lawyer seeks to resolve potentially conflicting interests by developing the parties' mutual interests. The

alternative can be that each party may have to obtain separate representation with the possibility in some situations of incurring additional cost, complication or even litigation. Given these and other relevant factors, all the clients may prefer that the lawyer act as intermediary.

[4] In considering whether to act as intermediary between clients, a lawyer should be mindful that if the intermediation fails the result can be additional cost, embarrassment and recrimination. In some situations the risk of failure is so great that intermediation is plainly impossible. For example, a lawyer cannot undertake common representation of clients between whom contentious litigation is imminent or who contemplate contentious negotiations. More generally, if the relationship between the parties has already assumed definite antagonism, the possibility that the clients' interests can be adjusted by intermediation ordinarily is not very good.

[5] The appropriateness of intermediation can depend on its form. Forms of intermediation range from informal arbitration, where each client's case is presented by the respective client and the lawyer decides the outcome, to mediation, to common representation where the clients' interests are substantially though not entirely compatible. One form may be appropriate in circumstances where another would not. Other relevant factors are whether the lawyer subsequently will represent both parties on a continuing basis and whether the situation involves creating a relationship between the parties or terminating one.

Confidentiality and Privilege

[6] A particularly important factor in determining the appropriateness of intermediation is the effect on client-lawyer confidentiality and the attorney-client privilege. In a common representation, the lawyer is still required both to keep each client adequately informed and to maintain confidentiality of information relating to the representation.

See Rules 1.4 and 1.6. Complying with both requirements while acting as intermediary requires a delicate balance. If the balance cannot be maintained, the common representation is improper. With regard to the attorney-client privilege, the prevailing rule is that as between commonly represented clients the privilege does not attach. Hence, it must be assumed that if litigation eventuates between the clients, the privilege will not protect any such communications, and the client should be so advised.

[7] Since the lawyer is required to be impartial between commonly represented clients, intermediation is improper when that impartiality cannot be maintained. For example, a lawyer who has represented one of the clients for a long period and in a variety of matters might have difficulty being impartial between that client and one to whom the lawyer has only recently been introduced.

Consultation

[8] In acting as intermediary between the clients, the lawyer is required to consult with the clients on the implications of doing so, and proceed only upon

consent based on such a consultation. The consultation should make clear that the lawyer's role is not that of partisanship normally expected in other circumstances.

[9] Paragraph (b) is an application of the principle expressed in Rule 1.4. Where the lawyer is intermediary, the clients ordinarily must assume greater responsibility for decisions than when each client is independently represented.

Withdrawal

[10] Common representation does not diminish the rights of each client in the client-lawyer relationship. Each has the right to loyal and diligent representation, the right to discharge the lawyer as stated in Rule 1.16, and the protection of Rule 1.9 concerning obligations to a former client.

Model Code Comparison

There was no direct counterpart to this Rule in the Disciplinary Rules of the Model Code. EC 5-20 stated that a "lawyer is often asked to serve as an impartial arbitrator or mediator in matters which involve present or former relationships." DR 5-105(B) provided that a lawyer "shall not continue multiple employment if the exercise of his independent judgment on behalf of a client will be or is likely to be adversely affected by his representation of another client, or if it would be likely to involve him in representation of differing interests, except to the extent permitted under DR 5-105(C)." DR 5-105(C) provided that "a lawyer may represent multiple clients if it is obvious that he can adequately represent the interests of each and if each consents to the representation after full disclosure of the possible effect of such representation on the exercise of his independent professional judgment on behalf of each."

Table of Cases and Other Materials

Principle cases and accompanying page numbers, are in italic type. Cases cited or
discussed, and the accompanying page numbers, are in roman type. Articles are
in italic type. Books and other materials are in roman type. Non-case
materials appear alphabetically by author's names.

A

B

C

G

H

I

J

K

Index

A

B

1077